The Cambridge History of
Literary Criticism

VOLUME 4

The Eighteenth Century

The Cambridge History of
Literary Criticism

GENERAL EDITORS

Professor H. B. Nisbet
University of Cambridge
Professor Claude Rawson
Yale University

The Cambridge History of Literary Criticism will provide a comprehensive historical account of Western literary criticism from classical antiquity to the present day, dealing with both literary theory and critical practice. The *History* is intended as an authoritative work of reference and exposition, but more than a mere chronicle of facts. While remaining broadly non-partisan it will, where appropriate, address controversial issues of current critical debate without evasion or false pretences of neutrality. Each volume is a self-contained unit designed to be used independently as well as in conjunction with the others in the series. Substantial bibliographical material in each volume will provide the foundation for further study of the subjects in question.

VOLUMES PUBLISHED

Volume 1: *Classical Criticism*, edited by George A. Kennedy
Volume 8: *From Formalism to Poststructuralism*, edited by Raman Selden

OTHER VOLUMES IN PREPARATION

Volume 2: *The Middle Ages*, edited by Alastair Minnis
Volume 3: *The Renaissance*, edited by Glyn Norton
Volume 5: *Romanticism*, edited by Ernst Behler and Marshall Brown
Volume 7: *The Twentieth Century: Modernism and New Criticism*,
edited by A. Walton Litz, Luke Menand, and Lawrence Rainey

The Cambridge History of
Literary Criticism

VOLUME 4
The Eighteenth Century

Edited by

H. B. NISBET AND
CLAUDE RAWSON

CAMBRIDGE
UNIVERSITY PRESS

Published by the Press Syndicate of the University of Cambridge
The Pitt Building, Trumpington Street, Cambridge CB2 1RP
40 West 20th Street, New York, NY 10011–4211, USA
10 Stamford Road, Oakleigh, Melbourne 3166, Australia

First published 1997

Printed in Great Britain at the University Press, Cambridge

Typeset in 10/12 pt Sabon, in QuarkXPress™ [GC]

A catalogue record for this book is available from the British Library

ISBN 0 521 30009 6 hardback

Contents

Notes on contributors viii

Editors' preface xiv

INTRODUCTION: CRITICISM AND TRADITION

1 The institution of criticism in the eighteenth century   3
   DOUGLAS LANE PATEY

2 Ancients and Moderns   32
   DOUGLAS LANE PATEY

GENRES

3 Poetry, 1660–1740   75
   JAMES SAMBROOK

4 Poetry, after 1740   117
   WILLIAM KEACH

5 Drama, 1660–1740   167
   MAXIMILLIAN E. NOVAK

6 Drama, after 1740   184
   JOHN OSBORNE

7 Prose fiction: France   210
   ENGLISH SHOWALTER

8 Prose fiction: Great Britain   238
   MICHAEL MCKEON

9 Prose fiction: Germany and the Netherlands   264
   C. W. SCHONEVELD

10 Historiography   282
    MICHEL BARIDON

11 Biography and autobiography   302
    FELICITY A. NUSSBAUM

12 Criticism and the rise of periodical literature   316
    JAMES BASKER

                  LANGUAGE AND STYLE

13 Theories of language   335
    NICHOLAS HUDSON

14 The contributions of rhetoric to literary criticism   349
    GEORGE A. KENNEDY

15 Theories of style   365
    PAT ROGERS

16 Generality and particularity   381
    LEO DAMROSCH

17 The sublime   394
    JONATHAN LAMB

                  THEMES AND MOVEMENTS

18 Sensibility and literary criticism   419
    JOHN MULLAN

19 Women and literary criticism   434
    TERRY CASTLE

20 Primitivism   456
    MAXIMILLIAN E. NOVAK

21 Medieval revival and the Gothic   470
    PETER SABOR

22 Voltaire, Diderot, Rousseau and the *Encyclopédie*   489
    CHARLES A. PORTER

23 German literary theory from Gottsched to Goethe   522
    KLAUS L. BERGHAHN

24 The Scottish Enlightenment   546
    JOAN H. PITTOCK

25 Canons and canon formation   560
    JAN GORAK

        LITERATURE AND OTHER DISCIPLINES

26 Literature and philosophy   587
    SUSAN MANNING

27 The psychology of literary creation and literary response 614
    JAMES SAMBROOK

28 Taste and aesthetics   633
    (i)   Shaftesbury and Addison: criticism and the public
          taste   633
          DAVID MARSHALL
    (ii) The rise of aesthetics from Baumgarten to
          Humboldt   658
          HANS REISS

29 Literature and the other arts   681
    (i)   Ut pictura poesis   681
          DAVID MARSHALL
    (ii) The picturesque   700
          DAVID MARSHALL
    (iii) Literature and music   719
          DEAN MACE
    (iv) Parallels between the arts   730
          DEAN MACE

30 Classical scholarship and literary criticism   742
    GLENN W. MOST

31 Biblical scholarship and literary criticism   758
    MARCUS WALSH

32 Science and literary criticism   778
    MICHEL BARIDON

Bibliography   798

Index   901

Notes on contributors

Michel Baridon is Emeritus Professor of English Literature at the Université de Bourgogne, Dijon. He specializes in the interrelation of forms and ideas. His publications include *Edward Gibbon et le Mythe de Rome* (1977), *Le gothique des Lumiéres* (1991) and numerous articles dealing with the cultural history of the period 1650–1850. He is completing an anthology of garden texts due to be published in 1998. He is the founding editor of *Interfaces*, a bilingual review focusing on the Image/Language relationship and the visual arts.

James G. Basker is Professor of English at Barnard College, Columbia University. His publications include *Tobias Smollett, Critic and Journalist* (1988) and *Tradition in Transition* (ed. with Alvaro Ribeiro, S.J., 1996). He is currently preparing a scholarly edition of *Roderick Random* and completing a book on *Samuel Johnson and the Common Reader*.

Klaus L. Berghahn has been Professor of German at the University of Wisconsin-Madison since 1967. He has published widely on eighteenth-century German literature, poetics, and aesthetics and on Schiller, Classicism, criticism, Utopian literature and German-Jewish Culture. His latest book is entitled *The German-Jewish Dialogue – Reconsidered* (1996).

Terry Castle is Professor of English at Stanford University and has written widely on eighteenth-century literature. Her recent books include *The Female Thermometer: Eighteenth-Century Culture and the Invention of the Uncanny* (1995); *Noel Coward and Radclyffe Hall: Kindred Spirits* (1996); and an edition of Ann Radcliffe's *The Mysteries of Udolpho*.

Leo Damrosch is Ernest Bernbaum Professor of Literature at Harvard University, and was chairman of the Department of English from 1993 to 1998. He is the author of *Samuel Johnson and the Tragic Sense* (1972); *The Uses of Johnson's Criticism* (1976); *Symbol and Truth in*

Blake's Myth (1980); *God's Plot and Man's Stories: Studies in the Fictional Imagination from Milton to Fielding* (1985); *The Imaginative World of Alexander Pope* (1987); *Fictions of Reality in the Age of Hume and Johnson* (1989); and *The Sorrows of the Quaker Jesus: James Nayler and the Puritan Crackdown on the Free Spirit* (1996).

Jan Gorak is currently Professor of English at the University of Denver, where he has taught since 1988. He is the author of *The Making of the Modern Canon* (1991); *The Alien Mind of Raymond Williams* (1988); *Critic of Crisis* (1987); and *God the Artist* (1987). He is currently writing a study of the idea of civilization 'in emigration' from European capitals to colonial outposts. He has contributed reviews and essays to *Modern Philology*, *Denver Quarterly*, *English Studies in Africa*, and *Theater Journal*.

Nicholas Hudson is Professor of English at the University of British Columbia. He is the author of *Samuel Johnson and Eighteenth-Century Thought* (1988) and *Writing and European Thought 1600–1830* (1994).

William Keach teaches English at Brown University. He is the author of *Shelley's Style* (1984) and of articles on late eighteenth- and early nineteenth-century British literature and culture. His edition of the *Poems of Coleridge* will appear soon in the Penguin English Poets series.

George A. Kennedy is Paddison Professor of Classics Emeritus at the University of North Carolina. His recent books include *Aristotle, On Rhetoric* (1991); *A New History of Classical Rhetoric* (1994); and *Comparative Rhetoric: An Historical and Cross-Cultural Introduction* (1997), and he is the editor of *The Cambridge History of Literary Criticism, Volume 1: Classical Criticism*.

Jonathan Lamb is a Professor of English Literature at Princeton University. He is the author of *Sterne's Fiction and the Double Principle* (1989); *The Rhetoric of Suffering: Reading the Book of Job in the 18th Century* (1995) and co-editor of *Voyages and Beaches: Contact in the Pacific 1769–1840* (forthcoming), and is currently working on cross-cultural themes in narratives of British voyages in the Pacific, 1680–1779.

Dean T. Mace is Professor Emeritus of English at Vassar College. He has also served as Visiting Reader in English at the University of York (England) and as Visiting Professor of English at Bedford College. He has published numerous essays on painting, music, and poetry as they have invaded one another's realms in various ways from the Italian

Renaissance to the European eighteenth century. His essays include: 'Pietro Bembo and the Literary Origins of the Italian Madrigal' in *The Garland Library of the History of Western Music* (1985); 'Tasso, La Gerusalemme Liberata, and Monteverdi' in *Studies in the History of Music Vol. 1, Music and Language* (1983).

Susan Manning is a Lecturer in English at Cambridge University and a Fellow of Newnham College. Her work includes a book on Scottish and American literature, *The Puritan-Provincial Vision* (1990), and she has edited Scott's *Quentin Durward* (1992), Irving's *Sketch-Book* and Crevecoeur's *Letters from an American Farmer*. She has also recently published articles on Boswell and Hume, on Robert Burns, and on Henry Mackenzie. She completed a term as President of the Eighteenth-Century Scottish Studies Society in 1996.

David Marshall is currently Professor of English and Comparative Literature at Yale University. He is the author of *The Figure of Theater: Shaftesbury, Defoe, Adam Smith, and George Eliot* (1986); *The Surprising Effects of Sympathy: Marivaux, Defoe, Rousseau, and Mary Shelley* (1988); and articles on Rilke, Shakespeare, Austen, Hume, and a forthcoming work on eighteenth-century fiction and aesthetics.

Michael McKeon is Professor of English literature at Rutgers University. He is the author of *Poetry and Politics in Restoration England* (1975) and *The Origins of the English Novel* (1987). He is currently working on a study of the domestic novel and the early-modern transformation of the relation between the public and the private.

Glenn W. Most is Professor of Ancient Greek at the University of Heidelberg and Professor of Social Thought at the University of Chicago. He has published widely on ancient and modern poetry and philosophy and on the classical tradition and the history of classical scholarship. His publications include *F.A. Wolf: Prolegomena to Homer* (co-edited with A.T. Grafton and J.E.G. Zetzel, 1985); *Collecting Fragments – Fragmente sammeln. Aporemata 1* (1997), *Studies on the Derveni Papyrus* (co-edited with A. Laks, 1997); and *Raffael, Die Schule von Athen. Bild und Text* (1997).

John Mullan is Lecturer in English at University College London. He is the author of *Sentiment and Sociability. The Language of Feeling in the Eighteenth Century* (1988). He has edited Daniel Defoe's *Memoirs of a Cavalier* (1991) and *Roxana* (1996), and an anthology of memoirs of

Shelley (1996) in the series *Lives of the Great Romantics by their Contemporaries*, of which he is General Editor.

H.B. Nisbet was formerly Professor of German at the University of St Andrews and is currently Professor of Modern Languages at the University of Cambridge, and Fellow of Sidney Sussex College. He has written extensively on the history of ideas and of science, and on literature – especially that of eighteenth-century Germany, including works on Herder, Goethe, and Lessing – and has translated works of Kant and Hegel. He has contributed to numerous journals and was formerly the General Editor of the *Modern Language Review*.

Max Novak is Professor of English Literature at the University of California, Los Angeles. He is presently finishing a biography of Daniel Defoe, having published books on Defoe (1962) and Congreve (1971), a history of English literature during the eighteenth century (1983), edited several volumes in the California Dryden edition and two collections of essays, *English Literature in the Age of Disguise* (1977), and (with Ed Dudley) *The Wild Man Within* (1972). He is also a co-editor of Defoe's *An Essay upon Projects* which will soon appear as the first volume of the Stoke Newington Edition of Defoe's writings.

Felicity A. Nussbaum, Professor of English at the University of California, Los Angeles, is the author of *'The Brink of all we Hate': English Satires on Women, 1660–1750* (1984); *The New Eighteenth Century: Theory, Politics, English Literature* (co-edited with Laura Brown, 1987); *The Autobiographical Subject: Gender and Ideology in Eighteenth-Century England* (1989); and *Torrid Zones: Maternity, Sexuality, and Empire in Eighteenth-Century English Narratives* (1995). She currently holds a National Endowment for the Humanities Fellowship to complete a book on mid-eighteenth-century conjunctions of race, defect, and gender.

John Osborne is Professor of German at the University of Warwick. He has published widely on German literature and theatre of the eighteenth and nineteenth centuries. His books include: *The Naturalist Drama in Germany* (1971); *J.M.R. Lenz: the Renunciation of Heroism*, (1975); *Meyer or Fontane? German Literature after the Franco-Prussian War* (1983); *The Meiningen Court Theatre* (1988); *Vom Nutzen der Geschichte: Studien zum Werk Conrad Ferdinand Meyers* (1994).

Douglas Lane Patey, Professor of English at Smith College, Northampton, Massachusetts, is the author of *Probability and Literary Form:*

Philosophic Theory and Literary Practice in the Augustan Age (1984) and, most recently, of *Evelyn Waugh: A Critical Biography*.

Joan Pittock Wesson has been an Honorary Research Fellow in English in the University of Aberdeen since she retired as Director of Cultural History and of the Thomas Reid Institute for Research at that university. She has recently written on 'Thomas Hearne and the Narratives of Englishness' (forthcoming) and contributed a chapter on the teaching of literature and rhetoric in Aberdeen to Robert Crawford's *Scottish Invention of English Literature* (forthcoming). Her book on *Poetry and the Redemption of History: The Life of Henry Birkhead* (Founder of the Oxford Poetry Chair) is in press.

Charles A. Porter has taught in the French Department of Yale University since 1960. He is the author of *Restif's Novels, or an Autobiography in Search of an Author* (1967) and *Chateaubriand: Composition, Imagination, and Poetry* (1978), and has edited special numbers of *Yale French Studies* on 'Men/Women of Letters'; 'After the Age of Suspicion: the French Novel Today'; and 'Same Sex/Different Text? Gay and Lesbian Writing in French'.

Claude Rawson is Maynard Mack Professor of English at Yale University and Honorary Professor at the University of Warwick. His publications include *Henry Fielding and the Augustan Ideal Under Stress* (1972); *Gulliver and the Gentle Reader* (1973); *Order from Confusion Sprung* (1985); *Satire and Sentiment 1660–1830* (1994). He was formerly the English Editor of the *Modern Language Review* and of the *Yearbook of English Studies* and has lectured widely not only in the United Kingdom and United States, but throughout Europe, the Americas, Asia, Australasia and North Africa.

Hans Reiss is Emeritus Professor of German and Senior Research Fellow, University of Bristol. Amongst other works he is author of *Franz Kafka* (1952; 1956); *Goethes Romane* (1963); *Politisches Denken in der deutschen Romantik* (1966); *Goethe's Novels* (1969); *Kants politisches Denken* (1977); *The Writer's Task from Nietzsche to Brecht* (1978); and *Formgestaltung und Politik. Goethe-Studien* (1995), and is the editor of *Kant, Political Writings* (1970; 1991). He has also published more than fifty articles on German literature and thought as well as on aesthetics.

Pat Rogers, DeBartolo Professor in the Liberal Arts at the University of South Florida, has written and edited some thirty books on the eighteenth century, most recently *The Samuel Johnson Encyclopedia* (1996) and *The Text of Great Britain: Theme and Design in Defoe's 'Tour'* (1997).

Peter Sabor is Professor of English at Laval University, Quebec. He has edited Richardson's *Pamela* (1980); Cleland's *Memoirs of a Woman of Pleasure* (1985); Sarah Fielding's *The Adventures of David Simple* (1998); and *Samuel Richardson: Tercentenary Essays* (co-edited with Margaret Anne Doody, 1989). Other publications include two books on Horace Walpole and (in collaboration) editions of Frances Burney's *Cecilia* and *The Wanderer*, and her collected plays.

James Sambrook is Emeritus Professor of English in the University of Southampton. He has edited James Thomson for Oxford English Texts and William Cowper for Longman Annotated Texts; his other recent publications include *James Thomson, a Life* (1991) and *The Eighteenth Century: The Intellectual and Cultural Context of English Literature, 1700–1789* (1986).

Cornelis W. Schoneveld teaches English Literature at the University of Leiden, the Netherlands. He has specialized in the history of Anglo-Dutch literary relations and translation. His publications include *Intertraffic of the Mind: Studies in Seventeenth-Century Anglo-Dutch Translation* (1983), and *Sea-Changes: Studies in Three Centuries of Anglo-Dutch Cultural Transmission* (1996).

English Showalter is a Professor of French at Rutgers University, Camden. He is the author of *The Evolution of the French Novel, 1641–1782* (1972) and numerous articles on early French fiction. He is one of the editors of the correspondence of Madame de Graffigny and has written extensively about her life and works.

Marcus Walsh, who is Reader in English at the University of Birmingham, has written extensively on Smart, Swift, Johnson, and Sterne, on the history and theory of editing, and on biblical interpretation and scholarship in the seventeenth and eighteenth centuries. He has edited, with Karina Williamson, the Oxford University Press *Poetical Works of Christopher Smart* (1983–). His study of *Shakespeare, Milton, and Eighteenth-Century Literary Editing* will be published in 1997.

Editors' preface

The period covered by this volume begins around 1670, roughly at the time of the Quarrel of the Ancients and Moderns in France. This was followed by its more specialized British sequel, inaugurated by Sir William Temple's 'Essay upon the Ancient and Modern Learning' (1690), and enlisting the polemical energies of the great classical scholar Richard Bentley on the Modern side (a seeming paradox, rich in significance), and those of the satirist Jonathan Swift (in perhaps his most brilliant work, *A Tale of a Tub* and its appendix, the *Battle of the Books*) on the side of the Ancients, defending Temple, his patron. The volume ends around 1800, a decade or so after the outbreak of the French Revolution, and at the time of some of the most important early achievements of European Romanticism, although the main intellectual impact of these events is the subject of Volume 5 of *The Cambridge History of Literary Criticism*, now in preparation. The seventeenth-century *querelle* also crosses volume-divisions. It is a late and unusually explicit phase of a cultural preoccupation which had, in a variety of forms, been actively debated throughout the Renaissance, and which will receive attention in Volume 3, now in press. Volumes of this series have overlapping chronologies: our 'periods' are not sealed units but parts of a continuous intellectual history.

The late seventeenth and eighteenth centuries, or specific portions of them, have been spoken of as an age of Reason (now largely discredited), or of Neo-classicism (indeed of several successive Neo-classicisms), or of Enlightenment. They have also, like some other periods, been thought of as an age of transition, most specifically in their 'pre-Romantic' aspects. Northrop Frye commented on this in a famous essay, 'Towards Defining an Age of Sensibility' (1956), pleading for the recognition of the later part of the period as having an integrity of its own, marked by a new self-consciousness, an intensified intimacy and 'sympathy' between author and reader, and the creation of a literature concerned, as part of its radical subject-matter, to register the processes of its own composition. Frye was right to be impatient with the truisms and confusions of the pre-Romantic scenario, and to repudiate the second-class status which attaches to 'ages of transition'. His essay seems to us seminal, however, not because it introduced an alternative label, but partly for its challenge to a previous one and mainly for its substantive insights into the modes of a literature of process. The present volume has in general sought to avoid categorisations, whether of the traditional or revisionist varieties (though the Enlightenment appears as a special exception from time to time), while recognising that such categories are themselves sometimes part of the intellectual history they attempt to describe.

The period covered by this volume is one in which many changes in literary history can be recorded, not all of which received the same degree of critical attention or recognition at the time. (Our primary concern is with the history of this critical response, rather than with the primary phenomena, to the limited extent that the two are separable.) The most conspicuous literary development of the period is perhaps the evolution of prose fiction into what we now think of as the novel, its extension of the subject-matter of narrative into private life, its heightened preoccupation with circumstantial 'realism', and the vastly increased scope which it offered for the exploration of individual sensibility. A large body of criticism, both of specific works and of what would now be called theoretical issues, grew up around this, some of it concerned with the differences between the new novel and the various older forms of prose romance. But this criticism generally failed to keep pace with the more remarkable works of fiction, and the novelists had themselves not yet evolved the habits of extended and sophisticated critical exploration of the resources and objectives of narrative art which we associate with Flaubert or James, or even with Sir Walter Scott. 'Romance', moreover, was not simply dislodged. Some of its older forms remained strong, and others passed into specialised branches of the new fiction, notably the Gothic novel, which was in turn the product of a 'medieval' revival in the second half of the eighteenth century.

In poetry and drama a familiar gradual shift is perceptible from strictly demarcated conceptions of genre, and from the assumption that poems or plays must or can be written within a framework of prescriptive rules. The 'organic' conception of the work of art sometimes makes a preliminary or 'pre-Romantic' appearance, usually sub-textual, but doctrines of the 'Grace beyond the Reach of Art', or 'nameless Graces which no Methods teach', were themselves part of the older prescriptive system or readily accommodated within it. If the 'Licence' answered 'th' Intent proposed', or was sanctioned by a great master, that licence, as Pope said, was itself a rule. Much of the impact of the Longinian Sublime, in the earlier part of the period especially, has to do with an authoritative sanction for supposedly unsanctioned, ostensibly transgressive, effects.

Longinus' treatise *On the Sublime* was translated into French by
Boileau (1674). It passed quickly into English, translated, as Swift put
it, from Boileau's translation, and into other languages. (At least one
English translation preceded Boileau's, but it was Boileau who made
Longinus familiar in seventeenth- and eighteenth-century Europe.) Pope
thought of Longinus as being '*himself* the great *Sublime* he draws',
perhaps the most important case of licence becoming rule, except that
Longinus (like Aristotle) was a critic, the source of prescription rather
than a poetic model. Or rather, Longinus was found to be both, though
not quite in the sense in which the Horace of the *Art of Poetry* was
both. His writing, like Plato's, was sometimes thought of as having
primary poetic qualities, but there is also a special sense, made evident
throughout Pope's *Essay on Criticism*, in which 'just *Precepts*' and 'great
Examples' are seen to interpenetrate more deeply than later critical
discourse might acknowledge:

> Those RULES of old, *discover'd*, not *devis'd*,
> Are *Nature* still, but *Nature Methodiz'd*.

Pope's fable of a young Virgil, scorning the 'Critick's Law' and drawing
only on '*Nature's Fountains*', is instructive in this regard. For when
Virgil matured, in Pope's account, and

> ...t' examine ev'ry Part he came,
> *Nature* and *Homer* were, he found, the *same*

the point is not that Homer dislodged Aristotle, or the poet the critic:
it is that when Virgil knew better, he realised that the precepts of the
one and the example of the other came to the same thing.

Between this outlook and the notion that a poem can be understood
only by laws generated from within itself, there is a considerable conceptual distance, just as there is a considerable distance between the
Longinian Sublime as understood by Boileau or Pope, and the Romantic
Sublime as it appears, for example, in Wordsworth or in Turner. The
differences may in some cases be less than they seem: Addison's response to Alpine grandeurs, for example, suggests some important continuities, much-invoked by proponents of pre-Romantic origins. It
has been our aim, moreover, to maintain a general awareness that ideas
about poetry bear an indirect and usually elusive relation to the poetry
itself, and that 'literary theories' at particular times are often fictions by
which poets seek to make sense of what they do, rather than firmly
believed doctrines with literal and direct operational consequences.

It is also in this period that we witness the beginnings of what might
be called critical careers, of whole lifetimes devoted to extensive consideration both of literary principles and of the practice of authors. Dryden

and Johnson in England, Voltaire, Diderot, and some of the lesser *Encyclopédistes* in France, and Lessing in Germany are examples. In all these cases, however, criticism remained an ancillary, or at least a secondary, activity. It accompanied primary composition, or more general philosophical pursuits, as an active component of the intellectual life, but not as an end in itself. The Arnoldian idea of the function of criticism, and its attendant sense of the importance of the critic's calling, seldom appear. The phenomenon of a prestigious career mainly devoted to critical activity, like Sainte-Beuve's in the nineteenth century, or Edmund Wilson's or F. R. Leavis's in the twentieth, depended on developments in the history of intellectual journalism, and the teaching of literature in universities, which belong to later times. Reviewing journals had existed since the seventeenth century. Their early function was mainly informative, consisting of abstracts, quotations, and perhaps a brief judicial comment. By 1714, the *Tatler* and especially the *Spectator*, had popularised a form of periodical essay sometimes given over to the discussion of an author, a genre, or even an individual work (Addison's papers on *Paradise Lost* are perhaps the most important example). The discussion of literary works and of issues arising from them established itself in several periodical media throughout the eighteenth century, and by the time of the *Correspondence littéraire* of Grimm and Diderot serious critical journalism was well on the way to recognition as an important feature of intellectual culture.

But the era of the great journals of opinion and of the influential reviewer was still some decades away. Universities did not begin the systematic teaching of vernacular literatures until well into the nineteenth century, and the academic critic as we know him or her today is even more recent. Some teaching of the literatures of modern Europe took place, notably in Edinburgh and Glasgow, from the 1740s. Adam Smith lectured on 'rhetoric and belles-lettres' in Edinburgh in 1748–1751, and subsequently as Professor of Logic and Rhetoric and then of Moral Philosophy at the University of Glasgow, emphasising the value of polite letters in the intellectual formation of his audience, and drawing heavily on 'the best English classics' and on Italian and French as well as ancient writers. Smith's lectures remained unpublished until a version of 1762–3, drawn from student notes, appeared in two scholarly editions of 1963 and 1983. They were heard by Hugh Blair in 1748, and may have been used in the lectures Blair gave in Edinburgh from December 1759 and then as the first Regius Professor of Rhetoric and Belles-Lettres at the University of Edinburgh. The Chair, described by J. C. Bryce as 'in effect the first Chair of English Literature in the world', had been established in 1762 in recognition of Blair's success as a lecturer, and Blair's *Lectures on Rhetoric and Belles-Lettres*, unlike

Adam Smith's, were published in his own full text in 1783. Like Smith's, they draw significantly on modern English and European authors. Nevertheless, the widespread institutional adoption of modern literary studies as a prominent part of the curriculum belongs to a later time.

We have not, for these and other reasons, devoted separate chapters to academic or institutional aspects of critical activity, or to the careers of individual critics, though we recognise the interest and pertinence of the life-work of Dryden or Johnson, Diderot or Lessing, taken as individual wholes. It has seemed to us more fruitful to arrange this volume of the *History* according to the topics and modes of critical activity and the intellectual influences upon it, its various theoretical preoccupations (including especially issues of genre and style) and its treatment of individual authors and works, its relations with other branches of knowledge and inquiry and with the criticism of other arts, its media of dissemination.

The aim of this volume, and of the *History* as a whole, is informative rather than polemical. It is not, however, a chronicle, but a historical account of issues and debates. Our contributors have been invited, where appropriate, to engage with these issues as well as to report them. On controversial questions, contributors have not been encouraged to adopt a false neutrality, but to be scrupulous in the fair reporting of alternative points of view.

We wish to thank Sebastian Frede for his help with the preparation of copy, and Phyllis Gibson for drafting the index and supplying a valuable extra pair of eyes in the process of proof-correction.

Introduction:
Criticism and Tradition

The institution of criticism in the eighteenth century

Douglas Lane Patey

I

Starting in the late seventeenth century, observers throughout Europe agree that never before had the world seen so many critics. '[T]ill of late years *England* was as free from Criticks, as it is from *Wolves*', Thomas Rymer attests in his Preface to Rapin (1674) – the work that launched the word's popularity in England – though 'our Neighbour Nations have got far the start of us'. 'Criticism' had entered the vernacular languages from Latin around 1600, first in France and later in England, where Dryden was the first to use it; it arrived in Germany only about 1700, but by 1781 we have the testimony of Kant's first *Critique*, testimony as well to the term's extraordinary breadth of meaning for the period: 'Our age is in every sense of the word the age of criticism [*Kritik*], and everything must submit to it.'[1]

The eighteenth century inherited from the seventeenth a primary meaning of 'criticism' as a range of activities including grammar, rhetoric, history, geography, and such newly named studies as 'palaeography' – the whole range of textually based learning pursued by Renaissance humanists; as Bayle said, 'le règne de la critique' began with the revival of letters. This is how the term is defined from Bacon to Jean Le Clerc's great *Ars critica*, first published in 1697 and much reprinted.[2] In this

---

[1] Rymer, *Works* (Rymer's translation appeared in the same year as Rapin's *Réflexions sur la poétique d'Aristote*), pp. 1–2; Kant, *Schriften*, III, p. 9 ('Unser Zeitalter ist das eigentliche Zeitalter der Kritik, der sich alles unterwerfen muß'). Cf. J. G. Buhle in 1790: 'Our age deserves the credit of having examined, explained, and enlightened more critically than previous ages; therefore some have rightly called ours the *critical* age' (*Grundzüge*, p. 39). Wellek supplies general histories of 'critic' and 'criticism' in 'Literary criticism' and 'The term and concept of literary criticism' (*Concepts*, pp. 21–36).

[2] Bayle, *Dictionary*, s.v. 'Aconte', note D (Bayle here equates 'Criticism' and 'Philology'). The term 'palaeography' originated in Bernard de Montfaucon's *Palaeographia Graeca* (1708). Le Clerc's *Ars critica*, still celebrated by Gibbon in his *Essay on the Study of Literature* in 1761, appeared in augmented editions in 1698, 1700, and 1712, and continued to be reprinted after Le Clerc's death (1736). It treats essentially the same range of 'critical' inquiry Bacon had detailed in the *Advancement of Learning* (1605): '(1) concerning the true correction and edition of authors, (2) concerning the exposition and explication of authors, (3) concerning the

sense 'criticism' appears as a synonym for 'grammar', 'philology', 'erudition', and even 'literature', as it still does for instance in Marmontel's entry 'Critique, s.f.' in the *Encyclopédie*; in the *Dictionary* of 1755, Johnson defines 'Philology' simply as 'Criticism; grammatical learning'. Eighteenth-century writers both refine and extend this definition. Purely textual matters become the special province of 'verbal criticism', whose narrowness Alexander Pope memorably castigates. As Johann Christoph Gottsched writes in his *Versuch einer Critischen Dichtkunst*, 'Over the last several years, the practice of criticism has become more common in Germany than it had been hitherto', and

thus the true concept of criticism has become more familiar. Today even young people know that a critic or judge of art deals not just with words but also with ideas; not just with syllables and letters but also with the rules underpinning entire arts and works of art. It has already become clear that such a critic must be a philosopher and must understand more than the mere philologists.[3]

'Criticism' came to include social and political inquiry, indeed the application of reason to any field (as in Kant's 'critical philosophy') – what we generally mean by 'Enlightenment critique'. Thus by 1765 Voltaire can celebrate criticism as a tenth Muse come to rid the world of unreason; he writes in the *Encyclopédie*, '*critique* no longer occupies itself solely with dead Greeks and Romans but, joined with a healthy philosophy, destroys all the prejudices with which society is infected'.[4] Kant's similar comment of 1781 continues, neither 'religion through its sanctity' nor 'law-giving through its majesty' can 'exempt themselves from it'.

The term's extension in these directions began in the seventeenth century with textual studies of the Bible such as Louis Cappel's *Critica*

times, which in many cases give great light to true interpretations, (4) concerning some brief censure and judgment of authors, and (5) concerning the syntax and disposition of studies' (182).

[3] 'Das Critisieren ist seit einigen Jahren schon gewöhnlicher in Deutschland geworden, als es vorhin gewesen: und dadurch ist auch der wahre Begriff davon schon bekannter geworden. Auch junge Leute wissens nunmehro schon, daß ein Criticus oder Kunstrichter nicht nur mit Worten, sondern auch mit Gedanken; nicht nur mit Sylben und Buchstaben, sondern auch mit den Regeln ganzer Künste und Kunstwerke zu thun hat. Man begreift es schon, daß ein solcher Criticus ein Philosoph seyn, und etwas mehr verstehen müsse, als ein Buchstäbler.' Preface to 2nd (1737) edn, n.p. For Pope on 'verbal criticism', see *Dunciad* IV, ll. 101–74 ('Words are Man's province, Words we teach alone': l. 150), and *Epistle to Arbuthnot*, ll. 157–72 ('Comma's and points they set exactly right'; 'Pains, reading, study, are their just pretence, / And all they want is spirit, taste, and sense': ll. 159–61).

[4] Voltaire, *Oeuvres*, XX, p. 218; *Encyclopédie*, s.v. 'Gens de lettres' ('leur critique ne s'est plus consumée sur des mots grecs & latins; mais appuyée d'une saine philosophie, elle a détruit tous les préjugés dont la société étoit infectée').

sacra (1650) and Richard Simon's *Histoire critique du Vieux Testament* (1678). Criticism had always included 'judgement', but these exercises in philological judgement so disturbed the orthodox as to engender attacks on 'criticism' for irreligion (and as late as 1711 to lead Pope to make clear that his *Essay on Criticism* would not engage such concerns). The new sense is enshrined in Bayle's *Dictionnaire historique et critique* (1695), where the critic is defined as one who 'shows what can be said for and against authors; he adopts successively the persona of prosecutor and defender'; because of this new meaning, though 'criticism' had always suggested some degree of captious censoriousness, both Bayle and Voltaire are especially concerned to distinguish 'critique' from 'satire' and 'libel'.[5] Richard Alves mixes all the term's senses when he writes in his *Sketches of a History of Literature* (1794) that after the death of Pope 'the English language' entered its 'fourth age', an 'age of criticism', characterized by 'the study of criticism, philosophy, and the rules of good composition' (p. 151). Our concern here is of course primarily with Alves's third sense of criticism, but in this period the term's varied meanings cannot wholly be disentangled – not least because of what were criticism's larger 'ideological' functions for the period: criticism, like literature itself, served as a forum for discussion of a wide range of social, political, and religious issues as critics sought to create, through the education of taste, a body of polite popular opinion in all these areas (especially in countries where censorship of more direct forms of commentary remained rigorous).[6]

Partly because so many aspired to the title of critic (eventually doing so in print), partly because of the period's conception of criticism itself, eighteenth-century texts persistently raise as a central question one not asked so pointedly before and posed very differently since: what are the qualifications of the critic? Addison and Johnson, Du Bos and Voltaire, Gottsched and Schiller devote pages to the crucial question of self-identification and definition. Thus Hume asks in 'Of the Standard of Taste' (1757): 'But where are such critics to be found? By what marks are they to be known? How distinguish them from pretenders?' For all Hume's rhetoric of immediacy, his formulations in fact echo Alexander Pope's *Essay on Criticism* (1711), his chief model in that essay.[7] Through-

---

[5] Pope, *Essay on Criticism*, ll. 545–59 (on those 'Monsters', the irreligious 'Criticks' of the Restoration); Bayle, s.v. 'Archelaus'; s.v. 'Catius'; Voltaire, *Oeuvres*, VIII, p. 551.

[6] This mode of analysis, stressing the role of criticism in creating a 'public sphere' of political discourse, was pioneered by Reinhart Koselleck (in *Critique and Crisis*, 1959) and Jürgen Habermas (*The Structural Transformation of the Public Sphere*, 1962).

[7] Hume, *Works*, p. 279; cf. Pope, *Essay on Criticism*, ll. 631f. ('But where's the Man?').

out the century 'true' critics guide the public in identifying 'pretenders', for instance in that series of composite satiric portraits of 'false' critics from Addison's Sir Timothy Tittle to Martinus Scriblerus to Johnson's Dick Minim.[8] An account of why the qualifications of the critic became a central question for criticism, and why the answers given to it varied – in their varied balancings of leisure and labour, polite companionship and combativeness, knowing enough and not knowing too much, natural endowment and what the age called 'culture' – might constitute one history of eighteenth-century criticism, or at least of the question: what did it mean to be a critic in the eighteenth century?

For the question of how the history of criticism is itself to be written has become a deeply contested matter, and eighteenth-century criticism has provided the chief battleground. Detailed academic histories of criticism began to appear in the late nineteenth century, with the era of specialist journals, when criticism became in its modern way an academic affair; behind the modern debate stands most commandingly George Saintsbury's *History of Criticism and Literary Taste in Europe* (1900–4), parts of which were later excerpted to form a *History of English Criticism* (1911). It was Saintsbury and his followers (such as J. W. H. Adkins) whom more recent writers, most notably René Wellek in his *Rise of English Literary History* (1941) and *History of Modern Criticism* (1955–92), sought to replace (though Wellek while writing the latter came to despair that a history of criticism is even possible).[9] Since those first efforts at revision, the eighteenth century has come fully to the centre of debate: when R. S. Crane proposed replacing the tradition of Saintsbury with a more adequate kind of history, he did so in an essay 'On writing the history of criticism in England, 1650–1800'; it is with Saintsbury and our understanding of the eighteenth century that Peter Hohendahl's 'Prolegomena to a history of literary criticism' begins; and when Ralph Cohen proposes reconceiving the history of criticism, he does so in 'Some thoughts on the problems of literary change 1750–1800'. Programmes of reconstruction are so various, and have proceeded so briskly, that at the moment, as Hohendahl remarks, 'there are little more than beginnings for a history of the institution of criticism' (p. 240) – suggesting that for our time, collaborative volumes such as those in *The Cambridge History of Literary Criticism* must form the site at which a newly adequate history of criticism is worked out.

---

[8] Addison, *Tatler* 165 (1710; cf. Steele, *Guardian* 12 (1713)); Pope *et al.*, *Memoirs of Martinus Scriblerus*; Johnson, *Idler* 60, 61 (1759). James Basker has recently suggested Tobias Smollett as the original of Johnson's Dick Minim (*Smollett*, ch. 2).

[9] Wellek lamented in 'The fall of literary history' (1970): 'attempts at an evolutionary history have failed. I myself failed in *The History of Modern Criticism* to construe a convincing scheme of development ... Croce and Ker are right. There is no progress, no development, no history of art' (p. 341).

Eighteenth-century criticism has become central to this debate because, as Cohen has most fully explained, the first problems the historian must face are those of continuity and change (innovation and variation),[10] and because it was the romantic figuration of literary change as revolutionary discontinuity, in manifestoes such as Wordsworth's Preface to *Lyrical Ballads* (1800), whose norms have in one form or another governed most criticism ever since. To a remarkable extent, how the history of criticism in any period is written has depended on the historian's understanding of how criticism evolved from the eighteenth century to the nineteenth, while this evolution itself (and thus the eighteenth century from which it began) has been construed according to Romanticism's own account of its nature and origins.

There is first of all the problem that it is only in this period that the term 'literature' (and a host of related words) take on something like their modern meanings, making the eighteenth-century critic's question of self-identification seem all too reasonable, and making historical attention to questions of continuity and change especially pressing. The phrase 'literary criticism' is itself to be found scarcely anywhere in the eighteenth century: in a variety of ways, the phrase suggests a realignment of disciplines and institutions only just occurring. The term 'literature' still meant, primarily, as Johnson defines it in the *Dictionary* (1755), 'learning; skill in letters' – erudition in whatever field; the concept was only gradually being reformulated (and contracted) to its modern sense of literary 'art' or 'imaginative' literature (literature as fundamentally aesthetic in purpose and effect: poems, novels, and plays), a process of redefinition occurring in the context of much larger reconceptualizations of such categories and terms as 'art', 'science', and 'humanities', and one not complete until the nineteenth century. Hence we do not hear until very late in the eighteenth century of any specifically *literary* 'canons' or 'criticism'.[11]

For most of the period, furthermore, 'literature' still carried primarily an active sense of learning gained through reading, of human attainment won by the effort of cultivation, as it does when Johnson refers in his *Life of Milton* (1779) to the poet's father as a man of 'more than common literature', or as it does as late as 1840 in the title of John Petherham's *Sketches of the Progress and Present State of Anglo-Saxon Literature in England*, where 'literature' means what we would call the

---

[10] See Cohen, 'Innovation and variation' and 'Some thoughts'.

[11] See Patey, 'The canon', and Gossman, 'Literature'. In early eighteenth-century France, *belles-lettres* remained, as Richelet's *Dictionnaire* had defined it in 1680, '*knowledge of* the orators, poets, and historians'; d'Alembert is among the first consciously to contract the term merely to 'eloquence' and 'poetry', though he still defines it as 'knowledge of' these (*Encyclopédie*, s.v. 'Érudition').

study of literature (of all varieties). (In Britain it is only at mid-century that the adjective 'literary', previously reserved to discussion of the letters of the alphabet, takes on a larger sense, as it does for instance in the title of the *Literary Magazine, or Universal Review,* founded in 1756; the word does not appear in the *Dictionary,* though Johnson came to use it and may have been one of its chief popularizers.) This reconfiguring of the 'literary' forms part, as Patrick Parrinder has shown, of that larger eighteenth-century shift by which (in the context of a new marketplace for authors) 'literature' came to mean *works of* literature, to take on its 'passive, institutional sense, to denote a body of works already in existence'; the change can be related as well to the period's conception of criticism as centred in the response of taste, 'literature' in its passive sense 'reflecting the attitude of the consumer rather than the literary producer' (*Authors,* pp. 20–1).

But it is not only because we have not attended to the changing meanings of words (or to the causes of such change) that Romantic norms have governed the history of eighteenth-century criticism, as students of the period well know. On a much larger scale, acceptance as normative of romantic doctrines of literature and change has produced teleological 'histories' of criticism framed as tales of the gradual emergence of modern (romantic) categories and institutions (categories and institutions which had been more or less obstructed or occluded in the century before) – has produced, as Clifford Siskin puts it in his exploration of *The Historicity of Romantic Discourse,* romantic histories of criticism, from Saintsbury through the works of Ernst Cassirer and M. H. Abrams to W. J. Bate and James Engell.[12] Among Anglophone historians especially, romantic categories have escaped interrogation, so that dichotomies such as 'originality' and 'imitation', and even 'organic' and 'mechanical', continue to organize histories, concealing important continuities and changes from us. Thus historians who romantically conceive imitation as mere formal and generic recapitulation fail to see that Augustan imitation was a mode of cultural transmission that crucially involved correction of a tradition from within: in this way, writes Joseph Trapp, poetry 'by lively Copies produces new Originals': as Jaucourt explains in the *Encyclopédie,* 'Good imitation is continual invention'.[13] Dryden and Pope extol imitation because they recognize both the referentiality of literature and the condition we now call 'intertextuality': copying nature by imitating Homer entails selecting and recombining elements of previous works, thereby both correcting

---

[12] See, in addition to Siskin, Robert Griffin's critique of Romantic constructions of the transition from 'Classic' to 'Romantic' in *Wordsworth's Pope.*

[13] Trapp, *Lectures,* p. 9; *Encyclopédie,* s.v. 'Imitation' ('La bonne *imitation* est une continuelle invention'). On the concept of imitation in the period, see Weinbrot, 'Emulation'; Weinsheimer, *Imitation;* and Morrison, *Mimetic Tradition,* chs. 12–13.

our understanding of nature and refining – recreating by changing – a literary tradition. Johnson may have written that 'No man ever yet became great by imitation', but he equally understood – as in his remarks on Sterne – that no one becomes great without it.[14]

Similarly, histories that read Romantic notions of the organic and mechanical backward through the eighteenth century hide from us the fact that *all* eighteenth-century writers liken successful literary works to living creatures, but do so in the context of their own notions of organism (notions preceding those governing the consolidation and naming of 'biology' in about 1800). For most eighteenth-century writers, the organism was first of all a 'system', and 'since all *System* involves *Subordination*' (as Soame Jenyns puts it in a useful phrase), a hierarchy. Its levels of organization stand to each other, and so are unified, in the relation of soul to body: higher levels are the formal cause of lower ones, which the lower in turn 'express' (as thoughts are expressed in the face, for instance). So too in the literary work, whose organization thus becomes a particularly Augustan version of the Aristotelian hierarchy of moral, fable, characters, sentiments, and language – the categories through which generations of critics approach particular works (a logical hierarchy in the sense of that which presents itself to readers, whatever the critic may believe to be the chronological or psychological order of composition). This model of the literary work obtains in critics from Hobbes, who speaks in his 'Answer' to Davenant (1650) of the 'Body and Soul' of a poem, to James Harris, who writes in 1752 that 'Every *legitimate* Work should be ONE, as much as a Vegetable, or an Animal; and, to be ONE like them, it should be a WHOLE, *consisting* of PARTS, and be in nothing *redundant*, in nothing *deficient*.'[15]

In the literary work so conceived – as it is for instance by Pope in the *Essay on Criticism* – reading is the movement from lower levels to higher (thus joining parts into wholes). For reading and the work to be successful, all relations among levels – all relations of form to meaning – must be adequate relations of *expression*, the term Pope and others repeatedly employ (and which is too often associated only with later poetics). And for expression to occur, for the reader to be able to move from form to intended meaning at any level in the work, formal choices must be *appropriate* and *natural*. As Dryden puts it in his Preface to *Albion and Albanius* (1685), 'Propriety of thought is that fancy which arises naturally from the subject. Propriety of words is the clothing of those thoughts with such expressions as are naturally proper to them;

[14] *Rambler* 154 (1751); Boswell, *Life*, II, p. 449. Cohen makes the point in 'Dryden's criticism', pp. 72–3.
[15] Hobbes, 'Answer', p. 60; Harris, *Inquiries*, II, p. 116. I give a fuller account of this model of the literary work and the theory of form upon which it rests in *Probability*, ch. 4.

and from both these, if they are judiciously performed, the delight of poetry results' (*Essays*, II, pp. 34–5). In this way – in terms of this Augustan hierarchic conception of the literary organism and its consequent account of interpretation – a chief meaning for those much discussed eighteenth-century literary-critical terms 'nature' and 'decorum' is precisely *expressiveness*. This model of course begs what were to become crucial questions about the relation of history to human nature and so to changes in literary response, but for those who held it, a 'natural style' was one 'appropriate to its subject', and the 'rules of art' – conceived as formulations of successful relations of means to ends, form to meaning – were embodiments of critical *judgement*; all are attempts to describe relations of form to meaning that critical judgement has found to be expressive, and hence appropriate. And for modern historians of criticism, finally, understanding these norms of literary form and interpretation reveals that the eighteenth century (probably like all periods) had its own theories of 'organic' unity, different from, but not wholly discontinuous with, the romantic.

I have so far been arguing for a history which seeks to understand eighteenth-century criticism in its own terms, but it must equally be acknowledged that all modern histories are precisely that – modern histories – written from the interests and points of view of the historian; all history is in some sense the genealogy of its writers, a history of ourselves. Such reflection provides us with another reason why the eighteenth century has provided the major site of conflict in recent attempts to reformulate a history of criticism. Nearly all historians, looking backward from the vantage of their desks in colleges and universities, have found eighteenth-century criticism pivotal in the genealogy of modernity: it is here, we read, that 'modern' criticism – criticism in its modern 'institutional', 'specialized', 'professional', 'disciplinary', or 'autonomous' sense – emerges. (Thus, to take a small instance, Scott Elledge includes in his collection of *Eighteenth-Century Critical Essays* the *Praelectiones Poeticae* (1711–19) of Joseph Trapp, whom he finds 'a dull poet and an unoriginal critic', because as Oxford's first Professor of Poetry Trapp was 'the first professional academic critic' (p. ix).) Yet even historians professedly seeking the origins of modernity differ about whether 'modern' criticism emerges in the late seventeenth century (with the 'Enlightenment' itself), or in the course of the eighteenth (with new institutional arrangements such as authorship as a paying profession, periodicals as vehicles for criticism, and university posts in literary fields), or only after and because of eighteenth-century developments (such as the invention of 'aesthetics' or the breakdown of an eighteenth-century 'public sphere' of social, including critical, discourse).

And it is here most of all, we should note, that the fact of varied national traditions complicates the historian's task, not merely in matters of dating (different rates of change in different countries). National traditions differ more profoundly than this: as Goldsmith argues in his *Enquiry into the Present State of Polite Learning in Europe* (1759), in a chapter entitled 'The polite learning of England and France incapable of comparison', 'if criticism be at all requisite to promote the interests of learning, its rules should be taken from among the inhabitants, and adapted to the genius and temper of the country it attempts to refine' (*Works*, I, pp. 294–5). We are only beginning, for instance, to understand the different political motivations and effects of what in eighteenth-century Britain was a discourse of 'taste', serving there a vision of civil society, and what in the German states was 'aesthetics', serving as Howard Caygill argues in his *Art of Judgement* a very different vision of the state. In the remainder of this introduction I shall examine two moments of transition in conceptions of criticism and the critic: the first in the opening years of the century, which take us from John Dennis to Addison and Pope; the second in the years after mid-century, the era of Goldsmith and Johnson. These transitions occur first in Britain, but analogues can be found in France and Germany. In the first, an older, more court-centred and rationalist criticism gives way, under the pressure of a new, sensationalist theory of taste (elaborated especially by Joseph Addison and the Abbé Du Bos), to a broader-based empirical inquiry, one that by qualifying the critic in terms of 'taste' – a sensation potentially present in all – extends the literary 'public' beyond the realms of scholarship and the court to include what in *Spectator* 592 Addison called the 'Town', and Du Bos in his *Réflexions critiques* (1719) called the 'parterre'. In the second, the critical 'public' again contracts: under such pressures as an explosion of new publication and a consequent sharpening of distinctions between 'high' and 'low' literature, the qualifications of the critic again become stringently exclusive in something like the old manner: the critic must once again be either scholar or member of a new quasi-aristocracy of 'fine taste'.

II

What does it mean to be a critic in the eighteenth century? In Britain John Dennis was widely hailed in the first decade of the century as, in Giles Jacob's words, 'the greatest Critick of this Age'; in an anonymous book of 1704 called *The Tryal of Skill* he was nicknamed 'the Critick', and the label stuck. Like most writers of his time, however, Dennis engaged a vast range of subjects and genres – he produced pamphlets and treatises on matters historical, political, religious, and naval, as well as' plays, poems, translations, and works of criticism; but he could not live on the proceeds of publication, depending instead on frequent acts of patronage (from an equally wide range of individuals, from peers to fellow writers) and the small sinecure of a waitership in the customs (worth £52 a year). In 1702 he provides the century's first list of the qualifications of the critic, in a letter to George Granville published as *A Large Account of the Taste in Poetry, and the Causes of Degeneracy of It*:

> This, I think, Sir, need not be disputed, that for the judging of any sort of Writings, those talents are in some measure requisite, which were necessary to produce them . . . Now there are three things required for the succeeding in Poetry: 1. Great parts. 2. A generous Education. 3. A due Application . . . But now, as Parts, Education, and Application are necessary to succeed in the writing Poetry, they are requisite in some degree for the forming a true judgment of it.
>
> (*Works*, I, p. 290)

We should note here first of all that the critic as Dennis characterizes him is not necessarily a *writer*. As one of his enemies pointed out, Dennis was in the habit of sharpening his arguments by developing them orally, 'at the head of a Club' – a coffeehouse gathering such as David Fordyce had in mind when he wrote in 1745 that 'we are of all nations the most forward to run into clubs, parties, and societies'.[16] So too when Pope complains in the *Essay on Criticism* of those new-hatched swarms of critics who plague the modern poet, he can hardly have publishing critics in mind; his references to the act of criticism suggest not written but oral communication, whether in pit, coffeehouse, or polite social gathering. Many of Dennis's critical works, furthermore, though written, originate as letters to friends – to Henry Cromwell ('Of Simplicity in Poetical Compositions'), to Matthew Prior (*Upon the Roman Satirists*), to William Congreve (on Ben Jonson, to which Congreve replies with a letter 'Concerning Humor in Comedy') – letters written for some circulation, but not all for print. (Collections of such letters comprise some of the century's first books of criticism, such as Abel Boyer's *Letters of Wit, Politicks and Morality* (1701), and provide as well a model for later collections such as the *Spectator*.) Criticism might find its way into print mimicking the forms of polite speech in dialogue form, as in Dryden's only independent critical work, *Of Dramatic Poesy* (1668), and Dennis's first, *The Impartial Critick* (1693). Criticism in 1700, then, is a social act, one branch of what the age called 'polite conversation' – as it remains in large part through the time of Johnson.

---

[16] Dennis, *Works*, II, p. xxv; Fordyce, *Education*, pp. 60–1.

As participants in an ongoing polite conversation, critics must at least affect the forms of polite discourse, rejecting 'method' with its air of the schools, of French rationalism, and particularly its implied claim of special expertise. The ideal critic, like Pope's Horace, 'without Method *talks* us into Sense' (*Essay on Criticism*, l. 654). Thus Bouhours sets his *Art of Criticism* in the polite locale of a country house, and casts it not as 'a Treatise' but in the 'free and easy manner' of a dialogue ('To the Reader'). Thus is enacted the *Spectator*'s project to bring 'Philosophy out of Closets and Libraries, Schools and Colleges, to dwell in Clubs and Assemblies, at Tea-Tables, and in Coffee-Houses' (*Spectator*, 10 (1711)), and Shaftesbury's of freeing philosophy from the learned tome. Dennis and even Rymer strike this pose often, though a later generation will include them under Addison's censure that 'There is nothing so tiresome as the Works of those Criticks, who write in a positive Dogmatick way.'[17] In criticism as in poetry, 'politeness' fosters short rather than long works (Dennis's most ambitious plan for a critical treatise failed when it found only seventy-seven subscribers, and so dwindled into *The Grounds of Criticism in Poetry* (1704)). Through much of the century treatises must affect not to be treatises, as when Trapp casts his *Lectures* – 'Read', as the title goes on to tell us, 'in the Schools of Natural Philosophy at Oxford' – as individual conversations. Trapp promises especially to avoid the academic vice of learned long-windedness: 'For *Brevity as such* (to use the Language of the Schoolmen) and considered in its own Nature, is by no means a Fault; but rather an Excellence' (p. v; thus does pedantry deny pedantry when even the phrase *per se* is suspect). Even after mid-century, when the polite critic has become the teacher and scholar, Kames announces at the start of his long and systematic *Elements of Criticism* (1762): 'What the author has collected upon that subject, he chooses to impart in the gay and agreeable form of criticism; imagining that this form will be more relished, and perhaps be no less instructive, than a regular and labored disquisition' (I, p. 17). For by mid-century, as Goldsmith complains in his *Enquiry* (having established that in France, the love of system has damaged taste), the critic as scholar has invaded even that vehicle by which Addison had taught a nation politeness, the periodicals:

The most diminutive son of fame, or of famine, has his *we* and his *us*, his *firstlys* and his *secondlys* as methodical, as if bound in cow-hide, and closed with clasps of brass. Were these Monthly Reviewers frothy, pert, or absurd,

---

[17] Addison, *Spectator* 253 (1711). Rymer begins *The Tragedies of the Last Age* ('in a Letter to Fleetwood Shepheard, Esq.') (1677): 'And you know I am not cut out for writing a *Treatise*, nor have a *genius* to *pen* anything *exactly*' (*Works*, p. 21). Among recent works on politeness in the period, see Pocock, *Virtue*; France, *Politeness*; Klein, *Shaftesbury and Politeness*; Staves, 'Refinement'; and Woodman, *Politeness*.

they might find some pardon; but to be dull and dronish, is an
encroachment on the prerogative of a folio.

(I, pp. 304–5)

The critic as Dennis describes him, secondly, need not be a poet
himself. Rather, Dennis is concerned to establish the reverse, that 'there
never was a great Poet in the World, who was not an accomplished
Critick' (I, p. 197). Dryden and Pope would press the ancient claim –
'Let such teach others who themselves excell, / And *censure freely* who
have *written well*' – partly (like Dennis) to suggest the continuity of the
two roles (in both the shared knowledge and shared social space of
author and qualified reader), but partly also to distance themselves from
and buttress their authority against unworthy opponents, especially that
growing number of critics who set up not as the muses' handmaids but
in the independent business of judging for themselves.[18] Dennis's own
poetry of course gave him no such claim to authority, even had he
wished for it. But more important, Dennis's critic is first of all a judge,
a man of taste qualified to judge particular works by his natural ability
('parts') and 'generous' education. Membership in the republic of taste,
in the polite realm, is in principle open to all. According to Hume, 'The
general principles of taste are uniform in human nature'; thus Burke
can write, 'the true standard of the arts is in every man's power', and
Bouhours, 'The humblest Man in the World is touched with these Beauties as much as any Body else, provided that he understands them, and
is able to relish them.'[19]

The very nature of criticism as the eighteenth century understands it,
then, places the critic and the question of his qualifications at the centre
of attention. Criticism – the response of taste – is ability in judgement:
when Bouhours's *Manière de bien penser dans les ouvrages d'esprit*
(1687) is translated into English, it becomes *The Art of Criticism* (1705).
Whether in the more rationalist model of Dennis, Shaftesbury's theory
of an internal sense, or Pope's effort to harmonize all alternatives, criticism has standards (the 'rules') – the republic of taste is no anarchy –
but these are internal to taste itself; as Goldsmith says in the *Enquiry*,
'English taste, like English liberty, should be restrained only by laws of
its own making' (p. 295), while for Dennis, man's 'Mind is a Law to
itself' (I, p. 202). Writers throughout the century make clear that Homer
and Aristotle (or whoever one chooses) are authorities because they

---

[18] For accounts of the proper relation of critics to poets, see Dryden, *Essays*, I,
p. 225, and Pope's complaint about the corruption of that relation in *Criticism*,
ll. 100–17; Dennis takes exception to these views, defending the critic's
independence, in *Works*, II, pp. 398–9.

[19] Hume, *Works*, III, p. 280; Burke, *Enquiry*, p. 54; Bouhours, *Art*, p. 32.

embody or have come to understand the rules, not vice versa. Had Homer not pleased many and long, or Aristotle not seemed to codify shared responses, neither would enjoy such status; the final court of appeal for both is not any particular formulation of the rules, but taste itself. Necessarily then the nature of criticism can be ascertained in no other way than through inquiry into the identity of the critic. This is why Pope concludes *An Essay on Criticism* not with abstract principles but 'rules for the Conduct of Manners in a Critic', including especially a 'Character of a good Critic'. Differing judgements can be validated by no external authority, but only according to criticism's internal demands (the demands of taste), and so can only be more or less 'educated' or 'cultivated', more or less 'impartial' or 'disinterested' (free from external constraint) – more or less in conformity with taste (or politeness) itself. Writers of the late seventeenth and eighteenth centuries thus ask more often than ever before, do we like what we should? In other words, are we what we should be? Do we meet the qualifications of the critic?

What finally the critic should be, as all these formulations suggest, is a *gentleman*. The point becomes clear when Dennis unpacks what he means by the critic's third qualification, 'due Application': not labour of any kind, but 'Leisure' and 'Serenity' – the critic as polite man of taste must 'have his mind free from all avocations of Business, and from all real vexatious Passions'. The *Large Account*, a contribution to the movement for reform that swept England in the years around 1700, closes with a socio-historical explanation for what Dennis sees as the decline of taste since the Restoration which starkly reveals his notion of the critic as gentleman of taste. In the better days of 'King *Charles* the Second', he writes, 'a considerable part of an Audience had that due application, which is requisite for the judging of Comedy':

They had first of all leisure to attend to it. For that was an age of Pleasure, and not of Business. They were serene enough to receive its impressions: for they were in Ease and Plenty ... [And] they who had it not, were influenced by the Authority of those who had.

(p. 294)

But the present is 'a Reign of Politicks and Business', of 'Interest' and 'Faction': 'Younger brothers, Gentlemen born', no longer frequent the theatre, having 'been kept at home, by reason of the pressure of the Taxes', while their seats are taken by 'Foreigners' and unborn 'People, who made their Fortunes in the last War' – uneducated folk not properly 'influenced' by 'Authority'. Even the gentry who remain have lost their critical credentials: 'want throws them upon employments, and there are ten times more Gentlemen now in business, than there were in King *Charles* his Reign'.

Dennis is not alone in his conception of the critic as gentleman, however old-fashioned some of his social views must have seemed in 1702. All early eighteenth-century characterizations of the critic closely parallel, on the one hand, descriptions of the poet, and on the other, definitions of the 'gentleman' – efforts to define the latter being, as John Barrell has found, a persistent concern in early Augustan writing (appropriately so in a time of social change).[20] Thus Steele's 'fine Gentleman', characterized in *Guardian* 34 (1713), is cut on the model both of the true poet (the man of 'comprehensive soul' described by writers from Dryden through Johnson's Imlac) and of Dennis's true critic:

By a Fine Gentleman, I mean a Man compleatly qualify'd as well for the Service and Good, as for the Ornament and Delight, of Society. When I consider the Frame of Mind peculiar to a Gentleman, I suppose it graced with all the Dignity and Elevation of Spirit that Human Nature is capable of: To this I would have joined a clear Understanding, a Reason free from Prejudice, a steady Judgment, and an extensive Knowledge ... Besides the natural Endowments with which this distinguished Man is to be born, he must run through a long Series of Education. Before he makes his Appearance and shines in the World, he must be principled in Religion, instructed in all the moral Virtues, and led through the whole Course of the polite Arts and Sciences.

The gentleman's extensive knowledge has freed him from all merely partial views ('as a work is conducted under the influence of general ideas, or partial', writes Reynolds in his seventh *Discourse*, 'it is principally to be considered as the effect of a good or bad taste'). He has studied 'the polite Arts and Sciences', but as Barrell notes, he need not *practise* them (p. 38). In the same way, the critic need not (as did the Renaissance courtier) produce verse himself: as Trapp tells his university audience of 'Gentlemen of the most distinguish'd Wit, Birth, and good Manners', the 'Courtier' who appointed him professor 'knew, by Experience, that no Pleasure was equal to the reading ancient Poets, except that of imitating them. Happy they, that can partake of both; but the former ought to be the Employment of all, that desire to have any Taste for Letters, or Politeness' (p. 4). Taste (in the empirical tradition of Britain and France) is a receptive faculty (Goldsmith defines it as 'a capacity of *receiving* pleasure'); in its exercise the man of taste stands only as contemplative spectator (to use the term favoured from Addison and Shaftesbury to Adam Smith) – not producer but consumer.[21] But like Cincinnatus, the gentleman is qualified by what the exercise of taste has

---

[20] Barrell, *Literature*, pp. 17–51.
[21] Goldsmith, *Works*, I, p. 296; on the fate of the pruducer in the new economy of taste, see Caygill, *Judgement*, pp. 53–62.

taught him – by his disinterested, extensive views – to leave his estate behind in order more actively to serve civic virtue by leading the polity. Thus, too, Dennis's poet may serve the state, though such opportunity come perhaps only through patronage: 'For whenever a good Poet has laid aside Poetry for any other employment, he has seldom failed of succeeding in that employment, tho it has been of never so great importance' (I, p. 290).

Later in the century, when these equations will have become more difficult to sustain – when the critic has again become a scholar and the writer not part of any system of aristocratic patronage but visibly what in *Rambler* 93 Johnson calls a 'general challenger' in the literary marketplace (1751) – the faith Dennis expresses here will also fade. Goldsmith will write, 'Not that I think a writer incapable of filling an employment with dignity, I would only insinuate, that when made a bishop or a statesman, he will continue to please us as a writer no longer', and others that 'It is a prejudice now generally receiv'd, that men of letters are good for nothing but making books.'[22] But while the equations last, the critic can serve the same functions in civil society as does the properly qualified gentleman who leads it. Not only art but criticism can be conceived as structured by analogy with the state (as Addison's Spectator Club fosters discussion among representatives of all its enfranchised interests); not only the experience of art but also of criticism (such as the *Spectator*) can be understood as providing education in the values of that society. Literature, morals, and politics – to borrow the terms of Abel Boyer's title – will form a single, continuous polite realm, where the critic as much as the poet may range freely, a common ground from which both can assert, with a directness not possible since the eighteenth century, that their activities serve the state.

It is this vision of the critic's role in civil society that Terry Eagleton has in mind when he begins *The Function of Criticism*, expressing one of the most useful rediscoveries of its modern historians: 'Modern European criticism was born of a struggle against the absolutist state' (p. 9). In poetry as in politics, Peter Hohendahl explains, such criticism 'is based on the idea of restricting the power of authority through the concept of law' (p. 49), laws accessible to all qualified interpreters: 'Mind is a Law to itself.' In this new 'public sphere' carved out of the absolutist state, gentlemen of taste could govern themselves. Just as the societies for the reformation of manners which sprang up in England after 1688 appear to their modern historian Dudley Bahlman as 'signs of English freedom', 'of the withdrawal of the government from certain

---

[22] Goldsmith, *Works*, I, p. 308; L. A. de La Beaumelle, *Mes Pensées*, quoted in Goldsmith.

important aspects of life, allowing private persons and organizations to take on functions that might have been or had once been functions of the government' (*Moral Revolution*, pp. 106–7), Goldsmith can write in the *Enquiry*: 'An author may be considered a merciful substitute to the legislature' (pp. 313–14).[23]

Dennis's critic does not yet fully embody this Addisonian vision. By 1710, just a few years after the height of his fame, John Dennis appeared hopelessly old-fashioned, a man of the 1690s rather than of the new age. This was not because of any substantial disagreement the generation of Addison and Steele may have had with him over such matters as the evaluation of particular works or the need to reform England's religion and manners, but for the same reason he enters Pope's *Essay on Criticism* as Appius: Dennis now appeared impolite. Though he had rejected method, a new generation found him too methodic; though like Pope, Addison, and Steele, he had sought to rescue the name of 'critic' from its reputation of captious censoriousness, he now appeared just such a carping censor. Dennis had failed to keep pace with the progress of politeness, and in the new context his smallest critical gestures took on new social and political meaning. Beneath the gestures, there were his old-fashioned views of commerce and of the state.

To its lists of the qualifications of the critic, the new generation adds a characterization of the critic as 'companion' and 'friend' (not merely of poets but also of readers). The failed critic, Steele writes in *Tatler* 29 (1709), 'is never a Companion, but always a Censor'; according to the *Essay on Criticism*,

> 'Tis not enough, Taste, Judgment, Learning join;
> In all you speak, let Truth and Candor shine:
> That not alone what to your *Sense* is due,
> All may allow; but seek your *Friendship* too.
>
> (ll. 562–6)

Goldsmith captures the new qualification perfectly in a notice of the newly collected papers from *The Connoisseur. By Mr Town, Critic and Censor General*: 'This Writer may be stiled the *Friend* of Society, in the most agreeable acceptation of that term: For he rather converses with all the ease of a chearful companion, than dictates, as other Writers in this class have done, with the affected superiority of an Author': he is

---

[23] Under Germany's more stringent conditions of censorship, Schiller writes in an essay on 'Die Schaubühne als eine moralische Anstalt' (1784), 'The jurisdiction of the stage begins where the realm of secular law comes to an end' ('Die Gerichtsbarkeit der Bühne fängt an, wo das Gebiet der weltlichen Gesetze sich endigt') (*Werke*, V, p. 823).

'perfectly satyrical, but perfectly good natured' (I, p. 14). The critic as polite companion and friend engages in what Addison and Steele so often call the 'commerce' of conversation not from above but from within the social group he seeks to guide (another application of the principle of imitation as correction from within). If he teaches, it is only as Pope's critic does, by seeming to remind his audience of what it already knows:

> Men must be *taught* as if you *taught* them not;
> And Things *unknown* propos'd as Things *forgot*.
>
> (ll. 575–6)

An amateur speaking to fellow amateurs, his claim is not to expertise but good breeding (since, as Thomas Reid says, 'in matters which relate to human conduct, good taste and good breeding are the same'); since his authority stems from the shared values of the group of which he is part, his rhetorical pose even when writing a work such as *Elements of Criticism* is that of solidarity and consensus: 'the author assumes no merit for his performance, but that of evincing [his principles], perhaps more distinctly than has hitherto been done'. Even James Harris, for all his famous stiffness, yet manages to capture something of the pose: 'Indeed CRITICS (if I may be allowed a metaphor) are a sort of *Masters of the ceremony* in the Court of Letters, thro' whose Assistance we are introduced into some of the first and best company.'[24]

Dennis's critic may seem to employ these polite gestures, as when he addresses Granville in the *Large Account*: 'I am glad that this is addrest to a Gentleman, who needs only to be put in mind of this [and] who is perfectly well acquainted with *Horace* and *Boileau*'. But the encomium continues, explaining that such a reader as Granville understands that modern writers must like ancient address only a 'knowing few', a few whose cultural 'Authority' will come ultimately to 'influence' the 'many'. 'Few are qualified to judge of the greater poetry, but works which please the best judges will ultimately please all.' (Meanwhile, Horace and Boileau properly 'laugh at the taste of the Vulgar', including the vulgar of 'Rank'.) Dennis's critic speaks not from within but from above those whose taste he means to guide. He writes to the Earl of Mulgrave in dedicating *The Advancement and Reformation of Modern Poetry* (1701):

I should be wanting to that noble Cause, if I should Address myself to the Reader in general; and I should be thought by all discerning Persons to proceed as absurdly, as would a Lawyer, who upon a solemn Pleading,

---

[24] Reid, *Lectures*, p. 47; Kames, *Elements*, I, p. 16; Harris, *Inquiries*, I, p. 38.

should apply himself to the Multitude, who have little Knowledge of his Affair, and no Authority to determine it; instead of speaking to his Awful Judge, who has a perfect Knowledge of his Cause, and a Sovereign Authority to decide it.

(I, pp. 199–200)

Prefatory comments such as this do more than enlist patrons in critical combat; they make clear that criticism is itself a form of combat. The critic's polite gestures take on meaning only within a structure of 'Authority', a structure capable of providing some assurance that the views of the 'best judges' will have their proper 'influence'. And the only state of affairs Dennis can conceive as providing such assurance is one in which authority is maintained congruently in the realm of taste and in the state. The realm of taste is thus properly no republic but an aristocracy, a hierarchy ruled ideally by the taste of its monarch (the *Large Account* ends by celebrating the superior taste of Charles II). Modern writers should imitate Horace and Boileau, who 'directed their writings to the knowing few, and were neither exalted by the approbation, nor dejected by the censure of the rest' (p. 288) – that is, they should participate in a system of aristocratic patronage, 'free from all avocations of Business', which according to the familiar model can only corrupt both taste and the state. Where superior reason and the hierarchic embodiments of taste fail, finally, there is always force: *The Grounds of Criticism in Poetry* begins by seeking 'an effectual way of Reconciling People to a Regulated Stage' (I, p. 325).

Addison, Steele, and the younger Pope do not speak this way because their conceptions of politeness and taste – and so of the critic – exist within, take their meaning from, a new conception of civil society and hence of the state, one founded in large part on a rethinking of the nature and role of 'commerce'. A. O. Hirschman and others have traced a shift from the seventeenth century's notion of what was called (by Colbert and Josiah Child, respectively) 'perpetual combat' and 'a kind of warfare' to an eighteenth-century *doux commerce*, a system of exchange in which, as William Robertson writes in his *View of the Progress of Society in Europe* (1769), 'Commerce . . . softens and polishes the manners of men'. Providence has made us in such a way that commerce can be reconciled with, indeed be the engine of virtue, apart from (and even by restraining) the powers of the state.[25] It is within this reconception of commerce, as the site no longer of Dennis's 'vexatious Passions' but of Hutcheson's benign 'calm passion', that early eighteenth-century accounts of the formative power of 'polite conversation' and of the critic

[25] See Hirschman, *Passions* (the passages cited appear on pp. 79, 61), and Pocock, *Virtue*.

as 'friend' should be understood.[26] The most influential early exponent of these views in England was Shaftesbury, whose *Characteristicks* (1705–11) proposes free exchange – 'liberty' – as everywhere the 'hinge and bottom' of social progress, 'Liberty in Thought and Action' as a mechanism of healthy self-regulation in the arts as in the state:

When the free spirit of a nation turns itself this way, judgments are formed; critics arise; the public ear and eye improve; a right taste prevails, and in a manner forces its way. Nothing is so improving, nothing so natural, so congenial to the liberal arts, as that reigning liberty and high spirit of a people, which from the habit of judging in the highest matters for themselves, makes them freely judge of other subjects, and enter thoroughly into the characters as well of men and manners, as of the products or works of men, in art and science.[27]

Not stable relations of authority – Dennis's 'Serenity' – but social tensions rendered peaceful and productive through the mechanisms of commerce serve taste and the state, and so Shaftesbury initiates (and later writers such as Thomson and Akenside develop) a critic of aristocratic patronage – not of patronage misplaced or misused, but of the institution itself.[28]

But of course Shaftesbury's (and Addison's) 'public sphere' does not comprehend the nation as a whole any more than Dennis's does. Taste is not a republic. In his English embodiment, the gentleman of taste appears always to bear the imprint of 1688. 'English taste, like English liberty, should be restrained only by laws of its own making', but as John Cannon has argued, 'affirmation of the liberal and open nature of English society' could in practice serve as 'one of the most potent ways by which the aristocracy reinforced its privileged position' (*Aristocratic Century*, p. ix). (Even the reformation societies depended on a system of magistrates, informers, and blank warrants.) Enfranchisement in the realm of taste, though a new vision of civil society allows it to be extended, remains limited. Few theorists allow women a vote.[29] And as Kames writes in *The Elements of Criticism*, having first argued like Hume that taste is 'rooted in human nature, and governed by principles common to all men',

Those who depend for food on bodily labor are totally devoid of taste, of such a taste as can be of use in the fine arts. This consideration bars the greater part of mankind; and of the remaining part, many by corrupted taste

[26] Hutcheson, *Works*, V, p. 12; on Steele's elaboration of polite companionship, see Leites, 'Good humor'.
[27] Shaftesbury, *Letters*, p. 449; *Second Characters*, pp. 22–3.
[28] See Meehan, *Liberty*, for Shaftesbury and his influence.
[29] See especially Barrell, *Painting*, pp. 63–8.

are unqualified for voting. The common sense of mankind must be confined
to the few that fall not under these exemptions.

(I, p. 7; III, p. 369)

Taste, like gentility, may depend more than ever before on ability and
education rather than birth, but as has often been pointed out, only
some elements in society can afford to take a 'disinterested' view of the
objects that surround them (or, in Hume's and Goldsmith's variant, to
survey all their uses). 'Only when need is satisfied', Kant puts the point
gently in the third *Critique*, 'can we decide who among the many does
or does not have taste.'[30]

III

Eighteenth-century critics were well aware that in writing history they
traced their own genealogy. In that mid-century nationalist movement
of revisionist literary history by which Milton's *Paradise Lost* came to
be reclassified as a Renaissance rather than an Augustan poem (as a
work of a previous age rather than of that of Dryden and Pope), poet-
critics such as Gray and the Wartons sought to align themselves with
what they thought to be a literary tradition both native and 'universal',
but distinct from the intervening era of practices imported from France.[31]
In the historical catalogue of previous authorities with which *An Essay
on Criticism* closes (including finally his own teachers and friends, and
last the author himself), Pope explains and justifies himself – provides
his own qualifications as a critic. (A modified version of this procedure
will govern the opening chapters of Coleridge's *Biographia Literaria*.)
Yet when twentieth-century scholars look back to the eighteenth for its
own histories of criticism, such self-identifications are often overlooked;
the scholar does not recognize histories of criticism which are embedded
in other genres, or which present themselves in other than a scholarly
guise. Thus we often hear that eighteenth-century criticism did not write
its own history: no Augustan left a book on the subject. (Dr Johnson
projected one, but never wrote it.) Perhaps the only history of criticism
unambiguously recognizable as such by modern eyes is to be found in
James Harris's *Upon the Rise and Progress of Criticism* (1752), Part I
of which announces itself as 'an investigation into the Rise and different

---

[30] 'Nur wenn das Bedürfnis befriedigt ist, kann man unterscheiden, wer unter vielen
Geschmack habe, oder nicht.' *Schriften*, V, p. 210.

[31] See Patey, 'The canon', and Hurd, 'On the Idea of a Universal Poetry', in *Works*,
II, pp. 1–26; on the political context of this revisionary history, see Newman,
Nationalism, ch. 5.

Species of CRITICISM and CRITICS'. Harris's account deserves attention not as a unique historical effort (which it is not), but for what it shows us of the mid-century transformation of the Augustan critic from polite gentleman back into teacher and scholar, and some of the contradictions that transformation brought with it.

Harris locates the ground on which he himself stands by distinguishing roles that in the previous century had been equivalent – by identifying himself not as a critic but a philologist: 'PHILOLOGY should hence appear to be of a most *comprehensive* character, and to include not only all Accounts both of *Criticism* and *Critics*, but of every thing connected with *Letters*, be it *Speculative* or *Historical*' (*Inquiries*, p. 3). His gesture here is different from that of Hobbes a century before, who in his 'Answer' to Davenant had distinguished the 'critic', the judge of particular works, from the 'philosopher', who is in a position to analyse in general 'the Nature and differences of Poesy'. Hobbes's 'philosophical' concerns have become firmly part of criticism itself (p. 54). Rather, in subsuming criticism in a larger 'philology', Harris identifies himself as a scholar rather than a gentleman critic in the Addisonian mould, and as someone able to stand outside the activity of criticism in order to survey its history.[32]

Modifying Bacon's account in *The Advancement of Learning*, Harris divides criticism into three types, in the order of their emergence: 'philosophical', 'historical', and 'corrective' criticism. In the beginning, there were only authors; from the social process of recitation and response arose the first and most general kind of criticism: 'HERE therefore we have the RISE and ORIGIN of CRITICISM, which in its beginning was a deep and philosophical Search into the primary Laws and Elements of good Writing [what Harris elsewhere calls 'the rules'], as far as they could be collected from the most approved Performances.' Such criticism is philosophical in that it searches into causes: 'This led them at once into the most curious of subjects; the nature of *Man* in general; the *different characters of Men* . . . their *Reason* and their *Passions*' (p. 7). Criticism is born with rhetoric, but Harris means more than this; he goes on to censure most ancient philosophical critics for their excessive concern with oratory. Rather, Harris believes with those writers from Thomas Blackwell and John ('Estimate') Brown to the Scots 'philosophical historians' that all learning was born originally in poetry, and that the various disciplines separated from it and from each other by a kind of (what Mandeville was the first to call) division of labour. As

---

[32] In 1776 George Campbell also makes 'criticism' a branch of 'philology', which he defines as including 'history, civil, ecclesiastic and literary: grammar, languages, jurisprudence and criticism' (*Rhetoric*, p. 56). On the fortunes of 'philology' in the decades to follow, see Burrow, 'Philology'.

Blackwell wrote in his *Letters on Mythology* (1748), 'POETRY, PHILOSO-PHY and LEGISLATION, originally conjoined in one and the same Person, came in a few Generations to be separated into three different Charac-ters' (p. 294); Harris follows the genealogy to the birth of criticism.

When he comes to list the 'modern' masters of philosophical criti-cism, Harris cites Vida and the elder Scaliger, and from France, Rapin, Boileau, Le Bossu, and Bouhours. The English tradition does not reach back before the Restoration (before the influence of continental mod-els): here Harris cites only Mulgrave's *Essay upon Poetry* (1692), Ros-common's *Essay on Translated Verse* (1684), Shaftesbury's *Advice to an Author* (1710), and Pope's *Essay on Criticism*. (To this list he later adds Reynolds's *Discourses on Art*, the first seven of which had been pub-lished in 1778, to show 'that all *the liberal arts* in their Principles are congenial'.) Harris's list seems remarkable mainly for its omissions. No writers after Pope appear, no Burke or Kames or Johnson; but by philo-sophical criticism Harris means what we would call literary theory, and his list proposes to us a list of founders; such omissions are testimony to his sense that by about 1710 a distinct tradition of critical theory had been established in England, upon which later critics provide only vari-ations. Like Pope (whose catalogue contains no Briton before Roscom-mon), Harris omits Dryden, presumably because the genres in which Dryden's criticism is embedded make him appear to Harris no theorist; Harris died before Johnson established Dryden in his *Life* of the poet (1779) as 'the father of English criticism' (*Lives*, I, p. 410). And like nearly all Augustan historians, finally, Harris omits native works writ-ten before 1660, works he knew well such as Jonson's *Timber* and Puttenham's *Arte of English Poesie*: these works appear to Harris part of a different tradition, one not 'philosophical'.[33]

Harris's 'second Species' of criticism, the historical, includes (as he explains in the expanded *Rise and Progress* published in his posthumous *Philological Inquiries* (1781)) 'the tribe of *Scholiasts, Commentators,* and *Explainers*'. These roles emerged even in antiquity, as a result of time itself: because of changes in language and customs, old texts grew dark. Among great modern works of historical criticism Harris instances John Upton's edition of Spenser (1758), Addison's *Spectator* papers on *Paradise Lost* (1712), and Joseph Warton's *Essay on the Genius and Writings of Pope* (the first volume of which had appeared in 1756). Such a varied list of works, and their place as examples of the 'second Species' of criticism, suggest two of Harris's fundamental principles: that concern for individual authors and texts takes place within the context of a tradition of critical theory (of 'philosophical' criticism), and that within

---

[33] George Dyer provides a contemporary discussion of Harris's concept of 'philosophical criticism', in *Poetics* (1812), II, pp. 86–92.

this tradition the interpretation and evaluation of individual works are matters of scholarship, acts of 'historical' criticism. Harris goes on to include in the same category such other kinds of historical critics as 'the Compilers of *Lexicons* and *Dictionaries*' (most notably Johnson), 'Authors upon *Grammar*', 'Writers of *Philological Epistles*', and 'Writers of *Library Catalogues*' (works such as Johnson's on the Harleian library), as well as translators, whose work is also 'a Species of Explanation'. It is from this large second branch of criticism that Harris traces his own genealogy, citing among its modern exemplars his own relatives, teachers, and friends.

By 'corrective', Harris means what we call textual criticism. Its main instrument is 'collation'; it may equally be called 'authoritative' criticism (it yields us authors). Its abuse is 'Conjecture', wherein the editor – Harris cites Bentley's Milton – indulges in 'intemperate excess', not restoring his author but vaingloriously giving 'a testimony to the Editor and his Art'. This whole history of criticism ends with a paean to critics as preservers of knowledge, transmitters of wisdom: 'were it not for their acute and learned labours, we should be in danger of degenerating into an age of dunces' (p. 38). Thus the old sense of literature as erudition persists, although nearly all the particular texts Harris cites are 'literary' in the newer sense; Harris's criticism is very much, in fact if not in name, *literary* criticism.

Harris's history has the merit of taking into account most of the term's historical applications: grammar and textual editing (what the previous century called indifferently 'grammar' and 'criticism'); judgement of individual authors and works; critical theory. By 1781 a new and varied institution of criticism had become sufficiently established and familiar for its historian to have no difficulty recognizing it, knowing what it is. Thus Harris need no longer address such questions as the relation between critic and poet, or the critic's qualifications; the critic is a scholar. But this confidence is won only at a price: Harris's history is not really a history. All three of his species of criticism, he admits, emerged in antiquity; all criticism's history occurred then, and events since have been simply the national migrations of these timeless categories. Thus Harris can be as confident that his tradition in criticism is the only one, the true one – he has no trouble excluding Jonson and Puttenham from the ranks of philosophical critics – as he is of the canon of England's greatest authors as delivered by the philosophical critic to the historical (he lists 'our capital authors': Shakespeare, Milton, Cowley, Pope (p. 25)). Like the identity of criticism itself, these are timeless truths. Now that philosophical criticism has come to England and settled fundamental issues – including issues of value – the practising critic becomes a historical scholar. Thus the way is open to criticism as Herder would conceive it, as that branch of history which unfolds the inner meaning of particular works (criticism as interpretation), and as well to that new distinction pioneered by the later eighteenth century between critical and another kind of reading, what we call 'appreciation'.[34]

To put the point another way: there is a contradiction in how Harris locates himself in relation to the developments he traces. Is he part of the unfolding of events (as would appear from his genealogy as a critic of the second species), or is he above and outside them – is he philologist or (historical) critic? Dilemmas of this sort, concerning what possible vantage the surveyor can take on complex systems of which he is himself part, become pressing in the later eighteenth century as society itself comes to be understood as a whole too complex for any single element within it (and shaped by it) to comprehend.[35] The gentleman can no longer be understood as capable of taking an extensive and impartial view of the whole by virtue of his social position – a position which supposedly frees him from such shaping; it is the later eighteenth century's hope that such vision may, however, be the possession of the scholar – what the next century would call the 'intellectual'. (Scholarly surveys tend to be lengthy, and so the major critical works of the later eighteenth century tend to much greater length than those of the earlier.) Some students of society such as Adam Ferguson and Adam Smith may have been aware that this critique of the gentleman applied equally to themselves – that they no more than he could claim independent vision; but most were not so troubled. Harris is typical here. He 'solves' the problem of his contradictory vantage – or rather avoids it – through the same kind of cultural confidence that had secured the gentleman in his taste: through a confidence that the interests of his part and of the whole are fundamentally the same. Historical criticism can rely on the truths of philosophical criticism, which it in turn embodies. And, to repeat, Harris can make this equation, can feel this confidence, because by 1781 the institution of criticism has become a recognizable social formation.

If James Harris looks forward historically, embracing the transformation of critic into scholar (and eventually intellectual), Oliver Goldsmith looks backward, mourning scholarly intrusions into what he wishes to preserve as the polite realm of taste. The *Enquiry into the Present State of Polite Learning* seeks to explain what after mid-century was widely perceived to be another decline in English taste by reference to the transformation of critic into scholar, which Goldsmith further links

---

[34] On Herder and on the split between 'critical' and 'appreciative' reading (which first clearly appears in England in Archibald Alison's *Essays on Taste* of 1790), see Hohendahl, *Institution*, pp. 56–8, Berghahn, 'Classicist to classical,' pp. 72–3, and Patey, 'The canon', p. 24.

[35] See Barrell, *Literature*, pp. 17–51.

with the spread of what he calls 'the profession of an author' (p. 314) as part of the economic marketplace.[36] Yet the same contradictions emerge in both: while Harris writes history that is not really history, Goldsmith writes criticism that claims not to be criticism: 'I have assumed the critic only to dissuade from criticism' (p. 317).

Joseph Warton might well have Goldsmith in mind when he observes in the *Essay on Pope*, defending his own practice as a historical critic, 'The dread of pedantry is a characteristic folly of the present age' (II, p. 127), while Goldsmith may equally have Warton in his eye when he describes in the *Enquiry* how the critics of his age have turned 'pedants':

To acquire a character for learning among the English at present it is necessary to know much more than is either important or useful. The absurd passion of being deemed profound, has done more injury to all kinds of science, than is generally imagined. Some thus exhaust their natural sagacity in exploring the intricacies of another man's thought ... others have carried on learning from that stage, where the good sense of our ancestors thought it too minute or too speculate to instruct or to amuse.

(p. 306)

Turned pedant, the critic can no longer fulfil the offices of taste:

The ingenious Mr Hogarth used to assert, that every one, except the connoisseur, was a judge of painting. The same may be asserted of writing; the public in general set the whole piece in the proper point of view; the critic lays his eye close to all its minutenesses, and condemns or approves in detail. And this may be the reason why so many writers at present are apt to appeal from the tribunal of criticism to that of the people.   (p. 318)

Pedantry – microscopic attention rather than extensive views – rushes in where politeness does not receive proper encouragement: 'When the link between patronage and learning was entire, then all who deserved fame were in a capacity of attaining it ... The middle ranks of mankind, who generally imitate the Great, then followed their example ... But this link now seems entirely broken' (pp. 310–11). Addison's great educational scheme has succeeded only too well: there has emerged a large and diverse reading public (what in a few years Francis Jeffrey will

---

[36] On the popularity of such views in Britain from mid-century onward, see Plumb, 'The public'. I take Goldsmith's *Enquiry* as my example precisely because, as William Kenrick said of it in the *Monthly Review*, it consists 'of little else ... than trite commonplace observations' (quoted in Goldsmith, *Works*, I, p. 247). Among recent studies of eighteenth-century authorship in the marketplace, see (for Britain): Kernan, *Printing Technology*; Rose, *Authors and Owners*; (for Germany): Woodmansee, *The Author, Art, and the Market*, and McCarthy, 'Art of reading'; (for France): John Lough, *Writer and Public*; Robert Darnton, *Literary Underground* and *Revolution*.

call in a significant plural 'the reading classes'),[37] which has in turn helped to generate too many writers, too many, that is, of the wrong social alignments (lacking polite taste): 'If tradesmen happen to want skill in conducting their own business, yet they are able to write a book; if mechanics want money, or ladies shame, they write books and solicit subscriptions.' Thus the very extension of taste to a wide public damages taste; and it does so by its extension of those very mechanisms Addison himself employed – by turning from patronage to the marketplace in periodical publications:

> The author, when unpatronized by the Great, has naturally recourse to the bookseller. There cannot be, perhaps, imagined a combination more prejudicial to taste than this. It is the interest of the one to allow as little time for writing, and of the other to write as much as possible; accordingly, tedious compilations, and periodical magazines, are the result of their joint endeavours. In these circumstances, the author bids adieu to fame [and] writes for bread ... A long habitude of writing for bread, thus turns the ambition of every author at last to avarice ... he despairs of applause, and turns to profit ... Thus the man who under the protection of the Great, might have done honour to human nature, when only patronized by the bookseller, becomes a thing little superior to the fellow who works at the press.
>
> (p. 316)

Of course, Goldsmith does not see that it has been the very success of the programme of taste that has led to this state of affairs, any more than he sees the contradiction between condemning those hacks who 'write for the public' and his claim that when critics turn pedants, there will be an 'appeal from the tribunal of criticism to that of the people'. The 'public' – the reading public – has become too diverse for any easy identification of education with taste such as the Abbé Du Bos could stipulate earlier in the century when he wrote in his *Réflexions critiques* (1719), 'The word "public" here includes only those persons who have acquired enlightenment'; Dr Johnson will speak more circumspectly than Goldsmith of 'an appeal open from criticism to *nature*'.[38] The critic who disclaims criticism, who prefers the polite discourse of 'agreeable trifling' to modern 'solemnity' (p. 319), does not see any contradiction when he writes of the proper qualifications of the critic:

> Some such law should be enacted in the republic of letters, as we find take place in the house of commons. As no man there can shew his wisdom,

[37] Quoted in Eagleton, *Criticism*, p. 49.

[38] Du Bos, II, p. 351 ('Le mot de publique ne renferme ici que les personnes qui ont acquis des lumières' – in contrast to 'le bas peuple'); Johnson, Preface to Shakespeare (1765; *Works*, VII, p. 67). On the political significance of Du Bos's construction of the 'public', see Kaiser, 'Rhetoric'.

unless first qualified by three hundred pounds a year, so none here should profess gravity, unless his work amounted to three hundred pages.

(p. 320)

Nor can Goldsmith see any way to arrest the decline of taste but to exhort 'gentleman writers', as he does at the conclusion of his chapter 'Upon criticism', to exert their 'power to lead the taste of the times' (p. 322). But the rhetorical space in which such reforming gentlemen-critics must now stand inevitably differs from that occupied by the earlier eighteenth-century 'companion' and 'friend':

The man of taste, however, stands ... in a middle station, between the world and the cell, between learning and common sense. He teaches the vulgar on what part of a character to lay emphasis of praise, and the scholar where to point his application so as to deserve it. By this means, even the philosopher, acquires popular applause ...

(p. 306)

Neither common sense nor learning ('philosophy') is any longer the distinctive property of the man of taste or of the class he represents. Goldsmith's critic is first of all a *teacher*, a member now neither of that public he must instruct nor of the world of scholarship he must mediate to it. His is the posture of a Hugh Blair, initiating generations of Scotsmen into British culture through a course of *Lectures in Rhetoric and Belles Lettres* (1783), or more famously of a Johnson – though Johnson, with his high valuation of 'labour', his defence of the 'innocent employment' of commerce, and celebration of the writer as labourer in the literary marketplace, manages even more impressively to embody the roles both of teacher and scholar. (In the years after publishing the *Enquiry* – by the time of *The Vicar of Wakefield* (1766) – Goldsmith has himself come round to Johnson's point of view.)[39] As mediator (even popularizer), this new, un-Addisonian critic is the parent of the nineteenth-century

[39] Hirsch gives a useful account of Blair's cultural purposes in *Literacy*, pp. 84–7. On Johnson's 'innocent' commerce and celebration of the business of authorship, see Hirschman, *Passions*, pp. 57–8; Parrinder, *Authors*, pp. 27f.; and Kernan, *Printing Technology*; for Goldsmith's eventual acceptance of such views, see *The Vicar*, ch. 19.
     Mark Rose has made clear that it was partly in the context of the debate on copyright, culminating in the decision of *Donaldson v. Becket* (1774), that authorship fully won public recognition as a species of economic labour. Whereas Edward Young could still in his *Conjectures on Original Composition* (1759) distinguish 'imitations' from 'original' works on the ground that the former are merely 'a sort of *Manufacture* wrought up by ... *Labour*', in the debate culminating in *Donaldson* literature came to be construed as a market commodity subject to appropriate legal protections because it qualified as property on traditional Lockean grounds: like other workers, the writer – as Locke put it in the *Two Treatises of Government* – 'hath mixed his *Labour* with, and joyned to it something that is his own, and thereby makes it his *Property*' (Rose, *Authors*, ch. 1).

quarterly reviewer. And in the tensions of his twin roles as teacher and scholar we can trace much of the critical persona's fortunes since the eighteenth century.

Analogues of our two moments of change in the institution of criticism may be found throughout Europe in the eighteenth century. The first transition, that which separates Addison from Dennis, occurs clearly in France when in his *Réflexions critiques* (1719) Du Bos espouses Addison's sensationalist account of taste (with its consequent widening of the critical 'public'); it is visible later in Germany, in the transition from the generation of Bodmer, Breitinger, and Gottsched to that of Lessing and Friedrich Nicolai. The earlier generation instructed from above through treatises, such as Gottsched's *Versuch einer Critischen Dichtkunst* (1730) and Breitinger's *Critische Dichtkunst* (1740); the later one opposes such 'system' (as Lessing explains at the conclusion of his *Hamburgische Dramaturgie* (1767–9)), favouring instead more conversational genres such as letters, as in the *Briefe, die neueste Literatur betreffend* (1759–65) edited by Lessing, Nicolai, and Moses Mendelssohn. (This work emerges as a conversational form not only as it answers letters from readers, but also in 1767, when Herder publishes his own 'supplement' to the *Briefe* under the title *Über die neuere deutsche Literatur*.)

Gottsched's *Versuch* is an especially interesting transitional document, in effect a reply to the new theories of Addison and Du Bos with which Dennis might have sympathized. Though he sets out to extend the qualifications of the critic beyond membership of either the world of scholarship or of the court, Gottsched like Dennis is too fully committed to a rationalist criticism – to the 'rules' as revealed by educated reason, rules to which all works should cleave, whatever response to such works the mass of readers may have – to carry his project through. For Gottsched the judgement of taste remains a cognitive judgement, and so all merely sensory responses (in the manner of Addison or Du Bos) remain so far defective. J. J. Bodmer replies to Du Bos even more pointedly, insisting that taste is no receptive faculty – no mere matter of sense – but rather an active power of the understanding: 'Thus the sensualistic judgement of taste is rejected, and with it the judgement of the "majority". Only the educated specialist can judge the true value of an artwork, since only he is familiar with the "fundamentals of science". The scholar is the true judge of art.'[40]

---

[40] Berghahn, 'Classicist to classical', pp. 36–7. Arguments such as Bodmer's suggest the special direction literary theory was to take in early eighteenth-century Germany, where there did not yet exist that sizable literary public – Addison's 'Town' – for which French and English critics wrote, and from which they drew support.

Just as Germany experiences, later and in its own pronounced way, our first moment of transition in the institution of criticism, so it experiences the second. By the end of the eighteenth century, in response to the very success of writers and critics in creating a large and diverse literary public, the qualifications of the critic come once again to be construed in Dennis's manner, his relation to the public once again defined as that of privileged speaker not from within but from above. Faced with an explosion in the volume of publication and in numbers of writers and readers, as well as a new populism propagated by critics of the *Sturm und Drang* such as Herder and Gottfried August Bürger (author in 1784 of a manifesto 'Von der Popularität der Poesie'), many observers diagnose a new German 'reading mania' potentially pernicious both to taste and to the state – to all of which Goethe responds in the revolutionary context of 1795 with an essay attacking 'Literarischer Sansculottismus'.[41] Finally, in the context of Weimar classicism, Friedrich Schiller adopts a style deliberately too complex and philosophical for any but those Schiller identified as the 'elect' (the 'educated' and 'connoisseurs') to understand. Just as in 1704 Dennis had listed among the qualifications of the critic a 'due Application' which in fact meant 'leisure' and freedom from 'Business', Schiller in his *Über naive und sentimentalische Dichtung* (1795–6) defines a central purpose of art as providing 'relaxation' – a state often misinterpreted, Schiller notes, as mere passivity. Schiller's 'relaxation' turns out instead to be an 'active' condition, one inaccessible to those who 'work': the public to which Schiller as critic speaks is sharply limited to those 'who, without working, are nevertheless active ... Only such a class can preserve the beautiful wholeness of human nature, which ever labor temporarily disrupts, and which a laboring *life* permanently destroys.'[42]

[41] On Bürger and the new 'reading mania', see Woodmansee, *The Author, Art, and the Market*.

[42] *Werke*, V, 768, quoted in Berghahn, 'Classicist to classical', p. 89.

2

Ancients and Moderns

Douglas Lane Patey

> What the ancients have taught is so scanty and for the
> most part so lacking in credibility that I may not hope for
> any kind of approach toward truth except by rejecting all
> the paths which they have followed.
>
> Descartes, Traité des passions de l'âme (1649)

> It is the disease of the times, reigning in all places. New
> Sects: new religions: new philosophie: new methods: all
> new, till all be lost.
>
> Meric Casaubon, Treatise concerning Enthusiasme (1656)

It has become almost a cliché among historians of our century to say
that, although once dismissed by the likes of Macaulay as a trivial spat
confined to literary folk (a mere Battle of the Books), the Quarrel between the Ancients and the Moderns (as it was named by Hippolyte
Rigault in his *Histoire de la Querelle* of 1859) was in fact a watershed
– that in the Moderns' rejection of the authority of the Ancients, their
texts, and the rules drawn from them, we can locate the birthplace not
only of eighteenth-century criticism but of modern thought. In 1920
J. B. Bury (following the lead of French scholars) identified the seventeenth-century Quarrel, especially the works of Fontenelle, as the site
where 'the first clear assertions of a doctrine of progress in knowledge
were provoked', making possible the full-scale theories of human progress
of the Abbé de Saint-Pierre, Turgot, and Condorcet, which Bury found
characteristic of the period.[1] In parallel with Bury, Richard Foster Jones

---

[1] Macaulay, 'Atterbury'; Bury, *Progress*, p. 79. Bury's work grew from an inquiry
pursued in France from Auguste Javary's *De l'idée du progrès* (1851) to Jules
Dalvaille's *Essai sur l'histoire de l'idée du progrès jusqu'à la fin du XVIIIe siècle*
(1910); on Bury's influence, see Wagar, 'Origins'. Bury's views quickly penetrated
eighteenth-century studies (in works such as Carl Becker's *Heavenly City of the
Eighteenth-Century Philosophers* (1932)), but especially after World War II
produced their negative response in the form of denials of Enlightenment 'optimism'
such as Carlo Antoni's *Die Kampf wider die Vernunft* (1951), Henry Vyverberg's
Historical Pessimism in the French Enlightenment (1958), and most generally
Peter Gay's *The Party of Humanity* (1964) and *The Enlightenment: An
Interpretation* (1966–9). (We can usefully understand Judith Plotz's *Ideas of Decline
in English Poetry* (1965) and W. J. Bate's *Burden of the Past and the English Poet*

began an inquiry into the background of the English Battle of the Books, which resulted in his thesis that with their rejection of the Ancients' doctrines of authority, imitation, and degeneration, the Moderns – pre-eminently Bacon and his puritan followers – produced the activity we know as modern experimental science; in the process, Jones sought to establish both that the Quarrel was not solely a 'literary' matter, and that its origins were not in the France of Descartes and Fontenelle but in England.[2] For both Bury and Jones, what the seventeenth-century Moderns had to overcome was 'humanism' – as Bury put it, 'the intellectual yoke of the Renaissance' (p. 78).

Other scholars soon began to undermine these large claims by showing that the Quarrel, even as applied to literature, did not begin in the seventeenth century at all – that earlier texts, once viewed only as precursors to the debate, in fact form a coherent and continuous tradition to which the well-known late seventeenth-century texts are merely a coda. Hans Baron found the Quarrel of Ancient and Modern at the heart of the the self-understanding of the Italian Renaissance, part of the humanist project itself (indeed, throughout the seventeenth and eighteenth centuries, 'Modern' generally meant since the revival of learning). Others traced the conflict (and its attendant, the idea of progress) back into the Middle Ages and even to classical antiquity.[3] Oppositions of Ancient and Modern emerge as part of the way any age constructs its identity, particularly the way it understands itself as a distinct 'age'. For the past twenty-five or so years, then, it has become a concern to define what was really new in the late seventeenth- and eighteenth-century Quarrel, traditionally conceived as having three phases: the French debate

---

(1970) as instances of this reaction.) Meanwhile in two vast and overlapping literatures, (1) the 'idea' of progress itself came under increasing scrutiny, and (2) belief in progress was traced backward, first to the Renaissance and finally to antiquity. Yet the thesis of Bury and Jones, albeit in more sophisticated form, remains very much alive: for Nannerl Keohane (1977) it is still 'in the era of Bacon and Descartes [that] we first recognize a pattern of argument that can sensibly be labelled 'the idea of progress' (p. 29); the thesis receives its fullest reformulation in David Spadafora's *Idea of Progress in Eighteenth-Century Britain* (1990).

[2] Jones began his inquiry with *The Background of the Battle of the Books* (1920), and extended it in *Ancients and Moderns: A Study of the Rise of the Scientific Movement in 17th-Century England* (1936); according to the latter, 'our modern scientific utilitarianism is the offspring of Bacon begot upon Puritanism' (p. 91; thus Jones opened the large and ongoing debate about the role of puritanism in the rise of modern science). Jones has been widely criticized for his insular focus (see Rattansi's review of *Ancients and Moderns*) as well as for his reading of seventeenth-century science (despite its Puritan background) as a fundamentally secular and secularizing activity (see especially Hutchison, 'Supernaturalism').

[3] See among this large literature Baron, 'The *querelle*'; Buck, 'Aus der Vorgeschichte der Querelle'; Margiotta, *Le Origini Italiane*; Gössman, 'Antiqui und Moderni'; and Curtius, *European Literature*, pp. 251–5 and *passim*.

leading up to the works of Perrault and Fontenelle; the English Battle
of the Books sparked by Sir William Temple and continued most notably by William Wotton and Jonathan Swift; and a rekindling of hostil-
ities at the opening of the eighteenth century in the form of debates
about Homer (begun in France but quickly engaging all Europe). Nearly
all recent studies of the Quarrel have found its importance in fostering
and diffusing a new understanding of history: one that contributed to
an understanding of all human works as historical products (cultural
constructions) and consequently to a relativization of taste, increased
interest in non-classical cultures both past and present, and ultimately
to that late eighteenth-century body of thinking we have come to call
'historicism'.[4] It was also the site at which the modern distinction between the arts and the sciences emerged. In what follows I shall trace
the main phases of the Quarrel with an eye to the ways in which these
historical concerns shape the institution of literary criticism, continuing
in fact to do so long after the 'official' battles had concluded.

Perrault and Fontenelle: emergence of the modern division between 'art' and 'science'

La belle Antiquité fut toujours vénérable,
Mais je ne crus jamais qu'elle fust adorable.
Je voy les Anciens, sans plier les genoux,
Ils sont grands, il est vray, mais hommes commes nous:
Et l'on peut comparer sans craindre d'estre injuste,
Le Siècle de LOUIS au beau Siècle d'Auguste.

Charles Perrault, *Le Siècle de Louis le Grand* (1687)

On 27 January 1687, sitting in celebration of Louis XIV's recovery from
a fistula, the French Academy heard Perrault's poem celebrating the
achievements of Louis's age – accomplishments so great as to rival those
of antiquity. The response was an uproar: Racine thought the poem a
joke; Boileau, after grumbling through the opening lines, shouted for
the reading to stop – the poem 'brought shame on the Academy'; only
the intervention of his friend Huet (a convinced believer that both man
and nature had degenerated since ancient times) quieted him. As the
famous story makes clear, by 1687 battle lines in the French Quarrel,
both intellectual and personal, were already drawn.[5] Perrault had risen

---

[4] The most important of these recent treatments are by Krauss, Kortum, Jauss,
Kapitza, Lachterman, and Levine (see as well Meyer, 'Recent German studies').
[5] Narratives of these events can be found in Rigault and Gillot; Perrault himself
described his poem's reception in his *Memoirs*, p. 115. For Huet's belief that (*pace*
Fontenelle) modern trees (as well as men) are actually meaner than those of
antiquity, see *Huetiana*, pp. 26–30.

to prominence in the 1660s through Colbert, who secured for him in 1671 membership in the Academy (despite his small literary output) and in 1672 the important post of *Contrôleur des Bâtiments de Sa Majesté*, a source of patronage, power, and wealth; as late as 1691, though Colbert had died and Perrault fallen from royal favour, Perrault was still influential enough to help secure a seat in the Academy for his friend Bernard de Fontenelle (a seat Fontenelle had four times been refused, through the united efforts of the Ancient party, including Boileau, Racine, Molière, La Fontaine, and La Bruyère). From the start, participants in the Quarrel were aware of its political dimension: as would also be true in Temple's England, most French Moderns stood far closer to centralized power (whose greatness Perrault had celebrated) than did more independent humanists such as Boileau.[6]

Battle lines had been drawn in the years since Chapelain and Corneille, especially as critics disagreed over the use of Christian materials in the higher genres of poetry (the so-called *querelle du merveilleux*). Epic in particular must instruct as well as please; so, though Homer and Virgil provide no models for it, must not modern poetry make use of Christian revelation?[7] Boileau defended the great ancients as standards for imitation in his *Art poétique* (1674) – to which he added attacks on some of his old enemies: Charles Perrault's brother Claude, designer of the new façade of the Louvre and physician to Boileau's recently deceased fiancée (as an 'assassin' in both architecture and medicine), and Jean Desmarets de Saint-Sorlin, author of the Christian epic *Clovis* (1657). Desmarets had already defended modern poetry, vernacular language, and *le merveilleux chrétien* in many works, most lengthily in a *Comparaison de la langue et de la poésie françoise avec la grecque et la latine* (1670); in a reply to Boileau of 1674, he called on his friend Charles Perrault to 'defend France' against 'that rebel troop which prefers ancient works to our own'.

---

[6] Thus Temple suggested that the French Moderns adopted their opinions 'at first only to make their court, and at second hand to flatter those who flattered their king' (*Works*, III, p. 473), and Jean Le Clerc wrote from Amsterdam in 1699 in an effort to explain 'the decay of belles-lettres' by reference to the Quarrel: 'No one will any longer listen to those who quote antiquity and who have principles independent of the will of the sovereign' (*Parrhasiana*, I, pp. 259–60). The class bases of the French Quarrel have been analysed by Kortum (*Perrault und Boileau*) and Niderst (*Fontenelle*, pp. 365–99); the same analysis has long been given of Boileau's forebears, the humanists of the Renaissance, of whom Felix Gilbert observes, 'they hardly ever took part at a policymaking level . . . There remained a gap between the humanists and the ruling classes of their time' ('Bernardo Ruccelai', p. 242).

[7] In Britain defenders of Christian epic and marvels could of course point to the example of Milton, rapidly becoming a classic, but Modern principles were none the less felt to require defence in John Dennis's *Grounds of Criticism in Poetry* (1704) and Richard Blackmore's *Essay upon Epick Poetry* (1716).

Nor were the 'works' in question just books: the quarrel encompassed the whole reputation of France, then reaching an apogee of self-
sufficiency in its cultural nationalism. It extended for instance to the
question of which language public inscriptions should use, Latin or
French (to which in his *Deffense de la langue françoise* (1676) François
Charpentier answered unequivocally: the language of the culturally
superior nation – France). By 1688, the year after Perrault answered
Desmarets's call, the quarrel was so familiar that François de Callières
could publish an *Histoire poëtique de la guerre nouvellement declarée
entre les anciens et les modernes*. But the most important texts of the
Quarrel were to come: not from Boileau, who dealt less in the principles
at issue than in personal attacks on Perrault and criticisms of his
misreadings of Homer, but from the Moderns, in the four volumes of
Perrault's *Parallèle des anciens et des modernes* (1688–96) and especially in Fontenelle's *Digression sur les anciens et les modernes*, first
published in a volume of his *Poésies pastorales* (1688). (This first phase
of the Quarrel is often said to conclude with the publication in 1699 of
Fénelon's *Télémaque*, an epic classically inspired but written in modern
French prose.)

Perrault's *Parallèle* is cast in a dialogue between a pedantically learned
provincial Président who has not been to Paris for twenty years, is out
of touch with recent cultural developments, and believes that nothing
truly great and new has been achieved since antiquity; a worldly, ironical Abbé (spokesman for Perrault), at home in philosophy and science
(Perrault had called for help on his friend Huyghens), and an admirer
of the age of Louis XIV; and a Chevalier, a Parisian wit supposedly
undecided, but who usually sides with the Abbé. The setting is a visit
to Versailles, the visible symbol of Modern accomplishment. In the
course of their five dialogues, Perrault panoramically surveys ancient
and modern achievement in all fields, raising nearly all the topics of the
Quarrel, past and future.[8] In all fields except sculpture – 'the simplest
and most limited of all the arts' (I, p. 183) – the Abbé finds progress:
time is the parent of politeness and good taste as of natural knowledge;
not only in physics and astronomy but also in poetry, eloquence, and
ethics has the seventeenth century outdone the ancients, for these activities depend like the natural sciences on justness of reasoning as well as

---

[8] Perrault had models for this procedure of systematic comparison through assembly
of long lists of ancient and modern accomplishments in Alessandro Tassoni's
Pensieri diversi (1620), Book X, George Hakewill's *Apologie of the Power and
Providence of God* (1627), and Joseph Glanvill's *Plus Ultra: or, the Progress and
Advancement of Knowledge since the Days of Aristotle* (1668); the *Parallèle* would
itself serve as a model for Wotton's *Reflections* (1694) and Vico's *De mente heroica*
(1732). On the Renaissance origins of this rhetorical procedure, see Black, 'Ancients
and Moderns'.

on detailed knowledge of human nature, both of which have been *perfectionnés* in the century of Descartes.[9] If, as was still generally believed, it is the task of the highest poetry, especially epic, to convey wisdom in all fields, then it is absurd now to claim Homer's greatness: just as in *Le Siècle* Perrault had suggested that Homer would have been a better poet had he lived in Louis's age, here, in a series of disadvantageous comparisons with Virgil and later poets, he finds Homer defective not only formally – in what, according to Perrault, his untutored 'genius' supplied – but especially in the limitations imposed by his primitive culture. Homer was no naturalist; in manners, 'the princes of his age resemble modern peasants' (III, p. 98).[10]

In 1688 Fontenelle, a nephew of Corneille, was at the beginning of his long career as a popularizer of Cartesian science; he had already defended the Modern cause in his *Dialogues des morts* (1683).[11] His *Digression* presents the Modern argument in sharp relief, and with unalloyed contempt for the ancients (taken as a group, Fontenelle writes, their chief merit is in having 'driven us to truth' by providing a spectacle of all possible errors and follies). All human works must be understood as cultural products: nature, including human nature, has not changed since antiquity (as Fontenelle puts it, the whole Quarrel turns on the question whether ancient trees were taller than those of today); whatever differences distinguish men's minds, then, 'must be caused by exterior

---

[9] 'Pourquoy voulez-vous Mr le President que l'Eloquence & la Poësie n'ayent pas eu besoin d'autant de siecles pour se perfectionner que la Physique & l'Astronomie? Le coeur de l'homme qu'il faut connoistre pour le persuader [rhetoric] & pour luy plaire [poetry], est-il plus aisé à penetrer que les secrets de la Nature ... où l'on découvre tous les jours quelque chose de nouveau [?]' The ancients knew nature and 'les passions de l'ame' 'en gros', to which we have added a more detailed knowledge and thousands of 'belles & curieuses découvertes', to be found especially in the novels, tragedies, and moral treatises of our (seventeenth-century) authors (II, pp. 29–31).

[10] Ancients and Moderns both agreed that the epic must be, in Le Bossu's phrase, a 'corps de doctrine'; to Desmarets, the epic poet must know and teach 'history, geography, astronomy, matters of nature, logic, ethics, rhetoric, fables, agriculture, architecture, painting, sculpture, perspective and music'. For Perrault, 'Un Poëte & particulierement un Poëte épique doit parler pertinemment de toutes les matieres qu'il traite dans son poëme, ou bien il se mesle d'un métier dont il est indigne. Il faut qu'il connoisse les choses de la Nature' – from which Perrault draws the conclusion that progress since antiquity has rendered absurd the view that 'Homere n'a rien ignoré des choses de la Nature, & qu'il est le pere de tous les Arts' (III, pp. 93, 95). Perrault like Fontenelle borrows his criticism of Homer's formal and ethical defects in comparison with Virgil from Vida's *De arte poetica* (1527) and especially J. C. Scaliger's *Poetices libri septem* (1561); what is new in both is the detailed criticism of Homer's science.

[11] Especially in Dialogue III, between Socrates and Montaigne, in which Socrates argues, 'Est-ce que la nature s'est épuisée, et qu'elle n'a plus la force de produire ces grandes âmes? Et pourquoi se serait-elle encore épuisée en rien, hormis en hommes raisonnables?' (*Oeuvres*, II, p. 190).

circumstances, such as the historical moment, the government, and the state of things in general' (trans. Hughes, p. 360). Fontenelle is not so sure as Perrault that modern poetry can outdo ancient: he too cites new vernacular genres, especially the novel and the fairy tale (a form Perrault practised), but he also suggests both that the great age of French literature may be over, and that poetry may have been perfected in Augustus' time (so that a Virgil can only be equalled, not surpassed).[12] Most important for the century to follow, Fontenelle in the course of considering the nature of progress in various disciplines makes explicit what Perrault only sketched, a fundamental distinction between fields which progress by slow cumulation of knowledge (such as physics, astronomy, and mathematics) and those wherein genius can reach the heights almost at once (such as poetry and eloquence). He transforms, in other words, traditional distinctions between poetry (or rhetoric) and philosophy into the seventeenth century's most fully elaborated division of what we have come to call the arts and the sciences:

However, if the moderns are to be able to improve continually on the ancients, the fields in which they are working must be of a kind which allows progress. Eloquence and poetry required only a certain number of rather narrow ideas as compared with other arts, and they depend for their effect primarily upon the liveliness of the imagination. Now mankind could easily amass in a few centuries a small number of ideas, and liveliness of imagination has no need of a long sequence of experiences nor many rules before it reaches the furthest perfection of which it is capable. But physics, medicine, mathematics, are composed of numberless ideas and depend upon precision of thought which improves with extreme slowness, yet is always improving ... It is obvious that all this is endless and that the last physicists or mathematicians will naturally have to be the ablest.[13]

---

[12] *Digression*, pp. 364–5, 368. By the time of his later *Sur la poésie en général* (published 1751), Fontenelle concluded that poetic progress remains possible: see Krauss, *Fontenelle*, Preface. Perrault's and Fontenelle's defences of vernacular forms continued humanist defences of modernity as these were conducted in the Renaissance phase of the quarrel: see Baron, 'The querelle', and Gravelle, 'The Latin-Vernacular Question'.

[13] Cependant, afin que les Modernes puissent toujours enchérir sur les Anciens, il faut que les choses soient d'une espèce à le permettre. L'Eloquence & la Poësie ne demandent qu'un certain nombre de vûes assez borné par rapport à d'autres Arts, & elles dépendent principalement de la vivacité de l'imagination. Or les hommes peuvent avoir amassé en peu de siècles un petit nombre de vûes; & la vivacité de l'imagination n'a pas besoin d'une longue suite d'expériences, ni d'une grande quantité de règles, pour avoir toute la perfection dont celle est capable. Mais la Physique, la Médecine, les Mathématiques, sont composées d'un nombre infini de vûes, & dependent de la justesse du raisonnement, qui se perfectionne toujours ... Il est evident que tout cela n'a point de fin, & que les derniers Physiciens ou Mathématiciens devront naturellement être les plus habiles.

(p. 357; trans. Hughes, p. 362, altered).

Neither Tassoni, Hakewill, nor even Perrault had sorted their varied examples in this way;[14] after the *Digression*, Fontenelle's division would quickly be taken up throughout Europe, by writers on both sides of the Quarrel – as early as 1694 by such Moderns as Wotton and Charles Gildon, and later by such Ancients as Du Bos.[15] These writers do not yet use the *terms* 'art' and 'science' to mark their divisions; to the extent that these terms were distinguished (and many conflated them), they continued to carry the senses they had had since antiquity – 'science' still meant theoretical understanding, 'art' practical activity, a making done according to rules. Modern usage of these terms would not emerge fully until the nineteenth century.[16] But already Perrault and Fontenelle, almost as a by-product of the Quarrel – in considering whether all fields progress in the same way – had created the division of disciplines upon which the next century would depend in formulating the new category of the 'aesthetic', a category that thus emerges correlatively with modern

[14] On the extent to which Perrault's *Parallèle* suggests the new division of knowledge, see Davidson, 'Realignment of the arts'. (In his *Cabinet des Beaux-Arts* (1690), a catalogue of these arts as they were represented in allegorical paintings on the ceiling of a room in his house, Perrault listed together eloquence, poetry, music, architecture, painting, and sculpture, but also optics, mechanics, and the crafts (pp. 1–2)). R. S. Crane discusses Bacon's contribution to the new division, his distinction between the disciplines of 'cultivation' and those of 'invention' or 'increase', in *The Idea of the Humanities*, I, pp. 55–72; see also Levine, *Humanism and History*, ch. 5.

[15] Wotton writes in his *Reflections*:

of [kinds of knowledge] there are two sorts: One, of those wherein the gravest part of those Learned Men who have compared Ancient and Modern Performances, either give up the Cause to the Ancients quite, or think, at least, that the Moderns have not gone beyond them. The other of those, where the Advocates for the Moderns think the Case so clear on their Side, that they wonder how any Man can dispute it with them. Poesie, Oratory, Architecture, Painting, and Statuary, are of the First Sort: Natural History, Physiology, and Mathematicks, with all their Dependencies, are of the second.

(p. 19)

Gildon draws a similar division in his *Miscellaneous Letters and Essays* of the same year.

[16] Spadafora surveys eighteenth-century usage of these terms in *Progress*, pp. 26–34. Because the term 'art' continued even in the early nineteenth century to suggest, in d'Alembert's words, 'any system of knowledge which can be reduced to positive and invariable rules independent of caprice or opinion' ('On peut en général donner le nom *Art* à tout système de connoissances qu'il est possible de réduire à des regles positives') (*Preliminary Discourse*, p. 40), Goethe was to deny that poetry is an 'art' (see Kristeller, 'Modern system', p. 222). By 1750 the older phrase 'natural philosophy' had been supplemented by 'natural science' and 'exact science'; the unmodified singular 'science' appears first to have gained its limited modern sense of biology, chemistry, physics (and studies that model themselves on these) in England, in the context of professional societies such as the British Association for the Advancement of Science (founded 1831; see Ross, 'Scientist').

conceptions of 'science' in the course of the Quarrel between Ancients and Moderns.[17]

By 1700 nearly everyone ceded superiority in science to the Moderns and in arts to the Ancients. Even for the utopian progressivist Turgot,

Time constantly brings to light new discoveries in the sciences; but poetry, painting and music have a fixed limit which the genius of languages, the imitation of nature, and the limited sensibility of an organ determine, which they obtain by slow steps, and which they cannot surpass. The great men of the Augustan Age reached it, and are still our models.[18]

Nearly everyone, in other words, accepted the new division of knowledge. That poetry and eloquence now took their place among the arts, in opposition to the sciences, had far-reaching implications for literary criticism, three of which in particular merit our attention here. (1) The remapping of disciplines accomplished in the Quarrel contributed to the distinctive logical structure of eighteenth-century criticism; (2) it brought on a crisis in conceptions of the sense in which any 'art' can have a *history*; and (3) it led to the construction of a new category of 'literature' (as literary 'art') – resulting ultimately in a newly pressing need for criticism to *defend* literature.

The Quarrel contributed first of all that redefinition of critical 'rules' that separates Chapelain and Pascal – for whom the rules of writing can be demonstrated in Cartesian fashion, *a priori* – from Pope and Du Bos, for whom criticism is a probabilistic, *a posteriori*, 'experimental' affair. For all but a few extreme (usually Cartesian) Moderns, criticism in the eighteenth century was understood as an *a posteriori* attempt to discover what in literary works was the source of their particular merits or effects, the means by which authors achieved their ends. Formulations of these relations between means and ends continued to be called 'rules', but such rules could not be known *a priori* or with certainty; the critic could only conjecture them with probability from the effects (ends) he had experienced – as Du Bos said, rules 'only teach us to know the

---

[17] The role of the Quarrel in the emergence of 'aesthetics' – essentially a Modern category – has been examined by Kristeller, 'The modern system'; Saisselin, 'Critical reflections'; and Patey, 'The canon'. Eighteenth-century architects of the 'aesthetic' such as Addison and Baumgarten are thus primarily engaged in theorizing distinctions which were already emerging in the previous century and were first given a rationale by Perrault and Fontenelle.

[18] 'Le temps fait sans cesse éclore de nouvelles découvertes dans les sciences; mais la poësie, la peinture, la musique, ont un point fixe, que le génie des langues, l'imitation de la nature, la sensibilité limitée de nos organes déterminent; qu'elles atteignent à pas lents et qu'elles ne peuvent passer. Les grands-hommes du siècle d'Auguste y arrivèrent et sont encore nos modèles.' 'Discours', p. 78.

cause of an effect, which was already felt'.[19] At the same time, because literary standards cannot be known *a priori*, the critic cannot demonstrate which are the works of commanding merit: as Boileau, Pope, and Du Bos argue fully, only the test of time (the combined weight of many probable opinions) can sort them out. Johnson makes the point: 'To works, however, of which the excellence is not absolute and definite, but gradual and comparative; to works not raised upon principles demonstrative and scientifick, but appealing wholly to observation and experience, no other test can be applied than length of duration and continuance of esteem.' Criticism cannot be a 'science' like geometry (in the old sense of a field in which we have demonstrative knowledge of causes), because, as Addison argues in discussing 'The pleasures of the imagination', we simply do not and cannot know the mechanisms by which works affect us.[20] Thus the critic, Gibbon tells us, must be satisfied with that kind of proof his subject admits of – whether that subject is poetry or history: 'Geometry is employed only in demonstrations peculiar to itself: criticism deliberates between the different degrees of probability.' Eighteenth-century writers extend the point to every field in which demonstration is impossible: such fields can only be *a posteriori* (experimental) sciences. Thus Burke in discussing the art of government employs the same argument Addison had used of imaginative works.[21]

[19] *Reflections*, II, p. 325 ('ils apprendront seulement à connoître la cause d'un effet qu'on sentoit déjà': III, p. 467). For Pope as well, 'Rules were made but to promote their End'; where writers have succeeded in achieving their ends, rules (*'unseen*, but in th'*Effects'*) are to be conjectured ('Just *Precepts* thus from great *Examples* giv'n') (*Essay on Criticism*, ll. 147, 79, 98). For Richard Hurd, 'Rules themselves are indeed nothing else but an appeal to *experience*; conclusions drawn from wide and general observation of the aptness and efficacy of certain *means* to produce those *impressions*'; Hurd presents critical method as the analogue of inductive generalization in experimental science (*Works*, I, pp. 390–2).

[20] Johnson, Preface to Shakespeare, pp. 59–60; Addison, *Spectator* 413:

> Though in Yesterday's Paper we considered how every thing that is *Great, New*, or *Beautiful*, is apt to affect the Imagination with Pleasure, we must own that it is impossible for us to assign the necessary Cause of this Pleasure, because we know neither the Nature of an Idea, nor the Substance of a Human Soul, which might help us to discover the Conformity or Disagreeableness of the one to the other; and therefore, for want of such a Light, all that we can do in Speculations of this kind, is to reflect on those Operations of the Soul that are most agreeable, and to range, under their proper Heads, what is pleasing or displeasing to the Mind, without being able to trace out the several necessary and efficient Causes from whence the Pleasure or Displeasure arises.

> Hutcheson makes the same argument of the 'sense of beauty' in his *Inquiry into … Beauty*, ch. 1.

[21] Gibbon, *Essay*, pp. 50, 51 (echoing Aristotle, *Nicomachean Ethics*, I.iii. 1–4); Burke, *Reflections*:

These arguments began to be applied to literary (and other) studies in and because of the Quarrel. Fontenelle distinguishes the two cultures not merely according to how extensive a view each requires, but also by the method and governing mental faculty of each. Poetry and eloquence depend on 'imagination', the sciences on 'reason', especially Descartes's 'new method of reasoning' which has so much 'improved the way we think ... in this century' (and which he hopes will come to reign even in 'criticism' (pp. 362–3). Thus physics yields truths while poetry possesses only imagination's traditional status: opinion.[22] Wotton makes the point, calling on the language of logic:

The Generality of the Learned have given *the Ancients* the Preference in those Arts and Sciences which have hitherto been considered [painting, poetry, eloquence, sculpture, and architecture]: But for the Precedency in those Parts of Learning which still remain to be enquired into, *the Moderns* have put in their Claim, with great Briskness. Among this Sort, I reckon *Mathematical* and *Physical Sciences*, considered in their largest Extent. These are Things which have no Dependence upon the Opinions of Men for their Truth; they will admit of fixed and undisputed *Mediums* of Comparison and Judgment: So that, though it may always be debated, who have been the best Orators, or who the best Poets; yet it cannot always be a Matter of Controversie, who have been the greatest *Geometers, Arithmeticians, Astronomers, Musicians, Anatomists, Chymists, Botanists*, or the like ...[23]

Thus even the Modern Wotton is content to concede the necessity that 'The Masters of Writing, in all their several Ways, to this Day, appeal to the Ancients, as their Guides; and still fetch Rules from them, for the Art of Writing'.

The science of constructing a commonwealth, or renovating it, or reforming it, is, like every other experimental science, not to be taught *a priori*. Nor is it a short experience that can instruct us in that practical science; because the real effects of moral causes are not always immediate; but that which in the first instance is prejudicial may be excellent in its remoter operation; and its excellence may arise even from the ill effects it produces in the beginning.

(p. 53)

[22] Fontenelle implies as much in contrasting the 'endless' disputes of 'rhetoric' with the terminable disagreements of 'science'; not only is the former the traditional home of the merely probable (opinion), but Fontenelle describes the main 'trick of eloquence' as balancing opinions on both sides of a question (p. 360) – a fair description of argument *in utramque partem* as Academic sceptics such as Cicero understood it, and a method that yields only probabilities. (See Patey, *Probability*, ch. 1, and on the connection of imagination and opinion, pp. 134–6.)

[23] *Reflections*, pp. 77–8 (Addison makes the same division in the *Spectator*, no. 160). In including music with arithmetic and geometry, Wotton has in mind *musica theoretica* – the study of ratios and other numeric relations – rather than *musica practica* (composition and performance).

Secondly, the new division of knowledge precipitated a crisis in conceptions of the 'history' of any art. It was implicit in the new division that science, now that a proper method was in place, progresses cumulatively; the arts do not. Eventually – in the context of the century's many debates about imitation and originality – this implication of the new division would force a rejection of the old conception of 'art' itself. 'Art' ceases to be a methodic activity (one governed by 'rules'); this becomes the defining feature of 'science' (whose method becomes – simply – 'scientific method'). And when 'art' no longer means 'rule-governed', the very notion of artistic 'progress' becomes unintelligible. Once the meaning of 'art' changes, John Aikin can write: the 'excellence of a particular artist cannot be transmitted to a successor; hence a later age does not stand on the shoulders of an earlier one with respect to [the arts]'.[24] Grasping the means by which great practitioners had achieved their effects – that is, grasping rules – had once been understood as the way young writers learned their art (though of course only the gifted writer – the 'genius' – could improve on his models): rules thus supply continuity in the transmission of any art. Histories of art, in turn, took the form of histories of given genres: like Vasari's *Lives of the Artists* and even Johnson's *Lives of the Poets*, they were organized as the story of succeeding artists seeking new means the better to achieve given ends, ends which had been established by the founders of the genre. (In this way critics such as Du Bos could speak of one author as 'successor' to another, whom the new author 'replaces' or 'substitutes', because he has produced 'better performances of the same kind': *Critical Reflections*, II, pp. 313, 400.) For Vasari and Du Bos, every work of art forms part of a continuous tradition extending through time and space, even across national boundaries – wherever that kind is practised; thus in his *Essay on Criticism* Pope traces the development of criticism from Aristotle to his own time, organizing his history according to each critic's

---

[24] 'On Attachment to the Ancients', in *Letters*, pp. 18–19 (Aikin of course calls on the famous phrase for cumulative progress achieved by building on the work of predecessors whose long history is traced in, among others, Merton's *On the Shoulders of Giants* and Jones's *Ancients and Moderns*). Hazlitt makes the same point in his 'Why the arts are not progressive? – a fragment' (1814); indeed, he makes it the more clearly because by his time, the terms (as well as the categories) 'art' and 'science' had very nearly taken on their modern senses:

the complaint itself, that the arts do not attain that progressive degree of perfection which might reasonably be expected from them, proceeds on a false notion, for the analogy appealed to in support of the regular advances of art to higher degrees of excellence, totally fails; it applies to science, not to art ... What is mechanical, reducible to rule, or capable of demonstration, is progressive, and admits of gradual improvement: what is not mechanical or definite, but depends on genius, taste, and feeling, very soon becomes stationary or retrograde.

(*Round Table*, pp. 160, 161)

particular excellence within the universal ends of criticism itself. But the Modern notion of art spelt the rejection of such organization. This is one reason why arguments such as the following, by Voltaire, were to have such significance:

The greatest Part of the Critics have fetch'd the Rules of *Epick* Poetry from the Books of *Homer*, according to the Custom, or rather, to the Weakness of Men, who mistake commonly the beginning of an Art, for the Principles of the Art itself, and are apt to believe, that everything must be by its own Nature, what it was, when contriv'd at first.[25]

With the end of the old understanding of art as rule-governed and of its attendant theory of genre, how the history of any art was conceived has to change. Histories of given arts, as we shall see, are assimilated to more general intellectual, cultural, or national history. If Fontenelle's distribution of disciplines by faculty stems ultimately from Bacon's account in the *Advancement of Learning* of memory, imagination, and reason (the faculties of history, poetry, and philosophy, respectively), he has added a theory of the progressive unfolding of the mind through the historical succession of these faculties: 'there is an order which regulates our progress. Every science develops after a certain number of preceding sciences have developed and only then; it has to await its turn to burst its shell.' Fontenelle's historical model is taken up along with his division of knowledge by nearly all subsequent Moderns; it provides d'Alembert, for instance – for whom imagination has become the faculty governing not merely poetry but all the fine arts (the *beaux-arts* and *belles-lettres*) – with an explanation of the development of European culture since 'the renaissance of letters': 'When we consider the progress of the mind since that memorable epoch, we find that this progress was made in the sequence it should naturally have followed. It was begun with erudition, continued with belles-lettres, and completed with philosophy.'[26] Others will chart a progress from sense through imagination and finally reason; this is the model that guides Thomas

---

[25] *Essay on Epick Poetry* (1727), p. 38; Voltaire goes so far as to argue that

An *Epick* poem is a Discourse in Verse. Use alone has prefix'd the Name of *Epick*, particularly to those Poems which relate some great action' (p. 39). Swift parodies arguments like Voltaire's in *A Tale of a Tub*: 'But I here think fit to lay hold on that great and honourable Privilege of being the *Last Writer*; I claim an absolute Authority in Right, as the *freshest Modern*, which gives me a Despotick Power over all Authors before me.

(p. 130)

[26] *Preliminary Discourse*, p. 60 ('Quand on considère les progrès de l'esprit depuis cette époque mémorable, on trouve que ces progrès se sont faits dans l'ordre qu'ils devoient naturellement suivre. On a commencé par l'Erudition, continué par les Belles-lettres, & fini par la Philosophie').

Warton in writing the history of English poetry as an aspect of the history of England itself, and that leads Hugh Blair as he distinguishes and orders variant national traditions in rhetoric and *belles-lettres*.[27] The history of any art becomes a history of stages – periods – corresponding to, because informed by, larger movements of the national mind and institutions. Such new kinds of history – of the sort discussed for example by René Wellek in *The Rise of English Literary History* – were thus made necessary by the new division of knowledge (as well as the deepened sense of historical difference) that emerged in the Quarrel.

Finally, the new division led to a reconception of the category of the 'literary' itself, one that we can see completed in the eighteenth century when literature was brought into the ambit of the new category of the 'aesthetic'. When Perrault and Fontenelle class poetry under the heading of 'imagination', they call upon a faculty whose meaning had changed since Bacon's time: imagination had lost what in the Renaissance had been its major intellective functions, especially its connection with judgement; the understanding alone now performs those tasks. Hence Fontenelle's dismissive treatment of the arts in the *Digression*: he contrasts the 'tricks of eloquence' with the dependability of *la physique*, 'liveliness' with 'precision'; poetry and eloquence, he writes, 'are not very important in themselves' – eloquence may once have had a political function, but 'Poetry, on the other hand, was good for nothing, as it has always been under all kinds of governments; that failing is of the essence of poetry'.[28] There follows a stream of works reiterating such criticisms, from Tanneguy Lefebvre's *De futilitate poetices* (1697) until well into the eighteenth century.[29]

The eighteenth-century consolidation of the category of the aesthetic, as is well known, serves even further to sharpen Fontenelle's division of mental labour: for Batteux, writing in 1746 about what constitutes the fine arts as a category – *Les Beaux-Arts réduits à un même principe* – 'Taste is in the arts what intelligence is in the sciences'; 'Truth is the object of the sciences; that of the arts is the beautiful' (p. 56). Thus will emerge Schiller's complaint in *The Aesthetic Education of Man* (p. 17) that in his time the mental faculties have begun to seem 'as separate in practice as they are distinguished by the psychologist in theory' – a point of which the most circumspect Ancients, suspicious of the Modern

---

[27] See Crane, *Humanities*, I, pp. 73–4, 87–8 and, on the older history these writers replace, Gombrich, 'Artistic progress'.

[28] Trans. Hughes, pp. 359–64 ('La poésie, au contraire, n'était bonne à rien, et ça a toujours été la même chose dans toutes sortes de gouvernement: ce vice-là est bien essentiel': p. 359).

[29] See Le Clerc, *Parrhasiana* I, pp. 28–9; Pons, *Dissertation sur le poème épique*, in *Oeuvres*, pp. 143–4; and Cartaud de la Villate, *Essai sur le goût*.

system of the arts, had long been aware.[30] The concept of literature itself, under such pressure, changes: '*belles-lettres*', once a capacious category including all polite written learning, contracts until it comprises only 'imaginative' literature – the poetic, dramatic, and narrative kinds that in the next century were to form its main divisions; as Johann Bergk writes in 1799, 'The function of polite literature is thus not to increase our knowledge, for this it would share with the sciences, but to cultivate our taste.'[31] The result by the end of the eighteenth century is a widespread sense that though literary art may once, in another cultural context, have served a useful function, it does so no longer – that it no longer, as Hegel says of all the arts, can 'serve our highest need'; and the defence of poetry becomes once again a major project.

The Battle of the Books: the conflict of wit and learning

There is a difference between erudition and literature ... Literature is the knowledge of letters; erudition is the knowledge of facts, places, times, and the monuments of antiquity ... The erudite may or may not be a good *littérateur*, for exquisite discernment and a good and carefully furnished memory require more than study alone. In the same way, a *littérateur* may lack erudition. Should both of these qualities be present, the result is a learned and cultivated man.
                                    Jaucourt, 'Littérature' (*Encyclopédie*)

In 1690 the retired diplomat Sir William Temple published 'An Essay upon the Ancient and Modern Learning', opening a debate that was to consume the learned, provide Swift and Pope with the leading concerns of several of their greatest works, and set the terms of much of English

---

[30] Schiller, *Aesthetic Education*, p. 33. Much earlier Alexander Pope registered his awareness of the Moderns' division of labour (and made full use of the new notion, first so named by Mandeville, to castigate their reduction of learning and the arts to trades). He writes in *Peri Bathous* (1728): 'our Art ought to be put upon the same foot with other Arts of this age. The vast improvement of modern manufactures ariseth from their being divided into several branches, and parcel'd out to several trades ... To this œconomy we owe the perfection of our modern watches; and doubtless we also might that of our modern Poetry and Rhetoric, were the several parts branched out in the like manner' (p. 242).

[31] Bergk, *Die Kunst*, p. 176. It was in the old sense of *belles-lettres* – inclusive of all the 'sciences', especially historical learning – that the 'Little Academy', founded by Colbert in 1663, changed its name in 1716 to that of Académie des Inscriptions et Belles-Lettres; by the time of d'Alembert, the term has shrunk: 'On a réservé le nom de *science* pour les connoissances qui ont plus immédiatement besoin du raisonnement & de la réflexion, telles que la Physique, les Mathématiques, &c & celui de *belles-lettres* pour les productions agréables de l'esprit, dans lesquelles l'imagination a plus de part, telles que l'Eloquence, la Poésie, &c.' (*Encyclopédie*, s.v. 'Erudition').

Augustan literary debate. Having read defences of Modern learning in Thomas Burnet's *Sacred Theory of the Earth* and Fontenelle's *Digression*, Temple set out in a *parallèle* of his own to demonstrate that 'the oldest books we have are still in their kinds the best' – books, that is, in Greek and Latin, 'to which we owe all that we have of learning' – so that even the greatest Moderns 'do but trace over the paths that have been beaten by the ancients ... and are at best but copies of those originals'.[32] As the terms of Temple's argument suggest, the English Battle, though like the French Quarrel framed as a debate about the relative merits of ancient and modern literature, was from the start more concerned with *books* themselves: with their production, uses and users, and especially with the rules and functions of the critic.

Temple never adopted the new division of arts and sciences. He argues against Fontenelle that there may indeed (as archaeological evidence suggested) have been literal giants in former ages, then proceeds in his *parallèle* through the mingled headings of 'philosophy', including especially astronomy and physiology (here Temple dismisses the new theories of Copernicus and Harvey as of little moment and no practical use); 'magic'; architecture (including the applications of mathematics to architecture in 'fortification'); navigation and geography (where even the lodestone has not led to modern superiority); painting and statuary; mechanics (in which 'Gresham College' has not exceeded the ancients); and poetry (works in both verse and prose, including histories).[33] In all these fields, learning since its revival 'within these hundred and fifty years' has failed even to equal that of the ancients; to prove oldest is best in the last category, Temple cites Phalaris' letters and Aesop's fables, which he dates – despite earlier critics' doubts – to the time of Pythagoras. Finally, Temple cites four causes of modern inferiority: the Reformation, which distracted attention too much to religion; a decline of patronage; avarice – men pursue money where they once sought 'honour'; and a false 'scorn of pedantry'.

The first to reply in detail to Temple was William Wotton, twenty-eight years old when his *Reflections upon Ancient and Modern Learning* appeared in 1694. Unlike Temple, Wotton was an expert linguist – he

[32] 'An Essay' (first published in Temple's 1690 *Miscellanea*), in *Works*, III, pp. 463, 431. On Burnet's Modern argument in the *Sacred Theory* (published first in Latin in 1681 and 1684, then in English in 1684 and 1690), see Tuveson.

[33] By 'magic' Temple means what since the Middle Ages was called 'natural magic', an applied natural philosophy crucial in the development of modern science (see Hutchison, 'Occult qualities', and Eaman, *Science*). In denying the significance of the lodestone (and later suggesting that the ancients themselves perhaps possessed explosives), Temple calls in question what for centuries had been the trinity of great modern inventions: printing, gunpowder, and the compass (see Wolper, 'The rhetoric of gunpowder').

had been raised like the young John Stuart Mill, starting Latin, Greek, and Hebrew at four (he entered Oxford before he was ten); in scientific matters, he confesses calling for help on members of the Royal Society such as John Craige and Edmund Halley. Wotton casts himself as mediator between Ancient and Modern, dividing the honours through his elaborate division of arts and sciences, to each of which he devotes a chapter. In fact he dispatches poetry and eloquence – the ethical fields of concern to Temple – in five short introductory chapters, devoting the bulk of the *Reflections* to cataloguing Modern accomplishment in the physical sciences.

Among those fields in which Wotton cites Modern superiority is one not previously central to the Quarrel: 'philology' ('criticism'), a study brought to perfection since and because of the revival of learning. Through the efforts of modern editors in establishing the small details of dates and names, 'the *Old Chronology* and *Geography*' – work too often dismissed as pedantic drudgery – we now know the shape of ancient history better than could anyone in antiquity itself. Wotton grows eloquent in celebrating such scholarship, using phrases Swift would recall when he came to write *A Tale of a Tub*: 'the Annotations of Modern Criticks', Wotton writes, 'required more Fineness of Thought, and Happiness of Invention, than, perhaps, Twenty such Volumes as those were, upon which these very Criticisms were made'; such monumental efforts of learning 'raise a judicious Critick very often as much above the Author upon whom he tries his Skill, as he that discerns another Man's Thoughts, is therein greater than he that thinks' (p. 318).

Temple entered the Battle only once more, in a reply to Wotton written about 1695 but not published until after his death in the edition of his works assembled in 1701 by his longtime secretary, Jonathan Swift. Here, explaining that he writes to persuade university scholars not to give up study of the classics, Temple registers his awareness of the pedagogic side of the Quarrel: at issue is what disciplines and approaches will capture the curriculum. Here too he faces, though without understanding it, the new division of knowledge. Temple sees that the learning his opponents mean most to celebrate is not simply that which has arisen since the revival of learning, but especially those advances made possible by the 'new philosophy', which is only 'fifty or sixty years' old – i.e., the philosophy of Descartes. (Temple cites Paracelsus as Descartes's precursor and 'Gresham' as his successor; Bacon nowhere enters this account.) Since Wotton admits ancient superiority in fields such as poetry and eloquence, Temple finds that the dispute now rests with 'chemistry, anatomy, natural history of minerals, plants, and animals; astronomy, and optics; music; physic; natural philosophy; philology; and theology; of all of which I shall take a short survey . . .' – but here his manuscript breaks off, leading Wotton to comment, 'Just where the

Pinch of the Question lay, there the Copy fails.'[34] Instead, Temple proceeds only to reiterate his views on 'eloquence' (including especially history), and to question how philology came to be dignified as a 'science'. Critics did once perform the useful function of restoring ancient texts, but now they concern themselves only with 'vain niceties', dates and the 'antiquated names of persons or places, with many such worthy trifles'. Worse yet they make 'captious cavils about words and syllables in the judgment of style', thus setting up as judges of their betters and becoming 'a sort of levellers' in the republic of learning. Throughout, Temple speaks of critics in terms that make clear they are not gentlemen (they are mere 'brokers' who 'set up a trade' in learning) and that theirs are not the concerns of gentlemen (they are 'a race of scholars I am very little acquainted with') (pp. 490–2).

In all this Temple was to inspire Swift's treatment of critics in his 'Battle of the Books' and throughout *A Tale of a Tub* (begun in the mid-1690s and first published in 1704). In the 'Digression concerning Criticks' Swift's upstart, ungenteel Modern speaker distinguishes two past critical personae – the ancient critic, concerned only to 'Praise or Acquit' works and expound the rules of good writing, and the Renaissance 'Restorers of Antient Learning' – from the 'Heroick Virtue' of the 'TRUE CRITICK', 'a Discoverer and Collector of Writers Faults'; 'A *True Critick* is a sort of Mechanick, set up with a Stock and Tools for his Trade.' In the 'Battle', a mock-*parallèle* in which Homer slays Perrault by 'hurl[ing] him at *Fontenelle*, with the same Blow dashing out both their Brains', modern critics are characterized by '*Noise* and *Impudence, Dulness* and *Vanity, Positiveness, Pedantry*, and *Ill-Manners*' and seek to 'level' the peaks of Parnassus. And Swift, like Temple, associates modern critics with 'method': in his famous Aesopic episode, the humane Ancient Bee warns the vulgar, ill-spoken, mathematical Modern Spider: 'In that Building of yours, there might, for ought I know, have been Labor and Method enough, but by woful Experience for us both, 'tis too plain, the Materials are nought, and I hope, you will henceforth take Warning, and consider Duration and matter, as well as method and Art.'[35] Alongside

---

[34] Temple, 'Some thoughts upon reviewing the essay of Ancient and Modern Learning', *Works*, III, pp. 472, 481 (Temple does distinguish the 'arts' of 'pleasure' and of 'use', but this does not correspond to Wotton's division); Wotton, *A Defence of the Reflections upon Ancient and Modern Learning* (1705; rpt in the Guthkelch and Nicol Smith edition of Swift's *Tale*), p. 316.

[35] Swift, *Tale*, pp. 93–5, 246, 240, 232 (Aesop returns to the question of 'method': 'Erect your Schemes with as much Method and Skill as you please' (p. 234). The fullest explication of Swift's satire on critics remains Starkman, *Swift's Satire on Learning*, now supplemented by Real's edition of 'The Battle'; a narrative of the quarrel leading up to 'The Battle', with full bibliography, may be found in Guthkelch's 1908 edition. Throughout the *Tale*, Swift ignores the new division of knowledge; later, in *Gulliver*, he would make it a specific target of his satire on the Moderns (see Patey, 'Swift's satire on "science"').

Wotton in 'The Battle' appears his 'lover' Bentley, who steals the armour of Phalaris and Aesop – a reference to the Phalaris controversy, the most important (and most acrimonious) element of the English Quarrel. Following Temple's praise of Phalaris and Aesop in 1690, an undergraduate at Christ Church, Charles Boyle (later earl of Orrery), was set the task of editing Phalaris; the edition was eventually published in 1695, though only after Richard Bentley, recently named Keeper of the King's Libraries, had refused Boyle access to some relevant manuscripts. Meanwhile Bentley, soon to emerge as the greatest classical scholar of the age, undertook to prove both Phalaris and Aesop not classical at all, but Hellenistic forgeries; his efforts appeared first in a short appendix to the second edition of Wotton's *Reflections* in 1697, then two years later as *A Dissertation upon the Epistles of Phalaris*. (In the interim Francis Atterbury and others published under Boyle's name an attack on Bentley, both on his scholarship and his manners.)

Temple, no linguist, had argued the antiquity and genuineness of Phalaris' letters wholly by reference to their content, to the moral nobility and usefulness to the statesman (by definition, a gentleman) of what they have to say; Bentley proved them late forgeries by brilliantly bringing to bear all the apparatus of philology. As Swift suggests in 'The Battle', Bentley had stolen only Phalaris' armour – the merely external matter of his date; the man – the great works themselves – remained. Like the spider and the bee, Ancients and Moderns in the Phalaris controversy differ over the proper approach to reading and composing texts. Temple reads ancient texts in the time-honoured humanistic way, for the useful knowledge they contain. For him, the great ancients speak directly to us, and because of their direct relevance can also serve as models for imitation, a way of assimilating past models for present use. (In this way Augustan mock forms, such as the mock epics *Mac Flecknoe* and *The Rape of the Lock*, not only imitate past models but make proper modes of imitation their explicit subject.) Temple refers to books and reading as a form of 'conversation', just as at the inception of humanism Petrarch not only imitated Cicero but composed familiar letters to the Roman who had died centuries before.[36] But soon the humanist project of recovery had proceeded so far – especially in antiquarian learning, gained not merely through texts but also material remains such as coins and medals – that those who at first appeared friends were becoming foreigners: difference between past and present

---

[36] Temple, III, p. 461 ('For the books we have in prose, do any of the moderns we converse with appear of such a spirit and force, as if they would live longer than the ancients have done?'); on Petrarch, see Minnis, *Medieval Theory of Authorship*, pp. 211–17.

rendered problematic both the direct accessibility and continuing relevance of ancient texts. For the philologist Bentley, Phalaris' letters are not a source of wisdom to be conversed with but a historical document in need of decoding; as such, they can hardly serve as models for assimilative imitation. The problem was not new; already in the Renaissance, humanism had divided on the issue of history, and the word *copy* shifted in meaning from copiousness to mere recapitulation; but in the seventeenth century, precisely because of the success of the humanist project in advancing historical knowledge – and through the very spread of printed materials – it reached a crisis.[37]

The problem thus finds clearest expression, as Joseph Levine has argued, in conceptions of history, of what purposes history serves and how it should be written. In the older view, history – especially of the Greeks and Romans – was to be, in Mably's phrase, 'a great school of morals and politics'.[38] Thus for Ancients such as Temple, history is still a branch of 'eloquence' (as Sidney had said, 'the best of the historian is subject to the poet'); its 'great ends' and 'the chief Care of all Historians' are to 'argue the Virtues and Vices of Princes' and 'serve for Example and Instruction to Posterity', tasks to be accomplished through the construction of shapely historical narratives. But with their elaborate apparatus of footnotes, glossaries, quotations, and appendices – all subjects of Scriblerian attack as signs of triviality and disarray – antiquarian Moderns produce a different, non-narrative kind of history. Wotton likens his own *History of Rome* (1701) to 'Mosaic': 'Affectation of Eloquence becomes History the least of anything, especially such a History as this, which like Mosaic Work must be made up and interwoven with the Thoughts and Sentences of other Men, and where to add to, or diminish from one's Authors, may be of ill consequence.' Just as he had classed philology as a 'science', Wotton here conceives history

---

[37] On the emergence of this split within humanism, see Grafton, 'Renaissance readers', and Wencelius, 'La querelle'; G. W. Pigman argues from numerous examples, however, that for most Renaissance readers, 'when a historical awareness of the difference between present and past threatens to subvert the exemplarity of history, the past loses some of its difference, not its exemplarity' ('Imitation', p. 177). Eisenstein connects the Quarrel with the spread of print in *The Printing Press*, pp. 289–90; Ancients such as Swift and Pope throughout works such as *A Tale* and the *Dunciad* register their uncomfortable awareness of an explosion in the number, availability, and new composition of printed books, and Temple had already noted with concern how the numbers of ungentle 'porers upon books' had grown in England in the past 'fifty years' ('I have had several servants far gone in divinity, others in poetry; have known, in the families of some friends, a keeper deep in the Rosycrucian principles, and a laundress firm in those of Epicurus': 'Of Poetry', in *Works*, III, pp. 426–7).

[38] Mably, *Observations*, prefatory epistle ('ce seroit un grand malheur si on se lassoit d'étudier les Grecs et les Romains; l'histoire de ces deux peuples est une grande école de morale et de politique'.

not as moral guide but as scientific research.[39] Thus in 'The Battle of the Books', Swift presents Bentley, the Scriblerian epitome of index-learning rather than humane letters, in armour 'patch'd up of a thousand different Pieces' and has Scaliger say to him, '*Thy* Learning *makes thee more* Barbarous, *thy Study of* Humanity, *more* Inhuman' (pp. 250–2). Worse was to come when critics exercised their skills in editing modern authors (as in Bentley's Milton of 1732), whereby moderns in effect became ancients – and the discipline of 'modern philology' was created.

In this way emerges the opposition of 'wit' and 'learning' (or gentility and pedantry), of which so many contemporaries speak – between taste and that historical and grammatical learning known especially in France as 'érudition'. In 1699 Le Clerc mourns the absence of any modern Scaliger or Lipsius as evidence of a 'decay of letters', while for Pierre Bayle 'A change in taste is all that is involved in what you call the decline of erudition ... The mind is cultivated more than the memory. The desire now is to think with delicacy and to express oneself politely'; 'certain so-called (or real) wits have made it a custom to condemn quotations from the Greeks and erudition as pedantic'.[40] In 1762, continuing the same debate, Gibbon would trace the conflict of wit and erudition specifically to 'the famous dispute, concerning the ancients and the moderns' and devote his *Essay on Literature* to their reconciliation (p. 11). In the same effort to reconcile ancient and modern, Gibbon manages in the *Decline and Fall* to construct a shapely and instructive narrative while also including over 8,362 specific textual references – this in a century in which Condillac could write the three volumes of his *Histoire ancienne* without a single citation – though a later century would condemn even Gibbon's history as not scientific enough.[41]

The Querelle d'Homère: geometry vs history

However, being extreamly sollicitous, that every accomplished Person who has got into the Taste of Wit, calculated for this present Month of *August*,

---

[39] Wotton, *History*, and Temple, *An Introduction to the History of England* (1695), quoted in Levine, *Humanism*, pp. 172, 166; Sidney, *Defense of Poesy*, quoted in Tinkler, 'Splitting of humanism', p. 461.

[40] Le Clerc, *Parrhasiana*, I, pp. 223–4; Bayle, *Dictionnaire*, s.v. 'Alegambe' (note D), 'Meziriac' (note C). Cf. Swift in *A Tale* on 'Criticks and Wits', into 'which two Factions, I think, all present Readers may justly be divided' and who differ over their 'Way of using Books' (pp. 131–2, 145).

[41] Gibbon's self-conscious attempt to reconcile Ancient and Modern is traced by Levine in *Humanism and History*, ch. 7, and Porter, *Gibbon*, ch. 1; on Ancient vs Modern theories of history in France, see Gossman, *Medievalism*, pp. 107–25.

1697, should descend to the very *bottom* of all the *Sublime* throughout this Treatise; I hold fit to lay down this general Maxim. Whatever Reader desires to have a thorow Comprehension of an Author's Thoughts, cannot take a better Method, than by putting himself into the Circumstances and Postures of Life, that the Writer was in, upon every important Passage as it flow'd from his Pen; For this will introduce a Parity and strict Correspondence of Idea's between the Reader and the Author. Now, to assist the diligent Reader in so delicate an Affair, as far as brevity will permit, I have recollected, that the shrewdest Pieces of this Treatise, were conceived in Bed, in a Garret: At other times (for a Reason best known to myself) I thought fit to sharpen my Invention with Hunger; and in general, the whole Work was begun, continued, and ended, under a long Course of Physick, and a great want of Money. Now, I do affirm, it will be absolutely impossible for the candid Peruser to go along with me in a great many bright Passages, unless upon the several Difficulties emergent, he will please to capacitate and prepare himself by these Directions. And this I lay down as my principal *Postulatum.*

Jonathan Swift, A Tale of a Tub (1704, Preface)

On 5 April, 1716, Jean-Baptiste de Valincourt held a supper party for two members of the Academy and translators of Homer, Anne Dacier and Antoine Houdar de La Motte, along with their friends and support-ers. 'We drank to the health of Homer', one of the guests reported, 'and all went off well', thus ending (according to older textbooks) the *querelle d'Homère* which for five years had occupied first France, then all of Europe.[42] This phase of the Quarrel between Ancients and Moderns had begun in 1711 when Madame Dacier – daughter of the classical scholar Tanneguy Lefebvre, who had taught her Greek; wife since 1683 of the classicist André Dacier; and already editor of Dictys, Florus, and Callimachus, and translator of Anacreon, Sappho, Aristophanes, Plautus, and Terence – published the prose translation of Homer's *Iliad* on which she had been working for fifteen years. To Mme Dacier Homer repre-sented the 'perfection' of poetry: 'taste is never so false and corrupted as when it leaves behind the spirit and ideas of Homer'; 'It has ever been my Ambition', she wrote in her preface, 'to present our Age such a Translation of Homer as, by preserving the main Beauties of that Noble Poet, might recover the great Part of Mankind from the disad-vantageous Prejudice infus'd into them by the monstrous Copies that have been made of him'.[43]

But in 1714 the court poet Houdart de La Motte published such a monster in the form of an 'improved' Homer on which he had been

---

[42] Mlle Delaunay, quoted in Tilley, *Decline*, p. 349.
[43] *Des causes*, p. 11; *Homère défendu*, p. 4; *The Iliad*, I, p. i.

working since 1701, in which he 'corrects' Homer's 'puerilités' and 'inutilités' and clarifies, modernizes, shortens, rearranges, and sometimes simply rewrites passages to form an *Iliad* in twelve books of hexameter couplets. The whole appeared with a *Discours sur Homère*, defending his procedure – 'j'ai changé sans scrupule', he wrote – on the grounds that Homer unaltered would be as tedious to modern French readers as a romance by d'Urfé, and defending himself – he knew no Greek – on the grounds that no one knows the classical languages well enough to grasp all the details of ancient texts, and that 'reason' alone would reveal whatever was of value in Homer. Like geometry, 'the art of poetry has its axioms, its theorems, its corollaries, and its demonstrations', against which Boileau's test of time can carry no weight: 'if the critic's reasons are evident, three thousand years of contrary opinion has no more force than one day' (*Oeuvres*, II, p. 135; III, pp. 162–3).

Mme Dacier replied with her most ambitious work of criticism, *Des Causes de la corruption du goût* (1714), defending her approach to Homer on the traditional humanist grounds of the useful knowledge his work contains. La Motte's popularity, she argues, itself stems from a general decline in taste everywhere visible, from new, effeminate musical forms to the taste for novels; the 'simple', 'direct', and 'original' manners of Homer's 'heroic age' (a concept she did much to consolidate) will, she hopes, shame and educate falsely 'delicate' modern readers. For this reason her translation had made little of textual matters; her many notes explicate mainly Homer's 'beauties' and his wisdom. The epic is still for her a 'corps de doctrine' – not of scientific doctrine, to be sure; the Moderns had won that battle – but in all other fields, including even religion. Mme Dacier is quick to allegorize, and even calls on the tradition of *prisca theologia* to argue that Homer had intimations of the Christian dispensation. If Perrault and La Motte find 'low' the scene in which Achilles seeks to keep flies from the body of Patroclus, Mme Dacier follows Le Bossu in finding the scene a useful lesson in hygiene. 'Homer's faults', she tells La Motte, 'you have put there yourself': properly understood, the *Iliad* is throughout as 'logical', 'reasonable', and 'philosophical' as any *géomètre* could wish (*Corruption*, pp. 110, 144).

In 1715 as well, the most extreme of all the Cartesian Moderns, the Abbé Jean Terrasson, published the two long volumes of his *Dissertation critique sur l'Iliade, où, à l'occasion de ce poëme, on cherche des règles d'une poétique fondée sur la raison*. When Mme Dacier heard this work announced, she cried 'A geometer! the scourge of poetry, a geo-meter!' Terrasson maintained that because the soul is one, not two, divisions between the arts and sciences have been overdrawn; progress occurs equally in both, as 'a necessary effect of the human constitution':

> The exact mind discovers truth, and taste finds the way of saying it well. Such exactness is the fruit of philosophy applied to belles-lettres, just as to physical nature. For lack of this, the ancients said very elegantly so much that is false, in morals as in physics.

According to this law of progress, 'The Greeks knew how to speak, the Romans knew how to think, but the French know how to reason.'[44] Terrasson's *Dissertation* is a relentless attack on Homer's 'barbarism', intended 'to introduce the same Light of Reason and true Philosophy, by Help and Assistance of which there has of late been such Great and Noble Discoveries in the Study and Knowledge of Nature, into ... Eloquence and Poetry, Criticism and Philology, in a word ... Belles Lettres'. Even though Descartes had not yet come on the scene, Homer should through simple 'Common Sense, and natural Morality' have been able 'to have corrected the false Taste of his Age'. 'Nothing human is infallible but reason, and to reason sentiment itself must submit'; in this spirit Terrasson employed Descartes's analytic geometry to prove certain of Homer's descriptions physically impossible and constructed a definition of epic which, he said, fit all the greatest practitioners – except Homer.[45]

By this time many others had joined in, the Abbé Pons (who characterized Homer as a 'beau monstre') on the side of La Motte, Jean Boivin in defence of Mme Dacier with an *Apologie d'Homère*; both André and Anne Dacier produced further pamphlets; La Motte in turn replied in *Réflexions sur la critique* (1715); others made fun of the quarrel or sought a reconciliation. And the quarrel had become international: in England, Alexander Pope could not but be affected by it in his own project of translating Homer (Mme Dacier found him insufficiently Ancient), and Richard Blackmore, an English La Motte, published 'An Account of the Present Controversy concerning Homer's Iliad' (1716); in Italy, Vico was radically recasting the whole debate. A century of intensive historical investigation into Homer and his age had begun.[46]

Like the English Battle of the Books, this *querelle* had its roots in the era of Perrault and Fontenelle, both of whom had sought to dethrone the 'prince of poets' in their defences of modernity. Perrault especially,

---

[44] Mme Dacier, quoted in Tilley, p. 348 ('Un géomètre! quel fléau pour la poésie qu'un géomètre!'); Terrasson, *La Philosophie*, pp. 120, 21.

[45] Terrasson, *Critical Dissertations*, I, p. xxxiii; I, p. lxi; *Dissertation critique*, I, p. li.

[46] See the surveys by Foerster, Hepp, and Simonsuuri.

in his fourth *Parallèle*, had made much of Homer's coarse language, indecorous heroes, indecent gods, outdated science, and trivial and repetitious details: he wondered who was more miserable, Homer or his heroes, and made use of as yet unpublished speculations by d'Aubignac to suggest that 'Homer' had never existed at all.[47] André Dacier had already replied to Perrault in a new edition of his translation of Aristotle's *Poetics* (1692), Boileau in the critical apparatus to a new edition of his translation of Longinus (1693), which attacked Perrault especially for his ignorance of Greek; in fact it was partly his account of Homer's sublimity that had drawn Boileau to Longinus from the first. But in the years to follow, while the Modern position hardened into an extreme rationalism, the Ancients found themselves shifting ground. The seventeenth-century Quarrel had emerged from a division of what in Chapelain's time had seemed to coincide, rational principle and ancient practice; when because of scientific progress, cultural nationalism, and the claims of a new philosophy these appeared to coincide no longer, Moderns like Perrault opted for the former, while Ancients such as Boileau appealed to what had stood the test of time – to universal taste as revealed in ancient works of continuing popularity among readers of taste. What had secured 'l'approbation de plusieurs siècles' must represent 'le sentiment de tous les hommes', and so must finally be conformable with reason, even if not demonstrable scientifically.[48] Both sides thus agreed on the universality of their claims. Both stressed, whatever their views of progress, that human nature is always and everywhere the same. (Universal human nature could of course for both sides too easily collapse into the nature of man in Louis's France: when Moderns like Perrault challenged the status of ancient works in the name of universal reason, that reason usually corresponded in practice to modern French taste – for Perrault, the perfection of that of the ancients (*Parallèle*, I, pp. 98–9). In the same spirit an Ancient such as Bouhours can establish the 'rational' superiority of classical literary standards by showing modern French authors superior to any in Italy or Spain.)[49] But in the next phase of the dispute, faced by the *géomètres*, Ancients from Mme Dacier to

---

[47] Written in the mid-1690s, d'Aubignac's *Conjectures académiques, ou dissertation sur l'Iliade* were twice suppressed by the state before appearing posthumously in 1715; they were, however, widely circulated, and were known both to Perrault and later to Bentley, who for a time planned a new edition of Homer which would reflect his acceptance of d'Aubignac's view that the Homeric poems were merely a collection assembled at the time of Pisistratus.

[48] Boileau, *Réflexions critiques sur quelques passages du rhéteur Longin*, in *Oeuvres*, V, pp. 83, 97. On the uses of 'taste' in this context, see Moriarty, *Taste and Ideology*, and the introduction to this volume, pp. 14–15 above.

[49] In *La Manière de bien penser* (1687) – a work thought by many to continue the arguments of Boileau's *Art poétique* – when Philanthe defends the right of each

Du Bos began to defend Homer on the grounds of cultural and historical *difference*. This nascent historicism consorted ill with their continuing claims for a universal taste; later eighteenth-century thinkers such as Herder would call upon it to dismantle those claims and so to change the structure of criticism altogether.

'I find ancient times more beautiful', argues Mme Dacier, 'as they resemble ours less'; for her supporter Boivin, 'What pleases me in the Chinese is Chinese manners ... If the heroes of Homer's age do not resemble those of our own, that difference should give us pleasure.' The poet is a representative of his time, and so interpretation must not elide difference:

In a word, the poet imitates what is, not what came into being only later. Homer could not have embodied the customs of later centuries; it is for later centuries to recapture the customs of his. It is a primary precept of poetics that manners be well marked.[50]

Thus in her preface to the *Iliad* Mme Dacier stresses above all the other difficulties of translating such a work Homer's foreignness, and establishes the hermeneutic principle that it is the interpreter's task to place himself as far as possible in the historical position of the author. This principle, devised by the new generation of Ancients, quickly becomes commonplace: 'we should transform ourselves, as it were, into those for whom the poem was written, if we intend to form a sound judgment of its images, figures, and sentiments' (Du Bos); 'to judge the beauties of Homer, one must put oneself into the Greek camp, not into a French army' (Montesquieu); 'reason, good sense and equity demand that in reading ancient authors one transport oneself into the time and country they speak from' (Rollin). Gibbon, for whom 'want of being able to place ourselves in the same point of view with the Greeks and Romans' hides their 'beauties' from us, equates historical reconstruction with literary study itself, which is in turn a key component in the formation of a true 'philosophical spirit': 'I conceive, however, that the Study of Literature, the habit of becoming by turns, a Greek, a Roman, the

nation to its own literary taste, Bouhours gives his own spokesman Eudoxe, the defender of classical standards, a crushing reply in the name of universal 'raison' (p. 41). It was this work, J. G. Robinson has argued, through its parallel of historical and cultural difference and defence of classical French taste against Italian 'tinsel', that brought the Quarrel between Ancients and Moderns to Italy (*Studies in the Genesis*, pp. 6–15).

[50] Dacier, *L'Iliade*, p. xxv; Boivin, *Apologie d'Homère*, quoted in Lombard, p. 24; Dacier, p. xxiv. Vyverberg has recently provided a survey of *Human Nature, Cultural Diversity, and the French Enlightenment*, though without mention of the Quarrel.

disciple of Zeno and of Epicurus, is extremely proper to exercise its powers and display its merits.'[51]

There could hardly be a more conspicuous reversal from the position of seventeenth-century Ancients such as Boileau – humanist readers concerned with the universally valid lessons to be drawn from texts; no 'principal *Postulatum*' for these readers such as Swift's Modern author prescribes in *A Tale of a Tub*, a prescription that would guarantee the uniqueness of every author, and so the uselessness of all reading. The historical position taken by eighteenth-century Ancients from Mme Dacier onward of course reflects their own tastes, as opposed to that of the *géomètres*: while La Motte defends his modernized *Iliad* on the grounds that 'only a few savants are pleased to admire Homer in Greek, because they take a merely historical pleasure in it and in their understanding a learned language, rather than a purely poetic pleasure', Fénelon confides to Du Bos his fears that La Motte will cheat him of that same 'historical pleasure'.[52] But La Motte's defence suggests as well two paradoxes in Mme Dacier's stance: with her attention to historical detail, she runs the risk of appearing less the ally of Boileau than of such other 'savants' as the antiquarian Modern Bentley – as she does in stressing the foreignness of Homer's age, thereby endangering humanist reading of his works for the useful knowledge they contain. La Motte himself had defended the reading of Homer for what he has to teach us, and so also his own duty in presenting Homer to the public by selecting for presentation only those parts of the text from which we can genuinely learn: as Boileau would have agreed, what is universally true in Homer will remain so in a new context. La Motte in fact called his *Iliad* not a translation but an 'imitation', and if he knew no Greek, doesn't Homer's wisdom reside in what he has to say rather than in the language in which his thoughts are dressed? Perhaps Perrault had meant to condemn the ancients when he suggested that prose is a more exact medium than

---

[51] Du Bos, *Critical Reflections*, II, p. 394; Montesquieu, 'Mes pensées', in *Oeuvres*, p. 1,023; Rollin, *Manière d'enseigner les belles lettres*, p. 400; Gibbon, *Essay on the Study of Literature*, pp. 25, 91. Wellek lists further British instances in *Literary History*, pp. 52–4. For the development of this hermeneutic in Germany, see Reill, *Historicism*, esp. pp. 109–18; according to Bergk, proper reading of a text 'places our minds in the same state as that of its creator when he brought it into being' (*Kunst*, p. 200).

[52] Fénelon writes to Du Bos in 1713:

Je suis ravi de ce qu'il travaille à nous donner une édition de l'*Iliade*, mais s'il y change tout ce qui n'est pas accommodé aux moeurs et aux préjugés des modernes, son *Iliade* sera la sienne et non celle du poète grec. ... Ce que je souhaite, par zèle pour le public et pour le traducteur, c'est qu'il ne diminue rien de cette simplicité originale, de ce degré de naturel, de ces caractères forts et ingénus, qui peignent les temps, *qui sont historiques* et qui font tant de plaisir.

(Quoted in Lombard, pp. 24–5)

poetry, but had not Mme Dacier herself defended the fidelity of her prose to Homer's verse, arguing that 'A translator can say in prose everything that Homer said'?[53] La Motte like Dacier saw himself as a preserver of ancient values; he, not she, chose poetry as his vehicle. His complaints about Mme Dacier's pedantry occasionally recall Swift on Bentley; his differences with her ironically recapitulate the English conflict between wit and learning, this time with courtly Moderns such as La Motte representing the wits. Whereas England's best classicists (such as Bentley) were led by their new philological and antiquarian methods and learning to side with the Moderns, French classicists – in the face of the *géomètres*' claims to a monopoly on reason and method – side with erudition and 'ancienneté'.[54]

Finally, the nascent historicism of the Ancients conflicts with that other Ancient premise, universal taste. And if universal taste comes in question – if, as Batteux was to suggest, a different taste is not necessarily a bad one – so too does the premise on which taste rests: the uniformity of human nature. As Du Bos says in defending the test of time, 'There is one only supposition admitted in this reasoning, which is, that men of all ages and countries resemble one another with respect to the heart.'[55] The problem is only implicit in Mme Dacier, given her view of Homer's heroic age as a model for moderns; it becomes acute in Du Bos, whose *Réflexions critiques* (1719) contain both the most thorough early eighteenth-century attack on the *esprit de géometrie* in criticism, and the subtlest French formulation of the Ancient position. The *Réflexions* are filled throughout with echoes of earlier participants

---

[53] Perrault, *Parallèle*, II, pp. 5, 12; III, p. 62; Dacier, *L'Iliade*, I, p. xxxviii ('Un traducteur peut dire en prose tout ce qu'Homère a dit'). La Motte elsewhere defines poetry in terms that specifically exclude metre: 'la poésie, qui n'est autre chose que la hardiesse des pensées, la vivacité des images et l'énergie de l'expression, demeurera toujours ce qu'elle est indépendamment de toute mesure' (*Oeuvres*, III, p. 31).

[54] Roy Porter explains this difference by reference as well to the relatively more highly developed professionalization of historical study in early eighteenth-century France, where historical research and publication were actively sponsored not only by the Catholic Church but also through prestigious professional societies such as the Académie des Inscriptions and their subsidized learned journals; in England at the same time no such societies or journals existed, and even in the universities historical study languished (*Gibbon*, pp. 31–8).

[55] Du Bos, *Reflections*, II, pp. 356–7; Batteux, *Les Beaux Arts*, p. 108: 'Serons-nous assez hardis, pour préférer celui que nous avons à des autres, & pour les condamner? Ce seroit une témérité, & même une injustice parce que les Goûts en particulier peuvent être différens, ou même opposés, sans cesser d'être bons en soi.' Dr Johnson's well-known historical scepticism ('Why, Sir, we know very little about the Romans'; 'That certain Kings reigned and certain battles were fought, we can depend upon as true; but all the colouring, all the philosophy of history is conjecture') may be explained in part as an attempt to counter the threat of human difference lurking within historicism, and so to shore up the continuing relevance of ancient literature.

in the Quarrel whose views Du Bos seeks to mediate, especially by making use of Locke and of the new doctrine of sensory beauty Du Bos had learnt from Addison.

Du Bos opens his challenge to the *géomètres* by posing a question: will the *Iliad* go the way of Ptolemy's astronomy? Must poems, like scientific theories, eventually be exploded? To deny that they must, Du Bos returns to the new division between art and science – which, as we have seen, he accepts – in order to disprove the implications the Moderns had drawn from it: that science is the realm of reason, art of opinion. He does this by substituting an extreme Lockean view of the sciences (as based on accumulated sense experience) for the Cartesianism of Fontenelle and Terrasson (science as method). No difference of 'method' – in the sense of any supposed 'perfection to which we have brought the art of reasoning' in 'the last seventy years' (since Descartes, 'who passes for the father of the new philosophy') – distinguishes 'natural science'. Thought itself has not changed; 'tis imperceptible in practice, whether . . . Barbey's logic, or that of Port Royal' makes any difference in how one thinks. 'We do not reason better than the ancients in history, politics, or morals' (thus Du Bos reclaims 'reason' for the Ancients); 'The only cause of the perfection of natural sciences, or to speak more exactly, the only cause of these sciences being less imperfect at present than they were in former days, is our knowing more facts than they were acquainted with.' Natural science has progressed, then, 'not by any methodical research, but by . . . mere fortuitous experiment', 'time and chance' – a happy accumulation of sense experience in which 'reasoning has had very little share'.[56] In natural science as in art and criticism, then, there are no *a priori* rules: in Du Bos's Lockean view, the impressions of sense must decide in both, and where sense does not extend we can have no more than (more or less probable) opinion. And so, finally, it is in the realm of reason, not sense, that 'prejudice' and 'authority' have their sway; and since judgements of literary merit are reports of sense impressions, 'natural facts' given us in experience which 'we know without meditating' – here Du Bos makes use of Addison – it is not in the world of letters that their effects have most been felt.

---

[56] In an extended example, Du Bos traces Galileo's, Torricelli's, and Pascal's experiments leading to the theory of the vacuum, concluding: 'This is an uncontestable proof that the learned did not proceed from one principle to another, and in a speculative way to the discovery of this truth' (II, p. 340). The new 'philosophical spirit' of the 'geometricians', he writes in a passage that could come from Vico (or from Swift on his Laputans), has in fact retarded progress: it has caused 'necessary arts [to be] neglected; the most useful systems for the preservation of society abolished; and speculative reasonings preferred to practice. We behave without any regard to experience, the best director of mankind' (p. 331).

Instead, Du Bos claims, relishing the irony of using the Moderns' own arguments against them, they have been the attendants of science: to the extent that natural science must depend on reason, prejudice and authority will afflict it and we will 'have fashions in sciences as well as in cloaths'.[57]

Du Bos thus helps initiate in France a century of defences of erudition against what were seen as the encroachments not only of wit (as had already begun in England) but also of natural science. Especially in that haven of *ancienneté*, the Académie des Inscriptions, appears a succession of discourses such as the Abbé du Resnel's 'Réflexions générales sur l'utilité des Belles-Lettres; et sur les inconvéniens du goût exclusif qui paroit s'établir en faveur des mathématiques et de la physique' (1741):

We must be careful not to confuse the philosophical mind with the calculating mind ... We will not hide the fact that our century is beginning to lose sight of this distinction; that in taking pride in geometry – or rather, in its desire to reduce everything to calculation, to apply that method everywhere, or to erect it as a universal instrument – our century has practically ceased to be philosophical ... Letters are the only barrier capable of stopping the progress of false wit, of limiting the conquests of the calculating mind: the first tries to seduce us, the second to subjugate us. By maintaining the taste for truth which the Ancients gave us, letters will teach us not to mistake the tinsel of the first for gold: in the same way, they will teach us to contain the second within its limits.[58]

The theme is taken up by Fréret; Juvigny traces to Fontenelle the moment when 'Geometry was attacked by Wit's disease', 'to imagine that

[57] II, p. 357 (prejudice), p. 355 (authority), pp. 356–8 (the judgement of taste), p. 326 (fashion). Du Bos (like other Ancients who considered the question, such as Jonathan Swift) thus comes closer to that view of science which has emerged in the late twentieth century than do Moderns such as Wotton, who speculates in the *Reflections* that, given the wealth of new discoveries and theorizing that had followed development of proper method, natural science may soon like poetry be complete: 'such Swarms of Great men in every Part of Natural and Mathematical Knowledge have within these few Years appeared, that it may, perhaps, without Vanity, be believed, that ... the next Age will not find very much Work of this Kind to do' (p. 348). Cf. Swift, *A Tale of a Tub*, ed. A. C. Guthkelch and David Nichol Smith, 2nd edn (Oxford, 1958), pp. 44–5.

[58] '... l'esprit philosophique ... il faut bien ne le confondre avec l'*esprit de calcul*, qui de sa nature est renfermé dans un cercle, au delà duquel on ne doit pas lui permettre de s'étendre. Nous ne dissimulerons pas que notre siècle commence à perdre de vûe cette distinction; & qu'à force de piquer d'être Géomètre, ou plustôt de vouloir tout ramener au calcul, d'en appliquer par-tout la méthode, de l'ériger en instrument universel, il cesse presque d'être Philosophe ... les Lettres sont la seule barrière qui puisse arrêter les progrès du faux bel esprit, & borner les conquêtes de l'esprit de calcul: l'un cherche à nous séduire; l'autre voudroit nous subjuger. Les lettres, en maintenant le goût du vrai que les Anciens nous ont donné, nous enseigneront à ne pas prendre pour de l'or le clinquant du premier: elles nous enseigneront de même à contenir le second dans les limites ...' (pp. 23–4, 36).

it could set the laws for poetry and eloquence'; in an essay 'Sur la Guerre des sciences et des lettres', Bonald predicts 'the imminent fall of the republic of letters, and the universal domination of the exact natural sciences'.[59] It is this debate that Gibbon takes up in his *Essay on the Study of Literature* (in which 'literature' includes all learning, especially history), complaining that 'Natural Philosophy and the Mathematics are now in possession of the throne', tracing the conflict to Descartes and Fontenelle, and outlining a 'philosophy' of 'criticism' which will reunite erudition, wit, and geometry, science and letters, Ancient and Modern. But all these writers, having routed the *géomètres*, fall prey as had Du Bos to the conflicts of historicism with both humanist reading and taste.[60]

Like Mme Dacier, Du Bos demands historical knowledge of readers, since 'the poet's task is not to purge his age of its errors in physics, but to give a faithful description of the customs and manners of his country, in order to render his imitation as likely as possible' (pp. 395–6). 'Life and manners' are the poet's province – not science, or even natural description, which can please only those familiar with the scenes described. (Having spent pages describing the effects of differing climates on different nations, Du Bos writes, 'As we are indifferent in respect to delights which we never wish for, we cannot be sensibly affected by the description of them, were it drawn even by Virgil' (pp. 378–9)). But even assuming we can, as readers, 'become' Greeks or Romans in manners, to what end do we do so? If we moderns find it low or eccentric to talk to horses, we must recall that 'these discourses were very suitable in the *Iliad*, a poem written for a nation, among whom a horse was, as it were, a fellow-boarder with its master'; 'Homer, in this very passage for which he has been so frequently censured, would still have pleased several nations of Asia and Afric, who have not changed their ancient method of managing their horses' (pp. 395–6). But how is such

---

[59] Juvigny, *Décadence*, pp. 348, 385 (he adds on p. 476: 'the more the positive sciences, geometry, algebra, and mathematics, and the rest, rise and become perfected, the more we lose in sentiment, the more taste will be lost, the more letters will waste away, and the more genius for the fine arts will die'); Bonald, *Oeuvres*, pp. 394–6 ('les sciences *exactes* et *naturelles*').

[60] Gibbon, *Essay*, pp. 4, 11, 45–51. (We can most clearly see Gibbon falling prey to the conflicts when, having spent many pages demonstrating the use of historically informed 'criticism' through a reading of Virgil's *Georgics*, he can conclude no more than that understanding the poet's historical context shows us Virgil was not a 'mere Writer': p. 44.) On this debate in France see, besides Starobinski, Lorimer, 'A neglected aspect of the "Querelle"', and Seznec, 'Le Singe antiquaire'; it had its German equivalent in the reaction against Wolff and his school, under whose influence, according to the great jurist Pütter, writers 'began to neglect languages, philology, antiquities, history, experience, observations, laws, and sources of all kinds whose mastery was more difficult than just considering postulated definitions and demonstrations' (*Litteratur*, I, p. 445).

a passage to please *us* – to do more than serve for us as a curious historical document? Nor, given his Addisonian account of the sensory nature of aesthetic pleasure, can knowledge of any sort finally partake of what for Du Bos is the defining nature and purpose of poetry: 'The chief merit of history is to inrich our memory, and to form our judgment; but that of a poem consists in moving us, and 'tis the very charm of the emotion that makes us read it' (pp. 382–3). It is this strain in Du Bos's thought that leads him to explain poetry as a mere 'divertissement' from 'ennui', and to identify the 'poetic' specifically with 'expression'.[61] Siding with Mme Dacier against La Motte, Du Bos falls into the arms of Bentley; siding with Locke and Addison against Terrasson, he fails to escape Fontenelle.

Nachleben of the Quarrel: alternative traditions, periodization, and the naming of 'classicism'

That futile quarrel is well known which raged for half a century in France, England, and Germany, especially in the first, over the preferences of the Ancients over the Moderns. Although much was said by both parties that was good, the quarrel could nevertheless not come to an end, because it had been started without a clear perspective on the question, and because almost always it was vanity that carried the day.

Johann Gottfried Herder, *Adrastea* (1801)

Historians of the Quarrel of the Ancients and the Moderns from Rigault onward have made much of the 'solution of 1717', a reconciliation based on both sides' acceptance of a general historicist relativism; this reconciliation would hold until the 1790s, when Schiller and Friedrich Schlegel, concerned to provide a positive account of what by then was modernity – one that would not simply judge modern culture in ancient terms – reconceive the dispute.[62] In the process of this reconception were created the terms by which eighteenth-century literary culture has so long been known: 'classicism' and, later, 'neo-classicism'. But it is hardly clear that in 1717 the Quarrel was 'resolved': we have seen how fragile was Du Bos's mediation; few of the *géomètres* were convinced. 'Relativism' is always unstable, threatening at any moment to revert to the absolutes that motivated it: the same Winckelmann who wrote so stirringly of the uniqueness of Greece wrote as well, 'The only way for

---

[61] I, pp. 4–10 (ennui); II, p. 382: 'the merit of things in poetry is almost always identified (if I be allowed the expression) with the merit of expression', echoing Mme Dacier ('Jamais poète ne paraîtra excellent poète, indépendamment de l'expression': *Corruption*, p. 164).
[62] Rigault, *Histoire*, ch. 7; Jauss, 'Schiller und Schlegel'.

us to become great, and, indeed – if this is possible – inimitable, is by imitating the ancients.'[63] Through the rest of the century all major critics return to the Quarrel, with the result that much eighteenth-century criticism seems 'a prolonged epilogue' to it.[64] These recurrences can be as naive as Mark Akenside's 'Ballance of Poets' (1746), a *parallèle* which awards 167 'points' to the modern poets, 105 to the ancients, or as thoughtful as Voltaire's lifelong meditation on the problem, but all major critics, especially after mid-century, display a far greater and more central interest in history than had critics a century before.[65]

The Quarrel would persist as long as, and along with, debate over imitation, emulation, and originality. Thus Edward Young calls upon the arguments of Perrault and Fontenelle in championing the possibilities of Modern literature in his *Conjectures on Original Composition* (1759): 'knowledge physical, mathematical, moral, and divine increases; all arts and sciences are making considerable advance'; 'the day may come' for literature as well 'when the moderns may proudly look back on the comparative darkness of former ages' (p. 74). But where his French sources had cited philosophic advance as the ground of modern literary progress, Young adduces the Christian dispensation, unknown to Homer and Virgil: 'a marvelous light, unenjoy'd of old, is pour'd on us by revelation, with larger prospects extending our Understanding, with brighter objects enriching our Imagination, with an inestimable prize setting our Passions on fire, thus strengthening every power that enables composition to shine' (p. 72). Young in fact owed much of this argument to his friend and fellow-Modern Samuel Richardson, editor or author of much of the *Conjectures*.[66] In his correspondence and novels Richardson had long called upon arguments familiar from the *querelle d'Homère* to defend modern literature against ancient, and in particular the piety and politeness to be found in that genre long thought original with the Moderns, the novel, against the brutality and superstition of ancient epic. He writes for instance to Lady Bradshaigh in about 1749:

I admire you for what you say of the fierce, fighting Iliad. Scholars, judicious scholars, dared they to speak out, against a prejudice of thousands

---

[63] 'Thoughts on the imitation of the painting and sculpture of the Greeks' (1755), p. 33.

[64] Nisbet, *German Criticism*, p. 3.

[65] Akenside's essay is discussed by Spadafora in *Progress* (pp. 67–8); on Voltaire's concern with the Quarrel over half a century, see David Williams, *Voltaire*. Spadafora provides ample evidence that the Quarrel occupied Britain throughout the eighteenth century (*Progress*, ch. 1); see Lorimer and Kapitza for France and Germany, respectively.

[66] Richardson's contribution to the *Conjectures* was first made clear by McKillop in 'Richardson, Young, and the *Conjectures*'.

of years in its favour, I am persuaded would find it possible for Homer to nod, at least. I am afraid this poem, noble as it truly is, has done infinite mischief for a series of ages; since to it, and its copy the Eneid, is owing, in a great measure, the savage spirit that has actuated, from the earliest ages to this time, the fighting fellows, that, worse than lions or tigers, have ravaged the earth, and made it a field for blood.

On the basis of passages such as this, Ian Watt has suggested a conscious rejection by Defoe, Richardson, and even Fielding of classical, especially epic, models for their experiments with the novel.[67]

The 'solution of 1717', however ambiguous, guided a century of historical literary studies: inquiries into the 'true Homer', most notably by Vico, the Scotsmen Thomas Blackwell and Robert Wood, and the Germans C. G. Heyne and F. A. Wolf, as well as manifold inquiries into alternative (non-classical) traditions, most notably into 'Gothic' and other Northern European medieval traditions, but also into 'the East' and the pre-classical Mediterranean (where, with Homer, writers such as Pindar and others came to be associated). As Lionel Gossman has observed, eighteenth-century 'medievalism' was but one 'part of a wider movement of curiosity about and sympathy for earlier and more "primitive" cultures'.[68] That all these inquiries comprise in effect one search for an alternative, non-classical literary tradition – a new *ancienneté* – is testified both by the facility of critics and of poets in mixing them together (for instance, in the frequent, and frequently criticized, conflation of Celtic and Scandinavian materials into a single, so-called 'runic' tradition), and by what for many antiquarians was the virtual interchangeability of their interests. Thomas Percy, for instance, outlines in 1762 his plans for an anthology of 'Specimens of the ancient Poetry of different nations' that would include:

the *Erse Poetry*: the *Runic Poetry*: and some *Chinese Poetry* that was published last winter at the end of a book called *Hau Kiou choaan* or *the Pleasing History* 4 vol. Besides these, I have procured a MS. translation of the celebrated *Tograi Carmen* from the Arabic: and have set a friend to translate *Solomon's Song* afresh from the Hebrew, chiefly with a view to the poetry ... I have myself gleaned up specimens of *East-Indian Poetry*: *Peruvian Poetry*: *Lapland Poetry*: *Greenland Poetry*: and inclosed I send you one specimen of *Saxon Poetry*.[69]

---

[67] Richardson, *Correspondence*, IV, p. 287, quoted in Watt, *Rise of the Novel*, p. 243.

[68] *Medievalism*, p. 334. On the 'Gothic', see Peter Sabor's contribution in this volume; on Vico's Homeric studies as a novel reconciliation of Ancient and Modern, see Levine, 'Vico and the Quarrel'.

[69] Letter to Evan Evans, *Correspondence*, p. 31. On mixture and confusion of Norse and Celtic materials, see Snyder, *Celtic Revival*, pp. 9–12.

Study of non-classical traditions was of course a project of more than scholarly interest: it was to serve as the source of inspiration for a new poetry. Freed from classical models (from Greek and Roman mythology especially, now seen as exhausted or immoral), able to pursue a historically well-grounded marvellous, poetry was to be reinvigorated through emulation of the newly recovered alternative *ancienneté*. 'Tis such pieces', William Shenstone wrote to Percy in 1760, 'that contain ye true *Chemical* Spirit or Essence of *Poetry*'; Thomas Warton reveals part of his purpose in writing his long study of Spenser's precursors, the *History of English Poetry* (1774–81): 'the manners of romance are better calculated to answer the purposes of true poetry, to captivate the imagination, and to produce surprise, than the fictions of classical antiquity'.[70] Poets join critics in becoming literary historians, producing over the last half of the eighteenth century hundreds of volumes of historical verse, complete with detailed, learned (or pseudo-learned) annotation. Nor, again, was the new *ancienneté* to be of use in understanding (and composing) poetry alone: varied lists (like Percy's) of Northern and Eastern materials loom large in the age's many inquiries into the origins of 'romance' specifically in the sense of prose fiction, in works from Bishop Huet's *Traité de l'origine des romans* (1670) and the essays of the Comte de Caylus through Clara Reeve's *The Progress of Romance* (1785) and John Moore's 'Upon the Original of Romances' (1797).[71]

Inquiry into non-classical traditions served nationalist ends as well, especially as literary and other antiquarians joined in what Herbert Butterfield has called 'the greatest creative achievement of historical understanding' in all of scholarship: 'the recovery and exposition of the medieval world' (*Historical Scholarship*, p. 33). As John Aikin asked in 1773, 'Shall we feel the fire of heroic poetry in translations from Greece and Rome, and never search for it in the native products of our own country?' (*Prose*, p. 140). Elaboration of a historic national identity through examination of medieval literary remains could serve varied political purposes: in Britain (where medieval texts were often found to express English 'liberty') and in Germany (where they conveyed the sense of a Germanic 'people'), scholars such as Richard Hurd and J. J. Bodmer sought to establish a national identity independent of what they saw as the cultural domination not merely of the Ancients, but of the Ancients especially as they had been interpreted in France; in France

---

[70] Shenstone to Percy, 10 Nov. 1760, in *Letters*, p. 401; Warton, *History*, I, p. 434. On eighteenth-century reconsiderations of Spenser, culminating in Richard Hurd's reclassification of *The Faerie Queene* 'as a Gothic, not a classic poem', see Johnston, *Enchanted Ground*, pp. 62–5.

[71] Johnston surveys theories of the origin of romance from Huet to Walter Scott in *Enchanted Ground*, ch. 1.

itself – with its longer tradition of scholarly interest in *le genre trouba-dour* – medievalism could serve equally well the ends either of radical critique or conservative defence of the 'bon vieux temps de notre Monarchie', with its 'brave, pious, and simple chevaliers'.[72] But in all three nations, medieval texts, which had until recently been classified as modern (i.e., post-classical), came, in order to serve as the basis of a new *ancienneté*, to be labelled 'ancient'. Thus for instance the kinds of texts such as ballads that in the *Spectator* Joseph Addison had elevated by comparison with the great 'ancients' come fifty years later to take their place in collections such as Evan Evans's *Specimens of the Poetry of the Ancient Welsh Bards* (1764) and Percy's *Reliques of Ancient English Poetry* (1765).[73]

In the course of these inquiries was elaborated one of the most sig-nificant legacies of the long debate between Ancient and Modern: the concept of distinct historical periods. 'It is the *different Periods* or Steps, naturally succeeding in the *Progression of Manners*', Thomas Blackwell writes in 1735, 'that can only account for the Succession of Wit and Literature' (*Homer*, p. 77). From mid-century onward Turgot, Rousseau, Condorcet, and all the many authors of what Dugald Stewart would call 'conjectural history' divide history into such developmental stages. Du Bos had already in 1719 paused to explain that by 'siècle' he did not mean simply a century: 'Before I enter upon my subject, I must beg leave of the reader to use the word *age* in a signification somewhat different from that in which it is rigorously understood. The word age, in the civil sense thereof, implies a duration of one hundred years; but sometimes I shall make it import a duration of sixty or seventy only.'[74] His example of 'sixty or seventy' years – the length of a human life – suggests that principle which would govern the development of the new concept: the period as a stage in the life of a people, understood as an interconnected whole – a 'culture', in the eighteenth century's newly weighted historical (rather than simply cultivational) sense of that word.[75]

---

[72] The phrases are Sabathier de Castres's, from his *Les trois siècles de la littérature françoise* (1773), quoted in Gossman, *Medievalism*, pp. 340–1.

[73] Addison, *Spectator* nos. 70, 74 (1711). Evans and Percy take the word 'ancient' for their titles from James Macpherson's first Ossianic volume, *Fragments of Ancient Poetry, Collected in the Highlands of Scotland* (1760).

[74] *Reflections*, II, p. 95 ('Avant que d'entrer en matière, je dois demander à mon lecteur qu'il me soit permis de prendre ici le mot de siècle dans une signification un peu différente de celle qu'il doit avoir à la rigueur. Le mot de siècle pris dans son sens précis, signifie une durée de cent années, & quelquefois je l'employerai pour signifier une durée de soixante ou de soixante & dix ans': *Réflexions*, II, p. 135).

[75] On the emergence of periodization, see Bergner, *Formalism*, ch. 2, and (on the 'four stages' theory of the conjectural historians in particular) Meek, *Social Science*; on changes in the meaning of 'culture' (especially in Germany), see Kroeber, and Kluckhohn, *Culture*, pt. 1. P. H. Reill traces the emergence of German historicism in the context both of the Quarrel and of the rise of 'aesthetics' in *Historicism*.

The relativist historicism implicit in such periodization becomes most apparent in the work of Herder, who like Voltaire meditated on the Quarrel throughout his life. According to his *Ideen zur Philosophie der Geschichte* (1784–91), 'every nation [*Volk*] is one people, having its own national form, as well as its own language'; 'nations modify themselves, according to time, place, and their internal character: each bears in itself the standard of its perfection, totally independent of all comparison with that of others' (pp. 7, 98). Such a view means the end of the uniformity of human nature: whereas Hobbes claimed each man to be able 'to read in himself, not this or that particular man; but mankind' (*Leviathan*, p. 6) – and from the laws of physics to develop a political analysis that would describe all men at all times in all places – for Herder, just as individuals change in the course of their lives, 'the whole species is one continued metamorphosis' (p. 4). Thus Herder subscribes to the hermeneutic developed by Ancients from Mme Dacier onwards: the task of the interpreter is not first of all evaluation, but to enter into the spirit of works, to understand them from inside and in their own terms – to 'become for a while an ancient Caledonian', as he says in his essay on Ossian (p. 157). Most of all must we read poetry this way, for it is the poet's achievement to 'express' the culture from which he arises – to write *Volkspoesie*, works that in their special literary unity mirror the unity of the cultural period that they express.

Thus in his many comments on the 'ridiculous Quarrel', Herder condemns the genre of the *parallèle* as fundamentally ahistorical – it seeks to compare incommensurables – and singles out for special abuse 'the Perraults of France and Germany', self-righteous 'sycophants of their century' who write only to celebrate the standards of their own age. Their mode of evaluation is in fact impossible; since we, like those we read, are the products of our cultures, the critic has no neutral ground on which to stand.[76] Yet despite all this, Herder does engage in *parallèles* of his own. In his essay on 'Ossian', he likens Ossian both to ancient Scandinavian and American Indian bards; in 'Shakespeare', having just explained that drama is a unique cultural product – 'In Greece drama developed in a way in which it could not develop in the north', and so 'Sophocles's drama and Shakespeare's are two things which in a certain respect have scarcely the name in common' – he proceeds to a comparison. All wrote at a similar early stage in their nations' development, and so all display in the same ways parallel historical processes: what in the

---

[76] Herder writes with bitter irony of one 'Latin Perrault', Christian Klotz, who had presumed to praise Homer: 'Such praise has a monstrous dimension; for if Homer is indeed a supreme power and a measure, as it were, of the human mind, then it seems that the one who is able to judge and criticise him must be altogether superhuman! . . . In this case, I step back in order to admire the critical god' (quoted in Menges, 'Herder', pp. 160–1).

Ideen Herder would call 'laws' of history, whose task it is to understand not merely static states, but processes of change. All wrote, too, at a moment fortunate for *Volkspoesie*, a moment that has been lost: 'Our poetry does not emerge from a living world.'[77]

For the conjectural historians, all cultures, in their own way, follow a similar sequence of stages, an autonomous yet analogous pattern of growth – usually in the direction of economic and political progress. One Scottish conjecturalist, James Gordon, writes in 1762:

It is agreed that Human affairs in general have proceeded from very small beginnings. I shall venture to suppose, that by attending to their progress, a certain uniform course might be discovered, which they all pursue; and that consequently by knowing to what particular stage they had in any instance advanced, the state of perfection in which they then were, might with some probability be guessed at.

(*Thoughts*, p. 12)

We should no doubt be grateful, as Blackwell had suggested, not to live in a time that could become the subject of an epic – an age as barbarous as Homer's. But equally often these historians testify to a sense of loss, especially in arts such as poetry. Throughout Europe can be heard such comments about the difference between past and present as: 'What we have gotten by this revolution, you will say, is a great deal of good sense. What we have lost, is a world of fine fabling' (Richard Hurd, 1762); 'We lose taste, but we acquire thought' (Voltaire, 1775); 'Our time, the death of poetry!' (Herder, 1764).[78] A culture which once sustained great poetry seemed to have passed. For many, the earliest period in any culture was one of savage spontaneity, the latest of rich but enervating refinement; only a middle period could sustain a Homer or a Shakespeare – a poised balance of 'civilized superstition', as Thomas Warton called it (*History*, IV, p. 328).

Historicism, then, continued to favour 'ancient' writing, even while opening that category to texts earlier Ancients had rejected (and if a new generation celebrated 'runic' or 'Hebrew' poetry, the Nibelungenlied, popular balladry, or Ossian, it was largely classical scholarship, especially through its development of antiquarianism and revised understanding of Homer, that had shown them how). But the widening of the historical

---

[77] 'Shakespeare', p. 162; 'Ossian', p. 159. Within a tradition both understanding and evaluation are possible: Herder says of Shakespeare, 'Happy am I that, though time is running out, I still live at a time when it is possible for me to understand him' (p. 176).

[78] Blackwell, *Homer*, p. 28 (Hume develops the same view in 'Of eloquence', Gibbon in his *Essay on Literature*, pp. 21–3); Hurd, *Letters on Chivalry*, p. 120; Voltaire, letter to Frederick the Great, quoted in Williams, *Voltaire*, p. 111; Herder, quoted in Menges, 'Herder', p. 169. Judith Plotz surveys such ideas in Britain, 1700–1830, in *Ideas of Decline*.

categories of 'ancient' and 'modern' into stages in the development of any culture – in effect, stages or states of consciousness – led in the 1790s to a transformation of the Quarrel: Schiller's *Über naive und sentimentalische Dichtung* (1796) transforms the categories into 'naive' and 'sentimental', Friedrich Schlegel's *Über das Studium der griechischen Poesie* (1796–7) into the 'objective' and the 'characteristic', 'individual', or *'interessant'* – terms the Schlegel brothers would soon reformulate as the 'classic' and 'romantic' and which, through writers such as Madame de Staël, would gain European currency. The first historic stage and state of consciousness was characterized by harmonious unity with nature such as Winckelmann had found in the Greeks (and which Schiller found in his friend Goethe), the second by the division, alienation, and complexity of the modern self. To the extent that the poet expresses his culture, both are necessary and even justified, but it was the aim of both Schiller and Schlegel to point the way to a higher modernity that reconciles Ancient and Modern: 'the problem of our literature', Schlegel wrote in 1794, 'seems to me the unification of the essentially modern with the essentially classical' (*Briefe*, p. 170).

It is thus in the final eighteenth-century stage of the Quarrel, in the romantic construction of an 'other' against which to define itself but also to be recaptured, that our own period terminology for speaking of the eighteenth century is created. First, seventeenth-century French writers such as Corneille, Racine, and La Fontaine become 'classic' not in their excellence (as the term had meant since Aulus Gellius' famous formula 'classicus scriptor, non proletarius'), canonical authority, or even antiquity, but in Schlegel's new sense. The term was quickly applied to English writers as well (long seen as dominated by the French), so that in 1800 Schlegel can refer to 'the so-called classical [*klassischen*] poets of the English: Pope, Dryden and whoever else'. 'Classicism', a more value-laden term, is coined about 1820, slowly to make its way, given the early nineteenth century's animus against the eighteenth, amongst competing labels such as 'classicalism', 'classicality', and 'pseudo-classicism', until at the turn of our century an anti-romantic reaction established the term for good. (Meanwhile, mainly in Britain, to avoid the negative connotations of the neologism 'classicism', some nineteenth-century historians revive the label 'Augustan' to designate the still uncertainly labelled era in English letters that falls, in Leslie Stephen's words, 'midway between the taste of the Renaissance and that of modern times'.)[79]

---

[79] Stephen, *History of English Thought*, I, p. 355. On the history of 'Augustan' in England and recent debate surrounding its use, see Johnson, Weinbrot, and Erskine-Hill; no similar studies exist of the term in other literatures, or in the non-literary arts (Schueller cites references to an 'Augustan age' of music in 'The Quarrel', p. 326).

Finally, to distinguish the French eighteenth century – since Voltaire, seen as inferior – from the seventeenth, literary historians from about 1900 use the initially even more pejorative 'neo-classicism', which again soon spreads beyond France; among American academics especially, it comes by the 1920s to designate eighteenth-century English practice as well.[80] Our terms 'classic' and 'neo-classic', then, though suggestive of antiquity, are the last, delayed contribution of eighteenth-century Moderns to the Quarrel. Most recently, following Schlegel's stated purpose in studying Greek poetry to find 'the origin of modern poetry among the Ancients' (II, p. 48) – that is, to trace the genesis of romanticism – the French literary historians Daniel Mornet (1909) and Paul Van Tieghem (1924) devise *préromantisme*, which quickly achieves international application to name eighteenth-century harbingers of the nineteenth. Though long in disfavour in Anglo-American circles because of its implication of a teleological ('Whig') theory of literary history, the term 'preromanticism' now appears even here to be reviving.[81]

[80] See Howarth, 'Neo-classicism' – who in 1978 finds that term not yet fully established in French studies – and Wellek, 'The term and concept of classicism' and 'French classicist criticism', who traces the importance of political conservatives such as Charles Maurras and Julien Benda (and in England T. S. Eliot and T. E. Hulme) in finally establishing 'classicism'.

[81] On the invention of 'preromanticism' see Scouten, 'The Warton forgeries', and for criticisms of the concept Miller, 'Whig interpretation', pp. 78–9, and Stone, *Art of Poetry*, pp. 84–97. After some twenty years of suspicion, testimony to the term's reviving popularity in English may be found in Rolf Lessenich's *Aspects of English Preromanticism* (1989), J. R. Watson's *Pre-Romanticism in English Poetry of the Eighteenth Century* (1989), and Marshall Brown's *Preromanticism* (1991).

Genres

3

Poetry, 1660–1740

James Sambrook

French: to 1700

Critic Learning flourish'd most in *France*

(Pope, *Essay on Criticism*)

With one of those left-handed compliments that are often directed across
the English Channel Dryden in his *Dedication of the Aeneid*, 1697,
candidly concedes that, 'impartially speaking, the French are as much
better critics than the English, as they are worse poets'; he calls Le
Bossu 'the best of modern critics', allows the critical writings of Boileau
and Rapin to be 'the greatest of this age', and speaks respectfully of
Bouhours and Saint-Évremond (Dryden, *Of Dramatic Poesy*, I, pp. 246,
199, II, pp. 56–8).

The *Traité du poème épique* (1675) of René Le Bossu (1631–89)
provided for its period the most authoritative modern treatise on what,
it was generally agreed, was the highest genre of poetry. Le Bossu shares
the neo-classical view that poetry was brought to perfection by the
ancients, 'therefore they who practise afterwards the same art are obliged
to tread in their footsteps, and to search in their writings the foundation
of them; for it is not just that new rules should destroy the authority
of the old' (Dryden, *Of Dramatic Poesy*, I, p. 246). Le Bossu's moderate
tone, more judicious than judicial, appealed to the scientific temper of
his age. The anonymous English translator of the *Traité* in 1695 said of
him:

What he takes from Aristotle and Horace he explains, improves and refines:
What is his own, though never so judicious and rational, he lays down not
in a dogmatical, magisterial way, but by way of problem; and what he
asserts with an air of confidence, though not his masters' thoughts, yet seem
to be natural deductions from what they have wrote about it.

(Clark, *Boileau*, p. 250)

The first rule that Le Bossu lays down for the writer of an epic poem
is to determine what the work's moral end will be. The moral

is the first business of the poet, as being the groundwork of his instruction. This being formed, he contrives such a design, or fable, as may be most suitable to the moral. After this he begins to think of the persons whom he is to employ in carrying on his design; and gives them the manners which are most proper to their several characters. The thoughts and words are the last parts, which give beauty and colouring to the piece.

(Dryden, *Of Dramatic Poesy*, II, p. 186)

Dryden here summarizes Le Bossu's central doctrine as to how an epic is made and lists in order Le Bossu's headings under which an epic may be systematically criticized. Pope ridiculed this 'recipe for making an epic poem' in *An Essay on Criticism*, lines 114–15, and in a Scriblerian parody, but he used it for the schematic criticism of epic in the preface to his own translation of Homer; so did Addison in his important and influential criticism of Milton's *Paradise Lost* in the *Spectator*.

The humbler but no less well-trodden field of pastoral sprouted its authoritative treatise in the *Dissertatio de Carmine Pastorali* (1659) of René Rapin (1621–87). This too is a neo-classical primer: it extracts a set of principles from the pastorals of Theocritus and Virgil and from what might be applied to pastoral poetry in the criticism of Aristotle and Horace. Rapin lays it down that pastoral is the imitation of the actions of a shepherd, or one considered under that character, living in a remote or fictitious Golden Age. In writing this kind of poetry, 'we must consult unstain'd, uncorrupted Nature', and, as simplicity was the principal virtue of the Golden Age, so 'the Fable, Manners, Thought, and Expression ought to be full of the most innocent simplicity imaginable' (Rapin, *Dissertatio*, pp. 33, 37). Between 1668 and 1681 Rapin published a series of comparisons between writers (Virgil and Homer, Horace and Virgil, Demosthenes and Cicero, Plato and Aristotle, Thucydides and Livy) which did much to establish a distinct mode of criticism which contemporaries, including Saint-Évremond and Dryden, employed to good effect.

Rapin's most important work, *Réflexions sur la poétique d'Aristote et sur les ouvrages des poètes anciens et modernes* (1674) is best known as a work of dramatic critical theory, but it dealt with non-dramatic poetry too. Rapin takes for granted the traditional hierarchy of kinds, headed by the epic and tragedy. Satire finds a place in this hierarchy as the non-dramatic counterpart to comedy, its function being to instruct its readers by discrediting vice. The satirist is one who speaks out with true zeal against the evils of his times, but he should not tear the mask from vice too rudely. Rapin therefore rates Horace's art above Juvenal's by virtue of its greater delicacy: smiling satire is to be preferred to savage satire. Descending the hierarchy of kinds, Rapin treats the lower forms with an unusual degree of contempt: 'A Sonnet, Ode, Elegy, Epigram, and those little Verses that often make so much noise in the world, are ordinarily no more than the meer productions of imagination; a superficial wit, with a little conversation of the world, is capable of these things'; in them there is 'nothing of that celestial fire which only is the portion of an extraordinary Genius' (Rapin, *Réflexions*, I, p. 3). The true genius is bold, therefore Rapin complains of 'a too scrupulous care of purity of language' among modern poets: 'they have begun to take from Poesie all its nerves and all its majesty by a too timorous reservedness and false modesty, which some thought to make the Character of the French tongue, by robbing it of all those wise and judicious boldnesses that Poesie demands' (Rapin, *Réflexions*, I, p. 31). A balance of art and power, of imagination and judgement, is implied in 'wise and judicious boldnesses'.

Rapin reaffirms the 'rules' not because Aristotle dictated them but because good sense and reason (*bon sens* and *raison*) did. The rules, as Pope would agree, were nature methodized:

If the rules be well considered, we shall find them to be made only to reduce nature into method, to trace her step by step, and not to suffer the least mark of her to escape us: 'tis only by these that probability in fiction is maintained, which is the soul of poetry. They are founded upon good sense, and sound reason, rather than on authority; for though Aristotle and Horace are produced, yet no man must argue that what they write is true because they writ it.
  (Dryden, *Of Dramatic Poesy*, I, pp. 260–1)

However, like most other critics of his generation, Rapin recognized that poetry could not be taught: 'Yet is there in *Poetry*, as in other Arts, certain things that *cannot be* expressed, which are (as it were) *mysteries*. There are no precepts, to teach the hidden *graces*, the insensible *charms*, and all that secret *power* of *Poetry* which passes to the heart' (Rapin, *Réflexions*, I, p. 57).

For these things that cannot be expressed the French already had a *mot juste*, which they had taken from the Spanish in the first half of the seventeenth century and translated as *je ne sais quoi*. This *je ne sais quoi*, the indefinable quality that can be felt in a work of art but cannot be described, is the subject of one of the dialogues in *Les entretiens d'Ariste et d'Eugène* (1671) by Dominique Bouhours (1628–1702). The phrase, more a slogan than a critical tool, recurs in another collection of dialogues by Bouhours, *La manière de bien penser dans les ouvrages de l'esprit* (1687), during a discussion of true and false wit. Bouhours, like other French critics of his day, claims that the Italian and Spanish poets, with their far-fetched conceits, are the enemies of true wit. He advocates the 'natural' thought, that directs the reader's mind towards the object or idea in view rather than towards the ingenuity of the writer. The true *pensée naturelle* has, *Je ne sais quelle beauté simple, sans fard et sans artifice*: 'a Natural thought should come into any body's Mind ... it was in our Head before we read it, it seems easie to be found and costs nothing where e'er we meet it, they come less in some manner out of the Mind of him that thinks than the things that was spoke of' (Bouhours, *La manière*, p. 156). The importance of Bouhours' discussion of wit was recognized by Addison in *Spectator* 62, in a passage which greatly advanced the French critic's reputation in England:

Bouhours, whom I look upon to be the most penetrating of all the *French* Criticks, has taken Pains to show, that it is impossible for any Thought to be beautiful which is not just, and has not its Foundation in the Nature of things: that the Basis of all Wit is Truth; and that no Thought can be valuable, of which good Sense is not the Ground-work.

Good sense, in Bouhours's view, could sometimes operate instinctively and rapidly but with great certainty: in such cases it was the same as good taste.

Good sense, taste, and reason, not unexpectedly, are key terms in the writings of the aristocratic Charles de Marguetel de Saint-Denis de Saint-Évremond (1610–1703), who spent most of his last forty years as a political exile in England and was known personally to Dryden. Though his critical essays were published in his lifetime and widely admired, they were intended by their author to be no more than *bagatelles* for the enjoyment of a coterie of friends, not the general reading public. They do not constitute a treatise or a system, but they show some common tendencies. Saint-Évremond, like Dryden, often studies or speculates upon the individual personalities of the authors whose work he is criticizing. He attempts to see literature in its historical context and he recognizes that the history and customs of different countries will shape their literature differently. His own criticism claims to convey no more than one discriminating, reasonable man's tastes and opinions. His free use of that relatively new critical term 'taste' (*le bon goût*) was influential, as too was his undogmatic, even nonchalant manner. Like Dryden, he conveys to the reader an engaging personality: the critic, while analysing the poet's art to please, also himself cultivates the art of pleasing.

Nicolas Boileau-Despréaux (1636–1711) cultivates this art too. *L'Art poétique* (1674) is a prescriptive treatise, but it is written in highly polished, witty couplet verse; it is a modern version of Horace's *Ars Poetica*, and it resembles its model in form and mood as well as in the

Lessons, that my infant Muse
Learnt, when she *Horace* for her Guide did chuse[1]
(Dryden, *Art of Poetry*, p. 156, ll. 1084–5)

The first and last cantos of Boileau's poem deal with general principles
of poetry and criticism and offer general advice to authors; the middle
two cantos outline the principles of good writing in the various genres,
including some (for example, sonnet, rondeau, madrigal) not known to
Horace. Each genre has its appropriate style and language-register; every
type of poem has a beauty of its own.

Boileau was himself an admired and skilful verse-satirist, so his comments on satire in Canto II are perhaps of most interest. He opens his
account of this genre with the proud claim that satire is the weapon of
virtue and truth:

Desire to show it self, and not to wrong,
Arm'd Virtue first with Satyr in its Tongue
(Dryden, *Art of Poetry*, p. 135, ll. 371–2)[2]

He then praises the ancient Roman satirists, each for some essential
quality of satire – courage, wit, sense, truthfulness, fire – but observes
that much in their writings is too indecent for the taste of modern
readers. As for Boileau:

I love sharp Satyr, from obsceneness free;
Not Impudence, that Preaches Modesty.

With the caveat:

Our freedom in our Poetry we see,
That Child of Joy, begot by Liberty
(Dryden, *Art of Poetry*, p. 136,
ll. 403–4, 409–10)[3]

Delight in freedom of expression is implicit in Boileau's *Satire* VII
(1666), where he describes his exhilaration when writing satires that
he knows might endanger his own safety. In *Satire* IX (1668), a more

[1]   ces leçons que ma Muse au Parnasse
Rapporta jeune encor du commerce d'Horace
                    (*Art poétique*, IV, 227–8)
[2]   L'ardeur de se montrer, et non pas de médire,
Arma la Verité du vers de la Satire.
                    (*Art poétique*, II, 145–6)
[3]   Je veux dans la Satire un esprit de candeur,
Et fuis un effronté qui prêche la pudeur ...
La liberté Françoise en ses vers se déploye.
Cet enfant de plaisir veut naistre dans la joye
                    (*Art poétique*, II, 179–80, 185–6)

extended defence of his chosen art, he admits that satire is ineffective and ephemeral; the satirist's literary life is endless warfare; though he might please a few readers he earns the hatred of hundreds; he even runs the risk of being thrashed or drowned. Nevertheless, satire is rich in good sense and pleasing moral instruction; it is a moral preceptor and an arbiter of literary taste. *Satire* IX was published with a *Discours sur la satire*, in which Boileau appeals to classical precedent for the naming of names in order to carry out effectively the corrective purposes of satire.

Much of Canto III of *L'Art poétique* is concerned with tragedy and comedy, but there is a long section on epic, which, surprisingly in the light of the moral claims made for satire, does not emphasize the didactic purpose of epic. What is stressed, rather, is that epic is fiction and that it must, above all else, give pleasure.

Returning to Canto I, we find that Boileau advises the poet to think before he attempts to write; he should seek only to express clear and distinct ideas:

> As your Idea's, clear or else obscure,
> Th' Expression follows perfect, or impure:
> What we conceive, with ease we can express;
> Words to the Notions flow with readiness[4]
>
> (Dryden, *Art of Poetry*, p. 128, ll. 151–4)

Poetry is a craft: the poet should not be facile, but should work slowly and with great care, considering a hundred times what he is saying and constantly revising:

> Polish, repolish, every Colour lay,
> And sometimes add; but oft'ner take away[5]
>
> (Dryden, *Art of Poetry*, p. 129, ll. 173–4)

In this couplet there is an unforced analogy between poetry and the sister art of painting.

Early in the first canto Boileau offers a sketchy history of French versification, according to which Malherbe (1555–1628) was the first correct poet. Boileau discussed other seventeenth-century French writers

---

[4]
Selon que nostre idée est plus ou moins obscure
L'expression la suit, ou moins nette, ou plus pure.
Ce que l'on conçoit bien s'énonce clairement,
Et les mots pour le dire arrivent aisément
(*Art poètique*, I, 150–3)

[5]
Polissez-le sans cesse, et le repolissez.
Ajoûtez quelques fois, et souvent effacez
(*Art poètique*, I, 172–3)

elsewhere in *L'Art poétique*, always ridiculing the elaborate word-play, the extravagant affectation, the *préciosité* of earlier poets and vindicating the practice of his great modern contemporaries. He calls for a clear, concise, noble, pure style:

> Chuse a just Stile; be Grave without constraint,
> Great without Pride, and Lovely without Paint[6]
>
> (Dryden, *Art of Poetry*, p. 127, ll. 103–4)

and, like other French critics of his generation, he castigates Italian poets:

> Most writers, mounted on a resty Muse,
> Extravagant and Senceless Objects chuse;
> They think they erre, if in their Verse they fall
> On any thought that's Plain, or Natural:
> Fly this excess; and let *Italians* be
> Vain Authors of false glitt'ring Poetry[7]
>
> (Dryden, *Art of Poetry*, p. 125, ll. 39–43)

In one of his satires he ridicules the fool who prefers Tasso's tinsel to Virgil's gold.[8]

The ideal, then, is good sense and natural thoughts, but these are not the possession of all reasoning men. Reason, as Boileau conceives it, is a high and uncommon power which supplies what is striking in great poetry:

> Love Reason then: and let what e'er you Write
> Borrow from her its Beauty, Force, and Light[9]
>
> (Dryden, *Art of Poetry*, p. 125, ll. 37–8)

Reason is a power that enlightens: it is associated with 'Descartes's "lumière naturelle" – a fugitive reflection on earth of the "lumière pure,

---

[6]   Soyez simple avec art,
Sublime sans orgueil, agréable sans fard
             (*Art poètique*, I, 101–2)

[7] La pluspart emportez d'une fougue insensée
Toûjours loin du droit sens vont chercher leur pensée.
Ils croiroient s'abaisser, dans leurs vers monstrueux,
S'ils pensoient ce qu'un autre a pû penser comme eux.
Evitons ces excez. Laissons à l'Italie
De tous ces faux brillans l'éclatante folie
                    (*Art poètique*, I, 39–43)

[8] le clinquant du Tasse á tout l'or de Virgile (*Satire* IX, 176).

[9] Aimez donc la Raison. Que toûjours vos écrits
Empruntent d'elle seule et leur lustre et leur prix
             (*Art poètique*, I, 37–8)

constante, claire, certaine ... et toujours présente" of beatific vision –
the "clarté" which for Boileau guarantees the infallibility of the ideal
critic's "raison" is but a secularisation of that *clarté* by which human
reason is made spiritually sentient' (Brody, *Boileau and Longinus*, p.
84). Reason is swift and intuitive; it is good sense (*le bon sens*), which
is at the same time the end and the means of art; without this exalted
power of reason it is futile to attempt to write poetry. Boileau insists
from the opening of *L'art poétique* that a poet is born, not made, and
that in poetry there can be no medium between triumph and disaster.

A comparable all-or-nothing conception of poetry is implicit in
Longinus, so it comes as no surprise that alongside *L'Art poétique*
Boileau published his prose translation of Longinus' *On the Sublime*, a
work that he called 'one of the most precious relics of antiquity': his
was the first translation that brought widespread attention to Longinus.
He explained in the preface to the 1674 volume which contained both
works that they complemented one another and that he had drawn
some of the precepts of his own criticism from Longinus. Before Boileau
the French word *sublime* generally signified an elaborate, high style, but
in the influential preface to his *Traité* he effectively redefines the word,
with reference to Longinus' famous citation of the opening of Genesis:

By the 'sublime' Longinus did not mean what orators call 'the sublime
style', he meant the element of the extraordinary in discourse, the
marvellous, the striking, that in virtue of which a work exalts, ravishes,
transports. The sublime *style* needs lofty language; but the *sublime* may
appear in a single thought, a figure, a phrase ... *Le souverain arbitre de la
nature d'une seule parole forma la lumière*: there is the sublime *style* for
you ... But, *Dieu dit, Que la lumière se fasse; et la lumière se fit*. This
extraordinary expression ... is genuinely sublime; it has something divine
about it.
                          (Wimsatt and Brooks, *Literary Criticism*, p. 285)

Boileau elaborated his views on the sublime in his prose *Réflexions sur
Longin* (1694), where he lists the sources of the sublime, but concludes
that the sublime cannot be analysed, it can only be felt. Sublimity is that
sovereign perfection, that inexplicable force in poetry that transports us:
when we feel it we are aware of the mysteriousness of the creative
process.

L'Art poétique, by virtue of its compact, polished, witty verse, was
the most memorable of that group of critical handbooks in the 1670s
and 1680s which were intended to make modern poetic practice accord
more closely with norms and ideals deduced from ancient poetry and
criticism (especially Aristotle, Horace and Longinus), now read in the
light of modern reason. That opaque, inclusive, overused epithet

'neo-classical' can fairly be applied to Boileau and other French critics of his time, for their theories and precepts were elaborated with modern poetry in view and they made a determined effort to follow what they took to be classical practice. They agreed that poetry had a moral end and that there was a hierarchy of definable genres of poetry, distinct from one another, each with its own function and form. They agreed that genius was a prerequisite for good poetry and that the poet's art could best be learned by a study of the ancients, because the ancients' practice and precepts were in accord with nature, truth, and reason. Nature, truth, and reason implied order, harmony, simplicity, and common knowledge. The rules derived from the ancients were nature methodized, but there was something in poetry, a *je ne sais quoi*, recognized by the heart rather than the mind, which the rules could not account for.

Boileau, Bouhours, and other French critics disparaged the poetry of Italy and Spain, though they drew rather more than they cared to acknowledge from sixteenth-century Italian critics. By the last quarter of the seventeenth century France had assumed a leadership in literary criticism which the rest of Europe, including even Italy, acknowledged.

There appears to have been little original critical activity in Spain towards the end of the seventeenth century, though Boileau's *L'Art poétique* was translated into Spanish in 1687 and remained an authority in that country for over 100 years; it was still being adapted and imitated in the 1820s: Juan Bautista Arriaza, the translator of *L'Art poétique* into Spanish blank verse in 1807, called it a code of laws for modern literature. Italy produced such unoriginal compilations as Benedetto Menzini's verse *Poetica* (1688), but nothing of significance until after the foundation of Arcadian academies during the 1690s. In Germany, whose poetry up to that time had been negligible in comparison with the achievements of Spain and Italy, Georg Neumarck, before Boileau, reduced Aristotle, Horace, Scaliger, Heinsius and other ancient and Renaissance authorities to a wholly derivative poetical primer in his *Poetics* (1667). After Boileau, French neo-classical principles were most fully and rigorously restated in German by Johann Christoph Gottsched (1700–66) in his *Critische Dichtkunst* (1730). Gottsched built his system upon reason; he castigated the ornamentation and far-fetched conceits of German baroque poetry along the same lines of attack as those used by his co-thinkers in France, Italy, and Spain in their assaults upon *préciosité*, Marinism, and Gongorism. Boileau influenced an Art of Poetry by a Dutch literary academy, 'Horace's Poetics applied to our Time and Manners' (1677), and there was a Danish *Ars Poetica* (1701), modelled on Boileau, by one Toger Reenberg; both these Dutch and Danish poetics made the customary call for clarity and simplicity.

English: to 1700

Dryden may be properly considered the father of English criticism

(Johnson, *Life of Dryden*)

The critical writings of Le Bossu, Rapin, Bouhours, and Boileau discussed above were republished in England not long after their first
appearance in France and most of them were translated into English
before the end of the century. Rapin's *Réflexions* were translated in
1674, in the same year as their first publication in France, and in a more
dogmatic spirit than that of the original author. The translator was
Thomas Rymer (1641–1713), best known for his criticism of *Othello* in
A Short View of Tragedy (1693). In his preface to Rapin's *Réflexions* he
enjoins modern poets to follow Aristotelian principles for reasons as
'convincing and clear as any demonstration in *Mathematicks*' (Spingarn,
Critical Essays, II, p. 165); these principles were, after all, nature reduced to method. Rymer's conception of nature requires that the poet
should follow empirical truth, so he condemns the use of the
'impossibilities' of Old Testament miracles in Cowley's *Davideis* and
censures Spenser, who, admittedly, 'had a large spirit, a sharp judgment,
and a *Genius* for *Heroic Poesie*, perhaps above any that ever writ since
Virgil', but who, instead of keeping to the paths marked by Homer and
Virgil, allowed himself to be misled by Ariosto; so 'All is fanciful and
chimerical, without any uniformity, without any foundation in truth; his
Poem is perfect *Fairy-land*' (Spingarn, *Critical Essays*, II, pp. 167–8).
Spenser's judgement was debauched by the Italians. In Rymer's view
reason must predominate over fancy, and the standard of reason is
unchanging. So much is implied in the title of his *Tragedies of the Last
Age Consider'd and Examin'd by the Practice of the Ancients and by
the Common Sense of all Ages* (1677), where Rymer, with characteristic
vigour, draws images from Church, Law, and Bedlam to define the right
relationship between reason and fancy:

But *Fancy*, I think, in Poetry, is like *Faith* in Religion: it makes for
discoveries, and soars above reason, but never clashes or runs against it.
Fancy leaps and frisks, and away she's gone, whilst *reason* rattles the chains
and follows after. *Reason* must consent and ratify what-ever by *fancy* is
attempted in its absence, or else 'tis all *null* and void in law.

(Spingarn, *Critical Essays*, II, p. 185)

Rymer's praise of Spenser's spirit and genius is heavily qualified, but
Edward Phillips (1630–96), whose critical opinions may have been in-
fluenced by his uncle John Milton, asserts in the preface to his *Theatrum
Poetarum* (1675) that Spenser is, alongside Shakespeare, one of the rare

possessors of true poetic energy: 'with all his Rustie, obsolete words, with all his rough-hewn, clowterly Verses, yet take him throughout, and we shall find in him a gracefull and Poetic Majesty' (Spingarn, *Critical Essays*, II, p. 271). Phillips wonders why English poets of his own day used Italian verse forms ('the Italian *Stanza* in Heroic Poem, and the Sonnet, Canzon, and Madrigal in the Lyric') so little, when their predecessors had employed them successfully, 'so except in their own proper Language they become none better than ours'. *Ottava rima* and its 'Improvement' the Spenserian stanza are more stately than the couplet or the alternate-rhyme, four-line stanza, though, of course, the nephew of Milton has to add that blank verse gives 'far more ample Scope and liberty both to Style and fancy than can possibly be observed in Rime' (Spingarn, *Critical Essays*, II, pp. 265–6). Contrasting with his praise of the Italians, Phillips's references to the French are brief and depreciatory, setting him outside the main current of English criticism in the 1670s.

The masterwork of French criticism, Boileau's *L'Art poétique*, was translated by Sir William Soames in 1680 and was published as *The Art of Poetry* in 1683, after Dryden had revised it and substituted English analogues, not all of them happy, for the French authors named by Boileau. Similarly John Oldham, in *Horace's Art of Poetry, imitated in English* (1681), put Horace into modern dress 'by making him speak, as if he were living and writing now', altering the scene from Rome to London, and making use of English names of men, places, and customs, 'where the parallel would decently permit'. Horace's own precept in the *Ars poetica* provided Oldham with a warrant against a word-for-word rendering, but he claims to be 'religiously strict' to Horace's sense. Dryden and Oldham both approach Boileau and Horace in the context of a debate on translation begun in England about thirty years earlier, when Sir John Denham, in commendatory verses prefixed to Sir Richard Fanshawe's version of Guarini's *Pastor Fido* (1647), and Abraham Cowley, in the Preface to his *Pindarique Odes* (1656), argued for a far freer mode of translation than the literalism of, for instance, Ben Jonson's version of the *Ars poetica*.

Dryden distinguishes, in his Preface to a translation of Ovid's *Epistles*, between three ways of turning another poet into English. The first is metaphrase, word by word and line by line. This way is inherently so difficult as never to produce successful results: it is 'like dancing on ropes with fettered legs: a man may shun a fall by using caution; but the gracefulness of motion is not to be expected: and when we have said the best of it, 'tis but a foolish task'. The second way is paraphrase, 'or translation with latitude, where the author is kept in view by the translator, so as never to be lost, but his words are not so strictly followed, as his sense, and that too is admitted to be amplified, but not altered'.

The third is imitation, 'where the translator (if he now has not lost that name) assumes the liberty not only to vary from the words and sense, but to forsake them both as he sees occasion; and taking only some general hints from the original' may, as it were, invent variations upon a theme, as musicians do. It is 'an endeavour of a later poet to write like one who has written before him on the same subject; that is, not to translate his words, or to be confined to his sense, but only to set him as a pattern, and to write, as he supposes that author would have done, had he lived in our age, and in our country' (Dryden, *Of Dramatic Poesy*, I, pp. 268–70). The important difference between the second and third methods is that imitation can play upon differences between itself and the original and is therefore fully effective only if the reader already knows the original; such knowledge is not so necessary in the case of paraphrase. Dryden declares in his Preface to Ovid that he prefers the second way, but, in practice, the many translations and imitations he wrote during the following twenty years move freely back and forth across the indistinct boundary between the two methods.

Implicit in the theory and practice of Dryden and his contemporaries is the notion of a respectful but easy companionship between the translator or imitator and his original. This is neatly expressed by Wentworth Dillon, Earl of Roscommon (1633?–85), in *An Essay on Translated Verse* (1684), when he proclaims that the translator should 'chuse an *Author* as you chuse a *Friend*' and grow so familiar with him that

> Your *thoughts*, your *Words*, your *Stiles*, your *Souls* agree,
> No Longer his *Interpreter*, but *He*

> (Spingarn, *Critical Essays*, II, p. 300)

As befits a work claiming that English verse is superior to the prose customarily favoured by French translators of the Greek and Roman classics Roscommon's *Essay* is in heroic couplets. In the second edition (1685), however, Roscommon adds a passsage of blank verse which is at once a panegyric upon *Paradise Lost* and an argument that this metre is more suited than the couplet for truthful translation of the ancients. On a hint from Milton's prefatory note to the second edition of *Paradise Lost* Roscommon declares that rhyme is a Gothic device, unknown to the ancient Greeks and Romans; so only by refusing its 'barb'rous aid' can English verse translation of the classics arrive at '*Roman* majesty'. This is a contentious claim in the light of the widespread belief that translation of the classics formed part of the process of cultural refinement upon which the age congratulated itself, a belief held alongside another, equally widespread, that one of the finest literary fruits of modern refinement was a polishing of the heroic couplet by Waller and Denham.

Roscommon's own translation of Horace's *Art of Poetry* (1680) was in blank verse, but the fashion did not catch on. A freer version of Boileau and Horace by John Sheffield, Earl of Mulgrave and later Duke of Buckingham (1648–1721), *An Essay upon Poetry* (1682), is in the usual heroic couplets. Mulgrave runs dutifully through the genres, much after Boileau's fashion but naming English representative authors; for the most part he repeats the precepts gathered together by Boileau, sometimes adapting them to the recent history of English poetry. Dealing with a major genre of his own period Mulgrave, like Rapin, advocates that satire should be 'smiling', rather than savage, Horatian, rather than Juvenalian: 'A Satyr's Smile is sharper than his Frown'. It should also be decent, as Boileau claimed; so Mulgrave censures what he calls the Earl of Rochester's 'Bawdry barefac'd, that poor pretence to Wit' (Spingarn, *Critical Essays*, II, pp. 290, 288).

Perhaps the only significance of this attack is that it provoked Robert Wolseley, in his Preface to *Valentinian* (1685), to defend Rochester and then go on to make an unusually bold affirmation of artistic freedom:

it never yet came into any man's Head, who pretended to be a Critick, except this *Essayer's*, that the Wit of a Poet was to be measur'd by the worth of his Subject, and that when this was bad, that must be so too: the manner of treating his Subject has been hitherto thought the true Test, for as an ill Poet will depresse and disgrace the highest, so a good one will raise and dignifie the lowest.   (Spingarn, *Critical Essays*, III, pp. 15–16)

This was to prove a good working principle for the satirists and, indeed, the georgic poets of this and the following generation.

Mulgrave, though, is committed in his *Essay upon Poetry* to the familiar subject-based hierarchy of the genres, so he naturally regards epic as the highest kind and 'the chief effort of human sense'. The world has so far brought forth only two epic poets, the 'gigantic' souls of Homer and Virgil. Homer is the object of wonder, but his explainer Le Bossu evokes admiration too:

> Had *Bossu* never writ, the world had still
> Like *Indians* view'd this wondrous piece of Skill;
> As something of Divine the work admired,
> Hoped not to be Instructed, but Inspired;
> Till he, disclosing sacred Mysteries,
> Has shewn where all the mighty Magick lies
>
> (Spingarn, *Critical Essays*, III, pp. 295–6)

Mulgrave's general observations on poetry are the commonplaces that stem from Boileau's injunction *Aimez donc la Raison*, 'without judgement, fancy is but mad' (line 6), but they also agree with Rymer, and, in

common with much English criticism of the 1670s and 1680s, echo
Thomas Hobbes's psychological account of the process of poetic com-
position, in which 'Judgment begets the strength and structure, and
Fancy begets the ornaments of a Poem' (see pp. 614–15 below).

Hobbes's psychology of judgement and inspiration is implicit too in
the criticism of John Dryden (see pp. 615–16 below). Dryden is the
most comprehensive English critic in this period, even though, unlike
the greatest of his classical and continental mentors, he never attempted
a systematic critical treatise (at least in the non-dramatic criticism which
is the subject of this chapter). As we have seen, he showered unstinted
praise upon Boileau, Rapin, and Le Bossu, and, as we have also seen,
took a considerable hand in Soames's English translation of Boileau's
L'Art poétique. Like the French critics of his day, Dryden places himself
very firmly within the classical tradition: 'Aristotle with his interpreters,
and Horace, and Longinus, are the authors to whom I owe my lights'
(Dryden, *Of Dramatic Poesy*, I, p. 243). However, he challenges, in the
Apology for Heroic Poetry and Poetic Licence, prefixed to *The State of
Innocence* (1677), the modern legislative use of ancient critics, when he
traces his own kind of appreciative, rather than prescriptive, criticism
back to the ancients: 'they wholly mistake the nature of criticism who
think its business is principally to find fault. Criticism, as it was first
instituted by Aristotle, was meant a standard of judging well; the chiefest
part of which is to observe those excellencies which should delight a
reasonable reader' (Dryden, *Of Dramatic Poesy*, I, pp. 196–7).

All Dryden's criticism of poetry is occasional, nearly all of it is in
prefaces to his original poetry or translations, much of it is concerned
with the practical problems of writing. As one might expect in the light
of his own poetry, he often discusses verse satire. Referring to the prime
models of ancient satire in his Preface to *Sylvae* (1685), he declares that
Horace's satires 'are incomparably beyond Juvenal's, if to laugh and
rally is to be preferred to railing and declaiming' (Dryden, *Of Dramatic
Poesy*, II, p. 31). He enlarges upon the advantages of rallying or 'raillery'
(the use of good-humoured ridicule) in the *Discourse concerning Satire*
(1693), prefixed to his own verse translations of Juvenal and Persius.
There he compares the different satirical weapons employed by Horace
and Juvenal, each appropriate to the age and circumstances in which it
was wielded, and concludes:

Let the chastisements of Juvenal be never so necessary for his new kind of
satire; let him declaim as wittily and sharply as he pleases: yet still the
nicest and most delicate touches of satire consist in fine raillery ... How
easy is it to call rogue and villain, and that wittily! But how hard to make
a man appear a fool, a blockhead, or a knave, without using any of those
opprobrious terms! To spare the grossness of the names, and to do the thing

yet more severely ... A man may be capable, as Jack Ketch's wife said of his servant, of a plain piece of work, a bare hanging; but to make a malefactor die sweetly was only belonging to her husband. I wish I could apply it to myself, if the reader would be kind enough to think it belongs to me. The character of *Zimri* in my *Absalom* is, in my opinion, worth the whole poem: 'tis not bloody, but 'tis ridiculous enough.

(Dryden, *Of Dramatic Poesy*, II, pp. 136–7)

By this token he is now not so sure of Horace's primacy:

This manner of Horace is indeed the best; but Horace has not executed it altogether so happily, at least not often. The manner of Juvenal is confessed to be inferior to the former; but Juvenal has excelled him in his performance. Juvenal has railed more wittily than Horace has rallied.

(Dryden, *Of Dramatic Poesy*, II, p. 138)

Dryden explains that Horace laboured under the great disadvantage of being a 'Court-slave' to the tyrannical Augustus, so, 'as he was a courtier, complied with the interest of his master, and, avoiding the lashing of greater crimes, confined himself to the ridiculing of petty vices, and common follies' (Dryden, *Of Dramatic Poesy*, II, pp. 134–5). Dryden's changed critical valuation of his great forebears may perhaps be connected with his own loss of court favour after 1689.

It is perhaps a reflection of the growing importance of the genre that Dryden's *Discourse concerning Satire* is his longest piece of criticism (though about a quarter of it is on epic, not satire) and is the only one honoured with the title 'discourse'. Of all his works it is the one most heavily loaded with scholarship: all second-hand and acknowledged. Dryden learnedly weighs up the case for each of the contending etymologies for satire – from the mythical satyr or from the culinary *satura*, a mixture – and favours the latter. He traces the history of satire in great detail from its shadowy origins to the present. He compares the poetical characters of Horace, Persius, and Juvenal, showing how the work of each was shaped by its social and political context; as a 'public' poet himself he was well qualified to do this. He claims that in satire, as too in tragedy, the moderns have excelled the ancients, and he singles out Boileau's 'famous *Lutrin*' as 'the most beautiful and noble kind of satire'. In this mock-epic 'we see Boileau pursuing [Virgil] in the same flights; and scarcely yielding to his master ... Here is the majesty of the heroic, finely mixed with the venom of the other; and raising the delight which otherwise would be flat and vulgar, by the sublimity of the expression' (Dryden, *Of Dramatic Poesy*, II, p. 149). He could well be describing his own *Absalom and Achitophel*.

Considering the perennial problem of personal satire, Dryden admits the principle that 'We have no moral right on the reputation of other men. 'Tis taking from them what we cannot restore to them', but then he allows that, in practice, lampoons are justified for motives either of personal revenge or the exposure of a public nuisance. Such justifications would be wide enough to accommodate Dryden's own satires: *Mac Flecknoe* being an example of the first and *Absalom and Achitophel* of the second. The Preface to *Absalom and Achitophel* (1681) asserts the classic moral case for satire: 'The true end of satire is the amendment of vices by correction. And he who writes honestly is no more an enemy to the offender than the physician to the patient when he prescribes harsh remedies to an inveterate disease'. He returns to that familiar physician metaphor in the 'Postscript' to his *Aeneis* (1697), when he writes of his own renunciation of satire after 1689: 'For who would give physic to the great, when he is uncalled? To do his patient no good, and endanger himself for his prescription?' (Dryden, *Of Dramatic Poesy*, II, p. 259). Whether the Ancients, the Moderns, or his own verse is under view, Dryden criticizes as a practising poet; his constant concern is to ascertain and analyse what it is that reader and author have found effective.

Dryden rarely concerns himself with the principles of poetry in the abstract. He is aware, to an unusual degree for his time, that any poem is the particular creation of an individual poet and that its distinctive character arises from and reflects the character of its creator. The object of Dryden's criticism is not so much the analysis of a corpus of writings as a personal engagement with a living fellow-poet. So, in the preface to his *Fables, Ancient and Modern* (1700), after discussing Homer and Virgil, both of whom he had translated, and giving high praise to the latter, he writes:

the Grecian is more according to my genius than the Latin poet. In the works of the two authors we may read their manners and natural inclinations, which are wholly different. Virgil was of a quiet, sedate temper: Homer was violent, impetuous, and full of fire. The chief talent of Virgil was propriety of thoughts, and ornament of words: Homer was rapid in his thoughts, and took all the liberties, both of numbers and of expressions, which his language, and the age in which he lived, allowed him. Homer's invention was more copious, Virgil's more confined.

(Dryden, *Of Dramatic Poesy*, II, p. 274)

We might infer that Dryden has special insight and authority as the translator of the poets he criticizes, but he does not force such considerations upon us: rather he implies that the common reader makes the same degree of engagement with the poetry and its creators. He concludes his discussion of Homer and Virgil in the preface to the *Fables*:

From all I have said, I will only draw this inference, that the action of
Homer, being more full of vigour than that of Virgil, according to the
temper of the writer, is of consequence more pleasing to the reader. One
warms you by degrees; the other sets you on fire all at once, and never
intermits his heat. 'Tis the same difference which Longinus makes betwixt
the effects of eloquence in Demosthenes and Tully; one persuades, the other
commands. You never cool while you read Homer . . . This vehemence of
his, I confess, is more suitable to my temper; and, therefore, I have
translated his first book with a greater pleasure than any part of Virgil. But
it was not a pleasure without pains: the continual agitations of the spirits
must needs be a weakening of any constitution.

(Dryden, *Of Dramatic Poesy*, II, p. 276)

Poetry is appreciated by its psychological effects, by the degree to which
it moves us and excites pleasure and admiration.

So, invoking Longinus again, in the *Apology for Heroic Poetry*, Dryden
writes:

Imagining is, in itself, the very height and life of poetry. It is, as Longinus
describes it, a discourse which, by a kind of enthusiasm, or extraordinary
emotion of the soul, makes it seem to us that we behold those things which
the poet paints, so as to be pleased with them, and to admire them.

(Dryden, *Of Dramatic Poesy*, I, p. 203)

Such works of heightened imagination can be accommodated to the
ancient and still valid primary critical principle that art should imitate
nature, but this principle must be interpreted with a liberal disregard of
mere *vraisemblance*. Dryden takes issue with unnamed modern 'correct'
critics: 'all that is dull, insipid, languishing, and without sinews, in a
poem they call an imitation of nature'. However, 'those things which
delight all ages must have been an imitation of nature', and those things
include the daring metaphors and hyperboles of great poets from Homer
to Milton (Dryden, *Of Dramatic Poesy*, I, pp. 200–3). Also, as we
discover from Dryden's preface to his play *The Conquest of Granada*,
they include visionary objects:

neither Homer, Virgil, Statius, Ariosto, Tasso, nor our English Spenser could
have formed their poems half so beautiful without those gods and spirits,
and those enthusiastic parts of poetry which compose the most noble parts
of all their writings . . . And if any man object the improbabilities of a spirit
appearing or of a palace raised by magic, I boldly answer him that an
heroic poet is not tied to a bare representation of what is true, or exceeding
probable: but that he may let himself loose to visionary objects, and to the
representation of such things as depending not on sense, and therefore not to
be comprehended by knowledge, may give him a freer scope for imagination.

(Dryden, *Of Dramatic Poesy*, I, pp. 160–1)

The touch of pride with which he introduces 'our English Spenser' among the great poets is characteristic of Dryden's nationalism. As T. S. Eliot said: 'The great work of Dryden in criticism is that at the right moment he became conscious of the necessity of affirming the native element in literature' (Eliot, *Use of Poetry*, p. 14). We have seen that Dryden engages himself with the individual personalities of authors whose work excites him, but his awareness of kinship between poets becomes particularly explicit when he reflects upon national literature. Thus in the Preface to *Fables* (1700) 'Milton was the poetical son of Spenser, and Mr Waller of Fairfax; for we have our lineal descents and clans as well as other families: Spenser more than once insinuates that the soul of Chaucer was transfused into his body; and that he was begotten by him two hundred years after his decease' (Dryden, *Of Dramatic Poesy*, II, p. 270). Dryden implies that he is a son of this clan when he acknowledges Spenser as his own master in English versification, and, more intimately, when he translates and praises Chaucer, whom he venerates as 'the father of English poetry ... a perpetual fountain of good sense ... a man of a most wonderful comprehensive nature' (Dryden, *Of Dramatic Poesy*, II, pp. 237–8, 280, 284). Chaucer's qualities are brought out in Dryden's typical fashion by way of an extended comparison between his work and Ovid's, all done in a casually incisive manner: 'For an example, I see Baucis and Philemon as perfectly before me, as if some ancient painter had drawn them; and all the Pilgrims in the *Canterbury Tales*, their humours, their features, and the very dress, as distinctly as if I had supped with them at the Tabard in Southwark'. The distinction between 'sup' and 'see' conveys a sense of Dryden's own gusto and makes the point that Chaucer's characters are more lively than Ovid's, to which Dryden disarmingly adds, 'though I have not time to prove, yet I appeal to the reader, and I am sure he will clear me from partiality' (Dryden, *Of Dramatic Poesy*, II, p. 278).

Dryden's placing of English poets in genealogies is accompanied by some awareness of evolution, an evolution he sees largely in terms of the refinement of language and versification, with appropriate gains and losses. He assumes that refinement of language will continue; so after describing his own modernization of Chaucer he adds: 'Another poet in another age, may take the same liberty with my writings; if at least they live long enough to deserve correction' (Dryden, *Of Dramatic Poesy*, II, p. 287). He sees his own criticism in similar terms as a possible contribution to progress: 'we live in an age so sceptical, that as it determines little, so it takes nothing from antiquity on trust. And I profess to have no other ambition in this essay than that poetry may not go backward, when all other arts and sciences are advancing' (Dryden, *Of Dramatic Poesy*, I, p. 169). Such belief in progress aligns Dryden with the Moderns in the quarrel between the Ancients and the Moderns which erupted in France and spread to England in the last twelve years of his life, but, apart from occasional references (Dryden, *Of Dramatic Poesy*, II, pp. 161, 177–8), he did not become involved.

Ancients versus Moderns

... we cannot learn to which side the victory fell.

(Swift, *The Battle of the Books*: the Bookseller to the Reader)

The large intellectual and cultural context of the quarrel between Ancients and Moderns is explored in Chapter 2 by D. L. Patey, who discusses, *inter alia*, the two key works by advocates of the Moderns: Perrault's *Parallèle des anciens et des modernes* (1688–97) and Fontenelle's *Digression sur les anciens et les modernes* (1688). Both these works consider the possibility that modern poetry has benefited from the general advance of knowledge that, it was claimed by the Moderns, had occurred between ancient times and the present.

Perrault has no doubt that poetry has gained by such an advance. He argues that the business of the poet is to delight and move the hearts of his readers. As knowledge of the human heart has increased, so the modern poet has an advantage over his predecessors. Homer would have written a better epic if he had lived in the age of Louis XIV; in any case, 'Homer' was perhaps no more than the collective name for a series of disconnected rhapsodies by one or more primitive singers, eventually collected arbitrarily under the titles of 'Iliad' and 'Odyssey'. Nature is still the same: just as lions today are as fierce as they were in the days of Alexander the Great, so the best of men today are equal in talent and genius to the best of the ancients. Perrault illustrates this claim in a discussion of his own contemporaries in *Les hommes illustres* (1697–1700), translated by John Ozell as *Characters Historical and Panegyrical of the Greatest Men that have appeared in France, during the last Century* (1704–5). Praising Racine, he declares that genius is inborn: 'Genius is a Gift of Nature which cannot be hid, and which shews itself in Children almost as early as Reason'. In the case of La Fontaine, Perrault praises originality: 'Never did a Person merit more to be looked upon as an Original, and as the first in his kind' (Perrault, *Characters*, I, p. 189; II, p. 158).

There are, of course, few geniuses in any age. Perrault had already published his ideas on genius in *Le Génie* (1686), a verse epistle to that more moderate and philosophical advocate of the Moderns, Bernard le Bovier de Fontenelle (1657–1757). True genius, which may be manifested in eloquence, painting, sculpture, music, or poetry, has the power, Perrault declares, to ignite every passion of the heart (*Allume dans le coeur toutes les passions*); it is the Promethean fire, once audaciously seized from heaven, now bestowed on a few choice spirits favoured by the gods. Perrault is beginning to see poetry and the other arts in terms of emotion rather than form, but his epistle did not become widely known and seems not to have been particularly influential. The effect of the fairy stories, for which he is so famous, is another matter.

Fontenelle put the case for the Moderns in his *Digression* with more qualifications than Perrault had permitted himself, for he accepted that poetry, which depends upon imagination, does not progress in the way that the sciences do, and where Perrault had claimed that the human mind is the same in all ages, Fontenelle allows that it differs in different countries on account of the influence of climate:

Different ideas, are like plants and flowers which do not grow alike in all kinds of climates. Perhaps our French soil is no more fit for the reasoning used by the Aegyptians, than it is proper for their palms; and without travelling so far, probably our orange-trees which do not grow with such ease here as in Italy, are an indication that there is a certain turn of mind in Italy, which is not altogether like that of France. 'Tis absolutely certain, that by the concatenation and reciprocal dependance between all the parts of the material world, the difference of climate which shews itself sensibly in the plants, must extend itself likewise to the brain, and be productive there of some effect or other.   (in Le Bossu, *Treatise*, II, pp. 110–11)

Such a climatic theory had already been put forward by Bouhours in the dialogues on *le bel esprit* in his *Entretiens d'Ariste et d'Eugène*, where it is suggested that the scarcity of *les beaux esprits* in northern countries is owing to the cold, damp climate, and that climate is responsible for the particular nature of the French genius. The notion that climate affects mental development is at least as old as Aristotle; it was restated for English readers in our period by Thomas Sprat among others. His discussion of the question in his *History of the Royal Society* (1667) opens with a truism that complements Fontenelle's: 'the *English Genius* is not so airy and discoursive as that of some of our neighbors' (Spingarn, *Critical Essays*, II, p. 112).

Fontenelle's *Digression* was published as an appendix to his treatise on the pastoral, *Discours sur la nature de l'eglogue* (1688), where he is concerned to establish a truthful and rational psychological basis for that ancient genre. He finds that the rationale of pastoral is in the natural pleasure that men have in leisure and in love, so this form of writing is founded upon the illusion or half-truth of a 'quiet Life, with no other business but Love' (Fontenelle, *Discours*, p. 282). The language of literary pastoral should be simple but not rustic; the sentiments of innocent love should be refined; this is the particular power of pastoral to please: 'We are amaz'd to find something that is fine and delicate in common unaffected terms; and on that account the more the thing is fine, without ceasing to be Natural; and the Expression common, without being low, the deeper we ought to be struck' (Fontenelle, *Discours*, p. 290). Unlike Rapin on the pastoral, Fontenelle does not refer to the critical authority of the ancients; his authority is what he calls the natural light of reason. He declares that he will treat Theocritus and Virgil (from whose practice Rapin derived most of his rules for pastoral) just as he would treat modern authors, with the result that he takes Theocritus to task for indecorum and outright clownishness. Fontenelle's theory was an alternative to Rapin's. In practice, the late seventeenth-century pastorals written according to one theory were not very different from those written according to the other but Fontenelle's ideas, cutting entirely free from ancient models, opened the way to a further development of subjective theories, to accompany the gradual naturalization of pastoral in the eighteenth century.

Devotees of the ancients responded to the more extremely modernist declarations of Perrault of course. Jean de La Fontaine (1621–95) almost immediately brought out his *Epître à Huet* (1687), in which he agrees that France now excels in the arts, praises modern French writers and, unusually for a Frenchman of this period, praises Ariosto, Tasso, and other Italians too; but he reaffirms that the ancients are the best models to follow. Writing of his own literary career, he tells how his style was almost ruined by his imitation of a highly esteemed, unnamed, exaggeratedly clever, over-ornamental modern poet (perhaps Malherbe or Voiture), until 'Horace fortunately opened my eyes' (*Horace, par bonheur, me dessilla les yeux*).

Jean de la Bruyère (1645–96) added some remarks to the section 'Des ouvrages de l'esprit' in his *Caractères* (1694). Probably with Fontenelle in mind, he writes of a modern author, nurtured on the ancients who, when he believes he can stand on his own two feet, turns against them and abuses them, 'like those children who, having grown robust and strong by sucking good milk, beat their nurse' (La Bruyère, *Characters*, p. 27). For La Bruyère the test of art is not rules but effect: 'when a good book exalts your mind and inspires it with lofty and courageous feelings, seek no other rule to judge it by: it is good, and made by the hand of a master' (La Bruyère, *Characters*, p. 31). This is to give taste great authority, but from what La Bruyère says elsewhere in 'Des Ouvrages de l'esprit' it is clear that he believes there are uniform standards of taste and that good taste is as rare a possession as Boileau found reason to be:

There is in art a point of perfection, just as there is in nature a point of excellence or of ripeness. The man who feels it and loves it has perfect taste; the man who does not feel it, and who loves what falls short of it or is in excess of it, has defective taste. So there is good taste and there is bad taste, and we are justified in arguing about our tastes ... there are few men in whom native wit is combined with a sure taste and a judicious critical sense.

(La Bruyère, *Characters*, p. 26)

Fontenelle's *Digression sur les anciens et les modernes* caught the attention of Sir William Temple (1628–99), whose essay *Upon Ancient and Modern Learning* (in *Miscellanea*, 1690) is a response both to Fontenelle and to English proponents of modern science and devotees of the Royal Society; in due course it prompted the replies of Wotton and Bentley, which, in turn, provoked Swift's *Battle of the Books* (1704). Though Temple declares at the beginning of his essay that he was partly motivated by indignation at Fontenelle's 'censure of the Old Poetry and preference of the New', his only references to poetry are during the briefest skirmish with straw men, when he asks rhetorically if the flights of Boileau are above those of Virgil and adds that, if this is allowed, 'I will then yield *Gondibert* to have excelled *Homer*, as it pretended, and the modern *French* Poetry, all that of the Ancients' (Spingarn, *Critical Essays*, III, pp. 33, 63).

Temple defers fuller consideration of such matters to his essay *Of Poetry* (also in *Miscellanea*, 1690), where, in the familiar English fashion, he disparages French elaboration of the rules, because, he writes, 'there is something in the *Genius* of Poetry too Libertine to be confined to so many Rules'. He observes moreover that the codification of rules is itself a symptom of literary decline: 'I do not know that there was any great Poet in *Greece* after the Rules of that Art layd down by *Aristotle*, nor in *Rome* after those by *Horace*, which yet none of our Moderns pretend to have outdone'. He assesses conventionally the relative merits of the two supreme poets, Homer and Virgil, and, equally conventionally, he sets out the balance of powers requisite for true poetry: 'Besides the heat of Invention and liveliness of Wit, there must be the coldness of good Sense and soundness of Judgment ... a true Poem must have something both Sublime and Just, Amazing and Agreeable'. Like Rapin he expresses contempt for the lyric, and, also like Rapin, he complains that modern poetry has only 'Smoothness of Language or Style' to set against the 'Spirit and Strength' of the ancients (Spingarn, *Critical Essays*, III, pp. 83–4, 81, 102).

Temple's most influential, and for English readers most original, remarks occur during a discussion of the great antiquity of poetry, when he refers to the 'runic' verse of ancient Scandinavia. Along with passages

from another Temple essay, *Upon Heroick Virtue*, these references provided eighteenth-century English readers with their first exciting glimpses
of northern literature. The Hebrews, Norsemen, Greeks, and Romans
of whom Temple writes in *Of Poetry* associated poetry variously with
prophecy or magic, but he declares that poetry is not the product of
divine inspiration: rather it is due to 'the greatest Excellency of natural
Temper or the greatest Race [i.e. liveliness] of Native Genius' (Spingarn,
Critical Essays, III, p. 75). He advances the old familiar climatic theory,
but, in contrast with Sprat, he argues that the effect of the English
climate is to make the national character mercurial and various, so
providing that wealth of varied humours presented on the English stage.

Climate is also an important factor for John Dennis (1657–1734). In
The Impartial Critic (1693) he details some conventions of ancient
Greek drama that would 'be very ill receiv'd amongst us, upon the
account of the differences of our Religion, Climate, and Customs'; he
also argues, less convincingly, that the motif of love, almost universal in
English drama, 'could but rarely be brought upon the *Grecian* Stage
without the violation of probability, considering that their Scene lay
generally in their own, or a warmer Country' (Spingarn, *Critical Essays*,
III, pp. 150–1).

Dennis is more significant, though, as the major English proponent of
the sublime in this period. The intentions of his ambitious treatise, *The
Advancement and Reformation of Modern Poetry* (1701), are stated
with reference to the French quarrel between the Ancients and the
Moderns: Dennis notes that Boileau, discerning the actual pre-eminence
of ancient poets, wrongly concluded that they were superior to the
moderns by nature, and that Perrault, disdaining to acknowledge any
natural superiority to the ancients, no less wrongly denied their actual
superiority; Dennis, for his part, intends to show that the ancient poets'
pre-eminence was derived from joining religion with poetry, and that
'the Moderns, by incorporating Poetry with the Religion reveal'd to us
in Sacred Writ, may come to equal the Ancients' (Dennis, *Critical Works*,
I, p. 207).

Dennis investigates the nature of poetic genius and uses the notions
of Longinus to build up a theory of poetry based upon emotion. He
argues that all art is the expression of passion; its object is to excite
passion in order to satisfy and improve the mind; the more passion
there is, the better the poetry; and the highest art, the sublime, is the
expression of the most enthusiastic passion. As Longinus taught, the
sublime is recognized by its effects upon the mind and feelings of men:
'it causes in them Admiration and Surprize; a noble Pride, and a noble
Vigour, an invincible Force, transporting the Soul from its ordinary Situation, and a Transport, and a Fulness of Joy mingled with Astonishment'

(Dennis, *Critical Works*, I, p. 223). As religious subjects give us more frequent and stronger enthusiastic passions than any others, the modern poet should turn to these, taking Milton as his great example: further-more, to the extent that Christianity is true and classical paganism is false, the modern will have the advantage of the ancient.

In his no less ambitious, but unfinished, *Grounds of Criticism in Poetry* (1704) Dennis sets out to analyse the kinds of enthusiastic passion, which he believes are six in number: admiration, terror, horror, joy, sadness, and desire. He also develops his criticism of Milton in greater detail; he enumerates the beauties and defects of *Paradise Lost* by comparison with other epics: for instance, he compares descriptions of Hell by Homer, Virgil, and Milton, very much to Milton's advantage. He also praises the great modern poet for deliberately breaking through the rules of Aristotle and rising above them: Milton

had observ'd, that *Aristotle* had drawn his Rules which he has given us for Epick Poetry from the Reflections which he had made upon *Homer*. Now he knew very well, that in *Homer* the Action lay chiefly between Man and Man: for *Achilles* and *Hector* are properly the Principals, and the Gods are but Seconds. He was resolved therefore, that his Principals should be the Devil on one side and Man on the other: and the Devil is properly his Hero, because he gets the better. All the persons in his Poem, excepting two, are either Divine or Infernal. So that most of the Persons and particularly one of the Principals, being so very different from what *Homer* or *Aristotle* ever thought of, could not possibly be subjected to their Rules, either for the Characters or the Incidents.   (Dennis, *Critical Works*, I, pp. 333–4)

Milton is a daring genius who has written 'the most lofty, but most irregular Poem, that has been produc'd by the Mind of Man', but even he succeeded only in *Paradise Lost*, for Dennis regards *Paradise Regained* as a relative failure. Lesser mortals who aspire to write noble poetry do require rules however, and Dennis proceeds to lay down these rules in accordance with his theories concerning the enthusiastic passions, the superiority of religious ideas over profane ideas, and the great end of art, which is conceived in the light of the Platonic ideal, for it is 'to restore the Decays that happen'd to human Nature by the Fall, by restoring Order' (Dennis, *Critical Works*, I, p. 336).

Dennis spanned the ages of Dryden and Pope, as did Charles Gildon (1665–1724). In 1694 Gildon edited a volume of *Miscellaneous Letters and Essays* containing some pieces of his own in which he joins in the battle of the books on Perrault's side, with 'Vindications' of Shakespeare, Cowley, and Waller, and a letter 'for the Modern Poets against the Ancients'. This collection also contains a letter of uncertain authorship 'in Vindication of *Paradise Lost*', which marks an early stage in the growth of Milton's fame. The author of this letter hints at some physiological explanation of imagination (nearly always in this period conceived as visual) when he speculates that Milton's mental visionary power was the corollary of his physical blindness; which made him 'capable of much *continued Strenuous Inward Speculations* as he who has the use of his *Bodily Eyes* cannot possibly become possest with' (Spingarn, *Critical Essays*, III, p. 200). Gildon's undoubted contributions to the 1684 collection of essays generally disparage the rules, but his later work, *The Complete Art of Poetry* (1718), justifies 'the Use and Necessity of Rules in Poetry'. Swimming against the critical current of Georgian England, he insists that 'no *Modern* has any Merit but what he owes to the Rules and Precedents of the *Ancients*'. This, he claims, is equally true of poets and critics, so the only piece of modern criticism worthy of note is Addison's 'excellent Examination of *Milton*, which is every where directed by the Rules of *Aristotle*, and the receiv'd *Critics*' (Durham, *Critical Essays*, p. 61).

Addison and Pope

... a Master-piece in its Kind

    (Addison, *Spectator* No. 253, on Pope's *Essay on Criticism*)

The examination to which Gildon refers was a series of eighteen *Spectator* papers published weekly from January to May 1712. At the beginning of the series Addison announces that he will examine *Paradise Lost* according to 'the Rules of Epic Poetry'; so the first few papers (nos. 267, 273, 279, and 285), confessedly following the methods of Aristotle, 'the best Critic' according to *Spectator* 291, and Le Bossu (see pp. 75f. above), deal with, respectively, the fable or action, the characters or manners, the sentiments, and the language of Milton's poem. Under these headings Addison judges according to what he describes as Aristotle's particular requirements: for instance, that the action of an epic poem should be single, entire, and great, and that its language should be perspicuous and sublime. However, when he warms to his subject he evinces a modern notion of the imagination and an admiration for originality. In *Spectator* 279 he observes that, whereas Homer and Virgil introduced persons whose characters were commonly known, Milton's characters, for the most part,

lie out of Nature, and were to be formed purely by his own Invention. It shews a greater Genius in *Shakespeare* to have drawn his *Caliban* than his *Hotspur* or *Julius Caesar*: The one was to be supplied out of his own

Imagination, whereas the other might have been formed upon Tradition, History and Observation. It was much easier therefore for *Homer* to find proper Sentiments for an Assembly of *Grecian* Generals, than for *Milton* to diversifie his Infernal Council with proper Characters, and inspire them with a variety of Sentiments. The Loves of *Dido* and *Aeneas* are only Copies of what has passed between other Persons. *Adam* and *Eve*, before the Fall, are a different Species from that of Mankind, who are descended from them; and none but a Poet of the most unbounded Invention, and the most exquisite Judgment, cou'd have filled their Conversation and Behaviour with so many apt Circumstances during their State of Innocence.

Dryden had praised Shakespeare's Caliban over thirty years earlier, but he allowed for some popular tradition and observation in its creation.

In the last twelve of his papers on *Paradise Lost* (beginning with no. 303) Addison takes each book of the poem in turn, endeavouring to show 'how some Passages are beautiful by being Sublime, others by being Soft, others by being Natural; which of them are recommended by the Passion, which by the Moral, which by the Sentiment, and which by the Expression'; also 'how the Genius of the Poet shines by a happy Invention, a distant Allusion, or a judicious Imitation; how he has copied or improved *Homer* or *Virgil*, and raised his own Imaginations by the use which he has made of several Poetical Passages in Scripture' (*Spectator* 369). These twelve essays are more than sufficient to over-balance the effect of *Spectator* 297, where the faults and blemishes of *Paradise Lost* are detailed; for Addison's task as a true critic in the Dryden tradition is 'to dwell rather upon Excellencies than Imperfections, to discover the concealed Beauties of a Writer, and communicate to the World such things as are worth their Observation'.

As it is Addison's intention to show that *Paradise Lost* is as much of a great classic as Homer's and Virgil's epics he continues to use Aristotle as his guide; thus in *Spectator* 315: '*Aristotle* observes, that the Fable of an Epic Poem should abound in Circumstances that are both credible and astonishing; or as the *French* Critics chuse to phrase it, the Fable should be filled with the Probable and Marvellous. This Rule is as fine and just as any in *Aristotle's* whole art of poetry'. This paradoxical combination of qualities is to be found in Homer, Virgil, and Milton alike; it produces delightful astonishment in the reader: 'the most pleasing Passion that can rise in the Mind of Man, which is Admiration'. Here, as frequently elsewhere in the *Paradise Lost* papers, Addison echoes Le Bossu, but the critic most often mentioned after Aristotle is Longinus. Time and again Addison finds in Milton just those devices and qualities that Longinus had praised in Homer; he constantly stresses the sublimity of Milton's epic.

Milton's sublimity is the product of genius, but he possesses learning and judgement too; he belongs to that class of geniuses, such as Plato, Aristotle, Virgil, and Cicero, who 'have formed themselves by Rules, and submitted the Greatness of their natural Talents to the Corrections and Restraints of Art' (*Spectator* 160). In this *Spectator* essay Addison distinguishes this kind of genius from the great natural geniuses 'never disciplined and broken by Rules of Art' in whose work 'appears something nobly wild and extravagant' that is 'infinitely more beautiful than all the Turn and Polishing of what the *French* call a *Bel Esprit*, by which they would express a Genius refined by Conversation, Reflection, and the Reading of the most polite Authors'. Shakespeare, needless to say, is one of the greatest of these natural geniuses, but in ancient times natural genius was prominent particularly among the 'eastern' writers of the Old Testament and, of course, Homer. Addison relishes the primitive qualities of Homer, the effect of which he conveys in picturesque terms: 'Reading the *Iliad* is like travelling through a Country uninhabited, where the Fancy is entertained with a thousand Savage Prospects of vast Desarts, wide uncultivated Marshes, huge Forests, misshapen Rocks and Precipies'. Virgil's *Aeneid*, by contrast, is likened to a beautiful well-ordered garden, and Ovid's *Metamorphoses* is 'enchanted Ground', where we 'see nothing but Scenes of Magick lying round us' (*Spectator* 417).

These comparisons occur in Addison's *Spectator* papers on the pleasures of the imagination (discussed more fully on pp. 618–22 below), where Shakespeare is praised again as the poet whose 'noble Extravagance of Fancy' made him capable of 'succeeding where he had nothing to support him besides the Strength of his own Genius'. He is the greatest master of what Addison, following Dryden, calls 'the Fairy kind of writing', the art 'Wherein the Poet quite loses sight of Nature, and entertains his Reader's Imagination with the Characters and Actions of such Persons as have many of them no Existence, but what he bestows on them'. In bringing to life imaginary beings, such as fairies, witches, demons, and personified abstractions, the poet 'must work altogether out of his own Invention', so the fairy way is the most difficult way of writing. In such writing the imagination displays to the full its creative power; it 'makes new Worlds of its own', by it 'we are led, as it were, into a new Creation'. Those who would succeed in the fairy way of writing ought to be 'very well vers'd in Legends and Fables, antiquated Romances, and the Traditions of Nurses and old Women, that he may fall in with our natural Prejudices, and humour those Notions which we have imbib'd in our Infancy' (*Spectator* 419).

The implied genteel primitivism of these remarks on the fairy way of writing is applied to simpler forms of romantic poetry in Addison's earlier papers on traditional ballads. In *Spectator* 85 he praises 'The Two Children in the Wood' (i.e. 'Babes in the Wood') as 'a plain simple

Copy of Nature, destitute of all the Helps and Ornaments of Art. The Tale of it is a pretty Tragical Story, and pleases for no other Reason, but because it is a copy of Nature' (*Spectator*, I, p. 362). In *Spectator* 70 and 74 he offers a fuller discussion and higher praise for the equally popular ballad of 'Chevy Chase', which he criticizes according to the rules of heroic poetry laid down by Le Bossu and other modern critics. He draws telling parallels between the *Aeneid* and the heroic medieval ballad, the sentiments of which, he declares, 'are extremely natural and poetical, and full of the majestick Simplicity which we admire in the greatest of the ancient Poets'. He concludes: 'If this Song had been written in the *Gothic* Manner, which is the Delight of all our little Wits, whether Writers or Readers, it would not have hit the Taste of so many Ages, and have pleased the Readers of all Ranks and Conditions'. This is a disconcerting and challenging use of 'Gothic': Addison asserts that, though 'Chevy Chase' is a work from the medieval or 'Gothic' period, it is not 'Gothic'; that is, it is not in bad taste.

The 'Gothic Manner' of which Addison disapproves is evidently what appeals to that 'Gothic' taste for epigrams, turns of wit, and forced conceits which he condemns in *Spectator* 409; it embraces all the ways of writing discussed in four early papers, *Spectator* 58 to *Spectator* 61, where Addison provides a history and anatomy of 'false wit', ancient and modern, in all its varieties, including acrostics, 'emblem' poems in typographical shapes, anagrams, *bouts rimés*, and puns. At the end of *Spectator* 61 Addison declares that the only way to test a piece of wit is to translate it into another language: false wit depends merely upon a resemblance of words and cannot be translated whereas true wit can, for, as Addison elaborates in *Spectator* 62, it lies in resemblance and congruity of ideas. He quotes Locke on the difference between wit and judgement and approves of Locke's account of wit as the putting together, with quickness and variety, of those ideas 'wherein can be found any Resemblance or Congruity thereby to make up pleasant Pictures and agreeable Visions in the Fancy', but he ignores the disapproving context of Locke's account (see pp. 616f. below) and adds the important rider that 'every Resemblance of Ideas is not that which we call Wit, unless it be such an one that gives Delight and Surprise to the Reader'. Addison notes also that not only the resemblance but the opposition of ideas can on occasion produce wit.

In addition to true and false wit there is, according to Addison, an amphibious kind of 'mixed wit' which consists partly in the resemblance of ideas and partly in the resemblance of words. It is a composition of pun and true wit: 'Reason puts in her Claim, for one half of it, and Extravagance for the other'. Ovid, Martial, Cowley, and Waller had much of this mixed kind of wit, the Italians, even in their epic poetry were full of it, Horace and Dryden had a little, but Virgil, Spenser, and Milton had a genius much above it. Boileau and Bouhours rejected mixed wit, because they believed that the basis of wit is truth and that no thought can be valuable of which good sense is not the groundwork: 'This is that natural Way of Writing, that beautiful Simplicity, which we so much admire in the Compositions of the Ancients'. In attacking verbal conceits Addison allies himself with the French critics of the previous generation; indeed, as early as *Spectator* 5, in his attack on the absurdity of Italian opera, he endorsed Boileau's opinion that one verse of Virgil is worth all the tinsel of Tasso. However, one important area where Addison does not follow Boileau is the defence of satire. In *Spectator* 23 he declares: 'Lampoons and Satyrs, that are written with Wit and Spirit, are like poison'd Darts, which not only inflict a Wound, but make it incurable ... So pernicious a thing is Wit, when it is not tempered with Virtue and Humanity'. No modern satirist is named in this essay; if Addison had anyone particularly in mind it was probably Swift and certainly not Boileau. Addison always writes of Boileau with great admiration, so it is a mark of respect to the younger poet when Addison invokes Boileau in *Spectator* 253, which is a review of Alexander Pope's *Essay on Criticism*.

Despite its title, Pope's poem is as much an art of poetry as of criticism: in form as well as content it challenges comparison with Boileau's *L'Art poétique* and Horace's *Ars Poetica*, both of which it deliberately echoes from time to time. Like his two great predecessors Pope justifies his principles by his practice; he exemplifies his critical pronouncements when, for instance, offering advice on prosody, he first proclaims a principle, 'The *Sound* must seem an *Eccho* to the *Sense*' (line 365), then illustrates it:

> When *Ajax* strives, some Rock's vast Weight to throw,
> The line too *labours*, and the Words move *slow*;
> Not so, when swift *Camilla* scours the Plain,
> Flies o'er th'unbending Corn, and skims along the Main.
>
> (ll. 370–3)

The *Essay on Criticism* is not, like most of Pope's other criticism or like most of Dryden's, an 'occasional' piece, attached as a preface to some original work by the poet, but it is not a systematic treatise either. It has an easy, discursive manner of proceeding, as if of an animated, serious conversation circling round some key words: nature, wit, judgement.

At the opening of his poem Pope asks whether, in view of the great varieties of human understanding, true judgements about literature are possible, but he answers confidently that there is a norm 'Nature', against which the truth of critical judgements may be tested. Nature is

an immutable standard: poetry imitates nature, that is, the universal
order of things:

> First follow NATURE, and your Judgment frame
> By her just Standard, which is still the same:
> *Unerring Nature*, still divinely bright,
> One *clear*, *unchang'd*, and *Universal* Light,
> Life, Force, and Beauty, must to all impart,
> At once the *Source*, and *End*, and *Test* of *Art*.
>
> (ll. 68–73)

Conveniently, as Rapin and others had pointed out, the principles of
that natural order which the poet's work should reflect if he was to
imitate nature were readily available in the ancient rules:

> Those RULES of old *discover'd*, not *devis'd*,
> Are *Nature* still, but *Nature Methodiz'd*.
>
> (ll. 88–9)

According to Pope, Virgil found that Nature and Homer were the same;
if a modern poet properly considered the matter he would make the
same discovery:

> Learn hence for Ancient *Rules* a just Esteem;
> To copy *Nature* is to copy *Them*.
>
> (ll. 139–40)

This said, Pope agrees with Rapin and the rest that there is a nameless
grace, not attainable by obedience to the rules:

> Which, without passing thro' the *Judgment*, gains
> The *Heart*, and all its End *at once* attains ...
> Those oft are *Stratagems* which *Errors* seem,
> Nor is it *Homer Nods*, but *We* that *Dream*.
>
> (ll. 156–7, 179–80)

The conclusion and climax of this first movement of the *Essay* is a
noble expression of almost religious veneration for the ancients, to
whose guidance Pope commits himself as a humble disciple:

> Still green with Bays each *ancient* Altar stands,
> Above the reach of *Sacrilegious* Hands ...
> Hail *Bards Triumphant*! born in *happier Days*;
> *Immortal* Heirs of *Universal* Praise!
> Whose Honours with Increase of Ages *grow*,
> As Streams roll down, *enlarging* as they flow!
>
> (ll. 181–2, 189–92)

Then follows a long section where Pope investigates the causes hindering a true judgement of poetry and where he gives freest rein to his predilection for satire, but he also continues to make explicit his positive principles, always relating them to the norm of 'nature'. Thus:

> *True Wit* is *Nature* to Advantage drest,
> What oft was *Thought*, but ne'er so well *Exprest*,
> *Something*, whose Truth convinc'd at Sight we find,
> That gives us back the Image of our Mind.

(ll. 297–300)

'True wit' here embraces the whole creative activity of the poet, which strikes the reader with immediate conviction in the clear and universal light of nature. An earlier passage in the *Essay* shows that wit is not to be opposed to judgement, as Locke declared and some literary critics allowed, but is complementary to it:

> *Wit* and *Judgment* often are at strife,
> Tho' meant each other's Aid, like *Man and Wife*.

(ll. 82–3)

Pope concludes his poem with a sketch of the character of a good critic and a short history of criticism from Aristotle to his own times, when '*Critic Learning* flourish'd most in *France*'. He continues:

> The *Rules*, a Nation born to serve, obeys,
> And *Boileau* still in Right of *Horace* sways.
> But *we*, brave *Britons, Foreign Laws* despis'd,
> And kept *unconquer'd*, and *unciviliz'd*,
> Fierce for the *Liberties of Wit*, and bold,
> We still defy'd the *Romans*, as *of old*.

(ll. 713–18)

In order to contrive a culturally nationalist taunt against the French, Pope momentarily and oddly associates himself with woad-painted ancient Britons, but his own critical principles are very much in line with Boileau.

What is perhaps the highest explicit tribute to Boileau in Pope's writings occurs in the 'Letter to the Publisher' prefixed to *The Dunciad Variorum* (1729), where the Frenchman is described as 'the greatest Poet and most judicious Critic of his age and country', and it is implied that Pope is to be Boileau's English counterpart as a 'candid' (i.e., impartial and unmalicious) satirist. This letter, attributed to William Cleland but written by Pope himself, makes the traditional moral defence of satire and argues that the satirist's arm can strike against some kinds of wrongdoing that otherwise would go unpunished: 'Law can pronounce judgment only on open Facts, Morality alone can pass censure on Intentions of mischief;

so that for secret calumny or the arrow flying in the dark, there is no publick punishment left, but what a good writer inflicts.' For some readers, though, *The Dunciad* itself lacked moral justification. Ambrose Philips, in *Codrus: or The Dunciad Dissected* (1728), declares that calamities are not crimes and that Pope has no moral right to attack writers merely because they are dull and poverty-stricken. Pope defends himself in the 'Cleland' letter by asserting that 'in all ages, all vain pretenders, were they ever so poor or ever so dull, have been constantly the topicks of the most candid Satyrists, from the Codrus of *Juvenal* to the Damon of *Boileau*' (Pope, Twickenham Edition, VI, p. 17).

Pope's *Imitations of Horace* are to a considerable extent an implicit, and at times explicit, defence of satire, where that defence is at the same time a defence of Pope's own character and motives. In the *Epistle to Augustus* (1737) he asserts that satire 'heals with Morals what it hurts with Wit' (line 262); he reaffirms satire's moral utility with the greatest energy, confidence, and self-righteousness in the second dialogue of the *Epilogue to the Satires* (1738):

> Yes, I am proud; I must be proud to see
> Men not afraid of God, afraid of me:
> Safe from the Bar, the Pulpit, and the Throne,
> Yet touch'd and sham'd by Ridicule alone.
> O sacred Weapon! left for Truth's defence,
> Sole Dread of Folly, Vice and Insolence!
> To all but Heav'n-directed hands deny'd,
> The Muse may give thee, but the Gods must guide.

No one maintained the moral defence of satire with more skill and passion than Pope did. Nevertheless some of his most devoted admirers were dismayed that the greatest English poet of their generation should, as they saw it, dissipate his genius in libels against government ministers of the day, their hacks, and other servants, when he was so well fitted to write the national epic that, it was thought, the age required. It seems that Pope himself saw the force of their argument, because not long before his death he was at work on a four-book epic poem in blank verse, taking the legendary progenitor of the British people as his hero. Had Pope lived a few years longer his crowning achievement might not have been *The Dunciad in Four Books*, but *Brutus*. The choice of blank verse, inescapably associated with Milton, would have placed his poem firmly in the English tradition. As it is, despite the nationalist flourish that concludes his *Essay on Criticism*, Pope's critical keepings are rather with ancient Rome, Italy, and France.

Pope is the most self-regarding of the leading critics in this period. One might claim that his justifiably very high valuation of his own poetry becomes a kind of moral rectitude, though this would be truer of his satires than his pastorals, where self-praise is again an important strand of criticism. This is the case in an anonymous essay, *Guardian* 40 (1713), when Pope employs a transparent irony to praise his own pastorals while dispraising those of Ambrose Philips and, incidentally, Philips's model Spenser. The issue of principle between the poets is Philips's naturalizing of the pastoral by including English scenery, folklore, and dialect, as against the elegant literariness favoured by Pope, whose primary model was Virgil. Pope's theory, briefly sketched in this *Guardian* essay and laid out more fully in the 'Discourse on Pastoral Poetry', first published in his *Works* (1717) but probably written in 1709 (if not 1704), leans heavily upon modern French critics. Some concessions are made in the 'Discourse' to Fontenelle's psychological account of the origin and motive of pastoral, but the heart of Pope's theory comes from Rapin. Pope writes:

If we would copy Nature, it may be useful to take this Idea along with us, that pastoral is an image of what they call the Golden age. So that we are not to describe our shepherds as shepherds at this day really are, but as they may be conceiv'd then to have been; when the best of men follow'd the employment.

(Pope, *Pastoral Poetry*, p. 25)

'Nature' is ideal, not common nature.

Pope returns to French critical models when he praises Le Bossu in the Preface to his own translation of Homer's *Iliad* (1715) and attaches to his translation of the *Odyssey* (1726) 'A General View of the Epic Poem, and of the *Iliad* and *Odyssey*, extracted from *Bossu*'. Pope's Preface to the *Iliad* is much taken up with the vital importance of invention which he calls 'the very Foundation of Poetry'. Invention is the poet's power to create something that did not exist before: in effect it is the imagination itself. Invention is to judgement as nature is to art: 'Art is only like a prudent Steward that lives on managing the Riches of Nature. Whatever Praises may be given to Works of Judgment, there is not even a single Beauty in them to which Invention must not contribute.' Homer's invention is unrivalled; therefore Homer 'has ever been acknowledged the greatest of Poets'. Taking up Dryden's remarks on Homer's fire, Pope declares: 'It is to the Strength of this amazing Invention we are to attribute that unequal'd Fire and Rapture, which is so forcible in *Homer*, that no Man of a true Poetical Spirit is Master of himself while he reads him . . . The Reader is hurry'd out of himself by the Force of the Poet's Imagination' (Pope, *Iliad*, pp. 3, 4). This 'fire' makes a bond between poet and reader, linking together the acts of creating and of experiencing great poetry.

Pope's translation of Homer itself attained classic status and was very soon the subject of detailed and sympathetic study in *An Essay on*

Pope's Odyssey (1726) by Joseph Spence (1699–1768). One of Spence's speakers (for the *Essay* is in dialogue form) praises the 'pleasing Terrour' of a 'horribly delightful' speech in Pope's translation, but another speaker finds Pope's version not equal to Homer's '*True Sublime*', which gives a quality that can be conveyed only by a neologism, '*orientalism*', which is then defined by a series of quotations from sublime passages in the Old Testament (Spence, *Essay*, II, pp. 56–7).

Spence was the third holder of the Oxford University Professorship of Poetry, founded in 1708, that foundation being an early pointer to the institutionalizing of literary criticism in England as it was being institutionalized in literary academies all over Europe. The first holder of the Oxford chair, Joseph Trapp (1679–1747), was, like Spence, a devotee of oriental poetry; his lectures constantly insist on the merit and antiquity of Old Testament poetry. He claims that poetry flourished among the Hebrews before the Trojan war, that Old Testament lyric poetry antedates Pindar, and that pastoral was invented by the Hebrews long before Theocritus, who indeed borrowed from the Song of Solomon. In a similar vein, the author of *Guardian* 86 (1713), probably Edward Young (1683–1765), claims that the Book of Job is the most ancient poem in the world and that it possesses much greater spirit in thought and energy in style than the epics of Homer and Virgil. Sir William Temple had speculated in his essay *Of Poetry* (1690) that the Book of Job was written before the time of Moses, being a translation from the Chaldean or Arabic.

English speculations about ancient literature are amateurish and superficial in comparison with the reflections of the Italian philosopher Giambattista Vico (1668–1744), who argues in his 'new science' of history, the *Scienza nuova* (1725, expanded 1730), that human society passes through three ages of, successively, the senses, the imagination, and the reason, rather as individual men do; before men obtained any rational knowledge of nature they employed their imaginations upon it; their imaginings are the ancient fables or poetic wisdom (*sapienza poetica*); thus the poetic imagination is the embodiment of a formative epoch in the history of man. 'Homer' was the collective mind of the Greeks describing their early history in poetry.

Continental: after 1700

Boileau still in Right of *Horace* sways
(Pope, *Essay on Criticism*)

Italian criticism of contemporary literature at this period was much occupied in a regular campaign to refine taste. Among the principal agencies of this refinement were the Arcadian academies, the first of which was founded in 1690 with the object of renewing 'the sweet studies and innocent customs which the ancient Arcadians cultivated' (Robertson, *Studies*, p. 17). Pastoral simplicity was to be substituted for the excesses of 'Marinism', the conceitful verse made fashionable by Marino and his followers in the seventeenth century. Italian Arcadianism was thus part of a general movement towards that classic simplicity advocated by Boileau.

Boileau and his fellows prompted other critical activity in Italy by their attacks on Italian poetry in general and Tasso in particular. In 1703 the Marchese Orsi responded to Bouhours's *La manière de bien penser* with voluminous and pedantic *Considerazione*, which Voltaire justly dismissed as 'deux gros volumes pour justifier quelques vers du Tasse'. A far more temperate, stylish, and constructive defence was offered by Ludovico Antonio Muratori (1672–1750) in his *Della perfetta poesia italiana* (1706), in which he moves beyond immediate, particular criticism in order to develop a general theory of the imagination (*fantasia* or *immaginazione*). According to Muratori, imagination apprehends images without itself judging whether what these images represent is true or false: such judgement is the work of the intellect. The imagination or 'fantasy' has the power to conceive new images or 'idols'. 'The fantasy thus controls the private arsenal and secret treasury of our soul'; 'idols' are 'set out like so much merchandise in a great square or market, in more or less order – sometimes in disorder – and from these, at one time the fantasy, at another the intellect, swiftly selects appropriate embodiments for its thoughts' (Robertson, *Studies*, pp. 78–9). True poetry is the joint work of imagination and intellect, so that the capriciousness of the fantasy harmonizes with the intellect's love of truth to create 'lively painting' (*viva dipintura*).

The nature of poetry is also the subject of *Della Ragion poetica* (1708) by Gian Vincenzo Gravina (1663–1718), who seeks to determine some underlying principle (*ragion* or 'reason') on which a science of poetry may be erected. This principle is not to be found in Aristotelian rules because each new generation must adapt the idea of poetry to its own rational needs. Though in one part of this treatise Gravina draws a parallel between the rules of poetry and the rules of architecture, he asserts that the most impressive poetry has novelty (*novità*) and marvellousness (*maraviglia*). Ordinary, familiar facts do not impress themselves upon the mind as novel poetic fictions do; the poet-magician's siege of the reader's imagination must therefore be armed with what is novel and striking in order to capture attention and then drive home a moral lesson. The value of these fictions emerges when the mind reflects upon them and finds the moral truths that they embody. Poetry is an enchantress, but the success of its enchantment depends, as the ancients had declared, upon probability (*verisimile*), so that what the compelling power of poetry creates must be true and natural: 'of all the wise enchanters Homer is the most powerful and wisest (*il mago più potente e l'incantatore più sagace*); he is the supreme poet of the natural' (Robertson, *Studies*, p. 39).

Muratori declared that the imitation of nature presented by poetry 'to the eyes of the soul' is a parallel with what is seen by the eyes of a painter. The parallel between poetry and painting, based upon the Horatian tag *ut pictura poesis*, is treated in Chapter 29 below. Dryden's 'Parallel of Poetry and Painting' (1695) combines French, Italian, and English thinking on this theme, for it is a preface to his own translation of Du Fresnoy's Latin poem *De arte graphica* (written 1637, published 1667) and it incorporates extensive quotation from a discussion of the parallel between the arts in *Le vite de' pittori, scultori, et architetti moderni* (1672) by Giovanni Pietro Bellori. Dryden agrees with Du Fresnoy and Bellori that in the highest forms of art, such as epic poetry and history painting, the artist 'should form to himself an idea of perfect nature'; then Dryden speculates on the process by which imitations of ideal nature affect the viewer or reader:

They present us with images more perfect than the life in any individual; and we have the pleasure to see all the scattered beauties of nature united by a happy chemistry, without its deformities or faults. They are imitations of the passions which always move, and therefore consequently please; for without motion there can be no delight, which cannot be considered but as an active passion. When we view these elevated ideas of nature, the result of that view is admiration, which is always the cause of pleasure.

(Dryden, *Of Dramatic Poesy*, II, pp. 183, 194)

The best-known and most influential treatise on the sister arts in the early eighteenth century was *Réflexions critiques sur la poésie et sur la peinture* (1719) by Jean-Baptiste Du Bos (1670–1742). This work deals also with sculpture, engraving, and music: when it was translated into English in 1748, by Thomas Nugent, the word 'Music' was added to the book's title. The *Réflexions* carries Horace's tag on its title-page. Du Bos declares that both arts are imitative and present images of sight to the mind, but whereas poetry can build up a character and action over time, painting must apprehend them in an instant, so the painter is limited to the representation of such feelings and ideas as find immediate natural expression in a single image. The poet can work upon his reader's feelings with a linked succession of impressions, but each impression will in itself be more faint than the painter's, for the painter uses signs that are more like the original, and therefore arouse a response more immediately; he addresses the predominant sense of sight directly, not indirectly.

Comments by Du Bos on parallels between the arts are only a part of his general theory, the key terms of which are passion, genius, and climate. He declares that men are naturally led by instinct to pursue objects capable of exciting their passions, despite the unhappiness that such pursuit often causes, but the value of art is that it can create objects which 'excite artificial passions, sufficient to occupy us while we are actually affected by them, and incapable of giving us afterwards any real pain or affliction' (*Critical Reflections*, I, p. 21). Art, then, satisfies one of our deepest instincts: it exists to move us and it is known by its effects. That being so, its best judges are ordinary readers of poetry and viewers of pictures:

> The public gives not only a disinterested judgment of a work, but judges likewise what opinion we are to entertain of it in general, by means of the sense, and according to the impression made thereon by the poem or picture. Since the chief end of poetry and painting is to move us, the productions of these arts can be valuable only in proportion as they touch and engage us. A work that is exquisitely moving, must be an excellent piece, take it all together. For the same reason, a work which does not move and engage us, is good for nothing; and if it be not obnoxious to criticism for trespassing against rules, 'tis because it may be bad, without any violation of rules; as on the contrary one full of faults against rules, may be an excellent performance.   (*Critical Reflections*, II, p. 237)

The organ by which a work of art is judged is a 'sixth sense', which responds without deliberation or reflection:

> The heart is agitated of itself, by a motion previous to all deliberation, when the object presented is really affecting; whether this object has received its being from nature, or from an imitation made by art. Our heart is made and organized for this very purpose: Its operation therefore runs before our reasoning, as the action of the eye and ear precedes it in their sensations. 'Tis as rare to see men born without the sense here mentioned, as 'tis to meet with people born blind.   (*Critical Reflections*, II, pp. 239–40)

This last statement runs counter to the commonly accepted notion, expressed by Boileau and Pope among others, that very few men possess the true taste that is required for sound critical judgements. Du Bos therefore devotes his next four chapters to overcoming objections and reaffirming that an immediate sense-impression is better than discussion for distinguishing the merit of poems and pictures, and that common public judgements prevail at length over those of artists and critics.

Du Bos's conception of genius is conventional enough: it is 'the fire which elevates painters above themselves . . . 'Tis the enthusiasm which seizes poets' (*Critical Reflections*, II, p. 13). Genius is rare, and even where it exists may not always be displayed. This notion of innate genius is half-way towards the sentiments of Gray's *Elegy* when he writes: 'Men born with the genius which forms the great general, or the magistrate worthy of enacting laws, frequently die before their abilities are discovered' (*Critical Reflections*, II, p. 15). Du Bos conjectures that genius in the individual consists

in a happy arrangement of the organs of the brain, in a just conformation of each of these organs, as also in the quality of blood which disposes it to ferment during exercise, so as to furnish a plenty of spirits to the springs employed in the functions of the imagination. In fact, the excessive lassitude and wasting of spirits, which attend a long application of mind, are sufficient to evince, that the fatigues of the imagination considerably exhaust the strength of the body.

(*Critical Reflections*, II, pp. 10–11)

There may also be physical explanations as to why the arts have flourished in certain periods and places, and not in others. Du Bos shares the general opinion that very cold and very hot climates are inimical to the flowering of genius; he goes so far as to claim that the arts and sciences have not flourished north of 52° or south of 25° of northern latitude. England is on the very frontier of genius, having produced good native scientists, philosophers, poets, and even musicians, but no native painters of any note: Du Bos declares that 'poetry is not so much afraid of the cold as painting' (*Critical Reflections*, II, p. 110). The air differs from country to country and from time to time, consequently men differ, just as 'two grains from the same plant, produce a fruit of a different quality when they are sown in different soils, or even when they are sown in the same soil but in different years' (*Critical Reflections*, II, p. 177). Du Bos enters into lengthy speculations upon the physical causes for these differences.

Voltaire greatly admired the criticism of Du Bos and took up the cause of critical relativism himself in the *Essay on Epick Poetry* (1727), written in English. Voltaire takes issue with the notion that we should go to the ancients for the immutable laws of epic poetry:

The same Fancy which hath invented Poetry, changes every Day all its Productions, because it is liable itself to eternal Vicissitudes. The Poetry and Musick of the *Persians*, differ as much from ours, as their Language. Even a Nation differs from itself in less than a Century. There are not more Revolutions in Governments, than in Arts. They are shifting, and gliding away from our Pursuit, when we endeavour to fix them by our Rules and Definitions.

(*Essay*, p. 82)

The *Essay* is an exercise in comparative criticism, based upon the notion that it is necessary to take account of the distinct genius of each nation and epoch before passing judgement upon its literature. So Voltaire offers a rapid and lively survey of eight epic poems from Homer to Milton, promising that his reader

will mark the Progresses, the Sinking of the Art, its Raising again, and pursue it through its various Changes ... He will not be tyranniz'd by *Aristotle*, *Castelvetro*, *Dacier*, *Le Bossu*, but he will extract his own Rules from the various Examples he shall have before his Eyes, and governed by his good Sense alone, be a Judge between the Gods of *Homer*, and the God of *Milton*, and between *Calipso*, *Dido*, *Armida*, and *Eve*.

(*Essay*, p. 88)

There is no French epic among the chosen eight, because Voltaire hoped that his own *Henriade* would fill that vacancy. The *Essay* is a piece of virtuosity characteristic of its author. Voltaire greatly prefers Virgil to Homer: the *Iliad* reflected the primitive values and manners of Homeric society; Homer's authority now hindered progress in the writing of epic poetry because French critics of the previous generation, such as Le Bossu, had mistakenly read Homer's poems as if they were a repository of the rules for epic. Turning to modern poetry, Voltaire repeats some of the usual French criticisms of Italian taste, but he partly rehabilitates the reputation of Tasso in France; he praises Milton's *Paradise Lost*, acknowledging that he draws upon the work of Addison, 'the best Critick as well as the best Writer of his Age' (*Essay*, p. 134). In the expanded, greatly revised French edition of his *Essay* (1732), though, Voltaire qualified his praise of Milton and elaborated upon the defects of *Paradise Lost*, which in its French translation was a formidable rival to *La Henriade*. There was a comparable hardening of his attitude towards Shakespeare over the years following the *Letters concerning the English Nation* (1733). The main literary-critical interest of these essentially political letters lies in Voltaire's view of the English drama, but they contain praise of modern English wit as embodied especially in Rochester and Pope. 1733 also saw the publication of Voltaire's *Le Temple du goût*, the title of which testifies to the universality of 'taste' as the critical norm by this date. This sprightly allegory in prose and verse represents a temple, like Pope's Temple of Fame; it is besieged by French authors, from the times of Rabelais and Marot to Voltaire's own day; all clamour for admission, each is judged by the standards of truth, nature, and simplicity, and only eight admitted; these are the neo-classical masters, mostly of the generation just before Voltaire's, Fénelon, Bossuet, Corneille, Racine, La Fontaine, Boileau, Molière, and Quinault. Meanwhile the pedantic commentators, 'Baldus, Scioppius, Lexicocrassus, and Scriblerius', have been consigned to Hell. However much Voltaire is prepared to take account of the distinct genius of other nations and other epochs, his own taste is firm, consistent, and conservative.

The English influences that are so evident in the criticism of Voltaire scarcely penetrated to Spain. Addison had acknowledged in *Spectator* 409 that it was a Spaniard, Baltasar Gracián, who first used the term taste (*gusto*) to mean a special function of the mind. This he did in his *Arte de ingenio* (1642), where, as it happens, he praises the taste for elaborate conceits in the manner of Góngora and his followers, or what Addison himself would have called the Gothic taste and false wit. (Góngora was the Spanish contemporary of and counterpart to Marino in Italy.) The Spaniards were also credited with having invented the notion of the *je ne sais quoi*, for when the idea is introduced by the French critic Vincent Voiture in 1642 he employs the Spanish form: 'ce que les Espagnols appellent *el no sé qué*' (Spingarn, *Critical Essays*, I, p. c.). By the end of the century, though, Spain was plunged into intellectual torpor, from which there was only a slow revival in the 1720s and '30s.

The revival of literary criticism in Spain was begun by Benito Jerónimo Feijóo (1676–1764) in a series of essays, *Teatro crítico universal* (1726–41). One of these essays, published in 1734, is on *El no sé qué*, now long naturalized in France and England as the *je ne sais quoi*; Feijóo offers the usual observations: it is outside the sphere of reason, it can be felt but not analysed, its cause remains a mystery, it is more often found in irregular than in regular works. The most substantial critical treatise of the period was by Ignacio de Luzán (1702–54): *La Poética, o reglas de la poésia en general, y de sus principales especies* (1737), that is 'Poetics, or Rules of Poetry in General and of the Principal Genres'. This work in elegant prose is an elaborate, schematized codification of classical and neo-classical critical precepts, which was intended to be a full, perfect, and complete treatise on poetics. Luzán discusses the theories of nearly 100 critics from Aristotle and Horace to Boileau, Rapin, Le Bossu, Orsi, Muratori, and Gravina; his primary authority is Aristotle, whose reasoned pronouncements are said to be almost as old as reason itself. Luzán ridicules the obscurity, ingenuity, and over-elaboration of Góngorism in Spanish poetry and attacks the irregularity of Spanish drama in the previous century. He recommends clarity, simplicity, good sense, and truth to nature, in precepts that had by now become all too familiar north of the Pyrenees. Not surprisingly, he became known as the 'Spanish Boileau'.

Conclusion

If one person dominates literary criticism during the period 1660–1740 it is Boileau. As the imitator of Horace and translator of Longinus he consciously links himself with the ancients, but his style and critical posture are those of a sociable man of the contemporary world, a man of polished wit, sound sense, and refined taste. His aesthetic ideal is clarity and noble simplicity: his watchwords are nature, truth, and reason.

All critics agreed that poetry is an imitation of nature, but 'nature' admitted some breadth of interpretation. It might be what Dryden, following Bellori, calls the idea of perfect nature, in which the scattered beauties of ordinary observed nature are united, while nature's deformities and faults are excluded. This same notion of perfect nature might be regarded in specifically Christian terms as prelapsarian nature, so that the great end of poetry becomes, for Dennis for instance, to restore that natural order which was lost at the Fall. Art is necessary to complete nature, so, as Fontenelle, followed by Pope, observed, in order to follow nature it is necessary to be artificial. Nature, though, could also be defined in terms of what is not shaped by art: for instance when Addison praises the old ballad of the Babes in the Wood as a plain simple copy of nature, destitute of all the helps and ornaments of art. Nature might be, in Pope's terms, one clear, unchanged, and universal light, or it might comprise the local, concrete, and individual, such as the humours, the features, and the very dress of Chaucer's pilgrims, realized as distinctively for Dryden as if he had supped with them at the Tabard in Southwark. Nature in Rymer's view is empirical truth, so he condemns Spenser's fanciful and chimerical fictions; but for Dryden those things which delight all ages, for instance the visionary objects of poets from Homer to Milton, including 'our English Spenser', must have been an imitation of nature.

For many critics of this period the surest way of following nature was to follow the ancients. The poets of ancient Greece and Rome were still very much alive: 'Still green with Bays each *ancient* Altar stands', wrote Pope; Dryden's criticism conveys a very personal engagement with Virgil and Homer, the latter being more suitable to Dryden's temper. Homer, Pindar, Theocritus, Virgil, Ovid, and Horace are the prime authoritative examples, but some English critics elevated Milton and even Spenser to the ranks of classical poets worthy of imitation; moreover there was a growing interest in older poetic models, such as Chaucer, the ballads, northern runic verse, and the ancient poetry of the Hebrews.

Growing admiration for non-classical models would eventually blur the clear distinctions between literary genres inherited from the ancients, but distinct notions of genre held good in the period 1660–1740: Addison was content to discuss even the ballad of 'Chevy Chase' in accordance with the classical rules for heroic poetry. Critics agreed that there was a hierarchy of the genres, headed in the case of non-dramatic poetry, by the epic. Forms unknown to the ancients could always be fitted into this hierarchy, as, for instance, Boileau shows in *L'Art poétique*. Each genre had an appropriate style, form, and function, corresponding to some different aspect of nature, though critics might differ as to the detail of such correspondence: for instance pastoral is related to historical factors by Rapin and to general human psychology by Fontenelle.

Boileau called upon poets to love reason; critics of the period invariably stress the need for judgement in the writing of poetry, but no one argued that poetic creation was a wholly rational activity. Creative power still lay where it always had lain – in the fancy or imagination, terms regarded as synonymous by most critics. The relationship between reason and imagination is represented metaphorically by Dryden's clogged spaniel or the bridled Pegasus in Pope's *Essay on Criticism*. Imagination controlled by judgement constitutes 'true wit', which, as Pope said, 'is *Nature* to Advantage drest'. True wit produces the natural thought or image, which directs the reader's mind towards the idea or object in view, rather than towards the ingenuity of the poet. Possessors of true wit can sometimes be witty out of season, as Dryden says of Ovid, when they ignore the cooler dictates of judgement and allow the false applause of fancy to influence them.

The degree to which a poet might ignore the cooler dictates of judgement was a matter of debate. Critics as a matter of course praise the original genius of poets such as Homer and Shakespeare, who equalled or even excelled poets of manifestly greater learning, such as Virgil and Milton. In the poetry they most admire they are eager to find mysteries, nameless graces, Promethean fire, and the sublime. The sublime, as Boileau, the popularizer of Longinus, declared, cannot be analysed; it can only be felt in what exalts, ravishes, transports the reader and sets him on fire. This is also the case with those nameless graces beyond the reach of art which were comprehended in the *je ne sais quoi* or *el no sé qué*. There is a secret power in poetry that is recognized by the heart, and not the mind, so that even criticism in the last analysis is not a wholly rational matter. Despite continuing respectful acknowledgement of the rules of poetry, taste becomes a more significant critical touchstone in the period 1660–1740. In the following years the doctrine of taste would open up ways towards greater critical relativity and towards a criticism focusing more upon the subjective effects of poetry.

4

Poetry, after 1740

William Keach

The proliferation, dissolution, and crossing of genres

The poetry produced during the middle and later eighteenth century confronts us with an impressive formal and thematic diversity. Simply listing some of the more influential verse published in England during the 1740s will indicate the protean situation: Collins's *Persian Eclogues* (1742) and *Odes on Several Descriptive and Allegorical Subjects* (1746); Pope's *New Dunciad*, Robert Blair's *The Grave*, and Hammond's *Love Elegies* (all 1743); Akenside's *The Pleasures of Imagination* (1744) and *Odes* (1745); Joseph Warton's *The Enthusiast: or The Lover of Nature* (1744–8) and *Odes on Various Subjects* (1746); Young's *Night Thoughts* (1742–5); the final edition of Thomson's *The Seasons* (1746) and *The Castle of Indolence* (1748); Thomas Warton's *The Pleasures of Melancholy* and Gray's *Ode on a Distant Prospect of Eton College* (both 1747); Shenstone's *The School-Mistress* (1748); Johnson's *The Vanity of Human Wishes* (1749). The first edition of Robert Dodsley's *A Collection of Poems, by Several Hands* in 1748 is in itself a demonstration of generic profusion as well as authorial range. The influence of Pope and Augustan satire is still evident alongside the newer poetry of Akenside, Collins, the Wartons, Gray, Mason, Shenstone; there are satires, epigrams, and verse epistles as well as hymns, odes, and elegies. The success of Dodsley's collection in its first and subsequent editions testifies to a remarkably flexible, eclectic mid-century readership. On the continent, neo-classical preferences sustained their predominance somewhat longer and more pervasively, but there too poetry was moving towards generic variety and crossing.

What, then, is the relation of criticism and theory to these post-1740 developments? Johnson himself lays out a sceptically generalized prospect in *Rambler* 158 (21 September 1751):

we owe few of the rules of writing to the acuteness of criticks ... practice has introduced rules, rather than rules have directed practice. For this reason the laws of every species of writing have been settled by the ideas of him who first raised it to reputation, without enquiry whether his performances were not susceptible of improvement.

(*Works*, V, p. 76)

In contrast to this view, W. K. Wimsatt – Johnson's most acutely admiring modern critic – observes that 'the age of Pope witnessed a strange lag between poetry and theory – a success for poetry which consisted in its being a hundred years behind the most advanced theory' (*Short History*, p. 233).[1] By mid-century, poetic practice was beginning to reduce, even eliminate, this lag, and a relaxing of neo-classical assumptions about genre was one of the conspicuous results. Dennis's emphasis on the sublime intensity of the sacred ode, and Addison's valuing of the popular ballad, were being taken up by poets aroused by fresh generic possibilities. At the same time, in response to deep social and cultural changes, critical theory was moving still further in directions that encouraged generic complication.

The history of criticism has evolved a consensus on the question of genre in later eighteenth-century poetry, and it rests on two basic convictions. The first is that in the high Augustan period, as Geoffrey Tillotson puts it, 'The kinds were ready waiting for [the poet], and, if the rules for the kinds . . . were properly complied with, the products were recognizable as poems of those kinds . . . epic, tragedy in verse, pindaric, elegy, heroic and familiar epistle, pastoral, georgic, occasional verse, translation and imitation'. 'Mixing the kinds', Tillotson adds, a poet 'knew what he was doing and marked off the component parts by the use of different kinds of diction' (*Poetic Diction*, p. 25). Tillotson illustrates the basic attitude with a quotation from Joseph Spence's *Anecdotes* (begun in 1726); a range of representative positions might be located in the second canto of Boileau's *Art poétique* (1674), in Edward Bysshe's frequently reprinted *Art of Poetry* (1701), and in Gottsched's *Versuch einer kritischen Dichtkunst* (1730).

The second conviction pertinent to the evolving critical attitude towards poetic genre asserts that the lyric gradually replaced more didactic kinds such as satire and epic as the paradigmatic mode. The case is set out forcefully in Abrams's *The Mirror and the Lamp*, where the eventual ascendancy of lyric in the course of the eighteenth century is seen as the primary cultural sign that neo-classical mimetic theory had been supplanted by romantic expressivism. With respect to poetic practice Abrams writes of the 'lyric revival in the generation of Gray, Collins, and the Wartons' (p. 98). Within the sphere of critical theory, characteristic mid-century celebrations of lyric in England are those of Joseph Warton, Robert Lowth, Edward Young, John Brown, and Sir William

---

[1] Wimsatt continues: 'The numerous and varied figures (mixed wit and false wit), antithesis, metaphor, pun and quasi-pun, Gothic rhyme, alliteration, turn, tranlacer, and agnomination, which actually mark the highly artful poetry of Alexander Pope, are scarcely alluded to in the reigning poetic treatise of his day, the *Art of Poetry* by Edward Bysshe' (*Short History*, p. 233).

Jones; in France those of Rousseau and Diderot; in Germany, only a little later, those of Johann Georg Sulzer and Herder. From this point of view, *Lyrical Ballads* at the end of the century concludes rather than initiates a massive shift in generic priority, despite Wordsworth's emphasis in the Preface on the publication as an 'experiment'.

We may now go back to the conviction that neo-classical assumptions about poetic genre were clear and distinct and ask whether the critical situation was as straightforward as it seems. Perhaps our assumption that early eighteenth-century writers operated from a premise of rigid, discrete, continuous genres has been too narrowly and inflexibly held. This is precisely what Ralph Cohen argues in 'On the interrelations of eighteenth-century literary forms'. The 'poetic kinds were identified in terms of a hierarchy that may not have been all-inclusive (since not all possible forms were specified)', Cohen writes, 'but were all interrelated' (p. 35). Lower forms in the hierarchy were understood to be included in higher – epigram in satire or georgic, for instance, or ode in epic. Cohen accepts that there was a shift in the course of the century from a hierarchy dominated by didactic forms to a hierarchy dominated by lyrical forms, but he discovers an enthusiasm for generic interrelation that persists through this shift. So when Lowth praises the poetry of the Bible in his *Lectures on the Sacred Poetry of the Hebrews* (Latin edn 1753, English trans. 1787), he sees the Book of Psalms as 'a collection, under the general title of hymns to the praise of God, containing poems of different kinds, and elegies among the rest' (II, p. 144). Much earlier in the century the first professor of poetry at Oxford, Joseph Trapp, was already emphasizing that the 'Epic Poem ... comprehends within its Sphere all the other Kinds of Poetry whatever' (*Lectures on Poetry*; Latin edn 1711–19, English trans. 1742, p. 10).

When Cohen argues that eighteenth-century poetic forms 'had their genesis in social forms so that subsequently successful interrelations became instances of civilized harmony' (p. 67), he anticipates Marshall Brown's essay on 'The urbane sublime' (*English Literary History*, 1978), and more explicitly John Barrell's work on generic crossing, mixing, and integration. In *English Literature in History* (1983), Barrell sees the development of generic hybrids as a reflection of the increasing diversity of English society in the eighteenth century. The mixture of pastoral and georgic elements in Thomson's *The Castle of Indolence*, for instance, or more crudely in Dyer's *Grongar Hill* and *The Fleece*, is motivated by a pressing and conflicting need to idealize both the rural landscape and the forms of economic activity that were changing it. This perspective on poetic genre and socio-economic change is incisively extended in the essay Barrell co-authored with Harriet Guest 'On the use of contradiction: economics and morality in the eighteenth-century long poem'.

Here the very absence of a generically distinct principle of formal order 'exhibited especially by long poems in the newly invented genres of poetry – the meditative poem, the descriptive poem, the moral essay' (p. 122) is seen as serving the need to assemble 'disparate discourses ... into an aesthetic whole' (p. 123) and thus enabling ideological contradictions to be uttered. Barrell and Guest show how generic fluidity works in 'the characteristic vehicle of eighteenth-century poetry, the poem of mixed genre, variously mingling satire, the epistle, and the didactic poem whether philosophical or georgic' (p. 133). So Thomson's 'Spring' combines the pastoral idea of a remote Golden Age from which society has declined and a georgic celebration of present economic activity and progress; Young's *Night Thoughts* makes use of comparable generic fusions to negotiate a way around the conflict between patriotic self-sacrifice and economic self-interest.

As a fundamental part of their argument, Barrell and Guest document a 'criticism that legitimates the employment of a variety of discourses within a poem' (p. 136) – that is, a criticism that sanctions and encourages generic openness. Addison's admiration of Virgil's digressive flexibility looks forward to Joseph Warton's remarks along the same lines in his 'Reflections on Didactic Poetry' (in *The Works of Virgil*, 1778). Both emphasize the importance of transitions in managing shifts in discursive registers, an emphasis found earlier in Trapp's *Lectures on Poetry* and in the anonymous *Art of Poetry* (1762). In France the Abbé Du Bos had recognized in his *Réflexions critiques sur la poësie et sur la peinture* (1719) that successful writers of didactic poetry had to draw eclectically upon a range of generic conventions so as to please the reader's 'heart' as well as 'understanding'. But in English criticism there is more specific support for the sorts of generic interrelations charted by Cohen, and as Barrell and Guest show, this reveals the cultural pressures of a rapidly expanding and changing economic environment.

It would be misleading to suggest, however, that the neo-classical system of generic distinctions had dissolved completely by mid-century. The characteristic critical position combines a basic acceptance of the inherited hierarchy of genres with a disposition to approve of blending and deviation. In his *Essay on the Genius and Writings of Pope* (1756, 1782), Joseph Warton's parallel theory of genres and of human faculties takes in the classical hierarchy, with its exaltation of epic and tragedy. Richard Hurd's position on genre in *Letters on Chivalry and Romance* (1762) is similar: he stays with the traditional neo-classical hierarchy but works hard to accommodate Ariosto, Tasso and Spenser, with all their digressive exuberance and generic impurity, into a history that sees the loss of 'fine fabling' as the price paid for civilized refinement (*Works*, IV, p. 350). Like Warton, Hurd sees the preferred Augustan forms of satire and ethical epistle as 'humbler sorts of poetry'. But in this he is entirely consistent with neo-classical priorities.

Thomas Warton's *History of English Poetry* (1774–81) is indebted to Hurd on these as on many points. While he begins with a Dissertation 'Of the origin of romantic fiction in Europe', he makes clear in his Preface that he thinks his own age has 'advanced to the highest degree of refinement', and that the elevation 'from rudeness to elegance' is based in part on the discriminating observance of generic decorum (1824 edn, I, p. 3). And Hugh Blair, in his widely influential *Lectures on Rhetoric and Belles-Lettres* (1782), still takes for granted an order 'of the chief kinds of Poetical Composition' that ranges from 'the lesser forms of Poetry' (that 'which is most simple and natural', pastoral and lyric) 'to the Epic and Dramatic, as the most dignified' (II, p. 335) – even though he defines poetry as 'the language of passion, or of enlivened imagination, formed, most commonly, into regular numbers' (II, p. 312).

Blair also asserts that poetry was originally inseparable from music (II, pp. 314–18), thus indicating his relation to that gradual ascendancy of the lyric that Abrams emphasizes and that Wimsatt says 'had been in serious preparation throughout the eighteenth century' in England, 'not only in the writings of the theorists but in the practice of numerous "Great Ode" and elegy writers' (*Short History*, p. 382). Even while the old hierarchy of genres was retained with an increasing acceptance of generic fluidity, then, a belief in the primacy of the lyric impulse was gathering force.

From the late seventeenth century on, the idea of reconstituting the imagined primitive unity of poetry and music was a motive force in opera, oratorio, and song as well as in poetic practice and in literary theory (see Wimsatt, *Short History*, p. 275). The basic commitment to lyric primacy could be variously inflected and complicated. Even Charles Batteux's effort to account for lyric within his rigorous scheme of neo-classical mimesis in *Les Beaux-Arts réduits à un même principe* (1747) – 'Lyric poetry . . . enters naturally and even necessarily into imitation; with a single difference . . . The other species of poetry have actions for their principal object: lyric poetry is entirely devoted to sentiments' (pp. 248–9)[2] – will find an echo in Thomas Twining's 1789 edition of Aristotle's *Poetics*. For a more representative elaboration we may look to John Brown's *A Dissertation on the Rise, Union, and Power . . . of Poetry and Music* (1763), which posits an original 'union of song, dance, and poetry' and sees lyric poems such as odes and hymns as the first forms to arise because 'these in their simple stage, are but a kind

---

[2] 'La Poësie lyrique . . . entre naturellement & même nécessairement dans l'imitation; avec une seule différence . . . Les autres espèces de Poësie ont pour objet principal les Actions: la Poësie lyrique est toute consacrée aux sentiments.'

of rapturous exclamations' (pp. 55, 41). The influence of Rousseau's *Essai sur l'origine des langues* (1749) is apparent in Brown's *Dissertation*; through him that influence was transmitted to such writers as Blair and Adam Ferguson. The most interesting English advocate of lyric primacy, however, was the Orientalist scholar, linguist and translator Sir William Jones. In his *Essay on the Arts Commonly Called Imitative*, appended to a volume of translations and adaptations of Indian, Arabic and Persian poems published in 1772, Jones rejects completely mimetic theories of poetry, asserts that 'poetry was originally no more than a strong and animated expression of the human passions', and claims the lyric both as the original poetic form and as the prototype for all poetry (see Abrams, *Mirror and Lamp*, p. 87). Jones was to be an influential figure for later lyric enthusiasts; Shelley placed an urgent order for Jones's work with his bookseller in 1811.

Another aspect of the connection between music and poetry should be mentioned here as reinforcing the move towards granting the lyric generic priority. Emotional intensity of a specifically religious kind formed the link between music and verse in the tradition of Nonconformist and Methodist hymns of the eighteenth century. Isaac Watts's hymns from early in the century would have a significant later influence on the lyrics of Anna Laetitia Barbauld and of William Blake; John Wesley's collections of hymns from 1737 on helped make the communal singing of verse a familiar experience for many people who would otherwise have read little if any lyric poetry.

From the primitivist emphasis on lyric in Rousseau, Brown, and Jones it is only a short step to the exuberances of Herder and the *Stürmer und Dränger*. Before taking that step, though, we must consider two other mid-century phenomena that made a powerful impact on thinking about poetic genre: the ballad revival and the excitement over Ossian. Thomas Percy's *Reliques of Ancient English Poetry* (1765) makes clear its commitment to a musical and performative sense of lyric in the introductory 'Essay on the Ancient Minstrels in England', and in the engraved frontispiece showing a bard strumming his harp. In his Preface, however, Percy advertises his collection's way of mediating between ancient bards and modern poets: 'To atone for the rudeness of the more obsolete poems, each volume concludes with a few modern attempts in the same kind of writing: and, to take off from the tediousness of the longer narratives, they are every where intermingled with little elegant pieces of the lyric kind' (4th edn, 1794, I, p. xiv). Percy's editorial negotiations between the 'rough majestic force' of his relics and the 'elegant' tastes of 'a polished age, like the present', are deeply characteristic of mid-eighteenth-century efforts to reorient generic priorities towards the lyric while accommodating the genteel taste of an expanding middle-class

readership. Percy's Preface also illustrates an adjustment of lyric intensity to extended narrative interests that was important in the ballad
revival. His critical mediations between different – and potentially even
contradictory – poetic registers are connected to the procedures examined by Barrell and Guest in georgic and didactic poetry, and doubtless
reflect related social and economic changes.[3] Joseph Ritson's attacks on
Percy in 1783 may be taken as one eccentric – and republican – scholar's resistance to Percy's exploitation of the vogue for tastefully archaizing
lyricism. Still, Percy's *Reliques* significantly influenced the later work of
Chatterton, Burns, Tickell and Scott in Britain, and of Goethe, Schiller,
Gottfried August Bürger and subsequent Romantic writers in Germany.

   That other great invention of the eighteenth-century primitivist imagination, James Macpherson's Ossian forgeries (1760–3), overlapped with
the ballad revival in its influence and affected attitudes towards poetic
genre primarily by reawakening a belief in the epic dimension of ancient
bardic song. Macpherson himself calls attention to 'the rules of the
epopoea' (Preface to *Fingal*), and in the notes points out rhetorical
parallels between his epic and those of Homer, Virgil, and Milton. Hugh
Blair goes further in his *Critical Dissertation on the Poems of Ossian*
(1763; expanded 1765): 'Examined even according to Aristotle's rules, it
would be found to have all the essential requisites of a true and regular
epic'. This synthesis of generic conformity and regularity with romantic
wildness and sublimity is of course familiar and represents the Ossianic
version of those negotiated contradictions we have observed in critical
responses to other kinds of eighteenth-century poetry. The cultural support for Macpherson's fabrications provided by criticism was substantial: Blair and Henry Home, Lord Kames, had strongly encouraged
Macpherson's project from the beginning, and it was initially greeted as
a genuine rediscovery of ancient Gaelic epic by such prominent figures
in the Scottish Enlightenment as David Hume and Adam Smith.

   In considering the effect of the Ossian texts on subsequent thinking
about poetic genre, we must not take for granted the fact that Macpherson wrote mainly in prose. Macpherson himself does not take it for
granted: in the Preface he says that his 'intention was to publish in
verse', but he decided that 'the harmony which these Poems might
derive from rhime ... could [not] atone for the simplicity and energy
which they would lose' (*Ossian*, 1809, pp. xxxii–xxxiii). The implications of Macpherson's logic here for eighteenth-century verse are worth
taking seriously. That Roger Lonsdale includes a prose passage from
Fragments of Ancient Poetry, Collected in the Highlands of Scotland
(1760) in *The New Oxford Book of Eighteenth-Century Verse* suggests

---

[3] See 'On the use of contradiction', esp. pp. 132–5, 139–43.

that Macpherson's prose has been accepted into English poetry to a
degree that is quite extraordinary (prose translations of *Beowulf* and
of *Sir Gawain and the Green Knight* represent a related but distinct
phenomenon). The consequences for eighteenth-century poetic practice,
as Maximillian Novak has pointed out, are extremely interesting:
Macpherson's poetic prose 'opened the possibility of verse based on
very different principles than customary English metre' (*Eighteenth-
Century English Literature*, p. 147). Related prosodic possibilities were
emerging from the new awareness of the structures of Hebrew biblical
verse encouraged by Lowth in his *Lectures* and brilliantly explored by
Christopher Smart in *Jubilate Agno*. Near the end of the century Ossianic
and Hebrew influences would converge in the versification of Blake's
'prophetic books'. There is no working through of these formal developments in eighteenth-century criticism, however, despite the remarkable vogue of Ossian in France (Pierre Letourneur's translation appeared
in 1777), Germany (Michael Denis's translation appeared in 1768–9),
and Italy (the influential adaptation into unrhymed verse by Melchiorre
Cesarotti appeared in 1763).

Turning now to Herder, we find in him a drive to disregard the distinctions and conventions of poetic genre that is quite unlike the adjust-
ments between neo-classical and anti-neo-classical attitudes characteristic
of English, and to a lesser degree of French and Italian, criticism. To be
sure, even more radical perceptions of the conventional, non-essential
status of genre may be found in the 1760s and 1770s. If a firmly
conservative critic such as Lord Kames could acknowledge that 'Literary compositions run into each other, precisely like colours' (*Elements
of Criticism*, p. 329, note), it is hardly surprising that a philosophically
scrupulous writer such as Condillac would argue that 'the names of
epic, tragedy, comedy have been preserved, but the ideas connected with
them are not at all the same: and every people has assigned different
styles, different traits to each different species of poem' (*L'Art d'écrire*,
1775, *Oeuvres philosophiques*, I, p. 610).[4] From yet a different perspective, that of sentimental bourgeois drama, Louis-Sébastien Mercier makes
the famous proclamation: 'Tombez, tombez, murailles, qui séparez les
genres' (*Du Théâtre, ou nouvel essai sur l'art dramatique*, 1773, p. 105).
With Herder, however, disregard for traditional generic distinctions is
the consequence of a more sustained and positive affirmation of an ideal
of poetry as natural, spontaneous, passionate. 'Epic, drama, and lyric are
almost the same to him', Wellek observes (*Modern Criticism*, I, p. 200);
the important differences are historically specific ones of national culture

---

[4] 'Les noms d'épopée, de tragédie, de comédie se sont conservés; mais les idées qu'on
y attache ne sont plus absolument les mêmes, et chaque peuple a donné, à chaque
espèce de ces poëmes, différents styles, comme différents caractères.'

and language, rather than allegedly universal ones of formal ordering and representation.[5]

Herder is, of course, a crucial early influence on Goethe and Schiller. And the antagonistic dynamic of that influence is especially evident in their distinctive attitudes towards genre. Whereas genre is mainly a secondary, even peripheral issue in Herder's criticism, in Goethe's it is centrally important throughout his career. Herder's lead essay in *Von deutscher Art und Kunst* (1773), the manifesto of the *Sturm und Drang* group, celebrates Ossian, folk-song and folk-poetry without the slightest worry about generic distinctions, and in ways that had a profound impact on Goethe's writing in the 1770s. Yet Goethe's own poetry of this period demonstrates a sensitivity to lyric, narrative and epic decorum that sets him off, even at this early stage, from Herder. Goethe's reflections on genre in the relatively late essay on 'Natural forms of poetry' ('Naturformen der Dichtkunst', part of the 'Noten und Abhandlungen' to the *West-Östlicher Divan*, 1819) pointedly look back to questions posed by Herder and his friends in the 1770s. 'There are only three natural forms of poetry', Goethe writes: 'The clearly telling, the enthusiastically excited, and the personally acting: Epic, Lyric, and Drama. These three poetic modes can work together or separately' (*Werke*, III, p. 480). Goethe's starting point is still deeply organicist ('Naturformen'), but the elaboration of the argument depends on his carefully discriminating among historically specific generic formations, and finally on a schema in which 'the external arbitrary forms and these internal necessary origins might be offered in a comprehensible order' (*Werke*, III, p. 482).[6] In his correspondence with Schiller during the 1790s, genre is, Wellek observes, a 'constant preoccupation' (*Modern Criticism*, I, p. 213). Goethe attempts to explain, in a letter of 23 December 1797, 'how it is, that we moderns are so much inclined to mix genres': 'everything strives towards drama, towards the representation of *complete immediacy*' (*Werke*, XX, p. 472).[7] Such recognitions in Goethe are almost always accompanied by a resistance to total generic dissolution, by an insistence on formal and representational discriminations.

Schiller, even more resolutely than Goethe, refuses to accept the

---

[5] See Victor Lange, *The Classical Age of German Literature*, pp. 61–4.

[6] 'Es gibt nur drei echte Naturformen der Poesie: die klar erzählende, die enthusiastisch aufgeregte und die persönlich handelnde: Epos, Lyrik und Drama. Diese drei Dichtweisen können zusammen oder abgesondert wirken' (p. 480); 'die äußeren zufälligen Formen und diese inneren notwendigen Uranfänge in faßlicher Ordnung darbrächte' (p. 482). The English translations are those of Julius A. Elias (1966).

[7] '... wie es kommt, daß wir Moderne die Genres so sehr zu vermischen geneigt sind ... alles zum Drama, zur Darstellung des *vollkommen Gegenwärtigen* sich hindrängt'.

Herderian disregard for differences in poetic genre. In *Über naive und sentimentalische Dichtung* (1795–6), he works not so much to supplant the old neo-classical categories as to sublate them in a new typology based on 'modes of perception' ('Empfindungsarten'). The basic distinction between 'naive' (primarily ancient and spontaneous) and 'sentimental' (primarily modern and reflective) leads to a rethinking of poetic genre ('Gattung'). In so far as poetry is able to retain a 'naive' relation to innocent nature, Schiller says, it is exempt from the strictures of generic decorum. But insofar as it operates within the 'modern', 'sentimental' modes of reflective mediation across the gap between ideal and real, it is bound by laws no less 'sacred' for being generated out of cultural 'corruption' ('Verderbnis') and artifice.

Schiller eventually declares that there are three 'species of sentimental poetry' ('Species sentimentalischer Dichtung') – 'satire', 'elegy' and 'idyll' – corresponding to three modes of perceiving the relationship between actuality and the ideal (*Werke*, XX, p. 466). These modes can be combined and are, pre-eminently, in two English texts: *Paradise Lost* and *The Seasons*. 'Idyll' emerges only gradually in Schiller's schema: it is initially a sub-species of 'elegy', but by the end of the essay it becomes the highest kind of 'sentimental' poetry, the genre in which the modern poet rediscovers and reconstitutes a lost 'naive' innocence. Schiller says little theoretically about lyric, despite his own practice in the form: Wellek cites a letter of 1789 to Christian Gottfried Körner in which lyric is characterized as 'the pettiest and most ungrateful' ('das kleinlichste und auch undankbarste') of poetic forms (*Werke*, XXV, pp. 211–12). 'The concept of this Idyll', by contrast, 'is the concept of a conflict fully reconciled not only in the individual, but in society, of a free uniting of inclination with the law, of a nature illuminated by the highest moral dignity, briefly, none other than the ideal of beauty applied to actual life' (*Werke*, XX, p. 472).[8] We have here, in Schiller's Kantian terminology, a theorized reflection of those 'uses of contradiction' which Barrell and Guest recognize as pervasive in mid- and late-eighteenth-century English writing.

The efforts of Goethe and Schiller to re-establish a theory of generic hierarchy as a counter-response to the primitivist, lyricist and historicist extremes of Herder and the *Sturm und Drang* are fundamental to their positions at the centre of German *Klassik*. There are no critical treatments of genre in late-eighteenth-century English literature – not even

---

[8] 'Der Begriff dieser Idylle ist der Begriff eines völlig aufgelösten Kampfes sowohl in dem einzelnen Menschen, als in der Gesellschaft, einer freyen Vereinigung der Neigungen mit dem Gesetze, einer zur höchsten sittlichen Würde hinauf geläuterten Natur, kurz, er ist kein andrer als das Ideal der Schönheit auf das wirkliche Leben angewendet.'

those of Wordsworth and Coleridge – that have a comparable centrality and authority. In English poetic practice, however, both centrifugal and centripetal generic pressures were intense. On the one side, as Donald Davie has said, many poets came to believe 'that no subjects are outside the scope of poetry' (*Late Augustans*, p. ix). He cites William Falconer's *The Shipwreck* (1762) and Erasmus Darwin's *The Loves of the Plants* (1789) as instances in which untraditional material put the decorum of eighteenth-century verse under extreme stress. The impact of science – particularly of optics, meteorology and chemistry – on poetry, as Marjorie Hope Nicolson so influentially demonstrated in *Newton Demands the Muse*, stretched the capacity of eighteenth-century diction and imagery. From the middle of the century the cult of the picturesque led towards what Martin Price has termed a 'democratization of subject matter' (*Palace of Wisdom*, p. 381). The word 'Picturesque', writes Uvedale Price in 1794, 'is applied to every object, and every kind of scenery, which has been, or might be represented with good effect in painting, and that without any exclusion' (*An Essay on the Picturesque, as Compared with the Sublime and the Beautiful*, 1794, p. 34). Such an aesthetic perspective, carried over into poetry, had far-reaching implications for genre.

Parallel to these various tendencies towards the dissolution of genre were myriad purposes that continued to be served, if only through burlesque or parody, by holding on to the traditional kinds. Though Christopher Smart has been depicted as a mystical eccentric whose writing moves outside the accepted forms, he was also, as Claude Rawson reminds us, 'the translator and imitator of Horace, admirer of Pope . . . author of georgic and mock-epic poems, and of lyrics in the line of Prior, Gay, Gray, and Goldsmith' (*Order from Confusion Sprung*, p. 373). Working-class and peasant poets such as Stephen Duck, Mary Collier and Ann Yearsley had their own strong reasons for looking to conventional generic norms as sources of cultural legitimation, cultural oppression, or both.[9] In French poetry André Chénier has come to epitomize the passionate intensity of the idealizing pro-Revolutionary imagination. Yet in his verse – most of which was published after his execution on 25 July 1794, two days before the fall of Robespierre – he demonstrates a tenacious loyalty to the forms of classical poetry: eclogues, idylls, odes, elegies (see Wellek, *Modern Criticism*, I, p. 76). In *L'Invention* he makes the case for preserving generic difference and decorum:

[9] See Raymond Williams, *The Country and the City* (London, 1973), pp. 87–95, 127–41, and Donna Landry, 'The resignation of Mary Collier', pp. 90–120.

Mais inventer n'est pas, en un brusque abandon,
Blesser la vérité, le bon sens, la raison;
Ce n'est pas entasser, sans dessein et sans forme,
Des membres ennemis en un colosse énorme ...
    La nature dicta vingt genres opposés
D'un fil léger entre eux chez les Grecs divisés.
Nul genre, s'échappant de ses bornes prescrites,
N'aurait osé d'un autre envahir les limites.[10]

[But to invent is not, in brusque abandon, to wound truth, good sense, reason; it is not to accumulate, without design and without form, incompatible limbs into a monstrous colossus ...
    Nature dictated twenty separate genres, divided among themselves by a fine line devised by the Greeks. No genre, breaking loose from its prescribed boundaries, would have dared to invade the limits of another.]

When we look back from a passage like this to Pope's pronouncements in *An Essay on Criticism* about how 'Nature to all things fix'd the Limits fit' (I, l. 52) and 'how learn'd *Greece* her useful Rules indites' (I, l. 92), we have at least a rough emblem of the way in which neo-classical convictions about genre persisted through all the impulses to do away with or obscure them.

The language of poetry

The changing historical and social pressures that complicated the under-standing of poetic genre in the latter half of the century also disrupted neo-classical assumptions about poetic language. The expansion of the reading public, the burgeoning of commercial and mercantile life, the influx of new scientific perspectives and discourse into 'literature', the consolidation and development of dissenting religious practice – these and other changes in western European culture variously affected criti-cal discussion of the kind or kinds of language appropriate to poetry. This discussion was largely conducted in relation to – and often directly within – an extraordinary flourishing of formal philosophies of lan-guage. From the great debate between Locke and Leibniz in the 1690s and the far-reaching speculations of Vico's *Scienza Nuova* (1725–44), through the crucial mid-century interventions of Condillac, Rousseau and Herder, to the radical extensions of Horne Tooke and Destutt de Tracy during the period of the French Revolution, eighteenth-century philosophy made language a more prominent topic of inquiry than it had ever been before. This philosophical preoccupation informs in very

---

[10] *Oeuvres complètes*, ed. Gerard Walter (Bruges, 1940), p. 10.

important ways more restricted and pragmatic critical treatments of the language of poetry.

Working our way back from Wordsworth's Preface to the middle of the century, we may begin to orient ourselves conceptually and historically by looking at Johnson's definition of 'diction' in the *Dictionary* (1755) – the first such work, as Tillotson points out, to provide an entry for its own root concept-word.[11] 'Style; language; expression' is the one succinctly broad meaning Johnson offers, and he cites Dryden on Virgil: 'There appears in every part of his *diction*, or expression, a kind of noble and bold purity' (*Essays*, II, p. 148). Dryden's notion of 'purity' of diction has its relation to Donald Davie's important reassessment of the language of English poetry in the eighteenth century, *Purity of Diction in English Verse* (1955). As far as Johnson's own understanding of 'diction' is concerned, two points may be noted. On the one hand, he follows Dryden and identifies 'diction' with 'expression', thereby establishing a less obvious contrast to romantic convictions than is usually assumed. But on the other, he subsequently criticizes Dryden (in *Lives of the Poets*) for using specialized colloquial and technical terms, articulating, as Wimsatt emphasizes, an authoritative universalist standard: 'It is a general rule in poetry that all appropriated terms of art should be sunk in *general* expressions, because poetry is to speak an universal language' (*Lives*, I, pp. 433–4; see *Short History*, p. 328).

Wimsatt is of course right to argue, citing a parallel in Buffon's *Discours sur le style* (1753), that the 'norm of style which Johnson was expounding was close to the metaphysics and the science of his age'. But the ideal of poetry's speaking 'an universal language' that privileges '*general* expressions' already encounters resistance and complication in the most important philosophical treatment of language for the eighteenth century, Book III of Locke's *Essay concerning Human Understanding*. Many readers, still burdened by nineteenth-century distortions of Locke, think of him first as the philosopher who denounces 'all the artificial and figurative application of Words Eloquence hath invented' as being intended 'for nothing else but to insinuate wrong *Ideas*, move the Passions, and thereby mislead the Judgment; and so indeed are perfect cheat' (*Essay* III.x.34). But in fact Locke's philosophy of language establishes principles and defines problems that come to play an important role in later eighteenth-century critical thinking about poetic language.[12]

---

[11] *Augustan Poetic Diction*, p. 46.

[12] See John Yolton's study *John Locke and the Way of Ideas* (Oxford, 1956); also Yolton's *Locke and the Compass of Human Understanding* (Cambridge, 1970), esp. pp. 196–223. Indispensable for an understanding of Locke's philosophy of language and its influence is the work of Hans Aarsleff: see *The Study of Language in England 1780–1860* (1967) and the essays collected in *From Locke to Saussure: Essays on the Study of Language and Intellectual History* (1982).

He consolidates and elaborates the principle that words are the *arbitrary* signs of ideas, not the *natural* signs of things. And while it is the mind that makes arbitrary signs for its ideas and, through processes of social interaction, organizes them into a language, these signs in turn acquire a constitutive function with regard to thinking. When it comes to the 'general Names' assigned to those collective ideas which Locke terms 'mixed Modes', 'Though ... it be the Mind that makes the Collection, 'tis the Name which is, as it were the Knot, that ties them fast together' (III.v.10). If the *'general* expressions' insisted on by Johnson depend on the knotting power of arbitrarily instituted verbal signs, rather than on transcendent rational categories, then the claim of poetry or any other linguistic practice to speak a 'universal language' is of course severely compromised.

Locke's theory 'Of Words' was the point of departure for virtually all later eighteenth-century philosophies of language, including philosophies opposed to his. And as can be seen from the ideas just summarized, the implications of Locke's theory for poetic language are more far-reaching, and potentially more unsettling, than they are usually taken to be. Most accounts of the influence on poetry of Locke and the empiricist tradition have emphasized not the problems of linguistic institution, signification and reference, but a presumed preoccupation with sensory detail and scientific description. What has come to be known as the 'doctrine of particularity' and the poetry of minute description it valued and encouraged, in contrast to Johnson's championing of *'general* expressions', certainly does have a basis in one aspect of Lockean empiricism. We find this doctrine in Joseph Warton's praise of Thomson's *Seasons* and its 'minute and particular enumeration of circumstances judiciously selected' (*Essay on the Genius and Writings of Pope*, 1782, II, p. 168), in Kames's urging the poet to 'avoid as much as possible abstract and general terms' (*Elements of Criticism*, 1762, I, p. 307), in Hugh Blair's insistence that 'Description is the great test of a Poet's imagination' because it 'makes us imagine that we see [the object] before our eyes' (*Lectures on Rhetoric and Belles Lettres*, 1783, II, p. 371) – and, to cite a contemporary instance from Italian criticism, in Cesare Beccaria's celebration of concrete detail and vivid sensation in *Ricerche intorno alla natura dello stile* (1770). This critical stress on descriptive particularity is broadly related to what W. J. Bate means when he says that by mid-century 'problems of diction, metaphor, sentence-structure, and prose-rhythm were investigated in great detail, with continual reference to concrete illustrations' (*From Classic to Romantic*, p. 95; Bate cites Joshua Steele's innovative work on metre).

To understand the practical import of the 'doctrine of particularity' for eighteenth-century poetic diction, we have to see it operating in relation to the principles of generic decorum, classical allusiveness and scientific ordering spelled out by Tillotson, Josephine Miles, John Arthos and others who have taught us not to dismiss as empty circumlocutions epithetical formations such as 'fleecy care' or 'finny tribe'. By mid-century these stylistic principles were being altered by new, or newly appropriated, intellectual currents and cultural changes. Some of Nicolson's most enlightening analysis in *Newton Demands the Muse* is focused on mid-century examples from Akenside, Thomson, Young and Jago in which a critical justification for poetry's appropriation of the new empirical science is built into the verse, reflected in the vocabulary and phrasing. But if the scientific, observational dimension of empiricist philosophy led criticism to value descriptive particularity and accuracy, its subjectivist, mentalistic dimension led in other directions. There is a famous passage in Akenside's *The Pleasures of Imagination* (1743) where Lockean epistemology and Addisonian poetic converge in a celebration of the poet's power 'to behold in lifeless things, / The inexpressive semblance of himself, / Of thought and passion' (III, ll. 284–6). As Price points out (*Palace of Wisdom*, p. 344), Akenside includes a note on this passage in which he says that it describes 'the foundation of almost all the ornaments of poetic diction'. Though 'inexpressive' and 'ornaments' are not Wordsworthian words, Akenside looks forward here to later ideas about language, landscape, and subjectivity that will link Wordsworth's Preface back to Lockean principles. Locke had given the mind an active role in constructing experience, and recurrent evidence for that role was to be found in language itself.

Eighteenth-century criticism responded to Locke's 'way of ideas' and to subsequent developments in empiricist philosophy by becoming preoccupied with the representation of mental experience in writing – with the capacity of poetic language to register 'the association of ideas', for example. Locke himself deals very sceptically with the association of ideas and refers to it as an irrational 'sort of Madness' (*Essay* II.xxxiii.1–5). But through the philosophy of Hume and Hartley in England and of Condillac in France, what we now call associationism became a conspicuous force in critical discussions of poetic language. Hartley's ideas were taken up by Joseph Priestley and Erasmus Darwin, and with greater critical influence by Alexander Gerard, Archibald Alison and Abraham Tucker. Tucker argued that 'nothing is beautiful in itself', that beauty depended on the associational habits and activities of individual minds (*Light of Nature Pursued*, 1768–78; 2nd edn, 1805, II, p. 147). One implication of this kind of position for poetry was a new interest in synaesthetic language, in the verbal representation of one kind of sensory experience in terms of another. Philosophical and scientific interest in synaesthesia goes back directly to Newton and Locke, but in the course of the eighteenth century it came to be valued aesthetically as a special potential of the language of poetry and its relation to feeling. 'Soft or Strong, Mild or Bold, Gay or Gloomy', writes Alison in his *Essays on Taste* (1790), 'are terms in all languages applied to Colours ... and indicate their connection with particular qualities of Mind' (pp. 131–2). In the assumed common ground of human emotion, empiricist criticism discovered its own route through sensationalist particularity back to Johnson's notion of a 'universal language'.

There were, however, antagonistic developments within the line of critical thinking that sprang from Lockean empiricism. In *De l'Art d'écrire* (1775), Condillac distinguishes carefully between the 'association of ideas', which he sees as the peculiar province of poetry's discourse of emotion, and the 'connection [*liaison*] of ideas', which he understands to be characteristic of prose and rationalist discourse. The association of ideas in poetry gets expressed, according to Condillac, through features peculiar to each national language-culture; it does not, as Alison would claim, transcend linguistic differences. Condillac's articulation of what has come to be known as the principle of linguistic relativity has its roots in Locke's argument that words function as the signs of ideas 'arbitrarily' and 'not by any natural connexion, ... for then there would be but one Language amongst all Men' (*Essay* III.ii.1). This principle, commonly associated with the emphasis on local linguistic colour held to be typical of romantic poetry and criticism, is in fact a development of eighteenth-century empiricist thinking, though in Herder and other writers of the last quarter of the century it gets powerfully reinforced by mystical notions of primitive cultural origins.

The influence of empiricist theory on later eighteenth-century critical ideas about the language of poetry is rich, complex – and often contradictory, especially in relation to the universalizing language of general nature advocated by Johnson and neo-classical rationalists. Consider that very prominent and subsequently contested feature of mid-century poetic style, personification. The valuing of personification has a strong, continuous history in eighteenth-century criticism, from Addison's claiming that it 'makes new worlds of its own, shews us persons who are not to be found in being', and 'has something in it like creation' (*Spectator* 419, 421); through Joseph Warton's assertion that 'personification, conducted with dignity and propriety, may be justly esteemed one of the greatest efforts of the creative power of a warm and lively imagination' (*Adventurer* 57); to Anna Laetitia Barbauld's recognition that through personification poetry is 'peopled with beings of its own creation'.[13] Abrams sees personification as the most important sign of a developing

[13] Quoted in Chester Fisher Chapin, *Personification in Eighteenth-Century English Poetry* (New York, 1955), p. 84.

belief in the creative imagination during the eighteenth century, and understands Wordsworth's and Coleridge's critique of certain modes of personification as an indication of its deep importance to their own concerns (*Mirror and the Lamp*, pp. 288–97). More recently, Clifford Siskin has examined personification as an 'exemplary feature' of eighteenth-century poetry, and the romantic 'turn from personification' as a key to understanding a major shift in the literary 'workings of social power'.[14] At stake in all forms of personification are relations of the specific to the general, of the particular to the universal. Wordsworth polemically avoids 'personification of abstract ideas' in *Lyrical Ballads* because to him this had become 'a mechanical device of style', a false and trite way of attempting to realize in poetic language what Wimsatt calls the 'concrete universal' (*Prose Works*, I, pp. 130–3; *Short History*, pp. 313–36). But as Davie has shown, and as eighteenth-century writers themselves certainly realized, personification can generate surprising forms of metaphorical life for readers alert to its distinctive stylistic potentialities – to the shifting of figurative force from noun to verb, for instance, in Johnson's 'London':

> Till Want now following, fraudulent and slow,
> Shall spring to seize thee, like an ambush'd foe.

At issue here is the particularizing power of figurative rhetoric operating within a poetics of '*general* expressions' and universalizing objectives.

We should also consider what becomes of the doctrine of particularity and detailed description in theories of the literary sublime. In contrast to the kind of valuing of precise descriptive detail evident in the criticism of Joseph Warton, Kames and Blair, Edmund Burke claims that 'obscurity' is the greatest and most distinctive source of poetic power: 'the most lively and spirited verbal description I can give, raises a very obscure and imperfect *idea* of ... objects; but then it is in my power to raise a stronger *emotion* by the description than I could do by the best painting' (*A Philosophical Enquiry into the Origin of our Ideas of the Sublime and Beautiful*, 1757, ed. Boulton, p. 60). Burke's supreme example of a poet whose language operates through sublime obscurity is Milton: in this he is joined by Thomas Warton, who says of a passage in *Lycidas* that the poet, 'in obscure and mysterious expressions, leaves something to be supplied or explained by the reader's imagination';[15] and on somewhat different grounds by Lessing, who praises Milton's non-visual imagination and relates it to his blindness (*Laokoon*, appendix 2). From one perspective Burke's analysis of poetic language overtly contradicts the Lockean principle that words only have meaning as the

---

[14] *Historicity of Romantic Discourse*, pp. 68–84.
[15] Quoted in Price, *To the Palace of Wisdom*, p. 369.

signs of ideas. Following Berkeley's critique of Locke in *A Treatise
concerning the Principles of Human Knowledge*, Burke argues that in
poetry words affect us as 'mere sounds; but they are sounds, which
being used on particular occasions . . . produce in the mind, whenever
they are afterwards mentioned, effects similar to those of their occasions . . . the sound without any annexed notion continues to operate
as before' (*Enquiry*, p. 165). Particularity, for Burke, is a matter of
rhetorical 'occasion' rather than of representational accuracy. Understanding this may help us see that from another perspective, Burke's
emphasis on the reader's active response to the 'obscurity' of sublime
language in fact owes much to the subjectivist strain in empiricist theory.

Blake saw and protested against these connections in his attack on
'obscurity' in the 'Annotations' to Sir Joshua Reynolds's *Discourses*
(1798–1808): 'Burke's Treatise on the Sublime & Beautiful is founded
on the Opinions of Newton & Locke' (*Poetry and Prose*, p. 660). In his
conviction that 'All Sublimity is founded on Minute Discrimination',
that 'Obscurity is Neither the Source of the Sublime nor of any thing
Else' (*Poetry and Prose*, pp. 643, 658), Blake recognized that the aesthetic valuing of indefiniteness in Burke leads back to Locke. What he
did not or could not recognize is that this aspect of Locke's influence
derives from Locke's seeing the mind as active and constitutive, not
passively mechanical.

The divergent, sometimes contradictory influence of Lockean theory
on critical ideas about poetic language is strikingly evident in Diderot,
who like Condillac developed a theory of language as a system of signs
which had evolved from the concretely sensuous and natural to the
arbitrary and conventional. On the one hand Diderot sees the poet as
returning civilized language to its 'natural' condition of particularized
sensory immediacy. At an intriguing point in his *Lettre sur les Sourds
et Muets* (1751), Diderot argues that in poetry we are presented 'not
merely with a chain of strong terms which express the idea with force
and nobility, but with a tissue of hieroglyphs heaped one above the
other which picture it. I could say, in this sense, that all poetry is
emblematic' (*Oeuvres*, I, p. 374).[16] This notion of language as hieroglyph
may owe something to a broader eighteenth-century interest in hieroglyphs, and specifically to William Warburton's ground-breaking
account of how Egyptian hieroglyphs, originally natural signs, came to
be used as arbitrary signs. Diderot's immediate purpose, though, is to

[16] '. . . n'est plus seulement un enchainement de termes énergiques qui exposent la
pensée avec force et noblesse, mais c'est encore un tissu d'hiéroglyphes entassés les
uns sur les autres qui la peignent. Je pourrais dire, en ce sens, que toute poésie est
emblématique.' The most important text for eighteenth-century understanding of
ancient hieroglyphs in relation to the philosophy of language is William

foreground sound, metre and other material properties of poetic language. His ideas on such matters are echoed late in the century in the counter-revolutionary criticism of Antoine de Rivarol, who is reported to have said in 1795: 'The poet is nothing but a very ingenious and animated savage ... Both the savage and the poet ... speak only in hieroglyphs'.[17] It is worth noting that in 1784 Rivarol had published a prize-winning essay entitled *Discours sur l'universalité de la langue française*, in which he celebrated the clarity of French over English. Diderot too, although with a very different political agenda, had argued that French prose syntax corresponds more closely than other languages to the 'natural' order of thought. When it came to poetry, however, he could follow Burke in an emotivist celebration of indefiniteness: 'Clarity of whatever kind damages enthusiasm. Poets, speak incessantly of eternity, infinitude, immensity, time, space, divinity ... Be dark!' (*Oeuvres*, XI, p. 147: 'La clarté de quelque manière ... nuit à l'enthousiasme. Poètes, parlez sans cesse de l'éternité, d'infini, d'immensité, du temps, d'espace, de la divinité ... Soyez ténébreux!'). Rationalist, sensationalist and mentalistic positions on poetic language compete for dominance in Diderot's criticism, as they do in much of the criticism that takes Book III of Locke's *Essay* as a theoretical point of departure.

The primitivist inflections in what Condillac, Diderot and Rivarol say about poetic utterance are characteristic of critical thinking in this period and should also be seen in a broader philosophical context: eighteenth-century philosophies of language recurrently present themselves genealogically, as accounts of the origin and development of human language. The extent to which such accounts are either self-consciously conjectural or credulously literalist varies a good deal. Locke, Condillac, Diderot and Rousseau himself make us aware that they are constructing philosophical fictions when they suppose that human beings first uttered 'natural cries' of desire or fear and then gradually evolved the use of artificial signs. Thomas Blackwell, on the other hand, in *An Enquiry into the Life and Writings of Homer* (1735), seems to accept as historical truth the view that language had its origin in 'certain rude accidental sounds, which that naked Company of scrambling Mortals emitted by Chance', that 'at first they uttered these Sounds in a much higher Note than we do our Words now; occasioned, perhaps, by their falling on them under some Passion, Fear, Wonder or Pain' (pp. 37–8). What

---

Warburton's *The Divine Legation of Moses* (1737–8); see Maurice Pope, *The Story of Archaeological Decipherment* (New York, 1975), pp. 43–53, and Jacques Derrida's reflections on the 1744 French translation of a section of Warburton's book in 'Scribble (writing-power)', *Yale French Studies*, 58 (1979), 117–47.

[17] 'Le poète n'est qu'un sauvage très ingénieux et très animé ... Le sauvage et le poète font le cercle; l'un et l'autre ne parlent que par hiéroglyphes' (quoted in Sainte-Beuve, *Chateaubriand et son groupe littéraire*, II, p. 128).

proved to be critically influential in Blackwell's *Enquiry* was that such
beliefs led him to assert that language was originally 'full of Metaphor;
and that Metaphor of the boldest, daring, and most natural kind' (p.
41). Blackwell's primitivism is not without qualification: such metaphor
in the 'broken, unequal and boisterous' condition of primitive speech is
not in itself a 'Strength and Expression', he says – 'it is a real Defect'.
But when 'the rude Community' is 'a little advanced . . . *Admiration* and
Wonder will succeed', allowing language to become more fully 'poetical'. Blackwell goes on to contrast the rude emotive power of language
in its early phases of evolution with that '*Polishing*' which 'diminishes
a Language; it makes many Words obsolete; . . . allows [the poet] but
one set of Phrases, and deprives him of many significant terms, and
strong beautiful Expressions' (pp. 58–9). We enter the period 1740–
1800 with many of the terms set for an attitude that will culminate,
historically, in the Preface to *Lyrical Ballads* and in the Wordsworth/
Coleridge debate about poetic language that followed.

The case of Vico, whose *Principi di Scienza Nuova* appeared in a
third edition in 1744, bears controversially on the line of critical thinking we are now surveying. It is right that Vico should figure prominently
in Abrams's discussion of 'Primitive language and primitive poetry'.
With greater attention to Biblical myth than Blackwell, Vico claims that
after the Flood the earth was populated by a race of giants whose
perception of reality was 'not rational and abstract like that of learned
men now, but felt and imagined . . . these first men . . . were all robust
sense and vigorous imagination'. Their 'metaphysics was their poetry',
and from such immediately sensuous, imaginative, non-ratiocinative
thought 'poetic wisdom' derives (trans. Bergin and Fisch, p. 116; *Opere*,
p. 502). 'Thus our Science comes to be at once a history of the ideas,
the customs, and the deeds of mankind', Vico says, and 'poetic wisdom'
constitutes its basis (p. 112; *Opere*, p. 497).[18] Vico's project is undeni-
ably provocative and forward-looking in its convictions that the primary processes of thought are at once imaginative and verbal, and that
the key to understanding the history of civilizations lies in a study of the
forms of language. True, as Hans Aarsleff has argued, many of Vico's
ideas are less original than his modern proponents have assumed: much
of his speculative argument is already suggested in Bacon, Leibniz and
Locke. And Wellek has demonstrated both that Vico's ideas about the
role of metaphor in primitive language and poetry are basically the
same as those found in Blackwell, Warburton, Blair and many other

---

[18] (1) '. . . non ragionata ed astratta qual è questa or degli addottrinati, ma sentita ed
immaginata . . . siccome quelli ch'erano . . . tutti robusti sensi e vigorosissime
fantasie . . . Questa fu la loro propria poesia . . .' (2) 'Di tal maniera questa Scienza
vien ad essere ad un fiato una storia dell'idee, costumi e fatti del gener umano.'

mid-century writers, and that there is no explicit evidence of Vico's influence on philosophy and criticism until the nineteenth century.[19] Still, Vico's elaboration of widely held primitivist ideas into a speculative history and science of human culture remains a singularly powerful contribution to eighteenth-century thinking about poetic discourse.

In England, as noted earlier, one of the most influential articulations of emotivist primitivism was Lowth's *De sacra poesi Hebraeorum*, published in Latin in 1753 and in English, under the title *Lectures on the Sacred Poetry of the Hebrews*, in 1787. Though much in Lowth's argument had been anticipated in Blackwell, he was the first, as Stephen Land puts it, 'to make an unqualified division between the rational and the passionate in language' (*Signs to Propositions*, p. 63). And in arguing for the passionate sublimity of the Hebrew poetry of the Bible, Lowth attached the idea of ancient emotive power in language to a sacred authority that even Homer and Pindar could not match. His distinction between prose as the language of reason and poetry as the language of emotion has much in common with Condillac and Diderot, and of course looks forward to the debate on this question between Wordsworth and Coleridge. Lowth's ideas were widely influential on Scottish critics and theorists such as Ferguson, Blair, Duff and Monboddo, and on the extended elaboration of lyrical primitivism in Brown's *Dissertation on the Rise, Union, and Power ... of Poetry and Music* (1763), where the intersection of primitivist ideas about poetic language and generic hierarchy is especially apparent.

Within the broader spectrum of primitivist theory, the biblical and theological variety represented most emphatically in Lowth inevitably found a place in eighteenth-century religious controversy. Debates such as the one over the 'gift of tongues' in 1763 (see Monk, *The Sublime*, pp. 78–9) are of limited significance in the history of criticism, but they bear instructively on the stylistic practice of poets such as Smart and later Blake who wrote out of a conviction that their language had a special emotive relation to the word of God. Smart's *A Song to David* (1763) enacts its celebration of the poet of the Psalms in ways that are entirely consistent with, if not immediately influenced by, the arguments of Lowth, Warburton and Hurd; his *Jubilate Agno* (written c. 1759–66) combines the antiphonal structure of Hebrew verse with what Rawson describes as a literalistic plainness of diction and imagery,

---

[19] See Wellek, 'The supposed influence of Vico on England and Scotland in the eighteenth century', *Giambattista Vico: an International Symposium*, ed. Giorgio Tagliacozzo and Hayden V. White (Baltimore, 1969), and the various references to Vico in Aarsleff's *From Locke to Saussure*; also Stuart Hampshire, 'Vico and language', *The New York Review of Books* (13 February 1969), 19–22 and Aarsleff, 'Vico and Berlin', *The London Review of Books* (5–18 November 1981), 6–8 (includes Isaiah Berlin's reply to Aarsleff).

in an eccentrically brilliant and critically self-conscious effort to revital-
ize visionary poetic language.[20]

In Germany the most influential writer on the language of poetry was
Herder, whose prize-winning *Abhandlung über den Ursprung der Sprache*
(*Essay on the Origin of Language*) was written in 1770 in response to
a topic set by the Berlin Academy. The intellectual context of Herder's
essay has been examined in rich detail by Aarsleff, who stresses the
significance of Condillac's *Essai sur l'origine des connoissances humaines*
(1746) not just for Herder but for the extended debate within the Berlin
Academy on the origin-of-language question. We know that Herder was
also influenced by Blackwell and by Lowth; the latter's *Lectures* are
acknowledged in Herder's own *Vom Geist der Ebräischen Poesie* (1782).
The young Herder's immediate mentor in some respects was the religious mystic Johann Georg Hamann, whose *Kreuzzüge des Philologen*
(*Crusades of the Philologist*) appeared in 1762. Hamann's aphoristic
pronouncements include a series of linguistic precepts that will sound
strikingly familiar to anyone who has read Coleridge and other proponents of a romantic *Logos*: the natural world is itself the language of
God, a kind of divine text; poetry is the imitation, more or less inspired,
of this language and expresses itself through images ('all our knowledge
is sensuous, figurative', *Werke*, I, p. 159); poetry is coeval with human
language, religion, myth. Culturally Hamann reveres the ancient Hebrews specifically and the East more generally as repositories, along
with Homer and Shakespeare, of that fusion of poetry with language
itself and with religious inspiration.

What Herder specifically takes over from Hamann and develops along
distinctive lines is the idea that poetic language reenacts the divine
creation of the world understood as *Logos*, as expressive verbal act.
Where he departs most sharply from Hamann is in his attitude towards
the survival of language's conjectured original creative vitality in modern native languages, and above all in *Volkspoesie*. Hamann had referred to Lowth, as Wellek observes, but not to Percy or to Ossian
(*Modern Criticism*, p. 180). For Herder, however, the revival of ancient
British popular poetry by Percy and Macpherson offered substantiation
of the philosophical position argued in the *Essay*, that the inherent
human capacity for reflective thought made the invention of language
not just a social but a metaphysical necessity. In his later writing Herder
elaborated his version of the identification of primitive language with
poetry according to his conviction that the subsequent history of a particular language, reflected most vividly in its poetry, reveals the deep
spiritual identity – the *Volksgeist* – of a particular national culture.

[20] Rawson, *Order From Confusion Sprung*, pp. 378–9.

Many of the characteristic accents of nineteenth-century historical philology are already sounded in Herder. Though the concept of historical relativity in language study had already been established by Condillac, as Aarsleff shows, it was the spiritualized and organicist inflection of that concept in Herder that would play such an influential role in the next century.

With the theory of poetic language as with many other late eighteenth-century cultural phenomena, British developments made their mark on continental writing and then returned home with fresh metaphysical amplification. Some of the key ideas about language in the Preface to *Lyrical Ballads* – the notion of a poetry based on 'the real language of men' living in a condition of 'humble or rustic life' and therefore free to express 'the spontaneous overflow of powerful feeling' (Wordsworth, *Prose Works*, I, pp. 124–6) – are anticipated in Herder and in Sulzer, who asserted that the poet's 'thoughts and feelings irresistibly stream out in speech' (*Allgemeine Theorie*, I, p. 609). Nor was Wordsworth alone in his effort to derive from the primitivist, emotivist and nativist strands characteristic of so much mid- and late-eighteenth-century critical theory a new agenda for poetic language. A series of essays that appeared in the 1796 *Monthly Magazine*, signed 'The Enquirer' and written by William Enfield, cites Hugh Blair's *Lectures on Rhetoric and Belles Lettres* and various French (rather than German) theorists in claiming that poetry has its origins in a 'rude state of nature' when language was inherently 'bold and figurative' and would often 'flow in a kind of wild and unfettered melody'. Enfield contradicts Lowth and Herder and anticipates Wordsworth in insisting that 'the natural and proper expression of any conception or feeling in metre or rhyme, is its natural and proper expression in prose'. Condemning the 'modern' preference for 'the meretricious ornaments of art to the genuine simplicity of nature', he goes on to replace the traditional distinction between poetry and prose with a distinction between 'the language of fancy, passion, and sentiment' on the one hand, and 'the language of reason' on the other.[21]

The various primitivist dispositions towards poetic language are complexly related to the rise of literary nationalism and imperialism in the course of the century. Enthusiasm for the alleged emotive spontaneity and figurative power of language in its chronologically remote and culturally unsophisticated condition was often accompanied by strong nationalist sentiment, yet it stands in obvious contrast to the neo-classical nationalism of Voltaire and later of Rivarol, with their differently motivated celebrations of the 'essential' clarity and idiomatic propriety of modern French. At the same time, the nationalistic implications in

---

[21] *Monthly Magazine*, 2 (1796), 453–6.

accounts of ancient bardic sublimity such as those of Lowth and Macpherson need to be distinguished from what we find in Enfield's and Wordsworth's praise for the contemporary English common idiom. We have to contend with a plurality of contradictions on all sides. The difficulty involved in Wordsworth's identifying 'the real language of men' with a rustic speech that neither he nor his readers actually used – his having to acknowledge that such speech must be 'purified' by the poet 'from what appear to be its real defects, from all lasting and rational causes of dislike or disgust' (*Prose Works*, I, p. 124) – has deep if disguised analogues in earlier critical pronouncements, some of which Wordsworth claimed to disdain. In 1742 Gray said that 'the language of the age is never the language of poetry',[22] an assertion which at first seems entirely in keeping with the negative role Wordsworth assigns him in the Preface. But Gray's assertion is ambiguous: everything depends on what is meant by 'the language of the age'. To the extent that Wordsworth understood 'the language of the age' to be a corrupted urban parlance which was vitiating poetic expression, he could have agreed with Gray's formulation. Yet in practice his project of giving English poetry a new linguistic integrity by returning to its native rustic roots differs fundamentally from Gray's effort to cultivate an ancient bardic vitality while accommodating it to the eighteenth-century taste for urbane artifice.

Closer to Wordsworth's ideal in most respects, and yet at the same time sharing in the deceptive generality of Gray's remark, is William Cowper's often-quoted ideal in a letter to the Rev. William Unwin of 17 January 1782: 'To make verse speak the language of prose, without being prosaic, to marshall the words of it in such an order, as they might naturally take in falling from the lips of an extemporary speaker, yet without meanness; harmoniously, elegantly, and without seeming to displace a syllable for the sake of rhyme, is one of the most arduous tasks a poet can undertake' (*Letters and Prose*, II, p. 10). Who is Cowper's 'extemporary speaker' whose conversation 'naturally' produces the prose that poetry should emulate in all but versification? Neither Wordsworth's idealized Cumberland peasant nor the ancient British Bard of primitivist fantasy – but a well-educated, morally sensitive member of the middle class, whose identity has become so transparently fundamental to the institution of English literature that it need not be specified. Cowper advances nothing less than a modest version of Johnson's authoritative maxim that 'poetry is to speak an universal language'. Shifting the ideal of what language 'naturally' expresses from musical numbers to prose still evades the problematic challenges posed

[22] To West, 8 April 1742, *Correspondence of Thomas Gray*, I, p. 192.

by the evolving Lockean principle that words 'arbitrarily' signify ideas through processes of historical and cultural exchange.

Genius, originality, and sympathy

By the time Samuel Johnson began writing the *Lives of the English Poets* in 1779, 'genius' had become a pre-eminent topic in late eighteenth-century criticism. William's Sharpe's *A Dissertation upon Genius* (1755) marked the onset of an English, and especially a Scottish, theoretical concern that quickly developed into a preoccupation with the publication in 1759 of Edward Young's *Conjectures on Original Composition*, Alexander Gerard's *Essay on Taste* and – with a more selective but still powerfully influential relevance – Adam Smith's *Theory of Moral Sentiments*. Mid-century poets themselves had made 'genius' a recurring feature of their desire to revive ancient sources of bardic vitality: Collins's 'Ode on the Poetical Character', Gray's 'The Progress of Poetry' and 'The Bard', and Beattie's *The Minstrel; or, the Progress of Genius* are probably the most familiar instances.

If Johnson acquiesces in the new fascination with genius and originality, as Wimsatt claims,[23] it is with more than a little temperamental resistance. In the *Life of Cowley*, for instance, his attitude is distanced, sceptical, and hints at Johnson's irritation with critical fashion as he approached the age of seventy (ed. Hill, I, p. 2). In some respects Johnson is theoretically up-to-date: the question of genius's being 'accidentally determined', as he says, was a major point of debate. But when in the *Life of Pope* Johnson designates 'in proportions very nicely adjusted to each other, all the qualities that constitute genius', he expounds ideas current in contemporary discussions along lines that would have seemed distinctly old-fashioned to many of his readers. He finds in Pope's verse 'new trains of events', 'energies of passion', 'representation more powerful than the reality', and 'wonderful multiplicity' – but such recognitions of superior poetic capacity are more than counterbalanced by appeals to adjustment, accommodation, decoration, elegance (ed. Hill, III, p. 247). However aptly applied to Pope, these latter qualities were not the signs of genius that Young, Gerard and other writers on the subject were urging readers to trace back to Homer and, much less remotely, to Shakespeare.

Beginning with Johnson's *Lives*, we may approach what German writers of the 1770s were elaborating into a *Geniezeit* and *Genielehre* from an historically rooted vantage point critically distanced from the

---

[23] *Short History*, p. 323 and note citing *Rambler* 121, 'on the evils of imitating'.

main line of theoretical exuberance. Other aspects of this vantage point pertinent to the production and reception of poetry emerge when we look back from *Lives of the Poets* to Johnson's earlier handling of 'genius' in the *Dictionary*. Five senses of the word are distinguished, none of them (as the *OED* notes) fully corresponding to that modern sense of original and exalted mental power that became dominant in England – and then in France and Germany – between the 1750s and the 1770s. Johnson's first definition, 'the protecting or ruling power of men, places, or things', though in some respects obsolete, would actually gain a new lease of life by lurking within the new and elevated sense of 'genius' that does not yet appear in the *Dictionary*. Kant explains what Ken Frieden has termed the 'introjection of genius'[24] in the *Critique of Judgment* (1790): 'if an author owes a product to his genius, he himself does not know how he came by the ideas for it; nor is it in his power [*Gewalt*] to devise such products at his pleasure . . . (Indeed, that is presumably why the word genius is derived from [Latin] *genius*, [which means] the guardian and guiding spirit that each person is given as his own at birth, and to whose inspiration [*Eingebung*] those original ideas are due)' (sec. 46, trans. Pluhar, p. 175; *Akademie* ed., V, p. 308).[25] In this respect Young's famous characterization of genius as 'that god within' is not just the hyperbolic claim of an English eccentric, but an acknowledgement of inexplicable mental power to be found at the very heart of late Enlightenment aesthetics. More informal recognitions of the convergence of the new with the ancient 'genius' abound in late-eighteenth-century criticism – as in Anna Barbauld's praise of Mark Akenside as a writer at once 'prepared by nature with genius' and imbued with 'the genius of the place' where he was educated (Edinburgh University).[26] This kind of sliding from a self-conscious adaptation of the mythological *genius loci* to a psychological and aesthetic reference to natural genius was still common at the end of the century.

Barbauld contrasts Akenside's 'liberal, cheerful, and sublime' genius with the 'Gothic' genius of Edward Young, which 'was clouded over with the deepest glooms of Calvinism, to which system however he owed some of his most striking beauties' (p. 15). Though Barbauld's immediate reference is to Young's *Night Thoughts* (1742–5), the counterposing of Akenside's Scottish Enlightenment intellectualism to Young's

---

[24] *Genius and Monologue*, pp. 66–83.

[25] '. . . daher der Urheber eines Products, welches er seinem Genie verdankt, selbst nicht weiß, wie sich in ihm die Ideen dazu herbei finden, auch es nicht in seiner Gewalt hat, dergleichen nach Belieben oder planmäßig auszudenken . . . (daher denn auch vermuthlich das Wort Genie von *genius*, dem eigenthümlichen, einem Menschen bei der Geburt mitgegebenen, schützenden und leitenden Geist, von deßen Eingebung jene originalen Ideen herrührten, abgeleitet ist.)'

[26] 'Critical Essay' prefixed to Akenside's *The Pleasures of Imagination* (1794), pp. 8–9.

darkly individualist sensibility applies with equal justness to the *Conjectures*, one of the most unaccommodating critical texts of the century. Johnson must have been defending himself against this very aspect of Young's epistolary essay if, as Boswell reports, he responded to hearing Young read the *Conjectures* at the house of Samuel Richardson (to whom they are formally addressed) by saying that 'he was surprized to find Young receive as novelties, what he thought very common maxims' (*Life of Johnson*, V, p. 269). True, there are moments in Shaftesbury's *Characteristicks* (and in his *Soliloquy; or, Advice to an Author* of 1710) and in some of Addison's *Spectator* essays (especially Nos. 62, 159–60, 414, and 419) that anticipate Young's main points of emphasis, as there are more generally in the Longinian tradition of transcendent poetic inspiration transmitted to the eighteenth century through Boileau and Pope. But Young's claims on behalf of an originality rooted in natural subjective intensity and in an active disregard for literary precedents and models initiate a new phase of development in an old tradition.

Beyond Young's extravagant appeals to recognize and 'reverence' individual genius, the *Conjectures* exerted more specific kinds of influence on later eighteenth-century poetics. First, there are the figurative patterns, sometimes entertwined, of genius as magical power and genius as vegetative growth. 'The pen of an *Original* Writer', Young says, in a passage which contains strikingly contradictory gender implications, 'like *Armida's* wand, out of a barren waste calls a blooming spring' (p. 10); and later, 'an original may be said to be of a vegetable nature; it rises spontaneously from the vital root of genius; it grows, it is not made' (p. 12). Secondly, there are Young's explicit comments on poetry. His celebration of Homer, Pindar, Shakespeare, and Milton is less interesting than his more generalized understanding of language and style. The early assertion that 'There is something in Poetry beyond Prose-reason; there are Mysteries in it not to be explained, but admired' does not, in its immediate context in the *Conjectures*, lead anywhere. But when Young focuses more sharply on the matter of rhyme late in the *Conjectures* and argues that Dryden and Pope 'were no great friends to those solemn ornaments which the nature of their works required', the contrast between 'Poetry' and 'Prose-reason' resonates: 'Must rhyme then, say you, be banished? I wish the nature of our language could bear its entire expulsion; but our lesser poetry stands in need of a toleration for it; it raises that, but it sinks the Great' (p. 84). Young is, of course, echoing one of his own heroic originals here, Milton's statement at the beginning of *Paradise Lost* about rhyme's 'being no necessary adjunct or true ornament of poem or good verse ... but the invention of a barbarous age, to set off wretched matter and lame metre'. There is more to notice here than simply the irony of Young's borrowing from

Milton in the cause of original composition. Genius has a very complex relation to formal convention, as Young must have realized in posing without resolving the problem of what it means to speak of 'true ornament', or 'ornaments . . . which the nature of [poetic] works required'.

Young's account of poetic genius is usually set in opposition to Gerard's, and it is certainly true that the self-dramatizing idiosyncrasy of the *Conjectures* seems very distant indeed from the intellectual milieu that produced *An Essay on Taste* (1759) and *An Essay on Genius* (1774). The first of Gerard's essays was a prize-winning response to a question set by the Select Society of Edinburgh for the Encouragement of Arts, Sciences, Manufactures, and Agriculture; the latter grew out of debates within the Aberdeen Philosophical Society that formally began in November, 1758. Gerard's analysis is conspicuously engaged with empiricist, and particularly with associationist, epistemology.

In some respects, though, Gerard's late Enlightenment method belies what he and Young have in common. They both make 'invention' primary. 'Genius is properly the faculty of *invention*', Gerard writes in *An Essay on Genius* (p. 8), extending his argument in the *Essay on Taste* that 'the first and leading quality of genius is *invention*, which consists in a great extent and comprehensiveness of imagination, in a readiness of associating the remotest ideas that are in any way related' (2nd edn, 1780, p. 163). In the *Essay on Genius* this passionate responsiveness gets articulated as a theory of 'enthusiasm', 'a very common, if not an inseparable attendant of genius'. 'When an ingenious track of thinking presents itself, though but casually, to true genius . . . imagination darts amongst it with great rapidity; and by this rapidity its ardour is more inflamed. The velocity of its motion sets it on fire, like a chariot wheel which is kindled by the quickness of its revolution . . . Its motions become still more impetuous, till the mind is enraptured with the subject, and exalted into an extasy. In this manner the fire of genius, like a divine impulse, raises the mind above itself, and by the natural influence of imagination actuates it as if it were supernaturally inspired' (pp. 67–9). The linking here of associationist and even mechanistic figures of mental activity with ancient tropes of inspiration is characteristic of Gerard – but so is a critical vocabulary of inflammation, infection, and revolution that, especially in historical retrospect, opens up surprising possibilities. In some passages of the *Essay on Genius* Gerard's well-mannered professorial prose yields some striking analogues to Young's 'Gothic' images of magic and of vegetative growth (see especially the comparison of the operations of genius to 'a vegetable draw[ing] in moisture from the earth', p. 167).

Gerard's rival for primacy among the Scottish theoreticians of original genius was William Duff, who lived in Aberdeenshire and must have been aware of the discussions within the Aberdeen Philosophical Society, though there is no evidence of his actually being a member. Influence between Duff and Gerard almost certainly runs both ways; Duff's *An Essay on Original Genius* (1767) displays a similar emphasis on 'invention' as the 'vital spirit' of genius (pp. 124–5), on 'an extreme sensibility both of pain and pleasure' (p. 152), and on 'enthusiasm', which he recommends by taking the word back to its etymological root in the image of being breathed into by a god. What especially distinguishes Duff from Gerard and makes him relevant to the present discussion is his more sustained focus on poetry. 'Poetry, of all the liberal Arts, affords the most extensive scope for the display of a Genius truly Original', he writes at the beginning of the section devoted to this topic, and he goes on to analyse poetic invention under the headings 'Incidents', 'Characters', 'Imagery', and 'Sentiment'. The discussion of 'Imagery' begins with the familiar argument that the 'ordinary modes of speech' are 'unable to express the grandeur or the strength of [the original poetic genius's] conceptions'; 'to supply the poverty of common language, he has recourse to *Metaphors* and *Images*' (p. 143). What is of interest in the discussion that follows is Duff's concern for 'common Readers' who are challenged by the genius's impatience with 'common language': 'An original Author indeed will frequently be apt to exceed in the use of this ornament, by pouring forth such a blaze of imagery, as to dazzle and overpower the mental sight; the effect of which is, that his Writings become obscure, if not unintelligible to common Readers' (p. 145). Though Duff cites access to the sublime as a distinguishing mark of poetic genius, his worry that it may lead to figurative obscurity contrasts sharply and deliberately with Burke's *Philosophical Enquiry*, with its declaration that there are 'many descriptions in the poets and orators which owe their sublimity to a richness and profusion of images, in which the mind is so dazzled as to make it impossible to attend to that exact coherence and agreement of allusions, which we should require on every other occasion' (I. xiii, ed. Boulton, p. 78).

The sheer volume of English and Scottish theorizing about original genius reveals a good deal about changing conceptions of and attitudes towards subjectivity in the late eighteenth century. An extraordinary range of writers extend, amplify, debate the principal emphasis we have noted in Johnson, Young, Gerard, and Duff. In essays on 'Genius of Poetry' and 'Originality' in a collection called *Gleanings* (1785), the Rev. John Moir challenges conventional Augustan beliefs in the 'Uniformity of temper and manners'. 'The mind of man is equally fond and full of variety', he writes; 'every new inspection of the most common and familiar phenomena of nature discovers a thousand new variations, distinctions, and resemblances . . . original genius never rests in generals,

... but gives, in vivid, glowing, and permanent characters, the identical impression it receives' (I, pp. 29–30, 107). The closely linked doctrines of diversity and particularism are obviously of great import for poetry: arguments related to those advanced by Moir may be found in John Aikin's *An Essay on the Application of Natural History to Poetry* (1777), in Thomas Percival's *Moral and Literary Dissertations* (1784), in W. L. Brown's *Essay on Sensibility* (1789), in James Hurdis's *Lectures Shewing the Several Sources of that Pleasure which the Human Mind Receives from Poetry* (1797), in Nathan Drake's *Literary Hours* (1798) – as well as in better-known texts by Hurd, Kames, Joseph Warton, Hugh Blair, Priestley. Most of these writers also join Moir in proclaiming the unique personal individuality of geniuses, who 'perceive every object through a medium peculiar to themselves' (*Gleanings*, I, p. 104).

The notion of an 'era of genius' figures prominently in French critical discussions, which show ample awareness of the evolving British tradition but also establish their own distinctive patterns of focus and debate. That true genius comes into being 'pour faire époque' – to make or mark an era – is a recurrent claim of one of the most important, and notorious, contributions to French theories of genius, Helvétius's *De L'Esprit*, which was published a year before Young's *Conjectures* in 1758, immediately condemned as dangerously heretical by both church and state, and vigorously suppressed. An anonymous English translation appeared in London in 1759 under the title *De L'Esprit: or, Essays on the Mind and its Several Faculties*. In a note on the title of Helvétius's 'Discours IV: Des Differents Noms Donnés À L'Esprit', the translator remarks: 'The subject of this discourse as expressed by our author is, "The different names given to the Esprit", a word, which cannot be literally translated, and signifies not only the mind, but its faculties' (p. 241). In fact this translator renders *esprit* as 'genius' throughout the English version, even though Helvétius himself distinguishes *esprit* and *génie* in calling the first chapter of Discours IV 'Du génie'.

It is in this chapter, which builds upon the inquiry of Discours III 'Si L'Esprit Doit Être Considéré Comme un Don de la Nature, ou Comme un Effect de L'Éducation' ('Whether Genius ought to be considered as a natural gift; or, as an effect of education' in the 1759 translation), that Helvétius intervenes most significantly in the discussion by insisting on the role of chance ('le hasard') in producing the inventions and discoveries that everyone takes to be characteristic of genius. Helvétius opens up a radical alternative perspective, one that cuts against the celebrations of transcendent individual power and that leads to a particular kind of subordination of such individual power to historical circumstances. But the stress on 'le hasard' is only one side of Helvétius's account of genius. 'What part soever I give to chance', he writes, 'whatever share it has in the reputation of great men, it . . . can do nothing for those who are not animated by a lively desire of glory' (1759 trans., p. 244).[27] Chance convergence with historical change on the one side; a desire for fame which 'is the soul of the man of genius' on the other: no wonder Helvétius provoked – in this as in other aspects of De L'Esprit – such a torrent of defensive reaction.

Helvétius decisively elaborates a scepticism towards the emerging cult of individual genius that we also find in Voltaire and Condillac. Diderot, on the other hand, dissents from this line of thinking and claims, in explicit opposition to his friend Helvétius, that genius does constitute a distinctive, and often a tormenting, mode of subjective power. He speaks of the 'tyrannical impulse of genius' (Réfutation suivie de l'ouvrage d'Helvétius, written 1773–4 but unpublished), of an inner emotional intensity and drive so great that it amounts to a kind of madness.[28] The poet of genius, in the moment of inspired composition, 'no longer knows what he says, what he does; he is mad' ('ne sait plus ce qu'il dit, ce qu'il fait; il est fou'). But this impulse in Diderot to identify genius with passions so extreme that they amount to a kind of psychopathology or monstrosity has to be understood in relation to other, sometimes contradictory strands in his thinking. In the Paradoxe sur le Comédien the genius is, by contrast, a figure of supreme self-control and self-possession, whose originality and inventiveness derive from the power of observation ('l'esprit observateur'). When he elaborates on this power in a fragment that has been given the title Sur le génie, Diderot takes up Helvétius's stress on 'le hasard' and turns it along a different trajectory (Oeuvres complètes, IV, p. 27). The contradictoriness of Diderot's endorsements of genius – the swings between inspired but tormented passion on the one hand, and poised but unpredictable observation on the other – give his remarks a destabilizing critical force with respect to the dominant lines of thinking on the subject.

From a political perspective the preoccupation with genius, even among the philosophes, carried ambiguous implications. The idea of the supremely gifted individual, inspired and inspiring, could be seen to conflict with democratic, egalitarian, or republican ideals. (This is one of the complications that Wordsworth will have to negotiate when he defines 'the poet' in the Preface to Lyrical Ballads as 'a man speaking to men . . . endued with a more lively sensibility . . . a greater knowledge of human nature, and a more comprehensive soul, than are supposed

---

[27] 'Quelque rôle que je fasse jouer au hasard, quelque part qu'il ait à la reputation des grands hommes, le hasard cependant ne fait rien qu'en faveur de ceux qu'anime le désir vif de la gloire.'

[28] See Herbert Dieckmann, 'Diderot's conception of genius', Journal of the History of Ideas, 2 (1941), 151–82 (164–6).

to be common among mankind', yet not 'differing in kind from other men, but only in degree'; *Prose Works*, I, p. 138). In France near the end of the century, as L. M. Findlay has recently shown,[29] the older uses of *genius* to refer to the distinctive character or spirit of a nation and to the prevailing character or spirit of a language, law, or institution (see *OED* 2 b. and c.) were deployed by counterrevolutionary and reactionary writers to reassert royalist and Catholic ideals of French cultural superiority. Chateaubriand's *Génie du Christianisme* (1802) is the best known of these efforts, but Rivarol's *Discours sur l'universalité de la langue française* (1784) bears more immediately on questions concerning poetic genius. Appropriating and transforming Condillac's idea of a particular language as expressing the 'genius' of a national culture, Rivarol finds in the very structure of the French language evidence of a long-evolving cultural superiority under threat from revolutionary innovation: 'What distinguishes our language from ancient and modern languages is the organization and construction of its sentences. This organization must always be direct and of necessity clear. A Frenchman begins by naming the *subject* of any speech, then the *verb* which expresses the action, and lastly the *object* of this action: here is the logic natural to all men ... THAT WHICH IS NOT CLEAR IS NOT FRENCH; that which is not clear remains English, Italian, Greek or Latin' (*Oeuvres complètes*, II, pp. 48–9).[30] Specious and contradictory though this celebration of French linguistic superiority is, Rivarol's *Discours* nevertheless marks out one of the more disturbing and influential directions in which theories of national 'genius' could tend. The 'imagination of the poet', he goes so far as to claim, must be 'confined by the circumspect genius of the language' (II, p. 51). Figurative boldness, the very sign of poetic genius for theorists such as Gerard and Duff, poses for Rivarol a danger to the essential clarity of French and must therefore submit to the established 'hierarchy of styles ... classed ... like the subjects in our monarchy' (II, p. 62).

Rivarol was, among other things, mounting a conservative defence against imported British accounts of poetic genius: Young's *Conjectures* and Gerard's *Essay on Taste* had both been translated into French shortly

[29] 'The genius of the French language: towards a poetics of political reaction during the Revolutionary period', *Studies in Romanticism*, 28 (1989), 531–57.

[30] 'Ce qui distingue notre langue des langues anciennes et modernes, c'est l'ordre et la construction de la phrase. Et cet ordre doit toujours être direct et necéssairement clair. Le Français nomme d'abord le *sujet* du discours, ensuite le *verbe* qui est l'action, et enfin l'*objet* de cette action: voilà la logique naturelle à tous les hommes ... Le Français, par un privilège unique, est seul resté fidèle à l'ordre direct ... la syntaxe française est incorruptible. C'est de là que résulte cette admirable clarté, base éternelle de notre langue. CE QUI N'EST PAS CLAIR N'EST PAS FRANÇAIS; ce qui n'est pas clair, est encore anglais, italien, grec ou latin.' I have followed L. M. Findlay's English translation of this passage in 'The genius of the French language', pp. 542–3.

after their initial publication.[31] But it was in Germany that English and Scottish writing about genius made its greatest impact. The *Conjectures* was translated into German twice within two years of its publication in 1759; Karl Friedrich Flögel translated Gerard's *Essay on Taste* in 1766 and Christian Garve the *Essay on Genius* in 1776.[32] Young's *Conjectures* became, as Abrams says, 'a primary document in the canon of the Storm and Stress'. Sulzer's article on *Erfindung* (Invention) in his *Allgemeine Theorie der schönen Künste* emphasizes the 'happy expressions of . . . genius' ('glückliche Äußerungen des Genies'), and Herder's enormously influential essay of 1778, 'On Cognition and Sensation of the Human Soul' ('Vom Erkennen und Empfinden der menschlichen Seele') expands on Young's and Gerard's figurings of genius as a biological process, as a germinating and growing plant. Directed to the *Conjectures* by his mentor Hamann, Herder saw a particular significance for the project of consolidating a German national literature in Young's insistence that poetic genius was not only independent of but antithetical to the imitation of canonical greatness. Though full of enthusiasm for what he took to be the intuitive power of Shakespeare, Milton, and Ossian, Herder urges contemporary German poets to shun foreign models and instead turn simultaneously to the native 'genius' of German folk poetry (a very different kind of nationalist appeal from Rivarol's celebration of French clarity and hierarchical order) and to their own spontaneous emotional resources. And his exhortation to poets extends to critics as well: he calls for 'living reading' ('lebendiges Lesen'), which he defines as the 'divination of the soul of an author' (*Sämmtliche Werke*, VIII, p. 208), and insists that 'criticism without genius is nothing. Only a genius can judge and teach another' (VIII, p. 131).

The influence on Goethe of Herder's call for an original, emotive, and profoundly German 'genius' can readily be detected in Goethe's essay *On German Architecture* and in his other early critical writings, with their stress on spontaneous intuition as the source of an organized aesthetic unity, of an 'inner form' that can neither be achieved nor grasped through deliberate artifice. Michael Beddow has recently called attention to the ways in which such Herderian ideals are enacted in Goethe's own lyric poems of the early 1770s. In his drama of 1773, *Götz von Berlichingen*, and in *Die Leiden des jungen Werthers* of 1774, Goethe did more than anyone else to establish the *Sturm und Drang* as, in Beddow's words, 'a modish cult of original genius'.[33] In *Werther*, however, Goethe simultaneously initiates a more critical and historically self-conscious perspective on this same literary ideology: he calls attention

---

[31] See Fabian's edition of *An Essay on Genius*, p. ix.
[32] Engell, *Creative Imagination*, pp. 80, 88, 114.   [33] 'Goethe on genius', p. 103.

to his protagonist's fascination with British writing that celebrates spontaneous feeling, and he shows him being driven to suicide by the excessive cultivation of his own subjectivity. So in the very text that represents the culmination of Goethe's investment in the *Sturm und Drang* fascination with original genius, Goethe opens up questions that he would continue to rethink during the 1780s and 1790s.

Goethe's protracted working through of the question of genius may be seen, in this sense, as encompassing the more systematic and formal terms of Kant's famous account in the *Critique of Judgement* (*Kritik der Urteilskraft*, 1790), and of his remarks on genius in *Anthropology from a Pragmatic Point of View* (*Anthropologie in pragmatischer Hinsicht*, 1798). Kant followed the debates over genius, both inside and outside Germany, with keen interest. He read Gerard's *Essay on Genius* with admiration, and while he disagrees with Gerard's claim that genius is a separate faculty or power in its own right and parodies the reliance on analogies to vegetative growth, he praises Gerard as having produced the best treatment of the subject then available. For Kant as for Goethe, the crucial question posed by the concept of genius concerns the relation between the purposiveness of organic growth on the one hand, and the rules necessary for art on the other. Genius, Kant argues in the 'Analytic of the Sublime', is precisely the realm where nature and art converge (sec. 46; *Akademie* edn, V, p. 307). And while art and judgements of art presuppose rules, these rules cannot have concepts for their 'determining basis, i.e., the judgement must not be based on a concept of the way in which the product is possible'. It follows for Kant that 'genius must be considered the very opposite of a *spirit of imitation*'. Yet this opposition is ambiguous: 'no *Homer* or *Wieland* can show how his ideas, rich in fancy and yet also in thought, arise and meet in his mind; the reason is that he himself does not know, and hence also cannot teach it to anyone else ... the artist's skill cannot be communicated but must be conferred directly on each person by the hand of nature ... the rule must be abstracted from what the artist has done, i.e., from the product, which others may use to test their own talent, letting it serve them as their model, not to be *copied* [*Nachmachung*] but to be *imitated* [*Nachahmung*]' (sec. 47; trans. Pluhar, pp. 176–7; *Akademie* edn, V, p. 309).[34]

If from the perspective of Kantian aesthetics genius had become a

---

[34] '... kein Homer aber oder Wieland anzeigen kann, wie sich seine phantasiereichen und doch zugleich gedankenvollen Ideen in seinem Kopfe hervor und zusammen finden, darum weil er es selbst nicht weiß und es also auch keinen andern lehren kann ... eine solche Geschicklichkeit sich auch nicht mittheilen läßt, sondern jedem unmittelbar von der Hand der Natur ertheilt sein will ... die Regel muß von der That, d.i. vom Product, abstrahirt werden, an welchem andere ihr eigenes Talent prüfen mögen, um sich jenes zum Muster nicht der Nachmachung, sondern der Nachahmung dienen zu lassen.'

pre-eminently synthetic and mediating category of subjectivity, from a social and political perspective it was an extraordinarily contradictory ideological formation. Commenting on the volatile and, given the course of historical events, uncertain political implications of the concept of genius in the 1790s, Simon Schaffer notes a tendency to counterbalance cultural influence with idealized removal: 'It was precisely the power of sympathy with the course of history which allowed the true genius to liberate himself from public culture'.[35] We can see this tendency at work in Schiller's On Naive and Sentimental Poetry (1795–6), even as he attempts to claim for the necessarily 'naive' poetic genius a heroic ethical and cultural position. Schiller celebrates poetic genius in terms that are close to, and importantly influenced by, Kant's: 'It proceeds not by the accepted principles, but by flashes of insight and feeling; but ... its feelings are laws for all ages and for all races of men' (Werke, XX, p. 424).[36] A bit later in Schiller's essay we learn, though, that to find such genius we must look not to those engaged in practical activity and struggle, but 'for a class of men which, without toiling, is active, and capable of formulating ideals without fanaticism; a class that unites within itself all the realities of life with its least possible limitations and is borne by the currents of events without becoming its victim. Only such a class can preserve the beautiful unity of human nature that is destroyed for the moment by any particular task, and continuously by a life of such toil, and decide, in everything that is purely human, by their feelings the rule of common opinion' (Werke, XX, p. 490).[37] Schiller is conscious that 'such a class might [not] actually exist', that he is offering 'only an idea'. Still, the motivation and implication of Schiller's 'idea' – his extending the concept of genius to an entire 'class' ('Klasse'), which he sets in stark contrast to the 'labouring class' ('arbeitende Klasse') – constitutes a significant and influential transformation of earlier eighteenth-century ideas of primitive natural genius. Schiller's formulation is fascinatingly connected to the ideals of Wordsworth's Preface, where poetic genius appropriates the language and experience of rustic labour and transforms them through the culturally privileged work of writing.

Throughout the late eighteenth century what we might broadly call

---

[35] Schaffer, 'Genius in Romantic natural philosophy', p. 93.

[36] 'Es verfährt nicht nach erkannten Prinzipien sondern nach Einfällen und Gefühlen ... seine Gefühle sind Gesetze für alle Zeiten und für alle Geschlechter der Menschen.'

[37] '... nach einer Klaße von Menschen umsehen, welche ohne zu arbeiten thätig ist, und idealisiren kann, ohne zu schwärmen; welche alle Realitäten des Lebens mit den wenigstmöglichen Schranken desselben in sich vereiniget, und vom Strome der Begebenheiten getragen wird, ohne der Raub deßelben zu werden. Nur eine solche Klaße kann das schöne Ganze menschlicher Natur, welches durch jede Arbeit augenblicklich, und durch ein arbeitendes Leben anhaltend zerstört wird, aufbewahren, und in allem, was rein menschlich ist, durch ihre Gefühle dem allgemeinen Urtheil Gesetze geben.'

an elitist or vanguard image of sublime poetic genius contended for prominence with a more congenial and proto-populist ideal of sympathetic, compassionate giftedness. The seminal philosophical text in this regard is Adam Smith's *Theory of Moral Sentiments*. Elaborating on earlier discussions of the primacy of feeling in the writings of Shaftesbury, Francis Hutcheson, and James Arbuckle, and on the shrewd analysis of sympathy in Hume's *A Treatise of Human Nature* (1739), Smith devotes his first chapter to arguing that 'How selfish soever man may be supposed, there are evidently some principles in his nature, which interest him in the fortune of others', and to designating 'sympathy' as 'our fellow-feeling with any passion whatever' (I.i.1, paras. 1 and 5). The reasoning here is closely analogous to Smith's later account of the interplay of economic self-interest and co-operation in *The Wealth of Nations* (1776). Though he says nothing directly about poetic genius in *Moral Sentiments*, Smith's emphasis on the distinctively human ability to identify our own feelings with the feelings of others was vastly influential on poets, critics, and theorists for whom genius was a primary concern. For John Ogilvie in his *Philosophical and Critical Observations on the Nature, Character, and Various Species of Composition* (1774), the great poet must be capable of 'entering deeply into the characters of those with whom he is conversant. He gains a facility of reading in the countenance those sensations, however closely concealed, that actuate the heart' (I, pp. 282–3). James Beattie, whose *Essays on Poetry and Music, as They Affect the Mind* appeared some five years after his poem on *The Progress of Genius*, insists that the sympathetic power must extend to non-human beings and objects: the poet 'must not only study nature, and know the reality of things; but must also possess ... sensibility, to enter with ardent emotions into every part of his subject, so as to transfuse into his work a pathos and energy sufficient to raise corresponding emotions in his reader' (2nd edn, 1778, p. 53). Poetic efforts to enact this understanding of the sympathetic imagination were profuse: Beattie's own poem, 'Sympathy', appeared in 1776 along with the *Essays on Poetry and Music*. Nearer the end of the century, Erasmus Darwin offers something like a materialist version of this power and characteristically links it to the ancient mythopoeic tradition when, near the beginning of *The Botanic Garden*, a personified 'GENIUS' appeals to both poet and reader:

> But THOU! whose mind the well-attemper'd ray
> Of Taste and Virtue lights with purer days;
> Whose finer sense each soft vibration owns
> With sweet responsive sympathy of tones ...

> ('The Economy of Vegetation',
> Canto 1, ll. 9–12)

The notion of a 'finer sense' coexists with a 'sweet responsive sympathy' – a hierarchy of sensibility with a community of feeling.

Finally, we may note the extent to which the latent tension between gifted superiority and giving compassion runs throughout theories of the sublime. Burke devotes three sections of Part I of his *Enquiry* to 'sympathy' and returns to the idea in Part V, where he is particularly concerned to explain the sublimity of poetic language. After looking at examples of poetic power from Virgil, Homer, and Lucretius, he concludes that the 'business' of poetry and rhetoric 'is to affect rather by sympathy than imitation; to display rather the effect of things on the mind of the speaker, or of others, than to present a clear idea of the things themselves' (V.v, ed. Boulton, p. 172). Further on Burke links his decisively affective argument to the distinctive potential of words: 'we take an extraordinary part in the passions of others . . . and . . . are easily affected and brought into sympathy by any tokens which are shewn of them; and there are no tokens which can express all the circumstances of most passions so fully as words. . . . We yield to sympathy, what we refuse to description' (V.vii, ed. Boulton, pp. 173, 175). Burke offers a dramatic consolidation of the view expressed by Joseph Warton in the *Essay on Pope*: 'The sublime and the pathetic are the two chief nerves of all genuine poetry' (I, pp. i–ii, vi). We see why Wimsatt says in retrospect, despite Johnson's resistance,[38] that 'The 18th-century notion of sublimity as a subjective experience of genius had gotten along well enough with the emerging principle of association by emotive congruity' (*Short History*, p. 407).

Imagination

'Nature's kindling breath / Must fire the chosen genius', writes Mark Akenside near the beginning of *The Pleasures of Imagination* (ll. 37–8). But what this turns out to mean is that 'From Heaven my strains begin; from Heaven descends / The flame of genius to the human breast' (ll. 56–7). Akenside had only recently completed his studies in theology and medicine at the University of Edinburgh when, in 1744, he published his most popular and successful poem; the course of Akenside's academic career – the accretive movement from religion to science – is evident in the conceptual perspective and synthesis his poem offers. Though focused throughout the opening verse paragraphs on the rich diversity of earthly existence – the word 'things' threads its way recurrently through Book the First and emphatically concludes two of the

---

[38] Cf. Wimsatt, *Short History*, p. 323, on Johnson's refusal 'to merge the pathetic with that other emotive keynote, the sublime'.

first three verse paragraphs – Akenside is eager to establish himself
among those of 'finer mold' whom Nature has 'tempered with a purer
flame':

> To these the Sire Omnipotent unfolds
> The world's harmonious volume, there to read
> The transcript of himself.

(ll. 99–101)

That old category the 'pre-romantic' certainly has its limitations, but
there is an important and undeniable link between Akenside's sense of
a universe of things to be read as the 'transcript' of 'the Almighty One'
(l. 64) and the world of nature to which Coleridge desires his infant son
to have access in 'Frost at Midnight' (1798):

> so shalt thou see and hear
> The lovely shapes and sounds intelligible
> Of that eternal language, which thy God
> Utters, who from eternity doth teach
> Himself in all, and all things in himself.

(ll. 58–62)

For Akenside as for Coleridge (writing more than fifty years later, and
before German transcendentalist discourse had made its great impact on
his thinking), the material world provokes and yields to the human
imagination because that world is itself created by imagination in its
supreme and infinite form.[39] In this respect imagination has an originary
as well as the more obvious and familiar mediating function that
Akenside, following Addison, assigns it in his prose 'Design'.[40] Both in
nature and in art, writes Akenside, beauty dwells

> Where dawns the high expression of a mind:
> By steps conducting our enraptured search
> To the eternal origin, whose power,
> Through all the unbounded symmetry of things,
> Like rays effulging from the parent sun,
> This endless mixture of her charms diffused.

(I, ll. 475–83)

Addison's *Spectator* papers on The Pleasures of Imagination, Thomson's
versified appropriations of new scientific descriptions of the natural world,

---

[39] See Engell, *Creative Imagination*, p. 45, who also notes Akenside's reference to
'plastic powers', a phrase with major significance for Coleridge's critical vocabulary.
[40] 'There are certain powers in human nature which seem to hold a middle place
between the organs of bodily sense and the faculties of moral perception: they have
been called by a very general name, the Powers of Imagination'.

and Shaftesbury's vision of Platonic harmony converge in Akenside's celebration of imagination as a moral and political as well as an aesthetic power.

The political implications of Akenside's poem are worth noting at this early stage in the discussion, since their contradictory aspect will emerge often in later writing about the imagination. On the one hand imagination leads both to 'Truth' and to 'Her sister Liberty' (I, ll. 23–4); on the other, it is a power exercised by the 'high-born-soul' (I, l. 183) whom Nature has wrought 'within a finer mold', has 'tempered with a purer frame' (I, ll. 97–8). Further, within a related but somewhat different frame of reference, while 'the bounteous providence of Heaven' has implanted 'this desire / Of objects new and strange, to urge us on / With unremitted labour' (I, ll. 239–42), this imaginative labour 'mocks possession' (I, l. 169), 'Disdains to rest her heaven-aspiring wing / Beneath its native quarry' (I, ll. 184–5). 'Work', like 'thing', is recurrent and semantically mobile in Akenside's diction. We can already see quite clearly the ideological function of imagination as a category of desire that puts the drive to self-assertion and self-expansion into play while idealizing its relation to socio-economic class and detaching it from anything so vulgar and finite as material acquisition. At this level of articulation and reception no less than in its overtly self-conscious synthesis of prevailing critical ideas, *The Pleasures of Imagination* is a valuable mid-century point of reference for tracing the development of imagination's role in emerging ideologies of the aesthetic.

James Engell gives Akenside conspicuous prominence in his capacious history of eighteenth- and early nineteenth-century ideas of the creative imagination, noting that Akenside not only 'predates ... the descriptions of Gerard and Tetens' as well as of Coleridge 'concerning the imaginative process of combining ideas into a new and harmonized whole' but anticipates what will become some of their favourite verbs: 'blend/divide', 'mingle', 'join', 'converge', 'enlarge', 'extenuate', 'vary'. It is important to acknowledge, however, that the word 'imagination' had begun to take on more elevated and imposing inflections throughout the early decades of the century. The elevation of 'imagination' over 'fancy' was already under way in Hobbes's *Leviathan*, although there the elevation depends upon a concept of imagination rooted in sensory and especially visual experience, both immediate and recollected. As Wimsatt explains, 'whenever the distinction between "imagination" and "fancy" was being made – and it often was – honors were likely to fall to the term "imagination." A certain softness and warmth and depth of good feeling grew around the term "imagination" in its Addisonian sense' (*Short History*, p. 385). The connection with sense experience, particularly with seeing, remained prominent, though – and for this very reason – 'fancy' sometimes became the privileged term when a more inventive, less earthbound mental power was being asserted. Joseph Warton's ode 'To Fancy' of 1746 illustrates this latter turn through unabashedly eroticized and exotic personification. Warton is more committed to primitivist and emotivist ideals of poetic transport than is Akenside, and his 'fancy' is a relatively more aural, less visual, mode of psychic intensity. But the striving for a transcendent and unifying mental faculty is common to both (see ll. 87–92). The emphasis on the formal verbal manifestations of Fancy's 'energy divine' is a striking feature of Warton's ode:

> Like lightning, let his mighty verse
> The bosom's inmost foldings pierce.

> (ll. 115–16)

So is the concluding gesture linking native British with ancient classical genius – 'O bid Britannia rival Greece!' (l. 120) – with its somewhat less deferential echo of Akenside's desire at the end of *The Pleasures of Imagination*, Book I, to 'tune to Attic themes the British lyre'.

While British poetry of the 1740s was giving fresh scope to enthusiastic and inclusive notions of imagination and fancy, British philosophy was assigning to the former word a different but no less central mental function. In Hume's *Treatise of Human Nature* (1739), imagination, defined as 'the vivacity of our ideas', is made the principal active and integrating force in the mind's processing of experience: 'The memory, senses, and understanding are . . . all of them founded on the imagination, or the vivacity of our ideas' (ed. Selby-Bigge, p. 265). Imagination for Hume not only enriches and complicates the association of ideas; it is the capacity of the mind to reproduce the 'impressions' of sense as 'ideas' in the first place. And as Engell says, 'in reproducing impressions as ideas, the imagination may transpose, wrench them out of sequence, divide, or even fuse them' (*Creative Imagination*, p. 53). Humean imagination is at once indispensable and unpredictable, constantly vulnerable to and often in conflict with the 'passions', which the imagination is responsible for provoking but only in part capable of controlling or directing. It is as powerful and necessary to human life as it is deceptive and endangering. And Humean imagination is not always so ambivalent. Hume prefigures Adam Smith in regarding 'Sympathy' as 'the conversion of an idea into an impression [reversing the initial process of mental construction] by the force of imagination' (*Treatise*, ed. Selby-Bigge, p. 427). Later, in his essay 'On Tragedy' of 1757, Hume assigns to imagination the key role in unifying a literary text. The events of a narrative 'must be connected together by some bond or tie', he writes: 'They must be related to each other in the imagination, and form a kind of *unity*' (*Philosophical Works*, 1854, III, pp. 26–8). It is the poetic genius, Hume claims, who demonstrates this aspect of imaginative activity most compellingly.

It is evident in Hume that imagination is not confined, as romantic and post-romantic critics of empiricist epistemology so often allege, to either an entirely negative or an exclusively visualist role. The same may be said about the place of imagination in the philosophy of Hume's great French contemporary Condillac, whose materialist and sensationalist inflections of the Lockean tradition have sometimes led to his being dismissed as mechanistic and irrelevant to an understanding of literary discourse.[41] In the *Traité des Sensations* (1754) Condillac elevates 'imagination' above memory and argues that in its most extended sense it is 'the name of the mental process that combines the properties of various objects to create groups for which there are no models in nature ... it provides pleasures which in certain respects are preferable to reality itself' (II.xi.6; *Oeuvres philosophiques*, I, p. 271). Though dependent for its constructive role in discourse and culture on being integrated with reflection and analysis, imagination for Condillac is never merely a source of delusion. In the *Essai sur l'origine des connoissances humaines* (1746) 'imagination' is initially understood through its activity in reviving and preserving perceptions (I.ii.2 – 'Imagination, Contemplation, and Memory'). But when he turns to 'Reflection' and the production of language, Condillac sees reflection as arising from imagination and memory and then 'reacting back on the imagination and memory that produced it' (I.ii.5, para. 49; *Oeuvres philosophiques*, I, p. 22). Later the operation of 'Giving Signs to our Ideas' is strikingly shown to result 'from the imagination's presenting the mind with signs which are not yet in use, and from the attention's connecting these signs with ideas' (I.iv.1, introduction; *Oeuvres philosophiques*, I, p. 41).[42] The positive place of imagination in Condillac's account of mental life and development is one of the marks of his critical relation to the Lockean position he so brilliantly extends.

Elsewhere in French criticism of the mid-eighteenth century there is

---

[41] See Aarsleff, 'The tradition of Condillac: the problem of the origin of language in the eighteenth century and the debate in the Berlin Academy before Herder' and 'Condillac's speechless statue', in *From Locke to Saussure*, pp. 146–224. See also Derrida's discussion of 'productive' and 'reproductive' imagination in Condillac, in *The Archaeology of the Frivolous*, pp. 66–79.

[42] (1) '... le nom d'une faculté, qui combine les qualités des objets, pour en faire des ensembles, dont la nature n'offre point de modèles ... elle procure des jouissances, qui, à certains égards, l'emportent sur la réalité même'. (2) '... réagissant sur l'imagination et la mémoire qui l'ont produite' (3) '... de l'imagination qui présente à l'esprit des signes dont on n'avoit point encore l'usage, et de l'attention qui les lie avec les idées'. The English translations are those of Franklin Philip and Harlan Lane (1982).

less developed theory of the poetic imagination than one might expect. Wellek can list 'imagination' along with 'individuality', 'revery', and 'nature' as a positive term in Rousseau's critical writings (*History of Modern Criticism*, I, p. 63), but he does not bother to pause over any specifically Rousseauvian contribution to the formal discourse on the imagination. Diderot, however, is another matter: the *Rêve de d'Alembert* (written in 1769 but not published until 1830) contains an important meditation on 'l'imagination métaphorique' as the apprehension of hidden analogies between different spheres or registers of experience. While Diderot's figure of memory as a kind of vault of *images* suggests a strong visualist orientation, his most striking critical trope – the metaphoric imagination functions like the sympathetic vibrations of a string instrument (*Oeuvres*, II, p. 113) – is more interesting and more forward-looking.[43] At times he writes about imagination as if it were an entirely physiological phenomenon, speaking of 'nerve centres' and of the poetic 'organism'. Diderot's speculations on imagination in the *Rêve de d'Alembert* are left tantalizingly incomplete; Wellek is perhaps right to claim that 'No theory of poetry may be derived from these passages' (*History of Modern Criticism*, I, p. 52). Yet Diderot has left a distinctive if inchoate account of metaphorical apprehension as the primary function of the imagination, a function that is at once mysterious and material in its basis.

All of the writers we have looked at so far, and especially Hume, see imagination as working in close connection with 'the association of ideas', a concept that gradually emerges from the negative status given it in Locke's *Essay* to become the dominant preoccupation of mid-century philosophy (see James Sambrook's discussion below, pp. 616–26). While associationism may appear to have constrained imagination, if not to a mechanistically physiological matter of neurological vibration then to an ineluctably supplementary relation to sense experience, it in fact allowed for quite expansive and exuberant critical elaborations. Still, the problem of what Coleridge would call the 'despotism of the eye' (*Biographia Literaria*, ch. 6, p. 107) persisted; 'imagination' continued to be regarded, quite understandably, as having principally to do with 'images', which were in turn conceived as the result of visual sensations. Addison's remark that 'We cannot indeed have a single Image in the Fancy that did not make its first Entrance through the Sight' (*Spectator* 416) lives on in Kames's argument that in 'fabricating images of things that have no existence', the imagination is limited to 'ideas of sight' (*Elements of Criticism*, II, pp. 403–4).

---

[43] See *Oeuvres complètes*, II, p. 113: 'ce qui m'a fait quelquefois comparer les fibres de nos organes à des cordes vibrantes sensibles ... Cet instrument a des sauts étonnants, et une idée réveillée va faire quelquefois frémir une harmonique qui en est à un intervalle incompréhensible.'

Even writing that appears to move boldly towards recognizing imagination as an independent power remains tied to a fundamentally visualist
discourse of ideas and images. Wellek says that 'The shift away from
Addison's meaning of imagination as visualization seems first accomplished in Edmund Burke's *Philosophical Inquiry* . . .' (*History of Modern Criticism*, I, p. 111). Burke does begin the *Enquiry* by seeming to
offer a different perspective: 'the mind of man possesses a sort of creative power of its own; either in representing at pleasure the images of
things in the order and manner in which they are received by the senses,
or in combining those images in a new manner, and according to a
different order. This power is called Imagination, and to this belongs
whatever is called wit, fancy, invention, and the like' ('Introduction', ed.
Boulton, p. 16). Yet Burke goes on to say that 'the imagination is only
the representation of the senses' (p. 17). The initial gesture signals a
shift – but it is a shift at odds with what turns out to be Burke's own
premise, as well as with Addison. In the important discussion of poetic
obscurity as a source of the sublime which we looked at earlier, Burke
shows himself still to be operating, albeit negatively, in relation to a
visualist paradigm: it is still in 'description' that the language of *Paradise Lost* produces those effects of sublime obscurity that demonstrate
a 'power to raise a stronger *emotion*' than even 'the best painting'. The
argument that words can affect us as 'mere sounds' without the signification of ideas diverges dramatically from the visualist paradigm, but
it does so in contradiction to the predominant representational assumptions of the *Enquiry*. Burke's claim that imagination exerts its creativity
by 'combining . . . images in a new manner, and according to a different
order' never breaks entirely from a visualist understanding of what
constitutes an 'image'.

In German criticism the grounding of 'imagination' in the visual 'image' appears as an analogous etymological configuration: *Einbildungskraft*
rests on the concept of *das Bild*, the picture or picturable image. As
Engell shows, however, Leibniz and Christian Wolff had attempted to
distinguish systematically between the Latin terms *imaginatio* and *Facultas
fingendi* in ways that opened up fresh critical perspectives on *Einbildungskraft* well before Burke's *Enquiry* was translated into German. Lessing
was keenly interested in the *Enquiry* and thought seriously of translating it during the period leading up to the publication of *Laokoon* (1766),
the most famous Enlightenment argument against identifying the poetic
with the pictorial imagination. One finds in Lessing's appeal to the 'free
play of the imagination' ('freyes Spiel der Einbildungskraft') the basis of
what will become a major trajectory in German critical discourse. While
Lessing himself retains the term *Einbildungskraft*, his influence must
have been determinative in promoting the ascendancy of *Dichtungskraft*
(or sometimes *Dichtungsvermögen*) as alternative equivalents to English

and French 'imagination' – equivalents that grant poetry, *Dichtung*, a privileged relation to creative mental power.

Einbildungskraft is never completely displaced by its alternatives – Kant, for example, gives it new and elevated life but holds on to it because, like 'imagination', it can designate an epistemological category that is not limited to a specific artistic mode and medium. Yet as Engell says, 'From 1770 on, the tendency to separate *Phantasie*, *Einbildungskraft*, and *Dichtungskraft* . . . is a common practice in German thought' (*Creative Imagination*, pp. 105–6). Many theorists beyond the familiar names of the *Sturm und Drang* circle contributed to the new critical initiative: Ernst Platner in his *Anthropologie für Aerzte und Weltweise* (1772, enlarged in 1790), Leonhard Meister in *Versuch über die Einbildungskraft* (1778) and in three other studies published between 1775 and 1795, and Sulzer, whose articles on *Einbildungskraft* and *Dichtungskraft* in his *Allgemeine Theorie* are especially relevant to the bearing of new German thinking about imagination on theories of poetry. Sulzer insists on distinguishing *Einbildungskraft*, the more generalized capacity of the mind to perceive the world as its own construction, from *Dichtungskraft* because the latter 'is a special attribute of the imagination, and is more extended and vivid' (*Allgemeine Theorie*, I, p. 684). Sulzer says that the poetic imagination has 'the power to create images from objects of the senses and of internal sensation, that have never been immediately perceived before', and in phrasing certainly echoed by Coleridge in his famous definition of the Secondary Imagination, he argues that in creating these new images the imagination must often dissolve and disconnect the perceptions of commonly received experience on its way to integrating them into a perfected organic totality (I, p. 683). Sulzer's discussion anticipates Shelley's *Defence* more strikingly even than Coleridge's *Biographia* in its idealizing emphasis on the distinctive power of language to engage the mind directly, independently of sensory mediation: 'Among artists the poet requires the power [of *Dichtungskraft*] in the highest degree, because . . . he never works for the senses, but for the imagination' (I, p. 638).[44] Here we really do see a break with the empiricist tradition, even as Burke and Lessing had absorbed and transformed it.

This tendency towards severing the poetic imagination from physical sensation has its limits – as Sulzer himself recognizes in saying that

---

[44] (1) 'Die Dichtungskraft ist eine Eigenschaft der Einbildungskraft, und ist desto ausgedehnter, je lebhafter diese ist.' (2) 'Das Vermögen, Vorstellungen von Gegenständen der Sinnen und der innern Empfindung, die man nie unmittelbar gefühlt hat, in sich hervorzubringen.' (3) 'Unter den Künstlern hat der Dichter dieses Vermögen im höchsten Grad nöthig, weil . . . er niemals für die Sinnen, sondern für die Einbildungskraft arbeitet.'

through imagination in its highest form 'the spiritual being of things becomes *visible* to us' ('wird das geistliche Wesen der Dinge uns *sichtbar*', my emphasis). Writers committed to a poetics of emotive immediacy and dense historical referentiality continued to promote an idea of imagination in which sense experience is transformed and intensified rather than marginalized and evaded. In Herder the drive to set poetry apart as the only art of pure imagination is powerful: poetry is 'the only fine art immediately for the soul' ('Die einzig schöne Kunst unmittelbar für die Seele', *Sämtliche Werke*, IV, p. 163); 'it works on the inner sense, not on the external eye of the artist' ('Auf den inneren Sinn wirket sie, nicht auf das äußere Künstlerauge', XVIII, p. 140). But as we have seen, Herder's devotion to lyric and to folk poetry and song always led him back to an emphasis on sound, voice, rhythm – from *Über den Ursprung der Sprache* of 1772 to 'Von der Natur und Wirkung der lyrischen Dichtkunst' in *Terpsichore* II of 1795 (*Sämtliche Werke*, XXVII, pp. 163–76). The sensuous dimension of language – primarily for Herder a matter of the ear and not of the eye – becomes a vital part of imaginative energy by being grounded in the emotive spontaneity of ancient cultural tradition.

It may be noted at this juncture that Herder is probably the most important literary figure of the late eighteenth century who definitely read Vico's *Scienza Nuova*, with its positing of a post-diluvian age of sensuous imagination.[45] More widely influential on later eighteenth-century theories of the imagination was Vico's contemporary Ludovico Muratori, whose *Della forza della Fantasia Umana* was published in Venice in 1740. Muratori's revival of Italian Renaissance notions of imaginative invention and fiction is mentioned prominently by Sulzer and by Friedrich von Blanckenburg, whose *Litterarische Zusätze zu Johann Georg Sulzers allgemeiner Theorie der schönen Künste* (1796) provides an inclusive survey of the German theoretical discourse on imagination in which Goethe, Kant, Schiller, and Tetens made their interventions.

Johann Nicolaus Tetens is never mentioned by Wellek, Wimsatt and Brooks, or Abrams, but Engell gives his *Philosophische Versuche über die Menschliche Natur und ihre Entwicklung* (1776–7) prominent attention and says that he and Kant 'stand like two colossi in their concepts of the imagination' (*Creative Imagination*, p. 118). In Engell's view, Tetens is Kant's most important forerunner – and later an important direct influence on Coleridge – primarily because of the ways in which he 'links together British associationists and investigators of genius, especially Gerard, with German transcendental thinkers' (p. 119). Tetens introduces a new term for 'imagination' in its most comprehensive sense:

---

[45] Wellek, *History of Modern Criticism*, p. 135.

Vorstellungskraft, literally 'presentation power', or as Tetens specifically understands it, the mind's power of 'presenting images internally' (I, p. 26). Included in Tetens's *Vorstellungskraft* are immediate perception ('Perceptionsvermogen' or 'Fassungskraft'), the arrangement of immediate perception in representation ('Wiederstellungkraft', or alternatively 'Phantasie' or 'Einbildungskraft'), and – in its highest manifestion – the formation of new images and ideas, which Tetens calls *Dichtungsvermögen* or *Dichtkraft*. Imagination as *Dichtkraft* is, for Tetens, 'a forming, creating power' ('ein bildende, schaffende Kraft'), a formulation that clearly privileges poetry as a mode of imaginative articulation, even though Tetens often adduces instances from the visual arts. His instances of *Dichtkraft* in writing are sometimes surprising, as in his praise of Swift's Brobdingnagians and Lilliputians (see Engell, *Creative Imagination*, p. 121). *Dichtkraft* is above all else plastic, unifying, vitalizing ('lebhaft') for Tetens. Explicitly following Gerard in connecting imaginative genius with willed intentionality, Tetens explains that in *Dichtkraft* the lower or more basic modes of imaginative activity rise to a higher level and become 'selbsthätige' – 'self-activating', 'self-generating', or even 'self-willed'.[46]

Nowhere is Tetens's importance for Kant more apparent than in his insistence on the imagination's critical epistemological role in representation, in imaging – through the function that Tetens calls 'das Bildliche' – the mind's otherwise entirely internalized concepts.[47] Kant's remarks on poetry in the *Critique of Judgement* are not extensive, but they are substantial enough to suggest how the increasingly central place of imagination in his philosophy of mind might apply to the production and reception of verbal works of art. In the section 'On the Division of the Fine Arts' which immediately follows his account of genius, Kant divides the 'arts of SPEECH' into *oratory* and *poetry* with axiomatic philosophical wit: 'Oratory is the art of engaging in a task of the understanding as [if it were] a free play of the imagination; *poetry* is the art of conducting a free play of the imagination as [if it were] a task of the understanding' (sec. 51, trans. Pluhar, p. 190; *Akademie* edn, V, p. 321). This intriguing distinction leads Kant to claim for poetry a kind of cognitive productivity in disguise: 'The poet . . . promises little and announces a mere play with ideas; but he accomplishes something worthy of [being called] a task, for in playing he provides food for the under-

---

[46] Engell, *Creative Imagination*, p. 124, quotes Tetens: '[Dichtungsvermögen] ist die selbsthätige Phantasie; das Genie nach Hrn. Girards [*sic*] Erklärung.' He goes on to note Coleridge's keen interest in the term *selbsthätige* in his marginalia to Friedrich Jacobi's *Über die Lehre des Spinoza* (1785).

[47] See Engell, *Creative Imagination*, p. 134: 'After reading Tetens (on 17 May 1779, Hamann wrote to Herder that Kant had Tetens always before his eyes, and Kant himself mentioned the use of Tetens) . . .'

standing and gives life to its concepts by means of the imagination' (p. 191).[48] Kant continues in this vein in section 53, 'Comparison of the Aesthetic Value of the Various Fine Arts': 'Among all the arts *poetry* holds the highest rank. (It owes its origin almost entirely to genius and is least open to guidance by precept or examples.) It expands the mind: for it sets the imagination free, and offers us, from among the unlimited variety of possible forms that harmonize with a given concept, though within that concept's limits, that form which links the exhibition of the concept with a wealth of thought to which no linguistic expression is completely adequate, and so poetry rises aesthetically to ideas' (trans. Pluhar, p. 196; *Akademie* edn, V, p. 326).[49] Kant goes on to argue for the intimate connection between poetry and music that we have come to see as characteristic of the ascendancy of lyric in the late eighteenth century. Though lacking the kind of specific exemplification – and more crucially the explicit philosophy of language – that would enable his observations to become immediately applicable in critical interpretation, Kant's celebration of poetry in the third *Critique* brings us to the verge of those romantic accounts of imaginative transcendence and aesthetic value of which he has come to be seen as the main philosophical progenitor.

More immediately, the third *Critique* brings us to the verge of that great philosophical and critical ferment of the German 1790s in which Herder, Fichte, Schiller, Tieck, Wackenroder, Schelling, and the Schlegels would contest and extend the Kantian position. This ferment is far too complex even to be sketched out here: Fichte's identification of Spirit with Imagination, *Geist* with *Einbildungskraft*, to cite just one of the major philosophical interventions, is too abstractly connected to poetry and poetics to be effectively digested in a survey of this kind, and in any case its bearings on theories of the poetic imagination are best grasped within the historical context of early nineteenth-century romanticism.[50]

---

[48] (1) 'Beredsamkeit ist die Kunst, ein Geschäft des Verstandes als ein freies Spiel der Einbildungskraft zu betreiben; Dichtkunst, ein freies Spiel der Einbildungskraft als ein Geschäft des Verstandes auszuführen.' (2) 'Der Dichter ... verspricht wenig und kündigt ein bloßes Spiel mit Ideen an, leistet aber etwas, was eines Geschäftes würdig ist, nämlich dem Verstande spielend Nahrung zu verschaffen und seinen Begriffen durch Einbildungskraft Leben zu geben.'

[49] 'Unter allen behauptet die Dichtkunst (die fast gänzlich dem Genie ihren Ursprung verdankt und am wenigsten durch Vorschrift, oder durch Beispiele geleitet sein will) den obersten Rang. Sie erweitert das Gemüth dadurch, daß sie die Einbildungskraft in Freiheit setzt und innerhalb den Schranken eines gegebenen Begriffes unter der unbegränzten Mannigfaltigkeit möglicher damit zusammenstimmender Formen diejenige darbietet, welche die Darstellung desselben, mit einer Gedankenfülle verknüpft, der kein Sprachausdruck völlig adäquat ist, und sich also ästhetisch zu Ideen erhebt.'

[50] Chapter 16 in Engell's *Creative Imagination* provides a good introductory discussion of Fichte's contribution.

But something does need to be said about Schiller's and Goethe's contributions to end-of-the-century discourse on imagination. Though Goethe read Kant as early as the 1780s and began commenting on him then, his more important critical pronouncements on imagination belong primarily to the later phase of his career. As part of his critical representation of *Sturm und Drang* ideology in *Werther*, however, Goethe articulates a concern with the dangerous, destructive power of poetic imagination that stands in sharp contrast to the transcendental enthusiasm we have just been examining: 'Our imagination, forced by its very nature to unfold, nourished by the fantastic visions of poetry, gives shape to a whole order of creatures of which we are the lowliest, and everything around us seems to be more glorious, everyone else more perfect' (*Werke*, IV, p. 440).[51] Schiller's thinking is, in part, an explicit attempt to address Goethe's concerns by locating a culturally and psychologically healthy alternative to the morbid instability of imaginative desire. In his *Letters on the Aesthetic Education of Man* (1795), Schiller rethinks Kant's recurrent appeal to 'the free play of the cognitive faculties' and introduces the concept of *Spieltrieb*, literally 'play-drive' or 'play-impulse', in an effort to name a mental force even more fundamental than *Dichtungskraft* and less troubled by accumulated problematic implications than *Einbildungskraft*. *Spieltrieb* creates the condition that Schiller calls 'lebende Gestalt', 'living form' (letter 15, *Werke*, XX, p. 355), in which the sensuous and historical content of a work of art is transvalued by being overtly detached from reality and from practical motivation and purpose. We can see Schiller working towards these enormously influential formulations – and begin to grasp some of their implications for the writing and reading of poetry – in his 1789 poem 'Die Künstler' (*Werke*, II [1], pp. 383–96).

Coleridge read Schiller's *Die Räuber* with great excitement when he was at Cambridge in the early 1790s. But it was not until after he and the Wordsworths went to Germany for ten months in 1798–9 that German literary and philosophical writing exerted a decisive influence on his thinking about the imagination. As we have seen, however, the poems written between 1795 and *Lyrical Ballads* (1798) contain speculative seeds that would later spring to full theoretical life after his reading of Tetens and Kant, Fichte and Schelling. There is a famous instance in 'The Aeolian Harp' (1795):

---

[51] 'Unsere Einbildungskraft, durch ihre Natur gedrungen, sich zu erheben, durch die phantastischen Bilder der Dichtkunst genährt, bildet sich eine Reihe Wesen hinauf, wo wir das unterste sind, und alles außer uns herrlicher erscheint, jeder andere vollkommener ist.' The English translation is that of Catherine Hunter, Signet Classic edition (1962).

Full many a thought uncall'd and undetain'd,
And many idle flitting phantasies,
Traverse my indolent and passive brain,
As wild and various as the random gales
That swell and flutter on this subject Lute!
   And what if all of animated nature
Be but organic Harps diversely fram'd,
That tremble into thought, as o'er them sweeps
Plastic and vast, one intellectual breeze,
At once the Soul of each, and God of all?

(ll. 39–48)

Coleridge revised this poem many times for subsequent editions (it first appeared in *Poems*, 1796), and it is often argued that his addition of an eight-line passage about 'The one Life within us and abroad' in 1817 demonstrates how undeveloped his thinking about the creative imagination still was in the late 1790s. Yet the original text – despite an emphasis on the mind's receptive passivity – does use the tropes of human artifice ('Lute') and natural energy ('random gales') to link the mind of the poet-speaker with an active cosmic power identified at once as 'Soul' and 'God'. The conceptual perspective, and even such terms as 'Plastic' and 'intellectual', may look back to Akenside, but Coleridge is already discovering a new potential in well-established patterns.

As for Wordsworth, it comes as a shock of perhaps more than mild surprise to notice that the word 'imagination' does not appear at all in the Advertisement to the first edition of *Lyrical Ballads* (1798), and that it appears just once in the 1800 Preface, with reference to 'Goody Blake and Harry Gill': 'I wished to draw attention to the truth that the power of the human imagination is sufficient to produce such changes even in our physical nature as might almost appear miraculous' (*Prose Works*, I, p. 150). We may assume that imagination had yet to acquire the awesome sublimity Wordsworth will attribute to it in Book VI of the 1805 *Prelude*, where its power is revealed in the poetic recollection of a moment in which the physical experience of the natural world is thwarted and negated, in which 'the light of sense / Goes out in flashes that have shewn to us / The invisible world' (VI, ll. 534–6). The linking of 'The power of the human imagination' with 'changes even in our physical nature' in the 1800 Preface is all the more arresting for the contrast it offers to the increasingly spiritualized and idealized emphasis of the later writing. For the Wordsworth of the Preface, imagination is still very much a matter of 'the mighty world / Of eye and ear'; it is these senses that 'half-create' the world they 'perceive' in the famous lines from *Tintern Abbey* (ll. 106–8). Wordsworth's own note on these lines tells us that they have 'a close resemblance to an admirable line of Young, the exact expression of which I cannot recollect'. What Wordsworth here half-remembers is *Night Thoughts* VI, l. 424, where the 'senses' 'half create the wondrous world they see'.[52] Wordsworth's borrowing from Young, at this moment in *Tintern Abbey* and in this way, is poised between implications that reach back to the extravagant mid-century birth of the cult of genius and forward into Wordsworth's own later moments of imaginative extremity.

For Blake, illustrator of Young's *Night Thoughts* (1796–8), imagination was also always a matter of eye and ear – but in a very different sense from Wordsworth's 'natural piety'. 'I know that This World Is a World of Imagination & Vision', Blake wrote to the Rev. John Trussler on 23 August 1799; 'I see Every thing I paint In This World, but Every body does not see alike ... to the Eyes of the Man of Imagination Nature is Imagination itself ... to Me This World is all One continued Vision of Fancy or Imagination' (*Poetry and Prose*, p. 702). To claim that Blake's visionary belief in the sensory imagination was in any formal sense influential on late eighteenth-century critical discourse would be mistaken: even his specially printed work was known to very few people. But Blake's art and ideas came to prominence in the late nineteenth century and have played a major role in this century in defining the revolutionary as well as the romantic imagination. For this very reason it is well to recognize how deeply responsive Blake was to his own late-eighteenth-century context. His convictions about human imagination were mystical and extreme, but they grew out of Blake's familiarity with the key eighteenth-century debates about the imagination's relation to sense experience, to emotion, to cultural norms, and to social conflict. Blake's astonishing vision of 'fearful symmetry' in 'The Tyger' (*Songs of Innocence and Experience*, 1794) is complexly connected to Akenside's vision of 'The unbounded symmetry of things' in *The Pleasures of Imagination* (I, l. 478). That the connection should turn on Blake's affirmation of a symmetry that is at once bounded or framed *and* fearful, politically as well as aesthetically, is just one of the surprising ways in which his radical figurings of imagination recall even as they challenge figurings which have come to epitomize the dominant tradition of critical thinking.

[52] See *Lyrical Ballads*, ed. Brett and Jones, pp. 116, 297.

5
Drama, 1660–1740

Maximillian E. Novak

In general, during this period of the drama, critical theory moved from a formal analysis of dramatic structure based on what critics thought to be rationalist principles to an affective theory in which the feelingful response of the audience was the crucial test of a play. In short, it changed from the prescriptive theories of François Hédelin, Abbé D'Aubignac, to those of the Abbé Du Bos with their rejection of mechanical principles of taste. The practical question of audience response to a medium such as the drama, however, was crucial. What the court or the city audience liked often had to be rationalized into a theoretical position. Few critics went so far as George Farquhar, who dismissed Aristotle as an amateur without any practical grasp of the real structure of a play,[1] but so practical a matter as how many days a play was performed might exert a not so subtle pressure on current dramatic theory.

Somewhat more complicated but still significant were the ways in which national power and contemporary fashions fascinated audience and critic alike. The period here under consideration saw the hegemony of French taste and French literature throughout Europe. Spain, which had dominated Europe militarily during the sixteenth and early seventeenth centuries, still had some influence over European taste; but just as the battle of the ambassadors in 1661 settled once and for all the relative status of these two nations, so French dramatic theory and practice was to triumph over the less regular forms of the Spanish theatre. For a small nation such as England, there was a constant pressure from the continent to conform to the taste of the age – a taste that was often inimical to British sensibilities.

I

Although published three years before the start of our period, the treatise of d'Aubignac, *La Pratique du théâtre* (translated into English in 1686

---

[1] Farquhar, *Works*, II, pp. 326–36.

as *The Whole Art of the Stage*), had a major influence upon dramatic presentations. While it may be regarded by some, more as a critical consensus of the quarrel over *Le Cid* that raged long between Corneille and the forces of Richelieu,[2] *La Pratique* argues its points with such assurance and authority that it would have taken a critic who was both learned in the literature of the theatre and fully experienced in staging plays to argue against d'Aubignac with any force. D'Aubignac appeals not directly to Aristotle's *Poetics*, but to reason as the basis for what he calls the 'Regles du Theatre'. His arguments need not depend upon the discredited authority of the ancients:

As to the first Objection; I answer, That the Rules of the Stage are not founded upon Authority, but upon Reason; they are not so much settled by Example, as by the natural Judgment of Mankind.[3]

What d'Aubignac regards as reasonable involves much more than the usual three unities that demanded that a single action take place at a single location within a twenty-four-hour period.

Probably the most striking statements of d'Aubignac arise out of his comparisons of the delusions created by the stage to those presented in a painting. The painting has no depth – there is nothing beneath the picture but the canvas – yet the viewer accepts what is perceived as a form of reality. The same is true of the matter presented on a stage. The figures seen are actually actors, but the audience by convention accepts them for what they appear to be. D'Aubignac argues that an individual who had never before viewed a play would have to learn how to understand it; otherwise, he would be unable to tell whether the kings on the stage were real kings or merely representations. According to d'Aubignac, just as perspective in painting has its scientific laws, so must the action of the drama have its reasonable laws. Marion Hobson suggests, and rightfully, that behind such pronouncements lies a profound distrust of illusion, a desire to control the imagination and limit the field of representation.[4]

According to d'Aubignac, our reason would tell us that time on the stage must be actual time; therefore, our sense of time should not be distorted. D'Aubignac thinks not merely in terms of the reality of the action, but also in terms of the experience of the viewer. Thus, time may be somewhat extended during an intermission between acts, when the imagination may be allowed some room. On the whole, however,

---

[2] See Gasté, *La Querelle du Cid, passim; Les sentiments de l'académie française sur le Cid*; Batiffol, *Richelieu et Corneille*.

[3] Quant à la premiere objection, je dis que les Regles du Theatre ne sont pas fondées en autorité, mais en raison. Elles ne sont pas établies sur l'example, mais sur le Jugement naturel d'Aubignac (*La Pratique du théâtre*, p. 26; English trans. as *The Whole Art of the Stage*, p. 22).

[4] Hobson, *The Object of Arts*, pp. 33–7.

d'Aubignac believes that the six hours for an action suggested by Scaliger are more in keeping with our sense of reality than the twenty-four allowed by the classicists.

D'Aubignac also elevates the concept of *liaisons des scènes* – the tying together of scenes by having an actor continuously on stage occupying space and thus creating a kind of fourth unity. This is referred to as 'vray-semblance' in the original and rendered 'Probability and Decency' by the English translator. Following the principles implicit in this concept, d'Aubignac sets out rules for character and action that must seem somewhat odd to readers of literature schooled in notions that began in the eighteenth century and that remain part of the realist movement in the novel – notions of psychological depth and ambiguity. In place of the latter, d'Aubignac offers rules of decorum based in part on rank and class. Whatever may happen in a play, kings must never be depicted as performing an action beneath the dignity of what might be expected of a monarch, and other figures in the drama are bound by similar strictures based on class and sex. This theory of d'Aubignac was not so much literary and critical as an ideological view of society transposed to stage productions.[5] D'Aubignac insisted on a world in which a hierarchical vision of the strictest order restrained the dangerous aspects of illusion.

Although Aristotle is often the authority for his arguments, d'Aubignac presents as his model the theatre of Corneille with its emphasis upon the conflict between love and an heroic ideal of 'gloire'. Love, or the kind of love depicted in seventeenth-century French tragedy, was hardly a subject treated in Greek tragedy, and some special pleading was necessary to justify such an innovation. D'Aubignac sees tragedy as a series of pathetic discourses; he notes that the French have their national emotions and that these exclude an interest in the death of a tyrant and specialize in an appreciation of the sacrifice of love for honour. The French, he further notes, prefer tragedy to comedy, and his discussion of comedy stresses its inferiority as a genre:

Comedy among us has remain'd long, not only in meanness and obscurity, but look'd upon as infamous, being chang'd into that sort of *Farce*, which we still retain at the end of some of our Tragedys; though they are certainly things without Art, or Grace, and only recommendable to the Rascally sort of Mankind, who delight in obscene, infamous words and actions.[6]

---

[5] Reiss, *Tragedy and Truth*, pp. 3–34.
[6] La Comedie est long-temps demeurée parmy nous non seulement dans la bassesse, mais dans l'infamie; car elle s'est changée en cette Farce ou impertinente bouffonnerie que nos Theatres ont soufferte en suite des Tragédies: Ouvrages indignes d'estre mis au rang des Poëmes Dramatiques, sans art, sans parties, sans raison, et qui n'estoient recommandables qu'aux maraux et aux infames, à raison des paroles deshonnestes et des actions impudentes qui en faisoient toutes les graces (d'Aubignac, *La Pratique du théâtre*, p. 146; English trans. as *The Whole Art of the Stage*, p. 143).

Corneille himself in his *Trois discours* (1660) was somewhat less appreciative of Aristotle, of the rules that were supposedly drawn from his
Poetics, and of ancient ideas of the appropriate passions for tragedy.
Corneille rejects the violence of Greek tragedy as inappropriate for
modern audiences – who would find incest to be almost inconceivable
– and, in general, defends his own practice of writing a type of tragedy
based on love and honour rather than on the exclusive passions of fear
and pity. Such an idea suggests the confidence that France had in its
own cultural values during the seventeenth and eighteenth centuries (a
confidence which, as shall be seen, is not at all evident in England).[7]

Saint-Évremond, for example, in his 'Dissertation sur le *Grand
Alexandre*', writes:

> To banish Love out of our Tragedies as unworthy of Heroes is to take away
> that secret Charm which unites our Souls to theirs by a certain Tie that
> continues between them. But then to bring them down to us by this
> common Sentiment, don't let us make them descend beneath themselves, nor
> destroy what they possess above Men. Provided this Discretion be observed,
> I dare affirm that there are no Subjects where so universal a Passion as love
> is may not be introduced naturally and without Violence.[8]

Saint-Évremond maintains that since the audience enjoys seeing women
on the stage, women should be shown expressing the emotions that
make them the most attractive and for which they are supposed to have
the greatest affinity. Similarly, he argues, in common with Corneille and
against Aristotle, that the age enjoyed seeing exemplary virtue in distress. Saint-Évremond ended his essay 'Of Ancient and Modern Tragedy' with what he called 'un sentiment hardi et nouveau':

> a new and daring thought of my own ... we ought, in tragedy, before all
> things whatever, to look after a greatness of soul well expressed, which
> excites in us a tender admiration. By this sort of admiration our minds are
> sensibly ravished, our courages elevated, and our souls deeply affected.[9]

---

[7] For a discussion of the particular nature of seventeenth-century tragedy as discourse,
'a kind of machine for attaching the right and true meaning to the activities of man
in society and of man in nature', see Reiss, *Tragedy and Truth*, pp. 9–26, 240–82.

[8] Rejetter l'amour de nos Tragedies comme indigne des Heros, c'est oster ce qui leur
reste de plus humain, ce qui nous fait tenir encore à eux par un secret rapport, et je
ne sçay quelle liaison qui demeure encore entre leurs ames et les nostres; mais pour
les vouloir ramener à nous par ce sentiment commun, ne les faisons pas descendre
au dessous d'eux, ne ruinons pas ce qu'ils ont au dessus des hommes. Avec cette
retenuë, j'avoüray qu'il n'y a point de sujets où une passion generale que la Nature
a melée en tout, ne puisse entrer sans peine et sans violence ('Le Grand Alexandre',
Oeuvres en prose, II, p. 96, lines 210–20; English trans. from *Works*).

[9] C'est qu'on doit rechercher à la Tragédie, devant toutes choses, une grandeur d'ame
bien exprimée, qui excite en nous une tendre Admiration. Il y a dans cette sorte
d'Admiration quelque ravissement pour l'esprit; le courage y est élevé, l'âme y est
touchée (Saint-Évremond, *Oeuvres en prose*, IV, p. 184; English trans. *The Works of
Monsieur de St Évremond*, II, p. 111).

With this advocacy of 'tender' admiration, Saint-Évremond sets the critical tone for the new theatre of Racine with its stress on character and the passions, a theatre that prepared the way for the thinking of Du Bos in the eighteenth century.

Meanwhile, in the writings of René Rapin a more rigid 'classical' doctrine held sway. While it would be a mistake to think that Rapin's Aristotle was any less a seventeenth-century creation than the French plays he critiqued, his unflinching loyalty to Aristotle and the models of the ancients still had considerable force. Rapin was particularly hard on the French propensity for making love the central element in their tragedies. He led up to his attack on 'gallantry' by praising the national character of the French:

Perhaps our *Nation*, which is naturally *Gallant*, has been oblig'd by the necessity of our *Character* to frame for our selves a *New System* of *Tragedy* to suit with our *Humor*. The Greeks, who were *popular Estates*, and who hated *Monarchy*, took delight in their *Spectacles*, to see Kings humbled, and High Fortunes cast down, because the Exaltation griev'd them. The *English*, our Neighbours, love Blood in their Sports by the Quality of their Temperament: These are *Insulaires*, separated from the rest of Men; we are more *Humane*. *Gallantry* moreover agrees with our *Manners*, and our Poets believ'd that they could not succeed well on the *Theatre*, but by sweet and tender *Sentiments*; in which, perhaps, they had some reason: For, in effect, the Passions represented become deform'd and insipid, unless they are founded on *Sentiments* conformable to those of the *Spectator*. 'Tis this that obliges our Poets to stand up so strongly for the Privilege of *Gallantry* on the *Theatre*, and to bend all their *Subjects* to *Love* and *Tenderness*; the rather, to please the Women, who have made themselves Judges of these *Divertissements*, and usurped the Right to pass Sentence.[10]

Rapin pretends to yield to the taste of his age, while in fact he is lamenting the loss of the Greek genius. He blames Spanish influence for introducing love intrigues and suggests that the French might well try

---

[10] Peut-estre que nostre nation, qui est naturellement galante, a esté obligée par la necessitée de son caractere à se faire un Systeme nouveau de Tragedie pour s'accommoder à son humeur. Les Grecs qui estoient des Estats populaires, & qui haissoient la Monarchie, prenoient plaisir, dans leurs spectacles, à voir les Rois humilés, & les grandes fortunes renversées: parce que l'élevation les choquoit. Les Anglois nos voisins aiment le sang, dans leurs jeux, par la qualité de leur temperament, ce sont des insulaires, separés du reste des hommes; nous sommes plus humains, la galanterie est davantage selon nos moeurs: & nos Poëtes ont crû ne pouvoir plaire sur le theatre, que par des sentimens doux & tendres: en quoy ils ont peut-estre eu quelque sorte de raison. Car en effet les passions qu'on represente deviennent fades & de nul goust, si elles ne sont fondées sur des sentimens conformes à ceux du spectateur. C'est ce que oblige nos Poëtes à privilegier si fort la galanterie sur le theatre, & à tourner tous leurs sujets sur des tendresses outrées, pour plaire davantage aux femmes, qui se sont érigées en arbitres de ces divertissemens, & qui ont usurpé le droit d'en decider (Rapin, *Réflexions*, II, Section XX, pp. 182–3; English translation from Rymer, *Reflections on Aristotle's Treatise*).

to do without such frivolities. It was Rapin's stand against such contemporary practices that may have inspired his translator, Thomas Rymer, to make a much more severe attack upon English theatrical productions.

Rymer found in Rapin a high moral tone. Although at first glance Rapin's approach would seem to offset Horace's persuasive and ubiquitous discussion of the profitable and the pleasurable, Rapin vigorously emphasizes the moral end of poetry, arguing that

> All *Poetry* that tends to the Corruption of Manners, is Irregular and Vicious; and *Poets* are to be look'd on as a publick Contagion, whose Morals are not pure.[11]

Rapin's tragic theatre is indeed a lecture hall in which the audience are taught to make the ethical distinction between a Clytemnestra who deserves to be slain for her killing of Agamemnon and a Hippolytus who dies despite being wholly virtuous. Thus tragedy serves as a homeopathic cure for pride and hardness of heart. For those who feel too much pity or are too fearful in their natures, tragedy serves as a regulator of these feelings by teaching the viewer to pity only those who deserve it and to show, by a revelation of the terrible things suffered by great men, that what is so common to all of humanity need not be feared. To teach these lessons, tragedy must stir the passions of the soul. Like so many writers on tragedy, Rapin seems to find in this activity of the passions – in the relief from their ordinary sluggishness – a source of genuine pleasure. Rapin ends his discussion on an ethical note. Like Le Bossu, who insisted that all literary plots, no matter how complex, have at their core a relatively simple, didactic moral lesson,[12] Rapin stresses the obligation of the theatre to raise the minds of its audience by providing examples of great actions. Although it was left to Rymer to develop the formula of 'poetic justice', the idea was inherent in the prescriptive rules of the seventeenth-century French critics.

Rapin implies a concept that found a more ardent exponent in Goldsmith during the next century – the notion that tragedy and other literatures are not truly international and that each national literature has its own unique essence expressing its own individual national character. Thus, when speaking of comedy, Rapin assigns it to the Italians, whom he finds 'naturellement Comediens'. Despite the genius of Molière, Italian *commedia dell'arte* dominated the image of comedy throughout the seventeenth century, and Watteau's magnificent paintings of the figures

---

[11] Toute Poësie qui est contre les moeurs est déreglée & vicieuse: l'on doit mesme traitter les Poëtes de corrupteurs & d'empoisonneurs publics, quand leur Morale n'est pas pure (Rapin's *Réflexions*, I, Section IX, p. 19; English trans. Rymer, *Reflections on Aristotle's Treatise*, II, Section IX, p. 143).

[12] Le Bossu, *Traité du poème épique*, *passim*.

from the Italian company in Paris offer almost an encyclopaedia of rococo iconography and artistry. Molière, of course, had his early training in the Italian mode, but broke away to create some of the most brilliant comedic theatre of the age. Along with his triumphs on the stage and their example, he left a few comments that became important for the theory of comedy. In the Preface to *Le Tartuffe*, Molière presented his play as an innocent amusement, at the same time defending the serious role of comedy as a social corrective – particularly of those who had attempted to repress the play. Once these ends were granted, Molière was in a position to defend a form of literary imitation in which a hypocrite must be portrayed as he is if the work is to be successful. In some sense, Molière appeals to a practical, realist aesthetic rather than to the prevailing rationalist model as the cornerstone of his defence. (This defence was similar to that employed by the English playwrights when Collier accused them of immorality and profaneness at the end of the seventeenth century.) A second document, *Lettre sur la comédie de l'imposteur* (1667), sometimes ascribed to Molière but probably by Cureau de la Chambre, was a defence of Molière's practice in writing comedy and an analysis of the psychological elements that produce laughter. The *Lettre* insisted on the essential coldness of comedy, its ability to detach the spectator from sympathy. In an area in which critical ideas have been in short supply, this contribution to a theory of comedy retains its significance.

II

With the exception of Jonson's version of Aristotle's *Poetics*, it may be said that there was almost nothing resembling a theory of drama in England before 1660 and little consistent in the drama of the 'Last Age' from which a theory might have been extracted. When Charles II returned to England, the monarchy was once again restored, and in dating his reign, the legal fiction of his having assumed the throne immediately after the beheading of his father, Charles I, appeared in all of the documents. But no such fiction could prevail in the world of theatre. The stage had been shut down for close to twenty years, and the thinking that went into James Shirley's remarks to the reader in the Beaumont and Fletcher folio of 1647 was that plays might be enjoyed more in the reading than in the seeing, since the theatre of the mind allowed for endless imaginative projections while the theatre of the stage prescribed the fantasy. Despite such consolation at a time when there were no plays to be seen, various attempts were made to start theatrical performances even before the King had arrived, and the companies of Thomas Killigrew and William Davenant moved rapidly toward establishing their theatrical repertories. The stock of old plays was divided up and remained a repertory to draw upon, but what of the new? What kind of play did the new Restoration audience want? Dramatic theory, particularly in the hands of John Dryden, its most ingenious practitioner in England, often appeared in the form of a preface accompanying the printed versions of his plays by way of justifying his written practices. Such pieces, when they became part of collected editions after 1700, formed a brilliant but often inconsistent body of criticism.

But if theory was to be invented to defend a given practice, what practice would best suit the Restoration audience? To some extent, English drama still depended on its native traditions. In his prologue to *The Tempest* (1667), Dryden presents Shakespeare as a force of nature – a tree whose abundant fruits nourished Jonson and Fletcher.

> *So from old* Shakespeare's *honour'd dust, this day*
> *Springs up and buds a new reviving play:*
> Shakespeare, *who (taught by none) did first impart*
> To Fletcher *wit, to laboring* Jonson *art.*
> *He, monarch-like, gave those, his subjects, law;*
> *And is that nature which they paint and draw,*
> Fletcher *reach'd that which on his heights did grow,*
> *Whilst* Jonson *crept, and gather'd all below*
> *This did his love, and this his mirth digest:*
> *One imitates him most, the other best.*[13]

Shakespeare seems to get high marks for a unique kind of magic in this play intended to boost his reputation along with that of his supposed descendant, Sir William Davenant, but at this date the jury was still out on which of this triumvirate would obtain the place as the great genius of the English theatre. Jonson was considered the most learned, but he was also the least popular; Fletcher was the most popular, but the playwright Dryden seems to have found him least imitable.

All three wrote plays that were less tightly organized than French plays and less exciting than contemporary Spanish plays with their plots of intrigue and disguise. Dryden and his contemporaries defended native drama for its variety. But with the attacks upon English plays beginning with Sorbière in 1663 and continuing with those of Voltaire and Riccoboni in the eighteenth century, English writers were made to feel a certain provinciality in their admiration of Shakespeare. Sorbière mocked the violation of the unities of time, place, and action and the lack of decorum in creating character:

[13] *The Works of John Dryden*, X, p. 6.

In representing a Miser, they make him guilty of all the basest Actions that have been practised in several Ages, upon divers Occasions and indifferent Professions: They do not matter tho' it be a Hotch Potch, for they say, they mind only the Parts as they come on one after another, and have no regard to the whole Composition.[14]

In this reply to Sorbière, Thomas Sprat defended the originality of English plays, their 'greater variety of actions', and their closer approximation to real life both in the use of blank verse rather than poetry and in the mingling of low and high characters. The French, on the other hand, Sprat argued, seem, oddly enough, to enjoy 'the grave Delight of Heroick Poetry; which the *French* Tragedies do resemble'.[15]

Although Sprat might wax furious about the insult to England – to the extent of defending English food as more sincere than French cooking – this was a period in which French dominance in politics and the arts had to leave defenders of English drama distinctly uneasy. Sprat may have thought the heroic boring and un-English, but it was nevertheless a passionate preoccupation of the age. Davenant, in the Preface to *Gondibert* (1650) addressed to Hobbes, argued that heroic poetry would inspire the people to show obedience to their superiors by creating an image of greatness to which princes and nobles might aspire and to which the ordinary citizen would react with a sense of awe. Davenant thought that the heroic could be conveyed through the drama as well as through the heroic poem.

In searching for images of greatness, English dramatists could find them both in the Spanish plays of *capa y espada* in which the heroic figures maintained a lofty sense of honour or in French drama with its heroes and heroines who pursued a sense of *gloire* or personal honour. The remarkable success of Samuel Tuke's *The Adventure of Five Hours* in 1663 seemed to suggest that the serious plays of Spain would be the major influence on English drama and theory, but the French model prevailed, with the major Spanish influence emerging in the comedy of the period. Versions of Corneille's *Le Cid* and *Pompey* were acted in 1662 and 1663, and Roger Boyle, Earl of Orrery, had the first English rhymed heroic play produced in Dublin in 1662, thereby initiating a form that dominated serious drama in England until 1677.

In defending the new rhymed heroic play, Dryden, in his *Essay of*

---

[14] Pour depeindre un avare, ils en font faire à un homme toutes les plus basses actions qui se prattiquent en divers âges, en diverses rencontres, & en diverses professions; Et il ne leur importe que ce soit un pot pourry; parce qu'ils n'en regardent disent-ils, qu'une partie apres l'autre, sans se soucier du total (Sorbière, *Relation d'un voyage en Angleterre*, p. 168; English trans. *A Voyage to England*, pp. 69–70).

[15] Sprat, *Observations*, in Sorbière's *A Voyage into England*, p. 168.

Dramatic Poesie, gave most of the best arguments among his four debaters to his spokesman Neander, although, in pursuit of a sceptical method of arranging an argument, the others, representing ancient drama (Crites), modern French drama (Lesideus), and the older English drama (Eugenius), also score some excellent points. Before beginning the debate, the four agree on the definition of a play as: '*A just and lively image of human nature, representing its passions and humours, and the changes of fortune to which it is subject, for the delight and instruction of mankind.*'[16] Both Eugenius and Neander argue that English drama is more lively than that either of the ancients or the modern French, despite the evident failure of the English to observe the unities of time, place, and action. By his careful examination of Jonson's *Epicene*, Neander suggests that the English dramatists could follow these mechanical rules of the drama if they wished, but points out that the French writings lack the variety and richness of the English. There is a certain irony in this, for just as Dryden was engaged in borrowing his dramatic plots from French and Spanish plays, so his theoretical positions are drawn mainly from French and continental sources. In much the same way, he abandons the 'natural' that Sprat had used to counter Sorbière, in favour of a heightened artistic effect, most notably in his defence of rhyme in serious plays. And of course, there was nothing more French about Dryden's heroic plays than this very use of rhyme.

After the success of *The Conquest of Granada* in 1672, Dryden proclaimed the triumph of the heroic play as a form over the drama of the 'Last Age', both in his witty epilogue to the second part of that play and also in 'An Essay on the Dramatic Poetry of the Last Age'. The latter attacks Shakespeare as often writing 'below the dullest writer' of the Restoration, Jonson for his lack of wit, and Fletcher for his inconsistency, and in return aroused a storm of criticism against himself.[17] But Dryden's triumphant new form hardly lasted out the decade. Among the effects of the form as Dryden practised it were moments in which the heroic figures dared to represent themselves in postures of greatness so extreme that the audience responded with nervous laughter. It was an effect that might easily slip into farce when practised by a lesser playwright, and with the reasonable facsimile of a Dryden heroic play, *The Empress of Morocco* (1673) by Elkanah Settle, and even more laughter, the end was in sight. Buckingham had already parodied the heroic play in *The Rehearsal* (1671), but what really finished it off was the debate between Settle and the triumvirate of Dryden, Shadwell, and Crowne. Against the accusation of using metaphor in an extreme and absurd manner, Settle was able to show that he was hardly doing anything that Dryden himself had not done. The effort to paint Settle as 'an enthusiast

---

[16] *Works*, XVII, p. 15.   [17] *Works*, XI, p. 213.

in poetry', who used metaphor in a wild and imprecise manner, ended by showing that the laureate, John Dryden, did much the same as his rival. From a theoretical standpoint, it directed English drama away from the heroic ideal recommended by Davenant and Hobbes, back to blank verse and toward a more 'natural' rendering of the passions. Not only Dryden, but Thomas Otway and Nathaniel Lee followed this path.

Although Dryden continued to be the most important critical spokesman for the drama, his failure to establish the highly artificial form of the heroic play left him vulnerable to a systematic critic such as Thomas Rymer. When Rymer's *The Tragedies of the Last Age* was published in the fall of 1678, Dryden had finished writing his *All for Love*, a blank verse play in which he thought he had discovered in the ample use of metaphor by Shakespeare, Daniel, and other Elizabethan playwrights a crucial new clue to writing poetic drama. His first response was critical of Rymer's ideas, and in some notes, 'Heads of an Answer to Rymer', he advanced a number of bold positions on the superiority of English theatre in raising the passions through a much higher level of poetry than might be discovered in French drama and through exploring a rich and varied selection of tragic subjects unburdened by the French insistence on always treating love. By the time he came to publish his 'Grounds of Criticism in Tragedy', which was prefixed to his *Troilus and Cressida*, an attempt to turn Shakespeare's tragic satire into a tragedy along contemporary French lines, Dryden had caved in to Rymer's rigid insistence that the tragedies of the 'Last Age' were successful on the stage only because of excellent acting and that it was irrational for a modern English audience to continue to be entertained by a literary form that displayed violence on the stage, broke all the reasonable rules of the drama, and violated 'poetic justice'.

In Rymer's approach may be found some elements of the battle between the Ancients and the Moderns, in which the Moderns are seen as improving themselves by learning directly from the authors of Greek tragedy and ridding themselves of their 'Gothic' past. Since Dryden had boasted of the superiority of modern drama to the writers of the 'Last Age', he had to see some part of his own critical position in Rymer's *Tragedies of the Last Age*. Rather than repeat what Rymer had asserted so dogmatically, Dryden chose to go to Rymer's French sources, particularly the criticism of René Rapin, Nicolas Boileau, and René Le Bossu. Under their influence, he throws out irregular 'Spanish *Plots, where accident is heap'd upon accident, and that which is first might as reasonably be last*',[18] accepts a theory of character in which one passion is clearly dominant and decorum maintained according to the position of

---

[18] *Works*, XIII, p. 230.

the character in society, and criticizes Shakespeare for obscurity of language and thought. Under the influence of Boileau, he also accuses Shakespeare of bombast – of a distortion of the true sublime.[19] Although he throws in a little criticism of Racine and some praise of Shakespeare, Dryden clearly brings his criticism into line with the French on almost all important concepts. After this commitment to French ideals, Dryden, in his later critical comments, relaxed his stance and gave in to the practical demands of the theatre audience. Although he occasionally appears to comply with good grace, overall Dryden did not conceal his unhappiness at this triumph of popular taste.

Rymer's attempt at tragedy, *Edgar*, proved to be a notable failure, but his critical demand that tragedy reveal 'poetic justice' at the end with the good rewarded and the evil punished, along with his insistence upon the rationality of the rules, was influential in shaping English tragedy during the eighteenth century. Nicholas Rowe, the most popular writer of tragedies in England during the eighteenth century, may have championed Shakespeare, but his own form of 'providential tragedy' was exemplarily moral in its purpose and, for the most part, French in its design. The popularity of Shakespeare on the stage seemed a living rebuke to the theories of the drama put forth by the French critics, but it is notable that efforts were made to revise tragedies such as *Hamlet* and *Othello* so as to satisfy the three unities of action, time and place and that plays such as *Antony and Cleopatra* not amenable to revisions of this kind were never popular.

What the great actor Edmund Kean found when playing tragedy, as compared to comedy – that tragedy was easy, but comedy hard – might be applied to the critical statements about comedy. Since the Aristotelian approach made comedy a species of the ugly, a critic such as Dryden might well complain at having to work in such a debased medium. One way of elevating the status of comedy was to distinguish it from farce, though it may be said that, except where it was applied to the grotesque mimes of characters from *commedia dell'arte*, the term 'farce' was generally used in a vague manner to denigrate the comedies of other playwrights. (*I* write comedy; *they* write farce.) The earliest controversy over comedy in Restoration England involved Shadwell, who advocated a continuation of Jonson's comedy of the humours and opposed the new writers of wit comedy such as Sedley and Dryden. Shadwell complained about plays in which the 'Wit . . . consisted in bringing two persons upon the Stage to break jests, and to bob one another, which they call Repartie, not considering that there is more wit and invention requir'd in the f[ind?]ing out good Humor, and Matter proper for it,

---

[19] See Boileau-Despréaux, *Oeuvres*, pp. 342–5, 405–8.

than in all their smart reparties.'[20] Shadwell claimed for his comedies a higher moral purpose as well as a superior artistry, which required the playwright to satirize vices and to create characters dominated by a single humour. Dryden's preface to *An Evening's Love* sets out his view of the achievement of Restoration comedy in '*refining . . . Courtship, Raillery, and Conversation*' far beyond anything that Jonson managed. He appeals to a type of urbane comedy as the ideal and argues that the amusement arising from the conversation of witty characters is produced by 'a pleasure that is more noble' than the laughter arising from farce.[21] Like the author of *Lettre sur la comédie de l'imposteur*, Dryden sees comedy as creating a certain distance between the objects of laughter in the play and the audience. As for the morality of comedy, its ethical points are made indirectly:

For it works first on the ill nature of the Audience; they are mov'd to laugh by the representation of deformity; and the shame of that laughter, teaches us to amend what is ridiculous in our manners. This being, then establish'd, that the first end of Comedie is delight, and instruction only the second; it may reasonably be inferr'd that Comedy is not so much oblig'd to the punishment of the faults which it represents, as Tragedy.[22]

Dryden's discomfort with laughter, as an action that creates a form of shame or embarrassment, is echoed in contemporary books on manners. If farce causes open guffaws, wit comedy produces intellectual delight and only occasional laughter. Dryden's preface, with its variety of quotes from the classics, attempts to overwhelm his enemies with a kind of hauteur, and his final statement on craft and artistry suggests that only he and a few other writers are capable of producing true comedy.

Congreve may be regarded as the master of the kind of comedy Dryden admired, but Congreve's rhetoric makes no effort to disparage the form itself. Like Dryden, Congreve argued for the artful construction of comedy, but in his letter to John Dennis on humour in comedy, he refines the theories of the ridiculous as set out by Molière and Dryden: 'Humour is neither Wit, nor Folly, nor Personal defect; nor Affectation, nor habit', writes Congreve, 'and yet each . . . have been both written and received for Humour'.[23] What Congreve has to say on humour – that it is rooted in a dominant and fixed character trait – is less interesting than his concept of comedy as a mixture of elements

---

[20] Shadwell, Preface to *The Sullen Lovers*, *Works*, I, p. 11.
[21] *Works*, X, p. 209. Dryden sees comedy as creating a certain distance between the objects of laughter in the play and the audience. As for the morality of comedy, its ethical points are made indirectly.
[22] *Works*, X, p. 209.   [23] In Congreve, *Letters & Documents*, p. 177.

from the 'Personal defect' associated with farce and low comedy to 'Habit', by which he means the comedy arising from taking characters with particular occupations and a concomitant vernacular and placing them in an estranging context.[24] Although he made use of all the elements of comedy in his plays, for Congreve, the essence of comedy arises from affectation – from social pretence. When characters pretend to a form of behaviour (often an ideal which Congreve upholds) and then reveal to the audience the degree to which their real behaviour is entirely different, they subject themselves to laughter. Thus, in a play such as *The Double Dealer*, almost all of the characters open themselves to ridicule and to laughter by affecting virtues they do not possess. In the following century, this approach to comedy had a major influence upon Fielding, refining both his comedies and farces and his novels.

III

A few years after Congreve's letter to Dennis, a non-juring clergyman, Jeremy Collier, published *A Short View of the Profaneness and Immorality of the English Stage* (1697 [1698]). This attack upon Restoration drama, particularly Restoration comedy, produced a major change in English drama, although Collier's *Short View* contained little in the way of moral condemnation that had not been set forth by William Prynne a half century earlier. What was new was the combination of a typical jeremiad against the stage with a Rymeresque type of literary criticism that discovered immorality in violations of decorum in the treatment of almost all the couples of Restoration comedy. Collier took the stage as a direct representation of the world and managed to discover statements that were in general demeaning of the clergy in almost every play. Since he regarded any use of language that had a prior use in the Bible as sacrilegious, almost every dialogue in every play fell under suspicion. More significantly, Collier questioned whether the theatre had any right to make serious moral statements about society when the same might more appropriately be done by a clergyman. Collier's bombast had the very real effect of causing actors to be physically attacked and theatres threatened with riots. Revised to suit a more stringent moral code, many Restoration plays, particularly comedies, were rendered innocuous and worthless. The new comedies tended to avoid offending; lacking any satiric bite, they often became dull.[25]

[24] Congreve mentions the use of '*Humour*' and '*Humourously*' in its present meaning, but in an essay which resembles some of Saint-Évremond's on a given critical term, Congreve prefers to narrow the meaning of the complex of words associated with 'humour'.

[25] For a general account of Collier's attack on the stage in the context of similar attacks, see Barish, *The Antitheatrical Prejudice*, especially pp. 221–55.

At the same time that Congreve was writing what was clearly a continuation of the mode generally known as Restoration Comedy (and would go on to conclude with the classic *The Way of the World* written after Collier's attack), some playwrights began introducing into their work a pathetic strain, which was to lead to the form of comedy known as 'Sentimental Comedy'. While Colley Cibber may be given credit for creating the first comedy that attempted to achieve an effect that may be described as *joyous sadness*, the theorist and practitioner of the new movement must be identified as Richard Steele. His plays, written during the first decade of the eighteenth century, presented scenes involving tearful reunions, and his attacks on the indecency of Etherege's *Man of Mode* in the *Spectator* suggested an approach to comedy that might almost have satisfied Jeremy Collier. Steele's essays prepared his readers for the preface to *The Conscious Lovers*, in which he defended a 'Joy too exquisite for Laughter' as being a superior form of comedy and the tears shed by the audience as a response better than laughter.[26] The production of sentimentality is a complex matter, but the appeal to stock types of situations, such as the meeting between the long lost child and her father, along with masking ideological attitudes toward women and the poor, make up a blend of elements that were not purely literary.

When Du Bos published his *Réflexions critiques sur la poësie et sur la peinture* in 1719, the movement toward a new age of sentiment, sincerity, and sympathy was already well established. In Britain, John Dennis had already settled upon the emotions aroused by the sublime as the most important element of the drama and had nominated Shakespeare as one of the 'greatest Geniuses that the World e'er saw for the Tragick Stage' as well as one of the greatest writers of comedy. Dennis's *Essay on the Genius and Writings of Shakespeare* (1712) leaves no doubt that a familiarity with the rules of dramatic writing would have improved Shakespeare's works, but in quoting Milton's image of Shakespeare as the playwright 'warbling his native woodnotes wild', Dennis still extols Shakespeare as a genius 'touching the passions', particularly 'the Master Passion . . . Terror' and allows him great powers of judgement and great poetic gifts.[27] Similarly, John Hughes, in *Guardian* 37, illustrated how Shakespeare had triumphed by the power of his psychological insight into the passion and character of Othello.[28] Hughes's essay begins the praise for Shakespeare's power of characterization, a quality that was to dominate Shakespeare criticism throughout the century and that even

---

[26] Steele, *Plays*, p. 299.   [27] In *Critical Works*, II (4), pp. 1,939–43.

[28] Hughes dismissed Rymer's extended attack on *Othello* in his *Short View of Tragedy* (1692) as the result of the 'Mechanical Judgment' by a critic lacking both sensitivity and a knowledge of psychology. See *The Guardian*, ed. Stephens, pp. 150–3.

Pope allows in his unenthusiastic Preface to his edition of Shakespeare (1725). For all of these critics – Dennis, Hughes, and even Pope – the grounds of criticism were the same as they would later be for Voltaire, but whereas Voltaire saw only a monster, these British critics still managed to recognize Shakespeare's brilliance.

Jean-Baptiste Du Bos was the first to create a systematic theory of tragedy based on realistic representation and the moving of the passions. He remarked at the beginning of his treatise, 'Tis observable, that we feel in general a greater pleasure in weeping, than in laughing at a theatrical representation' ('Généralement parlant les hommes trouvent encore plus de plaisir à pleurer, qu'à rire au théâtre').[29] Like Hume, later in the century, Du Bos saw the passions as sluggish and the human psyche in need of sense impressions. Tragedy, to a lesser extent, duplicates the violent arousal of the passions experienced by the witnesses to an execution, and whatever the lesson to be learned from such a spectacle, there is a spillover of sheer feeling. And if viewing an execution had its pleasures for the eighteenth century, tragedy, Du Bos believed, provided even more enjoyment insofar as it was uncontaminated by sorrow.

Curiously enough, Du Bos draws upon English critics to make some of his points. He defers to an English poet's (Dryden's?) mockery of an excessive use of love in French tragedy and uses Addison once more to object to Corneille's use of ornate language, rather than noble and natural sentiment, to drive home a point. What is needed from great art is a force of impression. But Du Bos maintains a position familiar to those treating Shakespeare in England, when he argues that the pleasure of reading is so great that

the best poem is that which engages us most; that which bewitches us so far, as to conceal from us the greatest part of its faults, and to make us even willingly forget those we have seen, and with which we have been offended.[30]

Since what is involved is feeling and not reason, the theatrical audience is generally as good a judge of the drama as the learned critic. Despite this theory which suggests that the audience is involved with the work of art to the extent that the critical faculties are suspended, Du Bos did not believe that the audience ever lost its sense of being in a theatre for more than a few moments. Pleasure is possible even though we know that we are witnessing art rather than life; and as with the hypothetical

---

[29] Du Bos, *Réflexions critiques*, I, p. 2; trans. Thomas Nugent, *Critical Reflections*, I, p. 2.

[30] Le meilleur poëme est celui dont la lecture nous interesse davantage; que c'est celui que nous séduit au point de nous cacher la plus grande partie de ses fautes, & de nous faire oublier volontiers celles mêmes que nous avons vûes, & que nous ont choquez. (Du Bos, *Réflexions critiques*, I, p. 287; English trans. I, p. 242.)

execution discussed above, the experience may be untainted by the complex passions aroused by real events.

In Du Bos's discussion of the drama appear many of the critical concepts that did not become commonplace in British criticism until mid-century. Indeed, some of his remarks seem to prepare the way for Coleridge's pronouncements in the nineteenth century. The comparative method of Du Bos allowed him to import, into his discussion of the drama, ideas that had long been familiar in the treatment of painting or music. Thus, the idea of individual genius was common in the criticism of painting, where the emergence of Renaissance artists of undeniable brilliance had removed any necessity for deferring to the greatness of the ancients, but less common in literary criticism. This notion of genius arising without apparent explanation from hovel or court allowed a more satisfactory treatment of Shakespeare than that proclaiming him to be 'divine' or an emanation of 'nature'. Similarly, Du Bos praises originality and invention as the chief gifts of genius and establishes his points with illustrations from the drama as well as from the other arts. His account of ancient drama, by analysing the development of human speech and language itself, suggests a theatre that embodied dance, gesture, and music. He quotes Dacier, who suggested that were one to follow Aristotle too closely, one might believe that the Greek drama was similar to opera, which both Dacier and Du Bos considered a grotesque mode.[31] Despite this seeming agreement with Dacier, Du Bos conceives of ancient drama as a perfect blend of music, dance, gesture, and words, all interactive and extraordinarily effective.

It would be a mistake to see Du Bos as the father of something like the dramatic opera of a Wagner or Verdi, but certainly the effect of his theories led to a broader concept of the possibilities of the stage. If the contemporary theatregoers he imagined still kept their awareness of the stage as delusion, Du Bos prepared the way for the audience of consumers that Hobson sees developing around the middle of the century, an audience completely immersed in the illusion of the theatre.[32]

[31] 'Les opéras sont, si je l'ose dire, les grotesques de la Poésie'. Du Bos III, p. 9; English trans. III, p. 67.A.
[32] See Hobson, *The Object of Arts*, pp. 180–93.

6

Drama, after 1740

John Osborne

The theory and criticism of neo-classical drama at its height had been based on principles of generic purity and exclusiveness; the three dramatic genres, tragedy, comedy and pastoral together were held to provide a complete picture of human life in its three forms; the life of the court, the life of the town and the life of the country (d'Aubignac, *Pratique*, p. 142). Such notions, which had previously been subject to only isolated questioning, came increasingly under fire during the earlier part of the eighteenth century and, from 1740 onwards, the overriding tendency was towards convergence rather than distinction of the genres. As the aristocratic court societies were confronted by an increasingly self-confident urban bourgeoisie, the theatre, the most public of literary media, became increasingly exposed to the demands of a social group looking for the serious treatment of its own values and feelings, and finding its spokesmen as much among the theorists and critics of drama as among the practising dramatists. Initially the debate took place with reference to the definitions provided by Aristotle, which earlier commentators had taken to refer to the social status of the participants in the drama. Only with the emergence of a new historicist aesthetics in the 1770s did the absolute validity of the Aristotelian model come to be called in question; this signalled the end of one line of dramatic criticism and opened the way for a bolder and more innovative approach to drama than had been adopted in the eighteenth century.

Throughout this period politics, society and culture did, of course, develop in different ways and at different speeds in the various countries of Europe. At the time of the English Revolution of 1688 Germany was barely beginning to recover from the ravages of the Thirty Years War; even a century later, when France was experiencing its Revolution, Germany remained a fragmented and politically underdeveloped country, where literary criticism was only just beginning to flourish in a still limited bourgeois public sphere. Equally diverse were the literary traditions of the major European countries and the character of their respective 'classical', that is to say national, drama. In Britain the massive presence of Shakespeare as the dominant playwright in the live theatre and as the major focus of dramatic criticism had made it difficult for

Aristotelian theories of drama to secure a firm hold. The Restoration was the first period to have witnessed a serious discussion of the neo-classical position; though, of course, this continued into the eighteenth century. By contrast, in the France of the early eighteenth century the tragedies of Racine (d. 1699; *Phèdre*, 1677) and the criticism of Boileau (d. 1711; *L'Art poétique*, 1674) were still fresh in the memory and represented classical norms which had to be swept aside before new avenues could be freely explored. In Italy, on the other hand, the obstacle to renewal took the form of the indigenous *commedia dell'arte*, with its tradition of improvisation around a conventional scenario; whilst in Germany the great classics, the Weimar dramas of Goethe and Schiller, would not be written until after the domestic tragedies of the eighteenth century.

So far ahead was England that its major domestic tragedy, George Lillo's *The London Merchant*, had made its appearance as early as 1731, its author claiming in his prologue a line of descent through Southerne, Rowe and Otway. Neither the play itself, nor the short critical essay which constitutes its dedication, had a great deal of influence on the development of drama in its country of origin, but it was to catch the attention of the major French dramatic theorist of the age, Diderot, and – partly through him – his German counterpart, Lessing. The issues identified by Lillo, implicitly or explicitly, will have to be discussed further below, for they are constants in dramatic criticism in Europe over the next fifty years. These issues include: the question of the moral or didactic function of drama; the social restrictions conventionally applied to characters in tragedy and the consequent limitation of the subject matter of serious drama so as to exclude 'moral tales in private life'; the emotional relationship between the dramatic characters and the audience and how this might be furthered; and in the background there is the related question of scenic illusion (Lillo, *London Merchant*, pp. 3f.).

It is possible to find traces of the ideas behind Lillo's attempt to 'enlarge the province of the graver kind of poetry' even in the France of the classical period. The most notable example occurs in the *Épître dédicatoire* to Corneille's *Don Sanche d'Aragon* (1650). Citing Aristotle's definition of tragedy, Corneille rightly insists that in the *Poetics* the hero is characterized only in terms of his personal moral qualities and the effects these might produce, and without any reference at all to his social rank: 'when [Aristotle] examines the qualities necessary in the hero of a tragedy, he does not mention birth at all, but emphasises only the events of his life and his conduct'. He then proceeds to anticipate certain of the arguments which were to become current in the eighteenth century by claiming that the effectiveness of tragedy will be increased if the audience is permitted to witness the sufferings of those who resemble them in social terms:

now if it is true that this latter feeling [fear] is aroused in us by its representation only when we see the suffering of people like ourselves, and that their misfortunes make us feel similar ones, is it not also true that fear could be aroused more strongly by our witnessing misfortunes which befall people of our own rank, whom we resemble completely?[1]

Corneille's primary purpose here was not, in fact, to contribute to the theory of tragedy, but to provide, by analogy, the justification for a new kind of comedy, *comédie héroïque*, which infringes the conventions by taking its characters from the ranks of the nobility and whose genre is determined solely by the nature of its action: '*Don Sanche* is in truth a comedy, although all the actors in it are either kings or Spanish noblemen, since there arises in it no peril by which we could be moved to pity or fear'.[2] In doing this Corneille anticipates in an exemplary manner the necessary convergence of two mutually exclusive genres, the one hitherto concerned with the heroism of noble public persons, the other with the ridicule of lowly private persons. It was to be left to a later generation, however, to fill the space between these extremes with a comedy without ridicule or a tragedy lacking any far-reaching public catastrophe, both instead being devoted to the serious treatment of the private lives of men and women of average condition. Corneille himself did not persevere with this mixed genre. The dedicatory essay was omitted from the later edition of *Don Sanche d'Aragon*; and in his *Discours de la Tragédie* (1660), when he returns to the passage from the *Poetics* which he had discussed previously: 'We have pity ... for those whom we see suffering an undeserved misfortune and we fear that a similar misfortune might overtake us when we see people like ourselves suffering', he redefines identity in terms of common humanity rather than social equality between dramatic characters and audience: 'these kings are men just like the members of the audience'.[3] For all that he is reverting

---

[1] '... quand il examine lui-même les qualités nécessaires au héros de la tragédie, il ne touche point du tout à sa naissance, et ne s'attache qu'aux incidents de sa vie et à ses moeurs ... Or, s'il est vrai que ce dernier sentiment ne s'excite en nous par sa représentation que quand nous voyons souffrir nos semblables, et que leurs infortunes nous en font appréhender de pareilles, n'est-il pas vrai aussi qu'il y pourrait être excité plus fortement par la vue des malheurs arrivés aux personnes de notre condition, à qui nous ressemblons tout à fait?' (Corneille, *Théâtre*, II, pp. 606–8).

[2] '*Don Sanche* est une véritable comédie, quoique tous les acteurs y soient ou rois ou grands d'Espagne, puisqu'on n'y voit naître aucun péril par qui nous puissions être portés à la pitié ou à la crainte' (Corneille, *Théâtre*, II, p. 609).

[3] 'Nous avons pitié ... de ceux que nous voyons souffrir un malheur qu'ils ne méritent pas, et nous craignons qu'il ne nous en arrive un pareil, quand nous le voyons souffrir à nos semblables ... ces rois sont hommes comme les auditeurs' (Corneille, *Trois Discours*, pp. 76–8; see also Adams, *Dramatic Essays*, pp. 2f.).

here to a more conservative position, and notwithstanding his essentially stoic attitude towards the emotions, in emphasizing the shared experience of passion as the source of empathy Corneille is anticipating another of the principles which will underlie the new drama of eighteenth-century Europe: the aesthetic of sentimentalism. We have already seen traces of this in the dedication to *The London Merchant*; but before then this central principle will have received one of its clearest and most influential statements in the *Réflexions critiques sur la poësie et sur la peinture* (*Critical Reflections on Poetry and Painting*, 1719) by the Abbé Du Bos:

> we are principally sensitive to the troubles and afflictions of those who resemble us in their passions. All the discourses which bring us back to ourselves and confront us with our own feelings have a special attraction for us. It is therefore natural to have a predilection for imitations which depict other versions of ourselves, that is to say persons consumed by passions which we feel at present or which we have felt in the past.[4]

Even as late as 1740, however, these new ideas and their dramaturgical consequences had not begun to penetrate into Germany. Here the principal dramatic critic of the time, Johann Christoph Gottsched, saw it as his task to improve the condition of dramatic literature and the theatre by communicating to the German-speaking world those rational and absolute principles which were perceived to have informed the great neo-classical dramas of the admired and envied French neighbour. There is a certain analogy with the attempts of Luigi Riccoboni and subsequently Goldoni to adapt the *commedia dell'arte* to literary drama, except that the native German tradition lacked the vitality and durability of the *commedia*. Gottsched's *Versuch einer Critischen Dichtkunst* (*An Essay in Critical Poetics*, 1731) was a work of great authority in its day, although it lacked originality and did not advance significantly beyond André Dacier's commentary on the *Poetics* (1692). For all his efforts at the integration of literature into the life of the German middle classes, Gottsched happily argues for the perpetuation of the convention which excluded this very stratum of society from tragedy:

> A tragedy ... is an instructive moral poem in which an important action among noble persons is imitated and presented on the stage.... Tragedy is an image of the misfortunes encountered by the great men of this world

---

[4] '... nous sommes sensibles principalement aux inquiétudes comme aux afflictions de ceux qui nous ressemblent par leurs passions. Tous les discours qui nous ramènent à nous-mêmes, et qui nous entretiennent de nos propres sentimens, ont pour nous un attrait particulier. Il est donc naturel d'avoir de la prédilection pour les imitations qui dépeignent d'autres nous-mêmes, c'est à dire, des personnages livrez à des passions que nous ressentons actuellement, ou que nous avons ressenties autrefois' (Du Bos, *Réflexions*, II, p. 123).

and which are either borne steadfastly and courageously or heroically overcome.[5]

Similarly he accepts that comedy should be reserved for those lower down the social hierarchy, although Gottsched, like most of the critics of this period, does not exclude the lower aristocracy when acting in a private capacity:

The persons who belong in comedy are common citizens or people of modest rank. Not because the great individuals of this world are not in the habit of committing follies which are ridiculous: no, but because it is not compatible with the respect which is due to them to depict them as ridiculous.[6]

In this latter instance, however, Gottsched offers an essentially pragmatic and politically conservative justification for the exclusiveness of the genre, and this is indicative of a certain weakening of the aesthetic principle. This is further evident in Gottsched's own subsequent practice as a critic, even though he did not prove flexible enough to adapt completely to the changing situation after 1740. Nevertheless, in reasserting the moral function of drama, the principle of *mimesis* and the importance of adherence to a set of normative rules, he set the agenda for the theoretical and critical discussion of drama in Germany at least up to the 1770s. Even Lessing, Gottsched's most trenchant critic, will still conduct the debate on Gottsched's Aristotelian terms.

It is a paradox that the conscious, if limited, attempts of the tragedian, Corneille, to provide a theoretical basis for, and a practical example of, the new intermediate form of drama, which he described with an oxymoron as *comédie héroïque*, should have had little or no direct impact, whereas the comedian, Molière, should have been such a productive stimulus to criticism during the following century, for Molière had no theoretical ambitions and his plays not only adhered firmly to the principle enunciated by Batteux and others that the function of comedy was the representation of the ridiculous aspects of the life of the bourgeoisie, but did so quite mercilessly and without any sentimental softening. It is true that the satirical dimension of Molière's comedy embraced much that might have been expected to appeal to progressive

---

[5] 'Ein Trauerspiel ... ist ein lehrreiches moralisches Gedichte, darin eine wichtige Handlung vornehmer Personen auf der Schaubühne nachgeahmet und vorgestellt wird ... Die Tragödie ist also ein Bild der Unglücksfälle, die den Großen dieser Welt begegnen und von ihnen entweder heldenmütig und standhaft ertragen oder großmütig überwunden werden' (Gottsched, *Schriften*, p. 5).

[6] 'Die Personen, so zur Komödie gehören, sind ordentliche Bürger oder doch Leute von mäßigem Stande. Nicht als ob die Großen dieser Welt etwa keine Torheiten zu begehen pflegten, die lächerlich wären: Nein, sondern weil es wider die Ehrerbietung läuft, die man ihnen schuldig ist, sie als auslachenswürdig vorzustellen' (Gottsched, *Schriften*, p. 189).

Enlightenment rationalism: the criticism of religious hypocrisy or the depiction of tensions between the social classes, but the point of view is that of the court. There is a strongly conservative basis to Molière's comic characterization of figures such as Alceste (*Le Misanthrope*) and M. Jourdain (*Le Bourgeois gentilhomme*). Unlike Corneille's oxymoron, Molière's ('le bourgeois gentilhomme') does not represent a challenge to convention, but indicates a discrepancy whose acceptance is the source of the ridicule. Satire is designed not so much to educate the bourgeois as to demonstrate the limits of his educability. In the long run this could not but prove provocative to a criticism inspired by a new bourgeois self-confidence.[7]

Shortly after the middle of the century, in fact, the moral indifference of the 'perfidious' comedy of Molière provoked an indignant rejection of his work. This extreme response had been anticipated in England by the Collier controversy at the turn of the century, for several of the examples cited by Jeremy Collier in his attack on the Restoration comedy of wit, *A Short View of the Profaneness and Immorality of the English Stage*, are taken from English plays inspired directly by Molière, such as Wycherley's *The Country Wife* and *The Plain Dealer*. The English dramatists were able to offer very little defence against Collier's charges, lacking as they did any theory of comedy which did not rest on the assumption of moral purpose in a rather narrow sense, and from now on the tide ran very much against them as criticism sought to establish the basis of comedy in sentiment and pathos rather than wit and satire. One consequence of this has been the reputation of the eighteenth century as a barren era for the comic muse. Only in the last third of the century did the critical tide begin to turn, as Goldsmith led the protest against the narrowing of the range of dramatic art by its convergence in the area between tragedy and comedy as traditionally understood. Beginning in 1768 with the Preface to *The Good-Natured Man*, Goldsmith argued that comedy in England had lost touch with its roots and become too refined. In his own dramatic practice in *She Stoops to Conquer* (1773) and in his critical *Essay on the Theatre; or A Comparison between Laughing and Sentimental Comedy* (1773) Goldsmith would vigorously – though not entirely successfully – press the case for the return of humour to the stage.

As early as 1592 the Italian dramatist, Sforza Oddi, had argued in the prologue to his *Prigione d'amore* (*The Prison of Love*) for a form of comedy which presented virtuous characters in sentimental actions, capable of provoking both laughter and sympathetic tears.[8] It was over

---

[7] J. Brody, 'Esthétique et société', pp. 315f. and Szondi, *Theorie*, pp. 223–35.
[8] Martino, *Geschichte*, pp. 375f.

a century before such hitherto isolated ideas were to be taken up, but they then very soon became the dominant ideas and were developed at great length in several European countries. After Collier had cleared the ground with his attack on the coldly intellectual comedy of the Restoration it was one of the leading exponents of sentimentalism in England, Sir Richard Steele, who provided both the major example of a sentimental comedy, *The Conscious Lovers* (1723), and a preface justifying this new but, by now, widely practised form. The principal arguments implicit in this brief preface are not unlike those shortly to be used by Lillo in the preface to his tragedy, *The London Merchant*: the need to extend the range of the genre beyond the boundaries imposed by existing conventions, the value of the expression of the emotions, particularly the more delicate and melancholy ones, and the importance of audience involvement through identification with the characters and their feelings. Underlying the theory and development of sentimental comedy in England is the familiar principle of moral utility, the notion that the drama should have 'the effect of example and precept' and that 'to give way to the impressions of humanity is the excellence of a right disposition and the natural working of a well-turned spirit' (Adams, *Dramatic Essays*, p. 236).

In mid-century England it was not in the drama but in the lyric and, above all, the novel that the principles of sentimentalism found their most powerful literary expression. This has been attributed in part to the deficiencies of English dramatic criticism in failing to build on the early discussions of the new style by Vanbrugh, Dennis and Steele; the prologues, epilogues and reviews written between 1720 and 1750 are dismissed by Bernbaum as superficial, repetitious and perfunctory.[9]

In France views similar to those of Steele began to find expression a decade later, and leadership in the systematic discussion of the new drama shifted decisively to mainland Europe. The sentimental comedy was first introduced to the French with *Le Philosophe Marié* (*The Married Philosopher*, 1727) by Destouches, who had acquired familiarity with the English theatre from earlier visits to London. The focal point for discussion of the new developments was, however, provided by the dramas of Nivelle de la Chaussée, and his *La Fausse Antipathie* (*False Antipathy*, 1733) is usually regarded as the point of departure. In the prologue to this play there is the same emphasis as in Collier on the need to avoid impropriety or indecency, and on the importance of appealing directly to the emotions of the audience; at the same time there is a markedly greater emphasis on realistic plausibility, which is to be furthered by the avoidance of satirical exaggeration and unnecessary

---

[9] Bernbaum, *Sensibility*, pp. 199–200.

complexity of intrigue – the plausible is becoming increasingly equated with the rationally comprehensible. One of those to respond to Nivelle de la Chaussée's innovations was Luigi Riccoboni, whose *Lettre sur la comédie de l'Ecole des amis* (*Letter on 'The School of Friendship'*, published in Paris in 1737) provides a fuller and more analytical discussion of the trend. Riccoboni speaks of a new system of comedy which he expressly associates with the emergence of a social class which is too low to be represented in traditional heroic tragedy, but too elevated to be the object of ridicule in traditional comedy. The depiction of characters who resemble the members of the audience in terms of their social rank and their code of values is seen as contributing to emotional identification on the part of the audience and so to their receptivity to the moral implicit in the drama; it is thus particularly conducive to the fulfilment of the function of the theatre as a school of virtue. Writing in 1754 Bougainville recognizes the same qualities in the work of Nivelle de la Chaussée, and still sees the moral utility of the theatre in the same rather narrow way:

the pure and sweet impression extends to his [the spectator's] own conduct because it is communicated to him by characters whom he re-encounters after the performance in the world outside among his friends, his peers, his rivals. Just as their sphere is his own, he feels himself capable of aspiring to their virtues; since nothing happens to them which he cannot also experience, he appropriates their experience, he learns from them to protect himself from the same dangers.[10]

Seeking to place the emergent dramatic form more systematically within the context of the established literary genres, Fontenelle, writing in 1751, defines the space between tragedy and comedy in terms of the emotions aroused. Running from the extremes of 'le terrible' and 'le grand', the proper province of tragedy, to 'le plaisant' and 'le ridicule', the realm of comedy, Fontenelle draws up a scale which includes 'le pitoyable' and 'le tendre'; on this scale the various emotions, like the spectral colours with which he compares them, are encountered more frequently in mixed than in unadulterated form. His conclusion, which goes quite a long way in anticipating views to be developed by Diderot, is an argument in favour of a 'comédie mixte', located at the mid-point of the scale and partaking of all that is most piquant and refined in

---

[10] '... plaisir dont l'impression douce et pure s'étend à ses moeurs, parce qu'elle lui est communiqué par des personnages qu'après le spectacle il retrouve dans le monde sous les noms de ses amis, de ses pareils, de ses rivaux. Comme leur sphère est la sienne, il se sent capable d'atteindre à leurs vertus; comme il ne leur arrive rien qu'il ne puisse éprouver, il s'approprie leur expérience, il apprend d'eux à se garantir des mêmes écueils' ('Discours de réception à l'Académie francaise', quoted from Vial, *Idées*, p. 224).

comedy, and all that is most touching and agreeable in tragedy. It is characteristic of the newly dominant sentimental cast of mind that the extreme comic end of the scale, 'le bouffon', should be excluded, whereas the pitiful and tender are to be admitted without restraint. Once again it is the principle of moral utility which provides the basis for the argument and is seen as calling for a type of drama that conforms most closely to the everyday experience of the audience:

This kind of comedy . . . would possess all the more utility inasmuch as it would increase the conformity of what is depicted to ordinary life. I do not believe I need to relate the actions of emperors to myself, they are too lofty for me; I do not deign to relate the actions of clowns to myself, they are too lowly; and they both constitute exceptional cases in which I never find myself: the implications of this are self-evident.[11]

In England it had been practising dramatists such as Vanbrugh, Congreve and Farquhar who had resisted the ideas of Collier; in France, where court and academy still held sway, resistance to the new senti-mental comedy was of a more theoretical kind and found its spokesman in Chassiron, Treasurer of France and Executive Counsellor to the Academy of La Rochelle. Chassiron's restatement of the principle of generic purity in his *Réflexions sur le comique larmoyant* (*Reflections on Sentimental Comedy*, 1749) immediately secured the support of Voltaire, whose own comedy, *Nanine* (1749), inspired by Richardson's *Pamela*, displayed many of the characteristics of the new genre. Writing from an almost provocatively aristocratic standpoint, Voltaire joined Chassiron in attacking the emergent concept of bourgeois tragedy:

what would a tragic intrigue among common people amount to? It would be nothing but a debasement of tragic style; it would fail to achieve the aim of tragedy or comedy; it would be a bastard form, a monstrosity born of the inability to create either a true comedy or a true tragedy.[12]

On the subject of comedy Voltaire is less rigid; here he is willing to allow the claims of the more tender passions, provided only that the dramatist does not lose sight of the basic aim of the genre: to make honest people laugh.

---

[11] 'Il auroit d'autant plus d'utilité, qu'il rendroit la représentation plus conforme à la vie ordinaire. Je me crois dispensé de m'appliquer ce que font des Empéreurs, ils sont trop hauts pour moi: je ne daigne pas m'appliquer ce que font des Saltimbanques, ils sont trop bas; et les uns et les autres ne sont que des cas extraordinaires, où je ne me trouve jamais: la conséquence se tire d'elle-même' (Fontenelle, *Oeuvres*, VII, p. 11).

[12] '. . . que serait-ce qu'une intrigue tragique entre des hommes du commun? Ce serait seulement avilir le cothurne; ce serait manquer à la fois l'objet de la tragédie et de la comédie; ce serait une espèce bâtarde, un monstre né de l'impuissance de faire une comédie et une tragédie véritable' (Voltaire, *Oeuvres*, V, p. 6).

The substance of Chassiron's criticism of the mixture of laughter and tears in the drama is accepted even more readily by Fréron in his *Lettres sur quelques écrits de ce temps* (*Letters on Some Contemporary Writings*, 1751). However, the conviction of the value of emotional empathy is by now so deeply rooted that there can be no going back. The logical consequence for Fréron is therefore the renunciation of the comic, and the exclusively serious presentation in the drama – as in the novel – of the ordinary course of the life of contemporary private persons of average condition (Vial, *Idées*, p. 225).

The German critics of the second quarter of the century were a further decade behind in the shift from satirical to sentimental comedy and the progressive reduction in the emphasis on wit. In 1741 Adam Daniel Richter was one of the first to seek to modify Gottsched's traditional definition of comedy as the ridicule of vice in the interest of moral improvement, by arguing for the extension of its subject-matter to include virtuous as well as vicious actions and by seeking to change its effect from provoking laughter to giving pleasure (Martino, *Geschichte*, pp. 384–6). Richter was a rather limited critic and some of his disagreements with Gottsched were a consequence of misunderstanding, but they are symptomatic of the incipient penetration of sentiment into the criticism of drama in Germany. Richter, like Gottsched, was concerned with the effect of the drama on the audience, but whereas Gottsched, the neo-classic stoic, was looking for practice in the resistance to fear or the unemotional rejection of vice, Richter sought from comedy the evocation of pleasant inward feelings of delight. A similar demand for comedy that achieves its effects by realistically portrayed example rather than by satire came from Georg Friedrich Meier in his *Beurtheilung der Gottschedischen Dichtkunst* (*An Assessment of Gottsched's Poetics*, 1747–8). Accepting the convention that the characters of comedy be drawn from the middle ranks of society, Meier nevertheless claims the tragic emotions, subject to a certain degree of restraint, as an essential component of middle-class experience and therefore as an appropriate subject of comedy. By this time Gottsched himself had begun to modify his earlier position a little. Although still unwilling to allow the new mixed forms as full and equal representatives of the dramatic genre, he did not deny their validity alongside tragedy and comedy; he insisted, however, that they be given distinct names, and in doing so, Gottsched was one of the first in Germany to propose the use of the term *bürgerliches Trauerspiel*.[13]

The major theoretical statement in favour of the sentimental comedy, Christian Fürchtegott Gellert's *Abhandlung für das rührende Lustspiel*

---

[13] Gottsched, *Schriften*, p. 385.

(*An Essay in Defence of Sentimental Comedy*), appeared in 1751, the same year as the fourth edition of Gottsched's modified, but still authoritative *Versuch einer Critischen Dichtkunst*. The leading German exponent of this genre with plays such as *Die Betschwester* (*The Pious Woman*, 1745) and *Die zärtlichen Schwestern* (*The Tender Sisters*, 1747), Gellert had already spoken out for the new genre in the preface to his comedies (1747). In this longer piece, an inaugural lecture delivered in Latin, Gellert set out to defend the *comédie larmoyante*, as it had developed in France, against the restrictions imposed by traditional Aristotelians such as Dacier, and the mockery of contemporary critics such as Voltaire. From the *Praelectiones Poeticae* (1722) of Joseph Trapp he draws a broader definition of comedy: 'a dramatic poem which contains descriptions of ordinary private life, which praises virtue and deals with the various vices and inconsistencies of mankind in a humorous and refined manner'.[14] Within this field, the private sphere, he sees a space for the exercise of sentiment in a way which had not figured in Trapp's more detached view of the effects of drama. For Gellert the experience of comedy is distinguished from that of tragedy by the avoidance of extremes in actions, emotions and expression, by the absence of any intensely passionate sense of pity, sadness or loss; that is to say, for those men and women of average condition who constitute its actors, the great exemplary deeds and adventures of public life are renounced. Instead the melancholy sadness which is now accepted as the norm of comedy is alleviated by the sense of participation in a common world of feeling and in a common admiration of shared values.

Gellert's essay of 1751 is not, in European terms, a central document in the history of dramatic criticism, but it none the less marks a turning point. The considered seriousness with which he treats his subject, the consciousness of a tradition of exponents of the genre he is discussing (Destouches, Fontenelle, de la Chaussée, Marivaux, Voltaire, Fagan), and the confidence with which the virtues it celebrates are proclaimed as universal human values, suggest that the sentimental comedy has come of age. This is confirmed by the revival of sentimental comedy in England in the second half of the century, beginning with Philip Francis's *Eugenia* (1752). In plays such as William Whitehead's *The School for Lovers* (1762), Mrs Frances Sheridan's *The Discovery* (1763) and George Colman's *The English Merchant* (1767) the substance and methods of French sentimental drama were absorbed, but without any original critical discussion. Journalistic criticism did not seek to conceal a certain reserve

---

[14] '... ein dramatisches Gedicht, welches Abschilderungen von dem gemeinen Privatleben enthalte, die Tugend anpreise, und verschiedene Laster und Ungereimtheiten der Menschen, auf eine scherzhafte und feine Art durchziehe'. Quoted in Lessing's translation, Lessing, *Schriften*, VI, p. 34.

about the more extreme aspects of the sentimental style: its gravity, its moralizing, the absence of the comic, but the genre was now sufficiently established and popular to survive the attacks of Goldsmith, referred to above, and to emerge triumphant in the 1770s.[15] The development of Richard Cumberland epitomizes this episode: in 1751 he had taken issue with Johnson's account of Rowe's *The Fair Penitent*, arguing for the superiority of *The Fatal Dowry* by Massinger and Field on sentimentalist grounds: 'Is there a man who has any feeling for real nature, dramatic character, moral sentiment, tragic pathos, or nervous diction who can hesitate, even for a moment, where to bestow the palm?'[16] Over a long and prolific career, however, his own prologues and epilogues – and indeed his plays – are not without a certain ambivalence. In *The Brothers* (1769) and *The West Indian* (1771) he argues in favour of humorous laughter rather than sentimental tears, and on occasion he even indulges in satirical criticism of that sentimentalism which is generally felt to have reached its climax in the latter play, and which otherwise so informed his work that it was he who, as Sir Fretful Plagiary, was the principal focus of Sheridan's attack on the conventions of emotional comedy in the French style in *The Critic* (1779).

Such attacks were designed to reclaim some of the ground lost by the 'laughing comedy' and were successful in clearing the way for the major English comedies of the later part of the century: *She Stoops to Conquer* (1773) and *The School for Scandal* (1777). In general, however, English dramatic criticism was doing little more than modifying earlier developments. In mid-century France and Germany there were now coming forward a number of critics who had not been closely associated with sentimental comedy; having assessed the situation, they now began to move on to a new stage, centred on the appropriation of tragedy. Such was clearly Lessing's intention when he translated Gellert's essay and published it alongside Chassiron's critique of the *comédie larmoyante* in the first number of the *Theatralische Bibliothek* (1754), conceived by Lessing as a continuation of his earlier project on the history of the theatre, *Beyträge zur Historie und Aufnahme des Theaters* (*Essays on the History and Development of the Theatre*, 1750).

Chassiron's essay of 1749 was a conservative piece written from a rationalist point of view in opposition to the dominant emotional trend. While Lessing makes clear his view that Gellert had satisfactorily rebutted most of Chassiron's objections to the new form, he nevertheless voices serious criticism of his own. Preserving the moral standpoint which would be abandoned by the English champions of the 'laughing

---

[15] Sherbo, *Sentimental Drama*, p. 152.
[16] Elledge, *Eighteenth-Century Critical Essays*, II, p. 970.

comedy', he casts serious doubt on the moral efficaciousness of a kind of drama – and he insists he is thinking of the work of the Frenchman, de la Chaussée, rather than the German, Gellert – which, dispensing with satire, uses only one of the weapons available to the comedian. In concentrating on the exemplary as an object for identification, the *comédie larmoyante* runs the risk of becoming no more than a vehicle for self-flattery:

The attention with which the audience listens is ... only a compliment it pays to its own self-love, a nourishment of its own pride. I do not see how any improvement can come from this. Each one of them believes himself to be all the more capable of the noble sentiments and magnanimous deeds which he sees and of which he hears the less he has the opportunity to think of the opposite and to compare himself with it.[17]

Lessing, dedicated to realistic principles, and rejecting both satirical exaggeration and sentimental idealization, was looking for a new dramatic form of more seriously moral character than the *comédie larmoyante*. This much was already clear from the introduction he had written to his translations of the essays of Chassiron and Gellert. Here he had expressly noted that process of convergence which was resulting from the modification of the principal dramatic genres, leading, on the French side, to the *comédie larmoyante*, and on the English side to the – in Lessing's view – more promising domestic tragedy (*Schriften*, VI, pp. 6f.). For the next quarter of a century, up to the publication of his *Emilia Galotti* (1772), this form will occupy a central position in Lessing's dramaturgical writings, but the initial English inspiration will not remain exclusively dominant. Only six years after his publication and criticism of Gellert's lecture, Lessing turned to translation again to advance his theoretical views. In 1760 he published his versions of Diderot's dramas, *Le Fils naturel* (*The Natural Son*, 1757) and *Le Père de Famille* (*The Father of the Family*, 1758), together with Diderot's two major dramaturgical essays, *Entretiens sur le Fils naturel* (*Conversations on 'The Natural Son'*, 1757) and *Discours de la Poésie dramatique* (1758), commending them to his fellow countrymen as, respectively, examples and justifications of a new dramatic genre, and as support from France itself for Lessing's attacks on Gottsched and the imitation of French neo-classical models.

The term *tragédie bourgeoise* had been used in France well before

---

[17] 'Die Aufmerksamkeit, mit der sie zuhören, ist ... doch nur ein Kompliment, welches sie ihrer Eigenliebe machen; eine Nahrung ihres Stolzes. Wie aber hieraus eine Beßrung erfolgen könne, sehe ich nicht ein. Jeder von ihnen glaubt der edlen Gesinnungen, und der großmüthigen Thaten, die er siehet und höret, desto eher fähig zu seyn, je weniger er an das Gegentheil zu denken, und sich mit demselben zu vergleichen Gelegenheit findet' (Lessing, *Schriften*, VI, pp. 52f).

Diderot to describe a play by Paul Landois, *Sylvie* (1742), mentioned approvingly in the *Entretiens*, for its prologue does go some way to anticipate Diderot's own justification of a realistic style of theatre. The latter's two essays, however, are works of incomparably greater substance, which deal both with central questions of the contemporary state of dramatic art and with more general questions of theatrical production which will continue to be relevant until the advent of naturalism at the end of the nineteenth century. The two essays are quite different in form and structure: the *Entretiens* consist of a dialogue between 'Dorval', the mouthpiece of Diderot as author of *Le Fils naturel*, and 'Moi', Diderot as a dramatic critic. The essay is conceived very much as an apology for the one play and certain of its arguments arise from the claim that it consists of the dramatization of a factual occurrence; only in the third section does Diderot extend the argument significantly and consistently beyond issues raised directly by his own play. The *Discours*, though referring occasionally to both of Diderot's plays, is an autonomous dramaturgical essay written in an almost ostentatiously systematic fashion. Together the two essays advance a consistent programme which was to have considerable impact on the development of dramatic theory and rather less direct impact on the writing of drama; and in this latter respect outside rather than inside their country of origin.

Common to both essays is that concern with the distinction between the dramatic genres which exercised most of the dramatic critics of this period. Like Fontenelle, Diderot thinks in terms of a hierarchy descending from tragedy to comedy, with these ideal forms marking the boundaries outside of which stand the burlesque, which falls below the comic, and the marvellous, which extends above the tragic. Between these two extremes Diderot locates not tragi-comedy, a hybrid mixture of remote opposites, but the form which he describes in the *Entretiens* as the *genre sérieux*. The various distinctions are given greater precision in the *Discours* where Diderot sets out to identify a whole range of genres according to content:

Here, then, is the system of drama in its whole extent: gay comedy, which has for its object ridicule and vice; serious comedy, which has for its object virtue and the duties of man; the kind of tragedy which would have for its object our domestic afflictions; and tragedy which has for its object public catastrophes and the afflictions of the great.[18]

---

[18] 'Voici donc le système dramatique dans toute son étendue. La comédie gaie, qui a pour objet le ridicule et le vice, la comédie sérieuse, qui a pour objet la vertu et les devoirs de l'homme. La tragédie, qui aurait pour objet nos malheurs domestiques; la tragédie, qui a pour objet les catastrophes publiques et les malheurs des grands' (Diderot, *Oeuvres Esthétiques*, p. 191; see also Adams, *Dramatic Essays*, p. 351).

Like his creative interests, Diderot's critical interest is focused on the space between the two extremes and his chief aim is to broaden the range and deepen the claim to truth of what falls within it. He thus argues that the exceptional characters of heroic tragedy only ever act as unrepresentative individuals, while the characters of traditional comedy are only ever types; he challenges the conventional court setting of tragic (i.e. sad) events, arguing that these are more plausibly located amid the pressures of the everyday life of the subject than of the ruler; moreover, in such a setting they are more likely to prove effective and useful because they are brought closer to the situation of the audience. In short, Diderot begins to argue as a social determinist for a form of drama in which conditions are more crucial than character, and in which individual psychology or literary stereotyping are therefore less significant than occupation and status within the family.

Diderot takes up a fairly advanced position in the elaboration of a theory of social drama but, like Corneille a century earlier, he does not press his thoughts to the most radical conclusion. As an illustration of tragic grief he cites, among several examples, the scene (V, 4) from Racine's *Iphigénie* where Clytemnèstre expresses her despair at the sacrifice of her daughter. Diderot here insists that Clytemnèstre is portrayed as a mother rather than as a queen, and that therein lies the truth of this scene. A few pages later he describes another scene of female grief in a family setting, but in a more humble social environment, and poses the question: 'Do you believe that a woman of different rank would have displayed more pathos?'[19] Diderot's own reply to his question, that the same situation would have inspired the same discourse, reveals him as an adherent of an emotionalist theory of tragedy: response is achieved through a sense of common humanity in shared emotions, and to this extent the traditional class distinctions are irrelevant; as Corneille put it: 'these kings are men just like the members of the audience'. There is not, at least not in the analyses of such cases offered by Diderot, any element of social solidarity about this sympathetic response to suffering humanity; the *genre sérieux* is not yet the programmatic *tragédie bourgeoise*. From a different point of view, of course, it might well be argued that there is something deeply and distinctly bourgeois about Diderot's absolutization of the sentimental ties of the nuclear family into ahistorical, universally human values; but it is equally evident that this can be no part of Diderot's own argument.

The empirical reality to which Diderot appeals in justification of his dramaturgy may seem somewhat restricted in socio-political terms, for

---

[19] 'Croyez-vous qu'une femme d'un autre rang aurait été plus pathétique?' (Diderot, *Oeuvres Esthétiques*, p. 99).

in the last analysis very little importance is attached to the social condition of the individual in the public sphere. However, the appeal is carried through with a persistence which enables Diderot to question details of dramatic and theatrical convention to a greater degree than any of his predecessors. It is to this end that Diderot exploits the dialogue in the *Entretiens*. Dorval, speaking as the author of the play, is characterized as only a dilettante dramatist defending his work before a 'moi' who speaks for the public and the critics. His authority derives from the fact of his own participation in the events of the drama; he can thus appeal to the authenticity of lived experience when confronted by his interlocutor with the norms and conventions of theory and tradition. Conformity to nature, as understood from an undogmatic, commonsense point of view, is the essential criterion: the plausibility of rationally comprehensible causation is preferred to complexity of intrigue; everyday prose speech, inarticulate cries or even silent playing to polished verse or the rhetorical tirade; actors like the Italian comedians, who appear to be totally absorbed in their own actions as if separated from the audience by a fourth wall, are preferred to those who address the audience directly; static tableaux to sudden *coups de théâtre*. In the name of realism Diderot is thus advocating the renunciation of all that is most 'theatrical' about the theatre. He and his successors, authors of domestic tragedies and social problem plays, adhere to the form of the 'well-made play', but Diderot's theory already points beyond this to a much more loosely structured form of drama which, it should be said, drew inspiration from the sentimental narrative of the eighteenth century as well as the theatrical arts. In the *Eloge de Richardson* (*In Praise of Richardson*, 1762) Diderot presents the English novelist as a painter of the passions, a master of scenic presentation and as a fertile creator of 'situation'; and this last concept is the crucial one in Diderot's idea of pictorial drama (and, incidentally, in Puff's in Sheridan's *The Critic*), consisting of a rapidly changing sequence of tableaux.[20] It was this alternative model of drama which came to dominate popular theatrical forms in the nineteenth century; but it was also to be embodied in the seminal work of unorthodox non-Aristotelian dramatists such as the Germans Lenz and Büchner. The twentieth century would see these two strands merge in the work of Brecht.[21]

---

[20] Diderot, *Oeuvres Esthétiques*, p. 30; p. 277. See also Meisel, *Realizations*, pp. 41f., 83–6.

[21] In his *Paradoxe sur le Comédien*, where he focuses on the self-consciousness of the actor, Diderot provided a basis for the critique of the idea of emotional sincerity in theatrical performance which, at least superficially, is at odds with the dramatic tradition he fathered. Diderot's essay came to be an important document in the discussion of theatricality and also points towards the Brechtian theory of the alienation effect, but it was not published until 1830.

By the time of Diderot the interest of the major critics and the ambitions of the major theorists had shifted decisively away from comedy to tragedy. While Diderot did not raise such high claims as the Englishman, Lillo, for the significance of the bourgeois merchant ethic in the development of public life, he was fairly assertive in his claims for the superior authenticity and seriousness of the contemporary familial sphere in comparison to the court life of the historical past as represented in classical tragedy:

Can you not conceive of the effect which would be produced on you by a real scene, authentic costume, speech appropriate to the action, simple actions, dangers which you cannot but have feared for your relations, your friends, yourself? A reversal of fortune, the fear of disgrace, the consequences of misery, a passion which leads man to his ruin, from ruin to despair, from despair to violent death, these are not unusual occurrences; and so you think that they would not move you as much as the legendary death of a tyrant or the sacrifice of a child on the altars of the gods of Athens or Rome?[22]

It was just such an assertiveness which inspired, at almost the same time, an extreme assault on the 'laughing comedy', which is at once anachronistic in the narrowness of the utilitarian demands it makes on the theatre and fully representative of contemporary pride in sentiment expressed within the private sphere.

Anticipating the historicist position that was soon to become central in aesthetic discussion, Diderot had suggested in the *Entretiens* that Molière's *Le Misanthrope* could well be rewritten every fifty years in order to reflect changing conditions. In the *Lettre à d'Alembert* of 1758 Rousseau indicates how a mid-eighteenth-century sentimentalist might have set about this by proposing a tragic reading from the point of view of Alceste, whom he sees as a virtuous man confronting the vice of society, a man seeking friendship and finding only self-interest, seeking love and finding coquetry, seeking justice and finding corruption. Rousseau's hostility to the theatre is comprehensive, but it is directed less fiercely against tragedy precisely because, he argues, the social and historical remoteness, which contemporary critics were attempting to break down, prevents all possible sense of identification, so rendering

---

[22] '... vous ne concevez pas l'effet que produiraient sur vous une scène réelle, des habits vrais, des discours proportionnés aux actions, des actions simples, des dangers dont il est impossible que vous n'ayez tremblé pour vos parents, vos amis, pour vous-même? Un renversement de fortune, la crainte de l'ignominie, les suites de la misère, une passion qui conduit l'homme à sa ruine, de sa ruine au désespoir, du désespoir à une mort violente, ne sont pas des évènements rares; et vous croyez qu'ils ne vous affecteraient pas autant que la mort fabuleuse d'un tyran, ou le sacrifice d'un enfant aux autels des dieux d'Athènes ou de Rome?' (Diderot, *Oeuvres Esthétiques*, p. 149).

tragedy manifestly uninstructive, but harmless (pp. 92–110). In Rousseau's idiosyncratic readings of Molière's comedies, however, it is clearly the tragic emotion of pity (for Alceste, for M. Jourdain in *Le Bourgeois gentilhomme*) which is brought into play; and it is pity which was now to provide the basis for the theoretical justification of the domestic tragedy as it developed in Germany. The achievement of Lessing was to bring together the more general concept of pity advanced by Rousseau in the *Discours sur l'inégalité* (*Discourse on the Origin of Inequality*, 1755) and the concept of tragic compassion, pity as it figures in the *Poetics* of Aristotle, which once again come to the forefront of critical debate.[23]

In 1754, on the occasion of his translation of the essays of Chassiron and Gellert, Lessing had stated his intention of contributing further to the critical discussion of domestic tragedy. First, and partly in response to Lillo's *The London Merchant*, which he had seen performed in a German translation in 1752, he wrote his own play, *Miß Sara Sampson* (1755), which he expressly designated as a *bürgerliches Trauerspiel*. His critical works were to follow and, wide-ranging though they are, they nevertheless show a continuous preoccupation with this subject. Lessing's central conviction is stated very early and remains constant: in a preface to the tragedies of James Thomson he contrasts the stoicism of Gottsched's *Der sterbende Cato* (*The Death of Cato*) with the emotionalism of *The London Merchant* and concludes that the evocation of such tears of pity, which exemplify feeling humanity, is the sole possible aim of tragedy; its purpose is clearly defined in terms of its effect on the audience (*Schriften*, VII, p. 68). In the subsequent correspondence with Nicolai and Mendelssohn, *Briefwechsel über das Trauerspiel* (*Correspondence on Tragedy*, 1756–7) Lessing then develops a theoretical justification for this sentimentalist position.

The consequence of Lessing's basic conviction is a radical attack on heroic tragedy, which his more conservative and rationalist correspondents wish to preserve. In the eyes of Lessing the feelings of fear and admiration which, according to Mendelssohn, properly belong among the emotions aroused by tragedy, are secondary expressions of the primary emotion of pity; cultivated as ends in themselves, they are actually capable of detracting from the sensibility – and so the humanity and the plausibility – of the tragic hero and can in this way positively undermine the sensitizing effect of tragedy. This is important to Lessing because, in contrast to his correspondents, Lessing is a moralist in his theory and criticism, although not a moralist of the old kind requiring from drama the condemnation of vice and the proclamation of virtue. For Lessing the moral effect of tragedy lies not in the teaching of any

---

[23] Schings, *Der mitleidigste Mensch*, p. 38.

specific lesson, but in its extension of the sensibility, the capacity for sharing in the feelings of one's fellow men:

the best man is the man who pities most, he is the one who is the most outstanding in all social virtues and most disposed to generosity. Therefore, whoever makes us sympathetic, makes us better and more virtuous; and tragedy which does the former does the latter too, or it does the former in order to do the latter.[24]

Lessing's most important and extensive work of dramatic criticism appeared in periodical form under the title *Hamburgische Dramaturgie* from May 1767 to April 1768. In it Lessing combined the *ad hoc* criticism of plays in performance at the new Hamburg National Theatre with the discussion of basic theoretical problems. A continuous thread is provided by the arguments already rehearsed in the discussion with Mendelssohn and Nicolai, but the place of Lessing's two Berlin friends is, in this more polemic work, taken by the theorists of French classicism and their followers. Not without a certain mischievousness, Lessing is here inclined to present himself as the faithful interpreter of Aristotle, although in certain respects he mounts a challenge to Aristotelian principles by developing the historicist position we have already noted in the work of Diderot.

The intention to arouse sympathy in the sense in which Lessing uses the term requires identification between *dramatis personae* and audience, and so realism in the manner of Diderot. Lessing therefore also demands characters who fall between the outstanding and the insignificant, the individual and the stereotype. It follows that for Lessing the characters in the several dramatic sub-genres need not be drawn exclusively from distinct social classes, but he goes no further than Diderot in recognizing a specifically social-historical determinism as an element in characterization and a stimulus to audience identification. Like Diderot in his response to the 'tableau of maternal love' in Racine's *Iphigénie*, he focuses on universal human qualities which seem to transcend social differences. Again like Diderot, Lessing is inclined to recognize these universal human qualities in the private life of the bourgeois family:

The names of princes and heroes can lend a play pomp and majesty; but they do nothing to render it more moving. The misfortune of those whose circumstances most closely resemble our own will naturally penetrate most deeply into our soul; and if we feel pity for kings, we feel it for them as

---

[24] 'Der mitleidigste Mensch ist der beste Mensch, zu allen gesellschaftlichen Tugenden, zu allen Arten der Großmut der Aufgelegteste. Wer uns also mitleidig macht, macht uns besser und tugendhafter, und das Trauerspiel, das jenes tut, tut auch dieses, oder – es tut jenes, um dies tun zu können' (Lessing, *Briefwechsel*, p. 55; see also Adams, *Dramatic Essays*, p. 331).

men and not as kings . . . 'One does the human heart an injustice', says
Marmontel, 'one misunderstands nature, if one thinks that titles are
necessary in order for us to be moved and touched. The sacred names of
friend, father, beloved, husband, son, mother, or just man: these have more
power to move than anything else; they will always assert their claims'.[25]

The best-known sections of the *Hamburgische Dramaturgie* are those
(74–8) in which Lessing redefines the Aristotelian concept of *catharsis*,
so bringing to a conclusion the line of argument initiated in the *Correspondence*. Arguing that the tragedy of *Richard III* by the little-known
German dramatist Christian Felix Weisse failed to achieve the effects of
true tragedy because the central character was so unrelievedly vicious,
Lessing concludes that the fear required in Aristotle's definition has been
misunderstood and in some cases mistranslated as 'terror'. Lessing proposes that it should be understood not as fear at some misfortune likely
to overtake another, but as the fear which affects the spectator for
himself, and which will only be felt if he can recognize a real similarity
between himself and the suffering character presented on stage. Fear is
seen as a subdivision of the emotion of pity, whose primacy is thereby
emphasized and whose scope is increased: pity is directed outwards
towards others; fear is its reflexive form, pity directed back upon the self.
A second problem arises from the notion of purification; for the neo-
classic stoics from Corneille to Gottsched the purification of the passions had meant the rational process of moderating or eliminating them
and their unhappy consequences. Lessing, on the other hand, sees the
theatre as an arena in which the practice of the emotions should be
positively encouraged because thereby, in accordance with the principles
enunciated in the correspondence with Nicolai and Mendelssohn, the
virtuous disposition of man is fostered and prepared for virtuous activity in the social world (*Schriften*, X, p. 117).

This – albeit fairly restrained – argument for a drama which will
intervene in the world outside the theatre heralds the politically more
forceful style of drama which was to emerge in the next decade, with
Beaumarchais's *Le Mariage de Figaro*, Lessing's own *Emilia Galotti* and
Schiller's *Kabale und Liebe* (*Intrigue and Love*). At this stage even

---

[25] 'Die Namen von Fürsten und Helden können einem Stücke Pomp und Majestät
geben; aber zur Rührung tragen sie nichts bey. Das Unglück derjenigen, deren
Umstände den unsrigen am nächsten kommen, muß natürlicher Weise am tiefsten
in unsere Seele dringen; und wenn wir mit Königen Mitleiden haben, so haben wir
es mit ihnen als mit Menschen, und nicht als mit Königen . . . "Man thut dem
menschlichen Herze Unrecht, sagt auch Marmontel, und verkennt die Natur, wenn
man glaubt, daß sie Titel bedürfe, uns zu bewegen und zu rühren. Die geheiligten
Namen des Freundes, des Vaters, des Geliebten, des Gatten, des Sohnes, der Mutter,
des Menschen überhaupt: diese sind pathetischer, als alles; diese behaupten ihre
Rechte immer und ewig"' (Lessing, *Schriften*, IX, pp. 239f).

Beaumarchais, in his contemporaneous *Essai sur le genre dramatique sérieux* (*Essay on the Serious Genre of Drama*, 1767) was still concerned only to establish the aesthetic validity of the *genre sérieux* against heroic tragedy. The injection of a recognizably revolutionary element into sentimental theories of drama came first with an essay of 1773 by Louis Sebastien Mercier, *Du Théâtre ou Nouvel Essai sur l'Art Dramatique* (*On the Theatre, or New Essay on Dramatic Art*).

With a directness that is anticipated only in the criticism of Rousseau, Mercier launches an attack on the literary forms of classicism which is at the same time an attack on the social structures of the *ancien régime*. Heroic tragedy is seen as alien to the life of the nation at large, a glorification of the absolute power of the monarchy and an instrument in the suppression of the people. Classical comedy fares no better than it did at the hands of Rousseau. On the constructive side sentiment is held to provide the basis for a committed social and political drama whose function is to intervene in public life on behalf of oppressed humanity:

[the dramatic poet] reigns by means of sentiment – sentiment, that invincible and mighty force that demands the submission even of the most rebellious of men. By the exquisite and repeated sensations with which it attacks the human heart, it relieves the vicious of their prey, despots of their clubs, and the wicked of the ability to be deaf to their remorse.[26]

Mercier sees the need for the development of a new idealistic form of national tragedy which would have an educational and inspirational function in a republican state, but for the present he advocates a form of drama which is in most respects similar to the *genre sérieux* of Diderot, and would take the form of a series of sentimental tableaux of bourgeois life. The social range which Mercier would see represented extends much further than with Diderot, but the really crucial difference resides in the specificity of Mercier's understanding of political conflict and the determinative force of social conditions. No longer is it simply a question of identifying with the tragic sufferings of kings and princes out of a sense of shared humanity; Mercier sees the source of tragedy very precisely in the social and political conditions of a particular time and place.[27]

Mercier's essay was warmly received in Germany among the young critics and dramatists of the *Sturm und Drang*. In 1776 Heinrich Leopold

---

[26] '... il regne par le sentiment, le sentiment, cette force invincible et puissante, qui soumet les êtres les plus rebelles: c'est par des sensations exquises et répétées qu'il bat le coeur humain, il enleve au vice sa proie, au despotisme sa massue, au méchant le pouvoir d'étourdir ses remords' (Mercier, *Du Théâtre*, pp. 9f.; see also Adams, *Dramatic Essays*, p. 388).

[27] Martino, *Geschichte*, p. 412; McInnes, *Theater*, pp. 28–31.

Wagner translated the *Nouvel Essai*, while at the same time as Mercier
J. M. R. Lenz had been reflecting along similar lines about the development of the dramatic genres. In his *Anmerkungen übers Theater*
(*Remarks on the Theatre*, 1774) he also turns away from the classical
model of tragedy and, finding his model in Shakespeare and the German
tradition, proposes an ideal form in which the great personality will be
celebrated as master of his own destiny; comedy, on the other hand, is
concerned with individuals bound up in the contingency of social life.
The reasons for the attraction of Mercier in the eyes of this group of
writers lay partly in a shared social commitment and revolutionary
fervour, but partly also in their enthusiasm for the new relativist attitude evident in Mercier's sense of the significance not just of conditions,
but of changes in conditions.[28]

It is paradoxical that, at a crucial point in the *Hamburgische
Dramaturgie*, Lessing should have called up the authority of Aristotle to
support his dramatic criticism, for the empirical basis of Lessing's work
in the criticism of drama in performance had inevitably forced him to
confront the discrepancy between practical effectiveness and conformity
to the rules. In fact he had confronted it earlier in the celebrated seventeenth *Literaturbrief* (*Letter on Literature*, 1760), where he had made
the strange claim that 'even when judged by the standards of the ancients, Shakespeare is a far greater tragic poet than Corneille'.[29] By this
Lessing meant that Shakespeare achieved his effects by unorthodox
means, implying that rules are not static, permanent and eternal, and
that genius is superior to them, especially when inspired by nature. In
the later criticism Lessing adds the charge that the upholders of the
authority of Aristotle have detached his work from its base in the
ancient Greek theatre and illegitimately claimed for it an absolute validity. These arguments, which slowly emerged from the historical thought
of the eighteenth century, were to be developed further by Gerstenberg
in his *Briefe über Merkwürdigkeiten der Literatur* (*Letters on Literary
Memorabilia*, 1766) and by Herder. In doing so Gerstenberg in particular was able to build on critical discussion of Shakespeare which had
taken place in England during the previous two decades, notably the
Elements of Criticism (1762) by Henry Home, Lord Kames.

In England, where it was not a question of absorbing Shakespeare
into the canon, the changes in critical approach had taken place within
the context of a more moderate and continuous debate. By the middle
of the century the climate of opinion, as expressed by critics such as
Arthur Murphy and Joseph Warton, was favourable to the view of

---

[28] Szondi, *Theorie*, pp. 185f.
[29] 'Auch nach den Mustern der Alten die Sache zu entscheiden, ist Shakespear ein
weit größerer tragischer Dichter als Corneille' (Lessing, *Schriften*, VIII, p. 43).

Shakespeare as a poet of nature, inspired by genius in the sublime expression of the passions. The neo-classical position was not, however, so far transcended that it was felt unnecessary to excuse his transgressions against the formal (Aristotelian) rules nor his infringement against the principle of moral utility in the portrayal of evil characters. Nor indeed was the firmly Aristotelian position taken up by Mrs Charlotte Lennox (*Shakespeare Illustrated*, 1753–4) lacking in distinguished supporters such as Johnson, Goldsmith and Smollett. By the early 1770s, however, the liberal attitude to the unities, based on newly emerging historicist principles and the emancipation of the imagination of the spectator, were clearly in the ascendancy, allowing the work of Shakespeare to be appreciated on its own terms. This change is exemplified in important critical essays by, among others, Richard Hurd, Daniel Webb and Kames:

> Modern critics, who for our drama pretend to establish rules founded on the practice of the Greeks, are guilty of an egregious blunder. The unities of place and time were in Greece, as we see, a matter of necessity not of choice; and I am now ready to show that if we submit to such fetters it must be from choice, not necessity. This will be evident upon taking a view of the constitution of our drama, which differs widely from that of Greece ... The spectator ... may be conscious that the real time and place are not the same with what are employed in the representation: but this is a work of reflection; and by the same reflection he may also be conscious that Garrick is not King Lear, that the playhouse is not Dover cliffs, nor the noise he hears thunder and lightning. In a word, after an interruption of the representation it is no more difficult for a spectator to imagine a new place or a different time than at the commencement of the play to imagine himself at Rome, or in a period of time two thousand years back.

(Critical Heritage, IV, pp. 495–6)

In the present context the major English contribution to Shakespeare criticism, Samuel Johnson's Preface to his edition of the plays (1765) is less important. For although Johnson lends his authority to the challenge to the unities, he foregoes the appeal to imaginative participation in dramatic illusion which was to be so essential to those younger dramatists and critics who came to see themselves as renewers of the Shakespearean tradition. In other respects his criticism tended to adhere to neo-classical principles of generic purity, decorum and poetic justice which had been dominant over the extended period he had devoted to the work of editorship, and which continued to play a part in dramatic criticism, alongside the various innovations, until the end of the century.

Like Lessing before him, Herder aimed to free German literature from what he saw as the constraining influence of the classical tradition, as mediated by French drama and dramatic criticism. He did this in an essay on Shakespeare (1771–3) which cannot properly be regarded as dramatic criticism or theory, by arguing that the form of all cultural manifestations, and specifically the dramas of ancient Greece and Elizabethan England, is necessarily determined by the full set of historical, cultural and geographical conditions under which they emerged and developed. Aristotle is now seen as an essentially descriptive aesthetician, drawing his standards from the phenomena which lay before him in his own day. Herder's achievement was to complete the work of those dramatic critics who had been slowly chipping away at the neo-classical tradition throughout the eighteenth century. In doing so he provided an approach which permitted the work of Shakespeare to be accepted without the rejection of the great dramas of antiquity which Herder knew and admired. This achievement was obscured – in the short term, at least – by the enthusiasm with which his younger contemporaries responded to the rediscovery and popularization of Shakespeare, and seized on his work as an alternative model of heroic tragedy.

First Goethe, in *Zum Schäkespears Tag* (*On Shakespeare's Name-Day*, 1771), and then Lenz, in his *Anmerkungen übers Theater*, wrote a rhapsodic essay in praise of Shakespeare's creative power, emphasizing above all his genius in drawing full, complex and convincing characters, who reflected nature rather than an ideal: 'Nature! Nature! Nothing as natural as Shakespeare's men and women', proclaimed Goethe.[30] They then both followed the Shakespearian example, as they understood it, by developing an anti-Aristotelian drama in which character took primacy over action; Lenz did so directly in an adaptation of *Coriolanus* (1775), Goethe more distantly in *Götz von Berlichingen* (1772) – but not so distantly as to avoid Herder's criticism that he had been totally spoiled by Shakespeare.[31] A decade later Schiller was to do the same in his first drama, *Die Räuber* (*The Robbers*, 1781), renewing in his preface the now familiar attacks on the Unities, on Aristotle, Batteux and the French neo-classical drama, and calling up Shakespeare in justification of his portrayal of large-scale, morally flawed characters.

The tendency of the young German critics of the 1770s to regard Shakespeare as a force of nature and his characters as natural creations had been developing steadily in England since the middle of the century when it had been heralded by Joseph Warton in essays on *The Tempest* and *King Lear* (1753–4). It received further impetus in the 1770s and 1780s with the work of Thomas Whately, *Remarks on some of the*

---

[30] 'Natur! Natur! nichts so Natur als Shakespeares Menschen' (Loewenthal, *Sturm und Drang*, p. 697).

[31] See Goethe's letter to Herder, *c.* 10 July 1772, in Goethe, *Werke*, ed. Beutler, XVIII, p. 175.

Characters of Shakespeare (published 1785), William Richardson, *Philosophical Analysis and Illustration of some of Shakespeare's Remarkable Characters* (1774) and, above all, Maurice Morgann.[32] In his *Essay on the Dramatic Character of Sir John Falstaff* (1777), which for rapture of tone approaches the work of his German contemporaries, Morgann sets out to defend the character against the moralistic charge of cowardice, as if he had an independent existence outside the action of the drama; the dangers of such criticism have been pointed out often enough; its effect was to extend significantly the understanding of the dramatist's psychological insights. The principal Shakespearean character to become subject to this new approach was, of course, Hamlet, on whom Richardson had included a chapter in his book of 1774. He was followed by Henry Mackenzie with two essays on the character of Hamlet in *The Mirror* in 1780 before the first episode of this discussion was brought to a climax in Germany with Goethe's celebrated image of Hamlet as an oak tree in a costly vase. *Wilhelm Meister's Apprenticeship* (1795–6), which contains Goethe's account of *Hamlet*, marks the threshold of a new era of criticism both in England and in Germany. In the one country through the lectures of Coleridge, in the other through the essays of Friedrich Schlegel, the combination of Goethe's novel and Shakespeare's play exercised enormous influence on the emergence of the Romantic movement. Both Goethe and Schiller, however, stood aside from this development to produce during the last decade of the century a body of dramatic masterpieces tending much more to the neo-classical than to the Shakespearean style.

The major dramaturgical writings of Weimar Classicism are largely Schiller's, and they are rooted in an epistemological scepticism of a kind which did not occur to earlier dramatic critics; they provide a theoretical underpinning to his own works rather than contributing to the wider development of dramatic criticism, but in that context they are of crucial importance.

Schiller's dramatic theory and practice are informed by an idealism which remains consistent, but which takes a new form in the works of his post-Kantian maturity. Younger than the principal dramatists of the *Sturm und Drang*, he nevertheless assented, in the preface to *Die Räuber*, to the belief, espoused by Mercier, in the connection between art and social action, and the realistic implications of this for dramatic composition. In an essay of 1785, *Die Schaubühne als eine moralische Anstalt betrachtet* (*The Theatre Considered as a Moral Institution*), he perseveres with the Enlightenment notion of utility, following Lessing in the advocacy of a national theatre as a contribution to the development of

---

[32] Nichol Smith, *Shakespeare* (1928), pp. 82–5.

the bourgeois public sphere, but adding the newer ideas on the role of dramatic literature in providing instruction in psychological insight. By the 1790s, however, as a consequence of a long struggle with Kantian philosophy and that sense which affected so many of his contemporaries that for modern man a wedge had been driven between belief and knowledge, art and nature, ideal and reality, he was advocating – and practising – the renunciation of contemporary subject-matter and realistic techniques, and the reversion to verse drama and Aristotelian norms.

In a series of essays beginning in 1792 with *Über den Grund des Vergnügens an tragischen Gegenständen* (*On the Source of Pleasure in Tragic Subjects*), and including *Über die tragische Kunst* (*On the Art of Tragedy*, 1792), *Über das Pathetische* (*On Pathos*, 1793) and *Vom Erhabenen* (*On the Sublime*, 1793), Schiller presents the essence of tragedy as the conflict between suffering nature, that is the mental or physical compulsion to which men and women are uncomprehendingly subject in the real world of experience, and moral resistance to suffering, that is the imaginary possibility of the triumph of the mind over material circumstances: the sublimity to which the tragic hero aspires is the preservation of the moral self in the face of physical defeat. As a theorist of tragedy the mature Schiller operates with a very firm notion of what men and women ought to be, although it should be said that as a practising dramatist and suspicious psychologist he has a clear sense that they are not what they ought to be. It follows from this that he should advocate in his classicist tragedy, *Die Braut von Messina* (*The Bride of Messina*, 1803), a radical renunciation of illusionism in the theatre and the adoption of a technique which makes it clear that the world of the stage is a contrasting image to the real world. The chorus of ancient Greek tragedy, which he reintroduces here, functions as a living wall around the action, to emphasize that it is completely cut off from empirical reality.

The vibrant and radical idealism of these theories bore fruit in dramas which constitute the classical core of the repertoire of the German stage. Ultimately, however, it was to be the other lines of criticism which were to prove more productive and inspirational. It is to Diderot's theory of a drama of constantly changing tableaux and, above all, to Shakespeare that the progressive critics – like the innovative dramatists – of the nineteenth century will turn.

7
Prose fiction: France

English Showalter

The debate in the classical era: *roman* and *nouvelle*

Introduction

Fictional prose narratives of several types were popular in France throughout the Middle Ages and Renaissance. Some have always been called
romans, the standard word for the English term 'novel'. The history of
the French novel therefore begins in the early medieval period; in the
seventeenth and eighteenth centuries the genre achieved new prominence
and stature. A serious critical discourse on the novel existed in France
well before 1670. *Romans* – especially those of d'Urfé, Gomberville, La
Calprenède, Georges and Madeleine de Scudéry – were discussed in the
salons, in authors' prefaces, and even in writings by scholars and academicians like Chapelain, Ménage, Segrais, Boileau, Furetière, and Huet.

A different but equally significant concern for the theory and practice
of fiction appears in French imitations of Cervantes's *Don Quixote*
(translated in 1614) by writers such as Charles Sorel and Paul Scarron.
Spain also introduced France to the *novela*, a shorter and less exotic
genre than the heroic *romans*. Early translations and imitations emphasized the verisimilitude of the new form; Segrais's *Nouvelles françoises*
(1656) stated succinctly a key problem for theorists of the novel: 'the
difference between the *Roman* and the *Nouvelle* [is] that the *Roman*
writes things as propriety wishes them and in the manner of a poet; but
the *Nouvelle* must take a bit more from History, and try rather to give
the images of things as we ordinarily see them happen, than as our
imagination figures them' (I, p. 146).[1]

In the decade of the 1660s, the long heroic *romans* lost favour, while
the *nouvelles* flourished, a change in taste that coincided with the golden
age of French classicism. In 1678 Marie-Madeleine de Lafayette published *La Princesse de Clèves*, an instant popular success still considered

---

[1] '... la différence qu'il y a entre le Roman et la Nouvelle ... que le Roman écrit ces
choses comme la bienseance le veut, et à la maniere du Poëte; mais que la Nouvelle
doit un peu davantage tenir de l'Histoire, et s'attacher plûtôt à donner les images
des choses comme d'ordinaire nous les voyons arriver, que comme notre imagination
se les figure' (Segrais, *Nouvelles françoises*, I, p. 146).

a classical masterpiece. The proliferation of criticism surrounding Lafayette's novels constitutes the first phase of French theory of the novel. Although theory is closely related to practice, this discussion will concentrate on theoretical statements – essays and books about the genre – sketching only enough history of the novel to situate the ideas.

Huet's Lettre-traité sur l'origine des romans, *1670*

Pierre-Daniel Huet was an erudite academician, a member of Lafayette's circle, and Bishop of Avranches. His *Traité*, the first history of the genre, was published with Lafayette's *Zayde*; it enjoyed great prestige, with eleven printings by 1711, when the last revised version appeared. Huet's ostensible purpose was to trace the origins of the *roman*, but in doing so he had to define it and discuss the relationship between the *roman* and truth or reality, and the purpose of the *roman*. The search for origins, moreover, implied a quest for legitimacy. Without ancient precedents, the *roman* had no models and no rules; Huet's historical research set out to supply both.

Huet defines *romans* as 'fictive stories of amorous adventures, written in prose with art, for the pleasure and instruction of readers'.[2] Pleasure is a subordinate goal, a device to overcome natural human resistance to instruction, which is the main goal. Huet offers the standard formula for this instruction: 'show virtue rewarded and vice punished'.[3] The whole definition is motivated by his eventual argument that the *roman* is a form of epic and should follow the same rules.

Although Huet accepts the *roman*'s fictionality and disagrees with moralists who condemn it as lies, he remains concerned with its relationship to historical veracity. He dismisses 'relations of imaginary origins of nations'[4] and fulminates against Annius Viterbus for having fabricated histories. The *roman*, in short, must declare its fictional status and not imitate truth so well that scholars might be deceived. Furthermore, the *roman* is bound by the principle of verisimilitude; consequently, pure fiction is unacceptable in the *grands romans*, because it is implausible that great deeds should have escaped the notice of historians. Huet thus situates French theories of the novel within the Aristotelian tradition contrasting history to poetry. He distinguishes between *grands romans* and *romans comiques* like *Don Quixote*: in the latter, pure fiction is acceptable. Writing before the vogue of the *nouvelle*,

---

[2] 'histoires feintes d'aventures amoureuses, écrites en prose avec art, pour le plaisir et l'instruction des lecteurs' (Huet, *Lettre-traité*, p. 46).
[3] 'la vertu couronnée et le vice puni' (p. 47).
[4] 'origines imaginaires de la plupart des nations' (p. 49).

he ignored the new genre, but did not revise his argument in later editions, and probably objected to the *nouvelle* as fraudulent history.

Huet locates the *roman*'s ultimate source in the prehistoric 'Orient' (North Africa, the eastern Mediterranean, the Middle East); from there, it eventually passed to the Greeks, who perfected it, and transmitted it to Rome. This linear genealogy, however, is only one of many parallel histories, for, according to Huet, the desire to know is universal and the acquisition of sure knowledge is difficult. Hence the impulse to rely on fiction can be found everywhere, and there is no reason to doubt that the French, German, and English *romans* are native to the region: 'they have no other origin than the histories filled with falsehoods that were produced in obscure ages, full of ignorance ... these histories mingling truth and falsehood having been accepted by half-barbarian peoples, historians had the boldness to compose purely supposititious ones which are the *romans*'.[5]

Huet consigns the medieval *romans* to critical oblivion, despite their popularity throughout Europe, because they owed their success to readers' mental weakness, and 'good judges are perhaps rarer than good novelists and good poets'.[6] Then Huet turns to the epic tradition he would rediscover, or more accurately, invent for the *roman*: 'The Greeks ... cultivated the art of the *roman*, and from the raw and unpolished thing it was among the Orientals they gave it a better form, bringing it under the rules of the epic, and joining in a perfect body the various disorderly and unrelated parts that composed the *romans* before them'.[7] In the end, however, Huet can find only seven novelists adhering to the Homeric outline; they form a meagre tradition.

Huet's erudition masks a persistent anxiety about the genre's epistemological status. Even the seventeenth-century *romans*, which followed his model and which he admired, inspired reservations. French preeminence in the field he attributes to women's influence. But women made *romans* their exclusive preoccupation, and to conceal their ignorance they scorned history; to please women, men followed their example. Thus, laments Huet, 'a good cause produced a very bad effect and the beauty of our romances brought about contempt for belles-lettres,

---

[5] '... elles n'ont point d'autre origine que les histoires remplies de faussetés qui furent faites dans des temps obscurs, pleins d'ignorance ... ces histoires mêlées du vrai et du faux ayant été reçues par des peuples demi-barbares, les historiens eurent la hardiesse d'en faire de purement supposées qui sont les romans' (pp. 133–4).

[6] '... les bons juges sont peut-être plus rares que les bons romanciers ou les bons poètes' (p. 88).

[7] 'Les Grecs ... ont aussi cultivé l'art romanesque, et de brut et inculte qu'il était parmi les Orientaux, ils lui ont fait prendre une meilleure forme, en le resserrant sous les règles de l'épopée, et joignant en un corps parfait les diverses parties sans ordre et sans rapport qui composaient les romans avant eux' (p. 102).

and just as ignorance led to their birth, they led to the rebirth of ignorance'.[8]

Despite Huet's conservatism, elitism, and misogyny, he was worried about ignorance and not immorality. He concludes with a strong defence of the genre. After quoting critical attacks on *romans*: 'they dry up religious faith, inspire illicit passions, and corrupt morals', he admits that such things may happen; but evil minds, he says, turn everything to evil uses. He recognizes that some readers will distort the formula ending; however, 'The cause of this disorder is not in the work, but in the bad inclination of the reader'. He argues that young people need to know about love, and that experience shows 'those who know love least' to be 'the most susceptible', and 'the most ignorant' to be 'the most easily duped'.[9] Moreover, *romans* are 'silent preceptors' which prepare young men for society.

Despite his prestige, Huet had little direct influence on the future course of the novel. His poetics derived from an already moribund subgenre, the heroic romance. His history founded that genre on a fabricated epic tradition. Placing the *roman* under the rules of the epic solved the epistemological problem by maintaining an absolute distinction between fiction and history, and providing familiar rules for respecting that division. Even the epic, however, used history, and their problematic relationship would not be so easily dismissed.

Valincour's Lettres sur la Princesse de Clèves, *1679*

The year after the appearance of *La Princesse de Clèves*, a minor man of letters, Jean-Baptiste Trousset de Valincour, published an anonymous book-length criticism of it, cast in the form of three letters, addressed to 'Marquise ***'. Each letter takes up a different aspect of the novel: the 'conduite' (organization or structure), the 'sentiments' (psychology and morality), and the style; and each one proceeds through the novel from beginning to end, commenting on the parts. Valincour argues no consistent interpretation; rather, the letters purportedly reproduce conversations among the writer's friends. The second and third letters have less interest than the first; the letter on style consists largely of cavils and the letter on sentiments anticlimactically repeats many subjects from the

---

[8] '... une bonne cause a produit un très mauvais effet et la beauté de nos romans a attiré le mépris des belles-lettres, et comme l'ignorance les avait fait naître, ils ont aussi fait renaître l'ignorance' (p. 140).

[9] '... ils dessèchent la dévotion, ils inspirent des passions déréglées, ils corrompent les mœurs.... La cause de ce désordre n'est pas dans l'ouvrage, mais dans la mauvaise disposition du lecteur ... celles qui connaissent moins l'amour en sont les plus susceptibles et ... les plus ignorantes sont les plus dupes' (pp. 140, 141, 142).

letter on structure, where Valincour makes his most important arguments: the key scenes succeed in involving the reader's sympathy; the sources of the sympathy lie in the work's verisimilitude and structure; the lapses from historical accuracy and psychological plausibility are warranted by the overall plan; the epic is not the proper model; the episodic digressions are therefore a mistake and the action should be even more tightly unified.

The repeated standard of judgement for Valincour is the psychological truth and emotional force of the scene. Of the Princess's early attraction to the Duke, he writes: 'That expresses admirably the nature of certain feelings that form in our heart, that we hide from our closest friends, and that we try to hide from ourselves, for fear of being forced to combat them'.[10] In similar terms he defends the scenes where the Princess allows Nemours to steal her portrait and where she learns that the story of her confession is known. Even the controversial confession seems justifiable because of the interesting situations that result. But Valincour adds, 'it would not have been less pleasurable if it had been less contrived. It is a question of not having so much the air of a great adventure, for I confess that where history is concerned the verisimilar touches me more than anything else'.[11]

As Gérard Genette has said, Valincour outlines an economics of narrative plausibility. Infractions of verisimilitude are costs, but may be balanced by the gain. Valincour condemns the failed encounter between the Duke and the Princess near the end, partly as improbable, but more pointedly as 'useless'. Regarding the Prince's death, he observes: 'some blame an Author for having a Hero die too soon, without guessing the reasons he had for it, nor what purpose that death was to serve in the rest of the story'.[12]

The first letter contains three voices: 'Valincour', who defends verisimilitude and structural coherence; a lady, who defends morality and propriety; and a pedant, who defends the epic rules 'with that air of self-satisfaction Scholars cannot avoid'.[13] The pedant repeats Huet's principles, especially concerning a proper use of history. 'Valincour' argues that despite its flaws the work gives pleasure, and so its historical

---

[10] '... cela exprime admirablement bien la nature de certains mouvemens qui se forment dans nostre cœur, que nous cachons à nos plus intimes amis, & que nous taschons de nous cacher à nous-mesmes, de peur d'estre obligez de les combatre' (Valincour, *Lettres sur la Princesse de Clèves*, pp. 16–17).

[11] '... la chose n'en eust pas esté moins agréable, si elle eust esté moins concertée. C'est à faire à n'avoir pas tant l'air de grande aventure: car je vous avoûë, qu'en matiere d'histoire, le vray-semblable me touche plus que tout le reste' (p. 46).

[12] '... tel blasme un Auteur d'avoir fait mourir un Heros de trop bonne heure, qui ne peut pas deviner les raisons qu'il en a eû, ni à quoy cette mort devoit servir dans la suite de son histoire' (pp. 258–9).

[13] 'avec cet air de suffisance dont les Sçavans ne sçauroient se défaire' (p. 90).

veracity should not matter; but the pedant compares the novel to a concert where some voices are not in tune and demands perfect conformity to the rules.

The letter ends saying that the scholar is not right about everything, but not wrong about everything, either. Two more letters follow, mingling praise and criticism. It is unfair, as some have done, to take the pedant's views as Valincour's. On the contrary, 'Valincour's' sensitive appreciations, his intelligent analysis of the composition, and the mere existence of such extended commentary, reveal a new theory emerging, which rejects the epic model, emphasizes the reader's belief in the story, and calls the relation of fiction to history back into question.

Charnes's Conversations sur la critique de la Princesse de Clèves, *1679*

Within months the Abbé Jean-Antoine Charnes published a book to rebut Valincour, except that Charnes assumed his target to be the famous grammarian Bouhours. This mistaken assumption led Charnes to misdirect some of his remarks. In addition, Charnes disputes Valincour point by point, compounding the incoherence of Valincour's piecemeal approach. Finally, it is harder to affirm a work's flawlessness than to denounce its weaknesses. On the whole, then, Charnes's *Conversations* are less readable than Valincour's *Letters*.

Charnes, however, foregrounds a theme advanced but contested in Valincour: that *La Princesse de Clèves* is a new kind of literature, neither latter-day epic nor degraded history. Rather, 'it is a third genre in which one invents a subject or takes one that is not universally known; and one enhances it with several historical references that sustain its credibility and awaken the reader's curiosity and attention'.[14] He leaves the name of the genre in doubt, using interchangeably the terms *histoire galante, petite histoire, petite nouvelle,* and occasionally *roman.* Charnes harbours no qualms about confusion resulting from works of the third kind: 'They are simple and faithful copies of true history, often so similar to it that they are mistaken for history itself'.[15] And he professes a thoroughgoing modernism: 'our poets would not do badly to abandon antiquity, whose subjects are exhausted by now, to put on our stages

---

[14] '... c'en est une troisième espèce dans laquelle ou l'on invente un sujet, ou l'on en prend un qui ne soit pas universellement connu; et on l'orne de plusieurs traits d'histoire qui en appuyent la vraisemblance, et réveillent la curiosité et l'attention du lecteur' (Charnes, *Conversations*, p. 130).

[15] 'Ce sont des copies simples & fidelles de la veritable histoire, souvent si ressemblantes, qu'on les prend pour l'histoire mesme' (p. 135).

heroes for our times'; 'it is up to the rules to adapt themselves to the taste of a century as refined as ours'.[16]

Charnes generally agrees with Valincour about what works best in *La Princesse de Clèves* and why: readers believe that the scenes are real, feel as if they were there, and are moved. Both critics attribute the effect to faithful depiction of familiar subjects. Both take conversation as the appropriate stylistic model and both deem language's function to be clear communication; on specific cases Charnes simply denies the ambiguities that troubled Valincour's grammarian. Charnes's aesthetic principle is pure French classicism: 'it is easy to abridge by omitting half; the question is to abridge and say everything, as the Author does so well';[17] but his enthusiasm for the *nouvelle* leads him to a progressive modernist position.

Du Plaisir's Sentiments sur l'histoire, *1683*

Du Plaisir still remains an unknown figure, except as the author of a *nouvelle* and a treatise, of which the full title is, *Sentiments sur les lettres et sur l'histoire, avec des scrupules sur le style*. The section on 'history' begins by stating that there are few rules for writing true history ('histoire véritable'). Therefore the author will discuss the *histoire galante*, and point out how it resembles, and differs from, true history. What follows is a 'poetics of the *nouvelle*', which had become the dominant fictional form. Du Plaisir offers no new ideas; his merit consists in having synthesized theoretical statements and the authors' practices in a succinct essay.

In the first four paragraphs Du Plaisir uses four different names for the genre: 'histoire galante', 'petite histoire', 'nouvelle', and 'nouveau roman', to be distinguished from 'ancien roman' and 'fable à dix ou douze volumes' on one side, and from 'histoire véritable' on the other. The new genre has 'destroyed' the old, he says, and describes the new: it is short, with a single main action, no digressions, a setting neither far in the past nor distant in space, no narrations by confidants, no beginning *in medias res*, and verisimilitude founded on credibility rather than historical facts.

The final point leads to the paradox that history can relate more

---

[16] '... nos Poëtes ne feroient pas mal d'abandonner cette antiquité, dont les sujets sont desormais épuisez, pour mettre sur nos theatres des Heros de nostre façon ... C'est aux regles à s'accommoder au goust d'un siecle aussi poli que le nostre ...' (pp. 144, 145).

[17] 'Il est facile d'abreger, dit Cleante, en ne disant que la moitié des choses. La question est d'abreger & de tout exprimer, comme fait si bien l'Auteur ...' (p. 321).

extraordinary events than fiction, because history deals with true events; but the beauty of a fiction lies in its ability to make an untrue event seem true, and for Du Plaisir its merit is all the greater if the event is extraordinary. Both old and new novels seek to please by the invention of incidents, the constancy of characters, the nobility of the thoughts, and the appropriateness of the feelings. The *nouvelles* succeed because of their familiarity; the situations apply to everyone.

Finally, Du Plaisir presents a practical guide for writing *nouvelles*, although he disclaims any intention to legislate. The author should begin by setting the scene and introducing the characters, individualizing their personal qualities but shunning physical detail; principal characters should be revealed through deeds rather than portraits. Scenes should not be interrupted arbitrarily and motivations should be credible. The author may narrate inner states of mind but should avoid conventional soliloquies. Conversations are important; the style should be fluent and natural, and may be freer than normal literary style. Action should accelerate near the end. The story should conclude with death or the union of the couple and it should include an obvious moral lesson, based on distributive justice.

Du Plaisir's most restrictive principle concerns the author's impartiality. Viewing the novelist as a historian, he would forbid any expression whatsoever of the author's opinion: no irony, no moralizing, no politics, no maxims, 'not even any general reflections added to a description or to a narrative'.[18] Ultimately he sounds like Flaubert, arguing that detachment is so necessary that it is forbidden 'even to join to a name some flattering adjective, however easy to justify ... even of the King they could not say *this great Prince*'.[19]

Du Plaisir's work was not reprinted after 1683. His name remained in obscurity and he was not cited as an authority. None the less, his essay proves the level of interest and sophistication that the theoretical discussion of fiction had attained in the late seventeenth century. Du Plaisir accurately described the state of the genre as practised by Lafayette and others, formulating a free and modern relationship between the novel and reality. Anxiety persisted, however, over the novelist's role as historian. In fact novelists turned increasingly to first-person genres – fictitious memoirs, imaginary voyages, letter-novels – to the outrage of scholars like Pierre Bayle, who were trying to found a scientific method of historical investigation.

---

[18] '... l'on n'ajoûte plus mesme de réflexions generales à une description, ou un recit' Du Plaisir, *Sentiments*, p. 61.

[19] '... défend aux Historiens de joindre mesme à un nom quelque terme flateur, quoy que facile à justifier ... Parlassent-ils mesme du Roy, ils ne pourroient pas dire *ce grand Prince*' (p. 56).

The debate in the 1730s, the ban on novels, and the moral formula

Introduction

An extraordinary burst of creativity in prose fiction occurred near the end of the seventeenth century and the start of the eighteenth. Old genres flourished, new ones proliferated – fairy tales and oriental tales, as well as first-person narratives. Obviously, Huet's dream of defining and regulating the novel failed. Despite the activity among novelists, there was not much significant critical and theoretical writing until the 1730s. Boileau's *Dialogue des héros de roman* (1688, reprinted 1710) had been written in the 1660s, and Boileau's attacks were directed against a type of *roman* long since gone out of fashion with writers, although not with readers. The Abbé Faydit's *Télémacomanie* (1700), a vehement denunciation of Fénelon's *Télémaque* (1699), gives a foretaste of things to come. Faydit argues that a few moral reflections do not compensate for the licentious descriptions. The Church, he says, has always 'believed *Romans* and *Romanciers* more pernicious and more criminal than books full of heresies and heretics themselves'.[20]

Finally, periodical criticism was beginning to prosper. The *Mercure galant* had begun publication in 1672. In 1701 the Jesuits began issuing their *Mémoires pour l'histoire des sciences et des beaux-arts*, better known as the *Mémoires de Trévoux*. In 1713 a group of men of letters in Holland started the *Journal littéraire*; by the late 1720s it reviewed novels regularly. A host of ephemeral periodicals contained reviews and comments. It is difficult to synthesize any consistent conception of the novel from this journalism; for the most part, the reviewers applied classical standards of verisimilitude and propriety, and often found the work deficient in both, as well as threatening to society, morals, taste, and a proper understanding of history.

Even authors with a personal stake in the genres of fiction failed or refused to discuss theoretical questions. The Abbé Desfontaines translated Swift's *Gulliver's Travels* in 1727 but attempted no theoretical justification of fantasy or science fiction, nor did Voltaire when he began writing in the genre toward mid-century. Crébillon wrote 'oriental' tales, fairy tales, and an epistolary novel; but his prefaces take up the traditional theme of morality, not the specific qualities and problems of the genres. Aubert de La Chesnaye Des Bois first translated *Pamela* in 1741; but like Prévost, who translated *Clarissa* in 1751 and *Sir Charles*

---

[20] '... elle a crû les Romans & les Romanciers plus pernicieux & plus criminels que les Livres pleins d'heresies, & les Heretiques mêmes' (Faydit, *Télémacomanie*, pp. 18–19).

Grandison in 1755–6, he treated some of the most original aspects as problems and adapted Richardson to French taste. English novels enjoyed great popularity in France but the numerous imitations differ little from the standard French fare, except for the characters' names. Despite a vigorous tradition of letter-novels dating from Guilleragues's *Lettres portugaises* (1669) and extending to Laclos's *Liaisons dangereuses* (1782) and beyond, neither authors nor critics paid much attention to the specificity of a fictional correspondence, subsuming epistolary novels under the general questions of verisimilitude and morality.

The moralists attack

The novel had come under attack for immorality in the seventeenth century. Huet's tolerant attitude carried the day, however, even though a fundamental condition of his defence was soon undermined. For Huet, the *roman* was an admitted fiction, seeming true (*vrai*), as opposed to real (*réel*). In ordinary French usage as in English, the two terms are often used interchangeably; in the critical debate, the *vrai* as in *vraisemblable* came to be associated with the abstract concepts of what was possible, whereas the *réel* referred to actual events attested by reliable documents. For purposes of clarity, in this discussion the English terms 'true' and 'real' will be used consistently to reflect that contrast. According to Huet, novelists working in the gaps and shadows of historical reality could evade the historian's obligation to relate ignoble and offensive facts, and concentrate on the morally and spiritually uplifting truth. Writers, however, found that Huet's abstract verisimilitude pleased readers less than practical credibility, not dependent on verifiable documents, but on accurate observation of familiar character-types and situations. The indecorous and corrupting matter that propriety banished from the old *roman* found its way back into the various forms of the new. The alarm and outrage Faydit expressed over *Télémaque* intensified and reached crisis level in the 1730s.

The decade of the 1730s was a golden age for the French novel. Several major novelists – Lesage, Prévost, Marivaux, Crébillon *fils* – were writing at the peak of their powers. New fiction titles had averaged about twelve a year from 1700 to 1729; from 1730 to 1739, the annual average was almost twenty-three, nearly double the previous rate. Accompanying the novels was a growing critical literature. Many novels included a justificatory preface. Prévost and Desfontaines edited periodicals, which gave regular and knowledgeable attention to fiction. Within the novels, authors carried on rivalries, parodying and criticizing each other. A flurry of critical essays appeared: Lenglet-Du Fresnoy's *De l'usage des romans* (1734) and d'Argens's 'Discours sur les nouvelles' in

his *Lectures amusantes* (1739), both supporting the novel; and opposing it, Lenglet-Du Fresnoy's *L'Histoire justifiée contre les romans* (1735)
and Porée's sermon 'On Novels' (1736). These books had neither the
perspicuity nor the originality of the four works that accompanied the
rise of the *nouvelle*; rather than discuss them individually, it seems more
useful to synthesize the positions in a polarized debate, and to include
some works that extended the debate well past 1740, such as Aubert de
La Chesnaye Des Bois's *Lettres amusantes et critiques sur les romans en
général* (1743), Baculard d'Arnaud's 'Discours sur le roman' (1745) and
later prefaces, Abbé Jaquin's *Entretiens sur les romans* (1755), and
Marmontel's *Essai sur les romans* (1786).

Recent scholarship, especially the work of Georges May and Françoise
Weil, has established that in 1737 the French government silently ceased
authorizing the publication of novels, effectively banning the genre. The
political figure responsible was apparently the chancellor of France,
Daguesseau. May argued that hostile critics brought about the ban and
that their action had a profound influence on the genre; Weil contends
that the literary arguments were merely pretexts in a secret campaign to
exert stricter control. In any case, a lively debate took place and preoccupied critics for decades. A sermon by the Jesuit Porée, delivered in
Latin at the Collège Louis-le-Grand on 25 February 1736, exemplifies
the negative side. The *Mémoires de Trévoux* summarized Porée's arguments a few weeks later: 'By contagion [novels] spoil all the kinds of
literature with which they have any relationship. By their quantity they
stifle the taste for good literature, even for genres with which they have
no relationship ... They harm morality in two ways, by inspiring a
taste for vice and by stifling the seeds of virtue'.[21]

Porée's most original argument is that the quantity of bad novels is
driving out good literature. The perception of an increase in the number
of novels published was accurate, and the line of argument makes the
novelists' very success count against them. Some critics added the complaint that market forces alone were dictating literary taste; writers
wrote and printers printed whatever would sell, not what would improve the mind and soul of the reader. The alleged audience of women,
children, and fops was cited to prove the genre's unworthiness and
superficiality. The diversity of fictional genres supposedly substantiated
that charge; unlike great literature, novels enjoyed fleeting vogues and
sank into oblivion.

---

[21] 'Par leur contagion, ils gâtent tous les genres de littérature auxquels ils ont quelque
rapport. Par leur fécondité, ils étouffent le goût des bonnes lettres, et même des
genres auxquels ils ne se rapportent point.... les romans nuisent doublement aux
moeurs, en inspirant le goût du vice et en étouffant les semences de la vertu'
(quoted in May, *Dilemme*, p. 9).

Porée's fear that novels would corrupt other genres resembles Huet's concern to distinguish between fiction and history. The novelists' discovery of genres like the fictional memoir and the imaginary voyage, however, gave new urgency to the problem. Furthermore, as a strict observer of propriety, Huet would have been horrified by some of the characters depicted by 'realist' writers – hypocritical churchmen, corrupt statesmen, promiscuous actresses, cynical seducers, coarse coachmen, vulgar shopkeepers, thieves, even a whore and a rascal as Montesquieu called *Manon*'s protagonists.

The most persistent and strenuous diatribes were directed at the recurrent portrayal of love. Even the edifying love stories presented in *Télémaque* and *La Princesse de Clèves* raised the spectre of seduction and lost innocence; any image of ardent passion risked inflaming the reader's heart with culpable desire. In the view of hostile critics, the novel had become a school for libertines. Jaquin paired the charge of licentiousness with one of irreligion; writing in 1755, after the flood of pornographic and satirical tales of the 1740s, he had reasonable grounds to complain, although years earlier the charge had been brought against serious novels like *Cleveland*. Still another accusation held that novels threatened society and the state by ridiculing real people under the mask of fiction.

In short, enemies claimed that the practice of novelists had transformed the genre into a vehicle of contestation and subversion. By and large, the writers themselves denied any transgressive intentions, but the attacks describe the fiction of the times better than the authors' apologias. According to its adversaries, the novel could not help calling established values into question; the self-indulgent narratives of criminal behaviour contained more seductive power than the formulaic, and often long-delayed, distribution of rewards and chastisements in the dénouement. Moreover, the anti-novelists' accusatory portrait of the genre bears a striking resemblance to the programme advocated by many later theorists: a vehicle of contestation and subversion is precisely what many twentieth-century readers want the novel to be, and to have been.

The case for the defence

When one turns to the defenders of the genre, one is astonished to realize that they concede most of their opponents' points. An ostensible friend like Lenglet-Du Fresnoy rejects the whole picaresque genre, and even Scarron, because the works lack dignity and nobility; the whole heroic romance tradition, because the works lacked a clear structure and have gone out of style; and the whole corpus of *nouvelles galantes*, because they make love too seductive. D'Argens, himself a prolific novelist, endorses the interdiction, dating back to Huet, on the supernatural and on fictional events involving famous persons, but goes well beyond Huet in condemning *La Princesse de Clèves* as morally dangerous. Even the boldest novelists pay lip service to the ideal of a morally edifying novel based on the principle of distributive justice at the conclusion.

In certain cases the pious homily of vice punished and virtue rewarded clashes so with the novel itself that it seems ironic. Defences based on faithfulness to reality carry more conviction. They fall under several broad headings: the tableau of human behaviour; the superiority of concrete examples over abstract preaching; the preparation of young people for entry into society, both as a school of etiquette and as a warning against the dangers. Despite some superficial resemblances, this reasoning diametrically opposes the premise of Huet's rationale; it proclaims the precedence of the observably real over the ideally true. The best novelists claim faithfulness to reality in their prefaces and sometimes within the work itself. Prévost, Marivaux, and Crébillon all defend their subjects as drawn from actual contemporary society, and their art as useful precisely because of its accurate portrayal of reality.

These 'realist' arguments were not, however, unanimously supported. D'Argens, whose condemnation of *La Princesse de Clèves* has already been noted, offers a paragraph of conventional advice to would-be novelists, concluding: 'Above all, respect religion and morals. If in the plot there be any acts that set a bad example, let them receive a punishment that takes away the desire to imitate them'.[22] Lenglet-Du Fresnoy explicitly reasserts the claim that the *roman* is truer than history, adding that history is full of events and characters better left unmentioned. He is all too obviously talking about a hypothetical genre, an idealized version of the novel. When he proposes some principles for writing, he begins with the negatives: one must not give offence to religion, censure kings, attack those in public office, or affront morality; as for the affirmatives, one should choose a noble subject, respect verisimilitude, form the mind, and propagate morality – that is to say, depict well-behaved people who come to an honest end; include pleasing portraits of virtue, honour, and probity; express favourable ideas on chastity and modesty; teach more by images of perfection than of human misery. In his *Lettres sur les romans* Aubert de La Chesnaye Des Bois repeats verbatim key points from Huet, especially concerning the moral utility of novels with edifying conclusions – apparently the only lesson he retained from translating *Pamela* in 1741. He reiterates the charge that excessive numbers of novels have been published and have diverted

---

[22] 'Sur-tout, respectez la Religion et les bonnes moeurs. Si dans votre intrigue, il entre des actions de mauvais exemple, qu'elles y reçoivent un châtiment qui ôte l'envie de les imiter' (quoted in Coulet, *Roman*, II, p. 114).

both writers and readers from higher pursuits and he regrets that an irrational prejudice leads French men of learning to disparage the genre instead of illustrating it.

The consequence of the 1737 ban on novels in France was not at all to stop fiction from being written, sold, and read. The ban apparently drove some authors away from the genre; it may explain why Marivaux and Crébillon left works unfinished. It certainly created a windfall for the foreign presses that specialized in smuggling books into France. It induced a certain number of French publishers to risk prosecution for printing unauthorized works. And by favouring this underground network, it facilitated a far more transgressive literature than the one it was intended to suppress. The 1740s were thus marked by a strong upsurge in the publication of licentious and even pornographic fiction, alongside and sometimes overlapping a growing body of satirical and philosophical works aimed at the sacrosanct institutions of the church and the state.

The end of the proscription and the moralist consensus

When Malesherbes replaced Daguesseau as chancellor in 1751, the government's official posture toward novels became more tolerant. The tacit ban on novels was apparently lifted almost immediately. The debates of the 1730s had left a mark, however; the argument that novels served a high moral purpose became dogma. For the rest of the century, even the most independent-minded geniuses retained a strong dose of morality in their otherwise original prescriptions for the genre. Lesser writers and thinkers parroted the requirement endlessly, in the most conventional and superficial terms.

In 1761 Rousseau's *Julie, ou la Nouvelle Héloïse* aroused unprecedented public enthusiasm. It scarcely met the old formula for distributive justice, and was widely attacked, but the vast majority of readers thought it fused a powerful illusion of reality with a moving moral instruction. It seemed the masterpiece of the genre, and made the novel respectable. Novels, prefaces, periodical criticism, and essays poured forth as never before. Many recited the same basic lesson: fiction is similar to history, but fiction is superior to history, because fiction is moral, whereas history is not. Huet had advocated an idea that sounds the same, but there is a crucial difference. For Huet, the *roman* aimed to be true, whereas history was bound to the real. But the *roman* itself was a subsidiary form of history, confined to its interstices. Huet's rules forbade changing any known facts and inventing any that historians would presumably have known. As a consequence, only remote and exotic subjects were available to the authors of *romans*. Moreover, the true was always considered immanent in the real; the real was an imperfect embodiment of the true. The real and the true did not conflict, although the historian might have to labour to make the truth perceptible, whereas the *romancier* could freely construct a situation where truth manifested itself. In effect, Huet's *roman* evaded the Aristotelian choice between history and poetry by deriving its matter from history, its form from poetry.

By 1730 the theory had to accommodate subjects that were close to home, and seemed – because of the familiar details – real rather than true. In effect, the formula just mentioned was reversed: the *nouvelle* derived its matter from poetry, its form from history. That is, the characters, situations, and events were imaginary, but the story was recounted as if it were historical fact. Provided that the characters were not historically illustrious and that the story respected propriety, such a *nouvelle* might not violate Huet's precepts. Moreover, the theory tolerated fantasy and the supernatural as easily as realism. It became clear, however, that the illusion of reality depended on attributes of the narrative, which might easily override objections based on historical error ('This never happened'), narrative impossibility ('No one could know this'), or moral or psychological implausibility ('This could never have happened'). The last is an ambiguous and alarming category in which natural and ethical laws tend to merge. It is no doubt a natural law that girls do not drop gems from their mouths when they speak; what sort of law is it that Providence does not reward the wicked? or that virtuous women do not love men they are not married to?

The moralists' crusade against the novel arose from anxiety over the latter issue. Novels were persuasively presenting stories that were morally wrong. The novelists defended themselves by claiming fidelity to reality; the debate thus constructed and emphasized a difference between reality and truth. It is somewhat paradoxical that in the heyday of rationalism edifying fables should have been preferred to documented histories; yet such was the case, because moral 'truth' was deemed superior to empirical 'reality'. Baculard d'Arnaud's 'Discours sur le roman' (1745) provides an early version of the new moral dogmatism, asserting that readers will be entertained and instructed in reading *romans* 'much better than in going through all the volumes of history'.[23] Baculard did not go far beyond Huet there, but was still seeking his voice.

Thirty years later, with a score of titles to his credit, he wrote in the preface to his *Nouvelles historiques* (1774):

how will we love virtue if everything we read, everything we see, shows it trampled underfoot, unrewarded, unrespected, gathering dust and forgotten?

---

[23] 'beaucoup mieux qu'en parcourant tous les volumes d'histoire' (quoted in May, *Dilemme*, p. 149).

Let us have recourse, if necessary, to the artifices of fiction; that is the situation where one must take care not to expose the true in a nakedness dangerous to behold; let men believe that virtue will lead them to pleasure, wealth, power; it's a novel: very well! ardent partisans of truth, do not take our novel away from us . . .[24]

In 1786, with another score of titles in print, he prefaced his *Délassemens de l'homme sensible* with a fierce diatribe against history, describing it as 'disgusting compilations of prostituted praise, calumniatory satires, false judgments, criminal lies, humanity everywhere insulted, everywhere suffering, trampled underfoot, vice everywhere heaped with eulogies, fawned upon, rewarded . . . No, you will never persuade me that history can be of any use to most men . . .'[25] Although Baculard d'Arnaud is one of the most vehement and prolific, numerous other writers of the time echo his denunciations of history – Dorat, Mercier, De La Solle, Rétif de la Bretonne, Marmontel, and Sade.

Clearly, for such critics, history's prestige has sunk as much as the novel's has risen. The past is a book of horrors; a record of crime and savagery, not of heroic figures and epic deeds; a compendium of ignorance and superstition, not of unsurpassable achievements and noble origins. In part this attitude stems from their belief in progress; society and humanity were evolving toward a superior state, so that the past had to be transcended, if not obliterated. Whereas the seventeenth century located the 'true' in an essence not always visible but always present, these writers, sentimental and frustrated, locate the 'true' in a perfection not yet attained, but visible. Fiction's formidable power to make the imaginary seem real was thus enlisted in the cause of a project for reform.

Marmontel's Essai sur les romans, considérés du côté moral, *1787*

Among the conventional moralists, Marmontel is the most impressive figure. A protégé of Voltaire and Madame de Pompadour, he edited

---

[24] '. . . comment l'aimera-t-on cette vertu, si tout ce que nous lisons, tout ce que nous voyons, la montre foulée aux pieds, sans récompense, sans considération, dans la poussière de l'oubli? Ayons donc, s'il le faut, recours aux artifices de la fiction; c'est dans cette circonstance qu'il faut bien se garder d'exposer le vrai dans une nudité dangereuse à voir; laissons croire aux hommes que cette vertu les menera aux plaisirs, aux richesses, aux dignités; c'est un roman: eh bien! ardents sectateurs de la vérité, ne nous ôtez point notre roman' (Baculard, *Nouvelles historiques*, I, p. x).

[25] '. . . des compilations dégoûtantes de flatteries prostituées, de satyres calomnieuses, de faux jugemens, de mensonges punissables, l'humanité par-tout outragée, par-tout souffrante, foulée aux pieds, le vice par-tout comblé d'éloges, caressé, récompensé . . . Non, vous ne me persuaderez jamais que l'histoire puisse être de quelqu'utilité pour la plupart des hommes' (quoted in Coulet, *Roman*, II, p. 172).

the *Mercure* and succeeded d'Alembert as secretary of the Académie Française. He wrote tragedies, literary articles for the *Encyclopedia*, and numerous short stories collected as *Contes moraux*, a genre he was credited with inventing. Here, 'moral' means 'relating to mores'; some of the stories treat rather licentious themes. Late in his career, he wrote the *Essai sur les romans, considérés du côté moral*. It opens with the line, 'The worthiest object of literature, the only one that ennobles and honours it, is its moral usefulness'.[26]

Like Huet, Marmontel begins with a genealogy, extending back to antiquity. Even more than Huet's, Marmontel's account stigmatizes the genre. Part of his 'history' is the hypothesis that prose narratives preceded artful poetic epics; another part is that novels have always arisen in periods of decadence. Marmontel dismisses seventeenth-century *romans* as a worthless vogue, because they lacked moral utility. Still following and distorting Huet's thought, Marmontel turns to feminine influence. Observing that 'of all goods, the only one that remains to an obscure, indigent, and weak man is the property of his wife and children', he argues that chivalric romances taught men to devote their valour to the 'protection of weakness and innocence, beauty and love'.[27] Thus, in their time, they had a moral usefulness. By contrast, the 'long, boring' seventeenth-century romances celebrated a trivial *galanterie*. Molière's satire killed the old romances, by Marmontel's account; then the novel went to the other extreme with *La Princesse de Clèves*, 'composed by a woman as if to mark the limit to which illegitimate love could go in a well-born heart without degrading it and without depriving it of its right to esteem and pity'.[28] Moreover, it is a dangerous novel, because few women could resist as the Princess did. Imperceptibly, Marmontel has replaced men with women as the primary targets for the novel's moral teaching, while giving women's role in shaping the genre a purely negative cast.

In fact, for Marmontel the moral utility of the novel comes down to its efficacy in regulating women's desire. Fiction's ability to stir up emotion gives it unusual power over women, with attendant risks; badly used, it could unloose chaos. Marmontel reduces the instructional function to the conclusion. He would rewrite *La Princesse de Clèves* to show the heroine 'guilty and unhappy through the sole temerity of her confidence

---

[26] 'Le plus digne objet de la littérature, le seul même qui l'ennoblisse et qui l'honore, c'est son utilité morale' (Marmontel, *Essai*, p. 558).

[27] 'De tous les biens, le seul qui reste à l'homme obscur, indigent et faible, c'est la propriété domestique de sa femme et de ses enfans ... la protection de la faiblesse et de l'innocence, de la beauté et de l'amour' (p. 563).

[28] '... composé par une femme, comme pour marquer la limite jusqu'à laquelle l'amour illégitime pouvait aller dans un cœur bien né, sans l'avilir, et sans lui ôter ses droits à l'estime et à la pitié' (p. 570).

in herself and her own resolve'.[29] In a similar spirit he criticizes *Manon Lescaut* and he would revise *Julie* to banish Saint-Preux and leave Julie 'condemned to weep in humiliation and never marry'.[30] His formula for the plot is that, 'in the main character, unhappiness should be the result of crime, crime the result of error, error the result of passion, and passion should arise from a fundamental natural goodness'.[31]

For all his misgivings about the novels that had been written, Marmontel joined enthusiastically in the chorus ranking fiction above history:

> Such is [the historian's] condition that, at the risk even of being immoral, he must conceal nothing, neither these iniquitous prosperities, nor these disgraceful calamities which are the shame and the crime of fate: and that is what makes his job so critical and so painful ... it is more inconsequential than is thought for most people, whether it is really the truth that is transmitted to them; and if one consults them, one will see that the usefulness of the example, the importance of the lesson, the interest of the event, are what concerns them most.[32]

Marmontel makes uncomfortable reading today. The most authoritative, in some ways the most authoritarian and the most explicit spokesman for the moral critics, he exposes his fundamental arrogance in his very style. Whenever possible, he replaces a character's name with a characterizing epithet; he then treats those so characterized as a class; and finally represents the class by the abstract common quality: 'virtue', 'vice', 'weakness', 'innocence', 'beauty', 'love', 'gallantry', etc. The last line of the essay contains an insight few would dispute today: 'persuasion does not depend exclusively on certainty; it depends on the need to believe'.[33] Unfortunately, it seems never to have entered Marmontel's mind that his confident assertions might owe something to his own need to believe.

---

[29] 'devenue coupable et malheureuse par la seule témérité de sa confiance en elle-même et en ses propres résolutions' (p. 570).

[30] 'condamnée à pleurer dans l'humiliation, et à ne se marier jamais' (p. 582).

[31] 'dans le personnage intéressant, le malheur soit l'effet du crime, le crime l'effet de l'égarement, l'égarement l'effet de la passion, et que la passion prenne sa source dans un fonds de bonté naturelle' (pp. 577–8).

[32] 'Telle est donc sa condition, qu'au risque même d'être immoral, il ne doit rien dissimuler, ni de ces prospérités iniques, ni de ces indignes calamités qui sont la honte et le crime du sort: et c'est ce qui rend ses fonctions si critiques et si pénibles ... il est plus indifférent qu'on ne pense pour le plus grand nombre des hommes, que ce soit bien réellement la vérité qui leur est transmise; et si on les consulte, on verra que l'utilité de l'exemple, l'importance de la leçon, l'intérêt de l'événement, sont ce qui les touche le plus' (pp. 591–4).

[33] 'La persuasion ne tient pas exclusivement à la certitude; elle tient au besoin de croire ...' (p. 595).

The novel in Spain and Italy

It is scarcely an exaggeration to say that in the seventeenth century the French derived most of their ideas of the novel from Spain, which gave rise to three powerful models: the comic novel, based on *Don Quixote*; the 'nouvelle', based on the 'novela'; and the picaresque. Other forms, like the pastoral and the heroic romance, also owed a debt to Spanish models. The Italian influence was more distant, but Boccaccio's *Decameron* lay at the source of a significant tradition of tales. Aretino, Ariosto, Tasso, and others were also read and regularly retranslated throughout the eighteenth century in France. In both Spain and Italy, however, the period from 1660 to 1800 is remarkably barren in new fiction and in critical writing on the subject.

In Spain, after the Golden Age, literature passed through a prolonged decline. The influence of the Inquisition and censorship exercised by a reactionary government combined with a generally conservative society to resist the social and intellectual changes associated with the rise of the novel. In the first half of the eighteenth century, almost no new fiction was written in Spain. Beginning with Diego de Torres Villaroel's *Vida* in 1743, a few interesting fictions were published; and the public continued to read both translations of English and French novels and reprintings of earlier Spanish fiction. For critics, nevertheless, the over-riding concern remained the moral acceptability of fictions. To some extent, the arguments echoed those of France in the 1730s, but in Spain the enemies of the novel held a far stronger position politically and a more extreme position morally. In their view entertainment and diversion were never innocent; to defend itself the novel would have had to demonstrate its superiority as a method of moral improvement. French and English critics had already rehearsed the fundamental arguments on both sides, and Spain produced no important criticism.

Italy's political climate differed from Spain's, and although the eighteenth century was not one of Italian literature's great periods, some genres fared better than prose fiction. French fictional theory made its influence felt in the middle of the eighteenth century, when a debate on the moral value of novels and on the relative merits of history and fiction took place among a group of Italian intellectuals, all of whom had read Huet. Notable among them were Pietro Chiari, who first denounced novels in 1749 and then became a defender in 1753; Giuseppe Antonio Costantini, who held in 1748 that the genre could be instructive and edifying; and Gasparo Patriarchi, who in 1759 sent a translation of Huet's *Traité* in a letter to Francesco Algarotti, published in Algarotti's *Opere* in 1794. Patriarchi urged a more inclusive definition of 'romanzo' than Huet, so as to legitimize philosophical and allegorical fictions. Carlo Gozzi in 1761 and Giuseppe Maria Galanti in 1780 defended novels on still broader grounds, as superior to history, capable of making people virtuous, happy, and productive citizens.

In both Spain and Italy, the state of the novel languished far behind its position in England or France, in number of novelists, number of novels published, and influence of the novels on later writers. The reading public depended in large measure on translations of English or French novels. It is not surprising, then, that the critical and theoretical discourse also lagged, and in fact borrowed most of its substance from works produced in England and France. The critical orthodoxy of the mid-eighteenth century never silenced dissent in France, as will be seen in the next section; and in England the powerful models provided by Fielding, Richardson, and Sterne led to a different dynamic altogether. In Spain and Italy, however, critical discussion of prose fiction in this period was little more than a repetition of already familiar and even conventional French ideas.

Theories of the late eighteenth century

Rousseau's preface to Julie, 1761

The most enduring fiction of the last half of the eighteenth century was produced outside the mainstream, and the most interesting theoretical texts were likewise written outside the critical consensus. Rousseau played the paradoxical role of leading novelist and outspoken enemy of the genre; he explained his ideas most explicitly in the two prefaces to *Julie, ou la Nouvelle Héloïse*. A brief one, full of lapidary formulas – 'Spectacles are necessary in big cities, and novels for corrupt peoples'; 'Never has a chaste maiden read novels'[34] – appeared with the first edition; in it, Rousseau speaks as the editor of the collection of letters constituting the novel. The second, longer preface takes the form of a dialogue between the editor, who identifies himself as Rousseau, and a man of letters called 'N'.

The man of letters raises a host of objections, reflecting the standard concerns of the age: the interest of the story and characters; the truth of the world portrayed; the moral effect of reading the work. In each case, Rousseau accepts the validity of the concern and responds by affirming that *Julie* obeys the rules; but he interprets the rules in his own way. Simultaneously, he piques the potential reader's curiosity, especially by his evasion of the first question, 'Is the correspondence real

---

[34] 'Il faut des spectacles dans les grandes villes, et des Romans aux peuples corrompus ... Jamais fille chaste n'a lu de Romans' (Rousseau, *Julie*, pp. 5, 6).

or a fiction?'.[35] For 'N', the difference matters: if the letters are real, then the work is a portrait, to be judged by its resemblance to the original events and people; if the letters are fiction, then the work is a novel, to be judged by its fidelity to universal truth. Rousseau foresees the trap: if it is a portrait, then it is a perfect likeness, but the subject is base and uninteresting; if it is a fiction, then the story violates the principles of verisimilitude and propriety. The pretence that letters or memoirs were real was a cliché; Rousseau, however, leaves the answer ambiguous, challenging 'N' and the reader to decide for themselves, adding that he has been to the region and found no trace of the people, admitting that there are geographical mistakes. Thus Rousseau carves out a new space for the novel, neither true nor false, neither real nor fictional.

Regarding interest, Rousseau reverses Huet's position, that a scholarly elite can judge best and that polite Parisian society had led to French pre-eminence in the novel. Rousseau waives any appeal to the urban sophisticates, professing to write only for a provincial audience. Solitude and tranquillity are required to appreciate a work like *Julie* and Rousseau asserts that the provinces are populated with people, especially women, who while away their time reading novels. Evoking a figure resembling Emma Bovary, he imagines a novel that would sustain such readers in their real lives, rather than feed their dissatisfactions. Instead of idealized ('true') characters in extraordinary actions, Rousseau proposes unique ('real') characters in commonplace situations; instead of lofty heroic virtues, attainable ones. Although Rousseau measures his distance from Richardson, the English novel had established the genre's right to narrate the lives of common folk.

Stressing attainable virtues leads to moral questions. Conservative moralists rejected any portrayal of waywardness; the conventional solution of moderates was distributive justice. In *Julie*, despite having sinned, the heroine and her lover escape punishment, and Rousseau underscores the absence of villains. This is, then, a new kind of moral teaching, based on sympathetic and familiar characters whose moral growth can be emulated. Rousseau emphasizes the need to read the whole story, the fall as well as the redemption; in this also he owes a great deal to the English model, and he looks toward the future course of the genre, with its interplay between time and human consciousness. Fiction before him had followed a character – in the dual sense of a fictional person and a set of stable moral traits – through a sequence of dramatic events; Rousseau located the drama in the inner life and violated the precept that character should remain uniform throughout.

Rousseau brings to his theory of the novel many of the themes of his

---

[35] 'Cette correspondance est-elle réelle, ou si c'est une fiction?' (p. 11).

thought: the value of the individual, the anxiety of the self in the flux
of time, the transmutation of guilt, the denunciation of the city and
civilization, the return to the country and nature. In many respects these
are the future preoccupations of the novel. They are illustrated throughout Rousseau's works, and his theoretical commentary on the novel is
quite brief. Far from celebrating a bold new way of writing, he returns
to his pessimistic view of human history. The novel must be tolerated
only because society has already declined so far that nothing else has
any chance of success. He repeats the old simile of the sugar-coated pill,
albeit with a new intensity, for Rousseau diagnoses humanity as stricken
with a mortal illness, curable only by drastic measures. His posture as
the misunderstood outsider, the lonely voice of conscience in a corrupt
world, would have great appeal for decades to come; and a certain kind
of novel, lyrical and pathetic, would be one of his followers' ideal
modes of self-expression.

Diderot's Éloge de Richardson, 1762

Enthusiasm for the novel came late to Diderot. The original English
versions of Richardson's novels converted him to the ranks of the pro-
novelists; but he discovered Richardson late, too. By 1755 the anti-
novelist Jaquin was already wishfully claiming that Richardson's vogue
had subsided. The Eulogy contains perceptive appreciations of Richardson,
but its primary value is that it contains Diderot's most explicit statements on the aesthetics of the novel.

The Eulogy begins with a contentious definition of the roman as 'it
has been understood' until then: 'a tissue of chimerical and frivolous
events, the reading of which is dangerous for taste and for morals'.[36]
One recognizes the rhetoric of anti-novelists from the seventeenth century on and a blithe disregard for the genre's many defenders and
practitioners. Diderot extols Richardson's effectiveness as a moral influence; this call for moral edification is what is most outdated in his
theory. At least he undertakes to demonstrate how it might take place,
instead of relying on poetic justice to indoctrinate the reader. The key
is a representational realism so powerful that the reader is caught up in
the illusion. Diderot himself succumbed readily to this effect; in the
Eulogy he relates several incidents in which readers reacted to the characters as if to living people. Once this powerful illusion is established,
the dramatic structure then awakens feelings through sympathetic

---

[36] 'Par un roman, on a entendu jusqu'à ce jour un tissu d'événements chimériques et
frivoles, dont la lecture était dangereuse pour le goût et pour les mœurs' (Diderot,
Éloge, p. 29).

identification. For the materialist Diderot, this process is almost automatic; the writer's appeal to the reader's senses, by way of the imagination, sets in motion – literally – the fibres or nerves, which in turn
generate consciousness, ideation, and most importantly, moral sensibility. Furthermore, Diderot believes that feelings – in particular, pity and
sympathy, the imaginative sharing of the feelings of others – lie at the
basis of morality. To arouse the emotions is to fertilize the seeds of
virtue innate in all human beings.

After Richardson, Diderot wishes to rename the genre, although doing
so implies that *roman* remains the term in use. In the epilogue to *Les
Deux Amis de Bourbonne* Diderot uses a different word: *conte*, generally translated as 'tale', and normally reserved for short fictions, told in
the third person by a distinctly perceptible narrator. Diderot distinguishes three types of *conte*, however: the *conte merveilleux*, 'supernatural (or miraculous) tale', in the manner of Homer, Virgil, and Tasso;
the *conte plaisant*, 'humorous tale', in the manner of Vergier, Ariosto,
and Hamilton; and finally the *conte historique*, 'historical tale', as in the
nouvelles of Scarron, Cervantes, and Marmontel. The historical tale
interests Diderot most, but he is one of the first critics to consider these
sub-genres and to recognize criteria for excellence in each. The supernatural tale inhabits an exaggerated and idealized world of its own; if
that world is well imagined and consistent, the work succeeds. The
humorous tale does not aim at plausibility or the illusion of reality; if
it amuses through wit, charm, and imagination, the author has fulfilled
his aim. For Diderot, those two sub-genres raise few problems; the historical tale, however, must be defended against the dual accusations of
lying and platitude – exactly the dilemma Rousseau faced. If it is a copy
of reality, it is dull; if it is invented, it is a lie, not a work of literature.

In response, Diderot develops a complex theory of mimesis. The key
elements are the accumulation of small details; the artist's eye for significant particulars; the inclusion of arbitrary items; and a technique of
representation in which the reader understands better than the characters. Diderot scolds Prévost for having abridged Richardson's text in
translating it; he regards immersion in the fictional world as crucial.
Although the massive quantities of minutiae might sound tedious, the
genius perceives things others overlook. In some cases, the detail may
exist simply to make the reader think 'One just doesn't invent that sort
of thing';[37] here Diderot anticipates what Roland Barthes called the
'effet de réel'. Finally, he prizes certain ambiguities and keywords, in
which a hidden or repressed truth can be glimpsed. When Richardson
introduces a character with a secret feeling, Diderot says, 'listen well,

---

[37] 'on n'invente pas ces choses-là' (Diderot, *Deux Amis*, p. 791).

and you will hear a dissonance that betrays him' (*Eulogy*, p. 32).[38] Deciphering such passages engages the reader's mind.

Moreover, Diderot embraces the power of the imagination. The illusion cannot be created without 'eloquence and poetry', both forms of falsehood which inspire mistrust. The techniques of verisimilitude will overcome that mistrust, so that eloquence and poetry can 'interest, touch, sweep along, move, make the skin crawl and tears flow'.[39] For Richardson is at the opposite remove from someone who merely copies reality. Diderot is captivated by the immensity and variety of his world. Diderot responded to dramatic contrast, both in character and in situation. He welcomed the self-contradictory and unpredictable characters in English novels, as more lifelike than the unified and consistent characters of classical theory, but unlike Rousseau he did not develop a theory of character development and education. Diderot's conception of the novel demands strong characters with powerful and variable emotions; but narrative time serves only to place these characters in dramatic situations that test their feelings. He does not show the self as a fluid entity changing and maturing as a result of experience.

Diderot's verisimilitude derives from a way of structuring the text rather than from an external principle, whether respect for historical fact, or plausible sources of information. The use of the word *conte* is significant in that regard; Diderot ignores the question, 'How could the narrator know that?' – a question that lay behind such contrivances as confidants, eavesdropping, soliloquies, perfect memory, and even the first-person forms. The persuasive narrative becomes self-justifying. Diderot's theory of verisimilitude could be applied to the great novels of the nineteenth century.

Staël's Essai sur les fictions, 1795

Germaine de Staël belongs to a different generation, indeed to a different era, from Marmontel, whose essay predates hers by only eight years. Whereas he represents an ossified and exhausted Enlightenment, she represents a nascent and vigorous Romanticism. Her *Essai sur les fictions*, published in 1795 to preface a collection of her stories, is a youthful work, but brilliantly fresh. From the outset, Staël distinguishes herself from her predecessors by privileging the imagination over reason. To place the novel above history was a commonplace, but the grounds for its priority were utilitarian: literature's purpose was to teach morality;

---

[38] 'écoutez bien, et vous entendrez un ton dissonant qui le décèlera' (Diderot, *Eulogy*, p. 32).

[39] 'intéresser, toucher, entraîner, émouvoir, faire frissonner la peau et couler les larmes' (Diderot, *Deux Amis*, p. 791).

the novel worked better than history, so it was preferable to history. For Staël the value of the imagination lies in its capacity to bestow happiness. It can both distract and move; thus a work of imagination can both entertain and teach. However, it must entertain, but it need not teach.

She divides fiction into three kinds: *fictions merveilleuses*, which traditionally meant fiction involving the supernatural, but to which she gives a new meaning; historical fictions; and natural fictions, where 'everything is at the same time invented and imitated, where nothing is true but everything seems true'.[40] Of the first group, Staël has little good to say. In her opinion, even the best epics, allegories, fables, and oriental tales are weakened by the use of fantasy and supernatural elements. To this point, Staël is original only in deigning to consider all these forms; most previous theorists simply ignored fables and oriental tales. Here, though, she makes a bold move, and includes 'allusion', by which she means topical satire and works with a key, and which she regards as ephemeral; and analogy, or extended comparisons, which she thinks should be avoided for much the same reasons as allegory. And finally she remarks that the clever tales of Swift and Voltaire are delightful, but that the charm of the story overpowers the philosophical message. Staël perceives deeper structural relationships among works and genres than anyone before her. It is not by chance that she entitled her broad-ranging essay 'sur les fictions' rather than 'sur les romans'. The term 'merveilleux' is less suitable, but she was pursuing a subtle distinction between genres that are overtly figural and those that try not to be.

A second novelty separates Staël from her immediate forerunners: the range of her reference. She cites recent German and English authors they could not have known, but only parochialism prevented them from including Dante, Spenser, Milton, and Swift alongside Homer, Virgil, Boileau, and Fénelon. Unlike the dogmatic critics, who measured all works by the same rule, Staël displays great generosity and flexibility, as well as an impressive learning. Later in the essay, she displays the same open-mindedness toward French novels.

At this stage, she still formulated aesthetic ideas in classical terms. Her ideas on composition, structure, and order contain nothing new. She still professes a sort of classical minimalism regarding details; to say more with less, is the ideal. Moral edification remains an important function, and she thinks the novel can insinuate a stricter sense of duty than any other form, because it engages the reader's feelings. Her most prescient recommendation is that the novel should broaden its range of

---

[40] 'tout est à la fois inventé et imité; où rien n'est vrai, mais où tout est vraisemblable' (Staël, *Essai*, p. 63).

subjects. Besides love, novels could be written about ambition, pride, avarice, and vanity; 'the Lovelace of ambition' would be an especially fine figure.

The tension between Staël's classical education and emergent Romantic sensibility bursts out in the closing paragraphs, where she recalls four works – Pope's *Epistle of Abelard, Les Lettres portugaises, Werther,* and *Julie* – which do not conform to the moral pattern. They depict, in vivid and inflammatory language, the most fervid excesses of love. But, she asks, 'would anyone want to ban these miracles of language?'[41] And she resolves the question by valorizing an elite of sentimental readers, who alone will be affected by such novels:

Let sensitive and ardent souls enjoy them, they cannot make their language heard. The feelings with which they are agitated are barely understood; and constantly condemned, they might think themselves alone in the world, they would soon detest their own nature that isolates them, if a few passionate and melancholy works did not make them hear a voice in the desert of life, did not make them find, in solitude, a few glimmers of the happiness that escapes them amid the world.[42]

Staël's brief essay brings the boldest new concepts into the discussion of fiction since the rise of the *nouvelle*; it recognizes other options than the tired effort to locate the novel among Aristotelian categories; it moves outside the well-worn polarities of history and poetry, truth and lies, reality and imagination, moral and immoral; it becomes expansive, and to the goals of pleasure and usefulness adds others like solace and exaltation, to the theme of love adds other passions, to the heritage of the classics both French and ancient adds the medieval and the northern. In short, it points to a new era.

Sade's Idée sur les romans, *1800*

Sade conceived his essay on the novel in the 1780s and published it with the first edition of *Les Crimes de l'amour*. He repeats many of the clichés of his time. Structurally, he thinks in terms of episodes and a well-prepared dénouement, like Huet or Du Plaisir. As a novelist, in fact, Sade is decidedly conventional, even necessarily so; the impact of

---

[41] 'mais voudrait-on interdire ces miracles de la parole?' (p. 70).

[42] 'Laissez-en jouir les âmes ardentes et sensibles, elles ne peuvent faire entendre leur langue. Les sentiments dont elles sont agitées sont à peine compris; et sans cesse condamnées, elles se croiraient seules au monde, elles détesteraient bientôt leur propre nature qui les isole, si quelques ouvrages passionnés et mélancoliques ne leur faisaient pas entendre une voix dans le désert de la vie, ne leur faisaient pas trouver, dans la solitude, quelques rayons du bonheur qui leur échappe au milieu du monde' (p. 71).

his transgressive imagination depends on the existence of clear codes to violate. He needs targets for his blasphemy, sacrilege, and scandal – a moral order, with institutions, taboos, and deep-seated beliefs. Among these is a conventional plot where immanent justice rewards the virtuous and punishes the wicked.

Sade begins with an original idea: the appetite for fiction is universal, and arises from deep human desires to pray and to love. After a century of pontification about humanity's natural affection for the truth, it is refreshing to hear that people have other more urgent drives. Having only touched on the idea, however, Sade reverts to tradition and recapitulates Huet's history of the genre. When he comes to the theme of moral utility, however, he advances another arresting observation. Having virtue triumph, he says, is something 'one should aim for as much as one can', but 'that rule is neither in nature, nor in Aristotle, but only the one we wish all men were subject to for our own happiness'. Then he argues that if readers see virtue victorious they will conclude that 'things are what they should be'; whereas 'if after the rudest trials we finally see virtue overthrown by vice, unfailingly our souls are rent, and the work having violently moved us ... must undoubtedly produce that involvement which alone assures the laurels'.[43] Sade has performed a deconstructive reading of providential justice in fiction. Posterity proved him right, moreover, for the pathetic ending has had a richer tradition than the happy ending.

Referring to the terrifying and diabolical Gothic genre, Sade explains it as a consequence of the times: 'the novel became as hard to write as monotonous to read; there was no one who had not experienced in four or five years more misfortunes than the most famous novelist could depict in a century ...'[44] Here again, Sade reverses the standard argument; instead of offering a refuge from history, the novel competes with its horror, an impossible contest, because reality has outstripped the imagination. Sade's argument appears to anticipate contemporary discourse on representing the Holocaust, but long before the Terror, he had sought to legitimize violence in fiction, and in 1788 a perversely conventional morality supplied as good a pretext as history: forced marriages

---

[43] 'il faut y tendre bien certainement autant qu'on le peut, ... cette règle, ni dans la nature, ni dans Aristote, mais seulement celle à laquelle nous voudrions que tous les hommes s'assujettissent pour notre bonheur'; 'les choses étant ce qu'elles doivent être'; 'si après les plus rudes épreuves, nous voyons la vertu enfin terrassée par le vice, indispensablement nos âmes se déchirent, et l'ouvrage nous ayant excessivement émus ... doit indubitablement produire l'intérêt qui seul assure les lauriers' (Sade, *Idée*, p. 49).

[44] 'le roman devenait aussi difficile à faire que monotone à lire; il n'y avait point d'individu qui n'eût plus éprouvé d'infortunes en quatre ou cinq ans que n'en pouvait peindre en un siècle le plus fameux romancier de la littérature' (p. 53).

no longer distress women readers, he claims, because they know that 'a little make-up and a young lover soon make them forget these momentary troubles'; so to drive the moral home, Sade will put his female characters into the clutches of a man who 'by a process of inconceivable depravity, abominable conduct, bizarre tastes, cruel and shameful whims, threatens the young and tender victim he pursues with an eternal sequence of spiritual and physical unhappiness'.[45]

Sade's conception of the novelist's function also starts from an orthodox statement. The writer should know the human heart, have experience, look, listen, and learn, rather than talk. He should paint things as they are. The hackneyed image of the painter soon gives way, however, to a hallucinatory mixture of metaphors, combining Sade's familiar obsessions with sex, incest, and mayhem: 'the novelist is nature's man, she created him to be her painter; if he does not become his mother's lover as soon as she has given birth to him, let him never write, for we will not read him; but if he feels that burning thirst to paint everything, if with a shudder he opens up nature's breast, to seek his art and obtain his models there',[46] then he will succeed. Sade's vision of the artist, if one may call it that, has already gone far beyond the lonely prophet or self-sacrificing Prometheus of the Romantics; he looks ahead at least to the *poètes maudits*, to an avant-garde that expects the artist to risk damnation venturing into forbidden zones and bringing back shocking and outrageous knowledge.

Only in the twentieth century have Sade's works been widely and respectfully read. Now, the central theme of his *Idea* seems not only welcome, but actually more characteristic of nineteenth-century novelists than they would have admitted. Sade calls for a novel filled with energy and capable of filling the reader with awe. The only excuse for replacing truth with fiction is to dazzle. The novelist's imagination should constantly overstep normal limits of all kinds and disseminate excess. Addressing himself to an imaginary author, Sade writes: 'We want outbursts from you, not rules; exceed your plans, change them, expand them . . .'[47]

---

[45] 'une toilette et un jeune amant peuvent faire oublier aussitot ces petites traverses momentanées . . . Par une suite d'inconcevable dépravation, de conduite affreuse, de gouts bisarres, de caprices cruels, et ignominieux, menace d'une suite eternelle de malheurs moraux et phisiques la jeune et tendre victime qu'il poursuit' (p. 72).

[46] 'le romancier est l'homme de la nature, elle l'a créé pour être son peintre; s'il ne devient pas l'amant de sa mère dès que celle-ci l'a mis au monde, qu'il n'écrive jamais, nous ne le lirons point; mais s'il éprouve cette soif ardente de tout peindre, s'il entrouvre avec frémissement le sein de la nature, pour y chercher son art et y puiser des modèles' (p. 55).

[47] 'ce sont des élans que nous voulons de toi, et non pas des règles; dépasse tes plans, varie-les, augmente-les' (p. 56).

8

Prose fiction: Great Britain

Michael McKeon

In the following essay I will pursue the theory of prose fiction by attending to the emergent theory of the novel. The theory of a genre in the process of coming into being is discovered in unpredictable places, many of them extra-'literary'. During the first half of our period, the theory of the novel appears in a variety of discourses in which the epistemology of fiction is being treated, and often in the interstices of narrative itself. Later on, novel theory ceases to be so commonly embedded in practice itself because it is being separated out and institutionalized within the discourse of the periodical review.[1] I will draw upon these several sources in order to suggest the expansive character of a theory whose terms have not yet been securely formulated.

I

For those who take the novel to be an ancient form given new life in the eighteenth century, the history both of prose fiction and of its theory in this period will cohere as the complicating development of what is none the less a familiar and continuous genre. Contemporaries, however, tended not to see things this way. For them, the novelty of the novel was an essential feature of the form – hence its theory and its poetics (the rules for composing novels) were at best uncertain. This meant different things to different people. In some it aroused apprehension: 'I know not whether [the] novel, like the *epopee*, has any rules, peculiar to itself. – If it has, I may have innocently erred against them all . . .' Others were untroubled: 'How fortunate it is for us Historians [i.e., novelists] . . . that no modern *Aristotle* has stept forth, and laid down Rules for the Conduct of History, like the Unities of Action, Time, and Place, prescribed by the Ancients to all dramatic Writers. I hug myself when I think of it' (Elizabeth Griffith, *The Delicate Distress* (1769), I, pp. ix–x; Herbert Lawrence, *The Contemplative Man* (1771), I, p. 213:

---

[1] On the institutionalization of the periodical novel review, see Bartolomeo, *New Species*, chs. 4, 5 (hereafter cited as 'Bartolomeo').

Bartolomeo, pp. 104–5). Nevertheless, much early novel theory consists of efforts to familiarize the new by the standards of older forms, efforts that sometimes only underscore its strangeness.

William Congreve provides the best-known early instance of this with respect to drama: 'Since ... there is no possibility of giving that life to the Writing or Repetition of a Story which it has in the Action, I resolved ... to imitate *Dramatick* Writing, namely, in the Design, Contexture and Result of the Plot. I have not observed it before in a Novel.' Samuel Richardson and his friends remarked more than once on the affinity between his epistolary narration and dramatic form; readers praised the Aristotelian unity of Henry Fielding's plots; Horace Walpole claimed Shakespeare as his model in the management of narrative 'catastrophe' (Congreve, Preface to *Incognita* (1691), Williams (ed.), *Novel and Romance*, p. 27 [hereafter cited as Williams]; and see Williams, pp. 104, 117, 166; 152–3, 251, 260, 294n., 337; 264, 267). With respect to epic, Fielding's early coinage, the 'comic epic-poem in prose', is the most celebrated effort at accommodation, but his later novels also seemed intelligible by epic criteria (Preface to *Joseph Andrews* (1742); and see Williams, pp. 163, 253–4, 327). Some writers, like Clara Reeve and Lord Monboddo, were quite comfortable with the idea of the novel or the romance as an epic poem in prose. Others, like Bishop Hurd, saw such narratives as at best 'hasty, imperfect, and abortive poems ... [, the] sure prognostic of expiring Letters' (Reeve, Preface to *Old English Baron* (1778), Monboddo, vol. III of *Origin and Progress of Language* (1776), Richard Hurd, 'Dissertation on the Idea of Universal Poetry' (1766): Williams, pp. 299, 291, 271).

Novels began to be written in the United States only toward the very end of our period. Like their English counterparts, American authors were to some extent preoccupied with formal precedents. They were additionally faced, however, with the problem of European, and especially English, precedence. Over ninety per cent of the fictional narratives published in the United States between 1789 and 1800 were not by American authors, and those that were tended to be highly indebted to popular English precursors (Gilmore, 'Literature', pp. 625–6). In other words, the problem for American novelists was one not of establishing a new genre, but of extending that genre in a novel fashion. Of course, this is also the paradox of the modern 'novel tradition' as such, which, unlike traditions of the past, achieves continuity only through the appearance of profound innovation and discontinuity. The invention of American 'romance' in the early nineteenth century may plausibly be seen as one consequence of this requirement.

In the United States, however, the paradox of the 'novel tradition' was reinforced by the problem of American 'exceptionalism'. Until the middle of the nineteenth century, the American theory of the novel may be said to be inseparable from the theory of the American novel. Can the novel be accommodated to the physical and cultural arena of the New World, radically different as it is from that of the Old? *Should* it be so accommodated, given its grounding in 'the levity and vices of the mother country, the false splendours of a social world that had no bearing on, or counterpart in, America . . .'? (Perosa, *American Theories*, p. 4). Rhetorical and heuristic, these perennial doubts aim not so much at confirmation as at eliciting efforts – like those of Charles Brockden Brown – to naturalize the novel through 'engaging the sympathy of the reader by means hitherto unemployed by preceding authors. Puerile superstition and exploded manners, Gothic castles and chimeras, are the material usually employed for this end. The incidents of Indian hostility, and the perils of the western wilderness, are far more suitable; and for a native of America to overlook these would admit of no apology' (Preface to *Edgar Huntly* (1799), quoted in Ruland, *Native Muse*, p. 64).[2]

To return to the English context: Bishop Hurd's vision of literary devolution makes explicit his doubts regarding the compatibility of the new forms with the old generic models. More commonly, such doubts were expressed through the subtly parodic suggestiveness that often coloured efforts at generic classification. Parody is a complex effect that takes place between the antithetical poles of pious imitation and subversive critique, and it is central to contemporary efforts at theorizing the emergent novel as that which is strange by virtue of the way it recalls the familiar. Certainly readers knew that Fielding's narratives were not only epic, but mock-epic departures from the form (see Williams, pp. 153, 258, 293). Indeed, modern theorists of the novel have tended to designate the epic as the great literary genre of antiquity in parodic relation to which the novel comes into being (see Lukacs, *Theory*; Ortega y Gasset, *Meditations*; Bakhtin, *Dialogic Imagination*). Despite this, contemporary readers – of *Don Quixote* (1604, 1614), of *Shamela* (1741), of *Northanger Abbey* (1818) – were overwhelmingly persuaded that not epic, but romance, was the novel's most important literary precedent and foil.

This can be seen on several levels. One level is that of generic history. Some commentators saw the history of prose narrative as a movement from the old to the new – from the ancient to the modern – romance (see Williams, pp. 101, 142–3). Others saw that history as a qualitative shift from romance to novel (e.g. Reeve, *Progress of Romance*, I, p. 8; George Canning, *Microcosm*, 26 (14 May 1787); Williams, pp. 341–2).

[2] See also Edward Tyrell Channing, *North American Review* (1818) and James Kirke Paulding, *National Literature* (1819–20) in defence of Brown's efforts at accommodation: Ruland, *Native Muse*, pp. 118–30, 132–6.

Moreover, superficially similar schemes might express very different views of the relation between romance and novel. Reeve aimed to show 'how the Modern novel sprung up out of [the romance's] ruins', whereas Canning thought that 'the novel is but a more modern modification of the same ingredients which constitute the romance'. This sort of disparity confirms (on another level) the great fluidity of contemporary usage, which frequently employed 'novel' and 'romance' as synonymous terms. Most pervasively, however, 'romance' served as an all-purpose generic touchstone for the negative definition of an emergent form whose positive denomination – 'the novel' – remained unstable even at the end of the eighteenth century.

This negative use of the term 'romance' appears quite early, and its local, generic function partakes of a more general, epistemological aim to designate the category of narrative falsehood. Although with diverse valences, the repudiation of 'romance' falsehood plays a central role in the way all those authors we are accustomed to associate with the early novel – Aphra Behn, Congreve, Delarivier Manley, Daniel Defoe, Eliza Haywood, Richardson, Fielding – characterize the truth of their narratives. By the same token, their 'true' narratives are most commonly described as some version of 'history' or 'true history' (see McKeon, *Origins*, chs. 1, 3, 9, 11–12). Especially in the prefaces that introduce them, this claim to historicity dominates the emergent novel until the middle of the eighteenth century. Its implications are by no means uniform. Still, its essence entails the insistence that the events about to be narrated really happened. In its strong form, the claim to historicity was not to be confused either with the claim to antiquity or with the claim to probability. As one contemporary pointed out, 'A Romance, or an Imposture, may be as ancient and more ancient than a true History, this is nothing to the purpose'. Another protested: 'It is no argument to me, that a thing is true, because it is possible; no, nor because probable: nay, it is certain, that many lyes and falshoods are founded upon this very thing, *probability*' ([Simon Tyssot de Patot], *Travels and Adventures of James Massey* (1710, trans. 1733), p. 287; Meric Casaubon, *Of Credulity and Incredulity* (1668), p. 155).

The claim that narrated events really happened is of fundamental importance in the early theory of the novel, for it signifies the commitment of the nascent genre to a rigorously empirical model of truth that was distinct (contemporaries believed) from traditional standards of truth-telling. By this way of thinking, the as-yet-unnamed genre might coexist with traditional literary genres like romance and epic, but it was sharply distinguished from them by its strict fidelity to, its immediate representation of, the realm of the real. 'I do not pretend,' said Behn, 'in giving you the history of this royal slave, to entertain my reader with the adventures of a feign'd hero, whose life and fortunes fancy may manage at the poet's pleasure; nor in relating the truth, design to adorn it with any accidents, but such as arrived in earnest to him ... I was myself an eye-witness to a great part of what you will find here set down' (Behn, *Oroonoko; or, The Royal Slave. A True History* (1688), p. 147). Of *Robinson Crusoe* (1719) Defoe said, 'the Editor believes the thing to be a just History of Fact; neither is there any Appearance of Fiction in it ...' (Preface, in Williams, p. 56). Even works whose larger aim would appear diametrically opposed to that of faithful historical narration were nonetheless ready to claim it: early on in part II, one of Bunyan's allegorical personifications soberly provides eye-witness confirmation of the fact that Christiana and her children have gone on pilgrimage (*Pilgrim's Progress* (1678, 1682), II, p. 145).

The claim to historicity may therefore be seen as the most important early effort to establish a standard of judgement and rules of composition that might separate the novel from more traditional fictional practices – to establish, as it were, the novel convention of unconventionality. It was a dominant strategy in the early American novel as well (Orians, 'Censure', p. 204; Martin, *Instructed Vision*, pp. 79–80). And because the claim was grounded in an empirical epistemology, narratives that embraced it had recourse to a range of documents – reports, records, memoirs, journals, letters – whose possession of literal objecthood seemed to ensure the empirical objectivity of the narratives that relied upon them. The most important such document for the early history of the novel is the letter, which provided the basis for the most popular novelistic mode of this time, epistolary form.

The complex authenticity of the letter form lies both in its documentary objectivity and in its affective subjectivity – the truth of the heart – but these potentially contradictory appeals were able to coexist in the early epistolary novel (see Day, *Told in Letters*, ch. 6). In *Love-Letters between a Nobleman and his Sister* (1684–7), Behn exploited epistolary form both to disclose the interiority of her protagonists and to establish their documentary historicity: 'After this flight, these Letters were found in their Cabinets, at their house at St *Denice*, where they both liv'd together for the space of a year, and they are as exactly as possible plac'd in the order they were sent' (*Love-Letters*, p. 10). Richardson's *Pamela* (1740) extended this technique: 'The Letters being written under the immediate Impression of every Circumstance which occasioned them ... the several Passions of the Mind must, of course, be more affectingly described ... [I]t will appear from several Things mentioned in the Letters, that the story must have happened within these Thirty Years past' (*Pamela*, pp. 4–5). Perhaps because of its versatility in providing both objective and subjective authentication, epistolary form remained the most visible novelistic mode in England until about 1785 (see Tompkins, *Popular Novel*, p. 34 [hereafter cited as Tompkins]).

Implicit in the claim to historicity was the promise of a plain style purged of its 'romance' excrescences and offering unmediated access to reality. But how does one gain access to a plain style? As Defoe observed, it is easy enough 'to relate real Stories with innumerable Omissions and Additions: I mean, Stories which have a real Existence in Fact, but which by the barbarous Way of relating, become as romantick and false, as if they had no Original ... nothing is more common, than to have two Men tell the same Story quite differing one from another, yet both of them Eye-witnesses to the Fact related' (Defoe, *Serious Reflections*, pp. 116, 113). In this way, the anti-romance scepticism of the empirical claim to historicity tended to promote a deeper scepticism about the very possibility of a transparently 'historical' narration, of any escape from the narrative mediations of 'romance'. Defoe himself became increasingly circumspect in his use of the claim to historicity and stylistic authenticity (see prefaces to *Colonel Jack* (1722), *Moll Flanders* (1722), and *Roxana* (1724), in Williams, pp. 73–8, 80–1). It did not take long for readers to detect, in the quickly conventionalized topoi of historicity, the unintentionally parodic return of the old romance in a new guise. Nowhere was this so evident as in the cult of the travel narrative. 'These are in our present Days', said Shaftesbury, 'what *Books of Chivalry* were, in those of our Forefathers'. This is the reflexive logic of the novelistic parody of romance: the earnest critique of romance falsehood is critically unmasked as the stealthy imitation of romance in other terms.

In some authors, the parody was manifestly intentional. Like his follower Fielding, Congreve combined the naive claim to historical transparency with third-person intrusions so ostentatious and manipulative that they implied the sheer conventionality of the claim. In his famous experiment in the epistolary mode, Fielding exploded *Pamela*'s double authenticity by reducing Richardson's epistolary present-tense to absurdity ('Odsbobs! I hear him just coming in at the door ... Well, he is in bed between us') even as the 'real' letters *Shamela* purports to print reveal *Pamela*'s most intimate truths to be clever counterfeits (*Shamela* (1741), p. 313). Modernists were convinced that Laurence Sterne's *Tristram Shandy* (1759–67) was a brilliant anomaly that proleptically anticipated their own epistemological sophistication. A more plausible view must recognize Sterne's brilliance to be deeply rooted in the self-conscious formal experimentation of his immediate predecessors.

Yet as Shaftesbury intimated, the sceptical demystification of the 'true history' need not abandon us to romance falsehood. 'For *Facts* unably related, tho with the greatest Sincerity, and good Faith, may prove the worst sort of Deceit: and mere *Lyes*, judiciously compos'd, can teach us the Truth of Things, beyond any other manner' (Anthony Ashley Cooper, Third Earl of Shaftesbury, *Characteristicks*, 2nd edn (1714), I, pp. 344–7). The naive claim to an immediate historical truth was a crucial (and ultimately expendable) means by which contemporaries learned to formulate a different standard of truth – 'realism' – that by the end of the century would be increasingly embraced as characteristically novelistic. I will return below to this formulation.

II

The discovery that the novel might be no more than a new way of romancing is only one expression of the paradox that is central to the notion of a 'novel tradition'. By the latter part of the eighteenth century, readers were already finding that the new genre had become *too* conventional. 'All the variety of which this species of literary entertainment is capable, seems almost exhausted, and even novels themselves no longer charm us with novelty'. '[E]very novel that appears . . . renders the task of this species of writing more arduous . . .'. 'Since almost every track is become beaten, authors are obliged to make the most of what is left them'. Elizabeth Inchbald whimsically took a more positive view: utter conventionality has in fact been embraced by novel readers, who 'admire one novel because it puts them in mind of another, which they admired a few days before. By them it is required, that a novel should be like a novel' (*Monthly Review*, 6 (March 1752), 231, quoted in Taylor, *Early Opposition*, p. 13 [hereafter cited as Taylor]; *Monthly Review*, 2nd ser., 2 (Aug. 1790), 463–4, Bartolomeo, p. 130; Inchbald, article in the *Artist* (June 1807), Taylor, p. 48).

The new genre in search of its own rules had quickly become so rule-bound as to appear utterly formulaic. One method contemporaries used to register this predictability was the trope of the 'recipe' to make a novel. In one of these recipes, the prospective author is charged to 'go to Middle Row, Holborn . . . buy any old forgotten novel, the older the better; give new names to the personages and places, reform the dates, modernize such circumstances as may happen to be antiquated . . . All this may be done with a pen, in the margin of the printed book, without the trouble of transcribing the whole' (*Monthly Review*, 2nd ser., 5 (July 1791), Williams, p. 374; for other recipes see Williams, p. 368, Taylor, pp. 45–8). The recipe trope underscores the interdependence of writing and its 'consumption' in the contemporary literary scene; it also suggests that the crisis was seen to extend beyond this particular genre. In 1728, Alexander Pope had used the recipe trope to reflect upon the modern epic poem and its entanglement in the economy of supply and demand that was seen to control the emergent literary marketplace (Pope, *Peri Bathous* (1728), XV; see also II, XIII, XVI). Later commentators on the novel showed a similar interest. The enervation and degradation of the novel were linked, crucially, to the fact of its being an article of 'manufacture' for the 'market' (see Taylor, p. 42, Tompkins, p. 5, Bartolomeo, p. 141). Clara Reeve was not the only commentator to connect the flourishing of the novel market with that of the circulating library, 'in consequence [of which] the manufacturers of Novels were constantly at work for them, and were very poorly paid for their labours' (*Progress of Romance*, II, pp. 38–9; cf. Williams, p. 333 and Taylor, ch. 2).

The contemporary analysis of the literary marketplace has a central relevance to the theory and poetics of the novel because it suggested that the source of the 'rules' that had quickly rendered novels so conventional was the market itself: the production, consumption, and circulation of novels as commodities. The rules of the market, as contemporaries discovered them, were those of quantification, abstract equalization, the transformation of use- into exchange-value, and instantaneous obsolescence. Its cardinal rule was the replacement of qualitative distinctions of value by the absolute criterion of quantity. It is perhaps unsurprising that Lord Chesterfield, like many others, was tempted to distinguish between novels and romances on the basis of quantity alone: of size and number of volumes (letter of 1740–1, Williams, p. 100). Yet the universal reign of quantity might, on the other hand, be felt to confound novel and romance by inspiring (as in one satirical scheme) a simple table of equivalences that could, 'like machinery in factories', permit a novel to 'be made out of a romance, or a romance out of a novel with the greatest ease, by scratching out a few terms, and inserting others'. The attached table authorizes a simple substitution: 'Where you find – / A castle ... put An house. / A cavern ... A bower. / A groan ... A sigh. / A giant ... A father' (*The Age; A Poem* ... (1810), pp. 209–10, n.1, quoted in Napier, *Failure of Gothic*, pp. 27–8). Another satirical vision of the novel-writing process imagined it to consist in the undiscriminating composition of mere sentences: 'and when a *very great quantity* of them ... are wedged together after a particular form and manner, they are denominated a NOVEL' (*Sylph*, 19 (5 Dec. 1795), pp. 147–8, Taylor, p. 43).

In one novel, a character advises his eager friend that 'the booksellers pay mechanically at the rate of so much per sheet ... Sit down and write as fast as you can. Nine sheets make a volume, and eighteen sheets two volumes. It's very easily calculated; never trouble yourself about meaning, it can't be too bad to be admired, when you have finished it'

(*The Egg* (1772), Tompkins, p. 8). 'The booksellers', said a reviewer, 'take care every winter to procure a sufficient quantity of tales, memoirs, and romances for the entertainment of their customers, many of whom, not capable of distinguishing between good and bad, are mighty well satisfied with whatever is provided for them' (*Critical Review*, 16 (Dec. 1763), p. 449, Taylor, p. 42). Elizabeth Griffith complained of her first novel, 'I find the Booksellers will give nothing worth taking for it ... They say they do not dispute the Merit of it, but that while the Public continue equally to buy a bad thing as a good one, they do not think an Author can reasonably expect that they will make a Difference in the Price' (to Richard Griffith, *Genuine Letters* (1770), V, p. 15, Tompkins, pp. 6–7). Robert Bage thought the futility of novel reviewing was self-evident, since 'books of this class are printed, published, bought, read, and deposited in the lumber garret, three months before the reviewers say a syllable of the matter' (Preface to *Mount Henneth* (1781), Tompkins, p. 6).

As these remarks suggest, the problem was systemic: the theory of the novel had ultimate recourse to a theory of ideology whereby modern culture was understood as a comprehensive determination of modern economy. Thus William Godwin confirmed the impossibility of affixing special blame for the quantification of value and the homogenization of technique (is it the fault of the bookseller? the author? the reading public?) by finding complicity even in the reviewer: 'The critic and the moralist, in their estimate of romances, have borrowed the principle that regulates the speculations of trade. They have weighed novels by the great [i.e., in the mass] and taken into their view the whole scum and surcharge of the press' (Godwin, 'Of History and Romance', p. 369). A broad sketch of this system was provided by a reviewer who wittily imagined 'the modern novel' as a 'species of goods' first fabricated by Defoe and Haywood, then perfected by Richardson, Fielding, Smollett, and Sterne, who 'were the Wedgwoods of their days' (*Monthly Review*, 2nd ser., 5 (July 1791), Williams, pp. 373–4).

Framed in irony, the retrospection of this reviewer none the less echoes a sober refrain heard increasingly toward the end of the century. This is the refrain of the 'novel tradition', paradoxical but inevitable, compressed into four decades as the emergent canon of (with some variations in personnel) Richardson, Fielding, Smollett, and Sterne (see Williams, pp. 301, 412, 440, 448; see Bartolomeo, pp. 130–2 for a discussion of this retrospect). Inseparable from its negative counterpart, the mid-century novel canon defined the uncertain moment of quality before the modest 'modern' decline into quantification. The dependence of novelistic form (length, seriality, conventionality) on the form of the market would continue to preoccupy commentators in the following century.

III

If contemporaries were sensitive to the novel's participation in a system of economic production and consumption, who, more specifically, did they imagine its authors and readers to be? What bearing might this have on contemporary novel theory? Modern criticism has reached a consensus that women dominated the authorship and readership of the eighteenth-century novel. Certainly the remarks of contemporaries – especially their anxiety about female readership – support this consensus.[3] The condescension commonly shown female authors by male reviewers obliquely acknowledged and even encouraged their prevalence (see Williams, p. 368, Tompkins, pp. 127–8, Taylor, pp. 83–4, Bartolomeo, pp. 119–20). Gendering the association of novelistic and industrial production, a reviewer of 1773 claimed that 'this branch of the literary *trade* appears, now, to be almost entirely engrossed by the Ladies' (*Monthly Review*, 48 (Feb. 1773), p. 154, Taylor, p. 84). Another believed, less equivocally, that the 'prosaic epic, which ... arose to its meridian in the hands of Fielding and Smollett ... has continued with a milder, but not less captivating splendour, in those of Miss Burney, Mrs Smith, and Mrs Lennox' (*Critical Review*, 70 (Oct. 1790), pp. 424–5, Bartolomeo, p. 122). And a third reviewer confirmed women's recent canonical elevation: 'Of the various species of composition that in course come before us, there are none in which *our* writers of the male sex have less excelled, since the days of Richardson and Fielding, than in the arrangement of a novel. Ladies seem to appropriate to themselves an exclusive privilege in this kind of writing' (*Monthly Review*, 2nd ser., 3 (Dec. 1790), Williams, p. 370).

What about female readership? Attributing to women a peculiarly 'keen ... relish for novels' and a powerful 'identifying propensity', commentators feared that female readers would be filled with 'vapours', 'seduced' first by fantasy and then by real men, their 'imaginations' 'perverted' by 'chimerical ideas' and 'alienated' from 'social life' – or, on the contrary, inflamed with upwardly mobile ambitions (*Monthly Review*, 48 (May 1773), p. 417, Bartolomeo, p. 116; *Eclectic Review*, 8 (June 1812), p. 606, Taylor, p. 69; *Monthly Review*, 48 (July 1773), Williams, p. 279; J. L. Chirol, *Inquiry* (1809), p. 234, *Lady's Magazine*, 11 (Supplement, 1780), 693, Taylor, p. 77; Richard Berenger, *World*, 79 (4 July 1754), Williams, p. 214; Fielding, *Shamela*, pp. 305, 307, 338). In *The Female Quixote* (1752), Charlotte Lennox gave the world an enduring

---

[3] On the other hand, there is no basis for the belief, common among modern scholars, that early modern commentators associated romance (as explicitly distinguished from the novel) with women.

if ambiguous portrait of one such female reader, and other novelists followed her example (see Tompkins, p. 207n.). American commentators expressed comparable fears (see Orians, 'Censure', pp. 198, 212–13; Gilmore, 'Literature', p. 624).

On this evidence, we may well be justified in seeing, in the joint spectacle of female authorship and readership, a respectively positive and negative assessment of women's sensible powers – their capacity both to inculcate and to stray from virtue (see Mullan, *Sentiment*, p. 104, who suggests this is Richardson's double lesson). What lies behind this spectacle is a profound concern with the novel as a powerful instrument of pedagogy and socialization. Women were seen as a likely object of this concern, but they were not the only one. In fact, fears of female novel readership were echoed, and fully equalled, by fears of novel readership by the young of both sexes. Henry Mackenzie saw 'the young and the indolent, to whom the exercise of imagination is delightful' as the principal readership of the novel. Samuel Johnson believed that novels 'are written chiefly to the young, the ignorant, and the idle, to whom they serve as lectures of conduct, and introductions into life. They are the entertainment of minds unfurnished with ideas, and therefore easily susceptible of impressions'. Speaking of novels and romances, Hugh Blair argued that 'any kind of writing ... that obtains a general currency, and especially that early pre-occupies the imagination of the youth of both sexes, must demand particular attention' (*Lounger*, 20 (18 June 1785), *Rambler*, 4 (31 March 1750), *Lectures on Rhetoric and Poetry* (1762): Williams, pp. 328, 143, 247).

Novels 'enervate the [youthful] mind', and send 'young readers' 'into the world debauched'. Through them 'the youth of both sexes' are 'rendered liable to the grossest illusions'. They induce 'a bloated imagination, sickly judgment, and disgust towards all the real businesses of life'. 'In vain is youth secluded from the corruptions of the living world' if novels are allowed to 'pollute the heart', 'inflame the passions', 'and teach all the malignity of vice in solitude' (*Gentleman's Magazine*, 58 (Nov. 1788), Vicesimus Knox, *Essays Moral and Literary*, 14 (1778): Williams, pp. 367, 306; Thomas Jefferson to Nathaniel Burwell, 14 March 1818, quoted in Martin, *Instructed Vision*, p. 158; *Critical Review*, 20 (Oct. 1765), p. 288, Taylor, p. 66; on the American scene, see Orians, 'Censure', p. 205, Davidson, *Revolution*, p. 47). Although the young of a certain social standing 'depend much upon the early impressions they receive from books, which captivate the imagination, and interest the heart', commentators were particularly preoccupied with the novel-reading practices of 'Vulgar' youth – apprentices, chambermaids, 'green girls'. Only the propertied 'have a right to fling away their time as they please; the works of the loom receive no impediment from their idleness' (Anna Seward, *Variety*, 25 (1787), *Athenian Mercury* (17 Dec. 1692), Thomas Monroe, *Olla Podrida*, 15 (23 June 1787): Williams, pp. 357, 29, 349–50; *Critical Review*, 2 (Nov. 1756), p. 379, Bartolomeo, p. 116). Some writers began with the problem of youthful readers and moved from there to the special case of girls (see Williams, pp. 333–5, Reeve, *Progress of Romance*, II, pp. 77–98). This sort of development confirms one's sense that women, and especially common girls, who read distil the quintessence of a more general anxiety about the social and moral effects of novel reading on those thought to be most unformed, susceptible, impressionable – most vulnerable to the formidable powers of novelistic pedagogy.

Yet the logic of the argument would seem to allow to novels the possibility of an affirmative pedagogy as well. One tolerant reviewer, conscious of the attendant dangers, none the less would only wish 'young minds ... to be fond of books, and I should have no doubt of being able to lead their taste, from the pursuit of mere amusement, to solid improvement' (*Analytical Review*, 16, (1793, Appendix): Williams, pp. 382–3). Another makes a more synoptic and suggestive observation:

Among the various proofs which the present age affords, that the female character is advancing in cultivation, and rising in dignity, may be justly reckoned the improvements that are making in the kind of writing which is more immediately adapted to the amusement of female readers. Novels, which were formerly little more than simple tales of love, are gradually taking a higher and more masculine tone, and are becoming the vehicles of useful instruction.

(*Monthly Review*, 2nd ser., 9 (Dec. 1792), p. 406, Bartolomeo, pp. 122–3)

How is the association of women with novels related to the putative gendering of their component elements – to the correlation of 'amusing tales' with the feminine, and of 'useful instruction' with the masculine? The rule of the market encouraged an appeal to the lowest common denominator. Novels were the focus of intense concern about education and socialization because novels, more than other genres, were accessible to the unformed and impressionable – to women, youth, and commoners. But what does the accessibility of novels, their danger but also their promise, have to do with their 'novel' form? What does their accessibility have to do with the formulation of a novelistic standard of 'realistic' truth-telling alternative to the empirical?

IV

According to Hugh Blair, 'the wisest men in all ages have more or less employed fables and fictions, as the vehicles of knowledge. These have ever been the basis of both epic and dramatic poetry. It is not, therefore, the nature of this sort of writing, considered in itself, but the faulty manner of its execution, that can expose it to any contempt' (*Lectures on Rhetoric and Belles Lettres* (1783), Williams, pp. 247–8). 'It is owing, no doubt, to the weakness of human nature', wrote James Beattie, 'that fable should ever have been found a necessary, or a convenient, vehicle for truth'. Beattie analysed this strategy as a mode of historical, moral, or political 'allegory' evident in the writings of both ancients and moderns, like Swift and Bunyan (*On Fable and Romance* (1783), Williams, pp. 309, 310–18). A century earlier, the most influential modern treatise on romance had associated it with this same strategy: 'The first Occasion of Introducing *Romance* into the World, was, without Dispute, to mollify the Rigour of Precepts, by the Allurements of Example' (Pierre Daniel Huet, Bishop of Avranches, *History of Romances* (1670, trans. 1715), Williams, p. 43).

Protestant thought sought to improve 'moral allegory' by making its 'fable' or 'example' more concrete and substantial. In John Bunyan's eyes, this was the novel 'method' of *The Pilgrim's Progress* (1678, 1682) (I, 'Author's Apology', l. 31, p. 1; see McKeon, *Origins*, pp. 75–6, 295–7). When Defoe undertook to reform the traditional technique of catechizing children, he replaced abstract doctrine by casuistical stories or domestic 'cases': 'The Way I have taken for this, is *intirely new*, and at first *perhaps* it may appear something *odd*, and the method may be contemned'. But if 'this mean and familiar Method, should, by its Novelty, prevail, this will be a happy Undertaking' (*Family Instructor* (1715), pp. 8, 9). Five years later Defoe defended *Robinson Crusoe* in similar terms, as a 'fable' that needs to be 'moralized': for 'the fable is always made for the moral, not the moral for the fable' (*Serious Reflections*, sig. A2r).

As these passages will suggest, the maxim that morals (or precepts) are best taught through fables (or examples) was a commonplace in eighteenth-century novel theory. Eliza Haywood thought the romancers of the previous age had 'found it most proper to cloath Instruction with Delight'. By this means, 'Precepts ... steal themselves into the Soul ... We become virtuous ere we are aware, and by admiring the great Examples which in the Narrative appear so amiable, are led to an Endeavour of imitating them' (*The Tea-Table* (1725), Williams, p. 84). Setting the familiar Horatian categories in instrumental relation, Clara Reeve observed that mid-century novelists had 'tempered the *utile* with the *dulce*, and under the disguise of Novels, gave examples of virtue rewarded, and vice punished' (*Progress of Romance*, II, p. 41). According to John Hawkesworth, 'precept becomes more forcible and striking as it is connected with example. Precept gains only the cold approbation of reason, and compels an assent which judgment frequently yields with reluctance, even when delay is impossible: but by example the passions are roused ... the affections are drawn out into the field: they learn their exercise in a mock fight, and are trained for the service of virtue' (*Adventurer*, 16 (30 Dec. 1752), Williams, pp. 196–7). Novelistic example is accessible because it is a mode of knowledge that requires no knowledge. 'To follow the chain of perplexed ratiocination ... or weigh the merits of opposite hypotheses, requires perspicacity, and presupposes learning. Works of this kind, therefore, are not so well adapted to the generality of readers as familiar and colloquial composition; for few can reason, but all can feel, and many who cannot enter into an argument may yet listen to a tale'. Indeed, novels 'teach us to think, by inuring us to feel' (John and Anna Laetitia [Barbauld] Aikin, *Miscellaneous Pieces in Prose and Verse* (1773), Williams, pp. 281, 282; see also p. 240).

When Haywood began publishing *The Female Spectator*, she promised her readers access to public news, a promise for which she was soon berated by one of her correspondents:

Tho' I never had any very great Opinion of your Sex as Authors, yet I thought, whenever you set up for such, you had Cunning enough to confine yourselves within your own Sphere, or at least not to raise the Expectations of the Public by such *mountainous* Promises as you have done ... Are you not under most terrible Apprehensions that ... you should be taken for an idle, prating, gossiping old Woman, fit only to tell long Stories by the Fireside for the Entertainment of little Children or Matrons, more antiquated than yourself?

Haywood defended herself against this charge of the female triviality of stories by defending their pedagogic seriousness. 'Many little Histories, it is true, are interspers'd, but then they are only such as serve to enforce *Precept* by *Example* ... it was necessary to engage the Attention of those I endeavoured to reform, by giving them such Things as I knew would please them: Tales, and little Stories to which every one might flatter themselves with being able to find a Key, seemed to me the most effectual Method ... For this End it was I chose to assume the Name of the *Female Spectator* rather than that of *Monitor*, as thinking the latter by discovering too plainly my Design, might in a great Measure have frustrated it with the Gay and Unreflecting' (*Female Spectator* (1744–6), II, pp. 118, 120, 125, 362–3; see I, p. 80). Haywood does not dismiss the association of stories with women. Rather, she revalues both by arguing the pedagogical utility of appearing to be without pedagogical design. By the same token, the 'feminine' character of the novel form lies in its deceptive indirection, its easy access to the 'female'

realm of concrete affective example as the most dependable if stealthy
route to the 'male' realm of abstract rational precept.

Only the latest in a long history of forms that teach precept by
example, novels none the less improve upon tradition in the closeness
with which their examples are accommodated to our experience; in
Congreve's words, they 'come near us, and represent to us Intrigues in
practice' ('Preface' to *Incognita* (1691), Williams, p. 27). The claim to
historicity appealed to contemporaries in part because its concentration
of this sort of proximity into a species of virtual 'presence' seemed
greatly to enhance the novel's pedagogic powers. As Arabella, the female Quixote, protests to her Doctor, 'he that writes without Intention
to be credited, must write to little Purpose; for what Pleasure or Advantage can arise from Facts that never happened? What Examples can be
afforded by the Patience of those who never suffered, or the Chastity of
those who were never solicited?' (Lennox, *The Female Quixote* (1752),
Bk IX, ch. 11, Williams, p. 185). But the claim to historicity was fraught
with difficulties. If, to moral ends, we narrate what really happens, we
cannot avoid (such is the world) narrating immorality. In the claim to
historicity that prefaces *Moll Flanders* (1722), Defoe acknowledged (not
only the epistemological, but also) the moral necessity of selectiveness:
'some of the vicious part of her Life, which could not be modestly told,
is quite left out, and several other Parts are very much shortened'
(Williams, p. 75). But Defoe also wrestled mightily with the moral
contradiction of making a false claim to historicity – of claiming for
moral purposes that Moll Flanders was a real person – and by the
middle of the century, most people were likely to agree with Godwin:
'I ask not, as a principal point, whether it be true or false? My first
enquiry is, "Can I derive instruction from it?"' ('Of History and
Romance', p. 367).[4]

However, jettisoning the claim to historicity did not solve the problem of selectiveness. As Johnson famously affirmed, the accessibility of
novelistic example, its sheer proximity to us, entails both a pedagogic
promise and a pedagogic danger:

[T]hese familiar histories may perhaps be made of greater use than the
solemnities of professed morality, and convey the knowledge of vice and
virtue with more efficacy than axioms and definitions. But if the power of
example is so great, as to take possession of the memory by a kind of
violence, and produce effects almost without the intervention of the will,
care ought to be taken, that when the choice is unrestrained, the best
examples only should be exhibited ... It is justly considered as the greatest

---

[4] Defoe's wrestling may be seen retrospectively as an effort to formulate a theory of
realism: see McKeon, *Origins*, pp. 120–2.

excellency of art, to imitate nature; but it is necessary to distinguish those parts of nature, which are most proper for imitation . . .

(*Rambler*, 4 (31 March 1750), Williams, p. 144)

It is this dilemma to which *Pamela's* title-page alludes in characterizing what follows as 'a Narrative which has its Foundation in TRUTH and NATURE; and at the same time . . . is intirely divested of all those Images, which, in too many Pieces calculated for Amusement only, tend to *inflame* the Minds they should *instruct*' (see Richardson, *Pamela*, p. 1).

In its most extreme form, the problem may extend beyond even the imperative of moral selection. Novelistic example may be so powerfully seductive in its appeal that, however cleansed, it tends to usurp the place of precept altogether. Bunyan had warned his readers against '*playing with the* out-side *of my Dream*' (*Pilgrim's Progress* (1678, 1682), I, 'Conclusion', l. 8, p. 134). Richardson discouraged all prospective readers who might '*dip* into' *Clarissa*, 'expecting a *light Novel, or transitory Romance*; and look upon Story . . . as its *sole end*, rather than as a vehicle to the Instruction' (Preface to *Clarissa* (1751), Williams, p. 167). Haywood might well indict the hostile reader of *The Female Spectator* of precisely this error, of neglecting the precept for the example. Yet by 1810, Barbauld was content to say that 'when I take up a novel, my end and object is entertainment' ('On the Origin and Progress of Novel-Writing', prefixed to *The British Novelists* (1810), I, p. 46, Taylor, p. 112). Is this because the novel had by now learned fully to 'internalize' instruction within entertainment, reason within feeling, precept within example? Beattie's historical account of narrative pedagogy as a matter of the 'allegorical' signification of 'truth' by 'fable' seems so sweeping that it comes as some surprise that this signifying structure should appear to collapse once he arrives at modernity and the novel, in which 'we attend only to the events that are before us . . . when I read *Robinson Crusoe*, or *Tom Jones*, I attend singly to the narrative; and no key is necessary to make me comprehend the author's meaning' (*On Fable and Romance* (1783), Williams, p. 318). Is this because 'meaning' has been successfully incorporated into 'narrative' as 'truth' into 'fable'? Or has the novel so embraced its exemplary access that the pedagogical precept has somehow been left behind?

Championed as an improved method of teaching precept by example, the novel succeeded so well that it turned the tension that had been contained by that maxim into an explicit competition between precept and example, 'morality' and 'naturalness'. There is some justice in seeing the conflict between morality and naturalness as the central problem in novel theory at this time; certainly it controlled the terms of the rivalry between Richardson and Fielding during the 1740s (see McKeon,

Origins, pp. 410–17). The debate blossomed over important matters of novelistic technique like poetic justice or 'mixed' characters. Is moral precept best conveyed when characters are drawn with a purity that is perspicuous but experientially unnatural, or when they are drawn as a mixture that is lifelike but ethically obscure? However, the rivalry between Richardson and Fielding was also crucial in the development of an attempted solution to the conflict between morality and naturalness.

V

Although early novelistic narrative was dominated by the claim to historicity, it also partook of a standard of truth-telling alternative to the empirical. Especially in France, where experimentation with the 'anti-romance' possibilities of romance was most inventive, the claim to historicity often coexisted uneasily with the doctrine of *vraisemblance*, translated as 'verisimilitude' and conceived as a quasi-Aristotelian mode of 'probability' (see McKeon, *Origins*, pp. 54–5, 59). The well-known Preface to Delarivier Manley's *Secret History of Queen Zarah* (1705) – recently found to be copied from a French source[5] – aptly distinguished between 'True History' and 'the Probability of Truth' without clearly associating the narrative that followed with either (Williams, p. 34).

Richardson's first novel ostentatiously claimed epistolary historicity. But it also featured an antagonist who knows that the truth of history depends entirely on 'the Light you put Things in', and whose ultimate 'belief' in Pamela's 'pretty Novel' is less an acceptance of its strict historicity than an acknowledgement that 'you have touch'd me sensibly with your mournful Relation' (Richardson, *Pamela* (1740), pp. 201, 207, 208). The 'Editor's' preface to volume III of *Clarissa* (1748) admitted the fictionality of its epistolary form (Williams, p. 124), although Richardson soon wished 'that the *Air* of Genuineness had been kept up, tho' I want not the letters to be *thought* genuine; only so far kept up, I mean, as that they should not prefatically be owned *not* to be genuine: and this for fear of weakening their Influence where any of them are aimed to be exemplary: as well as to avoid hurting that kind of Historical Faith which Fiction itself is generally read with, tho' we know it to be Fiction' (Richardson to Warburton, 19 April 1748, in Carroll, *Selected Letters*, p. 85). This is not far from Fielding's famous claim that *Joseph Andrews* (1742) is a 'true history' because in it 'I describe not men, but manners; not an individual, but a species' (III, i, pp. 159, 161),

---

[5] See John L. Sutton, Jr., 'The Source of Mrs Manley's Preface to *Queen Zarah*', *Modern Philology*, 82, 2 (Nov. 1984), 167–72.

or from his anonymous supporter's remark concerning this 'probable' story that "'twas thought necessary, to give it a greater Air of Truth, to entitle it *an History*' (*Essay on the New Species of Writing* (1751), Williams, p. 153). By 1783 the claim to historicity was becoming obsolete, a dead convention: although novelists 'study to make their inventions probable, they do not even pretend that they are true: at least, what they may pretend in this way is considered only as words of course, to which nobody pays any regard' (Beattie, *On Fable and Romance*, Williams, p. 309). The claim to historicity became moribund at the same time as the decline in the epistolary mode of propounding an 'objectively' external narration.

Was probability understood as a mechanism for internalizing instruction within entertainment, reason within feeling, precept within example? To some degree: in contrast to romance, at least, novelistic probability was commonly conceived as a constraint upon the latter elements in the service of the former. 'The Novel, though it bears a nearer resemblance to truth, has yet less power of entertainment; for it is confined within the narrower bounds of probability'; the novel 'is shackled with a thousand restraints; is checked in her most rapid progress by the barriers of reason; and bounded in her most excursive flights by the limits of probability' (Hawkesworth, *Adventurer*, 4 (18 Nov. 1752), Canning, *Microcosm*, 26 (14 May 1787): Williams, pp. 193, 341). But how do the constraints of a probabilistic 'naturalness' affect the teaching of 'morality'?

To answer this question we must first observe that contemporaries recognized two different sorts of probability, which might be called 'external' and 'internal' probability (for a full discussion see Patey, *Probability*, ch. 5). In the first instance, reference is made to the correspondence between fictional action or characterization and real experience as we know it. It is in this sense that Charles Gildon found Defoe's account of Robinson Crusoe 'not very probable'; that Richardson and his critics debated the 'probability' of Lovelace's character; and that in his portrait of Squire Allworthy, Fielding was credited with having 'soberly restrained himself within the bounds of probability' (*Epistle to Daniel Defoe* (1719), *Gentleman's Magazine*, 19 (July 1749), Murphy, Intro. to *Works of Henry Fielding* (1762), Williams, pp. 61, 139–40, 257). Radcliffe's effect of the 'explained supernatural', whereby Gothic terror is achieved while remaining 'within the limits of nature and probability', is similarly a case of external probability (*Monthly Review*, 2nd ser., 15 (Nov. 1794), Williams, p. 393).[6]

---

[6] Compare Charles Brockden Brown's 'Advertisement' to *Wieland* (1798), quoted in Perosa, *American Theories*, p. 8.

Richard Payne Knight discriminated this sense of probability from internal (or 'poetical') probability:

[T]hat sort of semblance to truth, which ... we will call *poetical probability*, does not arise so much from the resemblance of the fictions to real events, as from the consistence of the language with the sentiments, of the sentiments and actions with the characters, and of the different parts of the fable, with each other: for, if the mind be deeply interested ... it will never turn aside to any extraneous matter for rules of comparison; but judge of the probability of the events merely by their connection with, and dependence upon each other.

(*Analytical Inquiry into the Principles of Taste* (1805), p. 267)

By this more strictly Aristotelian standard, Knight (p. 283) found the impossibilities of *Gulliver's Travels* more probable than the possible plot of *Clarissa*. Fielding had made a similar distinction when he argued that 'the Actions should be such as may not only be within the Compass of human Agency, and which human Agents may probably be supposed to do; but they should be likely for the very Actors and Characters themselves to have performed' (*Tom Jones* (1749), VIII, i; I, p. 405). Invoking the theory of another, older genre, Fielding identified this principle as 'what the dramatic Critics call Conservation of Character'. It is in this spirit of internal probability that a reader of *The Mysteries of Udolpho* (1794) thought Valancourt's 'disgraceful indiscretions' uncharacteristic and therefore '*unnatural*'; that a reader of *Pamela* deemed crucial Pamela's service to Mr B.'s mother: 'for if she had always remain'd a Fellow-cottager with her Father, it must have carried an Air of Romantick Improbability to account for her polite Education'; that readers praised Richardson and Smollett for an epistolary mode that precisely distinguished among a host of letter-writers by correlating with each a style 'excellently adapted to the character of the writer' (*Monthly Review*, 2nd ser., 15 (Nov. 1794), prefaces to *Pamela* (1740), *Gentleman's Magazine*, 19 (July 1749): Williams, pp. 394–5, 114, 135).

'Conservation of character' partakes of the more general Aristotelian principle of unity of action, which requires that plots proceed with probability and necessity. Godwin makes this connection when he asserts that it is really 'romance' (i.e., fiction) that is 'true history'. Unlike history-writing, which must be responsible to the ultimate unknowability of external experience, romance is able to achieve the consistency of internal probability, 'showing how character increases and assimilates new substances to its own, and how it decays, together with the catastrophe into which by its own gravity it naturally declines' ('Of History and Romance' (composed 1797), p. 372). This does not contradict Godwin's grounding political tenet that 'The Characters of Men Originate in Their External Circumstances' (*Enquiry* (1793), I, iv, chapter heading). It recapitulates that tenet in the analogous but distinct sphere of fictional activity (see Kelly, *English*, pp. 15–16).

External probability concerns the reflection of reality by fiction; internal probability reconceives this concern as an autonomous structural principle internal to fiction itself. Modern doctrines of realism are fed by both species of probability. Although internal probability is an 'ancient', because Aristotelian, principle, modern theory could rediscover and embrace its revolutionary formalism only when the ground had been thoroughly prepared by the discourse of external probability and the claim to historicity (see McKeon, *Origins*, pp. 119–20). Of course, the formal sophistication of internal probability disregards the accountability of fiction to external experience. Does it follow that this effort at 'naturalness' must also undermine fiction's efforts at an externally effective 'morality'? Perhaps not; still, some contemporaries thought much current fiction did indeed discourage the mechanism through which novelistic 'example' was driven and justified by moral 'precept'.

VI

What does it mean to say that novels 'teach us to think, by inuring us to feel'? The association between the novel and its reader's emotional transport had been gathering momentum from Richardson onward. But many commentators recognized that if a transported reader is to remain morally thoughtful and responsible, she or he must also be a detached and active reader (see Bartolomeo, pp. 34, 127). One effect of the cult of sensibility was to sensitize commentators to the way the circuit between feeling and thought, example and precept, fictional distress and active moral response, could be shorted out by the very textual pleasures that were supposed to complete it.

'In the enthusiasm of sentiment there is much the same danger as in the enthusiasm of religion, of substituting certain impulses and feelings of what may be called a visionary kind, in the place of real practical duties, which, in morals, as in theology, we might not improperly denominate good works.' 'But in these writings our sensibility is strongly called forth without any possibility of exerting itself in virtuous action, and those emotions, which we shall never feel again with equal force, are wasted without advantage.' 'I am afraid lest the same eye which is so prone to give its tributary tear to the well-told history of fancied woe, should be able to look upon real misery without emotion, because its tale is told without plot, incident, or ornament.' 'Young people are all imitation, and when a girl assumes the pathos of Clarissa without experiencing the same afflictions, or being put to the same trials, the result will be a most insufferable affectation and pedantry'. 'I have actually seen mothers, in miserable garrets, *crying for the imaginary distress of an heroine*, while their children were *crying for bread*' (Mackenzie, *Lounger*, 20 (18 June 1785), J. and A. L. Aikin [Barbauld], *Miscellaneous Pieces in Prose and Verse* (1773), Monroe, *Olla Podrida*, 15 (23 June 1787), Cumberland, *Observer*, 27 (1785): Williams, pp. 330, 289, 350, 335; *Sylph*, 5 (6 Oct. 1795), pp. 35–6, Taylor, p. 53). On the evidence of these passages, contemporaries discovered simultaneously the Aristotelian doctrine of catharsis, and the Brechtian insight that catharsis militates against, by substituting for, moral behaviour.

Like probability, the renovated doctrine of catharsis made a vital contribution to the eighteenth-century theory of realism. Realism may be understood as that branch of the emergent notion of aesthetic autonomy that had reference to imaginative productions, like prose narratives, that appeared most directly implicated in the sphere of real experience. To some degree, of course, all aesthetic objects were understood to be so implicated. From Addison through Burke and beyond, commentators had been increasingly preoccupied with the apparent fact that the pleasure we take in aesthetic experience is dependent upon, yet absent from, the real experience of what that art depicts – that aesthetic experience therefore must come close, but not too close, to real experience. Coleridge made the case specifically for prose fiction:

The merit of a novelist is in direct proportion . . . to the *pleasurable* effect which he produces. Situations of torment, and images of naked horror, are easily conceived; and a writer in whose works they abound, deserves our gratitude equally with him who should drag us by way of sport through a military hospital, or force us to sit at the dissecting-table of a natural philosopher. To trace the nice boundaries, beyond which terror and sympathy are deserted by the pleasurable emotions, – to reach those limits, yet never to pass them, – *hic labor, hoc opus est.*

(*Critical Review*, 2nd ser., 19 (Feb. 1797), p. 195, Bartolomeo, p. 140)

In the attention shown to the moral expense of emotional transport was underscored the dangerous power of the novel to appear so much like reality as to challenge the priority of the real. Probability named that element of likeness, while also insisting (unlike the claim to historicity) on the crucial fact of difference. The third major tributary to the flood of realism, the explication of aesthetic belief as the willing suspension of disbelief, addressed the affective corollary of probability, that peculiarly doubled state of consciousness which refined and complicated the otherwise monolithic effects of emotional transport. Coleridge's famous formulation of that consciousness as it arises in response to poetry was well preceded by theorizations of it deriving rather from the experience of reading novels. Both Richardson and Fielding self-consciously created for their readers the aesthetic effect of the willing suspension of disbelief – Richardson through the reader-surrogate (for example, Mr B.), Fielding through his omniscient narrator (see McKeon, *Origins*, pp. 361–2, 406–8). But neither theorized this effect as explicitly as did their followers.

One reviewer maintained that 'when a person sits down with a novel in his hand, he knows he is going to read a fiction; but if it be well written, he soon forgets that circumstance, under an agreeable imposition; and becomes interested in the narrative, as a history of real events' (*Monthly Review*, 42 (Jan. 1770), p. 70, Bartolomeo, p. 148). Richard Cumberland argued that novelists 'are no otherwise *impostors*, than those fair-dealing jugglers are, who candidly warn their spectators beforehand, that their tricks are nothing more than mere slight of hand, the effect of nimble art and practised adroitness, by which they cheat the sight, but aim not to impose upon the understanding; like them, the novelist professes to deal in ingenious deceptions, but deceptions so like truth and nature, that, whilst his performances have all the vivacity of a romance to excite admiration, they have the harmony of a history to engage approbation' (*Henry* (1795), VI, i, Williams, p. 415; contrast Fielding's darker comparison of romance 'imposition' to that of a puppet master, in *Jonathan Wild* (1743), III, xi, pp. 154–5). Describing the effect of Radcliffe's explained supernatural, a reviewer claimed that 'the reader experiences in perfection the strange luxury of artificial terror, without being obliged for a moment to hoodwink his reason, or to yield to the weakness of superstitious credulity' (*Monthly Review*, 2nd ser., 15 (Nov. 1794), Williams, p. 393).

The emergence of realism during the latter decades of the eighteenth century (the term itself did not appear until the following century) has a close bearing on a contemporary innovation in the technology of narration that was to have a crucial importance in the history of the novel. Even before Richardson perfected the epistolary mode, it had been prized as a method of achieving, in narrative, the close characterization available in drama through dialogue and monologue (see Day, *Told in Letters*, ch. 7). Richardson seemed to bring all of its potential to fruition. For him epistolary form provided

the only natural opportunity that could be had, of representing with any grace those lively and delicate impressions which *Things present* are known to make upon the minds of those affected by them. And [the author] apprehends, that, in the study of Human Nature, the knowledge of those apprehensions leads us farther into the recesses of the Human Mind, than the colder and more general reflections suited to a continued and more contracted Narrative.

All the Letters are written while the hearts of the writers must be supposed to be wholly engaged in their subjects ... So that they abound not only with critical Situations, but with what may be called *instantaneous* Descriptions and Reflections ... [This is highly preferable to] 'the dry, narrative, unanimated Style of a person relating difficulties and dangers surmounted ... the relater perfectly at ease; and if himself unmoved by his own Story, not likely greatly to affect the Reader'.

(Warburton, Preface to *Clarissa* (1748), III; Richardson, Preface to *Clarissa* (1751): Williams, pp. 124, 166)

Epistolary form gives immediate access to the deepest emotions of its characters. Its 'naturalness' lies not only in the impression it creates of an 'instantaneous' 'present', but inseparably in the fact that it employs the words, the very consciousness, of those characters: 'Slight strokes, and gentle touches, seemingly frivolous and impertinent, have an astonishing effect in strengthening the resemblance of the portraiture ... [E]very character speaks in his own person, utters his feelings, and delivers his sentiments warm from the heart. It admits of an infinity of natural moral reflections' (*Critical Review*, 11 (March 1761), Williams, p. 234). In accord with the general theory of teaching precept by example, this reviewer affirmed the utility of first-person emotion in stimulating moral instruction. The reward of detached reflection depends upon the prior experience of immediate identification. Epistolary form 'keeps the reader in the same suspense, in which the persons themselves are supposed to be'. 'The illusion is lasting, and complete ... I interrupt the unhappy Clarissa, in order to mix my tears with hers: I accost her, as if she was present with me. No Author, I believe, ever metamorphosed himself into his characters so perfectly as Richardson' (Beattie, *On Fable and Romance* (1783), *Gentleman's Magazine*, 40 (Oct. 1770): Williams, pp. 323, 274–5). If, on the other hand, we begin with the 'general reflections' of a 'contracted narrative', we are denied the foundation in emotional sympathy on which our moral improvement depends.[7]

However, even Richardson's supporters had to acknowledge the liabilities of epistolary form. It encouraged repetition, prolixity, and the absurdity of universal and incessant letter-writing, even between characters for whom 'conversation was within their reach' (Cumberland, *Henry* (1795), III, i, Williams, p. 406). It also promoted the spectacle of vanity. One of Richardson's friends wrote to him that self-praise in characters 'should be as much avoided as possible'. True, 'when the scenes represented are passionate, they must come from the persons concerned, or they lose their spirit'. Still, 'I am persuaded you can point

---

[7] See Godwin's account of his replacement of third- by first-person narration in composing *Caleb Williams* (1794): *Fleetwood* (1805), Preface, p. xi.

[out] to us' those virtues that may be abstracted from such scenes of passion (Mrs Donellan to Richardson (25 Sept. 1750), Williams, p. 148). Fielding was rather more trenchant. Alluding to Richardson's formulation of the pedagogical maxim (story should be considered little more than a vehicle to instruction), he derided the immodest ambition 'of reforming a whole people, by making use of a vehicular story, to wheel in among them worse manners than their own' (Preface to *Journal* (1755), p. 30; for Richardson's formulation see Williams, p. 167). The danger of the first person, of unmediated letters – and this is at the parodic heart of *Shamela* – is that they deny the author all third-person opportunity to reflect upon and improve the fully articulated morals of characters who may themselves be vicious.

Although it was practised by Fielding himself, as well as by a number of novelists of the later eighteenth century (most notably Frances Burney), the narrative technique English-speaking critics have come most commonly to call 'free indirect discourse' was not named or fully theorized until the early twentieth century. It may be understood as a method of refining access to character interiority in conjunction with an exteriority free (unlike epistolary form) of the naive claim to historicity. Recently defined as 'the technique for rendering a character's thought in his own idiom while maintaining the third-person reference and the basic tense of narration', free indirect discourse combines the virtues of first- and third-person narration by allowing the narrator as it were to enter and speak from within the mind of the character, but also to vacate that internal locale in order to reflect externally upon its contents (Cohn, *Transparent Minds*, p. 100). And yet if the earliest novel theorists never attained this level of definitional precision, the debate concerning the virtues and liabilities of epistolary form came very close – as though to combine the best of both Richardson and Fielding – to evoking the narrative method that was even then being invented. In the present context, free indirect discourse may also be seen as a sophisticated technique, like the method of realism to whose store it contributed, for balancing the claims of example and precept, entertainment and instruction, feeling and reason, first and third person, illusionary artifice and its self-conscious display.

The investment of early realism in achieving this equilibrium between illusion and its display was recognized by the great novel theorists when they affirmed, each in his own way, that the thematization of formal matters on the level of content is central to the novel genre (see Lukacs, *Theory*, pp. 60–2, 71–3; Ortega y Gasset, *Meditations*, pp. 143–4; Bakhtin, *Dialogic Imagination*, pp. 45–9). By this means, novelistic practice has maintained its characteristic reflexivity, its tendency to reflect 'theoretically' upon itself, even in the absence of explicit prefatory commentary.

In recharacterizing realism as illusionary artifice alone – as an effort to achieve the transparency effect of immediate representation – post-structuralist theory tells us more about itself than about realism (see Coward and Ellis, *Language and Materialism*, pp. 45–60; Belsey, *Critical Practice*, pp. 47–55, 67–84). For the retrospective simplification of realism only fulfils the paradoxical imperative of the 'novel tradition' to conceive each stage of its continuity as though it were wholly innovative upon and discontinuous with what came before.

This having been said, however, we are surely justified in asking how far the doctrine of realism – of transport, probability, and aesthetic belief – preserved the pedagogical end of teaching precept by example that contemporaries associated with the new genre. By eschewing the antithetical improbabilities of both romance and history, realism clearly extends and sophisticates the aim and accomplishment of 'naturalness'. What is its relationship to 'morality'?

On the foregoing evidence, those novelistic categories we now understand as formal and intrinsic – character consistency, unity of design, internal probability – were first elaborated in the express service of an extrinsic moral end to which they now appear irrelevant. The eighteenth-century novel may well be said to 'internalize' pedagogy in the way it characteristically conceives the education of the protagonist as a lesson in probabilistic knowledge ideally replicated in the formal experience of the reader (see Patey, *Probability*, chs. 7, 8). But to affirm, more generally, that the teaching of precept in the modern novel has been internalized within the enjoyment of example – so that a pleasurable response is taken to signify the moral worth of the reader – is perhaps only another way of acknowledging the relative unimportance of the moral in the modern evaluation of literature. In the 1790s, probability was characteristically justified not only by its naturalness, but also (therefore) by its capacity for moral instruction. Fifty years later, the pedagogic function of probability is much less likely to be acknowledged by its practitioners.

This is a result of the modern division of knowledge. Modernity is accustomed to see in the eighteenth century an anomalous devotion to moral instruction, to the 'didactic'. It is important to recognize, however, that this phenomenon represents not so much an increased investment in moral pedagogy as the coalescence of moral pedagogy as one among several categories of knowledge, rather than (as in the customary view) the purpose that superintends them all. The didactic was not simply endorsed at this time; it was constituted as the mode of ostentatiously explicit instruction out of the debris of an older system in which all knowledge had been tacitly and pervasively 'didactic'. By the same token, contemporary anxiety about the effects of novels on impressionable readers signifies an increase not in the impulse toward social regulation and discursive discipline, but in the apprehension that customary (and highly effective) regulatory discourses were being enervated by social instability.

Most pertinently, the didactic was now separated out over against another Enlightenment invention, the aesthetic. The model of the novel as example teaching precept would carry little conviction once modernity conceived pleasure and instruction, the 'aesthetic' and the 'didactic', as essentially incompatible ends. That the novel – the 'modern' genre – was none the less first theorized in just these terms suggests its central role in the experimental effort to co-ordinate categories that had been traditionally and tacitly understood as inseparable. And modern novel theory may be said with some plausibility to 'internalize' the didactic within the aesthetic in so far as it perpetuates the problem of their emergent opposition in its own more thoroughly formalized terms: character versus plot, description versus narration, showing versus telling, spatial form versus seriality, *jouissance* versus *plaisir*, etc. A comparable effect is achieved when modern novel theory translates the problematic relationship of the aesthetic and the didactic into an extended diachronic series of opposed forms: realism versus the claim to historicity, modernism versus realism, post-modernism versus modernism, etc. (Of course, this argument of period opposition is tacitly undermined by the relativizing continuity of the series itself – that is, by the imperative of an implacably 'novel tradition'.) Analogously, if (by the logic of gender differentiation) the novel is a 'feminized' form, its feminization entails the full internalization of the masculine as a sublimation or refinement of pedagogy, a mitigating 'domestication' of a blunt male moralism.

This development may also be adumbrated in the terms of genre history. The traditional prose literary genres – the epic, the romance – had been conceived as narrative fictions that taught a truth higher or deeper than, yet fully compatible with, their fictional form. When empirical and historical truth were accorded their special privilege in the early modern period, fiction was discredited as incompatible with truth. Required to justify itself in turn by its service to morality, by its guise of historicity, by its maintenance of probability, fiction was now explicitly revalued according to criteria that had once been tacitly operative. The novel ceased to be fundamentally opposed to romance once the theory of realism had mastered, in highly sophisticated terms, the basic lesson that fiction might be compatible with truth. This was a lesson romance had always known. And yet the terms in which it could now once again become intelligible were the terms of a complex theory of affective response that had no equivalent for – or appeal to – those who had consumed narrative before the novel's emergence.

9
Prose fiction: Germany and the Netherlands

C. W. Schoneveld

For practical reasons, the developments in the critical debate about prose fiction in two separate languages are here placed under a single chapter heading. In fact, the differences and resemblances between German and Dutch criticism are no greater or smaller than those between English and French. In all four there is much common ground, originally based on the classical heritage of the European Renaissance, with Latin as its shared language, but subsequently continued through an ever increasing intertraffic of translations between the vernacular languages. Ultimately, it was very much a European debate, with regional, yet sometimes quite significant, differences. The first section will deal with the German-speaking world, the second with the Dutch Republic.

German theory and criticism

In general it can be said that German theorizing about prose fiction in the seventeenth and eighteenth centuries showed greater sophistication than that in England. There are also more treatises written independently of particular specimens of the genre. But until the latter part of the eighteenth century the terms of the debate were similar to those elsewhere. German criticism in the second half of the seventeenth century, then, just like its French and English counterparts, ignored lower and popular forms of contemporary prose fiction and concerned itself with the pastoral and the heroic romance, as practised in Italy, Spain, France and England and reaching Germany in translation. Until the 1680s criticism was aimed at legitimizing these works, and integrating them into a hierarchy of existing genres. In the field of terminology there was to be less confusion than in English, since, as in France, the term *Roman* was accepted from the beginning and hardly ever questioned as the proper overall generic term. Its defenders claimed for the *Roman* a place alongside the epic, or indeed they equated it with that prestigious genre. In France, Bishop Huet had been at great pains to establish the ancestry and noble status of the romance, on a level with the epic, in a treatise, translated into English as *A Treatise of Romances and their*

Originals within two years of its first appearance in 1670.[1] With German theorists, Huet's defence gained even more authority and it in fact pointed the way for them. But even before the text was translated from the French by Eberhard Werner Happel in 1682, Sigmund von Birken's *Dichtkunst* (1679), the first German poetics to pay full attention to the *Roman*, put it on a par with the epic. Before this work was published, Birken himself and others had already suggested two sub-genres, subtly labelled *GeschichtGedicht* and *GedichtGeschicht* ('historical poem' and 'poetical history') respectively, to distinguish between on the one hand prose narratives in which the main story is true but embellished by invented episodes and non-chronological narration and differing from the epic only in their use of prose, and on the other hand stories which are either fully true to fact but hide their truth by invented names and circumstances, or which are entirely fictional but designed to teach a moral.[2]

Other writers such as Morhof, Omeis and Roth also followed Huet in distinguishing the *Roman* from the epic only by virtue of being written in prose (L, p. 29).[3] But soon, further sub-genres with other criteria were being identified, particularly by Christian Thomasius in his *Spectator avant la lettre*, the *Monats-Gespräche* (1688ff.), and elsewhere. In the wake of French criticism Thomasius distinguished between a long and a short variety. He treated the latter form as merely another sub-genre of the *Roman* dealing with the private love between two people, as opposed to the long variety which had the history of a whole nation as its subject. Later he added the chapbook (*Volksbuch*), the pastoral romance, and the prose satire to his classification. In his critical assessment he had already moved away from the *utile dulci* approach to the artistic appreciation of verisimilitude (L, p. 39).

Gotthard Heidegger, as a Protestant Swiss minister and a representative of continental puritanism, nourished a radical distrust of all fiction and of the poetic imagination in general. In his *Mythoscopia Romantica, oder Discours von den so benanten Romans* (1698), he saw the appearance of the shorter form in France, the *nouvelle*, as an indication that the genre would soon dwindle out of existence (L, p. 38). To him partially invented stories were even worse than totally fictional ones, since they pretended to correct God's work as reflected in history. Such a view was

---

[1] See for Huet the section on France, pp. 211–13.
[2] Birken used these terms in his Preface to Herzog Anton Ulrich's *Aramena* (1669; L, p. 23; see note 3 for this abbreviation) and in *Teutsche Redebind- und Dichtkunst* (1679; L, p. 26). Cf. Johann Rist, *Zeit-Verkürtzung* (1668), who makes a distinction between 'Fabelhaffte Historien' and 'wahrscheinliche Geschichten' (L, p. 16).
[3] The abbreviation L. refers to Eberhard Lämmert *et al.* (eds), *Romantheorie: Dokumentation ihrer Geschichte in Deutschland 1620–1880* (Köln/Berlin, 1971), followed by the first page-number of the passage concerned.

bound to elicit reactions. Total agreement was voiced by some; others, like Leibniz, gave only partial support, but there were strong opponents too, like Nicolaus Hieronymus Gundling and Erdmann Neumeister, who continued to defend the *Roman*. Leibniz, in a review of Heidegger's treatise, condemned the new *histoires galantes* from France as mere 'old wives' tales', but did stress the usefulness of inventing beautiful and utopian ideas, to be found in the French heroic romance, as vehicles for moral improvement (L, p. 57). Gundling's reaction was based on the distinction between good and bad fiction, either long or short, depending on whether it treated of 'lewd' love or of 'reasonable' love, and in general he stressed the difference between *fingere* and *mentiri*, to fictionalize and to lie (L, p. 58). Neumeister, if he is indeed the author of the anonymous *Raisonnement über die Romanen* (1708), was more appreciative than the others of the *galante Roman*, especially in its comic and satiric varieties, which he treated as conduct books, useful for achieving *prudentia civilis* or the true character of a *galant* man in society (L, p. 66).

Until half way through the eighteenth century criticism and theory continued to build on the earlier established categories. One of the traditional issues, the criterion of verisimilitude, now even became central in the discussions of Gottsched, Breitinger and Bodmer. Johann Jacob Breitinger dealt with it in the context of poetry (in the sense of literature) in general, defining it as everything that a critical mind considers possible and non-self-contradictory in a given situation. Bodmer's discussion of *Don Quixote* in his *Critische Betrachtungen über die Poetischen Gemählde der Dichter* (1741) introduced a new refinement to the criterion of verisimilitude, in that he allowed for the subjective and false truths in the hero's mind, which even as species of 'the marvellous' remained within the boundaries of probability. Paradoxically, he held that these delusions actually foster more belief in the reader than the medieval romances from which Don Quixote derives them. Bodmer also philosophized about the relativity of the truth of history, as necessarily based on reports only, when compared with the truth of mathematics. This argument allowed him to elevate the *Roman* potentially to the (still highly rated) level of history. Johann Christoph Gottsched had merely reviewed some works of prose fiction before he added a chapter on the subject to the fourth edition of his *Versuch einer Critischen Dichtkunst* (1751). Throughout, he still based himself on Huet, writing, in a strongly prescriptive tone, about consistency of characterization, starting the narration *in medias res*, the punishment of vice and reward of virtue, and the imitation of nature (defined as resemblance to what is known to happen in real life); to this last criterion a *Roman* should adhere even more strictly than an epic should.

Gottsched relegated the *Roman* to a low position in the hierarchy of genres. That he finally did pay attention to it in his *Dichtkunst* is no doubt due to the impact which Richardson and Fielding had been making in German translation from the middle of the 1740s. The 'moral weeklies' and even the learned periodicals welcomed the combination of credible characters and situations and the inculcation of virtue. The analysis of the most secret human emotions and the deepest springs of moral behaviour in Richardson and Fielding were seen as educational tools of the first order. However, in 1751 Johann Adolf Schlegel argued the equality of the *Roman* with poetry as a form of art, locating its value in its capacity to please rather than merely instruct (L, p. 96), and more traditionally, but also more pragmatically, Karl Friedrich Troeltsch compared the *Roman* with drama and even recommended the application of the Aristotelian rules for drama to the writing of prose fiction (L, p. 98). As in England, where Richardson and Fielding became the leading figures in a debate about idealism and realism in the portrayal of characters, in the German-speaking world a similar controversy developed, in which Rousseau served as Richardson's opposite number. But even a decade before the appearance of Rousseau's *Nouvelle Héloïse* (1761), there had been two strong pleas – by Gotthold Ephraim Lessing (L, p. 91) and Johann Carl Dähnert (L, p. 89) – on behalf of description of the personal lives of characters of everyday stature, with life-size virtues as well as vices.

Rousseau's defence – against Richardson (in Letter 11 of his *Confessions*, 1761) – of his method of concentrating on a few characters only, and those not 'above nature', and a simple subject that should continue to engage the attention without the distraction of a multiplicity of incidents and 'episodes' was the starting point of a seminal debate between Moses Mendelssohn and Johann Georg Hamann. Ironically, the former, in the *Briefe, die Neueste Litteratur betreffend* (1761), accused Rousseau precisely of presenting idealistic characters without showing any knowledge of the human heart, the quality that he admired in Richardson; further, Rousseau was lacking in narrative skill, the power to write dialogue and the ability to engage the reader's imagination (L, p. 108). Hamann, in a bantering reply to Mendelssohn (1762), allowed the artist the use of a kind of improbability to achieve poetic beauty, *incredibile sed verum*, and referring to Edward Young's *Conjectures on Original Composition* more than once, stressed the value of originality, as opposed to imitation (L, p. 113).

All these discussions centred round foreign authors. The few German attempts at imitation remained very much in the shadow or received only adverse criticism.[4] Christian Fürchtegott Gellert's *Schwedische Gräfin*

---

[4] Vosskamp, *Romantheorie*, pp. 143, 225.

of 1746 was later recognized as the first German *Original-Roman*, although it failed to elicit much enthusiasm. But during the 1760s critics began to advocate the writing of a national form of prose fiction. Christoph Martin Wieland's *Geschichte des Agathon* (1767) was to gain a lasting reputation as the first great German novel ('the first and only *Roman* for the thinking mind', as Lessing observed; L, p. 132). It was praised for its combination of imaginative appeal and profound thought, but the fact that its scene was set in antiquity was seen as a disadvantage, especially since the 'peculiar character of our nation and the resulting manners would provide much material for novels', as Friedrich Gabriel Resewitz wrote; and he regretted that no one dared to move the scene to Germany (L, p. 122). Even so, Wieland's fiction marks a turning point in the history of the German novel as well as novel theory. In imitation of Fielding he employs a narrator who argues about the work he is engaged in. This is also the case in his first published novel, *Die Abenteuer des Don Sylvio* (1764), for instance, in Book 5, chapter 1, 'in which the author has the pleasure of speaking about himself'. As a follower of Bodmer and Breitinger, Wieland there stressed 'the marvellous' as an essential element in art. But whereas with Breitinger this had been juxtaposed with 'the probable' or 'the natural', Wieland found a way to combine the two in *Don Sylvio*. The hero's quixotic fantasies are made probable by narration as realities in the character's mind, so the narrator himself argues, insisting that whatever happens to Don Sylvio lies strictly within the ordinary course of nature. In Book 1, chapter 12 the narrator generalizes about this paradox as the theme of his work. When Bodmer had characterized *Don Quixote* in the same way, he contrasted it with the medieval romances in which the fantastic adventures themselves were presented as having really happened.

Again like Fielding, Wieland presents his narrator paradoxically as someone telling the history of real events and at the same time as someone who creates the story, but always in accordance with the principles of nature. Mentioning Fielding by name, he defends the historical character of his *Agathon*, arguing in the preface to the second edition (1773) that its truth is not that of historical fact but of human nature in general. Thus, as he insists more than once in the novel itself, it is much more in accordance with life than those 'ephemeral' or even 'moral romances' in which the hero never changes.[5]

Soon after Wieland's work, Johann Timotheus Hermes's *Sophiens Reise von Memel nach Sachsen* (1770) appeared, in which, as the title indicates, the scene was finally moved to Germany itself. A dialogue in one of the early letters in this novel (very much on the author's behalf, it

---

[5] Preisendanz, 'Auseinandersetzung', pp. 82–91.

seems) invites the co-operation of the critics in creating a truly original German novel, to be modelled on Richardson and Fielding but making sure not to imitate them directly. That ideal novel should be characterized by a serious purpose, episodes with a hidden connection to the equally hidden main design, and an element of mystery in the hero's identity to maintain the reader's interest throughout, but without making the main character unnaturally perfect (L, p. 124). A reviewer in the *Teutsche Merkur* (1773) wondered whether the emphasis on surprise was a viable way of attaining originality. He did believe that Hermes's main purpose was to further the cause of social morality, but at the same time he implied that it might be better to tell the history of the human heart and to present 'psychological' (a very early use of this adjective in novel criticism) discoveries (L, p. 129).

This reaction is representative of new directions in German novel theory and criticism, to which both the *Teutsche Merkur* and the *Neue Bibliothek der schönen Wissenschaften und der freyen Künste* were important contributors. In the latter Christian Garve, professor of philosophy in Leipzig, had already argued (1770) that, whereas the ancients had dealt with the visible aspects of nature, it was the task of the moderns to reveal the inner motivation of human behaviour, and to find effective ways to express these sentiments and sensibilities in art. In these views he was influenced by British thinkers such as Edmund Burke and Henry Home (L, p. 136). In a more pragmatic contribution to the same periodical, entitled 'Ueber Handlung, Gespräch und Erzählung' (1774), Johann Jakob Engel translated this and related concepts into a treatise on aspects of the novel. He wished to extend 'action' to cover the expression of whatever goes on in the soul, and in this respect he displayed a strong preference for dialogue over narration as being a more direct and subtly expressive and therefore much more effective mode of presentation. On the other hand, narrative allows infinitely greater freedom in the treatment of time, by dwelling at length on one particular moment or at the other extreme by hurrying over an entire episode, as in a summary phrase like 'I came, I saw, I conquered'. It also gives much greater scope than dialogue for presenting a point of view on the part of the narrator (L, p. 139).

Influenced by both Garve and Engel, it was Friedrich von Blanckenburg who in the same year (1774) produced the first German book-length theory of the novel, *Versuch über den Roman*. Lacking any originality of thought, its importance lies in its synthesizing of previous approaches to prose fiction into a consistent whole. Blanckenburg saw the *Roman* as successor to the epic, taking the totality of life for its province rather than dealing only with love; he wholeheartedly adopted Fielding's term 'comic epic poem in prose' and rejected Richardson's 'perfect heroes'.

Next to Fielding, he based himself on Wieland's *Agathon* as his major example. Instead of concerning himself with outward actions as in the epic, it was the novelist's special task to portray the inner history of a man, but according to a carefully worked-out design, or plot, in such a way that the whole would serve as a moral example to the reader.[6]

Although it is largely backward-looking, Blanckenburg's *Versuch* also contains the seeds of what is often seen as the typically German variety of the form as it developed in the work of Goethe and after: the concentration on the inner life of an individual, more often than not in opposition to or in isolation from society. However, before this flowering came about there continued to be a number of sceptical opinions concerning the possibilities of freeing the genre from foreign, especially English, elements and classical, especially epic, influence. The *Neue Bibliothek* allowed, in addition to the 'moral' *Roman*, a small opening for the 'political' *Roman*, as practised by Albrecht von Haller in his *Fabius und Cato* (1774), but the full meaning of such works would be understood only by the philosophically and politically erudite reader (L, p. 154). Johann Heinrich Merck, on the other hand, blamed the poor quality of German fiction on the lack of maturity and real-life experience in its (mostly youthful) practitioners (*Der Teutsche Merkur*, 1778). Even if it remained for him essentially epic in spirit, the novel should deal with genuine human emotions (L, p. 156).[7] Two years later Johann Carl Wezel launched the phrase 'wahre bürgerliche Epopee' (truly civic epic) to characterize the ideal modern novel, in the preface to his *Herrmann und Ulrike* (1780). The term has remained current in describing the craving for a typically national character in the German novel. Wezel sought the solution in a combination of the genres of comedy and biography, with the introduction of 'the marvellous', based on an uncommon combination of events or the intensity of their impact on the main character's emotions and behaviour, but always with the intention of creating an artistic whole, and, in his own case, of edifying the reader (L, p. 160).

For a while afterwards, the discussion on the relation of the novel to the other genres was continued by others. In a long essay of 1791 in the *Neue Bibliothek* the anonymous author argued for a combination of the dramatic presentation of dialogues with an epic or narrative approach to action in the gradual delineation of a character. The thrust of his argument, however, was to show the limitations of the predominantly dramatic method, that is, a succession of dialogue scenes; the reader also wishes to be informed and taught, through narration, about the circumstances, and the influence of society, places and times. It is also

[6] Wölfel, 'Schlegels Theorie', pp. 29–60.   [7] See Vaget's article in *PMLA*.

the only way of filling up the gaps between important episodes so as to create a harmonious whole (L, p. 165).

In the fifth Book of Goethe's *Wilhelm Meisters Lehrjahre* (1795) we also find a comparative discussion of the characteristics of the novel and drama. Here the stress is on the essential differences, implying that the two should be kept separate. The discussion was continued outside this novel by Schiller, in an exchange of letters with Goethe on epic and dramatic *Dichtung*.[8] Together with Herder, who stressed the comprehensive and versatile nature of the novel (L, p. 175), Schiller was also able to shift the discussion away from the prescriptive Enlightenment approach, which concentrates on the nature of the finished product, towards the Romantically inspired recognition of the novelist as an individual creator whose genius would enable him to create true beauty in adherence both to Nature and the Ideal; it is this which makes him essentially a poet (L, p. 173). From these beginnings, Friedrich Schlegel, Novalis and their successors were to develop views of the novel which placed the genre and its theory at the centre of German Romanticism.

Dutch theory and criticism

In the Netherlands the publication of prose fiction before the last quarter of the seventeenth century was largely confined to translations from French, Italian and Spanish originals. Nor was there much independent reflection upon it. Amyot's French version of Heliodorus' *Aethiopica* was translated into Dutch in 1610, but its poetological preface was modified into a mere commendation of the text for its moral usefulness (Pol I, pp. 21–9). More often the original prefaces were left out, even in the case of Georges de Scudéry's important preface to *Ibrahim* (1641; translated 1679). Clearly, the virtual absence of original texts made it unnecessary to engage in defences of prose fiction in relation to other genres, such as the epic – a major concern of French practitioners. In fact, the few prefaces that do occur concentrate on moral effects, stimulating the reader to imitate good characters and their behaviour and to shun their opposites. One critical issue that occasionally came up was that of the degree of truth of the narrative. One N.B.A., translator of Palaephatus, *Van de Ongelooflijcke Historiën* (1661), distinguishes fictionality from falsehood, and defends the former as an attractive way (provided it is made to resemble reality) of advocating the truth (Pol I, p. 33). Incidental remarks about form seem to indicate an early dislike of elaborate structures, with episodes, as in D'Urfé's *L'Astrée* and Sidney's *Arcadia*

---

[8] Schiller, *Briefwechsel*, Bd. I, nos. 177, 186, 367.

– which would explain why, initially, both were translated only in part. The term *roman*, today in Dutch as elsewhere on the continent the undisputed generic term, did not gain this general currency nearly as soon as in Germany. Before 1700 it was used only sporadically, and mostly, except in some prefaces translated from the German, in a derogatory sense to indicate lack of veracity in a narrative. But further specification of types of prose fiction and their characteristics or requirements remained absent for a long time. However, at the end of the 1660s two writers, in a dedication and a preliminary verse respectively, did treat the short *nouvelle* form as a welcome reaction to the long heroic romance (Pol I, p. 47). At the same time some preface writers began to recommend Dutch authors like Johan van Heemskerk, Lambertus van den Bos and Jan Brune de Jonge as equalling foreign fiction-writers in quality (Pol I, p. 49). But apart from this, the *nouvelle* never gained any foothold in Dutch as a reaction to the heroic romance and neither of these two forms became the subject of much reflection or controversy.

In this light it may seem strange that Huet's *Traité* was translated twice (in 1679 and 1715). This can hardly be due to any other reason than its international prestige. Its content, as a defence of the dignity and high pedigree of the heroic romance, played no role in the gradually developing debates about prose narratives in Holland. The Dutch discussion took a quite different direction, resembling that in England more than that in France or Germany, even though translations from English were still rare. Almost all prefaces to prose narratives in the period between the two Huet translations claim factual truth for the events they report, instead of mere verisimilitude. After all, there was a distrust of all fiction in the still dominant orthodox Protestant circles. In addition, literary claims for prose fiction were precluded by the strongly prevailing idea, voiced among others by the leading Dutch poet Joost van den Vondel and the philologist and playwright Lodewijk Meijer, that literary texts should use verse (Pol I, pp. 71–6). Not surprisingly, the prefaces continued to stress the moral instruction to be derived from the work they introduced, especially by the young. A representative example is the preface by the anonymous female author of *D'Openhertige Juffrouw* of 1699. She claimed to write about the 'common' affairs of women, who were real but whose names she had hidden, in a matching, that is unadorned and unelevated, style and in the simple chronological form of memoirs. Hendrik Smeeks posed as the editor of an account of a South Sea island by the name of 'Krinke Kesmes', written by a traveller named Juan de Posos (1708). He defended his style as reflecting the simplicity of a sailor, 'for whom it is more natural to present matters of fact than employ florid language' (Smeeks, p. 74). In some cases such 'geschiedenissen' or 'historiën' (histories), 'gevallen' (adventures, fortunes) or 'levens' (lives) may have had a basis in fact, but many readers, like those who recognized the name of the kingdom of 'Krinke Kesmes' as a near-anagram of the 'editor's' name, must have appreciated such works first and foremost as fiction.

Until the early 1750s no great changes in these positions took place. They were largely confirmed and strengthened by the translations of Defoe's fiction. The translator of *Robinson Crusoe* (1721) contributed a preface of his own with lengthy elaborations on the author's original preface. Defoe's influence was further prolonged by many imitations, the so-called 'robinsonades'. Both translators and imitators continued to stress the veracity of their stories, their moral effect, and the naturalness of their style. However, in addition to this continuing trend, there were occasional prefaces – most of them translated – which did admit and defend the fictionality of the narratives they introduced. One direction taken in such defences was that probability was all that was required to reach the same aim as in true stories, which was likewise to give moral instruction. Another tendency was to follow Huet in claiming literary respectability on account of epic qualities in style and structure. Fénelon's *Télémaque* served here as a touchstone. Although its being in prose was considered pardonable by one translator, a later one felt he had to do the story full justice by translating it into Dutch alexandrine verse and so removing the last obstacle to full epic status.[9]

But changing prose into verse could not, of course, raise the status of prose fiction as such. To bring this about the examples of Richardson and Fielding were required and were indeed gradually taken to heart. Fielding's Preface and introductory chapters to the Books of *Joseph Andrews* were translated (anonymously) along with the text as early as 1744. The same is true of *Tom Jones* in 1749–50, turned into Dutch by the experienced and respected translator Pieter Le Clercq.[10] *Pamela* had already appeared in Dutch in 1741–2 (including Richardson's own short preface but omitting the letters of praise).[11] Such translated prefaces are, not of course, necessarily a faithful reflection of native Dutch thought but must at least have stimulated it. This seems to have happened in the preface to a (non-translated) anonymous Dutch 'robinsonade', *De Walcherse Robinson* of 1752. Even as late as this, it claimed to introduce a true account but, while still paying lip service to the idea that fictional 'romances' may have an evil influence on the young, at the same time it praised the moral teaching of Homer and Virgil, no matter whether their stories were historical or fictional (Pol II, pp. 113–15). If

[9] Compare Pol II, pp. 74–6 (F. de Salignac de la Mothe Fénelon, *De Gevallen van Telemachus*, trans. Isaak Verburg (Amsterdam, 1715)) with *Telemachus, uit het Fransch . . . in Nederduitche Vaerzen Overgebracht*, trans. Sybrand Feitama (Amsterdam, 1733), Voorrede, pp. I–X.

[10] See De Voogd, 'Fielding', *passim*.

[11] For Dutch translations and imitations of Richardson see Mattheij, 'Bibliography'.

this is still a voice wavering between the old and the new, a fresh note was struck in the same year by Pieter Adriaan Verwer, a translator who provided his own preface to defend the fictionality of Charlotte Lennox's *Het Leven van Henriette Stuart*.[12] He begins by attacking writers of history for including invented stories in their accounts. Furthermore, diversity of possible interpretations of history makes historical truth uncertain. Theology, law and philosophy also have their fables: 'Consider the outlines sketched of a spiritual life ... in which many produce more of a spiritual romance than catching the truth. Why then may not a quick and witty mind invent adventures which have the shape of a history and by which he is able to entertain his fellow man?' (Pol II, p. 112)

But, again in 1752, the real and even internationally recognized turning point in Dutch novel theory came about with the extensive reflections by the Mennonite minister Johannes Stinstra which accompanied his translation of the first two volumes of *Clarissa*. These were followed until 1755 by further prefaces to the later volumes, for which, ironically, he claimed the example of Fielding's introductory chapters to *Tom Jones* (Slattery, *Stinstra*, p. 131). In fact, his thinking was based on both Richardson and Fielding. The first, thirty-seven-page-long, preface has a strongly persuasive intention, being organized on the rhetorical principles of a classical oration. Its purpose comes out at the start when Stinstra anticipates the reader's surprise that a clergyman should occupy himself with prose fiction. After reminding his readers that both Huet and Fénelon were divines, he develops his main argument that fiction, when it has the right characteristics, is morally more effective, by furnishing examples, than books of moral and religious instruction, which provide precept only. The absence of factual truth is no hindrance, as long as the fiction adheres to what is probable and natural (p. 110). Histories or biographies of prominent men usually provide stories of famous events only; a novel can show the actions of common, plain and domestic life together with their motivations and intentions and thus serve as an example to all (p. 109). In *Clarissa* the characters, although representative of virtues and vices, are not entirely perfect or evil and show greater individuality than those of Fielding who 'stays more with the general, sketches more a rough and external outline' (pp. 115–16). They preserve their character consistently and can be identified by the style and manner of their letters (p. 117). This feature especially shows a penetrating knowledge of human nature on the part of the author (Stinstra could as yet only guess that it was Richardson), which he applies with a wonderful combination of imaginative power, sharp wit and solid judgement (p. 125).

[12] Amsterdam, 1752, translation of *The Life of Harriot Stewart*.

In the second preface Stinstra stressed the value of relaxation and reading for enjoyment. As a result, good reading will give us pleasure in virtue, provided we read with care and attention, since it is the smaller details that reveal most about people. By applying this in life to other people we learn prudence and by applying it to ourselves we gain self-knowledge as a source of wisdom. The rich materials themselves will moreover enlarge our understanding, enliven our wit and sharpen our judgement (pp. 163f.). The third preface is a justification of the imagination as a means to acquiring virtue and the fourth defends the tragic ending of *Clarissa* along the same lines as Richardson himself had done.

From an international viewpoint none of his arguments was quite original, but for Dutch literary history Stinstra's importance lies in the fact that he succeeded in making the novel respectable, not so much artistically as morally, thereby educating serious Christian believers in the reading of fiction of a moral type. A modern feature of his approach was his explicit focus on the effect that the various components of a moral novel would have on the reader. His extensive reflections far exceeded the format of a mere preface and they soon began to exert an influence of their own, forming a bridge to other, non-prefatory, criticism in reviews and *Spectator*-like essays.

Stinstra's pivotal role comes out once more if we look back to before his time. In the case of reviews of Richardson the situation had been quite different. *Pamela* received no mention in the Dutch-language press at all, even though its translation (1741–3) was immediately followed by translations of both *Pamela Censured* (as *Pamela Bespiegeld* in 1742, even before the translation of *Pamela* itself was complete), and Mrs Haywood's(?) *Anti-Pamela* (1743). And as far as essays are concerned, the father of the Dutch moral weekly, Justus van Effen, in his *Hollandsche Spectator* of 1734 had ridiculed the heroic romance for the extravagance of its characters and adventures, and in his earlier French-language *Misanthrope*, now translated into Dutch by Pieter Le Clercq (1742–5), had criticized its falsity and its effect of infecting people with idle and dangerous ideas.[13] By contrast, in the year after Stinstra's first preface, Elie Luzac, in his *Nederlandsche Spectator*, replied to the bantering question of a reader (a half-literate army officer) whether any moral lessons could be derived from novels that he should read *Clarissa* and consult Stinstra's preface.[14] As late as 1788 another periodical essayist, wishing to provide some thoughts on novel reading, felt that

---

[13] Justus van Effen, *De Hollandsche Spectator*, x (1734), no. 255; *De Misantrope of Gestrenge Zedenmeester* (3 vols., Amsterdam, 1742–5), I, pp. 422–5, III, pp. 457f.
[14] 'Brief van Lugthart of er zedenpreken uit romans te haalen zyn', *De Nederlandsche Spectator*, 5 (1753), pp. 137–40; reply pp. 141f.

he could do no better than produce a lengthy summary of Stinstra's ideas.[15]

Although Stinstra preferred Richardson's character portrayal to Fielding's, he certainly did not share Richardson's dislike of his rival. In fact, Fielding's reception in the Netherlands in general was as favourable as Richardson's and no need was felt to take sides as in England, even though the differences between them were fully acknowledged. Their work was recognized as a new kind of *roman* which came to be bracketed as 'moral': the *zedelyke roman*[16] or *zedekundige roman*. And if for the translators of *Joseph Andrews* and *Tom Jones*, coming before Stinstra, Fielding's own extensive reflections had rendered any introductions of their own unnecessary, J. A. Verwer, after his Lennox translation of 1752, and again in his Dutch version of *Amelia* of 1753, inserted prefaces before both the first and the sixth volumes of his translation. In the first, Fielding is accorded the highest praise for the naturalness with which he portrays the inner workings of the soul. In the last, Verwer discusses this novel's unfavourable reception in England and argues in its defence that it is the natural sequel to *Tom Jones* and that Booth is a maturer version of Jones.[17]

Tom Jones itself had already received an uncommonly enthusiastic reception in *De Boekzaal* (1751),[18] an established review periodical, which usually provided only summaries and extracts. Although, tellingly, the reviewer believed that *Pamela* was by the same author, he did go into the differences between the two works in the type of plot and narrative method used, and subsequently outlined Fielding's educational and moral message, gave a summary of the story, and praised the characters for their naturalness and consistency; the incidents for being so wittily invented, artfully woven together and naturally linked (p. 297); the form for the cleverness of its inimitable introductory chapters; and the style as 'very pleasant, smooth, and at once natural and in keeping with the subjects' (p. 299).

Thus in the 1750s and 1760s Dutch criticism became increasingly impressed by serious English narrative fiction in contrast to the French variety which was often dismissed as frivolous,[19] even with support coming from France itself: Diderot's *Eloge de Richardson* (although attributed to Arnaud) was published in translation twice (in 1763 and

---

[15] 'Gedagten over 't leezen van vercierde geschiedenissen en romans', *Algemeene Vaderlandsche Letteroefeningen*, 3, 2 (1788), pp. 97–110.
[16] E.g., Cornelis van Engelen in *De Philosooph*, no. 42 (1766).
[17] De Voogd, 'Fielding', pp. 181f.
[18] *De Boekzaal der Geleerde Wereld*, 73 (Sept. 1753), pp. 284–302; Boheemen, 'Fielding and Richardson', pp. 298f.
[19] See e.g., the periodical *De Gryzaard*, 1 (1767), p. 46.

1770).[20] But in view of the many translations of English novels now appearing on the market there was also a painful awareness of the absence of any native Dutch equivalents.[21] One Dutch critic, Rijklof Michael Van Goens, suggested that prospective novelists should begin by writing short moral narratives ('zedekundige verhalen'). In the absence of any English examples here, he recommended Marmontel as a good model.[22]

Van Goens is one in a continuous line of Dutch thinkers and critics who shared a liberal outlook in religion (mostly Mennonites and Remonstrants). Although a small minority in opposition to an orthodox majority, they had great influence in cultural matters, especially through the many moral weeklies edited by them.[23] They all had a high opinion of the English novel. Thus the Remonstrant A. A. van de Meersch in *De Denker* looked to *Grandison* for guidance on travel and the definition of a good Christian.[24] *De Philosooph*, run by Stinstra's friend Cornelis van Engelen, recommended to young ladies 'the principles of common sense and virtue' found in Richardson and Fielding.[25] *De Onderzoeker* written by A. J. W. Van Dielen, who probably belonged to the circle of Van Goens,[26] in 1771 devoted a whole issue (no. 154) to the reading and writing of fiction. He carefully distinguishes several types. The love affairs of some knight-errant or lady of pleasure might be read for entertainment without any effort of the mind, and the impossible adventures of semi-divine heroes and heroines should please only those under sixteen. These are *romans* proper, but Fielding's, and especially Richardson's works, lack such extravagant and miraculous adventures. They might be called 'verdigte leevensgevallen' (fictional life adventures)

---

[20] 'Lofrede op den Heer Richardson, schryver van de Pamela, Clarissa en Grandison', *Vaderlandsche Letteroefeningen*, 3, 2 (1763), pp. 135–43, 165–75; and *Algemeene Oefenschoole*, 10, 6 (1770), pp. 303–24. The introduction to the former compares the French piece, as showing 'the immediate effect of the strong impression ... on a sensitive heart and a lively mind', with Stinstra's manner which is 'more in a concatenated and sedate Dutch way of thinking' (p. 135).

[21] An attempt was made to produce a Dutch equivalent to *Pamela*, the anonymous *De Hollandsche Pamela* (2 vols., Amsterdam, 1754). But this was backward-looking, for the 'editor' explicitly denied its fictionality by claiming in his preface that the letters by the poor uneducated Zoetje Gerbrants were genuine, and he laid the scene at the court of Stadtholder-King William III, where the virtuous girl behaved passively but successfully like the heroine of a heroic romance.

[22] 'Het zedenkundig verhael' in *Nieuwe Bydragen tot de Opbouw der Vaderlandsche Letterkunde*, 2 (1766), pp. 485–505, where it is defined as 'an original and succinct presentation of a fictional occurrence, for improving the morals or satirizing the follies of the people for whom it is written' (p. 487).

[23] Boheemen, 'Reception', *passim*.

[24] *De Denker*, 2 (1765), p. 80; 6 (1768), p. 306, quoted by Mattheij, 'Ontvangst', p. 150.

[25] *De Philosooph*, 1 (1766), pp. 331f.; cf. 2 (1767), p. 37, where Fielding is considered somewhat less safe reading than Richardson.

[26] Zwaneveld, 'De Opmerker', *passim*.

containing more moderate and sensible stories. The desire to read these is excellently suited 'to make the principles of religion and virtue known in a pleasant and clever way' (p. 397). The author then makes a special plea for the character of Grandison:

Where you are to give an example to be imitated should you not make that example as perfect as you can? ... I confess that you do not find such men, but I do not see that it is impossible that such a one could be found. For a character like this to be absolutely impossible it would have to contain an element of contradiction against the characteristics of human nature.

(p. 398)

This pronouncement clearly puts him in the camp of those who believed in the idea of the imitation of ideal nature which was gaining support from some Dutch critics in the last part of the century. Even so, Van Dielen ended his essay by repeating Van Goens's preference for the short moral tale *à la* Marmontel, as the best way 'to teach the young in a pleasant and hence powerful way' (p. 399).

In a footnote Van Dielen also advertised the imminent appearance of a Dutch translation of Sophie von La Roche's *Geschichte des Fraüleins von Sternheim* (attributed to Wieland, however), which indicates a growing interest in German moral fiction in the wake of the popularity of Richardson. The review periodicals of the 1760s and 1770s increasingly paid appreciative attention to Dutch translations of these works from Germany. In the early 1780s Goethe's *Werther* (next to Sterne's *Sentimental Journey* and *Tristram Shandy*) began to influence Dutch critical thought, of which more later.

For the Dutch novel the great breakthrough finally came in 1782, with the publication of *De Historie van Sara Burgerhart*, by Betje Wolff and Aagje Deken. Just as in Germany, here was at last an original national novel – an 'oorspronkelyk Vaderlandschen Roman' – as the female authors proudly wrote in their long preface (p. iv). It was 'a novel designed for the meridian of domestic life. We paint Dutch characters for you; people whom you really find in our fatherland',[27] and, in contrast to most fiction published at the time, it was 'not translated' ('Niet Vertaalt') as the title page explicitly announced. In spite of the term 'Historie' and the phrase 'edited by' ('uitgegeven door') in the title there is no attempt in the preface to hide the story's fictionality, nor do the writers pose there as editors. They in fact make extensive use of the

---

[27] 'Een Roman, die berekent is voor den Meridiaan des Huyselyken levens. Wy schilderen u Nederlandsche karakters; menschen, die men in ons Vaderland werkelyk vindt', p. vii. As Breekveldt (*Wildschut*, p. 76) points out, the term 'meridian' also occurs in *Clarissa* (letter 68): 'How artfully has Lovelace ... calculated to your meridian'.

opportunity of providing interpretative comment on the characters, which they could not place within the text itself, since it is an epistolary novel, modelled on Richardson's technique (but more Fielding-like in spirit).[28] Their moral aim is to educate young girls in the direction of domestic, i.e. married, bliss, as opposed to the dangers of extra-marital relationships. And although they admire *Clarissa* they are careful to stress the native character of their work in its portrayal of an immediately recognizable world, where 'everything remains in the realm of the natural' ('alles blyft in het natuurlyke', p. xii) with no 'divine Clarissa' (p. vi) or a Lovelace who probably could only occur 'in the world of the imagination' (p. x).

Just as Wolff and Deken were writing and publishing their first novel, a debate arose about the new vogue of Sternean sentimentalism. In 1783 Rijnvis Feith published *Julia*, which he called 'a simple scene of two tender hearts which are sincerely in love', with 'no suggestive incidents, no unexpected coincidences' and in which 'I preach a love that does not exist without virtue'.[29] It gave rise to a debate between him and Willem Emmery, Baron de Perponcher. The latter objected to the exalted way in which love was presented in fiction, since it would cause a serious disease of the soul, threatening to upset the whole order of society. To him such writing was quite different from 'the true sentimental [which] is like sunshine to the soul, it is warming, cherishing, clear and calm; it nourishes, strengthens and produces healthy fruits'.[30] Feith in his turn defined sentimental writings as those in which 'private perceptions are expressed in a style that speaks more to the heart and the imagination than to the head, in such a way that these perceptions are transferred to the reader's soul and create similar tender feelings there'.[31] In the characters presented it is their emotions rather than the events of their lives which are described, but these emotions might range from noble to criminal and from happy to sad. Taking Sterne's *Sentimental Journey* as the point of reference, each opponent in his own way stressed the moral potential as well as the dangers of sentimentalism and showed himself sensitive to the new trend, although both entirely overlooked Sterne's humour. Wolff and Deken, in the meantime, still adhered strongly to their enlightened rationalistic moralism and in their second novel, *Willem Leevend*, inserted a long episode demonstrating the disastrous

---

[28] In the preface to a later novel Wolff wrote: 'what is gained by *Clarissa* in richness and composition is perhaps balanced in *Tom Jones* by no lesser signs of art and knowledge of humanity' ('het geen Clarisse in rykheid en compositie wint, wordt misschien in Tom Jones opgewogen, door geene mindere trekken van kunst en menschkennis'), *De Gevaaren van de Laster* (The Hague, 1791), p. xii.

[29] Reprint ed. Het Spectrum (Utrecht, 1981), pp. 11f.

[30] Van den Toorn, 'Sentimentaliteit', pp. 266, 269.   [31] *Ibid.*, p. 267.

effects of sentimentalism on a young girl named Lotje Roulin, as 'an instructive example to everyone who is inclined to exaggerated sensibility' (VIII, p. 220). It was their protest against 'the dictatorship of a weakened moral sense', as they put it in the preface to the fifth volume.

But a theoretically more fundamental difference between Wolff (and Deken) and Feith concerned their attitude to the imitation of nature. Feith wished to create pictures of ideal nature, partly by selecting and combining existing elements, partly by consulting his own feelings, and by avoiding the particular in representing times and places, although he admitted that if one wished to write for a particular audience and reflect their own manners and morals (he mentions *Sara Burgerhart*), description of the particular cannot be avoided.[32] The two women, on the other hand, wanted 'to show the world as it really is' by portraying it in a 'lively, striking and touching way' as they explained in a preface to a later novel (*Cornelia Wildschut*, I, pp. v, vi) and by keeping to the nation's 'own, particular character' as Wolff wrote in yet another preface.[33]

The same division of opinion can be identified in the reception and criticism of Goethe's *Werther*. The novel's fundamental ambivalence was invariably overlooked, and the periodicals especially warned of the dangers of Werther's character, particularly for the young (who were voicing their admiration in the literary ephemera of the day).[34] However, a new tone of voice was heard in a preface to an amended Dutch edition of 1793. Its anonymous author has recently been identified as Johannes Lublink. He argued that the portrayal of the main character's inner self should not be judged in terms of any moral purpose, but is an end in itself, presenting a psychological analysis in the form of a story. He was probably influenced by German ideas and remained an isolated voice for a considerable time to come, except for a similar argument developed by Petrus Nieuwland, who denied that even Tom Jones was a model for everybody's behaviour; novels simply illustrate 'how human nature can work in some persons and some circumstances' and if we imitate such characters we shall have only ourselves to blame for the results, not the novel in question.[35]

The late 1790s witnessed a rejection of sentimentalism and a return to earlier enlightened Christian morality, with reprints appearing of Stinstra's translation of *Clarissa* (1797–1802) and *Grandison* (1797–1802), to the latter of which the same Lublink again added a preface, but a more traditional one this time.[36] New impulses and ideas were to arrive with

[32] Feith, *Ideaal*, Buijnster's 'Inleiding', pp. 56f. Van den Berg, 'Burgerhart', pp. 173f.
[33] *De Gevaaren van de Laster* (The Hague, 1791).
[34] Kloek, *Werther, passim*; Kloek, 'Lublink', p. 342.
[35] Nieuwland, 'Gevoeligheid', pp. 546f.   [36] Kloek, 'Lublink', pp. 344–7.

the influence of Sir Walter Scott, but by then we have moved well into the nineteenth century.

Thus we can conclude that the Dutch through the openness of their culture were influenced at first by French, later by English and finally also by German fiction and its concomitant theorizing and in the development of their native thought remained in close contact with European trends.

10

Historiography

Michel Baridon

No English historian at the time of the Restoration would ever have prophesied that a century later one of his successors would be bold enough to proclaim: 'History is the most popular species of writing'.[1] Nor could he have foreseen that, in the words of Hume, Britain would become 'the historical nation'. On the contrary, he might have been inclined to think that France or Italy with their Oratorians, their Benedictines, their Jansenists and their long tradition of scholarship would be more likely to distinguish themselves in the field. Besides, in England and elsewhere in Europe, the drama was favoured above all other species of writing, and booksellers had not yet created the conditions which were to make history what it is now, one of the very few literary genres that finds its way on to railway bookstalls. The Restoration historian, like so many historians before and since, made the wrong guess about the future because, with all his knowledge of the past, he could not free himself from the present.

In seventeenth-century England, an antiquarian might write about long-forgotten events and a statesman in disgrace might relate the history of his life and times. What they had in common was their love of the past, their scholarly turn of mind, their common preoccupation with documents; but society did not consider them as belonging to the same walk of life and they attached their loyalties to different milieus. Most highly distinguished among them all were the King's historiographers in France and in England. Racine received this title 'as a grace from God', knowing that he (like Dryden) had better claims to literary fame, and he saw the appointment as a social rather than an intellectual distinction. He would probably have agreed with Père Le Moyne that history was a 'continuous narration of great events relating to state affairs' written 'with candour, with eloquence and with judgement' in order 'to instruct private citizens and princes, and to benefit civil society'.[2]

Bossuet echoed this definition of history in his *Adresse à Mgr le*

---

[1] Gibbon, *Memoirs*, p. 157.

[2] 'L'histoire est une narration continue de choses vraies grandes et publiques, écrites avec esprit, avec éloquence et avec jugement pour l'instruction des particuliers et des princes et pour le bien de la société civile.'

Dauphin which opens his *Abrégé de l'Histoire universelle*. According to him, since religion and the state are 'the two poles round which human affairs revolve', the business of the historian is to reveal 'what is great among men' by following 'the thread which runs through human affairs'.[3] The similarities between these two texts are evident since both use the adjective 'great' and stress the dignity of historical writing. They present the historian as an official figure to whom the fasti of the state are entrusted.[4] In the same way, Caxton said he wished to relate 'the brave deeds which our ancestors accomplished', implying by 'our ancestors' the great in both the nation and the Church. The idea that the past belonged to those who ruled the state was so strongly rooted in the minds of the humble that the chapbooks reflect an almost total lack of historical sense, confusing all periods – and even all styles of dress in their illustrations – as if to convey an impression of antiquity vague enough to give access to the regions where things happened 'once upon a time'.

Such was not the case with the chronicles in which state affairs were gravely recorded; they adjusted their language to their learned readers and their method of composition reflected the influence of the great historians of Rome. This was the 'real, solemn history' which Catherine Morland could not read because it devoted so much space 'to the quarrels of popes and kings, with wars and pestilences, in every page; the men all so good for nothing and hardly any women at all'.[5] Of course, she spoke in such a way as to make Henry Tilney rise to the defence of 'Mr Hume and Mr Robertson', for even 'real, solemn history' was no longer what it had been in the days of Dugdale and Tillemont. In Catherine Morland's time, the new public mentioned by Hume and Gibbon was already in existence.

This new public had not come into being as if by magic. It had begun to appear in the sixteenth century, when the works of the great Florentine historians, Machiavelli and Guicciardini, were discussed by the learned all over Europe. Their books revealed to the world that history could concern itself, not only with the relation of events, but with their causes discussed from the civic humanist's point of view. Even more important

---

[3] 'Comme la religion et le gouvernement sont les points sur lesquels roulent les choses humaines, voir ce qui regarde ces deux choses dans un abrégé et en découvrir par ce moyen tout l'ordre et toute la suite, c'est comprendre par la pensée tout ce qu'il y a de grand parmi les hommes et tenir pour ainsi dire le fil de toutes les affaires de l'univers.'

[4] On seventeenth-century French historiography, see O. Ranum, *Artisans of Glory*, particularly chapters 5, 6, 7, 9, on patronage and on Racine.

[5] 'I can read poetry and plays and things of that sort, and do not dislike travels. But history, real, solemn history, I cannot read'. Jane Austen, *Northanger Abbey*, chapter XIV.

to the formation of a potentially large public, was the popularization of the public disputations which took place after the Reformation. They dealt with such subjects as the early history of the Papacy, the nature of miracles after the second century, or the encroachments of ecclesiastical power on civil government[6] and as such they could not fail to develop an historical approach to the great questions related to state affairs. These two trends, both tending to develop a new way of considering the past as a force still shaping the present, both stressing the political implications of religious factors, converge in such important books as Hotman's *Franco-gallia* and Harrington's *Oceana*.

At the same time, in the leading protestant countries, the combined efforts of the Arminians and of the 'Presbyterians turned Latitudinarians' were able to liberalize the regimes established by the iron hand of the Calvinists. In both Holland and England, for example, the development of the book trade and of popular education gradually modified the image of historians. They came to be seen as practical philosophers whose views on politics, ethics and economics raised questions of general interest to the common reader. Grotius and Pufendorf would not have gone through so many translations had things been otherwise. Harrington, neglected and persecuted though he was in his own time, finally came into his own in the eighteenth century and the politicians of the Bolingbroke school, so aptly called neo-Harringtonians by J. G. A. Pocock,[7] derived from *Oceana* most of their ideas concerning 'antique balance' and 'the mixed constitution'.

If the object of his studies were to be brought closer to the public, the historian could no longer adhere to the kind of writing associated with 'real, solemn history'. Saint-Évremond, for instance, who admired Grotius for his brilliant handling of state affairs and economic factors, was well aware that historiography was changing and that there was a need for a more literary approach to the relation of the past. Nobody, he thought, seemed to answer the challenge in his own country. 'One must admit that the merit of our historians is still of the mediocre kind',[8] was his somewhat dispirited comment on the situation prevailing there. He probably had a more favourable opinion of Clarendon and of Sir William Temple who provided food for thought at the same time as they called up a vivid image of the past. The latter had had long personal experience of high politics, and the former, although he wrote about events still remembered by his readers, had interesting views on what he called

---

[6] See R. Snoeks, *L'Argument de tradition dans la controverse eucharistique entre Catholiques et Réformés français au XVIIᵉ siècle* (Gembloux, 1961).

[7] See Pocock, *The Machiavellian Moment* and his 'Machiavelli, Harrington and English political ideologies in the eighteenth century' in *Politics, Language and Time*.

[8] 'Il faut avouer que nos historiens n'ont eu qu'un mérite bien médiocre.'

'the character of the times' and the necessity of 'knowing the genius that prevailed when the matters of fact were transacted'.[9]

These new priorities were to play an important part in the genesis of eighteenth-century historiography for, once they were grafted on to the Tillemont school of pure erudition, a change in the tone and atmosphere of historiography became possible. Cartesianism played a part in this combination of erudition with more worldly concerns. This is evident in the works of Bayle, but Tillemont had shown the way. Although he repeatedly professed his complete faith in the Scriptures, he had always collected, sifted and tested his documents as if he were applying the lessons of the *Discourse on Method* to the writing of history. He treated historical documents with the circumspection recommended by Descartes who compared himself to a man 'who walks alone in the dark', 'qui marche seul et dans les ténèbres'. Bayle followed in his steps, calling into question not the nature of the document itself but its spirit and its connection with 'the character of the times'. At the same time his concrete approach to history and the tone he imparted to his *Dictionnaire historique et critique* bridged the gap between scholarly annals and personal records.

Much has been said on the subject of Bayle's Cartesianism. But a historian is not a philosopher, and once the influence of the Cartesian method has been duly acknowledged in his use of documentary evidence, it must also be said that he made good use of the possibilities offered by the Baconian school with its insistence on concrete data and minute observation. Holland was not so far from England, and many of his friends belonged to the empirical school that Locke had already begun to publicize by circulating his manuscripts in the Le Clerc–Limborch circle. To trace the importance of Baconian influence in the very texture of his prose, one need only compare his style with Tillemont's.

The two men belong virtually to the same generation since Bayle was only ten years younger, but between them lies the distance which separates Holland from France and the beginnings of the Enlightenment from a much more traditional outlook. Referring in a letter to his *Histoire des Empereurs*, Tillemont describes it as 'wholly ecclesiastical', adding that he does his best 'not to give it a worldly tone'.[10] This explains why the sober quality of his style reminds the reader of Philippe de Champaigne. His book is the very image of the Jansenist soul, studiously balanced, undemonstrative and sparing of effect. Such is not at all

---

[9] Clarendon, *History of My Own Time*, Introduction.

[10] '... il faut l'éloigner autant qu'il se peut de l'air profane.' Quoted by Bruno Neveu, 'Sébastien Le Nain de Tillemont (1637–1698) et l'érudition écclésiastique de son temps', in Neveu, Religion, Erudition et Critique à la fin du XVIIe et at au début du XVIIIe siècles (Strasbourg, 1968), p. 31.

Bayle's conception of historical narration. In his dictionary, he praised Suetonius for having collected not only 'the documents concerning wars and other public affairs' ('les matériaux des guerres et des autres affaires publiques') but also 'the monarch's own activities and his tastes ... his aversions, his whims, his habits and his food'.[11] This inevitably gave his style a lively character which was in strong contrast with Tillemont's austere manner.

Once Bayle had established a new conception of historical writing, it became evident that the *Dictionnaire* and the *Pensées sur la Comète* were very efficient instruments of intellectual exploration. Fontenelle lost no time in assessing the possibilities offered to the philosophes – whom, it will be remembered, the *Encyclopédie* defines as 'investigators of causes' – by this new way of writing history. Fontenelle was born and educated in Rouen, a city in which Calvinistic influence was great and in which trade relations with England remained substantial even after the repeal of the Edict of Nantes. He was also in a position to reconcile the Cartesian critique of documents with the empirical approach and a practical sense of human affairs. His *Sur l'Histoire* is a manifesto which prepared the way for what historiography was to become in the hands of Voltaire and Montesquieu: a literary genre which captured the interest of an ever-growing public by making its vision of the past more consistent and all-embracing. He explained his conception of historiography in a passage which proved influential among the philosophes. The historian's task, Fontenelle insisted, was to concentrate on the character and motivations of the men about whom he wrote. Tacitus, who lived in a 'polite, enlightened age', had shown that events could be accounted for by the psychology of the actors of history. At this point, Fontenelle drew a parallel between Tacitus and Descartes whom he presented as 'two system-builders' ('deux inventeurs de systèmes'). The philosopher and the historian were confronted with a number of 'effects' whose causes they must connect in order to compose an harmonious whole ('un tout bien lié'). If they succeeded, they could frame a system which ascribed definite causes to definite events and which related these causes to the

---

[11] '... les inclinations et les actions particulières du monarque ... ses dégouts, ses caprices, ses habits et ses repas'. *Dictionnaire historique et critique*, Art. Suétone.

[12] 'A cette manière d'écrire l'histoire [Fontenelle is alluding to medieval chronicles] en succéda une plus parfaite qui entrait dans les motifs et dans les caractères et c'est celle qui a toujours été en usage dans les siècles polis et savans. Elle ressemble assez à celle dont on fait un sistème de philosophie. Le Philosophe a devant lui un certain nombre d'effets de la nature et d'expériences; il faut qu'il en devine les causes vraisemblables, et de ce qu'il voyait, il en compose un tout bien lié; voilà le sistème. L'Historien a aussi un certain nombre de faits dont il imagine les motifs et sur lesquels il bâtit le mieux qu'il peut son sistème de l'histoire, plus incertain encore et plus sujet à caution que son sistème de philosophie. Tacite et Descartes me paraissent deux grands inventeurs de sistèmes en deux espèces bien différentes.' Fontenelle, *Sur l'Histoire*, pp. 363–4.

nature of man.[12] In expounding his views on history, Fontenelle made frequent use of a concept which proved essential to the eighteenth-century historian, the concept of 'connection' ('liaison') which he uses in relation to what he called 'little things'. His advice to historians was to find the small origin of great things ('Donner de petites origines aux grandes choses') by using details concerning customs and manners. He knew that little things could provide the 'hidden natural connection', the 'liaison nécessaire mais cachée' which is the warp and woof of history.[13] They alone could make the past come to life again; but they could do more: they could connect elements which had hitherto been considered unrelated, and by so doing they could supply the causes of events.

But little things could establish fruitful connections only when the historian knew how to free documents from the accretions deposited by the credulity of men. He could do so only by being thoroughly acquainted with human nature whose general characteristics are invariable ('je n'ai supposé dans les hommes que ce qui leur est commun à tous')[14] and which has been accurately depicted by the 'polite, enlightened ages'. If human nature was everywhere the same, it became possible to establish principles valid for all types of societies in all climates. Human nature thus provided the substance of a system in which the actions of man were to be ascribed to causes discoverable by the philosopher. Tacitus was the Descartes of history because he traced the causes of events to the passions of man.

If the historian learnt from the best sources – and the age of Louis XIV might have as much to teach as the age of Augustus – he would be in a position to compare the variations imposed upon human nature by local conditions. He would know how to appreciate and to relate the motives of princes and the reactions of slaves. To say that Constantine could not be suspected of the murder of Priscus 'because he was a good Christian' was good enough for Tillemont, but totally unacceptable to the modern historian. Racine had learnt from Tacitus what Fontenelle would, in turn, learn from both: jealousy exists in the heart of an ageing emperor, whether he be a Christian or not.

This inevitably led to a new way of conceiving historical narration. The stress was no longer on the 'dignity' of history; it was on the 'small things'. And the vocabulary which had so long elicited a feeling of reverence in the reader became the occasion for gibes and jokes which stimulated his critical sense and urged him to derive practical lessons from past events. History could then divest itself of its antiquated trappings. It must become, it actually had already become, part of the general culture of the men actively employed in promoting the wealth and prestige of the nation. This was much to the taste of men of letters

---

[13] Ibid., p. 379.   [14] De l'origine des fables, p. 30.

at a time when literacy was spreading fast[15] and France's greatest writers turned to history as a means of expressing their views and of contributing to the formation of a new mental framework.

Whereas their English counterparts were still enmeshed in political arguments concerning the Glorious Revolution (hence Pope's and Fielding's disparaging views on historians)[16] they knew that their ideas would gain added impetus by ricochetting off the past. The *Lettres anglaises* and the *Histoire de Charles XII* have much in common. So have the *Lettres persanes* and the *Considérations*. But it would not be historically sound to present the satirical bent of such important works as detrimental to their stimulating power. Without them the Enlightenment would never have accomplished so much in the field of anthropology.

To appreciate the changes which resulted from this general reconsideration of the object and aim of history a comparison between Bossuet and Montesquieu will be more revealing than a long discussion. Both of the following texts deal with early Roman history.

Bossuet:

To feed their cattle, to plough the earth, to deny themselves all but the bare essentials, to live sparingly and laboriously – such was their existence, such was the way they supported their families which they brought up accordingly. Livy speaks the truth when he says that no nation ever honoured frugality, thrift and poverty over a longer period of time.[17]

Montesquieu:

We must not base our impression of the City of Rome in its infancy on the City which exists at the present time, unless we have in view the towns of the Crimean Tartars built for storing and securing plunder, cattle, fruits and other produce of the country. The ancient names of the chief places in Rome are all relative to this use.[18]

---

[15] On literacy in the eighteenth century, see F. Furet and M. Ozouf, *Lire et ecrire*.

[16] Pope ridiculed Caxton's English in an appendix to the 1729 edition of the *Dunciad* (*The Twickenham Edition of the Poems of A. Pope*, V, pp. 213ff.), and Fielding found fault with history for being 'too particular' in *Joseph Andrews*, III, i. I am indebted to Claude Rawson for these two points.

[17] 'Nourrir du bétail, labourer la terre, se dérober à eux-mêmes tout ce qu'ils pouvaient, vivre d'épargne et de travail: voilà quelle était leur vie; c'est de quoi ils soutenaient leur famille qu'ils accoutumaient à de semblables travaux. Tite-Live a raison de dire qu'il n'y eut jamais de peuple où la frugalité, où l'épargne, où la pauvreté aient été plus longtemps en honneur.' *Discours sur l'Histoire universelle*, p. 347.

[18] 'Il ne faut pas prendre de la ville de Rome, dans ses commencements, l'idée que nous donnent les villes que nous voyons aujourd'hui; à moins que ce ne soit celles de la Crimée, faites pour renfermer le butin, les bestiaux et les fruits de la campagne. Les noms anciens des principaux lieux de Rome ont tous du rapport à cette image.' *Considérations sur les Causes de la Grandeur des Romains et de leur Décadence*. Opening sentence.

Whereas Bossuet speaks of the Romans as if they were men of his own time, rounding off his description by an allusion to Livy, Montesquieu broadens considerably the scope of history. His reader needs to have seen quite a few towns to understand what ancient Rome was like; he must have read about the Crimea in order to form his own sense of history by geographical distance; he must also remember the toponyms of ancient Rome to connect them with the living conditions of the times. The very terms 'storing and securing' convey a concrete impression of the atmosphere which must have prevailed in a city engaged in a constant struggle for survival. However briefly we compare the two texts, our conclusion must be that the second uses a vocabulary at once more familiar and more technical, and that its sentences do not flow so majestically as those of the *Histoire universelle*. Montesquieu's description of Rome does not aim at the moral edification of the reader; it aims at his instruction. His oracular brevity is truly Palladian while the orotund periods of Bossuet preserve the ample movement of the baroque.

But neither of these styles was to Voltaire's liking. His own works were so popular that they must be examined separately in order to account for their remarkable success. His criticism of Montesquieu offers a good starting point. In a letter to Thiériot written in November 1734 he described the *Considérations* as 'an ingenious table of contents written in the Roman style'.[19] He criticized *L'Esprit des Lois* for displaying a great irregularity in its composition, and he lamented 'the singular affectation' which made Montesquieu 'write chapters of only three or four lines, and make a joke even of these'.[20] On another occasion he described Montesquieu as 'Michel de Montaigne législateur', as if *L'Esprit des Lois* affected the quaint irregularity of sixteenth-century prose.

In fact, what Voltaire was attacking was the Palladian character of Montesquieu's style. The Palladian wave had swept over England in the 1720s, spreading the fame of Pope, Burlington and Kent. While it made a powerful contribution to the development of the English garden and was in no way averse to Gothic ruins, it favoured a different architectural style based on a combination of Palladio and Inigo Jones. This style, like all other styles, promoted values which had both positive and negative aspects. It aimed at sobriety and at the harmony of geometrical proportions, implicitly negating the spectacular effects of the baroque and seeking the true image of *Roma antica* under the mask of *Roma moderna*. In the eyes of the Palladians, grace achieved what beauty could not always devise. Reason became 'the most exquisite of our

[19] Letter to Thiériot, November 1734.
[20] '... la singulière affectation de ne mettre souvent que trois ou quatre lignes dans un chapitre, et encore de ne faire de ces quatre lignes qu'une plaisanterie.' *Siècle de Louis XIV*, Catalogue des écrivains.

senses' ('le plus exquis de nos sens') mentioned by Montesquieu in the 'Invocation to the Muses' which opens the second part of *L'Esprit des Lois*.

Voltaire had no patience with this Roman stance. He was more pragmatic and more attached to literary forms likely to please a wider public. His admiration for the age of Louis XIV remained intact and, in true neo-classical fashion, he composed tragedies and even an epic, in strict conformity with the classification of genres. It may indeed seem strange that Montesquieu should often be considered 'Cartesian' and Voltaire 'Newtonian' while their respective works appear to demonstrate the very reverse. Voltaire's adherence to the models of neo-classicism is evident in most of his works while Montesquieu, who belonged to the Royal Society and composed some of his scientific works in true Baconian fashion (see his *Mémoires sur les Mines*), seems to have understood the aesthetic import of the newly created English garden. For reasons which were both political (he was in favour of the 'antique balance' of the mixed constitution and he quoted the name of Harrington in his famous chapter on the English constitution) and personal (he was a member of the *noblesse de robe*), he felt attracted to the English version of Palladianism.

Voltaire saw things differently. He had more taste for intellectual drive than for mental elevation. Portraits remained essential to his view of history because they enabled him to moralize the cause of events and because he knew by experience what a great man can achieve by personal commitment. By nature and by taste he felt closer to the great creations of the age of Louis XIV and adhered strictly to the system described by Fontenelle. When he wrote: 'I have always believed that history required the same art as tragedy' or 'In a book of history as in a play, one must begin with the exposition, proceed to the central crisis and end up with the denouement',[21] he certainly did not mean that the spectacle of history was tragic, but, quite clearly, that human reason and a thorough knowledge of the passions which govern human nature can put some order into the chaos of history and make it both intelligible and instructive. In this respect he was faithful to the teaching of La Mesnardière, who advised tragedians to take as their subjects actions famous in history so that the spectator, knowing how the play would end, could concentrate on 'the order of events, their connection and the conduct of the play on which the poet's glory depends' ('l'ordre, l'agencement et la conduite d'où dépend la gloire du poète'). The

---

[21] 'J'ai toujours pensé que l'histoire demandait le même art que la tragédie', 'Il faut dans une histoire comme dans une pièce de théâtre, exposition, nœud et dénouement.' Quoted in Brumfitt, *Voltaire, Historian*, p. 161.

important thing in history was the way in which the succession of events was logically made to depend on the conflicts of human passions. This partial adherence to neo-classical aesthetics does not prevent Voltaire from constantly mixing concrete terms with a more elevated vocabulary. 'Elegance' is a term of which he is very fond but he has no time for complacency, and he urges his reader along by means of the brisk, compelling rhythm of his short sentences, combining description, analysis and comment as he goes. In the *Siècle de Louis XIV*, his description of France mentions 'the labour of twenty million inhabitants' whose hands can make 'stuffs, hats, rolls of braid, stockings', which does not prevent him from praising the great artistic creations to be seen at Versailles and elsewhere. His ambition is to paint a very broad canvas, a 'machine' in the manner of Rubens. 'What I want to paint is the last century, not one prince only', he wrote to Harvey, and he did so by making the important figures stand out from the crowd, while infusing into the whole picture a single all-embracing swirl. He considered that no attention should be paid to details because they are 'the vermin that kill great works' and because posterity neglects them.[22]

Montesquieu would never have endorsed such a statement. He was more interested in the theory of history than in the portraits of great men, and he was never so happy as when he could prove that whatever the men, whatever the circumstances, a given event was bound to happen. In chapter 11 of the *Considérations*, he wrote that since the Roman republic could not possibly survive, it mattered little who gave it the death blow. His taste for general ideas and for a broad view of history certainly explains the architectural quality of his style.

But the differences between *Les Considérations* and the *Essai sur les Moeurs* did not prevent them from contributing jointly to the rise of the British school of historians which, as Gibbon saw, owed so much to Voltaire and so much more to Montesquieu.

Reflecting on the general consequences of the Crusades, Gibbon wrote in one of his many footnotes: 'A Strong ray of philosophic light has broke from Scotland in our own times and it is with private as well as public regard that I repeat the names of Hume, Robertson and Adam Smith.'[23]

Since Gibbon was not in the habit of making rash pronouncements and since he rarely divorced taste from philosophy in his appreciation

---

[22] 'Les principaux personnages sont sur le devant de la toile; la foule est dans l'enfoncement. Malheur aux détails: la postérité les néglige tous; c'est une vermine qui tue les grands ouvrages.' Lettre à M. l'Abbé Du Bos, *Oeuvres historiques*, p. 160.

[23] *Decline and Fall*, VI, p. 445.

of other historians, what he said of the Scottish school deserves full
consideration. In his view, the best examples of what we now call intellectual prose came from Scotland. Hume, he thought, had mastered the
art of dealing with difficult subjects with ease and elegance. In many
ways, Hume remained a true Palladian, faithful to the values of antiquity whether he was at his desk or contemplating the gardens of Lord
Bathurst at Oakley Park which he defined, with characteristic perspicuity, as 'true classical ground'.[24]

To be on classical ground was to be able to preserve the 'elegance' of
one's vocabulary, the natural movement of one's sentences and the
balanced proportions of one's chapters in the general design of a long
work. All this, Hume had achieved in his *History of England,* since he
had written it in reverse chronology without ever losing the sense of
unity which presided over the whole work.[25] In the Advocates' Library
one could be on ground as truly 'classical' as that of Stowe or Oakley
Park because the intellectual elite of the 'Athens of the North' was
anxious to civilize a country which might easily become a prey to the
bigotry of the High Churchmen and to the 'zeal' of the Presbyterians.
Man's creative powers are never so stimulated as when he has to face
two enemies at the same time. It is one of the great paradoxes of
Scottish history that exactly when Hume was civilizing his compatriots
by drawing up a list of Scotticisms at the end of his *History,* Macpherson
should have barbarized Europe with his *Ossian.* But genres have their
laws, and when Macpherson wrote his *History of Great Britain from
the Restoration till the Accession of George I* he reverted to a more
'civilized' sort of style. Yet the rules which governed the writing of
history also changed, even if they were slower in their evolution than
those of poetry. Hume and his Scottish followers, Smith, Robertson and
Ferguson, tried to create a style which would be a match for the great
historians of France for whom they felt the highest respect, as Robertson's
views on Voltaire testify.[26]

Their ambition is all the more understandable as they were not mere
disciples of the French. They were applying new disciplines to the study
of history. Prominent among these was economics, an important addition to the philosophic conception of history and one which owed much

---

[24] Hume to Crawfurd: 'I am here at a kind of classical Place [Lord Bathurst's garden
at Oakley Park], celebrated by Pope, Swift, &c. and with a classical man, who
lived in intimacy with these two wits.' *New Letters of David Hume,* pp. 184–5.

[25] On Palladianism and the standard of taste, see my comments in the chapter
'Science and Literary Criticism' below.

[26] Of Voltaire, Robertson wrote that if he had taken more care to indicate his sources
'Many of his readers who now consider him only as an entertaining and lively
writer, would find that he is a learned and well informed historian.' *Works,* III,
p. 332.

to the British empirical tradition. If, in true Baconian fashion, history was to be grounded on the material facts which conditioned men's lives, then the production and the exchange of riches loomed very large in a 'philosophic' view of the past. Mandeville had once made a *succès de scandale* out of this evident truth, but the time had come for a more dispassionate, a more thorough examination of the economic factor. Hume managed to introduce such matter-of-fact topoi into his *History*. At the end of chapter 23, we find him discussing the decline of serfdom in the following terms:

> The villains were entirely occupied in the cultivation of their master's land, and paid their rent either in corn or in cattle, and other produce of the farm, or in servile offices, which they performed about the baron's family and upon the farms which he retained in his own possession. In proportion as agriculture improved and money increased, it was found that these services, though extremely burdensome to the villain, were of little advantage to the master; and that the produce of large estates could be much more conveniently disposed of by the peasants themselves ... A commutation was therefore made of rents for services, and of money-rent for those in kind; and as men, in a subsequent age, discovered that farms were better cultivated where the farmer enjoyed a security in his possession, the practice of granting leases to the peasant began to prevail, which entirely broke the bonds of servitude, already much relaxed from the former practices.

While explaining how 'the progress of the arts' increased the number of slaves in antiquity whereas it proved 'a source of liberty' in modern Europe, Hume achieves a perfect merging of technical terms ('servile offices', 'rent', 'the money increased') with the more elevated prose of his narrative ('subsequent age', 'bonds of servitude'). Such passages open the way for *The Wealth of Nations* and for a kind of historical narrative which would give more space to 'great revolutions and changes' and gradually lessen the part allotted to psychology. 'The describing of characters is no essential part of a historical narration', said Adam Smith in his *Lectures on Rhetoric and Belles Lettres*,[27] and the lesson was learnt not only by Ferguson, Millar and Robertson but also by the French *idéologues* of the turn of the century.

Although he was an admirer of the Scottish school, Gibbon allowed himself some time before permitting the innovations of *The Wealth of Nations* to percolate into the *Decline and Fall*. He certainly would not give up 'the describing of characters' on which he relied to trace the causes of great events – Constantine's conversion is one of the famous examples – or to ornament his narrative with purple patches which bear

---

[27] *Lectures on Rhetoric and Belles Lettres*, p. 89.

the Roman stamp of which Voltaire spoke. But with Gibbon, the Roman stamp became more pronounced, majestic and solemn. However paradoxical it may sound, Gibbon infused a good deal of baroque *copia* into the Palladian elegance of Montesquieu.[28] He may well have reverted to the seventeenth-century tradition because the pomp of the baroque had often served to magnify death[29] and because the ruins of Rome were the finest image of past greatness ever offered to the contemplation of empire-builders. Knowing, as he did, how extraordinary the destiny of England had been and was likely to be, he managed to invest his great theme with the grandeur and the melancholy inseparable from the contemplation of human affairs at a great distance and on a large scale. What religion had done for Bossuet, history would do for him. Hence the characteristics of his style which 'hits the middle tone between a dull chronicle and a rhetorical declamation';[30] and hence also his interest in history as the noblest of all literary genres. This aspect of Gibbon's style has been admirably characterized by Tillyard[31] who perceived that, whereas Milton had written the epic of the seventeenth-century common man, Gibbon composed the epic of empire-builders. He managed to be the Reynolds of English prose because, like Reynolds, he was convinced that true art had its origin in the imitation of antiquity:

I know that the classics have much to teach and I believe that the Orientals have much to learn; the temperate dignity of style, the graceful proportions of art, the forms of visible and intellectual beauty, the just delineation of character and passion, the rhetoric of narrative and argument, the regular fabric of epic and narrative poetry.[32]

This reads like the credo of those Grand Tourists who visited 'the ruins, not of superstition, but of empire' as Gibbon himself wrote in his memorable conclusion to the *Decline and Fall*. His own 'intellectual beauty' is a direct echo of Reynolds's *Discourse VI* with its call for a return to the proportions so finely established by antique models and by their neo-classical imitators. The 'temperate dignity of style' of which Gibbon speaks might also have been found in Hume's *History*. There again, the elegance of neo-classicism was at work: Hume and Gibbon had a common admiration for Racine and the Shakespeare jubilee organized by Garrick did not change their views. Hume wrote to John Home:

[28] 'Alas how fatal has been the imitation of Montesquieu', he said of his own prose style in the *Essai sur l'Etude de la Littérature, Memoirs*, p. 103.
[29] On the pomp of state funerals in baroque churches, see V. L. Tapié, *Baroque et Classicisme*, p. 269.
[30] *Ibid.*, pp. 155–6.   [31] *The English Epic and its Background*, ch. 11.
[32] *Decline and Fall*, VI, p. 33.

'For God's sake, read Shakespeare but get Racine and Sophocles by heart'[33] while Gibbon remarked in his *Memoirs*: 'taste has perhaps abated my idolatry for the Gigantic Genius of Shakespeare which is inculcated from our infancy as the first duty of an Englishman'.[34]

Gibbon was so great a poet of history, however, that while he professed his loyalty to neo-classicism and to Palladianism, he in fact allowed his style to be receptive to climates of sensibility which darken its colours and deepen its resonance. As a critic he might write: 'A simple naked statue finished by the hand of a Grecian artist is of more genuine value than all these rude and costly monuments of barbaric labour',[35] but as a historian he described the conquest of England by the Saxons with a sensitiveness to landscape poetry reminiscent of *Ossian*: 'The dark cloud which had been cleared by the Phoenician discoveries and finally dispelled by the arms of Caesar, again settled on the shores of the Atlantic, and a Roman province was again lost among the fabulous islands of the Ocean.'[36]

Such passages are closer to Turner and to the aesthetics of sublimity than to Reynolds. They explain why Gibbon, although he always proclaimed his faith in neo-classicism and in Palladian proportions, was in fact so fascinated with what he considered to be the rise of a new form of barbarism, that he finally accepted poetically what he refused rationally. His style is a creation which could be achieved only by a historian for it is the very embodiment of the eternal struggle between the order established by culture and the disruptive forces of innovation. Passages such as these explain why the *Decline and Fall*, although it could only have been written in the eighteenth century, finally passed so triumphantly into the nineteenth. Its Palladian inspiration and its baroque copiousness stretched the Latinization of English to its very limit, but the meditation of a solitary man absorbed in the contemplation of 'the winds, the waves and the barbarians' brought the book back to northern climes. As such, it is a unique combination in which pure erudition and poetic sensibility speak the language of culture with one common voice. To parody one of Gibbon's many endearing mannerisms, it could be said that the modern blurb-writers who call him a classic deserve to be forgiven for so 'abusing' the term.

Whether the Romantic tendencies at work in the second half of the eighteenth century were irrational or whether they were struggling to conquer a new rationality, the concept of sublimity with all its barbaric connotations was everywhere at work in the emergence of a new world-

[33] David Hume, *Letters*, I, p. 215.   [34] *Memoirs*, p. 84.
[35] *Decline and Fall*, II, p. 499.   [36] *Decline and Fall*, IV, p. 157.

image. In this context, one can understand why Vico, although he remained an obscure figure in his own lifetime, was hailed both in France and in Germany as one of the great forerunners of a new conception of history. Vico's opposition to the cold rationality of the Cartesian method cannot wholly be ascribed to the originality of a solitary genius. Naples was to be a strange quasar in the bright firmament of the Enlightenment. Great discoveries were made there with Shaftesbury enthusing over Salvator Rosa with all his *maudit* connotations, or with Giannone discovering new ways of establishing the 'liaison cachée' of human societies by legal history, or again with Herculaneum and Pompeii becoming the founts of archaeological learning from which Winckelmann, Vien, Wright of Derby and others drew so much to achieve the revaluation of the heritage of antiquity. Vico epitomizes the strange relation of Naples to the rest of the European Enlightenment.

His protest against Cartesianism must be seen in the context which was studied by Frank Manuel in his *The Eighteenth Century Confronts the Gods*. Newton's world-image was very far from being as clear as Voltaire made it, and one has only to read his *Optics* to realize that the audacity of his conceptions revealed unfathomed depths and the secret working of gigantic forces.[37] Like the Newtonians, like the Leibnizians, Vico saw time as an essential dimension of non-Cartesian epistemology. To him, history was the knowledge proper to man since man was the agent through which change occurred. And history, he thought, offered a key to the understanding of the world as it stood. Hence the development of a theory of cycles far removed from the Polybian conception in which changes result from political causes. Vico saw things more broadly and wrote the overall history of man's relation to his environment. To the three successive ages he defined corresponded three types of language and three types of civil nature. With such a conception of historical change, the *Scienza Nuova* inevitably proscribed from history the tracing of individual psychological motives so important to Fontenelle and to Voltaire; it also proscribed the general political causes envisaged by Montesquieu's civic humanist approach.

If men passed from one stage of development to another they owed it to a collective evolution. The fiction of an eternal human nature on which the great historians of the Enlightenment had relied since the days of Fontenelle was no longer viable. The views that Vico held implied that the historian must rely on his imagination rather than on the power of reason whose geometrical mode of progressing was now ruled out.

---

[37] On the Newtonian world-image as different from the Cartesian, see my comments in the chapter 'Science and Literary Criticism', below.

'This world of nations', he writes in Book I of the *Scienza Nuova*,

has certainly been made by men and its guise must therefore be found
within the modifications of our own human mind. And history cannot be
more certain than when he who creates the things also describes them. Thus
our science proceeds exactly as does geometry, which, while it constructs out
of its elements or contemplates the world of quantity, itself creates it; but
with reality greater in proportion to that of the orders having to do with
human affairs, in which there are neither points, lines nor figures.

Such affirmations, with their strange blend of radical empiricism (we
know only what we ourselves make and we can know history because
it is made by us) and visionary elements (we can imagine past ages
because they represent modifications of our own mind), provide the key
to Vico's theory of history and to the nature of his style.

Since he presents the imagination as a faculty strong enough to re-
model the contents of memory, and since the memory of man is more
capacious than volumes of print, our understanding of history lies in
our faculty to imagine it. To understand what polytheism could have
meant we have only to look at children when 'they take inanimate
things in their hands and play with them and talk with them as if they
were living persons'. The same capacity to conjure up the visible and
the visionary is evident in Vico's vivid description of what could be
called the birth of Zeus. When the ancient Greeks saw the sky which
'fearfully rolled with thunder and flashed with lightning' they thought
it was one great animated being 'who, by the whistling of his bolts and
the noise of his thunder was attempting to tell them something'.[38] By
striving to recreate the world-image of primitive men by empirical
observation, Vico gave his style a poetic quality which demonstrated the
validity of his views: history was indeed within the ambit of our imagination because it enabled us to resurrect the life of our ancestors and
to understand why they had in common 'una spezia di natura' which
held their societies together.

Since the nations which formed mankind passed from one stage of
development to another under the guidance of Providence, since man's
imagination enabled him to reconstitute the stages of a long evolution,
Vico's conception of history can be described as a theodicy which, in
many ways, provides an interesting link between Leibniz and the rise of
German historicism as it began to manifest itself in the writings of
Mascov and Möser. In both of these early precursors of the great German school, the importance of the genetic approach is stressed in such
a way as to suggest the basic idea that human societies grow and
develop like living organisms; they have their own individual characters

---

[38] Quoted by Frank E. Manuel in *The Eighteenth Century Confronts the Gods*, p. 155.

and their own particular laws of development, yet they contribute to the general progress of mankind. Continuity, individuality, organicism regulated the life of the monads, and the German historians conceived a general scheme of gradual development which supposed that history was on the march and that the Cartesian philosophy, with its insistence on geometry and static systems, must be radically rejected. If we bear in mind that Leibniz himself had been a friend of Boyle and applied the classificatory method of Bacon we can see that the same forces were at work in the *Scienza Nuova* and in the German historical school. The same combination of empiricism and bold metaphysics was clearly at work in both.

Möser put the emphasis on the epic as an important source for the early history of mankind because he knew that, as a literary genre, it revealed the living conditions and the world-image of primitive nations. He chose Homer to demonstrate his point. What Lowth, Hughes and Blackwell were doing in England, what Vico had done in Italy, was now being done in Germany. The growing influence of poetry as the form of literature which best liberated the powers of the imagination, the insistence on primitive forms of expression as likely to make emotions more infectious, the feeling that the past still shaped our innermost nature, all concurred in the creation of a new style, a style which made emotion and sympathy essential to a true understanding of history. Of Möser, Meinecke said:

He drew comfort from the overflow of new life produced by the awakening of German poetry, realising that words are not the only medium through which man can communicate with man. The competent reader can 'reach out sympathetically to the author, and draw out from his soul all that remained hidden in it'.[39]

This is equally true of Herder, who does not divorce history from the feelings he shares with its famous figures:

Here Plato stands before me: there I listen to the friendly interrogations of Socrates, and participate in his last fate. When Marcus Antoninus confers in secret with his own heart he confers also with mine ... How ample, yet how narrow is the human heart! How individual, yet how recurrent are all its passions and desires, its faults and its foibles, its home and its enjoyment![40]

---

[39] F. Meinecke, *Historism, The Rise of a New Historical Outlook*, p. 257.
[40] 'Hier stehet Plato vor mir: dort höre ich Sokrates freundliche Fragen und theile sein letztes Schiksal. Wenn Mark-Antonin im Verborgnen mit seinem Herzen spricht, redet er auch mit dem meinigen ... Wie weit und wie enge ist das menschliche Herz! Wie einerlei und wiederkommend sind alle seine Leiden und Wünsche, seine Schwachheiten und Fehler, sein Genuss und seine Hoffnung!' *Ideen*, XV, 4, *Sämtliche Werke*, XIV, pp. 251–2.

This impassioned rhetoric may sound antiquated, but it shows that Herder conceived emotion, not as a means of capturing the reader's attention by playing on his sensibility, but as a way of acting on both his sensibility and his understanding. In his view, vitalism contributed greatly to the development of the strong ties which bind man to man. Since 'no psychology is possible which is not physiology at every step',[41] the development of our mental life is an organic process in which vital forces develop the characteristics of individuality. But all individualities derive ultimately from one common origin, just as leaves, however diverse they may be, draw their life force from the same roots. 'The darkest regions of the soul, from which most human inventions arise' must be found somewhere among those dark roots where the language of the nation and the *Volksgeist* have their sources. Vitalism, then so influential in the world of poetry, was thus helping to make the concept of perfectibility central to the world-image of the period.[42] If the nature of man, if human societies, were susceptible of boundless improvement, they must have been subjected, like plants, to endless transformations. These transformations can only be brought to life by the sympathetic imagination of the historian since logical deduction is of no avail in accounting for the operations of nature.

Hence the link between the genetic principle, the power of the imagination and the style of sensibility. This was, of course, the heritage of Lockean psychology, which made sensations and modes of sensations the basic material from which thoughts were processed by the mind. It was also the heritage of the Scottish school with the importance it gave to sympathy as the prime mover of the ethical world. But it was also the heritage of post-Leibnizian physiology with its emphasis on vitalism and on the shaping power of organic forces. The historian must write the kind of prose which will make his readers receptive to the feelings generated by ideas, for ideas prove their validity by the emotions they elicit. If he can stir deep emotions, he can also recreate the shape and the colours of things past, he can resurrect the images which people the minds of men and make them glow with the life and the passions of the dead. What was true of the *Scienza Nuova* was also true of the *History of Osnabrück*, of the *Ideen* and of *Auch eine Philosophie der Geschichte*.

Also dependent on the general atmosphere generated by the use of a complex vocabulary expressive of feelings was the sentiment of nostalgia which permeated the description of bygone ages. By conveying to his reader this feeling of nostalgia, the historian also conveyed a true understanding of the past. He made the reader receptive to the fact that there was a sort of unity within the individuality of a given moment in

---

[41] Quoted by Clark Jr, *Herder*, p. 226.
[42] On perfectibility, see my comments in the chapter 'Science and Literary Criticism' below (pp. 791–7).

a given society and that this unity had now gone forever. Meinecke remarks quite rightly that this nostalgia also existed in Burke's attachment to the past.[43] The *Reflections* do indeed contain a number of passages written in this vein, such as the portrait of Marie-Antoinette or the famous indictment of the age of the calculators. But Meinecke might have added that Burke's feelings of anger and emotion at seeing the overthrow of the French monarchy merely give added force to the emotional style which was coming into being elsewhere in Europe because sensibility was essential to the development of historicism. If a given stage of development in the history of mankind is determined by the action of countless individuals whose feelings we can still share, then time takes on an affective dimension. A feeling of personal bereavement becomes part of our vision of the past, which we feel to be present and yet irretrievably lost.

However briefly, the name of Winckelmann must be mentioned here, for if any historian ever gave his reader the feeling of nostalgia for things past, it was he. Greece, to him, was an ideal land in which political liberty had generated the forms of beauty. The 'universal spirit' which was then at work in art, filling it 'with new life and enthusiasm', is poetically expressed in the *Geschichte der Kunst des Altertums*, a book which conveys the pleasure of aesthetic emotion and the nostalgia of historical distance. Such themes almost wiped out the distinction between literature and historiography, since they made the past part of the intellectual heritage of nations.

To compare Winckelmann's conception of antiquity to Gibbon's is to perceive the changes which intervened between Gray in England and the *Sturm und Drang* in Germany. It is also to realize how much closer to the romantic vision of the past the leading German historians had already advanced in the 1760s. When Gibbon described himself 'musing amidst the ruins of the Capitol', he conveyed to his readers the feelings of a historian who experienced the transient character of his existence and the impression of solitude generated by the sight of ruins. With German historicism the poetry of the past acquired a new existential dimension. Lost societies were still there, teeming with life in the mists of the past – only time had estranged them from us. If the solitary mind of the writer was capacious and sensitive enough to recreate the totality of a moment of history, then this moment would preserve its unique character. But the warmth of feelings which alone could fire his imagination and lend colour and movement to the pageant of the past could not be communicated to the figures that had been resurrected. They looked real, but theirs was a borrowed life. Romantic historiography could not

---

[43] Meinecke, *Historism*, p. 267.

be detached and ironical because however complete the emotional commitment it required, it left one with a feeling of irrecoverable loss. Keats's *Ode on a Grecian Urn* expresses the depth of this existential experience. It also shows why, as a genre, history now came closer to poetry and to music than it had ever been. One has only to hear Beethoven's *Eroica* or his Ninth Symphony to realize that in the days of Schiller and Goethe the death of a great man or the hopes of nations, even if only a single genius expressed them, found their proper resonance in the voices of the multitude.

This survey, however cursory, suggests two concluding remarks. The first is that historical writing is related to the general movement of ideas in the same way as all other types of literature. In the eighteenth century, Voltaire still felt that tragedy afforded the best model for bringing the past back to life, while Herder saw poetry as his surest guide. In both cases, the relation to the history of science is not so distant as it may seem, for the preference given to one literary form over another depends on critical assumptions which are determined by a particular theory of knowledge. The second observation derives from the first. In the case of Voltaire, as in the case of Herder and Winckelmann, the world image of the historian constantly appears as an organizing pattern in the representation of the past. Far from being an occasion for enlarging despondently on the impossibility of attaining any kind of objective knowledge, this should make us more confident in a discipline which corrects and sharpens the scholar's judgement by showing him that the writing of history is part of history itself.

Biography and autobiography

Felicity A. Nussbaum

Biography begins during the eighteenth century to develop a substantial body of critical assumptions and terminology, though a fully elaborated account of its form and subject-matter does not emerge until the nineteenth century. When the term 'biographer' first entered the English language, it was applied interchangeably to an historian or to a writer of individual lives. While the *Oxford English Dictionary* lists the first use of the word as John Dryden's in the 1683 introduction to his edition of Plutarch, 'biography' was earlier employed in the modern sense in the lives of Thomas Fuller (1661) and Oliver Cromwell (1663), where it meant the history of a particular individual.[1] Dryden, following Francis Bacon's earlier categorization, divides history into three types – annals or chronicles, general history or narrative, and biographia. Dryden imagined biography as a more circumscribed and less dignified (but more pleasurable) branch of history because it limited its treatment to aspects directly relevant to an individual man's fortune.

The formulation of biographical and autobiographical theory at first appears primarily in casual remarks occasioned by prefaces and reviews rather than in discrete essays. In addition, occasional critical comments are interspersed in criminal accounts, anecdotes, scandalous memoirs, fictional biographies, newspapers, and legal documents that incorporate biographical approaches and techniques. Biography in its earliest manifestations also frequently commingled with other genres of individuation such as novels, diaries and letters. The memoir, for example, with its daily record of public affairs, often interweaved fiction and history with biography and autobiography. Georges May's argument that the genealogies of English and French life-histories were different is convincing when he writes, 'British biography developed earlier and more fully than French biography . . . because it evolved more directly from historiography, whereas in France, it emerged primarily (and slowly) from memoir writing and fiction' (p. 156). Over the course of the century, biography and its theory became increasingly distinct from both history

---

[1] See Dryden, 'The Life of Plutarch', pp. 226–88, and Stauffer, *Biography Before 1700*, p. 219.

and fiction in techniques and methods at the same time that it borrowed substantially from them.

England led the continent in biographical innovations. The 1740s were something of a watershed in the criticism of biography, with the publication of many literary lives of Alexander Pope after his death (1744) and the first of Samuel Johnson's lives of the poets, *The Life of Savage* (1744). In addition, Johnson's masterful *Rambler* 60 (13 October 1750) and *Idler* 84 (24 November 1759) at mid-century, and Boswell's comments in the opening pages of the *Life of Johnson* (1791), stand as landmarks in biographical criticism. By the 1770s increasing numbers of regular reviews of recently published lives encouraged a more fully elaborated biographical criticism to emerge, and the early decades of the nineteenth century brought biographical dictionaries and multi-volume collections of lives throughout Europe. Biography is assumed to take its legitimate place within *belles-lettres* when it is called 'the most fascinating and instructive species of literary composition' in *Public Characters* (1803), but the first full-length book on the theory of biography in English did not appear until the early nineteenth century when James Field Stanfield published *An Essay on the Study and Composition of Biography* (1813). While Stanfield's piece lacks originality, it does provide a coherent synopsis of the literary opinions on biography at the turn of the century.

The earliest biographers throughout England, France, and Germany wrote to praise eminent men as saintly models. Most life-histories at the beginning of the eighteenth century either flattered their subjects in this well-established panegyrical tradition, or moved to the opposite extreme with unrelenting satire. Plutarch's lives, remarkable for their extraordinary learning and their attention to detail, were widely acclaimed throughout the eighteenth century in England and on the continent as the ideal biographical models. The lives of these fellow human beings offered exacting patterns for emulation, records of personal history, and edifying memorials of commendable men and their achievements. In addition, the French *éloge*, the panegyrical funeral eulogy, provided a satisfying biographical memorial of the eminent, as did the popular biographical notices that appeared in the collected works of recently deceased writers.

Oliver Goldsmith's edition of Plutarch's lives (1762) stressed that biography should inspire the nation's youth to patriotism. The reason why Plutarch's lives are instructive and pleasing, Gilbert Burnet similarly suggests in the preface to the memoirs of the Dukes of Hamilton and Castleherald (1677), is because they provide the details of great and worthy men's lives together with the country's history. Biographical criticism in its early stages frequently recommended linking the writing of individual histories to national interests. Joseph Addison, joining those who thought of biography as a species of history, conceived of it as the history of great generals. Conyers Middleton, author of *The Life of Cicero* (1741), concurred in believing that the best biographies encapsulated the lives of the great in spite of their tendency towards panegyric. In the biography of his father that introduced his *Dissertations upon the Aeneids* (1770), Thomas Martyn countered that

the lives and actions of illustrious warriors and statesmen have ever been esteemed worthy the attention of the public: but this age has been the first to enter the more private walks of life, to contemplate merit in the shades, and to admire the more silent virtues ... the world seldom condescended to look upon literary accomplishments even of the highest order; but wholly disdained the study of common life, and those characters which it would be of the most general use to be acquainted with, because they lie most open to imitation.

(p. i)

By the end of the century the fascination with the great gives way to the lives of ordinary men, but both could be mustered in the cause of nationalism.

In France in Pierre Bayle's scholarly *Dictionnaire historique et critique* (1697) the biographical articles focused on historical notables and asserted the impartiality of their chronicling by detailing the errors of earlier biographers. Appearing in eleven editions between 1697 and 1740, the biographical entries provided the model for other encyclopaedic projects in Germany and England and significantly influenced the philosophes. Bayle's frequent inclusion of scurrilous personal details was controversial and even innovative; his compendious footnote apparatus and appendices contain general reflections on the enterprise of learned biography and established future standards for accuracy with their thorough documentation. Following this exhaustive pattern, the massive *Biographia Britannica* (1747–66) also emphasized elevated and publicly recognized men of the English nation. The monumental volumes of biography represent themselves as 'a BRITISH TEMPLE OF HONOUR, sacred to the piety, learning, valour, publick-spirit, loyalty, and every other glorious virtue of our ancestors' (Preface). Similarly, in Germany, Johann Gottfried Herder argued in *Haben wir noch jetzt das Publikum und Vaterland der Alten?* (1765) that biography should reject classical models that fostered heroic action through biographies of Greek and Roman rulers and statesmen, and instead create national German heroes through pedagogical representation of public personages' lives.

In the biographical criticism that can be extracted from eighteenth-century writings, the various questions repeatedly confronted include truth and objectivity, the appropriate focus for biography, the relationship between biographer and subject, the affective functions of biography, and the relative merits of biography and autobiography. The debate in these first formulations often rehearses the issues of the universal and the particular. Writing in 1753, Gotthold Ephraim Lessing rejected claims that particular biography was the most useful study of human nature:

> Either one considers humans in particular or in general. Of the first approach one can hardly say it is the noblest pursuit. What is it to know humans in particular? It is to know fools and scoundrels. To what end do we benefit from this insight? to know ourselves thoroughly either in folly and wickedness or to fall into melancholy about the worthlessness that we share with other creatures.[2]

Lessing believed that the narrative representation of such a life in fiction or biography might even produce a wider and more permanent effect than the life itself. But unlike Lessing, most eighteenth-century critics of biography in its varied forms prefer the lives of particular individuals to general history as exemplary of human nature.

In a turn away from classical and Renaissance beliefs, John Dryden argues that the unity of action in a particular man's life, a single picture, affords greater moral benefit than a broader historical approach. His preface to Plutarch's lives, for example, emphasizes biography's more powerful allure, which, unlike history's diversity, compels us to virtue. It demonstrates that 'the vertues and actions of one Man, drawn together into a single story, strike upon our minds a stronger and more lively impression, than the scatter'd Relations of many Men, and many actions' (p. 274). The loss of variety is worth sacrificing to impress a single point upon the reader. Similarly, Samuel Johnson's *Rambler* 60 favours the powerful moral persuasion of intimate biography over larger historical narratives. In one of the early biographical notices of Samuel Johnson first published in the *Universal Magazine* for 1784, the author 'L' prefers biography because he believes that it, not history, should deal with 'calamities of private life and the elevated woes of royalty' (p. 30). Biographical criticism generally incorporates the plain prose of annals and the objective detail of dignified history even as it increasingly confines its scope to ordinary people and the commonplace.

While most eighteenth-century biographers wished to frame the individual personality within a larger human nature, the extent to which

---

[2] Lessing, V, p. 143: 'Entweder man betrachtet den Menschen im einzelnen oder überhaupt. Auf die erste Art kann der Ausspruch, daß es die edelste Beschäftigung sei, schwerlich gezogen werden. Den Menschen im einzelnen zu kennen; was kennt man? Thoren und Bösewichter. Und was nutzt diese Erkenntniß? uns entweder in der Thorheit und Bosheit recht stark oder über die Nichtswurdigkeit uns gleicher Geschöpfe melancholisch zu machen.' I am grateful to Ingeborg O'Sickey and Anna Quinn for help with the German translations.

particularity demanded the revelation of weaknesses and vices remained a lively subject of contention. Roger North, perhaps the first English-man to write a piece of sustained biographical criticism, maintained that a 'life should be a picture; which cannot be good, if the peculiar features, whereby the subject is distinguished from all others, are left out. Nay, scars and blemishes, as well as beauties, ought to be ex-pressed; otherwise, it is but an outline filled up with lillies and roses'.[3] John Toland in his *Life of Milton* (1698) also argues for full disclosure of weaknesses: 'For it is commonly seen, that Historians are suspected rather to make their Hero what they would have him to be, than such as he really was ... but I am neither writing a Satyr, nor a Panegyric upon *Milton*, but publishing the true History of his Actions, Works and Opinions' (p. 84). The proclivity towards an increasing individuation brings about new definitions of privacy and a fuller, more truthful revelation of personal eccentricities and flaws.

The keen interest in the individual that spurred biography and its criticism derived variously from increased attention to the political rights of the individual, the philosophical debates on identity concerning the substantiality of consciousness, an emergent mercantile capitalism that fostered independent consumer units, increased realism and its expres-sion in the novel, secularization, and the new science with its emphasis on empirical observation. In addition, the proliferation of newspapers and coffeehouses redefined the public and private realms, created soci-eties for conversation, and broadened the exchange of information which took its public form in increased consumer demand for published lives. The European bourgeoisie, separating itself from the aristocracy and the landed gentry, found in biography an experimental ground for shaping individual public identities.

England unquestionably led Europe in its intense interest in the per-sonal, the private, and the ordinary, turning for its biographical subjects from the lives of the eminent and learned to the middle ranks and below with tales of rogues and whores, painters, actors, the clergy, and mili-tary officers. Early in the century Roger North protested that even the life of a tinker could engage the reader if the author wrote a spirited memoir in figurative language and fictional style. As North puts it in his *Preface*, 'The history of private lives adapted to the perusal of common men is more beneficial (generally) than the most solemn registers of ages and nations, or the acts and monuments of famed governors, statesmen, prelates, or generals of armies'.[4] For North, writing the lives of private persons is especially difficult because there are fewer sources, and the

---

[3] North, *Lives of the Norths*, I, p. 154.
[4] North, 'General Preface', ed. Millard, p. 51.

competing versions which he would welcome seldom exist. 'For such controversies interpret enigmas, correct partial insinuations, supply defects, fill up blanks and omissions, and what is most of all, expose the knavery of writers ... In short all history of one form or other is like painting, never exactly true', argues North. 'That which comes nearest is best, and however discrepant, there may be some use or other that makes it reasonable not to slight, but to preserve it' (p. 77).

Precise detail contributes to making personal biography more definitive and authoritative, and for later eighteenth-century biographical theorists, the jury of readers increasingly bears the burden of deciphering narrative meanings. Jean-Jacques Rousseau and later Boswell asserted the significance of engaging the reader in the evaluative task: 'It is not up to me to judge the importance of the facts; I must tell them all, and leave it up to him [the reader] to choose.'[5] For the most part eighteenth-century biography consists of loosely compiled materials (as in Mason's *Memoirs of the Life of Gray*, 1755), and when biographical criticism emerges, it often contests this failure to discriminate between relevant and irrelevant details. Johnson displays contempt for those biographers who simply 'exhibit a chronological series of actions or preferments' rather than showing the real character of a man. Owen Ruffhead in the *Monthly Review* (1758) inveighed against relating minutiae such as paring one's nails:

As the business of biographical writing, however, consists principally in the art of *compiling*, the seeming facility of the employment, has induced many laborious drones to commence biographies, who have neither been blest with genius, taste, or learning. They have collected materials without discernment, put them together without order, and commented upon them without judgment.

Mason was among those accused of being inclusive to a fault, apparently believing that everything which a man of genius writes deserves preservation – but it was precisely this inclusiveness that Boswell proudly imitated in the *Life of Johnson*.

The question as to whether the life of an ordinary individual was truly worthy of a biography continued to be a persistent source of critical debate. Of course the most significant defence of the common man as subject of biography appeared in *Rambler* 60 when Samuel Johnson argued that the life of the ordinary person best reveals the vicissitudes of human nature: 'There has rarely passed a life of which a judicious and faithful narrative would not be useful.' He continued, 'We are all prompted by the same motives, all deceived by the same

[5] Rousseau, *Confessions*, IV, p. 175: 'Ce n'est pas à moi de juger de l'importance des faits, je les dois tous dire, et lui laisser le soin de choisir.'

fallacies, all animated by hope, obstructed by danger, entangled by desire, and seduced by pleasure' (p. 320). In an act of sympathetic imagination, biography allowed readers to place themselves, for a moment, within the life of another.

While biography's authors and readers increasingly included more private individuals by the end of the century, women figured considerably less often than men as biographical subjects. More commonly the subject of biographical writing in Italy, France, and Germany than in England, women throughout Europe rarely published biographies themselves. George Ballard's *Memoirs of Several Ladies of Great Britain* (1755), the *Biographium Faemineum* (1766), and James Granger's *A Biographical History of England* (1769–74) were among the innovative few that reflect on the method for representing female character in biography. Granger, for example, moved from the highest ranks to the lowest and included as his penultimate category 'Ladies, and others, of the Female Sex, according to their Rank'. Ballard, employing antiquarian methods, acquired detailed information concerning learned ladies from the fourteenth century onwards in a break from the hagiographic tradition of saints' lives and from panegyrics that honour women simply because of the achievements of their husbands.[6] In his preface to the *Memoirs*, Ballard's goal was 'to inform us of those particulars in their lives and manners which best deserve our imitation, and to transmit to posterity even those peculiar ties which afford us no inconsiderable entertainment'. Women such as Madame de Staal de Launay were numbered among those who composed memoirs, and others contributed *chroniques scandaleuses, journaux intimes*, and letters. For the first time in history, women's lives and achievements were judged worthy of public attention and permanent record, and women began to pen their own autobiographical accounts.

Biographical theory as it emerged, then, came to terms with the fact that life-history increasingly focused on subjects who did not possess hereditary privilege or great wealth. The increased market demand often spawned hasty publications based on crude research and insufficient information. North cautioned biographers against succumbing to bribery or to flattery in the hope of gaining favour with the friends and family of the subject. Biographers, according to North, must be of undisputed honesty and clearly ought to write without hope of gain or preferment. In *The Freeholder* Addison lamented the current extension of biography to Grub Street hacks who expeditiously exposed the secrets of recently deceased notable men in catchpenny pamphlets in order to line their own pockets.[7] Vicesimus Knox, in *Winter Evenings: or, Lucubrations*

---

[6] Ballard, *Memoirs*, ed. Perry, p. 28.
[7] Addison, *The Freeholder*, no. 35, ed. Leheny, p. xx.

on Life and Letters (1788), argued that biography should be more discreet, declaring 'Biography is every day descending from its dignity. Instead of an instructive recital, it is becoming an instrument to the mere gratification of an impertinent, not to say malignant, curiosity'. Men's foibles should be buried with them, and the blemishes hidden from sight. Knox contends that the present fashion for 'biographical anatomy', for the dissection of people into bits, violates the memory of the great.[8]

Among the culprits was the infamous Edmund Curll, a biographical scavenger, who produced forty to fifty lives written immediately after their subjects' deaths. Curll's biographies were riddled with fabrications, and they reprinted unreliable newspaper accounts and sections stolen from miscellanies of poetry. Gilbert Burnet somewhat cynically cautioned in the preface to his life of Hale, that biographers often corrupt the truth for their own questionable ends so that 'the lives of princes are either writ with so much flattery, by those who intended to merit by [the flattery] at their own hands, or others concerned with them: or with so much spite' that the biographers successfully revenge themselves on the memory of their subjects. In addition to his caution against writing for commercial advantage, Addison advises impartiality, accuracy, and discretion, all of which he believes cannot be achieved unless the subject of the biography is not personally known to his biographer. Addison finally determined that lives should not be written until a respectable amount of time had elapsed after death, 'till Envy and Friendship are laid asleep, and the Prejudice both of his Antagonists and Adherents be, in some Degree, softened and subdued' (p. 196).

Roger North's preface, written between 1718 and 1722 but unpublished during his lifetime, broke with previous assumptions about biographical writing in expanding it from prominent to ordinary people, and in encouraging more personal and anecdotal accounts. One commentator has called it 'revolutionary in its implications' in its anticipation of 'the vivid, full, and personal biography that developed later in the century'.[9] North, like Addison, anticipates Boswell in his recommendation that the biographer be close friends with his subject, that he keep extensive notes, exercise his imagination, include minute particulars and employ his subject's own words. A scrupulously reliable author must command the reader's confidence by knowing the subject intimately. Johnson's dictum on the subject of the relation of the biographer to his subject is well-known: 'nobody can write the life of a man, but those who have eat, and drunk and lived in social intercourse with him', a comment Boswell cites with self-congratulatory pleasure (*Life of Johnson,*

[8] Knox, *Winter Evenings*, I, p. 105.
[9] North, 'General Preface', ed. Millard, p. 17.

II, p. 166). Yet Johnson and others thought that the best biography affords the opportunity for the subject to be his own witness. Mason's *Memoirs of the Life of Gray* pioneered the method of including Gray's letters in his biography as a way of allowing the biographical subject to speak for himself. The biographer, according to John Toland, and later Conyers Middleton, should make every attempt to provide primary documents in support of all assumptions. For this reason Middleton researches all of Cicero's writings and includes excerpts from his letters in an effort to interweave Cicero's own words into the biography.

Increasing attention to minute details, anecdote, and private conversation during the century continually ignited debate over how much a biography should reveal. In spite of the necessity for concealing matters that would offend the relatives of the deceased Johnson preferred writing the life of a subject immediately upon his death rather than waiting until the passage of time allowed greater objectivity. 'If a life be delayed till interest and envy are at an end, we may hope for impartiality, but must expect little intelligence', he notes in the *Lives of the Poets* (1781). The potentially hurtful aspects of character contribute something useful to mankind, and Johnson apparently believed they should be divulged because 'many invisible circumstances' may reveal more of a man's character than his public activities (*Rambler* 60).

Boswell's *Life of Johnson* was without parallel in its attention to detail and authenticity. Boswell, never unduly modest, recognized his unprecedented achievement in offering a view of the whole man, by which he meant the private as well as public. He wrote to William Temple on 24 February 1788, 'I am absolutely certain that *my* mode of biography, which gives not only a *history* of Johnson's *visible* progress through the world, and of his publications, but a *view* of his mind, in his letters and conversations is the most perfect that can be conceived, and will be *more* of a *Life* than any work that has ever yet appeared'.[10] In addition to using Mason's *Memoirs* as his model for incorporating letters and diaries verbatim to display the subject's character, Boswell also emphasizes the importance of a chronological approach, a sense of development in living 'o'er each scene' and in showing the 'shade as well as light' to escape the dangers of panegyrical models of biography. His principle of biography is inclusion rather than rigorous selection, the accumulation of a mass of material with minimal narrative intervention.

David Mallet antedated Boswell in his support for 'scrupulous attachment to truth' in his biography of Francis Bacon (1740): 'Whoever undertakes to write the life of any person, deserving to be remembered [sic] by posterity, ought to look upon this law as prescribed to him. He

---

[10] *Letters of James Boswell*, ed. Tinker, II, p. 422.

is fairly to record the faults as well as the good qualities, the failings as well as the perfections, of the dead' (p. 2). On the other hand, Samuel Whyte charged that trifling anecdotes were a 'flagrant breach of private confidence, and an infringement of the rules of good breeding'. In fact, he found minute details to be 'a vicious indulgence of inquisitive impertinence', and 'a disgrace to the pages of history' (Preface, pp. vi–vii). Hester Lynch Piozzi's (Mrs Thrale's) anecdotes of Johnson were criticized in the *Monthly Review* (May 1786): 'Was it necessary for her to record the boiled pork, or the salt beef, the port wine with capillaire [*sic*], or the peaches at Ombersley?' (p. 373). But one can also find many descriptions of the pleasures that biographical particulars afford. In the *Monthly Review* of 1799 the author commends such detail: 'how grateful must be the pleasure imparted by particular biography, which, placing the object of contemplation at the proper distance for distinct vision, enables the mind to observe its minutest parts, to trace its most delicate features, and to catch the symmetry and beauty of the whole' (p. 241). This attention to detail assumed that the subject's peculiarities would still allow him to participate in a universal nature.

At the end of the century the publication of the *Life of Johnson* (1791) acted as a catalyst for renewed discussions of the familiar critical questions, especially the use of anecdotes, objectivity, and the extent of privacy. After the publication of the *Life*, some reviewers criticized Boswell's techniques and, in voicing opinions about biographical writing, helped to formulate its theory. At the same time in Germany, Herder argued against the flood of necrologies that mythologized the dead and turned them to stone: '*Let the dead bury their dead*; we want to look upon the dead as living, we want to enjoy their presence which lives on through their work even after their departure and precisely because of their lasting achievements we want to show our appreciation by recording them for future generations'.[11] He wanted to create a concept of the interaction between the dead and the living in biography; rather than a pious remembrance of the dead, he wanted to make such biographies vivacious, dynamic, and enduring to their readers. Biography ought to be a mimetic substitute for the life instead of a spectral vision or a gravemarker.

Herder also offered coherent reflections on biography in the preface to *Ueber Thomas Abbts Schriften* (1768) in which he maintained that the historian is best advised to regard his subject's exterior as the mirror of his soul (p. 18). Rejecting pietistic and philosophical confessions as excessively introspective and sentimental, he put forward instead the

---

[11] Herder, '5. Humanitätsbrief', XVII, p. 19: '*Laß Todte ihre Todten begraben*: wir wollen die Gestorbenen als Lebende betrachten, uns ihres Lebens, ihres auch nach dem Hingange noch fortwirkenden Lebens freuen und eben deßhalb ihr bleibendes Verdienst dankbar für die Nachwelt aufzeichnen.'

idea of life-descriptions that would connect the soul and the world, and inspire one's fellow men. By the end of the eighteenth century, the display of this interiority identified biography and autobiography as demonstrably different from earlier forms of the genres, for these newly conceptualized versions reflected shifts in the boundaries between public and private.

Schubart, like Herder, preferred authentic life-history to fiction because the 'real' had much greater impact than descriptions in novels which the world recognizes as fictional, and biographical fiction throughout Europe often indiscriminately combined historical accounts with mythology. At about the same time that Johnson was writing the *Rambler* essays, Thomas Abbt in his *161. Literaturbrief* (1768) further distinguishes biography from history by turning away from biography's investigation of the connections between the individual and his time towards a soul-searching probing of the self. For others in Germany, this attention to the psyche, prominent in spiritual autobiography (1670–1720), yielded to an alternative view that autobiography is not so much a knowledge of self as a representation of the process of becoming oneself in the world. In *Dichtung und Wahrheit*, Goethe writes:

> For this seems to be the chief task of biography, to depict a man in the circumstances of his times, and to show to what extent they alienate him, to what extent they work in his favour, to show in which ways he used them to shape a world-view and a view of human beings, and how, if he is an artist, poet, or writer, he in turn reflects them back to the world. For this, however, something scarcely attainable is demanded, namely that the individual should know himself and his century.[12]

Thus, he, like Herder, stresses the extent to which human beings are confined by their historical and external circumstances.

Scientific attempts to uncover universal laws of human nature drew increasing attention to the interiority of the individual. In fact, North believed that biography had analogies with science, and he imagined it as 'being exactly True ... part of ye Natural history of Mankind'.[13] Directives from the *Philosophical Transactions of the Royal Society* in England during the Restoration separated composition into 'ongoing action and retrospective narration', encouraging the development of narrative perspective.[14] Introspective individualism in some fashion imitated

---

[12] Goethe, 'Preface' to *Dichtung und Wahrheit*: 'Denn dieses scheint die Hauptaufgabe der Biographie zu sein, den Menschen in seinen Zeitverhältnissen darzustellen, und zu zeigen, in wiefern ihm das Ganze widerstrebt, in wiefern es ihn begünstigt, wie er sich eine Welt- und Menschenansicht daraus gebildet, und wie er sie, wenn er Künstler, Dichter, Schriftsteller ist, wieder nach außen abgespiegelt.'

[13] North, [Early draft of the life of the Lord Keeper] B.M. Add MS. 32,509 f9v.

[14] McKeon, *The Origins of the English Novel, 1600–1740* (Baltimore, 1987), p. 103.

scientific investigation of the body's interior as the individual became a spectator of himself.

During most of the eighteenth century, autobiography is assumed to be part of biography, not sufficiently distinct to bear another appellation. When biography first began to be contrasted with autobiographical accounts rather than history, critics cautioned that gaps in understanding could occur no matter how intimately acquainted the biographer and subject might be. Many critics believed autobiography provided transparent access to one's own truth while biography inevitably created distortions. Autobiography was first conceptualized as a separate form when publications of personal accounts proliferated late in the eighteenth century. Isaac D'Israeli was among the first to use the English term 'self-biography' in one of the few essays in the period devoted to the art of writing oneself.[15]

Autobiographical writing, like biography, was assumed to have a moral purpose, to depict the traits and predicaments common to all humans, and to be read for diversion. From the earliest expressions of faith in the conversion narratives, the Dissenters confessed their belief in order to define their identity in Christ. Though the criticism of autobiography in the eighteenth century is less plentiful than that of biography, North recommends keeping an autobiographical journal as a key to accuracy for future biographers, as a moral guide for oneself, as vindication against future detractors, and occasionally as a pattern for other men. William Houstoun among many others argues that autobiography is closer to the truth than biography and thus superior to it, for 'none know the original Source and secret Springs of those Actions and Transactions but the Actor himself' and, he adds, 'in my humble Opinion, every Man of tolerable Understanding, with common Honour and Honesty, is the fittest Man to write his *own Memoirs*' (p. 8).

While many acknowledge the worth of the diary as a monitor of behaviour in the well-established tradition of spiritual autobiography, others echo the sentiment of the review of Peter Daniel Huet's *Memoirs* (August 1810) that 'self-biography' lacks truth and is excessively conscious of its audience (p. 104). Thomas Warton in *Idler* 33 (2 December 1758) parodies the triviality of published diaries, especially those of the Methodists, and later in the century D'Israeli repeats the warning against publishing dull private detail. The attention to subjective states was especially pronounced in France. Rousseau's influential *Confessions* (1782) conceived of autobiography as an unprecedentedly truthful revelation of inner feeling, no matter how disreputable: 'The true object of

---

[15] D'Israeli, 'Some observations on diaries, self-biography, and self-characters', pp. 95–110.

my confessions is to reveal my inner thoughts exactly in all the situations of my life. It is the history of my soul that I have promised to
recount, and to write it faithfully I have need of no other memories; it
is enough if I enter again into my inner self, as I have done till now'.[16]
Rousseau's autobiography was arguably the first of its kind. His stark
unveiling claimed to invent both a new language of sentiment and a
new style which linked past events to present remembrances of them. In
its self-conscious baring of his soul, he insisted that fidelity to his feelings equated with truthfulness even if facts or dates proved inaccurate.
In the confessional mode, newly secularized emotive display substituted
for strong narrative line.

For Johnson, on the contrary, autobiography was more likely to reveal the truth of character, 'for he that sits down calmly and voluntarily
to review his life for the admonition of posterity, or to amuse himself,
and leaves this account unpublished, may be commonly presumed to
tell truth, since falshood [sic] cannot appease his own mind, and fame
will not be heard beneath the tomb' (*Idler* 84, p. 264). Rousseau shares
the view that a man is his own best witness: 'No one can write a man's
life other than himself. His inner way of being, his true life, is known
only to himself'.[17] Rousseau openly acknowledges, however, that truth
is always filtered through self-posturings and disguise.

Johnson advises Boswell to keep a journal as a remembrance of
amusing and instructive anecdotes, and as a spur to happiness. But
diary-writing is a laborious endeavour, Boswell finds, and the principles
of selection may be very difficult to determine: 'Sometimes it has occurred to me that a man should not live more than he can record, as
a farmer should not have a larger crop than he can gather in'.[18] Boswell,
like Johnson, D'Israeli, and Warton, contends that diaries should remain unpublished, and the diarist must guard against divulging hurtful
remarks or recording mindless particulars. Johnson believes that, though
no man is a hero to himself, most men will attempt to reveal the truth
of their own character. The best biography imitates the truthfulness,
private detail, and didactic quality that the diary form often provides:

The writer of his own life has at least the first qualification of an historian,
the knowledge of the truth; and though it may be plausibly objected that his

---

[16] Rousseau, *Confessions*, VII, p. 278: 'L'object propre de mes confessions est de faire
connoitre [sic] exactement mon interieur dans toutes les situations de ma vie. C'est
l'histoire de mon âme que j'ai promis, et pour l'écrire fidellement [sic] je n'ai pas
besoin d'autres mémoires: il me suffit, comme j'ai fait jusqu'ici, de rentrer au
dedans de moi.'

[17] Rousseau, 'La première rédaction des Confessions', *Annales*, IV, p. 3: 'Nul ne peut
écrire la vie d'un homme que lui-même. Sa manière d'être intérieure, sa véritable
vie n'est connue que de lui...' [page 1 of autograph ms.].

[18] Boswell, *Hypochondriack*, no. 66 (March 1783).

temptations to disguise it are equal to his opportunities of knowing it, yet I cannot but think that impartiality may be expected with equal confidence from him that relates the passages of his own life as from him that delivers the transactions of another.

(Idler 84, p. 263)

At the end of the century Isaac D'Israeli seems to share Johnson's belief in the humanist impulse to read and write diaries: 'Nothing which presents a faithful relation of humanity is inconsiderable to a human being' ('Observations', pp. 97–8). The diary testifies to truth, according to D'Israeli, and it becomes a way to address oneself, to communicate with 'that other Self, which Shaftesbury has described every thinking being to possess' (p. 101).

Biography and autobiography were no longer considered in the Enlightenment to be lesser categories of history, but instead they begin to be conceptualized as genres that possess literary merit in their own right. Biographical theory and criticism for the first time help discriminate between hack-writing and serious attempts to render a life in text. The formation of a biographical criticism brings an aesthetic shift in which critical opinion finally embraces biography as a form of *belles-lettres*, and it paradoxically marks the entrance of the history of the common individual into the privileged realm of the literary.

12

Criticism and the rise of
periodical literature

James Basker

The rise of periodical literature changed the face of criticism between
1660 and 1800. The genres and publishing vehicles that came to dominate critical discourse by 1800, particularly review criticism and the
review journal, would have been all but unrecognizable to Dryden and
his contemporaries. The impact of journalism on critical practice, and
on its underlying principles, was broad and complex. It introduced new,
more accessible forums for critical discussion; it multiplied and diversi-
fied the opportunities for critical expression; it fostered new critical
values, drew attention to new literary genres, systematized the treatment of established ones, and expanded the audience for criticism. Its
impact was felt by authors, readers, and publishers, as well as institutions ranging from scholarly libraries to rural reading societies; in subtler ways it affected canon formation, reception history, the emergence
of affective criticism, the assimilation of foreign influences, the segrega-
tion of 'women's literature', and ultimately the politics of culture.

Because of the sheer mass and complexity of material involved in the
history of journalism, this chapter will focus primarily on major patterns in English critical history, with intermittent attention to the parallel developments elsewhere in Europe. In tandem with the growth of
print culture generally, the rapid expansion of the periodical press was
a pan-European phenomenon. Scholars differ on definitions and methods
of counting, but by any measure there was a dramatic increase in the
number of periodicals between 1660 and 1800. In England political
upheaval and various licensing acts caused erratic shifts during the seventeenth century – three periodicals in print during 1641, then fifty-nine
in 1642, for example, or thirty-four in 1660 and then seven in 1661 –
but the average of five periodicals per year from 1661 to 1678 grew to
twenty-five titles by 1700, ninety in 1750, and 264 in 1800.[1] In France
and Germany, trends were similar: for France scholarly authorities list
thirty-six titles in 1700, seventy in 1730, 114 in 1750, 173 in 1770 and
an explosion to 250 or 300 per year after 1789, while in Germany,

---

[1] Golden, 'Introduction', in Sullivan (ed.), *British Literary Magazines*, I, xv; Crane
and Kaye, *Census*, pp. 179–201.

using a slightly different emphasis, Fabian locates the first 'scholarly' journal in 1682, lists fifty-four in print by 1720, and between 1760 and 1800 counts 740 more titles appearing at one time or another.[2]

With the burgeoning numbers comes a multiplication of kinds and specializations that in its fecundity might rival nature itself. A reader in the 1790s could choose a periodical that specialized in botany, politics, music, fashion, art, jokes, poetry, business, children, drama, the military, law, magic, medicine, horse-racing, biography, French culture, women, orientalism, Italian literature, mathematics, Methodism, novels, or agriculture, among scores of other possibilities (*NCBEL*, 1305–12). That reader could take up a daily (morning or evening), thrice-weekly, bi-weekly, weekly, fortnightly, monthly or quarterly periodical, in formats that ranged from a single sheet to hundreds of pages.

To chart a course through this jungle of literary growth and its implications for the history of criticism, it is useful to look at three basic periods within which slightly different genres of periodical predominated and left their mark on literary culture. The first, from the mid-1600s to 1700, saw the infancy of the newspaper and, from about 1665, the establishment of the learned journal; during the second, from 1700 to 1750, the periodical essay enjoyed its greatest influence, and the magazine or monthly miscellany, with all its popular appeal, came to prominence; in the third, from about 1750 to 1800, the literary review journal emerged in a recognizably modern form and rapidly came to dominate the practice of criticism.

Pre-1700

The two journalistic genres of this period that contributed most to the history of criticism – the newspaper and the learned journal – epitomize the dualism that lies behind literary criticism as a cultural practice: that is, criticism has commercial/consumerist as well as intellectual/aesthetic roots in cultural history. Newspapers, which had been around in some form early enough to provoke Ben Jonson's wit in the 1620s (e.g., *News from the New World*, 1620), did not contain criticism *per se* and neither Dryden nor his continental counterparts such as Boileau, Rapin, and Le Bossu would have dreamed of publishing serious criticism in a newspaper. Book publishers and other interested parties, however, regularly printed short notices and advertisements for their books in the newspapers; works by Milton, Davenant, Izaak Walton, Browne, and Cowley

---

[2] Sgard, *Bibliographie*, p. 202; Hatin, *Bibliographie*, p. xci; Fabian, *Widening Circle*, pp. 145–7.

were promoted or 'reviewed' in this way as early as the 1640s.[3] Book-sellers published catalogues – many of them annotated with descriptive prose ('puffs') – that functioned similarly. Commercial interests not-withstanding, both of these practices served to raise the general public's awareness of recent books and to habituate even the lowest common denominator of literate people to reading something about them. (What is often called the first modern literary review journal, *The Monthly Review* (1749), sprang into being partly to serve the commercial inter-ests of its founder, the bookseller and publisher Ralph Griffiths.)

In these ways, newspapers laid the groundwork for changes in the sociology of literature that were to follow. They fostered literacy and created the consumer appetite that would drive the commodification of information – its mass production, distribution, and consumption – that lies at the centre of modern print culture. They instilled in readers a craving for news – 'freshest advices' – that conferred value on the most recent, the new and immediate. This hunger for newness or novelty spilled over, so that new books and other cultural developments were treated as 'news events' that had to be described and evaluated like other phenomena. As time passed, the numbers of publications would outgrow the reader's ability to keep up and the necessity for some kind of consumer guide – such as a periodical devoted solely to new books – became steadily more apparent.

More directly influential on the practice of criticism were the learned journals that emerged in the late 1600s, beginning with de Sallo's *Jour-nal des savants* in 1665. Unlike the *Philosophical Transactions of the Royal Society* (London, 1665), which published only original findings, the *Journal des savants* devoted some of its contents to abstracts of books. In imitating the *Journal* (and later the *Mercure galant*, 1672) in this attention to books and literary topics, a whole generation of Euro-pean journals moved to the threshold of fully fledged literary criticism: the *Giornale de' letterati* (1668) in Italy, *Acta eruditorum* (1682) in Leipzig, and Bayle's *Nouvelles de la République des Lettres* (1684) in Amsterdam, along with the *Philosophical Collections* (1679), *Weekly Memorials of the Ingenious* (1682), and the first of several learned journals founded by Jean de la Crose, the *Universal Historical Biblio-thèque* (1685) in London. These journals were still very limited. They tended to cover only a few books, some quite arcane, and to offer abstracts rather than critical evaluation; original literary essays were rare and those by writers of Pierre Bayle's stature even rarer; the con-tents were too esoteric and dry for non-specialist readers, and the *Acta eruditorum* were even published in Latin.

---

[3] Graham, *English Literary Periodicals*, p. 22.

Yet in small incremental ways, these learned journals point to a time when writers and readers would turn automatically to periodicals as the major vehicles of criticism, rather than to the occasional prefaces, prologues, and pamphlets that even for Dryden – so clearly the dominant critic of the period that Johnson termed him 'the Father of English criticism' – constituted his critical œuvre. Gradually such journals regularized and systematized criticism, just as learned bodies were systematizing other fields of knowledge during the Enlightenment. (Indeed, had Dryden and Roscommon succeeded in founding an English Academy of Letters in the 1660s, it would inevitably have started a journal to disseminate its views and extend its authority.)[4] With their regularity of publication, journals were natural forums for ongoing critical discussion. They were more convenient and capacious, and more conducive to broadbased participation, than the haphazard, isolated utterances of critics writing in prefaces and pamphlets.

From learned journals, the literary periodical evolved by degrees. In 1679 Robert Hooke's *Philosophical Collections* included the kind of section on recent books that the *Philosophical Transactions* lacked. In 1682 the *Weekly Memorials for the Ingenious* began to offer abstracts of foreign publications; in 1684 Bayle made foreign coverage a primary aim of his *Nouvelles de la République des Lettres* and in 1685 de la Crose expanded on that idea by setting out to provide in the *Universal Historical Bibliothèque* 'an account of the most considerable books printed in all languages'.[5] De la Crose's journal also became the first to invite submissions from its readership, foreshadowing the point in the mid-eighteenth century when reader participation had become so routine that, for example, Hume's writings on language could be the subject of critical exchange with members of the general public in the pages of the *Scots Magazine* (26 (1764), pp. 187–8). It was a service to the less learned among their readers, as well as a sign of broader trends in the sociology of literary criticism, that many journals began to translate their excerpts from foreign publications; eventually the *Acta eruditorum* were succeeded by a similar journal, the *Neue Zeitungen von gelehrten Sachen*, written in German rather than Latin.

At the same time, the learned journals sought to maintain critical discussion at the highest level. They were highly selective about their subject-matter, and in 1691 de la Crose went so far as to bar any discussion of light literature – 'plays, satyrs, romances, and the like' – from his journal. As a result the literary contents of the journal seldom went beyond articles on L'Estrange's *Fables*, Raleigh's *Arts of Empire*,

---

[4] Basker, *Tobias Smollett*, pp. 18–20.
[5] Graham, *English Literary Periodicals*, pp. 29–30.

William Temple's *Memoirs,* and Wood's *Athenae Oxonienses.*[6] If this
had the ironic effect of excluding Dryden's works (which were after all
mostly 'plays, satyrs, and the like') from critical discussion, it none the
less signalled the seriousness with which men like de la Crose sought to
promote learning and *belles-lettres.* The popularizers would come, and
the marriage of their influence with that of the learned journals would
lead to the fully developed critical journals of the later eighteenth century. But the highest aims of the learned journals – objectivity of treatment through abstract and summary, elevation of tone, selectivity of
material, and above all the international cosmopolitanism that transcends national boundaries and defines enlightenment – would leave
their mark on periodical criticism and its inner struggles ever after.

1700–1750

Whereas before 1700 important critical writings seemed to appear in
every form except periodicals – prefaces, dedications, prologues, epilogues, pamphlets, treatises, even verse epistles – after 1700 it is impossible to discuss the history of criticism without dwelling on major critical
writings that appeared in periodicals, from the *Tatler* (1709–11) and
Spectator (1711–15) to Johnson's articles in the *Gentleman's Magazine*
in the 1730s and '40s and his *Rambler* essays (1750–2). The two genres of
periodical that most influenced the history of criticism during the early
eighteenth century – the *periodical essay* and the *magazine* or monthly
miscellany – both came from the popular (as opposed to the learned)
end of the spectrum. Both derived their power to affect the practice of
criticism from their enormous popularity, a popularity reflected not only
in the numbers and composition of their readership, but in the subject-
matter, shape, tone, and idiom of their contents. Both genres are too
well known and too well covered in the scholarly literature to warrant
rehearsing their histories here, except in passing, and so the immediate
concern is how they contributed to the history of criticism.

Suited in size to the attention span of a typical middle-class reader
taking a break from a busy life, the periodical essay represented a
respite or diversion rather than a serious intellectual exercise. The need
to be entertaining was paramount, yet amidst the stream of witty sketches,
political satire, and social commentary, the essayists chose to include
considerable literary criticism. The results could be quite curious. Defoe,
in one of the few literary essays in his largely political periodical *The
Review* (1704–13), focused his discussion of *Paradise Lost* on the question

[6] Graham, *English Literary Periodicals,* p. 40.

of whether Adam and Eve had sex in Eden before the Fall (VIII, p. 159 (29 March 1712)). Pope contributed to Steele's *Guardian* a mock serious critique of pastoral poetry that simultaneously ravages the poems of his rival Ambrose Phillips and, with a flourish of the double-edge, undercuts the rule-bound methods of the critics he himself is imitating (40 (27 April 1713)). In the *Covent-Garden Journal* (1752), Fielding allegorized his views on contemporary literature, particularly Smollett's novels, in his own 'battle of the books', serialized as 'A Journal of the Present Paper War' (nos. 1–3 (4–11 January 1752)).

Beneath the levity, there are important implications for literary history. These periodical essays opened up the subject of criticism to a readership far more diverse and numerous than that of the learned journals. The subscription lists of the *Tatler* and *Spectator*, for example, show not only literati and aristocrats but merchants, professionals, military officers, and bureaucrats, as well as a large number of women and a sprinkling of apothecaries, druggists, goldsmiths, watchmakers, and dyers.[7] In later years large numbers of students became part of the readership, whether following the advice of Hugh Blair and Benjamin Franklin (who both recommended the *Tatler* and *Spectator* as models for style) or simply finding the essays reprinted in their schoolbooks. On the basis of multiple readerships of single copies in such places as coffeehouses (there were 2,000 coffeehouses in London in 1710) and an estimated print-run of 3,000–4,000, some have estimated an immediate readership for the *Tatler* of 10,000. Generation after generation joined that readership as scores, perhaps hundreds, of collected editions of the *Tatler* and *Spectator* were reprinted over the course of the century. Another measure of influence is the number of imitators: in Britain alone, by one count, more than fifty-five different journals had tried to imitate the *Tatler* by 1790. There was extensive international influence too. The *Spectator* was translated into French (1714), Dutch (1720), and German (1739); there were innumerable imitations in other countries, especially Germany where the *Spectator* was particularly influential, but also in Denmark, Poland, and France. Marivaux's *Le Spectateur français* (1722–3) was perhaps the most distinguished, while Bodmer's and Breitinger's *Discourse der Mahlern* (Zurich, 1721–3) and Gottsched's *Die vernünftigen Tadlerinnen* (Leipzig, 1725–7) exemplify hundreds of German imitators. The first Russian literary journal, *Monthly Papers for Profit and Entertainment* (1757–62), featured translations of *Spectator* essays.[8] As the *Tatler* and *Spectator* show, successful periodicals could reach many publics, across class and national boundaries, and over time.

[7] Ross, *Selections*, pp. 487–9.
[8] Sullivan, *Literary Magazines*, I, pp. 393–400; Ross, *Selections*, pp. 52–5; Martens, *Die Botschaft, passim*.

The influence thus extended had many ramifications. There is, first, the simple fact that these periodicals brought literary topics and critical issues into the everyday conversation and consciousness of ordinary middle-class people, whether in the salon, the coffeehouse, the schoolroom or the family diningroom. As Addison and Fielding and Johnson introduced literary topics such as Shakespeare, Milton, tragedy, pastoral poetry, and the novel into the banter of their essays, some knowledge of literary issues became part of 'keeping up' and thus helped define the norms and horizons of middle-class culture.

Of course the sense of context and audience affected the idiom in which this criticism was presented, making it lighter and more entertaining than straight critical discourse. Swift, for example, scarcely sounds the solemn philologist in his *Tatler* essay on the corruption of English when, to argue for a standardized orthography, he says of bad spellers: 'The usual pretence is, that they spell as they speak: A noble standard for a language! To depend upon the caprice of every coxcomb, who because words are the cloathing of our thoughts, cuts them and shapes them as he pleases, and changes them oftener than his dress' (230 (28 September 1710)). Or Pope in a mock-essay on poetic genius: 'What Molière observes of making a dinner, that any man can do it with money, and if a profest cook cannot without, he has his art for nothing; the same may be said of making a poem, 'tis easily brought about by him that has a genius, but the skill lies in doing it without one' (*Guardian* 78 (10 June 1713)).

Throughout their critical writings, playful or serious, the essayists tended to resist the rules and theory of strict neo-classical orthodoxy in favour of a more reader-centred common-sense criticism. Thus Addison on Tate's 'corrected' version of *Lear*:

> *King Lear* is an admirable tragedy of the same kind, as Shakespeare wrote
> it; but as it is reformed according to the chymerical notions of poetical
> justice, in my humble opinion it has lost half its beauty ... I do not
> therefore dispute against this way of writing tragedies, but against the
> criticism that would establish this as the only method.
>
> > (*Spectator* 40 (16 April 1711))

Often this attitude (too inchoate to qualify as a movement) is described in terms of a transition from genre rules to psychological or 'affective' criticism, a shift from the classical emphasis on the ideals of form and their codification by critics, to a focus on the power of art to affect its beholders. The best example is Addison's series of essays on 'the pleasures of the imagination' (*Spectator* 409 and 411–21 (19 June and 21 June– 3 July, 1712)), though the attitude surfaces in most of the essayists from Steele to Johnson and Goldsmith.

Johnson provided a kind of manifesto for this critical spirit at the end of *Rambler* 156 (14 September 1751). There, having argued from psychology and common sense to attack rigid adherence to the dramatic unities, Johnson declares:

It ought to be the first endeavour of a writer to distinguish nature from custom, or that which is established because it is right, from that which is right only because it is established; that he may neither violate essential principles by a desire of novelty, nor debar himself from the attainment of beauties within his view by a needless fear of breaking rules which no literary dictator had authority to enact.

Here is a rallying cry for the 'common reader', Johnson's imaginary critical arbiter, famous for being 'uncorrupted with literary prejudices' and free from 'the refinements of subtlety and the dogmatism of learning'. It is significant, therefore, that Johnson first conceived of this 'common reader' not in the *Life of Gray* (1781), but thirty years earlier, in the crucible of his *Rambler* writings, where he used the term repeatedly (e.g., nos. 4 and 57, 31 March and 2 October 1750). In short, the common reader – so essential to Virginia Woolf and other modern critics – entered the history of criticism through periodical literature. The resistance of Addison, Johnson, and others to strict neo-classical rules and theory in favour of affective criticism, usually ascribed to the influence of Locke, may owe as much to the journalistic context in which its authors conceived and articulated it. Certainly no other context offered a more immediate and sustained sense of real reader response – its thrust, its underlying psychodynamics, its collective force – than the day-to-day interplay between journalists and readers.

The openness and variety of the essay form also enabled writers to bring into critical discussion literary genres that, because regarded as too new or low or unimportant, had received little formal attention. Addison's enthusiastic treatment of the popular ballad 'Chevy Chase' in *Spectator*s 70 and 74 (21 May and 25 May 1711) is a famous example. The critical principles he urges in its defence – warning the literati against forming 'a wrong artificial taste' and extolling 'the plain common sense' of ordinary readers – foretell the shift in poetic values to come in the later eighteenth century. The most important new genre to gain attention in this way was the novel. Fielding's essay on Charlotte Lennox's *Female Quixote*, for example, brought her novel to the public's attention and linked it to the comic tradition of Cervantes, a welcome boost for a woman writer in 1752 (*Covent-Garden Journal* 24 (24 March 1752)). Though by mid-century the novel was so well established as a genre that even Johnson would devote an early *Rambler* (4 (31 March 1750)) to its artful powers, it is telling that almost no book-length criticism on the novel as a genre appeared until the next century. To map the early critical reception of the novel, therefore, modern literary historians have had to do as the editors of the Critical Heritage volume on Fielding did: turn for material to the periodical press where almost all of that critical activity was happening. One modern literary theorist, in exploring what he calls the 'interesting set of relationships ... between literary theory and the form of criticism', observes that 'it is difficult to write an engaging *long* piece of criticism: virtually none exist in any language' and he reminds us that 'since the inception of systematic criticism ... most criticism falls in the category of the *periodical*'.[9]

The magazine, like the periodical essay, was an enormously popular vehicle that was only partly concerned with literary topics. Its form, though, was utterly different, consisting of a wide array of departments covering everything from politics and foreign affairs to lists of deaths, crimes and crop prices. Miscellaneity was its chief characteristic, a quality that dated back in rudimentary form to such monthly miscellanies as the *Gentleman's Journal* (1692) and the *Mercure galant* in the seventeenth century, but which only came into its own with the *Gentleman's Magazine* (1731) and *London Magazine* (1732). The rivalry of these two defined the magazine as a form which, though it continued to evolve, is still remarkably similar today.

The magazine's contributions to the progress of criticism are many. With its capacity to include literary articles of whatever kind the editors chose, it was able, like the periodical essay, to present light and occasional pieces of criticism, plus biography, fiction, and poetry. A whole section devoted to poetry was a standard feature. Often the magazines would reprint pieces from the periodical essays and newspapers, a practice that inadvertently facilitated the demise of the essay as a separate publication: it was simply swallowed up and incorporated into larger publications. By 1760, for example, Johnson was publishing his *Idler* essays in the *Universal Chronicle* and Goldsmith was contributing a serial on *belles-lettres* to Smollett's *British Magazine*.[10]

Like the periodical essay, the magazine expanded the audience for literary criticism, however lighthearted or fragmentary, and promoted awareness of it among those who read primarily to get the stock prices or society news. It brought marginal genres into view, especially new or lowbrow forms such as the novel, farce, and popular verse. It could affect contemporary critical tastes, and perhaps by extension the trajectory of canon formation. Who can say what effect the *London Magazine*'s frequent publication of poems by the 'thresher poet' Stephen Duck had

---

[9] Paulson, *Henry Fielding*, pp. vii–xix and *passim*; Engell, *Critical Mind*, pp. 166–8.
[10] Basker, *Tobias Smollett*, pp. 194–6.

on the eighteenth-century taste for working-class poets? Or what formative influence magazine poetry had on the young Wordsworth, who at the age of sixteen published his first poem in the *European Magazine*? Given that more than half the 107 women poets collected in the new Oxford anthology *Eighteenth-Century Women Poets* (1989) originally published significant pieces of their work (often their first) in magazines, how does one measure the impact of periodicals on the place of women in literary history?[11]

Magazines also played a role in the international reception of literature and the assimilation of foreign influences. The *London Magazine* might publish translations of several pieces by Voltaire in a single year, for example, while Johnson – no friend to Voltaire – none the less tried to make coverage of foreign literature a high priority when he edited the *Gentleman's* and later the *Literary* magazine.[12] The influence flowed both ways. In France the *Journal étranger* reprinted copiously from English magazines and the *Journal encyclopédique*, when it reprinted instalments of Smollett's *Sir Launcelot Greaves* from the *British Magazine*, presented the French reading public with the first serialized novel in English literary history. In Germany the *Göttinger Musenalmanach* (1769), modelled on the French journal *Almanach des muses* (1765), pursued Klopstock's vision of German culture by publishing such poets as Bürger, J. H. Voss, L. C. Holty, and Friedrich Leopold Graf von Stolberg. Still another example points up the value of periodical literature to the study of post-colonialism: not only British but French writers (Voltaire, Montesquieu, Rousseau) appear regularly in eighteenth-century American magazines, from the colonial period (e.g., the *American Magazine* in the 1740s) right through Independence and the early republic (e.g., the *Columbian Magazine* in the 1780s and '90s).[13] And so it went, along an infinitely complex and fertile web of international connection and cross-pollination.

With its voracious monthly appetite for copy, the magazine had a major impact on the profession of authors. Where the periodical essay tended to support a single author at a time, the magazine generated huge and varied amounts of work for a large number of writers. It contributed as much as any other single cause to the rapid transition from patronage to professional writing; there is no more famous example

---

[11] Sullivan, *Literary Magazines*, I, p. 203; Basker, *Tobias Smollett*, pp. 192 and 312; *European Magazine*, 11 (1787), p. 202; Roger Lonsdale (ed.), *Eighteenth-Century Women Poets* (Oxford, 1989), pp. xxii, xxvi, and 516–38.

[12] *London Magazine*, 26 (1757), pp. 78–9, 82–5, 129–32, 590–99; Kaminski, *Johnson*, pp. 146–8.

[13] *Journal étranger*, Dec. 1761; Janssens, *Matthieu Maty*, p. 126; *Journal encyclopédique* II (1760), pt. 3, 154; IV (1761), pt. 3, pp. 101–15; V (1761), pt. 2, pp. 101–11. Richardson, *History*, pp. 48, 289, and *passim*.

than young Samuel Johnson – college dropout, failed schoolmaster, patronless playwright – coming to London in the 1730s to start his career as a writer for Cave's *Gentleman's Magazine*. Similarly in Germany, Lessing began his professional writing career as a review critic for the *Berlinische privilegierte Zeitung* in 1748 and the young Goethe wrote for the *Frankfurter gelehrte Anzeigen* in the 1770s. Journalism could be the testing ground for authorial talent but it could also influence writers' achievements in other genres. Goldsmith, for example, discovered the public's taste for sentimental fiction in the response to a story he wrote for a magazine, and expanded that story into a fulllength novel, *The Vicar of Wakefield*.[14]

New genres were born and others revived in the magazine. The emergence of the short story as a major literary genre in the nineteenth century, for example, owes everything to its long gestation in the thousands of short fictions that filled the eighteenth-century magazines. Similarly the resurgence of the short lyric poem in the late eighteenth century may have been in part an authorial response to the vast new opportunities to publish short poems in the magazines and, correspondingly, the public's growing attention to poems in magazines rather than the long, separately published poems of earlier eras. In terms of poetry readers and publishing vehicles, this has remained a fact of poetic life ever since.

The greatest significance of the magazine to criticism, however, may lie in one of its meagrest features: the book list. From their beginning in the 1730s, the *Gentleman's* and *London* magazines printed simple lists of the new books published each month. Occasionally a critical comment or excerpt was attached, but usually they appeared in stark form – a list of thirty or forty titles, with author, publisher, price. Competition over this feature put a premium on promptness and completeness, and this would carry forward as a concern into book review journalism later on. More importantly, the standardization of this feature in a form so similar to the lists of stock prices, ships in port, foreign exchange rates, births, deaths, marriages, promotions, etc. which were regularly printed in every issue, suggests that the commodification of information was becoming also the commodification of culture. The contents of the magazine were like an inventory of middle-class consciousness. In an age that was soon to begin producing anthologies and standard collections for mass consumption, a superficial awareness of literature was becoming a component of social and cultural competence.

Recently, scholars have begun to consider the ways in which periodicals define and inform 'imagined communities', whether those communities are based on ethnicity, geography, language, gender, class, ideology, or other factors.[15] Throughout the eighteenth century, and increasingly so

---

[14] Basker, *Tobias Smollett*, p. 196.   [15] Sollors, 'Immigrants', pp. 568–9.

after 1750, periodicals emerged that began to articulate the views – including the critical views – of sub-groups within society, whether of women (e.g., Frances Brooke's *Old Maid*, 1755) or the lower-middle classes (e.g., *General Magazine*, 1787) or political radicals (e.g., *Analytical Review*, 1788).[16] The learned journals, which have continued as a separate and increasingly elite kind of periodical down to the present, identified another 'imagined community', one that was perhaps as alienated from middle-class culture as any other. Nevertheless, in the middle of the eighteenth century the energies of the learned journal and the general magazine merged in a new kind of periodical. The *review journal* combined the popular reach and cultural aspirations of the magazines with the higher pretensions of the learned journals, with lasting consequences for the function of criticism in society.

1750–1800

In the 1750s, with the emergence of the *Monthly Review* (1749) and the *Critical Review* (1756), modern review criticism really began. The distinctive properties of the review journal, descended from two different traditions of periodical literature, made it the most widely influential organ of criticism in the history of periodical literature. Like some of the learned or abstract journals, it was devoted exclusively to reviewing published works but unlike them, it aimed to provide prompt and universal coverage of *all* new publications, learned and common, belletristic and prosaic. These journals had large circulations and a degree of popular appeal, like the magazines: they each printed 2,500 to 3,500 copies a month and they were read in coffeehouses, reading societies, and homes everywhere.[17] The reviews covered plays, novels, popular poems, political pamphlets – all the works the man or woman in the street wanted to hear about – and their reviewers could be lively, witty, entertaining. Yet they covered the most scholarly works too, providing detailed accounts of each volume of the *Philosophical Transactions*, for example, and they periodically expressed the high seriousness of a learned journal, as in their determination to correct and regulate the use of English or their efforts to maintain a correspondence with other cultural centres in Europe. From this mixture of ideals and pragmatism, tempered by editorial experiment and adjustment, came an uneven but voluminous archive of eighteenth-century critical thinking in action. For literary historians and theorists, the collected volumes of the *Monthly* and *Critical* reviews, and their continental counterparts such

---

[16] Sullivan, *Literary Magazines*, I, pp. 11–14 and 131–6.
[17] Basker, *Tobias Smollett*, pp. 172–3. Unless otherwise noted, the following derives from Basker, pp. 1–38, 164–87, and 211–19.

as *France littéraire* and the *Journal encyclopédique* or Germany's *Allgemeine deutsche Bibliothek* and the *Göttingische Anzeigen von gelehrten Sachen*, provide an unprecedented depth of perspective on the intellectual and cultural life of the century.

In their own time, the impact of these review journals was immediate, multi-faceted and profound. One of the most obvious effects is also a reminder of criticism's ties to the marketplace: publishers and booksellers began quoting reviews in advertisements for books. Beginning about 1750, the practice quickly spread and soon became routine. The reviews were used in this way, it should be noted, by booksellers in the English provinces as well as in Edinburgh, Dublin, and the American colonies; critical authority in this culture clearly extended from London outward to the periphery of the English-speaking world. In a century that also saw extensive Dutch, French, Spanish, and Portuguese colonial activity, the broader role of periodicals as conveyors of cultural authority is full of implication for theorists and historians alike. In the specific practice of citing reviews in book advertisements, what the publishers had jumped to exploit, the review journals tacitly conceded by listing 'publisher' and 'price' at the head of each article: at this level the review journal was a consumer's guide for what was, after all, the first mass-production industry in history. Reviewers' opinions prompted canny publishers to commission more books in certain genres or by certain authors, or translations of new foreign publications. Literary fads flourished. Opinion fed on opinion until it had the force of reality.

The impact on authors was equally dramatic. Although reviews were published anonymously, authors began to read them attentively and even, as scholars have shown, to revise the texts of their works according to the criticisms of the reviewers. Not just novices or minor writers reacted in this way, but a surprising number of major ones too, including David Hume, Edmund Burke, Thomas Gray, Frances Burney, Horace Walpole, and even Samuel Johnson himself. Review critics, it seems, were quietly editing the text of eighteenth-century literature. Writers began to address prefaces and postscripts to the reviewers, some began to send complimentary copies or ingratiating letters to the journals, and others to complain in print about negative reviews. All the evidence points to a rapid realignment of power and influence in the literary world, with authors conceding authority to the review critics and looking to them, rather than to an amorphous and unpredictable public, to articulate critical standards.

The impact on readers is harder to summarize but it can be indicated. Already in the 1750s and '60s the *Monthly* and *Critical* reviews circulated nationally and internationally. Known individual subscribers came from a variety of class backgrounds, including large and small landowners, merchants, traders, professionals, and clergy, but by far the largest and most heterogeneous readership was reached through community institutions, lending libraries and reading societies. These flourished everywhere, from lending libraries in provincial cities like Ely and Salisbury, to proprietary libraries in Liverpool, Manchester, and Leeds, to community libraries in Aberdeen and Innerpefray in Scotland, to the Library Company of Philadelphia and the Charleston Society Library in America, to the Göttingen Library in Germany: records prove that all these bodies subscribed to the reviews as, by extension, must have hundreds or thousands of similar institutions. Where borrowing records are available, such as for Innerpefray, the reviews were constantly among the works most frequently circulated. Equally telling is the common practice among these libraries of prohibiting the review journals – alone of all their holdings – from circulating. They were too much in demand.

The implications for reception history and canon formation are striking. Archival records show that these groups actually used the review journals to decide what books to acquire. In the Liverpool Library, a typical membership library with (in 1770) 300 members, readers recommending a new book for acquisition were *required* to cite the *Monthly* or *Critical* article that would support such an acquisition. At other libraries, such as Warrington and colonial Charleston, members of the book selection committee brought the review journals to their meetings and used them as the basis for their decisions. Thus, to an extraordinary degree review criticism not only shaped public opinion, but actually determined the contents of libraries, public and private, throughout the English-speaking world. As powerful an influence as this might be in the metropolis (the London Library subscribed to both journals from its inception in 1785), it was virtually inescapable in places like rural Scotland and South Carolina, where there was little or no other access to books.

Similar forces affected international reception. It fulfilled one kind of Enlightenment ideal, for example, that more than a third of the subscribers to the *Journal étranger* in 1755 lived far from Paris, in the provinces of France or in foreign cities. Its international circulation was impressive: London had sixty-three subscribers, Leipzig fifty, Warsaw thirty-five, Lisbon thirty-one, Florence twenty-five, The Hague twenty, Madrid eleven, and so forth in more than twenty other European cities.[18] Because the English reviews regularly 'covered' foreign books simply by translating articles from journals such as the *Journal étranger*, the *Journal's* influence abroad extended well beyond those who could read the original in French. The reality of that influence is suggested in an example

---

[18] *Journal étranger*, April 1755, pp. xxxi–xxxii.

from the *Monthly Review* for May 1757, in which Oliver Goldsmith
compiled the 'Foreign Section' by translating twenty-six notices of books
from foreign journals. One of those was a glowing report on a book –
Les Mémoires d'un Protestant – whose wider readership in England was
assured a few months later when Goldsmith translated it into English
and published it in London, doubtless as a result of that foreign article.
If *canon* can be taken to mean the approved books available in a society
at a given moment, then review criticism shaped canons.

A more far-reaching example comes from Göttingen, where the acquisition records show that the eighteenth-century librarians relied for
years on the London review journals to decide what books to order
from England. As the Göttingen librarians were building what would
become the largest archive of English books in Germany and the one
to which Haller, Lichtenberg and other German literati would come
to read English literature, the pattern of their acquisitions affected the
reception of English literature in Germany on the highest levels. And
that pattern was largely determined by the opinions of review critics.

But again, the traffic went both ways. The review journals imported
and exported influence. A recent composite index of review journals in
London during the years 1749–74 offers some insight into the level of
'foreign exposure' among the English reading public. Despite the 'John
Bull' image, during the mid-century a typical English reader was exposed to hundreds of articles in the main London review journals about
contemporary foreign authors: specifically, forty-nine (two per year)
about literary works by Voltaire and another eight about Montesquieu,
as well as five on Goldoni, six on Haller, seven on Klopstock, ten on
Salomon Gessner, and so forth.[19] Later in the century, review journals
would perform the crucially important function of importing the ideas
of German romanticism, as English reviewers transmitted works by
Lessing, Goethe and others to an English reading public for whom
German was generally less accessible than French or even Italian. Meanwhile in Germany, through such journals as the *Theatralische Bibliothek*
(1754–8), Lessing had been importing Dryden's critical ideas and other
English influences since the 1750s. Indeed, as the many journals in
England, France, Germany, Holland, Italy, Russia and elsewhere imitated and cited and reprinted each other, they made themselves the
natural circuitry through which national literatures were transmitted
and foreign influences received.

Beyond these kinds of institutional and sociological impact, review
journals affected criticism on other levels. Practical criticism forged new
critical ideas. The necessity to evaluate and compare, month after month,

[19] Forster, *Index, passim.*

a succession of works in the same genre encouraged reviewers to begin to evolve criteria and critical terminology to apply systematically, especially in genres like the novel for which there was a lot of new material but little established critical theory. The reviews habituated ordinary readers to thinking about literature in certain categories and terms. Feminist literary historians have shown, for example, how reviewers rapidly developed the habit of relegating women writers to the category of 'female pens', and then either politely declined to engage in serious criticism or dismissed them altogether. In turn, popular taste shaped critical discussion as reviewers were forced, in reviewing wildly new kinds of writing such as Sterne's *Tristram Shandy*, to reconcile popular response with their own preconceived critical ideas. Review journalism became a vast laboratory of non-stop critical activity, too frenetic to develop its own coherent theories but productive of results applicable to every area of critical thinking.

This species of criticism is important also for its impact on the careers and achievements of individual critics, the work it drew from them and the ways in which it contributed to their creative or intellectual development. Among the tens of thousands of review articles generated, some individual pieces stand on their own as important critical documents. One thinks of Johnson's brilliant treatment of Soame Jenyns's *Inquiry into the Nature and Origins of Evil*; or of Lessing's momentous argument in 1759, in the *Briefe, die neueste Literatur betreffend*, that the Germans take Shakespeare rather than the French classical drama as the model for their national theatre; or, less obviously, of Cleland's theory of the novel expounded in reviewing works by Fielding and Smollett. Collectively, some of these critical writings had the potential to shape history. When Diderot and Grimm and Madame d'Épinay wrote for the clandestine journal *Correspondance littéraire* in the 1750s, '60s, and '70s, they spread enlightenment ideas among a small but extraordinarily powerful group (fifteen members) that included the King of Poland, Frederick of Prussia, the Queen of Sweden, and Catherine the Great.[20] But the process itself of grinding out so much critical work – hundreds of reviews each by writers like Johnson and Diderot and Smollett, reportedly 9,000 by the German critic Haller – had its effects in subtler ways.[21] Goethe, who from his early twenties had written regularly for periodicals, turned again to them in the 1780s and '90s, to express some of his most important aesthetic ideas in such journals as *Der Teutsche Merkur* and *Die Horen* (1795–7). In England Coleridge, whose critical genius rests on a profound understanding of the reader's

---

[20] *Literary Magazine*, 2 (1757), pp. 171–5, 251–3, 301–6; *Monthly Review*, 4 (1751), pp. 355–64 and V (1751), pp. 510–15; Weinreb, p. 389.
[21] Fabian, *Widening Circle*, p. 150.

experience in literature, first began to think as a practical critic during his early years reviewing for the *Critical Review* in the 1790s. Similarly, out of her early labours reviewing trash fiction for the *Analytical Review*, Mary Wollstonecraft formed many of the ideas about women's fiction and other literature that were to fuel her great treatise, *A Vindication of the Rights of Woman*.

By the end of the century, periodical criticism as a field of writing commands attention simply by the roll of names who have practised it: Diderot, Voltaire, Marmontel, Desfontaines, Rousseau, Grimm, and Madame d'Épinay in France; Lessing, Goethe, Haller, Herder, Fichte, Schiller, and the Schlegels in Germany; Addison, Steele, Fielding, Johnson, Goldsmith, Smollett, Godwin, Wollstonecraft, and Coleridge in England, among hundreds of others. The entrance of these writers into the field of criticism – practical if not theoretical criticism – is primarily due to the opportunities and inducements of periodical writing. As it educated and enfranchised readers, periodical writing also formed and empowered critics.

If journalism can be said to have had one overarching effect on literary criticism, it would be that it fostered the democratization of culture. The widespread circulation of periodicals enabled readers who might otherwise be excluded from mainstream cultural life – whether by geographic distance, socio-economic or educational deprivation, lack of leisure time, or other indisposition – to read and know about contemporary literature and criticism, and even to contribute to the ongoing public conversation themselves. Periodicals, as Sollors pointed out, not only helped define sub-groups within larger heterogeneous societies; they also 'nationalized' disparate groups of people and 'created national unity'.[22] Not only our inheritance of a unified culture (or our shared illusion of it), but so much of the power structure and conventions of the modern literary world hark back to the rise of periodical literature in the eighteenth century. In the history of criticism as in other areas of cultural life, the impact of periodical literature is difficult to map but impossible to ignore.

[22] Sollors, 'Immigrants', p. 569.

Language and Style

13

Theories of language

Nicholas Hudson

The natural point at which to begin a discussion of eighteenth-century theories of language is John Locke's 1690 *Essay concerning Human Understanding*. Virtually every theorist of language and literature over the next century owed something to Book 3 in Locke's *Essay*, 'Of Words'. Locke's influence was not, however, to popularize any single doctrine. There were, in fact, two major interpretations of Locke's theory of language, each leading to a quite different conception of its nature and history. The first interpretation looked no deeper than Locke's explicit statements that words were merely arbitrary 'signs' of ideas. The second interpretation took inspiration from Locke's unclear but challenging suggestions that words were much more than outward signs, but had a fundamental role in the formation of ideas and their organization in rational thought. These provocative insights into the mental function of language led to the theories of Vico, Condillac, Rousseau, Herder and other philosophers of the mid- and late eighteenth century. These authors would argue that the history of literature had been closely connected with the joint evolution of language and reason.[1]

The 'arbitrary sign' and its literary implications

Locke's name is now closely associated with the doctrine that words '*signify* only Men's peculiar *Ideas*, and that by a *perfectly arbitrary Imposition*'.[2] Impelled by their natural sociability, argued Locke, the first humans invented 'external sensible Signs' to communicate their 'invisible *Ideas*' to others.[3] Locke's insistence that words refer only to ideas in the mind of the speaker, and not to 'things' in the world, corrected the habit of many seventeenth-century grammarians and philosophers

---

[1] Good discussions of Locke's linguistics include Norman Kretzmann, 'Locke's semantic theory', in Parret (ed.), *History*, pp. 331–47; Hans Aarsleff, 'Leibniz on Locke on language', in *From Locke to Saussure*, pp. 42–83; Land, *Philosophy*, pp. 31–77; Formigari, *Language*, pp. 99–131.
[2] Locke, *Essay*, bk 3, ch. 2, p. 408.   [3] Locke, *Essay*, bk 3, ch. 2, p. 405.

of using the terms 'idea' and 'thing' almost interchangeably: Locke's admirers were more careful to specify that words referred only to thoughts in the mind of the speaker, and not to physical objects. Locke's claim that words were 'perfectly arbitrary' repudiated the doctrine of some mystical and hermetic philosophers that language – particularly the characters of written Hebrew – was originally instituted by God and signified objects in the world by natural resemblance. By the end of the seventeenth century, however, few disagreed with Locke that language signified by human convention rather than by a divinely ordained resemblance between words and things.

By stressing that words signified only by convention, and not by natural affinity to the objects they denoted, Locke intended to warn his readers against confusing hollow verbiage with substantial knowledge. Like his predecessors Bacon and Descartes, Locke blamed the confusion between words and knowledge for the emptiness of scholastic philosophy, and for a wide range of intellectual errors. 'How many are there', he complained, 'that when they would think on Things, fix their Thoughts only on Words?'[4] Locke repeatedly declared that words were utterly worthless unless used as agreed by speakers to denote the same ideas in their minds. He also cautioned against the inherent instability and uncertainty of language. In the last three sections in Book 3 'Of Words', he dwelt on the great 'imperfection' of words, their frequent 'abuse', and the need for constant vigilance against their perpetual slide into meaninglessness and ambiguity. Because linguistic signs were arbitrary, he warned, they easily shifted meaning, leading unwary speakers into using the same words to refer to different ideas. Locke's deep distrust of language left little room for figurative language and other rhetorical devices. Although figures were tolerable 'where we seek rather Pleasure and Delight, than Information and Improvement', they were nothing but a 'perfect cheat' in serious language. The dangerous tendency of 'Eloquence' was 'to insinuate wrong *Ideas*, move the Passions, and thereby mislead the Judgment'.[5] As this statement suggests, Locke was wary of any use of language to incite or express the passions. He valued words only as signs of ideas, and he aspired above all to make language more lucid, logical and unchanging.

Here was an ideal widely shared by eighteenth-century lexicographers and grammarians: works such as Samuel Johnson's great *Dictionary of the English Language* in 1754 set out professedly to fulfil Locke's ambition of a more stable and consistent lexicon. Moreover, while Locke himself had very little appreciation for literature, his general suspicions of empty verbiage found a sympathetic audience among critics and

[4] Locke, *Essay*, bk 3, ch. 11, p. 510.   [5] Locke, *Essay*, bk 3, ch. 10, p. 508.

authors of the Restoration and early eighteenth century. Rapin, Dryden, Addison, Du Bos and many other critics condemned puns, word-play and all kinds of 'harmonious nonsense' as characteristic of 'false Wit'.[6] Like Locke, these critics typically reduced figurative language to the status of mere 'ornament', useful for dignifying and enlivening pleasurable writing, but always at fault when it drew attention from the essential 'thought' or 'design' of the author. Moreover, many critics reflected the habit of empiricist philosophers after Locke of assuming that ideas were discrete, static and largely *visual* images in the mind. As a consequence of their 'specular' conception of mind, Jonathan Richardson, Jean-Baptiste Du Bos and others considered poetic language to be less realistic and effective than painting, which represented visual images by resemblance rather than convention.[7]

Locke's *Essay* had provided the classic statement for this view of language as arbitrary, delusive and external to the mind. Yet Locke's *Essay* also inspired quite different insights, especially among philosophers of the mid- and late eighteenth century. For Condillac, Rousseau, Herder, Adam Smith and others who advocated a new linguistic philosophy, speech was inseparable from knowledge, essential to thinking, and naturally expressive of the human passions.

Condillac and the mental role of language

Early drafts of the *Essay concerning Human Understanding* indicate that Locke originally intended only to warn briefly against the imperfection and abuse of words, and did not plan to make language a central part of his philosophy.[8] His final decision to devote the entire third book of the *Essay* to language reflects insights that he reached during the course of his research into the origin and nature of ideas. Locke found repeatedly that language played a more important role in the understanding than he had initially suspected. Indeed, 'Words . . . seem'd scarce separable from our general Knowledge.'[9] Indispensable for the creation of moral concepts, a tool for collecting and organizing our disparate sensations, language was linked in fundamental ways to the primary activities of the understanding.

According to some of his eighteenth-century interpreters, however, Locke had recognized the mental role of language too late to give this

---

[6] Cf. Rapin, *Reflections*, p. 47; Dryden, 'MacFlecknoe' (1678), ll. 83–4, 203–10; Addison, *Spectator* Nos. 58 and 61 (1711); Du Bos, *Reflections*, I, p. 60.
[7] Cf. Richardson, *Essay* (1715), *Works*, pp. 5–6; Du Bos, *Reflections*, I, pp. 321–2.
[8] Cf. *An Early Draft of Locke's Essay*, ed. R. I. Aaron and Jocelyn Gibb (Oxford, 1936), pp. 42, 48–9.
[9] Locke, *Essay*, bk 3, ch. 9, p. 488.

subject the centrality it deserved. This was the view taken by Locke's most original commentator in France, Etienne Bonnot, abbé de Condillac, in *Essai sur l'origine des connoissances humaines* (1746): Locke 'saw ... that the consideration of words, and of our manner of using them, might give some light into the principle of our ideas: but because he perceived it too late, he handled this subject in his third book, which ought to have been discussed in the second'.[10] Condillac therefore set out to carry Locke's linguistic ideas to their logical conclusion, arguing that the articulate word is essential to our ability to reason coherently about the world and ourselves. Condillac stressed particularly that words give humans the power to recall and control their ideas. Before the discovery of language, primitive humans passively followed their instincts and appetites. With the discovery of the word, they became conscious of these appetites, and gained the power to direct their actions with freedom and efficiency towards the satisfaction of their wants.[11]

With Condillac, we genuinely turn the corner into a new era in the history of linguistic thought. When later authors such as Jean-Jacques Rousseau noted similarly 'how many ideas we owe to the use of speech',[12] they were clearly indebted to the now famous abbé. Philosophers of the mid- and late century became especially fascinated with two related functions for language in rational thought. They argued, first, that language was necessary to 'decompose' and organize our jumbled thoughts into coherent propositions or sentences. Secondly, philosophers maintained that we cannot form general concepts without words. And without general concepts, we can hardly be said to 'reason' at all.

The first theory was developed with great sophistication by Goethe's early mentor, Johann Gottfried Herder, in his *Abhandlung über den Ursprung der Sprache* (1772). For Herder, as for Condillac and Maupertuis, language and reason had originated simultaneously, for it was language that imposed a regular 'syntax' on our impressions, reducing them to order. Before language, the primitive mind was flooded with an incoherent mass of sensations and relations; language disentangled and ordered this mass into a comprehensible 'world' of discrete objects and

---

[10] Condillac, *Essay*, p. 10. The importance of Condillac in the history of linguistic thought was largely overlooked until the work of Hans Aarsleff. Cf. 'The tradition of Condillac: the problem of the origin of language in the eighteenth century and the debate in the Berlin Academy before Herder', in Aarsleff, *From Locke to Saussure*, pp. 146–209. Cf. also Robinet, *Le language*, pp. 203–30; G. A. Wells, 'Condillac, Rousseau and Herder on the origin of language', *Studies on Voltaire and the Eighteenth Century*, 230 (1985), 233–46; 'Condillac on the origin of language and thought', in Harris and Taylor, *Landmarks*, pp. 120–35. The English grammarian John Horne Tooke later shared Condillac's opinion that Locke had only belatedly and incompletely realized the importance of language to thinking. Cf. *The Diversions of Purley* (1786), 2 vols. (2nd edn, London, 1798), pp. 36–7.
[11] Cf. Condillac, *Essay*, pt. 2, and *passim*.   [12] Rousseau, *Discourse*, p. 152.

thoughts.[13] Such a thesis, we should note, makes the sentence rather than the single word the basic unit of meaning: the sentence corresponds to an entire perception in the primitive mind ('I see the tree') which is broken down and organized by language. A second and associated consideration pointed similarly to a primal connection between language and reason: only with language, philosophers argued, could humans reach general conclusions about the world, rather than unrelated observations about particular objects. 'Abstract and general ideas are nothing but names', wrote Condillac, in his posthumously published *Logique* (1780).[14] It followed from this view that there could be no reason without language, for rational thought was impossible without general terms. As Lord Kames wrote in his *Elements of Criticism* (1762), 'there is scarce any reasoning without making use of general terms. Hence it follows, that without language man would scarce be a rational being.'[15]

Long before the 'linguistic turn' of our time, therefore, language had attained a new and central role in epistemology and cognitive philosophy. Indeed, at the end of the century, Joseph Marie Degérando would claim that the study of the mental use of linguistic signs constituted the most important difference between ancient metaphysics and philosophy after Locke.[16] The new theories of language also had important implications for literature and criticism. The linguistic doctrine that the sentence was the basic unit of meaning corresponded, as recent scholars have noted, with a stronger preference for narrative and the organized connection of ideas in both poetry and prose.[17] Inspired by the new linguistics, authors also found reason to question the long accepted superiority of painting to poetry. Was not language, in fact, much more closely related to human thoughts and emotions than was visual representation? This was the position advanced by Edmund Burke in the concluding section of his *Philosophical Enquiry into the Origin of our Ideas of the Sublime and Beautiful* (1757). Countering an assumption common in Locke's time, Burke denied that words normally signified mental pictures. Indeed, many ordinary statements *cannot* be accurately reduced to a series of mental images.[18] The statement 'I shall go to Italy

---

[13] Herder, *Essay*, in Moran and Gode (eds.), *Origin*, pp. 115–16. Cf. also Pierre Louis Moreau de Maupertuis, *Réflexions philosophiques sur l'origine des langues* (1748), in Grimsby (ed.), *Sur l'origine*.

[14] In *Philosophical Writings*, pt 2, ch. 2, 1.388.

[15] Lord Kames, *Elements*, III, p. 406.   [16] Cf. Degérando, *Des signes*, I, p. xi.

[17] Cf. Land, *From Signs to Propositions*, and Cohen, *Sensible Words*.

[18] Cf. Burke, *Philosophical Enquiry*, pt 5 'Of Words'. Some historians have credited Berkeley with first recognizing that words can be used meaningfully without corresponding 'ideas'. Cf. Berkeley's *Alciphron; or the Minute Philosopher* (1732), 7th discourse. Cf. also Mugnai, *George Berkeley*; Daniel E. Flage, *Berkeley's Doctrine of Notions* (London, 1987).

next summer', for example, could not be represented by the most ingenious painter. Similar considerations led Gotthold Ephraim Lessing, in *Laokoon* (1766), to indicate that language was more closely akin to human thought than any visual medium, and far better adapted than statuary or painting to the representation of human ideas and activities.[19] For theorists of language and art, therefore, speech gained a new dignity and importance as the very medium of thought. Attention turned increasingly to the origin of language, for that event marked the birth of reason and the first spark of poetry.

The origin of language

Few subjects so fascinated philosophers of the eighteenth century as the origin of language. Condillac, Vico, Mandeville, Rousseau, Adam Smith and many others presented theories on how language was invented, approaching this issue not by way of empirical research – for example, by tracing the roots of words – but rather by imagining how primitive people, totally without speech, might have discovered language, given the unchanging and universal truths of human nature. With the ascendance of empirical and comparative philology early in the nineteenth century, this methodology fell into disrepute. Adam Smith's first biographer, Dugald Stewart, dismissed these works as '*Theoretical* or *Conjectural* Histories', a term meant to suggest that they were of no scientific value compared with the factual linguistic research of his own day.[20] Stewart's dismissal was not, however, entirely fair. Eighteenth-century philosophers were *not* attempting to establish an authentic history of language; rather, their re-creations of the origin of speech were intended to shed light on the nature of language in its modern form. With this methodology, philosophers had a means to isolate those fundamental elements that no language could do without. The authors of so-called 'Conjectural Histories' also made substantial contributions to the understanding of language, determining that language was a far more complex and sophisticated mechanism than had been previously suspected.

Most seventeenth-century philosophers had concurred publicly that God had given Adam speech in the Garden of Eden, though this orthodox doctrine had little impact on their understanding of language. They thought of language as inefficient, unstable and inaccurate, despite its divine origin. They did not believe that it required any supernatural ability to invent arbitrary signs for ideas. But when eighteenth-century

---

[19] Cf. *Laokoon*, ch. 16. For discussion of Lessing's place in linguistic thought during the eighteenth century, cf. Wellbery, *Lessing's Laocoön*.

[20] Stewart, *Smith*, in Smith, *Essays*, p. 293.

authors tried to imagine exactly how speechless humans would invent a language, they encountered some perplexing difficulties. Reason, it was widely agreed, was dependent on language. How then could totally irrational humans, bereft of speech, have contrived such a subtle tool as language in the first place? Rousseau provided the classic formulation of this paradox in his 1755 *Discours sur l'origine et les fondements de l'inégalité parmi les hommes*: 'if Men needed speech in order to learn how to think, they needed even more to know how to think in order to find the art of speech'.[21] This problem deeply impressed many philosophers of the time. An interesting work inspired by Rousseau's statement, Adam Smith's *Considerations concerning the First Formation of Language* (1761), raised a number of difficulties that would have confronted the inventors of language. How, for example, could the speechless and primitive inventors of language have conceived of the adjective? The adjective requires the speaker to conceive of a property, such as colour or size, in abstraction from physical objects. While this way of thinking has become natural to us, it was surely too 'metaphysical' for people at the dawn of reason. For Smith, as for Rousseau, language was not the great source of error and delusion castigated in parts of Locke's *Essay*, but rather a mental tool of enormous subtlety and precision.

The challenge faced by the conjectural historians was therefore as follows: discover the means by which humans at the most primitive level of mental development could have gradually created the noblest and most difficult invention in history. Solutions to this problem were extremely varied. Rousseau himself threw up his hands, stating bluntly that language was far too complex to have 'arisen and been established by purely human means'.[22] This hint that God first bestowed language was enthusiastically pursued by Nicolas Beauzée in his 1765 article 'Langue' for the *Encyclopédie*, and by a large number of authors around Europe, including James Beattie in Scotland and Johann Peter Süssmilch in Germany.[23] Contrary to what has sometimes been assumed, the eighteenth century witnessed the widespread revival of belief in a divinely wrought 'Adamic' language. Other authors adopted some version of Condillac's thesis that the first language consisted of spontaneous cries of fear or desire, supplemented by vigorous gestures. Cries and gestures were considered the natural and spontaneous signs of human feeling, universally comprehensible even by the most primitive people. It thus seemed plausible to assume that language had begun with this simple form of communication, which had gradually evolved, over many centuries, into modern grammatical speech.

[21] Rousseau, *Discourse*, p. 154.   [22] Rousseau, *Discourse*, p. 157.
[23] Cf. Beattie, *Theory* (1788); Süssmilch, *Versuch eines Beweises* (1766).

This theory concerning the origin of language had important implications not only for linguistics, but also for many other fields of knowledge. In studies of language and rhetoric, there was renewed interest in the role of 'natural' signs – that is, sounds or marks with some discernible relation with human motives or physical objects. Indeed, many authors insisted that it was simply illogical to believe that the first words were 'perfectly arbitrary', in Locke's phrase. As Hugh Blair argued in *Lectures on Rhetoric and Belles Lettres* (1783), 'To suppose words invented, or names given, to things, in a manner purely arbitrary, without any ground or reason, is to suppose an effect without a cause.'[24] According to some authors of the mid- and late eighteenth century, language had never lost this basis in 'natural' signification. Our words still faintly echoed the spontaneous cries of our primitive ancestors. Johann Wachter, Charles de Brosses, Rowland Jones, Antoine Court de Gébelin and others contrived ingenious proofs that modern languages, and even the symbols of the Roman alphabet, continue to signify natural objects and human ideas by resemblance rather than merely by convention.[25]

Again, linguistic theory began to influence, directly and explicitly, new trends in literary criticism. With the challenge to theories insisting on the arbitrary nature of language, critics and rhetoricians began to explore the possibilities of a poetic language or eloquence that was immediately and naturally related to the human soul. This natural language, it was thought, would be like the ordinary speech of primitive people. In the passionate songs of pre-civilized cultures lay a simplicity, expressiveness and power that poets in a civilized age could only weakly recapture.

The historical decline of poetic language

According to Condillac, the history of language was closely interconnected with the history of poetry, drama and music. The earliest speakers, he conjectured, combined natural cries of passion with 'a language of action' – vigorous gestures that reinforced their sentiments and pointed out objects of fear or desire. The earliest drama similarly combined music, derived directly from natural cries, with gestures and dances developed from the 'language of action'. Moreover, the Greeks and other ancient peoples never thought of separating words from music, for their vocal language, modulated by passionate tones, was naturally melodic. They 'sang' rather than clearly articulated their words. But

---

[24] Blair, *Lectures* (1785), I, p. 129.
[25] Cf. Wachter, *Naturae* (1752); Brosses, *Traité* (1765); Jones, *Hieroglyfic* (1769); Nelme, *Essay* (1772); Gébelin, *Origine*, in *Monde primitif* (1777–93), III.

gradually, as new words were invented and grammar was perfected, people relied less on gesture and tone to make their meaning clear. Language became less musical and poetic, while becoming more exact and clear: 'in proportion as languages became more copious, the mode of speaking by action was abolished by degrees, the voice admitted of less variety of tone . . . and their style began to resemble our prose'.[26]

For a few authors, the process described by Condillac represented an unmitigated and tragic decline. In *Essai sur l'origine des langues*, published posthumously in 1781, Rousseau lamented the corruption of the early melodic tongues, and their transformation into the lucid, harsh and dispassionate languages of the present. Such cold and rational languages, he claimed, were suitable to European nations that had become increasingly avaricious, selfish, and reliant on force rather than eloquence.[27] But for most authors, as for Condillac, the evolution of language had been marked by both gain and loss, the increase of precision being proportionate to the decrease in poetic vigour. In the words of Hugh Blair, 'Language is become, in modern times, more correct indeed; but, however, less striking and animated: In its ancient state, more favourable to poetry and oratory; in its present, to reason and philosophy.'[28]

Language had become less suited to poetry because it had lost much of its original power to express and incite the passions. According to many critics of the mid-century, the language of poetry was closely akin to the language of people stirred by deep feelings. As Kames wrote in *The Elements of Criticism* (1764):

each passion has by nature peculiar tones and expressions suited to it . . . Thus the unpremeditated tones of admiration, are the same in all men; as also of compassion, resentment, and despair . . . The chief talent of a fine writer, is a ready command of the expression that nature dictates to every man when any vivid emotion struggles for utterance; and the chief talent of a fine reader, is a ready command of the tones suited to these expressions.[29]

Kames's statement points to a number of the central differences between the new and the old theories of poetic language. In the more traditional view, still advocated by some authors of the late century, the role of language was to convey the artist's 'thought' or 'design' as clearly and as unobtrusively as possible. As we remarked, Locke distrusted 'Eloquence' that moved the passions rather than instructed the reason. In Kames's time, however, Locke was criticized for ignoring the communication of passions. In a series of lectures on elocution delivered in

---

[26] Condillac, *Essay*, pt 2, sec. 1, ch. 8, p. 229.
[27] Rousseau's history of language is analysed in great detail by Jacques Derrida in *Of Grammatology*, pp. 165–316.
[28] Blair, *Lectures*, I, p. 159.   [29] Lord Kames, *Elements*, II, pp. 119–20.

1758–9, for example, Thomas Sheridan castigated Locke for examining only 'the nature of words, as symbols of ideas: Whilst the nobler branch of language, which consists of the signs of internal emotions, was untouched by him as foreign to his purpose'.[30] Typical of authors in his day, Sheridan distinguished sharply between 'ideas' and 'sentiments'. He agreed that 'ideas' were best communicated by conventional symbols. Nevertheless, the signs of emotions were not arbitrary symbols, but those 'tones, looks, and gestures' universally expressive of our sentiments.

This new interest in tones and accents meant that philosophers and critics increasingly looked to *speech*, rather than writing, as the ideal medium of literary expression. The task of the reader, Kames indicated, was to return the author's text to its original oral form, reintroducing the impassioned tones lost when the words were written down. In *Essai sur l'origine des langues*, Rousseau echoed the common view in his time that only speech was capable of expressing passions – 'Feelings are expressed in speaking, ideas in writing'.[31] He also claimed that where literacy was common, as in Europe, speech had lost its primitive melody of expressive tones, becoming harsh and inexpressive. The rise of literacy was similarly criticized as harmful to the expressive power of speech by Thomas Sheridan, Thomas Reid, Monboddo and J. G. Herder.[32] The distrust of written language shown by these authors – reminiscent of Plato's ancient attack on writing in the *Phaedrus* – marked a significant change in linguistic thought since the seventeenth century. Authors of an earlier time, such as Locke, Dryden, Du Bos, and Addison, rarely placed much importance on the difference between spoken and written discourse. They assumed that speech, no less than writing, consisted merely of arbitrary and outward signs for ideas.[33]

Nostalgia for the more impassioned, poetic language before the rise of 'letters' and modern civilization inspired much of the most popular poetry of late eighteenth century. James Macpherson presented his *Poems of Ossian* (1762–3) as the product of an age in which the heroic stories were recited to music by bards and passed down mainly through the oral traditions of the Highlands.[34] The bold metaphors, broken syntax and archaic inversions of the Ossian poems conformed with late eighteenth-century conceptions of the 'primitive' beauty of early language. Not all scholars were persuaded by the new theories: Samuel Johnson condemned

---

[30] Sheridan, *Course* (1762), p. 92.
[31] Rousseau, *Essay*, in Moran and Gode (eds.), ch. 5, p. 21.
[32] Cf. Sheridan, *Course*, pp. 16–17, and *passim*; Reid, *Inquiry* (1764), in *Works* (1863), ch. 4, sec. 2, pp. 118–19; Monboddo, *Origin*, II, p. 25; Herder, *Essay*, in Moran and Gode (eds.), pp. 92–3.
[33] On changing attitudes to written language, cf. Hudson, *Writing*.
[34] Cf. Macpherson's 'Dissertation concerning the Antiquity, &c. of the Poems of Ossian the Son of Fingal', which prefaced the epic *Fingal* (1762).

the Ossian 'translations' as forgeries because, in part, he doubted that even bad poetry of this sort could exist before writing and literary criticism.[35] But Johnson was out of step with his time. The poems of Thomas Chatterton, Thomas Percy and Robert Burns reveal that many authors found great interest in the belief that older languages, and rustic idiolects, were more spontaneous and 'natural' than modern tongues. Not long after the publication of *The Poems of Ossian*, the English traveller Robert Wood argued that even Homer, founder of the Western literary tradition, belonged to a primitive 'oral tradition'.[36] By the end of the century, Wood's initially egregious thesis was widely accepted, buttressed by the redoubtable historical and philological scholarship of the German classicist F. A. Wolf.[37]

The figurative origins of language

Another way of differentiating between older and new languages concerned their varying reliance on metaphors and other tropes. It was widely concluded that ancient languages are more metaphoric than modern languages. Moreover, it was believed that some languages of the present day – especially Arabic, Persian, and other 'Oriental' languages – continue to rely heavily on figures, a quality that was associated with the supposedly more passionate and 'poetic' souls of non-Europeans. Discussions of figurative language thus led to one of the most important doctrines of late eighteenth-century linguistics – the doctrine that language reflects the innate character of a people or culture.

The theory that language was originally figurative was propounded with great eloquence early in the century by the Neapolitan scholar Giambattista Vico in his *Scienza nuova* (1725; final version 1744). Having received deserved fame only in our age, Vico is now often considered well ahead of his time in appreciating the joint development of language and culture. In fact, Vico's linguistic thought was in many ways highly characteristic of his age. Not only is *Scienza nuova* among the earliest 'Conjectural Histories', but its central philosophical issue, the origin and development of general or abstract concepts, was also central to the linguistic philosophy of Condillac, Rousseau, Smith and many others throughout the century. Like these thinkers, Vico assumed that general concepts, or what he called 'abstract universals', were far beyond the capacities of savages before the invention of language. Vico's conclusion was that these speechless and primitive people must therefore have

---

[35] Cf. Samuel Johnson, *A Journey to the Western Isles of Scotland*, pp. 114–16. This is vol. 9 of *The Yale Works of Samuel Johnson*.
[36] Wood, *Essay* (1769).   [37] Wolf, *Prolegomena to Homer* (1795).

communicated and reasoned by means of tropes. The invention of tropes marked the beginning of reason.

No eighteenth-century thinker developed this thesis with such sophistication and learning. Nevertheless, other authors arrived at similar conclusions about the metaphorical origin of modern language. In a widely cited section of the *Essay concerning Human Understanding*, for example, Locke remarked that most words for mental operations and phenomena were originally metaphors derived from the material world. The word 'spirit', for example, derives from 'breath'.[38] During the late 1730s, when Vico was writing a second version of his *Scienza nuova*, the English bishop William Warburton produced a widely admired study of the figurative origin and evolution of hieroglyphics. Warburton argued that the first writing must have consisted of simple pictures, and that these pictures were later used tropically to represent abstract or non-material concepts.[39] The figurative basis of language was widely examined later in the century, as in J. G. Herder's *Abhandlung über den Ursprung der Sprache* (1772). Having conjectured that the first words were onomatopoeic – the first word for 'lamb', for example, would have sounded like 'ba-a-a' – Herder wondered how the first speakers would denote 'unsounding' objects, like those perceived solely through touch or sight. His answer was that speakers drew analogies between sound and the other senses. For a roughly textured object, they found a rough sound; for a vivid colour, they chose a sharp sound. Herder believed that such metaphorical leaps between the senses, a process at the origin of both language and reason, is especially typical of 'Oriental' languages like Hebrew or Persian: 'Open at random an Oriental dictionary, and you will see the urge to express! How these inventors tore ideas away from one feeling to use them in the expression of another!'[40]

Herder's theory exemplified some important characteristics of the new linguistic philosophy of the eighteenth century. Whereas Locke had been suspicious of all metaphorical language, which betrayed the properly denotative function of linguistic signs, Herder thought of metaphors as expressive of deep and original properties of the human mind. Moreover, Herder thought of language not as a set of external signs for ideas, but rather as 'distinguishing marks' internal to thinking, and fundamental

---

[38] Cf. Locke, *Essay*, bk 3, ch. 1, p. 403.

[39] Warburton's dissertation on the origin of writing and hieroglyphs was included, incongruously, in his work of Christian apologetics, *The Divine Legation of Moses Demonstrated*, 2 vols. (London, 1738–41). This section was separately translated into French by Marc-Antoine Léonard des Malpeines in 1744, and was subsequently more admired and influential in France than in England. On Warburton's place in the development of linguistic thought, cf. V.-David, *Le débat*, pp. 93–103.

[40] Herder, *Essay*, in Moran and Gode (eds.), p. 149.

to the basic operations of reason. He also totally rejected the belief that the first language was 'arbitrary'.[41] In these positions Herder was thoroughly typical of late eighteenth-century thought. In other ways, however, he looked ahead to trends in linguistics that would be fully realized only in the nineteenth century. Most of the philosophers whom we have discussed – Condillac, Vico, Rousseau, Smith – constantly had in mind the difference between 'primitive' people and 'civilized' people. They thought of linguistic history as progressive in one sense, though regressive in another: language, like humanity, had become more rational and philosophical, but less poetic, impassioned and imaginative. But Herder was moving away from this model of linguistic development. Unlike his predecessors, he had no strong interest in the dichotomy of 'primitive' peoples and 'civilized' peoples. Instead, Herder thought of language as reflective of the innate characteristics of a 'people' or a 'nation'. He indicated that Oriental people have produced a more figurative language not because they are less 'civilized', but because they are innately *different* from Europeans – more imaginative and spontaneous, less rational and restrained. Implicitly questioning eighteenth-century beliefs concerning the universality of human nature, Herder treated differences in language as reflective of inherent differences in national character.

It was a short step from this thesis to a form of linguistic analysis based on the concept of *race*. Herder himself was cautious of this term,[42] but it would be central to the linguistics of August and Friedrich Schlegel, and of Wilhelm von Humboldt, in the early nineteenth century. An earlier tradition, as we have seen, thought of poetry as expressing fundamental passions of humanity in a language naturally and universally suited to this task. A new brand of criticism, however, would be more inclined to think of literature as expressive of national character, and as more or less successful depending on the innate genius of the people. In linguistic philosophy and literary criticism, as in other areas of culture, Enlightenment universalism was giving way to the fervent nationalism and sense of racial identity typical of a new era.

In summary, theories of language were quickly changing throughout the century. At the fountainhead of these changes was John Locke, whose discussions of language gave rise to widely divergent currents of linguistic thought. On the one hand, Locke's *Essay* provided a classic statement of the doctrine that words are arbitrary signs of ideas, and should never be confused with real knowledge. Locke's warnings against the 'imperfections' and 'abuse' of words helped to inspire a great age of linguistic consolidation, as grammarians and lexicographers sought to

---

[41] Cf. Herder, *Essay*, in Moran and Gode (eds.), p. 139.
[42] Cf. Barnard (ed.), *Herder*, p. 284.

make the spelling and construction of their languages more consistent and logical. A second branch of linguistic theory grew from Locke's suggestions concerning the mental function of language. Many of the most interesting methodologies developed by eighteenth-century philosophers – the investigations into the origin of language, the contrasts between primitive and modern languages, the speculations concerning the figurative basis of language – were designed to establish and to analyse the close connection between words and reason. In the work of these philosophers, we discover much of our own sense of the importance of language in all areas of human life. We find that eighteenth-century authors saw language not simply as an inefficient tool for communicating thoughts, but rather as the fabric of thought itself, spun from the deepest urges of the human spirit, and intricately interwoven with the evolution of reason and society.

14

The contributions of rhetoric to literary criticism

George A. Kennedy

The importance of rhetoric in the seventeenth and eighteenth centuries results, in the first place, from the attention given it in formal education, beginning in grammar schools for students at the age of about ten and continuing into studies at universities. Late medieval scholasticism had much reduced the emphasis on rhetoric in higher education, but the humanists brought it back, first in Italy, by 1500 in France, Germany, the Low Countries, and Britain. Most of the hundreds of books on rhetoric published and republished throughout the Early Modern period were intended as school texts, from elementary to advanced levels, or represent lectures given in universities. Though rhetoric was always intended to teach composition (often including verse composition) and public speaking, its teachers regularly engaged in rhetorical analyses of literary texts, including the poets, and required their students to do so as well. Directly or indirectly, the study of rhetoric provided the general literate public with a theoretical basis for reading, interpreting, and evaluating texts, including theories of the nature and uses of language, a formidable technical vocabulary, and concepts of style and genre, and it constantly coloured the writings of critics whose major interests were in poetry and drama.

In approaching the literature of the Renaissance and Early Modern period, we need to remember that for most readers of the time the most important literary genre was oratory, specifically Christian preaching: thousands of sermons were not only heard but published and subjected to intensive criticism, both theological and aesthetic. Nor should we forget that for most readers what made composition artistic, in any genre, was the use of tropes, or 'turns', figures, or 'schemes', and topoi, or 'places'. An educated person instinctively recognized and appreciated these, had been practised in their use, and could give them Greek or Latin names. In addition to rules for invention and style, rhetoric provided rules for arrangement, memory, and delivery, and a number of the most popular critical techniques were adapted from ancient writers on rhetoric, including *synkrisis*, judging the merit of an author's works by comparing them with those of another. Comparison of Homer and

Virgil, Demosthenes and Cicero, pagan and patristic writings, and ancients and moderns is a commonplace of the times.

The history of rhetoric in the seventeenth and eighteenth centuries is a complex one, and not yet completely studied. There are at least seven identifiable threads or trends. First, during the seventeenth century, and especially in Protestant countries, Ramism remained a strong influence.[1] It sought to provide a method of binary division in exposition of theory, severely limited each of the disciplines of grammar, rhetoric, and dialectic to avoid any overlap, and dogmatically restricted rhetoric to the study of style and delivery.[2] The general result was to give a higher order of importance to the study of logic, but within rhetoric itself to concentrate attention almost solely on ornamentation, as in the figures of speech. A second major thread was the continued debate over Ciceronianism: the extent to which Cicero was to be taken as the one authoritative model for prose composition, not only in Latin but in the vernacular languages, or whether other models were more appropriate to the times.[3] A third is the impact of the development of the new science and the new logic of Bacon and later Locke in England, or Descartes and later the Port-Royalists in France, with its preference for induction over the syllogism and its rejection of the theory of 'topics'. Bacon had allotted a place for rhetoric in *The Advancement of Learning* (2.18) as the 'art of illustration of transmission' of knowledge, and defined its function as 'to apply reason to imagination for the better moving of the will'. Locke, in the *Third Essay Concerning Human Understanding* righteously rejected rhetoric as an 'art of deceit and errour', 'a perfect cheat'. Although in the *Discours* Descartes had rejected rhetoric as an art of persuasion, he subsequently came to admit that clear and distinct ideas were not always sufficient to persuade and recognized a rhetoric of philosophical discourse, leaving to his successors definition of the precise role of rhetoric, description of its psychological processes, and analysis of the functions of language.[4] Descartes's successors in this sense include Lamy, to be discussed below, Claude Buffier, and César Chesneau Du Marsais.[5] The formation of the French

---

[1] Petrus Ramus, or Pierre de La Ramée (1515–1572), died in the St Bartholomew's Day Massacre and became a kind of Protestant saint. The Jesuits, however, were the major influence on French rhetoric in the seventeenth century; see Fumaroli, *L'Age de l'éloquence*, pp. 223–391.
[2] See Ong, *Ramus*, and for the seventeenth-century influence, Howell, *Logic and Rhetoric*, pp. 146–281.
[3] See Howell, *Logic and Rhetoric*, pp. 282–341, and Vickers, *Francis Bacon*, pp. 96–140.
[4] See Carr, *Descartes*, pp. 26–61 and 169–70.
[5] See Conley, *Rhetoric*, pp. 194–9.

and British Academies, with their encouragement of a fresh approach to learning, literature, and language, can also be associated with these movements. Fourth, and related to the third, is the development of *belles-lettres*, the teaching of literature, including the vernacular literatures, at an advanced level and as literature rather than as a facet of grammar or rhetoric. A fifth is the growing interest in 'the sublime', in which the most important stage was the publication of Boileau's translation of Longinus and his essays thereon (1694). A sixth is the 'elocutionary movement', with its system of oratorical delivery adapted to the drama and to public reading and interpretation of literature. Though there are some Italian and French antecedents, this had its greatest development in Britain.[6] And a final phenomenon is the Scottish Enlightenment of the second half of the eighteenth century, with its extension to England, Ireland, and the American colonies; it provided a synthesis of Ciceronianism, the new logic, 'faculty psychology', and *belles-lettres* in a context where political oratory again became an important force, though preaching remained a concern. Whereas Italy had been the rhetorical leader in the fifteenth century, in the sixteenth the focus began to move north of the Alps, by the seventeenth it centres on France, and by the eighteenth century some of the most important developments are to be found in Britain, but there are writings on rhetoric in our period in all European languages as well as much still in Latin.[7]

Since the body of writing on rhetoric in this period is so extensive, and the interrelationships among works so complex, the function of this chapter will be best served if we leave aside the history of rhetoric as a discipline and try to explore what some important rhetorical treatises have to say about literature and criticism as we understand those terms today. It is worth noting that rhetoric made similar contributions to the theoretical development and terminology of the other arts. Its influence on musical theory was strong, especially among Lutherans, in the sixteenth century, but then somewhat fades; its adaptation to the theory of painting also begins in the sixteenth century, and continues through the eighteenth. Among works in the period here under discussion this can be seen in G. J. Vossius's *De artium et scientiarum natura ac constitutione* (1697), George Trumbull's *Treatise on Ancient Painting* (1740), and Sir Joshua Reynolds's yearly *Discourses* to the Royal Academy between 1768 and 1790.

---

[6] As in John Bulwer's *Chirologia and Chironomia* of 1644 and especially Thomas Sheridan's *Course of Lectures on Elocution* of 1762.
[7] The last of these, still in use in modern reprints, are the two handbooks of J. C. T. Ernesti, *Lexicon technologiae Graecorum rhetoricae* (Leipzig, 1795) and *Lexicon technologiae Latinorum rhetoricae* (Leipzig, 1797).

La Rhétorique, ou L'Art de parler, by Bernard Lamy

Vernacular rhetorics began to appear in western Europe in the sixteenth century,[8] and are relatively common in the seventeenth. Their appearance in France was somewhat slower than elsewhere, but in the second half of the seventeenth century French writers made a major effort to recast rhetoric in a form appropriate to the needs of the time and applicable to their own language. Examples include *La Rhétorique françoise* by René Bary (1659) and *Réflexions sur l'usage de l'éloquence de ce temps* by René Rapin (1671), the latter important in the early development of the concept of *belles-lettres*. A much more widely read work was *De l'Art de parler*, published anonymously by Bernard Lamy (1640–1715) in Paris in 1675.[9] Anonymity is assumed to have been sought to protect Lamy, and the Congregation of the Oratory of Jesus of which he was a member, from well-deserved charges of Cartesianism.[10] In 1676 an English version (with some departures from the French text and omitting the chapter on preaching) was published in London. The translators, who cannot be identified with certainty, attributed the French original to 'Messieurs du Port-Royal'. Lamy was not a Port-Royalist, but he had benefited from some of their thinking, and readers easily accepted the new rhetoric as the counterpart of the well-known Port-Royal *Logic* and grammars, thus greatly increasing its sale. The English edition was repeatedly republished in the eighteenth century, but without inclusion of Lamy's revisions of the French text.

Although he admired and repeatedly quotes Cicero, Lamy's rhetoric is not traditional Ciceronianism. Quintilian and St Augustine are important authorities for him; the general approach to rhetoric is dialectical and thus almost Aristotelian, though Aristotle is dismissed with little notice; the influence of Ramism is slight, that of Cartesian method strong; and there are many points of contact with the Port-Royal *Logic*, beginning with the title.[11] The rhetorical theory is extensively illustrated, not only with Greek and Latin quotations, many of them from poets, but with examples from the Bible and from French poetry. Some of the latter cannot be identified and may be Lamy's own work.

---

[8] The first in English was *The Arte or Crafte of Rhetoryke*, by Leonard Cox (London, 1530?), based on Philipp Melanchthon's *Elementorum Rhetorices Libri Duo* of 1519.

[9] He is first identified as the author in the third edition (1688), where the title is changed to *La Rhétorique, ou L'Art de parler*, and continued to revise the work through five editions until his death in 1715.

[10] On the influence of Descartes, see Lamy, *Rhetorics*, pp. 131–9, and Carr, *Descartes*, pp. 125–67.

[11] It parallels *La Logique, ou L'Art de penser*, by Antoine Arnauld and Pierre Nicole, first published in 1662.

Lamy reorganized the subject of rhetoric from its traditional Ciceronian structure (invention, arrangement, style, memory, and delivery) to begin with the nature of language:

The Idea's present to our Mind (when it commands the Organs of the Voice to form such Sounds as are the signs of those Idea's) are the Soul of our Words: the Sounds form'd by the Organs of our Voice (which, though of themselves they have nothing resembling those Idea's, do notwithstanding represent them) are the material part, and may be called the Body of our words.[12]

The whole process of expression, whether in conversation or literary composition, is one of finding the most precise way to convey the ideas and images present in the mind of the author. Although the nature of language makes complete control impossible, authorial intent is basic to Lamy's view of composition and interpretation, as it was to all others in this period. He does not consider the possibility, even in poetry, that there is some way in which thought might follow words rather than the other way around.

'It is the nature of a Sign, to be known to those who make use of it' (p. 203). 'And as good Men are the properest Examples to those who desire to live well; so the practice of Speakers is the fittest Rule for those who would speak well ... But it is no hard matter to discern betwixt the good and the bad; betwixt the depraved Language of the comon people, and the noble and refin'd Expressions of the Gentry, whose condition and merits have advanced them above the others' (p. 204). Yet it is 'impossible to contrive words for all the forms of our thoughts: The ordinary terms are not always adequate, they are either too strong or too weak' (p. 213). Thus in speaking and writing we must resort to tropes: 'These Tropes do not signifie the things to which they are applied, otherwise than by reason of the connexion and reference that those things have with the things whose Names they do properly bear' (p. 214). The basic trope is metonymy, 'the putting off of one Name for another' (p. 214). In metonymy there is a 'strong relation' between the word used and the thing indicated, as when we say 'Paris is allarm'd'. In contrast, metaphor 'is a Trope by which we put a strange and remote word' for another, as in Deuteronomy 28:23 where it is said, 'The heavens were brass', meaning there was a drought.

The only use of tropes 'is to make us more intelligible' (p. 219). In contrast, the primary function of figures is to convey emotion; thus characteristic figures are exclamation, doubt, ellipsis, aposiopesis, etc. Figures can, however, also illustrate obscure truths and render the mind

---

[12] Quotations are from Harwood's edition of the English translation of 1676, pp. 181–2.

attentive. 'Figures proper to perswade are not to be sought for: It is the heat wherewith we are animated for the defence of Truth that produces them, and continues them in our Discourse; so that indeed Eloquence is nothing but the Effect of our Zeal' (p. 249). These are called 'figures in discourse', but there are also figures that 'are traced at leisure by a mind that is quiet' (p. 274), such as anaphora. These are used for ornamentation and give pleasure. The discussion of tropes and figures then leads to questions of style in a larger way, and only in a final section on the art of persuasion does Lamy briefly take up rhetorical invention, grudgingly allowing some possible utility to 'topics', and arrangement. The tendency of rhetoric to turn its attention from public address to literary composition is a recurring phenomenon in the history of the subject, beginning in classical times, only occasionally reversed in periods when opportunities for political oratory opened up, as in the early Renaissance in Italy and in the seventeenth and eighteenth centuries in Britain.

Lamy provides an extended discussion of versification, comparing the usage of French with that of Greek and Latin. Rhyme is 'very proper for the better distinction of the measures of Verse', but historically resulted from the loss of a sense of the quantity of vowels and becomes 'quickly tyresome, unless we be careful to occupy the mind of the Reader by the richness and variety of our thoughts, so as it may not be sensible of their simplicity' (p. 289). Lamy is much interested in what he calls the 'strange sympathy betwixt the Soul and Numbers' (p. 291), and also in the effects of different sounds. Style depends on imagination, memory, and judgement; it reflects the character of the mind of the author, of the climate, and of the age (p. 310). He adapts the classical theory of the three styles, lofty (or grand), middle, and plain, applying them, as others had done, both to prose and poetry. Style should be easy, strong, pleasant, and appropriate. The genres of prose are given priority in the way traditional with rhetoricians: oratory has pride of place, followed by history and philosophy (pp. 320–5). Then comes a section on the style of a poet (pp. 325–8):

A Poet is unconfin'd; we give him what liberty he pleases, and do not pin him up to the Laws of Custom: This liberty is easily justified. Poets are desirous to delight and surprise us by things that are great, wonderful, extraordinary: they cannot arrive at their designed end, unless they maintain the grandeur of things by the grandeur of words. All that they say being extraordinary, their expressions being to equal the dignity of their matter, ought likewise to be extraordinary; for this cause in Poetry we say nothing without hyperboles and metaphors ... We are so accustomed to conceive only by the mediation of our senses, that we are not able to comprehend barely with our minds, unless what we would understand be grounded and established upon some sensible experiment. Hence it is that abstracted Expressions are Enigma's to most people; and those only please which are sensible, and do form in the Imagination the picture of the thing that is to be conceived.

(pp. 325–6)

In the ensuing chapter Lamy sets out what might be called the dogma of neo-classicism, and the critical importance of his work is to a considerable extent the codification he gives to neo-classical aesthetic values, as they were understood by students for the next century:

A discourse is beautiful when it is compos'd according to the Rules of Art; it is great when it is more than ordinary [sic] perspicuous; when there is not one equivocation; no sentence unintelligible; no expression ambiguous; when it is well-disposed, and the mind of the Reader led directly to the end of the design, without the *remora* or impediment of impertinent words. Such clearness like a Torch dispells all obscurity, and makes every thing visible.

(p. 329)

But in the same chapter Lamy quotes Longinus, *On the Sublime*, with approval; Boileau's translation had been published the previous year and was already laying the groundwork for a critical development that would lead past neo-classical clarity to Romanticism.

A final section with interest for literary criticism is what Lamy has to say about comedy in his discussion of the use of the emotions to persuade, its traditional place in a rhetorical treatise since Cicero's *De oratore*. (Lamy does not discuss tragedy.)

The Poets in their Comedy's pretend to mock people out of their Vices; yet their pretensions are vain, experience making too evident that a Reader of this sort of Plays never made any serious conversion. The cause is plain, we despise and laugh at only such things as we think below us, and such as are but trifles in our estimation ... Poets in their Comedies labour not to give an aversion for Vice; their business is only to make it ridiculous; so they accustom their Readers to look upon Debauches as inconsiderable offenses ... The descriptions of an Adulterer never made any man chast [sic], and yet those sort of Crimes are generally the subject of Comedy's.

(pp. 367–8)

Fénelon's *Dialogues*

Within the tradition of classical rhetoric, Ciceronianism, both in its view of the 'duties of the orator' as to teach, to please, and to move, and in its preference for amplification and periodicity, is the dominant pattern, but as Greek works became better known the philosophical strand that had begun with Plato and Aristotle and that demanded a rhetoric of truth begins to re-emerge. There are some signs of this in Lamy's work, but its greatest expression in French comes in the *Dialogues sur l'éloquence en général et celle de la chaire en particulier*, written by François Fénelon in the late 1670s, though not published until 1718. It had numerous later editions and was translated into German, Spanish, Dutch, and English. It also represents the climax of the discussions of preaching that had engaged so much of the attention of rhetorically minded critics in seventeenth-century France. Fénelon saw the fashion for elegant preaching in terms of the dangers Plato had seen in the speeches of the sophists, and his *Dialogues* are a neo-classical version of the *Phaedrus*, with some debt to Cicero's *On the Orator*. Again Boileau's translation of Longinus as well as his *L'Art poétique*, is an influence, and again the authority of St Augustine is appealed to and use made of the insistence of the Port-Royalists on logical integrity of thought.

Although Fénelon denies he is writing a 'complete rhetoric', in fact he touches on all the traditional parts of the discipline; and although his subject is specifically preaching, he has much to say about eloquence generally, including observations on poetry. George Saintsbury, author of the first real history of criticism, thought highly of Fénelon as a critic,[13] but Fénelon's remarks about Homer and Virgil, Isocrates, Demosthenes, Cicero, the Bible, and the Fathers are perhaps better regarded as elegant phrasings of ideas that had often been expressed before. He is an austere judge, whose values are fidelity to the truths of religion and nature. In the first dialogue he seems willing to join Plato in expelling the poets from any ideal state and makes one of the speakers remark 'I wish to know whether things are true before I find them beautiful'.[14]

The Ciceronian 'duties of the orator' (to teach, to please, and to move) are recast by Fénelon as 'proving, portraying, and striking' (p. 92). 'To portray is not only to describe things but to represent their surrounding features in so lively and so concrete a way that the listener imagines himself almost seeing them.' As an example, he instances Virgil's description of the death of Dido in *Aeneid* VI. This is followed by a passage which is perhaps the most specific statement of literary theory in the *Dialogues*. Poetry is not a matter of the use of verse:

In the last analysis, poetry is nothing but a lively fiction which portrays nature. If one does not have this genius to portray, never can one impress things upon the soul of the listener – all is dry, flat, boring. Since the time of the original thing, man has been entirely enmeshed in palpable things. It

[13] Saintsbury, *History*, II, pp. 305–6.
[14] Quotations are from Fénelon, *Dialogues*, p. 60.

is his master misfortune that he cannot for long be attentive to that which is abstract. It is necessary to give a physical body to all the instructions which one wishes to inject into his soul. It is necessary to have images to beguile him. Thus it comes about that, soon after the fall of man, poetry and idolatry, always joined together, entirely made up the religion of the ancients. But let us not digress. You well understand that poetry, that is to say, the lively portraiture of things, is as it were the soul of eloquence ... If true orators are poets ... poets are also orators, because poetry is by rights persuasive.

(p. 94)

Some ideas similar to these were to be treated in greater depth by the only important Italian writer on rhetoric of the eighteenth century, Giambattista Vico, in his *Scienza nuova* (1725 and later), though Vico's systematic rhetoric, *Institutiones oratoriae* (1711), is a work in the tradition of Cicero and Quintilian.

European rhetorics of the eighteenth century

Reform of the educational system, with greater attention to composition in the national language, study of modern authors, and cultivation of taste and elegance of style, became popular causes on the continent of Europe by the middle of the eighteenth century. The most influential work, with many editions throughout Europe, was that by Charles Rollin: *Traité des études: De la manière d'enseigner et d'étudier les Belles-Lettres* (1726–8). It provided teachers with guidelines of what to look for in the reading and explication of texts in terms of traditional rhetoric: arguments, ideas, word choice, arrangement, figures, and emotion.[15] Models are quoted from the eloquence of the bar, the pulpit, and the Scriptures. The German counterpart is J. C. Gottsched's *Ausführliche Redekunst* of 1728 and later, with its models of German eloquence, to which is added a discussion of the faculty psychology of Christian Wolff.[16] The major Spanish rhetoric of the eighteenth century is the work of Gregorio Mayans y Siscar (1757, 1786), basically Ciceronian, but also seeking to adapt rhetoric to the perceived needs of the national language.[17] The subsequent history of French rhetoric, and of European rhetoric generally, was a narrowing of focus into an exclusive concern with tropes and figures. That at least is the view of most observers, including Gérard Genette, who describes the tradition as established by the *Traité des tropes* by César Chesneau Du Marsais (1730) and continued

---

[15] See Conley, *Rhetoric*, pp. 201–3 and 230–1.
[16] See Conley, *Rhetoric*, pp. 205–7 and 231–2.
[17] See Conley, *Rhetoric*, pp. 207–10 and 232–4.

in the authoritative handbooks of Pierre Fontanier, *Commentaire raisonné des tropes* (1818) and *Traité générale des figures du discours* (1821–7).[18] In the twentieth century this has led to such work as that of the 'Groupe *mu*' in Liège. The Anglo-American tradition, now represented by American research in speech communication, has been rather different, preserving the Ciceronian tradition of focus on public address and argumentation, an inheritance of eighteenth-century British rhetorics.

The 'lectures' of Adam Smith

Opportunities for political oratory were greater in Britain than in France, and perhaps for this reason it is in Britain, and in the excitable British colonies of North America, that the classical tradition in rhetoric as public address enjoyed a major revival in the second half of the eighteenth century. Though predominantly Ciceronian in its conception of rhetoric as centrally concerned with civic oratory, the revival is accompanied by appreciation of the new logic and study of psychology and by an interest in *belles-lettres*. Eventually the latter interest predominated, and the professorships of rhetoric that were established in the eighteenth century became by the mid-nineteenth professorships of English literature. The new synthesis can perhaps be said to begin with John Ward's appointment as Professor of Rhetoric at Gresham College in London in 1720, but came of age in Aberdeen, Edinburgh, and Glasgow in the middle of the century.[19]

Adam Smith, later to achieve fame as the author of *The Wealth of Nations*, lectured on rhetoric in Edinburgh in 1748–9 and perhaps in the two following academic years as well, and continued regular lectures on the subject as Professor of Logic and Moral Philosophy in Glasgow from 1751 to 1763. Though a little of the material was published during Smith's lifetime, the lectures as a whole are known from student notebooks containing fairly full transcriptions of them, of which the most important, from 1762–3, was discovered by J. M. Lothian in 1958. Though the lectures were thus known only to those who heard them, that included many of the intellectual leaders of Scotland in this and the next generation, including Hugh Blair.[20]

---

[18] See Genette, *Figures*, pp. 103–26. As he indicates, however, there were neo-classical French rhetorics that conceived the subject more broadly: e.g., J. B. L. Crevier's *Rhétorique françoise* of 1765. See Varga, *Rhétorique*, pp. 16–17.

[19] Howell, *Eighteenth-Century Rhetoric*, pp. 83–124, 536–74. An Irish example is John Lawson's *Lectures concerning Oratory Delivered in Trinity College, Dublin* (1758); the first American version was John Witherspoon's *Lectures on Moral Philosophy and Eloquence*, given at Princeton between 1768 and 1794.

[20] Smith, ed. Lothian, p. xxi.

Smith begins with observations on the nature and history of language, resembling what Lamy had said and similarly leading into discussion of tropes and figures, but this is not a subject to which he accords much importance. 'It is, however, from the consideration of these figures, and divisions and subdivisions of them, that so many systems of rhetoric, both ancient and modern, have been formed. They are generally a very silly set of books and not at all instructive', and he quotes, slightly inaccurately, Butler's couplet in *Hudibras* (1.1.89–90): 'For all the rhetoricians rules / Are but the naming of his tools.'[21] Smith's notion of a metaphor is an alteration in the signification of a word on the basis of some resemblance or analogy, e.g. 'the slings and arrows of adverse fortune';[22] metonymy is an alteration that involves some kind of connection but lacks resemblance: 'drinks off a *bowl*'. Beauty does not consist in the use of figures; style is beautiful 'when the words neatly and properly expressed the thing to be described, and conveyed the sentiment the author entertained of it and desired to communicate to his hearers' (p. 36). He then proceeds in the eighth and ninth lectures to consider the style of Jonathan Swift, whose real worth, he says (p. 37) has not been appreciated. 'All his words shew a complete knowledge of his subject. He does not, indeed, introduce anything foreign to his subject, in order to display his knowledge of his subject; but then he never omits anything necessary' (p. 38). Swift's form of ridicule consists in exposing mean objects by considering them grand; the Greek satirist Lucian, in contrast, exposed meanness or littleness in grand objects (p. 44). Joseph Addison, the subject of the tenth lecture, more resembles Lucian in his 'gaiety', but is hindered by his 'modesty'. The eleventh lecture is devoted to the style of Shaftesbury, whose reputation Smith regards as much inflated. Shaftesbury's style is much too abstract and results ultimately from his 'very puny and weakly constitution' (p. 52; cf. p. 54).

After examining these three exemplars, two favourably, one adversely, Smith moves on to the subject of composition in general, with appraisals, occasionally extensive, of ancient and modern authors. Though he does not expressly do so, it would be possible to construct a 'canon' from his lectures. In addition to the standard classical authors, especially Homer, Sophocles, Demosthenes, Cicero, and Virgil (Smith, predictably for his time and place, has a low opinion of Plato and Euripides, but his preference for Gray over Horace (p. 122) is something of a surprise), it would apparently include 'Ossian' in James Macpherson's (fictitious) 'translation' (p. 131), but not Chaucer, who is never mentioned;

---

[21] Smith, ed. Lothian, pp. 23–4.
[22] Again he slightly misquotes, from *Hamlet*. He seems to have spoken without notes, and sometimes without texts of the authors he discussed.

probably Shakespeare, though he has his faults, but not Jonson or Marlowe (unmentioned); Milton, but not Bunyan (unmentioned); Racine (preferred to Shakespeare, p. 118), but not Corneille, 'whom the French prefer' (p. 121); Swift, but not Defoe (unmentioned); Pope, but not Dryden (tragi-comedy is 'monstrous', and Dryden's *Spanish Friar*, his only work cited, would have been better as a separate tragedy and comedy, p. 117). Romances, including Ariosto's (p. 91), are scorned; Smith's one mention of Cervantes is ambiguous (p. 127), and he does not have a very high opinion of Spenser (p. 63). As to the novel, its only merit is 'newness' (p. 91). The judgements throughout reflect a dislike of the fanciful and a preference for formal regularity.

Though historiography is regularly the second prose genre after oratory in the view of writers on rhetoric, Smith gives it more than usual emphasis, devoting lectures 16–20 to the subject and often citing historians elsewhere in his work. Intense emotion, he claims, cannot be described adequately in narrative writing and it is best not to attempt an indirect description, 'but barely relate the circumstances the persons were in' (p. 82). Causes of historical events are to be explored only in proportion to the importance of the event. 'Describing characters is no essential part of a historical narrative' (p. 89). The greatest historians are Thucydides and Livy; among the moderns, the best is Machiavelli (pp. 110–11); Clarendon is too interested in representing character, the language of Burnet is what one would expect from 'an old nurse, rather than a gentleman', and Rapin, though not without some merit, is too concerned with the private affairs of monarchs and great men (pp. 112–13). Gibbon, of course, was not yet known.

The twenty-first lecture deals with poetry, which Smith regards as intended solely to amuse: no one reads Homer to be instructed about the Trojan War, or Milton to increase his Christian faith (pp. 116–17). Since the subjects of poetry are distant from reality, the reader is not offended at ridiculous stories and embellishments. The unities of plot, time, and place are not required in epic but are in drama. The problem in violating unity of time and place is not that it interrupts the deception of the audience: 'We know that we are in the playhouse, that the persons before us are actors, and that the thing represented either happened before, or perhaps never happened at all' (p. 118). Dr Johnson makes a similar point in his *Preface to Shakespeare*, published two years later. The real objection to violation of the unities, according to Smith, is that we become uneasy to know what has happened in the intervening time or space. Kings and nobles make the best characters in tragedy because 'we are too much accustomed to the misfortunes of people below or equal with us to be greatly affected by them' (p. 120). Lyric, elegiac, and pastoral poetry should not deal with great passions because such poems are too short to give them adequate development. 'A temper of mind that differs very little from the common tranquillity of mind is what we can best enter into, by the perusal of a small piece' (p. 122). Fine examples are 'The Church-yard' or 'Eton College' by 'Mr Gray'.

At this point Smith's student should have an understanding of language, style, narrative, characterization, and the chief features of the literary genres. It was thus now possible to move on to the climactic discussion of oratory in the last ten chapters, toward which the whole series has been moving. Although it was one of Smith's objectives to prepare his students for activity in public address, he concentrated on giving them an understanding of great classical oratory, especially the works of Demosthenes and Cicero, and there is surprisingly little reference to modern oratory, nor anything at all about preaching. This reflects Smith's own interests rather than a pervasive secularization of rhetoric. Even odder, when at the end of the last lecture he does make some remarks about speech in contemporary conditions, contrasting that of the House of Lords to the House of Commons, he seems to regard the Demosthenic and Ciceronian models as unsuitable for modern conditions. A final oddity is that he takes no account of the essay *Of Eloquence* that his fellow Scot, David Hume, had published in 1743 and in which he had tried to explain the reasons why British oratory fell so far below the classical. Hume's conclusion was that modern speakers simply do not make the effort, or lack the genius and judgement of the past: 'A few successful attempts of this nature might rouse the genius of the nation, excite the emulation of the youth, and accustom our ears to a more sublime and more pathetic elocution, than what we have been hitherto entertained with.'[23] Our record of Smith's lectures is incomplete, ending with what he said on Friday, 18 February 1763; it is probable that he continued with observations on the current scene, and he may well have sought to inspire the motivation Hume looked for. In fact, eloquence in the English tongue was about to enter a new golden age, represented by Edmund Burke, William Pitt, and their nineteenth-century successors, and in America by Patrick Henry and later Daniel Webster.

Hugh Blair's *Lectures on Rhetoric and Belles Lettres*

The most original work on rhetoric published by a Scot is probably *The Philosophy of Rhetoric* (1776) by an Aberdonian, George Campbell.

[23] 'Of Eloquence', *Essays*, p. 170.

Working in the tradition of British empiricism, he tried to define the basic principles of rhetoric in terms of the 'faculties' of human psychology, and he has rather little to say about literature. In the preface he acknowledges a debt to Kames's *Elements of Criticism* (1762). That work is primarily a psychological study of the emotions and their expression in all the arts. Though it contains a extended account of the psychology of figures, the author seems deliberately to avoid making any connections with rhetoric as understood at the time and in discussing literary genres ignores oratory. The works of Kames and Campbell were widely studied, but by far the most influential late eighteenth-century contributions to rhetorical criticism were the *Lectures on Rhetoric and Belles Lettres* of Hugh Blair, minister of the High Church of St Giles in Edinburgh, editor of the *Works of Shakespear* in eight volumes (1753), and author of an appreciative *Dissertation on Ossian*. He had heard Adam Smith's lectures, knew the works of Lord Kames and Campbell, and began to give a course on rhetoric in 1759. In 1762 George III appointed him Regius Professor of Rhetoric and Belles Lettres at the University of Edinburgh, a chair he held until retirement in 1783, when the *Lectures* were published. They were to see at least 130 editions over more than a century, and especially in America were the basic textbook of rhetoric and criticism for generations of students, only partially displaced by the last of the neo-classical rhetorics, Archbishop Whately's *Elements of Rhetoric* of 1828. Thus again they provide an insight into what may be called the standard academic view of literature, against which the innovations of the romantics and their successors should be viewed.

Blair followed the general structure of the subject he had heard from Adam Smith, moving from an investigation of the nature of language to style, to civic oratory, and to literature generally, but he emphasizes literary criticism from the beginning by introductory lectures on taste, criticism, the sublime, and beauty, and he greatly amplifies the final discussion of *belles-lettres*. 'True Criticism', he says, 'is the application of Taste and of good sense to the several fine arts. The object which it proposes is, to distinguish what is beautiful and what is faulty in every performance; from particular instances to ascend to general principles; and so to form rules or conclusions concerning the several kinds of beauty in the works of Genius.'[24] Criticism is founded on experience, on observation of such beauties as have been found to please mankind most generally. 'Critical rules are designed chiefly to shew the faults that ought to be avoided' (p. 38).

---

[24] Blair, ed. Harding, I, p. 36.

The public is the supreme judge, but the genuine public Taste does not always appear in the first applause given upon the publication of any new work. There are both a great vulgar and a small, apt to be catched and dazzled by very superficial beauties, the admiration of which in a little time passes away: and sometimes a writer may acquire great temporary reputation merely by his compliance with the passions and prejudices, with the party-spirit or superstitious notions, that may chance to rule for a time almost a whole nation. In such cases, though the Public may seem to praise, true Criticism may with reason condemn; and it will in progress of time gain the ascendant: for the judgment of true criticism, and the voice of the Public, when once become unprejudiced and dispassionate, will ever coincide at last.

(p. 39)

A twentieth-century reader might reasonably see here, in the first generation of professors of literature, the beginnings of an academic authority that, in its confidence in its own objectivity, was fully prepared to tell students what was good and what was bad and to outlast vulgar enthusiasms. Blair has to admit, however, that there are problems in his view. Sometimes the public wins!

Such are the plays of Shakespeare, which, considered as dramatic poems, are irregular in the highest degree. But then we are to remark, that they have gained the public admiration, not by their being irregular, not by their transgressions of the rules of art, but in spite of such transgressions. They possess other beauties which are conformable to just rules; and the force of these beauties has been so great as to overpower all censure, and to give the Public a degree of satisfaction superior to the disgust arising from their blemishes. Shakespeare pleases, not by his bringing the transactions of many years into one play; not by his grotesque mixtures of Tragedy and Comedy in one piece, nor by the strained thoughts and affected witticisms, which he sometimes employs. These we consider as blemishes, and impute them to the grossness of the age in which he lived. But he pleases by his animated and masterly representations of character, by the liveliness of his descriptions, the force of his sentiments, and his possessing, beyond all writers, the natural language of passion.

(p. 40)

Thus the rules still apply and the professor wins.

As this might suggest, perhaps the biggest blind spot in Blair's discussion of literature is his lack of appreciation of the Elizabethans. He proceeds genre by genre and within the genres historically, but he clearly regards the history of literature as having only two great periods: the classical, which is his first love, and the neo-classical in France and England. The prose author whom he discusses in the greatest detail (four whole lectures) and whom he admires with only minor reservations is Joseph

Addison. A positive result of this is Blair's sponsorship for generations of students of an elegant, natural style, trimmed of the excesses of rhetorical ornament – like Smith's, his interest in tropes and figures is remarkably slight – seeking clarity and vigour. If he is one of the last major spokesmen for classicism, a kind of British Quintilian (an authority he revered), he is also perhaps the one that contributed most to what afterlife it was to have among the public in the next century.

Formal education, even at the university level, tends to be conservative, and for much of the nineteenth century textbooks on rhetoric continued along neo-classical lines, but rhetoric as a traditional discipline with a highly structured system gradually lost ground to romantic ideas of free composition and distaste for poetic diction and conventional ornament. The decline of the study of Greek and Latin in the late nineteenth century further contributed to the demise of rhetoric as a part of the curriculum. In the second half of the twentieth century, however, rhetoric has begun to reemerge in a variety of ways, and for the first time since Cicero its history has been seriously studied in terms of its relationship to literature and other arts. A fully satisfactory way, however, has not yet been found to bridge the gap that widened in the eighteenth century between rhetoric as the study of tropes and figures and rhetoric as speech communication, between Europe and the English-speaking world.

15

Theories of style

Pat Rogers

I

Whilst recognizing the need to avoid crude evolutionary formulas, a volume of this kind must chart broad patterns and large-scale movements of thought. It is therefore a useful simplification, rather than a savage caricature, to describe the development of theorizing about literary style in this period as following a fairly steady progression. At the end of the seventeenth century, the prime centre of influence in European criticism remained France. Equally, the main attention still concentrated on epic and, to a slightly lesser extent, tragedy. Stylistic issues were derivative from broader moral questions about the import and bearing of a text, conceived as an exemplary and instructive (if not always precisely didactic) statement. In this phase of critical history, poetic language was not the heart of poetics – rather an instrument of a higher ordonnance which privileged doctrine and form.

All this is true despite the fact that the greatest practising critic of the later seventeenth century was an Englishman, John Dryden, who was himself a great master of language and a thinker about literature with no excessive reverence for neo-Aristotelian pieties. It is also true despite the fact that the famous quarrel of Ancients and Moderns dominated the last decade of the century, and here the Moderns seemed ready to overturn those traditional pieties which included a ranking of *elocutio* well beneath *inventio* and even *dispositio*.[1] It is true despite the fact that Boileau himself had translated Longinus in 1674 and begun the meteoric ascent of 'sublimity' as a critical watchword. It is true despite the fact that most of the forces which shifted the focus of stylistic discussion after 1700 were already present before that date; indeed, the founding fathers of the new movements, including Addison and Pope, were born in the old century and grew up in the brief window of history when neo-classicism really could be said to dominate the cultural and educational landscape. Orthodoxies last only a few years after they are enunciated,

---

[1] The best treatment of the subject as a whole is now that of Joseph M. Levine, *Ancients and Moderns* (Ithaca, 1991).

but those happened to be the years in which the formulators of high Augustan doctrine in England had grown up.

To be more explicit, the recognized lawgivers were four. They are included in those named by James Harris in the history of criticism which he set at the head of his *Philological Inquiries* (posthumously published, 1781). 'At length', Harris tells us, 'after a long and barbarous period, when the shades of Monkery began to retire, and the light of Humanity once again to dawn, the Arts also of CRITICISM insensibly revived.' But the 'Authors of THE PHILOSOPHICAL SORT' were 'not many in number' – the only names Harris can think of are Vida and the elder Scaliger among the Italians, and 'among the *French* . . . Rapin, Bouhours, Boileau*, together with *Bossu*, the most methodical and accurate of them all'.[2] The least known of these figures today is Dominique Bouhours (1628–1702), although in his time his work *La manière de bien penser dans les ouvrages d'esprit* (1687) commanded a good deal of respect and earned for its author a well-known commendation in *Spectator* 62 as 'the most penetrating of all the French critics'.[3] But this was an eccentric view. The other three critics were far more widely quoted, and whilst Boileau's *L'Art poétique* (1674) earned the most commendation as a treatise – especially among practising writers – the staple source of dogma, day in and day out, was rather René Le Bossu with his *Traité du poème épique* (1675), which set out the full grammar of neo-classical criticism. Le Bossu's emphasis is on the primacy of the fable, and on the structural consequences (e.g., how episodes are to be introduced without distracting us from the main plot). Both critics were deferred to with what now seems astonishing timidity; and Le Bossu had only the correctness of his doctrine to support his character, whereas Boileau could also be regarded as a significant poet. (In Dodsley's *Museum* of 1746, a table is drawn up showing 'The Balance of Poets'; Boileau gets pretty good grades all round, including an 18 out of 20 for 'critical ordonnance' which was matched only by Homer, Sophocles and Terence.)[4]

The crucial figure in the next phase is certainly Joseph Addison, another pre-eminence which might surprise us today. Along with Pope, his intervention ensured that the previous French dominance in critical thought gradually disappeared; that Milton joined the ancients as a prime site for the analysis of epic; and that a wider range of issues was explored, with an increasing tendency for writers to discuss localized effects (especially verbal habits and devices such as puns). At the same moment John Dennis was producing a mode of criticism as starkly legislative as anything in the previous era, and many of the minor English authors

---

[2] Harris, *Inquiries*, pp. 17–18.   [3] Elledge, *Essays*, I, p. 15.
[4] See Clark, *Boileau*, p. 461.

were following up specialisms and enthusiasms – Leonard Welsted the sublime vogue, John Hughes the Spenserian, Joseph Spence the antiquarian and archaeological, Lewis Theobald the Shakespearian. In a different vein Shaftesbury was taking criticism in the direction of the yet unchristened (and maybe unborn) field of aesthetics. None the less, the essential initiatives were those of Addison, in particular, and Pope. Elsewhere the language evolves but the issues remain the same: that could be said both of Gian Vicenzo Gravina, with his search for epic roots in *Della ragion poetica* (1708), and of Voltaire, with his attempt to historicize and contextualize Homer in his 'Essay on Epick Poetry' (first published in English, 1727).

The third, and for our purposes decisive, phase occurs in the middle of the eighteenth century. The initiative remains in Britain, and the most distinguished critic of the age is clearly Samuel Johnson. However, the wider movement hinges on the effort to found a new 'philosophic' criticism, otherwise describable as a neo-rhetorical approach to literature. Its intellectual origins go back in most cases to Locke, although in the case of James Harris the effort is to displace empiricism with a poetic based on idealist and Platonic models.[5] At the heart of the movement lie Scottish thinkers, developing criticism as one more branch of the science of man in the wake of the Edinburgh Enlightenment. Although David Hume wrote a number of interesting critical essays, his relevance is mainly that of providing a philosophic support-system, since he compiled no sustained body of his own theory regarding literature. The Scots who filled this gap included Lord Kames, Hugh Blair and George Campbell, all of whom wrote full-blown handbooks of the new poetic. Other critics, rhetoricians and philosophers who augmented the Scottish push were James Beattie, Alexander Gerard, Archibald Alison and even Monboddo, whose theories on the origins of human speech bore occasionally on the more narrowly literary issues of style which came under review elsewhere. Equally, theorizing about epic diction in this era could not always be separated from the contentious topic of Ossian, even though most commentators on Macpherson's prose poem, such as Blair, were able to take advantage of the work's 'translated' status to shy away from direct stylistic comment in the direction of broad cultural comment.[6] At a remote level, the general assumptions of the Scottish Enlightenment must have entered into the reckoning of critics in this category: Adam Smith had given his lectures on rhetoric and *belleslettres* before he pioneered his own version of cultural history or set out

---

[5] For Harris's general intellectual roots and attitudes, see Probyn, *Sociable Humanist*, esp. pp. 140–78, 239–86.
[6] See, for example, Blair's *Critical Dissertation on the Poems of Ossian* (1763), of which full extracts are given in Elledge, *Essays*, II, pp. 848–59.

his economic map of mankind, but he felt the impress of Hume in most stages of his career. Equally, Kames wrote much on law, history and anthropology outside of his *Elements of Criticism*.[7] But a line must be drawn somewhere, and here we are occupied by the contribution of these writers to the creation of a revived form of rhetoric.

Apart from Johnson, there were other notable critics at work in England at the same time, most notably those developing the historical study of literature by means of explorations of earlier English writing (Thomas Warton), sacred texts (Robert Lowth), or Celtic roots (Thomas Gray). Richard Hurd was forcing the classical tradition into a staged collision with chivalry and romance; Horace Walpole was endeavouring to import a desirable 'gothic' (as well as Gothick) element into taste. In France, outside the formalism of Vauvenargues, there is comparatively little until late in the century of direct importance, except Charles Batteux's *Les beaux arts réduits à un même principe* (1746). This joins a gradually swelling tide of works of broader aesthetic interest, considered elsewhere in this volume, which include Burke's *Enquiry into the Origin of Our Ideas of the Sublime and Beautiful* (1757) as well as Adam Smith's *Theory of Moral Sentiments* (1759). Ultimately the most fruitful ground for this vein of inquiry proved to be Germany, hitherto a relatively unadventurous corner of the critical map. Lessing, Baumgarten, Moses Mendelssohn and Hamann all explore the laws of aesthetic reception and help to evolve a branch of philosophy more concerned with the nature of that response than with the particular tune, texture or idiom of the work of art that provokes this response.[8] Necessarily this seldom engaged directly with stylistic expression, and so it belongs in a separate narrative. The main story of this discussion centres on what happened in Britain in the first eighty years of the eighteenth century and especially the way in which language was analysed as an index of literary tone and temper.

II

One way of describing the development of ideas on matters of style is to trace a shift from purely legislative and dogmatic approaches, as in Le Bossu and Boileau, through a more empirical and flexible manner exemplified by Addison and Pope, towards the increasingly technical

---

[7] The fullest review of Kames's career as a whole, including his criticism, is that of Ross, *Lord Kames*.

[8] Some of the most relevant texts are translated and excerpted in *German Aesthetic and Literary Criticism*, ed. H. B. Nisbet (Cambridge, 1985): apart from the more famous mainstream treatises in this collection, see Herder's discussion of 'Ossian and the songs of ancient peoples', pp. 154–61, a deeper and historically more sweeping survey of issues adumbrated by Hugh Blair (see note 6 above).

and philosophic treatment of literary language in critics like Harris and Kames. This is too simple a model to be wholly adequate, but it does point to the characteristic strengths of each group in turn. In his useful survey of *The Art of Poetry 1750–1820* (1967), P. W. K. Stone discerns 'a strong tendency among theorists in the latter half of the century to take over psychological doctrines as a foundation for their views, to displace rhetoric (in its widest acceptation as the "art of writing") from its traditional basis of classical authority and common-sense observation and establish it on a properly philosophic foundation'. Stone remarks elsewhere that 'much of this literary philosophizing or psychological analysis is jejune and trivial', adding that 'Kames, in particular, seems utterly unworthy in this respect of the reputation he achieved: when he is not being trite he is more often than not being merely silly.'[9] I think this is much too harsh. What happens is that the later critics approach stylistic issues from the point of view of effect on the reader, a consideration almost wholly absent in earlier criticism. The first volume of Kames's *Elements* is an analysis of the passions, strongly influenced by Hume and Adam Smith; only in the second volume does Kames apply this psychology of artistic response to such matters as 'beauty of language'. Thenceforth his concerns are almost entirely with literature, including drama, despite a notorious excursion on 'gardening and architecture' near the end. His opening sections concentrate on much the same issues as Burke's *Sublime and Beautiful*: but in Burke's case the author stays with the 'efficient cause' of artistic effects, and even in his final section devoted to 'Words' he remains at a safe distance from anything resembling practical criticism.[10] For most of the way Burke is not writing directly about literature at all. Kames pushes these psychological concerns into discussion of particular tropes, figures of speech, verbal devices and poetic forms. His apparent 'triteness' is a function of the detailed attention he gives to familiar linguistic phenomena such as metaphor, which had previously not been anatomized in such a thoroughgoing way.

It was Addison above all who had pioneered a theory of style which stressed the production of a particular level and kind of response in the reader, as against the previous emphasis on preordained levels of seriousness determined by the writer and the literary kind employed. For this reason any history of literary criticism must allot Addison a primacy which he would not attain if we were conducting an anatomy of criticism in terms of sheer interpretive power and philosophical depth. It was he who set forth in June 1712, with his papers on the pleasures of the

---

[9] Stone, *Art*, pp. 22, 14.
[10] See the edition by James T. Boulton (London, 1958), pp. 163–77.

imagination (*Spectator* 411–421), a fully articulated account of the affective qualities of literature. Standing largely outside the cult of Longinus, vigorously promoted at this precise juncture by John Dennis, he focuses particularly on poetic description, anticipating Burke with his view that 'Words, when well chosen, have so great a force in them that a description often gives us more lively ideas than the sight of things themselves.'[11] It is a limitation in Addison that sight predominates over the other senses to what now seems an unhelpful degree, with consequences for his understanding of poetic imagery. More generally, he works almost entirely within a Lockean epistemology, so that his account of the workings of the imagination can seem mechanical and positivistic when set beside that of Coleridge. But whatever reservations can be made along these lines, it is certain that the history of criticism was permanently transformed by these papers. The elegant arts of poetry thrown out by a succession of versifiers like Roscommon and Sheffield immediately came to look bellettristic and primitive; it became possible to see that Horace had been addressing particular concerns of his own literary period (and his own practice), and that this applied in some measure even to Boileau and Pope. Dryden's weighty critical observations had similarly appeared in an *ad hoc* context. With the papers on the pleasures of the imagination, we are entering a mode of something like professional criticism – more technical, less related to the critic's own literary circumstances, more consciously philosophical in language, and less reverential to the inert dogmas which had been handed down. Whilst many of Addison's individual judgements are conventional, the intellectual context in which they arrive is markedly different. Thus he refers in the fourth paper to experiments in optics, a sign of the penetration of Newtonian thought into wider areas of discourse.[12]

This is by no means the only way in which Addison opened out the field of criticism. His eighteen papers on *Paradise Lost* covered a wide range of issues, many of them stylistic; although the poetic underlying these discussions is again conventionally Aristotelian, the fact is that no vernacular classic had been given this amount of detailed attention – Dryden on Shakespeare and Ben Jonson is comparatively sketchy, Dryden on Chaucer almost over before it has started. Whilst there were few by 1712 who doubted that Milton was a great classic of the language (there were just a few who did still doubt this), it was only with Addison that the case was made substantively and demonstrably. The two papers

---

[11] Elledge, *Essays*, p. 60. Perhaps the most forward-looking and influential of all the papers is no. 418 (Elledge, *Essays*, pp. 65–8) on the 'action of the mind' determining the perception of beauty, and on the way in which the poet operates by 'mending and perfecting nature'.

[12] Elledge, *Essays*, I, p. 52.

on the ballad 'Chevy Chase' (*Spectator* 70 and 74) extend the standard 'rules' to incorporate a popular work from a 'Gothic' age; whilst the attempt to dignify the poem by imputing to it 'the majestic simplicity of the ancients', and by aligning it with classical epic, may not strike us as very convincing, the mere technique of parallel passages (especially where the texts concerned were so far apart in the old hierarchy) provided a tool which critics would find increasingly applicable to their needs.[13] Again, individual papers on genius, taste and ridicule set the agenda for later discussions by critics as notable as Hume and Johnson (who also supplemented the papers on Milton with his own analysis of the versification of *Paradise Lost*, a topic Addison had omitted, in *Rambler* 86, 88 and 90 (1751)). It is unsurprising to find that Addison's successors seem often to deploy a more sophisticated conceptual framework, and in particular Johnson's feel for linguistic propriety – as well as his ear for rhythmic effects – is more acute. Nevertheless, Addison had shown the way, not least in his papers on true and false wit (*Spectator* 58–63), where most of the grounds of Johnson's critique of the metaphysical poets are already in place. In fact, Addison's treatment of the pun supplies a negative definition of the high Augustan notion of poetic decorum: that is, the pun is the antithesis not merely of what is 'correct' in style, but also what is powerful, evocative and emotionally stirring. If we adopt a post-Romantic perspective and look for a sense of the 'creative' potential of divagations from propriety, we shall fail to see the cleansing effect of Addison's strictures on false wit.

In the same period, as already suggested, it was Pope who made the other substantial contribution to the evolution of critical approaches. Here the creative writer plainly was implicated in the critical judgements, and it is significant that the relative conventionality of the *Essay on Criticism* (1712) is modified by Pope's experience of working on his translations of Homer. For example, the preface to the *Iliad* (1715) shows the particular impress made on his mind by the actual task of finding appropriate English language to match the effects of the Greek: the notes are studded with passages reflecting this struggle. Pope lays chief emphasis on 'that unequaled fire and rapture' which characterize Homer's language; and he implicitly undermines much of the standard tenets of decorum when he writes, 'Exact disposition, just thought, correct elocution, polished numbers, may have been found in a thousand; but this poetical fire, this *vivida vis animi*, in a very few.'[14] Even in the 'very few' where it is admitted, the faculty is more spasmodic, as with Virgil, Milton and Shakespeare. Part of what is happening here is that linguistic energy as such is coming to supplant formal qualities of

---

[13] Elledge, *Essays*, I, pp. 17–27.   [14] Elledge, *Essays*, I, pp. 258–9.

'disposition', and tacitly even the basic task of 'invention'. It is not that Pope quarrels directly with the orthodoxy of Le Bossu and Boileau, rather that his most eloquent passages are those which relate Homer's 'invention' not to finding a plot, dressing up a suitable moral, or conceiving of a grand subject, but to finding apt words to stir the imagination and to bring his 'pictures' of the Greek world alive. Whilst Pope writes approvingly of the 'marvellous fable' underlying the *Iliad*, his sense of the deeper creativity of the poem emerges when he turns to the 'expression', the 'vast comprehension of images of every sort' displayed in Homer's work. Here, the central insistence for our purposes comes in the statement, 'We acknowledge him the father of poetical diction, the first who taught "that language of the gods" to men.' This is reflected in the warmth of the expression, the 'daring' metaphors, and the radically un-prose-like turns of speech.[15] It is clear that for Pope poetic diction is an enabling technique, a process of linguistic selection which frees the writer to write in a more heightened style, and a mode of emotional (as well as merely verbal) elevation.

Tillotson has traced the usage 'poetic diction' back to Dryden in 1685, through John Dennis in his *Remarks on Prince Arthur* (1696) and on to Pope. It remains a key concept for the whole of the next century: Johnson observes that Cowley, as representative metaphysical poet, offends because he 'makes no selection of words'. Tillotson provides what is still the fullest and best analysis of poetic diction, as it were, in practice: that is, the ways in which writers up to the time of Wordsworth exploited the potentialities of a special vocabulary demarcated for poetic use.[16] But the theory of the subject ran its own parallel course. It is important to realize that there had never been such stringent linguistic codes in ancient literature. Obviously, classical rhetoric had prescribed registers of style appropriate to particular literary tasks; and the threefold division of levels, usually traced back to Cicero's rhetorical scheme, was often applied to prose as well as verse. This decorum had its ultimate basis in Aristotle's epistemology, where the different capacity of objects of knowledge to be properly comprehended by the mind underlay a vision of that reality which art mimetically represented.[17] The high language of epic and tragedy aimed for a sense of wonder, drawing attention to its own effects so as to induce a consciousness in the reader of the scale of utterance attempted. The low style of comedy and occasional poems was meant to go relatively unobserved; it thus came closest to the familiar usages of everyday speech, and avoided 'choice' terms.

---

[15] Elledge, *Essays*, I, pp. 261, 263.
[16] See Tillotson, *Augustan Studies*, pp. 46–110.
[17] See S. Shankman, *Pope's Iliad: Homer in the Age of Passion* (Princeton, 1983), pp. 57–9.

However, as just remarked, there was no true diction in the sense of words expressly enjoined or banned. That came after the Renaissance, first from poetic legislators such as Malherbe, and then adopted in England with the enthronement of Denham and Waller as the masters of a new 'correctness' in style. The doctrine hinged on the view that the texture of literary language determined the mood and seriousness of what was being expressed. Johnson, who in this regard remained conservative for his entire career as a critic, set out the literary justification for the system in a famous portion of his *Life of Dryden*: starting from the observation that before the time of Dryden, 'there was ... no poetical diction', he goes on to gloss the expression: that is, 'no system of words at once refined from the grossness of domestick use and free from the harshness of terms appropriated to particular arts. Words too familiar or too remote defeat the purpose of a poet.' The poet shuns language 'which we hear on small or on coarse occasions'.[18] It is a technique of elevation by way of selection, refinement, suppression and substitution. Prior to the time of Dryden, Johnson states, with the exception of a few writers of outstanding natural gifts, poets had failed to observe this 'delicacy of selection'. It was at heart a negative doctrine, in the sense that we are always more conscious of what is forbidden or eliminated than what was allowed through. Hence the fact that the Scriblerian manual of anti-rhetoric, *Peri Bathous* (1728), provides an excellent model of eighteenth-century critical standards, as it pretends to laud the qualities needed to achieve 'the art of sinking' in poetry – thus the chapter on expression isolates and exemplifies 'florid', 'pert', 'alamode' and 'cumbrous' styles. Similarly James Harris praises the suitable use of language by saying, 'Here the DICTION is *Elegant*, without being *vulgar* or *affected*; the Words, tho' common, being taken under a *Metaphor*, are so far estranged by this *metaphorical use*, that they acquire thro' the change a competent dignity, and yet, *without becoming vulgar*, remain intelligible and *clear*.'[19] There are positives in place – clarity, order, dignity and so on – but it is the fear of what is common which seems to be uppermost. To 'estrange' vulgarity or meanness is the first function of Harris's poetic.

Critics sometimes envied the apparent, though of course illusory, propriety attaching to a dead language. For example, Johnson remarks that Addison was able to deal with low subjects in his Latin verses, 'which perhaps he would not have ventured to have written in his own language'. The explanation comes pat: 'When the matter is low ... a dead language, in which nothing is mean because nothing is familiar,

---

[18] Johnson, *Lives*, I, p. 420.
[19] Harris, *Inquiries*, p. 186: the passage in question is from Shakespeare's *Julius Caesar*.

affords great conveniences.'[20] This is no doubt one of the reasons why eighteenth-century poets made great use of Latin-based words and phrases as a key part of their diction, hoping to trap some of this neutrality of tone. It has often been pointed out that writers went to Edward Bysshe's *Art of English Poetry* (1700) as a repository of stock expressions and choice epithets – and so they did, for most of the century. But almost equally important, hovering in the background, was the Latin store contained in the manual *Gradus ad Parnassum*; and Christopher Smart was probably not the only author to use Latin dictionaries as an aid to composition. Smart found translatable and adaptable phrases in Ainsworth, whose dictionary was revised by the Rev. William Young in 1752; Young was the original of Parson Adams, and a friend of Harris as well as Henry Fielding. The role of lexicography in establishing stylistic norms in eighteenth-century English poetry has not yet been fully investigated.

'Diction', as considered up to this point, was almost exclusively a device of *poetic* elevation. The new form of the novel, largely written in the middle style, had not yet entered the domain of criticism in any serious way. It was acknowledged that prose might sometimes require a degree of rhetorical amplification to achieve a magnificent effect, and impassioned sections of writing in Thucydides, Cicero or Clarendon might be singled out for admiring comment. But most of the recent imperatives in prose had endorsed Thomas Sprat's plea for a simpler prose style, stressing the denotative rather than the connotative; Bacon was much more in fashion than Thomas Browne, and the recent English masters (Bunyan, Defoe, Swift) had eschewed the high style for the most part. It is not therefore surprising that, within this period, rhetoric has not yet caught up with the rise of the novel. Hugh Blair has a brief discussion of Marivaux, Rousseau and Defoe in his *Lectures* (1783), whilst James Beattie wrote an essay on fable and romance in his *Dissertations Moral and Critical* (1783) which marks the beginning of serious analysis of fiction – Clara Reeve's *The Progress of Romance* (1785) is a more fully developed and more wide-ranging successor. Beattie approaches the subject through the concept of allegory (not well treated in most of the rhetorical schemes based on poetry), and brings Bunyan, Swift, Arbuthnot and Defoe into consideration.[21] Existing models had little room for realistic fiction, whose low-mimetic basis seemed to exclude it from the topmost flights of literary creation, and hence to deny it a place in the serious business of criticism.

Initially, for example, prose was thought to be inimical to the sublime – a key concept analysed elsewhere in this volume. Sublimity was looked

---

[20] Johnson, *Lives*, II, p. 83.   [21] Elledge, *Essays*, II, pp. 920–31.

for, within literature, solely among the traditional high kinds – epic, tragedy, scriptural narratives, or at the lowest extreme, Pindaric odes. There is an interesting passage relevant to this situation in a letter from Fielding to Harris in 1742, just after the publication of *Joseph Andrews*. Fielding writes, 'I apprehend it will be readily admitted that every sort of Stile except the Sublime may be reached by Prose: And what if even this may not only be achieved by the Prose-Writer; but it should be found that the Dignity & Majesty of Prose should be superiour to that of Verse. Will you pardon me if I think Paradise lost is writ in Prose?'[22] Fielding is collapsing the usual distinctions, based on the fact that Milton had written in blank verse, and implying that the devices open to a prose-writer could likewise compensate for the absence of the embellishment of rhyme. Fielding himself is plainly a key figure in this entire story. His practice as a novelist forced a recognition of the way in which the new form utilized and subverted the traditional genres; only perhaps the practice of Marivaux counted for as much in this regard. But Marivaux had not theorized his procedures to the same degree as Fielding, whose preface to *Joseph Andrews* had raised major issues of classification and definition, and who would produce an even more reflexive and self-conscious text in *Tom Jones* within a few years. The critic who might have developed these insights was Diderot, but his taste lay rather with Richardson, and his most self-aware mode of fiction came in *Le neveu de Rameau*, which was not published until 1793 (*Jacques le fataliste* came out in 1796). It is worth adding that the entries on literary topics in the *Encyclopédie*, whether by Marmontel or Voltaire, are far less radical and forward-looking than those on social and political subjects. For all these reasons, the novel was never properly absorbed into mainstream criticism during the period; and questions of stylistics remain in the realm of 'poetics' in more than a technical or conventional sense.[23]

It became general doctrine to differentiate poetry on the basis of its vocabulary, although sometimes matters such as syntax were taken into account. Thus Robert Lowth in his *Lectures on the Sacred Poetry of the Hebrews* (1753 in Latin; tr. 1787) puts the issue in these terms: the nature of poetry is 'to be totally different from common language; and not only in the choice of words, but in the construction, to affect a peculiar and more exquisite mode of expression'. In general, theorists did not regard it as part of their task to specify the precise items of vocabulary which produced this heightening effect – it was for the poet

---

[22] *The Correspondence of Henry and Sarah Fielding*, ed. M. C. Battestin and C. T. Probyn (Oxford, 1993), p. 24.

[23] Harris in his *Inquiries* does deal with prose, but he had a peculiarly marked aversion for fiction, despite his close friendship with Henry and Sarah Fielding.

to compile his own list, by using his own taste (or, in practice, by consulting Bysshe or by assimilating Latin usages into English by reference to sources like *Gradus ad Parnassum*). Critics such as Beattie mention a number of special word-forms – archaic terms, compound epithets, and so on – but they cite these as illustrative rather than truly constitutive of 'the poetical style'.[24] The task of rhetoric was still, as it had been from ancient times, to indicate a broad level of approach, and to specify the apt linguistic register for particular tasks. The exercise is synthetic rather than analytic; 'practical criticism' of individual texts, such as Addison and Johnson had undertaken, is seldom felt to be appropriate in the context of a general critical handbook.

In crucial respects Kames is different. His range of allusion is exceptionally wide, drawing on French, Italian, and Latin texts; he normally confines himself to poetry, though Macpherson's rendition of Ossian is admitted. He quotes Shakespeare with great abundance. Moreover, Kames takes much more notice than his predecessors of recent literature, not just *Fingal* but also Dryden, Swift, Addison and Pope. His discussion provides an anthology of classical literary texts in an age where large-scale collections were still seldom published, a situation which would only change in the last decades of the century. Finally, whilst Kames analyses the same tropes as previous rhetoricians (apostrophe, hyperbole, and the like), he devotes more attention to the structure of devices such as parallelism and antithesis, and he spends longer on versification in the narrow sense. The result is that his *Elements* provide a fuller and a more directly *literary* account of stylistic matters than do the traditional manuals.

Kames has an especially interesting section on the various figures, especially metaphor. It is here that his philosophic approach seems to me, *pace* Stone, to add conviction to his approach. For example, his explanation of the way in which metaphor is distinguished from simile ('In a metaphor, the two subjects are kept distinct in the thought; only, not in the expression')[25] prefigures modern concepts of tenor and vehicle, or signifier and signified. It is not surprising that I. A. Richards should have devoted some pages to Kames in his *Philosophy of Rhetoric*, since the *Elements* do furnish quite a sophisticated view of figurative language. In addition, Kames treats poetic idiom less as a matter of isolated words and more in a context of verbal patterning, including syntax, rhythm and sound. His description of style moves the discourse from that of *parole* to that of *langue*. What happens in Kames in general is that metaphor ceases to be described purely in terms of its function as an embellishing or amplificatory device; the trope is seen as a transformative agent of

---

[24] Stone, *Art*, p. 79.   [25] Kames, *Elements*, II, p. 275.

thought, and whilst he retains the taxonomic method of standard rhetoric, the categories are more advanced – thus he provides a table of
various metaphoric substitutions, along the lines of '3. A word proper
to the cause, employed figuratively to explain the effect'.[26] Whilst earlier
critics had occasionally hit upon such formulations, they do not carry
out the task in such a thoroughgoing way, and their distinctions between metaphor, allegory, figures of speech and tropes are more formal
than those of Kames. Further, the extensive review in Kames of 'improper' figurative usages, and the aesthetic grounds for rejecting these,
moves into genuinely critical discriminations. It might be added that
Kames anticipates Johnson on a number of points; not only does he
make exactly the same point, in 1762, on dramatic verisimilitude as
Johnson was to make in his *Preface to Shakespeare* in 1765 – equally
his illustration of how 'a metaphor drawn out to any length ... becomes disagreeable by overstraining the mind', with a quotation from
Cowley, clearly points forward to the *Lives of the Poets.*[27]

Indeed, Johnson's entire discussion of the metaphysical poets draws
on the familiar notions of his age, although it is more eloquent, more
intelligent and more detailed than the run of commentaries. He admires
the energy of Cowley's poetry, and he defines wit with relation to the
metaphysicals in terms of 'a kind of *discordia concors*', a formula which
would permit an eighteenth-century critic to treat conceits as more than
mere word-play. However, he denies Cowley the key affective powers of
poetry when he remarks that 'he is never pathetick, and rarely sublime'.
The sustained consideration of what makes for a successful poetic simile
reaches a verdict close to that of Kames ('It has been observed, that a
simile cannot be agreeable where the resemblance is either too strong or
too faint').[28] To put a complicated matter simply, Johnson deepens and
refines the prevailing idea of propriety when he comes to examine stylistic
issues, but he certainly does not abandon the principle of correctness.
Cowley and his peers fall down because their linguistic means are not
in keeping with the poetic effects they propose: it is a breach of decorum.

The quality most commonly desiderated in eighteenth-century discussions of figurative language is vividness, the capacity to bring a lively
picture of what is being expressed to the reader's mind. Again the
underlying epistemology is that of Locke. Sometimes this quality of
pictorial vividness is traced back to Plutarch's use of the word ἐνάργεια.
Jean H. Hagstrum has shown how this concept originated in rhetoric,
and came to be applied more generally to literature and then to the
visual arts. It was adopted by disciples of Longinus, and then came to

---

[26] Kames, *Elements*, II, p. 307.   [27] Kames, *Elements*, II, pp. 415, 285.
[28] Kames, *Elements*, II, p. 282: Johnson, *Lives*, I, pp. 18–21, 56.

be confused on occasions with the Aristotelian term ἐνέργεια.[29] The distinction between *enargeia* and *energeia* may not be as clear-cut as a modern theorist would wish; in the eighteenth century, both terms were used to endorse writing which conveyed a feeling or a scene with force, immediacy and brilliance. In virtually all writers on style before the Romantic era, it was the job of metaphor (as of rhetorical tropes more generally) to deliver a predetermined message with added impact. There were disagreements between particular critics, and more and less conservative schools of rhetoric; but it was not normally in question that figurative language was designed to enhance, to adorn, to represent with special clarity. This proceeds from an overall attitude to style which judges language by its propriety, that is its suitability to a representational purpose, and which sees the verbal formulation as instrumental rather than originating. This was true of the old concept of *elocutio* as a model of expressive utterance: it is still true of the 'elocution' of writers like Campbell.

One critic who might have changed things was James Harris, who took a highly individual position on many issues. He adopted the firm evaluative stance – 'Now as to knowing, HOW TO LIKE, and then WHAT IS WORTH LIKING, the first of these, being the Object of *Critical* Disquisition'[30] – and he has some sketchily perceptive ideas on metaphor but ultimately falls back on the usual need to avoid bombast on one side and vulgarity on the other. Unfortunately his *Inquiries*, like everything he wrote, are jumpy and confusing in their arrangement, and he seldom settles long enough to any given task to be fully cogent. He quickly shifts from diction to metaphor, though proclaiming the crucial importance of maintaining such distinctions in criticism; and his fatal Cleopatra of etymologizing in and out of season ('As *the Poem* from its very *Name* respects various MATTERS RELATIVE TO LAND, (GEORGICA) . . .')[31] distracts the reader from the insights which do occur within the argument. Harris is an interesting case of a critic who wishes to reassert traditional Aristotelian norms, but who has rejected (or cannot command) the standard rhetorical methods of analysis. Dedicated to the task of reinstating the rules as permanently applicable to all good literature, even to the apparently lawless Shakespeare, he stands out against a current of criticism which was seeking to devise fresh norms to accommodate a wider range of texts. Addison had helped to set these movements under way with his praise of 'Chevy Chase' and his treatment of the 'fairy way of writing' (*Spectator* 419). Critics like Hurd and Warton

[29] Hagstrum, *Sister Arts*, pp. 11–12.   [30] Harris, *Inquiries*, p. 233.
[31] Harris, *Inquiries*, p. 121. For Harris's belief in 'this method of conveying Knowledge by discussing the meanings of Words & their Etymologies', see Fielding, *Correspondence*, p. 163.

had been trying to smuggle in Gothic and exotic elements into the critical pantheon, though almost entirely in respect of widening the subject-matter of poetry and loosening its ordonnance (neither of the authors named has much to say in detail about language as such). Harris is more observant about stylistic matters (e.g., alliteration, or the use of monosyllables), but he was not able to combine his assorted comments into anything more than a loose polemic in favour of conventional standards. He quotes widely and often appositely, but he has no operative sense of literary language which would forge a coherent stylistic from these materials.

In that respect Harris represents one end of the critical spectrum, as Kames does the other. Nearer to the centre is Johnson, who (as we have seen) offers unrevolutionary ideas on the nature of poetic diction, but who was able to move out of the categories of formal rhetoric into precise and detailed criticism of particular texts, notably in the *Lives of the Poets*. When Johnson says in his *Rambler* paper (no. 86) that Milton 'seems to have somewhat mistaken the nature of our language, of which the chief defect is ruggedness and asperity',[32] he is echoing a common complaint. What is different is the demonstrative technique, allowing Johnson to specify the exact location and cause of 'harsh cadences' in the Miltonic text; and the avoidance of schoolroom categories, in favour of a rapid, free-ranging and functional appraisal of the writer's style.

III

We are told nowadays that every historical narrative is a species of fiction, constructed for ideological purposes. No doubt the story of eighteenth-century theories of style told here could be seen in this way, as it has been selective and judgemental. But it would be a strange history of criticism which substituted a totally different narrative; the principal actors, in the phase between the dominance of Le Bossu and Boileau, and the rise of German aesthetic philosophy, were clearly British. Dryden, Addison, Pope and Johnson were the most distinguished literary minds applied to criticism, and Addison and Johnson were the most creative minds applied to the theory of the subject. It is hardly deniable, for that matter, that the new rhetoricians of the mid-century established a basis of theory which would endure right through the Romantic era and almost through to the present century. The role given to Kames in this chapter would not be accepted by all commentators, but he seems to me to have brought to the subject a degree of philosophic clarity, and

---

[32] Elledge, *Essays*, II, p. 591.

a measure of literary discernment, which give the *Elements* a particular significance. It is also true that the story traced here is only one sub-plot among a whole decameron of parallel tales, which are traced elsewhere in this volume. To abstract any one strand of the entire tapestry is to risk falsifying what actually happened. Nevertheless, the broad sequence of events is not in very much doubt. The investigation of literary language rested more and more, after Addison, on the notion of a 'mental act' performed by the reader; and stylistics, in the hands of a critic like Johnson or Kames, came to mean not slotting poetic expressions into various pre-labelled categories, but analysing the effectiveness of words in poetry by reference to their power to evoke a precise response in the reader – a matter to be explored in terms of their texture, their associations, their combination, and much else. There were still theories behind such an approach to style, but they were no longer the bespoke theories of traditional rhetoric.

16

Generality and particularity

Leo Damrosch

Writers in the eighteenth century had much to say about the relative status of the general and the particular, but if one were simply to summarize their views on this topic, the complications and contradictions would seem exasperating if not inexplicable. To make sense of what is going on, one has to recognize that in this instance a literary-critical question is inseparable from a philosophical one, and also that discussions of it usually carry a polemical charge.

Modern accounts of the topic have until recently been shaped by the assumptions of mid-twentieth-century poetics. René Wellek wrote in 1955:

> Most modern critics want poetry to be concrete, visual, precise, and not abstract or universal ... Some preromantic critics can be shown to be the first to have decidedly rejected the older view of poetry as abstract, universal, and wary of the 'streaks of the tulip, the shades of the verdure.' The shift happened late in the eighteenth century, and we have not returned to the neoclassical ideal.
>
> (*History*, I, p. 4)

In this formulation, a critic like Samuel Johnson (whose words Wellek is quoting) is understood to be a devotee of 'the neoclassical ideal', in which the universal is equated with the abstract, and is opposed to the concrete and visual which 'we', together with certain 'preromantic' critics, prefer.

Such an account seriously misrepresents Johnson in a way that is symptomatic of the New Critical recension of Romantic aesthetics, and that continues to colour accounts of the eighteenth century. Now that New Critical assumptions are fading into the past, however, it is possible to address the question more dispassionately. The literary, philosophical, and ethical questions that eighteenth-century critics sought to answer can be summarized as follows: (1) What sorts of things do poets describe? (2) What sorts of things *can* they describe? (3) What sorts of things *should* they describe?

For critics whose attitudes were formed in the seventeenth century and who retained an allegiance to Platonic ideas, there could be no problem of generality, since particulars have meaning only when they are seen in the light of the universal form or idea. Thus John Dennis writes in 1711 that Horace instructs poets 'not to draw after particular Men, who are but Copies and imperfect Copies of the great universal Pattern; but to consult that innate Original, and that universal Idea, which the Creator has fix'd in the minds of ev'ry reasonable Creature' (*Critical Works*, II, p. 418). Generality became a problem – in Britain far more than on the continent – when it became entangled with the issues of empiricism. It was because empiricism stressed the radical individuality of perception that aesthetics needed to reinvent a basis for collective categories and generalizable insights.

Empiricist thought takes it as axiomatic that all knowledge derives from experience, and that experience in turn is grounded in particulars. As Locke points out, the question then arises, 'Since all things that exist are merely particulars, how come we by general terms?' (*Human Understanding*, III.iii.6). Locke proposes two explanations that overlap but are not identical. According to one, a general idea is formed by a process of subtraction, which arrives at the concept 'man', for instance, by leaving out those features of individual men that are not common to all (III.iii). According to the other – which anticipates the position Berkeley soon developed – we can *know* only particulars, but when we generalize we choose to *attend* selectively to those features that they share with other particulars, for instance 'whiteness' as a property of both chalk and snow (II.xi.9).

In either of these explanations, abstraction or generalization is a subjective process. It refers to connections among particulars that exist only insofar as they are established within a person's mind (guided, as Hume would add, by linguistic expectations that are inculcated by social custom). Generalization does *not* refer, as Aristotle's theory of universals did, to really-existing universal categories in which particulars somehow participate. Categories of classification are merely human inventions: they make use of properties that particular things really have, but the same properties could just as well be grouped and described differently in other classificatory schemes.

In philosophical terms, these views reflect a great cultural shift from ontology to epistemology, emphasizing the discrete percepts of individual consciousness in what Richard Rorty has called 'the triumph of the quest for certainty over the quest for wisdom' (*Philosophy*, p. 61). But as Rorty shows, certainty is precisely what becomes impossible, since the empiricist account of the mind as interior spectator holds that what we perceive is not things themselves, but only our 'ideas' about them (which may or may not be reliable images of them). The uniformity of human nature is therefore an essential postulate, for Hume just as much as for Locke. Abstraction is a mental process of manipulating ideas, and to avoid solipsistic scepticism, it is essential to hold as well that their veridicality is guaranteed by the common experience of mankind.

It is plausible to detect a socio-political element in the eighteenth-century preoccupation with generality: just as continual appeals to 'order' and 'subordination' reflect an anxious sense of their breakdown, so the emphasis on general truths and the uniformity of human nature responds to the twin challenges of radical individualism and historical relativism. Hume declares, 'Would you know the sentiments, inclinations, and course of life of the Greeks and Romans? Study well the temper and actions of the French and English' (*Inquiry*, VIII.i, p. 93). It is here that the moral aspect of generality makes itself evident: Hume's scepticism is a propaedeutic to recognition of the secure basis of experience in social custom and in the 'passions' that inform it. Eighteenth-century theorists therefore seek, in William Edinger's words, 'a generality not of averages, as some scholars have thought, not of the colourless or abstract or vague, but of inclusiveness and moral community' (*Johnson*, p. 30).

This emphasis on community of experience underlies the process by which eighteenth-century theorists – following empiricist assumptions about the visual foundations of thinking – held that general terms receive specific and vivid embodiment in each reader's mind.[1] Post-Romantic calls for particularity have tended to overlook the fact that all words are general, referring to something that is not immediately present, and must therefore be imagined on the basis of the reader's own experience (whether of 'real' things or of the ways in which words are used). They also overlook the ways in which eighteenth-century poetic practice embodies a degree of specificity that pronouncements about generality might not suggest. For example, Pope's description of Buckingham's fate in the *Epistle to Bathurst* has as much density of detail as anything in Wordsworth:

> On once a flock-bed, but repair'd with straw,
> With tape-ty'd curtains, never meant to draw ...

Pope's note to Bk VI, line 595 of his translation of the *Iliad*, in which the infant Astyanax shrinks from his father's shining helmet, makes the theoretical point explicit:

There never was a finer Piece of Painting than this ... All these are but small circumstances, but so artfully chosen that every Reader immediately feels the force of them, and represents the whole in the utmost Liveliness to his Imagination. This alone might be a Confutation of that false Criticism some have fallen into, who affirm that a Poet ought only to collect the great

---

[1] See esp. William Youngren, 'Generality, science, and poetic language'.

and noble Particulars in his Paintings ... There is a vast difference betwixt a *small* Circumstance and a *trivial* one, and the smallest become important if they are well chosen, and not confused.

(Poems, VII, pp. 355–6)

Whenever a reader recreates the poetic 'painting' in his or her imagination, 'particulars' come to life, and so long as the poet has selected and organized them well, small as well as great may represent reality accurately.

The attempt to unite neo-classical universality with empiricist particularity is filled with complications, which may perhaps be best understood if they are examined in Johnson, Reynolds, and Blake, three writers who represent the full range of positions from Lockean empiricism to a renewed Platonism. In so far as neo-classicism implies a genre-specific system of 'rules', it was never fully naturalized in Britain, as is indicated by Johnson's contempt for Voltaire's 'minute and slender criticism' of Shakespeare (*Preface, Works*, VII, p. 80); but at the same time, Johnson calls for 'just representations of general nature' (p. 61) in a context that deserves to be called neo-classical.

The term 'general nature', in the usage of Johnson's contemporaries, refers ambiguously to a range of empiricist operations performed upon the data of experience. It may indicate (1) objects synthesized from parts that are found separately in nature, like Zeuxis' Juno, who was based on the features of various real women, (2) the statistical average of a biological species, (3) the generic human type, considered as a norm that transcends local differences, (4) aspects of the world that are widely familiar, poetic references to which will elicit shared recognition.[2] Of these formulations, the last seems to be the one that Johnson usually has in mind. 'The value of every story', he told Boswell, 'depends on its being true. A story is a picture either of an individual or of human nature in general: if it be false, it is a picture of nothing' (*Life*, II, p. 433). Whether the 'picture' represents a specific individual or the features that are common to a set of individuals, it can be understood and evaluated only by reference to what Johnson elsewhere calls 'the general sense or experience of mankind' (*Lives*, III, p. 345).

Johnsonian generality, then, rests upon an empiricist theory of perception that affirms a reliable congruence between outward phenomena and the processes of mind that organize and interpret them. 'General precepts', Johnson says in connection with Dryden's criticism, 'depend upon the nature of things and the structure of the human mind' (*Lives*, I, p. 413); and they can be reliably interpreted because 'human nature is always the same' (*Adventurer* 99, *Works*, II, p. 431). This insistence on shared experience dictates a resistance to the artificiality of literary

---

[2] This summary is indebted to Abrams, *The Mirror and the Lamp*, pp. 35–42.

genre, with a preference instead for comprehensive representations of the 'chaos of mingled purposes and casualties' that reflects 'the real state of sublunary nature' (*Preface*, p. 66). And it dictates as well a preference for whatever is widely familiar. All knowledge is particular, but some particulars are more general than others. In W. R. Keast's exposition, 'General nature is ... what all men everywhere recognize as like themselves, and particular nature is what men in general recognize as present only at certain times, under certain conditions, or among certain men' ('Theoretical foundations', p. 400). The occasional reminiscences in Johnson's writings of Platonic language are therefore rhetorical rather than substantive; as J. H. Hagstrum concludes, 'Plato wanted the particular to reveal the general and universal; Johnson wanted the general to recall the particular' (*Johnson's Literary Criticism*, p. 88).

Since the poet's task is to 'bring realities to mind' (*Preface*, p. 78), he must first extend his own 'observation' in an 'extensive view', as Johnson proposes in the opening lines of *The Vanity of Human Wishes*. Shakespeare's 'faithful mirrour of manners and of life' (*Preface*, p. 62) is the product of an empiricist process of accumulation: 'Nature gives no man knowledge, and when images are collected by study and experience, can only assist in combining or applying them. Shakespeare, however favoured by nature, could impart only what he had learned; and as he must increase his ideas, like other mortals, by gradual acquisition, he, like them, grew wiser as he grew older' (pp. 87–8).

Literary works are assembled from this fund of knowledge, and it is then the reader's task to revivify their images. As in Locke's account of general words or in Addison's *Spectator* papers on the pleasures of imagination, the reader gives imaginative existence to a poetic description with details drawn from personal experience. Cowley, Johnson says, weakens 'what might in general expressions be great and forcible' by excessive enumeration of detail. 'That Gabriel was invested with the softest or brightest colours of the sky we might have been told, and been dismissed to improve the idea in our different proportions of conception' (*Lives*, I, p. 53). It is in short-circuiting this collaboration between poet and reader that Cowley 'loses the grandeur of generality' (p. 45).

Johnson's (or his character Imlac's) remark in *Rasselas* that the poet should describe 'general properties', rather than numbering the streaks of the tulip, has exactly the same basis: 'He is to exhibit in his portraits of nature such prominent and striking features as recall the original to every mind, and must neglect the minuter discriminations, which one may have remarked and another have neglected' (ch. 10). Generality in this sense is the very opposite of vagueness, of the kind Johnson deplores in Rowe's plays where 'all is general and undefined' (*Lives*, II, p. 76), or in an epitaph by Pope that contains 'only a general indiscriminate character' (III, p. 263). Conversely, Shakespeare's characters represent 'species' rather than limited 'individuals' because they reflect 'those general passions and principles by which all minds are agitated' (*Preface*, p. 62). 'Shakespeare always makes nature predominate over accident; and if he preserves the essential character, is not very careful of distinctions super-induced and adventitious. His story requires Romans and Kings, but he thinks only on men' (p. 65). One might say, indeed, that Shakespeare's characters are individual *because* their characteristics are universally recognizable: 'Characters thus ample and general were not easily dis-criminated and preserved, yet perhaps no poet ever kept his personages more distinct from each other' (p. 64). In a quite similar way, Fielding's novels are filled with vivid details but rest upon a theory of character as generalizable and (like Hume's Greeks and French) as historically recurring. In *Joseph Andrews* (1742) Fielding's narrator declares,

I describe not men, but manners; not an individual, but a species. Perhaps it will be answered, Are not the characters then taken from life? To which I answer in the affirmative; nay, I believe I might aver, that I have writ little more than I have seen. The lawyer is not only alive, but hath been so these 4000 years.   (III.i)

For many of Johnson's contemporaries, however, the empiricist ac-count of experience was losing its force, and in keeping with the shift from mimesis to expressivism that Abrams describes in *The Mirror and the Lamp*, they demanded that art express the uniqueness of the poet's genius rather than conformity with the experience of his readers. 'Nature', Edward Young wrote in 1759, 'brings us into the world all *Originals*: No two faces, no two minds, are just alike; but all bear Nature's evident mark of Separation on them' (*Conjectures*, pp. 42–3).

This emphasis on the poet's individuality brought with it a corre-sponding emphasis on the individuality of the objects he describes. George Campbell directly reverses Johnson's position in his *Philosophy of Rhetoric* (1776): 'The more general any name is, as it comprehends the more individuals under it, and consequently requires the more extensive knowledge in the mind that would rightly apprehend it, the more it must have of indistinctness and obscurity' (II, p. 103). Similarly Lord Kames counsels the poet to 'avoid as much as possible abstract and general terms . . . Images, which are the life of poetry, cannot be raised in any perfection but by introducing particular objects' (*Elements*, I, p. 304).

Richard Hurd makes explicit the equation between the poet's indi-viduality and the specificity of his images: Shakespeare prefers 'the *specific* idea to the *general* in the *subjects* of his metaphors, and the *circum*-

stances of his description', so that 'every single property' of things is marked, 'and the poet's own image set in distinct *relief* before the view of his reader' (*Works*, II, p. 127). But critics like Hurd lacked a consistent theoretical basis for this preference for particulars, and often fell back incongruously on the language of Platonic idealism. Hurd himself, in his commentary on Horace's *Ars Poetica*, holds that the poet should not emphasize particulars at the expense of 'the general idea of the *kind*', an idea which should be gathered not from '*real* life' but from 'the nobler conception of it as subsisting only in the *mind*' (I, pp. 253–4).

The *Discourses* (1769–90) of Joshua Reynolds give sustained expression to these contradictions, which are so vexed and entangled as to deserve the name of antinomies, since incommensurable positions are felt to be somehow equally true. The fundamental issue is announced early in the first *Discourse*, when Reynolds describes the change that Raphael underwent after seeing Michelangelo's Sistine Chapel: 'He immediately from a dry, Gothick, and even insipid manner, which attends to the minute accidental discriminations of particular and individual objects, assumed that grand style of painting, which improves partial representation by the general and invariable ideas of nature' (pp. 15–16). Here a style of painting is given honoured status by virtue of its alleged conformity to 'general ideas' in the empiricist sense. In a later *Discourse* Reynolds asserts, just as Johnson does, an equation of outward images with mental interpretation: 'My notion of nature comprehends not only the forms which nature produces, but also the nature and internal fabrick and organization, as I may call it, of the human mind and imagination' (no. VII, p. 124). The painter, like Johnson's poet, proceeds by 'a new combination of those images which have been previously gathered and deposited in the memory' (no. II, p. 27).

Throughout the *Discourses* Reynolds invokes the whole range of meanings for the general that eighteenth-century critics had canvassed, seldom with any indication that they might not be entirely synonymous. It can mean whatever is widely familiar: 'No subject can be proper that is not generally interesting ... There must be something, either in the action, or in the object, in which men are universally concerned, and which powerfully strikes upon the publick sympathy' (no. IV, p. 57). It can mean the usual, as in the neo-classical concept of decorum: 'Care must be taken not to run into particularities. Those expressions alone should be given to the figures which their respective situations generally produce' (pp. 60–1). But it can also mean the ideal 'central form' (no. III, p. 45) to which existing phenomena are only partial approximations, either as a sort of average or as a quasi-Platonic ideal of 'perfection'.

Thus when Reynolds invokes abstraction in the Lockean sense, he does so with a significant difference: when the artist has learned 'to distinguish the accidental deficiencies, excrescences, and deformities of things, from their general figures, he makes out an abstract idea of their forms more perfect than any one original' (no. III, p. 44). Neither Locke nor Johnson would equate particularity with deformity and abstraction with perfection; Reynolds here introduces a value system that has closer affinities with Platonic aesthetics than with empiricism. So also in this *Discourse* he declares that the arts aspire to 'an ideal beauty, superior to what is to be found in individual nature' (p. 42), even while he continues to hold that 'this great ideal perfection and beauty are not to be sought in the heavens, but upon the earth', and 'can be acquired only by experience' (p. 44). As Hazard Adams comments, Reynolds is here attempting 'to force the inductive generalization from sense data to meet and become identical with the Platonic idea' ('Revisiting Reynolds' *Discourses*', p. 131), and the attempt is doomed to partial success at best.

Like Johnson's, Reynolds's aesthetic rests upon a moral basis: generality raises us above the limitations and obsessions of the world of particulars. But unlike Johnson, Reynolds is willing to describe this movement from particular to general as a quasi-Platonic 'elevation' in which we ascend to an ideal beauty that transcends the world of particulars:

As the senses, in the lowest state of nature, are necessary to direct us to our support, when that support is once secure there is danger in following them further ... it is therefore necessary to the happiness of individuals, and still more necessary to the security of society, that the mind should be elevated to the idea of general beauty, and the contemplation of general truth ...
The beauty of which we are in quest is general and intellectual; it is an idea that subsists only in the mind.
                                        (no. IX, pp. 170, 171)

The 'contemplation of perfect beauty', Reynolds concludes, 'is in many respects incompatible with what is merely addressed to the senses' (no. X, p. 177), and his anxiety about 'the security of society' suggests an extra-aesthetic basis for this aspiration.

These pronouncements are paradoxical not only because they contradict the empiricist premises that Reynolds elsewhere endorses, but also because they might appear to be incompatible with the very nature of visual representation. It was a commonplace of empiricist theory that words are arbitrary counters used to represent ideas, but that pictorial images have a closer relationship to the objects they imitate. As Johnson puts it in *Idler* 34, 'poetry and painting ... differ only as the one represents things by marks permanent and natural, the other by signs accidental and arbitrary' (*Works*, II, p. 106). In conversation Johnson added that 'the appearance of nature at large may be the province of poetry, but the form of particular objects must belong to the painter'.[3] Reynolds was a professional painter, for whom even the most 'universal' ideas had always to be conveyed by particular visual images. Like many theorists of art from the Renaissance on, he was drawn almost inevitably to Platonic rather than empiricist language that might suggest how particular images could embody truth.

Following this line, Reynolds asserts that 'the great end of art is to strike the imagination' (*Discourse* IV, p. 59), and that a painter stimulates the production of mental images just as the poet does:

Whenever a story is related, every man forms a picture in his mind of the action and expression of the persons employed. The power of representing this mental picture on canvass is what we call Invention in a Painter. And as in the conception of this ideal picture, the mind does not enter into the minute peculiarities of the dress, furniture, or scene of action; so when the Painter comes to represent it, he contrives those little necessary concomitant circumstances in such a manner, that they shall strike the spectator no more than they did himself in his first conception of the story.

(no. IV, p. 58)

Thus in a historical painting, human figures must be clothed, but their garments should nevertheless be generalized: 'the cloathing is neither woollen, nor linen, nor silk, sattin, or velvet: it is drapery; it is nothing more' (p. 62).

The 'grand style' is admirable, accordingly, not just because it depicts noble subjects, but because it evokes a sublimity that makes minute enumeration impossible. It is true that paintings, unlike poems, cannot indulge in the obscurity which according to Burke (*Philosophical Enquiry*, pp. 58–64) was essential to the sublime. As Reynolds observes, Burke praises Milton's description of Eve for permitting 'every reader to make out the detail according to his own particular imagination', whereas a painter 'is obliged to give a determined form, and his own idea of beauty distinctly expressed' (*Discourse* VIII, p. 164). But if that idea of beauty is universal in conception, 'the sublime in Painting, as in Poetry, so overpowers, and takes such a possession of the whole mind, that no room is left for attention to minute criticism' (no. XV, p. 276).

Reynolds, president of the Royal Academy, saw himself very much as a spokesman for his culture, and John Barrell's *Political Theory of Painting* throws light on the socio-political subtext of the *Discourses*. Reynolds's emphasis on the heroic generalities of history painting reflects the code of civic humanism, in which painting, as a 'liberal' rather than

---

[3] Quoted by John Hoole in the Biographical Preface to John Scott (of Amwell), *Critical Essays*, p. liii.

mechanic art, reinforces the public virtues of the human community at large – 'of every country and every age', as Reynolds puts it in *Discourse* III (p. 49). Most individuals, through poverty or through a narrow commitment to acquisition (like the Dutch merchants who commissioned the minutely circumstantial art that Reynolds ranks below the grand style) are unqualified to exercise the public virtues; these are the province of liberal gentlemen of leisure, the ideal patrons of Reynolds and his Academy.

In Barrell's exposition, Reynolds's commitment to generality represents an aesthetics of social unity, in which representations of 'central form' encourage the spectator to grasp and endorse the common interests that make 'the public' something more than a collection of individuals. Idiosyncrasy of taste is by definition aberrant, and just as in Hume's social thought, the empiricist doctrine of human uniformity underwrites a commitment to the values of the group. In Reynolds's words,

The internal fabrick of our minds, as well as the external form of our bodies, being nearly uniform; it seems then to follow of course, that as the imagination is incapable of producing any thing originally of itself, and can only vary and combine those ideas with which it is furnished by means of the senses, there will necessarily be an agreement in the imaginations as in the senses of men ... The well-disciplined mind acknowledges this authority, and submits its own opinion to the publick voice ... A general union of minds, like a general combination of the forces of all mankind, makes a strength that is irresistible.   (*Discourse*, VII p. 132)

To grasp general truths is to ratify the status quo.

The poet and painter William Blake, who was born in 1757 and whose attitudes were formed in the eighteenth century, filled a copy of Reynolds's *Discourses* with vehement marginalia that clarify the difficulties of eighteenth-century aesthetic theory. In addition, Blake's membership in radical political groups and his experience as a struggling commercial engraver filled him with rage against the social ethos for which the *Discourses* speak. As he wrote on the back of Reynolds's title page, 'Having spent the Vigour of my Youth & Genius under the Oppression of Sir Joshua & his Gang of Cunning Hired Knaves Without Employment & as much as could possibly be Without Bread, the Reader must Expect to Read in all my Remarks on these Books Nothing but Indignation & Resentment' (*Complete Poetry and Prose*, p. 636).

Blake's hatred of abstraction and his commitment to 'minute particulars' are well known, and are often seen as reflecting a Romantic preference for immediacy and diversity. But in fact Blake's position is at bottom Platonic, and his comments turn favourable whenever Reynolds uses Platonic language. As a visual artist he was committed to a 'distinct, sharp, and wirey ... bounding line' (*Descriptive Catalogue*, in *Poetry and Prose*, p. 550) but he abhorred naturalistic mimesis and called for universal images that often seem compatible with Reynolds's. In the *Descriptive Catalogue* (intended for an exhibition of his paintings) Blake talks about the universality of Chaucer's characters in ways that are fully compatible with Reynolds's views on history painting: 'The characters of Chaucer's Pilgrims are the characters which compose all ages and nations ... Accident ever varies, Substance can never suffer change nor decay' (p. 532).

From Blake's point of view, his disagreement with Reynolds stems from Reynolds's empiricist preoccupation with the thing perceived, as contrasted with Blake's expressivist emphasis on the mode of perceiving. An object can be simultaneously universal and distinct because it is *seeing* that confers distinctness: 'Vision is Determinate & Perfect' (Reynolds annotations, *Poetry and Prose*, p. 646); 'Nature has no Outline: but Imagination has' (*Ghost of Abel*, p. 270). But this vision of universality is very different from the empiricist account of perception that Reynolds endorses: 'Reynolds thinks that Man Learns all that he Knows I say on the Contrary That Man Brings All that he has or Can have Into the World with him. Man is Born Like a Garden ready Planted & Sown This World is too poor to produce one Seed' (p. 656).

In fundamental ways Blake's universals resemble Plato's forms, which are objects of intelligence rather than of perception – in Blakean terminology, of imaginative vision rather than of Lockean 'single vision' – and are eternal rather than transitory. But whereas Plato's forms are more real than their images in the world of change, Blake insists on the identity of the realms of eternity and time, infinity and particulars. In a way, therefore, Blake remains inside the empiricist system he so often denounces, believing that the only reality we can know is the reality of individual perception. Kant says in the *Critique of Pure Reason*, 'I understand by "Idea" a necessary concept of reason to which no corresponding object can be given in sensation' (*Transcendental Dialectic*, I. ii). Blake would dismiss this as a formulation of false Urizenic reason, and would insist that intuitions of universals can *only* be 'given in sensation' – though in a mode of imaginative sensation very different from the passive perception described by empiricist philosophy.

Blake is not a mystic who aspires to escape from the world of the senses to some higher realm, but he does constantly demand that the sensory world be transformed by a kind of interior apocalypse. It is because he retains the empiricist linking of thought and perception that he gets so angry about Lockean abstraction. Like Locke, Blake wants to say that everything we perceive flows directly from perception; but unlike Locke, he wants to say that we have spiritual modes of perception in which objects can be apprehended as embodiments of universal forms. As he writes in the *Descriptive Catalogue*, 'He who does not imagine in stronger and better lineaments, and in stronger and better light than his perishing mortal eye can see, does not imagine at all' (*Poetry and Prose*, p. 541).

Perhaps one might say that epistemologically Blake's position reflects the emphasis on particularity that is characteristic of empiricist thought (with closer affinities to the idealist Berkeley than to Locke, whom Blake despised) but that ontologically it grounds itself on the metaphors of neo-Platonism, in which Blake was widely read. 'All Knowledge is Particular', he writes in the margins of Reynolds's *Discourses*; but form is created in the imagination. 'All Forms are Perfect in the Poet's Mind, but these are not Abstracted nor Compounded from Nature but are from Imagination' (*Poetry and Prose*, p. 648). However fervently he may call for a regeneration of the world of the senses, Blake speaks of universal forms in a way that suggests a realm very different from that of the familiar world. 'Natural Objects', he comments in some annotations to Wordsworth, 'always did & now do Weaken deaden & obliterate Imagination in Me' (*Poetry and Prose*, p. 665). In *A Vision of the Last Judgment*, Blake's commentary on his (now lost) painting on that theme, he goes so far as to declare:

The Nature of Visionary Fancy of Imagination is very little Known & the Eternal nature & permanence of its ever Existent Images is considered as less permanent than the things of Vegetative & Generative Nature, yet the Oak dies as well as the Lettuce but Its Eternal Image & Individuality never dies, but renews by its seed. Just so the Imaginative Image returns by the seed of Contemplative Thought.

(*Poetry and Prose*, p. 555)

The true oak is the eternal form, as contrasted with the transitory oaks of 'vegetative' nature.

In the end, Blake achieves a union of general with particular only by an act of faith, in a conception of Jesus as the unifying principle in whom individual imaginations are subsumed. 'General Forms have their vitality in Particulars: & every / Particular is a Man; a Divine Member of the Divine Jesus' (*Jerusalem*, 91: 29–30, *Poetry and Prose*, p. 251). In the terms of Blake's myth, minute particulars have living existence only when they participate in this central form; if they do not so participate, they collapse into the disconnected atoms of empiricism.

[Los] saw every minute particular, the jewels of Albion, running down The kennels of the streets & lanes as if they were abhorrd.

Every Universal Form was become barren mountains of Moral
Virtue: and every Minute Particular hardend into grains of sand.

(*Jerusalem* 45: 17–20, p. 194)

As E. R. Wasserman has shown in *The Subtler Language*, Romantic
aesthetics develops as a reaction to the loss of a conceptual world that
can be felt to be autonomous and stable. Confronted with an atomistic
universe of 'objects of which his mere perceptive faculties can make no
whole, and in which no one object has special value' (p. 186), the artist
is forced to create his own order in an ever-renewed struggle of the
imagination. It is that struggle, rather than any narrow disagreement
with Reynolds about particularity and generality, that underlies Blake's
thinking about art.

17

The sublime

Jonathan Lamb

Francisco Robortello published the *editio princeps* of Longinus' first-century treatise, *Peri Hypsous*, in 1554. Although it was followed by the editions of Manuzio (1555) and Porta (1569), this remarkable work of criticism made no impression – that is to say, there was no attempt to assign the sublime more than a stylistic significance – until Boileau translated it into French, over a century later (1674). Despite three translations into English between 1652 and 1698, it was not until Welsted's in 1712 (reprinted in 1724) and Smith's popular *Dionysius Longinus on the Sublime* (1739) that Longinus and the sublime became thoroughly current in Britain. The long fallow period between the rediscovery of the Paris manuscript and the exploitation of the sublime in criticism and aesthetics can be accounted for in terms of a confidence among neo-classical critics that was interrupted in France, and terminated in Britain, by the quarrel over the Ancients and Moderns. When the pre-eminence of classical literature, together with the critical precepts it justifies, came under the hostile scrutiny of modernist writers the sublime simultaneously became an urgent issue; and Longinus was used by both sides as a champion, alternately playing the part of ancient exemplar and of modern usurper. The passage between these two points – between the sublime conceived to be the coincidence of rule and practice and the sublime in its more revolutionary aspect as an unprecedented event – will be traced in the following essay.

Ancients, moderns and patriots

Boileau drew on Longinus as a valuable ally with a good pedigree, capable of legislating, justifying, and above all embodying the taste for genres and expressions that seem at first sight to be lawless. His admiration for the sublime force which ravishes and transports its audience is founded on very firm notions of 'the rule of good sense' which is always Longinus' guide.[1] He keeps repeating that Longinus is

[1] Boileau, *Traité du Sublime*, p. ii.

a practising philosopher, like Cato or Socrates, whose beliefs and actions are always in harmony. In his most celebrated and often quoted estimate of the integrity of Longinus' performance, he says, 'Often he uses the very figure he is discussing, and in talking of the sublime, is most sublime himself' (*Traité*, p. ii). It is a judgement echoed down the eighteenth century because it effortlessly places what might have been a rebellious originality within an exemplary structure. For in accomplishing the same literary feat he is talking about (e.g. introducing the topic of rhetorical questions with a question) Longinus is understood by Boileau to transform each instance of independent boldness into a case that proves the rule; or, as Pope puts it in his redaction of neo-classical precepts, the *Essay on Criticism*, Longinus is a critic 'whose own Example strengthens all his Laws, / And is himself that great Sublime he draws.'[2] His hyperbaton on the hyperbaton is the simulation of disorder, the reduction of symptomatic agitation to the rule of art. He says nothing which is irrelevant to the case; he does nothing which is not conformable to the standard to which his own virtuosity perpetually appeals. His excess is redeemable as the symmetry of sublimity upon sublimity, example upon law, case upon precedent. His originalities are legible as citations of a grandeur whose antecedent authority may be disguised but never displaced by their panache.[3] Nor does the descent of sublimity from a great original to a bold imitator exclude a critic who judges with ardour. Boileau and Pope, being subtle enough to appreciate how gracefully Longinus has put the excess of his wit at the disposal of the law, inherit the excitement of adapting the surface irregularities of the sublime to the statutes of neo-classical orthodoxy.

There are two aspects of Boileau's critique that predominate in subsequent neo-classical discussions of the sublime. The first is Longinus' premier instance of it, Moses' story of the creation of light. The second is Boileau's judgement about Longinus' sublimity on the topic of sublimity. There are few critics within the broad neo-classical stream who omit to praise Longinus for his astuteness in grasping the importance of the *fiat lux*, or to protest that he exemplifies his precepts in the very act of uttering them. In fact, the two judgements are closely related, for they both concern the coincidence of words with deeds. Moses stands in the same relation to God as Longinus to Moses, and as Boileau (and all Boileau's imitators) to Longinus. Here is a vast hierarchy, reaching all the way from the divine *logos* to the latest critic, within which the most stunning outbursts of literary enthusiasm, and potentially the most disturbing manifestations of anarchy, are assimilable as exemplary mimesis.

[2] Pope, *Essay on Criticism*, ll. 679–80.
[3] See Wimsatt and Brooks, *Literary Criticism*, p. 100.

In his disagreements with Perrault, Le Clerc and Huet,[4] Boileau vigorously defends these positions as crucial to the concept of Longinus' 'judicious boldness'. In England a similar battle is fought and ultimately lost. First Dryden (*Apology for Heroic Poetry*, 1677) and then Pope attempt to imitate Boileau's neo-classical appropriation of Longinus; but they are outstripped by critics whose names make a rollcall of duncely modernism: William Wotton, Sir Richard Blackmore, Leonard Welsted, John Dennis. These men approach Longinus with a strong Whiggish belief in Revolution principles, and interpret his life and work as unremitting opposition to arbitrary rule, both in the spheres of politics and of literature. They read the last section of his treatise, where the mutualities of liberty and eloquence, and slavery and decadence, are loudly affirmed, literally as a defence of democracy, 'the Nurse of true Genius'.[5] Despite the contemptible parts they are made to play in Scriblerian satire, these Whig critics (particularly Dennis) emphasize resistance to oppression as true sublimity, as opposed to the summary and commanding sublime preferred by neo-classical readers. These libertarian interpretations prompt the most interesting contributions to aesthetics and criticism in the latter part of the century because they examine sublimity not as the confident exemplification of divine agency and the embodiment of the power of *a priori* rules, but as the mode of subverting power, and appropriating it.

The neo-classical interpretation underplays the sublime as a reaction, and in some cases a very lively one, to an overwhelming force. It is precisely this resistance the Whig interpretation stresses. Many of Longinus' examples treat the sublime as a crisis taking place between absolute power (of the gods, of the state, or even of a ruling passion) and a subjective state he calls *transport*. Confronted by an irresistible force (7.3), stricken with its 'compacted Might' (1.2), thrown into consternation by its vehemence (12.4), or writhing under its torments (10.2), the mind of the victim makes a comeback. It is 'so sensibly affected with [these] lively Strokes', that by a species of happy bruising, 'it swells in Transport and an inward Pride' (7.2). This swelling is an index of the mind's incorporation of the power that has just threatened to destroy or immobilize it. The threat is converted into a projection of its own initiative: 'as if what was only heard had been the Product of its own Invention' (7.2); and it is then free to turn the stream of its eloquence upon a fresh victim, or audience. In these fluxes and refluxes power does not dwindle from its solid and real agency to a fainter rhetorical simulacrum where the only thing at stake is a literary affair of imaginative

---

[4] See Monk, *The Sublime*, pp. 32–4, and Levine, *Battle of the Books*, pp. 121–47.
[5] Smith, *Longinus*, p. 103. Further references will be to section and paragraph of *On the Sublime*.

response or innovative reading. At all points rhetoric operates continuously with real power, and constitutes a political recoil upon authority: 'a Judge, from whose Sentence lies no Appeal . . . a Tyrant, a Monarch, or any one invested with arbitrary Power or unbounded Authority' (17.2). Figurative language – to which Longinus pays a great deal of attention – is both the sign and instrument of the power-shift.

The salient features of modernist resistance to the hierarchical model of the neo-classical sublime emerge in the conflict between Pope and Dennis about the language appropriate to God. ' "And God said" – What? – "Let there be Light, and there was Light" ' (9.13). Strictly speaking this is an example of quotation upon quotation – a 'finesse de l'élocution' Boileau taught the world to esteem – but this is not how Boileau and other neo-classicists choose to interpret this moment in Longinus, because to do so would be to connive in an evasion of the law and to undermine the hierarchy of command. Boileau himself uses the *fiat lux* to make a final distinction between the sublime considered merely as rhetorical skill, and the sublime as an astounding and peremptory demand for 'the obedience of the creature to the commands of its creator' (*Traité*, p. viii). As a devout adherent to the series which connects the *logos* to the true critic, Pope is rather more ambitious to acquire the reversion of such a commanding and jussive utterance. Often he is to be found experimenting with the phrasing of the *fiat lux*, sometimes seriously and sometimes comically, finally fashioning its counterpart – a sort of *fiat nox* – for the end of the *Dunciad*.[6] In every case Pope is preoccupied with the power of words to do what they say, rather than with the accumulation of figures. Queen Anne's announcement of peace creates peace; Belinda's calling of spades makes them trumps in that particular game of cards. He does not propose these as instances of quotation upon quotation, a modernist trope which his brother-Scriblerian Swift specifically held up for ridicule,[7] but as the rightful inheritance of true wit. Any figurative interference between the articulation of the word and its accomplishment as command breaches the line of mimetic descent which connects Pope to God, a connexion which occasionally acquires Mosaic dimensions in theodicies such as the *Essay on Man*. The mockery of rhetoric is plainly the task of his burlesque of Longinus, the *Peri Bathous, or the Art of Sinking in Poetry* (1727). There he takes particular aim at those excessive figures, such as

[6] See *The Rape of the Lock*, Canto III, ll. 45–6; 'Epitaph. Intended for Sir Isaac Newton'; and *Windsor-Forest*, ll. 327–8.

[7] On the rage of the 'forward Critick' for Longinus, he advises, 'Then, lest with Greek he over-run ye, / Procure the Book for Love or Money, / Translated from Boileau's Translation, / And quote *Quotation* on *Quotation*.' Swift, 'On Poetry: A Rapsody', *Poems*, II, pp. 648–9.

tautology, hyperbole, and pleonasm, whose redundancy might be confused with the double structure of performatives ('None but Himself
can be his Parallel', for example, or, 'Divide, and part, the sever'd World
in two').[8] Irony is the only trope allowed an instrumental function in
this catalogue of ineffectual rhetorical excess.[9]

Dennis is as careful to display the sublimity of figurative language as
Pope is to suppress it. His argument begins with the splendour of light,
how it leads the soul to its maker;[10] and it ends with a peremptory
question about the awesome nature of creative might: 'What can produce
a greater Terror, than the Idea of an angry God?' (I, p. 356). However,
the route between these two points is very different from Pope's. Dennis
takes the bulk of his examples from that 'lofty, but most irregular
Poem', *Paradise Lost* (I, p. 333). He quotes nothing but Milton's apostrophes and prosopopeias, figures which bring the 'World's Immensity'
within the scope of the human by personifying it (I, p. 349). He goes
on to show how the language of God is bereft of these figurative additions, and how, owing to its arrival at the ear *de haut en bas*, it must
strike us as flat and unmusical, without any stress of wonder or surprise. The speech of the Almighty acquires the force and elevation of the
sublime only when the poet transfers his own feelings to the Godhead,
'shifts Persons insensibly, and forgetting who speaks, expresses himself
with those Passions which indeed are proper enough in the Poet, but
never can be so in the Deity' (I, p. 353). Solely by the mediation of
figures (the prosopopeias of projected passion, or apostrophes addressed
to an imagined person) may the language of God put on passion. Dennis
has no interest in discussing the *fiat lux* in the terms proposed by
Boileau and Pope, as somehow intrinsically sublime because it represents the source of power each poet derives by virtue of obedience;
instead he turns to an anarchic instance, Homer's battle of the gods in
Longinus. He quotes Longinus' quotation, then quotes his commentary
on it, to show that passion, and its necessary accompaniment of accumulated figures, is inseparable from the sublime.

It is evident that Dennis is performing here the same appropriation
of his model as Longinus who, when he interjects his own 'What?' into
his quotation of Moses' quotation of God's creative word, substitutes a
trope for the action, drawing attention to himself, and to his own
rhetorical manipulation of the language of power. Dennis is not slow to
exploit the antagonism this implies between the original and the imitator. By mounting his quotation of Longinus upon Longinus' quotation
of Homer, he brings the instability of the sublime hierarchy home to the

---

[8] Pope, *The Art of Sinking*, pp. 31, 59.
[9] See Weiskel, *The Romantic Sublime*, p. 20.
[10] Dennis, 'Of the Grounds of Criticism in Poetry' (1704), *Works*, I, p. 348.

relation between the writer and reader of the sublime. The writer experiences a passion by reflecting on power beyond his comprehension, and by means of figurative language he impresses the reader with a force analogous to that idea inasmuch as it is 'impossible to be resisted' (I, p. 360). This force remains with the writer 'as long he remains master' of his rhetoric (I, p. 364). Dennis has already called it 'the united Force of a Writer', 'an invincible Force' which 'commits a pleasing Rape upon the very Soul of the Reader' (I, p. 359). Mastery will be lost as soon as the reader usurps the place of the writer. This occurs when the reader arrives at the exaltation Longinus associates with mimesis, when the soul swells 'with a certain noble Pride, as if it self had produc'd what it but barely reads' (I, p. 360; compare *On the Sublime*, 7.2). Such a transfer of force takes place when Longinus makes Moses' quotation his own, and when Dennis takes Longinus' for himself. In an essay attacking Pope for his low estimate of modern readers, Dennis defends this right of usurpation by applying Boileau's celebrated judgement to the instrumentality of figures: 'For why should not a modern Critick imitate the great Qualities of Longinus; and when he treats of a Subject which is sublime, treat of it sublimely?' ('Reflections on *An Essay on Criticism* [1711]', I, p. 409). For his own part, Dennis speaks as a writer newly emancipated from the pleasing servitude of reading Longinus and Milton, and no longer afraid of 'heaping too many Citations one upon another' (I, p. 350).

The profusion of publications in the 1750s devoted to taste, rhetoric and the sublime marks a new stage in modernist readings of Longinus. Despite his importance as Pope's literary executor, William Warburton's interpretation of the *fiat lux* is unfriendly to his patron's enthusiasm for it. Drawing on Le Clerc,[11] he argues that the original Hebrew is simple and unsurprising, and that it is only the accident of Longinus' Greek background that defamiliarizes a standard parallelism and gives it the sublime *éclat* Boileau talks of. Strangeness accomplishes the same transfiguration of the gelid language of omnipotence that prosopopeia is made to do in Dennis's account of Milton. This discloses nothing of the nature of divine power, but a good deal concerning the nature of eloquence which, Warburton infers, is itself merely 'accidental and arbitrary, and depends on custom and fashion'.[12] 'What is SUBLIMITY', he demands, 'but the application of such images, as arbitrary or casual connexions, rather than their own native grandeur, however dignified and ennobled?' (I, p. 70). Having considered the alliance of the arbitrary

---

[11] Of the *fiat lux*: 'If there is any Sublimity in these Expressions, as we own there is, it is to be ascribed to the Genius of the Hebrew Language, and not to the Eloquence of Moses, as Longinus, *peri hypsos*, imagined.' Le Clerc, *Twelve Dissertations*, p. 285.

[12] Warburton, *The Doctrine of Grace*, I, p. 69.

images and figurative language as characteristic both of eloquence and the sublime, he declares their end is only 'to stifle reason, and inflame the passions' (I, p. 75).

Warburton's unease with eloquence is focused on the word *arbitrary* and its relation to the 'groveling and puerile' state of Longinus' Greece. They indicate a correspondence between a weak polity and language that is powerful because it has lost any necessary connection with a divine originary principle. Unrestrained and unauthorized by anything more settled than custom, the orator thrives to the extent to which he makes factitious forms of words credible as native grandeur, laying claim to principles by which he is in fact unmotivated. What Warburton desiderates, Hume takes as the basis of his aesthetics and his political philosophy. Three of his essays – 'Of Eloquence' (1742), 'Of the Standard of Taste' (1757) and 'Of the Original Contract' (1748) – pursue the same conclusion, namely that all rules and criteria, if sifted to the bottom, are 'uncertain, ambiguous, and arbitrary'.[13] At the so-called origin of civil society is violence and usurpation; and at the root of taste there is nothing but caprice. However, out of the coalition of these two arbitrary elements, the finest language may spring. The disorders and crimes of ancient governments stimulate oratory that is both 'sublime and passionate' (Hume, 'Of Eloquence', p. 108), and capable of blunting or even seizing the despotic power of judges and tyrants. The 'much juster taste' of these speeches made amidst injustice is a matter not of a general convention about the criteria of judgement, however, but 'a proper violence' inflicted on any individual who is spellbound by another's facility for convincing an audience that his 'particular genius, interests, passions, and prejudices' have the force of general principles (Hume, 'Of the Standard of Taste', pp. 239–41).

Hume's arguments and Warburton's reservations establish the ground of a comparison between ancient sublimity and modern mid-century political oratory that has little in common with the neo-classical exemplary sublime, and which considerably modifies the sublime of Revolution principles to be found in the work of Williamite Whigs such as Blackmore and Welsted. Although they disagree about the sublime, both the Ancients and the early Moderns believe Longinus to be upholding and disinterestedly applying a standard of literary and moral excellence. Pope's 'ardent judge' and Welsted's 'great Statesman and Critick'[14] is faithful to a law above and beyond the singularity of taste. But Hume removes the ethical pathos from the calculus of that 'proper violence' which changes people's minds as it changes their relation to power. His

[13] Hume, 'Of the Original Contract', *Essays*, p. 482.
[14] Welsted, *Longinus*, p. xii.

Longinus, and eloquent patriot parliamentarians such as Pitt the elder, operate alike in political arenas from which positive principles have been expelled, together with their common substitute, factional slogans. They use the 'versatility'[15] of an idealist political rhetoric to conceal or dignify the particularity of private ends, manoeuvring within a context of arbitrary initiatives and customary tolerances Jeremy Bentham later summed up as follows: 'Right is conformity to a rule, wrong the deviation from it: but here there is no rule established, no measure to discern, no standard to appeal to: all is uncertainty, darkness, and confusion.'[16]

This is the era fit to assess the sophistic side of *On the Sublime*: the side that considers the sublime as a branch of political expedience. The praise lavished on Demosthenes by Longinus, not for his selfless devotion to the Athenian cause but for the rhetorical cunning with which he furthers his ambitions in the guise of a selfless patriot, is typical of the sort of sophist Plato attacks in the *Gorgias* and the *Protagoras*. Demosthenes' sublimity, Hume says, lies in artful impersonations of altruism that deceive his judges and elude the anger of the people ('Of Eloquence', pp. 100, 104). The Earl of Egmont defines a modern patriot as someone actuated by the principle of having no principles at all ('He will neither be fettered by general Maxims, nor tied to any chimerical System, but will be governed by Times and Circumstances'),[17] and the Earl of Shelburne drily explains Pitt's devotion to the study of eloquence in the same way: 'It gave him great advantages to serve a turn, by enabling him to change like lightning from one set of principles to another.'[18] It is interesting to observe how the archetype of the *fiat lux* is misapplied by such an adroit orator. In a speech on the Scottish magistracy, Pitt turns it specifically against what he takes to be the tyranny of definite principles and original laws: 'When master principles are concerned [Walpole is paraphrasing], he dreaded accuracy of distinction: he feared that sort of reasoning; if you class everything, you will soon reduce everything into a particular; you will then lose great general maxims ... He would not recur for precedents to the diabolic divans of the second Charles and James – he did not date his principles of the liberty of this country from the Revolution: they are eternal rights; and when God said, *let justice be justice*, he made it independent.'[19]

---

[15] A term applied by Godwin to the wayward element of the patriots' 'irresistible eloquence'. Of Pitt's ambition, he says it was 'the only part, that heaven had left vulnerable about him; and introduced a feebleness and versatility into his story, that must ever form the principal blemish of this immortal patriot' (Godwin, *Life of Pitt*, p. 150).

[16] Bentham, *Of Laws*, p. 184.

[17] *Faction Detected*, pp. 164–5; cited in Brewer, *Party Ideology*, p. 99.

[18] Cited in Clark, *The Dynamics of Change*, p. 283.

[19] Walpole, *Memoirs*, II, p. 39.

The circularity that affects the language of justification when there are no settled principles clearly to authenticate it, imparts a new valency to the Boilevian formula of sublimity upon sublimity, and Dennis's modification of it, quotation upon quotation. In a world where justice is justice, where 'the great patronise because they are great [and] the vulgar cavil because they are vulgar', where Sterne's uncle Toby will give no other explanation of why he rides a hobbyhorse than 'getting upon his back and riding him about', and where Henry Fox replies to his monarch's invitation to govern not with a principled yes or no, but a request for details ('I must know, Sir, what means I shall have, or I cannot answer for what I cannot answer'), the doubling up of the case with its rule is no more than a ruse to give a tautology the appearance of authority, and to turn the lack of principle into a persuasive explanation.[20] To be sublime upon the sublime in these terms is to make rhetoric an instrument of an excessive and unexemplary desire for power, and to offer no other justification for acting upon it than the success of the outcome.[21]

In France the sublime has relatively little to do until the Revolution. Before that period of violent change the pyramidal structure of political authority encounters the resistance only of Enlightenment reason, which does not disturb the regime of neo-classical criticism. Some astute reflections in Du Bos and Rousseau on the nature of our response to the representation of pain are the closest the French get to the issues preoccupying British and German critics of the sublime, apart from the astonishing contribution made to the theory and practice of the comic sublime in Diderot's *Le Neveu de Rameau*. The Revolution on the other hand provides numberless opportunities for the exponents of oratory and spectacle to discover in their capacity for resistance a boundless hunger for power. The careers of Robespierre, Danton and Saint-Just take place in the abyss between two regimes, where the rhetoric of self-sacrificing patriotism serves only to trace the sudden movement of power from one group to another. These exponents of a self-exemplifying revolutionary sublime share with Hume's Longinus – and with Longinus' Demosthenes – a clear-sightedness about the lack of principle necessary if rhetoric is to justify or to cause a rapid political change. The maxim of the Jacobin ascendancy – 'The most sacred duty and the most cherished law is to forget the law' – unfolds the tautology of Robespierre's rhetorical question to the Convention: 'Do you want a Revolution without a revolution?'[22] The doubling of the words mimics the insistent,

[20] Cited in Clark, *The Dynamics of Change*, p. 15; Sterne, *Tristram Shandy*, I, pp. 24, 78; Walpole, *Memoirs*, II, p. 30.
[21] See de Bolla, *Discourse of the Sublime*, pp. 143–82.
[22] Cited in Schama, *Citizens*, pp. 612, 649.

self-authorizing turn of a force exerted without law or precedent: each moment of such a force is its own example not by virtue of history or tradition, but by virtue of the reverberation of its own success. Robespierre's Mosaic posturings during the Festival of the Supreme Being, like Pitt's replay of the *fiat lux*, celebrate the authority the orator usurps by means of self-evident propositions. Hence Saint-Just on the guilt of overthrown monarchs: 'Every king is a usurper.'

Power and rhetoric

Burke's refinement of the Whig sublime in his *Enquiry* is usually interpreted as an historical irony, since forty years later he deprecates the resistance of the French to tyranny and oppression in a stream of lurid rhetoric that sentimentalizes the French monarchy as the last flowering of the age of chivalry.[23] But Burke's attitudes to power in the *Reflections* and the *Enquiry* are reasonably consistent. In both he finds the actual operation of unlimited power terrifying, whether it culminate in the unspeakable butchery of Damiens the regicide, or in the humiliation of a king and queen at the hands of their quondam subjects.[24] If the unlimited exercise of power is not to be intolerable to the spectator it must be disguised with 'all the pleasing illusions, which make power gentle' (*Reflections*, VIII, p. 128). In the *Enquiry* the sublime is the measure, if not of the illusion, then of the alteration that must take place if power is to produce delight instead of horror. This is exactly how he defines it: 'I know of nothing sublime which is not some modification of power' (*Enquiry*, p. 64). Unmodified power is God, and God is terrible, 'a force which nothing can withstand', before which 'we shrink into the minuteness of our own nature, and are ... annihilated' (p. 68).

The terms of this argument concerning the sublimity of a terrible God are already to some degree anticipated by Dennis, but Burke is equalled only by Hegel in the fear he supposes the Almighty to cause. As a Whig of the 1750s, power strikes him as the key issue, not figures (as for Dennis) or the lines of hierarchical descent (as for Pope). In the second edition of the *Enquiry* (1759) he explains his reticence on this topic as 'natural timidity with regard to power': 'I purposely avoided when I first considered this subject, to introduce the idea of that great and tremendous being, as an example in an argument so light as this' (pp. 67–8). His reasons for overcoming his reluctance are to be found in a

---

[23] See for example Paulson, *Representations of Revolution*, pp. 71–3; Kay, *Political Constructions*, pp. 266–78; Pocock, *Virtue, Commerce, Society*, pp. 193–212; and Mitchell, *Iconology*, p. 131.

[24] Burke, *Enquiry*, p. 39; *Reflections*, VIII, p. 122.

series of displacements from limited or imperfect definitions of the sublime, until he finally identifies the power of God as its true origin. In the first edition he says that the sublime is the cause of delight (p. 51). In the second, he begins by locating the cause of this cause in 'Terror [which] is in all cases whatsoever, either more openly or latently, the ruling principle of the sublime' (p. 58). Then he seeks the cause of the ruling principle. He defines it first as obscurity, 'this grand cause of terror . . . wrapt up in the shades of its own incomprehensible darkness' (p. 63), and finally as God, the 'capital source of the sublime' (p. 70).

These modifications to his argument about power are accompanied by a series of observations about images. Burke believes that images – especially painted images – are destructive of the sublime because they clarify and literalize 'fanciful and terrible ideas' that are better left obscure (p. 63). However, poetry can assemble 'a croud of great and confused images' that transport the reader with delight precisely because they resist any clear presentation to the mind's eye. His examples are Milton's descriptions of Death and Lucifer (pp. 59, 62). But the sole image Burke has supplied of God is of darkness wrapped up in itself, an image that does not stir the imagination but brings it to the point where it 'is finally lost' (pp. 63, 70). This is not quite the case with Milton's Death, however, of which Burke says, 'In this description all is dark, uncertain, confused, terrible, and sublime to the last degree' (p. 59). He is making a distinction he is unwilling to explore between the representation of terrible uncertainty and the experience of it, between a vivid poetic evocation of an idea of obscurity and the intuition of a force too darkly great to be presented in any distinct form at all. He cannot advance the distinction along Dennis's lines, contrasting the sublimity of the figurative representation of power with the flatness of the real thing, because he does not wish to consider figurative language other than as a fund of representational forms – images – whose difference lies solely in the degree of *vraisemblance* or distance in which they stand to power itself. But it would seem that an image is sublime for Burke not because it confuses the spectator but because it diffuses the annihilating light of God, modifying it with opacities and judicious obscurities until the eye is protected from the sheer light that would have blinded it. An image is the viewable shape printed on the screen that stands between the capital source of the sublime and the vulnerable spectator.

It is therefore in the spectator's interest to minimize the connection between the images and the force behind them, and if possible to assign them a function independent of it. Burke fills the section on Power with instances from the Book of Job – the war-horse, the wild ass, the unicorn, and the leviathan – none of which he produces as the vehicles of God's terrifying rhetoric but simply as empirical proof of the sublimity of animals of a certain order of strength and freedom.[25] Under this rubric Job himself can take his place not as a man made desperate by his unmediated relation to the annihilating force of God, but as one who has enjoyed power on his own account: ' "The young men saw me, and hid themselves" ' (p. 67). Like Burke's Lucifer, his Louis XVI – or possibly even more like his Marie Antoinette – Job is a figure of authority whose life's drapery has been rudely torn off. So in a consoling and ultimately literalizing gesture Burke turns to images as salves for the usurped body of the sovereign, and as garments to cover the nakedness of the victim of what would otherwise be an unimaginably terrifying exercise of power.[26]

This helps to explain why, when he arrives at the topic of language, Burke refuses to consider its obscurities as instruments of rhetoric. 'Those modes of speech that mark a strong and lively feeling in [the speaker] himself' (p. 175) do not even amount to the accidental rhetoric of complaint. They are the material of an obscurity that will eventually form an image whose purpose (at least for Burke) is to make power more gentle and the light less shatteringly bright. Dennis's treatment of Milton's prosopopeias is much subtler, owing to his clear division between 'speech' which might properly belong to God, and those rhetorical devices which permit writers to master readers and, conversely, enable readers to emancipate themselves. This is either too blasphemous or too revolutionary for Burke, who must consider power indirectly, 'at certain distances, and with modifications' (p. 40), veiled by images that pretend to be representations of ideas with an independent existence. Absent from his notion of the sublime is the reflective margin needed if a moment of terror or a desire for safety is to emerge as a calculated rhetorical effect. All that really engages his critical attention after the safety of the spectator has been secured is the nature of the sympathy that might unite the witness of power with the victim of it.

The only time he supposes something like a conscious reaction to power is when he talks of ambition and makes his single paraphrase of Longinus: 'Whatever either on good or upon bad grounds tends to raise a man in his own opinion, produces a sort of swelling and triumph that is extremely grateful to the human mind ... Hence proceeds what Longinus has observed of that glorying and sense of inward greatness, that always fills the reader of such passages in poets and orators as are sublime' (pp. 50–1).[27] He also compares the surge of ambition with the

---

[25] See Ferguson, 'The sublime of Edmund Burke', pp. 73–4.

[26] On Burke's relation to the eighteenth century's rhetoricization of history, see Hayden White, 'The politics of historical interpretation', p. 68.

[27] For a discussion of this apparent anomaly in the argument of the *Enquiry*, see Knapp, *Personification and the Sublime*, pp. 68–74.

effects of flattery, since both 'raise in a man's mind an idea of preference which he has not'. The instrumentality of rhetoric is therefore doubly unacceptable to him: it operates regardless of principle ('either on good or upon bad grounds'); and it deceives people about the likelihood of gaining power.

Burke's caution in the matter of sublime rhetoric cannot fully be appreciated without considering the flow and direction of political power in Britain at the time he was writing his essay. The versatility of men like Pitt and Townshend, their pragmatic but brilliant manoeuvring amidst the phantoms of ancient precedent, fascinates Burke as much as it repels him. If he were fully to confront the problem of sublime eloquence, and the figures the orator deliberately wields for a definite end, he could hardly avoid Hume's judgement that his control over his audience's tides of passion and credulity is inversely proportionate to 'the multiplicity and intricacy of laws' ('Of Eloquence', p. 100), and that it amounts to a species of violence. He makes that very judgement against Price and 'the gentlemen of the Society for Revolutions': 'They take the deviation from the principle for the principle' in order to justify political terror (*Reflections*, VIII, p. 73). Rather than be implicated in such lawlessness, Burke has no option but to believe as heartily as he can in the constitutional and legal fictions that warrant the fashionable language of power, and to honour the values that are arbitrarily or customarily associated with the name of chivalry: 'the unbought grace of life, the cheap defence of nations, the nurse of manly sentiment and heroic enterprise' (*Reflections*, VIII, p. 127). On all fronts Burke husbands the uncertainty, darkness and confusion that Bentham is to deprecate as inimical to law and that Hume says shroud the violence at the origin of civil society.

Kant's 'Analytic of the Sublime' in the third *Critique* is an extended consideration, some say a drama,[28] of the flux and reflux of sublime energy, ending with a rousing attack on political oratory. He is able to transcend the limitations of Burke's empirical treatment of power by abstracting the issues of violence, dominion and law from the arenas of nature and politics in order to resolve them at the level of mind, where a negotiation between the faculties results in the sublime adjustment of the particular to the general. With a single question, Kant despatches the preoccupations that lie behind the British fascination with landscape, Gothic novels and the picturesque: 'Who would apply the term "sublime" even to shapeless mountain masses towering one above the other in wild disorder, with their pyramids of ice, or to the dark tempestuous ocean, or such like things?'[29] He goes on to elucidate the reasons that

[28] Paul de Man, 'Phenomenality and materiality in Kant', pp. 140–1.

[29] Kant, *Critique of Judgment*, p. 104; for Kant's whole discussion of the sublime, see *Kritik der Urteilskraft*, in Kant, *Gesammelte Schriften*, V, 244–66. The political and aesthetic implications of the inadequacy of the Kantian imagination are handled well by Lyotard in 'The sublime and the avant-garde', and 'The sign of history'.

prevent our answering boldly, 'Mrs Radcliffe!'. These depend upon a distinction between fearing something (i.e., calmly assessing its might) and being afraid of it (i.e., being overwhelmed with terror at one's inability to resist it). Right-thinking and righteous individuals are afraid neither of nature nor of God; if they were they would be merely creatures of 'rude dominion', existing in a humiliating relation to external forces that would preclude any principled judgement of them (*Critique*, pp. 110–11). Kant is pointing out to Burke that there is no modification of power capable of modifying terror, and that terror is absolutely inimical to the sublime.

However, he allows that the urge to represent the 'violence of destruction', to reproduce it as an image in the brain, is the first instinct of the imagination when faced with waterfalls, volcanoes, and other prodigies of nature. In this vain effort, the imagination does a violence to itself because it tries to frame something that has already gone beyond the limit and arrived at 'the point of excess' (pp. 107–8). In effect it is committed to attaching a sensible image to the experience of infinite and incomparable greatness. It is destined always to fail, 'For the sublime, in the strict sense of the word, cannot be contained in any sensuous form, but rather concerns ideas of reason ... [It is] the mere capacity of thinking which evidences a faculty of mind transcending every standard of sense' (pp. 92, 98). After the imagination has suffered this check, renounced its interest in the representation of greatness in itself, the second, triumphant stage of the sublime experience becomes possible. The faculty of reason reads the inadequacy of the imagination as a negative symbolization of the illimitable idea: it grasps the failure of presentation as the 'equivalent to a presentation of ideas' (p. 119), that is, as a sign of a supersensible concept. This reading not only saves the subject from a humiliating submission to external force, it brings the experience of the sublime under the rule of law, 'for the rational idea of the supersensible is not excessive, but conformable to law' (p. 107). Instead of being complicit with the anarchy of arbitrary connections and the particularity of interested views, Kant's sublime achieves exemplary status, and conforms with precedents and laws established by the higher faculty of the mind itself. While this dispels the darkness and uncertainty of Burke's and Hume's sublime, it internalizes the hierarchy of legitimate descent on which Pope's and Boileau's relies, and does away with the need for a theodicy of the aesthetic.[30]

Once this legislative balance is achieved, the imagination can resume its business. It now plays as it were in perfect freedom under the law its failure has revealed. Among the arts that flourish under this regime, rhetoric stands out as an exception, for it deliberately undermines the government of the law which guarantees the freedom of the imagination.

[30] See Kant, *Theodicy*, pp. 233–5.

Even if its aim is virtuous, it damages the intuitive obedience to higher principles that makes even originality exemplary (p. 181). In a devastating footnote Kant despatches the sophistic cunning of orators such as Demosthenes and Pitt, and by implication impugns the candour of critics like Longinus or Hume who can approve of it: 'Oratory, being the art of playing for one's own purpose upon the weaknesses of men (let this purpose be ever so good in intention or even in fact) merits no *respect* whatever. Besides, both at Athens and at Rome, it attained its greatest height only at a time when the state was hastening to its decay, and genuine patriotic sentiment was a thing of the past' (p. 193, n.1). From quite the opposite side to Burke, in so far as he discounts the place of terror in the sublime, Kant arrives at a similar difficulty with rhetoric, holding it up as the element of the sublime that disturbs its relation to power and reintroduces threats of external danger and humiliation.

'Sublimity is only the representation of power.'[31] By that Hegel does not mean, any more than Kant means, that sublimity is representable in sensible images; on the other hand, the Hegelian sublime is not the result of a balance struck between two faculties within the subject, but arises when absolute power chooses to manifest itself as dominion: 'Sublimity is the shape of the powerful in the weak' (*Lectures*, II, p. 136). Its representation is its creation, what is called into being as the predicate of divine utterance, in order that its power may be acknowledged, feared and reflected back into itself as nothing but its own. The inadequacy of the subject is here registered not as a sign but as the experience of radical negativity.[32] Hegel's archetype is the *fiat lux*; and his exemplary text is Job, where the 'universal situation' of the Almighty confronting his own creature as 'perishing and powerless' is most dramatically and forcibly delineated, particularly in the theophany, where God overwhelms Job by listing the mightiest things in his creation as the inconsiderable surplus of his absolute will.[33]

Hegel's early fascination with Longinus may explain the prominence he gives to the overwhelming moment of the sublime.[34] In his account, the 'irresistible force' of creative words is literally unopposable, and the Longinian metaphors of blows, lightning strikes and wounds are literalized as the destruction of 'outward shaping' which takes place when power annihilates the material in which it has revealed itself (*Aesthetics*, I, p. 363). He leaves no room for the resistance of the Longinian sublime, or the resilience Burke accords ambition, which regards every exercise

[31] Hegel, *Lectures on the Philosophy of Religion*, II, p. 434.
[32] See Žižek, *Sublime Object*, p. 144.
[33] See *Lectures*, II, p. 424; and *Aesthetics*, I, p. 372.
[34] In 1786–7, at the age of sixteen, Hegel translated *On the Sublime*. See *Lectures*, II, p. 433 n.533.

of power potentially as its own. Hegel's sublime is rather like the blip on a radar screen. The illuminated dot is the ephemeral testimony of an invisible will, erased no sooner than it is made because it stands merely as the medium, not the object, of unlimited will. The things of the world may still be said to exist after God has finished speaking with them, but they are inert, or what Hegel calls *prosaic*, a collocation of 'powerless accidents' (*Aesthetics*, I, p. 374), until they are caught once more in the path of divine energy and gleam as if for the first time, like leviathan and the war-horse in the theophany of Job. In Hegel's argument the creature is not defended from the annihilating power of God by the image (as Burke suggests), the creature is the image.

The story of Job, like the best of the Psalms, reveals the sublime as the abjection of the creature of such a God. As the medium of a power that announces itself in the destruction of that very medium, Job cannot even discover the meaning of his own pain, inasmuch as it belongs to the representation of the sublime, which is always over and above the material by which it is (necessarily imperfectly) revealed. 'And we find depicted in a penetrating and affecting way grief over nullity, and the cry of the soul to God in complaint, suffering, and lament from the depths of the heart' (*Aesthetics*, I, p. 376). Hegel's Job is much more than Burke's the victim of an unmodified power, and Hegel is much less reticent than Burke in locating the chief principle of the sublime in a God whose power is vented solely in the annihilation of his creature. In his account of creatural inadequacy there is none of the voluntary acknowledgement of weakness made by Kant's imagination to the superior faculty of reason, nor any of the free collaboration between imagination and moral law that follows her capitulation. As Hegel's model of creatural abjection, Job stops resisting the inequities of providence: he stops complaining and bows before the might he no longer has the energy to question. 'It is his submission and renunciation that justifies Job, in that he recognises the boundless power of God' (*Lectures*, II, p. 447).

Although this unreserved submission concludes the story of Job as far as Hegel is concerned, his frequent citation of the maxim, 'the fear of the lord is the beginning of wisdom',[35] indicates the possibility of a dialectical recuperation of abjection. Job's unmodified sense of his own nullity gains him 'a freer and more independent position' within the negativity of his relation to God. His annihilation is partly the result of his own 'behaviour and action' (*Aesthetics*, I, p. 377), and the possibility of sublation – the nullification of nullity – is opened up, although not developed in these lectures. In the Psalms, Hegel finds an example of

[35] E.g., Hegel, *Pheomenology*, p. 117.

this capitulation-as-worship in the antiphonal response to the *fiat lux* in Psalm 104, where the lord is apostrophized as thou 'who coverest thyself with light as with a garment' (I, p. 375). Here the freer and more independent stand is expressed as the metaphor the Psalmist makes out of the predicate of the original utterance. As Paul de Man has pointed out, the language of positing has been transformed into a trope: a grammatical event has become something of a rhetorical feat.[36]

What Hegel starts to outline as a reflux of creatural energy in the *Lectures* and the *Aesthetics* is fully worked out in the *Phenomenology* as the dialectic of the lord and the bondsman, or the master and the slave. The rude dominion of the master requires as its trophy the fearful subjection of the slave, but only as a momentary and imperfect gleam of triumph. The slave begins like Job; he 'posits himself as a negative within the permanent order of things, and thereby becomes for himself, someone existing on his own account' (*Phenomenology*, p. 118). Unlike the master, whose enjoyment of things is sudden and destructive, the slave has time to work on matter and shape it heroically to his own ends. As his servitude becomes more and more self-conscious, he becomes aware of the tendency of all judgements and qualities to turn into their opposites. He begins to appreciate how imperceptibly his own heroism of service turns into the ignoble art of flattery, how the law merely disguises the caprices of an absolute force, and how every sentiment the honest man tries literally to utter turns out to be the opposite of what he intends because the universal order and the particular instance never dovetail (*Phenomenology*, pp. 66, 95; *Lectures*, II, p. 437). In these rapid oscillations speech has no longer anything immediately to do with truth. The plain mind can only adduce it by example, invoking its virtual existence as historical precedent (*Phenomenology*, p. 319); the more agile intellect resorts to language which is shamelessly 'clever and witty'.

Hegel turns for his own example of this witty, disrupted consciousness to Diderot's *Le Neveu de Rameau*, an exhibition of comic or reversed sublimity that includes all the tricks of sophistic and revolutionary oratory. Hegel's Rameau's nephew is a clowning Solomon, or a joking Moses, preaching and embodying the vanity and particularity of all things, and laying down the laws of an amoral existence, as he gambles for the dominion of consciousness over the dispersed field of human ambition (*Phenomenology*, p. 320). He is the slave who knows how to usurp the power of the master. This power is evident in his fragmentary performances of tragedy and his vignettes of the passions, which can transfix an audience that already knows they are mockeries. Specifically, he mocks Moses by citing the *fiat lux* whenever there is an urgent need

---

[36] De Man, 'Hegel on the Sublime', pp. 147–8.

to assert his mastery.[37] And here he winds Hegel's favourite example of the sublime of the creative positional statement into the realm of citation, figure and rhetoric.

Rameau's nephew rediscovers in rhetoric the caprice that character-izes all mastery, whether it is God's or a cunning orator's. Between the sophistic sublime of patriotic rhetoric and his brilliant mimetic swerves there is no difference except in the accent they place on the universal. Rameau bids openly for the measureless excess of particularity – 'acci-dental caprices and subjective desires'.[38] Pitt's bid is more guardedly made for the groundless and shapeless universal justice that warrants the 'versatility' of his principles; Robespierre's is for the 'patrie' that peremptorily requires all laws to fall before the sublime illegality of revolution. This is what Burke calls the principle of only deviating from principle, and it relies for its success on converting literal and positional language of primal mastery into the figures and tropes of usurpation: in turning 'Let there be light' into 'Light is the garment that you wear', for example, or into 'Let justice be justice'. Here sublimity is the represen-tation of power in a new and more resisting sense, by means of which Hegel recovers a Longinian appreciation of the potentiality of figurative language that eludes Burke and Kant.

Particularity and the sublime

Sappho's ode to her faithless lover (Lobel Page fr. 31) comes down to us only in the fragment quoted by Longinus in section 10 of his treatise, where he uses it to show how an exact attention to the physical circum-stances of passion, and a careful articulation of them in the represen-tation of it, will contribute largely to a sense of the sublime. Having listed the specific symptoms of jealousy as they affect severally her body, ears, tongue and eyes, he declares, 'The Excellence of this Ode ... consists in the judicious Choice and Connexion of the most notable Circumstances.'[39] He anticipates the defence of trifling details and vulgar expressions he will make in sections 30 and 31, and to some extent contradicts the negative judgements he makes about amplification in sections 12 and 43. The equivocal status of particularity in the aesthetics of the sublime explains why Sappho's ode was regarded as anomalous, especially by critics with conservative inclinations. Pope and Gay

---

[37] Diderot, *Le Neveu de Rameau*, ed. Jacques and Marie Chovillet (Paris, Livre de Poche, 1984), p. 39.

[38] Hegel, *Philosophy of Right*, pp. 185, 267.

[39] Smith, *Longinus*, p. 29. Sappho's disintegration provides the focus of one of the best modern essays on Longinus, Neil Hertz's 'A reading of Longinus', in *The End of the Line*, pp. 1–20.

burlesque the fragmentation of the female poet in their comedy *Three Hours after Marriage* (1717), where Phoebe Clinket disintegrates under the ferocious scrutiny of Sir Tremendous Longinus.[40] Gibbon observes, 'I hardly think the ode of Sappho was a proper example ... surely there is nothing in it which elevates the mind.'[41] Coleridge concedes that in the literature of excitement 'Sappho's Ode was, is, and probably ever will be, the most perfect specimen. But as to sublime you might as well call it blue or small-poxed.'[42]

Consistent with this hostile response to Sappho's poem is the line of criticism that applauds the totalizing tendency and the unitary impact of the sublime. Baillie is the first to give wide currency to the view that smallness is inimical to the sublime. Having shown how the vastness of the sublime object composes the mind to think 'one large, simple, and uniform Idea', he adds, 'No Object is so grand, but is attended with some *trifling* Circumstance, upon which a little Mind will surely fix; the Universe has its Cockle-shells, and its Butterflies, the ardent Pursuits of childish Geniuses.'[43] The sure way to ruin the sublime, Beattie warns, is 'by too minute descriptions, and too many words': you do not number the windows of a lofty building, or describe the state of a hero's teeth and nails.[44] 'One trifling circumstance, one mean idea, is sufficient to destroy the whole charm [of] Sublime description,' writes Blair.[45] In his opinion 'every superfluous decoration degrades a sublime idea'.[46] If a sublime emotion is to have free play, maintains Alison, the attention must be completely withdrawn from all 'trifling and ludicrous circumstances'.[47] These views are given their most majestic expression by Samuel Johnson in his essay on Cowley, where he states that 'sublimity is produced by aggregation' and that 'great thoughts are always general, and consist ... in descriptions not descending into minuteness'.[48] They are rehearsed finally by Coleridge in his deprecation of the 'matter-of-factness' of Wordsworth's poetry – 'a laborious minuteness ... the insertion of accidental circumstances' – and judges it to be 'incompatible with the steady fervour of a mind possessed and filled with the grandeur of its subject'.[49] Hogarth and Reynolds support the same standards in the

[40] Act II, ll. 111–48. See Trussler, *Burlesque Plays*, pp. 111–12.
[41] Gibbon, *Journal*, p. 156.   [42] Coleridge, *Miscellaneous Criticism*, p. 320.
[43] Baillie, *An Essay on the Sublime*, p. 13.
[44] Beattie, 'Illustrations on Sublimity', in *Dissertations*, p. 639.
[45] Blair, *Lectures*, I, p. 90.
[46] Blair, 'A Critical Dissertation on the Poems of Ossian', in Macpherson, *Ossian*, I, p. 230.
[47] Alison, *Essays on Taste*, I, pp. 138–9.
[48] Johnson, 'Cowley', in *Lives of the English Poets*, I, pp. 21.
[49] Coleridge, *Biographia Literaria*, II, pp. 68, 101. See Alan Liu, 'Local transcendence in cultural criticism, postmodernism, and the romanticism of detail', *Representations*, 32 (1990), 75–113.

field of the pictorial sublime. At the bottom of his mock-sublime piece *The Bathos*, Hogarth lays it down for a rule that the effect of sublime paintings is dissipated by the introduction of 'low, absurd, obscene and often prophane Circumstances into them'. Reynolds is no less emphatic: 'The Sublime impresses the mind at once with one great idea; it is a single blow: the Elegant, indeed, may be produced by repetition; by an accumulation of many minute circumstances.'[50] As far as he is concerned, minuteness and deformity are the same thing, a blurring of the idea of a general form (*Discourses* (no. 3), p. 47).

It is of course in his marginal commentary on the *Discourses* that Blake makes his celebrated retort: 'All Sublimity is founded on Minute Discrimination.'[51] Such a maxim puts Blake in company with a heterogeneous collection of critics in the eighteenth century who believe that particularity is an aspect of sublime representation not to be neglected.[52] Whether it is Blackwell and Gibbon talking about the circumstantial beauties of epic and history,[53] Lowth praising 'the minutest circumstances' and 'the exact and vivid delineation of the objects' which characterizes the scriptural sublime,[54] Priestley calculating the remarkable effects of 'a redundancy of particulars' upon the imaginations of readers,[55] Richard Payne Knight arguing that the truths which interest the feelings are 'naturally circumstantial',[56] or even a novelist such as Sterne explaining to his reader that the circumstances of things alone determine how they shall be judged – 'great—little—good—bad ... just as the case happens',[57] – the particularizing critics respond much more acutely to the singularity of the object of taste than their opponents, who would prefer it merely to exemplify a general rule about the indivisibility of sublime phenomena.

This disagreement lurks behind all theories of the sublime because the issue of sublimity upon sublimity – whether it is the coincidence of a loose circumstance with the rule that authorizes its appearance, or whether it is the excessive accumulation of contingent particulars that evade all regulation – is never fully confronted and never fully resolved at the level of taste until Kant broaches it in the third *Critique*, or at

[50] Reynolds, *Discourses* (no. 3), p. 47.
[51] *The Poetry and Prose of William Blake*, ed. Erdman, pp. 643, 185. See also Weiskel, *The Romantic Sublime*, p. 67; and de Luca, 'Blake and the two Sublimes', in Payne, *Studies in Eighteenth-Century Culture No. 11*, p. 98.
[52] This branch of the sublime tends to be dominated, however, by scriptural critics. See Abrams, *The Mirror and the Lamp*, and Morris, *The Religious Sublime*.
[53] Blackwell, *An Enquiry into Homer*, I, p. 12; Gibbon, *An Essay on Literature*, p. 30.
[54] Lowth, *Lectures on Sacred Poetry*, p. 51.
[55] Priestley, *Lectures on Oratory*, p. 85.
[56] Payne Knight, *Analytical Enquiry*, p. 277.
[57] *Tristram Shandy*, III, 2, p. 187. For a short history of particularity, or 'detailism' as it is now called, see Schor, *Reading in Detail*, pp. 3–37.

the level of politics until Hegel deals with it in the *Philosophy of Right*. The closest pre-critical aesthetics gets to a solution of the problem is the 'double principle' evolved by Addison in his *Spectator* papers on the pleasures of the imagination, and then developed in associationist models of perception. Very briefly, this involves a dual response to phenomena as both singular and representative, as free-standing impressions and as signs of universals. The intensity generated by this mutual relation of particle and form is experienced variously as awe, power and belief, and it is assigned by some of the more notable scriptural critics as the cause of the sublime in poetic language.[58]

Wordsworth describes the access of power deriving from the double principle as a privatized *fiat lux*, 'an auxiliar light ... which on the setting sun / Bestowed new splendor; the melodious birds, / The gentle breezes, fountains that ran on, / Murmuring so sweetly in themselves, obeyed / A like dominion; and the midnight storm / Grew darker in the presence of my eye' (*Prelude*, 2.288–293). In his versified exploration of Addison's theme, Akenside locates the source of poetic power likewise in the faculty that redoubles 'the native weight and energy of things' and makes language 'big with the very motion of the soul' (*Pleasures of the Imagination*, 2.149). Wordsworth is particularly struck by any phenomenon whose double quality projects or echoes this faculty. The boy of Winander's mimic hootings are returned by the owls on the far shore, and answered and retorted until 'long halloos, and screams, and echoes loud / Redoubled and redoubled' (*Prelude*, 5.402–3).[59] Wordsworth enjoyed the visual equivalent of this game of blurred differences whenever the air above a lake was still enough to confound the line of the surrounding hills with their reflections in the water, so that it would become 'scarcely possible to distinguish the point where the real object terminated, and its unsubstantial duplicate began'.[60]

In his essay 'The Sublime and the Beautiful' Wordsworth devotes a good deal of the argument to considering power not simply (like Burke) as a modification wrought upon nature by God, but as a 'twofold agency' involving a strong spectatorial bid to expand what he calls in the *Prelude* 'the empire of the sight': 'There is no sublimity excited by the contemplation of power thought of as a thing to be resisted & which the moral law enjoins us to resist, saving only as far as the mind ... conceives that that power may be overcome or rendered evanescent, and as far as it feels itself tending towards the unity that exists in security or absolute

[58] See Sitter, *Literary Loneliness*, pp. 9–29, and Ferguson, *Solitude and the Sublime*, pp. 98–101 where she tackles this 'self-haunting' quality of the sublime experience.
[59] See Hertz, *End of the Line*, pp. 233–9; Weiskel, *The Romantic Sublime*, p. 32.
[60] Wordsworth, *A Guide to the Lakes*, in *Prose Works*, II, p. 236. See Ferguson, *Solitude and the Sublime*, pp. 143–4.

triumph' (*Prose Works*, II, p. 356). However, when his recollections of the French Revolution literalize these metaphors of resistance and usurpation, Wordsworth faces enormous problems in trying to reconcile the patriot sublime of a largely individualist British creed with the bloody intractabilities of a real political upheaval. Between the unprecedented excesses of the Revolution and the tumult of Wordsworth's own mind there is generated an astounding and truly sublime sense of sheer instantaneity, when terror leaks through the divisions of temporality ('The fear gone by / Pressed on me almost like a fear to come' (10.64)) and the limitless particularity of the present moment overflows in advance the historical narrative that aims to make intelligible 'to future times the face of what now is' (9.177).

These moments when, as Wordsworth puts it in his *Essays on Epitaphs*, matters of fact emerge in their intensity,[61] are analysed by Lowth and Herder with great attention. They begin by stressing the prosaic elements of the scene, urging the reader of the Old Testament to appreciate the specific historical circumstances in which its passionate poems were composed. 'It is the first duty of a critic ... to remark, as far as possible, the situation and habits of the author, the natural history of his country, and the scene of the poem' (Lowth, *Sacred Poetry*, p. 77). Herder spends some time detailing the Arabian background to the book of Job, and concludes that not only images, but also maxims and proverbs are abstractions 'from particular occurrences, and many of these among the Orientals still include the particular case in the general expression'.[62] On this historical foundation they erect an analytic of the rhetoric of particularity, and of the figures of detailed misery. Lowth shows how the most energetic language of Job is consistent with the finest examples of the scriptural sublime in uniting the common and familiar cases of violence and suffering with the grandest ideas of divine power. He is careful to point out that in this sense of the sublime, Longinus is his authority, not those critics who reserve it solely to 'a magnificent display of imagery and diction' (p. 155).

Herder recurs to Dennis's opinion that the junction of the earthly and the particular with the boundless and the immense is especially fruitful in the figure of prosopopeia: 'The dawn appears in Job as a hero, who scatters the bands of misdoers, deprives the robber of the covering of darkness' (*Hebrew Poetry*, I, p. 67; *Sämtliche Werke*, XI, p. 267). The agency imparted to objects by this figure extends to the stricken patriarch himself, whose speech 'comes forth in rough and interrupted tones from among the rocks' (*Hebrew Poetry*, I, p. 108; *Sämtliche Werke*, XI, p. 309),

---

[61] Wordsworth, *Essays upon Epitaphs II*, *Prose Works*, II, p. 76.
[62] Herder, *Hebrew Poetry*, II, p. 15. *Herders Sämtliche Werke*, XII, p. 14.

achieving a timbre beyond the range of a mere recital of loss. Herder calls it 'a history of afflicted and suffering innocence', arguing that it acquires the relevance of a moral fable not by the abstraction but by the figuration of its particulars.

Like Lowth's notion of the Longinian sublime, Herder's treatment of the sublimity of Job emphazises the prosaic roots of of complaints such as Sappho's, and traces within it an alternation between the particular and the general that always returns to the particular for fresh supplies of energy. Their Job, like Longinus' Sappho, makes verse out of the impassioned articulation of bits and pieces. Lessing puts it very well when he says, 'The *coexistence* of the physical object comes into collision with the *consecutiveness* of speech, and the former being resolved into the latter, the dismemberment of the whole into its parts is certainly made easier, but the final reunion of those parts into a whole is made uncommonly difficult, and not seldom impossible.'[63] Wordsworth exploits this dislocation in his 'spots of time' by presenting heterogeneous particulars as the bare historical contingencies of passion at the same time as rehearsing them as the most compelling forms in which passion may be re-presented: 'The single sheep, and the one blasted tree, / And the bleak music of that old stone wall' (*Prelude*, 11.378–9).

[63] Lessing, *Laocoön*, p. 105.

Themes and Movements

18

Sensibility and literary criticism

John Mullan

Nay, mama, if he is not to be animated by Cowper! – but we must allow
for difference of taste. Elinor has not my feelings, and therefore she may
overlook it, and be happy with him. But it would have broke *my* heart had
I loved him, to hear him read with so little sensibility.[1]

Thus, in Jane Austen's *Sense and Sensibility*, Marianne Dashwood
criticizes the man who has been courting her sister. He lacks 'sensibility',
a faculty of which the novel is famously suspicious, and this lack is
shown in the way that he reads. 'Sensibility', in this example, is made
explicitly a matter of literary discrimination and performance. When
Marianne has her first conversation with Willoughby, she seems to be
discovering a shared 'sensibility' in their shared tastes in reading:

her favourite authors were brought forward and dwelt upon with so
rapturous a delight, that any young man of five and twenty must have been
insensible indeed, not to become an immediate convert to the excellence of
such works, however disregarded before.[2]

Austen's dry joke on the word 'insensible' only emphasizes the point:
sensibility is regarded by these characters as best tested and displayed
in the exercise of literary taste. *Sense and Sensibility*, published in 1811
but begun in the late 1790s, shows sensibility to be a dangerous indulgence rather than a natural sensitivity, and satirizes the effusive professions of 'taste' supposed to mark that indulgence. Significantly, the most
famous critic of sensibility chooses to identify it with a fashionable
vocabulary of literary appreciation.

This perception is common among the antagonists of Sensibility in
the late eighteenth and early nineteenth century. Mary Wollstonecraft's
Vindication of the Rights of Woman, first published in 1794, attacks
Sensibility from a position apparently very different from Austen's, but
shares the sense that it is a kind of responsiveness often encouraged by
and expressed in the reading of certain types of books. While writing
novels herself, Wollstonecraft convicts 'the herd of Novelists' of fostering

[1] Austen, *Sense and Sensibility*, p. 18. [2] *Ibid.*, p. 47.

in women 'a romantic unnatural delicacy of feeling'.[3] She depicts 'sensibility' as a fashionable female weakness encouraged by men, and by bad habits of reading, and despairs of 'fine ladies, brimful of sensibility, and teeming with capricious fancies' (ch. IV, p. 73):

Novels, music, poetry, and gallantry, all tend to make women the creatures of sensation, and their character is thus formed in the mould of folly during the time they are acquiring accomplishments ... This overstretched sensibility naturally relaxes the other powers of the mind, and prevents intellect from attaining that sovereignty which it ought to attain to render a rational creature useful to others.

(ch. IV, pp. 67–8)

Austen and Wollstonecraft turn into criticism what was a common proposition in later eighteenth-century discussions of Sensibility: that the finest and most delicate feelings might best be exercised in the activity of reading. We can sense the force of this proposition in an attempt to rebut it, Hannah More's poem *Sensibility. A Poetical Epistle* (1782). This text celebrates 'the finely-fashioned nerve' of the possessor of Sensibility, and provides an admiring catalogue of those writers who best stimulate that 'nerve' (Richardson, Sterne, Mackenzie, and Gray are prominent).[4] Yet it also has to attack those who know Sensibility only as an experience of reading. These imagined consumers of the texts that More herself most admires, while they are 'Alive to every woe by *fiction* dress'd', neglect 'The social sympathy, the sense humane' that is true Sensibility.

> While FEELING boasts her ever-tearful eye,
> Stern TRUTH, firm FAITH, and manly VIRTUE fly.[5]

Such an argument in favour of some versions of Sensibility and against others is not uncommon in the period, both in Britain and in France. It is central to the one work of Rousseau's that might be called 'literary criticism', his *Lettre à M. d'Alembert sur les spectacles* of 1758, translated into English in 1759. Rousseau wrote this in answer to d'Alembert's proposal for the establishment of a theatre in Geneva, and in it denounced 'the Effects of THEATRICAL ENTERTAINMENTS on the Manners of Mankind'.[6] What distinguishes his polemic from a long line of moralistic texts about the dangers of drama is its contention about the power of plays to arouse an impotent, and therefore harmful, Sensibility: 'The complaint against the stage, is not that it encourages criminal passions, but that it creates too great a sensibility, which is afterwards indulged at the expence of virtue' (p. 63). 'By shedding tears at those representations,

---

[3] Wollstonecraft, *A Vindication*, ch. II, p. 37.   [4] More, *Sacred Dramas*.
[5] *Ibid.*, p. 282.   [6] Rousseau, *A Letter*, p. 25.

we discharge all the duties of humanity, without any other inconveniency' (p. 24). The point of Rousseau's critique is that he does believe that there can be virtuous Sensibility. Indeed, he thinks that the virtue-loving citizens of Geneva are particularly susceptible to 'soft and moving representations' and 'have naturally an exquisite sensibility' (pp. 160–1). He applauds this faculty, which the theatre will only paralyse.

Rousseau went on to make Sensibility a crucial faculty (and source of pain) for the correspondents of his epistolary novel *Julie, ou La Nouvelle Héloïse* (1761). In the 'Dialogue ... on the Subject of Romances' prefaced to later editions, and English translations, of this novel, Sensibility is also imagined as a necessary possession of the discerning reader of such a text. 'Men of no sensibility', Rousseau argues, will not appreciate epistolary fiction, for they will look for stylistic sophistication, and miss the 'strength of sentiment' revealed by the clumsiness and repetitiveness of the letters.[7] Sensibility can sensitize – and it can incapacitate. Warnings about how the excitement of Sensibility in consumers of culture can paralyse any capacity for virtuous action are most often found in and around novels. Even advocates of Sensibility – indeed, perhaps especially they – are liable to warn of the dangers of an untutored sensitivity to fiction. Because novels are where Sensibility is most frequently displayed, with the tragic heroine of Richardson's *Clarissa* its most widely admired exemplar, they are often made to contain their own parables of the improper excitements of reading. Richardson himself famously wished 'to decry such Novels and Romances, as have a Tendency to inflame and corrupt',[8] and to distinguish a virtuous tenderness from an excessively susceptible imagination. (It is a distinction that Richardson himself makes difficult, allowing Lovelace, the villain of *Clarissa*, both to mock Clarissa for her 'sensibilities' and to claim such 'sensibilities' for himself.[9]) When the dramatist Richard Cumberland gently satirized the pious intentions of *Clarissa* in 1785, it was by expressing scepticism about just this distinction. While 'the moral' of the book is 'fundamentally good', 'sentimental Misses' are liable to be misguided by it:

Few female hearts in early youth can bear being softened by pathetic and affecting stories without prejudice. Young people are all imitation, and when a girl assumes the pathos of Clarissa without experiencing the same afflictions, or being put to the same trials, the result will be the most insufferable affectation.[10]

---

[7] See pp. xvii–xviii of *A Dialogue between a Man of Letters and M. J. J. Rousseau* in the Woodstock Facsimile reprint (1989) of Jean-Jacques Rousseau, *Eloisa, or a series of original letters*, trans. William Kenrick (1803).

[8] Letter from Richardson to George Cheyne, in Carroll (ed.), *Selected Letters of Samuel Richardson*, p. 46.

[9] Richardson, *Clarissa*, p. 609, 854.

[10] Cited in Williams (ed.), *Novel and Romance*, p. 335.

As Austen was mordantly to observe in *Northanger Abbey* (written in 1798–9), novels usually fended off the accusation that they encouraged the wrong kinds of emotional sensitivity by themselves sternly abjuring the dangerous excitements of novel-reading.

Yet Sensibility continued to be estimated as a desirable quality not only of fictional characters, but also of those who read about them and identified with them. The engagingly named *Sentimental Magazine* described the best fiction as 'tending to ennoble the passions, to awaken tenderness, sympathy and love (I mean virtuous love) to soften the finer feelings of the mind, and having for its object some important moral'.[11] Richardson's Preface to the first editions of *Pamela* described the aims of the novel as conveying instruction and moral edification 'in so probable, so natural, so *lively* a manner, as shall engage the Passions of every sensible reader'.[12] 'Sensible' here meant 'possessed of sensibility' – having the right degree of sensitivity to a text that was designed 'to raise a Distress from *natural* Causes, and to excite Compassion from *proper* Motives'. Such sensitivity could be imagined as being shared between characters and readers (and, implicitly, authors). While the tearfulness of novel readers begins to be mocked from about the 1770s, 'Sensibility' remains, until the end of the century, a standby of reviewers of fiction – a measure of the virtues of readers as well as of books.

The critical usefulness and influence of this measure can be seen in the reception of the fiction of Laurence Sterne, and especially in its treatment after the novelist's death in 1768.[13] 'The writings of YORICK bear visible marks of a great natural genius, seasoned with uncommon humour, and adorned with the most exquisite sensibility', wrote a typical follower.[14] The *Sentimental Magazine* described Sterne posthumously as a man with 'nerves too fine, that wound e'en while they bless', and John Ferriar, the first of a long line of Sterne scholars, celebrated him at the end of the century for his power to excite 'the quick tear, that checks our wond'ring smile'.[15] While *Tristram Shandy* and *A Sentimental Journey* are often taken by twentieth-century readers to satirize ready tears and convenient sympathies, eighteenth-century readers and reviewers worked hard to make Sterne into a writer of Sensibility, 'a master in the science of *human feelings*, and the art of describing them'.[16] The editor of *The*

---

[11] *The Sentimental Magazine* (1774), p. 31.

[12] Richardson, *Pamela* (1740), Preface.

[13] The story of how Sterne was made, sometimes against the grain, into a novelist of Sensibility can be followed in Howes, *Yorick*, and Howes (ed.), *Sterne*. See also Mullan, *Sentiment and Sociability*, ch. 4.

[14] *Yorick's Skull; or, College Oscitations* (1777), p. 34.

[15] *The Sentimental Magazine* (Jan. 1774), p. 7; Ferriar, *Illustrations of Sterne* (1798), Preface.

[16] *The Monthly Review*, 32 (Feb. 1765).

Beauties of Sterne, a popular anthology of selections from his work which was first published in 1782 and went through a dozen editions in the next decade, even claimed to have worried that 'the *feeling reader*' needed light relief from his pathetic episodes, which might otherwise 'wound the bosom of *sensibility* too deeply'.[17] The subtitle of the anthology is enough to suggest how a susceptibility to fine feelings could be treated as a qualification of the discriminating reader: 'Selected for the Heart of Sensibility'.

The selectiveness of *The Beauties of Sterne*, when placed alongside the often uncertain contemporary reviews of his fiction, allows one to see how critics found Sterne a problematic standard-bearer for Sensibility. His work had first to be sifted of its innuendo and irreverence. Until the turn of the century, Richardson appeared to critics an easier paragon, and was consistently celebrated for his capacity to arouse the Sensibility of his readers. (It should be emphasized that, in eighteenth-century discussions of fiction, Sensibility is described not so much in terms of the content of novels, but more as a type of effect upon a sensitive reader.) Because Richardson yokes feeling to virtue, he is the only novelist whom Clara Reeve can bear to recommend to young women in *The Progress of Romance* (1785), the first British attempt at a history of 'the Novel'. The critical text, however, that testifies most forcefully to Richardson's example is French rather than English: Denis Diderot's *Éloge de Richardson* (1761). As the title implies, this is less criticism than rhapsody; René Wellek says of Diderot's enthusiasm, 'This seems today the sheer madness of "sensibility"'.[18] The *Éloge* is not so much an analysis of Sensibility as an expression of it – thick with protestations and exclamation marks. Here is Diderot on his feelings when he reads of Clarissa's death:

ce qui m'étonne toujours, moi, quand je suis aux derniers instants de cette innocente, c'est que les pierres, les murs, les carreaux insensibles et froids sur lesquels je marche ne s'émeuvent pas et ne joignent pas leur plainte à la mienne.[19]

Astonishment, tears, and speechlessness are the instincts belonging as much to the good reader of the book as to its heroine.

Yet, for all the readiness to embrace pathos of his early criticism, Diderot has a more complex and ambitious theory of Sensibility than perhaps any other critic of the century, in either England or France. His materialism allows him to treat 'sensibilité' as an inherent property of matter, and that which, in its active form, is the principle of all life. In his early *Pensées sur l'interpretation de la nature* (1754), 'sensibilité' is

---

[17] *The Beauties of Sterne* (1782), p. vii.   [18] Wellek, *A History*, I, p. 60.
[19] Diderot, *Oeuvres*, p. 1,070.

described as the tendency of organic particles to seek out their proper situations.[20] It is not in the mind, but in the fabric of living matter. It is not therefore surprising that the entry on '*Sensibilité*' in Volume 15 of the *Encyclopédie* was written by a professional physician, Fouquet. In a letter of 1765, Diderot wrote that 'Sensibilité is a universal property of matter, inert in bodies ... made active in the same bodies by their assimilation with a living animal substance';[21] the importance of this life-giving property is discussed in the first section of *Le Rêve de d'Alembert* (written in 1769, but not published until 1830), where it also functions more conventionally as the capacity to be moved by suffering. Diderot recognizes that Sensibility has its origins in ideas of physical sensitivity, and he pursues the continuity between physical and emotional reflexes more rigorously than any other major figure. In his later critical writing, especially his *Paradoxe sur le Comédien* (written 1770–8, but not published until 1830), he comes to argue that those who would excite such reflexes should not themselves succumb to Sensibility (the best actor does *not* give himself over to the emotions of his character). It is a capacity to which the artist reaches out, but which he also transcends.

Elsewhere in Europe, the treatment of Sensibility in literature and criticism is derivative of that in Britain and France, for the simple reason that most of the exemplary works of Sensibility were produced by British or French writers – and especially novelists. In Germany, Richardson's fiction was a major influence throughout the 1750s and 1760s, not only on other novels, but also on drama, including Lessing's tragedy *Miss Sara Sampson* (1755). During this first phase of the German interest in Sensibility, critics attended to the morally edifying effects of sentimental literature. For theoretical backing, they no longer looked to the rationalistic ethics of Leibniz and Wolff (for whom the feelings were merely a lower and confused form of cognition), but increasingly to the 'moral sense' theories of Shaftesbury, Hutcheson, Hume, and Adam Smith. Thus, in his writings on tragedy, Lessing (who himself translated Hutcheson's *System of Moral Philosophy* into German in 1756) reinterprets Aristotle's theory of catharsis so as to minimize the importance of fear and magnify the therapeutic effects of pity or sympathy (the German word *Mitleid* does duty for both). Tragic theatre thereby becomes a school for humane sentiments.[22]

The second and climactic phase of the German appropriation of

[20] Diderot, *Oeuvres philosophiques*, Section LI.
[21] Cited in Mason, *The Irresistible Diderot*, p. 220.
[22] See Lessing, Mendelssohn, and Nicolai, *Briefwechsel* (1756–7) and Lessing's *Hamburgische Dramaturgie* (1767–9), sections 74–8, in Lessing, *Sämtliche Schriften*, IX.

Sensibility in literature coincides with the *Sturm und Drang* movement of the 1770s. Goethe's enormously successful novel *The Sorrows of Young Werther* (1774) – which owes its theme and many of its details to Rousseau's *La Nouvelle Héloïse*[23] – has a protagonist whose heightened sensitivities seem both cautionary and exemplary. On the one hand, the hero's cultivation of his feelings leads directly to his mental collapse and suicide; yet, on the other hand, he dies as a martyr of sensibility – a person who, like Richardson's Clarissa or Henry Mackenzie's Harley, has feelings that are too good for this world. Goethe himself sensed the moral ambiguity of this character, adding to later editions of his novel a motto enjoining its readers not to follow Werther. It was a warning that was necessary precisely because Sensibility was still being imagined as a capacity released by reading. Werther is first moved by Lotte, the object of his unrequitable affections, when he hears her express her enthusiasm for sentimental fiction. In the last decade of the eighteenth century, Goethe's novel came to stand for a morally suspect indulgence of this susceptibility to the literature of Sensibility. In response to the *Werther*-hysteria, critics began to regard this literature as a corrupting influence, a judgement strengthened by the wave of inferior imitations and parodies of Goethe's novel.[24] In Germany as in England, the supposed powers of a literature of Sensibility would eventually be condemned as symptoms of over-refinement and decadence.

Throughout criticism of the latter half of the eighteenth century, Sensibility is used to bring together the sensitivities depicted by literature and those experienced by readers. It has been said that it is possible to find in critical writing of the earliest decades of the eighteenth century an 'emphasis . . . on emotional response rather than rational judgement',[25] but it is really only from the 1750s, in a series of avowedly revisionist texts, that 'sensibility' is treated as a principle of literary taste. In novels contemporary with this criticism, Sensibility is usually represented as exceptional – a sensitivity that is admirable because few seem to possess or exercise it. In criticism too, this sense of exclusion is often important. Joseph Warton's *Essay on the Writings and Genius of Pope* (published in 1756; expanded in 1782) pits Sensibility against 'that philosophical, that geometrical, and systematical spirit so much in vogue, which has spread itself from the sciences even into polite literature'.[26] Warton asks his reader to consider whether this spirit 'has not diminished and destroyed SENTIMENT; and made our poets write from and to the HEAD rather than the HEART'. Sensibility has to be *re*discovered – and so

---

[23] See Schmidt, *Richardson, Rousseau und Goethe*.
[24] See, for example, the extracts in Doktor and Sauder (eds.), *Empfindsamkeit*, p. 214, and Sauder, *Empfindsamkeit*, III, pp. 254–68, 297, etc.
[25] Todd, *Sensibility*, p. 29.   [26] Warton, *Essay* (1756), p. 204.

Warton goes through the works not only of Pope, but also of other eighteenth-century poets, in quest of 'PATHETIC reflection' (p. 33). He tries to produce a new canon of outstanding texts, judged by the standards of 'the Sublime and the Pathetic' (p. v). (By these standards, Pope's most estimable poems are judged to be his previously marginal 'Elegy on the Death of an Unfortunate Lady' and 'Eloisa to Abelard'.)

In his search for what is 'tender and pathetic' (p. 249), Warton only rarely uses the word 'sensibility'. It is notable that when he does so it is to recover that quality from ancient writers or stories. So, while criticizing the 'method' of Longinus for being 'too loose', he says that his 'taste and sensibility ... were exquisite'; discussing the epistle of *Sapho to Phaon*, he regrets that Ovid 'has put into the mouth of his heroine, a greater number of pretty panegyrical epigrams, than of those tender and passionate sentiments, which suited her character, and made her SENSIBILITY in amours so famous' (pp. 171, 289). Yet, even if the word is rare, Warton's text can usefully be taken as the earliest important example of a critical discourse that takes 'tenderness' – a susceptibility to 'exquisite' feeling that is often called 'sensibility' in the period – as a governing principle of critical judgement.

This principle is useful because it can refer to the sensitivities of writers and readers as if they were shared. (Just as a novelist like Richardson could imagine sensibility to be the special possession of both his virtuous characters and his attentive readers.) In Warton's *Essay*, these sensitivities are excited through 'true poetry', which he tries to distinguish from mere 'wit' and 'sense'. In the book's Dedication, Warton declares that 'it is a creative and glowing IMAGINATION, "acer spiritus ac vis", and that alone, that can stamp a writer with this exalted and very uncommon character, which so few possess, and of which so few can properly judge' (p. v). This privilege is now something rarer than the connoisseurship of 'Imagination' that has been familiar since Addison's essays on 'the Pleasures of Imagination' in the *Spectator*. Using a metaphor that we have already encountered in writings on Sensibility, Warton says that 'the Sublime and the Pathetic are the two chief nerves of all genuine poetry'. The best readers are those who themselves have the most sensitive 'nerves'. Everywhere in his writing, the 'Pathetic' is the aspect of representation that is valued, and 'distress' and 'commiseration' are lauded as the best of reader responses – the surest signs of Sensibility.

Warton's text speaks clearly enough of the paradox at the heart of Sensibility: that it is a natural sensitivity which only a 'few' exercise. In David Hume's (almost exactly contemporary) 'Of the Standard of Taste', first published in 1757, 'sensibility' is named as exactly that principle whose relative development or suppression accounts for differences of taste. Eighteenth-century discussions of Taste begin from the supposed uniformity of human faculties (implicit in the very metaphor of 'taste'), and then attempt to account for cases of disagreement or incompatibility. In a characteristically sceptical (and amused) appeal to experience, Hume does the opposite, beginning with the differences of opinion that notoriously distinguish expressions of taste. These expressions present an appearance of 'variety and caprice', and only considerable philosophical reflection will reveal that 'there are certain general principles of approbation or blame, whose influence a careful eye may trace in all operations of the mind'.[27]

If 'human nature' is uniform (and this is the founding axiom of Hume's criticism), whence come the 'variety and caprice'? Initially, Hume's answer is to pursue the metaphor of taste to a logical conclusion, and talk of the differences between individuals as if they were variations of physical reflex – heightened or blunted in particular cases: 'Many and frequent are the defects in the internal organs, which prevent or weaken the influence of those general principles'. It is not therefore surprising that 'sensibility' should be an important item in his terminology. 'Sensibility' was a word that began by referring to specifically bodily sensitivities, and only in the mid-eighteenth century began commonly to denote an emotional, and even moral, faculty: 'Sensibility' with a capital 'S'. Like other writers of the period, Hume exploits a transition in the meaning of the word from a readiness of emotion to a desirable 'delicacy'. (By this transition, the capacity for 'feeling' was often translated as the capacity for fellow-feeling; the confusion of these two is what Hannah More attacks.)

The first explanation for differences of taste to which Hume turns is 'the want of that *delicacy* of imagination, which is requisite to convey a sensibility of . . . finer emotions' (Hume, *Essays*, p. 234). Like Warton, if less polemically, Hume imagines a heightened receptiveness to 'finer emotions' as a privilege (and a privilege that, although officially aesthetic, sounds something close to moral). 'One man has a strong sensibility to blemishes . . . Another has a more lively feeling of beauties . . .', and so on. Some of these differences seem to proceed merely from 'the different humours of particular men' (p. 244). 'Such preferences are innocent and unavoidable, and can never reasonably be the object of dispute'. But descriptions of 'variety' can also become descriptions of adequacy and inadequacy. (Hume remarks that the 'delicacy' to which he refers is something 'every one pretends to', even if few in reality possess it.) Sensibility is what varies between individuals, and in Hume's account it is easy to see how it can be understood as the achievement of a particular social class – or, at least, of that intellectually enlightened part of a class with which Hume was himself familiar.

[27] David Hume, *Essays*, p. 233.

On the one hand, Sensibility enables raw perception: 'The smaller the objects are, which become sensible to the eye, the finer is that organ'. On the other hand, it is the receptiveness of a tutored taste: 'the delicacy, which is requisite to make him sensible of every beauty and every blemish, in any composition or discourse' (p. 236). It is a natural potential, but apparently can be improved by refinement. In his earlier essay, 'Of the Delicacy of Taste and Passion' (1741), Hume had, indeed, distinguished between an 'incommodious' 'sensibility and delicacy of passion', and 'a *delicacy* of *taste* . . . which very much resembles this *delicacy* of *passion*, and produces the same sensibility to beauty and deformity of every kind, as that does to prosperity and adversity' (pp. 4–6). The former 'sensibility' is disabling, the latter is a characteristic of civilization, and Hume proposes that 'nothing is so proper to cure us of this delicacy of passion, as the cultivating of that higher and more refined taste'. A 'sensibility' to the objects of aesthetic appreciation will, Hume imagines, allow the philosophical citizen to conquer an excessive 'sensibility' to 'all the accidents of life'.

In his *Treatise of Human Nature* (1739–40), and to a lesser extent in his *Enquiry concerning the Principles of Morals* (1751), Hume had used the principle of 'sympathy' to explain how feelings could be communicated, and therefore shared moral judgements arrived at. (It is a principle developed in Adam Smith's *Theory of Moral Sentiments* (1759), which is likely to have been more directly influential on the critical and aesthetic arguments of the last decades of the eighteenth century.) It is not, however, Hume himself who turns to 'sympathy' in order to explain how texts affect readers of refined sensibility. First Edmund Burke, Alexander Gerard, and Lord Kames – later James Beattie and Archibald Alison – conflate aesthetic pleasure with the experience of sympathy. In the works of all these theorists, published through the second half of the eighteenth century, sympathy is a response to the best painting, poetry, and drama. Although notionally universal, it is interpreted as a fellow-feeling available most to those with sharpened sensibilities. James Beattie is representative when he declares in his chapter 'Of Sympathy' in *An Essay on Poetry and Music* that it is a faculty operated by those 'who have a lively imagination, keen feelings, and what we call a tender heart'.[28] For him and for others, 'sympathy' allows moral and aesthetic sensitivities to be equated. Feeling for others becomes the essential experience of literature and art. Unsurprisingly, then, critics of the second half of the eighteenth century are often preoccupied, like novelists of the time, with the representation of and response to suffering.

Alexander Gerard, in *An Essay on Taste* of 1759, describes how a

---

[28] Beattie, 'An Essay on Poetry and Music', *Essays* (1776), p. 198.

man of Taste requires 'such a *sensibility of heart*, as fits a man for being easily moved, and for readily catching, as by infection, any passion, that a work is fitted to excite'.[29] A tasteful reader is one whose sympathies are properly prepared, and, like Warton, Gerard identifies pathos as the quality he seeks: 'the pathetic is a quality of so great moment in works of taste, a man, who is destitute of sensibility of heart, must be a very imperfect judge of them' (Gerard, *Essay*, p. 88). Gerard's *Essay* is a representative product of the Scottish Enlightenment. It was the winner of a 'gold medal' offered by 'The Edinburgh Society for the encouragement of arts, sciences, manufactures, and agriculture' for the best explanation of the grounds of Taste. It explicitly presents itself as 'an Analysis of taste into those simple powers of human nature which are its principles' (p. 77), and wants to sanction its aesthetics by an anatomy of 'human nature'.

> There are qualities in things, determinate and stable, independent of humour or caprice, that are fit to operate on mental principles, common to all men, and, by operating on them, are naturally productive of the sentiments of taste in all its forms.

For Gerard as for Hume, 'sensibility' is what might vary between individuals, despite this envisaged uniformity.

The consumer of 'works of taste' must be gifted not only, therefore, with 'Judgment', which 'investigates the laws and causes of the works of *nature*' and 'compares and contrasts them with the more imperfect works of *art*', but also with 'Delicacy of passion' (pp. 89–91). A section of the *Essay* is indeed entitled 'Of sensibility of taste'. Here Gerard argues that this 'Sensibility of taste arises chiefly from the structure of our internal senses, and is but indirectly and remotely connected with the soundness or improvement of judgement. The want of it is but *one* ingredient in many sorts of false taste; but does not constitute so much one species of *wrong* taste, as a total *deficience* or great *weakness* of taste' (p. 113). Sensibility accounts for the vividness or intensity with which 'any excellence of art or nature' is experienced (p. 106). Gerard's discussion of the principle is largely an explanation of how a man of taste, by cultivation of his powers of aesthetic discrimination, may remain 'Feelingly alive' to such 'excellence', even as the excitement of novelty declines. 'In order to form a fine taste, the mental powers which compose it must possess exquisite *sensibility* and delicacy': sensibility begins as a natural capacity, but ends up as an artificially tutored and artfully sustained responsiveness.

Like Gerard, Edmund Burke, in the essay 'On Taste' that he prefaced

---

[29] Gerard, *An Essay on Taste* (1759), p. 86.

to the second edition of his *Philosophical Enquiry into the Origin of our Ideas of the Sublime and Beautiful*, takes 'sensibility' to be an explanation of variations in Taste. As the senses are uniform, he argues, so must be the working of 'imagination', which is 'only the representation of the senses': 'there must be just as close an agreement in the imaginations as in the senses of men'.[30] As long as 'we consider Taste merely according to its nature and species, we shall find its principles entirely uniform' – but 'sensibility and judgment, which are the qualities that compose what we commonly call a *taste*, vary exceedingly in various people. From a defect in the former of these qualities arises a want of Taste' (p. 23). All men's senses are the same, but their sensibilities differ. 'A rectitude of judgment in the arts . . . does in a great measure depend upon sensibility' (p. 24). Yet while Sensibility and judgement are combined in the composition of taste, they also allow Burke to represent taste as a divided principle. 'Judgement' is rational and comparative; 'Sensibility' is vividly responsive. The latter accounts for the immediate *pleasure* given by 'the arts', and, throughout eighteenth-century critical theory, allows pleasure to be separated off from other aspects of tasteful appreciation.

Burke's aesthetics famously privileged powerful emotions – especially fear. Any such theory gave prominence to the concept of 'sympathy', with which Sensibility was often closely connected. Just as David Hume and Adam Smith set theories of 'sympathy' at the centre of moral philosophy, so their fellow Scots James Beattie and Henry Home, Lord Kames, see an understanding of its operation as central to criticism. In his *Elements of Criticism* (first published in 1762) Kames only arrives at his critical theory after lengthy discussion of 'Emotions and Passions'. Indeed, his work seems closer to what we might call 'psychology' than to literary analysis. His criticism measures the capacity of texts to arouse 'sympathy' and communicate 'emotion' (it is not therefore surprising that he thinks drama the most 'powerful' of literary forms).[31] The exercise of taste will continually enhance our capacity for the 'sympathy' in which tasteful painting and writing would engage us: 'Such exercise, soothing and satisfactory in itself, is productive necessarily of mutual good-will and affection' (I, p. 13). By increasing 'sensibility', the development of taste can even be thought of as socially useful: 'delicacy of taste necessarily heightens our sensibility of pain and pleasure, and of course our sympathy, which is the capital branch of every social passion'. Discriminating consumers of art and literature make themselves better people.

The beneficial effects of 'the fine arts' are acclaimed in Kames's

---

[30] Burke, *Philosophical Enquiry*, p. 17.   [31] Lord Kames, *Elements*, I, p. 116.

Dedication to George III, which mingles conventional pieties with an apparently heartfelt grandiloquence: 'By uniting different ranks in the same elegant pleasures, they promote benevolence: by cherishing love of order, they inforce submission to government: and by inspiring delicacy of feeling, they make regular government a double blessing' (I, p. iii). It is this 'delicacy of feeling' that is Kames's special interest. He finds little difficulty in arguing that aesthetic sensitivity encourages 'social passions', for he believes that human emotions are engaged by fictions in exactly the same way that they are engaged by realities. In the section 'Emotions caused by fiction', he describes how fiction produces what he calls 'ideal presence', and how 'a lively and accurate description ... transforms me into a spectator'; 'Ideal presence supplies the want of real presence ... If our sympathy be engaged by the latter, it must also in some measure be engaged by the former' (I, pp. 110–12). The delicacy of feeling, or Sensibility, necessary to this operation of sympathy is, Kames acknowledges, restricted to the social class that can exercise taste. His high claims for the benefits of the exercise of taste lead him, however, to fend off the possibility that particular individuals might possess different degrees of Sensibility, and of the capacity to sympathize. For the privileged, an aesthetic training in fellow-feeling is always available.

James Beattie also treats 'sympathy' as the most important means by which literature excites and engages attention. He believes, though, that it needs to be harnessed to moral ends, and that 'sensibility' should only be exploited in an appropriate manner. 'As a great part of the pleasure we derive from poetry depends on our Sympathetic Feelings, the philosophy of Sympathy ought always to form a part of the science of Criticism', writes Beattie.[32] The writer worthy of admiration is one who turns this capacity for fellow-feeling (which is not in itself laudable) into an allegiance with virtuous characters and actions: 'Sympathy ... might be made a powerful instrument of moral discipline if poets and other writers of fable were careful to call forth our sensibility towards those emotions only that favour virtue and invigorate the human mind' (p. 201). Sensibility now designates a readiness to emotional identification that is aroused by fiction, and that is its power for good or for ill.

Beattie's critical theory becomes a discussion of the conditions of Sensibility. As is so often the case, the concept permits the critic to associate, or even conflate, the qualifications of readers and those of authors. On the one hand, we have the responsiveness of the reader – the 'human sensibility' to which the best writer will give 'proper direction' (p. 77); on the other, we have the merit of the poet, who, in order

[32] Beattie, *Essays*, p. 194.

to win Beattie's approval, must possess 'a peculiar liveliness of fancy and sensibility of heart' (p. 52). The poet's 'sensibility' allows him 'to enter with ardent emotions into every part of his subject, so as to transfuse into his work a pathos and energy sufficient to raise corresponding emotions in the reader' (p. 57). Beattie pauses to justify Shakespeare's mix of tragedy and comedy by referring to just this process: 'if he had made his tragedies uniformly mournful or terrible . . . no person of sensibility would have been able to support the representation' (pp. 203–4). His description is to be taken up in Archibald Alison's more systematic attempt to found criticism on a theory of 'emotions', his *Essays on the Nature and Principles of Taste* (1790), which explicitly recommends Beattie's work (p. 75).

More thoroughly than Beattie, Alison charts conditions of 'sensibility' in order to explain differences of taste. 'In proportion . . . as our sensibility is weak, with regard to any class of objects, it is observable, that our sense of Sublimity or Beauty in such objects, is weak in the same proportion' (p. 58). As 'Taste is that Faculty of the human Mind by which we perceive and enjoy, whatever is BEAUTIFUL or SUBLIME' (p. vii), it is necessary to describe 'the dependence of Taste upon Sensibility' (p. 68). The 'objects of taste' can only properly affect us in conditions of heightened sensibility. Alison will not be the last to argue that 'they who have been doomed, by their professions, to pass their earlier years in populous and commercial cities, and in the narrow and selfish pursuits which prevail there, soon lose that sensibility which is the most natural of all, – the sensibility to the beauties of the country' (p. 55). The critical discourse of Sensibility now concerns itself with all that hampers the exercise of taste.

Alison will use the word 'sensibility' to refer to any tendency to 'emotion', and in this sense sees it as a universal human property. But only 'the emotions of sublimity or beauty' characterize the effects of 'objects of taste', and Alison treats a sensitivity to these emotions as exceptional or exclusive. Aging itself produces a 'change of sensibility' – a diminution of the susceptibility to emotion essential in any experience of 'Sublimity and Beauty' (pp. 12, 53). Only those who diligently pursue the beauties of 'Nature or Art' can hope to remain 'men of sensibility' (p. 8). For Alison, 'sensibility to the beauties of nature' is fundamental to the appreciation of literature or painting, and is not available to 'the generality of mankind' (p. 38). An almost helpless intensity of feeling in the face of these beauties is taken as a model for aesthetic sensitivity (Alison recommends Rousseau's *Rêveries* to his reader, and fills his text with examples from the descriptive poetry of Thomson, Akenside, and Beattie). But an 'acquaintance with Poetry' also helps increase 'our sensibility to the beauties of nature'. The interest of Alison's argument lies less in his associationist psychology than in his attempts to reconcile the enervating and the educating effects of refinement. On the one hand, experience, cultivation, and even 'the labour of criticism' itself, sap that 'flow of imagination, in which youth, and men of sensibility, are so apt to indulge' (p. 8). On the other hand, a constant exercise of Taste – the sampling of Beauty and Sublimity 'in the works of Nature or Art' – teaches access to emotions of which most are 'little sensible' (p. 11). With Alison, as with other critics, the discourse of Sensibility is always concerned with whatever might blunt, impede, or preclude aesthetic appreciation. In theory, Sensibility is universal; in fact, it is often diminished or dead.

Given such pessimism, it seems appropriate to set, at the end of this account, a critical text at the edge of the century: Wordsworth's Preface to his 1800 *Lyrical Ballads*. For here Alison's equivocation is pursued to a new conclusion. Wordsworth presents his poetry as an antidote to the 'false refinement' of his contemporaries, claiming both to describe and to appeal to the fundamental 'sympathies of men'.[33] The poet should be a person of special intellectual strength, but must also be 'originally possessed of much organic sensibility'.[34] This 'organic sensibility' is his guarantee that his feelings are not merely personal, but can be generalized. Thus the poet reaches out to 'the being to whom we address ourselves'. This rather clumsy circumlocution for 'the reader' is telling: 'sensibility' now distinguishes fellow 'beings' rather than fellow members of a refined elite. Sensitivities are imagined to be 'organic' rather than polite. For several decades, Sensibility lived by being natural and refined; Wordsworth's text is evidence that this double life is, by the end of the century, almost over.

[33] Brett and Jones (eds.), *Wordsworth and Coleridge*, p. 240.
[34] *Ibid.*, p. 241.

19

Women and literary criticism

Terry Castle

Do women have the right to criticize? Throughout the eighteenth century it was commonly held that literary judgement was – or should be – a privilege reserved for men. A woman who set forth literary opinions in public exposed either her folly or her presumption. Women, according to Jonathan Swift, were the 'ill-judging Sex', inclined, like Echo, to take more delight in repeating 'offensive Noise' than in celebrating Philomela's song.[1] Henry Fielding, playing the role of 'Censor' to the 'great Empire of Letters' in the *Covent-Garden Journal*, debarred all 'fine Ladies' from admission to the lofty 'Realms of Criticism'. Women, he averred, spoke only a debased critical language, a repetitive modern lingo composed of the phrases, 'sad Stuff, low Stuff, mean Stuff, vile Stuff, dirty Stuff, and so-forth'. They were 'Gothic' marauders in the republic of letters, usurping authority 'without knowing one Word of the ancient Laws, and original Constitution of that Body of which they have professed themselves to be Members'.[2] In the 1750s Oliver Goldsmith and Tobias Smollett took turns reviling Isabella Griffiths, the wife of Ralph Griffiths, who had dared to emend Goldsmith's works and publish reviews of her own in her husband's *Monthly Review*. Smollett boasted that his own journal, the *Critical Review*, was free of the depredations of 'old women' like Griffiths, whom he dismissed, with palpable sexual disgust, as the 'Antiquated Female Critic'.[3] In 1769, when Elizabeth Montagu published her only critical work, *The Writings and Genius of Shakespeare*, James Boswell worried aloud about resentment which might be aroused by a woman 'intruding herself into the chair of criticism' and was eager to defend his mentor Samuel Johnson against charges of prejudice against his bluestocking rival. But Johnson's distaste for modern-day 'Amazons of the pen' was none the less apparent: 'I am very fond of the company of ladies', he observed in one conversation. 'I like their beauty, I like their delicacy, I like their vivacity, and I like their *silence*.'

[1] Swift, *The Battle of the Books*, p. 257.
[2] See Fielding, *Covent-Garden Journal*, pp. 18 and 96.
[3] Todd, *Dictionary of Women Writers*, p. 143.

Women were most pleasing, in Johnson's view, 'when they hold their tongues'.[4]

In the face of such relentless contempt, it is not surprising that many eighteenth-century women writers – including some who published works of criticism – should have internalized painful doubts about their own powers of taste and discernment. Early in her married life Mary Wortley Montagu produced – at the request of her husband (who merely wished to distract her from the travails of pregnancy) – a detailed critique of the plot and diction of Addison's then-unproduced tragedy *Cato*. Addison was impressed enough by her criticisms, which were both piquant and precise, to revise the play extensively along the lines she had suggested. Despite such implicit approbation, however, Montagu felt obliged to apologize for taking on a task 'so much above my skill' and in a letter to her husband, begged him to remember that she had done so only by his 'Command'. The essay itself (which at Addison's request was never circulated) bears Montagu's self-deprecating heading, 'Wrote at the desire of Mr Wortley; suppressed at the desire of Mr Addison'.[5]

In an even more paradoxical case of self-disparagement later in the century, the educational writer Hannah More (who also wrote a treatise on the theatre) judged women intrinsically incapable of critical thought. Because women were 'naturally more affectionate than fastidious', she wrote in *Strictures on the Modern System of Female Education* (1799), they were likely 'both to read and to hear with a less critical spirit than men, they will not be on the watch to detect errors, so much as to gather improvement; they have seldom that hardness which is acquired by dealing deeply in the books of controversy; but are more inclined to the perusal of works which quicken the devotional feelings, than to such as awaken a spirit of doubt or scepticism'. It was true, she allowed, that a female reader might display 'delicacy and quickness of perception', as well as an 'intuitive penetration' into character, but these were mere reactive powers, 'like the sensitive and tender organs of some timid animals', bestowed by Providence 'as a kind of natural guard, to warn of the approach of danger'. Women lacked 'the *wholeness* of mind' that critical judgement required and were defective in the crucial faculty of 'comparing, combining, analysing, and separating' ideas.[6]

It would require a separate study to explain adequately why the

---

[4] The phrase 'Amazons of the pen' comes from *The Adventurer*, 115 (11 December 1754). Johnson, it is true, often generously supported individual women writers (especially Charlotte Lennox and Anna Williams) but this did not keep him from making less charitable observations in public. For the context of the anti-female remarks cited, see Blunt, *Queen of the Blues*, II, pp. 140–1.

[5] See Halsband, 'Addison's *Cato* and Lady Mary Wortley Montagu', pp. 1123–4.

[6] More, *Strictures on Female Education*, in *Works*, IV, pp. 196–7 and 200–1.

prospect of women critics provoked so much anxiety in eighteenth-century commentators. Traditional misogynistic fears of female insubordination were at least partly responsible: a woman who assumed authority in the great 'Republic of Letters' (to adopt Fielding's political terminology) might be encouraged to train her critical faculties on the world at large. The persistent taboo against women criticizing *male* authors in particular – a prejudice which continues to influence reviewing practice in our own day – may have been motivated by deeper masculine anxieties about the 'Amazonian' sentiments a liberated women's criticism might be expected to unleash.

At the same time, women writers (of any sort) represented a new and destabilizing force in the eighteenth-century literary marketplace. Traditionally, of course, women had been granted a symbolic role in literary production: in the time-honoured formulations of classical rhetoric, masculine poetic genius owed its flights to the enabling inspiration of the Muses. But real women, in the prevailing archaic conception, were not supposed to take up the pen themselves. A few seventeenth-century feminists had complained of the exclusion. Bathsua Makin (?1612–?74) argued that the very cult of the Muses itself proved that women had once been – and could become again – creators in their own right. The arts were represented 'in Womens Shapes', she wrote in 1673, because women had in fact been their 'Inventors' and chief 'Promoters' in antiquity. 'Minerva and the nine Muses were women famous for learning whilst they lived, and therefore thus adored when dead.'[7] Other women, equally celebrated in their day, had invented the poetic genres: 'The Sybils could never have invented the heroic, nor Sappho the sapphic verses, had they been illiterate.'[8] It was time, wrote Makin, for women to make themselves pre-eminent once again in the 'Arts and Tongues' of civilization.

By the end of the seventeenth century, with a slow but perceptible rise in female literacy, the weakening of court patronage and the growing commercialization of literary activity throughout Western Europe, Makin's wish had begun to come partly true: more women than ever before were indeed becoming writers and getting paid for it. In early eighteenth-century London (somewhat later in Paris, Amsterdam and Berlin) the presence of a female literary subculture – a new class of 'scribbling females', composed of novelists, editors, hack journalists, booksellers and the like – was increasingly visible. Forced to compete with their new distaff rivals, the male literary establishment responded with alarm and resentment. The complaint against women critics drew much of its particular animus, one suspects, from larger impinging

---

[7] Makin, *Essay*, p. 9.   [8] Makin, *Essay*, p. 9.

professional jealousies; in the eyes of traditionalists, the female critic
was simply the most blatant example of women's new and overweening
literary ambition. She could easily be made to stand for any sort of
illegitimate hankering after authority. It is symptomatic of the deeper
sexual tensions in eighteenth-century intellectual culture that Swift, in
his diatribe against the corruption of learning in *The Battle of the
Books* (1704), should blame the collapse of traditional aesthetic values
on the feminization of contemporary taste. In the nightmare emblem-
world of the satirist, the 'malignant deity' Criticism takes shape as a
rampant, monstrous female, chaotically ruling over her offspring the
Moderns, who suckle on her nastiness and squalor:

She dwelt on the Top of a snowy Mountain in *Nova Zembla*; there *Momus*
found her extended in her Den, upon the Spoils of numberless Volumes half
devoured. At her right Hand sat *Ignorance*, her Father and Husband, blind
with Age; at her left, *Pride* her Mother, dressing her up in the Scraps of
Paper herself had torn. There was *Opinion* her Sister, light of Foot,
hoodwinkt, and headstrong, yet giddy and perpetually turning. About her
play'd her Children, *Noise* and *Impudence*, *Dullness* and *Vanity*,
Positiveness, *Pedantry*, and *Ill-Manners*. The Goddess herself had Claws like
a Cat; Her Head, and Ears, and Voice, resembled those of an *Ass*; Her
Teeth fallen out before; Her Eyes turned inward; as if she lookt only upon
herself; Her Diet was the overflowing of her own *Gall*; Her *Spleen* was so
large, as to stand prominent like a Dug of the first Rate, nor wanted
Excrescencies in form of Teats, at which a Crew of ugly Monsters were
greedily sucking; and, what is wonderful to conceive, the bulk of Spleen
encreased faster than the Sucking could diminish it.

One could hardly ask for a more flagrant image of a threatening gyno-
criticism.[9]

   Such vivid antipathy undoubtedly discouraged many women authors
from ever attempting the business of criticism at all. But even in the case
of women who did produce critical writing, particularly in the years between 1720 and 1780, one cannot avoid noticing in their works the often
distorting effects of cultural prejudice. Exaggerated self-consciousness –
a stylized display of authorial timidity or self-effacement – frequently
mars eighteenth-century feminine critical rhetoric. Frances Brooke,
introducing her theatre reviews and critical essays in *The Old Maid* in

---

[9] Swift, *Battle of the Books*, p. 240. A few exceptions to the general anti-feminist
sentiment of the period may be noted: George Ballard (1706–55) and John
Duncombe (1729–86) both wrote encomiastic works celebrating women's
contribution to the world of arts and letters; Thomas Seward (1708–90), the
father of the poet and letter-writer Anna Seward (1747–1809), published a poem
provocatively entitled 'The Female Right to Literature' in the second volume of
Dodsley's *Miscellany* in 1748.

1755, observed apologetically that such writing could only seem 'an odd attempt in a woman'. In the preface to her study of Shakespeare from 1769, Elizabeth Montagu deferred to the 'superiority of talents and learning' of Shakespeare's male editors and critics and abjured 'the vain presumption of attempting to correct any passages of this celebrated Author' herself. Even the usually forthright Marie-Jeanne Riccoboni, embarking in 1782 on what would become a celebrated epistolary debate with Choderlos de Laclos over his novel *Les Liaisons dangereuses*, disclaimed any right to criticize Laclos as a fellow *author*: her own novels, she said, were mere 'bagatelles'. She could only judge his work – and that diffidently – as a *woman* ('*en qualité de femme*'). Likewise, the recurrence of certain themes and issues in women's criticism – the obsession, for example, with the moralizing aspects of literary works – also signalled underlying self-doubt: female critics compensated for their profound sense of professional insecurity by paying exaggerated attention to the piety (or lack thereof) in the works they scrutinized. From Eliza Haywood on, eighteenth-century women critics made a cult of their moral respectability. Only near the end of the century, with the debut of charismatic literary figures like Germaine de Staël and Stephanie de Genlis in France, or Mary Wollstonecraft and Elizabeth Inchbald in England, did a less hidebound image of the female critic begin to emerge – the image of the woman confident enough in her intellectual abilities to pass judgement, without excessive scruple, on the great works of past and present.

Given such inhibitions, what sort of criticism did women actually write? Women critics employed a variety of rhetorical formats, reflecting the assortment of contexts in which the practice of criticism itself – which had yet to be defined in strictly professional or academic terms – was pursued in the period. Eighteenth-century critics worked in general in a hodge-podge of styles and genres; the formal critical essay, typified by Samuel Johnson's *Rambler* 4 'On Fiction' or Edward Young's *Conjectures on Original Composition*, was only one form among many. Prefaces, dedications, epilogues, linguistic treatises, translations, reviews, anthologies, biographical memoirs, private correspondence, and literary works themselves (one thinks of Austen's remarks on the novel in *Northanger Abbey*) all provided contexts in which a distinctly 'critical' discourse might flourish.

Certain styles and genres, of course, were more accessible than others. Generally speaking, the more formal critical sub-genres – the philological treatise, the learned dialogue, the refined verse epistle – were less popular with women than *ad hoc* forms, for obvious reasons. Owing to the defects of female education in the period, women seldom had the background in classical languages and literature necessary to engage in the erudite skirmishing of philological debate, though even here, it is important to note, a handful of exceptional women succeeded in making a mark. The seventeenth-century Dutch learned lady, Anna Maria van Schurman (1607–78), known to her contemporaries as the 'Star of Utrecht', was famous throughout Europe for her extraordinary linguistic accomplishments – besides learning all the modern languages, she had taught herself Hebrew, Greek, Latin, Arabic, Chaldee, Syriac and Ethiopian and written grammars for several languages – and her feats proved an inspiration to a number of eighteenth-century female scholars. The celebrated classicist Anne Lefèvre Dacier (1654–1720), for example, translated the *Iliad* and *Odyssey* into French in 1711 and took a vigorous part in the *querelle des Anciens et des Modernes*, publishing *Homère défendu contre l'Apologie du R. P. Hardouin; ou Suite des causes de la corruption du goust* in 1716. (So renowned were her Greek translations that even Fielding, some thirty years after her death, paid homage to the great 'Madam *Daciere*' in *Tom Jones*.[10]) Dacier's English contemporary Elizabeth Elstob (1683–1756), sometimes called the 'Saxon Muse', was another brilliant female scholar: after translating Aelfric's *English-Saxon Homily on the Birth-day of St Gregory* in 1709, she produced the first English Anglo-Saxon grammar, *Rudiments of Grammar for the English-Saxon Tongue . . . with an Apology for the Study of Northern Antiquities*, in 1715. Besides revealing Elstob's wide knowledge of English poetry, the *Rudiments* was noteworthy for its defence of Anglo-Saxon studies against the criticisms of Swift, who had complained that such knowledge was uselessly pedantic. Other gifted women followed in the footsteps of Dacier and Elstob: Constantia Grierson (1706–33), though born into a poor and illiterate family, mastered Greek and Latin and edited Virgil, Terence, and Tacitus in the 1720s; Elizabeth Carter (1717–1806), the friend of Samuel Johnson, produced a scholarly edition of Epictetus in 1758. In 1781 Ann Francis (1738–1800) published a poetic translation of the Song of Solomon, complete with historical and critical notes on the ancient Hebrew.

Several women in the second half of the century, likewise, produced learned books on the writings of Shakespeare. The novelist Charlotte Lennox (?1729–1804) published a source study of the plays, *Shakespear Illustrated*, in 1753. Samuel Johnson particularly admired this work, and drew upon it heavily (without acknowledgement) in his own *Preface to Shakespeare*. Montagu's *The Writings and Genius of Shakespeare* (1769) was primarily an attack on Voltaire, who had judged Shakespeare inferior to the French neo-classical dramatists and mistranslated (in Montagu's view) certain important passages in the plays. Elizabeth Griffith

---

[10] Fielding, *Tom Jones*, bk 7, ch. 12, p. 372.

(?1720–93) published her own lengthy vindication of the poet, *The Morality of Shakespeare's Drama Illustrated*, in 1775.

Yet the fact remains that such extended treatises were rare. As for verse epistles, critical dialogues, and the formal essay itself (as opposed to reviews or prefaces) – these too were primarily masculine forms in the period. Judith Madan (1702–81) published 'The Progress of Poetry' in 1731 – a 264-line verse essay on the development of poetry from Homer to Addison, which antedated Gray's similarly-titled poem on the same subject by twenty years. But her example seems not to have been followed by other women writers. Elizabeth Montagu's short work *Three Dialogues of the Dead* from 1769 (which includes a fanciful dialogue between Plutarch and a modern bookseller on the vagaries of taste) and Clara Reeve's *The Progress of Romance* (1785) were among the only literary-historical works written by women in the period in dialogue form.

Women occasionally published isolated critical essays and polemical pieces, though again rarely, and usually anonymously. Elizabeth Harrison (fl. 1756) published a pamphlet defence of Gay, *A Letter to Mr John Gay, on His Tragedy Call'd 'The Captives'*, in 1724, using the pretence of the private letter to expound her views. The novelist Sarah Fielding (1710–68) printed her influential *Remarks on 'Clarissa'* anonymously in 1749. Before her marriage, the editor-critic Anna Laetitia Barbauld (1743–1825) collaborated with her brother John Aikin on a collection of essays entitled *Miscellaneous Pieces in Prose* (1773), which included short articles on comedy and romance, a longer piece on Davenant's *Gondibert*, a vaguely Burkean meditation 'On the Pleasure derived from Objects of Terror', and commentaries on the *Arabian Nights, The Castle of Otranto* and other icons of contemporary taste. Barbauld did not distinguish her contributions from her brother's, however, and her name appears on the title page only as 'A. L. Aikin'. Only near the end of the century would a woman unhesitatingly embrace the independent essay format and produce a work of outstanding significance. Germaine de Staël's *Essai sur les fictions* (1795) – devoted to the novel's power of providing 'intimate understanding of the human heart' – remains one of the century's most thoughtful and impressive pieces of genre criticism.

The bulk of women's critical writing, however, was more impromptu – even haphazard – in style and scope; a great deal of it has undoubtedly been lost. Women tended to work in the ephemeral branches of criticism: the short review or squib (often unsigned) was a typically feminine genre throughout the century. Eliza Haywood published occasional pieces on Shakespeare and other poets in *The Female Spectator* in the 1740s; Frances Brooke reviewed theatrical productions in *The Old Maid* in the 1750s. (Reviewing the heavily doctored Garrick–Tate version of *King*

Lear in 1756, Brooke was one of the first critics to call for a return to authentic Shakespearean texts.) Charlotte Lennox wrote book reviews for the *Lady's Museum* in 1760–1, as did Mary Wollstonecraft (1759–97) and Mary Hays (1760–1843) for the *Analytical Review* and the *Monthly Review* at the end of the century. On the continent, Luise Adelgunde Victoria Gottsched (1713–62), the wife of Germany's best-known neo-classical critic, Johann Christoph Gottsched, almost certainly collaborated with her husband on his literary journal *Die vernünftigen Tadlerinnen* (modelled on *The Spectator*) in the 1720s, though the precise extent of her contributions cannot be determined. In the 1780s and 1790s, again in Germany, Sophie von La Roche (1731–1807) and Sophie Mereau (1770–1806) also produced occasional critical remarks for their influential publications *Pomona für Teutschlands Töchter* (1783–4) and *Kalathiskos* (1801–2).

Prefaces, usually written for popular anthologies or translations, were another female speciality. As a secondary or 'satellite' form, the preface, like the unsigned review, seems to have allowed women writers room for the kind of aggressive critical intervention they did not feel free to make elsewhere. Prefaces to works of drama were especially popular – perhaps because so many professional literary women had begun their careers as actresses or playwrights. Aphra Behn (1640–89) provided several memorable prefaces for the published editions of her own plays in the 1670s; her introduction to *The Dutch Lover* (1673) contains an important early comparison of Jonson and Shakespeare. The actress-playwright Susannah Centlivre (d. 1723) followed in Behn's path, producing a number of lively prefaces and dedications during her career, including one for her translation of Molière, *Love's Contrivance* (1703), in which she analysed the differences between French and English taste. The same theme was taken up later on the opposite side of the Channel by Riccoboni, in the introduction to the *Nouveau théâtre anglais*, the anthology of contemporary English comedies she edited in 1768.

Prefaces to works of poetry and fiction were fewer in number, but several important examples may be cited. In 1737 Elizabeth Cooper (fl. 1735–40) provided a lengthy scholarly introduction to *The Muses' Library*, an anthology of English poetry, in which she traced the history of English versification from its early 'Gothique Rudeness' in Langland and Chaucer up to the refinements of Spenser and Daniel. (Chatterton, it is thought, knew Cooper's work and drew on it during the fabrication of the notorious Rowley manuscripts.[11]) The industrious Anna Barbauld produced a number of prefatory pieces at the end of the century: she edited the poetry of Akenside and Collins in 1795 and 1797, wrote a

[11] Todd, *Dictionary of Women Writers*, p. 93.

critical and biographical introduction for Richardson's *Correspondence* in 1804, and composed the introductions for the 50-volume series *British Novelists* in 1810. The latter, together with the Richardson essay, make up a kind of embryonic genre history: Sir Walter Scott relied upon both heavily in his own *Lives of the Novelists* (1821–4). Occasionally, it should be noted, women novelists wrote prefaces for their own works: Françoise de Graffigny's impassioned 'Avertissement' to *Lettres d'une péruvienne* (1747), highlighting the anti-colonialist theme of her fiction, and Frances Burney's preface to *Evelina* (1778), condemning slavish imitation in authors, stand out as valuable critical statements in their own right.

In 1798 the Scottish dramatist Joanna Baillie (1762–1851) produced an unusually lengthy and ambitious critical introduction for her *Plays on the Passions*, in which she analysed the different 'passions' evoked by tragedy and comedy and outlined a psychological defence of dramatic spectacle. Tragedy, she wrote, aroused the 'sympathetic curiosity' of the viewer and offered 'an enlarged view of human nature'. Comedy, meanwhile, with its focus on love, revealed 'the human heart' in all its intricacy. Theatre itself was a school in which moral wisdom might be learnt. Baillie's dour contemporary Hannah More (1745–1833) shared none of these views. More's fiercely moralistic 'Observations on the Effect of Theatrical Representations with respect to Religion and Morals', advocating a ban on all theatrical performances, first appeared, paradoxically enough, as a preface to a collection of More's own dramatic works in 1804. Yet despite the oddity of the context, the essay remains a perversely appealing *tour de force* of anti-theatrical writing. Of particular note are More's comments on the differences between reading plays and seeing them performed on stage. The power of acting, she acknowledged sadly, was to heighten 'the semblance of real action' into 'a kind of enchantment'. The effect was to induce in spectators a state of 'unnerving pleasure'.[12]

The most incisive editorial prefaces of the period, however, were undoubtedly those of Elizabeth Inchbald (1753–1821), who wrote over a hundred introductory essays for Longman's 25-volume series *The British Theatre* between 1806 and 1809. These biographical and critical notes are little-known today, but as examples of practical criticism, bear comparison – in wit, style, and intellectual scope – with the prefaces of Johnson. Inchbald was as opinionated as her mighty predecessor: *Henry IV*, she wrote, 'is a play which all men admire; and which most women dislike'; Addison's *Cato*, while undoubtedly patriotic, suffered badly from its 'insipid' love scenes. And she could be as moralistic: *The Beggar's*

---

[12] More, 'Preface to the Tragedies', p. 23.

Opera, she thought, though superbly comic, had 'the fatal tendency to make vice alluring'. But Inchbald's own experience as a player led her to some interestingly unorthodox judgements. Centlivre's plays, she argued, were more successful on the stage than Congreve's; Colley Cibber's work had been persistently undervalued. While 'many a judicious critic', she wrote,

> boasted of knowing what kind of drama the public ought to like; Cibber was the lucky dramatist generally to know what they *would* like, whether they ought or not. If he secured their interest, he defied their understanding; and here, in the following scenes, so far he engages the heart in every event, that the head does not once reflect upon the improbabilities, with which the senses are delighted.[13]

Sampled at random, Inchbald's essays seldom fail to interest; taken in chronological sequence, they represent an outstanding intellectual achievement – the first truly critical history, in essence, of the English drama from the Renaissance to the late eighteenth century.

So far we have been dealing, of course, with 'official' kinds of critical activity – printed books, essays, reviews, prefaces and so on – yet many of the most interesting critical contributions by women during the century were made, it should be noted, in rather more spontaneous and informal contexts. Numerous miscellaneous reflections on books and poetry are to be found, for example, scattered through women's personal letters, journals, and private papers. This kind of impromptu, 'behind-the-scenes' commentary, despite its seemingly evanescent nature, occasionally had surprisingly immediate impact. Correspondence could itself become a form of critical intervention. Women readers, for example, sometimes wrote directly to authors – with provocative results. In 1749, soon after the publication of the first volumes of *Clarissa*, Lady Bradshaigh (Dorothy Bellingham) wrote to Samuel Richardson complaining about the plausibility of the novel and exhorting him to alter its projected ending: she wished for the heroine to marry her seducer instead of dying. Richardson rejected this drastic proposal, but made several changes in subsequent editions of the novel to forestall some of the other criticisms Bradshaigh had raised. Riccoboni provoked an even more celebrated *contretemps* with Laclos, author of *Les Liaisons dangereuses*, when she wrote to him in 1782 condemning his character Madame de Merteuil on moral and feminist grounds. He replied at length, and without her permission published the resulting correspondence in the 1787 edition of his novel. (Riccoboni protested, but may have secretly enjoyed the fray: she carried on similar epistolary disputes with Diderot and Garrick.) The 'letter to the author' format seems to have unleashed in a number

[13] Inchbald, preface to Cibber's *Love Makes a Man*, in *British Theatre*, XIV, p. 4.

of women writers a subversive fantasy of rewriting received (male) texts. This fantasy was itself at times realized. Lady Bradshaigh's sister, Elizabeth, Lady Echlin (?1704–82), produced a revised version of *Clarissa* (unpublished until 1982) in which the heroine indeed avoided being raped and succeeded in converting her persecutor. Later in the century the novelist Anne Eden (fl. 1790) rewrote Goethe's *The Sorrows of Young Werther* from the perspective of the husband Albert, stressing his sympathetic qualities, while Ann Francis published *A Poetical Epistle from Charlotte to Werther* (1788), focusing on Goethe's heroine's point of view.

We should not forget, finally, that some of the most important female criticism in the period was never written down at all. Eighteenth-century women *talked* about literature, even when they did not always feel free to write about it. Literary salons and bluestocking clubs became increasingly popular and influential over the course of the century. In England, Elizabeth Montagu, known to contemporaries as 'the Queen of the Blues', presided over a fashionable literary coterie in the 1760s and 1770s; Elizabeth Carter, Mary Delany (1700–88), Hester Mulso Chapone (1727–1801), Catherine Macaulay (1731–91) and Hannah More were also active bluestocking leaders. Important French *salonnières* included Claudine-Alexandre Guérin de Tencin (1682–1726), Marie-Thérèse Geoffrin (1697–1777), Emilie du Châtelet (1706–1749), Julie de Lespinasse (1732–1776), Suzanne Necker (1739–1794), and later Necker's daughter, Germaine de Staël. Salons developed somewhat later in Germany; none the less, as the letters and diaries of Sophie von La Roche, Dorothea Schlegel (1763–1839), Caroline (Schlegel) Schelling (1763–1809) and Rahel Varnhagen (1777–1833) indicate, women had begun to make a similar place for themselves in German literary society by the end of the century.

While not criticism in any conventional sense, the unofficial advocacy of the salon women was often instrumental in shaping contemporary literary taste. Richardson's circle of female admirers (including Hester Chapone and Mary Delany) did much, for example, to promote his literary reputation in the 1740s and 1750s; Suzanne Necker was a leading supporter of Rousseau. In Germany, the charismatic Rahel Varnhagen, leader of the most important salon in Berlin at the end of the century, almost single-handedly established Goethe's reputation as the reigning genius of European literature after the publication of *Wilhelm Meister's Apprenticeship* in 1796. Indeed, precisely when women's access to the official 'Republic of Letters' was so limited, the conversation of the salons provided them with a needed psychological outlet – a way of discharging aggressive intellectual energies. As Samuel Johnson grudgingly acknowledged of Elizabeth Montagu, his adversary in a number of verbal battles, '[she] is an extraordinary woman; she has a constant stream of conversation, and it is always impregnated; it has always meaning'.[14]

In order to give a full account of eighteenth-century female criticism, it is not enough, however, merely to enumerate the *kinds* of criticism women produced. What we might call the theoretical problem of women's criticism demands comment. How did women's new and somewhat vulnerable position in the 'Republic of Letters' shape their critical views? In what ways did women's literary values differ from those of men? And what impact did this minority criticism have on larger developments in contemporary critical thought? Let us begin by examining some of the characteristic themes of eighteenth-century women's criticism, paying particular attention to features that distinguished it from mainstream (male-authored) criticism. Then we can attempt, by way of conclusion, to address the larger question of historical influence.

The celebration of original or 'untutored' genius – coupled with a rejection of learning and decorum – was a favourite topic for women from the late seventeenth century on. That this should have been the case is hardly surprising, given that so many female critics were themselves untutored in the rules and prescriptions of classical rhetoric. Women writers turned their lack of erudition into a virtue. 'I do not repent that I spent not my time in learning', wrote Margaret Cavendish, the Duchess of Newcastle (1623–73), of her early years, 'for I consider it is better to write wittily than learnedly'.[15] True poetic genius, according to most female observers, did not inhere in erudition, or in the slavish concern with correctness, but in a spontaneous overflow of native wit and imagination.

Thus Aphra Behn argued that 'the immortal Shakespeare's plays' had 'better pleased the world than Jonson's works' precisely because Shakespeare (unlike Jonson) did not have much Greek or Latin – indeed 'was not guilty of much more of this than often falls to women's share'. The 'musty rules of unity' derived from classical literature were useless, according to Behn: 'methinks', she wrote sardonically, 'that they that disturb their heads with any other rule of plays besides the making them pleasant, and avoiding of scurrility, might much better be employed in studying how to improve men's too imperfect knowledge of that ancient English game which hight Long Laurence'.[16] Susannah Centlivre concurred: neo-classical critics might 'cavil most about Decorums, and crie up *Aristotle*'s Rules as the most essential part of the Play', yet

---

[14] Blunt, *Queen of the Blues*, II, p. 166.
[15] Cited in Mahl and Koon, *The Female Spectator*, pp. 136–7.
[16] Behn, preface to *The Dutch Lover* (1673). To 'play at Long Laurence', according to Wright's *English Dialect Dictionary*, meant to do nothing, to laze. St Laurence was the patron saint of idleness.

'they'll never persuade the Town to be of their Opinion, which relishes nothing so well as Humour lightly tost up with Wit, and drest with Modesty and Air'.[17]

The unconscious identification with Shakespeare – the great example of 'unlettered' genius – runs like a golden thread through eighteenth-century women's critical writing. Shakespeare's plays were so filled with moments of genius, wrote Elizabeth Montagu, that 'it avails little to prove, that the means by which he effects them are not those prescribed in any Art of Poetry'. Indeed, by deviating from the rules, the poet '[rose] *to faults true critics dare not mend*'.[18] Montagu's disciple Elizabeth Griffith went even further. Shakespeare, she argued, took the wreath from 'the whole collective Host of Greek or Roman writers, whether ethic, epic, dramatic, didactic or historic'. 'Though the dead languages are confessed to be superior to ours', Griffith observed, 'yet even here, in the very article of diction, our Author shall measure his pen with any of the ancient *styles* in their most admired compound and decompound epithets, descriptive phrases, or figurative epithets'. The 'living scene' of Shakespeare's plays exceeded 'the dead letter, as action is preferable to didacticism, or representation to declamation'.[19] Griffith was particularly attuned to the polymorphous, even feminist aspects of the poet's genius: fifty years ahead of Keats, she observed that 'our Author' could 'not only assume all characters, but even their sexes too'.[20]

Other untutored geniuses, however, inspired similar encomia. The persistent preference of women critics later in the century for Richardson over Fielding, for example, was at least partly due to the fact that Richardson was perceived as less educated – and hence more like a woman – than his rival. Richardson, wrote Anna Barbauld in her introduction to his *Correspondence*, exemplified 'natural talents making their way to eminence, under the pressure of narrow circumstances, the disadvantages of obscure birth, and the want of a liberal education'. He spoke no language besides English, she marvelled – 'not even French'. Later female critics would praise Robert Burns and other 'rustic' bards for similar reasons.

Not surprisingly, women had little sympathy for writers who cultivated an ostentatiously learned style. Samuel Johnson's prose, Elizabeth Montagu confided in a series of private letters to Elizabeth Carter, was '*trop recherché*'. He wrote like a 'parnassian beau', cramming his essays with so many 'ornaments of study' that his writing was more properly called 'writation'. This attack on Latinate diction, it should be noted,

---

[17] Centlivre, preface to *Love's Contrivance* (1703).
[18] Montagu, *Writings*, pp. xxii–xxiii. [19] Griffith, *Morality*, pp. 525–6.
[20] Griffith, *Morality*, p. 481.

often took on an explicitly chauvinistic edge. Women, Maria Edgeworth (1768–1849) asserted in her *Letters for Literary Ladies* (1795), wrote far more elegantly than men did, the female style being happily free of 'the melancholy apparatus of learning'.

Among the genres, women tended to prefer fiction, drama, and the popular essay to poetry – again, one suspects, because the received poetic styles were so imbued with masculine and elitist associations. Women critics seem to have had little interest in the epic or other exalted classical genres. Nor, despite their attachment to genius, did they share their male contemporaries' fascination with the poetical sublime. (Eighteenth-century women wrote relatively little, for example, about Milton.) On the whole, women preferred 'native wit' and accessibility – what could be called a domesticated poetic vision – to rhapsodic or visionary flights. They were suspicious of claims of mystical or vatic inspiration. This rejection of the hieratic mode would have interesting consequences at the end of the century: women often found themselves at odds with the more high-flown and visionary strains of Romanticism. There was a certain sexual logic in this resistance: besides disliking the solipsism and masculine conceit in high Romantic discourse – in the cult, for example, of the Wordsworthian 'egotistical sublime' – women could hardly afford to endorse its anti-intellectualism. Precisely because they had so often been accused of irrational flights themselves, they wanted little part of a poetic manner that seemed to value such things above all else.

By contrast, the more demotic and inclusive genres – plays, essays and prose fiction – won universal feminine approval. The drama, wrote Joanna Baillie, spoke more directly to the 'lower orders of society' than any other genre except the folk ballad; hence its value as a tool of moral instruction. Baillie saw no use in writing closet drama for an elite; had her own plays been more widely performed, she said, 'the spontaneous, untutored plaudits of the rude and uncultivated would have come to my heart as offerings of no mean value'.[21] Women cherished the popular essay for similar reasons; throughout the century female writers were especially attracted to the informal, ingratiating essay style perfected by Addison and Steele in the *Tatler* and the *Spectator*.[22]

Women's most heartfelt advocacy, however, as one might expect, was reserved for the novel – the literary form most powerfully grounded in everyday experience. Female critics were among the first to valorize the putative 'truthfulness to life' of the new genre. In a well-known passage in the *Progress of Romance*, Clara Reeve judged the novel superior to

[21] Baillie, preface to *Plays on the Passions* (1798).
[22] On the influence of Steele in particular, see Adburgham, pp. 53–66.

the older form of the romance precisely on account of its greater verisimilitude. While the romance, she wrote, was a 'heroic fable', treating
of 'fabulous persons and things', the novel was 'a picture of real life and
manners, and of the times in which it is written'. Its 'perfection' lay in
representing scenes 'in so easy and natural a manner, and [making] them
appear so probable, as to deceive us into a persuasion (at least while we
are reading) that all is real, until we are affected by the joys or distresses
of the persons in the story, as if they were our own'.[23] Barbauld agreed:
the novel had evolved, she argued in her essay on Richardson, out of
a desire for 'a closer imitation of nature'. Though it preserved the 'high
passion, and delicacy of sentiment of the old romance', it was superior
to the older form precisely because it depicted 'characters moving in the
same sphere of life with ourselves, and brought into action by incidents
of daily occurrence'. Unlike its precursor form, the novel was not concerned with 'giants and fairies', or even 'princes and princesses', but with
'people of our acquaintance'.[24]

Female critics were also the first to explore the technical aspects of
the new genre. Barbauld again, anticipating the concerns of twentieth-
century narratology, identified three types of fictional narration: the
kind in which an author related the whole adventure (as in Cervantes
and Fielding), the memoir, or first-person account (found in Marivaux
and Smollett), and the epistolary mode, in which characters addressed
one another in letters. Each narrative technique, she felt, had its draw-
backs. The authorial mode could seldom become 'dramatic' without the
introduction of dialogue; the memoir-novel made the reader wonder
how an 'imaginary narrator' could remember so precisely; the epistolary
novel had problems of exposition. In the end, however, she preferred
epistolary narration to the other two modes. Private letters, describing
the emotions of characters as they felt them '*at* the moment', had the
power, she thought, to make 'the whole work dramatic'.[25]

Women laboured to free the novel of its popular associations with
scandal and triviality. The great power of the novel, wrote Germaine de
Staël, was its capacity to 'move the heart'. Because it engaged the reader's
feelings directly, prose fiction could exert, Staël felt, an uplifting moral
and social force far greater than that of any abstract philosophy. Virtue,
she observed,

must be animated to struggle effectively against the passions, to create an
exalted feeling so that we may be attracted to sacrifice – in brief, to beautify
misfortune so that it will be preferred to sinful pleasures. Fiction that really

[23] Reeve, *Progress of Romance*, I, p. 111.
[24] Barbauld, *Richardson's Correspondence*, I, p. xvi.
[25] Barbauld, *Richardson's Correspondence*, I, p. xxvi.

moves us to noble emotions makes them habitual to us. It leads us unwittingly to make a pledge to ourselves that we would be ashamed to go back on.[26]

For Barbauld, the novel was likewise a kind of moral therapy: from the perusal of a serious work of fiction, she wrote, 'we rise better prepared to meet the ills of life with firmness, or to perform our respective parts in the great theatre of life'.[27]

Such claims were not merely rhetorical. A concern for the moral and social effects of literature was another standard feature in women's criticism throughout the century. Indeed, perhaps paradoxically (given their otherwise iconoclastic intellectual attitudes), female critics tended to moralize about works of literature far more often, and with greater fervour, than male critics did. This was due in part, as we saw earlier, to lingering professional insecurities: the best way to avoid reproach for trespassing in the masculine 'Republic of Letters', it seemed, was to pretend that one did so solely, as Clara Reeve put it, 'to promote the cause of religion and virtue'. And precisely because their literary tastes *were* somewhat unconventional, women may have felt obliged to emphasize their moral conservatism as a counterbalance. But female critics had also internalized the same sexual stereotypes that affected all women in the period: as members of the (supposedly) more delicate and refined sex, it was their duty, they believed, to uphold cultural standards of modesty and piety.

In particular, despite their professed regard for verisimilitude, women opposed the explicit depiction of the sexual passions. Female critics were quick to condemn works containing any hint of immorality or coarseness. Even 'with its worst pages curtailed', wrote Elizabeth Inchbald of Vanbrugh's *The Provoked Wife*, 'too much that is bad still lingers behind'.[28] Clara Reeve found Fielding's novels full of 'objectionable scenes'; Rousseau's *La Nouvelle Héloïse* was 'dangerous and improper'.[29] Even Shakespeare came under fire: the character of Doll Tearsheet, according to Elizabeth Montagu, was an 'obscenity' – 'not only indefensible but

---

[26] 'Il faut animer la vertu pour qu'elle combatte avec avantage contre les passions; il faut faire naître une sorte d'exaltation pour trouver du charme dans les sacrifices; il faut enfin parer le malheur pour qu'on le préfère à tous les prestiges des séductions coupables; et les fictions touchantes qui exercent l'âme à toutes les passions généreuses, lui en donnent l'habitude, et lui font prendre à son insu un engagement avec elle-même, qu'elle auroit honte de rétracter, si une situation semblable lui devenoit personelle' (Staël, *Essai sur les fictions* (1795), in *Oeuvres complètes*, II, p. 207). Here, as in subsequent citations from Staël's works, I have relied on the translation by Morroe Berger.

[27] Barbauld, *Richardson's Correspondence*, I, pp. xxi–xxii.

[28] Inchbald, preface to Vanbrugh's *The Provoked Wife*, in *British Theatre*, IX, p. 9.

[29] Reeve, *Progress of Romance*, I, p. 140 and II, p. 14.

inexcusable'.[30] 'Who can deny', wrote Hannah More, 'that all the excellencies we have attributed to [Shakespeare] are debased by passages
of offensive grossness?' His plays, she felt, were certainly too voluptu-
ous to be performed; only 'the discriminated, the guarded, the qualified
perusal of such an author' – i.e., reading a bowdlerized text in private
– could be permitted.[31] Nor were such puritanical comments confined
to British critics: Stephanie de Genlis (1746–1830), in her 1811 history
of French women writers, *De l'Influence des femmes sur la littérature
française*, condemned Madame de Lafayette's *La Princesse de Clèves* for
depicting 'une passion criminelle'. Far from being moral, it was too
dangerous a book to be put into the hands of 'les jeunes personnes'.[32]

Such views are easy enough to satirize; they seem to anticipate the
worse excesses of Victorian prudery. Yet it is also possible to interpret
some of this feminine resistance to the 'improper' in a more complex light.
Very often women's real objection seems to have been not so much to
the depiction of sexuality *per se*, but to the misogyny that frequently
accompanied the explicit representation of sexual themes. Riccoboni's
criticism of *Les Liaisons dangereuses* is a good case in point. In attacking Laclos's novel for what she saw as its 'revolting' picture of French
morals, Riccoboni took particular exception to the portrait of the female
villain, the wicked Madame de Merteuil. Merteuil's character was not
only implausible, she told Laclos, but insulting to women readers: he
had drawn a caricature of female iniquity. Laclos, with barely concealed
condescension, responded that he had simply presented nature with
'exactitude et fidélité' and that it was hypocritical to pretend that depraved creatures such as Merteuil did not exist.[33]

Laclos's defence has often been seen as a heroic vindication of realist
principles. Yet if we take Riccoboni's point of view seriously – and
indeed rehabilitate it as a *feminist* point of view – a number of interesting
theoretical and historical questions arise. To what extent is 'realism'
itself a gender-bound concept? How much so-called 'true-to-life' or
'naturalistic' writing has actually been grounded in the misogynistic
biases of Western culture? Without a doubt many of the most famous
exponents of the uncensored mode – Swift in his scatological poems,
Flaubert in *Madame Bovary*, Zola in *Nana*, Ernest Hemingway, D. H.
Lawrence, or Henry Miller in any of their various novels – have shown
themselves to be peculiarly obsessed with representing women as devious
and manipulative, physically or morally corrupt. For a woman to reject
the 'truth' of such writing, therefore, may not necessarily be a sign of

[30] Montagu, *Writings*, p. 105.
[31] More, 'Preface to the Tragedies', in *Works*, II, p. 24.
[32] Genlis, *De l'Influence des femmes*, p. 114.
[33] 'Correspondance de Laclos et de Madame Riccoboni', p. 759.

false modesty. In the case of Riccoboni, she seems to have been motivated less by prudishness than by a desire for a new kind of literary representation – a more exacting realism, unmarred by sexual prejudice, and faithful to the experience of all its readers.

Which brings us, by a somewhat paradoxical route, to the most subversive aspect of women's critical writing in the period: its implicitly adversarial content. Female critics, as we have seen, were acutely conscious of being interlopers in 'the Republic of Letters' – at times debilitatingly so. Yet on occasion they were able to transform this sense of marginality into a kind of covert intellectual resistance. While not feminists in the modern sense – few wished for a complete overhaul of male and female social roles – many eighteenth-century women critics resented the masculine bias of traditional literary discourse, and said so. A strain of incipient sexual protest informed their writing, becoming particularly pronounced as the century drew to a close.

This nascent feminism took a number of forms. Sometimes it surfaced only in a coded or oblique fashion – as in Eliza Haywood's praise of reading in *The Female Spectator*. Haywood describes a conversation between herself and two book-loving female friends. 'What clods of earth should we have been but for reading!' she is moved to exclaim, 'how ignorant of every thing but the spot we tread upon!' Mira and Euphrosyne agree: to reading – with its power of 'informing the mind, correcting the manners, and enlarging the understanding' – 'we owe all that distinguishes us from savages'.[34] The praise is couched in conventional terms, yet also has a curiously 'gendered' feeling to it: one cannot help sensing that Haywood's real subject is *female* literacy – still a relatively new and uncommon phenomenon in the 1740s. It was the idea of women reading, specifically, that excited her imagination. The passage can thus be read as an unconscious vindication of female mastery: for a woman to read books is to enter, at last, a world of knowledge and self-understanding.

At other times, feminist sentiments surfaced more directly – in complaints, for example, about the patronizing attitudes of male writers. At the end of her otherwise laudatory essay on Richardson, Barbauld could not help remarking, with ill-disguised irritation, that the author of *Clarissa* did not properly value intellectual women. Though she was willing to allow that 'the prejudice against any appearance of extraordinary cultivation in women, was, at that period, very strong', her hero's disdain clearly rankled. 'What can be more humiliating', she asked, 'than the necessity of affecting ignorance?' The only good result of such prejudice, she concluded, was that it gave 'female genius' something to overcome

[34] Haywood, *Female Spectator*, II, p. 39.

– 'so much, as to render it probable, before a woman steps out of the common walks of life, that her acquirements are solid, and her love for literature decided and irresistible'.[35]

Female critics were particularly affronted by what they perceived as the double standard informing masculine literary judgement: male writers were celebrated, whatever their talent, while women writers were almost always ignored. Because men alone assigned the ranks in literature, complained Stephanie de Genlis, female genius went unrecognized; praise was reserved for other men, including very mediocre talents. D'Alembert, she thought, was a blatant example of overrated mediocrity: he was considered important only because he had the support of the male-run Academy. If an academy of women existed, it would conduct itself better and judge more sanely.[36]

In an attempt to redress such injustice, women critics regularly commended the accomplishments of their fellow women writers. Susannah Centlivre, wrote Inchbald, 'ranks in the first class of our comic dramatists'. Hannah Cowley's *The Belle's Stratagem* was an 'extremely attractive' play, replete with 'forcible and pleasing occurrences'.[37] The novels of Sarah Fielding, wrote Clara Reeve, were eminently worthy of comparison with her brother Henry's: if they did not equal them in 'wit and learning', they excelled 'in some other material merits, that are more beneficial to their readers'.[38] Reeve also praised the fiction of Charlotte Lennox, Frances Brooke, Elizabeth Griffith, Frances Sheridan, Marie-Jeanne Riccoboni and Stephanie de Genlis. Barbauld's *British Novelists* series was in itself an act of feminist advocacy: out of the twenty-eight novels Barbauld included in the series, twelve were written by women.

Women critics conferred on certain 'female geniuses' an almost cult status. The acclaim bestowed on the seventeenth-century letter writer, Madame de Sévigné, for example, bordered on hero-worship. There was only one work in the French language no one had ever thought to criticize, declared Genlis, 'and that work was written by a woman'. Sévigné's letters were a 'perfect model' of style – superior in 'spirit, imagination and sensibility' to anything else in the epistolary genre.[39] Elizabeth Montagu agreed: the noble pen of Sévigné, she declared, had inscribed its wielder's character 'on every mind capable of receiving impressions of virtue, and of wit'. 'She was surely the most amiable of

---

[35] Barbauld, *Richardson's Correspondence*, p. clxiv.
[36] Genlis, *De l'Influence des femmes*, p. x.
[37] See Inchbald, preface to Centlivre's *The Wonder: A Woman Keeps a Secret*, in *British Theatre*, XI, p. 3; and her preface to Cowley's *The Belle's Stratagem*, in *British Theatre*, XIX, p. 2.
[38] Reeve, *Progress of Romance*, I, p. 142.
[39] Genlis, *De l'Influence des femmes*, p. 134.

Women', she told Elizabeth Carter. 'I am interested in every circumstance that relates to her.'[40] Similar encomia appeared in the works of contemporary German women writers – notably in the letters of Sophie von La Roche, herself a fluent and stylish correspondent.

Yet the eulogizing of individual women writers, however enthusiastic, did not for some female critics go far enough. At the end of the century two writers sought to reclaim for women a central role in literary history itself. In *De l'Influence des femmes sur la littérature française*, Genlis argued that women, not men, had been responsible for the development of French literature. Genlis was not deterred by the fact that few women had written before the seventeenth century: the role of 'protectrice', or literary patroness, was just as important, in her view, as actual authorship. Women exerted a civilizing force in culture; when women held power and social authority, genius and taste flourished. Among the great makers of French literature, therefore, she counted most of the early queens and princesses of France, as well as modern 'protectrices' such as Madame de Maintenon and the Marquise de Rambouillet. All of these women, she maintained, had used their status and prestige to cultivate 'les gens de lettres' and promote the arts: without them, French literature would not have come into existence.

A similar argument was put forth by the greatest female critic of the age, Germaine de Staël (1766–1817). Women, she believed, were the natural arbiters of taste. Thus advances in the arts took place in societies in which women were held in highest esteem. In her early masterpiece of literary sociology, *De la Littérature considérée dans ses rapports avec les institutions sociales* (1800), Staël made a direct connection between the status of women and the evolution of genres. The novel had developed in England, she said, because England was that country 'where women are most truly loved':

Tyrannical laws, coarse desires, or cynical ideas have settled the fate of women, whether in the ancient republics or in Asia or in France. Nowhere so much as in England have women enjoyed the happiness brought about by domestic affections.[41]

In France, by contrast, despite the upheavals of the Revolution, women were still treated with contempt. 'Men have thought it politically and morally useful to reduce women to the most absurd mediocrity', Staël complained. 'Women have had no incentive to develop their minds;

---

[40] Cited in Blunt, *Queen of the Blues*, II, p. 98.
[41] 'Des lois tyranniques, des désirs grossiers, ou des principes corrompus, ont disposé du sort des femmes, soit dans les républiques anciennes, soit en Asie, soit en France. Les femmes n'ont joui nulle part, comme en Angleterre, du bonheur causé par les affections domestiques' (Staël, *De la Littérature*, II, p. 228).

manners have thus not improved.'[42] French literature had stagnated as
a result. Rousseau's *La Nouvelle Héloïse*, she allowed, 'was an eloquent
and impassioned piece of writing', but 'all the other French novels we
like are imitations of the English'.[43]

Both Genlis and Staël defended women's writing and predicted that
female authors, and especially female critics, would play an increasingly
prominent role in the literature of the future. Women were not only
capable of producing great works of their own, wrote Genlis; their
natural 'finesse d'observation' and elegance of style made them excellent
judges of the works of others. According to Staël, as society moved
closer toward moral and social enlightenment and more and more women
took part in literary life, literature itself would evolve in a feminist
direction. While the comedy of the *ancien régime* had focused, for
example, on 'the immoral behaviour of men toward women' precisely
in order 'to ridicule the deceived women', in the perfected drama of the
future, male deception itself would become the satiric target. Corrupt
'purveyors of vice' – men who imposed on women – would themselves
be 'exposed as wretched beings, and abandoned to children's jeers'.[44]
Female critics, Staël implied, would play a crucial part in these uplifting
developments. As she would argue later in *De l'Allemagne* (1813), 'nature
and society have given women a great capacity for endurance, and it
seems to me that it cannot be denied that in our day they are in general
more meritorious than men'.[45]

Such heady sentiments, as one might expect, found little immediate
echo in mainstream criticism. Nor must it be said – in the decades to
come – did female critics find the acceptance that Staël and Genlis so
optimistically predicted. Indeed, as the study of literature became more
and more professionalized and institutionalized after 1800, the opposite
often seemed to be the case. For most of the nineteenth century, literary
criticism remained a predominantly male-identified activity: the early
contributions of women to critical thought were soon forgotten. Dryden,

---

[42] 'Néanmoins, depuis la révolution, les hommes ont pensé qu'il étoit politiquement et
moralement utile de réduire les femmes à la plus absurde médiocrité ... elles n'ont
plus eu de motifs pour développer leur raison: les moeurs n'en sont pas devenues
meilleures' (Staël, *De la Littérature*, II, p. 335).

[43] 'La Nouvelle Héloïse est un écrit éloquent et passionné, qui caractérise le génie
d'un homme, et non les moeurs de la nation. Tous les autres romans français que
nous aimons, nous les devons à l'imitation des Anglais' (Staël, *De la Littérature*, II,
p. 230).

[44] '... des hommes puissans, ces charlatans de vices, ces frondeurs de principes élevés,
ces moqueurs des âmes sensibles, c'est eux qu'il faut vouer au ridicule qu'ils
préparent, les dépouiller comme des êtres misérables, et les abandonner à la risée
des enfans' (Staël, *De la Littérature*, II, p. 350).

[45] 'La nature et la société donnent aux femmes une grande habitude de souffrir, et
l'on ne sauroit nier, ce me semble, que de nos jours elles ne vaillent, en général,
mieux que les hommes' (Staël, *De l'Allemagne*, I, p. 64).

Pope, Boileau, Johnson, Diderot, Wordsworth, Coleridge and other male writers were canonized as the great originators of the modern literary-critical tradition; the works of Behn, Montagu, Riccoboni, Inchbald, Barbauld, Genlis and even Staël herself (not to mention those of lesser figures) were consigned to oblivion.

Does this mean, therefore, that eighteenth-century women had relatively little impact on the early development of modern literary criticism? Here one must take issue with the masculinist biases of traditional literary history. The fact that individual women critics were so quickly forgotten does not mean that their influence on contemporary taste was itself negligible. Indeed, one might make a powerful revisionist claim on their behalf: that they represented the critical vanguard of their epoch. As we have seen, female critics regularly gravitated to the more iconoclastic topics of the day – the power of original genius, the rejection of classical models, the superiority of fiction and drama over poetry. They were impatient, by and large, with received styles and genres and turned instead to newer forms, such as the novel, which seemed to articulate in a powerful yet accessible way the moral and intellectual concerns of a growing middle-class (increasingly female) reading public. To borrow the language of the eighteenth century itself, women critics were almost always on the side of the 'Moderns' – in favour of novelty and experimentation, vernacular styles, and the democratization of reading and writing.

Over the next two centuries, of course, these literary values would gradually triumph. The history of modern criticism, one could argue, is a history of the feminization of taste. In the nineteenth century, with the continuing rise of female literacy, literature itself underwent a feminization: with the emergence of celebrated women writers – Jane Austen, George Eliot, George Sand, the Brontës, Emily Dickinson (and somewhat later, Edith Wharton, Virginia Woolf, Willa Cather, Colette and Gertrude Stein) – the 'Republic of Letters' seemed to evolve, if not into a women's domain, into a community in which women could at least claim an authority equal to that of men. In turn, what we might call 'female' literary values – informality, inventiveness, accessibility – gained a new prestige and importance. The canonization of the novel as the pre-eminent genre of 'modern life' was itself a testimony to women's growing critical influence.

Eighteenth-century women critics – who of course represented a much larger body of women readers – can be said to have anticipated this feminization of taste. Though unable to win legitimation for their own writing, they articulated for the first time an alternative to traditional male-oriented literary values. Fittingly, the process they initiated would culminate, in the twentieth century, in the vindication of women's role in the history of literary criticism itself – to which the existence of this essay may bear witness.

20

Primitivism

Maximillian E. Novak

Primitivism may be defined as the idealization of a way of life that differs from our own in being less complicated, less polished, and less self-aware. It may be found in an abstract state of nature, in the countryside where the influence of the city and the court has not been felt, in some land distant from the corruptions of western Europe, or in the historical past.[1] The most important critical debates associated with primitivism during the period between 1660 and 1800 involved a spectrum of positions which were intimately connected with political and social attitudes, and isolating the aesthetic from these contexts is neither possible nor useful. In England, the return of Charles II entailed a rejection of the past – literary as well as political – as a time of barbarism. In some ways, the defacing of the bodies of Oliver Cromwell and the regicides had its counterpart in the criticism of Thomas Rymer, who treated Shakespeare and his contemporaries as writers who knew nothing about art or decorum. The 'last age' was to make way for a time of order, control, and polish in both politics and poetry.[2]

Despite some notable exceptions, primitivism, when presented as an unmitigated ideal, functioned in the realm of criticism the same way as it operated in politics. It was invoked by those offering views of art and life that appealed to innovation and freedom. Although the main focus of this discussion will be upon critical debates over what might be considered primitive art forms, poetic figures, and language, none of this is intelligible without a brief discussion of the phenomenon of primitivism

[1] Following Arthur Lovejoy, Hayden White tries to distinguish between 'archaism' and primitivism. Although the impulse behind an idealization of the past may, under certain circumstances, be different from primitivism, it certainly shared the same general function of representing the 'other'. See Hayden White, 'The forms of wildness', in *The Wild Man Within*, ed. Edward Dudley and Maximillian Novak, pp. 25–8; and Lovejoy, *Documentary History of Primitivism*.

[2] The exchange between Sir William Davenant and Thomas Hobbes on the political purposes of heroic poetry suggests the degree to which poetry might be considered as a form of social propaganda for impressing the populace with the necessity for order. The emphasis upon polishing rather than creating as the true function of the artist, as stated by John Dryden in the preface to *An Evening's Love*, may also have political overtones, since it subordinates that very enthusiasm that later critics and poets attached to the bard to the image of the craftsman.

itself and its appearance in contemporary literature. For the flourishing of primitivism during this period raises a significant question. If the entire thrust of art and socio-political thinking was in the direction of polish and sophistication, why did so many works attempt to conjure up the image of an uncontaminated state of nature? Among the variety of answers to this question which will be suggested in this essay, two are essential: (1) That kind of criticism which placed a high value upon taste gradually accepted some 'primitive' works as possessing a certain natural power; (2) Despite the triumph of the ideals of politeness and polish, an admiration for the 'artless' work of genius was always present as an alternative.

There was hardly anything very new about the concepts of primitivism that flourished during the Restoration and eighteenth century. But the kind of thinking that tended to idealize a life lived close to nature assumed a very different flavour in a world dominated by new forms of thought and new social realities: by the advent of a consumer society, by an admiration for science and by quests after rational systems of law, morality, and theology. Nature itself had assumed the configuration of a complex system of signs in which God's presence had to be deciphered. And such a deciphering had to confront an obvious lack of those miracles that would have made such a search for God's power and influence unnecessary. Every idealized description of nature resounded with echoes of a long lost Eden or of a Golden Age, when God or the gods walked with humanity.

If the primitive might resonate with echoes from the past, it was also very much alive in the present with numerous travel accounts about exotic lands and their strange ways available to all. The earliest illustrations in books about the New World contained images of what may be distinguished as 'hard' and 'soft' primitivism – those pictures of savage life which tended to admire its ruggedness and simplicity (and to excuse its brutality) and those which sentimentalized it in the direction of pastoral. With their juxtaposition of depictions of American Indians against representations of the painted Picts encountered by the Romans in ancient Britain, these prints also suggested a concept of history, of human society moving forward haltingly within a cyclic pattern of the rise and fall of civilizations. Also present in both texts and illustrations were tendencies that ran counter to primitivism – pictures of cannibalism and descriptions of eating habits which suggested that the savages of the Americas were of questionable humanity. Columbus himself alternated between these views according to his moods.[3] The Caribs were sometimes the inhabitants of a Golden Age long lost to Europeans, sometimes

---

[3] See Tzvetan Todorov, *The Conquest of America*, pp. 34–50.

treacherous and vicious. The patterns were so well established that
writers of the period between 1660 and 1800 had no difficulty finding
an audience receptive to the variety of myths about the savage.

Present to all was the barbarism of the Spaniards who had wreaked
such havoc on the Indian populations of North and South America. Sir
William Davenant's one-act drama, *The Cruelty of the Spaniards in
Peru*, first produced in 1663, revealed natives who lived according to
the laws of nature in a type of Golden Age reminiscent of that depicted
in the ancient Greek and Latin poets. There is even a suggestion that
such an innocent life conveys eternal youth:

> We danc'd and we sung,
> And look'd ever young,
> And from restraints were free,
> As waves and winds at sea.
> . . .
> When garments were not worn,
> Nor shame did nakedness resent:
> Nor poverty bred scorn:
> When none could want, and all were innocent.[4]

The Incas and Aztecs were often given a somewhat different status from
less civilized tribes, but Davenant conflates noble savage and noble
barbarian. John Dryden, who coined the phrase 'noble savage' in *The
Conquest of Granada* (1672), tends to be more subtle in his distinctions,
but he had an opportunity to exploit many sides of primitivism in his
early poetry and plays, namely *The Indian Queen*, a collaboration with
Sir Robert Howard produced in 1664, *The Indian Emperor* (1665), and
a revision of Shakespeare's *The Tempest* following the suggestions of
Davenant (1667). Dryden's Almanzor, the hero of *The Conquest of
Granada*, is a noble savage in the sense that, like Dryden's Montezuma,
he is raised, in the manner of the mythical wild man of western European
folklore, in close contact with a savage nature. In Dryden's scheme,
these savage figures need to be tamed. Though admirable in many ways,
they must lose enough of their wildness and power to enable them to
enter society. This is the pattern of the child raised by a bear in the old
fable about nature and nurture, *Valentine and Orson*, and Dryden tames
his heroes by having them fall in love or by the more physical process
of having them lose some blood.

This baroque wild man has picked up some philosophical baggage
along the way. His egotism is not unlike that depicted by Hobbes in which
the solitary savage, ruled by self-interest, desire, the lust for power, and
fear, exists in such uncertainty that he abandons his freedom for the

[4] Sir William Davenant, *Dramatic Works*, I, pp. 79–80.

security afforded by the state. On the other hand, among another group, the adherents of philosophic Libertinism, the important point was conduct within society. The Libertine could accept the dull, secure life of the modern state only for the uninitiated, while he or she continued to live as a wild man or wild woman within society. It is in this context that the rake functioned in Restoration comedy – as a kind of natural man continuing to live for his animal pleasures and desires within a social structure that has abandoned true passion. Curiously enough, the way in which this concept was formulated bears some resemblance to that employed by Rousseau in *Émile* where the young hero was to embody the idea of the natural man within a corrupt society.

Hobbes's speculations on the state of nature produced a rash of reflections on the philosophical fiction of a model savage who was to illustrate the true nature of man. In response to Hobbes, writers as different as Cumberland, Pufendorf, and Locke posited archetypal man as naturally inclined to society – more sheeplike than lupine. And it was upon this vision of the human need to create communities that many treatises upon natural law were based. But Locke had read enough travel accounts about the encounters between Europeans and savage societies to make him sceptical of a pastoral view of primitive life. His former pupil, Shaftesbury, who, in his *Characteristicks,* specialized in a neo-stoic vision of a philosophic return to nature and natural principles, upbraided Locke for a certain naïveté in believing such lying travellers. But a degree of idealization, based on a faith that anyone brought up close to nature must be virtuous, existed alongside a more down-to-earth vision throughout the period. This 'realistic' or 'scientific' view could encompass the racist mentality that turned the sister of Caliban in the revised *Tempest* into the stereotyped vision of the hideously ugly black woman – Queen Blobberlips – or the naïve anthropology that produced David Hume's comments on the inferiority of blacks. Or it might make for the appreciative observations on the four Indian kings who visited Britain in the spring of 1710.

Steele's essay on the four kings in the *Tatler* (no. 171, 13 May 1710) depicted their natural dignity as an example of the absurdity of considering them barbaric. And Addison, in the *Spectator* (no. 50, 27 April 1711) pretended that one of the kings had left a commentary on London behind him. This presented Addison with the opportunity to view European behaviour through the eyes of a savage, a technique to be used by Voltaire in *L'Ingénu* and by Diderot in his *Supplément au Voyage de Bougainville.*[5] Addison's Indian finds British manners incomprehensible.

[5] For an excellent example of an earlier version of this literary device, see Baron de Lahontan, 'A Conference or Dialogue between the Author and Adario, a Noted Man among the Savages', *New Voyages to North America*, II, p. 618.

He cannot believe that St Paul's is truly a house of prayer, since everyone seemed asleep during the sermon. And he was shocked to find that the physical skills so admired by the Indians and which singled out the brave for leadership were practised by professional acrobats in Europe, while the leaders of the country were lazy. Such satire, as employed by both Addison and Voltaire, serves a dual purpose, mocking the naïveté of the savage while calling into question the values of European society. Diderot's dialogue, on the other hand, lends to the savage a nobility of vision which rejects European behaviour as evil in itself and corrupting to the natives of the South Seas.

Diderot's islander possesses a natural dignity of manner and an elegance of speech which, in its brevity and loftiness, approaches poetry. There were several reasons for this. (1) In searching for an equivalent to the status of the free savage, writers often resorted to a rhetoric associated with the Stoics of ancient Rome who aspired to a philosophical life that would bring them close to nature. The Indians in John Gay's _Polly_ offer a good example of this attempt to transform Indians into noble Romans. (2) It is likely, from accounts of explorers, that Indians were often heard in precisely this way. Joseph-François Lafitau describes at some length the solemn brevity and dignity in their manner of speaking. After interpreting their meetings in terms of the governments of contemporary western Europe, Lafitau notes that their orators are like those of ancient Sparta rather than of Athens or Rome (Demosthenes or Cicero).[6] An account reprinted in the _Gentleman's Magazine_ of August 1733 maintained that their orations were the equal of anything heard in ancient Greece or Rome, but also remarked on the appeal to reason in their councils and upon their 'Laconick and Concise' style.[7]

(3) It was thought that an explanation for this style had something to do with limitations upon the vocabularies of primitive nations. Lacking sufficient words, they speak in terse remarks and use metaphor to compensate for their inability to formulate difficult concepts. This idea lies behind the familiar statements made by Percy Bysshe Shelley, in his _Defence of Poetry_, that 'In the infancy of society every author is necessarily a poet, because language itself is poetry'. If this notion had currency among Romantic critics, it was, nevertheless, very much an idea of the Enlightenment. The reason for this is that, like Shelley, many writers of

[6] ... les Iroquois, comme les Lacédémoniens, veulent un discours vif et concis; leur style est cependant figuré et tout métaphorique: il est varié selon le différent caractère des affaires: en certaines occasions, il s'éloigne du langage ordinaire et resemble à notre style du Palais: en d'autres, il est soutenu d'une action plus vive que celle de nos acteurs sur le théâtre: ils ont en cela quelque chose de fort mimique; ils parlent autant du geste que de la voix, et ils représentent les choses si naturellement qu'elles semblent se passer sous les yeux des auditeurs (Lafitau, _Moeurs des sauvages Américains_, I, pp. 86–9).

[7] See _Gentleman's Magazine_, 3 (1733), p. 414.

the Enlightenment thought the language of primitive man to be 'vitally metaphorical'. Vico had made similar observations in his *New Science*, which first appeared in 1725, arguing that poetic speech preceded prose. For Vico, however, the productions were 'poetic monsters'.[8] Vico's approach reflects a division in contemporary thought. Almost everyone agreed that poetry was produced most naturally by people close to nature. But whereas the major French critics, Vico, and Dryden considered such poetry lacking in artistry, there were those who saw in the poetry of primitive people a key to producing a new and perhaps superior kind of poetry.

For the latter type of critics, the ballad, with its rich lode of traditional imagery, provided an important point of departure. Although there were always amateurs such as Samuel Pepys who appreciated and collected ballads, these traditional songs laboured under the double burden of being both the product of the rejected past and of being associated with the 'low' art of the rabble. Nevertheless, old and new ballads were sold on the streets of eighteenth-century European cities and carried by pedlars through the countryside. Though rejected as lacking the polish of high art, the ballad was part of the period's culture. Given the rise of nationalism and the repudiation of aristocratic values by those supporting the principles of the French Revolution, it was inevitable that someone like Johann Gottfried Herder should announce in his early writings that true poetry could *only* be found in works of this kind.[9]

The ballad 'Chevy Chase' had made several appearances in miscellanies of the time and had even been translated into Latin. To the amusement of a number of critics, Addison devoted two numbers of the *Spectator* during May of 1711 (70 and 74) to proving that it might be approached as an epic poem. Addison's arguments suggest that persons of true taste will be able to admire such works, since they have qualities pleasing to 'Readers of all Qualities and Conditions'. That they are also appreciated by the 'Multitude' ought not to disqualify them from being valued by more discerning critics. Whereas Shaftesbury and others had made good taste in the finished products of art into a litmus test for gentility, Addison was presenting a more Whiggish doctrine by which the simple and sincere productions of the people might be discovered to have genuine beauty for those who knew how to value them. Addison attempts to separate such works from those of bad ('Gothick') writers of clever verses (Martial and Cowley) who fail to capture that 'Perfection of Simplicity of Thought' to be discovered in the ballads of the common people throughout Europe. He quotes from 'Chevy Chase' at considerable length, comparing passages to those in Virgil's *Aeneid*. And he

[8] See Vico, *New Science*, pp. 129–132 (Bk 2, ch. 2).
[9] See Herder, *Sämtliche Werke*, V, pp. 160–6; and Lovejoy, 'Herder and the Philosophy of History', *Essays*, p. 167.

discusses it by using the categories established by Le Bossu, concluding, 'Thus we see how the Thoughts of this Poem, which naturally arise from the Subject, are always simple, and sometimes exquisitely noble; that the Language is often very sounding, and that the whole is written with a true poetical Spirit'. Given the influence of *The Spectator*, its translation into the major European languages and continuously high reputation throughout the eighteenth century, Addison's judgement should be viewed as carrying considerable weight and influence. His refusal to draw a hard line between high art and popular art and his appeal to the natural responses of all humankind had political ramifications. Although both Shaftesbury and Addison could appeal to a natural standard of beauty, Shaftesbury's concept of beauty was based on an enthusiastic appreciation of an ordered nature, the product of a purposeful creation that resembled nothing so much as a fine work of art to be appreciated best by an elite group of connoisseurs; Addison appealed to a nature in which real members of 'the Rabble of a Nation' could admire a song and poetry which spoke to emotions shared by all human beings.

The introduction to a collection of English ballads and lyrics published between 1723 and 1725 argued that Homer was merely a blind seller of old songs which he had somehow strung together into two great epic poems. To the extent that the ballads praised by Addison were still part of a living, popular literature that debate was meaningful in the context of a ballad revival. By allying the folk ballad with the ancient epic, these critics tried to give dignity to a popular form, but they also tended to minimize the special status of Homer and Virgil. The vision of Homer as a street-corner vendor of ballads was not uncommon even in the early seventeenth century, and although this somewhat down-at-heel Homer was to figure in the defence of ballads, he may also be seen as part of the battle between the Ancients and the Moderns – a battle which may have had its climax in the 1680s and 1690s but which involved minor skirmishes throughout the seventeenth and eighteenth centuries.[10] The editor of the preface to the volume of ballads may have been echoing the most recent outbreak of this literary quarrel in the exchange between Houdart de la Motte and Anne Dacier in 1715. La Motte argued that Homer's gods and goddesses were no longer meaningful to contemporary audiences while Dacier vindicated the greatness of Homer and the ancients. La Motte and the defenders of modern literature attempted to picture the great classical writers as inferior by representing the culture of ancient Greece and Rome as essentially primitive compared to the contemporary world with its astonishing scientific discoveries.

---

[10] The Abbé de Boisrobert made this comparison between Homer and a poor minstrel in 1734. For the *modernisme* of Boisrobert and for an account of the continuing quarrel of the Ancients and Moderns, see Antoine Adam, *Histoire de la littérature française au XVIIe siècle* (5 vols., Paris, 1948–56), I, p. 90, III, p. 125, V, p. 80.

The claim of ancient epic poetry to being the fountainhead of sublimity was also being undermined by a new literary approach to the Old Testament. Robert Lowth, who had been elected to the Poetry Professorship at Oxford in 1741, began lecturing during the 1740s on what he described as an 'almost ineffable sublimity' in Hebrew poetry. He argued that the poetry of ancient Israel had its origins in religion, and that the highest poetry came from religious inspiration. Although his *Lectures on the Sacred Poetry of the Hebrews* were not published in an English version until 1787, the lectures, a Latin edition of 1753 and his disagreements with Warburton gave his ideas wide currency. In addition to claiming a more sublime subject matter for Hebrew poetry than for that of Homer or Virgil, he set forth the ideal of a national poetry which was not based on Greek and Roman models. And while he argued that the Old Testament contained a verse system that had been lost, he gave status to a kind of inspired poetic prose, rich in metaphor and drawing its imagery from 'common life'.[11]

Such criticism prepared the way for the work of Macpherson and Chatterton. James Macpherson's earliest discoveries of poetry in the Highlands of Scotland amounted to a number of fragmentary songs and ballads published in 1760. But when in 1761 he began publishing the poems commonly attributed to Ossian, what he claimed to have discovered combined the materials of ballads – ghosts, warfare, violence, and love – with a pseudo-biblical style. If biblical figures seemed somehow to be outside the realm of the primitive, the same could not be said for Macpherson's recreation of a society ruled by savage chieftains.[12] Thomas Chatterton took another route. He claimed to have discovered some medieval manuscripts at St Mary Redcliffe Church, Bristol, containing poetry by hitherto unknown writers. The most impressive of these poets of his own imagining was the monk, Thomas Rowley. Like Macpherson, Chatterton occasionally 'translated' these works into modern English, but he also forged poems in a dialect, vocabulary and syntax which were intended to pass for English poetry of the fifteenth century. He appears to have drawn his subject-matter of brave knights and pampered priests mainly from Chaucer, but the world he projected belonged mainly to the kind of medievalism displayed by contemporary enthusiasts such as Horace Walpole. Chatterton, who died at the age of eighteen in 1770, may be viewed from any number of perspectives, but his attempt to recreate an earlier type of poetry belongs, at least in part, to the annals of primitivism. His act of returning to the past for poetic inspiration was anything but antiquarian. He was trying to give interest to contemporary poetry by conjuring up a world in which life could be

---

[11] Lowth, *Lectures*, I, p. 37.
[12] Whitney, 'Primitivistic theories', pp. 356–64.

depicted as more passionate, perhaps more natural than the lives of contemporary readers.

Between the publication of the poems of Ossian and of Chatterton at the end of the decade, appeared Thomas Percy's *Reliques of Ancient English Poetry* (1765), which was prefaced by lengthy critical introductions on the status of the bard and minstrel as predecessors of the modern poet. Thomas Percy, much like Addison, made claims for the value of the ballad as poetry. Johnson's mockery of the ballad's versification and his contempt for the art ballad that was growing in popularity as a literary form have to be understood in terms of his refusal to join Percy in considering the ballad as just another type of poetry. For him the ballad was a form of primitive art, and in his *Life of Gray* he criticized Gray's imitation of the abrupt beginning characteristic of the ballad in *The Bard* as 'below the grandeur of a poem that endeavours at sublimity'. Johnson obviously knew ballads by heart. He urged Percy to edit the manuscript that formed the basis of the *Reliques* and even promised to provide some notes. But aside from the pleasure they gave him, he seems to have regarded ballads as artifacts which were outside the boundaries of poetry and criticism.

Despite all this enthusiasm for the poetry of the Middle Ages and despite the success of Robert Burns in the 1780s, it should be remembered that the English reader was not accustomed to read his poetry with a glossary; Allan Ramsay's drama in Scottish dialect, *The Gentle Shepherd*, went into several translations at the end of the eighteenth century to make it accessible to English ears, and most readers probably preferred to read their Chaucer in some kind of modernized form. Percy modernized his ballads for this very reason. Chatterton's series of 'African Eclogues', ending in the love-death of Narva and the beautiful Mored, represented primitivism without problems of language and communication as did, indeed, Macpherson's *Fingal*, and most readers probably preferred an indulgence in primitivism that did not require labouring over strange words.

The poems of Macpherson's bard Ossian, however influential, were an oddity, and if Chatterton became something of a cult hero to poets of the time, it is not clear that he had a vast readership. Perhaps the most significant debate over primitive poetry concerned the poetic nature of the Old Testament which Longinus had quoted as a fine example of the sublime in one of the few connections between classical rhetoric and Hebrew literature. Theophilus Gale's *Court of the Gentiles* (1671–7) retained a traditional view of the matter. Primitive language still preserved some elements of the speech bequeathed to Adam by God with its quality of *onomathesia* (Vico's term), the exact relation between the word and its qualities. The poetic spirit found its fullest release in the poetry of the Old Testament, a poetry far superior in its power to the diabolic enthusiasm of Greek and Latin poetry and incomparably better than the work of modern poets who, living in a corrupt age, could never capture that 'masculine majestic Oratorie'.[13] According to Gale, it was from Moses that Homer had received most of his inspiration.

Gale's assumption that Hebrew retained some elements of a language that possessed the magical power of naming was not uncommon, but others argued that Adam's language represented a true language of nature – a language that might be found through some mystical quest or through a careful and profound analysis of the relationships between languages. As Hans Aarsleff has demonstrated, there were distinct similarities between Gottfried Wilhelm Leibniz's attempt to prove the existence of a single original language through etymological analogies and Jakob Boehme's attempt to discover the natural language used by Adam in the Garden of Eden. Leibniz would point to examples of onomatopoeia (the word 'nose' is pronounced in a nasal manner) that appear to suggest natural connections between the sound of a word and the intended meaning. Such words reflect the 'primitive root-language' for which he was searching. 'If we had the primitive language in its pure form', he wrote, 'or well enough preserved to be recognizable, the reasons for the connections [it involved] – whether they were grounded in reality or came from a wise "arbitrary imposition" worthy of the first author – would be bound to appear. But granted that our languages are derivative so far as origins are concerned, nevertheless considered in themselves they have something of the primitive about them.'[14] He mocked the language theories of Boehme and others as Platonic, but like them, he too toyed with the idea that hieroglyphics might embody a philosophic language.

Between Gale's work and the debates over poetry during the eighteenth century, Richard Simon's *Critical History* (1678) initiated a new awareness about the nature of biblical texts, their transmission and their reliability. By 1741, when William Warburton published his *Divine Legation of Moses*, the Enlightenment, with its criticism of enthusiasm and superstition, had succeeded in lessening the status of Jewish history and the importance of Hebrew as a language. Warburton approaches the poetry of the Old Testament as a primitive poetry by a primitive people. He pointed to the plethora of metaphor and to what he regarded as obscurity, arguing that Hebrew was a half-formed language of the kind found among the American Indians. For Warburton, language progressed from a state of nature when there were few words to the more 'sophisticated' languages such as those of western Europe. Metaphor, simile, and allegory were primitive forms created when there were insufficient words to allow for the development of difficult concepts. A language in this stage

---

[13] Gale, I, p. 96.
[14] See Leibniz, *New Essays on Human Understanding*, trans. Peter Remnant and Jonathan Bennett (Cambridge, 1981), pp. 278–88 (III, ii); and Aarsleff, *From Locke to Saussure*, pp. 59–69, 84–100.

of development – and this, Warburton, argued, was the state of Hebrew at the time of the writing of the Old Testament – may have a kind of dignity and strength, but it was not the kind of language conducive to the writing of great literature.

Warburton's arguments had wide circulation, and his comparison between the abundant use of metaphor by American Indians and by the authors of the Old Testament gave an anthropological cast to his discussion of Hebrew poetry that was adapted by numerous writers. But most writers on the Continent were interested in the ways in which language might reflect or initiate patterns of thought. This was certainly true of Etienne Bonnot de Condillac, whose *Essai sur l'origine des Connoissances humaines* (1746) appeared just five years after Warburton's work. Like Leibniz, he seems to have believed that the time needed for humans to progress toward speech was considerably more than any chronology allowed by Genesis. Relying heavily upon John Locke's dismissal of innate ideas, Condillac nevertheless argued that Locke had not realized that humans are capable of thought mainly through a powerful connection between memory and imagination. This connection, he argued, is triggered by a variety of signs but more particularly by spoken language.[15]

By way of avoiding any religious controversy, Condillac grants God's gift of language to Adam and Eve. But his subject is the origin of language, and therefore he will start with two children of different sexes, isolated, and without the knowledge of a single sign. The picture of the development of language and mind involves a slow evolution of a system of signs combining gesture, dance, music, and words. Borrowing from the Abbé Du Bos, Condillac notes that Greek and Roman drama, as the plays have come down to us in the manuscripts, retain elements of this related sign system. Gestures were so elaborate in Roman oratory and acting, that a famous actor decided to have a lesser actor handle the words while he performed the gestures.[16] Condillac imagines that the

[15] Condillac, *Essai*, in *Oeuvres*, I, pp. 154–5 (Part 1, chapter 11, section 107). Condillac presents the case of a young man who recovered his senses after being deaf and mute all of his life. He learned to speak, but recalled little of his twenty-three years. From this, Concillac concludes, 'ils confirment bien sensiblement que les opérations de l'esprit se dévelopent plus ou moins, à proportion qu'on a l'usage des signes' (*Essai*, p. 204). In a footnote which appeared only in the first edition, Condillac pointed to his own originality in this formulation, and Hans Aarsleff has agreed with him. But Condillac's historical model for the development of language allows for the gradual development from the 'language of action' to ordinary speech. He argues that during the early development of humanity, speech was expressive, often close to a form of song, and the largest burden of meaning fell upon a wide variety of gestures. Thus Condillac allows for the creation of human 'liaison des idées' by which the brain connects signs to things and ideas. For Aarsleff's argument that Condillac means oral language, see *From Locke to Saussure*, pp. 146–57.

[16] Abbé Du Bos, *Critical Reflections on Poetry, Painting and Music*, trans. Thomas Nugent (3 vols., London, 1748), III, pp. 132–4. Du Bos regards the joining

separation of this sign system into separate components – music without words, poetry without dance and gesture, dance without words – must have seemed remarkable innovations in the ancient world. Du Bos stressed the brilliance of ancient dance, gesture, and drama, but Condillac, like Warburton, regards this as a primitive system. The barbarism of excessive metaphor has been replaced by a superior kind of poetry, and the more gesture was replaced by words, the more humans became capable of thinking well.

Nine years later, Rousseau expressed his doubts about human progress. He speculated on the ways in which the savage first began using language to express his passions and on the savage's pleasure in a poetic dialect that must have been far more powerful than anything in modern languages. This was a language that antedated the corruptions of society's institutions and therefore had to be closer to natural human passions and feelings. Like the language sought by Boehme, it was closer to a purer source, but in Rousseau's account, that source was nature itself rather than God. And Herder was to argue in 1772 that language, which began in a highly metaphoric poetry, must be the product of a peculiarly human way of functioning and could not be the direct gift of God. In Herder's mind, ballads, the poems of Ossian, the *Odyssey* and *Iliad*, and the Old Testament were all great sources of poetic inspiration.[17] His grouping of these works, perceived as products of primitive and sublime genius, is suggestive of their connection in the minds of contemporary critics. Curiously enough, Hugh Blair, who was to write a long commentary on the poems of Ossian, refers to what he calls the 'American style' (i.e., the oratorical style of American Indians) as combining brevity and often elaborate metaphors.[18]

Contributing to this celebration of metaphor were the new directions of both poetic style and criticism. An appreciation for the sublime and for the kind of imaginative verse that had flourished during the Elizabethan period had almost entirely overcome the aversion for metaphor as an obscure figure that prevailed during the Restoration and early eighteenth century. Warburton's arguments about metaphor and the crudity of Hebrew poetry were demolished in 1765 by Robert Lowth, whom we have seen as the author of a series of well-known lectures on Hebrew poetry at Oxford. Lowth was able to show that Warburton often misunderstood his Hebrew texts, that far from being 'primitive', Hebrew poetry was the very greatest poetry – the poetry of the religious

together of dance, music, mime and speech as a superior artistic system. Condillac regards these combinations as part of primitive life.

[17] Herder, *Sämtliche Werke*, V, pp. 160–86.
[18] Blair, *Lectures on Rhetoric*, I, pp. 128–32. See also Herder, *Sämmtliche Werke*, V, p. 166, where he argues that Lafitau's account of poetry among the American Indians recalls the works of Ossian.

sublime.[19] In the hands of many writers of the Enlightenment, the Jews of ancient Israel were often depicted as sunk in idolatry and superstition. That the Old Testament should emerge as a model of the most profound poetry had important ramifications for the literature of the last half of the century, in which an exaltation of the primitive sublime emerged as an important aesthetic force in painting as well as poetry.

In respect of contemporary judgement, Warburton was also wrong in his discussion of writing. Following Bacon and a number of later critics, Warburton had judged hieroglyphics as a primitive form of communication, replaced by the (more or less) phonetic alphabet. He was apparently unimpressed by Locke's feeling that the pictures inherent in hieroglyphics would serve as a superior form of communication. And he dismissed the common argument offered by Defoe and others that writing was a divine gift to mankind, accompanying the making of the tablets of the law. If a phonetic alphabet seemed miraculous to orthodox Christians, hieroglyphics had a special place among those whose beliefs verged upon the occult. Among the admirers of Jakob Boehme such as William Law and those seeking that elusive key which would connect all the ancient religions, such as Jacob Bryant, hieroglyphics were viewed as a mysterious, arcane form of communication, embodying ideas that could not be communicated in writing. That element made them attractive to those searching for a universal myth which would make sense of spiritual history, and the hieroglyph, in its very indecipherability, had an attraction for the poetic temperament later in the century.

Toward the end of our period, some of the ideas on the primitive formation of language developed by Rousseau and Condillac were extended in directions that sometimes invited ridicule. In Britain, Lord Monboddo followed up on Rousseau's comments on the orang-utan as an example of man without language to develop a theory that, far from being natural, language was entirely the creation of civilized man. His investigation of wild children followed a pattern set by Condillac. He agreed with the notion that man began to speak by imitating the sounds of nature, but he dismissed Condillac's emphasis upon the importance of gestures ('langage d'action') in the early stage of communicating by signs. Once man began using words, he became a very different creature from the wild man of the woods. On the continent, Johann Gottfried Herder, an admirer of both Condillac and Lord Monboddo, contributed to the debate in his _Essay on the Origin of Language_ (1772). Herder argues that language is entirely natural to man as it is to the animals as a 'language of feeling'. It is from the simplest sounds expressing

---

[19] _A Letter to the Right Reverend Author of the Divine Legation_ (1765), pp. 91–4. See also _Lectures on the Sacred Poetry of the Hebrews_ (1787), I, p. 37, where he argued with reference to Hebrew poetry that 'the human mind can conceive nothing more elevated, more beautiful, or more elegant'.

emotion that language comes. Appealing to the languages of savage nations, Herder insists that these emotional sounds continue to be the genuine 'sap that enlivens the roots of language'. Just as he had admired *Ossian* a few years earlier, he could now write in praise of the poetry and music of the indians of America as embodying 'the language of nature'. No language is reducible to a few basic sounds and words; each language is essentially unique, the product of the people who speak it. The poetry of savage peoples, Herder argues, often moved European travellers to tears. Herder found both Condillac and Rousseau lacking. Both reflection and language are natural to man and would be part of him even if he were raised outside of society. And as for the metaphors that Warburton found so crude among the writers of the Old Testament and savage nations, Herder, exalting the primitive above the polished art of the Enlightenment, argued that these were the source of the greatest poetry.

If primitivism had a special status in the period between 1660 and 1800, its appeal continued into the following century unabated. But whereas the primitive ideal was to become an object of faith for the Romantics, it was more likely to be used during the eighteenth century as a satiric weapon against European ethnocentricity. With their faith in nature as a surrogate for the divine presence, eighteenth-century writers and readers were willing to grant a certain uncontaminated value to the natural and the primitive. If Rousseau's *Discourse on Inequality* (1755) is the most famous work of primitivism in the period, it has that status because it most fully stated some of the uneasiness that eighteenth-century thinkers felt about what was usually called 'luxury', and their hope for continuing improvements in the sciences and for an expansion of what we might call moral freedom. Rousseau's third stage of human development, a time when differences in property and the 'revolution' in metallurgy and agriculture had not yet destroyed happiness, saw mankind 'free, healthy, honest, and happy'. And if some readers found the freedom of the first stage, when there was no language, let alone writing, more attractive than contemporary civilization, he was not one to discourage such a view. In a tract on a wild boy discovered in 1725, one satirist suggested that the boy might lead his followers into the woods to live on vegetables. After 1755, the year in which Rousseau's *Discourse* appeared, not everyone would have found this proposition so amusing.[20] And from the ridicule that greeted Addison's advocacy of ballads at the start of the eighteenth century, criticism had moved to seeing the very essence of poetry in the concise and metaphoric style of less polished societies.

[20] Lord Monboddo made the case of Peter the Wild Boy an important part of his evidence for arguing the essential brutality of man in the state of nature. See *Of the Origins and Progress of Language*, I, p. 187.

21

Medieval revival and the Gothic

Peter Sabor

Criticism of Gothic fiction in English dates from 1765, when the first reviews of Horace Walpole's pioneering Gothic novel, *The Castle of Otranto*, were published. The medieval revival, which gave Walpole the impetus to write his pseudo-medieval novel, cannot be so precisely dated. A new reverence, however, towards medieval literature was displayed in Richard Hurd's impressionistic *Letters on Chivalry and Romance* (1762), and in the revised edition of Thomas Warton's *Observations on the Fairy Queen*, published in the same year. While this essay is concerned primarily with the work of later eighteenth-century English critics writing on medieval literature, on contemporary forgers of the medieval such as Macpherson and Chatterton, and on Gothic fiction and drama, a brief account of the attitudes toward medieval literature prevalent between the Restoration and the 1760s will provide a necessary background for subsequent developments.

In the preface to his translation of Rapin's *Réflexions sur la poëtique d'Aristote* (1674), Thomas Rymer devotes a paragraph to the Middle Ages, which he describes as 'the Age of *Tales*, *Ballads*, and *Roundelays*', and as such finds unworthy of critical consideration. Rymer also passes over Chaucer, 'in whose time our Language . . . was not capable of any Heroick Character' (*Critical Works*, p. 5). In *A Short View of Tragedy* (1693), Rymer was more explicit. For those who wrote before Chaucer, he still had only scorn; they 'made an heavy pudder, and are always miserably put to't for a word to clink'. Even though Chaucer himself is given credit for mingling Provençal, French and Latin vocabulary with English, 'our language retain'd something of the churl; something of the Stiff and Gothish did stick upon it, till long after Chaucer' (*Critical Works*, pp. 126–7).

Although Rymer, with his iconoclastic views on Shakespeare, is regarded today as an unconventional, if not quixotic, critic, his views on medieval literature were representative of his age. In 1668, both Denham and Waller published poems depicting Chaucer as a transitory light in medieval darkness.[1] For most Restoration and early eighteenth-century

---

[1] See Spurgeon, *Chaucer Criticism*, p. 244.

critics, the difficulties of understanding Middle English seemed over-whelming. In his 'Account of the Greatest English Poets' (1694), Addison lamented the inaccessibility of Chaucer's language:

> But age has rusted what the Poet writ,
> Worn out his language, and obscur'd his wit:
> In vain he jests in his unpolish'd strain,
> And tries to make his readers laugh in vain.

(Miscellaneous Works, I, p. 31)

Gower, Langland, Lydgate and other medieval poets were generally considered both more impenetrable and less worthy of attention than Chaucer, while *Sir Gawain and the Green Knight* was unknown until as late as 1824.[2]

There was, however, some significant criticism of medieval literature in the period before 1760. By far the most important Restoration commentator was Dryden, whose Preface to *Fables Ancient and Modern* (1700) contains an extensive and often perceptive discussion of Chaucer. After comparing Chaucer favourably to Ovid and Boccaccio and depicting him as 'the father of English poetry' (*Of Dramatic Poesy*, II, p. 280), Dryden considers his various shortcomings. In translating Chaucer into modern English for the *Fables*, Dryden has 'confined [his] choice to such tales . . . as savour nothing of immodesty' (II, p. 285); complaints against Chaucer's indecency were commonplace, and Dryden likewise condemns such 'profaneness'. Similarly, Dryden follows his age in assuming that Chaucer's language is inaccessible to all but a handful of learned scholars; he depicts Chaucer as 'a rough diamond', who 'must first be polished ere he shines' (II, p. 286). Paradoxically, Dryden's masterful adaptations made Chaucer's works themselves seem still more obscure. Pope, like Dryden an enthusiast for Chaucer, still felt the need to modernize the 'House of Fame' as the 'Temple of Fame' (1715), while regretting, in *An Essay on Criticism* (1711), both Chaucer's obsolete language and the increasing obscurity of Dryden himself:

> Our Sons their Fathers' *failing Language* see,
> And such as *Chaucer* is, shall *Dryden* be.

(ll. 482–3)

A century later, as we shall see, the efflorescence of interest in the Middle Ages made Pope's pessimism seem unwarranted.

A less conventional view of the medieval past is seen in Addison's three *Spectator* papers of the same year, 1711, written in praise of 'Chevy

---

[2] *Sir Gawain* was first discussed by Richard Price in his edition of Thomas Warton's *History of English Poetry* (London, 1824), I, p. 17 n.

Chase' (nos. 70 and 74) and 'The Two Children in the Wood' (no. 85). Addison's enthusiasm for medieval ballads was not, of course, unprecedented; as early as 1580, Sidney's *Apology for Poetry* expressed delight in the 'old song' of 'Chevy Chase' (*Apology*, p. 118). What is remarkable in Addison is not his pleasure in the old ballads but his devoting two essays to an analysis of a single example. In his papers on 'Chevy Chase', Addison places quotations from the ballad beside passages from the *Aeneid*, contending that both works display 'the same Kind of Poetical Genius' and 'the same Copyings after Nature' (*Spectator*, I, p. 316). In his subsequent *Spectator* paper on 'The Two Children in the Wood', Addison is more critical, acknowledging a 'despicable Simplicity in the Verse', which is written in 'such an abject Phrase, and poorness of Expression, that the quoting any part of it would look like a Design of turning it into Ridicule' (I, p. 362). Addison declares, however, that despite the deficiencies of its language, the ballad will appeal to those who 'have a true and unprejudiced Taste of Nature' (I, pp. 362–3). And in a trenchant final paragraph he turns on the 'little conceited Wits of the Age' who feel compelled to ridicule the 'Beauties of Nature' found in the medieval ballads (I, p. 364).

Unlike Thomas Percy and other later eighteenth-century critics, Addison admired the medieval ballads for what they have in common with the classics, rather than for qualities peculiar to themselves. Even so, as his closing remarks acknowledge, his position was vulnerable to attack; in 1711 analogies between Virgil and uncouth, anonymous balladeers seemed risible to many readers. Among the 'little conceited Wits' who responded satirically to his first two papers was William Wagstaffe, author of *A Comment upon the History of Tom Thumb* (1711), a pamphlet written as a mock encomium of the *History of Tom Thumb*, using the same technique of classical parallels deployed by Addison. Addison was also answered by John Dennis, whose essay 'Of Simplicity in Poetical Compositions' was written within days of the *Spectator* papers on 'Chevy Chase', but published only in 1721. Dennis's scorn here for the 'Imbecility, Affectation and Extravagance' (*Critical Works*, II, p. 33) of the old ballads was later to be echoed by that antagonist of the medieval revival, Samuel Johnson, in his *Life of Addison* (1781): 'In *Chevy Chase* there is not much of either bombast or affectation; but there is chill and lifeless imbecility' (*Lives*, II, pp. 147–8). When *A Collection of Old Ballads*, compiled by an anonymous editor, was published in 1723–5, two years after Dennis's essay, it was equipped with prefaces justifying the 'old Songs' on historical rather than literary grounds.

Like the ballads, medieval drama had few sympathetic critics before the later eighteenth century. Rymer's scorn for the morality play in his

A Short View of Tragedy (1693), as well as his ignorance of actual examples, is typical of his age. James Wright's pamphlet *Historia Histrionica* (1699) represents a considerable advance in knowledge and critical insight. Like Dryden on Chaucer and Addison on the ballads, Wright uses the strategy of analogy with the classics; his pamphlet concludes with the declaration that 'plays in England had a beginning much like those of Greece, the Monologues and Pageants drawn from place to place answer exactly to the cart of Thespis' (p. 27). Robert Dodsley's *Select Collection of Old Plays* (1745–6) made several medieval dramas widely available for the first time, but the critical comments in his 'Short Historical Essay on the Rise and Progress of the English Stage', a prefatory essay to the twelve volumes, are ill-informed and condescending. Characterizing the age of the Miracle plays as 'the Dead Sleep of the Muses', Dodsley finds that in the later Morality plays 'something of design appeared, a Fable and a Moral' (I, p. xiii). In a revealing architectural metaphor, Dodsley then shows his slight knowledge of his subject: 'I should have been glad to be more particular; but where Materials are not to be had, the Building must be deficient' (I, p. xv).

Criticism of the medieval romance in English before the later eighteenth century was similarly undeveloped, and lagged well behind that in France. Pierre Daniel Huet's *Traité de l'origine des romans* (1670), translated into English in 1672, surveyed the development of prose fiction from the Middle Ages to the seventeenth century. Other French critics, such as the Comte de Caylus, J. B. de la Curne de Sainte-Palaye, and Paul-Henri Mallet, examined the romances in much closer detail. There was, as Arthur Johnston observes, 'an almost unbroken tradition of the study of early French literature' from the late sixteenth to the eighteenth century (*Enchanted Ground*, p. 22). The work of later eighteenth-century English critics, such as Hurd, Percy, and Thomas Warton, was more indebted to French scholarship than to that of their English predecessors.

What impelled these critics to undertake their study of medieval literature in the 1760s will always be a subject for conjecture. The developing concept of historical relativism helped to overcome the long-established prejudice against the Middle Ages, allowing medieval works to be read without constant reference to classical standards. The early poetry of the brothers Warton (and of their father, Thomas Warton the elder), some of which celebrates the medieval past, predates their criticism by some fifteen years; an awakening creative interest in the Middle Ages by these and other poets, such as Gray and Collins, preceded analytical enquiry. When such enquiry was undertaken, critics of the 1760s possessed a crucial advantage over their predecessors: published catalogues of medieval manuscripts and access to the manuscripts themselves. The opening of the British Museum in January 1759 made available the

manuscript collections of Sir Robert Cotton and the Harleys, while the
Catalogue of the Harleian Collection of Manuscripts (dated 1759, published 1762), provided, as Arthur Johnston observes, 'a most valuable
tool to medievalists, and led Percy, Warton, and Ritson to many of the
romances for the first time' (*Enchanted Ground*, p. 42). An index to the
Harleian catalogue by Thomas Astle, published in 1763, was also of
major importance; as Percy acknowledged in a letter to Richard Farmer
of 10 January 1763, ''till that was done, the Collection was almost
useless' (*Correspondence of Percy and Farmer*, p. 30).

One of the features of the medieval revival was a new appreciation
of Chaucer. In his *Observations on the Fairy Queen* (1754), Thomas
Warton set the trend. Complaining that Chaucer 'seems to be regarded
rather as an old poet, than as a good one', he himself approached the
poems less as 'venerable relics, than as finish'd patterns', containing
'what later and more refin'd ages could hardly equal in true humour,
pathos, or sublimity' (p. 141). In the second edition of the *Observations*
(1762), Warton goes further in his praise, adding to the passage quoted
here a sentence characteristic of the new attitude to medievalism gathering
force in the 1760s: Chaucer's 'old manners, his romantic arguments, his
wildness of painting, his simplicity and antiquity of expression, transport
us into some fairy region, and are all highly pleasing to the imagination'
(I, p. 197). Some two years later, in his commonplace book, Thomas
Gray employed similar terminology in an account of Chaucer and his
contemporaries, written for a projected history of English poetry. Writing
of Lydgate, Gray remarks that 'in images of horrour & a certain terrible
Greatness, our author comes far behind Chaucer'.[3] Both Warton and Gray
extol Chaucer for the primitivism that Addison sought only to exculpate
in his remarks on the medieval ballads: rather than comparing a medieval
author to Virgil, they point out what qualities are uniquely his own.

The new approach to medieval literature in the 1760s was not, of
course, unchallenged. Other critics continued to insist on Chaucer's obscurity, although such complaints diminished considerably after Thomas
Tyrwhitt's edition of *The Canterbury Tales* was published in 1775–8,
providing at last a reasonably accurate text, together with a glossary.
Modernizations of Chaucer, however, remained popular. In the second
volume of his *Essay on the Genius and Writings of Pope*, largely written
by 1762 but published only in 1782, Joseph Warton commends Pope
for having 'omitted or softened the grosser and more offensive passages'
of Chaucer's 'Wife of Bath's Tale' (*Essay*, II, p. 7). And Horace Walpole,
in 1781, wrote to William Mason, rejecting his offer of a 'first edition'
(probably William Thynne's edition of 1532) of Chaucer: 'I am too,

---

[3] Gray's Commonplace Book, quoted from Brewer, *Chaucer Heritage*, p. 217.

though a Goth, so modern a Goth that I hate the black letter, and I love Chaucer better in Dryden and Baskerville, than in his own language and dress' (*Correspondence*, XXIX, p. 165). This preference, as we shall see, made its own contribution to the medieval revival; rather than studying authentic Middle English writings, Walpole and other Gothicists fabricated a pseudo-medievalism for modern tastes.

A less equivocal attitude to medievalism is found in Hurd's *Letters on Chivalry and Romance* (1762). As several recent critics have noted, Hurd's claims to authority are flimsy. He himself acknowledges, in the fourth letter, that his remarks on medieval romance are indebted to Sainte-Palaye's *Mémoires sur l'ancienne chevalerie* (1743–6), and like his English predecessors he displays little knowledge of the texts themselves. Lawrence Lipking, one of Hurd's harshest critics, believes that his 'appreciation for faery, the incredible, the marvellous, admiration and delirium, may be genuine, but it wilfully interferes with any objective search for the historical Gothic' (*Ordering*, p. 153). While Hurd's acquaintance with medieval literature was admittedly limited, his *Letters* are none the less a seminal work. From the outset, Hurd challenges the prevailing equation of Gothicism with barbarism, demanding 'what . . . is more remarkable than the Gothic CHIVALRY?' (*Letters*, p. 1). Written in the form of letters to an anonymous correspondent, and thus resembling an epistolary novel, the work reads more like a precursor of Gothic fiction than a sober piece of literary criticism. In depicting Hurd as a 'daring HERETIC', the *Monthly Review* perceived the innovative nature of his work (27 (1762), p. 81);[4] no previous critic had depicted medieval literature in so glamorous a fashion, or suggested that in reading it 'we are upon enchanted ground' (*Letters*, p. 54).

In contrast to Hurd, whose speculations about medieval literature outpaced his reading of primary texts, Percy's part in the medieval revival was based on a very palpable document: the famous mutilated folio manuscript, rescued by Percy, according to his own account, from negligent housemaids using it to light fires.[5] The manuscript, comprising transcripts, made in about 1650, of ballads, songs and metrical romances, dating from about the fourteenth to the seventeenth century, formed the basis of Percy's *Reliques of Ancient English Poetry* (1765), the single most important work of the medieval revival. As well as providing a rich source both of hitherto unknown poetry and of annotated versions of well-known ballads such as 'Chevy Chase', the *Reliques* contains several pioneering essays by Percy himself.

---

[4] For the reception of Hurd's treatise, see Hooker, 'The reviewers', pp. 194–5.
[5] For Percy's account of the rescue, written on the inside cover of the manuscript volume, see *Bishop Percy's Folio Manuscript*, ed. John W. Hales and Frederick J. Furnivall (London, 1867–8), I, p. lxxiv.

Percy's method of editing the texts he selected for his collection provoked a controversy that continues today. His foremost eighteenth-century adversary, Joseph Ritson, charged him with outright fraud, even claiming on several occasions that the folio manuscript was a mere fabrication of Percy's. In this Ritson was mistaken – the manuscript is extant in the British Library – but his indignation at Percy's cavalier treatment of his texts had some justification. Percy faced an unenviable task in attempting to reconcile the conflicting demands of scholars such as Ritson, who expected strict fidelity to the original manuscripts, and a general readership that sought not antiquarian scholarship but literary pleasure. Even William Shenstone, himself an antiquary and an enthusiast for the ballads, who encouraged Percy for many years in his plan of publishing the *Reliques*, expressed his doubts to the bookseller Robert Dodsley that the work could meet with popular approval: 'I am willing to *hope* that this collection will *still* have merit to engage the Publick: but am less sanguine than I should have been, had he shortened his notes, admitted more improvements, and rejected all such ballads as had no Plea but their *Antiquity*' (20 November 1762, *Correspondence of Dodsley*, p. 466).[6]

Shenstone's fears for the popularity of Percy's *Reliques* proved groundless. By 1794 it had gone into a fourth edition, and created a taste for several other such collections: David Herd's *Ancient and Modern Scots Songs* (1769), Thomas Evans's *Old Ballads* (1777–84), and John Pinkerton's *Scottish Tragic Ballads* (1781) are among its many successors. In the second edition of 1767, Percy lengthened one of his introductory essays, the 'Essay on the Ancient English Minstrels', from nine to twenty pages, as well as adding a plethora of additional notes. He did so to answer criticisms of the essay made by Samuel Pegge in a paper, 'Observations on Dr Percy's Account of Minstrels among the Saxons', read to the Society of Antiquaries in 1766, and belatedly published in *Archaeologia* in 1773. Pegge objected to Percy's contention that an order of minstrels existed among the Anglo-Saxons; in his revised preface, Percy modified his earlier claims, while providing copious new documentation. What is of interest in the controversy is that a detailed critical debate on medieval literature was being undertaken, in place of the sweeping generalizations about largely unread books prevalent in much of the earlier criticism. There is also much new information in Percy's three other essays in the *Reliques*, 'On the Origin of the English Stage', 'On the Metre of Pierce Plowman's Vision', and 'On the Ancient Metrical Romances', which, together with the essay on minstrels, were also published separately as *Four Essays* (1767).

---

[6] This passage, scored through in the manuscript, was printed for the first time in Tierney's 1988 edition of Dodsley's correspondence.

Percy's revisions to his essay on minstrels satisfied Pegge, who withdrew his objections in a second contribution to *Archaeologia* (1775). Joseph Ritson was a more formidable and persistent adversary. From 1782 until his death in 1803, Ritson challenged Percy's editorial practices and critical positions. Ironically, Ritson's almost pathological hostility to Percy's work succeeded in improving the *Reliques* considerably. The fourth edition of 1794 contains a much revised and expanded version of the minstrels essay, now equipped with a further battery of supplementary notes and running in all to some ninety pages. In his Preface Percy admits, for the first time, to having concealed his editorial interventions 'under some such general title, as a "Modern Copy", or the like' (*Reliques*, I, p. xvii); the new edition indicates by means of asterisks those passages where 'any considerable liberties' have been taken with the texts. The other critical essays are also revised and expanded in the fourth edition, with due acknowledgement made to such critics as Thomas Warton, Edmond Malone, and John Pinkerton, who had written on medieval poetry and drama since the *Reliques* first appeared. Ritson, whose name Percy deliberately excluded, was a pure antiquarian, rather than a literary critic. Most of his numerous publications took the form of editions, equipped with contentious prefatory essays taking issue with other scholars' views, and providing useful new information while avoiding critical analysis. In the Advertisement to his most important edition, *Metrical Romanceës* (1802), Ritson predicted darkly that the book would meet with 'little favour, and less profit', but be attacked by 'a base and prostitute gang of lurking assassins, who stab in the dark, and whose poison'd daggers he has already experienc'd' (*Metrical Romanceës*, I, pp. iii–iv). In the event, Ritson's work was less assaulted than neglected by contemporary reviewers; and for all his virulence, his censure of other scholars did little damage to their reputations. Critics in the later nineteenth century found his editorial concern for the accuracy of medieval texts exemplary; in his own time, however, it seemed merely eccentric.

Ritson's first publication was a typically violent treatise, *Observations on the Three First Volumes of the History of English Poetry* (1782), attacking Thomas Warton's monumental history. Warton had previously, as we have seen, outlined his views on medieval literature in his *Observations on the Fairy Queen* (1754, revised 1762), of which the second section deals with Spenser's debt to medieval romances, especially to Malory's *Morte D'Arthur*, and the fifth section with Spenser's debt to Chaucer. Warton's postscript to the much expanded second edition is of particular interest. Of the chivalric romances, he remarks that 'such are their Terrible Graces of magic and enchantment, so magnificently marvellous are their fictions and fablings, that they contribute, in a wonderful degree, to rouse and invigorate all the powers of imagination: to store the fancy with those sublime and alarming images, which true poetry best delights to display' (*Observations*, II, p. 268). The diction here is remarkably close to that of Hurd in his *Letters on Chivalry and Romance*, published in the same year. The two critics corresponded regularly at this time about their shared enthusiasm for the 'enchanted ground' that medieval literature occupied.

While the *Observations on the Fairy Queen* contains Warton's views on medieval literature in embryonic form, the three-volume *History of English Poetry* (1774–81), left incomplete on Warton's death in 1790, expands and refines his ideas. Volume One (1774) is prefixed by two dissertations, 'Of the Origin of Romantic Fiction in Europe' and 'On the Introduction of Learning into England'. The *History* proper begins with the eleventh century, passing rapidly over Anglo-Saxon and early Norman literature, but the two dissertations range much further back in time. The first, a speculative attempt to find Arabian sources for medieval romances, is led astray by William Warburton's theories, as René Wellek and others have noted. The second, a more sober essay, contends that there was little learning in England until after the Norman Conquest. The *History* improves dramatically when Warton reaches the thirteenth and fourteenth centuries, a period with which he was much more familiar. Even here, however, in a long and largely positive discussion of Chaucer, there is a limit to Warton's enthusiasm for the literature of a benighted age. After dwelling on Chaucer's 'vein of humour', Warton concludes this section with an apparent panegyric:

in elevation and elegance, in harmony and perspicuity of versification, he surpasses his predecessors in an infinite proportion ... his genius was universal, and adapted to themes of unbounded variety ... his merit was not less in painting familiar manners with humour and propriety, than in moving the passions, and in representing the beautiful or the grand objects of nature with grace and sublimity.
　　　　　　　　　　　　　　　　　　　　　(*History*, I, p. 457)

For Warton, however, it is remarkable that Chaucer 'appeared with all the lustre and dignity of a true poet, in an age which compelled him to struggle with a barbarous language'. Chaucer's writing is thus seen not as a product of his times, but as an exception to their general barbarism.

Although Warton regarded Chaucer as by far the most important medieval poet, his remarks on other authors, who had been largely neglected by previous critics, are also innovative. Volume Two of the *History* (1778) begins with a study of Gower, who has 'much good sense, solid reflection, and useful observation', but lacked 'Chaucer's spirit, imagination, and elegance' (*History*, II, p. 1). Warton is more generous towards Lydgate and the early sixteenth-century Scots poets, William Dunbar, Gavin Douglas, and David Lyndsay, but he is offended by Skelton and deplores his 'coarseness, obscenity, and scurrility' (II, p. 341). Warton also provides an account of early English drama, drawing on Percy's essay 'On the Origin of the English Stage' but devoting more attention than Percy to conditions of performance. Although his speculations about stage history are often ill-informed, Warton opened a profitable field of enquiry that Malone and other critics would subsequently develop.

Warton's greatest deficiency as a historian of English poetry was his inability to read Old English or Old Norse. Since most other critics of the medieval revival shared this handicap, little advance in Anglo-Saxon studies was made in the later eighteenth century. The massive philological researches undertaken earlier in the century by such Anglo-Saxon scholars as George Hickes, Edward Thwaites, Humfrey Wanley, Elizabeth Elstob and William Elstob had little impact on the medieval revival. As Richard C. Payne remarks, 'although the *idea* of Old English poetry had captivated literary men in the later eighteenth century, a corresponding interest in the individual texts known in England before 1800 had not emerged' (*Anglo-Saxon Scholarship*, p. 154). *Beowulf* was discussed for the first time only at the turn of the century, when Sharon Turner, in his *History of the Anglo-Saxons* (1799–1805), called it 'the most interesting relic of the Anglo-Saxon poetry which time has suffered us to receive' (*History*, II, p. 294).

While criticism of Old English poetry in the later eighteenth century was negligible, and while much criticism of Middle English took the form of broad generalizations, one strange form of medieval literature elicited a detailed and ever-increasing critical response. This was the pseudo-medieval, embodied most significantly in the Ossianic poetry of James Macpherson, published in the early 1760s, in the Rowleyan poems of Thomas Chatterton, published in the 1770s, and in the numerous Gothic novels and dramas that followed in the wake of Horace Walpole's *The Castle of Otranto* (1765) and *The Mysterious Mother* (1768). Even while the status of Macpherson's putative translations from the Gaelic of 'Ossian' was being questioned, his English renditions were being translated into Italian (1763), German (1764), and French (1774), and inspiring the hero of Goethe's *Die Leiden des jungen Werthers* (1774). Numerous treatises and articles argued for and against the poems' authenticity, both at the time of their first publication and, with renewed vigour, after Samuel Johnson's contemptuous dismissal of Macpherson in 1775: 'stubborn audacity is the last refuge of guilt' (*Journey*, p. 98). In contrast to these polemical works, Hugh Blair's *Critical Dissertation on the Poems of Ossian* (1763) is concerned with the poetry itself. A protracted comparison between Ossian and Homer is followed by an analysis of the poems in terms of their sublimity, spontaneity, and primitivism. Following Blair's lead, the comparison between Ossian and Homer became a commonplace. As late as 1818, Hazlitt could declare, in 'On Poetry in General', that Ossian was, together with Homer, the Bible and Dante, one of 'the principal works of poetry in the world' (*Works*, V, p. 15). In *The Progress of Romance* (1785), Clara Reeve took a more balanced approach. Acknowledging that Macpherson had used traditional Highland stories as a basis for his own compositions, Reeve none the less found that 'his works bear strong marks of genius and Originality; they are bold and figurative, and some of them are highly pleasing' (*Progress*, II, p. 67).

Chatterton's Rowley fabrications aroused still greater critical interest. Only two years after producing his edition of *The Canterbury Tales* (1775), Tyrwhitt edited the first collected edition of the Rowley poems. In doing so, he reinforced Chatterton's claims for Rowley as a major medieval author, despite withholding his own judgement on the poems' authenticity. A year later, in 1778, Tyrwhitt added an appendix to the third edition of his *Rowley*, conceding that the poems were Chatterton's creation, and in the same year Thomas Warton concluded an examination of Rowley's writings in the context of genuine fifteenth-century poetry with the pronouncement: 'It is with regret that I find myself obliged to pronounce Rowlie's poems to be spurious' (*History*, II, p. 164). Even while their authenticity as medieval writings was being denied, however, the significance of Chatterton's poems was being reinforced: Chatterton occupies far more space in Warton's *History* than any other eighteenth-century poet. Both Warton and Tyrwhitt, the two greatest medievalists of their age, went on to write substantial monographs on Chatterton – Warton's *Enquiry into the Authenticity of the Poems attributed to Rowley* (1782) and Tyrwhitt's *A Vindication of the Appendix to the Poems, called Rowley's* (1782) – and the same year saw the publication of a new edition of Rowley's poems and of several other critical treatises, including Malone's *Cursory Observations on the Poems Attributed to Thomas Rowley* (1782). As a reviewer of Jeremiah Milles's edition of Rowley noted astutely in the *Critical Review*, 'the rank and abilities of the disputants have rendered this controversy important, and invested it with a splendor, to which, from its own merits, it was not entitled' (*Critical Review*, 53 (1782), p. 401). A similarly restrained assessment of Chatterton's significance was made by Clara Reeve, who compared his method of composition with that of Macpherson: 'The groundwork his Manuscripts, the building his own' (*Progress*, II, p. 67).

Among the disputants investing the Rowley controversy with splendour was Horace Walpole, whose pamphlet, *A Letter to the Editor of the Miscellanies of Thomas Chatterton* (1779), first printed privately at

Strawberry Hill, was published in the *Gentleman's Magazine* for 1782. In his denunciation of Chatterton, as acerbic as Johnson's condemnation of Macpherson, Walpole makes outright accusations of fraudulence: 'All of the house of forgery are relations ... his ingenuity in counterfeiting styles, and, I believe, hands, might easily have led him to those more facile imitations of prose, promissory notes' (*Works*, IV, p. 218). For the author of *The Castle of Otranto*, first published under the guise of a translation 'by William Marshall, Gent. from the original Italian of Onuphrio Muralto', so to accuse the ostensible editor of Rowley's poems may seem unjust, and Chatterton himself connected the two impostures in a poem written in 1769, shortly before his death:

> thou mayst call me Cheat –
> Say, didst thou n'er indulge in such Deceit?
> Who wrote Otranto?
>
> (*Complete Works*, I, p. 341)

Unlike Chatterton, however, Walpole left a clue to his authorship ('Muralto', an Italianate rendition of Walpole) on the title page, and signed his initials to the preface of the second edition of 1765. Walpole's pseudo-medieval fiction was no more intended to be taken for an authentic medieval work than his remodelling of Strawberry Hill in Gothic style was designed to turn a former coachman's cottage into an authentic Gothic castle: the use of plaster for the battlements was evidently self-parodic.

The second edition of *The Castle of Otranto* (1765) is subtitled 'a Gothic story', the first time that an eighteenth-century novel had been so labelled by its author. In an important new preface, Walpole explained his intention of widening the scope of contemporary fiction, in which 'the great resources of fancy have been dammed up, by a strict adherence to common life'. His aim was to reconcile the inventiveness of ancient romance with the realism of the modern novel, making his characters 'think, speak and act, as it might be supposed mere men and women would do in extraordinary positions' (*Otranto*, pp. 7–8). Contemporary reviewers, however, were unsympathetic to this piece of modern Gothicism: John Langhorne marvelled that 'an Author, of a refined and polished genius, should be an advocate for re-establishing the barbarous superstitions of Gothic devilism!' (*Monthly Review*, 32 (1765), p. 394). Gothic fiction began to attract serious critical attention only in the following decade, beginning with a brief but seminal remark by William Warburton in his revised edition of Pope (1770), obscurely placed in a footnote to line 146 of 'An Epistle to Augustus'. Observing that *Otranto* is set 'in Gothic chivalry', Warburton contends that it effects 'the full purpose of the *ancient Tragedy*, that is, *to purge the passions by pity and terror*' (*Works of Pope*, IV, pp. 165–7). Although Walpole himself, in a letter of 1780, derided Warburton's account as 'an intention I am sure I do not pretend to have conceived' (*Correspondence*, XLI, pp. 409–10), the passage is of considerable importance. The editor of Pope, invoking the authority of Aristotle's theory of catharsis, had bestowed classical dignity on a new and still highly suspect literary genre, in the same way that critics such as Dennis and Addison had earlier invoked Longinus to support the growing interest in the sublime.

A more extensive attempt to valorize the Gothic was undertaken three years later by John Aikin and his sister, Anna Laetitia Aikin (later Barbauld), in an essay entitled 'On the Pleasure Derived from Objects of Terror' (1773). While the topic was by no means original, the Aikins were the first to make it the subject of an entire critical essay. And unlike previous critics, the Aikins had modern examples to consider: *Otranto* itself, and the Gothic episode in Smollett's *Ferdinand Count Fathom* (1753), which they summarize as follows: 'the hero, entertained in a lone house in a forest, finds a corpse just slaughtered in the room where he is sent to sleep, and the door of which is locked upon him' (*Miscellaneous Pieces*, pp. 126–7). The Aikins argue that we derive pleasure from objects of terror when they are connected with the marvellous or supernatural, whereas purely natural events will cause only revulsion and pain. *Otranto*, therefore, they regard as 'a very spirited modern attempt upon the . . . plan of mixed terror, adapted to the model of Gothic romance', whereas the scene in Smollett's novel, although 'strongly worked-up', is 'mere natural horror' and thus more painful than pleasurable for the reader (p. 126).

A second essay by the Aikins in the same volume, 'An Enquiry into those Kinds of Distress which excite Agreeable Sensations', sets out 'to distinguish those kinds of distress which are pleasing in the representation, from those which are really painful and disgusting' (pp. 192–3). Here again they distinguish actions which are merely repulsive, and 'only affect us with horror', from those which arouse feelings of tenderness and pity (p. 195). The modern novel held up for special praise is *Clarissa* (1747–8): 'Amidst scenes of suffering which rend the heart, in poverty, in a prison, under the most shocking outrages, the grace and delicacy of her character never suffers even for a moment' (p. 206). Later critics, as we shall see, also believed that Richardson's depictions of suffering afforded a model for writers of the Gothic: in combining the 'shocking' with 'grace and delicacy', Richardson created the 'agreeable sensations' that the Aikins sought in vain elsewhere.

Walpole's calling *The Castle of Otranto* 'a Gothic story', Warburton's praise of its 'Gothic chivalry', and the Aikins' admiring the use of 'mixed terror' in this example of 'Gothic romance' are all manifestations of a new use of the term 'Gothic' coloured by the works of Hurd, Thomas Warton and other critics of the medieval. After Gray had praised Chaucer for his 'images of horrour' and Warton had admired the 'Terrible

Graces' of chivalrous romances, critics began to perceive similar qualities in contemporary Gothic novels and dramas. John Langhorne's surprise that a respected modern author should be advocating 'Gothic
devilism' shows that the old use of 'Gothic' to mean barbarous was still
prevalent in 1765, but over the following decades his attitude came to
seem increasingly anachronistic. Borrowing the terminology of critics of
the medieval revival, criticism of modern Gothicism became increasingly
sophisticated; the authentic and the pseudo-medieval alike were felt to
occupy 'enchanted ground'.

In 1777 Clara Reeve published her novel *The Champion of Virtue*,
subtitled, like the second edition of *The Castle of Otranto*, 'A Gothic
Story'. It too was published anonymously, in the guise of a translation
from an old English manuscript, and like Walpole, Reeve revealed her
authorship in the second edition, published a year later as *The Old
English Baron*. Reeve's preface to the second edition is of considerable
interest, challenging both Walpole's mode of Gothicism in *Otranto* and
the Aikins' justification of that mode. While describing her novel as 'the
literary offspring of the castle of Otranto', Reeve criticizes Walpole's
work for its excessive use of the supernatural, and consequent disregard
for verisimilitude: 'Had the story been kept within the utmost *verge* of
probability, the effect had been preserved, without losing the least circumstance that excites or detains the attention' (*Baron*, p. 4). The argument
here thus contradicts the Aikins' advocacy of 'mixed terror'; in Reeve's
view, such a mixture of terror with the marvellous could only enfeeble the
Gothic. It is, however, notable that like the Aikins, Reeve holds up Richardson's novels for special praise. Her work is dedicated to Richardson's
daughter Martha Bridgen, who revised and corrected the first edition, and
Richardson himself is lauded in the Preface as an author who could both
'excite the attention' and 'direct it to some useful, or at least innocent,
end' (pp. [1], 4). The Gothic scenes in *Clarissa* and *Sir Charles Grandison*
(1753–4) – Clarissa using her own coffin as a writing desk on which to
compose her last will and testament, and the claustrophobic scenes of
imprisonment in Italian castles in *Grandison* – were probably among
Reeve's models for *The Old English Baron*, but unlike Richardson,
Reeve composed an entire novel from naturalistic Gothic episodes.

Horace Walpole disliked *The Old English Baron*, 'professedly written
in imitation of *Otranto*, but reduced to reason and probability! It is
probable, that any trial for murder at the Old Bailey would make a
more interesting story' (*Correspondence*, XXVIII, pp. 381–2). None the
less, the convention of ultimately attributing apparently supernatural
phenomena to natural causes became a staple device of subsequent
novelists, including Charlotte Smith, Ann Radcliffe, William Godwin,
and, of course, Jane Austen in *Northanger Abbey*. Reviewers of *The
Mysteries of Udolpho* admired this aspect of the novel, akin to that of

the modern detective story, in which 'mysterious terrors are continually exciting in the mind the idea of a supernatural appearance, keeping us, as it were, upon the very edge and confines of the world of spirits, and yet are ingeniously explained by familiar causes' (*Critical Review*, 2nd ser. 11 (1794), p. 361).[7] The device was of particular use to politically involved novelists such as Godwin, who used it to link the Gothic and the everyday world. The lack of 'familiar causes' explaining the supernaturalism of *Otranto* made the work attractive to readers such as Walpole himself, who regarded Gothic fiction less as a political device than as playful fantasy.

In criticism of the Gothic before the 1790s, there are few references to contemporary politics. Although Samuel Kliger and more recent critics have associated the vogue for medievalism and the Gothic in later eighteenth-century England with Whig politics and ideals of personal liberty, Whig enthusiasts for the Gothic such as Walpole rarely linked politics with aesthetic taste. Before the 1790s, the evocation of horror and terror, the proper use of the supernatural, and the necessity for imparting moral instruction, as well as mere entertainment, were the principal critical concerns. The outbreak of the French Revolution, however, utterly changed the terms of the discussion, so that in the 1790s criticism of the Gothic became inextricably linked with commentary on the current events in France. Ronald Paulson contends that the popularity of Gothic fiction in the 1790s 'was due in part to the widespread anxieties and fears in Europe aroused by the turmoil in France finding a kind of sublimation or catharsis in tales of darkness, confusion, blood and horror' (*Representations*, pp. 220–1).

In the preface to her final novel, *Memoirs of Sir Roger de Clarendon* (1793), Clara Reeve declares her intent of using the work as an anti-Revolutionary document, giving a 'faithful picture of a well governed kingdom, wherein a true subordination of ranks and degrees was observed, and of a great prince at the head of it' (*Memoirs*, I, p. xvi). Britain, she asserts, should 'shudder at the scene before her, and grasp her blessings the closer' (I, p. xx); 'shudder', a verb closely associated with readers' responses to the Gothic, is here transferred to the Terror in France. In another play on words at the end of the novel, Reeve declares that 'the late events have not only ruined France, but all Europe is injured by them' (III, p. 225); Gothic ruins have turned into the desecrated monuments of the *ancien régime*.

A similar transference takes place in an essay by Germaine de Staël, an *émigrée* in London from 1793 to 1795. Her political writings, *Réflexions sur le procès de la reine* (1793) and *Réflexions sur la paix* (1794), were followed by her *Essai sur les fictions* (1795), ostensibly

[7] The attribution of this review to Coleridge, made by several authorities, is refuted by Charles I. Patterson, 'The authenticity of Coleridge's reviews of Gothic Romances', *Journal of English and Germanic Philology*, 50 (1951), 517–21.

devoted to literary concerns. Like other writers of the 1790s, however, de Staël could not exclude political commentary from her critical remarks. Like Clara Reeve, she had little patience with the use of the supernatural in literature: 'The fiction of the marvelous gives us a pleasure that wears thin almost immediately' (*Selected Writings*, p. 62). But the reasons she gives for her strictures are new. In the face of the Terror, supernatural terrors have come to seem merely jejune: 'the bloody crimes we have just witnessed make Dante's underworld take second place' (p. 63).[8]

One result of such strictures was that Gothicists intensified the degree of horror and terror in their works to a new extreme, as Matthew Lewis did in his notorious novel, *The Monk* (1796). The consequence, however, was that rather than being accused of triviality and irrelevance, Lewis and other writers of high Gothic were said to have been corrupted by the excesses of the Terror. Such a charge was made by Thomas Mathias in his long splenetic poem, *The Pursuits of Literature* (1794–7), in which a trickle of verse is supported by a vast apparatus of notes and prefatory matter. In the preface to the third dialogue of his poem (1796), Mathias declares that 'literature, well or ill conducted, is the great engine by which . . . all civilized states must ultimately be supported or overthrown' (*Pursuits*, pp. 161–2). And in the preface to the fourth dialogue (1797), turning his attention to Lewis, Mathias identifies *The Monk* as just the kind of work by which the body politic was endangered. Demanding the suppression of the novel, Mathias enquires dramatically, 'Is this a time to poison the waters of our land in their springs and fountains? Are we to add incitement to incitement, and corruption to corruption?' (p. 242).

Another, wittier opponent of the high Gothic was the pseudonymous writer of an essay in the *Monthly Magazine* for 1797 on the 'Terrorist System of Novel-Writing'. We have, declares the author ironically, 'exactly and faithfully copied the SYSTEM OF TERROR, if not in our streets, and in our fields, at least in our circulating libraries, and in our closets' (*Monthly Magazine*, 4 (1797), p. 102). The author attributes the popularity of the Gothic novel at the end of the century to Robespierre, who, 'with his system of terror . . . taught our novelists that *fear* is the only passion they ought to cultivate . . . our genius has become hysterical, and our taste epileptic' (p. 103). The essay goes on to parody the typical adventures of a terrified Gothic heroine, trapped in a lonely ruined castle, in which she will encounter all that is 'horrible and terrible' (p. 104). Behind the wit is a serious charge; in using the signature 'A Jacobin Novelist', the author implies that the novel of terror has been an apologia for the Terror and its attendant horrors.

[8] 'La fiction merveilleuse cause un plaisir très-promptement épuisé'; 'les enfers du Dante ont été moins avant que les crimes sanguinaires dont nous venons d'être les témoins' (*Oeuvres complètes*, II, pp. 178, 182).

An attack on Gothic drama on similar grounds was made by another pseudonymous writer in the *Monthly Mirror* for 1800. 'Are we', he enquires, 'to have prodigies and monstrous omens, horrid shapes, and the fruits of brooding darkness forced on us at a place to which we resort to be instructed and amused?' (*Monthly Mirror*, 10 (1800), p. 181). This essay, 'On the Absurdities of the Modern Stage', is largely satirical, but at the end of the Revolutionary decade, 'monstrous omens' and 'horrid shapes' had inescapably political overtones. It is instructive to compare this piece with Henry Mackenzie's 'Account of the German Theatre', first delivered as a lecture in 1788 and published in 1790. Mackenzie had delighted in the powerful excesses of German drama, especially of Schiller's *Die Räuber* (1781), with its 'horrid sublimity' (*Transactions of the Royal Society of Edinburgh*, 2 (1790), p. 166). In German drama, unlike in English, 'horrors and . . . distress assault the imagination and the heart of the reader with unsparing force . . . and in its display of human passions and human sorrows, is little solicitous to mitigate the atrocity of the one, or the poignancy of the other' (pp. 167–8). In contrast to Mackenzie's enthusiasm for dramatic terror, reviewers of English Gothic drama a decade later were constantly deploring its dangerous wildness. In 1798, for example, the *Monthly Review*, *Analytical Review*, and *British Critic* all united in condemnation of Lewis's *Castle Spectre*, while the *Critical Review* and *European Magazine* outweighed their faint praise with censure.[9]

It is also notable that Mackenzie's high praise for the terrors of German drama had few counterparts in Germany itself. The outpouring of German Gothic fiction in the 1790s, classified under the categories of *Ritterroman*, *Räuberroman*, *Geisterroman*, *Schauerroman*, and *Gespensterroman*, was consistently dismissed as mere frivolity by German reviewers. There was more critical interest in authentic medieval literature, and in the supposedly medieval writings of Ossian, than in the pseudo-medievalism of modern Gothic productions. Rudolf Erich Raspe's 'Uber die Ritterzeiten und die Barbarey derselben', for example, prefixed to his verse romance *Hermin und Gunilde* (1766), drew on Hurd's *Letters on Chivalry and Romance* (1762). Like Hurd, Raspe contended that the achievements of the Middle Ages had been undervalued in comparison with those of Grecian and Roman antiquity. No writer of Raspe's stature in Germany made similar claims for contemporary Gothicism.[10]

In England some critics remained enthusiasts of the Gothic even after the Revolutionary decade, using various strategies to justify their taste. Its foremost advocate, Nathan Drake, included several essays on the Gothic, as well as examples of Gothic tales, in his collection *Literary Hours*, first published in 1798 and much expanded in editions of 1800

---

[9] For summaries of these reviews, see McNutt, *Gothic Novel*, pp. 248–51.
[10] For an account of German criticism of the Gothic, see Hadley, *The Undiscovered Genre*.

and 1804. In his essay 'On Gothic Superstition', Drake identifies two types of Gothic, 'the terrible and the sportive'; he contends that no author has yet 'availed himself of this circumstance, and thrown them into immediate contrast' (*Literary Hours*, I, p. 147). In both an 'Ode to Superstition' and a Gothic story, 'Henry Fitzowen', Drake creates just such a contrast. His ode, which opens with fine Gothic fervour – 'Saw ye that dreadful shape? heard ye the scream / That shook my trembling soul?' – progresses reassuringly to 'moon-light scenes, and woody vales, / Where Elves, and Fayes, and Sprites disport' (I, pp. 150, 152). In the story, likewise, 'loud howlings and lamentations' abruptly give way to 'the dying notes of distant harps, the gurgling of obstructed currents, and the sighings of the restless vapour' (I, pp. 195, 197).

Despite the example of these and other Gothic stories and poems in Drake's collection, few authors followed his lead. As Drake acknowledged, the major Gothic novelist who came closest to exemplifying his theory was Ann Radcliffe, who, he declared, 'to the wilder landscape of Salvator Rosa has added the softer graces of a Claude' (I, p. 359). By interposing picturesque description, Drake believed, Radcliffe was able to make the terrific aesthetically pleasing, so that her work 'never degenerates into horror, but pleasurable emotion is ever the predominating result' (I, p. 359). Radcliffe herself wrote a significant essay on the Gothic using a similar approach in 1802, four years after Drake's volume first appeared.[11] In an extensive discussion of Shakespeare's ability to enchant his audience, Radcliffe emphasizes above all his power to transform his scenes at will: 'a crowded Theatre has been changed to a lonely shore, to a witch's cave, to an enchanted island, to a murderer's castle ... to every various scene of the living world' (*New Monthly Magazine*, 16, pt 1 (1826), p. 150). Such dizzying changes of scene are a memorable feature of Radcliffe's own novels, in which characters are constantly on the move, often in flight from menacing pursuers. As well as invoking Shakespeare, Radcliffe draws heavily on Burke's theory of the sublime to justify her practice, finding the 'union of grandeur and obscurity ... a sort of tranquillity tinged with terror ... which causes the sublime' (p. 149) in *Hamlet* and, by implication, in her own works.

The examples of Drake and Radcliffe show that it was possible to theorize on Gothic terror after 1795 without alluding to the events in France, but such writing was unusual. More typical of the Revolutionary decade was the Marquis de Sade, whose *Idée sur les romans* was published in 1800. Like de Staël, de Sade was an admirer of the English

---

[11] First published in the *New Monthly Magazine* in 1826, three years after Radcliffe's death, the essay was originally written as an introductory dialogue to her novel *Gaston de Blondeville* (also first published in 1826). For the conjectural dating of 1802, see Alan D. McKillop, 'Mrs Radcliffe on the supernatural in poetry', *Journal of English and Germanic Philology*, 31 (1932), 352–9.

novel, in particular the works of Richardson and Fielding, 'who have taught us that the profound study of man's heart – Nature's veritable labyrinth – alone can inspire the novelist' (*The Marquis de Sade*, p. 106). And like de Staël, de Sade draws a comparison between Gothic and Revolutionary terror. De Sade's analysis of the connection, however, goes further. The Gothicist, he states, could scarcely depict events more appalling than those taking place in France: 'thus, to compose works of interest, one had to call upon the aid of hell itself, and to find in the world of make-believe things wherewith one was fully familiar merely by delving into man's daily life in this age of iron' (p. 109). While he admired *The Monk*, 'superior in all respects to the strange flights of Mrs Radcliffe's brilliant imagination' (p. 109), de Sade believed that the intensification of horror that Revolutionary terror necessitated had enfeebled the Gothic. By resorting to an excess of either the marvellous or mystification, Gothic novelists could only alienate their readers.[12]

In his preface to the second edition of *Lyrical Ballads* (1800), published in the same year as de Sade's treatise, Wordsworth deplored the proliferation of 'frantic novels' exploiting the public's 'degrading thirst after outrageous stimulation' (*Prose Works*, I, pp. 128, 130). At the turn of the century, critics in England and France believed that the Gothic was out of control; Wordsworth apprehended a 'general evil' that his *Lyrical Ballads* was designed to counteract. In the event, however, a post-Revolutionary phase of Gothic fiction and drama was to follow. Works such as Mary Shelley's *Frankenstein* (1818), and Charles Maturin's drama *Bertram* (1816) and novel *Melmoth the Wanderer* (1820), elicited a new wave of criticism. In the first decades of the nineteenth century too, George Ellis and Walter Scott were editing, introducing and modernizing a wide range of medieval literature, helping to make the Middle Ages more attractive to the popular imagination than ever before. Pope's prediction that 'such as *Chaucer* is, shall *Dryden* be' thus proved to be doubly mistaken. A century after his death, Dryden's works were being read with increasing attention in the new editions of Malone (1800) and Scott (1807), while the works of Chaucer and his contemporaries were being studied with the same intense critical interest as the productions of modern Gothicists. As Malone wrote to Percy in November 1809 (*Correspondence of Percy and Malone*, p. 260), 'the whole world is to be "bespread with the dust of antiquity" and what was formerly thought a good subject of ridicule, is now quite the fashion'.

---

[12] 'C'est Richardson, c'est Fielding qui nous ont appris que l'étude profonde du coeur de l'homme, véritable dédale de la nature, peut seule inspirer le romancier'; 'Il fallait donc appeler l'enfer à son secours, pour composer des titres à l'intérêt, et trouver dans le pays des chimères ce qu'on savait couramment, en ne fouillant que l'histoire de l'homme dans cet âge de fer'; '*le Moine*, supérieur, sous tous les rapports, aux bizarres élans de la brillante imagination de Radcliffe' (*Oeuvres complètes*, X, pp. 12, 15).

22

Voltaire, Diderot, Rousseau and the *Encyclopédie*

Charles A. Porter

Ideas about poetry changed almost completely during his time, Sainte-Beuve wrote in 1866: the poetic ideal of a 'most finished and beautiful work, the most clear and pleasant to read' had given way to the desire for a poetry offering 'the greatest latitude to [its] reader to imagine and to dream'. Quoting him Margaret Gilman noted that between the beginning of the eighteenth century and Sainte-Beuve's time 'the conception of poetry changed from that of embellished statement to "suggestive magic", to use Baudelaire's phrase'.[1] 'Merely decorative allegorization', as Paul de Man pointed out, using the terms of Wordsworth's reproach to Pope, came at the end of the eighteenth century to be seen as inferior to the 'imaginative use of figural diction. Meanwhile the term *imagination* steadily [grew] in importance and complexity in the critical as well as in the poetic texts of the period.' A 'profound change in the texture of poetic diction', often taking the form of greater concreteness, was paradoxically accompanied by the increasingly metaphorical structure of poetic language and 'the image – be it under the name of symbol or even of myth – [came] to be considered as the most prominent dimension of the style'.[2]

French literary criticism of the second half of the eighteenth century manifests a tension between, on the one hand, an uncompromising neo-classicism in its most characteristic dogmas and, on the other, frequent expressions of opinion that sound very unclassical. Some of the most original literature of the period is 'pre-romantic' in both subject and manner. Even the most backward-looking of the critics seem to be in search of different answers to the old questions: in this age of 'progress' they remark on the difficulty of finding suitable new subjects and suitable new ways of treating them, they note a perplexing absence of improvement in literary art, they seem increasingly aware of the difficulties of uniting the aesthetically most pleasing with maximal moral usefulness and at least some of them begin to question the suitability of

---

All translations in this article and its notes are by the author.

[1] Gilman, *Idea*, Preface, p. v.
[2] De Man, 'Intentional structure of the Romantic image', in *The Rhetoric of Romanticism* (New York, 1984), pp. 1–2.

judging the literary productions of all ages and all societies by the same standards.

As we follow below the evolution from 'embellishment' to 'image' in the comments of leading critics and some of the more original and imaginative writers of the time – Diderot, in particular – we shall see that, as literature is itself changing in the latter half of the eighteenth century, critics are making new demands: the reader's analytical ability to perceive clearly, compare, and judge decorative elements will be called upon less often than his sympathetic capacity to assimilate images.

The realm of 'literature' in this period included such domains as philosophy and history,[3] and 'criticism' was most often 'judgement'. Criticism consisted primarily of comparing those works considered literary to certain generally accepted models and standards. Similar kinds of comparison were used to judge poetry, drama and various kinds of prose. In the critical texts examined below Voltaire, his disciple Marmontel and, in general, the journalists will be seen to uphold the classical virtues: the 'rules', clarity, moral usefulness, propriety. Diderot makes an effort to understand why some artistic practices seem superior to others in their effect upon the reader, while Rousseau tries to map out the ways in which literature and the other arts change and are changed by society. However, it will be rapidly apparent that almost all the French critics remain characteristically backward-looking, prescriptive, moralistic, elitist, and understand their literary judgements to be universally applicable.

Voltaire

Pococurante's library

Voltaire devoted a chapter of *Candide* (1759) to art and literature. Visiting the Venetian Lord Pococurante's library, Candide is appalled to learn that his host is bored by the most esteemed literary monuments, dismissing Homer as repetitive and inconclusive and finding the *Aeneid* (with some exceptions) cold and disagreeable. Candide, 'who had been brought up never to judge anything for himself', is astonished, all the more when the denunciations go on to include Horace and Cicero. Candide, who 'rather liked Milton', is saddened to hear that Pococurante

---

[3] 'Littérature' is defined as the 'general term which designates erudition, the knowledge of *belles-lettres* and matters pertaining thereto', at the beginning of Jaucourt's article 'Littérature' in the *Encyclopédie*. Under 'LETTRES les' in the *Encyclopédie* one reads, for example, 'Grammar, Eloquence, Poetry, History, Criticism, in a word, all the parts of Literature . . .'

considers him a *barbare*, guilty of *tristes extravagances*: 'the marriage of Sin and Death, and snakes issuing from the womb of the former, are enough to sicken any person of slightly delicate taste'. In his satire of both Pococurante's blasé attitude and Candide's naïveté, Voltaire makes use of characteristic critical categories, categories typical of the critical attitude of his contemporaries, the 'philosophes', as well. Literature is judged – and the reader is expected to exercise judgement – on the interest and usefulness of its subject; the classical canons of taste (*le goût*) and propriety (*les bienséances*) are applied, and they define what kinds of decorative invention and poetic licence are acceptable. Since literary art knows neither national nor temporal frontiers the canons of criticism are applied universally, to Homer, Job, Shakespeare and Racine.

Voltaire was the leading literary figure in France in this period and the oldest of the major 'philosophes' of mid-century. Literary judgements abound throughout his massive work, including his pamphlets, books of history and personal correspondence, and his critical outlook appears consistent throughout his lengthy career. His judgements are corroborated by his own work in the classical genres – epic, tragedy, lyric poem – and by his more original works: stories, didactic poems and histories.

Lettres philosophiques, 1733–4

The *Philosophical Letters* contrast the society and thought of the England Voltaire lived in for several years in the late 1720s with the ways of contemporary France. The last quarter of the book is primarily concerned with English men of letters. Voltaire likes the comedies of writers like Wycherley because they remind him of Molière and 'observe rigorously the rules of the theatre'. He finds Pope, whom he will later translate, 'the most harmonious' of English poets: 'he can be translated because he is extremely clear and his subjects are mostly general and of concern to all nations'. Voltaire prefers Swift to Rabelais, because he has more *finesse* and taste and is more reasonable. But he finds that Shakespeare has ruined the English theatre, since 'Time, which alone makes men's reputations, in the end makes their defects respectable'. Voltaire is appalled that even recent writers can have imitated such 'silliness' (*sottises*) as Othello's strangling his wife on stage and the gravediggers' buffooneries in *Hamlet*. English tragic writers, including Shakespeare, excel only in detached passages, he claims; their plays,

almost all barbarous, deprived of propriety, order, verisimilitude, show strikingly bright spots amidst that night. The style is too inflated, too unnatural, too much copied from the Hebrew writers so full of Asiatic bombast; but nevertheless one must admit that the stilts of the figured style upon which the English language struts also raise the mind high, however irregular the step.[4]

Yet Voltaire admires Shakespeare's 'genius', however much he may be lacking in the 'least spark of good taste or the faintest knowledge of the rules'.

Thirty years later, in the article 'Enthusiasm' of the *Dictionnaire philosophique*, Voltaire tries to show how to reconcile the rules with the muse. 'Reasonable enthusiasm', he states, 'is the lot of great poets'.

How can reasoning govern enthusiasm? the poet first sketches out the arrangement of his picture, and then reason holds the pencil. But when he wants to animate his characters and give them the signs of passion, then imagination heats up, enthusiasm acts: it's like a charger bolting in its course, but the course is regularly laid out.[5]

In the *Lettres philosophiques*, also, the rules come first, but genius is what makes the difference.

Le Siècle de Louis XIV, *1751*

The French orators and writers of *The Age of Louis XIV* 'were the legislators of Europe'. Corneille, despite 'great faults', was a 'true genius' who, moreover, 'formed himself all alone' at a time when there were nothing but 'very bad models', whereas 'Louis XIV, Colbert, Sophocles and Euripides all contributed to forming Racine'. For Voltaire Racine's poetry has achieved perfection. He is 'always elegant, always correct, always true'. Corneille and Racine 'taught the nation how to think, feel and express itself'.

The existence of models poses a conundrum: without them it is hard to create anything fine, but once they have been commonly accepted it is hard for writers of a following generation to be anything more than imitators, for 'subjects and the embellishments appropriate to those subjects are much more limited than one would think'. Voltaire also notes that the French seventeenth century has given rise to new forms of eloquence (he cites Guez de Balzac's 'harmonious choice of words',

---

[4] '. . . presque toutes barbares, dépourvues de bienséance, d'ordre, de vraisemblance, ont des lueurs étonnantes au milieu de cette nuit. Le style est trop ampoulé, trop hors de la nature, trop copié des écrivains hébreux si remplis de l'enflure asiatique; mais aussi il faut avouer que les échasses du style figuré, sur lesquelles la langue anglaise est guindée, élèvent aussi l'esprit bien haut, quoique par une marche irrégulière'.

[5] 'Comment le raisonnement peut-il gouverner l'enthousiasme? c'est qu'un poète dessine d'abord l'ordonnance de son tableau; la raison alors tient le crayon. Mais veut-il animer ses personnages et leur donner le caractère des passions, alors l'imagination s'échauffe, l'enthousiasme agit; c'est un coursier qui s'emporte dans sa carrière; mais la carrière est régulièrement tracée.'

La Rochefoucauld's *Maximes* which 'accustomed one to think and give one's thoughts an animated, precise and delicate turn', Bossuet's funeral orations) and new literary genres, such as the *Caractères* of La Bruyère or Bossuet's *Discours sur l'histoire universelle*. Fénelon, in *Télémaque*, displays in a novel 'useful morals for mankind, a kind of morals completely neglected in almost all preceding fictions [*inventions fabuleuses*]'.

Voltaire is attentive to language and style. He praises Pascal for having, in the *Lettres provinciales*, established modern French prose[6] but criticizes the language of La Fontaine: young people and their mentors, he warns, must take care not to confuse his too frequent 'flaws' – use of 'familiar', 'low', 'careless', 'trivial' expressions – with his *beau naturel*, his natural simplicity.[7] In a rapid survey of the arts of the period in other countries Voltaire singles out Dryden and Pope, praising the latter's *Essay on Man* and concluding that 'No nation has treated morality in verse with more energy and depth than the English. There lies, I think, the greatest merit of her poets'.

Appended to Voltaire's History is an alphabetical 'Catalogue of the Majority of French Writers Who Appeared in the Age of Louis XIV in Order to Aid in the Establishment of a Literary History of This Time'. Mingling poets and playwrights, novelists, historians and journalists with philosophers and scientists (like Descartes and Gassendi), it includes biographical anecdotes as well as judgements of literary merit. The *Princesse de Clèves* and *Zaïde* of Madame de Lafayette were 'the first novels in which one saw polite manners and natural adventures described gracefully. Before her, writers wrote improbable things in a turgid style'.[8] A one-paragraph article on Madame de Sévigné praises her letters, 'written freely, in a style that paints and enlivens everything', but regrets that she 'lacks taste totally' and 'doesn't know how to treat Racine fairly'. The article 'Scarron', quoted here in its entirety, is an example of literary criticism in *The Age of Louis XIV*: historically detailed, judgemental, based on presumedly shared standards of taste, biting, pithy, anecdotal:

SCARRON (Paul), son of a counsellor of the Grand Chamber, born in 1610. His comedies are more burlesque than comic. Only a buffoon could be forgiven his *Virgile travesti*. His *Roman comique* is almost the only one of his works that people of taste still like; but they like it only as a gay,

---

[6] His remarks on the modernity of Pascal's language may be compared with his updating of language in his edition of Corneille, 1764.

[7] '... ne pas confondre avec son beau naturel le familier, le bas, le négligé, le trivial: défauts dans lesquels il tombe trop souvent.'

[8] '... les premiers romans où l'on vit les mœurs des honnêtes gens, et des aventures naturelles décrites avec grâce. Avant elle, on écrivait d'un style ampoulé des choses peu vraisemblables.'

amusing, mediocre work. This is what Boileau had predicted. Louis XIV
married his widow in 1685. Died in 1660.[9]

Dictionnaire philosophique, *1764*

In scattered remarks in the *Philosophical Dictionary* of 1764, supplemented in later editions,[10] Voltaire characterizes the good literary critic:
impartial and learned, a man of both taste and reason. In the article
'Criticism' Voltaire tells us that knowledgeable and tasteful but unenvious
artists would make 'excellent' critics but are 'hard to find'. In a later
revision he notes that successful works are almost always and everywhere attacked; a professional class of critics has arisen who, like

> inspectors of pigs, who were appointed to examine whether animals being
> brought to market were diseased ... don't find any author very healthy ...
> They earn some money at this craft, especially when they speak ill of good
> work and well of poor work.[11]

For Voltaire application of standards by the critic makes use of the
same *raison* (mind, reasoning, reasonableness) Voltaire requires of the
literary artist. Since reason 'consists of always seeing things as they
are',[12] the reasonable critic will be unlikely to approve certain kinds of
subject. Fantastic images, for example, are not justifiable in themselves,
though they may have their place in the category of the decorative. By
this bias Voltaire will reduce to allegory what other times regard as
myth:

> Are not the oldest fables clearly allegorical? ...
> Wisdom is conceived in the head of the master of the gods under the
> name of Minerva; man's soul is a divine fire which Minerva shows to
> Prometheus, who uses it to give life to man.

[9] 'SCARRON (Paul), fils d'un conseiller de la grand-chambre, né en 1610. Ses comédies
sont plus burlesques que comiques. Son *Virgile travesti* n'est pardonnable qu'à un
bouffon. Son *Roman comique* est presque le seul de ses ouvrages que les gens de
goût aiment encore; mais ils ne l'aiment que comme un ouvrage gai, amusant, et
médiocre. C'est ce que Boileau avait prédit. Louis XIV épousa sa veuve en 1685.
Mort en 1660.'

[10] The notes of the Classiques Garnier edition by Naves, Benda, and Étiemble, 1967,
supplement the original text with later additions. There is a useful translation of
the *Philosophical Dictionary* by Theodore Besterman in the Penguin edition.

[11] 'On a vu ... des gens qui se sont établis critiques de profession, comme on a créé
des langueyeurs de porcs pour examiner si ces animaux qu'on amène au marché ne
sont pas malades. Les langueyeurs de la littérature ne trouvent aucun auteur bien
sain ... Ils gagnent quelque argent à ce métier, surtout quand ils disent du mal des
bons ouvrages, et du bien des mauvais' (*Dictionnaire philosophique*, pp. 500–1).

[12] '... la raison consiste à voir toujours les choses comme elles sont' ('Enthousiasme',
Dictionnaire philosophique, p. 182).

It is impossible not to recognize in these fables a living portrait of all of nature. Most other fables are either a corruption of old stories or a caprice of the imagination.[13]

Such allegorization leads to a great homogenization of legends, myths, stories from past cultures. Voltaire places the Old Testament and Homer on the same plane: 'The story of Joseph ... appears to be the model of all the oriental writers; it is more affecting than Homer's *Odyssey*, for a hero who pardons is more touching than one who avenges himself.'[14] In an addition to 'Fables' Voltaire proposes that fables were invented in Asia even before Aesop by the first conquered peoples, since 'free men would not have always needed to disguise truth'. Aesop's fables 'are all emblems, instructions to the weak in order to preserve themselves against the strong as best they could'. Voltaire insistently seeks a moral allegory in poetic or legendary texts, assigning to the politically or socially 'useful' element an importance equal to that of the 'agreeable' or aesthetic element.

Voltaire's criticism exemplifies what Claude Pichois has called the 'tyranny of taste' of his period: 'Taste is opposed to genius ... as discernment, distinction, culture [are opposed] to instinct, inspiration, originality, as education [is] to nature, almost as the social [is] to the individual'.[15] His criticism is, on the whole, more 'classical', more conservative than his own literary practice. It has little place for those inventive works, such as his short 'philosophical' stories and parts of his personal correspondence, which have come to be considered his masterpieces: for him such works were essentially beneath criticism. Ironically his numerous works in the classical genres (epic, tragedy, lyric poetry), for which he was highly admired by his contemporaries, now seem quite unoriginal and conventional even where he believed he was innovating.

Diderot

Incisive comments on art and literature are scattered throughout Diderot's work. His earlier formulations were often abstract and theoretical, but

---

[13] 'Les plus anciennes fables ne sont-elles pas visiblement allégoriques? ...
   La sagesse est conçue dans le cerveau du maître des dieux sous le nom de Minerve; l'âme de l'homme est un feu divin que Minerve montre à Prométhée, qui se sert de ce feu divin pour animer l'homme.
   Il est impossible de ne pas reconnaître dans ces fables une peinture vivante de la nature entière. La plupart des autres fables sont ou la corruption des histoires anciennes, ou le caprice de l'imagination' ('Fables', *Dictionnaire philosophique*, pp. 195–6).
[14] 'L'histoire de Joseph ... paraît être le modèle de tous les écrivains orientaux; elle est plus attendrissante que l'*Odyssée* d'Homère, car un héros qui pardonne est plus touchant que celui qui se venge' ('Joseph', *Dictionnaire philosophique*, p. 261).
[15] Pichois, 'Voltaire et Shakespeare', p. 179.

as he composed more fiction, wrote plays and taught himself to be an
art critic by studying and then writing a description of the 'Salons', he
began to ask more and more original questions concerning specific cases.

The article 'Art', the Lettre sur les sourds et muets and the article 'Beau'

'Art' was first published in 1750, several months before the appearance
of Volume One of the *Encyclopédie*, as part of the editors' promotional
effort. Most of the article is concerned with the importance of the 'arts
mécaniques' (practical or manual arts, or crafts) and their usefulness to
society. The 'arts libéraux' are defined as those that are more the work of
the mind than the hand. For Diderot, at this early date, it would appear
that even the 'beaux-arts' were to be considered among the crafts, as a
praxis, involving rules and expertise: 'if the object [of man's effort] is
executed [rather than only contemplated] the collection and technical
disposition of the rules by which it is executed are called *Art*'.[16] Diderot
never ceased admiring craftsmanship; increasingly, however, he sought to
understand why it alone did not suffice. His critical comments, therefore,
would increasingly consider the subjects and intentions of the writer in
addition to his technique.

In his *Letter on the Blind for the Use of the Sighted* (1749) Diderot
had queried how being blind from birth might affect the thinking of an
intelligent man, particularly in regard to morals and religion; in the
companion *Letter on the Deaf and Dumb for the Use of Those Who
Hear and Speak* (1751) Diderot sought to imagine how the absence of
one or both of these faculties would affect the understanding, and the
understanding in particular of linguistic and literary values. Much of
the Letter is devoted to a discussion of style and language, and at one
point Diderot tries to characterize poetic language:

In all speech in general it is necessary to distinguish between thought and
expression; if the thought is rendered with clarity, purity and precision it
suffices for familiar conversation; join with these qualities careful word
choice and the rhythm and harmony of the period and you will have the
style appropriate to the pulpit; but you will still be far from poetry,
especially the kind of poetry that the ode and the epic poem display in their
descriptions. There a spirit passes into the speech of the poet which moves
and animates all its syllables. What is this spirit? I have sometimes felt its
presence, but all I know is that it is what causes things to be both stated

---

[16] 'Si l'object s'exécute, la collection et la disposition technique des règles selon
lesquelles il s'exécute s'appellent *Art* . . .' For a discussion of contemporary use of
the terms *art, artisan, artiste*, see Chouillet, *Formation*, pp. 373–5 and *passim*.

and represented at the same time, that in the same moment as the understanding grasps them the soul is moved by them, imagination sees them and the ear hears them, and that speech is no longer only a chain of energetic terms that set forth the thought with force and nobility but is also a tissue of hieroglyphics piled one on top of another that portray the thought. I might say that in this sense all poetry is emblematic.[17]

As examples of such portrayal he cites various texts, particularly from Virgil and Homer, and notes that one almost has to be a poet in order to grasp fully the poetic emblem. Margaret Gilman has emphasized the importance of Diderot's comments on poetry. He rethought the relation of art and reality and stressed that imagination is the poet's 'mediator between reality and art'. For Diderot 'the language of poetry has much the same relationship to natural language that the ideal model has to nature. It does not imitate, but suggests; it is not a copy, but a hieroglyph, a symbol.'[18]

Near the conclusion of the Letter, Diderot noted how he regretted the 'false delicacy' which had caused French to exclude 'a large number of energetic expressions': 'by dint of refinement we have impoverished our [language] and, frequently having but one fit term [*terme propre*] for an idea we prefer to weaken the idea rather than forego a noble expression'.[19] In his discussion of both the 'emblem' and 'false delicacy' one can see Diderot striving to articulate a basis for criticism that would both replace an automatic and reductive application of the rules of taste and make it possible to identify originality and new sources of beauty. In presenting

---

[17] 'Il faut distinguer dans tout discours en général la pensée et l'expression; si la pensée est rendue avec clarté, pureté et précision, c'en est assez pour la conversation familière; joignez à ces qualités le choix des termes, avec le nombre et l'harmonie de la période, et vous aurez le style qui convient à la chaire; mais vous serez encore loin de la poésie, surtout de la poésie que l'ode et le poème épique déploient dans leurs descriptions. Il passe alors dans le discours du poète un esprit qui en meut et vivifie toutes les syllabes. Qu'est-ce que cet esprit? j'en ai quelquefois senti la présence; mais tout ce que j'en sais, c'est que c'est lui qui fait que les choses sont dites et représentées tout à la fois; que dans le même temps que l'entendement les saisit, l'ame en est émue, l'imagination les voit et l'oreille les entend et que le discours n'est plus seulement un enchaînement de termes énergiques qui exposent la pensée avec force et noblesse, mais que c'est encore un tissu d'hiéroglyphes entassés les uns sur les autres qui la peignent. Je pourrais dire en ce sens que toute poésie est emblématique' (Diderot, *Sourds et muets*, ed. Meyer, p. 70). On the origins and concepts of the *Lettre* and 'Beau', see Chouillet, *Formation*, pp. 151–323.

[18] Gilman, *Idea*, p. 84.

[19] Diderot's regret is ahead of its time, as can be seen by comparing it to Rivarol's declaration in the *Discours sur l'universalité de la langue française* (1784), 'Les styles sont classés dans notre langue, comme les sujets dans notre monarchie. Deux expressions qui conviennent à la même chose, ne conviennent au même ordre de choses; et c'est à travers cette hiérarchie des styles que le bon goût sait marcher'. Cited by Brewer, *Discourse*, p. 268.

Diderot's 'emerging concept of the critic' Paul H. Meyer[20] pointed to
Sainte-Beuve's statement that 'it is indeed [Diderot] who has the honour
of having introduced first among us the fertile criticism of the beautiful
[*critique féconde des beautés*], which he substituted for that of faults'.

The article 'Beau' ('Beautiful'), which appeared first in the second
volume of the *Encyclopédie* (1752), defines the 'Beautiful' as that which
can 'awaken in my understanding the idea of *relationships*'.[21] 'Relationships' (*rapports*) include such notions as order, arrangement, symmetry.
Diderot takes particular care to distinguish his ideas from those of his
predecessors, from Plato and Saint Augustine to Shaftesbury (whose
Inquiry Concerning Virtue and Merit he had translated into French in
1745). Among the various kinds of 'beautiful' Diderot discusses is the
beau littéraire; he chooses a literary example to make the distinction
between *beau* and other categories such as 'pretty', 'sublime', or 'burlesque' or 'ugly'. He shows how in the situation of Corneille's tragedy
Horace the expression 'That he die' (*Qu'il mourût*) acquires its beauty,
and eventually its sublimity, from the spectator's increasing understanding
of the relationships among the several characters. He concludes by
considering various reasons for divergent judgements of works of art:
the quality and experience of the judge, his ability to distinguish among
differing kinds of relationships, the effects of custom and social situation, of prior knowledge or skill, the observer's skill at abstraction, his
education and prejudices, the effects of surrounding or incidental ideas,
of authority and tradition. Thus Diderot opens the way to a criticism
based on the individual observer and his perception of the play of forces
within the work of art.[22]

---

[20] Meyer, 'Lettre sur les sourds et muets', esp. pp. 140–7. He quotes a later statement
by Diderot in a letter which Sainte-Beuve cannot have known (Roth conjectures a
date of 1773 or 1774; it was first published in the twentieth century): 'a beauty of
the first order, such as those I find in Plato, covers a thousand flaws in an author,
ancient or modern; I am satisfied if I find several sublime spots. A critic who
gathers only faults and leaves the beauties behind is like a man walking along the
banks of a river which is carrying grains of gold dust and fills his pockets with
sand ... I will do otherwise.' Sainte-Beuve could perhaps have known the similar
passage from the *Correspondance littéraire* that is quoted below.
[21] 'réveiller dans mon entendement l'idée de rapports'.
[22] This has been further developed recently by Daniel Brewer in his *Discourse*, p. 252:
'In eighteenth-century fiction, drama, and art, the activity of reader and spectator
acquires heightened significance as the aesthetic object becomes part of a dialogical
relation... The meaning and value of things in general becomes relative, since all
objects susceptible to being known are related to the interpreting subject ... As a
result, one story concerning the eighteenth-century Enlightenment would recount the
emergence of a new and dialogical relation between subject and object, viewer and
painting, reader and text, individual and world. The monological, authoritative discourse
of a certain classicism and a certain classic subject gives way to a multiform discourse ...'
For the place of the 'emblème' and the articles 'Art', 'Beau' and others in the development
of Diderot's aesthetics, see Chouillet, *Formation*, Pt I, chs. 4–5; Pt II, ch. 1.

Writings concerning literary art

Some of the most often quoted of Diderot's remarks on fiction and literary technique appear in his novel *Jacques le Fataliste* (not published until 1796, but written in the 1770s) and story 'Les Deux amis de Bourbonne' (1772), but already in his writings on dramatic literature (*Entretiens sur le Fils naturel* (*Conversations on the Natural Son*, 1757), *De la poésie dramatique* (*On Dramatic Poetry*, 1758) and 'Éloge de Térence' (1769)) and his 'Éloge de Richardson' (1762) he was struggling to understand two of the major literary genres of his period. These essays mingle theorizing about the novel and drama with observations resulting from his experience as a reader of novels and as a playwright (the 1757 and 1758 essays are written to accompany his plays *Le Fils naturel* (*The Natural Son*) and *Le Père de Famille* (*The Father*)).

The most striking feature of Diderot's comments on the practice of reading is his emphasis on the reader's active involvement with the text.[23] Corneille forced him into dialogue: 'often I would close the book in the middle of a scene and seek for the reply: there's not much point in stating that my efforts were ordinarily of no use other than to frighten me with the logic and strength of mind of this poet'.[24] Richardson calls forth full emotional participation. 'Novel' had implied for Diderot 'a tissue of imaginary and silly events'[25] and reading one was a 'danger for both taste and morals', but he found that Richardson's novels 'elevate the mind, touch the soul and breathe out love of the good': 'O Richardson! however much one may try not to, one participates in your works, one joins in the conversation, one approves, blames, admires, becomes irritated or indignant'.[26] He admires the truth (the 'réalité') of Richardson's characters, backgrounds, motivations, comparing them to his own experience ('the passions he depicts are such that I feel them in me'); even more: in reading Richardson, he says, one 'acquires experience'.

Diderot inserts asides concerning narrative realism in two later short stories, 'Les Deux amis de Bourbonne' (1770) and 'Ceci n'est pas un conte' ('This Is Not a Story', 1773). At the end of 'Les Deux amis' he points out how the painter turns his 'ideal' figure into a portrait by adding 'a light scar on the forehead, a wart on one of the temples'; Diderot

---

[23] What Brewer calls the 'corporal aesthetic experience', *Discourse*, p. 128 and *passim*.
[24] '... souvent je fermais le livre au milieu d'une scène, et je cherchais la réponse: il est assez inutile de dire que mes efforts ne servaient communément qu'à m'effrayer sur la logique et sur la force de tête de ce poète' (*Oeuvres esthétiques*, p. 253).
[25] 'un tissu d'événements chimériques et frivoles'.
[26] 'O Richardson! on prend, malgré qu'on en ait, un rôle dans tes ouvrages, on se mêle à la conversation, on approuve, on blâme, on admire, on s'irrite, on s'indigne' (*Oeuvres esthétiques*, p. 30).

recommends a similar procedure to the teller of historical tales (*conteur historique*), who must strive both to conform rigorously to the 'truth' and to touch the reader, a 'result that is not obtained without eloquence and poetry'. But since 'eloquence is a kind of lie' and 'nothing runs so much counter to illusion as poetry', the *conteur historique* should

> strew his tale with little circumstances so closely bound to the thing, touches so simple, so natural, and nevertheless so difficult to imagine, that you will be forced to say to yourself, 'Well! that is true: things like that can't be invented'. In this way he will conceal the exaggerations of eloquence and poetry, the truth of nature will cover up the artifice, and he will satisfy the requirements of two seemingly contradictory states and be at one and the same time historian and poet, truthful and mendacious.[27]

In 'Ceci n'est pas un conte', having noted that the teller of a tale is often interrupted by his listeners, Diderot 'introduces ... a character who plays more or less the role of the reader'. Diderot uses a similar technique with great skill in his novel *Jacques le Fataliste et son maître*, to manipulate and guide the reader's reactions: for him it is one more way to foster the confusion of fiction with real life.

The imitation of nature

Probing and subtle comments on the imitation of nature are found in Diderot's writings on works of art in the *Salons* (1759–81) and on the theatre in his *Entretiens sur le Fils Naturel* (1757), *De la poésie dramatique* (1758), 'Éloge de Térence' (1769) and the *Paradoxe sur le comédien* (*Paradox concerning the Actor*, 1770–7). Successful imitation, for Diderot, requires a natural reality in the subject and mastery of the relevant art (or 'technique') in the execution. Diderot's admiration for mastery of technique allows the artist to choose his subject from among a much greater range of subjects than those traditionally admitted by classical taste. His requirement of natural subjects, on the other hand, eliminates implausible subjects, those that are not 'probable possibles'.[28] In describing one of Chardin's still lifes in the *Salon of 1765*, depicting a game bird, olives, a napkin and a glass of wine, he notes that 'there

[27] 'Il parsèmera son récit de petites circonstances si liées à la chose, de traits si simples, si naturels, et toutefois si difficiles à imaginer, que vous serez forcé de vous dire en vous-même: Ma foi, cela est vrai: on n'invente pas ces choses-là. C'est ainsi qu'il sauvera l'exagération de l'éloquence et de la poésie; que la vérité de la nature couvrira le prestige de l'art; et qu'il satisfera à deux conditions qui semblent contradictoires, d'être en même temps historien et poète, véridique et menteur.' *Oeuvres romanesques*, p. 791.

[28] 'les possibles vraisemblables' (*Essais sur la peinture*, in *Oeuvres esthétiques*, p. 691).

are no unworthy objects in nature, and the object is to render them'.[29] In Chardin all is 'nature and truth'; as a result the viewer is drawn into an almost physical relationship with the subject of the work: 'you would take the bottles by the neck if you were thirsty; the peaches and grapes arouse appetite and call to the hand'.

As the reader of Richardson 'joins in the conversation' of the characters, so the visitor to the *Salon* is called into the paintings' space. Viewing Poussin's *Paysage au serpent* (1767), Diderot exclaims, 'what an immense space, and in this space, what a succession of different passions, coming right up to you who are the ultimate object, the aim of the composition'.[30] Or, criticizing the excess of figures in a 'Grande Galerie éclairée du fond' of Hubert Robert: if there had been only one solitary figure wandering among these ruins, 'I would never have been able to keep myself from going in to daydream under that arch, sit among those columns, enter into your picture'.

In the *Paradoxe sur le comédien* Diderot develops the argument that the most convincing actor is not the one who actually feels the emotions he portrays but rather the one who, after studying a person in the sway of those emotions, then imitates that person on stage, while feeling nothing himself. Such imitation, mediated by the actor's art, represents a considerable change from the kind Diderot presented as an ideal in the *Fils naturel*: there he suggested that, at least in serious middle-class drama, the actor should be the very real-life person from the action imitated, his own salon having been 'transported' to the stage 'as it is'.

The *Entretiens* had presented Diderot's argument for the development of an 'intermediate genre' between tragedy and comedy. Among the virtues of 'serious comedy' or 'domestic tragedy' would be what he saw as the emotional persuasiveness of a 'real' *scène* (the word denotes both 'scene' and 'stage'), costumes that are true to life, 'simple actions, dangers that you have inevitably feared for your relatives, friends, yourself': 'Beauty, in the arts, has the same basis as Truth in philosophy. What is Truth? conformity of our judgements with things. What is beauty in imitation? conformity of the image with the thing.'[31] The subject of serious comedy would be the portrayal, no longer of 'characters', but

---

[29] '... on voit qu'il n'y a guère d'objets ingrats dans la nature, et que le point est de les rendre' (*Oeuvres esthétiques*, p. 490).

[30] In commenting on Diderot's art criticism (*Absorption and Theatricality. Painting and Beholder in the Age of Diderot* (Berkeley, 1980)), Michael Fried develops a theory of 'absorption and theatricality' based in part on the frequent passages in which Diderot 'enters' the picture; Fried relates Diderot's theatre and art criticism and places the latter in the context of contemporary French critics and painters.

[31] 'Les beautés ont, dans les arts, le même fondement que les vérités dans la philosophie. Qu'est-ce que la vérité? La conformité de nos jugements avec les êtres. Qu'est-ce que la beauté d'imitation? La conformité de l'image avec la chose' (*Oeuvres esthétiques*, p. 160).

of conditions (the man of letters, the merchant, the magistrate and so on) or relationships (like father, or brothers). We all have our own station in life and must deal with those of other stations: what then should interest us more? and how many new 'situations' could thus be found for the theatre!

In the *Entretiens* Diderot did not yet seem to have problematized the act of imitation; he began to do so the following year in *De la poésie dramatique*. He there links 'poet, novelist, actor' in describing their effort to strike the soul. But he is still concerned particularly with the subject and its effect. 'Poetry requires something huge, barbarous, wild.'[32] The ways of modern polite, civilized society are no longer as 'poetic' as once they were: 'everything is weakened by becoming gentler'.[33]

> When shall we see poets born? It will be after times of disaster and great misfortune, when exhausted peoples begin to breathe again. Then imaginations, agitated by terrible sights, will portray things unknown to those who did not witness them.[34]

Diderot shows here a clear predilection for a kind of sentimental horribilism that could easily lead away from the classical proprieties, towards either melodrama or realism. What is in question is the nature of the poetic, for the difference that Diderot draws in *De la poésie dramatique* between the historian and the poet is that the historian writes 'what happened, purely and simply, and that does not always bring out character as much as it could, and that does not affect and interest as much as it is possible to affect and interest. The poet would have written everything which seemed to him likely to affect his hearer the most.'[35]

Diderot then proceeds to suggest various means available to the dramatic poet for maximum effect (pantomime particularly), and he concludes with some considerations on 'Authors and Critics', recommending to both of these honest and diligent study of 'passions, manners, character, customs . . . history, philosophy, morality, science and the arts'.

---

[32] 'La poésie veut quelque chose d'énorme, de barbare et de sauvage' (*Oeuvres esthétiques*, p. 261).

[33] 'En général, plus un peuple est civilisé, poli, moins ses mœurs sont poétiques; tout s'affaiblit en s'adoucissant' (*Oeuvres esthétiques*, p. 260).

[34] 'Quant verra-t-on naître des poètes? Ce sera après les temps de désastres et de grands malheurs; lorsque les peuples harassés commenceront à respirer. Alors les imaginations, ébranlées par des spectacles terribles, peindront des choses inconnues à ceux qui n'en ont pas été les témoins' (*Oeuvres esthétiques*, pp. 261–2).

[35] '. . . l'historien a écrit ce qui est arrivé, purement et simplement, ce qui ne fait pas toujours sortir les caractères autant qu'ils pourraient; ce qui n'émeut ni n'intéresse pas autant qu'il est possible d'émouvoir et d'intéresser. Le poète eût écrit tout ce qui lui aurait semblé devoir affecter le plus' (*Oeuvres esthétiques*, p. 217).

In the *Essais sur la peinture* (*Essays on Painting*, 1766) Diderot defines 'taste' as 'a capacity acquired by repeated experience to grasp the true or the good, with the circumstance that makes it beautiful, and to be promptly and acutely touched by it', requiring 'experience', 'study' and 'sensibility' (*sensibilité*) for both artist and critic. He finds sensibility a mixed blessing, however: 'Cold men, stern and tranquil observers of nature, often know better the delicate strings that must be plucked.'[36] He mentions the mutual scorn genre painters and painters of historical subjects bear towards each other, the latter considering genre painting to be servile copying from nature, lacking 'ideas, poetry, grandeur, elevation, genius'; the former accusing the historical painter as novelistic, exaggerated and grandiloquent: 'You see, my friend, that it's the quarrel between prose and poetry, history and epic poetry, heroic and bourgeois tragedy, bourgeois tragedy and gay comedy.' Diderot finds that both require great art.

He makes a distinction in the *Essais* between disposition (*ordonnance*) and expression that rather parallels Voltaire's distinction between the roles of reason and enthusiasm; Diderot gives higher priority to emotion and imagination than did Voltaire:

Expression requires a strong imagination, fire and animation, the art of calling up ghosts, animating them, magnifying them; disposition, in poetry as in painting, implies a certain equilibrium between judgement and animation, warmth and wisdom, rapture and sang-froid of which there are few examples in nature. Without this rigorous balance, according to whether enthusiasm or reason predominates, the artist is extravagant or cold.[37]

Finally, in the *Paradoxe* Diderot argues specifically that what is required of the actor for effective imitation is required as well of the writer: that is to say, a calm and unemotional representing of the manifestations of passion.[38]

It is not the violent man beside himself who has us at his disposal; this is an advantage reserved for the self-controlled. The great dramatic poets especially are assiduous spectators of what is going on around them in the physical and the moral world ... Great poets, great actors, and perhaps in

---

[36] The dangers of *sensibilité* for great men, 'especially great actors, great philosophers, great poets, great musicians, great doctors' are developed further in a passage near the end of *D'Alembert's Dream*.

[37] 'L'expression exige une imagination forte, une verve brûlante, l'art de susciter des fantômes, de les animer, de les agrandir; l'ordonnance, en poésie ainsi qu'en peinture, suppose un certain tempérament de jugement et de verve, de chaleur et de sagesse, d'ivresse et de sang-froid, dont les exemples ne sont pas communs en nature. Sans cette balance rigoureuse, selon que l'enthousiasme ou la raison prédomine, l'artiste est extravagant ou froid' (*Oeuvres esthétiques*, p. 720).

[38] Cf. Wordsworth's expression, 'emotion recollected in tranquillity', from the Preface to the *Lyrical Ballads*.

general all the great imitators of nature, whoever they may be, endowed with a fine imagination, great judgement, tact and sensitivity, very assured taste, are the least susceptible of beings ... they are too busy looking, recognizing, imitating to be acutely affected within themselves.[39]

However much Diderot enjoys moral lessons in works of art, the ultimate literary value for Diderot, artist and critic, is finally not moral suasion by appeal to the sentiments but rather the convincing imitation of life. That imitation requires, on the one hand, study of both artistic and natural models and, on the other, imagination; as a practitioner himself Diderot does not fail to give both descriptions of such imitation (like his analysis of 'lassove papavera collo' from the *Aeneid* in the *Lettre sur les sourds et les muets*) and examples of it (for instance Rameau's panto-mimes of musical performance in *Le Neveu de Rameau*).

Rousseau

Jean-Jacques Rousseau's remarks concerning literature must be under-stood in the context of the role he assigned to himself in the debates of the philosophes. From his first great public success with the *Discours sur les sciences et les arts* (1751) through the increasingly autobiogra-phical writings of the latter part of his life, he took a position that in many respects opposed him to the majority of the philosophes of mid-century. Unlike them he argued that the progress made by modern society had degraded and enslaved mankind and caused general unhap-piness; he based his demonstration primarily on his personal history and his feelings. For Rousseau, much more than for his contemporaries, literature necessarily reflected its society; he included literature among the evils he denounced. For the other philosophes (if one may take the judgements of D'Alembert in the Preliminary Discourse of the *Ency-clopédie* as characteristic) the arts, and literature in particular, were one area which had not 'progressed' with the rest of society, at least not since the seventeenth century, whereas Rousseau finds that the arts continually reflect the decline brought by increasing civilization.

---

[39] 'Ce n'est pas l'homme violent qui est hors de lui-même qui dispose de nous; c'est un avantage réservé à l'homme qui se possède. Les grands poètes dramatiques surtout sont spectateurs assidus de ce qui se passe autour d'eux dans le monde physique et dans le monde moral ... Les grands poètes, les grands acteurs, et peut-être en général tous les grands imitateurs de la nature, quels qu'ils soient, doués d'une belle imagination, d'un grand jugement, d'un tact fin, d'un goût très sûr, sont les êtres les moins sensibles ... ils sont trop occupés à regarder, à reconnaître et à imiter, pour être vivement affectés au-dedans d'eux-mêmes' (*Oeuvres esthétiques*, pp. 309–10).

In the First Discourse Rousseau used literary evidence to show the debasement of man in contemporary society. He enlarged his examination of the relationship of literature – particularly dramatic literature – and society in the *Lettre à D'Alembert sur les spectacles* (1758), and there he described at some length the effects of dramatic literature on the individual. In his pedagogical treatise, *Émile* (1762) he essentially banished books (excepting *Robinson Crusoe*) from the child's education, and allowed only history and moralizing fables during adolescence; not until Émile is ready to enter into society does the time come for 'agreeable books'. Finally, in his *Confessions* (written 1764–71, published 1782 and 1789) he described both the effects of his own reading on himself and the intentions that lie behind his writings.

Criticism in the Discours sur les sciences et les arts *and the* Lettre à D'Alembert

'Letters' join the sciences and the arts at the beginning of the First Discourse as powerful enslaving forces that 'arrange garlands of flowers upon the iron chains that [men in society] bear'; they 'stifle in them the feeling of that original liberty for which they seem to have been born, make them love their slavery and form them into what are called regulated populations' (*des Peuples policés*). Like the other arts literature encourages uniformity and conformity and eventually hypocrisy and alienation: in the 'herd that is called society' one 'no longer dares to appear what one is ... One can thus never know for sure whom one is dealing with'.[40] In the body of the Discourse various aspects of contemporary literature are singled out as evidence of the sad state to which mankind has been reduced by civilization: 'how many male, strong beauties [Voltaire] has sacrificed to our false delicacy'. The result of excessive refinement of taste is that readers no longer ask if a book is 'useful but if it is well written', whereas Rousseau recommends that we seek rather to 'do good' than to 'speak well'.

The argument underlying the moral and psychological attack on literature is better focused in the *Discours sur l'origine et les fondements de l'inégalité parmi les hommes* (1755). In the state of nature as Rousseau hypothesizes it man did not 'reason about a condition different from his own' or suffer the 'ravages' of imagination. But early in the development

---

[40] 'On n'ose plus paraître ce qu'on est; et dans cette contrainte perpétuelle, les hommes qui forment ce troupeau qu'on appelle société, placés dans les mêmes circonstances, feront tous les mêmes choses si des motifs plus puissants ne les en détournent. On ne saura donc jamais bien à qui l'on a affaire ...' (*Oeuvres complètes*, III, p. 8).

of society certain characteristics came to be esteemed; 'it soon became necessary to have them or to affect them; it was necessary for one's own advantage to show oneself other than one actually was. To be and to seem came to be two completely different things . . .'. The result is a society made up of 'artificial men and imitation passions',[41] men whose needs and pleasures are no longer those of the state of nature. When Rousseau declares that 'social man' always draws from the judgement of others the 'feeling of his own existence', he establishes a basis for (among other things) what will be elsewhere his criticism of the arts of imitation and, in particular, a couple of years later, his denunciation of the theatre, in the *Lettre à D'Alembert*.

Stung by D'Alembert's proposal in the *Encyclopédie* article 'Genève' (1757) that Geneva would benefit from the establishment of a theatre, Rousseau passionately denounces the evils that have traditionally been associated with actors and plays[42] and goes on to claim that acting is by its very nature insincere and fraudulent. As for the traditional notions that tragedy 'purges the passions' and comedy *'castigat ridendo mores'*, Rousseau finds this so-called defence to be close to the opposite of the truth. Tragic heroes are not likely to affect any spectator with sympathy or pity, he writes, for these kings and warriors occupy a place too far above his. On the other hand passions are not 'corrected' but aroused by their theatrical portrayal, and Rousseau chooses to cite his own example: 'One need only . . . consult the state of one's heart at the end of a tragedy'. Since among opposing interests the author is forced to choose not 'those passions he wants us to love' but 'those that we love already',[43] Rousseau concludes that the 'general effect of the theatre is to reinforce national character, augment natural inclinations and give new energy to all the passions'. There is worse yet: in 'most of the plays of the French theatre you will find . . . abominable monsters and atrocious acts . . . [that] commoners . . . should not suppose possible', presented, moreover, 'garnished with all the brilliance of fine verse'.

Comedy, instead of correcting vices, teaches us to laugh at other people, and to prove it Rousseau chooses Molière, 'the most perfect comic author whose works are known to us'.

---

[41] 'un assemblage d'hommes artificiels et de passions factices' (*Oeuvres complètes*, III, p. 192).

[42] A detailed bibliography of the rekindled debate in France and Geneva in the seventeenth and eighteenth centuries on the old subject of the morality of the theatre is found in the Fuchs critical edition of the *Lettre*, pp. 195–204.

[43] 'Il ne faut . . . que consulter l'état de son cœur à la fin d'une Tragédie . . . Nous ne partageons pas les affections de tous les personnages, il est vrai; car leurs intérêts étant opposés, il faut bien que l'Auteur nous en fasse préférer quelqu'un, autrement nous n'en prendrions point du tout; mais, loin de choisir pour cela les passions qu'il veut nous faire aimer, il est forcé de choisir celles que nous aimons' (*Lettre*, pp. 27–8).

His greatest care is to make goodness and simplicity appear ridiculous, place wiles and lies on the side the spectator sympathizes with; his honourable characters do nothing but talk, while the unjust act and are usually rewarded with the most brilliant success ...[44]

In his notorious analysis of *The Misanthrope* Rousseau claims that Alceste, whom he finds sincere and upright, is made to appear ridiculous in a society he is really too good for. A variety of plays by Racine, Voltaire and others, present him with further examples of what he says will be a spectator's sympathy with the wicked or with extremes of passion in tragedy or willingness to gloat over the fate of a basically innocent comic victim.

There follows a denunciation of acting as imitation. Here Rousseau develops his attack on the theatre in a way consonant with his analysis of the alienation that man, according to him, necessarily experiences in modern society. Acting, he states, is

the art of feigning, of putting on a character not one's own, of appearing different from what one is, of showing emotion while feeling none, of saying something other than what one thinks as naturally as if one really thought it and finally forgetting one's own place through the habit of taking someone else's.[45]

The actor, who 'makes a spectacle of himself for money', is therefore worthy of the low esteem in which traditionally he has been held.

Although both Rousseau and Diderot in the *Paradoxe* hold that the actor, by conscious choice and by art, is imitating someone else, they draw from this radically opposed conclusions that serve as the bases for contrasting critical attitudes. For Diderot what counts is the *art* of imitation, as the spectator is affected by it: Diderot's approach to drama is thus, finally, aesthetic and interests itself primarily in the nature of the immediate effect of the acting upon the audience. For Rousseau what is important is the moral effect on the conduct of daily life of the ordinary spectator: an early 'sociological' mode of criticism. Moreover, what is important for Diderot, here as in the *Salons* or 'Les Deux amis de Bourbonne', is the artist's understanding, intelligence, technique; what concerns Rousseau is, rather, his sincerity.

---

[44] 'Son plus grand soin est de tourner la bonté et la simplicité en ridicule, et de mettre la ruse et le mensonge du parti pour lequel on prend intérêt; ses honnêtes gens ne sont que des gens qui parlent; ses vicieux sont des gens qui agissent, et que les plus brillants succès favorisent le plus souvent ...' (*Lettre*, p. 45).

[45] '... le talent du Comédien [est l]'art de se contrefaire, de revêtir un autre caractère que le sien, de paraître différent de ce qu'on est, de se passionner de sang-froid, de dire autre chose que ce qu'on pense aussi naturellement que si l'on le pensait réellement, et d'oublier enfin sa propre place à force de prendre celle d'autrui' (*Lettre*, p. 106).

Literature and education

Rousseau's moral approach to literature, his interest in education and his fascination with how he came to be what he is lead him naturally to consider the role of reading in childhood, and his remarks on that subject include reflections on such diverse subjects as authorial intention, the biographical roots of literature and the ways in which reading affects different social classes differently. His remarks on the effects of poetry or novels are as moralistic as the statements he makes concerning dramatic literature in the *Lettre à D'Alembert*, and they too are argued on the basis of personal experience.

La Nouvelle Héloïse (1761) does not contain a lengthy programme of education, and the role of books therein is barely mentioned. Saint-Preux proposes to his pupil, Julie, no 'books about love', for what could books teach them? 'our hearts tell us more about it than they'. For an example of the language and style of genuine passion Rousseau sends the reader to *La Nouvelle Héloïse* itself; his description in the Second Preface[46] of the language of true love is particularly significant when one considers that this is the period in which literary style is beginning to shift from the 'merely decorative' to 'suggestive magic':

Read a love letter written by an author in his study, by a *bel esprit* who wants to shine; if he has any fire at all in his head his letter will, as they say, burn the page; the heat won't go any further. You will be charmed, even moved, perhaps, but with a passing, dry emotion that will leave with you nothing more to remember than words. On the contrary, a letter that love really dictated, a letter from a truly impassioned lover, will be limp, diffuse, longwinded, disorderly, repetitious ... Nothing striking, nothing notable; you remember neither words, nor expressions, nor phrases; you admire nothing, you're not struck by anything. Nevertheless your soul is touched ...[47]

This is the effect of 'truth', Rousseau concludes, and his reader notes that that effect is based on style, a style that is not 'merely' concerned with 'decoration' and that is not in conformity with the laws of taste.

Books are largely banished from Émile's education. Rousseau develops

---

[46] 'Préface de Julie, ou Entretien sur les romans'.
[47] 'Lisez une lettre d'amour faite par un Auteur dans son cabinet, par un bel esprit qui veut briller. Pour peu qu'il ait de feu dans la tête, sa lettre va, comme on dit, brûler le papier; la chaleur n'ira pas plus loin. Vous serez enchanté, même agité peut-être; mais d'une agitation passagère et sèche, qui ne vous laissera que des mots pour tout souvenir. Au contraire, une lettre que l'amour a réellement dictée; une lettre d'un Amant vraiment passionné, sera lâche, diffuse, toute en longueurs, en désordre, en répétitions ... Rien de saillant, rien de remarquable; on ne retient ni mots, ni tours, ni phrases; on n'admire rien, l'on n'est frappé de rien. Cependant on se sent l'âme attendrie ...' (*Oeuvres complètes*, II, p. 15).

the reasons at length in his moral attack on La Fontaine's fable, 'The Crow and the Fox'. Children will readily understand from it, Rousseau says, not that they shouldn't let themselves be seduced by flattery, but rather that they can seduce others. Since 'reading is the scourge of childhood' his Émile will hardly know what a book is before the age of twelve. When the time comes Rousseau has a suitable book for him, and one alone: *Robinson Crusoe*, 'the most felicitous treatise concerning natural education'. But the tutor gives his pupil only the middle of the book, the part on the island, presenting it not as a good story but as a model of self-sufficiency.

Rousseau's wariness of books for children appears to stem from his reflections on his own childhood. He describes in his autobiography how in his earliest years his father and he would spend the night reading novels together, and how thus was formed in him 'an understanding of the passions unique for my age. I had no idea of things, and already I was acquainted with all the sentiments ... [developing in this way] bizarre and novelistic notions about human life which experience and reflection have never been able to cure me of.' When he was seven he began to read various historical works and Plutarch, Ovid, La Bruyère. Plutarch was his favourite and helped him develop his 'free, republican spirit, proud, indomitable character' which has never failed to 'torment' him. Here again, literature is valued as a source of moral reactions, but at least sometimes now those reactions are virtuous.

In his discussion of the origins of *La Nouvelle Héloïse* in Book IX of the *Confessions* Rousseau sketches the complicated intertwining of a novelist's life and writing; in retrospect it seems almost a model of romantic 'biographical' criticism. He began writing his novel to fill idle moments with the figment of 'an ideal world which my creative imagination soon peopled with beings in accord with my heart', including a lover and friend with whom Rousseau 'identified' himself 'as much as possible'. In the middle of his 'delirium', however, he encountered and fell in love with Madame d'Houdetot, and soon when he wanted to think about Julie he could only think of Madame d'Houdetot: first life imitates art, then art imitates life. But how could he, the severe enemy of 'those effeminate books that breathe love and sensuality', allow himself to publish a novel? Unable to stop himself, he hoped at least that 'the love of the good, which has never left my heart' had turned his 'folly' towards useful ends. He finds that his novel about a virtuous woman who has 'conquered' her youthful faults and 'become virtuous again' is in that respect 'useful', and he asks the reader to note also a useful allegory that he has tried to incorporate. At this particular time in which the Christian and the philosophical 'parties' were at each other's throats instead of 'reciprocally desiring to enlighten, to convince each other and lead each other into the path of truth', he aimed secretly with his portrayal of the mutual respect of Christian Julie and philosophe Wolmar to 'soften their reciprocal hatred by destroying their prejudices and showing to each party the merit and virtue of the other'.

Rousseau was not a literary critic like Voltaire or even Diderot: he did not write about authors or works in order to define their particular art or probe its aesthetic effect. But he was an important forerunner of Romantic literary criticism because of his awareness of the ways in which a society and its literary productions act on each other, his emphasis on the autobiographical and social origins of the literary text and his insistence on judging first by his own feelings.[48] His 'literary' works and his various treatises are in agreement on the ultimate social importance of literature; a general understanding of that importance had to replace the notion of literature as trivial entertainment (a notion held by many critics, particularly of the novel, in the eighteenth century) before Romantic writers like Victor Hugo[49] could hope to reclaim persuasively for the poet and writer a role of prophet and seer.

L'Encyclopédie, Marmontel, journalists, other writers

Few of the many other writers on literary matters in the second half of the eighteenth century in France wrote as memorably or with as much originality as Voltaire, Diderot and Rousseau. More often than not they merely repeated, or elaborated on, the thoughts of their predecessors. Yet as we trace their remarks from the 1750s through the 1780s we shall note a certain increasing disaffection with the 'rules' accompanied by increasing emphasis on imagination, the freedom of genius, originality.

L'Encyclopédie, 1751–65

The articles in the *Encyclopédie* devoted wholly or in part to literary matters take a conservative critical stance in general, insisting on models, rules and propriety, the hierarchy and the separation of genres. They make good taste the critic's criterion. An imaginative or creative use of

---

[48] Wellek (*Modern Criticism*, I, pp. 62–3) finds Rousseau 'hardly a literary critic in the strict sense' but notes that his 'importance for literary criticism is ... in the general impulse he gave to the primitivistic view of poetry and to the whole "conjectural" history of society ... To define what Rousseau contributed to criticism by his attack on civilization, his exaltation of individuality, imagination, and revery, and his insight into the connection between man and nature would be an almost impossible task, merging into the general history of ideas.'

[49] And numerous predecessors, traced extensively by Bénichou in *Sacre*.

decorative imagery is for them a writer's most acceptable kind of originality. The literary articles also note, however, several difficulties that such a stance cannot resolve. Firstly, in this advanced society, so confident in 'progress', the quality of contemporary literature seems to be in a state of stagnation or even decline; this seeming contradiction needs to be resolved. Secondly, it is observed that the requirements of taste and propriety and the desire for maximum moral or didactic usefulness do not always work well together. Thirdly, repeated examples continue to show that the 'genius' does not always abide by the rules, and increasingly substitutes for the rules are sought.

Writers and literary works are not treated as such in the *Encyclopédie*, but both aesthetics and literary genres are discussed under various headings; they are not, however, a principal subject and in general do not receive highly original treatment. D'Alembert, in his 'Discours préliminaire', sketched a rapid survey of French literature since the Renaissance, and wondered if it had not already peaked in the seventeenth century. Diderot wrote the article on 'Beau' and may have had a role in the composition of 'Génie', now attributed to Saint-Lambert. Marmontel and the Chevalier de Jaucourt, in particular, contributed numerous articles on literary subjects.

In the long article 'Critique, s.f., (*Belles-lettres*)' Marmontel tries to resolve the dilemma of taste versus creativity. He explains that the good critic assembles an ideal 'model' from the 'excellent qualities' of those works that constantly have been recognized as having superior 'merit' and then compares to this ideal the works under examination. A 'superior critic' will 'have in his imagination as many different models as there are genres'. He is thus obliged to be learned, but he must also possess qualities of imagination and sentiment:

Boileau, one of the men of his age who had most fully studied the ancients and had best mastered the art of applying their beauties to good effect, never judged well except by comparison. The result of this was that he did justice to Racine, the successful imitator of Euripides ... and gave faint praise to Corneille, who resembled no one else ... And how could Boileau, who imagined so little, have been a good judge in matters of imagination? How could he be truly expert in matters of the pathetic, since in his entire work not a trace of feeling has ever slipped out?[50]

---

[50] '... Boileau, l'un des hommes de son siècle qui avait le plus étudié les anciens, et qui possédait le mieux l'art de mettre leurs beautés en oeuvre ... n'a jamais bien jugé que par comparaison. De là vient qu'il a rendu justice à Racine, l'heureux imitateur d'Euripide ... et loué froidement Corneille, qui ne ressemblai[t] à rien ... Et comment Boileau, qui a si peu imaginé, aurait-il été un bon juge dans la partie de l'imagination? Comment aurait-il été un vrai connaisseur dans la partie du pathétique, lui à qui il n'est jamais échappé un trait de sentiment dans tout ce qu'il a pu produire?'

From this Marmontel draws the general rule that a superior critic will allow the genius his freedom, asking of him only great things and encouraging him to produce them, while an inferior critic requires only 'cold obedience' to the rules and 'servile imitation'.

Let us not then be surprised, Marmontel continues, if, as taste becomes more demanding, imagination becomes more timid, whereas almost all the great geniuses, from Homer and Lucretius to Milton and Corneille, appeared at a time when 'ignorance' on the part of an untutored public 'left them an open course ... Corneille would have sacrificed most of the beauties of his plays ... if he had been as severe in his composition as he was in his *examens*, but fortunately he composed his works in his own way and judged himself in the manner of Aristotle'.[51] Is good taste, then, an obstacle to genius? No, continues Marmontel: 'good taste is a brave and virile sentiment, which loves great things especially and fires up as well as enlightens genius. That taste that constricts and enervates it is a fearful and puerile taste, which in wanting to polish everything, ends up weakening it'.[52]

The article 'Génie' defines its subject as 'breadth of mind, strength of imagination and activity of soul':[53] the soul of 'the man of *genius* ... interested in all that is in nature, receives no idea that does not awaken a sentiment, everything animates it and everything is kept'. Genius often diverges from taste:

Genius is a pure gift of nature: what it produces is the work of a moment; taste is the work of study and time; it results from knowledge of a multitude of established or supposed rules; it brings into existence beauties which are only conventional. For something to be beautiful according to the rules of taste, it must be elegant, polished, wrought without the appearance of labour: to be a work of *genius* it must sometimes be careless, must have an appearance of irregularity, roughness, wildness. Sublimity and *genius* shine in Shakespeare like lightning in a long night, while Racine is always beautiful: Homer is full of *genius*, and Virgil full of elegance.[54]

[51] '... les temps où l'ignorance leur laissait une libre carrière ... Corneille eût sacrifié la plupart des beautés de ses pièces ... s'il eût été aussi sévère dans sa composition qu'il l'a été dans ses examens; mais heureusement il composait d'après lui, et se jugeait d'après Aristote'.

[52] '... le bon goût est un sentiment courageux et mâle qui aime surtout les grandes choses, et qui échauffe le génie en même temps qu'il l'éclaire. Le goût qui le gêne et qui l'amollit est un goût craintif et puérile qui veut tout polir et qui affaiblit tout.'

[53] 'l'étendu de l'esprit, la force de l'imagination, et l'activité de l'âme'.

[54] 'Le génie est un pur don de la nature; ce qu'il produit est l'ouvrage d'un moment; le goût est l'ouvrage de l'étude et du temps; il tient à la connaissance d'une multitude de règles ou établies ou supposées; il fait produire des beautés qui ne sont que de convention. Pour qu'une chose soit belle selon les règles du goût, il faut qu'elle soit élégante, finie, travaillée sans le paraître: pour être de génie, il faut quelquefois qu'elle soit négligée; qu'elle ait l'air irrégulier, escarpé, sauvage. Le sublime et le génie brillent dans Shakespeare comme des éclairs dans une longue nuit, et Racine est toujours beau; Homère est plein de génie, et Virgile d'élégance.'

Since the rules and laws of taste can hobble genius, it 'breaks them in order to fly to the sublime, pathetic, great'.

The troubling and unavoidable example of Shakespeare comes back once again in Jaucourt's article 'Stratford'. Despite Shakespeare's 'jokes in bad taste' (*mauvaises plaisanteries*) and juxtaposition of tragic and comic elements, Jaucourt strives to understand his greatness, in terms of his originality, bold imagination and eminent command of the art of stirring the passions. Jaucourt's article 'Roman' ('Novel') praises the new trends exemplified by the English novelists Richardson and Fielding; they have turned fiction toward useful ends and used it to inspire agreeably 'the love of good morals and virtue, through simple, natural and ingenious scenes of life's events'. Jaucourt finds that Rousseau's recent *La Nouvelle Héloïse* maintains the excellent tradition of novels written with 'this good taste', perhaps the only kind of 'instruction left for a nation so corrupt that any other kind would be useless'.[55] Social usefulness is a desirable goal of other literary forms as well, such as the ideal theatre that D'Alembert recommends for the city of Geneva in his article 'Genève', the article that occasioned Rousseau's *Lettre à D'Alembert*.

Marmontel

Voltaire's disciple, Jean-François Marmontel, is remembered principally as the author of the *Contes moraux*, of an autobiography and of a large number of articles, most of them written for the *Encyclopédie*, that he collected and published alphabetically in 1787 under the title, *Éléments de littérature*. He prefaced the latter with an 'Essai sur le goût'. After a definition that begins

Taste, in the narrowest sense of the word taken figuratively, is the keen and ready sentiment of the qualities of art, of its refinements, its most exquisite beauties, and even its most imperceptible and most seductive flaws.[56]

Marmontel goes on to examine the sources of taste, the rise and decadence of good taste and the role of the critic as its defender. There are both natural and cultivated tastes; the latter, he says, should strive to remain as close to the former as possible. As society becomes more demanding under the influence of its 'institutions, customs, opinions, fantasies', taste becomes 'variable and diverse', affected by notions of 'propriety [*bienséance*], nobility, dignity, politeness, elegance, attractiveness, delicacy, in

---

[55] Marmontel, on the other hand, strongly condemned Rousseau's novel on moral grounds in his 'Essai sur les romans, considérés du côté moral'.

[56] 'Le *goût*, dans l'acception la plus étroite de ce mot pris figurément, est le sentiment vif et prompt des finesses de l'art, de ses délicatesses, de ses beautés les plus exquises, et de même de ses défauts les plus imperceptibles et les plus séduisants' (*Oeuvres complètes*, XII, p. 1).

short all the refinements of the art of pleasure and enjoyment'. Marmontel traces a history of tasteful literature from Homer to contemporary times; like D'Alembert's history of philosophy in the *Preliminary Discourse* of the *Encyclopédie* it skips over the Middle Ages and Renaissance writers. Marmontel finds that the laws of good taste have become more severe in modern times than for the Greeks and Romans because the art of printing and the place of women in the modern audience make decency (*pudeur*) 'the first of the graces to which our writers must make sacrifice':

> And how greatly this art of eluding, veiling, dissimulating, of making the expression timid and modest, even when the thought is neither, how greatly this art must have had to refine itself in a language where gallantry and love have been so knowledgeably and subtly analysed![57]

He notes further that art does not 'run counter to nature' in order to achieve good taste but rather 'improves and embellishes it while imitating it', 'choosing in [nature] those traits, forms, aspects, accidents in which truth gives the most charm to imitation',[58] remembering always that the 'intention of art ... is to interest and please'.[59]

Among his examples of good taste in modern literature the following three are typical of him and his contemporaries: Madame de Sévigné shows an 'exquisite feeling for social convention [*le sentiment exquis des convenances sociales*]'; La Fontaine has a 'profound feeling for natural proprieties [*le sentiment profond des convenances naturelles*]'; one of the many genres in which Voltaire presents a model of good taste is tragedy:

> less finished than Racine, less polished, less pure, less attentive or, if one prefers, less skilled at binding together all the springs of the action, but more passionate, more fertile, more varied, more profoundly pathetic, and more faithful to local customs and manners, which Racine sometimes intermingled too much with our own.[60]

Certain critical attitudes reappear frequently in the *Éléments*; it would be possible to extract from the various articles devoted, largely, to the

---

[57] 'Et combien cet art d'éluder, de voiler, de dissimuler, de rendre l'expression timide et modeste, lors même que la pensée ne l'est pas, combien cet art a dû se raffiner dans une langue où la galanterie et l'amour ont été si subtilement et si savamment analysés!'(*Oeuvres complètes*, XII, p. 19).

[58] '... l'art ne consiste pas à contrarier la nature, mais à l'améliorer, à l'embellir en l'imitant ... en choisissant en elle les traits, les formes, les aspects, les accidents où la vérité donne le plus de charme à l'imitation' (*Oeuvres complètes*, XII, pp. 30–1).

[59] 'l'intention de l'art ... est d'intéresser et de plaire' (*Oeuvres complètes*, XII, p. 32).

[60] 'moins fini que Racine, moins châtié, moins pur, moins attentif, ou, si l'on veut, moins adroit à lier ensemble tous les ressorts de l'action; mais plus véhément, plus fécond, plus varié, plus profondément pathétique, et plus fidèle aux mœurs locales, auxquelles Racine, quelquefois, avait trop mêlé de nos mœurs' (*Oeuvres complètes*, XII, p. 63).

description of the parts of literary works ('Acte', 'Action', 'Alexandrin', 'Allégorie' and so on) and to various technical terms ('Amplification', 'Anacréontique', 'Anapeste', 'Antithèse') a set of prescriptions that form an excellent compendium[61] of the enduring legacy of classicism on the eve of the Revolution.

Journalists and critics

L'Année littéraire, the critical journal published from 1754 by Élie-Catherine Fréron and continued after his death in 1776 by his son, Stanislas, is today known best for Voltaire's enmity to its founder (the butt of his quatrain on the serpent who bit Fréron and died) and its hostility to the philosophic movement. Fréron was an outspoken defender of classical values and a sarcastic enemy of whatever he deemed irreligion, poor taste, illiterate versification, triteness, faults against usage. He defines the latter as 'the ways of speaking employed by good writers and polite society'.[62] He concerns himself with a broad range of published work, including periodicals and books on medicine, history and language as well as poetry, drama, fiction; his articles are largely descriptive and typically conclude with a critical evaluation.

Like the philosophes, Fréron recognizes that literary works of genius must be characterized both by imagination and by taste; the former rapidly and brilliantly assembles and compares ideas, while the latter 'chooses, polishes, rectifies'.[63] He finds the new, serious comedy, 'these dramatic portraits of *bourgeois* calamity, however much they are drawn from nature and humanity, however much more suitable perhaps than the misfortunes of kings for the stage, since they have a broader moral aim ... as inferior to good and true comedy as the novel is to the epic poem'.[64] Racine's imitators, wanting to copy the 'sustained elegance, inexpressible sweetness, enchanting style that characterize him' fall into the 'sweetish, the pastoral, and often the commonplace'.[65] On the appearance of *Candide*, which is rumoured to be by Voltaire despite the latter's denials, Fréron writes that it cannot be by Voltaire, because its pessimism is contrary to Voltaire's whole previous production, and because of

---

[61] Jacques Scherer, for example, in his *Dramaturgie classique en France* (Paris, n.d. [1950]) refers frequently to the *Eléments* to characterize various traits of classical theatre, noting that, in the case of the unity of action, Marmontel has expressed 'la doctrine à laquelle obéissent les œuvres classiques, mais qu'aucun classique n'a définie avec cette clarté' (p. 102).

[62] 'les manières de parler adoptées par les bons écrivains et par le monde poli' (*Année littéraire*, 1759, VIII, p. 151).

[63] *Année littéraire*, 1759, I, pp. 323–4.   [64] *Année littéraire*, 1759, I, p. 331.

[65] *Année littéraire*, 1759, IV, p. 7.

its extravagance and vulgarity.[66] In answering a provincial correspondent who has challenged his praise of a minor writer seven-eighths of whose works, he admits, are 'without wit and without style', Fréron reveals a characteristic critical attitude: the writer, the Abbé de l'Attaignant, 'knows it, he feels it, he sincerely agrees. Thus, the arm of Criticism should not bear down upon a writer like him but hold its thunder for the mediocre and insolent'.[67]

Since a principal aim of censorship under the Old Regime was to avoid controversy, published criticism tended to be conventional. The major interest of the monthly *Correspondance littéraire* of Grimm, Diderot and Meister stems from the quality of many of its contributions (particularly Diderot's, including his *Salons*), but the fact that it was an unpublished (and therefore uncensored) handwritten newsletter adds to its credibility as a witness and judge of the literary products of the time. The audience of the *Correspondance littéraire*, in most cases royalty and aristocrats in various courts scattered around central Europe, were eager to be kept informed about the latest developments: plays and operas, new actresses, debates in the French Academy, recent books. Unable to be in Paris, they were provided with a description and, sometimes, with various editorial asides on related subjects.

Criticism of literature in the *Correspondance littéraire* is varied and much less stuffy than Fréron's, as can be seen in several examples from the years 1775–7. In these years the bulk of the *Correspondance* was penned by Jacques-Henri Meister.[68] In March 1775, Meister reviewed the first performances of Beaumarchais's *Barber of Seville*. Although he seems to have liked the play, he certainly did not suspect that it would become a lasting classic: 'without having the madcap verve of Molière's farces [this comedy] is still the work of a very witty man'. In November of the same year the reviewer presented a most unusual new novel: Restif de la Bretonne's *Le Paysan perverti (The Perverted Peasant)*. He finds the book uneven and full of bad taste: 'this book leads the mind past the vilest and most disgusting scenes of life, and yet it is interesting, captivating', and concludes that 'while wishing that the author's brush had been more modest, the form of his composition

---

[66] *Année littéraire*, 1759, II, pp. 203–10. Fréron is probably being ironical here, but it is plain that he has no idea of how extraordinary *Candide* is. For a more perceptive and favourable criticism of *Candide* in Grimm's contemporary review of *Candide* in the *Correspondance littéraire*, 1 March 1759.

[67] *Année littéraire*, 1759, VI, p. 311.

[68] He had taken over the work of writer-editor Frédéric-Melchior Grimm a couple of years earlier. Kölving and Carriat, *Inventaire*, I, pp. xv–xl, give an excellent summary description of the publication, authorship and contents of the *Correspondance littéraire*. The place of this *correspondance littéraire* among numerous others is discussed in Schlobach, 'Literarische Korrespondenzen'.

more regular and especially the choice of his characters less low, we have to admit that it's been a long time since we read a French work with more spirit, invention and genius. Wherever is genius going to nest from now on?'

Comments like these are based more on an open-minded reader's or spectator's reactions than on comparison with 'models'; they also show that the writer of the *Correspondance* shared some of his colleague Diderot's thinking. Meister quoted Diderot in December 1775, complaining about critics who seem to seek only flaws in what they read. 'I compare them to a man walking along the seashore concerned with picking up only sand and pebbles. It's pure gold I look for there, and provided that I can find a few grains of it to gather carefully, I don't care about all the rest.' Such an attitude is the opposite of that of the critic La Harpe; the *Correspondance littéraire* describes the latter in January 1777 as 'supporting the cause of good taste' with an 'almost inquisitorial zeal'.

In March 1776, a considerable stir was occasioned by the appearance of the first volumes of Le Tourneur's Shakespeare translations. The writer tries to understand why Shakespeare is judged so differently in England and in France and to measure the effects of partiality and of the relative degree of cultural and literary development in each country. Then he makes a comparison that strives to be dispassionate, while at the same time respecting the views of Voltaire, considered the leading contemporary French writer of tragedy:

if Shakespeare's plots are vaster and more varied, those of Corneille and Racine have a nobler simplicity, a more sustained and more regular action. Would not [an impartial judge] also admit that the first, in their greater disorder, have a more theatrical and more arresting effect? How can it be denied, when M. de Voltaire himself agreed?[69]

The writer goes on to examine various aspects of Shakespeare's theatre – its undeniable interest, its unevenness and 'mixture of tones', the danger it represents for young French writers tempted to imitate 'a genre which will never suit either the manners or the spirit of the nation' – and he compares Shakespeare to 'a colossal statue, of an imposing and formidable conception but executed with sometimes unpolished, sometimes careless and sometimes the finest craftsmanship, inspiring in me even more astonishment than admiration', while Racine is 'like a statue as regular

[69] '. . . si les plans de Shakespeare sont plus vastes et plus variés, ceux de Corneille et de Racine ont une simplicité plus noble, une conduite plus soutenue et plus régulière[.] Mais n'avouerait-il pas aussi que les premiers, dans leur plus grand désordre, sont d'un effet plus théâtral et plus attachant? Comment le nier, lorsque M. de Voltaire en est convenu lui-même?' (*Correspondance littéraire*, XI, p. 217).

in its proportions as the Belvedere Apollo ... despite a few weak and
languid details, it at least always charms me by the nobility, elegance
and purity of its style'.[70]

The subject of Shakespeare versus French tragedy comes back at least
twice more in 1776; in November, apropos of a dispute between Voltaire
and a French-Irish writer named Rutlidge, the critic finds a particular
point of superiority in Shakespeare. French writers do not show mob
scenes, as Shakespeare does in *Julius Caesar*; if they are essential to the
plot they are described in a *récit*:

> we dare to suggest that such a *récit*, even if it were written by Racine,
> would never produce the effect of the scene in action. If this assertion is not
> incontestably true one might as well abandon dramatic art and limit our
> pleasures to hearing epic poetry declaimed. It follows that the action of the
> English theatre often offends our taste, and the *récits* of the French stage
> almost always weaken our interest.[71]

Wellek has called Jean-François de la Harpe, disciple and friend of
Voltaire, 'the most influential codifier of French taste' before and during
the revolutionary period.[72] In his extensive critical writings from the
1770s till his death in 1803, in many cases originally written for the
Mercure de France and later collected under the general title of 'Littérature
et Critique' in his published *Oeuvres*, he shows himself to be a harsh
judge of the unclassical and the unfamiliar. In reacting to a new translation of Dante he criticizes the poem even more than the translation.
The very title of the *Divine Comedy*, he says, is proof of the 'gross
ignorance [*ignorance grossière*] of Dante's century'. 'They call *comedy*
a work which has nothing in common with the dramatic genre, and
they give the epithet *divine* to a shapeless rhapsody that has no plan,
no interest, and is most boringly monotonous'.[73]

---

[70] '... une statue colossale dont l'idée est imposante et terrible, mais dont l'exécution
tantôt brute, tantôt négligée, et tantôt du travail le plus précieux, m'inspire encore
plus d'étonnement que [d']admiration. [Racine], comme une statue aussi régulière
dans ses proportions que l'Apollon du Belvédère ... malgré quelques détails faibles
et languissants, me charme au moins toujours par la noblesse, l'élégance et la
pureté de son style' (*Ibid.*, XI, p. 218).

[71] '... nous osons avancer qu'un tel récit, quand même il serait écrit par Racine, ne
produirait jamais l'effet de la scène en action. Si cette assertion n'est pas d'une
vérité incontestable, il faudrait abandonner l'art dramatique et borner nos plaisirs à
entendre déclamer l'épopée. Il en résulte que l'action du théâtre anglais blesse
souvent le goût, et que les récits de la scène française affaiblissent presque toujours
l'intérêt' (*Ibid.*, XI, pp. 380–1).

[72] Wellek, *Modern Criticism*, I, p. 66.

[73] 'On y appelle *comédie* un ouvrage qui n'a rien de commun avec le genre
dramatique; et l'on y donne l'épithète de *divine* à une rapsodie informe, sans aucun
plan, sans aucun intérêt, de la plus ennuyeuse monotonie ...' (*Oeuvres*, XV, p. 234).

Despite his conservatism La Harpe believes in progress in literature, often calling to task other critics (like Clément and Ginguené) who appear to find contemporary writers greatly inferior to their predecessors.

The role of translators

In the last third of the century two poets and translators, Jacques Delille, noted particularly for his translations of Virgil, and Pierre Le Tourneur, translator of Thomson, Young, and Shakespeare, prefaced their translations with essays of particular critical significance. They note various ways in which the French literature of their time is inadequate and intend to do something about it. Their commentaries provide a bridge between the France-centred neo-classical views of most of the critics of the age and the new spirit of internationalism and the new literary models that will be suggested at the turn of the century by Madame de Staël and Chateaubriand.

Le Tourneur's prefaces to his translations of Shakespeare 'completely destroy the classical aesthetic in the name of the rehabilitation of the rights of genius'.[74] In the Preliminary Discourse to his translation of Young's *Night Thoughts* (1769) Le Tourneur criticizes French poets for too often 'quenching their talent by dint of taste and servility'; he proposes the English poet as a model: struck by misfortune, Young is possessed of genius, imagination, sensitivity: 'Be apprised that he is English and that he lives in the country, that he writes what he feels and what he thinks as those feelings and ideas follow each other in his soul, and you will easily guess the tone, genre, beauties and flaws of the work.' This is an endorsement, however measured, for a personal and sentimental poetry little practised in France between the Renaissance and the end of the eighteenth century.

Delille begins the Preliminary Discourse of his translation of the *Georgics* (1769) with various remarks on the utility and beauty of the subject, on the art of Virgil, and also on French literary attitudes of his time and the general impoverishment of poetry other than dramatic poetry in his country. He agrees that the *Georgics* cannot be as interesting as dramatic poems but adds that the 'exclusive taste' of French writers for drama is

a veritable disaster for our literature. The English, more sensible than we, encourage all kinds of poetry, and so they have agreeable poems on all kinds of subjects and a literature that is infinitely more varied than ours ... Moreover we know that the style of tragedy is nothing other than that of noble conversation, the style of comedy, that of familiar conversation. Our

[74] Pichois, 'Voltaire et Shakespeare', p. 187.

language, confined hitherto within these two genres, has remained timid and needy and will never acquire wealth or strength if, always imprisoned on the stage, it does not dare to venture freely over all the subjects susceptible of great and beautiful poetry.[75]

He finds that the authors of poems on the arts or on the beauties of nature have opened for the French language 'a new world, from which it can bring back innumerable riches'.

In commenting on his own translation he notes several differences between Virgil's Latin and the literary French of his time: 'haughty delicacy' of taste has impoverished French by rejecting a number of words and images; the desire to ape the aristocrats has led to the exclusive use of their 'circumspect' way of speaking. He states that the Romans lived in the public eye, where 'the effervescence of ambition [and] the enthusiasm of liberty agitated their passions violently'; more than the French they lived in the country and knew how better to portray physical objects, while the French specialize in expressing moral ideas.

The great wellsprings of the soul, the great outbursts of passion, these they would paint powerfully; our language knows how to portray with subtlety the nuances of these same passions, the delicacy of sentiment and the most imperceptible fibres of the soul ... They had words for all the products of the earth, and we for all the movements of the heart.[76]

Delille complains of the difficulties the French language imposes on the poet: obligatory articles, pronouns, prepositions; rarely permissible inversion; rules for the alexandrine; obligatory rhyme. He concludes, though, that the example of Boileau and Racine shows that French, 'handled with skill, subjugated by effort, can indeed descend without being base to the most common objects'. He is confident that translations help to enrich a language with the 'treasures of foreign tongues'.

Stendhal's pamphlet *Racine et Shakespeare* was not to appear until 1823, but it is clear that these two great models served as polar opposites for

[75] '... un véritable malheur pour notre littérature. Les Anglais, plus sensés que nous, encouragent tous les genres de poésie; aussi ont-ils des poèmes agréables sur toutes sortes de sujets, et une littérature infiniment plus variée que la nôtre ... D'ailleurs, on sait que le style de la tragédie n'est guère que celui de la conversation noble; le style de la comédie, celui de la conversation familière. Notre langue, resserrée jusqu'ici dans ces deux genres, est restée timide et indigente, et n'acquerra jamais ni richesse ni force, si, toujours emprisonnée sur la scène, elle n'ose se promener librement sur tous les sujets susceptibles de la grande et belle poésie' (*Oeuvres complètes*, II, pp. xv–xvi).

[76] 'Les grands ressorts de l'ame, les grands éclats des passions, voilà ce qu'ils ont dû peindre avec force: les nuances de ces mêmes passions, la délicatesse des sentiments, et les fibres les plus imperceptibles de l'âme; voilà ce que notre langue sait rendre avec finesse ... ils ont eu des mots pour toutes les productions de la terre, et nous pour tous les mouvements du cœur' (*Oeuvres complètes*, II, pp. xxix–xxx).

critical meditation already throughout the middle and late eighteenth century in France, representing harmony versus excitement, rules versus innovation, embellishment versus imagination. With a few rare exceptions that have been noted above, French critical thought of this period appears to be caught in the dilemma of holding on to what all were still convinced was a tradition of incomparable perfection, while struggling at the same time with the desire to bring 'progress' and at least a measure of cosmopolitanism to the literary arts as well as to the rest of society.[77]

Criticism as it was applied in the period to particular literary texts is characteristically descriptive, hasty, judgemental, piquant; it recalls what Diderot described in the *Encyclopédie* as the role of the journalist: 'publish extracts and judgements of works of literature, science and art as they appear'.[78] The most far-reaching thoughts come from Diderot and Rousseau, but they are not so much critics as theorists, laying a ground for the kind of criticism that would be written in following generations: thus, when they do comment on literary texts, they seem so much closer to Sainte-Beuve – and to us – than do Voltaire, Marmontel and the other classical judges of taste and propriety.

[77] The shift about to take place at the beginning of the Romantic period can be seen clearly if one confronts D'Alembert's disillusioned statement in the Preliminary Discourse of the *Encyclopédie*, 'Ne soyons donc pas étonnés que nos Ouvrages d'esprit soient en général inférieurs à ceux du siècle précédent', with Stendhal's firmly modern declaration in *Racine et Shakespeare* that 'Le *romanticisme* est l'art de présenter aux peuples les œuvres littéraires qui, dans l'état actuel de leurs habitudes et de leurs croyances, sont susceptibles de leur donner le plus de plaisir possible. Le *classicisme*, au contraire, leur présente la littérature qui donnait le plus grand plaisir à leurs arrière-grands-pères' (*Encyclopédie* (1751), I, p. xxxii; Stendhal, *Racine et Shakespeare* (Paris, 1970), p. 71).

[78] Quoted in Trenard, 'Presse', p. 170. See also 'Critique, s.m. (Belles-lett.)' by Abbé Mallet in the *Encyclopédie*.

23

German literary theory
from Gottsched to Goethe

Klaus L. Berghahn

The history of modern literary theory begins in Germany with Johann Christoph Gottsched's *Versuch einer Critischen Dichtkunst (An Essay in Critical Poetics*, 1730), a poetics that is novel in spite of itself. Introduced by a translation and commentary on Horace's *De Arte Poetica*, the first, general part of the poetics contains doctrines still indebted to the neo-classical tradition. But Gottsched's views on the theory of genres, the concept of taste, and on the role of the critic all point towards an imminent break with this tradition. The time between 1730 and 1751, when the fourth edition of the *Critische Dichtkunst* appeared and when Lessing made his debut as a literary critic, was a time of transformation, during which literary discourse was still dominated by the old concepts while new approaches were not yet strong enough to transform the old into something explicitly new. René Wellek, from a twentieth-century perspective, proposes as a meaningful starting-point for the history of modern literary theory the middle of the eighteenth century.[1] This perspective is still generally accepted, but it requires some qualification in the case of Germany, where change was slow in coming. Not until the end of the eighteenth century was the *Querelle des Anciens et des Modernes*, which Perrault had started in France in 1687, finally decided in favour of the Moderns.

The fact that German theory lived so long under the spell of antiquity and neo-classicism had much to do with the miserable state of literary life in Germany. As late as 1795 Goethe complained about the back-wardness of Germany's literary conditions which did not allow a national author to emerge. In his polemical essay 'Literarischer Sansculottismus', he speculates about the ideal historical conditions for a classical national literature: a great national past, national unity, a mature public, a sup-ply of exemplary works, and finally 'a centre for the formation of social life'.[2] Measured against such prerequisites, which in England and France had led to the rise of great national literatures, the state of affairs in literary Germany was truly appalling. Political and cultural particularism,

---

[1] Wellek, *History*, I, p. V.
[2] Goethe, 'Literarischer Sansculottismus', in *Goethes Werke*, ed. Erich Trunz (14 vols., Hamburg, 1948–64), XII, pp. 240f.

the religious polarization of north and south, censorship, the lack of a general copyright law, the exploitation of writers by publishers, and a general lack of sophistication made it almost impossible for a unified literary public to emerge. Even the term 'public' (*Publikum*) was unknown before the middle of the century, and Lessing, who had been struggling to make a living as a freelance writer since 1748, advised his brother in 1770 to seek 'a serious bourgeois occupation'. 'Even the happiest authorship is the most miserable handicraft', he added.[3]

There were concrete reasons why the Enlightenment spread but slowly in Germany, and why the process displayed considerable regional differences. Without going into the details of all the structural transformations of literary life, and without reducing literary theory to a mere reflection of socio-historical changes, it is important to note the interconnections between the production, distribution, and reception of literature. Then and now theory was not only an intra-literary but also a social phenomenon.[4]

I

As Goethe knew from experience, Germany had no political or cultural centre comparable to Paris or London. The German-speaking world did, however, have several smaller cultural centres which contributed to the rise of a national literature that reached its height by the end of the eighteenth century. From today's vantage-point one could even say that the diversity and richness of this literature is the result of a regionalism that extended well into the nineteenth century. Free imperial and commercial cities like Hamburg, Leipzig, and Zurich were the centres of the early Enlightenment. Berlin, a city considered by many as nothing but a garrison town with a king who was himself alienated from German culture, became a centre of the Enlightenment proper. Strasbourg and Frankfurt, albeit briefly, were meeting-places of the writers of the Storm and Stress movement, while the tiny principality of Weimar was even called the *Athènes des lettres* by Mme de Staël. One can scarcely overestimate the importance of these places for the assimilation and transformation of foreign literature and theory, especially those of France and England, and for the development of a German national literature.

Hamburg, the most prominent and richest of the free cities, was oriented toward England. Its civic life and literary societies were modelled on the example set by London, from where the influential Moral Weeklies were imported to the continent. Leipzig, the leading trade city with its three annual fairs, became the northern capital of the book trade. An

[3] G. E. Lessing to Karl Lessing, 4 January 1770.
[4] Cf. Kiesel and Münch, *Gesellschaft und Literatur im 18. Jahrhundert*.

elegant city, sometimes called 'le petit Paris', it was the first to give a German articulation to the classicism and Enlightenment of France. It was here that Gottsched hoped to realize his plans for the education of the German bourgeoisie with the help of French neo-classicism. Conservative Zurich, where a theocratic government censured all worldly books and banned the theatre and a free press, was the centre of literary theory during the early phase of the Enlightenment in the German-speaking world. The Moral Weeklies were imitated, English authors translated, and the poetic imagination freed from religious constraints to conquer the sublime. Strasbourg, albeit by accident and only temporarily, became the centre of the literary revolt of the Storm and Stress, which reacted against neo-classicism and celebrated ancient English literature and Shakespeare. In Frankfurt, if only during the year 1772, the critical journal of this movement, the *Frankfurter Gelehrte Anzeigen*, was published.

Why Weimar of all places, neither a commercial, political, nor cultural centre, grew into the literary capital and home of German classicism is something of a mystery. Even Goethe, its foremost inhabitant, was not aware of its prominence. He only recognized the existence of an 'invisible school of writers' who paved the way for a viable literature. If political unity and a national culture could be achieved only at the price of a revolution, he reasoned, then he would rather forgo a national literature: 'We do not wish for Germany those political upheavals which might prepare the way for classical works.'[5] The spirit of the French Revolution, to which Goethe alludes here, was exorcized in Germany by philosophical and aesthetic means. The Germans' lack of political action was compensated for by a spiritual revolution that became known in literature as Weimar Classicism and in philosophy as German Idealism.

This spiritual revolution in Germany was a product of the Enlightenment. 'Ours is the true age of criticism, an activity to which all else must be subordinated', Kant wrote in the Preface to his first Critique of 1781,[6] giving expression to one of the most important principles of the German Enlightenment, the claim of reason to universality. Three years later, in his famous answer to Zöllner's question 'What is Enlightenment?', he summed up the tendencies of his age with the definition: 'Enlightenment is man's emergence from his self-incurred immaturity.' To free himself from immaturity, man had to have the courage 'to use his own reason' as well as the 'freedom to make public use of his reason in all matters.'[7] Although Kant's claim for the intellectual freedom of

---

[5] 'Literarischer Sansculottismus', in *Goethes Werke*, XII, p. 241.

[6] Kant, *Kritik der reinen Vernunft*, in *Gesammelte Schriften*, ed. Preussische Akademie der Wissenschaften (Berlin, 1902–), IV, p. 9.

[7] Kant, 'What is Enlightenment?', in *Kant's Political Writings*, ed. Hans Reiss (second edn, Cambridge, 1991), pp. 54f.

reason would ultimately raise the political issues of freedom of speech and formation of public opinion under enlightened absolutism, his criticism was chiefly confined to epistemology, morality, and aesthetics – areas which none the less have a bearing on the formation of a literary public.[8] For literary theory, the turn to critical thinking meant a questioning of tradition and authority in order to achieve autonomy from the guidance of antiquity and its norms. Reason, critical reflection, and aesthetic awareness became the foundations of modern literary theory.

Gottsched's *Critische Dichtkunst* contains these tendencies in embryo. As the title indicates, critical examination of the poetological tradition was the order of the day, even if the result of this revaluation remained a prescriptive poetics of rules. Gottsched understood his poetics to be both a definition of the essentials of poetry and a guide for the critic. By 1730, the concept and practice of criticism had in fact already taken hold in Germany, as Gottsched's definition of the critic in his Preface shows: 'A critic is [. . .] a scholar who has acquired philosophical insight into the rules of the liberal arts and is thus in a position to examine rationally and judge correctly the beauties and flaws of any masterpiece.'[9] What he wanted to provide, in other words, was a philosophical grounding for literary criticism.

Although this new criticism continued to acknowledge the traditional rules and regulations of poetry, it acquired a new philosophical foundation. It no longer sufficed to appeal to the authority of Aristotle or to ancient models; the rules had to agree with reason and possess general validity. Reason became criticism's intellectual currency. The loss of traditional authority was compensated for by the anthropological argument that human nature is the same at all times and that all forms of representation must conform to the principle of naturalness: nature is reasonable, and reason is natural. In practical terms this meant that all imitations of nature must possess verisimilitude, that is, they must be in accordance with reason. The judgement of art no longer depended on the concept of *decorum* (i.e., expectations of a patron or court) but was guided instead by a universally binding system of norms. Hans Mayer has compared this system of poetic laws to the division of powers in Montesquieu's political theory: 'The artist belongs to the executive, the critic is the judge. Both are subordinate to the laws of the beautiful, a

---

[8] Cf. Habermas, *Strukturwandel der Öffentlichkeit*. For a more detailed discussion of the connection between literary criticism and the emergence of a literary public, see Klaus L. Berghahn, 'From classicist to classical literary criticism, 1730–1806', in Hohendahl (ed.), *History*, pp. 16–28.

[9] Gottsched, *Versuch einer Critischen Dichtkunst*, preface (not paginated). Wellek underestimates the importance of Gottsched's literary reforms when he merely comments that his work 'established a ponderous and pedantic local version of French neoclassicism' (Wellek, *History*, I, p. 144).

legislature whose laws claim universal validity.'[10] The dangers inherent in such regulative poetics and normative judgements are, of course, dogmatism and pedantry, to which many critics since Gottsched have fallen prey.

Gottsched had barely completed his poetics when the debates on taste in Paris and London threatened to undermine its systematic approach. A keen observer of foreign trends, Gottsched could not remain aloof from this discussion and valiantly tried to integrate the concept of taste into his poetics – but only by neutralizing it altogether. In a separate chapter, entitled 'On the Good Taste of the Poet', he argued that the poet 'may never take his directions from the taste of the world', for this would open the floodgates to subjective and arbitrary opinion; instead he must follow objective rules in order 'to purify the taste of his fatherland'. Without an educated readership, Gottsched thus had to rely on the trained taste of the poet who would produce art by following the rules. Against Du Bos's 'sixth sense' and the judgement of taste, he erected his natural order of reason: 'That taste is good which conforms to the rules which have been established by reason.'[11] This reconciliation of taste and rules, of spontaneous and rational judgement lasted until the new philosophical discipline of aesthetics and a new poetics of effect (on reader and audience) emerged during the second half of the eighteenth century. The neo-classical standards of rules and reason, upheld until then, collapsed and gave way to a new understanding of art.

II

Change in the literary constellation of the eighteenth century in Germany was shaped by more than just the rise of a new poetics and the new philosophical discipline of aesthetics; even more important for the literary life of the Enlightenment was the surge of journals that reflected these theoretical developments and transformed them into critical practice. Indeed, it was during the eighteenth century that literary journals first emerged as the most important 'medium of the Enlightenment'.[12] When publishing was turning into 'a profitable industry' (Kant), reviewing journals informed readers about the ever-expanding book market, acting as a critical *vade mecum*. In their diversity and liveliness, these periodicals represent, as Robert Prutz noted long ago, 'a monologue which the age held concerning itself'.[13] Literary and philosophical trends were discernible,

[10] Mayer (ed.), *Deutsche Literaturkritik*, I, p. 25.
[11] Gottsched, *Critische Dichtkunst*, p. 125.
[12] P. Raabe, 'Die Zeitschrift als Medium der Aufklärung', in *Wolfenbüttler Studien zur Aufklärung*, I (1974), pp. 99ff.
[13] Prutz, *Geschichte*, p. 7.

for the journals placed current topics before the public in a manner both expressing and inviting opinion. The ideas of the Enlightenment were popularized and publicly discussed in their pages. As early as 1768, Just Riedel, in his 'Letters Concerning the Public', praised literary journals for providing the reading public with a guide, for encouraging a more sophisticated literature, and for shaping taste.[14]

If we disregard the Moral Weeklies, whose literary criticism consisted at best of recommendations for reading or 'basic instructions in poetics',[15] it was once again Gottsched who founded literary journalism and practical criticism in Germany. Upon his retirement in 1762, he could look back proudly on his accomplishments of thirty-five years: he had founded no fewer than five journals and had been instrumental in establishing several others. His *Beiträge zur kritischen Historie der deutschen Sprache, Poesie und Beredsamkeit* (*Contributions to the Critical History of German Language, Poetry, and Eloquence*, 1732–44) continued the practical criticism and polemics of his Moral Weekly *Der Biedermann* (1727–8) while at the same time popularizing the poetics of his *Critische Dichtkunst*. As already mentioned, however, his regulative poetics and normative criticism, important as they may have been for the development of literary theory during the early Enlightenment, grew increasingly dogmatic and became obsolete after 1750 with the emergence of the new poetics of effect.

Lessing made his debut as a critic in 1748, and the acuity of his judgement was soon recognized. Between the dogmatism of Aristotelian rules on the one hand and the aesthetics of reader response on the other, he developed a new form of criticism. In the introduction to his *Laokoon*, he distinguished three responses to art: that of the 'connoisseur' who enjoys art; of the philosopher who explains the conditions of the enjoyment; and of the 'judge of art' or critic who supports the emotional response with reason.[16] The critic is neither the legislator nor the disciplinarian of the poet (as Gottsched and the Swiss critics had been); he merely mediates between the individual work of art and the audience. He judges whether poetry achieves the effects specific to its genre, and in so doing he acts as an advocate as well as an educator of the public. As a critic, Lessing is always aware that he is speaking before a public, which gives his style its rhetorical, dialogical, and sometimes polemical dimension. He argues as a reader, for the reader, and with the reader by seeking to explain the reader's emotional response in terms of poetic principles. When he began publishing the *Briefe, die neueste Literatur betreffend* (*Letters concerning the Most Recent Literature*, 1759; in

[14] Kiesel and Münch, *Gesellschaft*, p. 165.   [15] Martens, *Die Botschaft*, p. 443.
[16] Lessing, *Gesammelte Werke*, ed. Paul Rilla (Berlin, 1968), V, p. 9.

collaboration with Moses Mendelssohn and Friedrich Nicolai), he presented this collection of reviews as a series of letters to a 'meritorious officer' wounded in the Seven Years War. The dialogical form corresponds to the fictitious addressee, lending the reviews a familiar, conversational tone. The same is true of most parts of Lessing's *Hamburgische Dramaturgie* (which is, after all, a theatrical journal). In its 'prospectus', he invited the public to contribute to the improvement of the German stage: 'The public's voice should never go unheard; its judgement should never be listened to without submission'.[17] But the ideal public he had hoped for in Hamburg kept silent, and the real public he had spoken for disappointed him.

What in Hamburg was already discernible in 1768, namely the polarization of the literary public into an educated elite and a broader audience, became more obvious towards the end of the century. Yet the mandarins of the Enlightenment held firm to the notion that the reading public could be directed, educated, and expanded through criticism. A case in point is Friedrich Nicolai's project of a journal to review the entire annual output of literature, the *Allgemeine Deutsche Bibliothek* (1765–92; continued as *NADB*, 1793–1806). Nicolai, editor and publisher of this periodical for forty years, truly lived for the Enlightenment – and from it. By 1769, the journal was scarcely able to keep up with the year's book-production, and over the years, it limped hopelessly further behind an ever-expanding book market. The Enlightenment's ideal of a homogeneous public that could be guided by criticism proved to be an illusion.

At the end of the *Hamburgische Dramaturgie*, Lessing not only polemicized against a lazy public that was ill-prepared for a national theatre, but also against a new generation of critics who seemed to abolish criticism in the name of 'genius'. Even worse, these critics considered themselves geniuses, or at least the equal of geniuses.[18] Lessing thereby grudgingly acknowledged a challenge to his form of criticism, one which turned out to be primarily a shift of emphasis and perspective on the part of the critic, who was now to serve as a congenial interpreter of the genius's work. In Johann Gottfried Herder's case, this change in criticism took the form of an indirect dialogue with Lessing, as his *Fragmente über die neuere deutsche Literatur* (*Fragments on Recent German Literature*, 1767) demonstrate. As its subtitle indicates, this work is a 'supplement' to the *Briefe, die neueste Literatur betreffend*. Herder now speaks of the role of the critic as a servant to the reader, the writer, and literature. His definition of the critic in relation to the reader is still based on the sensualistic aesthetics of effect, and he still hopes to guide the reader towards proper reading. But when he declares

[17] *Ibid.*, VI, p. 8.   [18] *Ibid.*, VI, p. 482.

that a 'true judge of art' acts as a servant and friend of the poet, he stands in open contradiction to Enlightenment criticism. It would never have occurred to Lessing 'to think always with and for his author', or 'to put himself in the mind of his author and read from his very spirit'.[19] Lessing's form of criticism was too surgical and polemical for Herder's taste. He preferred positive and creative criticism that seeks to understand the ideal intention of the author and his work. The essays on Shakespeare by Herder and the young Goethe are examples of this kind of genetic, emphatic criticism. Herder wants to be Shakespeare's 'interpreter and rhapsodist', while Goethe's speech is the hymn-like oracle of one genius ignited by another.

In his celebrated review of Bürger's poems (1791), Schiller not only rejected Bürger's (and Herder's) concept of *Volkstümlichkeit* (popularity) as a possible means of closing the gap between high and popular culture from below, but also abandoned the Enlightenment ideal of a homogeneous public. As a critic, he no longer speaks on behalf of a general public, and certainly not for the people, but for an educated elite which nevertheless should draw the people 'playfully' up to its own level. Schiller defends the absolute value of art as appreciated by an ideal public. His new aesthetic criticism defines art as independent of public taste and of contemporary interests; the critic stands with his back to the audience and conducts his critical conversation within a literary elite.

Schiller's *Die Horen* (*The Horae*, 1795–7) became the journal of a 'literary association' which he, as editor, assembled. According to the 'prospectus', which can be regarded as the manifesto of Weimar Classicism, the principles of the journal were to be 'above all temporal influences', to defend the 'ideals of a refined humanity', and 'to reunite the politically divided world under the banner of truth and beauty'.[20] The aesthetic education of *Die Horen* included philosophical reflections on art as well as exemplary items of poetry. In this way Schiller intended to reunite 'the previously dispersed public', but in a typically Schillerian manner: 'that which pleases the best' should make its way 'into the hands of everyone'. The taste of a literary elite was to become the model for the 'entire reading world'. Although he had the best of intentions, Schiller proved unable to bridge the gap between his literary society and the educated public. Although his publisher Cotta admonished him to think of the 'ordinary reader' too, he stuck to his aesthetic programme of educating the public through art and towards art – and lost his audience.

This development of practical criticism, as articulated in the journals

[19] *Herders Sämtliche Werke*, ed. B. Suphan (Berlin, 1877–1914), I, p. 247.
[20] Schiller, *Sämtliche Werke*, ed. G. Fricke and H. G. Göpfert (Munich, 1960), V, p. 870.

of the German Enlightenment, reflects the changes which took place in literary theory from Gottsched to Goethe. Together, these changes constitute the history of criticism in eighteenth-century Germany. But instead of reiterating a story told many times over in literary histories, the following account will concentrate on the development of some of the major concepts of the time, such as the creative process, the imitative quality of art, and the function of literature.[21]

III

The central concept of the neo-classical theory of literature was 'imitation of nature'. In the second half of the eighteenth century, however, this concept of imitation gradually lost its power. According to René Wellek, this breakdown came about 'partly under the impact of the shift toward the emotional effect of art and partly through the growing emphasis on the self-expression of the artist'.[22]

For Gottsched, however, the imitation of nature was still the key principle of literature, 'the inner spirit of poetry', as he states in the subtitle of his *Critische Dichtkunst*. But he gives this axiom a rationalist twist. He differentiates between three forms of imitation: the simple imitation of nature or natural objects, which he calls 'poetic paintings'; the scenic representation of actions on stage; and the highest form of poetic imitation, the fable, 'the narration of a useful moral truth'.[23] Although the fable is fictitious, 'an action which is possible under certain circumstances', it must also be probable. Since nature is organized according to the laws of reason, the precondition of poetic probability is to establish a symmetry between fable and reality. Probability for the sake of moral education is more important than mimesis in the literal sense. Gottsched's rationalism puts the lid on the sources of poetic inspiration, keeping the imaginary and the marvellous well out of sight.

In contrast, and later in opposition, to Gottsched's rationalistic regimentation of poetics, the Swiss critics Bodmer and Breitinger defended poetic painting, the pleasures of the imagination, and even the portrayal of the supernatural. They believed that the more closely literature imitated painting, the more readily it would reach perfection. True to Horace's dictum *ut pictura poesis*, they propagated 'painterly poetry' as early as 1721 in their tellingly titled journal *Discourse der Mahlern* (*Discourses of the Painters*). Both arts have the same purpose and produce a similar

---

[21] For a more detailed narrative of the history of German literary theory during this period (Lessing, Winckelmann, Herder, Goethe, Kant, and Schiller) see Wellek, *History*, I, pp. 144–256.
[22] Wellek, *History*, I, p. 25.   [23] Gottsched, *Critische Dichtkunst*, p. 150.

effect on us: they portray absent objects as though they were present and they captivate us as if we were experiencing nature itself. The poetic representation of reality, though not as convincing as its graphic counterpart (because it is confined to language), evokes the same emotional response to nature by means of the poetic image. Poetic imagery should, therefore, be vivid and heart-warming, employing a sensuously metaphorical language. The heart and sentiments are proclaimed the judge of the beautiful, and the response of the reader is valued more highly than the injunctions of a normative poetics. As for the imitation of nature, however, the natural signs of painting remain superior to the arbitrary signs of language. It was this, the weakest part of the Swiss critics' theory, that Lessing would criticize.

Gottsched severely limited the sphere of poetry by chaining it to the law of reason and the concept of probability, 'the similarity between the fictitious and those events that happen in real life'.[24] He could justify this principle with the help of the authority of Aristotle, who, in the ninth chapter of his *Poetics*, separated historical from poetic truth by distinguishing between the real, the probable, and the possible: 'The poet's job is not to tell what happened but the kind of things that can happen, i.e. the kind of events that are possible according to probability or necessity'.[25] The law of probability for Gottsched became the yardstick for the realm of poetry, and he restricted literature to the imitation of commonplace reality. What he neglected to see, or simply overlooked, was the poetic principle of possibility which justifies fiction as against reality. What Gottsched wanted to curtail was an imagination that transcended everyday reality, gave fantasy free rein, and explored not just probable but 'possible worlds'. Bodmer and Breitinger cautiously moved in this direction by opening up the all-too-restrictive concept of imitation, though they actually seemed to be more interested in a fantastic than in a real world, more in the 'possible probable' than in the merely probable: 'Poetry always prefers to take the material of imitation from the possible than from the existing world'.[26] In their writings, the poetic imagination, not restricted to the narrow interpretation of *imitatio naturae*, no longer has to justify its fancies before the court of reality. When the truth of the imagination has the licence to imitate even things or events that are not real, the marvellous, the wondrous and even the supernatural become objects of poetry. The debate between Leipzig and Zurich about 'das Wunderbare' would have been less heated if Gottsched had recognized the desire for the new and the unheard-of which is the 'mother of the miraculous'. The pleasure of poetry springs in no small

[24] *Ibid.*, p. 198.
[25] G. F. Else, *Aristotle's Poetics: The Argument* (Cambridge, 1957), p. 301.
[26] Bodmer, *Critische Abhandlung* (Zurich, 1740), pp. 31f.

measure from a novelty that goes beyond the quotidian and its tiresome routine. The imagination was free to use ancient mythology as well as the Christian supernatural (Dante, Milton) and even the 'heterocosmic' (Leibniz). This extension of the concept of fiction to 'possible worlds' not only allows the poet to represent what is hidden in the world and has not yet become real, but also anticipates the utopian intention of poetry which challenges the real world by confronting it with its unfulfilled potential. By defending the power of the imagination and by encouraging the creative genius of poets, Bodmer and Breitinger expanded and at the same time overcame the narrow confines of the imitation of nature.

Lessing marks the beginning of a new epoch in literary theory and criticism. He broke with dogmatic Aristotelianism and the pedantic poetics of rules and developed a new literary theory which did equal justice to the principles of art and to the emotional response of the audience. As a young critic, he was still influenced by Batteux's principle of the imitation of beautiful nature which he himself defended in a review of the German translation of Batteux's work in 1751. But he soon had doubts as to whether this concept would be of any practical use, for it seemed to offer little more than the meagre advice given to a cobbler's apprentice that shoes have to fit. Years later, after a development that can be traced through his writings as a practising critic, he found his own solution to the problems of mimetic theory in his *Laokoon oder über die Grenzen der Malerei und Poesie (Laocoön, or the Limits of Painting and Poetry*, 1766).

Painting and poetry make use of entirely different signs; painting uses forms and colours in space, poetry articulates sounds in time. 'Bodies with their visible properties are the peculiar subject of painting ... Actions are the peculiar subject of poetry.'[27] Poetry is transitory, i.e. it imitates actions in a temporal sequence, while painting can make use of only a single instant of an action in space. Painting is limited by space and has to choose the most fruitful or 'pregnant' moment for its imitation of an action; poetry is limited in its presentation of visual images but can imitate actions in time. Simple imitation of nature is, therefore, the domain of the painter, and poetry is relieved of the burden of description. Thus, Lessing not only determines the limits of the visual arts (and to a lesser degree also of poetry), but also frees poetry from its subjugation to painting. In fact, he inverts the old model and declares that poetry is 'the broader art form' with more possibilities of portraying the attitudes, motives, feelings, and desires of characters in action. It is true that Lessing has a far broader conception of literature

[27] Lessing, *Gesammelte Werke*, V, p. 10.

than of the fine arts; and his treatise (despite its many antiquarian digressions) actually does extend the literary horizon considerably. Horace's *ut pictura poesis* becomes an obsolete topos, and the idyllic quietism of poetic painting is replaced by the imitation of human nature and social conditions. In effect, drama now becomes the privileged genre.

One does not have to quote Lessing's famous attack on Gottsched in his seventeenth *Literaturbrief* (*Letter on Literature*, 1759) in order to appreciate how far he had come from Gottsched's neo-classicism. Nevertheless, he remained an Aristotelian. He criticized the simple imitation of nature in literature, but basically adhered to the principle of mimesis; he scorned any pedantic use of rules, but he did not discard them either. Yet scarcely had he liberalized the dogmatic interpretation of Aristotle than a new generation of writers rebelled against his own. 'We have now, thank heavens, a generation of critics', he fumed in 1769, 'whose highest criticism consists in making all criticism suspicious. They vociferate: Genius! Genius! . . . Thus they flatter genius, in order, I fancy, that we should regard them as geniuses too'.[28] This group of writers, who can hardly be described as literary theorists or critics, became known as the Storm and Stress movement. The cultivation of genius, for which Shakespeare was a synonym, was the order of the day. Lessing, however, viewed this revolt as just another 'fermentation of taste' that threatened all artistic rules.

Given their attitude, it is small wonder that these writers raged against Aristotle's principles and Batteux's imitation of beautiful nature. Jakob Michael Reinhold Lenz simply refused to waste his time on modelling an ideal of beauty, because he valued 'the characteristic, even the caricaturistic, painter more highly than the idealistic one'.[29] And Goethe, in a review of Johann Georg Sulzer's *Allgemeine Theorie der schönen Künste* (*General Theory of the Fine Arts*, 1771), doubted whether anybody could learn from its principles 'except a student seeking a basic primer'. Sulzer, he wrote, 'draws conclusions from nature about art' that trivialize 'imitation of nature' into 'prettification of objects'.[30] Neither the example of the Greek painter Zeuxis, whose painted cherries birds were supposed to have tried to peck, nor Aristotle's mimesis helped these writers to understand or imitate nature. 'What those gentlemen like to call nature', Lenz protested, 'is nothing but distorted nature'.[31] Nature

---

[28] *Ibid.*, VI, p. 482.
[29] J. M. R. Lenz, *Werke und Schriften*, ed. B. Titel and H. Haug (Stuttgart, 1966), I, p. 342.
[30] *Frankfurter Gelehrte Anzeigen vom Jahre 1772*, ed. W. Scherer (Heilbronn, 1883), p. 665.
[31] Lenz, *Werke und Schriften*, I, pp. 336f.

for him meant naturalness and naturalism. In his dramas he not only
rejected the traditional imitation of nature but also all rules, unities,
probability, and purity of genre. Instead he aimed for 'paintings of
human society' and genre scenes of *petit bourgeois* life, proclaiming that
when the real conditions of social life are depressing or ugly 'their
depiction cannot be cheerful'.[32] The naturalistic tendencies of the Storm
and Stress, no longer subsumable under the principle of *imitatio naturae*,
anticipate the realism of the nineteenth century.

In yet another respect, the principle of imitation drastically changed
its meaning during the 1770s. The new authors, if they spoke of it at
all, did not refer to mimesis but to the creative process as being similar
to that of nature. Nature is still the reference point, but only in so far
as art is created according to the universal laws of nature. Thus, poetry
is no longer an imitation of nature but an 'imitation of the creating,
name-giving Godhead', as Herder observed. The poet becomes 'a second
creator, *poietes*, maker'.[33] The genius needs no rules or models; he creates
his works spontaneously out of himself. This theory of genius, which
was not entirely original, can be traced back to the ancient idea of a
furor poeticus and to the rhetorical concept of *ingenium* as part of the
ars inveniendi. In the eighteenth century, Shaftesbury gave it its modern
meaning when he described the poet as 'a second maker', though the
emphatic cult of the 'original genius' in Germany was inspired by Edward
Young's *Conjectures on Original Composition* (1759). Young declared
the poet independent of tradition, learning, and rules, since the genius
has all that is needed within himself and produces art by a creative
process akin to that of nature. This book laid the foundation for the
German *Genie*-movement of the 1770s and contributed to the rise of
aesthetics in Germany.

Prometheus became the most powerful myth for this generation, and
Goethe's hymn to this idol is the purest expression of the independent,
assertive self which protests against any misuse of power. When Gottfried
August Bürger associated even 'freedom of thought and of the press'
with the deeds of Prometheus, the metaphorical protest became political.
Thus, Prometheus became a symbol of bourgeois emancipation, though
under conditions that were barely sufficient for a spiritual revolution.
The same is true of the subsequent development of German literature
and theory under the shadow of the French Revolution. The literary
theory of Weimar Classicism can be read as a response to this monumental
political event: art was divorced from life, and aesthetics from politics,
in order to save art from the hopeless conditions then prevalent in state
and society and to keep alive the hope for a better future. Thus, Schiller's

---

[32] *Ibid.*, I, p. 419.   [33] *Herders Sämtliche Werke*, XII, p. 7.

aesthetic theory has a utopian dimension, whereas Goethe's mimetic theory displays more realistic tendencies. In his autobiographical work *Dichtung und Wahrheit* (*Poetry and Truth*), Goethe recalls how influential Lessing's *Laokoon* had been for his generation: 'The concept of *ut pictura poesis*, misunderstood for such a long time, was abolished once and for all, and the difference between the pictorial and rhetorical arts was clearly delineated.'[34] He incorporated the results of Lessing's treatise into his own literary theory, as his short essay *Einfache Nachahmung der Natur, Manier, Stil* (*Simple Imitation of Nature, Manner, Style*, 1789) demonstrates. This essay contains in a nutshell Goethe's views on the problem of mimesis and anticipates the aesthetic programme of Weimar Classicism.

In brief, the first two concepts which Goethe employs in this essay simplify the old mimetic theories, while his understanding of 'style' constitutes a truly new concept. The 'simple imitation of nature' limits the artist to certain objects of inanimate nature which he copies with meticulous precision to produce still lifes or landscapes. Unlike Lessing, Goethe does not regard this tradition as problematic but recognizes it as a possible, if naive artistic method. Only much later did he criticize this form of imitation as 'portrait art' which merely duplicates nature without adding anything to it. What is missing in such works is art's 'truth', which is hidden in 'beautiful appearance'.[35] Although the term 'mannerism' already had a negative connotation in the eighteenth century, Goethe employs the concept 'in an elevated and respectable sense'. Under this rubric, he summarizes everything that belongs to the subjective side of the creative process, such as ingenuity, imagination, and invention. To imitate in a manneristic way means to produce fanciful works 'without having nature herself before us'. The artist creates his own world 'in order to express in his own manner that which has moved his soul'.[36] This characteristic expression of subjective emotional experience, however, must be subordinated to the totality and universality of the work of art. The danger of this artistic method lies in its tendency to lose sight of nature altogether and merely play with the material, in which case mannerism becomes 'more and more empty and meaningless'.

For Goethe, 'style' is the epitome of art. 'Style rests on the deepest foundation of knowledge, on the essence of things, inasmuch as we are allowed to know the latter in visible and tangible forms.'[37] Art depends on a profound understanding of nature; it is produced in an analogous manner to products of nature and in accordance with nature's laws. 'Through a deep and exacting study of the objects themselves', the artist

---

[34] *Goethes Werke*, IX, p. 316.   [35] *Ibid.*, XII, p. 89.   [36] *Ibid.*, XII, p. 31.
[37] *Ibid.*, p. 34.

arrives at 'an exact and ever finer knowledge of the quality of the things and the manner of their existence' which he can then represent in their purest and highest form. Great art expunges everything arbitrary, accidental, or individual for the sake of the regular and universal, so that beneath the surface 'the essence of things' may appear. It is no coincidence that Goethe developed this point of view after his return from Italy, where he experienced the classical perfection and ideality of ancient art. His exposure to Greek sculpture, under the guidance of Winckelmann's writings, was undoubtedly the intuitive basis for his concept of style, while his empirical research provided the epistemological foundation.

Despite the fact that Goethe continued to remain at a distance from Schiller after his return from Italy, the two were already in accord over the substantive matters of art. In a letter to Christian Gottfried Körner, Schiller defines style as the basis of the fine arts, 'the total elevation above the accidental to the universal and necessary'.[38] And several years later, clearly under the influence of Schiller, Goethe defines style as an 'idealizing' representation. Style, as a 'genuine method' of great art, becomes the foundation of the symbolic art form of Weimar Classicism. The two poets agreed that spiritual and intellectual matters attain expression in symbolic representation, without being reducible to concepts. For Goethe, however, this law of art is grounded in nature, whereas for Schiller it is a projection of an idea on to nature. Goethe's understanding of symbolic representation presupposes an object-related knowledge of essence, and it is an aesthetic imperative for the artist to make this 'essence of things' transparent in his presentation of nature. One of Goethe's many definitions of symbolic art in his *Maximen und Reflexionen* (*Maxims and Reflections*) states: 'It is the nature of poetry that it expresses the particular without thinking of the general or rawing attention to it. But whoever comprehends the particular vividly receives the general at the same time, without noticing it – or not until later.'[39] Goethe's symbolic representation of nature appears to be concrete and objective, but this makes its significance by no means easy to grasp, for his symbols are ambiguous, even mysterious – 'living, momentary revelations of the ineffable'.[40] The new symbolic form becomes for him a 'language for humanity', a language that allows the artist to elevate himself above the narrow confines of reality in order to represent the 'purely human'.

Goethe's symbolic representation of nature accords with his theoretical position, which lies between the mimetic concepts of imitation and realism. He ridicules both: the dead copy and the slavishly real. In the introduction to his art journal *Die Propyläen* (*The Propylaea*, 1798), he

---

[38] Schiller to Körner, 28 February 1793.   [39] *Goethes Werke*, XII, p. 471.   [40] *Ibid.*

returns once more to the distinction between nature and art, but in contrast to his essay of 1789 he draws the line more emphatically: 'The prime requirement for the artist is always that he should stick to nature, study it, and imitate it.' But in the same breath he also emphasizes that 'nature is separated from art by an enormous gap'.[41] He is no longer content with the axiom of 'simple imitation of nature' which he had once tolerated as a lower form of art. The naive art-lover who enjoys 'art as if it were a work of nature' allows himself to be deceived like 'the real sparrows who flew toward the painted cherries', while the connoisseur knows that 'what is true in art and what is naturally true are two completely different things'. Although the artist remains bound to nature and reality, the work of art, as 'product of the human spirit', goes beyond nature. The simple imitation of nature yields at best a superficial description of appearances, whereas true art transcends nature, lending it depth and significance. Goethe's statement at the end of the eighteenth century marks the limits of the traditional *imitatio naturae* and the beginning of a mimetic theory that points toward nineteenth-century realism.

It was Schiller who first used the term 'realism' in Germany. In a letter to Goethe in 1798, he characterized the national peculiarity of French literature as follows: 'It is no question that they are better realists than idealists, and I derive from this a conclusive argument that realism cannot make a poet.'[42] It was usually in this sense – and consequently pejoratively – that he used the term 'realism', and he described its more extreme form as 'naturalism'. For instance, in the preface to his last drama, *Die Braut von Messina* (*The Bride of Messina*), he defends his use of the classical chorus on the grounds that it 'transforms the modern, vulgar world into the ancient, poetical one', and he 'openly declares war on naturalism in art'.[43] There are, however, indications that he at times used the term 'realism' positively. Under the influence of Goethe, whose 'realistic tic' he came to tolerate, he discovered the aesthetic possibilities of the realistic method. An obvious example is his drama *Wallenstein*, whose hero he wants to portray as a 'genuine realistic character'. In order to take this 'realistic road', he decides 'to choose nothing but historical material', since this will force him to stay closer to reality and to restrain his imagination. He concludes that 'it is a completely different operation to idealize reality from what it is to realize the ideal'.[44] Even though his creative method seems to approximate to Goethe's here, Schiller still idealizes reality – or to put it another way, reality is merely the material that has to be sublated into art by means of form. The gulf

---

[41] *Ibid.*, XII, p. 42.   [42] Schiller to Goethe, 27 April 1798.
[43] Schiller, *Sämtliche Werke*, II, pp. 819f.   [44] Schiller to Goethe, 5 January 1798.

between Goethe and Schiller remains present, despite their efforts to bridge their differences through mutual 'fruitful misunderstandings'. To appreciate these differences, we must ask how Schiller reflects reality aesthetically and how he solves the mimetic problem historically.

Mimesis as commonly understood, or what Schiller describes as the 'servile' imitation of nature, is no longer valid for him. In a review of Matthisson's poems (1794) he argues, as Lessing had done in *Laokoon*, that landscape poetry can be justified only if the transformation of description into action is successful and if the significance of nature becomes transparent. To bring this about, a 'symbolic operation' is necessary which changes inanimate nature into human nature.[45] The 'symbolizing imagination' can achieve this in two ways: either by representing feelings by means of musical effects, or by representing ideas. But how can ideas be represented without falling into the trap of allegorical imagery? Schiller assumes that an analogy exists between the movements of the mind and appearances in nature. When the imagination discovers such an analogy, it connects the appearance of nature with an idea. This symbolic operation of the poet transforms the natural object, as seen through the subjective perception, into a symbolic one, thus making the landscape aesthetically pleasing. In this way, even the idea of freedom can be symbolized through nature, if we assume that the analogy between the work of art and nature consists in their shared quality of autonomy. 'Beauty is freedom in appearance'[46] – this is the axiom on which Schiller's poetics turns. Although he knows from Kant that the symbolic meaning is not a quality of the natural object (as was presupposed by Goethe's symbolism of nature), but a form of subjective perception and reflection, he nevertheless sees the symbolic operation as a possible means of representing ideas in terms of nature. But landscape poetry remains for Schiller an inferior form of poetry, and naive imitation of nature is something which belongs to the past.

The literary theory underlying this view was formulated in Schiller's famous treatise *Über naive und sentimentalische Dichtung* (*On Naive and Sentimental Poetry*, 1795). This work can be understood as a personal as well as a historical definition of Schiller's position in relation to Goethe and to antiquity. He wrote it after his important meeting with Goethe in August 1794, guided by what, for him, was the crucial question: 'What direction must the poet of our age and under conditions like ours choose?'[47] His starting point is nature, in its double meaning of sensuously experienced external nature on the one hand, and the inner experience of nature as human totality on the other. Modern culture has become

---

[45] Schiller, *Sämtliche Werke*, V, p. 998.   [46] *Ibid.*, V, p. 400.
[47] Schiller to Herder, 4 November 1794.

alienated from nature, a condition produced by the one-sided development of reason. Referring to our view of simple objects of nature, Schiller writes: 'They are what we were; they are what we ought to be. We were nature as they are: and our civilization must bring us back to nature by way of reason and freedom.'[48] The 'naive', as a mode of feeling, is characterized by closeness to nature and simplicity; its historical paradigm is Greek antiquity. The 'sentimental', as a form of reflection, is typical of modernity, which is characterized by alienation from nature and loss of totality. 'Our feeling for nature is similar to the longing of a sick man for health.'[49] Poets, as 'custodians of nature', differ in their relationship to nature: 'Either they *are* nature, or they will search for the lost one.'[50] The 'naive' poet *is* nature (the natural genius), and he merely has to imitate nature in order to move us by means of its sensuous truth. The 'sentimental' poet, who has lost the harmony with nature and for whom the totality of nature is 'merely an ideal', has to move us through ideas. The problem of the modern poet is his distance from nature, and he has to overcome this through art. He can no longer rely on simple imitation of nature; he must represent the lost ideal in order 'to give the most complete expression to humanity'.[51] 'Naive' poetry is the art of limitation, 'sentimental' poetry is the art of the infinite. The modern, 'sentimental' poet, divided within and in conflict with civilization, can react to the contradiction between the ideal and reality in a threefold fashion; his work can be satirical, elegiac, or idyllic. Schiller thus replaces the traditional classification of poetry in terms of genres by a new theory of poetic modes which reflect different attitudes towards reality. The satirical mode contrasts reality with the ideal in such a manner that reality appears wanting, as lacking totality; but neither 'punitive' nor 'laughing' satire need go on to construct that ideal reality which its satirical criticism implies. The elegy mourns the loss of the ideal in such a way that its enthusiasm for the lost ideal triggers a longing for it. In the idyll, however, as the highest 'sentimental' mode, the ideal is imagined in the past or projected into the future as if it were real. Such an idyll would represent the 'fulfilled ideal', the reconciliation of all contradictions and the utopian moment of perfection. This return to unity and harmony, which 'sentimental' poetry has yet to achieve, would also be the point of convergence between naive and sentimental poetry.[52]

Three aspects of Schiller's theory point to the future. He develops his poetics in relation to phenomena of modern society, such as alienation

[48] Schiller, *Sämtliche Werke*, V, p. 695.   [49] *Ibid.*, p. 711.   [50] *Ibid.*, p. 712.
[51] *Ibid.*, p. 717.
[52] Cf. Peter Szondi, 'Das Naive ist das Sentimentalische', in Szondi, *Lektüre und Lektionen* (Frankfurt, 1973), pp. 47–99.

from nature, division of labour, and specialization. On the basis of his social criticism, he replaces the old natural forms of poetry by new 'modes of feeling' or forms of consciousness which correspond to modern experiences of reality. And his new typology of 'naive' and 'sentimental' poetry not only defines modern in contrast to ancient literature, but also historicizes literary theory. There can be no return to 'naive' poetry; no simple imitation of nature can represent modern reality. The modern, 'sentimental' poet strives for a 'synthetic' poetry, which bridges the gap between reality and the ideal by representing ideas. The poet becomes the custodian of human totality and harmonious humanity. With Schiller's utopian concept of literature,[53] the century-old debate between Ancients and Moderns comes to a close in Germany and a truly modern theory of literature takes shape.

IV

The changes in the history of German theory during the eighteenth century can best be summarized in terms of the expectations that these theorists had with regard to the effects of literature on its audience. The neo-classical tradition adhered to Horace's famous dictum that poetry must be either useful or pleasurable (*aut prodesse volunt aut delectare poetae*), which is sound advice if both principles are of equal importance. For most critics, however, the pleasure of poetry merely served the purpose of moral or didactic usefulness (*utile dulci*). Poetry was generally considered a teacher of wisdom and virtue for those who were not sufficiently educated to achieve these qualities by other means; it was a 'sugar-coated pill', sweetening a truth or moral by means of allegories or fables. This crude rationalistic model, which was incapable of defining the specific nature of aesthetic pleasure, also had to deal with the fact that poetry can move the reader or audience, that it evokes an emotional response. The explanation of this phenomenon – at least in relation to tragedy – was Aristotle's much debated concept of catharsis, which was now equipped with a moral underpinning. The theatre, entertaining and emotionally stimulating, became a 'moral institution' in eighteenth-century Germany: tragedy was understood as a 'school of virtue' that taught moral lessons, comedy as a 'school of laughter' that corrected vices. Both served the same general purpose as other kinds of poetry: to

---

[53] On the utopian dimension of Schiller's literary theory, which Wellek also mentions – albeit with a critical aside (Wellek, *History*, I, pp. 242 and 254), see A. Gethmann-Seifert, 'Idylle und Utopie', in *Jahrbuch der deutschen Schiller-Gesellschaft*, 24 (1980), 32–67.

instruct, improve, and enlighten the audience. Like the problem of art's relation to nature and reality, the distinction between art and morality remained a hotly debated issue throughout the century. Only the advent of aesthetic theory enabled the theorists to distinguish between the pleasing, the good, and the beautiful, and to define the function of literature in new ways.

The theorists of the early Enlightenment in Leipzig, and even more so in Zurich, still had to cope with contemptuous attitudes towards poetry, whether on the part of pious clerics who could see in it only a dangerous stimulus to sinful fantasy, or of pragmatic patricians who considered it a wasteful diversion. In Zurich, Pastor Gotthard Heidegger polemicized against profane literature in his tedious book *Mythoscopia Romantica: oder Discours von den so benannten Romans* (*Mythoscopia Romantica or a Discourse on So-Called Novels*, 1798), in which he characterized the reading of novels as a useless amusement and sinful pleasure; and it is not surprising that the city's puritanical council did not allow any theatre-productions within its walls. Perhaps it was because of this backdrop of ignorance and hostility that the defenders of poetry had to stress its educational and moral value so forcefully, while playing down its pleasurable effects. In spite of the differences between the Leipzig and Zurich theorists regarding the power of the imagination and of the miraculous, there was general agreement when it came to the function of literature: it had to be useful, educational, and above all moral. Gottsched wanted to lend poetry the dignity of philosophy, and therefore stressed its moral value so much that he reduced it to didacticism. Thus the fable, as a didactic genre in its own right or as a plot paradigm for other kinds of poetry, was the centrepiece of his theory. Whether he talks about the imitation of nature or about the poetic genres, the fable is his necessary means of arriving at a moral end. His rule-governed poetics are notorious for their recipe character: 'First of all one has to choose an instructive moral maxim which lays the foundation of the whole poem ... Then one invents a very general event wherein an action occurs which demonstrates this maxim convincingly.'[54] The functions of tragedy and comedy are merely 'to instruct the audience through examples of virtues and vices'.[55] Tragedy cleanses the audience of the vices presented on stage, comedy exposes their folly through ridicule. But this didactic approach to literature (*fabula docet*) becomes even more moralistic and simplistic when it is applied to the classical works of antiquity. Thus, Gottsched reduces the tragedy of Oedipus to the moral lesson 'that God punishes even sins which are committed unwittingly',[56] and Bodmer sees in Antigone's tragedy merely a warning

---

[54] Gottsched, *Critische Dichtkunst*, p. 161.   [55] *Ibid.*, p. 91.   [56] *Ibid.*, p. 608.

against 'disobedience to rulers'.[57] For both critics, moral instruction was clearly more important than aesthetic pleasure.

In contrast to these critics, Lessing tried to distinguish between the peculiar effects which different arts and genres have on their audience. He is in agreement with Gottsched that poetry should ameliorate humanity, 'but all genres cannot improve all things . . . What each genre can improve most perfectly, and better than any other – that alone is its peculiar aim.'[58] Tragedy, for example, cannot correct all the passions presented on stage, nor can its objective be reduced to the presentation of a moral exemplum. The former would overstrain the possibilities of drama, the latter would be better served by reading an Aesopian fable. What matters to Lessing is not Gottsched's simple and generalized didacticism, but the specific effects of tragedy: 'The dramatic form is the only one in which fear and pity can be aroused.'[59] Lessing's famous reinterpretation of Aristotle's catharsis (*Hamburgische Dramaturgie*, §§ 74–9) not only discovers the importance of the emotional response of the audience, but also makes the arousal and exercise of pity the main function of tragedy. The fear that what happens on stage could also happen to us keeps compassion alive, even after the performance. As self-reflective pity, fear enhances the effect of pity and enables it to last. Hence the theatre has the function of improving our capacity for compassion and of transforming it into a habit; for 'the most compassionate person is the best person, the most inclined to all social virtues'.[60] This characterization of the theatre as a place where 'tears of pity and of feeling humanity' are cultivated marks a major shift in literary theory from rationalism to sensibility (*Empfindsamkeit*). But this discovery of the emotional dimension of art should be understood not as an irrationalism that runs counter to the Enlightenment, as historians of German literature used to argue, but rather as a complementary movement of the age. Thus, neo-classical poetics and their rational functionalism were replaced by an aesthetics of effect according to which emotional motives can be as important an impulse for human action as rational knowledge, if not an even stronger one. The heart as well as the head can prompt people to do what is right. This shift from rational didacticism to emotional motivation corresponds to the development of aesthetics during the second half of the eighteenth century, whereby the nature of aesthetic pleasure was explained and the concept of taste was further developed as a foundation of literary criticism.

The German Storm and Stress movement, which in the European context is sometimes also described as 'Pre-romanticism', nevertheless seems

---

[57] Bodmer, *Briefwechsel* (Zurich, 1736), p. 98.
[58] Lessing, *Gesammelte Werke*, VI, p. 395.   [59] *Ibid.*, p. 393.
[60] Lessing to Nicolai, November 1756.

to be directed against certain tendencies within the Enlightenment. Its literary rebellion, rejecting all formalized criticism, was mainly directed against French neo-classicism and dogmatic Aristotelianism. Nevertheless, in its social criticism, it continued and even intensified certain tendencies of the Enlightenment. A case in point is its views on the function of the theatre. For Lessing, the theatre is 'a school of the moral world', in which compassion is aroused and cultivated. But he also remarked that the theatre reaches its 'highest dignity' where it becomes 'the supplement of the law'.[61] The young Schiller echoed and radicalized this sentiment when he wrote in his essay *Die Schaubühne als eine moralische Anstalt betrachtet* (*The Stage Considered as a Moral Institution*, 1784): 'The jurisdiction of the stage begins where the realm of the secular laws ends.'[62] The theatre as a moral institution criticizes the unnatural conditions of society by confronting the corrupt courtly life with bourgeois virtues. The development of the domestic tragedy from Lessing to Schiller and Lenz clearly demonstrates how the theatre became a tool of social and political criticism.

When Schiller, in the same essay, calls the theatre 'a school of practical wisdom' and praises its civilizing effect on the people (*das Volk*) he touches upon yet another basic value associated with literature during the Storm and Stress period, namely the concept of *Volkstümlichkeit*. The standards of poetry should not be derived exclusively from the taste of an educated elite; they should also take into consideration the needs and feelings of simple people in order to create a homogeneous national culture. Herder, who became the champion of *Volkspoesie* and *Volkstümlichkeit*, reached back into history to legitimize popular literature. 'Unless we have a people [*Volk*]', he wrote, 'we lack a public, a nation, and a literature that are ours, that live and work in us.'[63] The so-called 'polished' society with all its conventions strangles what is natural and distinctive in a people. In the folksongs of the past, he finds evidence of naive and unspoiled feelings among the people that are missing in his own age. He rediscovered the aesthetic values of the popular literature of the past in order to develop a *Volkspoesie* for the present. Inspired by Herder's collection of folksongs and by his essays on *Volkspoesie*, Gottfried August Bürger became a passionate defender of this kind of poetry. His whole practice as a poet was determined by his 'poetic confession of faith' that 'all poetry should be in harmony with the people [*volksmäßig*], for that is the seal of its perfection'.[64] Although he aimed for a universal audience which would read his works in cottages as well as in palaces, his poetry clearly expressed the needs and feelings

---

[61] Lessing, *Gesammelte Werke*, VI, p. 41.   [62] Schiller, *Sämtliche Werke*, V, p. 823.
[63] Herder, *Sämtliche Werke*, IX, p. 529.
[64] *Bürgers Werke*, ed. L. Kaim and S. Streller (Weimar, 1956), p. 341.

of the simple people who were excluded from the privileges of polite society. The call for *Volkstümlichkeit* and the practice of *Volkspoesie* already contained the demand for equality – at least in the cultural sphere.

When Schiller reviewed the second edition of Bürger's poems in 1791, he rejected his emphatic claim to *Volkstümlichkeit* as well as most of his poems. Schiller's merciless review signals a turning-point in the understanding of literature and its function – the 'period of art' had begun. For Schiller, popularity in lyric poetry cannot be the 'seal of perfection', but only a fortunate addition. 'The perfection of a poem', he states categorically, 'is the first, indispensable condition' of art which possesses an absolute, inner value independent of its reader. He defends the 'highest demands of art' against the levelling taste of popular literature. The quality of poetry depends on the poet's artistic ability to distance himself from his personal experiences and to transform his subjective emotions into universal human feelings. Schiller explicitly warns that the poet must beware of singing 'his pain in the midst of pain'.[65] The other requirement of poetry, that the poet should idealize reality in order to transcend nature and individuality, already anticipates Schiller's and Goethe's theory of symbolic representation: the artist must objectify and idealize both his subjective experiences and contemporary reality in order to create works of universal validity. Art becomes autonomous, and yet its function is 'to unify the divided powers of the soul ... and as it were to restore the *whole human being* within us'.[66]

The separation of art from everyday life as a distinct and autonomous sphere received its philosophical justification in Kant's aesthetics, which Schiller made the foundation of his *Aesthetic Letters* (1795). 'Art is absolved from everything that is positive or that has been introduced by human conventions', he declared. '[I]t enjoys an absolute immunity from the arbitrariness of men.'[67] Art can no longer be used for religious, moral, or social purposes. 'Poetry never performs a specific task for human beings', reads another passage. '[I]ts sphere of activity is the totality of human nature.'[68] Art, as 'the pure product of separation', is freed from the restraints and expectations of bourgeois society, and only because it is autonomous can it use its critical potential to project the hope for a more humane society into the future. That Goethe shared this conviction is suggested by a letter to his friend Zelter, in which he praises Kant for the 'immeasurable merit' of having declared art to be autonomous.[69]

This functional transformation of art had tremendous consequences

---

[65] Schiller, *Sämtliche Werke*, V, p. 982.   [66] *Ibid.*, V, p. 971.   [67] *Ibid.*, V, p. 593.
[68] *Ibid.*, V, p. 535.   [69] Goethe to Zelter, 29 January 1830.

for literary theory and criticism. Art emerged as a cultural institution independent of its former representational and social functions; the aesthetic judgement was clearly distinguished from judgements concerning nature, morality, and society; the work of art occupied an autonomous sphere defined by its specific form of production and reception. Throughout the German Enlightenment, it had appeared self-evident that literature had a moral and social function, that it could influence the practical life of its audience. But the concept of autonomous art, as propagated by Kant and Weimar Classicism, detached literature from social practice. This loss, however, was compensated for by endowing poetry with a new critical and utopian function, with art assuming a new civilizing role in society: the aesthetic experience makes it possible for the individual to overcome the wounds of civilization, at least momentarily. Art unifies the divided powers of the soul and restores 'the whole human being within us'. It strengthens and motivates us and it illuminates the path to a better and more humane future.[70] Thus Schiller's utopian notion of literature eclipses the earlier theory of his century, and in so doing clears the way for modern criticism. As Wellek rightly observes, 'Schiller's theories proved to be the fountainhead of all later German critical theory.'[71]

[70] On the utopian dimension of Schiller's aesthetic theory, see K. L. Berghahn, 'Ästhetische Reflexion als Utopie des Ästhetischen', in *Utopie-Forschung*, ed. W. Voßkamp (Stuttgart, 1982), pp. 146–71.
[71] Wellek, *History*, I, p. 232.

24

The Scottish Enlightenment

Joan H. Pittock

'Among the ancients', wrote Robert Eden Scott, the first Professor of Moral Philosophy in King's College, Aberdeen, 'Criticism was chiefly cultivated as an art, and consisted rather in practical rules than in scientific investigation: it is to the Moderns, and those too of a very late date, that we owe a philosophical investigation of that science of Rhetoric, and an analysis of those faculties of the mind, upon which peculiar effects are produced, by literary composition, in its various kinds.'[1] 'Philosophical investigation' was the occupation of Scottish academics, ministers and lawyers in the heyday of the Enlightenment. It was rooted in the Scottish system of higher education, and it flowered in the concern for professional status, communal interests and national identity which evolved from the religious, political and cultural events of the recent past.

A strong sense of changing times, embodied in the Act of Union in 1707, of the superior refinement and politeness of metropolitian society, and of the need for efficiency in communication and consensus not only between countries but among regions (forcing to the periphery the issue of the large Gaelic-speaking population), determined the priorities of inquirers pursuing those 'inner formative forces' which for Cassirer distinguished the mind of the Enlightenment. Forces such as feeling, sympathy and taste, inherent in the writings of Shaftesbury and his popularizer Addison and grafted on to the stock of humanist speculation congenial to the religious temper of Scotland were expanded by Francis Hutcheson in the *Inquiry into the Origin of our Ideas of Beauty and Virtue* (1725). These found their way into the critical principles of Smith, Hume and their contemporaries.

A system of criticism for communication, interpretation and discrimination was developed along the lines of the empirical investigative principles of Bacon and Locke (facilitated by the methodology of Newton). This system, operating within the sphere of moral philosophy, became

---

[1] *Elements of Rhetoric for the Use of the Students of King's College, Aberdeen* (1802), p. iii. 'Rhetoric is that Science which professes to illustrate the different kinds of literary composition ... The same Science is also denominated Criticism, Eloquence, or the Belles Lettres. In this Science, as well as in most others, the poetical art has existed long before the foundation of the principles formed an object of enquiry' (pp. 1–2).

a priority within the highly institutionalized and closely wrought educational system of Scotland. When Dodsley looked for contributors on rhetoric and logic to his volumes of *The Preceptor* he chose the Aberdonians, David Fordyce and William Duncan – the latter of whom was later to influence Thomas Jefferson.[2]

Concern with the nature of language and feeling in action, event and perception, altered the more abstruse tradition of rhetoric, displacing its associate, logic, and incorporating issues of criticism as well as communication. This was in part due to the new attraction of the concept of *belles-lettres*. It was natural enough within an empirical tradition to introduce evidence and illustrations of human feelings and motivation (no richer repository than literature could be found, nor one so freely accessible). Commonsense assumptions and the evidence of the senses took the place of abstractions; this was a shift which the business of education and the impetus towards social refinement seemed with increasing obviousness to require.

It followed that a new rationale of discrimination might be established – one more securely grounded in human nature, in the discourse of common feelings and perceptions. In England, Johnson defined criticism as that which 'reduces the regions of Literature under the dominion of science' (*Rambler* 92). For Hogarth, Burke, Gerard, Kames and the generation concerned with analyses of the effects of beauty, sublimity and pathos, the possibilities of a science of criticism were explored. In Scotland, concern with the operations of taste was expressed with a social rather than an individualized voice. A favourite topic (particularly among Edinburgh literati) was that of the 'Standard of Taste' and a favourite exercise was to explore the importance of consensus in criticism as elsewhere in society.

Bacon's description of 'the duty and office of Rhetoric' is 'to apply Reason to Imagination for the better moving of the Will' (III, p. 409). The role of syllogistic reasoning in Dean Aldrich's short but enduring pedagogic treatise *Artis Logicae Compendium* (1691) and the University of Oxford's expulsion of Locke merge in Pope's attack on Oxford dons:

> Each staunch polemic, stubborn as a rock,
> Each fierce Logician, still expelling Locke

> (*Dunciad* IV, ll. 195–6)

No such comment could possibly be made on Scottish academic attitudes. There, the eighteenth-century concern with social communication and common standards of value is related to a philosophy of taste. In the

---

[2] Howell, pp. 345 ff. discusses the originality of Duncan's use of Locke's teaching in dealing with the problems of logic and his 'creative relation to Thomas Jefferson's great work, the Declaration of Independence'.

priorities of the Scottish pedagogic systems, teaching and learning were less subject to the demands of apparently ossified traditions of learning, on the one hand, or to the transient preoccupations of the fashions of the metropolis, on the other.

The network – for it was that – of Scottish universities had long-standing connections with their sister-establishments in France and the Low Countries: the professoriates were in close and respected communication with one another. The universities were ancient institutions: Glasgow founded in 1451, St Andrews in 1411, King's College, Aberdeen in 1495, Edinburgh in 1583 and Marischal, Aberdeen in 1593. Students were, as a rule, younger, and a far higher proportion of the population was educated at university than in England. Instruction was more generally in the vernacular, a grammarian was employed to assist those backward in their knowledge of the classical language, and the range of illustration would be more open and imaginative than under Latin instruction.[3]

In 1748 Adam Smith, coming from five years in Oxford to lecture on moral philosophy in Edinburgh, decided that the plan of teaching he had inherited from his predecessor was too dry and abstruse to be either of use or interest to his listeners. 'Accordingly', wrote the student who followed Smith to Glasgow to hear the lectures a second time and on whose notes Smith's editors rely:

after exhibiting a general view of the powers of the mind, and explaining so much of the ancient logic as was requisite to gratify curiosity with respect to an artificial method of reasoning, which had once occupied the universal attention of the learned, he dedicated all the rest of his time to the delivery of a system of rhetoric and belles lettres. The best method of explaining and illustrating the various powers of the human mind, the most useful part of metaphysics, arises from an examination of the several ways of communicating our thoughts by speech, and from an attention to the principles of those literary compositions which contribute to persuasion or entertainment. By those arts, everything that we perceive or feel, every operation of our minds, is expressed in such a manner, that it may be clearly distinguished and remembered. There is, at the same time, no branch of literature more suited to youth at their first entrance upon philosophy than this, which lays hold of their taste and their feelings.[4]

A similar undermining of the outworn if ingenious 'subtleties of logic' was effected by Alexander Gerard in his *Plan of Education* (1754) describing the reform of the syllabus in Marischal College. Where Gerard

---

[3] Roger Emerson, 'Scottish Universities in the Eighteenth Century'; Joan Pittock, 'Rhetoric and Belles Lettres in the North East', in Carter and Pittock (eds), *Aberdeen and the Enlightenment*, pp. 276–81.

[4] Cited by J. C. Bryce in Adam Smith, *Lectures on Rhetoric and Belles Lettres* (Oxford, 1983), p. 11.

is concerned with useful precepts which may be gleaned from literature to provide a system of rules of criticism and for the improvement of taste, Smith turns to explore rhetoric with reference to the assumptions of historians and lawyers, commenting on a wide variety of literary styles and on different (including contemporary) approaches to the art of communication. His exposition is practical and his manner easy: 'We in this country are most of us very sensible that the perfection of language is very different from what we commonly speak in. The idea we form of a good stile is almost contery [*sic*] to that which we generally hear' (p. 42). The result of this, suggests Smith, is that a refined style is supposed to be one remote from plainness. This is a pity: the most effective style is not the most ornamented, but the plainest. That of Swift is preferable to those of Shaftesbury and Addison, who are so much admired – 'Swift ... who is the plainest as well as the most proper and precise of all the English writers is despised as nothing out of the common road; each of us thinks he could have written as well.' Smith despises existing systems of rhetoric as 'a very silly set of books and not at all instructive'. As far as he is concerned, rules of criticism are a matter of common sense (p. 54).

In his overview of rules of composition (Lecture 12) Smith examines the different kinds of writing (including the novel) and means of persuasion as well as the structuring of the text – the use of suspense in narrative, for instance. In his account of the origins and elements of language Smith uses illustrations from ancient and modern literatures alike – from Homer and Herodotus, Cicero, Lucian and Quintilian, Horace, Tacitus and Juvenal, Dryden, Pope, Prior, Addison and Swift, Shaftesbury and Rowe, Voltaire, Rousseau, and so on. Considering different kinds of historical writing he is alert to the distances in time which separate the logical and rhetorical requirements of a Roman trial from those of a contemporary Scottish court.

Smith's pragmatic approach to the experience of communication and the structuring of literary kinds comes closer to the attempts at holistic criticism of the late twentieth century than we would expect. In a lecture delivered 'entirely without book', as the enthusiastic student's transcript records (Lecture 16), Smith discusses story-telling in terms of the suspension of disbelief, the different kinds of fiction, the preservation of decorum (easier, as he points out, in a short than in a long and complex piece and in simple rather than in complex structures – such as tragedy, for example). Shakespeare pleases more than Racine, though the latter has the greater command of decorum. The pleasure afforded by an ode or elegy in which sentiments differ hardly at all from the common state of mind are what most please us. 'Such is that on the Church yard, or Eton College, by Mr Gray' (p. 127).

Such unpretentious acuteness picks up the nature of reader response in determining genre at the same time as it opens literature to his hearers with imaginative breadth and enlightened perception. Smith displays the resources of literature as an educational force in terms of discrimination as well as communication. He offers it not only as a socializing experience but as one which extends the imagination and reflective resources of the reader. There are no artificial barriers interposed: ancients and moderns are of equal weight: decorum is merely a vehicle of analysis and has no mysterious authority, nor have the hypothetical refinements of taste. At his death Adam Smith left a system of criticism uncompleted.

The *Essays* of Hume direct attention to the role of feeling in experiencing literature: in tragedy

The whole art of the Poet is employed, in rouzing and supporting the compassion and indignation, the anxiety and resentment of his audience. They are pleased in proportion as they are afflicted, and never are so happy as when they employ tears, sobs, and cries to give vent to their sorrow, and relieve their heart, swoln with the tenderest sympathy and compassion.

(pp. 216–17)

Such pleasures are augmented by the sensations of taste, delicacy, refinement of feeling:

The impulse or vehemence, arising from sorrow, compassion, indignation, receives a new direction from the sentiments of beauty. The latter, being the predominant emotion, seize [*sic*] the whole mind, and convert the former into themselves, or at least tincture them so strongly as totally to alter their nature. And the soul, being at the same time, rouzed by passion, and charmed by eloquence, feels on the whole strong movement, which is altogether delightful.

(p. 220)

The difficulty of establishing a consensus of opinion, a standard of taste, with such driving forces is obvious. It had long been needed. Dryden had insisted in 'MacFlecknoe' and in the introduction to his *Essay of Dramatic Poesy*, how wit and good breeding might readily perceive the inanities and poverty-stricken clichés of a lower class of writers than his own – those who catered for the populace in general rather than for the cognoscenti.[5] The problem of popular taste had been

[5] 'Well, gentlemen', said Eugenius, 'You may speak your pleasure of these authors; but though I and some few more about the town may give you a peaceable hearing, yet, assure yourselves, there are multitudes who would think you malicious and them injured: especially him whom you first described; he is the very Withers of the city: they have bought more editions of his works than would serve to lay under all their pies at the Lord Mayor's Christmas' (John Dryden, *Of Dramatic Poesy*, ed. George Watson (2 vols., London, 1962), I, p. 22.

accepted and sidestepped by Addison who employed patriotic and primitive criteria in his paper on 'Chevy Chase'. For Shaftesbury and Addison
the principles of good taste were enshrined in Greek and Roman texts.
Johnson's co-operation with the booksellers resulted in a canon pragmatically geared to prospective sales.[6] In Scotland, however, the philosophical implications of a desired consensus attracted the educated
professionals who dominated the smaller and (partly because of a preoccupation with religious and political elements of discourse) culturally
homogeneous communities. It was thus an empirical solution to the
undoubted truth that tastes differ to which Hume arrived in his celebrated
essay 'On the Standard of Taste'. The idea of consensus was agreeable to
the civilized and civilizing impetus of Scottish society, especially in the
capital. Hume's assertion that 'Reason is and ever must be the slave of
the passions' is at once true and provocative. His pragmatic recommendation is for a consensus of educated opinion as the standard of taste.

The pleasures afforded by the arts are related to taste and sensibility
in a judgemental context: Hume's enlightened attitude resembles that of
Dr Johnson in his conclusion that 'Strong sense, united to delicate sentiment, improved by practice, perfected by comparison, and cleared of
all prejudice, can alone entitle criticism to this valuable character, and
the joint verdict of such, wherever they are to be found, is the true
standard of taste and beauty' (p. 306).

Hume repudiates the Gothic, the unwholesome and the decadent as
inimical to good taste. He deprecates as 'disagreeable' the 'gloomy disastrous stories, with which melancholy people entertain their companions'
(p. 282). Taste is both civilizing and educative and is a term sufficiently
pliable and ambivalent to stray into the paths of *belles-lettres* where the
appreciation of taste, sensibility and beauty acquire a broad and vaguely
elitist potential, or continue along a narrower track where the educational benefits of sentiments in various texts – especially those of antiquity, the classics – are put to use.

The first relates most clearly to developments in the teaching of
literature in Edinburgh where Hugh Blair was appointed to the first
Chair of Rhetoric and Belles Lettres in 1762 and where the expansion
of periodical comment on taste facilitated the growth of fashion and
opinion. The second is more characteristic of the humanist teaching
traditions prevailing in Aberdeen's two universities with their acknowledged responsibility for the education of clergy and schoolmasters within
a region at some distance from any large or sophisticated community.
Here Alexander Gerard and James Beattie, followed by Robert Eden

---

[6] See Lawrence Lipking, 'Inventing the common reader: Samuel Johnson and the
canon', in Pittock and Wear (eds.), *Interpretation*, pp. 153–74.

Scott, continued the tradition established by David Fordyce and the younger Thomas Blackwell early in the eighteenth century.

A student of David Fordyce, Alexander Gerard, was appointed to succeed him as Professor of Moral Philosophy at Marischal College in 1754. Gerard's reforms to the degree structure have already been referred to. Perhaps he was influenced by Fordyce's *Dialogues Concerning Education* (1745). Gerard's *Plan of Education* (1754) depends on an analogy between philosophy and criticism: as the rules of criticism are formed by an accurate scrutiny of the best works of poetry, so philosophy is best studied through the acquisition of knowledge and experience. In the Aberdeen Philosophical Society or 'Wise Club' (1756–77) Thomas Reid, George Campbell, Gerard, Beattie and others deliberated a variety of topics related to criticism and philosophy. Gerard's *Essay on Taste* (1756) and his *Essay on Genius* (1772) were influenced by these deliberations of this close-knit academic community of the north-east. Discussion of the arts and human knowledge of commonsense philosophy, of answers to the scepticism of Hume and on the philosophy of rhetoric reflected the sound moral preoccupations of this community of scholars. In Beattie's work, and especially in the widely popular *Essay on Truth* of 1782, the philosophy of taste supported traditional pietistic values as a defining preoccupation of the Scottish temperament.

In 1755 the Edinburgh Society for the Advancement of Arts, Manufacturers and Commerce offered a prize for the best essay on taste: in 1756 it was awarded to Alexander Gerard. His essay was published in 1758 and in 1759 was issued in a collection of essays on taste by Voltaire, d'Alembert and Montesquieu. The *Essay on Taste* is a central work of the Enlightenment.

According to Gerard's Introduction to the *Essay*, 'Taste consists chiefly in the improvement of those principles, which are commonly called the *powers of imagination*, and are considered by modern philosophers as *internal* or *reflex* senses.' A methodical identification of these as senses of novelty, sublimity, beauty, imitation, harmony, oddity, ridicule and virtue is followed by an account of their complicating factors – passion and judgement. The senses can be improved by attention to sensibility, refinement and correctness as well as a regard to proportion. Finally, the concerns of taste lie in matters relating to imagination, genius, criticism and pleasure and its effect on character. To these Beattie was to add the senses of shame and honour and Kames those of virtue and benevolence.

The confidence which Gerard and his contemporaries optimistically employed in analysing the operations of the human mind is methodical and suggestive. The reliance of the philosophers of taste on the ambivalences of these modes of identification of human feelings was to die a natural death as an identified branch of speculation in the early nineteenth century (see the article on 'Taste' in the *Encyclopedia Britannica*, 12th edn, 1917) though its discourse was relied on in the descriptive and impressionistic criticism of *belles-lettres*: its string of descriptive terms was the natural coinage of literary experience. Its practitioners attempted to establish a system of aesthetic analysis, but suffered from the effects of its own self-reflexive narrowness. Preoccupation with taste was a social factor. As Kant observed, in this kind of enlightenment man does not emerge from 'his self-imposed minority [which is] the ability to use one's own understanding without the guidance of another'.

In his Appendix to the third edition of the *Essay*, however, Gerard stirs other waters: the imitative nature of poetry and the limitations of language itself:

Poetry is not, nor can be properly imitation, as producing a resemblance of its immediate subject. Its employing language, or instituted signs, renders it absolutely incapable of being in this sense imitative. No combination of significant sounds can form an image or copy, either of sensible or of intellectual objects. An historical narration of any transaction, or a naturalist's description of any visible object, would not, by any man, be called an imitation, but a painting of the same transaction, or of the same object, would be termed an imitation by all men.

(p. 280)

The difference between poetry and other kinds of communication lies in the vivacity of the idea excited by poetry. The importance of taste is to identify the reflex senses and to foster such a sensibility of heart as will fit a man 'for being easily moved, and for readily catching, as by infection any passion that a work is fitted to excite' (1780, pp. 86–9). A standard of taste will hold any excesses in check by relying on principles of criticism. This differs from Hume's identification of a possible standard as a consensus of informed individuals. In such areas of discourse rigour and method were self-validating. A hermeneutic approach to literary experience was far off, but occasionally glimpsed in a growing awareness of the different roles and strategies of criticism.

Gerard's reforms at Marischal resulted in shifting the rhetoric syllabus from logic towards criticism and composition. This is clear from the notes taken by the students of that impeccably conscientious teacher, James Beattie. When Gerard moved from Marischal to take the Chair of Divinity at King's Beattie succeeded his teacher in the Chair of Moral Philosophy. In Edinburgh the business of criticism, fashion and belletrism might flourish: the moral benefits of reading literature were the sterner business of the north-east.[7] The *Philosophy of Rhetoric* (1776) of Beattie's

---

[7] See Dwyer, *Virtuous Discourse*, ch. 1 and *passim*, and Alexander, *Edinburgh Reviewers*.

contemporary, George Campbell, is founded on the human soul's disposition to be influenced by truth and virtue.

Several sets of lecture notes, all checked by Beattie himself, survive to
chart the kinds of criticism he taught in the second half of the eighteenth
century. Nor were his notes left unrevised or unchanged by shifting
circumstances. An early set is fairly predictable in the account of rhetoric,
poetry ('it imitates Nature by means of Language') and eloquence. Six
years later the notes show the influence of Campbell and Reid. In his
later lecture series of the seventies Beattie deals with the problem of
communication in terms of intelligibility and standard speech – he lists
the principal Scoticisms which his students must avoid if they are to
rank as educated and civilized members of society.

His interpretation of taste is based on Gerard's work. The role of
taste is significant as it relates to the effect of poetry on the feelings, and
as it awakens sympathy: 'If we were destitute of Sympathy, we should be
incapable of receiving from Poetry or Oratory those emotions ye Author
intended to excite, and consequently we could not judge of ye merit or
demerit of such performances'. Rhetoric is to be approached pragmatically in terms of the common ground between teacher and student:
literature brings students face to face with moral issues. 'A relish for the
sublime and beautiful elevates the mind above sensuality and meanness'.
Taste 'leads to a study of the works of Nature, and this study, attentively pursued, will lead an intelligent mind to contemplate the power,
wisdom and goodness of a Creator' (p. 181). In his poem *The Minstrel*,
Beattie shows, in ways which were to impress both Cowper and
Wordsworth, the effect of literature and landscape on the sensibilities of
his hero.[8]

There is a difference between Beattie's view that in literature, as in
life, the cultivation of the self through education can only be pursued
in the contexts of morality and religion, and the concentration on
'virtuous discourse' among the academics and literati of the cities of the
lowland belt. There, sentiment and sensibility move into the discourse
of sentimentality – notably in the work of Henry Mackenzie of course,
and where criticism as a business and a fashion are more frequently
evident.[9] The increasing use of the term 'belles lettres' became institutionalized in 1762 in the creation of the Edinburgh Chair. In the popular and widely influential lectures of Hugh Blair, published in 1783,
there is evidence of shifting priorities in rhetoric and criticism. The role
of literature (defined in Johnson's *Dictionary* of 1756 as 'learning')
moves into the discourse of feelings and taste. For Blair taste is 'the

[8] See Dwyer, *Virtuous Discourse*, and McGuirk, *Robert Burns and the Sentimental Era*.
[9] See Horner, *Present State*, ch. 4.

power of receiving pleasure from the beauties of nature and art, and so reducible to two characters, delicacy and correctness'. Blair's critical work is full of detailed illustration, citation of numerous authorities. He relies on the accepted genres, defers to the worn distinction between Ancients and Moderns. He is less challenging, less speculative, more improvingly packed with information and appreciation than his northern contemporaries. The most noteworthy example of his powers of admiration is his *Critical Dissertation on the Poems of Ossian* (1763). (Beattie's sceptical attitude to Macpherson and his epics is remarkable in the author of *The Minstrel*.)

Blair's self-imposed role was to find a match for Homer among the Scottish mountains. He voices a fashionable admiration for an acceptably voiced patriotism and primitivism in connection with the new area of poetic inspiration already tapped by Collins, Thomson and Gray. The aesthetic of the patriotic enabled Macpherson to make use of both nations to make his fortune. The cult of feeling, whether for times past in primitive vein or for star-crossed lovers and heroic deaths in which the epics abound, endowed with the elevating and repetitive notes of biblical poetry, was easily influential and fluently contagious. Blair's uncritical adulation of the text was endorsed by Lord Kames in his *Elements of Criticism* in 1762. The wise men of Edinburgh, not having much acquaintance with Macpherson's subject or theme, were for him as, roughly speaking, the home side, backed by Dr Johnson, was against.

Blair's transatlantic popularity as a guide to *belles-lettres* is due to the specificity of his guidance in matters of literary taste. His appreciation of the beauties of literature and his clear and basic rules for that appreciation were an encouragement to that flourishing growth industry of the 'beauties' of author after author which provided much profit for the booksellers and harmless 'culture' for the reading public.[10]

Lord Kames, on the other hand, retains the most enduring reputation for philosophical criticism in the Edinburgh milieu. 'I don't mean he has taught us any thing but he has told us old things in a new way', Dr Johnson said in his praise. In his *Philosophy of Rhetoric* I. A. Richards pinpointed Kames's misprision of the functioning of metaphor (because he restricts its propriety to the imaged nature of the poet's subject); he adds: 'Turning his [Kames's] pages you will again and again find points raised, which, if his treatment of them is unsatisfactory, are none the less points that no serious study of language should neglect' (p. 99). For Kames, also, the principles of criticism relate to the feeling heart which Gerard had prioritized and which was basic to the speculative excursions

[10] See Lehmann, *Henry Home*, ch. 14.

into social sympathy of Smith and Hume, as it had been to Ferguson. Dedicating the *Elements* to George III, Kames writes:

Fine arts [are] encouraged, not simply for private amusement, but for their beneficial influence in society. By uniting different ranks in the same elegant pleasures, they promote benevolence; by cherishing love of order, they inforce submission to government; and by inspiring delicacy of feeling, they make regular government a double blessing.

(Elements, I, p. v)

Education through sensitivity established the experience of literature (not specifically the experience of learning) as central to the civilizing and ordering process. The interpretation of its remit is in terms of an aesthetic of beauty. This is a follow-up to the sister-arts perspectives of the neo-classical influence, rather than an original voice. Kames's critical ideas are those of a strong-minded individual (according to Boswell Kames was a judge of hanging fame) who grasps the socializing potential of controlled feeling. Feeling in the context of taste – controlled and exercised perception and approved discrimination – may operate to the social good. The principles of association bind perception and idea which may be affected by emotions and passions to engender action. Kames notes that Montesquieu, in the *Esprit des Lois*, 'gives too great indulgence to imagination: the tone of his language swells frequently above his subject' *(Elements,* II, p. 346).

Kames concludes his work with his own interpretation of the standard of taste, in which his concern with the control of disorder is not far from his formulations. He writes with his eye on the perspectives of time and change from savagery to civilization which Vico had explored in his *Scienza Nuova* (1725):

Men, originally savage and brutal, acquire not rationality nor any delicacy of taste till they be long disciplined in society. To ascertain the rules of morality, we appeal not to the common sense of savages, but of men in their more perfect state, and we make the same appeal in forming the rules that ought to govern the fine arts: in neither can we safely rely on local or transitory taste; but on what is the most universal and the most lasting among polite Nations.

(Elements, II, p. 498)

Boswell's pursuit of 'transitory taste' in his flight to London to emulate the modish cynicism of the Nonsense Club was modified by his more fervent courtship of Dr Johnson. There is an interesting contrast between the dominant literary elite of Churchill, Wilkes and their associates in London and the Edinburgh elite of Kames, Hume and Lord Elibank.

The foregrounding of sympathy, sentiment and beauty was carried further in criticism, both psychological and aesthetic. The philosophy of taste expired under the pressures of German philosophy and more urgent religious and national passions than the Enlightenment could offer.

The probing of the interpenetrations of art and life has more far-reaching effects in marking differences of other kinds between Scotland and the southern kingdom. Kames narrowed the circle of those capable of developing taste. '[T]hose who depend for food on bodily labour [are] totally devoid of taste; of such a taste at least as can be of use in the fine arts' (*Elements*, II, p. 449). The world of folk culture, of 'Tam o' Shanter', was beyond this pale. The success of Ramsay in the use of the vernacular, of Smollett and Burns in undermining the conventionalities of politeness and decorum, make use of the parameters of social discourse and standards of taste. The susceptibilities of taste and feeling eschewed wit of any radical kind. In the 'hot bed of genius' which Smollett saw in Edinburgh the superior perceptiveness of a few was accessible through education, breeding and money. It was a state of affairs which imparted to the social upwardly mobile the need for a personal delicacy of perception, whether aesthetic or moral.

Where the concept of *belles-lettres* takes over from rhetoric, the affectations of culture tend to express their understanding of its social implications more lightly than in the past. The literati were more confident of their own capacity for responding to the primitive and uncivilized than one might have expected, in view of the recent past and the threat of risings in the Stuart cause. For Kames, Ossian is successful in drawing characters as he 'never fails to delight his reader with the beautiful attitudes of his heroes':

Dermid and Ossian were one: they reaped the battle together. Their friendship was as strong as their steel; and death walked between them to the field. They rush on the foe like two rocks falling from the brow of Ardven. Their swords are stained with the blood of the valiant: warriors faint at their names. Who is equal to Ossian but Dermid? Who to Dermid but Ossian?

(*Elements*, II, p. 330)

In terms of its political, religious and racial history, Scotland's culture and its landscapes were bound together in the history and myth of a distinct and recently blood-stained past. A contemporary poet like Gray perceived an untapped vein of myth and legend in the Highlands. The recollections of a lost and cherished independent past recurring in the defeats of the Stuart cause and the long traditions of the royal house of Scotland were both authentic and glamorous. The authenticity of different and more worthwhile ways of life had been memorably caught by Goldsmith in 'The Deserted Village' as it was by Fergusson in his 'Elegy on the Death of Scots Music', evoking an ancient independence and a republican virtue:

O Scotland! that cou'd yence afford
To bang the pith of Roman sword,
Winna your sons, wi' joint accord,
    To battle speed?
And fight till Music be restor'd,
    Which now lies dead.

No monarch could be restored to times of peace and plenty: there could be no 'Astræa Redux'. The music of Scotland is echoed in the elegiac fall of tears for the nature of things – 'mentem mortalia tangunt'. It is accordingly alien to the Enlightenment.

The need to retain a national identity, to reject the imported delicacies and fashionable refinements of the south, recurs in the works of Ramsay, Fergusson and Burns: it lets loose the satire of the Scots tongue, subverting the smoother tones of its neighbours; it inspires the collectors of songs and ballads. The sense of the past and the sense of place, of legend and story, are contrasted in their kind of authenticity with alternative realities, the refinement (and the sentiment) of modern societies. All the attractions of bravery and romance had illuminated the sufferings and escape of Charles Edward Stuart after the battle of Culloden Moor. Real dangers undergone, loyalty persevered in in spite of bribery and persecution, and courage displayed in the face of adversity brought back a scent of old values very different from those of the commercialism of modern times. The impact of the events challenged contemporary ideas of delicacy and politeness. Johnson's and Boswell's pilgrimage in the footsteps of the Prince in their journey to the Western Isles is a tribute to the force of history as legend. Earlier, in his *Enquiry into the Life and Writings of Homer* (1735) and his *Letters on Mythology* (1747) Thomas Blackwell, Principal of Marischal College, evokes the real circumstances of the life led by Homer while at the same time paying tribute to the magic of genius and the creative powers of myth in ways which seem far removed from the scientifically inspired analyses of Enlightenment criticism: 'What may be the Appearances or Aspects of Things natural or divine, which have the virtue thus to shake our frames and raise such a Commotion in the Soul, I will not so much as enquire. The Search, I should suspect, would be fruitless, if not *irreverent*' (p. 160).[11] The force of metaphor which transforms actual events and contemporary circumstances into myth and legend is the basis of Homer's magic. Blackwell invokes Bacon's opinion that the extravagancies of the imagination are 'the Wisdom of the Ancients, and a constant Source of Pleasure to a speculative Man, as they represent some of the grandest Ideas in Nature and Art' (p. 5). The

---

[11] Compare Simonsuuri, 'Blackwell and the myth of Orpheus', in Carter and Pittock (eds.), *Aberdeen and the Enlightenment*, pp. 199–206.

study of mythology, folklore and antiquities may reach into Romanticism more deeply than the philosophy of criticism of the Enlightenment.

The discourses of criticism fall within the idiom of self-conscious culture – social, academic – communicating appreciation, interpretation and discrimination. The possibilities of a science of criticism are established by the Scottish writers of the eighteenth century to meet the requirements of their society and its needs, as well as the problems of experiencing literature and the worlds it represents. Its cultural implications lie outside the scope of this chapter.

25

Canons and canon formation

Jan Gorak

Introduction

Criticism involves the selection, restoration, and evaluation of works retrieved from the past and the assessment, however tentatively offered, of works produced in the present. No doubt some societies can settle these tasks by an appeal to precedent, but where cultural production increases and audiences become less homogeneous – certainly the conditions that applied in Europe between 1660 and 1800 – more complex arrangements will become necessary for the estimation of cultural value and the provision of rational or plausible criteria of evaluation. In accomplishing both these tasks, a canon of some kind will prove useful.

For a long time the word *canon* had a restricted range of application. The most common usage referred to the collection of sacred writings accepted as authoritative by various Christian denominations. (Although Hebraic culture possessed its collection of sacred books, it did not call this catalogue a *canon*; however, European writers in the eighteenth century frequently did so.) Students of antiquity and sculpture were also familiar with the *canon* described by Pliny, whose discussion of the work of ancient sculptor Polycletus refers to 'a Canon, or Model Statue'[1] that set the standard for subsequent representations of the human body in that art. Polycletus also wrote a lost treatise *Canon*, which set out the theoretical basis for representing the human body adequately, and the high status this treatise once enjoyed may partly explain the long-standing usage that links canons to general principles, accepted rules and axioms.

Contemporary literary criticism restricts the meaning of *canon* almost exclusively to a list of valued secular works. Such a usage has a relatively brief history. Although scholars had long known that teaching in classical and Byzantine culture proceeded by the presentation of selected model examples, it was not until 1768 that David Ruhnken introduced the word *canon* to describe this process. Ruhnken's *Historia Critica Oratorum Graecorum* describes the radical pedagogical innovations

---

[1] Pliny, *Natural History*, trans. H. Rackham (10 vols., London, 1938–63), IX, pp. 168–9.

undertaken by two scholars of the early Alexandrian academy, Aristophanes of Byzantium (c. 257–180 BC) and Aristarchus of Samothrace (c. 215–c. 143 BC). These two men – 'critics of the highest intelligence and rarest learning' – recognized the dangers of cultural surplus, and acknowledged 'that the great number of writings was more harmful than beneficial to good letters'. They responded by drawing up 'a canon of only ten orators they thought the most important'.[2]

This innovative process of canon formation involves an act of choice sponsored by the agents of a powerful institution, the academy. The choice itself involves some element of convenience (there is too much material for the students to handle), but in making it, the teachers concern themselves chiefly with the value of their chosen works (they choose what is 'most important', not, for example, what is most 'teachable'). Ruhnken considers this an epoch-making act; as he sees it, these selected lists laid the foundations for the preservation of a foreign, extinguished culture.

Motivated initially by pedagogic convenience, Aristophanes and Aristarchus soon arrived at estimates of critical value. Their canons, Ruhnken notes, brought together writers 'of first rank' and to this canon of orators he (and his successors) soon added canons of tragedy, epic, comedy, history, elegy, and lyric. The provision of these selective lists, eighteenth-century scholars recognized, cleared the ground for a series of other operations – textual restoration, editorial redaction, allegorical exegesis – that are just as typical of critical institutions as the tasks of classroom instruction and literary evaluation.

In a way not at all unknown in the history of criticism, Ruhnken's coinage provides a word for issues already conceived of as pressingly important, and important in contexts far removed from the society he describes. His 'canon' provides a vessel for his own age's anxieties about the conditions of cultural survival, the institutions responsible for cultural choice, the criteria of critical appraisal, and the methods of critical selection. Ruhnken's momentous new usage highlights how two 'canons' interact. The 'canons of criticism' – the basic principles of critical judgement – provide the principles of selection that underlie the 'canon' itself – the list of exemplary texts. In so far as criticism is a

---

[2] Ruhnken's *Historia Critica Oratorum Graecorum* has been reprinted many times. However, I have quoted from the version found in the original edition of Rutilius Lupus that Ruhnken compiled under the title *P. Rutilii Lupi: De Figuris Sententiarum et Elocutionis Duo Libri* (Lyons, 1768), p. xcv. 'Exorti enim sunt duo summo ingenio et singulari doctrina critici, Aristarchus et Aristophanes Byzantus, qui, cum animadvertissent, ingentem scriptorum turbam plus obeisse bonis literis, quam prodesse, suum judicium secuti, certum omnis generis scriptorum delectum haberent. Itaque ex magna oratorum copia tamquam in canonem dumtaxat rettulerunt.'

rational activity or an activity capable of rationality, it will need its 'canons'; in so far as it is inevitably and increasingly a selective one, it will need a 'canon'.

Rules, canons, and canon

Critics from Wordsworth to Eliot have used the word *canons* interchangeably with the word *rules* in a conscious bid to associate both with the most frigid and conventional aspects of a superseded literary tradition. This view, which is influential throughout the history of modern criticism, ties *canon* to constraint rather than choice and turns the history of poetic movements into a series of revolutions. In 1801, when Wordsworth wants to distinguish the second edition of *Lyrical Ballads* from the rusty machinery of outdated critical custom, he points to the 'canon of criticism' that conventionally separates poetry from prose. This separation, Wordsworth warns, is one 'the Reader . . . must utterly reject if he wishes to be pleased with these volumes'.[3] Even so, by the time Wordsworth writes, the 'canon' he attacks could hardly claim self-evident truth or universal assent. Hugh Blair, for example, had offered an annual rebuttal of it to his students in the Rhetoric class at the University of Edinburgh. In his *Lectures on Rhetoric and Belles Lettres*, a volume published in 1783 that made available material long presented to undergraduate audiences, Blair announced that 'The truth is, Verse and Prose, on some occasions, run into one another, like light and shade'.[4]

This cautionary example points to the danger of trying to understand the history of *canon* through a series of manifestoes. Yet it does indicate the currents of deep-set resistance to rules and canons that ripple through the history of literary criticism from 1660 to 1800. In 1672 when, if at any time, one might expect rules to elicit considerable assent, Dryden reports that 'Many men are shocked at the name of rules.' They understand by the word only 'a kind of magisterial prescription upon poets',[5] he explains. Because this prescription was so frequently dispensed by some French affiliate of Aristotle – a Rapin or a Boileau – even greater mistrust followed. The mistrust persisted even into the mid-twentieth century, when E. R. Curtius suggested that *rules* constituted a French bid for intellectual hegemony, an attempt 'to promulgate the forms which correspond to her national mind as universally binding'.[6]

From 1635, French culture had not lacked the institutional means to make such a campaign possible. The French Academy, which for a time

---

[3] Wordsworth, *Lyrical Ballads*, p. 252.   [4] Blair, *Lectures*, II, p. 313.
[5] Dryden, *Of Dramatic Poesy*, I, p. 260.   [6] Curtius, *European Literature*, p. 265.

consolidated Curtius's three major agencies of literary canon formation – the church, state, and school – in the one formidable figure of Cardinal Richelieu, enjoyed enviable advantages in enforcing its cultural choices. Yet many French aims were also shared by writers in England, who often looked admiringly at French successes in regularizing usage, weeding out barbarisms, and raising the standards of politeness.

Swift's 'A Proposal for Correcting, Improving and Ascertaining the English Tongue' (1712) represents the best-known British contribution to the debate about a national academy. Swift's position can best be termed a cultural paternalism. He recognizes the importance of authoritative example at every level of the national culture, stressing the role of the Court in transmitting 'the Standard of Propriety and Correctness of Speech' to the aristocracy, and of 'the Bible and Common-Prayer-Book' in relaying 'a kind of Standard for Language' to the common people.[7] The joint alliance between power and learning embodied in a national academy will make its first priority the stabilization of language. This stabilization provides the necessary foundation for the nation's cultural life.

Some of the essay's most energetic passages imagine the fearful consequences of the current 'Age of Learning and Politeness'. A cult of fashion limits the opportunities to exercise a traditional craft. Historians in antiquity, Swift notes, enjoyed greater public esteem than their modern counterparts:

How then shall any Man, who hath a Genius for History, equal to the best of the Antients, be able to undertake such a Work with Spirit and Chearfulness, when he considers, that he will be read with Pleasure but a very few Years, and in an Age or two shall hardly be understood without an Interpreter? This is like employing an excellent Statuary to work upon mouldring Stone.[8]

But however keenly Swift feels the plight of talent buried under the rubble of fashion, he points to a far greater danger. For without the monuments to civic virtue collected by the canonical ancient historians, a modern commonwealth lacks an indispensable public resource. Who will immortalize the achievements of a latter-day Cato when the English language is capable only of recording the trivial, when English authors celebrate only the topical?

Swift's aspirations towards stability and permanence derived from a joint legacy of great bitterness. Europe had not long emerged from what Sir William Temple called 'the abyss of disputes about matters of religion',[9] an abyss commonly conceived of as a war of the Word. The zeal

---

[7] Swift, *Prose Works*, IV, pp. 5, 10, 14–15.
[8] Swift, *Prose Works*, IV, pp. 17–18. [9] Temple, *Five Essays*, p. 66.

for unrestricted access to the word of God, the exercise of unlimited ingenuity in its application, and the intensity of expectation projected on to canonical Scripture led many writers to agree with Shaftesbury that a separation of powers offered the best hope for civil peace. The sacred and the secular orders needed to mark out their territory, Shaftesbury suggested, in order to 'keep these provinces distinct and settle their just boundaries'.[10]

Neo-classical literature makes visible aspects of the relationship between politics and poetics that other traditions keep hidden. Accordingly, it comes as no surprise that the territorial metaphor also enjoyed currency inside the realm of literature proper. One of the most common images for the institution of letters between 1660 and 1800 refers to it as a 'republic', a 'province', or a 'commonwealth'. Boileau's *L'Art poétique* (1674) literalizes the metaphor in a remarkable way, allowing us to see beneath the conventional topos to a whole way of conceiving letters as a value-conferring activity. For Boileau, the history of art becomes a series of quasi-Virgilian annexations, in which the dangerous province of poetry must be harnessed to the civilizing force of correct rule. Boileau's Malherbe metamorphoses into a second Aeneas: 'Finally came Malherbe, who, for the first time in France, made us feel a just cadence in verse. He taught the power of a word put in its proper place and reduced the Muse to the rules of duty'.[11]

In Boileau's imagination, the world of letters contains a series of distinct, uncrossable boundaries, each controlled by an undisputed sovereign. Boileau singles out literature for special treatment, since its insurrectionary potential calls for the exercise of absolute powers. 'Every other art is ranked in different degrees and one can honourably fill the second rank. But in the perilous arts of verse and prose there are no degrees between the mediocre and the worthless.'[12]

For Boileau, genre and authorship become important institutional correctives to the inherently anarchic potential of literature. Genre guides author and audience along known public highways, so that no one,

---

[10] Shaftesbury, *Characteristics*, p. 232.
[11] Boileau, 'L'Art poétique', Chant I, ll. 131–4:

> Enfin Malherbe vint, et, le premier en France,
> Fit sentir dans les vers une juste cadence,
> D'un mot mis en sa place enseigna le pouvoir,
> Et réduisit la Muse aux règles du devoir.

[12] Boileau, 'L'Art poétique', Chant IV, ll. 29–33:

> Il est dans tout autre art des degrés différents.
> On peut avec honneur remplir les seconds rangs;
> Mais dans l'art dangereux de rimer et d'écrire,
> Il n'est point de degrés du médiocre au pire.
> Qui dit froid écrivain dit détestable auteur.

neither aspiring author nor expectant audience, will blunder into Racine's
Bérénice (1670) in search of an evening's mirth and spectacle. Authorship ensures that the commonwealth of letters exercises authority by
means of responsible officers able to transmit their craft to subsequent
generations. Moreover, if letters is to be acknowledged as a continuing
enterprise, it is important that not all roads to literary greatness be seen
as Roman in construction. Yet the great works of antiquity remain the
ultimate arbiters of cultural value, and the masterpieces of vernacular
traditions are ultimately weighed on the scales of Homer or Virgil.

The generic division that allotted each canonical artist a distinct region also stimulated other ways of organizing cultural achievement.
Thomas Blackwell's *An Enquiry into the Life and Writings of Homer*
(1735) notes that 'great Masters in every Profession and Science, always
appear in the same Period of Time, and are of the same Cast and
Model'.[13] In one way Blackwell reinforces the academic notion of a
period style, a prevailing set of norms inscribed in a limited catalogue
of canonical authorities. But his formulation also assimilates itself readily to the temporal division offered by Voltaire in *The Age of Louis XIV*
(1751). Here European cultural history divides neatly into four canonical epochs, each known by the name of a political ruler whose power
to impose peace (one suspects that such power was, like equality among
Orwell's animals, distributed somewhat unequally among Voltaire's rulers)
allows the arts to flourish. Hence Voltaire's 'cycles' bear the names of
Alexander, Augustus Caesar, the Medici, and Louis XIV.[14] The dynastic
names that Voltaire used for his 'cycles' were not, however, strictly
necessary to the organization of cultural history, which could be represented just as effectively by reference to the arts' own subject-matter or
formal organization. Accordingly, the tendency to group canonical works
around a distinctive style of culture (primitive, modern, and so on)
rather than around a royal sponsor, increased dramatically towards the
end of the century.

Karl Popper has advised social scientists to understand the 'logic of
situations' in assessing how 'ideas may spread and captivate individuals'.[15]
The logic of imagining the world of letters as a province or a Roman
republic lay chiefly in the large-scale institutional and moral continuities
it secured for eighteenth-century thinkers. To speak of a province is to
conceive of an empire, a centralized structure of authority that Reformation Europe appeared to have undermined permanently. To talk of a
'republic of letters' is to envisage an orderly disposal of cultural functions

---

[13] Blackwell, *Enquiry*, p. 74.
[14] See *Oeuvres*, XIV and XV, esp. XV, first ch., pp. 457–9.
[15] Popper, *The Poverty of Historicism* (London, 1957), p. 149.

that structural changes in the world of publishing appeared to threaten. To characterize the institution of letters as a 'commonwealth' is to credit letters with the legitimacy and continuity enjoyed by the larger polity. Citizens of a republic enjoy access to a common fund of civic benefits, ranging from military protection to uniform education. In the republic of letters, the canonical authors contribute to this fund, and successive generations become their beneficiaries. The commonwealth of letters furnishes its citizens with the *lingua franca* of literary expression, enabling them to cross literary frontiers without fearing any failure in communication. Even so, the idea of a 'republic', 'province', or 'commonwealth' of letters embodies aspirations to order that historical events could not support. These ideas belong to the logic of dream rather than the logic of *Realpolitik,* where, as recent studies have argued, the political analogies between Rome and eighteenth-century England could take a disturbing and unsettling turn. Only inside the logic of dream could a displaced intellectual class entertain the fictions of independence and civic concern so important to self-styled imperial or 'Augustan' authors. For this reason, it might be most accurate to think of the Augustan myth as a key element in the siege mentality of an eighteenth-century intellectual aristocracy.

These grand political metaphors for cultural transactions allowed the world of letters to attach itself to the authority of mighty precedent, where the security of a known, closed universe could exist alongside apparently endless spheres of extra-territorial influence. In this context, the republic of letters inevitably takes on the shape of an oligarchy, where a few writers of 'first rank' (Voltaire reduced these to just eight in *The Temple of Taste*) stand for the whole of a national culture. In time, as J. C. Maxwell once remarked, even 'antiquity itself can be stomached only in a rigidly selective presentation'.[16] Voltaire can stomach neither past nor present without drastic selection, but purges the republic of letters of a swarm of scribbling hacks, as well as reducing Rabelais by an eighth and Bayle to 'a single tome'. When Voltaire's narrator penetrates the inner sanctum of the temple to discover the canon-within-a-canon of eight authors who 'may serve as an example to posterity', he finds them still labouring assiduously at their texts, 'correcting faulty passages in their excellent writings which would be beauties in the works of their inferiors'.[17] At this point, the search for standards runs

---

[16] Maxwell, 'Demigods', p. 37.
[17] Voltaire, *Oeuvres*, VIII, p. 577. 'Enfin on nous fit passer dans l'intérieur du sanctuaire. Là, les mystères du dieu furent dévoilés; là, je vis ce qui doit servir d'exemple à la postérité: un petit nombre de véritablement grands hommes s'occupaient à corriger ces fautes de leurs écrits excellents, qui seraient des beautés dans les écrits médiocres.'

the risk of merging asceticism with aestheticism. Yet in a stronger version, as a vehicle for controlling cultural production as well as furnishing exemplary norms of correctness, the imperial metaphor had greater significance. The reduction of cultural suffrage that drastic selectiveness conferred on the past could also lend its authority to the present, where the activities of an intelligent, principled minority (one which, according to Johnson's hostile verdict, thought it 'had engrossed all the understanding and virtue of mankind')[18] could conceive of itself as continuing the civilizing mission of antiquity.

For some writers, however, Voltaire did not take his neo-classical assumptions far enough. In *Remarks upon M. Voltaire's Essay on the Epic Poetry of European Nations* (1728), Paul Rolli argues that the canonical achievements of European culture knit together into one unified narrative, readily comprehensible to a cultivated mind at any time:

> There is a degree of perfection and taste, which when authors and critics are arrived at, make them all of one nation, called the Commonwealth of Letters ... The Histories of Thucydides and Machiavelli seem to me as if they were writ by the same hand, and so do the Histories of Livy and Guiccardini. When I read Addison's work, I imagine I read Plato.[19]

Rolli's conviction that genius speaks a single language extends the tenure of his commonwealth of letters into eternity. Yet he achieves this by taking the cultural wish for the historic deed, dissolving what Guiccardini and Machiavelli employed as self-conscious analogy into a common identity.

Rolli's discussion offers no way of understanding cultural change, a problem that many eighteenth-century critics viewed as a potential threat to the unity of European letters. When Goldsmith considers this topic in *An Inquiry into the Present State of Polite Learning* (1759), he wonders whether the myth of a stellar canon in fact impoverishes a culture as a whole. 'Two poets in an age', he decides, 'are not sufficient to revive the splendour of decaying genius; nor should we consider the few as the national standard, by which to characterize the many'. Instead of a single restricted class of elite authors, Goldsmith argues the case for a standard fixed by the achievement of 'that numerous class of men who, placed above the vulgar, are yet beneath the great, and who confer fame on others without receiving any portion of it themselves'. He entrusts this second group with the treasury of public learning, pinning his hopes on the emergence of a more widely diffused bourgeois culture. Where Swift deploys his authors of 'first rank' as a shield to brandish against invading hordes of scribbling barbarians, Goldsmith

[18] Johnson, *Lives*, III, p. 61.
[19] Rolli, *Remarks upon M. Voltaire's Essay* (London, 1728), pp. 12–13.

hopes to educate public taste by means of an intelligent group of mid-dlemen, neither supremely gifted nor tortuously pedantic. These quali-ties allow them to serve as 'a proper standard, when others fail, to judge of a nation's improvement, or degeneracy in morals'.[20]

Yet from other directions the great ancients and the polite moderns faced a greater threat than the decay of the figures and institutions that once seemed to guarantee the continuity of European cultural life. In Britain, the expiry of the Licensing Act in 1695 lifted many printing restrictions and eased the way for a host of corporate undertakings among booksellers. Shared copyright, copyright transfer and purchase, strategic alliances among printing dynasties: these structural changes replace the republic with the market. In *A Tale of a Tub* (1704) Swift explores the threat this new order presents to accepted standards in letters. Swift's Grub Street represents a disturbing mixture of celebrity and anonymity where 'a corporation' of 'one hundred thirty six' poets 'of the first Rate' jostle aside 'a certain Author called Homer ... a Person not without some Abilities, and for an Ancient, of a tolerable Genius'.[21] Swift presents a world where the inability to understand Latin does not rule out contractual arrangement to translate it. The contrast between this world of commodity expansion and the common-wealth of learning celebrated in Book Three of *Gulliver's Travels* could hardly be more absolute. Inside the former, the question favoured by denizens of the republic of letters – 'How do you rank them, the most valued authors?' – has the status of a metaphysical question for a logical positivist.

When Swift pursues these problems to their source, in the 'rule and canon' of the Christian church, he finds that Scripture itself has become caught up in this mirage world of typographic constructs, so that the adjective 'canonical' loses any remaining threads of theological legitim-acy, becoming a tribute more to human ingenuity than divine authority. Like his favourite authors from antiquity, Scripture cannot remain untainted by hands eager to bend it to their purposes. The Puritans, who consider any word in the Bible potentially replete with significance, cannot build from Scripture a plausible narrative of what Christian culture means in human terms. Instead, they pull the threads of the text first in one direction, in an effort to enlarge its spiritual dimension through inspired interpretation, then in another, in a bid to press it into topical relevance. Since their 'rules' of interpretation veer from mysticism to factionalism, their 'canon' becomes at one end a zealot's divining rod, at the other a hollow reed swaying to any fashionable breeze. When Swift's three brothers decide to wear their coats in a fashion not permitted by

[20] Goldsmith, *Works*, I, pp. 276, 337.   [21] Swift, *Tale*, pp. 33, 127.

their father's will, they conveniently find a codicil that permits them to 'add certain Clauses for publick Emolument, though not deducible, *totidem verbis,* from the Letter of the Will'. 'This was understood for *Canonical*', the narrator observes, 'and therefore on the following *Sunday* they came to Church all covered with *Points*'.[22] By this time, the contradictions inherent in the status of *canon* and *rule*, as narrative of salvation and code of ecclesiastical authority, have become glaringly apparent.

Fielding's *Amelia* (1751) follows the same contradictions into the world of literature proper. Booth finds that both his familiar lists of favoured authors (Swift, Rabelais, Cervantes, Lucian) and his customary criteria for measuring their achievements have been swept into redundancy by the appearance of a new yardstick. Booth's cell-mate, 'the Author', measures only by demand, by 'the Price they pay by the sheet'.[23] This new world of public writing follows the market, reducing authors to paper and paper to profit in a process of valuation that leaves little room for Booth's informal tribunal of the great.

A further threat to the legitimacy of rules came from a source less easy to demolish through witty parody. Bernard Fontenelle's 'A Digression on the Ancients and Moderns' (1692) opposes the permanent lease extended to ancient pre-eminence, arguing for a more clearly demarcated division of cultural territory. He insists that although the ancients remain unequalled in poetry and rhetoric, in reasoning they do not embody 'ultimate perfection' since they allow 'vague and confused discourse to pass as proofs'. He then suggests a new governor for the realm of reason, arguing that Aristotle must make way for Descartes. 'Before Descartes', he avers, 'men argued more conveniently . . . He is the one who, it seems to me, has set out the new method of reasoning – a method much more estimable than his philosophy, of which a good part is false or uncertain – at least according to the correct rules he taught us.'[24]

What rules did Descartes teach? For Boileau or Rymer, rules operate by an appeal to precedent. But the very basis of Descartes's rules lay in their mistrust of precedent, and particularly the precedent of ancient letters. 'I was brought up on letters from my childhood', he recalls, 'and since it was urged on me that by means of them one could acquire clear and assured knowledge of all that is useful in life, I was extremely

---

[22] Swift, *Tale*, p. 90.   [23] Fielding, *Amelia*, p. 326.

[24] Fontenelle, *Oeuvres*, II, p. 358. 'Avant Descartes, on raisonnait plus commodément, les siècles passés sont bien heureux, de c'est lui, à ce qu'il me semble, qui a amené cette nouvelle méthode de raisonner, beaucoup plus estimable que sa philosophie même, dont une bonne partie se trouve fausse ou incertaine, selon les propres règles qu'il nous a apprises.'

eager to learn them'. However, all he discovered was 'the progressive discovery of my own ignorance'.[25]

For the rules of ancient wisdom collected in a catalogue of canonical texts, Descartes substitutes a canon of systematic self-doubt.

> As regards any subject we propose to investigate, we must inquire not what other people have thought, or what we ourselves conjecture, but what we can clearly and manifestly perceive by intuition or deduce with certainty. For there is no other way of acquiring knowledge.[26]

Descartes describes knowledge not as collectively transmitted but as individually acquired. In this way, he reduces the province of letters to a single, self-governing inhabitant, who constructs specific models in order to answer specific questions, in a manner that threatens to make obsolescent the case-law collected in a canon of guiding authorities.

Cartesian method assumed exemplary status. From 1475 to 1640, the *Short Title Catalogue* lists only five separate entries under the headings 'rule', 'standard', or 'canon'. But the volume for the years 1641 to 1700 includes thirty-one such entries, and this expansion continues throughout the eighteenth century. From now on, we see a rising number of works that promise to deliver the 'rules', 'canon', or 'standards' on activities ranging from 'true railing' to 'literal criticism'. Any critic who overlooks the ambiguous, not to say contradictory, status of 'rule', which by now embraces both established authority and sceptical method, will underestimate the unsettled nature of the province of letters during these years. When Christopher Smart decides to circulate his 'Horatian Canons of Friendship' (1750), he acknowledges that the very existence of such canons will not be conceded without prolonged introspection: 'Sift then yourself, I say, and sift again, / Glean the pernicious tares from out the grain'.[27]

For some eighteenth-century authors, Descartes promoted unusual degrees of self-scrutiny, to the point where no rule or canon could persist without the test of prolonged introspection. For other authors, the problem of rules triggers a sceptical exploration of the legitimate boundaries that define a given intellectual activity. The search that Lord Bolingbroke conducts in *Letters on the Study and Use of History* (1752) for 'the true standard of history' impels the author to consider 'the

---

[25] Descartes, *Oeuvres*, VI, p. 4. 'J'ai été nourri aux lettres dès mon enfance, et pour ce qu'on me persuadait que par leur moyen on pouvait acquérir une connaissance claire et assurée de tout ce qui est utile à la vie, j'avais un extrême désir de les apprendre.' (Spelling modernized)

[26] Descartes, *Oeuvres*, X, p. 366. 'Circa objecta proposita, non quid alii senserint, vel quid ipsi suspicemur, sed quid clare et evidenter possimus intueri, vel certo deducere quaerendum est; non aliter enim scientia acquiritur.'

[27] Smart, 'The Horatian Canons of Friendship', ll. 73–4, in *Works*, IV, p. 116.

rules ... necessary to be involved in the study of history' itself.[28] Such rules include consistent chronology, credible witnesses, and plausible occurrences, each of which Bolingbroke finds violated in the canon of the Old Testament.

Like Voltaire, Bolingbroke suggests that the canonical Scriptures serve the interests of the groups whose enterprises they narrate. Father Richard Simon does not go so far, but his *Critical History of the Old Testament* (1678) reminds his readers that the divine inspiration of Holy Scripture does not guarantee the authority of its every word. Simon advises them that the Scriptures have emerged as a result of human efforts, and encourages them to apply 'critical rules' to a text 'whose first originals have been lost'.[29] As John Evelyn lamented, Simon's work effectively destroyed the foundations of belief for all those who acknowledge 'the Holy Scriptures alone to be the canon and rule of faith'.[30]

Critical method challenged the authority of letters and Scripture alike. It also encouraged a new kind of reading and interpreting governed by rules and canons of evidence. Herbert Butterfield and Arnaldo Momigliano have pointed to the new directions that these methods opened for historical study. Butterfield notes that Abbé de Mabillon's *De Re Diplomatica* (1681) systematized the rules for the decipherment of material evidence, 'showing how the authenticity of charters could be tested by the examination of the parchment, the writing materials, the form of the seals, the way of describing dignitaries or recording dates', and so on.[31] Momigliano describes how antiquarian research extended the range of evidence quarried by the historian from 'good letters' to what the French antiquary Abbé de Montfaucon called the 'mute Histories, which Authors do not mention' – inscriptions, gems, vases, charters, statues, altars.[32]

Scholarly discussion has frequently spoken of these innovations in strictly dynastic terms, presenting Mabillon as a precursor of Ranke and Montfaucon as a precursor of Burckhardt. The student of canons of literary criticism may, however, view their achievements differently. For in drawing up the rules for distinguishing apocryphal from authentic documents, Mabillon cleared the way for the formation of a second canon, which would preserve an authentic remnant of secular history as

---

[28] Bolingbroke, *Historical Writings*, pp. 67, 3.
[29] Richard Simon, *Histoire Critique du Vieux Testament* (Rotterdam, 1685, repr. Frankfurt, 1967), p. 1. 'Mais comme les hommes ont été les depositaires des Livres Sacrés, aussi bien que de tous les autres Livres, et que les premiers Originaux ont été perdus.' Accordingly, Simon recommends his readers to 's'appliquer à la Critique de la Bible, et de corriger les fautes de leurs Exemplaires'.
[30] *Diary of John Evelyn*, ed. William Bray (4 vols., London, 1879), III, p. 411.
[31] Butterfield, 'Delays', p. 8; Momigliano, *Historiography*, pp. 1–55.
[32] Montfaucon, *Antiquity*, I, Preface.

authoritatively as an earlier canon had preserved the authentic remnant of its sacred counterpart. Ecclesiastical authority had sponsored the emergence of the sacred canon in the fourth century; during the seventeenth century, scientific authority regulates the appearance of a competing secular canon. Montfaucon emphasizes that such a canon would not be purely textual in composition, but might include physical materials as well. The authentic remnant established by science could promote the same informed commentary and expert investigations as its sacred predecessor. It could even, as later discussions from Vico to Winckelmann make clear, furnish an equally visionary identity narrative for its students.

Although Cartesian method initially threatened to annihilate canonical authority, it actually allowed for its accommodation to the demands of a scientific world view. To isolate literary criticism from these reconfigurations in the world of knowledge is to deny that changes in criticism participated in a wider reconstruction of the human sciences during these years. The long trail that takes Montfaucon's *Antiquity Explained* (translated into English in 1721) from the canonized texts of the Church Fathers to the drainage systems of the ancient world brings into bold relief the relationship between a canon of valued authorities and a canon that regulates an investigative empirical method. Behind Montfaucon's book lies a shift from a canon of public reputation to the decipherment of a deeper structure by means of canons of evidence systematically applied by a highly skilled researcher. In the introduction to his book, Montfaucon describes how he originally intended to compile an annotated text of the Church Fathers that would explain their classical allusions to a wider public. The allusions, however, led him further and further into a world that letters alone could never fully reconstruct. In 1698, he therefore set out for Italy, 'which alone furnishes more pieces of Antiquity than all the other Parts of Europe'. But an antiquity of limitless material objects is much more difficult to control than an antiquity restricted to a selection of valued texts, and three years did not suffice for Montfaucon to realize his ambition of inventorying knowledge of 'all the Parts of Antiquity',[33] and of remedying the errors caused by faulty etymologies and armchair conjectures.

Whereas a catalogue of canonized texts combined limited evidence and inexhaustible interpretation, a canonical culture of material artifacts involves limitless material and highly specific technical decipherment. As Montfaucon laments, the evidence never stops coming in. Monuments, cabinets, and collections are continually recovered, so that 'Every day there are some new ones found'. Even so, to reduce 'into one Body all

[33] *Ibid.*

Antiquity'[34] still remained the antiquary's goal, the driving force behind so many deciphered inscriptions and ambitious excavations.

All too often antiquarian research was alleged to have sunk beneath the weight of its own raw material. Gibbon's autobiographical reminiscences testify to the flagging capacities of later antiquaries to order their research discoveries into compelling unity. The well-known contrast between the antiquaries who had all the facts but no story to frame them, and the philosophers who had all the stories but none of the facts points to an absence of controlling narrative – of *canon,* in the sense of a schematic fiction – which was widely perceived as an inadequacy in antiquarian investigation. Yet at least one antiquarian, William Stukeley, tried to reconcile the material evidence yielded by his research to a grander narrative he takes from Scripture. Stukeley's *Stonehenge* (1740) endeavours to reconcile his national loyalties, ancient learning, and Christian orthodoxy into one overarching narrative. When Stukeley devises a 'Canon Mosaicae Chronologiae' ('Canon of Mosaic Chronology'), a system for measuring Old Testament time, he hopes to reconcile the material evidence of Stonehenge, inspected systematically and reported on in considerable detail, with a patriotic hope of proving that on British soil 'the patriarchal religion' turns out to be 'extremely like Christianity'. Like Sir Thomas Browne, and with similarly conciliatory intentions, Stukeley presents his study of Stonehenge as confirming 'that Religion is one system as old as the world'. But the impulse to confirm does not cancel out the need to explore and to report on those explorations systematically at a time when 'a spirit of Scepticism has of late become so fashionable'.[35] Accordingly, Stukeley presents many pages of diagrams, measurements, and illustrations. Wit and learning no longer suffice to convince an audience: the whole apparatus of scientific investigation must underpin any case presented in a post-Cartesian intellectual climate.

In Stukeley's work the guarantee of the rules by degrees becomes the trained eye rather than established authority. Yet established authority (or revered association) determines what the eye will train itself upon. An attempt to escape from this 'hermeneutic circle' lies behind the much bolder synthesis undertaken in Vico's *Scienza nuova* (1744), a work that adds a further dimension to the eighteenth-century understanding of *canon.* Vico observes that historical facts have a status different from scientific facts, and call forth different skills from their interpreters. It is 'a great canon of our mythology', he thinks, that 'whatever appertains to men but is doubtful or obscure, they naturally interpret according to their own natures and the passions and customs springing from them'. Vico begins his exploration of this 'mythology' by reiterating the

[34] *Ibid.* [35] Stukeley, *Stonehenge,* preface, p. 2.

traditional idea that the world of human knowledge divides itself into distinct provinces: the world of nature, created and governed by God; and the world of human societies. God alone can know the former, but since the world of civil society has been partly created by human hands, certain knowledge here is possible but difficult. 'The world of civil society has certainly been made by men, and . . . its principles are therefore to be found within the modifications of our human mind'.[36] However, the 'infirmity' of that mind makes the results of such introspection less certain and clear than René Descartes, for example, might submit. Moreover, Vico conceives of his new science as an historical one, and in this way stretches the Cartesian project of sustained introspection over a massive temporal and spatial frame. The potential for disorder in a field that accumulates so many separate subjectivities promises to be huge. And yet, Vico continues, viewed either diachronically or synchronically, human social organization does not proceed entirely fortuitously. Beneath the thicket of action and reaction that constitutes human history, he detects certain recurring principles that limit the possible forms of political organization, figurative expression, economic administration, and so on. As a student of the nascent social sciences, Vico focuses more on the supposed principles than on the political leaders who temporarily embody them. These principles he calls 'canons'. A 'chronological canon' fixes the origins of 'universal history', a 'mythological canon' represents the class structure of the ancient world through figurative representations of the gods. Vico's canons allow him to frame secular history in compelling hypotheses invested with the form and authority of logical axioms. In his work, science, not orthodoxy, becomes the buttress of human action.

Neither Vico's 'canon' nor his science offers close, empirical explanations of the phenomena it describes. Where the canons of evidence devised by historians and antiquaries allow us to inspect evidence with some precision, the canons of Vico and Stukeley point to the equally pressing need to integrate it memorably, to see the world's contingency as somehow answerable to human understanding. For these writers, a *canon* becomes once again a fictive construction that organizes events into memorable patterns.

---

[36] Vico, *Opere*, p. 455: 'Gli uomini le cose dubbie ovvero oscure, che lor appartengono, naturalmente interpetrano secondo le loro nature e quindi uscite passioni e costumi. Questa degnità è un gran canone della nostra mitologia.' p. 479: 'Lo che, a chiunque vi rifletta, dee recar maraviglia come tutti ì filosofi seriosamente si studiarono di conseguire la scienza di questo mondo naturale, del quale, perché Iddio egli il fece, esso solo ne ha la scienza; e traccurarono di meditare su questo mondo delle nazioni, o sia mondo civile, del quale, perché l'avevano fatto gli uomini, ne potevano conseguire la scienza gli uomini.' English trans. in *The New Science*, ed. Bergin and Fisch, p. 34; pp. 52–3.

As a result, eighteenth-century letters marks the convergence of several distinct canons. A canon designed to preserve 'the Augustan myth' hopes to regulate the republic of letters by means of a highly selective list of valued works whose qualities merit the perpetual esteem of the discerning. A scientific canon inaugurated by Descartes establishes standard rules for the authentication, analysis, and adjudication of written and material evidence. The first of these canons rests its authority on limitation, the restriction of value to a small number of accepted items. The second, in contrast, seeks perpetually to enlarge its territory. Richard Simon thinks that a 'critical' method must establish scientific principles for the analysis of the Scriptures. Mabillon and Montfaucon investigate historically physical and documentary evidence not previously considered worthy of attention. An expansion in raw historical material calls for a corresponding increase in the capacity to order this material. Canonical identity narratives that bridge the gap between accepted authority and empirical evidence provide one such order. The need for more reliable evidence, for a greater range of evidence, and for more compelling accounts of the evidence all modify the understanding of *canon* current in the world of art and literature during the later eighteenth century. From this point, the province of letters can no longer be divided among a few authoritative superpowers. More and more territories press for recognition, while at the same time the arbiter of value becomes the human consciousness embarked on a quest for self-actualization in history, culture, and tradition.

The literary canon

Literary criticism participates in each of the innovations in critical method described above. Textual scholarship attempts to move in a regular, 'scientific' manner to solve the problems of textual transmission, restoration, and emendation. Interpretation of national authors follows, in many cases, methods already devised for classical texts and Holy Scripture. In one famous instance, William Warburton will even endeavour to establish the *canons* of criticism that will separate amateur from professional activity in the editing of a vernacular classic. During the eighteenth century, a new generation of literary critics acknowledges the necessity of recovering the framework of expectations and the habits of perception of any artist's original audience, if an artistic production is to live again for future generations. The work of Robert Lowth, Hugh Blair, Thomas Warton, and Samuel Johnson takes this direction. Yet along with the effort to reconstruct the basic idioms, daily transactions, and cultural institutions of the past comes an effort to see that past as a construction of the human mind. In this task, which was initiated by Vico and Stukeley, works of art gain an enhanced importance. For in creating art the poet or painter works in seeming freedom; and it is also possible to see separate works of art not in terms of Voltaire's politically sponsored cycles but as an allegory of the creative mind operating across centuries, languages, and genres to create the new order that Goethe calls *Weltliteratur*.

In Germany, these routes were not divided, so that Winckelmann and Herder could knit these two kinds of investigation into a single historical discipline. And for both writers, a new understanding of canonicity inevitably follows. Canonical authors such as Homer and Virgil become exemplary not just in a formal or exhortatory sense (as spurs to the composition of epic or the achievement of *pietas*) but as vessels for a system of manners, symbols, and customs recoverable by historical investigation and archaeological excavation as well as by literary analysis. The ghostly framework of mythicized reconstruction and occult interpretation sketched out in Thomas Blackwell's *An Enquiry into the Life and Writings of Homer* (1735) yields to the much more substantial field inaugurated in Winckelmann's notion of *Altertumswissenschaft* ('knowledge of antiquity'), in which the scientific, archaeological, and mythic wings of the critical act combine in an unprecedented way. From the text and the world implicit in its words comes a third construct, the vanished, near-visionary society that the canonical work contains *in nuce*.

In the case of Shakespeare, professional expertise, patriotic sentiment, and mythopoeic interests unite. Eighteenth-century critics repeatedly emphasize how 'this extraordinary Man',[37] as John Dennis calls him in 1712, strained to the utmost the universal legitimacy claimed by the rules of criticism. Yet the obscurity and occasional confusions of Shakespeare's work threatened to seal off a national monument from national visibility without the aid supplied by the restoring activities of scientific scholarship. As Lewis Theobald remarked, Shakespeare slipped daily into the condition of 'a corrupt Classic'.[38] The spectacle of Shakespeare's canon being abandoned as a species of cultural orphan to what Warburton described in 1747 as 'the Care of Door-keepers and Prompters'[39] encouraged some of his editors to conceive themselves as continuing the battle against barbarism begun in the Renaissance. Yet the figures in this parable of civilization and barbarism were not to remain stable. Where Warburton hoped to deploy Shakespeare as a safe guide to the 'mother tongue', Herder abducts him from the salon to the forest. 'If

[37] Dennis, *Critical Works*, II, p. 16.
[38] Smith, *Eighteenth-Century Essays*, p. 80.   [39] *Ibid.*, p. 96.

there is any man to conjure up in our minds that tremendous image of one "seated high on the craggy hilltop, storm, tempest, and the roaring sea at his feet, but with the radiance of the heavens about his head", that man is Shakespeare'.[40] In Herder's writings, Shakespeare becomes a vehicle for the critical investigation of the symbols of civil society that began with Vico.

Shakespeare's new centrality, as the yardstick for each emerging scholarly, critical, and poetic category becomes ever clearer as the century progresses. One Shakespeare boosts the stock of a national literature that follows 'Gothic' rather than classical principles of composition. Another Shakespeare tears down the separate provinces of letters and heralds the emergence of a new critical-creative, scholarly-popular art which is both authentically primitive and absolutely modern. In 1797 Novalis praises the professional expertise that makes A. W. Schlegel's translation 'a more excellent canon for the scholarly onlooker',[41] the creative matrix for a modern poetry that is itself a translation.

In Britain, Warburton's edition of Shakespeare hopes to use the author as a test case for scientific 'Canons of literal Criticism' that establish clear criteria for emendatory commentary on a modern author. Warburton does not actually supply these canons, but he gives clear indications of their functions. He conceives that they will raise the status of textual criticism by setting forth 'scientific' principles of editorial method as well as practical guidance on the editing of Shakespeare in particular. He hopes to curb the 'Rage of Correcting' initiated by Sir Thomas Hanmer in his 1744 edition of Shakespeare. The formulation of general rules and the delimitation of the editor's proper sphere will in turn lend a new status to the labours of a textual editor. But this does not exhaust the limits of Warburton's ambition. He also cites Shakespeare as 'a Test or Standard to apply to' amid the waves of linguistic change. And even beyond this, he invokes criteria of a very different order when he describes another Shakespeare, whose 'resistless Splendor ... now shoots all around him'.[42] No wonder that Thomas Edwards, whose *A Supplement to Mr Warburton's Edition* (1748) appeared a year after Warburton's text, subjected his scientific canons to extended ridicule by setting forth a parodic list of twenty-five counter-canons. Edwards's 'Canons' imply that the sublimity of the author has

[40] Herder, *Werke*, II, p. 238. 'Wenn bei einem Manne mir jenes ungeheure Bild einfällt: "hoch auf einem Felsengipfel sitzend, zu seinen Füßen Sturm, Ungewitter und Brausen des Meers; aber sein Haupt in den Strahlen des Himmels!" so ists bei Shakespear!' (*Sämtliche Werke*, V, p. 208; trans. Nisbet, p. 161).

[41] Novalis, *Schriften*, IV, p. 237. 'Ihr Shakespear ist ein trefflicher Canon für den wissenschaftlichen Beobachter ... Am Ende ist alle Poësie Übersetzung.'

[42] Warburton, 'Preface', pp. 101, 100, 110, 97.

made its way into the working idioms of the editor, who, confronted by 'a difficult passage', substitutes for it 'words absolutely unintelligible'.[43]

The quarrel between Warburton and Edwards points to deep divisions in the province of letters. Edwards resents, for example, what he conceives as the presumption of offering to the public a national modern author wrapped in an interpretive apparatus usually associated with antiquity. As he sees it, Warburton's annotations do not fulfil his announced intention of helping a reader to understand Shakespeare's language. They seem designed 'not so much to explain the Author's meaning, as to display the Critic's knowledge'. Warburton's canons exhibit the critic's own 'universal learning' by elaborately pointing out 'from whence every metaphor and allusion is taken'.[44] Although Edwards's work has the effect of a rhetorical *tour de force*, its major implication – that a national canon cannot be hived off to professional textual editors nor even to the self-appointed guardians of national usage – becomes a major point of debate among later writers.

Samuel Johnson, one of Warburton's most important successors, addresses the problem of Shakespeare's canonical value in a more complex way than either Warburton or Edwards. The establishment of a vernacular canon requires an acknowledgement of the interlocking interests that inevitably converge on a valued modern author. Accordingly, Johnson's *Preface to the Plays of William Shakespeare* (1765) describes a Shakespeare able to satisfy neo-classical traditionalists, modern realists, historicists, and moralists in a canon as various as reality itself. Johnson emphasizes that Shakespeare is an author who 'has seen with his own eyes' and who 'gives the image which he receives, not weakened or distorted by the intervention of any other mind'. His drama 'has no heroes', but presents 'scenes from which a hermit may estimate the transactions of the world' through a method which Johnson calls 'the mirrour of life'. Moreover, the validation of Shakespeare's work calls for a suspension of 'the rules of criticism' in favour of the 'appeal open from criticism to nature'.[45] In short, Johnson accommodates Shakespeare to the structure of a post-Cartesian world.

It is clear that Johnson has no intention of abandoning the inventory of precepts, patterns, and case-law housed in the 'second nature' of a humanist canon. Yet he knows that whoever wants to understand Shakespeare must understand Shakespeare's England, with its very different view of what tragedy, comedy, or polite discourse meant. A canonical author is canonical partly because he can charge recurring crises in civil and private life with the authority of imaginative vision. But to understand that author fully demands knowledge of 'the state of the age in

---

[43] Edwards, *Canons*, pp. 25–8.   [44] *Ibid.*   [45] Johnson, 'Preface', pp. 89–90, 65, 67.

which he lived, and with his own particular opportunities ... to discover the instruments, as well as to survey the workmanship, know how
much is to be ascribed to original powers, and how much to casual and
adventitious help'. Acquaintanceship with the historical and biographical evidence requires a critic to shelve conventional prejudice masked as
universal norms. In Elizabethan England 'Tragedy was not ... a poem
of more general dignity or elevation than comedy' and 'the rules of the
ancients were yet known to few'. Even so, this historicist insight – the
sense that Shakespeare be judged only according to standards operable
in his own lifetime – does not rule out mythological investments of the
sort made by Johnson when he describes an author who, like a second
Adam, composed 'dramatick poetry with the world open before him'.[46]

Shakespeare's metamorphosis from abandoned Joseph to second Adam
forms part of a broader effort to extend the category of 'the first rank'
beyond existing boundaries and established hierarchies. The desire to
understand the conditions of Shakespeare's creativity reinforces the
effort to explore the origins of other 'primitive' poetic texts. Lowth, for
instance, in his *Lectures on the Sacred Poetry of the Hebrews* (published
in Latin in 1753) tells his Oxford audience that if they want to discover
'Poetry, in its very beginning', then they should study the canon of
Hebrew poetry discovered in Old Testament Scripture:

> Not only the antiquity of these writings forms a principal obstruction in
> many respects; but the manner of living, of speaking, of thinking, which
> prevailed in those times, will be found altogether different from our customs
> and habits. There is, therefore, great danger, lest, viewing them from an
> improper situation, and rashly estimating all things by our own standard,
> we form an erroneous judgment.[47]

Lowth's chapter-headings mark off his intention of conquering such
misapprehensions. One chapter announces 'the Song of Solomon not a
Regular Drama', another 'The Poem of Job not a Perfect Drama'. Yet
both works are 'eminent in the highest degree for elegance, sublimity',
and, he adds with regret, 'obscurity also'. The proper way to master so
dark a poem dissolves the boundary between the original audience and
its contemporary successor. The latter must sink into the former and 'in
one word ... see all things with their eyes, estimate all things by their
opinions'. Lowth then describes how the Book of Job violates the Aristotelian criteria encapsulated in Sophocles' *Oedipus*. To measure the
former by the latter is to allow the contingencies of a gentlemanly
education to block the reception of a work that occupies 'a distinct and
conspicuous station in the highest rank of the Hebrew poetry'.[48]

---

[46] Johnson, 'Preface', pp. 81, 68–9.
[47] Lowth, *Lectures*, p. 65.   [48] *Ibid.*, pp. 333, 65, 381.

Lowth's formulation signals a shift in critical paradigms that brings the understanding of *canonical* from 'exemplary' to 'originative'. In Lowth's eyes reception and reconstruction appear more important than judgement, and to understand these, critics must become 'even as the writers themselves'.[49] Future developments will show that such a view of literary criticism forces it further and further into the work it elects to investigate, to the point where criticism as a judicial activity threatens to cease. Lowth emphasizes the sovereign value of the works he chooses to analyse. However, his priorities, both as critic and as Christian, have effectively shifted from evaluation to reception, from judgement to understanding. If the way in which ancient texts construct their meanings is misunderstood, then to shore them up by recourse to canons their authors would not have recognized serves no purpose. The common thread that links the canonical texts to each other, the view that each represents a distinct province in a common empire, counts for less than the effort to uncover the larger properties of the world that brought it forth. Yet Lowth remains unwilling to press his arguments to their logical conclusion. To see Job as a poetic history, a narrative 'founded in fact' yet simultaneously embodying all 'the embellishments of poetry', involves major shifts in critical procedure. The Book of Job will not answer to accepted canons of Western literary composition. It is neither regular epic nor a conventional tragedy. But neither does it conform to the principles of modern 'civilized' society. To understand the world of Job is to adjust criticism to the point where it becomes an anthropological rather than a judicial discipline. Job bespeaks the mysterious origins of a history where 'the embellishments of poetry' came naturally to an early, and hence poetic, civilization.[50] Renewed contact with this aboriginal history promises to rekindle faculties dulled by endless reiteration of academic categories.

Literary criticism no longer rests content with the occasion-specific mode of Cartesian inquiry. Instead, for literary critics, the canonical work, viewed as an ever-deepening artifact from a mysterious vanished culture, takes on mythological properties. Increasingly, the province of letters looks out enviously at an imagined unity where, as Hugh Blair conceives it, 'All that we now call letters ... was then blended in one mass'. In these conditions, which are often referred to as 'the primitive', 'history, eloquence and poetry were the same'.[51] Homer and Greece, of all poets and worlds, epitomize this vision of mythical unity. The contrast between the territorial Rome and the organic Greece marks the sea-change that separates the scientific canons of the late seventeenth century from the mythic canons of a century later. Thomas Blackwell

[49] *Ibid.*, p. 66.   [50] *Ibid.*, p. 359.   [51] Blair, *Lectures*, II, p. 321.

sees Homer's writings as emerging from the junction where 'hard Beginnings, and jarring Interests' join in a more harmonious civil life. Blackwell's Greece is a fictive construct, a mythical, undissociated land created from Homer, Thucydides, and Herodotus. Where Eliot reconstructs seventeenth-century England from Lancelot Andrewes and John Donne, Blackwell speaks of a place 'where Nature was obstructed in none of her Operations; and no Rule or Prescription gave a check to Rapture and Enthusiasm'.[52]

The impulse to interpret Greek literature as a blueprint for a mythic world of unity finds its deepest fulfilment in Germany. Yet Germany is also the country where the study of ancient culture and art history reach new levels of scientific expertise. And Winckelmann, best of all, unites these two apparently separate activities. For Winckelmann, Greece itself becomes canonical, the yardstick of a lost unity. 'Much that might seem ideal to us was natural among them . . . All Greece may rightly be called the land of art'. Winckelmann measures ancient plenitude by modern vacancy, lamenting that 'we have no rule and canon of beauty according to which, as Euripides says, ugliness may be judged; and for this reason we differ about that which is beautiful, just as we differ about that which is truly good'.[53]

At this point, the canon of classical art no longer furnishes a yardstick for the measurement of a common culture, but registers rather the extent of a deep contemporary loss. To recover the material evidence of antiquity, to witness its existence with one's own eyes, to classify, and finally to decipher it is to engage in a kind of metaphysical repair, as Winckelmann and his successors realized. For Winckelmann, the separate items of Greek statuary compose a Hellenic canon expressly designed for a later generation's fulfilment. 'There is but one way for the moderns to become great and perhaps unequalled', he proclaims, 'by imitating the ancients'.[54] The impassioned commentary in which Winckelmann announces his scientific discoveries marks his passage from history to mythopoesis. The neo-classical myth of a civilization preserved in a core of major authorities recedes in the face of a Romantic myth that sees entire cultures replete with the symbols, institutions, and aspirations of an intense collective creativity. Moreover, who will be presumptuous

---

[52] Blackwell, *Enquiry*, pp. 22, 104.
[53] Winckelmann, *Geschichte*, p. 115: 'Vieles, was wir uns als idealisch vorstellen möchten, war die Natur bei ihnen.' p. 124: 'und es fehlt uns die Regel und der Kanon des Schönen, nach welchem, wie Euripides sagt, das Garstige beurteilt wird; und aus dieser Ursache sind wir so wie über das, was wahrhaftig gut ist, also auch über das, was schön ist, verschieden' (*History*, trans. Lodge, I, pp. 286, 299, 308).
[54] Winckelmann, *Gedanken*, p. 8: 'Der einzige Weg für uns, groß, ja, wenn es möglich ist, unnachahmlich zu werden, ist die Nachahmung der Alten' (trans. Irwin, p. 61).

enough to discriminate between these cultures? If, as Herder observes, 'The human race is destined to develop through a series of scenes in culture and customs',[55] then it becomes unnecessary to decide whether the age of Louis XIV or Valerius Maximinus contributes more to human development as a whole. Critics return to traditional historical periods looking for fulfilment more than judgement, as the French rules become German sympathies, ways of negotiating the gap between ancient and modern worlds.

Such a construction of the critical task merges the separate provinces of criticism and creation, the vocational categories of artist and critic, and even the practical division between canonical and non-canonical dissolves in the creative consciousness. According to Novalis,

> It is a great mistake to believe that such things as ancient worlds really exist. It is only now that Antiquity is coming into existence. This is brought about by the artist's eyes and soul. The relics of the ancient world are only the particular stimulus to our creation of Antiquity. Antiquity was not built with hands ... The mind produces it with the eye, and the hewn stone is but the body which acquires meaning only when imbued with the idea of Antiquity.[56]

When the canonical becomes a privileged way of seeing objects rather than a catalogue of privileged objects, then any object becomes potentially canonical and Novalis can confide to his diary his belief that 'the fairy tale is entirely the canon of poetry – everything poetical must be like a fairy tale'. Finally, drawing the logic of this argument to its rigorous conclusion, Novalis speaks of 'a truly canonical human being' whose life 'must be symbolic through and through'.[57]

But did the emergence of this 'canonical human being' herald the disappearance of a canon of valued works? A famous passage from Rousseau's *Confessions* makes it clear that this was not the case. We have seen that for Descartes, 'good letters' could not remain the source of clear and distinct knowledge. Yet Rousseau's recollections of his

---

[55] Herder, *Sämtliche Werke*, V, p. 168: 'Das menschliche Geschlecht ist zu einem Fortgange von Szenen, von Bildung, von Sitten bestimmt, wehe dem Menschen, dem die Szene mißfällt, in der er auftreten, handeln und sich verleben soll' (trans. Nisbet, p. 157).

[56] Novalis, *Schriften*, II, p. 640: 'denn man irrt sehr, wenn man glaubt, daß es Antiken giebt. Erst jezt fängt die Antike an zu entstehen. Sie wird unter den Augen und der Seele des Künstlers. Die Reste des Alterthums sind nur die specifischen Reitze zur Bildung der Antike. Nicht mit Händen wird die Antike gemacht. Der Geist bringt sie durch das Auge hervor – und der gehauene Stein ist nur der Körper, der erst durch sie Bedeutung erhält, und zur Erscheinung derselben wird' (trans. Wheeler, p. 103).

[57] Novalis, *Schriften*, III, p. 449. 'Das Mährchen ist gleichsam der Canon der Poësie – alles Poëtische muß mährchenhaft seyn.' *Schriften*, II, p. 418: 'Das Leben eines wahrhaft canonischen Menschen muß durchgehends symbolisch seyn.'

childhood reading prove that the traditional commonwealth of letters could stimulate the civic loyalties of a provincial adolescent. In the opening pages of his *Confessions*, Rousseau describes his education in reading, from his bewildered and dissatisfied immersion in romances to his liberating capture by canonical literature:

Ceaselessly occupied with Rome and Athens, living, so to speak, with their great men, born citizen of a republic, and son of a father whose love of his country was his strongest passion, I was inspired by his example. I believed that I was Greek or Roman. I became the person whose life I read. The account of steadfast and daring behaviour that had stirred me made my eyes shine and my voice strong. One day, at table, as I recounted the adventures of Scaevola, everyone present was afraid to see me go forward and put my hand on the stove in imitation of his action.[58]

For Rousseau, a canon is not so much a fund of potential knowledge as a repertoire of roles available to a modern and therefore histrionic identity. As he reads more and more about the canonical episodes and protagonists of the ancient world, Rousseau finds in them potential fragments of his own personality, a personality that turns classical *exempla* into romantic 'adventures'. Yet he is hardly unique in this. The canonical status of the *Confessions* itself underscores the continuing significance of antiquity for an audience sensitive enough to apprehend the structure of its identity by immersion in its inspiring examples. By breaking down the boundaries between art and life, the newly apprehended canonical work enlarges modern identity. Rousseau does not simply read about the heroes of ancient Rome, but participates in their actions even as he entrances his audience with his own performance. By reappropriating the ancient canon, Rousseau enlists it in the formation of a changeable, passionate personality. The same intensely unpredictable personality underpins Wordsworth's *Prelude* and Goethe's *Wilhelm Meister*. Yet the presence of Milton in Wordsworth, the patterns of ancient oratory that inform Rousseau's work, and the inspiration that Shakespeare's Hamlet supplies for Goethe's hero all make it clear that the new European poetics had not superannuated its predecessors. Instead, it had incorporated them in the blueprint for a canonical human society designed by a new generation of artist-visionaries. For artists

---

[58] Rousseau, *Oeuvres Complètes*, I, p. 9: 'Sans cesse occupé de Rome et d'Athènes, vivant, pour ainsi dire, avec leurs grands hommes, né moi-même citoyen d'une république, et fils d'un père dont l'amour de la patrie était la plus forte passion, je m'en enflammais à son exemple; je me croyais Grec ou Romain; je devenais le personnage dont je lisais la vie: le récit des traits de constance et d'intrépidité qui m'avaient frappé me rendait les yeux étincelants et la voix forte. Un jour que je racontais à table l'aventure de Scaevola, on fut effrayé de me voir avancer et tenir la main sur un réchaud pour représenter son action.' (Spelling modernized.)

like Schiller, Blake, and Chateaubriand, a literary canon becomes a regenerative as well as a conservative force, housing not just the best works of the past but a generation's visionary hopes for the future. In this way, the gap between the literary canon and its sacred precursor narrows drastically at a time, paradoxically, of intense heterodoxy.

Literature and Other Disciplines

26

Literature and philosophy

Susan Manning

> He who would at the present time write, or even dispute,
> about art, should have some idea of what philosophy has
> achieved and continues to achieve in our day.
>
> (Goethe, *Maxims and Reflections*)[1]

Philosophical writing was uniquely accessible in the eighteenth century: in 1711 Joseph Addison declared himself 'ambitious to have it said ... that I have brought Philosophy out of Closets and Libraries, Schools and Colleges, to dwell in Clubs and Assemblies, at Tea-Tables and in Coffee Houses' (*Spectator*, I, p. 44, no. 10). The philosophers of the mid-century followed him in their mutual confidence in themselves and their readers; philosophy did not become an irreversibly specialist profession until the publication of Kant's *Critique of Pure Reason* in 1781. For the bulk of the eighteenth century language had not divaricated into the specialized and mutually exclusive (if not incomprehensible) jargons which characterize the different disciplines in the modern age: scientists (natural philosophers), epistemological and ethical philosophers, theologians and literary critics all in an important sense described human experience in similar ways, and their language was, in the full contemporary sense of the word, a *literary* one. In his posthumously published autobiographical sketch, David Hume wrote 'a passion for literature ... has been the ruling passion of my life' ('My Own Life', in *Dialogues*, pp. 233ff.).

But this communicable synthesis did not come automatically or without effort; Hume engaged throughout his writing career with the problems of marrying expression and embodiment, form and content, which are central to the philosophy, literature and criticism of the period as a whole. An early letter to his mentor Francis Hutcheson expressed the opposing pulls of the analytic and the aesthetic in a graphic metaphor:

There are different ways of examining the Mind as well as the Body. One may consider it either as an Anatomist or as a Painter; either to discover its

[1] 'Wer gegenwärtig über Kunst schreiben oder gar streiten will, der sollte einige Ahndung haben von dem, was die Philosophie in unsern Tagen geleistet hat und zu leisten fortfährt' (*Werke*, XII, p. 490).

most secret Springs & Principles or to describe the Grace & Beauty of its Actions. I imagine it impossible to conjoin these two Views. When you pull off the Skin, & display all the minute Parts, there appears something trivial, even in the noblest Attitudes and most vigorous Actions: Nor can you ever render the Object graceful or engaging but by cloathing the Parts again with Skin & Flesh, & presenting only their bare Outside. An Anatomist, however, can give very good advice to a Painter or Statuary: And in like manner, I am perswaded, that a Metaphysician may be very helpful to a Moralist; tho' I cannot easily conceive these two Characters united in the same Work.

(*Letters*, I, pp. 32–3)

In Hume's opposition of anatomist and painter, the philosopher and literary critic would seem to stand at one extreme and the artist at the other. Eighteenth-century *writing*, however, everywhere seeks to know and to articulate these contradictory truths about human beings simultaneously, to find a continuous register of expression which is able to accommodate both extremes. At their best, philosophy, literature and criticism all employ the full range of human faculties from abstract logic to intuition as they attempt to find a language to approximate to reality, to a just estimation of the texture of life. The opposition of the 'anatomist' and the 'painter', and the possibility of bringing them together in writing, constantly unites the concerns of philosophy and literary criticism in the eighteenth century.

The empirical method

When Voltaire recommended contemporary English philosophy to his French compatriots in the *Lettres philosophiques* he reached, significantly, for an analogy. His point is strikingly similar to Hume's, in expression as in substance: 'Locke', he said, 'has expounded human understanding to mankind as an excellent anatomist explains the mechanism of the human body' (p. 63).[2] The empirical method made both philosophers and critics scientists of human nature; the language of metaphor and analogy offered the possibility of conjoining the functions of anatomist and painter through its flexibility and inclusive possibilities. 'Natural philosophy' – science – was the first and chief glory of the empirical method. Isaac Newton was the great anatomist of the natural world, discovering (to borrow Hume's phrase) the 'most secret springs and principles' of gravity and optics. Despite Pope's scepticism that science could in fact hold all the answers for man, and his ridicule in *An Essay on Man* of those who exalted Newton into a kind of demigod,

---

[2] 'Loke a developpé à l'homme la raison humaine, comme un excellent Anatomiste explique les ressorts du corps humain' (*Lettres philosophiques*, I, p. 168).

his 'Epitaph. Intended for Sir Isaac Newton' was representative in the way it celebrated the great scientist's revolutionary importance for contemporary understanding of their world:

> Nature, and Nature's Laws lay hid in Night.
> God said, *Let Newton be!* and All was *Light.*

Newton's work fostered a general confidence that the course of events is predictable and nature is controllable. All its general theories derived from particular observation:

In this philosophy particular propositions are inferred from the phenomena and afterward rendered general by deduction ... it is enough that gravity really does exist and act according to the laws which we have explained, and abundantly serves to account for all the motions of celestial bodies and of our sea.
(*Principia*, ed. Thayer, p. 45)

For Newton the empirical philosopher, the physical and the metaphysical, the mechanical and the imaginative, were not opposed; a single approach and a single language could – in theory – register everything that human beings could know of both the inner and outer worlds. This was the optimistic assumption of Locke and Hume and the moral empiricists who followed them – not that everything was objectively knowable, or reducible to certainty, but that everything that *could* be known by men of their world came of necessity through the empirical evidence of the senses. In fact, neither Newton nor Locke was in any way a materialist; Newton believed the fundamental 'ether' or essence of the universe to be spiritual rather than material, and Locke makes it clear in his *Essay concerning Human Understanding* that his investigation does not extend 'to examin[ing], wherein [the mind's] Essence consists', or its material or spiritual origins (Bk I, ch. 1, p. 43).

Locke, as Voltaire suggested, perceived the possibility of extending Newton's methods into the anatomy of human understanding, the secret springs and principles of human nature. His empirical epistemology rejected the concept of innate, pre-existing ideas in the mind in favour of a process of accretion of information through the senses. The mind at birth, so Locke thought, is a blank sheet, a *tabula rasa* upon which nothing is written. Objects and events in the external world impinge on this unwritten book through the impressions they make on the senses, and in this way imprint themselves on the mind. From these data the mind forms 'ideas' of sensation or reflection, which may be simple, complex or abstract. 'And thus all its General *Ideas* are made. This shews Man's Power and its way of Operation to be muchwhat the same in the Material and Intellectual World' (*Essay*, II, 12, p. 163).

Locke's *Essay* posits three types of knowledge about the world. The first is this empirical way of sensation whereby the 'ideas' of objects in the outside world strike the senses and subsequently combine in the mind to form our knowledge of reality. The second is the way of demonstration, by which we are convinced, for example, of the existence of God through the combined evidence of reason and the senses. The third and highest form of perception is intuition, which enables us to know ourselves, to be sure of our own existence. Locke finds no opposition or clash between these sources: all combine harmoniously to complete our picture of the world in its fullest sense. In England throughout the eighteenth century and in France increasingly, though to a lesser extent in Germany, the empirical methods of Locke's first form of understanding largely commanded the aims and methods of literary criticism.[3] So, for example, Samuel Johnson applies the test of experience to the standard criticism of the incorrectness of Shakespeare's 'mingled drama': 'That this is a practice contrary to the rules of criticism will be readily allowed; but there is always an appeal open from criticism to nature' (*Preface to Shakespeare*, Yale edn, VII, p. 67). Edmund Burke, too, accounted for our 'ideas' of the Sublime and the Beautiful in terms of the 'impressions' made on our senses by the external manifestations of nature.

Later, the internal workings of imagination, associated with intuition, took on an importance which diverted the language of criticism into investigations and judgements more akin to Locke's third form of knowledge. Locke's 'intuitive Certainty' (IV, 10, p. 620) of the immaterial existence of himself and God is not, after all, an immeasurable distance from Blake's discovery of God in the imaginative genius within the self, or Coleridge's view of the primary Imagination as a 'repetition in the finite mind of the eternal act of creation in the infinite I AM'.[4] The difference between the knowledge of sensation and the knowledge of intuition – Blake's 'Poetic Genius which is every where call'd the Spirit of Prophecy' – is one way of describing the route travelled by literary criticism through the eighteenth century.[5]

Locke's common-sense empiricism, which founded itself on an *a priori* assumption of the objective existence of an external world to be perceived by the senses, became then the starting-point of most British eighteenth-century thinking about human nature. Its crucial assumption, however, could not be sustained by its methods and came under immediate and continuing attack from fellow philosophers. If all our

---

[3] See ch. 28(ii) of this volume for a fuller treatment of German aesthetics.
[4] *Biographia Literaria* (1817), ed. James Engell and W. J. Bate (Princeton, 1983), ch. XIII, I, p. 304.
[5] *The Poetry and Prose of William Blake*, ed. David V. Erdman (New York, 1965), p. 2.

knowledge comes through the evidence of our senses, how do we know that anything exists beyond our senses? This deeply unsettling question led on the one hand to the idealism of Bishop Berkeley and on the other to the scepticism of Hume; its implications for eighteenth-century literature and literary criticism reached far into the incipient relativism of the mid-century aesthetics of sentiment and response (see below, ch. 27), and thence to the subjectivism that would find perhaps its most despairing expression in Coleridge's 'Dejection: An Ode' of 1802:

> O lady! we receive but what we give,
> And in our life alone does Nature live![6]

As early as 1710, however, Berkeley had declared sharply in his *Principles of Human Knowledge*

> Some truths there are so near and obvious to the mind that a man need only open his eyes to see them. Such I take this important one to be, viz. that all the choir of heaven and furniture of the earth, in a word all those bodies which compose the mighty frame of the world, have not any subsistence without a mind – that their *being* is *to be perceived or known*.

> (p. 67)

Hume's central insight that philosophy (thinking about knowledge, existence, being) could not – in the empirical tradition which he and his age inherited from Newton and Locke – be separated from psychology is clear from the full title of his *A Treatise of Human Nature: Being an Attempt to Introduce the Experimental Method of Reasoning into Moral Subjects* (1739–40). This thought provides the inextricable link between the metaphysician and the moralist in eighteenth-century philosophy, literature and literary criticism. It was quite natural, for example, for Fielding to announce his subject in *Tom Jones* (published within ten years of the *Treatise*) as – like Hume's – 'no other than HUMAN NATURE', thereby establishing it as an empirical enquiry in fiction into the fundamental springs of human action and motivation.[7] Indeed, one way of looking at Hume's writing is to see it as a sustained exercise in the demolition of literary 'categories': literary and philosophical, philosophical and psychological, psychological and critical, and so on.

Hume confronts head-on the epistemological problem of our complete dependence on the evidence of our senses: 'The difficulty, then, is how far we are *ourselves* the objects of our sense . . . 'Tis certain there is no question in philosophy more abstruse than that concerning identity,

---

[6] ll. 47–8; *The Poems of Samuel Taylor Coleridge*, ed. E. H. Coleridge (Oxford, 1912; 1988), p. 365.

[7] *The History of Tom Jones A Foundling*, ed. Fredson Bowers and Martin Battestin, intro. M. Battestin, 2 vols. (Oxford, 1974), I, p. 32 (Bk 1, ch. 1).

and the nature of the uniting principle, which constitutes a person' (*Treatise*, Bk I, part IV, sect. ii, p. 189). This leads him to the perception that the problems associated with the notion of personal identity are in reality grammatical rather than philosophical: 'All the disputes concerning the identity of connected objects are merely verbal, except so far as the relation of points gives rise to some fiction or imaginary principle of union' (*Treatise*, I, IV, vii, p. 262). Language, that is, may not only be our primary means of describing reality; its structures may actually be constitutive of that reality. Perception, articulation – and perhaps even existence – are mutually formative: in speaking, we do not merely know but create ourselves.

Problems of establishing personal identity were compounded by the atomizing procedures of the empirical method, which reduced the availability of knowledge about the world to the cumulation of fragmented data presented to human sense perception. Locke's account of how knowledge is acquired gradually through the accretion and combination of disparate perceptions leads smoothly into Hume's account of human nature, which flirts provocatively with atomism and its destructive implications for personal identity: individuals, says Hume, 'are nothing but a bundle or collection of different perceptions, which succeed each other with an inconceivable rapidity, and are in a perpetual flux and movement' (*Treatise*, I, IV, vi, p. 252). *Association* becomes the crucial bonding principle of atomistic perceptions:

These are the only links that bind the parts of the universe together, or connect us with any person or object exterior to ourselves. For as it is by means of thought only that any thing operates upon our passions, and as these are the only ties of our thoughts, they are really *to us* the cement of the universe, and all the operations of the mind must, in a great measure, depend on them.

(*Treatise, Abstract*, p. 662)

As gravity holds together the Newtonian physical universe, so the ties of association and sympathy bind the universe of human experience. This has profound implications for both literature and literary criticism in the eighteenth century. Archibald Alison's influential work *Essays on the Nature and Principles of Taste* (1790) founds an aesthetic on the 'trains of thought' induced in the imagination by the impression of an external object:

When we feel either the beauty or sublimity of natural scenery, – the gay lustre of a morning in spring, or the mild radiance of a summer evening, – the savage majesty of a wintry storm or the wild magnificence of a tempestuous ocean, – we are conscious of a variety of images in our minds, very different from those which the objects themselves can present to the eye. Trains of pleasing or of solemn thought arise spontaneously within our

minds; our hearts swell with emotions, of which the objects before us seem
to afford no adequate cause; and we are never so much satiated with
delight, as when, in recalling our attention, we are unable to trace either the
progress or the connection of those thoughts, which have passed with so
much rapidity through our imagination.

(Essays, I, pp. 4–6)

Alison develops his principle to account for the power of literary expression:

Language itself is another very important cause of the extent of such
associations . . . the use of Language gives, to every individual who employs
it, the possession of all the analogies which so many ages have observed,
between material qualities, and qualities capable of producing Emotion.

(Essays, I, p. 185)

Hume's reassessment of the implications of Locke's empiricism is fundamentally responsible for the recognition in later eighteenth-century and
Romantic literary criticism of (as Alison put it) 'the analogies between
the qualities of Matter, and the qualities of Mind'. The nature of things
– in so far as this is available to human perception – is acknowledged
to have two inextricable dimensions: a scientific or physical ('things'),
and a human or moral ('mind'); philosophers and literary critics
alike attempt to reunite these against the legacy of Cartesian dualism by
applying the methods and language of the one to the other in order to
establish a continuous register of philosophical discourse, a language
which unites metaphysician and moralist, the anatomist and the painter.

Philosophers construct a reality and then criticize it, just as literature
does. In Hume's writing, just as much as in any sentimental novel, the
presentness of sensation is vividly evoked, making the philosophical
point immediately available to the imagination of the reader. Here is
Hume analysing the constituents of our quite unprovable conviction
about the continuing reality of external objects and events:

I am here seated in my chamber with my face to the fire; and all the objects
that strike my senses are contained in a few yards around me. My memory,
indeed, informs me of the existence of many objects; but then this
information extends not beyond their past existence, nor do either my senses
or memory give any testimony to the continuance of their being. When
therefore I am thus seated, and revolve over these thoughts, I hear on a
sudden a noise as of a door turning upon its hinges; and a little after see
a porter who advances towards me. This gives occasion to many new
reflections and reasonings. First, I never have observed, that this noise could
proceed from any thing but the motion of a door; and therefore conclude,
that the present phenomenon is a contradiction to all past experience, unless
the door, which I remember on t'other side of the chamber, be still in being.
Again, I have always found that a human body was possessed of a quality,

which I call gravity, and which hinders it from mounting in the air, as this porter must have done to arrive at my chamber, unless the stairs I remember be not annihilated by my absence.

(*Treatise*, p. 196)

In its dramatic expectation, written as it is 'to the moment', this might almost be a paragraph from Richardson's *Pamela*, or *Clarissa*.

The French philosophe Denis Diderot achieves a comparable stylistic mastery and psychological immediacy in his engaging discussions of theoretically abstruse propositions. The world of his 'novel' *Jacques le fataliste* is one of dizzying variety and unpredictability, where philosophy, literature and criticism mingle and confound all categories and orders, approximating instead to the multifarious nature of experience. In one of its aspects, the book is a fictional exploration of the issues raised by Diderot's philosophical materialism – that the universe is completely explicable in terms of the properties and activities of matter, and that these are completely determined. But Diderot combined this systematic commitment with an intense preoccupation with ethical problems and the freedom of the individual. Like Hume, he found the mixture of metaphysics and morality in human thought to be an unstable, hugely comic compound. In the book Jacques constantly asserts a belief in fate and foreordination, but always acts resourcefully and feels impulsively, as if in contradiction of his own theory. The story becomes a medium for exploring and criticizing dilemmas and issues which are philosophically irreconcilable; no argument is developed, nor can any conclusion be reached: the criticism is literature, and the literature gives a tenable form to the philosophy. Throughout, the ironic, celebratory tone freewheels around the subject, playing with it, expanding its implications and giving it a human reference-point. If there is in the end any 'moral' to this story it is that of the first Book of Hume's *Treatise*: whatever the rightness of theory in abstract terms, experience will always be too strong for it. Just as we cannot believe that objects *do not* exist beyond our perception of them, we unavoidably feel and act as though we have free will. As Samuel Johnson declared to Boswell, 'all theory is against the freedom of the will; all experience for it'.[8] Similarly, Jacques's master is finally driven into a logical corner and finds an assertion which completely lets him off the hook: 'That is all too much for me. But in spite of your Captain and in spite of you, I shall believe that I want when I want' (*Jacques*, p. 236).[9]

---

[8] *The Life of Samuel Johnson LLD.* (1791), ed. George Birkbeck Hill, rev. edn L. F. Powell, 6 vols. (Oxford, 1934), III, p. 291 (entry for Wed. 15 April, 1778).

[9] 'Cela est trop fort pour moi; mais, en dépit de ton capitaine et de toi, je croirai que je veux quand je veux' (*Oeuvres romanesques*, p. 758).

Against Locke's anxious preservation of the province of human reason within his empirical epistemology, Hume had declared categorically that 'Reason is, and ought only to be the slave of the passions' (*Treatise*, p. 415); in *Jacques*, reason is merely another, self-justifying term for instinct: 'without knowing what is written above, none of us knows what we want or what we are doing, and we follow our whims which we call reason, or our reason which is often nothing but a dangerous whim which sometimes turns out well, sometimes badly' (p. 29).[10] In the face of necessarily imperfect and incomplete knowledge of what actually goes on in the mind and heart of another, all that can be known of life is its 'story'. When the hostess is chastised by Jacques's master for 'sinn[ing] against the rules of Aristotle, Horace, Vida and le Bossu' – the great critical authorities of neo-classicism – because she presents one of the figures in her tale in a disorientatingly inconsistent way, her reply, we feel, carries Diderot's own philosophical, literary and critical sanction behind it: 'I don't follow any rules. I told you the story as it happened, without leaving anything out and without adding anything. Who knows what was going on at the bottom of this young girl's heart, and whether perhaps in the moments when she appeared to us to be acting in the most carefree manner she was not secretly consumed with sorrow' (p. 149).[11]

This is similar to Johnson's reply to the rule-bound critics of Shakespeare who, like Voltaire, had puzzled over how, with all his natural sublimity and imaginative genius, Shakespeare was 'without the slightest spark of good taste or the least knowledge of the rules' (*Letters on England*, p. 92).[12] At issue here – and fully articulated in Diderot's literary scepticism – is one important consequence of philosophical empiricism for the possibility of 'objective' judgements in literature. Once it was accepted that all human knowledge is founded on the partial evidence of the senses and the governance of passion, the relative claims of 'rules' and 'inspiration' in literary composition could, as some of my quotations have been suggesting, no longer be settled on neo-classical principles. Aristotle, Horace, Vida and Le Bossu were no longer names to conjure with: the faithful rendition of emotions, however inconsistent or self-contradictory, came before the observance of rules.

[10] 'C'est que, faute de savoir ce qui est écrit la-haut, on ne sait ni ce qu'on veut ni ce qu'on fait, et qu'on suit sa fantaisie qu'on appelle raison, ou sa raison qui n'est souvent qu'une dangereuse fantaisie qui tourne tantôt bien, tantôt mal' (*Oeuvres romanesques*, p. 503).

[11] 'Je ne connais ni bossu ni droit: je vous ai dit la chose comme elle s'est passée, sans rien omettre, sans y rien ajouter. Et qui sait ce qui se passait au fond du coeur de cette jeune fille, et si, dans les moments où elle nous paraissait agir le plus lestement, elle n'etait pas secrètement devotée de chagrin?' (*Oeuvres romanesques*, p. 649).

[12] 'sans la moindre étincelle de bon gout & sans la moindre connoissance des règles' (*Lettres philosophiques*, II, p. 79).

The danger, eventually, seemed to be complete subjectivism. All is not lost to moral and critical anarchy, however, despite the fears of the critics of scepticism: in Diderot's writing as in Hume's the anecdote's good-humoured tone ensures that the wisdom it embodies gains a kind of assent which is not conditional on its logical consistency. In the imagination of the artist the contrarieties of human nature may find a single expression, a philosophical or critical truth may become a literary one. Eighteenth-century literature, criticism and philosophy all abandon absolutes, and search to find a basis rather in relation and relativity. In response to philosophical empiricism, criticism itself becomes historically based rather than rule-based for the first time, recognizing its dependence on human perception and its confinement to time and place. As Goethe put it, in – surprisingly – an almost Humean *aperçu*, 'The very thing in works of art which strikes uneducated persons as nature, is not nature (externally), but man (nature from within)' (*Werke*, XII, p. 478).[13]

To restrain the slide towards complete relativism philosophy, literature and criticism all clung to the idea of the shareable nature of experience. In his essay 'Of the Standard of Taste' (1757), Hume offers an extreme relativism of individual taste which none the less holds out the possibility of a consensus in critical judgements:

> no sentiment represents what is really in the object ... Beauty is no quality in things themselves: It exists merely in the mind which contemplates them; and each mind perceives a different beauty ... every individual ought to acquiesce in his own sentiment, without pretending to regulate those of others.   (*Essays*, pp. 234–5)

None the less, Hume goes on, some writing and some artists are, rightly, judged to be better than others, and the standard of judgement is based on a rather circular consensus of 'right-thinking' critics. Eighteenth-century writing is rescued from the perils of solipsism and subjectivity by its strenuous adherence to the power of shared experience. It should be noted, however, that Hume does not abate the rigour of his epistemological scepticism one iota during this discussion of taste: if we agree to call some works of literature good or bad, it is not because they are so on any objectively measurable scale, but only because we *do* agree that they are. 'All the general rules of art are founded only on experience' (p. 237). Once again, Hume commands his reader's assent through the persuasiveness of his literary language of metaphor and analogy; like Diderot, he clinches his critical and philosophical point with a story:

---

[13] 'Gerade das, was ungebildeten Menschen am Kunstwerk als Natur auffällt, das ist nicht Natur (von außen), sondern der Mensch (Natur von innen).'

It is with good reason, says Sancho to the squire with the great nose, that I pretend to have a judgment in wine: this is a quality hereditary in our family. Two of my kinsmen were once called to give their opinion of a hogshead, which was supposed to be excellent, being old and of a good vintage. One of them tastes it; considers it; and, after mature reflection, pronounces the wine to be good, were it not for a small taste of leather which he perceived in it. The other, after using the same precautions, gives also his verdict in favour of the wine; but with the reserve of a taste of iron, which he could easily distinguish. You cannot imagine how much they were both ridiculed for their judgment. But who laughed in the end? On emptying the hogshead, there was found at the bottom an old key with a leathern thong tied to it. The great resemblance between mental and bodily taste will easily teach us to apply this story ...

(pp. 239–40)

Hume's philosophy, like Diderot's, is inseparable from his narrative style and analogical cast of mind.

Despite Locke's attempt to limit the referential range of language, the connection between expression and knowledge is (long before Alison articulates it in a literary-critical context in his *Essays on the Nature and Principles of Taste*) inescapable in eighteenth-century philosophical writing. Locke's investigation into human understanding had depended upon a strictly denotative use of language: each word, he stresses, stands for a 'distinct idea':

I know there are not Words enough in any Language to answer all the variety of Ideas, that enter into Men's discourses and reasonings. But this hinders not, but that when any one uses any term, he may have in his Mind a determined Idea, which he makes it the sign of, and to which he should keep it steadily annex'd during that present discourse. Where he does not, or cannot do this, he in vain pretends to clear or distinct Ideas: 'Tis plain his are not so: and therefore there can be expected nothing but obscurity and confusion, where such terms are made use of, which have not such a precise determination.

(*Essay*, 'Epistle to the Reader', p. 13)

It is not unfair to say that much eighteenth-century literature is hampered by the legacy of Locke's distrust of 'the inexpressible'. His interest is in analytic discourse rather than in feelings or in imagination; the *Essay* disparages the ambiguity of 'indistinct ideas' in writing of any kind:

He that hath imagined to himself Substances such as have never been, and fill'd his Head with *Ideas* which have not any correspondence with the real Nature of Things, to which yet he gives settled and defined Names, may fill his Discourse, and, perhaps, another Man's Head, with the fantastical

Imaginations of his own Brain; but he will be very far from advancing thereby one jot in his real and true Knowledge.   (*Essay*, III, 10, p. 506)

From here, language's ability to obscure and confound as well as to reveal truth passes into eighteenth-century literature, philosophy and criticism. Theories of language have been the subject of Nicholas Hudson's chapter in this volume; the relevant point here is the way thinking – and anxiety – about the functions and shortcomings of language have substantial and similar effects on philosophical, critical and 'literary' *writing* in the eighteenth century. The implications of Locke's divorce of denotative and connotative language seem to be that the anatomist can only be hampered and misled by the skills of the painter – and, furthermore, that these latter may be thoroughly suspect seducers of sense. However, Locke's own writing reveals that the opposition between the referential and the evocative in expression cannot be sustained – or, at least, would not be until Kant – in even the most rigorous epistemological anatomy. Describing the philosophical process in the Introduction to the *Essay*, Locke writes in a richly metaphorical passage: 'It will be no Excuse to an idle and untoward Servant, who would not attend his Business by Candle-light, to plead that he had not bright Sun-shine. The Candle, that is set up in us, shines bright enough for all our Purposes' (I, 1, p. 46). 'Enlightenment' was no dead metaphor; for Locke, just as for Pope in his celebration of Newton, reason was the bringer of light to the darkness of our understanding. The early image of the flickering candle introduces a strain of light and visual imagery which runs through the *Essay* and is central not only to the clarity but to the content of Locke's exposition of human mind:

external and internal Sensation are the only passages that I can find of Knowledge, to the Understanding. These alone, as far as I can discover, are the Windows by which light is let into this *dark Room*. For, methinks, the *Understanding* is not much unlike a Closet wholly shut from light, with only some little openings left, to let in external visible Resemblances or *Ideas* of things without; would the Pictures coming in to such a dark Room but stay there, and lie so orderly as to be found upon occasion, it would very much resemble the Understanding of a Man in reference to all Objects of sight, and the *Ideas* of them.   (*Essay*, II, 12, pp. 162–3)

Locke's theory of the relationship between ideas and words, and his writing, seem at odds with each other here; the confusion is worth pausing over because it is the source of a false distinction between thought and expression which bedevils eighteenth-century criticism. Locke's *philosophy* of language tended to disparage care for words as such, in favour of the meanings they express (Pope picked up this thought in a couplet which Johnson approved so strongly that he used it twice in his *Dictionary*, under 'language' and under 'express': 'Others for language all their care express, / And value books, as women men, for dress').[14] But it is important to distinguish between the way Locke and his followers disparaged figures of speech as obscuring meaning and the way in which their own prose and poetry employ these to enlighten: to articulate and gain assent for their intentions. So Hume, who imagined himself 'affrighted and confus'd', set adrift in a leaky weatherbeaten vessel upon the seas of philosophic controversy, could also write that 'Many of the beauties of poetry, and even of eloquence, are founded on falsehood and fiction, on hyperboles, metaphors, and an abuse or perversion of terms from their natural meaning' ('Of the Standard of Taste', *Essays*, p. 236). In modern terms at least, eighteenth-century *writing*, whether philosophical or 'literary', is a great deal more sophisticated than its self-criticism. In the universe of the imagination, metaphor is an essential ingredient of understanding.

Locke's highly developed visual analogy of the basic unit of experience as a picture painted by the senses on the dark obscurities of the mind itself fostered a strain of literary criticism which tended to undervalue the creative and expressive powers of words. If experience proceeds in pictures, then language is at best a secondary descriptive medium for it, at a further remove than its impression from the experience or from reality itself. This thought passed quickly into aesthetics and criticism, where unfavourable comparison could be made with the more direct appeal to the senses of painting and music. Jonathan Richardson's view is representative:

Words paint to the Imagination, but every Man forms the thing to himself in his Own way: Language is very Imperfect: there are innumerable Colours and Figures for which we have no name, and an infinity of other Ideas which have no certain Words universally agreed upon as denoting them; whereas the Painter can convey his Ideas of these Things Clearly, and without Ambiguity; and what he says every one understands in the Sense he intends it.

Painting ... Pours Ideas into our Minds, Words only Drop 'em. The whole Scene opens at one View, whereas the other way lifts the Curtain up by little, and little.   (*Theory of Painting*, pp. 3–4)

---

[14] Locke's division between the functional and the ornamental in language is built on accepted classical and Renaissance literary-critical principles; in associating exclusively denotative language with the investigations of empiricism, he at once lends new power to the material perceived over the perceptive mind, and perpetuates the false division between substance and style into the empirical literary criticism of the eighteenth century.

The influence of Locke's denotative theory of language is direct, and potentially damaging to both literary expression and criticism.

In this strain, Samuel Johnson reiterates Locke's philosophical strictures on the abuse of words in the context of their specific bearing on criticism:

Among those who have endeavoured to promote learning, and rectify judgment, it has been long customary to complain of the abuse of words, which are so often admitted to signify things so different that, instead of assisting the understanding as vehicles of knowledge, they produce error, dissention, and perplexity, because what is affirmed in one sense, is received in another.

(Yale edn, V, p. 287)

The art of poets, Johnson says in this same *Rambler*, 'is imagined to consist in distorting words from their original meaning'.

These strictures on the poetic 'abuse' of language have strongly ethical overtones. Locke's *Essay* prompts its reader clearly to discriminate and compare ideas. The mind's true discipline consists in 'the severe Rules of Truth, and good Reason' (II, 11, p. 157). When it comes to matters of emotional response, which are gathered together in the Fourth Book of the *Essay* under the severe rubric of 'Enthusiasm', Locke is unequivocal that 'reason must be our last judge and guide in everything'. His caution in assenting to any of the movements of the mind which might be caused by or themselves give rise to irrational behaviour has profound implications for the literature and criticism of the eighteenth century:

In any truth that gets not possession of our minds by the irresistible light of self-evidence, or by the force of demonstration, the arguments that gain it assent are the vouchers and gage of its probability to us; and we can receive it for no other, than such as they deliver it to our understandings.

(*Essay*, IV, 19, p. 697)

Any claim for inspiration or supra-rational intuition receives an implicit but firm reproof from such robust common sense. Show us your credentials, enlighten our darkness, or be shown the door, such claimants are told.

Voltaire is the greatest exponent of that aspect of 'philosophic' thought which may be fully apprehended in a starkly clarifying use of language. His style is able to penetrate to the critical heart of an argument, or a philosophic position (such as optimism, in *Candide*) and with a single surgical stroke to lay bare its fallacies and absurdities. In this he is like Hume – whose own *Treatise* was largely composed in France while he moved in the circles of great *philosophes* like the Baron d'Holbach –

exposing the muddled thinking and incomplete logic of the '*modern philosophy*' which 'pretends . . . to arise only from the solid, permanent and consistent principles of the imagination' (*Treatise*, I, IV, iv, p. 226). The literary criticism implied by such a procedure is anatomical rather than hesitantly intuitive. It has, like the surgeon's wound, the virtues of clarity and precision, but also the limitations of these virtues. Thought, whether philosophical, literary or critical, is either true or false, and its status may be adequately tested by empirical enquiry. Haydn Mason has associated *Candide* with the great Chateau at Versailles: both, he says, 'are imperishable monuments to French classicism in a world to which the classical precepts do not speak with such immediate force'.[15] In this sense, then, Voltaire's thought represents the strongest form of a critical position and approach to human reasoning which other contemporary writers (among them Diderot and Hume himself) would increasingly complicate with a feel for all the shaping contours of life's ambiguities which are disregarded by the cut to the core. *Le Taureau blanc*, Voltaire's critical *conte* of the implausible or miraculous Old Testament tales, speaks for Voltaire's cherished critical principle of *vraisemblance* in conception and expression: 'I want a tale to be based on verisimilitude and not always resembling a dream. I wish it to contain nothing vulgar or extravagant'.[16]

In England, Johnson's *Dictionary* (1755) epitomizes the denotative, definitional aspects of the empirical attitude to language. His Preface outlines his experimental procedures: having

accumulated in time the materials of a dictionary . . . by degrees, I reduced [these] to method, establishing to myself, in the progress of the work, such rules as experience and analogy suggested to me; experience, which practice and observation were continually increasing; and analogy, which, though in some words obscure, was evident in others.

(*Preface to the Dictionary*, ed. Greene, pp. 307–8)

Such concern with – and confidence in – 'explanations' suggests that the main virtue of prose and poetic style would be found in *perspicuity*, but the variety of tone in the quotations Johnson adduces in support of his definitions itself immediately complicates any confidence that meaning could really be reduced to an identity of statement with implication. But despite the doubts of Johnson and others, perspicuity had by mid-century acquired a quasi-religious sanction in criticism. 'Truth', the critic John Dennis declared at the beginning of the period, '(like the Innocence

[15] *Voltaire* (London, 1975), p. 73.
[16] 'Je veux qu'un conte soit fondé sur la vraisemblance, et qu'il ne ressemble pas toujours à un rêve. Je désire qu'il n'ait rien de trivial ni d'extravagant' (*Zadig and Other Stories*, ed. H. T. Mason (Oxford, 1971), p. 224).

of our first Parents) loves to appear naked, and Solid Sense like perfect Beauty, is but hid by Ornament'.[17]

Since the turn of the century writers had increasingly felt the need to bring literary criticism into line with the advances made in philosophy by making it more 'scientific' in its aims and methods – 'scientific' understood as following the empirical method to the end of unvarying principle. Even within the works of the empiricists themselves, however, dissenting voices rose against this unmeasured tide of confidence in empiricism's ability to derive unequivocal rules from the observation of behaviour. Edmund Burke, who declared that the 'rules' derived from 'a careful survey of the property of things' might be successfully 'applied to the imitative arts', could also write in the same work without a sense of contradiction that 'a clear idea ... is another name for a little idea' (*Philosophical Inquiry into ... the Sublime and the Beautiful*, p. 63). One of the implications of empirical philosophy which it was increasingly difficult to ignore, was that with the abandonment of *a priori* categories of knowledge in the rationalist tradition and Locke's dismissal of innate ideas, knowledge of all kinds could only ever be relative and provisional. The implication of Lockean epistemology is individual isolation, the imprisonment of the individual within the random data of his or her own sense-impressions. The solution to the problem, Locke implies (and Hume's sociable manner of writing exemplifies), lies in the role the senses play in relating the mind to the outside world, and in the sympathetic movements of the senses towards the experience of others. This is that 'knowledge of the heart' so important to eighteenth-century literature and criticism: the imaginative capacity to make another's experience one's own, which links, once again, the researches of the anatomist into the 'most secret springs and principles' of the mind and the discoveries of the moralist about the 'Grace and Beauty of its [i.e., the mind's] Actions'. (See also chapters 18 and 27 of the present volume.)

More traditional ethical systems based on a rationalist theory of knowledge called for the control of reason to subdue the instincts of the imagination as much as possible; for Hume, the fundamental role of the imagination in the structure of human identity makes this not only impossible but undesirable; he therefore develops an ethical theory based on the sympathetic response which imagination arouses for certain actions and feelings between people. 'Sympathy', he says, 'is the conversion of an idea into an impression by the force of imagination' (*Treatise*, II, III, vi, p. 427). Imagination makes present to the senses what direct

---

[17] 'Remarks on ... Prince Arthur, An Heroick Poem' (1696), in *The Critical Works of John Dennis*, ed. E. N. Hooker, 2 vols. (Baltimore, 1939–43), I, p. 50.

observation cannot tell us. Hume's philosophical sense of the imagination as a completing agent in human experience influences later aesthetic and critical theories of the sublime, with its response to a similar sense of the partiality of what we can know and the immensity of what is not directly available. So there is an epistemological as well as a literary continuity between Locke's image of the peephole in a darkened room, the fictional games of Sterne's *Tristram Shandy* and that greatness beyond the power of language to express which characterizes the completing imaginative power of the Romantic sublime:

we live amongst riddles and mysteries – the most obvious things, which come in our way, have dark sides, which the quickest sight cannot penetrate into; and even the clearest and most exalted understandings amongst us find ourselves puzzled and at a loss in almost every cranny of nature's works.[18]

The imagination

Sympathy, as Adam Smith would put it, 'belongs' to the imagination, because it is the imagination alone which can 'carry us beyond our own person' to overcome the Cartesian dualism between self and other, the inner world and the outer (*The Theory of Moral Sentiments*, p. 9). The 'sympathetic' powers of the poet – philosophically and ethically understood – became vitally those of imagination, and literary criticism began explicitly to concern itself with the relationship between the two in the poetic process. Locke had given the imagination a bad name at the beginning of the century by classing it with falsehood as against truth, the fanciful product of an idle mind associating rather than discriminating between ideas. His famous opposition of wit and judgement, derived from this, was the cue for Addison's *Spectator* papers on 'True and False Wit', whence it became a highly influential critical orthodoxy: Locke finds

Wit lying most in the assemblage of *Ideas*, and putting those together with quickness and variety, wherein can be found any resemblance or congruity, thereby to make up pleasant Pictures, and agreeable Visions in the Fancy: *Judgment*, on the contrary, lies quite on the other side, in separating carefully, one from another, *Ideas*, wherein can be found the least Difference, thereby to avoid being misled by Similitude, and by affinity to take one thing for another.   (*Essay*, II, 11, p. 156)[19]

---

[18] *The Life and Opinions of Tristram Shandy, Gentleman*, ed. Ian Campbell Ross (Oxford, 1983), p. 233 (IV, ch. xvii).

[19] Locke's wit/judgement distinction may be traced to related passages in Hobbes; see James Sambrook's discussion of 'The Psychology of Literary Creation' in ch. 27 of this volume.

Following Locke, Addison would write

As true wit generally consists in th[e] resemblance and congruity of ideas,
false wit chiefly consists in the resemblance and congruity sometimes of
single letters, as in anagrams, chronograms [etc.] ... it is impossible for any
thought to be beautiful which is not just, and has not its foundation in the
nature of things: ... the basis of all wit is truth; and ... no thought can be
valuable, of which good sense is not the groundwork.

(Spectator 62)

Building on this notion of 'true wit' as somehow reflecting 'the nature
of things', Addison proceeded in later papers to derive the 'pleasures of
imagination' from another of Locke's distinctions, this time between
'primary' and 'secondary' qualities (*Essay*, Bk II, ch. 8). The 'true' pleasures of the imagination are 'only such pleasures as arise originally from
sight': firstly 'those primary pleasures ... which entirely proceed from
such objects as are before our eyes'; secondly, the secondary pleasures
'which flow from the ideas of visible objects, when the objects are not
actually before the eye, but are called up into our memories, or formed
into agreeable visions of things that are either absent or fictitious'.
Imagination, then, in its proper form, 'is but opening the eye, and the
scene enters' (*Spectator* 411). Thus tamed, it provides aesthetic pleasure; anything other is simply fantasy not proper to art.

Johnson's *Dictionary* gives one of its definitions of 'Imagination' as
'the power of representing things absent'; this is continuous both with
Addison's pleasurable aesthetic quality and with Hume's epistemological analysis of the workings of the mind, but its implications point in
much more disturbing directions, towards the perils of the 'false' indulged at the expense of truth. In *Rambler* 125, Johnson writes

Definitions have been no less difficult or uncertain in criticism than in law.
Imagination, a licentious and vagrant faculty, unsusceptible of limitations,
and impatient of restraint, has always endeavoured to baffle the logician, to
perplex the confines of distinction, and burst the inclosures of regularity.

(Yale edn, IV, p. 300)

Here are all the *dangers* of fiction, from the very source which to
Romantic writers would be its greatest sanction: its ability to bring the
intuitions from beyond the senses to attention. We may recall here the
untroubledness of Hume's 'universe of the Imagination' in which 'The
memory, senses, and understanding are therefore all of them founded on
the imagination, or the vivacity of our ideas' (*Treatise*, p. 265). *Rambler*
125 suggests, too, the necessary provisionality of *any* relationship between the products of the mind ('imagination') and the world. The way

is always open to idealism, or to the dualism of mind and world which (though it had been made explicit by Descartes) was kept in abeyance through the social stance of eighteenth-century philosophy until its re-enthronement in Romantic philosophy, literature and literary criticism. But though the prospect sometimes beckons both writers, neither Hume as philosopher nor Johnson as critic allows his writing to follow the road to the logical conclusions Kant would insist upon in his *Critique of Judgement*. For both Johnson and Hume, writing itself had the ability to hold the claims of mind and world in a communicable tension, to preserve a vital common ground between the potentially solipsistic imagination and the unverifiable external.

This pressing need for consensus begins to unravel the paradox that an age of philosophical concentration on particular fact and the units of experience should also have been the great age of generality in literary criticism. 'Great truths are always general', pronounced Johnson in his *Preface to Shakespeare*, drawing on the full weight of mid-eighteenth-century philosophy; 'Nothing can please long and please many but just representations of general nature' (Yale edn, VII, p. 61). Whatever the precepts of good writing (and within the body of his work Johnson advances or investigates many), nature – the empirical *facts* of the case – must always be the final arbiter. Nothing abstract or *a priori* can evade the test of experience: if Shakespeare has united 'the powers of exciting laughter and sorrow not only in one mind but in one composition', it is justified because that is what life itself is like. It may well be 'a practice contrary to the rules of criticism' but there is always an appeal open from criticism to nature (Yale edn, VII, p. 67).

The idea of 'general nature' is not a dogmatic standard of judgement, but a *critical* position which may be tentatively advanced as the meeting point between the mind and the external world, the point where inner and outer mutually confirm each other's reality and validity, where the perceptions of art may be tested against what Wordsworth would later call 'the beautiful and permanent forms of nature'.[20] In the absence of general *certainty*, Johnson emphasizes the primary validity of particular experience and its crucial ability to command general *assent*, a procedure which itself derives from the empirical method and has its influence on subsequent literature and criticism. In this Johnson holds a middle position between the dogmatic generality of a critic like Reynolds and the equally positive 'particularity' of Blake. The clashing of these extreme views on the source of aesthetic value is pointedly illustrated in Blake's annotations to Reynolds's *Discourses*:

---

[20] Preface to *Lyrical Ballads*, 2nd edn (1800), ed. R. L. Brett and A. R. Jones (London, 1963), p. 245.

[art (must) get above all singular forms, local customs, particularities, and
details of every kind.]
A folly
Singular & Particular Detail is the Foundation of the Sublime ...
[There is a rule, obtained out of general nature,]
What is General Nature is there Such a Thing
what is General Knowledge is there such a Thing [strictly speaking] all
Knowledge is Particular[21]

The relationship between empirical, atomistic evidence and general
reflection or synthesis was, therefore, problematic during the evolution
of both philosophical and critical thinking between the epistemological
gulf opened by Hume and Berkeley, and the point when Kant stepped
in to confront its implications with a theory which could assimilate the
radical possibilities of empiricism without finding itself reduced to despairing silence about objective knowledge of anything. For Reynolds,
art remedied the deficiencies of nature and the empirical processes of
the understanding by giving immediate access to the intuitions of the
imagination: 'The object and intention of all the Arts is to supply the
natural imperfection of things, and often to gratify the mind by realising
and embodying what never existed but in the imagination' (*Discourses*,
p. 244). Art and poetry are addressed 'to the desires of the mind, to that
spark of divinity which we have within'. The imagination is here the
residence of truth. The phrase recalls the episode in Johnson's *Rasselas*
where the travellers visit the pyramids, and Imlac is moved to comment
on 'that hunger of the imagination which preys incessantly upon life,
and must be always appeased by some employment. Those who have
already all that they can enjoy, must enlarge their desires' (*Rasselas*, p.
78). No 'reason' can be given for these massive monuments of human
art; they stand as an embodiment of all in human experience that evades
the philosophical analysis of mind. The parallel between Reynolds's and
Johnson's phrase is not merely a verbal or grammatical one; it points
to a kind of philosophical criticism which commits itself to a literary
understanding of experience in the fullest sense.

Philosophy as reason and as criticism

Alongside these empirically-based writings which describe, analyse and
finally celebrate the place of instinct and impulse in human behaviour,
eighteenth-century philosophical writing sustained a schematizing rational strain which was continuous with the major seventeenth-century
philosophical tradition of rationalism. The Earl of Shaftesbury, in his

---

[21] *The Poetry and Prose of William Blake*, p. 637.

'rhapsody' *The Moralists*, advances the thought that 'Nothing ... is more strongly imprinted on our Minds, or more closely interwoven with our Souls, than the Idea or Sense of *Order* and *Proportion*' (*Characteristicks*, II, p. 284). 'Harmony', he declares, 'is Harmony *by Nature*', and is therefore constant through art, morals and philosophy – which he defines as '*the Study of inward Numbers and Proportions*' (I, p. 353). Philosophy, aesthetics, ethics and literary criticism join in the rhapsodic unifying of his 'Miscellaneous Reflections' (1714): 'What is BEAUTIFUL is *Harmonious* and *Proportionable*; what is Harmonious and Proportionable, is TRUE; and what is at once both *Beautiful* and *True*, is, of consequence, *Agreeable* and GOOD' (*Characteristicks*, III, pp. 182–3). Looking back for a moment to Locke's 'God has made the intellectual world harmonious and beautiful without us; but it will never come into our heads all at once; we must bring it home piece-meal', the continuities and differences between empirical and rationalist thinking become clear. Locke and Shaftesbury agree that there is objective order in the external world, but where the latter believes that its principles are directly available to human consciousness through reason, Locke holds that it can become present to consciousness only through the accumulated observations of the senses. The rational integration of experience and larger 'Order' is (before Kant) largely confined to eighteenth-century aesthetics rather than epistemology, where empiricism held sway.

Founded as it is in perception, empirical philosophy makes all knowledge conditional upon the state of the knower and tends to relativism and ultimate scepticism about the state of human knowledge; rational philosophy, on the other hand, claims direct access to *a priori* truths through the exercise of reason and tends to belief in objective reality and absolutism. In his *Critique of Pure Reason* (1781), Kant sought to combine these views, to find a way of describing the world objectively (through the exercise of reason) which none the less took into account the subjectivity of human perception. For the primacy of sensation which was the cornerstone of Hume's empirical philosophy, Kant substitutes the primacy of logic; experience itself, he maintains, has *structure* and its order can be analysed. The shift has important implications for understanding human behaviour, which for Hume had been governed by impulse and instinct: Kant went on to consider these in his *Critique of Practical Reason* (1788).

If Hume had written philosophy as literature, Kant perhaps is the true heir of the 'critical' thrust of Enlightenment. His is, quintessentially, philosophy as criticism. 'Our age is', he writes, 'in an especial degree, the age of criticism' (*Critique of Pure Reason*, trans. Kemp Smith, p. 9).[22]

---

[22] Kant, AA IV, p. 9n.

He proposes to subject all doctrines not (as Hume and the empiricist writers had) to the test of experience, but to the test of reason. Five years before the publication of his *Critique of Pure Reason*, Kant wrote to his student Marcus Herz:

It must be possible to survey the field of pure reason, that is, of judgements that are independent of all empirical principles, since this lies *a priori* in ourselves and need not await any exposure from our experience ... we need a critique, a discipline, a canon, and an architecture of *pure reason*, a formal science, therefore, that can require nothing of those sciences already at hand and that needs for its foundations an entirely unique technical vocabulary.[23]

This signals the divorce of philosophical and literary language, the breaking apart of the delicate consensus that had kept the two disciplines continuous with one another through most of the eighteenth century. It heralds the age of the professional, university-based philosopher, committed to method and discipline as Hume (despite his mastery of both) never was; its implications for the professionalizing of literary criticism were to be profound (see chapter 28(ii), below, on the rise of aesthetics). Coleridge was no university professor, but – heavily influenced by German Romantic philosophy – he distinguished between his own abstract and philosophical aims in literary criticism and the empirical or descriptive intentions of Wordsworth. The lurking polarities of the anatomist and painter seem to surface once again:

it was Mr Wordsworth's purpose [in his 'Preface' to the *Lyrical Ballads*] to consider the influences of fancy and imagination as they are manifested in poetry, and from the different effects to conclude their diversity in kind; while it is my object to investigate the seminal principle, and then from the kind to deduce the degree.[24]

As the 'technical' chapters of Coleridge's *Biographia* demonstrate only too fully, arcane vocabulary and obscurity seem the necessary tools – and mysteries – of the trade of such an expert. Two years after *his* book's publication, Kant wrote in defence of its difficulty to Christian Garve, 'popularity cannot be attempted in studies of such high abstraction ... [an] unfamiliar language [is] indispensable'.[25]

For Kant both philosophy and life are rule-governed; these rules are determinable by the investigation of reason, and reason's findings must reflect their structure. He outlines the interaction between subject, method and expression in his new philosophy in 'The Transcendental Doctrine of Method' which concludes the *Critique of Pure Reason*:

---

[23] Kant, AA X, pp. 185f.; 24 November 1776.
[24] *Biographia Literaria*, I, pp. 87f.   [25] Kant, AA X, pp. 317f.; 7 August 1783.

In accordance with reason's legislative prescriptions, our diverse modes of knowledge must not be permitted to be a mere rhapsody, but must form a system. Only so can they further the essential ends of reason. By a system I understand the unity of the manifold modes of knowledge under one idea. This idea is the concept provided by reason – of the form of a whole – in so far as the concept determines *a priori* not only the scope of its manifold content, but also the positions which the parts occupy relatively to one another. The scientific concept of reason contains, therefore, the end and the form of that whole which is congruent with this requirement.

(trans. Kemp Smith, p. 653)[26]

The rule-governed base of every aspect of human behaviour extends to writing and language in Kant's belief in the grammatical primacy of verbal experience. This would imply a literary criticism fully devoted to formal and linguistic principles of judgement. Kant's later *Critique of Judgement* extends these principles specifically to aesthetics (cf. chapter 28(ii) below), where he defines 'genius' as the special quality 'which gives the rules to art'.

Equally important is the effect of these structuring principles on literary style: it is clear that at this point philosophy abandons the 'Grace & Beauty' of the painter and the 'Action' of the mind's story, for the analytic virtues of the anatomist. Kant (unlike Hume or Diderot) does not exemplify the complexity of human experience in the 'literary' shape of anecdote; he organizes it as 'critique'. Both forms of philosophy illuminate or (to evoke Locke's image) 'enlighten', but their implications for the form of literary criticism point in different directions in the nineteenth century.

There is another crucial difference, too, between broadly Lockean and Kantian enquiries. For Locke, the epistemological enquiry into 'human understanding' aimed to set *limits* to the comprehensible, to define what could be enlightened, and what must forever remain dark to human knowledge:

were the Capacities of our Understandings well considered, the Extent of our Knowledge once discovered, and the Horizon found, which sets the Bounds between the enlightned and dark Parts of Things; between what is, and what is not comprehensible by us, Men would perhaps with less Scruple acquiesce in the avow'd Ignorance of the one, and employ their Thoughts and Discourse, with more Advantage and Satisfaction in the other.

(*Essay*, I, i, p. 47)

Kant, on the other hand, declared in the Preface to the first edition of his *Critique of Pure Reason*,

---

[26] Kant, AA III, pp. 538f.

I flatter myself that . . . I have found a way of guarding against all those errors which have hitherto set reason . . . at variance with itself . . . I have made completeness my chief aim, and I venture to assert that there is not a single metaphysical problem which has not been solved, or for the solution of which the key has not been supplied.   (trans. Kemp Smith, pp. 9f.)[27]

This is not mad hubris on Kant's part. His 'transcendental method' recognizes from the outset that 'human reason . . . is burdened by questions which, as prescribed by the nature of reason itself, it is not able to ignore, but which, as transcending all its powers, it is also not able to answer' (p. 7). We strive to know, though we know that our tools are not adequate to the knowledge. It is in itself a proposition to which both Locke and Hume would have assented. Kant brings to its solution a crucial distinction between what he calls the 'thing-in-itself', its essence which cannot be recognized by the senses, and its empirical appearance – those aspects of it which are immediately available to sense perception. Our perceptual knowledge is of appearances only, but we seek to transcend the conditions of experience, to know the ideal 'thing-in-itself' which can never be present to perception. The state of human experience is of forever striving 'to find for the conditioned knowledge obtained through the understanding, the unconditioned whereby its unity is brought to completion' (*Critique of Pure Reason*, trans. Kemp Smith, p. 306).[28] Luckily, however, man is not merely the creature of his perceptions, dependent completely on the empirical evidence of the senses: there are, as Kant puts it, 'two stems of human knowledge, namely, *sensibility* and *understanding*, which perhaps spring from a common, but to us unknown, root. Through the former, objects are given to us; through the latter, they are thought' (*Ibid.*, pp. 61–2).[29] In the 'Transcendental Deduction' Kant clearly identifies this 'common root' of knowledge as the imagination:

while concepts, which belong to the understanding, are brought into play through relation of the manifold to the unity of apperception, it is only by means of the imagination that they can be brought into relation to sensible intuition.

A pure imagination, which conditions all *a priori* knowledge, is thus one of the fundamental faculties of the human soul . . . The two extremes, namely, sensibility and understanding, must stand in necessary connection with each other through the mediation of this transcendental function of the imagination.   (*Ibid.*, p. 146)[30]

---

[27] Kant, AA IV, pp. 9f.   [28] Kant, AA III, p. 242.
[29] Kant, AA III, p. 46.   [30] Kant, AA IV, p. 91.

Kant's thinking in this area gave a new philosophical rigour and impetus to the aesthetic concept of the sublime, which he defined as 'that, the mere capacity of thinking which, evidences a faculty of mind transcending every standard of taste' (*Critique of Aesthetic Judgement*, trans. Meredith, p. 98).[31] The sublime, then, became precisely that which overrode the Humean 'standard of taste', making an aesthetic leap from the empirical to the noumenal. The imagination is the faculty 'employ[ed] ... in the interests of mind's supersensible province' (*Ibid.*, p. 119).[32] Imagination points the way (as it would more emphatically in Romantic poetry and literary criticism) to the realms *beyond* rational or experiential comprehension, Coleridge's 'living power and prime agent of all human perception ... a representation in the finite mind of the eternal act of creation in the infinite I AM' (see above, p. 590).

Kant finds in his analysis authority to rank poetry first amongst the arts because

It expands the mind by giving freedom to the imagination and by offering, from among the boundless multiplicity of possible forms ... that one which couples with the presentation of the concept a wealth of thought to which no verbal expression is completely adequate, and by thus rising aesthetically to ideas. It invigorates the mind by letting it feel its faculty – free, spontaneous, and independent of determination by nature – of regarding and estimating nature as phenomenon in the light of aspects which nature of itself does not afford us in experience, either for sense or understanding, and of employing it accordingly in behalf of, and as a sort of schema for, the supersensible.

(*Critique of Aesthetic Judgement*, trans. Meredith, pp. 191f.)[33]

Kant called his philosophical combination of empirical experience and objective knowledge *in* the experience 'transcendental idealism'. Experience, in other words, has within it the capacity to transcend itself, to pass with the aid of imagination beyond the limits of empirical observation to the categorical or *a priori* in existence. The direct access to transcendent truths which Kant's philosophy seems to promise had an immense influence on Romantic literary criticism, though it was largely delayed until the nineteenth century. Its effect on poetry was surer and faster:

> ... Imagination, which, in truth,
> Is but another name for absolute strength
> And clearest insight, amplitude of mind,
> And Reason in her most exalted mood.
> This faculty hath been the moving soul
> Of our long labour: we have traced the stream
> From darkness, and the very place of birth

[31] Kant, AA V, p. 250. [32] Kant, AA V, p. 268. [33] Kant, AA V, p. 326.

> In its blind cavern, whence is faintly heard
> The sound of waters; followed it to light
> And open day; ...[34]

Against Locke's (and much of eighteenth-century criticism's) sense of the treachery of non-denotative language, Romantic philosophy, literature and criticism hold that poetry is best able to articulate the true essence of existence through the imaginative relationship it generates between individual experience and transcendent reality. This relationship is essentially private, visionary rather than visual, and it relies for its authority far less on the sanction of consensus, more on the vatic declarations of the inner voice. None the less, Kant felt it to be important to the validity of his 'objective' theory that the world it established was that accepted by contemporary scientific empiricism, conforming to Newton's laws. Indeed, he believed that his own metaphysical findings provided the theoretical ground and justification for the empirical principles of Newton's scientific methods.

Conclusion

The realm of science and that of imagination increasingly seemed to be opposed, the discourse and methods of empiricism dominant and inescapable, their materialistic tendencies obscuring and threatening to crush the province of imagination and the immaterial worlds of truth and beauty. In *Urizen* (1794) William Blake drew anguished figures, bound with the serpents of constricting imagination, falling into the abyss of Newtonian materialism, and his 'Vision of the Last Judgement' offered a poetic criticism of philosophy's procedures:

The Last Judgement is an Overwhelming of Bad Art & Science. Mental Things are alone Real; what is Calld Corporeal Nobody Knows of its dwelling Place <it> is in Fallacy, & its Existence an Imposture<.> Where is the Existence Out of Mind or Thought.[35]

In one sense, this is of course continuous with Hume's 'This is the universe of the imagination, nor have we any idea but what is there produc'd'; the difference between them may perhaps begin to give us a measure of the effects of the break-up of the eighteenth century's fragile consensus between 'metaphysics' and 'morality' on literature and philosophy, and its implications for literary criticism. Blake utterly rejects the consensus of taste in favour of the uniquely personal vision of genius: 'What it will be Questiond When the Sun rises do you not see a round Disk of fire somewhat like a Guinea O no no I see an Innumerable

---

[34] William Wordsworth, *The Prelude* [1805], XIII, ll. 167–76.
[35] *The Poetry and Prose of William Blake*, p. 555.

company of the Heavenly host crying Holy Holy Holy is the Lord God Almighty'.[36] An epistemology such as Locke's has no access to 'enlightenment' which comes in this form. For Blake, the imaginative, poetic perception is the *only* real one: here all knowledge and all vision unite. In this replacement of 'Enlightenment' by the 'light of vision', Blake's thought is continuous with Rousseau's description of the sudden flashes of inspiration which 'dazzled his mind with countless lights' prior to composition (*Oeuvres complètes*, I, p. 416). But where Rousseau had found true untrammelled vision in the state of Nature, Blake opposes Nature and Spirit: vision belongs only with Spirit; Nature is irretrievably contaminated by the atomistic procedures of empirical philosophy: 'I see in Wordsworth the Natural Man rising up against the Spiritual Man continually & then he is no Poet but a Heathen Philosopher at Enmity against all true Poetry or Inspiration.'[37]

But Blake remained and remains a lone voice. In 1789–91, Erasmus Darwin's poem *The Botanical Garden* aimed '*to enlist the Imagination under the banner of Science*'.[38] Fifty years earlier Hume had enlisted moral subjects under the same banner at the beginning of the *Treatise*, but in order to approximate psychology and ethics as closely as possible *to* a science; Darwin on the other hand saw it more as a matter of the imagination mediating *between* the insights of the senses ('poetry') and 'the ratiocination of philosophy'. Major writers of the Romantic period (Goethe and Schelling in Germany, for example, and Wordsworth and Coleridge in England) had faith in the union of science and art through the medium and methods of the imagination. 'The whole history of modern poetry', as Friedrich Schlegel put it, 'is a running commentary on the following brief philosophical text: all art should become science and all science art; poetry and philosophy should be made one' (*Critical Fragments*, no. 115; in Simpson (ed.), p. 191). The imagination now held an unambiguously primary role as the power able to uncover ideas and structures beyond the reach of ordinary sensory experience – in this sense, the laws of gravitation and the visions of Blake could be felt to belong to the same realm of inspirational insight. For Wordsworth, Newton became once more a great and noble figure, now the genius of imagination rather than of natural philosophy; *The Prelude*'s majestic vision comes back full circle to Pope's epitaph of the wondrous enlightener:

> Where the statue stood
> Of Newton, with his prism and silent face,
> The marble index of a mind for ever
> Voyaging through strange seas of Thought, alone.

> (*Prelude* [1850], III, ll. 61–3)

---

[36] *Ibid.*   [37] *Ibid.*, p. 654.
[38] *The Botanical Garden; A Poem in Two Parts* (London, 1791).

27

The psychology of literary creation and literary response

James Sambrook

The psychology of literary creation is clearly, concisely, and sturdily summarized in Thomas Hobbes's *Answer to Davenant's Preface to Gondibert* (1650):

Time and Education begets experience; Experience begets memory; Memory begets Judgment and Fancy: Judgment begets the strength and structure, and Fancy begets the ornaments of a Poem ... Judgment, the severer Sister, busieth her self in a grave and rigid examination of all the parts of Nature ... registring ... their order, causes, uses, differences, and resemblances; Whereby the Fancy, when any work of Art is to be performed, findes her materials at hand and prepared for use ... So that when she seemeth to fly from one *Indies* to the other, and from Heaven to Earth, and to penetrate into the hardest matter and obscurest places, into the future and into her self, and all this in a point of time, the voyage is not very great, her self being all she seeks; and her wonderful celerity consisteth not so much in motion as in copious Imagery discreetly ordered and perfectly registered in the memory.

(Spingarn, *Critical Essays*, II, pp. 59–60)

The images in the memory upon which judgement and fancy work are decaying sense-impressions retained in the mind after the object producing them is removed. Images run naturally into sequences within the mind, according to the contiguity in time and space of those sense-impressions of which they are the decaying residue. Such sequences, 'the train of imagination' or 'train of thought', may be unguided, as in dreams, or guided by the will, 'as one would sweep a room, to find a jewel; or as a spaniel ranges the field, till he finds a scent' (Hobbes, *Leviathan*, p. 22). The first guided train of thought is 'remembrance'; the second is 'invention'.

According to the familial metaphor in Hobbes's *Answer to Davenant*, fancy is a sister, not a serving-woman to judgement. The relationship between judgement and fancy will vary according to what kind of art the mind is performing:

In a good Poem, whether it be *epic* or *dramatic*; as also in *sonnets*, *epigrams*, and other pieces, both judgement and fancy are required: but the

fancy must be more eminent; because they please for the extravagancy; but
ought not to displease by indiscretion. In a good history, the judgement
must be eminent ... fancy has no place, but only in adorning the stile.
In orations of praise, and in invectives, the fancy is predominant.

(*Leviathan*, p. 51)

For Hobbes, judgement is the essential accompaniment to wit. For
Donne's generation the term 'wit' could embrace the notions of intelligence, cleverness, ingenuity, and the swift motions of fancy, but for the
generations of Dryden, Pope and Addison 'true wit' required judgement. Hobbes roundly declares: 'Judgement therefore without fancy is
wit, but fancy without judgement not' (*Leviathan*, p. 52).

Hobbes's psychology of judgement and inspiration, as well as his
spaniel simile, reappears in John Dryden's earliest piece of criticism, the
dedication of his play *The Rival Ladies* (1664): 'imagination in a poet
is a faculty so wild and lawless that like an high-ranging spaniel it must
have clogs tied to it, lest it outrun the judgment'. The very first sentence
of that same dedication offers a less fanciful but more telling and mysterious image of these mental powers: 'My Lord, This worthless present
was designed you long before it was a play; when it was only a confused mass of thoughts, tumbling over one another in the dark; when
the fancy was yet in its first work, moving the sleeping images of things
towards the light, there to be distinguished, and then either chosen or
rejected by the judgment' (Dryden, *Of Dramatic Poesy*, I, pp. 8, 2).
Evidently Hobbes's spaniel metaphor took Dryden's fancy, because he
uses it again in his next published critical essay, the preface to his historical poem *Annus Mirabilis* (1667): 'Wit in the poet, or *Wit-Writing*
... is no other than the faculty of imagination in the writer, which like
a humble spaniel beats over and ranges through the field of memory, till
it springs the quarry it hunted after'; that is, 'it searches over all the
memory for the species or ideas of those things which it designs to
represent' (Dryden, *Of Dramatic Poesy*, I, p. 98).

The preface to *Annus Mirabilis* continues with further elaboration of
the notion of imagination:

the first happiness of the poet's imagination is properly invention, or finding
of the thought; the second is fancy, or the variation, driving, or moulding
of that thought, as the judgment represents it proper to the subject; the
third is elocution, or the art of clothing and adorning that thought so found
and varied, in apt, significant, and sounding words; the quickness of the
imagination is seen in the invention, the fertility in the fancy, and the
accuracy in the expression.   (Dryden, *Of Dramatic Poesy*, I, p. 98)

This analysis produces a series consisting of three functions, but the attribution of all three to the single comprehensive power of the imagination indicates that the poetic creative process is one mental action, which Dryden aptly characterizes as the 'happiness of the poet's imagination'. Judgement of course plays a vital function in this process, as the arbiter of propriety.

Hobbes's philosophical heir John Locke (1632–1704) sharpened the antithesis between wit and judgement. According to Locke, in the *Essay concerning Human Understanding* (1690), wit is the facility for rapidly combining ideas which appear to have some congruity with one another, 'thereby to make up pleasant Pictures and agreeable Visions in the Fancy': judgement is the power to discriminate between ideas and to detect differences, so that one is not misled into mistaking one thing for another; the exercise of this power is the difficult and disciplined path to knowledge, 'a way of proceeding quite contrary to Metaphor and Allusion'. Implicit here is a contrast between the false, misleading, uncertain, metaphorical language of poetry and the clear, positive, plain, literal language of science. According to Locke, wit and judgement set out upon divergent courses, one away from, the other towards true knowledge. 'Wit and Fancy' are admissible 'in Discourses, where we seek rather Pleasure and Delight, than Information and Improvement . . . But yet, if we would speak of things as they are', we must allow that 'all the Art of Rhetorick, besides Order and Clearness, all the artificial and figurative application of Words Eloquence hath invented, are for nothing else but to insinuate wrong *Ideas*, move the Passions, and thereby mislead the Judgement, and so indeed are perfect cheat' (Locke, *Essay*, pp. 156, 508).

Similar suspicions underlie the chapter 'Of the Association of Ideas' which Locke added to his *Essay* in 1700. Locke concurs with Hobbes that there are natural associations of ideas in the mind which agree with the rational relations of things to one another, but he devotes most of his chapter to that irrational, unnatural association of ideas, wholly owing to chance or custom, which 'hinders Men from seeing and examining':

Ideas that in themselves are not at all of kin, come to be so united in some Mens Minds, that 'tis very hard to separate them . . . and the one no sooner at any time comes into the Understanding but . . . the whole gang always inseparable shew themselves together.

Habitual, chance trains of association, prompted by the same object, may be quite different in the minds of different people, 'according to their different Inclinations, Educations, Interest, *etc.*' (Locke, *Essay*, pp. 401, 395–6). For men who did not share Locke's view that 'unnatural' association of ideas led to error, the subjective and relativist features of association eventually encouraged the development of those same features in literary creation and response.

Locke's broader theory of perception and ideas had more rapid effects upon literary criticism, particularly when it was reinterpreted by Addison. Locke conceives of an idea as an intermediate object between the knowing mind and some ultimate object of perception. Such ideas include sense-data, memories, and more abstract conceptions; but Locke habitually refers to them all, whether sensory or conjectural, as 'pictures'. At one point he takes the *camera obscura* as a model for the way in which such pictures are painted in the mind: 'methinks the *Understanding* is not much unlike a Closet wholly shut from light, with only some little openings left, to let in external visible Resemblances, or *Ideas* of things without'. The dominant metaphor of ideas as pictures reinforces Locke's demonstration that our simple ideas are principally derived from sight, the most comprehensive of our senses and the chief intermediary between matter and mind. Locke also speaks of ideas being admitted through the senses and the nerves, 'which are the Conduits, to convey them from without to their Audience in the Brain, the Mind's Presence-room'. This presence-room metaphor implies that the understanding plays the role of a ruler or judge. According to Locke, there are no innate ideas, because the mind is like a sheet of blank paper at birth; only experience impresses it with ideas.

The powers by which external objects produce ideas in the mind are called by Locke qualities; of these he distinguishes two kinds, primary and secondary. Primary qualities are 'Solidity, Extension, Figure, Motion or Rest, and Number'. Secondary qualities 'in truth are nothing in the Objects themselves, but Powers to produce various Sensations in us by their *primary Qualities* ... as Colours, Sounds, Tasts [*sic*], etc.' (Locke, *Essay*, p. 135). Locke's primary qualities are exactly those presupposed by Newton for the mathematical model of the universe in his *Principia* (1687); their distinction from secondary qualities is paralleled in Newton's speculations concerning colour in his *Opticks* (1704). 'Rays of light', said Newton, 'to speak properly are not coloured ... Colours in the Object are nothing but a Disposition to reflect this or that sort of Rays more copiously than the rest; in the Rays they are nothing but their Dispositions to propagate this or that Motion into the Sensorium, and in the Sensorium they are Sensations of those Motions under the Forms of Colours' (Newton, *Opticks*, p. 125). The sensorium is that part of the brain where nerves terminate. In Locke's distinction primary qualities would exist if nobody perceived them; secondary qualities are inconceivable without perception. Even though our ideas of secondary qualities, unlike our ideas of primary qualities, are not exact resemblances of 'the thing in itself', Locke does not regard secondary qualities as subjective. Some of his popularizers, however, seem to allow this possibility.

Locke's influence in the eighteenth century was in no small measure due to the popularizing of his philosophy by Joseph Addison (1672–1719). In *Spectator* 291, one of the series of eighteen papers on *Paradise Lost* which for over a century constituted the best-known and most respected critical interpretation of Milton (see pp. 99–103 above), Addison claims that knowledge of Locke's *Essay concerning Human Understanding* is necessary for the literary critic; *Spectator* 62 takes for its text Locke's 'admirable Reflection upon the difference of Wit and Judgement'; but the influence of Locke is most pervasive and most important in a series of eleven papers on the pleasures of the imagination (*Spectators* 411–21, published in 1712). These papers, drawn from a treatise which Addison probably wrote in the 1690s, examine the psychological basis of aesthetic experience; they constitute an enquiry into the imagination less systematic than, but nevertheless comparable with, Locke's enquiry into the understanding.

Addison's aesthetic notions are based upon the premises of Lockean psychology. Firstly, that all ideas are traceable to sense impressions, and that sight is the principal sense: 'It is this sense which furnishes the Imagination with its Ideas; so that by the Pleasures of the Imagination or Fancy (which I shall use promiscuously) I here mean such as arise from visible objects, either when we have them actually in our view, or when we call up their Ideas into our Minds'. Secondly, that the mind has the power to retain, alter, and compound these ideas, so that by his imagination 'a Man in a Dungeon', for instance, 'is capable of entertaining himself with Scenes and Landskips more beautiful than any that can be found in the whole Compass of Nature' (*Spectator* 411). The mind is also able to associate one idea with another involuntarily; this capacity is regarded by Locke as dangerous but by Addison as highly beneficial:

We may observe, that any single Circumstance of what we have formerly seen often raises up a whole Scene of Imagery, and awakens numberless Ideas that before slept in the Imagination; such a particular Smell or Colour is able to fill the Mind, on a sudden, with the Picture of the Fields or Gardens where we first met with it, and to bring up into View all the Variety of Images that once attended it. Our imagination takes the Hint, and leads us unexpectedly into Cities or Theatres, Plains or Meadows. We may further observe, when the Fancy thus reflects on the Scenes that have past in it formerly, those, which were at first pleasant to behold, appear more so upon Reflection, that Memory heightens the Delightfulness of the Original.

(*Spectator*, III, p. 562)

This Proustian passage owes something to Hobbes's model of a mind where fancy makes an excursion through the stored images of memory.

Out of deference to Locke, Addison concedes that the pleasures of the understanding are more improving than those of the imagination. Yet,

> A beautiful Prospect delights the Soul, as much as a Demonstration; and a Description in *Homer* has charmed more Readers than a Chapter in *Aristotle*. Besides, the Pleasures of the Imagination have this Advantage, above those of the Understanding, that they are more obvious, and more easie to be acquired. It is but opening the Eye, and the Scene enters. The Colours paint themselves on the Fancy.   (*Spectator*, III, p. 538)

When he writes of colours painting themselves or circumstances raising a scene Addison seems to regard the imagination as a mirror or as a theatrical stage for the representation of sense impressions; when he comes to a discussion of metaphor and allegory in *Spectator* 421 he regards it in complementary terms as a mirror of the understanding:

> By these Allusions a Truth in the Understanding is as it were reflected by the Imagination; we are able to see something like Colour and Shape in a Notion, and to discover a Scheme of Thoughts traced out upon Matter. And here the Mind receives a great deal of Satisfaction, and has two of its Faculties gratified at the same time, while the Fancy is busy in copying after the Understanding and transcribing Ideas out of the Intellectual World into the Material.   (*Spectator*, III, p. 577)

Either way, the imagination is a sort of amphibious faculty which links together the worlds of intellect and of sensation.

The primary pleasures of the imagination arise from visible objects; the secondary pleasures arise from 'the Ideas of visible Objects, when the Objects are not actually before the Eye, but are called up into our Memories, or formed into agreeable Visions of Things that are either absent or Fictitious' (*Spectator*, III, p. 537). The terms of this distinction may well have been suggested by Locke's notion of the primary and secondary qualities of objects, also a very important concept for Addison: but essentially Addison's distinction is only the old one between nature and the art which imitates nature.

The natural objects which please the imagination are divided in *Spectator* 412 into three categories: the great, the uncommon, and the beautiful. The great corresponds to what men would soon afterwards agree to refer to as the sublime; examples of great objects include 'a vast uncultivated Desart ... high Rocks and Precipices, or a wide Expanse of Waters', where we are struck by a 'rude kind of Magnificence'. Such objects produce an effect of enlargement in the mind, for 'Our Imagination loves to be filled with an Object, or to grasp at any thing that is too big for its Capacity', and 'The Mind of Man naturally hates every thing that looks like a Restraint upon it'. That being so, 'wide and undetermined Prospects are as pleasing to the Fancy, as the Speculations of Eternity or Infinitude are to the Understanding'.

'Every thing that is *new* or *uncommon* raises a Pleasure in the Imagination, because it fills the Soul with an agreeable Surprise, gratifies its Curiosity, and gives it an Idea of which it was not before possest.' The new and the uncommon provide a form of mental refreshment which 'bestows Charms on a Monster' and 'recommends Variety'. The variety of some natural object in motion, such as a waterfall, is particularly pleasing:

We are quickly tired with looking upon Hills and Valleys, where everything
continues fixt and settled in the same Place and Posture, but find our
Thoughts a little agitated and relieved at the sight of such Objects as are
ever in Motion, and sliding away from beneath the Eye of the Beholder.

'But', Addison continues, 'there's nothing that makes its way more directly to the Soul than *Beauty*'; it instantly 'strikes the Mind with an inward Joy', giving immediate satisfaction to the imagination. We are so constituted as to find beauty in, for instance 'Gaiety or Variety of Colours, in the Symmetry and Proportion of Parts', but it must be admitted that 'There is not perhaps any real Beauty or Deformity more in one piece of Matter than another' (*Spectator*, III, p. 542).

The great, the uncommon, and the beautiful are known by their effects, so Addison's three categories are as much subjective as objective; like Locke his concern is with the operations of the mind. As he is unable, however, to proceed any further than Locke in explaining the efficient causes of mental events, he moves directly, in *Spectator* 413, to the consideration of their final causes, which are explained in accordance with Addison's belief that God has framed man so that he can act upon him through his imagination. Taking his categories in turn, Addison explains that God has made us naturally delight in what is great or unlimited in order to 'give our Souls a just Relish' of the contemplation of his divine being, and that God 'has annexed a secret Pleasure to the idea of any thing that is *new* or *uncommon*, that he might encourage us in the Pursuit after knowledge, and engage us to search into the Wonders of his Creation'; God's purpose in making us delight in beauty is explained in greatest detail, with an extraordinary application of Locke's 'great Discovery', confirmed by Newton, 'that Light and Colours, as apprehended by the Imagination, are only Ideas in the Mind, and not Qualities that have any Existence in Matter':

[God] has given almost every thing about us the Power of raising an agreeable Idea in the Imagination: So that it is impossible for us to behold his Works with Coldness or Indifference, and to survey so many Beauties without a secret Satisfaction and Complacency. Things would make a poor Appearance to the Eye if we saw them only in their proper Figures and Motions: And what Reason can we assign for their exciting in us many of those Ideas which are different from any thing that exists in the Objects themselves, (for such are Light and Colours) were it not to add Supernumerary Ornaments to the Universe, and make it more agreeable to the Imagination? We are every where entertained with pleasing Shows and Apparitions, we discover imaginary Glories in the Heavens, and in the Earth, and see some of this Visionary Beauty poured out upon the whole Creation; but what a rough unsightly Sketch of Nature should we be entertained with, did all her Colouring disappear, and the several Distinctions of Light and Shade vanish? In short, our Souls are at present delightfully lost and bewildered in a pleasing Delusion, and we walk about like the Enchanted Hero of a Romance, who sees beautiful Castles, Woods and Meadows; and at the same time hears the warbling of Birds, and the purling of Streams; but upon the finishing of some secret Spell, the fantastick Scene breaks up, and the disconsolate Knight finds himself on a barren Heath, or in a solitary Desart.   (*Spectator*, III, pp. 546–7)

The external world, philosophically considered, thus becomes a land-scape of romance.

What Addison makes of Locke's secondary qualities in his likening of the ordinary man's perception of the ordinary external world to a state of enchantment is not to be confused with his own concept of the secondary pleasures of imagination, the pleasures derived from art. He accepts the conventional view of his day that art imitates nature, but as he proceeds he tends to shift his ground a little. Sometimes he insists that art cannot compete with nature, even claiming at one point in *Spectator* 414 that the most perfect art he ever saw was the moving images (the unfixed photographs, as it were) of the river and park produced by the famous *camera obscura* in Greenwich Observatory, because such an art bears the closest possible resemblance to nature. On the other hand, by *Spectator* 418 he is allowing that art may excel nature,

because the Imagination can fancy to it self Things more Great, Strange, or Beautiful, than the Eye ever saw, and is still sensible of some Defect in what it has seen; on this account it is the part of a Poet to humour the Imagination in its own Notions, by mending and perfecting Nature where he describes a Reality, and by adding greater Beauties than are put together in Nature, where he describes a Fiction.   (*Spectator*, III, p. 569)

Other critics might describe such art as an imitation of ideal nature, but not Addison.

Ideal nature is the constant concern of Anthony Ashley Cooper, third Earl of Shaftesbury (1671–1713), whose Platonic belief that physical objects are merely shadows of the ideal world beyond themselves emerges most clearly in *The Moralists, a Philosophical Rhapsody* (1709), a series of dialogues on 'natural and Moral Subjects' between four characters, the most important of whom are the sceptic Philocles (the narrator) and the freethinker Theocles, who represents Shaftesbury's own viewpoint. Theocles launches himself into an imaginary journey through the sublime and beautiful wonders of the natural world, where he finds that even the deserts 'want not their peculiar Beautys. The Wildness pleases ... the scaly Serpents, the savage Beasts, and poisonous Insects, how terrible soever, or how contrary to human Nature, are beauteous in themselves, and fit to raise our Thoughts in Admiration of that *Divine Wisdom*, so far superior to our short Views.' Philocles, who has accompanied him on his mental excursion, checks himself, wondering why he is so 'deep in this *romantick* way', and asking what it was possessed him, when he was passionately struck with objects of this kind. 'No wonder, reply'd [Theocles], if we are at a loss when we pursue the *Shadow* for the *Substance*. For if we may trust to what our Reasoning has taught us; whatever in Nature is beautiful or charming, is only the faint Shadow of that *First Beauty*'. When contemplating beautiful objects and recognizing in them the shadow of transcendent intellectual beauty, the mind, which is man's divine part, apprehends itself in its truest nature:

there is nothing so divine as *Beauty*: which belonging not to *Body*, nor having any Principle or Existence except in *Mind* and *Reason*, is alone discover'd and acquir'd by this diviner Part, when it inspects *it-self* ... 'Tis thus the *improving Mind*, slightly surveying other Objects, and passing over Bodys, and the common Forms, (where only a Shadow of Beauty rests) ambitiously presses onward to Its *Source*, and views *the Original* of Form and Order in that which is intelligent.

In his 'Miscellaneous Reflections' of 1714, Shaftesbury sums up: 'What is *Beautiful* is *Harmonious* and *Proportionable*; what is Harmonious and Proportionable, is *True*; and what is at once both *Beautiful* and *True*, is, of consequence, *Agreeable* and *Good*' (*Characteristicks*, II, pp. 388, 395, 426–7, III, pp. 182–3). Those whom the wildness pleases, those who give way to their growing passion for 'Things of a *natural* kind', such as rude rocks, mossy caverns, unwrought grottoes, and waterfalls, are as deep in the '*romantick* way' as ordinary lovers are, because, whether they know it or not, they love ideal beauty. As the beauty of art is the expression of man's mind, so natural beauty is the expression of the universal, divine mind: beauty is truth. Beauty and truth are recognized by the same faculty, which is known as the 'moral sense' when it responds to human actions and discerns human affections and passions, but it is known as the sense of beauty when the eye opens upon shapes and the ear upon sounds.

When he insists that 'the Beautifying, not the Beautify'd, is the really Beautiful' (*Characteristicks*, II, p. 404) Shaftesbury directs our attention from the work of art to the artist by a critical manoeuvre just as decisive as, albeit less transparent than, the one by which Coleridge, near the end of chapter 14 of *Biographia Literaria*, substitutes the question 'what is a poet?' for 'what is poetry?'. The poet then described by Coleridge bears more than a chance resemblance to 'the Man who truly and in a just sense deserves the Name of *Poet*' described 100 years earlier by Shaftesbury in *Soliloquy: or Advice to an Author* (1710): 'Such a *Poet* is indeed a second *Maker*: a just *Prometheus*, under *Jove*. Like that Sovereign Artist or universal Plastick Nature, he forms *a Whole*, coherent and proportion'd in itself, with due Subjection and Subordinacy of constituent Parts'. The mythical allusion is to a familiar fable in Plato's *Protagoras*, 320–2, and Ovid's *Metamorphoses*, I, 78, telling how the Titan Prometheus stole the fire of creative power from the gods and mixed it with human clay, so that man became a partaker in the divine condition. Though this appealing myth of Prometheus as the 'plastick Artist', or as the allegorical representation of 'plastick Nature' (*Characteristicks*, I, p. 207, II, pp. 201, 203) is not as centrally important for Shaftesbury as it is for, say, the Shelleys, it plays a significant part elsewhere in his writings: for instance at the beginning of *The Moralists*, where it is used in the argument about whether a god is responsible for imperfections in nature.

The Promethean figure described in *Advice to an Author*, the 'Moral Artist, who can thus imitate the Creator', is very different from the 'insipid Race of Mortals ... whom we Moderns are contented to call *Poets*, for having attain'd the chiming Faculty of a Language, with an injudicious random use of Wit and Fancy'. As Shaftesbury does not include much specific literary criticism in his writings on aesthetics, we cannot be certain as to which contemporary rhymers are attacked here, in what appears to be a minor skirmish in the battle of the books between Ancients and Moderns; but later he ridicules the admirers of Dryden: 'the young *Fry* which you may see busily surrounding the grown Poet, or chief Play-house *Author*, at a *Coffee-House*' (*Characteristicks*, I, p. 207, III, p. 274). The Moderns under attack are mere contrivers who imitate the outward forms or mere body of nature, whereas the poet described in ideal perfection imitates the inworking, organizing, creative principle in nature. Using Spinoza's terminology, Coleridge makes the same distinction: 'If the artist copies the mere nature, the *natura naturata*, what idle rivalry! . . . you must master the essence, the *natura naturans*, which presupposes a bond between nature in the higher sense and the soul of man' (Coleridge, *Biographia Literaria*, II, p. 257). The creative principle, *natura naturans*, is what Shaftesbury calls 'the Sovereign Artist or universal Plastick Nature', taking the term 'plastic nature' from the Cambridge Platonist Ralph Cudworth, for whom it signifies the organic principle, subordinate to God rather than God himself, which animates matter and accounts for growth and purposive behaviour. It is not without passing interest that Shaftesbury, the freethinker, should find the terminology of Plato's myth, 'Prometheus under Jove', more congenial than Cudworth's. As 'plastic Nature' animates, forms, and shapes phenomena into an harmonious whole, so does the artist by his analogous 'plastic' (in Coleridge 'esemplastic') power.

Shaftesbury's notions concerning the creative imagination as analogous to 'the creatrix or sovereign plastic nature' reappear in a work entitled *Plastics, or the Original Progress and Power of Designing Art*, a treatise devoted largely to the visual arts and intended to be its author's crowning achievement, but left incomplete and fragmentary upon his early death and not published until the present century (Shaftesbury, *Second Characters*, p. 106). *Characteristicks*, though, was well known, frequently commented upon, and widely influential through the greater part of the eighteenth century. Shaftesbury's work made no claims to be a systematic philosophy; but it was important because it epitomized a unified sensibility, a harmony between the inner and the outer world at the point where the good, the true, and the beautiful are recognized to be one. His aesthetics confirmed the poets' traditional, instinctive beliefs in creative genius and an animated universe. In the first half of the century the direct, acknowledged debt of the 'new' poets Thomson and Akenside to Shaftesbury is obvious enough; but Pope, whether the debt is direct or not, stands in the same ancient intellectual tradition as Shaftesbury when, in the course of his account of the great chain of being at the opening of Book III of *An Essay on Man*, he writes about the activity of 'plastic Nature', and of a vital, not mechanical, harmony in which 'Parts relate to whole; / One all-extending, all-preserving Soul / Connects each being' (ll. 21–3). Shaftesbury's work was well known on the Continent. Diderot admired him, and Montesquieu numbered him as one of the four great poets among philosophers (the others being Montaigne, Malebranche, and Plato). In the second half of the century Shaftesbury's influence was considerable in Germany, where Winckelmann, Lessing, Wieland, Herder, Kant, Schiller, and Goethe knew his work. Though Coleridge makes no direct mention of him, much of Shaftesbury's doctrine is reimported in a modified form from Germany by Coleridge.

Coleridge acknowledged another philosophical debt, though, when he named his own eldest son in honour of David Hartley (1705–57), the author of *Observations on Man* (1749), a treatise which provided a mechanical account of the operation of the imagination. Hartley first considers what Locke had determined not to meddle with, the physical processes by which we have sensations and ideas. The immediate instrument of sensation, he claims, is a white medullary substance in the brain, the spinal marrow, and the nerves, consisting of tiny particles which respond to all motions of the ether, that subtle and elastic fluid which, according to Newton, is expanded through space and diffused through the pores of matter, and by which light is transmitted. Hartley theorizes that external objects have the power to propagate motions in the ether, which are then communicated, in the form of minute vibrations of the medullary particles, along the fibres of the nerves into the brain. When vibrations are moderate they give sensations of pleasure; when they are violent they cause pain. Sensory vibrations, thus communicated to the brain, soon fade, but if repeated they 'beget, in the medullary Substance of the Brain, a disposition to diminutive Vibrations, which may also be called Vibratiuncles', a term coined by Hartley. These vibratiuncles, being the vestiges or images of sensations, constitute ideas. Sensations arise mechanically from nervous vibrations and ideas arise equally mechanically from vibratiuncles. If several sensory vibrations are associated together in a series often enough, they attain a power over their corresponding series of ideal vibratiuncles so that any one sensory vibration of the series will immediately, mechanically, and necessarily excite the entire series of vibratiuncles, that is to say, ideas. Hartley thus offers a physiological theory of the association of ideas, where Locke and Hobbes had concerned themselves only with psychology. On this physiological basis Hartley erects an elaborate system in which the power of association accounts for our mental growth.

Our response to literature may be accounted for in terms of association. Thus the pleasures of imagination provided by good poetry arise from the harmony, variety, and regularity of metre and rhyme, the fitness and strength of diction, 'the Matter of the poem' and 'the Invention and Judgment exerted by the Poet, in regard to his Subject'; but these sources all have a mutual influence, so that the beauties of each 'are much transferred upon the other Two by Association'. Also, the pleasure derived from the 'Matter of the poem' is primarily from the object imitated, rather than the imitation itself: from, for instance, 'such Scenes as are beautiful, terrible, or otherwise strongly affecting, and such Characters as excite Love, Pity, just Indignation' (*Observations*, I, pp. 441–4). Turning from the psychology of literary response to literary 'creation', Hartley does not allow any special power to the poet's imagination, for in his view 'Invention' consists of the reordering and recombining of ideas: it calls for a strong and quick memory, so that 'the Ideas ... may depend upon, and be readily suggested by, each other', a large stock of the kinds of ideas proper to the writing of 'fictitious histories', and the 'Habit of forming and pursuing Analogies, the Deviations from these, and the subordinate Analogies visible in many of these first Deviations': that is, the mental activity of the poet is a refinement and intensification of a common, natural, and mechanical process; it 'seems as reconcileable with, and deducible from, the Power of Association, and the Mechanism, of the Mind here explained, as that of any other' (*Observations*, I, pp. 447–8).

The *Philosophical Enquiry into the Origin of our Ideas of the Sublime and Beautiful* (1757) of Edmund Burke (1729–97) is perhaps the best-known eighteenth-century account of the psychology of literary response. It systematically expands hints in Addison's papers on the pleasures of the imagination to establish the grounds of distinction between the sublime and the beautiful (deliberately refusing to treat novelty, Addison's third source of the pleasures of imagination, as a distinct category). Burke distinguishes two classes of agreeable sensations: one is positive pleasure, the other, which he calls 'delight', is that pleasure which arises from the ideas of pain and danger when we are not in actual pain and danger; the first pleasure is a social passion and is our emotional response to the beautiful, the second is a selfish passion (arising from our instinct for self-preservation) and is our response to the sublime. Both might be described as 'sympathy', which 'must be considered as a sort of substitution, by which we are put into the place of another man' and are made to feel in some respects as he feels. Sympathy 'turning on pain may be a source of the sublime', or 'it may turn upon ideas of pleasure', in which case it is a source of the beautiful. It is by sympathy and substitution 'that poetry, painting, and other affecting arts, transfuse their passions from one breast to another, and are often capable of grafting a delight on wretchedness, misery, and death itself' (Burke, *Philosophical Enquiry*, p. 44). Thus Burke accounts for our pleasure in tragedy, though he proceeds then to argue, in opposition to most theorists of tragedy, that we are more delighted by real distress (in others) than by its simulation in the theatre, as evidence of which he points out that a state execution is a far more popular spectacle than the very finest stage tragedy.

The strongest aesthetic emotion which the mind is capable of feeling, an emotion strong enough to deprive the mind of power to act or reason, is distanced or modified terror: immediate pain or danger 'are incapable of giving any delight, and are simply terrible; but at certain distances, and with certain modifications, they may be, and they are delightful'. The ideas which excite this species of terror are the source of the sublime, and they can be classified under certain headings. Obscurity is sublime because darkness and uncertainty arouse fear. In support, Burke quotes Milton's descriptions of Death, where 'all is dark, uncertain, confused, terrible, and sublime to the last degree', and of Satan, where the mind 'is hurried out of itself, by a croud of great and confused images; which affect because they are crouded and confused'; he concludes: 'A clear idea is therefore another name for a little idea' (Burke, *Philosophical Enquiry*, pp. 40, 59, 62, 63). So Burke continues through his other headings: power, where the idea of superior force excites fear; privations, such as vacuity, darkness, solitude (a foretaste of death), and silence; vastness of length, height, and depth, the last being the most frightening of the three, and so a particularly powerful source of the sublime; infinity, and such artificial forms of infinity as succession and uniformity (as in a colonnade) where imagination carries the mind beyond the actual limits of the object. So the list of headings continues down to 'bitters and stenches', which, admittedly, have a very tiny potential for sublimity.

The sublime is always founded, however distantly, upon the ideas of pain and terror, and so must always be fundamentally different from the beautiful, which is founded upon the ideas of love and pleasure. The experience of beauty is as immediate as that of the sublime: 'beauty demands no assistance from our reasoning; even the will is unconcerned; the appearance of beauty as effectually causes some degree of love in us, as the application of ice or fire produces the ideas of heat or cold' (Burke, *Philosophical Enquiry*, p. 92). Burke dismisses whimsical notions, such as those of Shaftesbury, which have arisen from the old habit of attaching the quality of beauty to virtue or to proportion, because such notions make beauty rely on reason and the will, rather than on immediate sense. Burke concludes that if beauty does not depend upon proportion, fitness, or virtue, it must reside in certain qualities which act mechanically upon the senses. These qualities include, for instance, smoothness, smallness, delicacy of texture, and that gradual variety of line which Hogarth called the 'line of beauty'; they are summed up in an analogy which became famous: 'Most people must have observed the sort of sense they have had, on being swiftly drawn in an easy coach, on a smooth turf, with gradual ascents and declivities. This will give a better idea of the beautiful, and point out its probable cause better than almost anything else'. This analogy is not a mere flight of fancy: Burke seeks to identify aesthetic feelings with physical sensations and to establish a mechanical theory of aesthetics in accordance with current notions of physiology. It was commonly believed that sensation is caused by vibration of the nerves or by vibration of minute particles along the nerves (as Hartley claimed).

It was also believed that one sense could cause others to react sympathetically, and this belief had already been incorporated into aesthetic theory with Addison's observation in *Spectator* 412 that the ideas of different senses 'recommend each other'. Burke claims 'There is a chain in all our sensations', so that what is 'beautiful in *Feeling* ... corresponds wonderfully with what causes the same species of pleasure to the sight' (Burke, *Philosophical Enquiry*, pp. 155, 120). Hence the coach analogy can stand as a literal account of a sensation of the beautiful. Dealing with the apparently more difficult case of the sublime, Burke observes that pain and fear alike produce in the body 'an unnatural tension and certain violent emotions of the nerves' (Burke, *Philosophical Enquiry*, p. 134). It follows, he argues, that any idea which produces the same physical tension and violent motions will produce a feeling akin to terror. To explain why such a feeling can be delightful, he claims that exercise refreshes and strengthens the nerves of 'finer organs' just as it does the limbs and larger, coarser organs of the body. Burke thus accounts for aesthetic responses in wholly physiological terms; we feel the sublime and the beautiful in the same way as we feel heat and cold. This is perhaps the eighteenth century's boldest attempt to bring aesthetics into line with the physical sciences.

The fifth and last part of Burke's *Enquiry* deals with the production of beauty and sublimity by means of words, and is directed against the common notion that words affect the mind by raising in it images of the objects for which they stand. Words in poetry and oratory may affect us more strongly than the things they represent because they carry a strong, impassioned expression:

We yield to sympathy, what we refuse to description. The truth is, all verbal description, merely as naked description, though never so exact, conveys so poor and insufficient an idea of the thing described, that it could scarcely have the smallest effect, if the speaker did not call in to his aid those modes of speech that mark a strong and lively feeling in himself. Then, by the contagion of our passions, we catch a fire already kindled in another, which probably might never have been struck out by the object described.

(Burke, *Philosophical Enquiry*, pp. 175–6)

Naked descriptions convey clear ideas, which, as we have seen, Burke believes to be little ideas.

For all this, when Burke discusses literary creation in the 'Introduction on Taste' added to the second edition of the *Philosophical Enquiry* in 1759, he sees it as no more than the capacity to recombine sense impressions:

The mind of man possesses a sort of creative power of its own; either in representing at pleasure the images of things in the order and manner in which they were received by the senses, or in combining those images in a new manner, and according to a different order. This power is called Imagination; and to this belongs whatever is called wit, fancy, invention, and the like.

(Burke, *Philosophical Enquiry*, p. 16)

Literary response is accounted for by a theory of taste similarly founded upon Locke's epistemology: 'as the senses are the great originals of all our ideas, and consequently of all our pleasures, if they are not uncertain and arbitrary, the whole ground-work of Taste is common to all' (Burke, *Philosophical Enquiry*, p. 23). As the imagination is only the representative of the senses there will be as much correspondence between the imaginative impressions of different normal human beings as between their sense impressions.

In his discussion of literary creation Burke accepts the traditional view that poetry is imitative, but there was a growing tendency in the eighteenth century to regard poetry as expressive. Such a view emerges in the wholesale attack on the notion of imitation in *Conjectures on Original Composition* (1759) by Edward Young (1683–1765). Anticipating by half a century Coleridge's distinction between mechanical making and organic growth, Young asserts that 'An *Original* may be said to be of a *vegetable* nature; it rises spontaneously from the vital root of Genius; it *grows*, it is not *made*: *Imitations* are often a sort of Manufacture wrought by those *Mechanics, Art*, and *Labour*, out of pre-existent materials not their own.' Young develops Addison's distinction, in *Spectator* 160, between natural genius and genius acquired by learning, but does so with a degree of contempt for learning ('Many a genius, probably, there has been, which could neither write, nor read') and with a far greater emphasis upon the mysterious process by which works of art come into being. He notes that most authors of distinction have been startled by 'the first beamings of their yet unsuspected genius on their hitherto dark Composition: The writer starts at it, as at a lucid meteor in the night; is much surprized; can scarce believe it true.' A man does not know the dimensions of his own mind. Young exhorts his readers to

Dive deep into thy bosom; learn the depth, extent, bias, and full fort of thy mind; contract full intimacy with the stranger within thee; excite and cherish every spark of intellectual light and heat, however smothered under former negligence, or scattered through the dull dark mass of common thoughts; and collecting them into a body, let thy genius rise (if a genius thou hast) as the sun from chaos.

Developing Addison's remarks, in *Spectator* 419, on the fairy way of writing Young again runs to the extreme of what would much later be called a Romantic aesthetic:

In the Fairyland of Fancy, Genius may wander wild; there it has creative power, and may reign arbitrarily over its own empire of Chimeras ... Moreover, so boundless are the bold excursions of the human mind, that in the vast void beyond real existence, it can call forth shadowy beings, and unknown worlds, as numerous, as bright, and, perhaps, as lasting, as the stars; such quite-original beauties we may call Paradisaical.

(Young, *Conjectures*, pp. 7, 17, 23, 24, 18, 31)

Like Shaftesbury's writings, Young's treatise became well known in Germany; consequently, like those, it enjoyed renewed influence in England when its ideas were reimported by Coleridge.

There is a soberer image of the imagination in *An Essay on Taste* by Alexander Gerard (1728–95), also first published in 1759. For Gerard, imagination, acting under the power of sympathy, is the central faculty of mind: it is not a mere receptor, for it has a kind of power, like a magnet:

As the magnet selects from a quantity of matter the ferruginous particles, which happen to be scattered through it, without making an impression on other substances; so imagination, by a similar sympathy, equally inexplicable, draws out from the whole compass of nature such ideas as we have occasion for, without attending to any others.

(Gerard, *Essay on Taste*, pp. 173–4)

An active power comparable with that of a magnet is hardly the kind of creativity that Young attributes to the imagination, but when Gerard turns from examination of the reader to examination of the writer, in his *Essay on Genius* (1774), he finds a less mechanical analogy for the imagination's activity. Genius, he says, 'bears a greater resemblance to *nature* in its operations, than to the less perfect energies of *art*'. He continues with a parallel described by M. H. Abrams as 'pregnant with implications for literary psychology' (*Mirror and Lamp*, p. 167), a parallel similar to Young's characterization of original works as vegetable growths from the root of genius, but developed with scientific precision:

When a vegetable draws in moisture from the earth, nature, by the same action by which it draws it in, and at the same time, converts it to the nourishment of the plant: it at once circulates through its vessels, and is assimilated to its several parts. In like manner, genius arranges its ideas by the same operation, and almost at the same time, that it collects them.

(Gerard, *Essay on Genius*, pp. 60, 64)

By that infallible principle of selection and organization known as sympathy, the imagination summons up both the parts and the whole of an artistic design in a single act of conjuration.

If such notions, and such a botanical analogy, point forward to Coleridge's theory of the secondary imagination, Gerard's notions about consciousness point forward to Coleridge's theory of the primary imagination. Gerard believes that self-consciousness is innate and is not the result of experience acting upon the Lockean *tabula rasa*: consciousness is a prerequisite to perception; every man is able 'without any information from experience, by a natural and inexplicable principle, to infer the existence of himself as the percipient and agent' (Gerard, *Essay on Genius*, p. 284).

Gerard is one of several Scottish thinkers who in the 1760s and 1770s investigated the act of imagination which underlies ordinary perception and related it to those special acts of imagination of which only original genius is capable. William Duff (1732–1815) argues in his *Essay on Original Genius* (1767) that the imagination (evidently something like Coleridge's primary imagination) accounts for differences between two persons' perception of the same objects, and that such differences in perception help to account for differences of character between people. 'The outward organ, by which these sensations are conveyed, is supposed to be equally perfect in both [persons]; but the internal feeling is extremely different. This difference must certainly proceed from the transforming power of Imagination, whose rays illuminate the objects we contemplate'. Duff anticipates Coleridge's distinction between the (secondary) imagination and the fancy. He characterizes fancy as a rambling and sportive form of association and memory; its function is merely to collect the materials of composition; in its ability to yoke disparate ideas together it is the parent of wit and humour. Imagination, which is the essence of genius, is inventive and plastic, and can discover truths that were formerly unknown. 'By the vigorous efforts of the creative Imagination [the poet] calls shadowy substances and unreal objects into existence. They are present to his view, and glide, like spectres, in silent, sullen majesty, before his astonished and intranced sight' (Duff, *Essay on Original Genius*, pp. 66–7, 177). Duff's notions about genius and imagination are coloured by the fashionable primitivism of the mid-eighteenth century (see chapter 20 of this volume). He believes that poetry of men far removed in time or place from the sophistications of civilization, 'being the effusion of a glowing fancy and an impassioned heart', is natural and original; the poetic genius of 'the uncultivated ages of the world' acknowledges no law 'excepting its own spontaneous impulse, which it obeys without control' (Duff, *Essay on Original Genius*, pp. 270, 282–4).

The notions of literary creation expressed by Gerard, Duff, and Young are far removed from those of Hobbes and Dryden. They imply a grander, albeit more problematic, process than Dryden's account of the fancy, 'moving the sleeping images of things towards the light, there to be distinguished, and then either chosen or rejected by the judgment'. Hobbes, Dryden, Addison, Pope, and their contemporaries contradicted one another (and indeed themselves from time to time) in their pronouncements upon the relationship between wit and judgement, but they agreed that it was important to take account of judgement in any attempt to analyse literary composition and response. Later analysts, though, tended to shift the focus of interest from judgement to sensation, particularly when they discussed literary response. Hartley, with his physiological theory of the association of ideas, linked aesthetic experience with sensation more directly than had been attempted before; Burke developed an elaborate and influential aesthetic theory in which it was claimed that the beautiful and the sublime reside in certain qualities of nature or art which act, directly or by association, upon the senses. Investigation of the sublime, beginning with Addison's assertion that 'Our Imagination loves . . . to grasp at anything that is too big for its Capacity', not only undermined whatever primacy was accorded to judgement; it brought into question the notion that literature is primarily imitative and opened the way for a fuller recognition of its expressive function and creative nature. The concepts of art as creation and as imitation were both commonplaces of earlier criticism, but with Shaftesbury's Promethean artist and, more strikingly, the genius figure adumbrated in the writings of Gerard, Duff, and Young, the emphasis is placed decisively upon creation.

28

Taste and aesthetics

(i) *Shaftesbury and Addison: criticism and the public taste*
David Marshall

With the possible exception of historians of the sublime, scholars rarely compare the contemporaneous contributions of Shaftesbury and Addison to eighteenth-century criticism and aesthetics.[1] Despite considerable over-lap between the political and literary circles in which they worked and travelled, there appears to be no direct biographical connection. There are major differences of focus, tone, subject-matter, and intellectual temperament in their work. Shaftesbury, whose three-volume collection of essays, *Characteristicks of Men, Manners, Opinions, Times*, was published in 1711, seems to address himself to fellow gentlemen-virtuosi; while Addison, whose writing appears largely in *The Tatler* and *The Spectator*, addresses the audience 'in Clubs and Assemblies, at Tea-Tables, and in Coffee-Houses'.[2] Yet the critical enterprises of Shaftesbury and Addison and their efforts to define a role for the critic have much in common, especially in so far as each is concerned with 'the public taste'.[3]

Shaftesbury, perhaps most ostentatiously, played critic to himself in the *Miscellaneous Reflections* he published on his own treatises in the *Characteristicks*. He creates a commentator to act as 'critic and interpreter to this new writer' (II, p. 161); but, describing his goals in his essay, *Soliloquy, or Advice to an Author*, Shaftesbury writes of himself: 'His pretence has been to advise authors and polish styles, but his aim has been to correct manners and regular lives. He has affected soliloquy, as pretending only to censure himself, but he has taken occasion to bring others into his company' (II, p. 272). This aim is consistent with Addison's critical and journalistic enterprise. As early as the *Tatler* (in

---

[1] See R. L. Brett, *The Third Earl of Shaftesbury: A Study in Eighteenth-Century Literary Theory*, p. 61, p. 86, p. 117, p. 152; and Samuel Monk, *The Sublime: A Study of Critical Theories in XVIII-Century England*. Parenthetical references in the text are to Shaftesbury's *Characteristicks*.

[2] *Spectator*, I, p. 44 (No. 10, 12 March 1711).

[3] *Second Characters*, p. 13.

the same year in which *Soliloquy* was published) Addison as Isaac Bickerstaffe identifies himself as the 'Censor of Great Britain'; modelling himself on the 'old Roman Censors' such as Cato, he describes his duty in 'frequent reviews of the people' to 'look into the manners of the people, and to check any growing luxury, whether in diet, dress, or building'.[4] In *Spectator* 16, he contemplates creating a *'Censor of small Wares'* to criticize various details of 'affected Dress', but reminds his readers that his purpose is to 'enter into the Passions of Mankind, and to correct those depraved Sentiments that give Birth to all those little Extravagancies'.[5] He explains in *Spectator* 135, 'I look upon my self as one set to watch the Manners and Behaviour of my Countrymen and Contemporaries.' Although Mr Spectator focuses on 'every absurd Fashion, ridiculous Custom, or affected Form of Speech',[6] he also expresses his desire 'to establish among us a Taste of polite Writing' with his 'Papers of Criticism' on such topics as opera, tragedy, and comedy.[7] This critical endeavour becomes increasingly central to the *Spectator*.

Like Shaftesbury, Addison reviews the manners, morals, and opinions of his time; although his publications consciously aim to create a community of readers, he can be counted on to censure rather than flatter them. Addison would not identify himself with those authors condemned by Shaftesbury, who 'are turned and modelled (as themselves confess) by the public relish and current humour of the times', who 'regulate themselves by the irregular fancy of the world' as 'the audience makes the poet, and the bookseller the author' (I, pp. 172–3). He is interested in regulating and, more importantly, in forming the public relish – or to use the term that, following Shaftesbury and Addison, would become crucial to eighteenth-century aesthetics: taste. The question of taste is central to the critical project of both Shaftesbury and Addison.

The discussion of taste in eighteenth-century aesthetics – a discussion to which Shaftesbury and Addison make important early contributions – to a great extent turns upon the possibility of a standard of taste. Addison, although still in the shadow of classical and neo-classical criticism, repudiates an overly literal adherence to rules in the evaluation of works of art. In the *Tatler*, he condemns the critic who, 'without entering into the soul of an author, has a few general rules, which, like mechanical instruments, he applies to the works of every writer'.[8] In the *Spectator* he insists that 'great natural Genius's' have never been 'disciplined and broken by Rules of Art'; naming Shakespeare as 'a Stumbling-block to

[4] *Tatler* II, pp. 142–3 (No. 162, 22 April 1710).
[5] *Spectator*, I, p. 70 (No. 16, 19 March 1711).
[6] *Spectator*, IV, p. 27 (No. 435, 19 July 1712).
[7] *Spectator*, I, p. 245 (No. 58, 7 May 1711).
[8] *Spectator*, II, p. 149 (No. 165, 29 April 1710).

the whole Tribe of these rigid Criticks', he asserts that 'there is sometimes a greater Judgment shewn in deviating from the Rules of Art, than in adhering to them'.[9] If one abandons *a priori* rules, however, one is faced with the problem of how to determine the quality of a work of art.

In 1719, the Abbé Du Bos would declare in the preface to his *Réflections critiques sur la poésie et sur la peinture*, 'Chacun a chez lui la règle ou le compas applicable à mes raisonnemens.'[10] One of Shaftesbury's characters in *The Moralists* says, 'All own the standard, rule and measure: but' – he immediately adds – 'in applying it to things disorder arises, ignorance prevails, interest and passion breed disturbance' (II, p. 138). Shaftesbury, whose notion of an internal moral sense would be elaborated into a notion of an aesthetic sense by Du Bos, Hutcheson, and others, is the first to formulate the concept of aesthetic disinterestedness.[11] He is especially concerned that (in the realms of art and morals) wholly subjective criteria would lead to false and capricious judgements and positions such as this one characterized in *The Moralists*: 'there can be no such thing as real valuableness or worth; nothing in itself is estimable or amiable, odious or shameful. All is opinion. 'Tis opinion which makes beauty, and unmakes it ... Opinion is the law and measure' (II, p. 139). Shaftesbury is particularly critical of the '*je ne sais quoi*', 'the unintelligible or the I know not what' that most people responding to a work of art, 'feeling only by the effect whilst ignorant of the cause ... suppose to be a kind of charm or enchantment of which the artist himself can give no account' (I, p. 214). Suspicious of the rise of an empirical aesthetics and an emphasis on subjective response that would subject taste to the whims of irregular fancy, he is contemptuous of those who would exclaim, 'I like! I fancy! I admire!' without knowing why or how – what he calls in the *Second Characters* 'the *je ne sais quoi* to which idiots and the ignorant would reduce everything'.[12]

If the standard, rule, and measure within each person is uninformed and unreliable, or leads to an unacceptably sceptical position that denies works any value in themselves and turns all judgement into accidental fancy, then an external standard of taste must be found if one is to judge works of art. Yet the parameters of the debate about the possibility of a standard of taste are set by the ambiguity in the very term *standard*, which

[9] *Spectator*, II, p. 127 (No. 160, 3 September 1711); V, pp. 27–8 (No. 592, 10 September 1714). See also Numbers 61, 321, 335.

[10] Du Bos, *Réflexions critiques*, II, p. 326.

[11] See Brett, *The Third Earl of Shaftesbury: A Study in Eighteenth-Century Literary Theory*; Stolnitz, 'On the origins of "aesthetic disinterestedness"'; Cassirer, *The Philosophy of the Enlightenment*, p. 325. See also Fowler, *Shaftesbury and Hutcheson*.

[12] *Second Characters*, p. 144. See Cassirer, *The Philosophy of the Enlightenment*, pp. 312–27.

vacillates between a sense of what is common, average, and shared by all and a notion of an exemplar or authority. Eighteenth-century writers sought to ground a standard of taste in a belief in universal agreement. If there generally is or at least has been universal agreement (or what passes for universal agreement) about the value of works of art, then the principle that there is good and bad art is established and individual examples can be recognized and identified. In his essay on taste in *Spectator* 409, Addison suggests that to discover whether one has taste (*'that Faculty of the Soul, which discerns the Beauties of an Author with Pleasure, and the Imperfections with Dislike'*) one should read those works 'which have stood the Test of so many different Ages and Countries' to see if one likes 'the admired Passages in such Authors' – taking care to confirm that one admires 'the Specifick Qualities' for which the authors have been praised and appreciated.[13] He apparently has enough confidence in this normative consensus to recommend (in *Spectator* 29) that the arts 'deduce their Laws and Rules from the general Sense and Taste of Mankind, and not from the Principles of those Arts themselves; or in other Words, the Taste is not to conform to the Art, but the Art to the Taste'.[14] Reynolds would later declare: 'What has pleased, and continues to please, is likely to please again: hence are derived the rules of art, and on this immoveable foundation they must ever stand'.[15]

Shaftesbury repeatedly notes in the *Second Characters* that 'the public always judges right . . . he who either fixes his taste or brief according to the universal judgment and public taste and confession of painters in works of the deceased will never be abused or come off a sufferer when he parts with his effects'.[16] Introducing one of his discussions of ballads, Addison writes, 'it is impossible that any thing should be universally tasted and approved by a Multitude, tho' they are only the Rabble of a Nation, what hath not in it some peculiar Aptness to please and gratify the Mind of Man'.[17] However, neither Shaftesbury nor Addison appears to trust the public taste. For the author who condemns other authors for being 'turned and modelled (as themselves confess) by the public relish and current humour of the times', the phrase *public relish* or *public taste* might seem to be an oxymoron. Whereas Addison describes a 'certain Unanimity of Taste and Judgment' in the court of Augustus, the *Spectator* is punctuated with references to 'the Corrupt Taste the Age is run into', 'the Depravity or Poverty of Taste the Town

---

[13] *Spectator*, III, p. 528 (No. 409, 19 June 1712).
[14] *Spectator*, I, p. 123 (No. 29, 3 April 1711).
[15] Reynolds, *Discourses on Art*, Discourse VII, p. 133. On Addison and taste, see also Elioseff, *Cultural Milieu*, pp. 181–8.
[16] *Second Characters*, p. 13.   [17] *Spectator*, I, p. 297 (No. 70, 21 May 1711).

is fallen into,' and 'the vicious Taste which prevails so much among Modern Writers'.[18]

The preoccupation with taste in the eighteenth century – it may not be an exaggeration to speak of a crisis about taste – is brought about by more than the shift in aesthetic criteria from rules to sensibility. It is also related to the very concept of the public taste, which of course is the logical result of the invention of the public by social and economic forces that include published books and papers like the *Spectator*. In the context of the seemingly depraved market relations and interpersonal relations denounced by Shaftesbury – which extend to the world of courtiers and profligate aristocrats as well as the participants of a nascent mass culture – the public taste does not seem trustworthy. The existence of a public itself seems to undermine the universal judgement and agreement upon which the standard of taste is founded.

If there is no standard in the sense of what is common, average, and shared by all, then those who would find a standard of taste must look to a standard in the sense of an exemplar or authority: an acknowledged judge who will determine and set the standard of taste. In 1757, in 'Of the Standard of Taste' (a notoriously complex essay that is indebted to Addison), Hume tries to displace the problem of the standard of taste by appealing to the authority of such judges, although he acknowledges the circularity of an argument that cannot guarantee universal agreement about who possesses the standard of taste any more than it can guarantee universal agreement about taste itself. None the less, he tries to identify the characteristics that would enable a 'true judge' to establish 'the true standard of taste and beauty'. Hume's elaboration of these characteristics ('Strong sense, united to delicate sentiment, improved by practice, perfected by comparison, and cleared of all prejudice')[19] recalls the characteristics that Addison prescribes in his discussion of verbal descriptions in his 'Pleasures of the Imagination' series. Discussing differences in 'Taste', he explains that 'to have a true Relish, and form a right Judgment of a Description, a Man should be born with a good Imagination, and must have weighed the Force and Energy that lie in the several Words of a Language ... The fancy must be warm, to retain the Print of those Images it hath received from outward Objects; and the Judgment discerning'.[20] (One also thinks of Shaftesbury's warnings about 'ignorance ... interest and passion' in the application of 'the standard, rule and measure' that one carries within.)

---

[18] *Spectator*, I, p. 592 (No. 280, 21 January 1712); II, p. 52 (No. 140, 10 August 1711); II, p. 314 (No. 208, 29 October 1711); II, p. 588 (No, 279, 19 January 1712).

[19] Hume, *Essays Moral, Political, and Literary*, p. 241.

[20] *Spectator*, III, p. 561 (No. 416, 27 June 1712).

Addison's context is more limited and his portrait of an ideal judge less developed than Hume's; but the crucial difference in Addison's approach to the problem of taste is that he focuses not on the 'true judge' whose authority would fix the standard but rather on 'a Man' who would 'have a true Relish, and form a right Judgment'. Indeed, Addison's discussion of *'the fine Taste'* in *Spectator* 409 (which, significantly, precedes the 'Pleasures of the Imagination' essays) begins by promising to 'lay down Rules how we may know whether we are possessed of it, and how we may acquire that fine Taste of Writing, which is so much talked of among the Polite World'. After recommending that one should compare one's own literary responses to universal opinion, he concedes, 'It is very difficult to lay down Rules for the acquirement of such a Taste as that I am here speaking of.' Yet despite this difficulty, and an acknowledgement that the 'Faculty must in some degree be born with us', Addison suggests that 'there are several Methods for Cultivating and Improving it'. These methods include 'becoming conversant among the Writings of the most Polite Authors', 'Conversation with Men of a Polite Genius', and becoming 'well versed in the Works of the best *Criticks* both Ancient and Modern'.

These methods of 'improving our Natural Taste' are indeed in a general sense what the *Spectator* has to offer. It aims not only to improve polite conversation in the world but also to draw its readers into the sort of conversation that will make them conversant with the best authors and critics. Addison's descriptions of the man of taste to a great extent describe himself – but more importantly, they describe his enterprise in his papers of criticism. After defining taste as *'that Faculty of the Soul, which discerns the Beauties of an Author with Pleasure, and the Imperfections with Dislike'*, he ends *Spectator* 409 by announcing his series *'on the Pleasures of the Imagination'*, which, he notes, 'will perhaps suggest to the Reader what it is that gives a Beauty to many Passages of the finest Writers both in Prose and Verse'.[21] This preview also recalls his papers on *Paradise Lost*, in which he has 'endeavoured to give a general idea of its Graces and Imperfections' since the poem 'deserves to be set before an *English* reader in its full Beauty'.[22] He has sought to 'shew the Defects' of Milton and, like a 'true Critick', to 'discover the concealed Beauties of a Writer' – since the 'most exquisite Words and finest Strokes of an Author are those which very often appear the most doubtful and exceptionable, to a Man who wants a relish for polite Learning'.[23] Addison's assertion in *Spectator* 409 that beyond 'the Mechanical Rules which a Man of very little Taste may

[21] *Spectator*, III, pp. 527–31 (No. 409, 19 June 1712).
[22] *Spectator*, III, p. 169 (No. 321, 8 March 1712).
[23] *Spectator*, III, pp. 36–7 (No. 291, 2 February 1712).

discourse upon', there is 'something more essential' that 'elevates and astonishes the Fancy, and gives a Greatness of Mind to the Reader'[24] also recalls his attempts to delineate the sublime in Milton and in general in aesthetic experience.

This is not to say that Addison presents himself (or Mr Spectator) as a literary Censor or as the 'true judge' that Hume imagines. By performing as a man of taste, Addison's demonstrations will inevitably help to determine public taste; but this is the point: if Addison can 'establish among us a Taste of polite Writing' with his 'Papers of Criticism',[25] it will be less because of the *Spectator*'s judgements or pronouncements than because of its investment in the 'Man' (or woman) who seeks to 'have a true Relish, and form a right Judgment'. Concerned with 'Cultivating and Improving' taste, the *Spectator* addresses itself to the reader 'who wants a relish for polite Learning' in both senses of the word *wants*. In this sense Addison and Steele seem to see the *Spectator* as the remedy for the very crisis that journalism and the eighteenth-century version of mass-market publishing have helped to precipitate.[26] In the absence of rules, universal consent, or judges whose authority will compel assent and establish rules, and in the presence of the reading public that it and other publications have called into being, the *Spectator* will seek to reform public taste by forming it.

This is where Shaftesbury perhaps unexpectedly allies himself with the *Spectator*. Whether or not the treatises of the *Characteristicks* are written in private conversation with the 'friend-Lord' that Shaftesbury often poses as the text's private interlocutor, they seem to address gentlemen who, with the benefit of 'a liberal education' (I, p. 125) might turn out to be gentlemen-philosophers or virtuosi. According to Shaftesbury, 'the taste of beauty and the relish of what is decent, just, and amiable perfects the character of the gentleman and the philosopher. And the study of such a taste or relish will, as we suppose, be ever the great employment and concern of him who covets as well to be wise and good as agreeable and polite' (II, p. 256). While the 'gallant' and 'privileged gentlemen' who 'set fashions' are 'no controllers in the commonwealth of Letters', Shaftesbury suggests that those who follow his advice might, 'having gained a mastery ... with the help of their genius and a right use of their art, command their audience and establish a good taste' (I, pp. 127, 181). Like Addison, however, Shaftesbury seems less interested

[24] *Spectator*, III, pp. 527–31 (No. 409, 19 June 1712).

[25] *Spectator*, I, p. 245 (No. 58, 7 May 1711).

[26] Writing in a somewhat different context about Addison's aim to 'establish ... a Taste of polite Writing', Neil Saccamano notes: 'The "great and only End" of *The Spectator* was to institute the very cultural subject to which it was supposedly addressed' ('The consolations of ambivalence: Habermas and the public sphere', p. 695).

in establishing arbiters of taste than in promoting the practice of taste. ''Tis we ourselves create and form our taste' (II, p. 271), he declares. As the narrator of the *Miscellaneous Reflections*, he describes the author's purpose in the preceding treatises as 'to discover how we may to best advantage form within ourselves what in the polite world is called a relish or good taste', recommending 'the narrowest of all conversations, that of soliloquy or self-discourse', the 'study of the highest politeness and elegance of ancient dialogue and debate', and 'modern conversation' with those who 'judge the best of what is perfect, and according to a just standard and true taste in every kind' (II, p. 252).

Like Addison (who seems to echo Shaftesbury's recommendations in *Spectator* 409) Shaftesbury emphasizes this cultivation of taste. Although 'good faculties, senses, or anticipating sensations and imagination may be Nature's growth', he writes, taste is not 'innate'. A 'taste or judgment', he suggests, 'can hardly come ready formed with us into the world'. Incorporating the same metaphors of nature and agriculture that Addison would use in advocating the cultivation of 'natural taste', Shaftesbury writes: 'Use, practice, and culture must precede the understanding and wit of such an advanced size and growth as this' (II, p. 257). In the letters he wrote to Michael Ainsworth (later collected in *Letters to a Student at the University*), Shaftesbury instructs the young man to 'check your own *eye* and fancy' and study admired works of art: 'when you have got one *glimpse*; improve it; copy it; cultivate the *idea*; and labour, till you have work'd yourself into a *right* TASTE, and form'd a relish and understanding of what is truly beautiful in the kind'.[27] In *The Moralists*, Theocles exclaims, 'How long ere a true taste is gained', and argues, ''tis not instantly we acquire the sense by which these beauties are discoverable. Labour and pains are required, and time to cultivate a natural genius ever so apt or forward. But who is there once thinks of cultivating the soil, or of improving any sense or faculty which nature may have given of this kind?' (II, p. 129). In the *Miscellaneous Reflections*, Shaftesbury declares, 'A legitimate and just taste can neither be begotten, made, conceived, or produced without the antecedent labour and pains of criticism.'

To the extent that he is concerned with self-criticism – the self-discoursing dialogic method through which one interrogates and regulates oneself – Shaftesbury's advice to authors appears to be directed to gentlemen. However, the introduction of *criticism* here in the context of the acquisition and cultivation of taste makes it clear that Shaftesbury is concerned with a wider audience. He continues: 'For this reason we presume not only to defend the cause of critics, but to declare open war

---

[27] *Letters to a Student at the University*, pp. 52–3.

against those indolent supine authors, performers, readers, auditors, actors or spectators who, making their humour alone the rule of what is beautiful and agreeable ... reject the criticising or examining art, by which alone they are able to discover the true beauty and worth of every object' (II, p. 257). At stake here is more than an attack on capricious fancy or the depravity of public taste. Like Addison, Shaftesbury looks to the critic (rather than a censor or authoritative judge) precisely because he is interested in the formation of public taste. Discussing the 'origin of critics' in *Soliloquy, or Advice to an Author*, he sketches a history of the first practitioners of the arts of persuasion, moving from 'orators and bards' to philosophers and 'learned critics' of various sorts who advanced their arts 'by revealing the hidden beauties which lay in the works of just performers, and by exposing the weak sides, false ornaments, and affected graces of mere pretenders'.

In a fiction of the origins of society, Shaftesbury explains that in 'free communities, made by consent and voluntary association', leaders could gain 'power' over the rest through 'force ... awe and terror'; but 'where persuasion was the chief means of guiding the society; where the people were to be convinced before they acted; there elocution became considerable, there orators and bards were heard'. The 'geniuses and sages of the nation' studied arts to make the people 'more treatable in a way of reason and understanding, and more subject to be led by men of science and erudition'. In this society the courtship of the public turns out to promote taste since ''twas the interest of the wise and the able that the community should be judges of ability and wisdom'; this self-interest leads them 'to promote that taste and relish to which they owed their personal distinction and pre-eminence'. Consequently, the 'more these artists courted the public, the more they instructed it'. Shaftesbury goes on to describe the study of the arts by geniuses who were 'less covetous of public applause, of power, or of influence over mankind' and of critics who 'were at length tempted to become authors and appear in public'. These critics assist the artists and geniuses by 'improving the public ear', by becoming 'interpreters to the people' as they teach 'the public to discover what was just and excellent in each performance' (I, pp. 154–6).

Shaftesbury imagines a counter-Hobbesian fiction in which self-interest leads to the cultivation and improvement of others; as if proleptically arguing against Rousseau, he creates a fiction in which the arts and sciences are introduced into the state of nature in such a way that does not lead to corruption and enslavement. If there is inequality here, it is that of an enlightened liberal republic in which the people consent to be governed by an intellectual aristocracy composed of benevolent leaders who govern by persuading the public through reason. This is what

Shaftesbury imagines in the *Letter concerning Design* when, discussing a 'national taste' and the 'improvement of art and science', he writes: 'When the free spirit of a nation turns itself this way, judgments are formed; critics arise; the public eye and ear improve; a right taste prevails; and in a manner forces its way.' (He rejects the patronage of 'court or ministry' since 'it is not in the nature of a court ... to improve, but rather corrupt a taste'.)[28]

In his idealized depictions of the past and the future, Shaftesbury imagines an alternative to the debased public world of commercial and theatrical relations that he denounces in the *Characteristicks*.[29] In the story of the origins of criticism, if authors are tempted to appear in public or to covet public applause, they cultivate, form, and advance public taste. The 'early poets of Greece', he writes, did not comply with the 'first relish and appetite' of their nation; rather, they 'formed their audience, polished the age, refined the public ear and framed it right, that in return they might be rightly and lastingly applauded' (I, p. 172). In the contemporary world the author seems to face a more difficult and even dangerous task since taste is ruled by a capricious and variable public, manipulated by booksellers rather than shaped and polished by geniuses. 'The great business in this (as in our lives, or in the whole of life) is "to correct our taste"', Shaftesbury writes in his notes for *Plastics*, 'For whither will not *taste* lead us?'[30] Taste itself, however, must be led; and this means that although Shaftesbury seems to limit his address to friends, authors, artists, and gentlemen, his eyes are on the public.

In the plan for the *Second Characters*, which Shaftesbury worked on between 1711 and 1713, he reminds himself that 'the precepts, demonstrations, etc. of real ethics' should be 'hid: not to be said except darkly or pleasantly with raillery upon self; or some such indirect way as in Miscellany'. However, he prescribes:

A rule, viz.: Nothing in the text but what shall be of easy, smooth, and polite reading, without seeming difficulty, or hard study; so that the better and gentler rank of painters and artists, the ladies, beaux, courtly gentlemen, and more refined sort of country and town wits, and notable talkers may comprehend, or be persuaded that they comprehend, what is there written in the text.

---

[28] *Second Characters*, pp. 21–3. In addition to sending young men such as Michael Ainsworth through Oxford, Shaftesbury 'was especially proud of the school he set up for the children of the parish in the chapel of the almshouse during his first autumn as an earl ... Gradually Shaftesbury took over the responsibility for paying the way of all the poor children of the parish through his school' (Voitle, *The Third Earl of Shaftesbury, 1671–1713*, p. 191).
[29] See Agnew, *Worlds Apart*.   [30] *Second Characters*, p. 114.

Foreign terms and 'more learned remarks' would be placed in notes, 'fit only for the critic, the real virtuoso, or philosopher'.[31] Shaftesbury's list of imagined readers is obviously more extensive than the 'friend-Lord' he plans to apostrophize on the same page; what is most striking, however, is that this list of characters and his strategy to reach them provide a good description of the audience and manner of the *Spectator*. The audience for the *Spectator* is, of course, even broader than this, extending, for example, to merchants and the growing middle class that is included and indeed defined as the very notion of the reading public – and consequently, the public – expands and changes. Shaftesbury's texts may seem more in dialogue with gentlemen and virtuosi than with the more promiscuous crowd constituted by the *Tatler* and *Spectator*; he may seem to speak more to those who might become 'interpreters to the people' than the public itself, but his concern with his reading public, his investment in the formation and reformation of public taste, and his efforts to ally himself with the method and audience of essay writers, all suggest his affinity with the project of the *Spectator*.

In other words, while it may be accurate to say that Shaftesbury's efforts to cultivate the aristocracy were appropriated by the *Spectator* and its middle-class audience in their effort to participate in cultural privileges and practices previously considered to be outside of their realm, one could argue that the seeds of this cross-pollination are already contained within Shaftesbury's intellectual and social project. Although writing within the aristocracy, as it were, he is also writing to and for the public with the aim of establishing public taste. Shaftesbury's characteristic assertion, 'To philosophise, in a just signification, is but to carry good-breeding a step higher', might be taken as a sign of an identification of philosophy and virtue with aristocratic blood.[32] However, the sentence which immediately follows in the *Miscellaneous Reflections* suggests what good breeding might mean for Shaftesbury: 'For the accomplishment of breeding is, to learn whatever is decent in company or beautiful in arts; and the sum of philosophy is, to learn what is just in society and beautiful in Nature and the order of the world' (II, p. 255).

Both breeding and philosophy involve *learning*. Shaftesbury writes at the moment in which the naturalizing metaphor of breeding as blood (which is itself a metaphor) gives way to the naturalizing metaphor of

---

[31] *Second Characters*, pp. 6–9. The first edition of the *Characteristicks* is prefaced with a note that tells 'the Reader' not to 'trouble' which the author's 'new Dress of Greek and Latin Quotations . . . unless he has the Curiosity to examine whether the Author has produc'd good Authorities for what he had before presum'd to advance' (*Characteristicks*, p. v).

[32] In the *Tatler*, Addison refers to 'a Philosopher, which is what I mean by a Gentleman' (I, p. 477, No. 69, 17 September 1709).

breeding as cultivation. Good breeding comes to represent the acquisition of culture and taste rather than the genetic issue of aristocratic
blood lines. Thus, when Shaftesbury declares in *Soliloquy, or Advice to
an Author*, 'One who aspires to the character of a man of breeding and
politeness is careful to form his judgment of arts and sciences upon
right models of perfection', he suggests that the character of a man of
breeding might be available to anyone capable of playing the part. He
concludes the next paragraph by asking: 'If a natural good taste be not
already formed in us, why should not we endeavour to form it, and
cultivate it till it become natural?' (I, p. 218). With roots in a metaphor
of nature, culture supplants nature until it seems natural.

'Good breeding' is used in the *Spectator* in relation to education. One
of Steele's correspondents, for example, speaks of his wife's accomplishments in singing, dancing, painting, music, French, Italian, and domestic sciences as that which 'we generally understand by good Breeding
and a polite Education'; while another tells Mr Spectator, 'your Writings have made Learning a more necessary Part of good Breeding than
it was before you appear'd'.[33] The phrase and concept, which appear to
be in transition in these years, are not used by Addison or Steele to refer
to aristocratic birth. Indeed, *Tatler* 204, instructing common people
how to address people of quality, associates good breeding with the
man who understands self-respect as well as respect for his social superiors: 'The highest Point of good Breeding, if any one can hit it, is to
show a very nice Regard to your own Dignity, and with that in your
Heart express your Value for the Man above you.'[34] In general in the
Tatler, good breeding is most often associated with good manners; in
the *Spectator*, writing about the manners of country and city people,
Addison explains: 'By Manners I do not mean Morals, but Behaviour
and Good Breeding'.[35] Indeed, he later asserts that in the absence of
what he calls 'Good-nature', 'Mankind have been forced to invent a
kind of artificial Humanity, which is what we express by the Word
Good-Breeding'. By defining good breeding as 'nothing else but an
Imitation and Mimickry of Good-nature', as 'exterior Shows and Appearances' which might be hypocritical or actually 'founded upon a real
Good-nature',[36] Addison turns the man of good breeding into a role. If
Shaftesbury suggests that the man of good breeding is a character that
must be personated, Addison suggests that it might be impersonated as
well.

[33] *Spectator*, III, p. 205 (No. 328, 17 March 1712); IV, p. 128 (No. 461, 19 August
1712).
[34] *Tatler* III, p. 87 (No. 204, 29 July 1710).
[35] *Spectator*, I, p. 486 (No. 119, 17 July 1711).
[36] *Spectator*, II, p. 165 (No. 169, 13 September 1711).

For Shaftesbury, the author of a book called *Characteristicks of Men Manners, Opinions, Times,* manners mean more than the codes of social politeness; manners are closely associated with morals, and both words have to be understood in the eighteenth-century sense of the French word *mœurs*.[37] The point here, however, is that in considering Shaftesbury's declarations in the context suggested by Addison, Steele, and Mr Spectator's alleged correspondents, it seems clear that his interest in good breeding is a sign of his investment in the cultivation and education of both private and public taste. Despite his theories about an innate moral sense, Shaftesbury in this context focuses on faculties and practices that can be learned and taught. It is for this reason that the *Characteristicks* is not in the end an instruction manual for gentlemen-virtuosi but rather a defence of criticism. If, as we have seen, Shaftesbury is to some extent engaged in an argument with both authors and readers about public taste, it is his belief that 'taste or judgment' is not 'innate' and therefore must follow 'the antecedent labour and pains of criticism' which compels him 'to defend the cause of critics' and 'to declare war upon those indolent supine authors, performers, readers, auditors, actors, or spectators' who 'reject the criticising or examining art' (II, p. 257).

As he presents 'an apology for authors and a defence of the literate tribe' (I, p. 139), and attacks 'critic-haters' (I, p. 153) who resent those 'severe judges' who 'are deaf to all courtship' (I, p. 150), he may seem like the 'man of sense' he imagines in the *Miscellaneous Reflections* who confronts 'some coffee-house committee' composed of a 'fraternity' of the wits who protect poets or playwrights from the attacks of critics; these wits are unable to understand 'that the greatest masters of art, in every kind of writing, were eminent in the critical practice' (II, p. 330). Yet despite the resistance to criticism in this 'coffee-house audience' and elsewhere, Shaftesbury insists that the critic is an ally of both artist and audience. His fictions about the origins of critics and his discussions about the formation of public taste identify critics as 'interpreters to the people ... who by their example taught the public to discover what was just and excellent in each performance' (I, p. 156). In this way good breeding and good taste can extend to the coffeehouse and beyond.

Addison, of course, places the critic in the coffeehouse. Whether or not he acted under the influence of Shaftesbury's advice to authors as he developed his literary and critical persona in the *Spectator*, his conception of the critic is similar as he both explicates and demonstrates '*that Faculty of the Soul, which discerns the Beauties of an Author with Pleasure, and the Imperfections with Dislike*'. Addison's early depictions

---

[37] See Gay, 'The Spectator as Actor', p. 29; and Bloom, Translator's Notes to Rousseau, *Politics and the Arts*, pp. 149–50.

of critics in the *Tatler* tend to be negative, attacking his own critics (as in *Tatler* 239) or associating them with pedantry, as in *Tatler* 165, where he writes, 'Of this shallow Species there is not a more importunate, empty, and conceited Animal than that which is generally known by the Name of a Critick.'[38] Shaftesbury also attacks scholars and pedants, recommending 'a just and liberal education by uniting the scholar-part with that of the real gentleman and man of breeding' as a way of avoiding both 'pedantry and school-learning' and 'the fashionable illiterate world' (I, p. 215). Addison is repeatedly contemptuous of pedantry in the *Spectator*,[39] but he tries to distinguish the 'true Critick' from the 'Critick who has neither Taste nor Learning'.[40] In *Spectator* 592, he condemns 'professed Criticks' and expresses 'great Esteem for a true Critick' – naming Aristotle, Longinus, Horace, Quintilian, Boileau, and Dacier.[41] His critical papers on *Paradise Lost*, for example, are not only demonstrations of criticism but also metacommentaries – essays about his own critical activity as well as the practice of good and bad criticism.

Indeed, the *Dialogue upon Medals* (one of Addison's earliest works, although it may have been revised later) defends critical analysis against a kind of anti-intellectual attack on pedantry by anyone who would 'ridicule those that valued themselves on their books and studies'. The medallist Philander converses with one interlocutor who suspects that it is easy 'to find out designs that never entered into the thoughts of the sculptor or the coiner', and another who declares, 'there is nothing more ridiculous than an antiquary's reading the Greek and Latin poets. He never thinks of the beauty of the thought or language, but is searching into what he calls the erudition of the author.' Philander sets out to convince his interlocutors not only that ancient medals are interesting but that they demand careful and detailed analysis of their historical and social function, their metaphors and allegories, their relation to the literary texts they allude to and cite, and the interplay between word and image they dramatize. 'I think there is a great affinity between coins and poetry, and that your medalist and critic are much nearer than the world generally imagines', explains Philander. In response to one of his demonstrations his interlocutor says, 'I find your women on medals do nothing without a meaning'.[42] Defending the medallist as a critic, Addison

[38] *Tatler*, II, p. 415 (No. 165, 29 April 1710); see also *Tatler*, III, pp. 227–32 (No. 239, 19 October 1710).
[39] *Spectator*, I, pp. 436–8, No. 105, 30 June 1711; IV, pp. 161–2, No. 470, 29 August 1712. See Elioseff, *Cultural Milieu*, pp. 21–48.
[40] *Spectator*, III, p. 36 (No. 291, 2 February 1712).
[41] *Spectator*, V, p. 26 (No. 592, 10 September 1714). Shaftesbury names, among others, Plato, Aristotle, Plutarch, Lucian, Cicero, Horace, Quintilian, Boileau, and Corneille (II, pp. 330–1).
[42] *Works*, I, pp. 255, 269, 271, 267–8, 278.

defends a critical practice that insists that every aspect of the verbal, graphic, and material text in question has a meaning and can be analysed.

This critical practice can be seen in the best-known and most influential practical criticism that Addison writes in the *Spectator*: the series on *Paradise Lost*. In these eighteen essays Addison takes on the role of interpreter to the people as he seeks to discover for the reader not only beauties and imperfections but especially 'concealed beauties' since the 'most exquisite Words and finest Strokes of an Author are those which very often appear the most doubtful and exceptionable, to a Man who wants a Relish for polite Learning'.[43] Writing of 'wonderful Incidents' in the Eighth Book of the poem, he declares, 'In a Word, though they are natural they are not obvious, which is the true Character of all fine Writing'.[44] Indeed, the critic must do more than point out beauties that 'are not so obvious to ordinary Readers'; even critics of Homer and Virgil have 'discovered several Master-Stroaks, which have escaped the Observation of the rest' – and Addison concedes that writers who follow him 'may find several Beauties in *Milton*, which I have not taken notice of'.[45]

Addison's efforts to discover and discern 'Beauties' and 'Imperfections' take him beyond the critical presuppositions and vocabulary he inherits from neo-classicism. Although he begins the series on *Paradise Lost* by proposing to 'examine it by the Rules of Epic Poetry, and see whether it falls short of the *Iliad* or *Aeneid* in the Beauties which are essential to that kind of Writing',[46] his interest in rules seems to diminish as his interest in *beauties* turns into an interest in *beauty*. This focus anticipates his examination of aesthetic experience in the 'Pleasures of the Imagination' series. Early in the *Paradise Lost* series Addison argues that 'a Man who sets up for a Judge in Criticism' should be acquainted not only with ancient and modern critics but also with Locke. He admits that the 'Essay on Human Understanding would be thought a very odd Book for a Man to make himself Master of, who would get a Reputation by Critical Writings' but he insists that 'an Author who has not learn'd the Art of distinguishing between Words and Things . . . will lose himself in Confusion and Obscurity'.[47] Addison, like many of his contemporaries, often misunderstands how he is being influenced by Locke. Although he repeatedly subscribes to Locke's theories of language, Addison's critical enterprise is finally closer to Tristram Shandy's reading of the *Essay concerning Human Understanding* as a book about

---

[43] *Spectator*, III, p. 37 (No. 291, 2 February 1712).
[44] *Spectator*, III, p. 284 (No. 345, 5 April 1712).
[45] *Spectator*, III, pp. 169–70 (No. 321, 8 March 1712). See Elioseff, *Cultural Milieu*, pp. 48–63.
[46] *Spectator*, II, p. 539 (No. 267, 5 January 1712).
[47] *Spectator*, III, p. 36 (No. 291, 2 February 1712).

what passes in a man's mind.[48] It is Steele who has Mr Spectator announce in the fourth issue that 'the workings of my own Mind, is the general Entertainment of my Life' but his declaration (and his following comment that his 'Pleasures are almost wholly confin'd to those of the Sight')[49] anticipates the aesthetic and critical investigations of Addison's Mr Spectator. Addison's interest in responding to *Paradise Lost* – and in showing himself responding to *Paradise Lost* – take him beyond a neo-classical evaluation and a belletristic appreciation of Milton to an effort to understand the experience and effect of reading the poem.

This can be seen in Addison's emphasis on Milton as a poet whose 'chief Talent, and indeed his distinguishing Excellence, lies in the Sublimity of his Thoughts'.[50] Longinus seems to supplant Aristotle as Addison depicts a Milton who not only chose a subject 'which was the most Sublime that could enter into the Thoughts of a Poet', but who also 'knew all the Arts of Affecting the Mind' of the reader.[51] With his inventory and analysis of similes, metaphors, allusions, and 'instances of Sublime Genius', he demonstrates how Milton can create 'some glorious Image or Sentiment, proper to inflame the Mind of the Reader'.[52] For Addison, Milton's greatness can be measured by mapping the experience of reading *Paradise Lost*, by tracing what happens in his mind – and by implication in the mind of the reader since his subjective experience (recounted in the third person) is offered as a model for his own reader. In *Spectator* 339, which begins with Longinus, he writes: 'The Sixth Book, like a troubled Ocean, represents Greatness in Confusion; the Seventh affects the Imagination like the Ocean in a Calm, and fills the Mind of the Reader without producing in it any thing like Tumult or Agitation.' If Addison's prose here seems uncharacteristically inflamed with poetry as he considers the effect of Homeric, Virgilian, and Miltonic similes, this may be because, as he suggests (following Longinus) in the next paragraph, 'one great Genius often catches the Flame from another, and writes in his Spirit, without copying servilely after him'.[53]

---

[48] According to Tristram, Locke's *Essay* is 'a history ... of what passes in a man's own mind' (p. 66). See Ketcham, *Transparent Designs*, pp. 98, 173; Elioseff, *Cultural Milieu*, pp. 150–88, and Kallich, 'Association of ideas'.

[49] *Spectator*, I, p. 21 (No. 4, 5 March 1711).

[50] *Spectator*, II, p. 587 (No. 279, 19 January 1712). See Monk, *The Sublime*; Damrosch, 'Addison's criticism', pp. 427–8; and Elioseff, *Cultural Milieu*, pp. 98–120. Dennis discusses the sublime in Milton's poetry in 'Grounds of criticism', published in 1704 (*The Critical Works of John Dennis*, I, pp. 325–73). See also Saccamano, 'Addison's "Pleasures"'.

[51] *Spectator*, III, p. 234 (No. 333, 22 March 1712).

[52] *Spectator*, III, p. 90 (No. 303, 16 February 1712).

[53] *Spectator*, III, p. 255 (No. 339, 29 March 1712).

Addison does not usually try to write in a Miltonic manner, but this principle is a major part of his theory and practice of reading Milton. Rather than invoking Homer and Virgil in order to examine *Paradise Lost* by the rules of epic poetry, he repeatedly calls attention to Milton's use of his precursors in his poem. Although he faults Milton's 'unnecessary Ostentation of Learning', Addison writes approvingly, 'no Poet seems ever to have studied *Homer* more'.[54] In comments such as, 'I must here take notice that *Milton* is every where full of Hints, and sometimes literal Translations, taken from the greatest of the *Greek* and *Latin* Poets',[55] he seems almost obligated to make such observations; but if he is at all troubled by Milton's allusions and translations, he is increasingly insistent about identifying textual parallels and supporting his observations with literary evidence. In *Spectator* 327 he writes, 'I cannot but take notice that *Milton*, in the Conferences between *Adam* and *Eve*, had his Eye very frequently upon the Book of *Canticles*', and, comparing a passage from Book 5 to passages from the 'Song of Solomon', he asserts that 'there is no question' that Milton 'remembred' them. A few paragraphs later he observes that Milton 'seems to have regarded two or three Passages' in the *Iliad* and insists that '*Milton* had this circumstance in his Thoughts'.[56]

If Addison's locutions reveal some anxiety (about Milton's borrowings or about whether his observations will be questioned) this anxiety seems to be balanced by the pleasure that the learned reader takes in perceiving these resemblances. In discussing Book 10, he declares that throughout the poem Milton 'has infinite Allusions to places of Scripture'.[57] In his last issue on the poem, looking back on his efforts 'to shew how the Genius of the Poet shines by a happy Invention, a distant Allusion, or judicious Imitation; how he has copied or improved *Homer* or *Virgil*, and raised his own Imaginations by the use which he has made of several Poetical Passages in Scripture', Addison cannot resist adding, 'I might have inserted also several Passages of *Tasso*, which our Author has imitated'.[58] He already has assured the reader that he has omitted 'many particular Lines and Expressions which are translated from the Greek *Poet*' since this would have 'appeared too minute and over-curious'. At times he seems to take so much pleasure in observing the 'Parallels'[59] that he has to restrain himself from observing more. As allusions to Homer, Virgil, the Bible, and Tasso seem to multiply and

---

[54] *Spectator*, III, p. 312 (No. 351, 12 April 1712).
[55] *Spectator*, III, p. 62 (No. 297, 9 February 1712); III, p. 173 (No. 321, 8 March 1712).
[56] *Spectator*, III, pp. 198–203 (No. 327, 15 March 1712).
[57] *Spectator*, III, p. 331 (No. 357, 19 April 1712).
[58] *Spectator*, III, p. 392 (No. 369, 3 May 1712).
[59] *Spectator*, III, p. 312 (No. 351, 12 April 1712).

resonate and become too numerous to enumerate, Addison anticipates what might be called the academic sublime.

Addison may wish to give Milton some of the authority and stature of the texts that are his models; but what is at stake here is also a way of reading. As Milton himself is repeatedly depicted 'with his Eye on' the *Iliad* or his imagination 'heated' with Homer,[60] we see the poet not only as a student of the sublime who seeks to affect the reader's imagination but also as a kind of critical reader himself: 'no Poet seems ever to have studied *Homer* more'.[61] Consequently, while Addison teaches us how to respond to Milton in describing what takes place in the reader's mind, he also suggests that to understand *Paradise Lost* the reader must view it next to a series of prior texts. Addison begins Number 291, 'Were I to chuse my Readers, by whose Judgment I would stand or fall', and goes on to describe the ideal reader's acquaintance with ancient and modern critics and poets.[62] Throughout the essays on *Paradise Lost*, Addison instructs his readers what they need to know in order to read both Milton and Milton criticism, and he suggests how to use this knowledge. In dramatizing these ways of reading (both the affective and the intellectual aspects of *Paradise Lost*) Addison suggests what to expect from the experience of reading. In doing so, he suggests what to expect from both readers and poets.

Addison's interest in the sublime and his investment in Milton as a reader and translator of the classics takes him beyond the narrowly Lockean view of language that underlies his criticism.[63] In his paper on Milton's language, he argues (following Aristotle) that 'the Language of an Heroic Poem should be both Perspicuous and Sublime'. In order to be sublime, he writes, 'it ought to deviate from the common Forms and ordinary Phrases of Speech. The Judgment of a Poet very much discovers it self in shunning the common Roads of Expression.' Praising Milton's '*Latinisms*, as well as *Graecisms*, and sometimes *Hebraisms*', he writes, 'Another way of raising the Language, and giving it a Poetical Turn, is to make use of the Idioms of other Tongues.'[64] Acknowledging in a subsequent essay that Milton's language is 'often too much laboured, and sometimes obscured by old Words, Transpositions, and Foreign Idioms', he nevertheless argues 'that *Milton*'s Sentiments and Ideas were so wonderfully Sublime, that it would have been impossible for him to have represented them in their full Strength and Beauty, without having recourse to these Foreign Assistances. Our Language sunk under him,

---

[60] *Spectator*, III, pp. 232–3 (No. 333, 22 March 1712).
[61] *Spectator*, III, p. 312 (No. 351, 12 April 1712).
[62] *Spectator*, III, p. 35 (No. 291, 2 February 1712).
[63] See Hansen, 'Ornament and poetic style'.
[64] *Spectator*, III, pp. 10–12 (No. 285, 26 January 1712).

and was unequal to that greatness of Soul, which furnished him with such glorious Conceptions.'[65]

At issue for Addison is a belief that poetry should be a foreign language, founded on an apparently rigid distinction between the languages of poetry and prose. This appears in his earliest works: in his *Remarks on Several Parts of Italy*, he discusses the 'advantage' that Italian poets have 'in the difference of their poetical and prose language' which allows them to use words 'that never enter into common discourse'. In contrast, the 'English and French, who always use the same words in verse as in ordinary conversation, are forced to raise their language with metaphors and figures'; this is why, he explains, 'Milton has made use of such frequent transpositions, Latinisms, antiquated words and phrases.'[66] The *Essay on Virgil's Georgics* praises Virgil in almost identical terms for his use of 'metaphors, Grecisms, and circumlocutions' and his decision to make his work appear 'in the pleasantest dress that poetry can bestow on it' rather than 'in the natural simplicity of its subject'.[67]

Addison's own figurative language here reflects the long rhetorical tradition of figuring poetry as ornament and dress, as well as Locke's more recent valuation of these terms in his recommendation to distinguish between words and things.[68] Addison favours blank verse in English tragedy and he recommends that a writer who valued sentiment over language should write 'his Dialogue in plain *English*, before he turned it into Blank Verse' so the reader could 'consider the naked Thought of every Speech in it, when divested of all its Tragick Ornaments'. Paraphrasing Locke, he continues: 'By this means, without being imposed upon by Words, we may judge impartially of the Thought'.[69] Addison proposes a similar test in his essays on wit: 'The only way therefore to try a Piece of Wit is to translate into a different Language, if it bears the Test you may pronounce it true; but if it vanishes in the Experiment, you may conclude it to have been a Punn.'[70] What is lost in the translation, in Addison's view, should be lost.

In one sense Addison seems to have a double standard; seeking to distinguish between words and things, language and sentiment, false wit and true wit, he wants to protect both poetry and prose by keeping them in separate realms. He defends 'plain English' in everyday discourse as well as in drama, suggesting at one point that 'certain Men might be set apart, as Superintendants of our Language, to hinder any

---

[65] *Spectator*, III, pp. 62–3 (No. 297, 9 February 1712).
[66] *Works*, I, p. 393.   [67] *Works*, I, p. 158.
[68] See Locke, *An Essay concerning Human Understanding*, II, p. 146.
[69] *Spectator*, I, p. 165 (No. 39, 14 April 1711).
[70] *Spectator*, I, p. 263 (No. 61, 10 May 1711).

Words of a Foreign Coin from passing among us'.[71] His papers on ballads (which follow the series on wit) praise their 'essential and inherent Perfection of Simplicity of Thought' and emphasize the appeal of a 'plain simple Copy of Nature, destitute of all the Helps and Ornaments of Art'.[72] He also praises Sappho (whose poetry he presents in translation) for containing 'genuine and natural Beauty, without any foreign or affected Ornaments'.[73] Yet although Addison would associate Milton with the natural simplicity of the ancients, his insistence on Milton's literary language and on a sublimity that is too great for the English language finally invests figurative language with meaning and power. Milton's sublime sentiments cannot be divested of their metaphorical expression; indeed, the sublime resides not in what is perspicuous but rather in the same figurative and foreign expressions that also can obscure. (Burke's codification of the sublime would later associate it with obscurity and oppose it to clarity.)

Consequently, although Addison maintains Locke's categories, at least in the realm of poetry he does not share Locke's distrust of figurative language. He maintains that '*Homer, Virgil,* or *Milton,* so far as the Language of their Poems is understood, will please a Reader of plain common Sense';[74] and paradoxically, both Milton's poem and Addison's papers of criticism lay the groundwork for a poetry that would speak in everyday language without foregoing figures – embodied by the end of the century in the preface and poems of the *Lyrical Ballads.* However, despite his belief that the critic should know how to distinguish language from sentiments and words from things, Addison's belief in poetry as a foreign language leads him to value Milton for his metaphors. As he says in his essay on taste in another outburst of figuration, 'there is as much difference in apprehending a Thought cloathed in *Cicero*'s Language, and that of a common Author, as in seeing an Object by the Light of a Taper, or by the Light of the Sun'.[75] It is precisely the clothing of figuration that provides the light by which we see objects. The power of poetry – especially in its embodiment of the sublime – seems to leave things behind. In Virgil's *Georgics,* Addison writes in his early essay, 'we receive more strong and lively ideas of things from his words, than we could have done from the objects themselves; and find our imaginations more affected by his descriptions, than they would have been by the very sight of what he describes'.[76] Addison would expand on this insight in the 'Pleasures of the Imagination' series: 'Words,

---

[71] *Spectator*, II, pp. 149–50 (No. 165, 8 September 1711).
[72] *Spectator*, I, p. 297 (No. 70, 21 May 1711); I, p. 362 (No. 85, 7 June 1711).
[73] *Spectator*, II, p. 367 (No. 223, 15 November 1711).
[74] *Spectator*, I, p. 297 (No. 70, 21 May 1711).
[75] *Spectator*, III, p. 528 (No. 409, 19 June 1712).   [76] *Works*, I, p. 158.

when well chosen, have so great a Force in them, that a Description often gives us more lively Ideas than the Sight of Things Themselves'.[77] Addison's attention to the power of Milton's language, especially as it enters foreign and figurative languages in order to affect the imagination, is part of his effort to attend to what is unobvious and difficult about the poem; interpreter to the people, he wants to train readers how to read Milton – especially 'ignorant Readers, who have formed their Taste upon the quaint Similes' of 'Modern Poets'.[78]

Addison's concept of the sublime seems to be informed by Shaftesbury's descriptions in *The Moralists*; there, the experience of the sublime is mainly confined to the realm of nature, although this experience is itself placed in the realm of aesthetic experience.[79] (Shaftesbury has been credited with translating the sublime from the realm of rhetoric to the realm of aesthetics.)[80] Despite his investment in aesthetic experience, however, Shaftesbury emphasizes the creation rather than the reception of the work of art and founds his notion of an aesthetic sense in an at once deistic and Platonic vision that views nature and beauty in terms of 'forms', 'the forms which form', and 'that third order of beauty, which forms not only such as we call mere forms but even the forms which form' (II, pp. 132–3). He is uninterested in and perhaps even hostile to the psychological or empirical aesthetics that Addison would develop. Despite his advice to authors, Shaftesbury does not engage in the sort of practical criticism in which Addison engaged, although at least one critic has seen in his brief account of *Hamlet* in *Soliloquy, or Advice to an Author* a ground-breaking reading of the play as an introspective monologue.[81]

Shaftesbury's advice, however, contains presuppositions about the design of a work of art and consequently how a work of art should be viewed or read. This is especially true of his writing about painting, which includes detailed close readings of hypothetical paintings. The influential 'Notion of the Historical Draught or Tablature of the Judgment of Hercules' (published in French in 1712 and in English in 1713) is written in the form of advice to an artist who sets out to depict the allegorical scene of Hercules' choice between Happiness and Vice. In addition to seminal discussions about the necessity of a unified tableau ('a single piece, comprehended in one view, and formed according to one

---

[77] *Spectator*, III, p. 560 (No. 416, 27 June 1712).
[78] *Spectator*, III, p. 90 (No. 303, 16 February 1712).
[79] See Cassirer, *Philosophy of the Enlightenment*, p. 84.
[80] See Brett, *The Third Earl of Shaftesbury*, p. 146. He writes, 'The reader of *The Moralists* is at once struck with the similarity between Shaftesbury's views and what Addison has to say about the sublime in the *Spectator*' (p. 150). See also Monk, *The Sublime*, and Fry, *Reach of Criticism*, pp. 87–124.
[81] See Tuveson, 'Importance of Shaftesbury'.

single intelligence, meaning, or design')[82] Shaftesbury presents a model of both conscious artistic design and careful analysis that presupposes a work of art in which every detail has a purpose and meaning. In the unpublished materials for the *Second Characters* there is also a translation of 'The Picture of Cebes, Disciple of Socrates' in which interlocutors faced with mysterious allegorical drawings discuss at length 'the meaning and explication of these fictions'.[83]

Perhaps the most explicit model of critical reading that Shaftesbury provides is found in his defence of criticism in the *Miscellaneous Reflections*. We saw that in the third volume of the *Characteristicks* Shaftesbury plays the role of 'critic or interpreter' (II, p. 160) to himself; having 'after our author's example, asserted the use of criticism in all literate works', the *Miscellaneous Reflections*' author proceeds to 'exercise this art upon our author himself, and by his own rules examine him' (II, p. 323). The last third of the book – the full title of which is *Miscellaneous Reflections on the preceding Treatises, and other Critical Subjects* – is devoted to explaining and defending himself, as he simultaneously submits himself to criticism and defends the preceding treatises against criticism. In addition to elaborating his previous arguments, and examining his own critical subject in a version of his dialectical self-discoursing method, Shaftesbury ends his general defence of criticism and particular defence of his own work with a defence of critical reading.

The context and occasion for this conclusion is a defence of the controversial speculations about religion in the preceding treatises, especially the characterization of a sceptical point of view. Asserting his 'critical liberty', the narrator enters into 'the form and manner of our dialogue author' and the character of the sceptic in order to present 'an open and free vindication not only of free-thinking but free professing and discoursing in matters relating to religion and faith' (II, p. 353). Within this context, however, the sceptic focuses on 'criticism of holy literature' and the notion that it could establish an absolute truth. He asserts that there are 'innumerable places that contain (no doubt) great mysteries, but so wrapped in clouds or hid in umbrages, so heightened with expressions or so covered with allegories and garments of rhetoric . . . that they may seem to have been left as trials of our industry'. He continues: 'For when there are found in the explications of these writings so many commentaries, so many senses and interpretations, so

---

[82] *Second Characters*, p. 32. This text originally was written in French and published in the Amsterdam edition of the *Journal des Sçavans* (November, 1712); it was subsequently published in English in 1713 and then included in the posthumous second edition of the *Characteristicks* in 1714. See also: Sweetman, 'Shaftesbury's last commission'; Paknadel, 'Shaftesbury's illustration'; and Fried, *Absorption and Theatricality*, pp. 83, 89, 92, 209, 214–15, 218–19, 223–4.

[83] *Second Characters*, p. 64.

many volumes in all ages, and all like men's faces, no one exactly like another: either this difference is absolutely no fault at all, or if it be, it is excusable.'

At issue here is more than the problem of establishing an authoritative or 'perfectly true' text; the problem is the absence of any

certain mark to determine whether the sense of these passages should be taken as literal or figurative. There is nothing in the nature of the thing to determine the sense or meaning ... 'tis unreasonably required, that what is of itself ambiguous should be understood in its own prime sense and intention, under the pain of a sin or an anathema.

There can be no authoritative text to dictate faith and belief because the absolute meaning of a text cannot be determined. It turns out that the sceptic is borrowing his argument from Bishop Taylor's argument about 'the liberty of criticism' in *Of the Liberty of Prophesying*. In a long footnote Shaftesbury includes Taylor's assertion that since in holy literature there are 'so many copies, with infinite varieties of reading' the sense of which can be altered by 'a parenthesis, a letter, an accent', and 'since some places have divers literal senses, many have spiritual, mystical, and allegorical meanings; since there are so many tropes, metonymies, ironies, hyperboles, proprieties and improprieties of language ... it is almost impossible to know the proper interpretation' (II, pp. 356–8).[84]

Although the stakes of Shaftesbury's arguments for freedom of thought, freedom of speech, and religious tolerance are obviously high in both political and personal terms and might in themselves justify concluding the *Characteristicks* with this sceptical coda, it none the less makes sense that Shaftesbury would end his final volume with a defence of 'critical liberty'. Throughout the *Miscellaneous Reflections*, as in *Soliloquy, or Advice to an Author*, he has argued for an active criticism that would not only evaluate but also interpret. Drawing on a long tradition of biblical exegesis (revived by the Puritan doctrine of reading both the Scriptures and the world allegorically and typologically) Shaftesbury's arguments against a kind of literal fundamentalism apply to secular literature as well. In the world of the *Characteristicks* – in which 'all turns upon the nature of a character'[85] and *characters* refer at once to printed marks or letters, the self, and a personated role – everything depends on critical reading and interpretation. Shaftesbury's sceptic does more than argue that a religion based on texts – 'founded on letters and Scripture' (II, p. 306) – must accept variant readings and multiple interpretations. Although he insists on his own 'faith and orthodox belief',

[84] See Taylor, *Discourse*. These ideas are developed at greater length in Marshall, *The Figure of Theater*, pp. 67–70.
[85] *The Life, Unpublished Letters, and Philosophical Regimen*, p. 189.

he suggests a view of a world in which the difficulty of knowing the proper interpretation necessitates the 'liberty of examining and searching' (II, p. 352).

In other words, given mysteries wrapped in clouds or hid in umbrages, covered with allegories and garments of rhetoric, explicated in so many senses and interpretations and volumes that like men's faces are never exactly like another, reading and readers are necessary. As he advocates 'the liberty to read', Shaftesbury interrupts himself to explain: 'that is to say, to examine, construe, and remark with understanding' (II, p. 306). *Examine* is the term he has used for a rigorous, sceptical, and self-conscious analysis; *remark* evokes the key senses of characterize, write, and recognize, as it calls on us to mark again with knowledge and comprehension. *Construe*, however, brings together several crucial senses, readings, and types of reading, including: to combine words or parts of speech grammatically; to trace the construction of a sentence to show its meaning; to translate a passage word for word or orally; to give the sense or meaning of, to explain, expound, or interpret; to deduce by interpretation, to judge by inference, to inform by way of explanation – and even to interpret wrongly, to misconstrue. This is what it means to read for Shaftesbury; this is what he demands for and of readers.

In this context we can see that Shaftesbury's attack on authors who flatter and court readers is actually based on an argument about the reader's inherent superiority. Boasting of 'the little courtship I have paid him', Shaftesbury asserts the 'reader's privilege above the author' and insists that he has assigned him 'the upper hand and place of honour' (II, pp. 306–7). Noting that Socrates and Jesus were not authors, declaring that to be an author is in itself to be only 'of the second rank of men', he redefines the capricious and variable relation formed between author and reader to reaffirm the place of the reader: the reader who 'unworthily resigns the place of honour, and surrenders his taste or judgment to an author ... not only betrays himself but withal the common cause of author and reader' (II, p. 312).[86] The critic may act as an interpreter to the people and try to form public taste, but Shaftesbury warns his reader not to be frightened by 'the proposal of giving him his liberty, of making him his own judge'; he declares his intention to 'raise the masterly spirit of just criticism in my readers and exalt them ever so little above the lazy, timorous, over-modest, or resigned state in which the generality of them remain', to invite his reader 'to criticise honestly', to give his reader 'the sharpest eye over his author' (II, pp. 312–13). The reader must also act as critic and accept the liberty of

[86] Shaftesbury writes: 'Of all the artificial Relations, formed between Mankind, the most capricious and variable is that of *Author* and *Reader*' (II, p. 296).

critical reading. Shaftesbury, who believes in the forms he both can and cannot see, finally stops short of scepticism; but like Addison he calls on the reader to be a spectator: to read with the sharpest eye. Shaftesbury and Addison both would teach us how to read. By viewing their critical projects and methods together, we can see how Shaftesbury and Addison each teaches us how to read the other's work as well as his own.

(ii) *The rise of aesthetics from Baumgarten to Humboldt*

Hans Reiss

Discourse on aesthetics has gone on at least since the Greeks. But in the second half of the eighteenth century writings on aesthetics took a decisive turn in Germany, since German thinkers – and they alone – sought to establish aesthetics as an independent discipline. The following account, therefore, necessarily deals primarily with their work and the consequences which resulted from the rise of the new discipline.

The term 'aesthetic' itself was coined by Alexander Gottlieb Baumgarten in 1735, when he introduced the word towards the end of his master's dissertation *Meditationes philosophicae de nonnullis ad poema pertinentibus* (*Philosophical Meditations concerning Some Conditions of Poetry*).[1] Fifteen years later, in a major work entitled *Aesthetica* (1750; 1758), he put forward the case for establishing a new philosophical discipline. Baumgarten wrote in Latin, and in difficult Latin at that. However, he had been lecturing on the subject since 1741, and many, but by no means all, of his central ideas had, before the publication of the *Aesthetica*, already been popularized (and misrepresented) by his pupil Georg Friedrich Meier in his *Foundations of All Fine Arts and Sciences* (*Anfangsgründe aller schönen Künste und Wissenschaften*) (1748–1750), a treatise which, since it was written in German, had a far wider appeal. As a result, Baumgarten's achievement was not fully appreciated for a very long time. Yet he had not merely created a new term, but taken a radical step. Indeed, the term 'aesthetics' would most probably not have become part of our common currency if it had not at the same time defined a new and separate sphere of philosophical enquiry. This represents a decisive departure from previous practice. Although Baumgarten is indebted to traditional poetics and rhetoric as well as to rationalism – he was a follower of Leibniz and Christian Wolff – his approach to the problem of ascertaining the philosophical status of the arts is highly original. Aesthetic judgements are, he maintains, autonomous judgements, independent of moral, metaphysical and theological thought. Admittedly, although his account is systematic, he at times appears not to pursue his original approach consistently. Sometimes he even writes as if he was not fully aware of the novelty of his thought.

By freeing aesthetics from the shackles imposed by theology Baumgarten showed himself a true champion of the Enlightenment; for he

---

[1] Cf. Baumgarten, *Meditationes*, §§ CXVIf., ed. Aschenbrenner and Holther, pp. 39f.

effectively secularized the subject. He was probably not aware of doing so, for he was a pious Christian who had also, however, imbibed the draught of rationalism and was relentlessly driven onward by philosophical inquiry to new ways of thought. His attention is focused not on the objects themselves, the works of art, whether of literature, fine art or music – or for that matter on the creative process – but on the mode of apprehending them. As he puts it succinctly in the *Aesthetica*, 'The concern of aesthetics is with the perfection of sensuous knowledge as such, that is, with beauty'.[2] Without cognition, there can, then, be no perfection. However, to apprehend works of art properly is mainly an intuitive act, though the intellect and reason are by no means excluded. It is a way of looking at the world different from that of scientific thought. Baumgarten calls intuitive or sensuous cognition a lower order, an inferior kind of knowledge in comparison to logical, rational, or intellectual knowledge, but we must not be misled by the term 'inferior'. It does not mean less important; it merely reflects a terminology taken over from Leibniz and Wolff, who distinguished between logical and mathematical knowledge on the one hand, and sensuous knowledge on the other. But the two modes of knowledge are not necessarily in conflict. Sensuous knowledge is analogous to reason, and Baumgarten appropriately uses the term 'the art of the analogy of reason'[3] to define its nature. Yet it is profoundly different; for whereas logic, mathematics, and science seek to achieve distinctness and clarity, aesthetics deals with phenomena which are, in the last resort, indefinable. However, sensuous cognition is not restricted to feelings, but is intellectual in character as well. It is both an art and a science (*Wissenschaft*), or rather an art raised to the level of a science.

Yet both modes of cognition, both logic and aesthetics, are concerned with truth. The whole truth can never be ascertained, and either mode will convey only a part of the truth (only God knows the whole truth). Since aesthetic judgements are independent of logical or moral judgements and not dependent on criteria belonging to these spheres, logical mistakes or moral defects are not capable of impairing aesthetic perception, though of course, logic and ethics will often agree with aesthetics. Likewise, 'aesthetic' or 'aestheticological truth'[4] must not contradict general perceptions of truth, but can safely ignore those assertions which are based only on reason. The concern of aesthetics is not to discover or define general or universal principles or laws, but to assist us in creating or apprehending the individual object or process. Its nature is, to some

[2] 'Aesthetices finis est perfectio cognitionis sensitiuae, qua talis ... Haec autem est pulcritudo' (Baumgarten, *Aesthetica*, §14, p. 6).
[3] 'Ars analogi rationis' (*ibid.*, § 1, p. 1).
[4] Veritas ... aesthetica' ['veritas ... aestheticologica'] (*ibid.*, § 427, pp. 269ff.).

extent, ambivalent since it will always retain some of the qualities characteristic of an art, however scientific it has become. For Baumgarten seeks
to give guidance both to the writer or artist who wishes to create works
of literature, music or art and to those who wish merely to appreciate
such works. In his opinion, creative aesthetic activity requires a suitable
natural disposition, keen sensitivity, imagination, insight, poetic talent,
memory, a sense of refined taste, the capacity for anticipating an expression and the ability to express representations, intellectual knowledge
and theoretical understanding, an inclination towards the arts, constant
training and above all an 'innate aesthetic temperament'.[5] These qualities
are needed to produce the truly creative artist (or aesthetician) – the
felix aestheticus.[6]

Like Leibniz and Wolff, Baumgarten distinguishes between those
impressions or ideas which are clear and distinct and thus belong to the
realm of mathematics, science or logic and those which are either obscure or indistinct, and which belong to the realm of the senses. If they
are indistinct they may yet be clear, but because they are indistinct, they
will appear confused – which means, in Baumgarten's terminology, that
their characteristics cannot be spelt out in distinct detail. In the realm
of aesthetics, confusion is confluence. It is not the origin of error, but
the necessary precondition for truth. 'The path to truth leads from night
through dawn to noon'.[7] Confusions which are incapable of being clari-
fied fall outside the scope of aesthetics. Baumgarten also differentiates
between intensive and extensive clarity. The former belongs to the realm
of mathematics and logic, the latter to that of aesthetics. Intensive clarity concentrates on general and distinct abstractions; extensive clarity
deals with individual objects whose magnitude and wealth determine
the extent of their particular individuality. Since Baumgarten focuses
attention on the mode of cognition, perception is what matters in the
realm of aesthetics. Appropriately the term 'aesthetics' itself is derived
from the Greek words 'αἰσθάνομαι' (I perceive), 'τὸ αἰσθητόν' (object
of [sense] perception) and 'αἰσθητικός' (perceptible).[8] Aesthetics is, however, more than perception. It also seeks to bring about or discern an
order for sensuous knowledge.

Since beauty does not reside in the object created or experienced but

---

[5] 'temperamentum aestheticum' (*ibid.*, § 44, p. 18).   [6] Cf. *ibid.*, § 27, p. 11.
[7] 'Ex nocte per auroram meridies' (*ibid.*, § 7, p. 3).
[8] Baumgarten uses the words 'αισθητα επιστημης αισθητιχης siue *aestheticae*'
('objects of [sense] perception [are to be known by the inferior faculty as objects] of
the science of [sense] perception or *aesthetics*') in *Meditationes*, § CXVI, p. 39 and
contrasts 'αἰσθητα' with 'νοητα' (objects of [mental] perception). He appears to
allude to the opposition of 'νοητά' and 'αἰσθητά' in Aristotle, *Nicomachean Ethics*,
X, iv, 1174 b, and perhaps also to Plato, *Timaeus*, 28a, as well as Plotinus, *Eneads*,
IV, 8, 7.

in the mental act of cognition, the object of cognition itself need not be 'beautiful' in the traditional sense of the word (or, to be more precise, suited to the creation or discernment of beauty) but could also be 'ugly'. That aesthetics, unlike science, deals not with abstractions but with individuality is not a disadvantage; for abstraction entails not only the gain of distinctness, but also the loss of individual significance. The greater the individuality, the greater the value or truth of the individual work created or experienced. Individuality gives rise to perfection which requires order and hence unity of thought. Beauty, then, is found in unity or harmony of thought.[9] To perceive or to know that unity, Baumgarten emphasizes, is the aesthetic phenomenon itself. Since we cannot apprehend that which is signified without signs, the signs, or means of expression, have to be brought into a harmonious order. That order needs to reflect a consensus, a unity or harmony of individual elements; for perfection of sensuous knowledge or beauty consists in our perceiving a harmony of different individual elements which Baumgarten lists. They are: plenitude (*ubertas*), magnitude (*magnitudo*), truth (*veritas*), clarity (*claritas*), certitude (*certitudo*), and a lively movement or living power of cognition (*vita cognitionis*).[10] Moreover, we must recognize the 'elegance of the object'.[11] These qualities, if brought into harmony, give us beauty of sensuous cognition from which we derive the pleasure of abundance (*copia*), nobility (*nobilitas*) and light (*lux*).[12] All this cannot be achieved without order which cannot itself arise without selection or concentration. Unity has to be perceived within diversity.

When Baumgarten left his university post in Halle for a chair in Frankfurt on the Oder, he was succeeded by his pupil Meier, who, although he expressed many of Baumgarten's views, does not appear to have fully grasped the main thrust of his argument, viz. that it is the act of cognition alone which creates perfection and thus constitutes the aesthetic experience; for while Meier, like Baumgarten, speaks of aesthetics as the cognition of sensuous thought, he also insists that beauty resides in the object perceived. Perfection is, for him, something that we perceive in the sense of noticing or discovering and not something that we bring about by the act of perception. Meier's list of the various characteristics which entitle objects to be called beautiful does not significantly differ from Baumgarten's. But he also believes that objects which are intrinsically incapable of conveying beauty have to be excluded from the realm of aesthetics. They fall below the 'aesthetic horizon'.[13] Thus, he deprives Baumgarten's theory of its major plank.

---

[9] 'consensus cogitationum' (Baumgarten, *Aesthetica*, § 18, p. 7).
[10] Cf. *ibid.*, § 22, p. 9.   [11] 'ipsa rerum elegantia' (*ibid.*, § 24, p. 9).
[12] Cf. *ibid.*, § 22, p. 9.
[13] 'ästhetischer Horizont' (Meier, *Anfangsgründe*, I, § 44, p. 75; cf. also I, § 55, p. 97).

Moreover, Meier's concern is utilitarian. For him aesthetics is not a truly independent discipline, but has to be justified on utilitarian grounds. For its purpose is to further virtue and bring about moral and psychological improvement. Furthermore, by its application to scientific discourse, it communicates the discoveries of science more forcefully. It also enhances taste. Thus, Meier no longer strictly separates aesthetics from other modes of thought, including ethics.

Baumgarten's conception of the *felix aestheticus* is closely linked to the novel status accorded to the artist of genius in eighteenth-century thought. In contrast to Renaissance thought, it was no longer expected that the *cortegiano* or *uomo universale* would occupy the pinnacle of human achievement. That place was accorded to the *homme de lettres* or the *philosophe*, and more particularly to the 'genius'. A new conception of genius arose. It harks back to the supernatural or divine inspiration often assigned to the poet in antiquity. However, it was given a peculiar twist in an age of increasing secularization. It expresses a turning against the prevailing poetics, the *doctrine classique* and the dogmatic belief in rules. In England Shakespeare had first been seen as an exception to this doctrine and then as the example of a special status assigned to the genius. That view was echoed and developed in Germany by Lessing and above all by Herder and the *Sturm und Drang* writers of the 1770s, including the young Goethe. Finally, Kant defended the role of the genius in aesthetics by a rigorous philosophical argument. In France Diderot, taking up suggestions made early in the century by the Abbé Du Bos, succeeded in fusing the notion of the *philosophe* and *homme de lettres*, on the one hand, and the artistic genius, on the other. His conception gained wide recognition.

Beauty, Diderot believes, results from a combination of morality and truth which is for him closely linked to the imitation of nature. For him 'nature never does anything wrong'.[14] The artist needs to discover and reproduce 'the relationships'[15] which obtain in nature and achieve the order, unity, symmetry and proportion which are concealed beneath the manifold diversity of nature.[16] Diderot, who was highly esteemed in Germany, waged war against the widely held rationalistic belief that reason alone is to provide the criteria of aesthetic judgement. Art ought to arouse feelings. The artist's exceptional powers are associated with enthusiasm – here Diderot harks back to the past – which is often pathological. But even more strongly, he emphasizes the creative power

---

[14] 'La nature ne fait rien d'incorrect' (*Essais sur la peinture* (1765); Diderot, *Oeuvres*, X, p. 461).

[15] 'des rapports' (*Recherches philosophiques sur l'origine et la nature du beau* (1751); *ibid.*, X, p. 24).

[16] Cf. *ibid.*, X, pp. 24f.

of the artist. Moreover, he believes that the genius necessarily comes into conflict with generally accepted ethical standards, and has, in this conflict, the right to insist on his own ethical values.

However, Diderot's beliefs are complex, perhaps even contradictory; for he also maintains that art should be in tune with the general moral climate and impart a moral message. Indeed, like Meier's, his conception of beauty is not free from utilitarianism. In Germany Johann Georg Sulzer, another author of an encyclopaedia – admittedly one devoted only to the arts, viz. his *General Theory of Fine Arts (Allgemeine Theorie der schönen Künste)* (1771–4) – also insisted on a utilitarian view of art. In his widely read work, written over a longish period – it was started in 1753 – this influential, but not profound, writer requires art to have a moral purpose, a view for which he was taken to task by no less than Goethe in one of the latter's early reviews.[17] For Sulzer, beauty is not the goal of art. On the contrary, art is to arouse feeling, which is in turn to promote moral sensibility. Sulzer is anything but consistent: sometimes feeling is regarded as independent of reason, at other times it is subordinated to it.

Johann Joachim Winckelmann, the great art historian, made a much more profound impact on eighteenth-century German taste, and thus indirectly on aesthetics, than Sulzer. By creating the myth of the superiority of Greek art and in promoting neo-classical values Winckelmann determined much of the aesthetic discussion in Germany, and not only in Germany, for more than a century. It is by no means inappropriate that Goethe called his essay on him *Winckelmann and his Century (Winckelmann und sein Jahrhundert)* (1805). For Winckelmann, taste is not a purely individual matter at all. It was formed in antiquity. What had been discerned and created in antiquity remains valid for later generations. The right taste arose in ancient Greece because social and political conditions had been favourable and proper respect was accorded to the artist; for, like Hume, Winckelmann believes that taste is shaped by historical circumstances. In the ancient Greek statues he finds the ideal of beauty. In his view, it is characterized by 'a *noble simplicity* and a *tranquil grandeur*',[18] qualities which the modern artist ought to emulate. Greek sculpture tells us of human self-sufficiency and autonomy, of spiritual strength, serenity, and nobility. Harmony and proportion are essential elements of beauty.

In contrast to Baumgarten, however, Winckelmann thinks that beauty,

---

[17] Cf. review of Sulzer's *Die schönen Künste, in ihrem Ursprung ihrer wahren Natur und besten Anwendung* (1772) (HA, XII, pp. 15–20).

[18] 'eine *edle Einfalt* und eine *stille Größe*'; *Gedanken über die Nachahmung der griechischen Werke in der Malerei und Bildhauerkunst* (1755) (§ 79; Winckelmann, *Sämtl. Werke*, I, p. 30).

'the *supreme end* and *centre* of art',[19] is a mystery, a secret of nature. It defies definition, and is a matter of individual discernment. However, in keeping with the moral outlook of his times, he also maintains that art should not only give pleasure but should teach as well. Indeed, instruction matters more than pleasure. Like Diderot, he considers 'the *good* and the *beautiful* to be only *one and the same thing*'.[20] For the idea inherent in a work determines its value. 'The *highest form of beauty* is found only in *God*'.[21] The more closely a work reflects God, the more beautiful it is. Beauty consists of unity within diversity. Winckelmann idealizes art, but his ideal is based on observation. He derives it from a judicious selection of the proportions of the human body as reflected in Greek art, which in turn reflects nature at its best.

Gotthold Ephraim Lessing, in his *Laocoön, or on the Limits of Painting and Poetry* (*Laokoon, oder über die Grenzen der Malerei und Dichtkunst*) (1766), took issue with some of Winckelmann's ideas. Like Winckelmann, he believed in universally valid rules. However, he did not believe that the Greeks had established a canon of rules and taste once and for all, but that rules and hence taste have to be modified in the light of new creations by writers or artists of genius. Beauty is for him the representation of perfection when the concept of unity prevails, that is, if we are able to survey the object as a whole and our view is not disturbed by diversity. In contrast, we call a work sublime when diversity prevails and we cannot apprehend the whole from one single point of view.[22] Moreover, each medium is governed by different rules. Visual art must concentrate on the pregnant moment of an action since it deals with coexistence in space. It uses figures, colours and space and employs 'natural' signs, which resemble the objects depicted. Poetry which articulates sounds in temporal succession employs 'arbitrary' signs, which do not have any necessary connection with the objects signified. Like Diderot, Lessing is a follower of the imitation theory of art, and believes that it is the task of poetry to use the arbitrary signs of words in such a way that they come close to appearing natural. This is achieved in drama in which the dramatic dialogue, as a sign, coincides with what is signified, the speech of the characters, an impression which can be further strengthened by the gestures of the actors. And because the signs of poetry are arbitrary, poetry also grants greater scope to the imagination.

---

[19] 'die *Schönheit*, als der *höchste* Endzweck, und als der *Mittelpunkt* der Kunst'; *Geschichte der Kunst des Altertums* (1763–8), IV, 2, § 9 (*ibid.*, IV, p. 45).

[20] '. . . daß das *Gute* und das *Schöne* nur *Eines* ist'; *Vorrede zu den Anmerkungen über die Geschichte der Kunst des Altertums* (1763–8), § 5 (*ibid.*, III, p. 35).

[21] 'Die *höchste Schönheit* ist in *Gott*'; *Geschichte der Kunst des Altertums*, IV, 2, § 22 (*ibid.*, IV, p. 60).

[22] 'Bemerkungen über Burke's philosophische Untersuchungen "Über den Ursprung unserer Begriffe vom Erhabenen und Schönen"' (1758–9) (Lessing, *Sämtl. Schr.*, XIV, p. 221).

Moses Mendelssohn, a close friend of Lessing's and an exceptionally lucid and pleasing philosophical stylist, is another thinker whose aesthetics are written in the shadow of Baumgarten. In his *On the Sources and Relations of the Fine Arts and Sciences* (*Über die Quellen und die Verbindungen der schönen Künste und Wissenschaften*) (1757) and in his *Philosophical Writings* (*Philosophische Schriften*) (1771), especially in the sections entitled *Rhapsody, or Additions to the Letters on Sensibility* (*Rhapsodie, oder Zusätze zu den Briefen über Empfindsamkeit*) and *On the Main Principles of the Fine Arts and Sciences* (*Über die Hauptgrundsätze der schönen Künste und Wissenschaften*), he defines beauty as cognition of perfection, which is perceived through intuition (*Anschauung*). The aim of art is to delight, and the character of the arts and sciences consists in an artificial perfect sensuous presentation (of phenomena) or in sensuous perfection presented by art. Aesthetic judgements arise from our ability to experience pleasure and displeasure; indeed, they are often based on a mixture of both emotions. But it is pleasure without desire. Anticipating Kant, Mendelssohn considers it 'an especial characteristic of beauty that we regard it with calm pleasure, that it pleases us, even if we do not possess it and are still far from any desire to do so'.[23] However, an aesthetic judgement does not merely spring from the emotions; it also contains an intellectual element, for it entails what, in *Morning Hours or Lectures on the Existence of God* (*Morgenstunden oder Vorlesungen über das Dasein Gottes*) (1785), he calls our 'capacity of approval'.[24]

An artist is entitled to depict an ugly object or evil action. Yet there are principles which he must not ignore. An object or action must be of a certain size or kind, for it has to reflect unity in diversity. If it is too uniform we fail to notice diversity; if it is too large unity eludes us. Perfection is achieved by harmonizing the various parts into a whole. Mendelssohn, anticipating Lessing's argument in *Laocoön*, distinguishes between the various media of art. Sculpture, painting, and architecture are appropriate to the organ of sight and make an impact by coexistence in space. Hogarth's view, expressed in *The Analysis of Beauty* (1753), that beauty is most convincingly found in a serpentine line, strikes him, as it did Lessing, as suggestive but inadequate. Music, dance, and poetry, on the other hand, are appropriate to hearing and their products exist in succession in time.

For Mendelssohn, art is more easily capable of arousing pleasure than nature, because a work of art is more than imitation (though imitation

---

[23] 'Es scheinet vielmehr ein besonderes Merkmal der Schönheit zu seyn, daß sie mit ruhigem Wohlgefallen betrachtet wird; daß sie gefällt, wenn wir sie auch nicht besitzen, und von dem Verlangen, sie zu besitzen, auch noch so weit entfernt sind' (*ibid.*, III, 2, p. 61).

[24] 'Billigungsvermögen' (Mendelssohn, *Ges. Schr.*, III, 2, p. 62).

may be a precondition of art). For the artist is able to improve on nature by selecting and focusing attention on what is conducive to moving us most. Beauty stimulates our obscure and latent impulses and, by providing us with examples, art – and in particular poetry – can arouse feelings, which matter as much as intellect and will. Moreover, a work of art also allows us to grasp something of the artist's spiritual qualities. We shall thus be encouraged to act morally and rise to a higher degree of perfection. But the impact is indirect. Art and morality are separate; the stage, for instance, has a morality of its own.

Johann Gottfried Herder, who greatly esteemed and was indebted to Baumgarten, Winckelmann, and Lessing, none the less challenged their conclusions and developed a different theory of art. In the wake of Locke and Hume and influenced by his Königsberg friend and mentor, Johann Georg Hamann (the most consistent German critic of Enlightenment thought), he rejected rationalism in aesthetics. For Herder, there cannot be any universally valid rules governing art. Herder is not a systematic, but an eclectic thinker, whose views on aesthetics, scattered throughout his voluminous writings, are not always consistent. But he always emphasizes the individuality and historical nature of all art. No one culture can establish a canon of aesthetic judgement. Each age, each nation, each individual is different and has to be appreciated accordingly. Arguing against Sulzer, he maintains that history is a process. He thus jettisons Winckelmann's conception of art based on the primacy of the Greek achievement. But the historical approach by itself is not adequate either. It is also imperative to study the origins of art in human nature, to approach art from the point of view of psychology (in Herder's view, associative psychology) and anthropology. Baumgarten's aesthetics had, in his view, been unduly restricted by his debt to traditional poetics and rhetoric. Art is rooted in the senses and expresses a spiritual energy and experience of which logic is ignorant. No extrinsic standard can do justice to a work of art; for each work contains its own rules. Herder, a Lutheran clergyman by profession, also sought to discover divine attributes in human artefacts. Analysis is to uncover what the senses have obscurely grasped, viz. the spiritual energy emanating from God inherent in a work of art.

Aesthetics can establish rules, but they are always empirical propositions based on the study of existing works of art. It cannot – and here he explicitly disagrees with Baumgarten – give any advice to artists. A man of genius is an artist of pronounced individuality. He is able to create a whole work which has originated in his mind. He gives coherence to manifold phenomena and thus endows his work with beauty. For beauty is the harmony between outward and inward existence. It is the sensuous expression of inner life. The richer an inner life a work of art conveys, the more perfect and the more beautiful it will appear. At its most striking, a genius has divine inspiration and thus original power and creates a coherent world in which we can and do believe. Shakespeare is the prime example. He creates illusion but we forget it is illusion; for everything appears to us natural, necessary, and real. We share the poet's ideas and identify ourselves with the hero of his work.

Although all artistic creations are individual, Herder still believes in certain general principles, albeit somewhat metaphysical ones. He holds that '*space, time* and *force* are the basic concepts'.[25] They are irreducible, as are the beautiful and the good. Indeed, '*beauty is the principal term of all aesthetics*'[26] and 'the outward appearance of truth'.[27] He even predicts that one day the '*science of beautiful semblance*'[28] will be based on mathematics and physics. He also insists that art is always permeated by reflective activity. In his *Critical Groves* (*Kritische Wälder*) (1769), particularly in the last and fourth part of the work, and in *On Plastic Art* (*Plastik*) (1778) he elaborates his ideas on the physiological basis of art. Each of the senses is related to a specific form of art, each of which has its own rules. Sight creates distance. Closest to the intellect, it is an organ of perception, but it is also the sense least capable of moving us. It deals with extension as well as with relationships and contrasts, especially with those between light and darkness in various gradations. The medium appropriate to it is painting. The sense of hearing is located deepest within us. Sound which exercises great power over our soul permits communication and allows us to experience phenomena in the form of succession in time. The appropriate medium is music.

The significance of touch, the third major sense, has not been properly understood, Herder claims. The sense of touch has developed a high sensitivity and allows us to ascertain the nature of our body and the bodies of others. Its medium is sculpture. The sculptor imitates touch by means of corporeal form which has no perspective; for its point of view resides within the work itself. A beautiful corporeal form constitutes an autonomous whole. In contrast to painting which is by comparison only a dream, it is truth, for 'the body which the eye sees is only surface; the surface which the hand feels is body'.[29] Thus, painting

---

[25] 'wie ... *Raum, Zeit* und *Kraft* drei Grundbegriffe sind'; *Erstes Kritisches Wäldchen*, § 16 (SW, III, p. 137; cf. also *Über die neuere Deutsche Literatur. Fragmente* (1766–7), III, 1, § 11; SW, I, pp. 419f.).

[26] '*Schönheit ist das Hauptwort aller Ästhetik*'; *Viertes Kritisches Wäldchen*, II, § 1 (SW, IV, p. 46).

[27] '*Schönheit ist nur die äußere Gestalt der Wahrheit*' *(Schulreden) Vom Begrif der schönen Wißenschaften, insonderheit für die Jugend* (1782?) (SW, XXX, p. 80).

[28] '*Wißenschaft des schönen Anscheins*', *Viertes Kritisches Wäldchen*, II, § 5 (SW, IV, p. 89).

[29] 'Der Körper, den das Auge sieht, ist nur Fläche: die Fläche, die die Hand tastet, ist Körper'; *Plastik* (1778), I, 2 (SW, VIII, p. 8).

relates to space, music to time, and sculpture to force which is the primary category.

Arguing against Lessing, he believes that poetry is not adequately defined as a succession in time. Its power resides in the energy inherent in the words which refuel the poetic spirit. It arouses the imagination. It makes us believe in the sensuous reality of its imagery. It is an energized succession of sounds in time, a melody of representation. It is sensuous speech and unites time and space. It also conveys the experience of the organic unity underlying artistic creation. Art is not in conflict with morality. Beauty is an expression of the good, but that does not mean a work of art ought to be avowedly didactic; for that would thwart its intention. The aim of art is to arouse pleasure. Only by doing so can it teach and make a moral impact. In his late treatise *Kalligone* (1800) Herder also attacks Kant and asserts that the beautiful corresponds to the (morally) good because it springs from an idea which reflects harmony of being.

Immanuel Kant, with whom Herder had studied at Königsberg, rigorously examined the philosophical foundations of aesthetics and successfully vindicated aesthetics as a philosophical discipline. In the first edition of the *Critique of Pure Reason* (1781) he had used the term 'transcendental aesthetics' to denote the 'science of all *a priori* principles of sensuousness'.[30] In the second edition of the *Critique of Pure Reason* (1787) he still dismissed as an impossible undertaking the attempt by Baumgarten (whom he greatly esteemed) to establish *a priori* principles (that is, principles which are logically independent of experience) of taste since he believed that aesthetics consists merely of empirical propositions.[31] But by 1790, only three years later, although aesthetics was, in his opinion, incapable of becoming a science, he thought it worthwhile coming to terms with the issue raised by Baumgarten and decided, in the *Critique of Judgement*, to provide a thorough account of the nature and status of aesthetic judgements. To understand Kant's account properly, one must view it in the context of his critical philosophy. He wrote the *Critique of Judgement* because he considered that it was not sufficient to have defined the limits of theoretical (or scientific) knowledge in the *Critique of Pure Reason* (1781), and the nature of moral decisions in the *Critique of Practical Reason* (1788). There is, in his view, a need to mediate between these two logically independent but compatible realms, nature and freedom, or scientific knowledge and moral action. For our freedom can be realized only in the world of nature. 'There must, therefore, be a ground for this *unity* of the supersensible

---

[30] 'Eine Wissenschaft von allen Prinzipien der Sinnlichkeit *a priori* nenne ich die *transcendentale Ästhetik*' (AA, IV, p. 30; repeated in second edition AA, III, p. 50).
[31] AA, III, p. 50 (originally stated in the first edition AA, IV, p. 30).

[the noumenal] which lies at the basis of nature with that which the notion of freedom contains as the practically real'.[32] This ground must be conceived in such a way that 'it makes possible the transition from the mode of thinking which is in accordance with the principles of nature to that which is in accordance with the principles of freedom'.[33] Reflective judgement (by which Kant means a judgement which is contemplative and does not set out to use determinate concepts to establish knowledge) provides *a priori* principles in order to establish the required unity between nature and freedom.

Kant wrote within the philosophical tradition of his time and used the conception, nowadays no longer in fashion, of three faculties, namely understanding, reason and judgement. Understanding provides determinate concepts which allow us to subsume the realm of nature under universally and objectively valid laws. Reason provides synthetic *a priori* propositions (that is, *a priori* propositions which are capable of contradiction) on which knowledge and moral decisions can be based. The faculties of understanding and reason accordingly deal with the problem of deriving particular laws from universal rules, but there is still the need to subsume particular phenomena under universal rules. That is the function of judgement. It does not deal with knowledge, which is the task of understanding, nor with freedom as reason does, but bases its activity on *a priori* principles which make us look for concepts which are not yet given.

In order to be able to discover general rules we have to assume that the phenomena which we encounter are part of a system which possesses unity and constitutes a whole; for if they were only individual, unrelated particular entities, we could not make sense of anything. Thus, we attribute 'purposiveness'[34] to them without maintaining, let alone knowing, that they are created for a purpose. For instance, we claim that all parts of an organism have a purpose in relation to the organism as a whole without maintaining that nature had a purpose in mind when it created the organism. But we use the notion of 'purposiveness' as a heuristic principle in order to enable us to understand the organism. This is a subjective principle in so far as it is not grounded in knowledge of the object. But it is also an objective principle since, in order to understand the object, we have no choice but to proceed in this way. Thus, when we attribute a purpose or an end to history, for instance,

---

[32] 'Also muß es doch einen Grund der *Einheit* des Übersinnlichen [des Noumenalen], welches der Natur zum Grunde liegt, mit dem, was den Freiheitsbegriff praktisch enthält, geben'; *Critique of Judgement*, [Second] Introduction, II (AA, V, p. 176).

[33] 'wovon der Begriff ... dennoch den Übergang von der Denkungsart nach den Prinzipien des einen [Natur] zu der nach den Prinzipien des andern [Freiheit] möglich macht'; *Critique of Judgement*, [Second] Introduction, II (AA, V, p. 176).

[34] Cf. *Critique of Judgement*, [Second] Introduction, IV (AA, V, p. 180).

we make a teleological judgement because we assume that this is the only way in which we can understand history. And it is profitable, and not only profitable but necessary, to employ this principle as a heuristic method. However, it does not confer objective knowledge since it is not based on determinate concepts. Similarly, when we make an aesthetic judgement – that is, a judgement whether an object is beautiful or not – we do not claim that the object has any specific properties; for that would be the task of the understanding. The judgement refers only to our feelings, the feelings of pleasure and pain, and is, therefore, merely reflective, not scientific or moral. The pleasure which we experience springs from the feeling that we imagine a sense of 'purposiveness' which we can assume to be subject to a law.[35] As Kant put it, 'beauty is the form of the purposiveness of an object in so far as it is perceived apart from the representation of a purpose'.[36]

Disinterestedness is a necessary feature of aesthetic judgements; for they are neither cognitive nor ethical. Hence they are indifferent to the purpose of the object. However, they are concerned with a particular object and fall under a universal rule. To explain his argument, Kant uses the example of a palace. When we call it beautiful we do not maintain that we refer to, or know anything about, any of its properties or characteristics, nor do we answer the question whether the palace ought to have been built or not – whether, for instance, the money spent on it was invested wisely or squandered.

Aesthetic judgements must be strictly distinguished from judgements concerning the agreeable. For a judgement of the latter kind is interested. We maintain, for instance, that the object concerned gratifies our appetites. But to call an object agreeable is a purely personal judgement and does not claim universal validity; for we have no right to claim that other people, too, ought to find it agreeable. We can merely discover the assent of other people by empirical observation and at best ascribe to our judgement some measure of general validity on empirical grounds. But we can put forward the claim that everyone ought to possess taste, which entails appraising an object independently of its content. When we maintain that someone lacks taste, we imply that taste is not a private matter, but a quality which can be universally communicated and which calls for universal approbation (though we may, of course, be mistaken in our appraisal). We call an object beautiful because it makes us conscious of the harmony between the imagination, on the one hand (which in Kant's terminology is the capacity that enables us to become aware of the manifold instances in the world of nature) and

---

[35] Cf. *Critique of Judgement*, § 35 (AA, V, p. 287).
[36] '*Schönheit* ist Form der *Zweckmäßigkeit* eines Gegenstandes, sofern sie *ohne Vorstellung eines Zweckes* an ihm wahrgenommen wird'; *Critique of Judgement*, § 7 (AA, V. p. 236).

the understanding on the other (the faculty which provides concepts for the purpose of uniting these instances). But the awareness of that harmony is not linked to concepts that can be defined or determined. It refers only to universal rules which we cannot name. Moreover, since it is not derived from experience it is not an empirical, but an *a priori* judgement.

Kant is concerned not merely with the beautiful, but, in accordance with the intellectual interests of the time, also with the sublime, which he had already discussed in his essay on *Observations on the Sense of the Beautiful and the Sublime* (*Beobachtungen über das Gefühl des Schönen und Erhabenen*) (1764). But in the *Critique of Judgement* he takes issue with Edmund Burke's treatise *A Philosophical Enquiry into the Origin of our Ideas of the Sublime and Beautiful* (1756) and explicitly rejects his empirical approach. For to call an object sublime is to make an aesthetic judgement, i.e. an *a priori* one. It is a very different judgement from that which calls an object beautiful, since the latter judgement entails awareness of form. For in calling an object sublime we imply that it lacks all form – indeed, it appears to do violence to the imagination. Yet it is precisely for that reason that we consider the object to be sublime: it transgresses the bounds of what we can conceive by the use of our imagination. It has magnitude or power, that is, it possesses either mathematical or dynamic sublimity. But it is never the object of nature as such which we call sublime – indeed, objects of nature cannot in themselves be sublime since they can be measured – but the view which we take of an object in our own mind.

When we call an object sublime our reaction is entirely mental and refers to the totality of things. Our judgement is based on our awareness of the faculty of reason which surpasses the limits of the world of sense. That experience renders our imagination and understanding helpless and we consequently suffer pain. Yet as rational beings, we simultaneously feel pleasure because we can fall back on reason, which derives its legitimacy from the noumenal world and which gives us freedom to feel superior to any object in the phenomenal world.

As to art itself, a work of art is created in accordance with rules, but when the artist creates a work of art he is incapable of knowing them. For if he knew them, they could be communicated and would belong to the realm of theoretical (scientific) knowledge. But art is not something that can be learnt. Nor can its characteristics in any way be defined. Kant here radically differs from Baumgarten, as he also does when he maintains that perfection is not a necessary trait of a work of art. In Kant's view, art is not like nature, but beautiful art conveys the impression that it is a product of nature. The genuinely original artist is a genius who creates his own rules, which are contained in the work of art. 'Genius is the talent (natural ability) which gives the rules to art'.[37] None of these rules can be spelt out – no artist knows the secret of his creative power – nor can they be imitated. They can serve only as an example to inspire other artists; for originality cannot be learnt. Yet originality, which is a necessary quality in an artist, is not sufficient either; for a work of art could be original nonsense. It has to contain an intellectual power of its own, that is, it should be pervaded by what Kant calls *Geist*.[38] We can expect from the artist the intention to make his work beautiful, but this is once again not a definite objective pur-pose, but merely points to his desire to bring about, with the help of intellectual power (*Geist*), the harmony of the faculties. If that is achieved, an 'Aesthetic Idea'[39] is embodied in his work. By an 'Aesthetic Idea' Kant understands a 'representation of the imagination which induces much thought, yet to which no definite thought whatsoever, that is, no *concept* can be adequate, and which cannot be fully and completely rendered intelligible in any language'.[40] An 'Aesthetic Idea' is, then, something that stirs up emotional forces, that is, it is a form of play which is autonomous, possesses evocative power, transcends the limits of the phenomenal world and serves as a symbol of the supersensible world. Kant thus goes beyond a purely rationalist conception of art and aesthetic experience. Moreover, he now once more links ethics and aesthetics, which, following Baumgarten, he had strictly separated. Aesthetic judgements can be symbols for moral decisions. In other words, although 'Aesthetic Ideas' can never be adequately exemplified, let alone defined, they can be symbolized. (This is also true of 'Practical Ideas'.) When we call an object beautiful we also imply that it is morally good. In support of his argument Kant cites examples which show that we tend to use analogies taken from the realm of morality when talking about beautiful objects just as we often use analogies from the realm of aesthetics when we describe moral actions, thus revealing our belief that awareness of beauty symbolizes the morally good.[41]

---

[37] '*Genie* ist das Talent (Naturgabe), welches der Kunst die Regel gibt'; *Critique of Judgement*, § 46 (AA, V, p. 307).

[38] *Critique of Judgement*, § 49 (AA, V, p. 313). 'Geist' is a word which is difficult to translate. It is usually best rendered by 'mind' or 'spirit', but here 'intellectual power' is more appropriate.

[39] 'Ästhetische Idee'; *Critique of Judgement*, § 49 (AA, V, pp. 314ff.).

[40] 'Unter einer ästhetischen Idee aber verstehe ich diejenige Vorstellung der Einbildungskraft, die viel zu denken veranlaßt, ohne daß ihr doch ein bestimmter Gedanke, d. i. *Begriff* adäquat sein kann, die folglich keine Sprache völlig erreicht und verständlich machen kann'; *Critique of Judgement*, § 49 (AA, V, p. 314).

[41] To draw political conclusions from Kant's aesthetics, as Terry Eagleton does in his *Ideology of the Aesthetic* (Oxford, 1990) is, however, ill-founded. For a discussion of Kant's politics, cf. Hans Reiss (ed.), *Kant: Political Writings* (2nd enlarged edn, Cambridge, 1991) and Patrick Riley, *Kant's Political Philosophy* (Totowa, NJ, 1983), particularly pp. 71ff. for a discussion of the role played by the *Critique of Judgement* in Kant's political thought.

Goethe strongly disliked philosophical rationalism, but greatly admired Kant's *Critique of Judgement*. His relatively infrequent comments on aesthetics are, in the main, merely incidental remarks or aphorisms. For him art needs to be rooted in tangible reality, but at the same time it should reflect the mind of the artist; for there needs to be a continuous interchange between mind and matter. The genuine artist chooses the material (*Stoff*) and gives it the appropriate form (*Form*) as well as the import (*Gehalt*) which comes from his inner life, but this import can be grasped only through the form. The import makes art dignified and important and ensures that the specific phenomenon implies general validity. But the general aspect is not an abstract idea foisted on to a specific phenomenon; it emerges from it quite naturally. For Goethe believes in the intrinsic unity of mind and matter. It is not the outer form that counts, but the inner form which comprises all forms within itself. It acts as a focus bringing unity to diversity and is thus able to affect our feelings.[42]

Beauty, for Goethe, is in fact a basic phenomenon of nature (*Urphänomen*) which the artist can express if he creates a work which possesses organic unity – that is, a work whose whole character is conveyed by each of its parts and all of whose parts point to the unity of the whole work, to a centre around which the whole work revolves, however much complexity and diversity and however many contrasts and gradations it reveals.[43] Great art, like nature, is organic and gives the impression of necessity. Yet it is also autonomous and has to be distinguished from nature. For in art truth and fiction are blended into a whole whose imaginary existence can cast a spell on us. Aesthetic judgements are about art and must not be influenced by extrinsic considerations, whether theological, philosophical or political. Art is didactic, but always indirectly so; to teach must never be its ostensible purpose.

Art brings to light the latent laws of nature which would otherwise have remained concealed. The Greeks knew the secret of art, which the genius intuitively grasps but which cannot be precisely defined. Hence the Greeks provide a model for modern artists to emulate. Their achievement suggests that the greatest product of art, as of nature, is the beautiful human being. Although Goethe wrote classicistic works only for a relatively short period – two decades at most – of a long creative life, his taste in the figurative arts remained wholly classical. Even when writing about a Gothic cathedral such as that of Strasbourg, he singles out those characteristics which correspond to the classicistic notions which he had learnt from his art teacher Adam Friedrich Oeser and imbibed from Winckelmann.

[42] Cf. *Aus Goethes Brieftasche* (1776) (HA, XII, p. 22).
[43] Cf. *Zum Shakespeares-Tag* (1771) (HA, XII, p. 226).

Friedrich Schiller, the other great German classical poet, in his early years strongly defended the moral purpose of theatre in a lecture entitled *Die Schaubühne als eine moralische Anstalt betrachtet* (*The Stage Considered as a Moral Institution*) (1784), perhaps in response to Rousseau's censure of the theatre in the *Lettre à d'Alembert sur les spectacles* (1758) (discussed on pp. 506f. of this volume). But in his mature years, after he had come under the influence of Kant, he developed a far more complex and subtle theory. At first he sought to improve on Kant's aesthetics by constructing a system which he intended to expand in a treatise entitled *Kallias or on Beauty* (*Kallias oder über die Schönheit*). He intended to argue that aesthetic judgements are objective synthetic *a priori* propositions.[44] But he did not complete that work, presumably because he realized that he had not succeeded in establishing the objectivity of aesthetic judgements. He did, however, give an outline of his projected theory in a series of letters to his friend Christian Gottfried Körner between 25 January and 28 February 1793, now usually referred to as the 'Kallias Letters', which were published only after his death. He hoped to develop a sensuous and objective conception of beauty, containing both rational and empirical components, which would provide us with objective principles of taste. For Schiller, aesthetic judgements belong to the realm of practical, and not theoretical, reason. But they differ from moral judgements, which are grounded in the realm of practical reason alone, since beautiful objects, although emanating from the realm of reason and thus of freedom, exist in the realm of nature. Hence, in a celebrated phrase, Schiller characterizes beauty as 'freedom in appearance'.[45]

In order to define beauty it is necessary to show that beauty is not, like morality, determined by reason alone, but also by nature; to define it, therefore, requires empirical principles as well. They are found in what Schiller calls the 'technical form' of the object. Freedom can be sensuously represented only with the help of the technical.[46] A 'technical' form is the form which is appropriate to the object: for instance, a certain size and a slender appearance are necessarily appropriate to a beech-tree if it is to be called beautiful. But another feature is equally essential, namely the 'heautonomy'[47] of an object, that is, its self-determination which is revealed to intuition (*Anschauung*). An object can be called beautiful only if its outer form determines its inner being and hence its own rules. Schiller strongly emphasizes – and he is here very close to

---

[44] Cf. his letter to Prince Friedrich Christian of Schleswig-Holstein-Augustenburg, 9 February 1793 (*Briefe*, III, pp. 247ff.).

[45] 'Freiheit in der Erscheinung'; letter of 23 February 1793 to Christian Gottfried Körner (*Briefe*, III, pp. 265ff.).

[46] 'Technik'; letter of 23 February 1793 to Körner (*Briefe*, III, pp. 268f.).

[47] 'Heautonomie'; letter of 23 February 1793 to Körner (*Briefe*, III, p. 274).

Kant – that beauty depends on form, but, in contrast to Kant, he believes that it is possible to identify the form of a beautiful object. He claims that a poem, for instance, is beautiful if each of its parts, each verse, each rhyme, appears independent and necessary and yet belongs to the whole. A work must appear beautiful to us without our having regard to its idea. Beauty is nature that has become art, an art that is like nature.

Schiller incorporated the material of the projected *Kallias* treatise in his major treatise *On the Aesthetic Education of Man, in a Series of Letters* (*Über die ästhetische Erziehung des Menschen in einer Reihe von Briefen* (generally referred to as the *Aesthetic Letters*) (1795). In this work, he went far beyond the customary limits of aesthetics, for he sought not merely to vindicate the autonomy of art and aesthetics by philosophical means, but also to define the role of the artist in the modern world and to show how art and aesthetic experience are capable of healing man's inward division and social disharmony. The *Aesthetic Letters* are an ambitious and complex work, much of whose argument consists of cultural and social analysis which is beyond the scope of this account. Suffice it to say that Schiller believed that aesthetic experience alone is able to promote social harmony and political stability. Moreover, he was convinced that Kant's conception of morality and politics is inadequate. The call of duty, both in public and in private life, can be effective only if it coincides with inclination – that is, morality and nature ought to be one.

More relevant to aesthetics proper is Schiller's view that human life is characterized by the antagonism of two drives (*Triebe*) which are in perpetual conflict. Schiller, who habitually sees life in the form of antitheses, calls them the 'sensuous drive', which arises from man's physical nature, and the 'formal drive' which arises from his rational nature. These two drives are in constant conflict, and only a third drive, the 'play-drive', is capable of uniting them by at the same time overcoming them. This drive brings form to matter, and matter to form, and thus creates beauty. It takes pleasure in semblance within which the living form (*Gestalt*) can prevail. Beautiful semblance is not just an imaginary fiction; it has an autonomous reality of its own, and is neither merely matter or sense, nor mind or form. The play-drive gives rise to aesthetic experience or an aesthetic condition which affects not just one or other part of our personality, but the 'whole man'. It conveys to us the feeling of being a whole person. 'With beauty man shall *only play*, and it is *only with beauty that he shall play*.'[48] In creating a beautiful object the artist imposes his will on matter without leaving the world of sense. To

[48] 'Der Mensch soll mit der Schönheit *nur spielen*, und er soll *nur mit der Schönheit* Spielen' (Schiller, *Über die ästhetische Erziehung*, ed. Wilkinson and Willoughby, 15th letter, pp. 106f.).

do this he must distance himself from his age, though such distancing does not entail his being indifferent to the age's problems. Indeed, the aesthetic experience, as well as the artist and art itself, can have a central and beneficial function in society, for without artistic creation, social life would not only be poorer, but also less cohesive. Schiller also attempts to solve the problem of the relationship between ethics and aesthetics by arguing that the aesthetic experience amounts to, or results from, a blending of moral thought and natural form into an autonomous whole.

Like Schiller, Wilhelm von Humboldt was also influenced by Kant, whose aesthetics he wished to develop further by establishing certain objective principles. He set these out in the *Essais esthétiques* (1799) which he wrote for Mme de Staël and in his essay on Goethe's epic poem *Hermann and Dorothea* (1798). For Humboldt, the basic problem to be solved by any artist is 'to turn into *image* that which is *real* in nature'.[49] The artist can do so with the help of the imagination, but he can do so only if his imagination arouses the imagination of the beholder or reader. This can be done only indirectly by an object which the artist creates. Art possesses the ability to make the imagination productive in accordance with laws. '*Art is the ability to represent nature by the imagination alone, which acts freely and independently.*'[50] Its task is to idealize reality, but that does not mean that it is purely intellectual. It ought to stimulate our imagination in such a way that we forget the imperfections of existence. (Humboldt may be indebted to Karl Philipp Moritz for this notion, for Moritz argued that a work of art ought to be 'something complete in itself'[51] which makes us forget ourselves.) Just as the artist's enthusiasm needs to be aroused so that he can create a genuine work of art, so our enthusiasm needs similarly to be kindled by the work of art. To do this, the imagination must be able to suppress all modes of cognition.

A work of art arouses a particular form of pleasure which involves both thought and feelings. If it fails to do so it cannot be beautiful. Indeed, it can be considered to be beautiful only if it is created in accordance with the laws which determine all genuine art. Humboldt lays down these laws in relation to the epic poem, but he also implies that they have general validity. A beautiful work of art must possess,

[49] 'Le problème général que ... tous les artistes ... ont à résoudre, c'est de transformer en *image* ce qui, dans la nature, est *réel*; *Essais esthétiques* (*Selbstanzeige über Hermann und Dorothea*) (GS, III, p. 1).

[50] 'L'art est le talent de représenter la nature par la seule imagination, libre et indépendante dans son action' (GS, III, p. 15).

[51] '*In sich selbst Vollendetes*'; *Versuch einer Verbindung aller schönen Künste und Wissenschaften unter dem Begriff des in sich selbst Vollendeten. An Herrn Moses Mendelssohn* (1785) (Moritz, *Schriften*, p. 3).

firstly, the highest possible degree of sensuousness; secondly, consistency; thirdly, unity, so that all its parts together make up a coherent whole; fourthly, equilibrium, so that the work can be viewed in a detached manner and our attention is not diverted by the material (*Stoff*); fifthly, it must possess totality, by which Humboldt means that we must not be attracted by a particular part of the work, but must feel free to view it as a whole; finally, the work of art must not contradict what he calls the laws of the imagination, since the imagination alone is capable of liberating us from the shackles of normal existence and dependence on the phenomena of nature.[52] A work of art creates illusion, a semblance which is more lasting than the products of nature. The work of art thus created does not exhibit anything superfluous; indeed, all its parts appear necessary. It is as it is, and it is wholly so. It does represent an idea, but the idea is inherent in the form and cannot be separated from it. It calms our passions, does not arouse desire, allows us to enjoy pure enthusiasm, and leads us back to ourselves. We recognize the work of a genius because our imagination overpowers our whole psyche. It can do so because the genius has followed his own bent fully and independently. He has transformed the representation of nature into something beautiful without consciously intending to do so. Humboldt applied these views to his discussion of *Hermann and Dorothea*, a classicistic verse epic by Goethe, to which they are indeed appropriate. It is, however, a moot point whether they can also be applied to different genres or different styles of writing.

In Germany aesthetics was, during the second half of the eighteenth century, not merely an academic discipline reserved for lecture-halls and learned journals but a topic which engaged the minds of the foremost writers and poets – Goethe and Schiller, Lessing and Herder. These men would not have written on aesthetics unless it had mattered to them. Aesthetics vindicated their imaginative achievement by philosophical means, for in a changing world they wished to come to terms with the character and standing of their work. This concern was undoubtedly part of the secularization of life in the Western world which gathered pace in the eighteenth century as scientists and philosophers sought to free themselves from the tutelage of theology. Poets, writers and artists, too, wanted to be no longer shackled by external restraint. Their belief in the power and function of the genius reinforced their conviction that art and literature ought to be appraised without reference to external criteria. Moreover, imaginative literature was gradually replacing writings on religion as the favourite reading matter. Since the tares had to

---

[52] *Ästhetische Versuche. Erster Teil. Über Goethes Hermann und Dorothea*, LXXXII–LXXXVII (GS, II, pp. 106f.).

be separated from the wheat, it appeared increasingly urgent to establish sound canons of literary criticism which did not need to be justified by reference either to established authorities or to theology, ethics and politics. In this respect, aesthetics also served to underpin literary criticism. Its philosophical rigour gave the critics confidence since it made criticism appear a serious and respectable undertaking. Not surprisingly, the leading writers and poets engaged in literary criticism, and their criticism, which is of the highest quality, was in turn greatly influenced by their views on aesthetics.

In seeking to establish the autonomy of art and literature, of criticism and aesthetics, these pioneers in philosophical aesthetics felt that it was imperative to define the relationship between ethics and aesthetics anew. The German Enlightenment or *Aufklärung* had acquired a strong moral tendency which also permeated its literature. (Even Lessing still expected tragedy to have a moral function; for him, 'catharsis' in Aristotle's *Poetics* has the meaning not of 'purging', but of 'purifying' the emotions of fear and pity.) Shaftesbury's and Hutcheson's conviction of the close analogy between the beautiful and the good (cf. pp. 622 and 635 above) made a powerful impact on German writers. Baumgarten's argument that beauty had a status equal to scientific truth and morality echoed and reinforced this conviction. Herder and Kant, Goethe and Schiller, while insisting on the autonomy of art and aesthetic judgement, maintained that ethics constituted an integral part of aesthetics but did not determine it. Their argument carried the day. To have established the primacy of the autonomous aesthetic judgement is, then, a central feature of German classical aesthetics and represents a genuine intellectual advance which has to be defended, even today, against those who, for reasons of ideology, seek to judge literature and art primarily by reference to moral or political criteria.

The rise of aesthetics has also to be seen in its social context. In the eighteenth century French taste prevailed at most German courts. As a consequence, the new aesthetics was in Germany first and foremost a middle-class concern. It was first promoted not by rulers, courtiers or aristocrats, but by university professors. This is not surprising, for the *Aufklärung* was far more professorial in tone and character than its English and French counterparts. Unlike those of England and France, some at least of the German universities played an important part in literary life throughout the eighteenth century. Admittedly, they were only marginally better than their English and French equivalents. Yet there were many of them, scattered among the many principalities of the Empire, and this increased the mobility of professors and their academic freedom. Moreover, special privileges made it relatively easy for professors to evade the censorship. No prince's writ was binding

throughout the German territories. Writers and artists were more likely
to take note of academic publications, especially since there were, in
comparison with England and France, so few men of letters who attracted public attention. For instance, major reforms of the German
language and of the German theatre were initiated by a Leipzig university professor, Johann Christoph Gottsched (cf. pp. 187f. and 522 *et
seq.* above). Gottsched's reforms laid the foundations of the classical
German theatre and led to the national theatre movement, a symbol of
German cultural aspirations. (Since the Holy Roman Empire was not a
unified state, culture became the focus of national aspirations long before
the demand for a politically unified state arose.) To discuss art and
literature was, therefore, of great topical relevance. There was in any
case little opportunity for anyone, apart from those who wrote on
constitutional or administrative law, to engage in public political debate
before the French Revolution, so that much intellectual energy was
devoted to cultivating the inner life. Thus, aesthetics could quickly become
a central issue in eighteenth-century German intellectual life. The fact
that well-known university teachers, such as Baumgarten, Meier and
Kant, championed the new discipline furthered the belief that the arts
mattered on their own account. German philosophers and writers thus
laid the philosophical foundations of that earlier scholarly study of
literature and the fine arts which, absorbing the tradition of poetics and
rhetoric, became institutionalized in the nineteenth-century German universities, now pre-eminent in the world. It has flourished ever since.

The establishment of aesthetics as a philosophical discipline was, despite Diderot's prestige and influence, essentially a German achievement.
Of course, reflections on art appeared outside Germany, too. For instance, some of the classicistic views which Winckelmann and his successors expressed correspond to ideas put forward in England by Sir
Joshua Reynolds in his *Discourses* (1769–90). According to Reynolds,
the artist has to correct, indeed to idealize, nature. It is the task of art
'to strike the imagination'.[53] The laws of art require that the parts be
subordinated to the whole. Variety, novelty and contrast are principles
which the artist should observe, but only within certain bounds; for if
they are taken to excess, they impair and even preclude pleasure. But
Reynolds writes mainly from the point of view of a practising artist; his
theoretical remarks are incidental and he does not use the word 'aesthetic'. For, characteristically, it was a long time before the term 'aesthetics' took root in the English language[54] – far longer than in France,

---

[53] Reynolds, *Discourses*, IV, p. 59.
[54] The first use of the term 'aesthetic' in English most probably occurs in *Thoughts of
Jesting, or the Merry Philosopher*, by George Frederick Meier (London, 1764), pp.
11f.; a second edition or reprint was published in 1765. This is a translation of

for instance, where it appears to have been introduced already in 1753 and, probably at the suggestion of J. G. Sulzer, found its way into the 1771 supplement of the *Encyclopédie*.[55] It took another few decades before the word became fully accepted as part of the common English linguistic and intellectual currency. Today it is so widely used that few people are aware of its relatively recent origin.

The rise of aesthetics is, then, a remarkable chapter of intellectual history which began in the pages of an obscure master's dissertation written in 1735 by a young philosophy student in the University of Halle and which led, within a century or so, to the general use of the term 'aesthetics' throughout the Western world and to a different way of thinking about the arts.[56]

Georg Friedrich Meier's *Gedancken von Schertzen* (Halle, 1744). However, since the *Oxford English Dictionary* lists a translation from Kant by the distinguished translator William Taylor of Norwich (1798) as the first occurrence, it appears to have become accepted in the English-speaking world only a generation later at the earliest. Euroscepticism is, thus, hardly of recent origin.

[55] *Supplément à l'Encyclopédie* (Amsterdam, 1771), II, pp. 872f. quoted by Chouillet, 'Littérature et esthétique', p. 1,644.

[56] Work for this essay was aided by a grant from the German Academic Exchange Service, for which I should like to record my thanks since it enabled me to study in the libraries of the University of Heidelberg.

29

Literature and the other arts

(i) *Ut pictura poesis*
David Marshall

In his *Philosophical Enquiry into the Origin of Our Ideas of the Sublime and Beautiful*, Burke argued that the effect of words 'does not arise by forming pictures of the several things they would represent in the imagination'. Insisting that 'on a very diligent examination of my own mind, and getting others to consider theirs, I do not find that once in twenty times any such picture is formed', Burke asserts: 'Indeed, so little does poetry depend for its effect on the power of raising sensible images, that I am convinced it would lose a very considerable part of its energy, if this were the necessary result of all description.'[1] As Burke's appeal to empiricism suggests, however, it was not at all uncommon in 1757 (the year the *Enquiry* was published) to assume that words, especially words in poems, could represent and even present pictures. Nine years later, in 1766, when Lessing set out to delineate the effects of painting and poetry in his *Laocoön*, he announced his intention to counteract the 'false taste' and 'unfounded judgements' that had converted Simonides' assertion that paintings were silent poems and poems were speaking pictures into a set of rules for artists and critics.[2]

Both Lessing and Burke sought to refute different aspects of the tradition known as *ut pictura poesis* – those famous words that were taken out of context from Horace's *Art of Poetry* to stand for the belief that poetry and painting were or should be alike.[3] Eventually arguments that disputed the power of description to produce images and the analogies between poetry and painting would lead to the undoing of this tradition; but Burke and Lessing were responding to views that had become pervasive

[1] Burke, *Enquiry*, pp. 167, 170.
[2] Lessing, *Laocoön*, p. 5; *Laokoon*, IX, p. 5.
[3] Horace, *Ars Poetica*, v. 361. The term 'poetry' in eighteenth-century comparisons generally was used in the way we would use 'literature'; it could refer to dramatic as well as epic poetry, as well as lyric modes. It also gradually encompassed the novel, although most treatises on aesthetics did not find it decorous to discuss novels.

by the second half of the eighteenth century. If the eighteenth century saw the demise of *ut pictura poesis*, it first saw its culmination. When the Abbé Du Bos chose the words 'Ut Pictura Poesis' as the epigraph for his influential *Réflexions critiques sur la poésie et sur la peinture*, published in 1719, he summarized and prefigured much eighteenth-century writing about art. By 1746, in *Les Beaux-Arts réduits à un même principe*, the Abbé Batteux could suggest that after having written a chapter on poetry, he hardly needed to write a chapter on painting. It would almost be enough, he wrote, to re-read his first chapter, substituting the word 'painting' wherever the word 'poetry' appeared.[4]

Representing the idea that works of literature and works of painting were or should be alike, *ut pictura poesis* overlapped with several related traditions, most importantly the tradition of viewing literature and painting as 'sister arts'.[5] The Renaissance enterprise of finding 'parallels' between the visual and verbal arts[6] was given new energy in the eighteenth century by the Enlightenment desire to discover universal principles. In the Renaissance, the humanistic attempt to elevate painting to the ranks of the liberal arts encouraged comparisons of the verbal and visual arts.[7] In the eighteenth century, the popularity, diffusion, and reproduction of paintings through prints and engravings contributed to the prestige of painting and an emphasis on the pictorial characteristics to which literary texts could and should aspire. Literary descriptions inspired by *ut pictura poesis* set out to rival paintings, following in the traditions of ekphrastic poetry (in which poems attempted to give voice to a work of graphic art)[8] and Renaissance *paragoni* or contests between the arts.

Yet there was uncertainty and controversy about where to place literature and painting in a hierarchy of the arts. Painting and poetry were each found to possess powers, properties, and effects that the other lacked. Lessing complained that the desire to find parallels and the subsequent confusion of the arts had caused a 'mania for allegory' in painting and a 'mania for description' in poetry.[9] *Ut pictura poesis*, however, was perhaps most influential as a call for literature to act like painting by presenting images and tableaux to the reader or listener. In Du Bos's formulation: 'Il faut donc que nous croïions voir, pour ainsi

---

[4] Batteux, *Les Beaux-Arts réduits à un même principe*, p. 247.
[5] See Hagstrum, *The Sister Arts*.
[6] See Howard, 'Ut pictura poesis', pp. 43–71. See also Hagstrum, *The Sister Arts*, pp. 57–92; and Bender, *Spenser and Literary Pictorialism*.
[7] See Bender, *Spenser and Literary Pictorialism*, p. 10; and Lee, *Ut Pictura Poesis*, pp. 201–2.
[8] See Hagstrum, *The Sister Arts*, p. 18n. See also Hollander, 'The poetics of *ekphrasis*', pp. 209–19.
[9] Lessing, *Laocoön*, p. 5.

dire, en écoutant des Vers: *Ut Pictura Poesis*, dit Horace.'[10] Despite the claims of writers such as Du Bos to reject rules and *a priori* principles, such declarations easily passed from descriptive to prescriptive accounts of art. Although less a formal school or doctrine than a set of beliefs and desires about aesthetic experience, the tradition represented by the slogan *ut pictura poesis* goes beyond the search for parallels between the arts to advocate that poetry should imitate painting.

Of course, Horace's original use of the words *ut pictura poesis* did not advocate the school of thought that came to be associated with the phrase. Discussing theatre in *The Art of Poetry*, he writes: 'Less vividly is the mind stirred by what finds entrance through the ears than by what is brought before the trusty eyes, and what the spectator sees for himself'; but *ut pictura poesis* appears in an innocuous context that is not concerned with a comparison between the verbal and visual arts.[11] As Jean Hagstrum explains, fifteenth- and sixteenth-century editions punctuated Horace's phrase differently: 'Ut pictura poesis erit . . .' rather than 'Ut pictura poesis: erit quae . . .' which makes the text read 'a poem *will be* like a painting' rather than 'it will sometimes happen that'.[12] The influential *De Arte Graphica* by Du Fresnoy, first published in 1667, begins with the words: 'Ut pictura poesis erit; similisque Poesi / Sit pictura . . .' turning Horace's casual comparison into a more programmatic pronouncement: 'As a picture, so a poem will be; likewise let a painting be similar to poetry.'[13] The important 1695 English translation of *The Art of Painting* appeared with 'ut pictura poesis erit' on its title page (fourteen years before Du Bos).[14] Written in Latin by the French critic Charles Alphonse Du Fresnoy in 1637, *De Arte Graphica* was published in French in 1667 with notes by Roger de Piles. The first English translation was published by Dryden in 1695, along with de Piles's commentary, and subsequent translations followed throughout the century, including a verse translation by Defoe in 1720 and an annotated translation by Sir Joshua Reynolds in 1783.[15] Du Fresnoy's often epigrammatic pronouncements are less a detailed comparison of the arts than a series of observations. Especially in Dryden's translation (which changes the opening 'As a picture, so a poem will be . . .'[16] to the less programmatic 'Painting and Poesy are two Sisters') the work emphasizes the general notion of parallels while discriminating between particular areas of superiority or inferiority.

[10] Du Bos, *Réflexions critiques*, I, pp. 278, 273, 274–5.
[11] Horace, *Ars Poetica*, vv. 180–2, 361.
[12] Hagstrum, *The Sister Arts*, pp. 9, 60.
[13] Du Fresnoy, *The Art of Painting*, p. 2; Hagstrum, *The Sister Arts*, p. 174.
[14] Hagstrum, *The Sister Arts*, p. 174.
[15] Hagstrum, *The Sister Arts*, pp. 174–5.
[16] Hagstrum, *The Sister Arts*, pp. 174–5.

'Painting and Poesy are two Sisters', begins the text, 'which are so like in all things, that they mutually lend to each other both their Name and Office. One is called dumb Poesy, and the other a speaking Picture.' They seem to be most alike, however, in their basic aims and standards: 'The Poets have never said any Thing but what they believ'd wou'd please the Ears. And it has been the constant Endeavour of the Painters to give Pleasure to the Eyes. In short, those things which the Poets have thought unworthy of their Pens, the Painters have judg'd to be unworthy of their Pencils.'[17] In his glosses on Du Fresnoy, de Piles cites Tertullian and Cicero to assert the relation, relatedness, and family resemblance between the arts but he emphasizes the concept of mimesis: 'They both of them aim at the same End, which is Imitation. Both of them excite our Passions; and we suffer willingly to be deceiv'd, both by the one, and by the other; our Eyes and Souls are so fixt to them, that we are ready to persuade our selves, that the painted Bodies breathe, and that the Fictions are Truths.'[18] In the eighteenth century the traditional concern with imitation increasingly means a demand for greater verisimilitude, which increasingly is expressed in terms of the effects of the work of art: the power of art not only to move readers or beholders but also to compel their belief.

Dryden prefaced *The Art of Painting* with an essay entitled 'Parallel between Poetry and Painting' (described by Saintsbury as 'the first writing at any length by a very distinguished Englishman of letters on the subject of pictorial art').[19] The actual parallels Dryden asserts between the arts are somewhat general. The essay emphasizes questions of subject-matter, decorum, propriety, and especially imitation. 'To imitate *Nature* well in whatever Subject, is the Perfection of *both Arts*; and that *Picture*, and that *Poem*, which comes nearest the Resemblance of *Nature* is the best.' Beyond these common goals, Dryden depends upon a series of translations or even correspondences between the two arts: for example, 'To make a Sketch, or a more perfect Model of a Picture, is in the language of Poets, to draw up the Scenery of a Play' or '*Expression*, and all that belongs to Words, is that in a *Poem*, which *Colouring* is in a *Picture*.'[20]

While the theories and aesthetic preoccupations grouped under the rubric of *ut pictura poesis* all share a fundamental interest in comparing the arts of literature and painting, the question of parallels invariably leads theorists to make fine distinctions between media, effects, and subject-matter; often a hierarchy is established which clearly demonstrates the superiority of one art over the other, at least in specified areas. In the domain of eighteenth-century literary criticism and aesthetic theory, *ut*

---

[17] *The Art of Painting*, p. 3. [18] *The Art of Painting*, p. 82. [19] Howard, p. 40.
[20] *The Art of Painting*, pp. xxxiv, xlvii, li.

pictura poesis generally involved a privileging of the sense of sight that posed the visual arts as an ideal. 'La vue a plus d'empire sur l'âme que les autres sens', wrote Du Bos. 'On peut dire, metamorphiquement parlant, que l'oeil est plus près de l'âme que l'oreille.'[21] Batteux, who declares, 'l'Homme est né spectateur', also asserts the primacy of sight: 'de tous nos sens, n'y en a-t-il point de plus vif, ni qui nous fournisse plus d'idées que cela de la vûe'.[22] Theories that asserted the power of visual perception did not necessarily conclude that painting was superior to poetry; but the alleged superiority of the visual, at least in terms of the experience of readers and beholders, led to the view that literature should imitate painting by speaking to the sense of sight.

In formulations characteristic of the tradition, Du Bos goes beyond parallels to insist that poetry imitate painting. Indeed, he argues that poetry should produce paintings. In order to move us, writes Du Bos, the writer must 'mettre sous nos yeux par des peintures, les objects dont il nous parle'. The representations of the poet should contain 'des images qui forment des tableaux dans notre imagination'. For Du Bos, 'il faut que ... le stile de la Poësie soit rempli de figures qui peignent si bien les objets décrits dans le vers, que nous ne puissions les entendre, sans que notre imagination soit continuellement remplie des tableaux qui s'y succedent les uns aux autres ... Il faut donc que nous croïions voir, pour ainsi dire, en écoutant des Vers: *Ut Pictura Poesis*, dit Horace.'[23] Kames's *Elements of Criticism*, first published in 1762, contains one of the most explicit and extensive formulations of Du Bos's position in English. Kames also calls for writers to present images and tableaux to their readers. According to Kames, 'Writers of genius, sensible that the eye is the best avenue to the heart, represent every thing as passing in our sight; and, from readers or hearers, transfrom us as it were into spectators.' Kames writes: 'A lively and accurate description ... raises in me ideas no less distinct than if I had been originally an eye-witness: I am insensibly transformed into a spectator; and have an impression that every incident is passing in my presence.' Not only is the reader *like* a spectator; as Kames portrays him the reader *is* a spectator, so strong is his sense of sight.

'The force of language', writes Kames, 'consists in raising complete images; which have the effect to transport the reader as by magic into the very place of the important action, and to convert him as it were into a spectator, beholding every thing that passes.'[24] *Transport*, of course, is a key term in eighteenth-century aesthetics and is particularly if not exclusively associated with the sublime. Longinus (in Welsted's 1724

---

[21] Du Bos, *Réflexions critiques*, I, pp. 386–7.
[22] Batteux, *Traité de la poésie dramatique*, in *Les Beaux-Arts*, p. 2.
[23] Du Bos, *Réflexions critiques*, I, pp. 278, 273, 274–5.
[24] Kames, *Elements of Criticism*, II, p. 248; I, p. 86; II, p. 232.

English translation) speaks of an 'extraordinary Transport of Mind' through which 'we seem to view the things we speak of, and . . . place them in their full light before those who hear us'.[25] Kames may be borrowing more directly from de Piles, who writes that both poetry and painting 'are intended to deceive; and if we do but give attention to them, they will transport us, as it were, magically, out of one country into another'.[26] Kames emphasizes the transport of readers who appear to be carried away by the power of images.

Precedents for such concepts of vivid illusion, especially the illusion of sight, are found in classical rhetoric and poetics, particularly in the recommendation that the orator speak with such vivid images that his listeners could see the objects he described – what came to be known as *enargeia*. In the *Rhetoric* Aristotle declares that words 'ought to set the scene before our eyes'. He praises 'expressions which set things before the eyes'.[27] In the *Poetics*, in terms that would echo in many eighteenth-century expressions of *ut pictura poesis*, especially the *Elements of Criticism*, Aristotle advises the poet to 'put the actual scenes as far as possible before his eyes. In this way, seeing everything with the vividness of an eye-witness as it were, he will devise what is appropriate'.[28] According to Cicero, 'every metaphor, provided it be a good one, has a direct appeal to the senses, especially the sense of sight, which is the keenest'. He instructs the orator that 'the metaphors drawn from the sense of sight are much more vivid, virtually placing within the range of our mental vision objects not actually visible to our sight'.[29]

Incorporating terms and concepts from classical rhetoric and poetics, eighteenth-century critics and theorists also expected writers to move their readers and listeners with vivid, clear, and perspicuous images. However, whereas Aristotle or Cicero may have used commonly understood idioms when they spoke of words placing a scene before the audience's eyes or addressing the sense of sight, after Descartes, Hobbes, Locke, Berkeley, and Hume terms and concepts such as *mental vision* and especially *images* acquired new, complex, and even technical meanings. In a note to the *Laocoön*, Lessing complained, 'What we call "poetic pictures" [*poetische Gemälde*] were *phantasiae* to the ancients . . . And what we call "illusion", the deceptive element of these pictures, they termed *enargeia*.' He argued that 'modern treatises on poetry' should have adopted Plutarch's use of the phrase 'waking dreams' and 'dropped the word "picture" altogether', in which case 'poetical *phantasiae* would not have been so readily confined to the limits of a material painting'.[30]

---

[25] Longinus, *Works*, p. 183.   [26] *The Principles of Painting*, pp. 257–8.
[27] Aristotle, *Rhetoric*, III.x, pp. 399, 405. On *enargeia* and *energeia*, see Hagstrum, *The Sister Arts*, pp. 11–12. See Bender, *Spenser*, pp. 8–10.
[28] *Poetics*, XVII.i, p. 65.   [29] Cicero, *De Oratore*, III, p. 127.
[30] Lessing, *Laocoön*, pp. 208–9; *Laokoon*, IX, p. 111.

Kames, in fact, describes his concept of ideal presence (the imaginary presence the reader perceives when transformed into a spectator) as '*a waking dream*', although he still insists, 'In narration as well as in description, objects ought to be painted so accurately as to form in the mind of the reader distinct and lively images ... The narrative in an epic poem ought to rival a picture in the liveliness and accuracy of its representations'.[31]

Addison's 1712 *Spectator* essays on the pleasures of imagination have been called the 'definitive statement in English of the doctrine of *enargeia*'. Noting the 'combination of ancient aesthetic principle and modern scientific psychology', Hagstrum suggests that *ut pictura poesis* 'rested on English empiricism – on Lockean epistemology and the related aesthetic tradition that ran from Hobbes to Addison'.[32] One could speculate that the growth of epistemology and theories of perception in the early eighteenth century contributed to the revival or at least the revitalization of aesthetic theories about the importance of images in literary works. The relation between the philosophical and nascent scientific investigations of the time and contemporary endorsements of *ut pictura poesis* may be less a sign of influence than an indication of related concerns and preoccupations. Yet the speculations of writers such as Locke and Hume were clearly important to the theorists of *ut pictura poesis*, at least in part because of the centrality of the status of *images* to Enlightenment epistemology and a preoccupation with acts of imagination, mimesis, and representation.

Locke writes in his *Essay concerning Human Understanding* of 'secondary perception' in discussing the retention of ideas – 'the Power to revive again in our Minds those *Ideas* which after imprinting, have disappeared, or have been as it were laid out of Sight'.[33] Addison writes about 'Primary Pleasures of the Imagination, which entirely proceed from such Objects as are before our Eyes' and 'Secondary Pleasures of the Imagination which flow from the Ideas of visible Objects, when the Objects are not actually before the Eye, but are called up into our Memories, or form'd into agreeable Visions of Things that are either Absent or Fictitious'.[34] More important than any specific correspondence of terms or categories is the concern with sensory perception, most notably sight, and a metaphorical strain that might be called the imagery of images. Addison is interested in the pleasures of the imagination that come from 'visible Objects, either when we have them actually

[31] Kames, *Elements of Criticism*, II, p. 232.
[32] Hagstrum, *The Sister Arts*, pp. 136, 150. See also Wimsatt and Brooks, *Literary Criticism: A Short History*, pp. 254–62.
[33] Locke, *Essay*, pp. 152, 149.
[34] Addison, *The Spectator*, III, p. 537 (No. 411, Saturday, 21 June 1712). Cf. Wimsatt and Brooks, *Literary Criticism*, p. 255n.

in our view, or when we call up their Ideas into our Minds by Paintings, Statues, Descriptions' but his descriptions of these experiences are located somewhere between primary and secondary pleasures precisely because he is interested in *images*.

Comparing the ease with which we acquire pleasures of the imagination to the more difficult pleasures of the understanding, he writes: 'It is but opening the Eye, and the Scene enters. The Colours paint themselves on the Fancy, with very little Attention of Thought or Application of Mind in the Beholder.'[35] Locke speaks of those with superior memory having 'constantly in view the whole Scene of all their former actions, wherein no one of the thoughts they have ever had, may slip out of their sight'. Angels, he imagines, have 'constantly set before them, as in one Picture, all their past knowledge at once'.[36] He describes the 'ability in the Mind' to 'as it were paint' ideas that were once there: what he calls 'those dormant Pictures'; and in an elaborate series of metaphors about the fading of memory he describes how in the mind 'the inscriptions are effaced by time, and the Imagery moulders away. *The Pictures drawn in our Minds, are laid in fading Colours.*'[37]

In speaking of the 'constant decay of all our ideas' Locke seems to be drawing on Hobbes, who describes imagination as 'nothing but *decaying sense*'.[38] What is most relevant in this context is the idea that we know and perceive the world around us through images in the mind. Every thought, writes Hobbes in his definition of sense in the *Leviathan*, is 'a *Representation* or *Apparence*, of some quality, or other Accident of a body without us; which is commonly called an *Object* ... this *seeming*, or *fancy*, is that which men call *Sense*; and consisteth, as to the Eye, in a *Light*, or *Colour figured*'. Imagination accounts for the presence of an image of the object after the object is gone:

> After the object is removed, or the eye shut, we still retain an image of the thing seen, though more obscure than when we see it. And this is it, the Latines call *Imagination*, from the image made in seeing ... But the Greeks call it *Fancy*; which signifies *apparence*, and is as proper to one sense, as to another. IMAGINATION therefore is nothing but *decaying sense*; and is found in men, and many other living Creatures, as well sleeping, as waking.

Memory and the ability to combine and change remembered images and thereby create new images are both examples of what Hobbes calls a 'fiction of the Mind'.[39] Berkeley, who also speaks of 'fictions of the mind', writes of 'ideas imprinted on the senses by the Author of Nature' which are called 'real things' and those less vivid ideas 'excited in the

---

[35] Addison, *The Spectator*, III, pp. 536–8.
[36] Locke, *Essay*, p. 154.   [37] Locke, *Essay*, pp. 150, 152.
[38] Locke, *Essay*, p. 151. See Hobbes, *Leviathan*, p. 15.
[39] Hobbes, *Leviathan*, pp. 15–16.

imagination' called ' "ideas" or "images of things" which they copy and represent'.[40]

In understanding the eighteenth-century investment in *ut pictura poesis*, then, we must recognize that for writers who tried to imagine, describe, or enact the visual experience of literature – the ability of words and texts to present scenes before the eyes of a reader – it was already possible and perhaps even necessary to think of ideas raised in the mind as images and pictures. Although they warn their readers about imprecise, improper, and figurative language, in describing the activities of perception and the mind (in particular, memory and imagination), Hobbes, Locke, Berkeley, and Hume invariably speak of images, representations, copies, pictures, and painting, as well as imprinting, inscriptions, impressions, and writing. The world imagined and described by eighteenth-century epistemology is conveyed by our senses through representations and images whether we are waking or sleeping, perceiving, remembering, or imagining. Memory and imagination (the contemplation of things that are absent or no longer present to the mind, or fictitious things that are combinations of things once experienced) are visual experiences from the outset. Even before considering the effects and conditions of a work of art, from the moment one opens one's eyes, so to speak, one is already in the realm of representation and mimesis.

It is not difficult to argue that texts should present images and pictures to the mind when one believes that the mind is normally filled with images and pictures painted and imprinted there by perception. According to one critic, 'our Thoughts are painted in the Imagination' and 'an articulated Voice' is 'the Picture of Thought' which is then 'immediately painted in the Imagination'. Pictures in the mind can be reproduced by words, which then paint pictures in the minds of others; 'the exterior Representation of anything by the Mediation of Words, is the same as that first painted in the Brain'.[41] Rhetorical notions of *enargeia*, a tradition of comparing the arts of literature and painting, and especially theories that called on literature to present images, pictures, and tableaux to the mind of the reader, were more than compatible with an epistemology that repeatedly describes perception and imagination in terms of fictions, images, pictures, and paintings.

These philosophical discussions of perception and imagination commonly make the distinction that the images generated by the imagination are more faint and obscure – less vivid and lively – than the things we actually perceive when they are present to us. However, eighteenth-century advocates of *ut pictura poesis*, *enargeia*, and description stress

[40] Berkeley, *Principles, Dialogues, and Philosophical Correspondence*, pp. 38, 36.
[41] Tamworth Reresby, *A Miscellany of Ingenious Thoughts and Reflections, In Verse and Prose*, pp. 20–1.

the vividness of fictions of the mind. Addison's distinction between primary and secondary pleasures of the imagination is surprisingly unhierarchical. Although he follows conventional formulations in stating that '*Description* runs yet further from the things it represents than Painting; for a Picture bears a real Resemblance to its Original, which Letters and Syllables are wholly void of', he elevates the status of the images that can be produced by words when he describes the power of language: 'Words, when well chosen, have so great a Force in them, that a Description often gives us more lively Ideas than the Sight of Things themselves. The Reader finds a Scene drawn in Stronger Colours, and painted more to the Life in his Imagination, by the help of Words, than by an actual Survey of the Scene which they describe.'

Indeed, taking the conventional terms of strength, vividness, and liveliness, Addison seems to reverse the conventional comparison of images produced by objects and images represented in the mind: 'In this Case the Poet seems to get the better of Nature; he takes, indeed, the Landskip after her, but gives it more vigourous Touches, heightens its Beauty, and so enlivens the whole Piece, that the Images which flow from the Objects themselves appear weak and faint, in Comparison of those that come from the Expressions.' Addison suggests that the 'reason, probably, may be, because in the Survey of any object, we have only so much of it painted on the Imagination, as comes in at the Eye; but in its Description, the Poet gives us as free a View of it as he pleases'.[42] Whatever the reason, in Addison's view the painting of a real thing on the imagination might not be as forceful as the images painted in the colours of art. Comparing two types of representations, copies, or paintings, he ascribes greater force to those in the poet's descriptions.

Hume, in his *Enquiry into the Human Understanding* (1748) warns that a 'blind and powerful instinct of nature' leads us to 'always suppose the very images, presented by the senses, to be the external objects, and never entertain any suspicion, that the one are nothing but representations of the other'.[43] However, he might be arguing against Addison's essays when he differentiates between the images of perception and those of imagination: 'These faculties may mimic or copy the perceptions of the senses; but they never can entirely reach the force and vivacity of the original sentiment. The utmost we say of them, even when they operate with greatest vigour, is, that they represent their object in so lively a manner, that we could *almost* say we feel or see it.' Hume insists, however, 'except the mind be disordered by disease or madness, they never can arrive at such a pitch of vivacity, as to render

[42] Addison, *The Spectator*, III, pp. 559–61 (No. 416, Friday, 27 June 1712).
[43] Hume, *Enquiry*, Section XII, Part I, p. 151.

these perceptions altogether undistinguishable. All the colours of poetry, however splendid, can never paint natural objects in such a manner as to make the description be taken for a real landskip. The most lively thought is still inferior to the dullest sensation.'[44] It is as if Hume is trying to reclaim a set of epistemological principles from an aesthetic tradition that has carried the power of images too far. Although he is part of a tradition that was accused of reducing the real world to images, he seems to resist the conflation of the fictions of art with the perceptions and even fictions of the mind.

Dedicated to exploring our fictions of the world, Hume is a sceptic when it comes to the world of fiction. He concedes the power of imagination: 'Nothing is more free than the imagination of man . . . in all the varieties of fiction and vision. It can feign a train of events, with all the appearance of reality, ascribe to them a particular time and place, conceive them as existent, and paint them out to itself with every circumstance, that belongs to any historical fact, which it believes with the greatest certainty.' However, when he asks what the difference is 'between such a fiction and belief', despite the similarity on some level of the images and representations produced in the mind by perception and imagination, Hume insists on the differences in the power of these images: 'belief is nothing but a more vivid, lively, forcible, firm, steady conception of an object, than what the imagination alone is ever able to attain. This variety of terms, which may seem so unphilosophical, is intended only to express that act of mind, which renders realities, or what is taken for such, more present to us than fictions.' For Hume, the imagination 'may conceive fictitious objects with all the circumstances of place and time. It may set them, in a manner, before our eyes, in their true colours, just as they might have existed. But as it is impossible that this faculty of imagination can ever, of itself, reach belief, it is evident that belief consists not in the peculiar nature or order of ideas, but in the *manner* of their conception, and in their *feeling* to the mind.' It is belief that 'distinguishes the ideas of the judgement from the fictions of the imagination'.[45]

For believers in the power of language such as Addison, who think that a description could present 'more lively Ideas than the Sight of Things themselves', it is possible to imagine believing in fiction. Advocates of the eighteenth-century versions of *ut pictura poesis*, partially founding their theories on a view of the world determined by post-Lockean epistemology, focused on what Hume described as the 'utmost' power of the imagination to 'mimic or copy the perception of the senses':

[44] Hume, *Enquiry*, Section II, p. 17.
[45] Hume, *Enquiry*, Section V, Part II, pp. 47, 49.

'they represent their object in so lively a manner, that we could *almost* say we feel or see it'. Transformed by *ut pictura poesis*, belief is no longer 'a more vivid, lively, forcible, firm, steady conception of an object, than what the imagination alone is ever able to attain'.[46] Fictions of the imagination, working through images presented to the mind, can compel belief by seeming to present (rather than represent) things themselves to the reader, who, in Kames's terms, is transformed into a spectator.

The emphasis on perspicuity, vividness, clarity, sight, and 'things themselves' found in eighteenth-century theories of *ut pictura poesis* brings the comparison of painting and poetry into the realm of semiotics, a province that was in the process of being charted by contemporary theories about the origins of language. Painting is seen to have an advantage over language because of its intelligibility, which was presumed to be both universal and immediate. Claiming that the painter speaks to 'men of all Nations . . . in their own Mother tongue', Jonathan Richardson wrote:

Words paint to the Imagination, but every Man forms the thing to himself in his own way: Language is very imperfect: There are innumerable Colours and Figures for which we have no name, and an Infinity of other Ideas which have no certain words universally agreed upon as denoting them; whereas the Painter can convey his Ideas of these things clearly, and without Ambiguity; and what he says every one understands in the Sense he intends it.[47]

In his notes on Du Fresnoy, de Piles writes that 'that amongst so great a Diversity of Languages', painting 'makes her self *understood* by all the *Nations of the World*'.[48] In *The Principles of Painting* (published in French in 1708, translated into English in 1743) he writes that 'painters have only one language, which imitates (if I may be suffered to say so) that which God gave to the apostles, and which all nations were to understand'. Poetry, according to this view, is inferior because the vision it presents and represents must be mediated through language. 'Words are only the signs of things', writes de Piles, 'whereas painting shews truth in a more lively manner, and moves and penetrates the heart more strongly, than can be done by discourse. In a word; 'tis the essence of painting to speak by things, as that of poesy is to paint by words.'[49]

The notion that painting speaks in the language of things while poetry communicates by signs is nuanced by later authors whose distinction between the arts follows from a recognition that both employ signs.

---

[46] Hume, *Enquiry*, Section V, Part II, p. 49.
[47] Richardson, *An Essay on the Theory of Painting*, pp. 5–6.
[48] *The Art of Painting*, p. 83.
[49] De Piles, *The Principles of Painting*, pp. 270, 283.

Du Bos distinguishes between the natural signs found in nature and the artificial signs fabricated by humans: 'la Peinture n'emploie pas des signes artificiels, ainsi que le fait la Poesie, mais bien des signes naturels. C'est avec des signes naturels que la Peinture fait ses imitations.' Since natural signs are immediately accessible and need not be learned or deciphered, they represent a more immediate and thus more powerful experience than verbal language. Even when we readily understand verbal signs, words first must awaken the ideas of which they are only the arbitrary signs: 'Il faut ensuite que ces idées s'arrangent dans l'imagination, & qu'elles y forment ces tableaux qui nous touchent, & ces peintures qui nous interessent.' Even Du Bos seems to step back, however, from his already mystified notion of natural signs to the almost pre-semiotic view of painting advanced by de Piles. 'Je parle peut-être mal, quand je dis que la peinture employe des signes; c'est la nature elle-même que la peinture met sous nos yeux.' Things present themselves 'dans un tableau sous la même forme où nous la voiions réellement'.[50] In his *Lettre sur les sourds et les muets*, Diderot also declares: 'C'est la chose même que le peintre montre; les expressions du musicien et du poète n'en sont que des hiéroglyphes.'[51] Despite this recurrent desire to claim for painting the ability to present nature or things themselves, Du Bos's distinction between natural and artificial signs (which, as linguistics and theories of language develop, are increasingly seen as *arbitrary* signs) becomes more commonplace. Discussing parallels in the *Idler* in 1758, Johnson notes in passing that poetry and painting 'differ only as the one represents things by marks permanent and natural, the other by signs accidental and arbitrary'.[52]

Many eighteenth-century writers can make such distinctions, adjudicating between the 'sister arts', while still endorsing the concept of parallels and advocating the goals represented by *ut pictura poesis*. Indeed, the semiotic distinctions between poetry and painting lead from an assertion of parallels to a more polemical advocacy of *ut pictura poesis* when the presupposition that painting is more natural, intelligible, and powerful leads to the conclusion that poetry should try to imitate painting. Such discriminations, however, also lead to the position that the arts do not operate in strictly analogous ways and therefore should be separated – a position that is argued most forcefully by Lessing. Here the understanding that poetry and painting employ different sorts of signs helps to form the basis for a rethinking of the relation between the arts.

Lessing, following Mendelssohn's discussion of natural and arbitrary

---

[50] Du Bos, *Réflexions critiques*, I, pp. 387–9.
[51] Diderot, *Lettre sur les sourds et les muets*, in *Oeuvres*, IV, p. 185.
[52] Johnson, *Idler*, No. 34, Saturday, 9 December 1758, p. 246.

symbols,[53] praises intelligibility ('when we recognize at first glance [*mit dem ersten Blick*] the intent and meaning of [the artist's] entire composition') and he assumes that speech and writing make use of 'arbitrary symbols'.[54] In a characteristically overdetermined example, he describes the difficult task of a painter copying a landscape from one of Thomson's descriptions who must create 'something beautiful out of indefinite and weak images of arbitrary symbols [*jener aus schwanken und schwachen Vorstellungen willkürlicher Zeichen*]'.[55] Although Lessing rejects the assumption that poetry should imitate painting, his desire for immediacy in the work of art makes him advocate poetry's use of its arbitrary signs to imitate natural signs. 'Poetry must try to raise its arbitrary signs to natural signs', declared Lessing in a letter written after the *Laocoön*; 'the highest kind of poetry will be that which transforms the arbitrary signs completely into natural signs'.[56] Yet Lessing emphasizes the distinctions between the signs of poetry and painting in order to separate the means and effects of the arts:

> if it is true that in its imitations painting uses completely different means or signs than does poetry, namely figures and colors in space rather than articulated sounds in time, and if these signs must indisputably bear a suitable relation to the thing signified, then signs existing in space can express only objects whose wholes or parts coexist, while signs that follow one another can express only objects whose wholes or parts are consecutive.

Thus, 'bodies' (or 'objects that exist in space') with 'their visible properties are the true subjects of painting' and 'actions are the true subjects of poetry'. With this distinction, and the insistence that painting employs signs (not things themselves) as much as poetry does, Lessing arrives at his claim that painting should represent 'only a single moment of an action [*nur einen einzigen Augenblick*]' while poetry should confine itself to progressive actions.[57] It is not simply an accident of etymology that Lessing uses the German word *Augenblick* in designating his concept of the 'moment' of painting.

These concepts are not entirely original to Lessing. As early as 1712 Shaftesbury advocated the term 'tablature' to designate a painting that is 'a single piece, comprehended in one view' and 'which constitutes a real whole'.[58] In *Tableaux tirés de l'Iliade* (an anthology of literary

---

[53] See Wellbery, *Lessing's Laocoon*, pp. 104–237.
[54] Lessing, *Laocoön*, pp. 64, 63; *Laokoon*, IX, p. 78.
[55] Lessing, *Laocoön*, p. 63; *Laokoon*, IX, p. 78.
[56] Cited in Wellek, *History*, I, pp. 164–5. Cf. Wellbery, *Lessing's Laocoon*, pp. 225–7.
[57] Lessing, *Laocoön*, pp. 78–9.
[58] See Fried, *Absorption and Theatricality*, p. 89. The 1712 essay, 'A Notion of the Historical Draught or Tablature of the Judgement of Hercules', was originally published in French in the Amsterdam edition of the *Journal des Sçavans*.

'tableaux' from classical texts intended as subjects for painters) Caylus writes that a 'Tableau, pour parler exactement, est la représentation du moment d'une action'.[59] The notion that painting should represent a moment had been used to delineate the temporal properties of writing and the spatial properties of painting. Discussing the signs of painting and poetry, Du Bos notes that a tableau can move us more than the image in a text: 'Nous voïons alors en un instant ce que les vers nous font seulement imaginer, & cela même en plusieurs instans.' A painting, representing only 'un instant de l'action', can make us understand 'en un moment'.[60]

James Harris, who declares that 'of necessity every picture is a *Punctum Temporis* or Instant', writes in his *Three Treatises*, 'The Subjects of Poetry, to which the Genius of Painting is not adapted, are – all Actions, whose Whole is of so lengthened a Duration, that no Point of time, in any part of the whole, can be given fit for Painting.'[61] In his *Lettre sur les sourds et muets* (which Lessing reviewed) Diderot discusses why 'une peinture admirable dans un poème deviendrait ridicule sur la toile'; pointing to 'le moment frappant' in a description from Virgil, he asks 'Comment arrive-t-il que ce qui ravit notre imagination déplaise à nos yeux?'[62] Lessing's contribution to these discussions, aside from consolidating observations from previous works into a systematic argument, is to use these distinctions to insist that painting and poetry should not try to imitate each other.

It is no coincidence that Lessing's central literary example in the *Laocoön* is the description of Achilles' shield in Book 18 of the *Iliad* – 'the famous picture [*Gemälde*] which more than anything else caused Homer to be considered by the ancients a master of painting [*ein Lehrer der Malerei*]'.[63] Lessing is most interested in the lessons that poets were learning from Homer. Pope, for example, in his translation of the *Iliad* praises Homer's ability to 'draw his characters with so visible and surprising a variety' that 'no painter could have distinguished them by more features'. He repeatedly refers to Homer as a 'painter' and identifies passages in the poem as 'Paintings'.[64] In a long note on the description of the shield, Pope sets out to 'consider it as a Work of *painting*,

---

[59] Comte de Caylus, *Tableaux tirés de l'Iliade*, p. ix (n). Cf. Fried, *Absorption and Theatricality*, p. 215.

[60] Du Bos, *Réflexions critiques*, I, pp. 390, 396, 391.

[61] Harris, p. 63; pp. 83–4.

[62] Diderot, *Oeuvres*, IV, p. 185. See the article 'Composition' in the *Encyclopédie*, III, pp. 772–4.

[63] Lessing, *Laocoön*, p. 94; *Laokoon*, IX, p. 133.

[64] See Alexander Pope, 'Preface' to *The Iliad of Homer*. See Hagstrum, *The Sister Arts*, pp. 229, 210–42; Williams, 'Alexander Pope and *Ut Pictura Poesis*', pp. 61–75; and Brownell, *Alexander Pope*, pp. 39–70.

and prove it in all respects conformable to the most just Ideas and establish'd Rules of that Art'. Calling the description of the shield 'a complete *Idea* of *Painting*, and a Sketch for what one may call an *universal Picture*', Pope insists that it realistically represents a plausible and imaginable work of art, that the shield as Homer describes it could really have existed. At stake is Homer's painting as much as his description and Pope includes an illustration and detailed plan to prove that the text could be exactly translated 'according to the Rules of Painting'.[65]

Lessing, in contrast, insists that 'Homer represents nothing but progressive actions'.[66] According to Lessing, he is able to achieve such a vivid representation precisely because he used narrative rather than images:

Homer does not paint the shield as finished and complete, but as a shield that is being made. Thus, here too he has made use of that admirable artistic device: transforming what is coexistent in his subject into what is consecutive, and thereby making the living picture [*Gemälde*] of an action out of the tedious painting [*Malerei*] of an object. We do not see the shield, but the divine master as he is making it.

This method is contrasted with Virgil's description of the shield of Aeneas in which, according to Lessing, 'the action comes to a standstill'. In a critique that can be read as an attack on eighteenth-century descriptive poetry, Lessing writes: 'By its eternal "here is" and "there is", "close by stands" and "not far off we see", the description becomes so cold and tedious that all the poetic beauty which a Virgil could give it was required to keep it from becoming intolerable.'[67]

It is here that we can see one of the main targets of Lessing's attack: what he calls in the preface the 'mania for description [*die Schilderungssucht*]'[68] that has been encouraged by the advocates of the sister arts. As he elaborates the different signs, subjects, and effects of poetry and painting, Lessing strategically enlists on his side Pope himself, who not only praised Homer's paintings but in poems such as 'Windsor Forest' had tried his hand at descriptive poetry. 'The mature Pope looked back on the descriptive attempts of the poetic works of his youth with great contempt', writes Lessing; 'He demanded expressly that whoever would bear the name of poet with dignity must renounce the mania for description as early as possible, and he called a purely descriptive poem a banquet of nothing but sauces.' In a long note, Lessing cites Pope's lines, 'who could take offence, / While pure Description held the place of Sense?' and offers 'Warburton's remark' as 'an authentic explanation by the poet himself' that to use 'a picturesque imagination . . . only in

---

[65] Pope, *Works*, VIII, pp. 363, 358, 363, 366.　　[66] Lessing, *Laocoön*, pp. 78–9.
[67] Lessing, *Laocoön*, pp. 95–6.　　[68] Lessing, *Laocoön*, p. 5; *Laokoon*, IX, p. 5.

Description, is like children's delighting in a prism for the sake of its gaudy colours'.[69]

Paradoxically, it may have been this mania for description that eventually brought about the demise of the very theories of *ut pictura poesis* that had encouraged it. 'Descriptive poetry', according to one late eighteenth-century writer, was meant 'to excite in the mind the clearest and most lively picture of the object imitated; and in proportion as the ideas forming that picture are vivid and the more they answer to the reality of the prototype or scene, the more complete is the imitation, and the more impressive the resemblance'.[70] The eighteenth century saw a proliferation of descriptive poetry, the most famous example of which is James Thomson's *The Seasons*, published in 1730. (*Winter, Summer,* and *Spring* had appeared in 1726, 1727, and 1728 respectively.) Writing in a tradition that was considered to be best exemplified by Virgil's *Georgics*, but seen even more as belonging to the genre of landscape painting, Thomson was praised as a master painter whose poetry contained poetical pictures.

In his *Essay on the Writings and Genius of Pope*, Joseph Warton declares that Thomson 'enriched poetry with a variety of new and original images which he painted from nature itself and from his actual observation: his descriptions have therefore a distinctness and truth'.[71] Other poets, such as Collins and Gray, also were praised for their literary pictorialism; but eventually both the excesses and the limitations of practitioners and less talented imitators led many readers to conclude that descriptive poetry was 'cold and tedious' rather than vivid and moving.

In his *Lectures on Rhetoric and Belles Lettres*, first published in 1783, Hugh Blair warns: 'We have reason always to distrust an Author's descriptive talents, when we find him laborious and turgid amassing common-place epithets and general expressions, to work up a high conception of some object, of which, after all, we can form but an indistinct idea.' According to Blair, when a 'second-rate Genius' tries to describe nature, he 'gives us words rather than ideas; we meet with the language indeed of poetical description, but we apprehend the object described very indistinctly. Whereas, a true Poet makes us imagine that we see it before our eyes ... he places it in such a light, that a Painter could copy after him.'[72] Indeed, even Kames attacks 'the language of a

---

[69] Lessing, *Laocoön*, p. 214. The lines are from Pope's *Epistle to Dr. Arbuthnot*. The note is to line 148.

[70] Dyer, *Poetics*, II, p. 116; cited in Cohen, *Art of Discrimination*, p. 160.

[71] [Warton,] *An Essay on the Genius and Writings of Pope*, I, p. 42. See Cohen, *Art of Discrimination*, pp. 131–247; and Spacks, *The Poetry of Vision*.

[72] Blair, *Lectures on Rhetoric and Belles Lettres*, II, pp. 383–4, 371.

spectator' and warns against the 'very humble flight of imagination' that will 'convert a writer into a spectator; so as to figure, in some obscure manner, an action as passing in his sight and hearing. In that figured situation, being led naturally to write like a spectator, he entertains his readers with his own reflections, with cool description, and florid declamation; instead of making them eye-witnesses, as it were, to a real event'. Going beyond classical rhetorical theories about *enargeia* in oratory, Kames asserts that if the writer himself is a spectator the reader will not see the scene. Even drama must avoid this 'descriptive manner of representing passion'; the 'descriptive tragedy' which conveys only 'cold description in the language of a bystander'[73] will place only description before our eyes. Paradoxically, for both Blair and Kames, the 'language of poetical description' finally presents itself to the sight of the reader rather than the things it is supposed to describe. The attempt to transcend the arbitrary signs of language and present unmediated nature can itself lead to the failure of *ut pictura poesis*.

An alternative to this impasse of descriptive writing was to some extent sought in the theatre; the preoccupation with *ut pictura poesis* in the eighteenth century should be seen in the context of the century's preoccupation not only with theatre but also with dramatic forms and theatrical relations. Theatre offered a model for – and a *literalization* of – the ideals of *ut pictura poesis* since it embodied literary texts in a visual medium. Jonathan Richardson, in comparing writing and painting, notes that the 'Theatre gives us Representations of Things different from both these, and a kind of Composition of both: There we see a sort of moving, speaking Pictures'.[74] For Kames, who writes that 'Painting seems to possess a middle place between reading and acting', 'theatrical representation is the most powerful' of 'all the means for making an impression of ideal presence'. An epic poem (which 'employs narration') or a 'narrative poem is a story told by another' whereas 'tragedy represents its facts as passing in our sight'.[75]

Du Bos sees dramatic poetry as possessing an advantage over painting since a tragedy 'renferme une infinité de tableaux'. The poet, he writes, 'nous présente successivement, pour ainsi dire, cinquante tableaux'.[76] In his article on 'Composition' in the *Encyclopédie*, Diderot writes: 'Un bon tableau ne fournira guere qu'un sujet, ou même qu'une scene de drame; & un seul drame peut fournir matiere à cent tableaux différens.'

---

[73] Kames, *Elements of Criticism*, I, pp. 355–6.
[74] Richardson, *An Essay on the Theory of Painting*, p. 7. Not surprisingly, he concludes that painting is superior: 'but these are transient; whereas Painting remains, and is always at hand. And what is more considerable, the Stage never represents things truly, especially if the Scene be remote, and the Story ancient.'
[75] Kames, *Elements of Criticism*, I, pp. 89–90; II, p. 262.
[76] Du Bos, *Réflexions critiques*, I, p. 396.

Diderot (who attacked the use of 'portraits' in novels) argued in his *Entretiens sur le Fils naturel* and *Essai sur la poésie dramatique* that plays should learn from painting and present tableaux to the spectators in the audience.[77] These attempts to imagine a literature that would literally present images and tableaux also must be understood in the context of the emergence of the published book and especially the novel in the eighteenth century. It is perhaps not a coincidence that theories of *ut pictura poesis* demanded that literary texts convey voice, presence, and especially *image* and *spectacle* – precisely what books lack – at a time when the novel increasingly was challenging theatre as a popular art form and the book as cultural fact and artifact was present and multiplying as never before.

The ideas represented by *ut pictura poesis*, however, had a significance beyond the fortunes of descriptive poetry, drama, or the novel. *Ut pictura poesis* represented not so much a doctrine or a formal school of thought as a set of beliefs about the experience of the work of art. In a sense it is a name for a cluster of aesthetic preoccupations about the effects of art and the power of both art and the imagination. It stands at the crossroads not only of literature and painting but also of aesthetics, epistemology, psychology, and even moral philosophy. Viewed in this context its importance in the history of criticism and aesthetics goes beyond the influence of a fashion for description or an effort to systematize elaborate analogies between the arts. Lessing's attempts to delineate the effects and semiotic properties of painting and poetry are in many ways similar to the comparisons that advocated the principles of *ut pictura poesis*. Both placed painting and poetry in juxtaposition in order to explore questions of subject-matter, imitation, intelligibility, temporality, action, and the power of art to move the passions. What is most important in tracing the overdetermined history of this tradition is not so much unravelling a controversy with many sides and variations as understanding what it means that so many writers and critics were compelled to address the relations between poetry and painting, text and spectacle, reader and beholder. *Ut pictura poesis* is part of the eighteenth-century investigation of the power and indeed the possibility of representation in both art and life.

[77] Diderot, *Encyclopédie*, III, p. 773; *Oeuvres*, X. See Diderot's description of the poet as a painter in the *Salon de 1767 (Oeuvres)*. See also Fried, *Absorption and Theatricality*.

(ii) *The picturesque*
David Marshall

The problem of the picturesque in eighteenth-century criticism and aesthetics might be approached through a *tableau* that appears in the conclusion to Uvedale Price's *Essay on the Picturesque* (first published in 1794 and then reprinted in the revised and expanded *Essays on the Picturesque* in 1810). Price recounts the following anecdote:

> Sir Joshua Reynolds told me, that when he and Wilson the landscape painter were looking at the view from Richmond terrace, Wilson was pointing out some particular part; and in order to direct his eye to it, 'There', said he, 'near those houses – there! where the *figures* are.' – Though a painter, said Sir Joshua, I was puzzled: I thought he meant statues, and was looking upon the *tops* of the houses; for I did not at first conceive that the men and women we plainly saw walking about, were by him only thought of as figures in the landscape.

Price's use of this story about Richard Wilson seems odd in the context of his polemic against the 'improvement school' of landscape design. Reynolds the portrait painter appears to be somewhat scandalized that Wilson the landscape painter should regard men and women as if they were figures in a painting. Yet Price seems to cite the story approvingly as an illustration of his claim that painting 'tends to humanize the mind'. Whereas the improvers practise despotism and destruction, he argues, 'the lover of painting, considers the dwellings, the inhabitants, and the marks of their intercourse, as ornaments to the landscape'.[1] Price is arguing that landscape design and gardening should be based on the principles of painting. In advocating the picturesque both in theory and practice, he is extending William Gilpin's admiration of 'that peculiar kind of beauty, which is agreeable in a picture' or is 'capable of being *illustrated in painting*'[2] to a way of looking at the landscape (and indeed composing the landscape) as if it *were* a painting. Despite Price's identification with Wilson's point of view, however, the story raises the question of what it means to see a scene from nature as if it were a work of art, what it means to look at the world through the frame of art.

For Raymond Williams, the 'very idea of landscape implies separation and observation'. In the late eighteenth century – a time when 'the proscenium frame and the movable flats were being simultaneously developed'[3] in the theatre – the idea that the landscape itself could be

[1] Price, *Essays on the Picturesque*, I, pp. 338–9.
[2] Gilpin, *An Essay upon Prints*, p. 2; *Three Essays*, p. 1.
[3] Williams, *The Country and the City*, pp. 149, 154.

a *scene* became inscribed in the language. The word 'scenery' seems to have been applied to the landscape for the first time (at least in print) in 1784 in William Cowper's *The Task*. Writers like Uvedale Price had to refer to 'natural scenery' and 'real scenery' in order to distinguish the views they were describing from the realm of art, but the terms 'scene' and 'scenery' implied a theatrical perspective from the outset.[4] According to John Barrell, the word 'scene', when 'applied to a landscape, assumed also that what was being described lay opposite the observer, *en face*: and this sense came with it from its theatrical origin'. In this context, a 'scene' 'is something opposite you and enclosed by the limits of your vision in very much the same way as a painting is enclosed within its frame, or, within the painting, the area beyond the foreground is marked off by the *coulisse* – the word can mean the wings of a stage. A "scene" directs attention to itself as a self-contained and separate entity, apart from the rest of the countryside, and apart from the observer.'[5] In Austen's novel *Mansfield Park* (1814), Fanny Price (the heroine who, like Uvedale Price, argues against the improvers and advocates picturesque principles) speaks of her tendency to rhapsodize when she is out of doors, but the speech in which she experiences the 'sublimity of Nature' in terms that recall the picturesque is spoken while 'standing at an open window' beholding what is described as a 'scene'. Her stance only literalizes the theatrical metaphor contained in the aesthetic category of the picturesque; the controversy about the theatricals rehearsed in the novel and the controversy about improvement and landscape design are both aspects of Austen's overall investigation of the problem of theatrical roles and relations.[6] In the same way, Goethe's novel *Elective Affinities* (1809) depicts characters engaged in extensive discussions of prospects, point of view, and landscape design (there is even an English lord who spends his time 'catching the picturesque views of the park in his portable *camera obscura* and in making drawings of these') *and* it dramatizes them posing in *tableaux vivants* in which they 'represent well-known paintings'.[7]

The picturesque represents a point of view that frames the world and turns nature into a series of *living tableaux*. Beginning as an appreciation

---

[4] Price, *Essays*, I, pp. 9–10; III, pp. 247–8.
[5] Barrell, *The Idea of Landscape*, pp. 23–4.
[6] Austen, *Mansfield Park*, in *Novels*, III, pp. 209, 113, 108. See Marshall, 'True acting', pp. 87–106 for related remarks about the picturesque in the context of a discussion about theatre and theatricality in *Mansfield Park*. On the picturesque and Austen, see Martin Price, 'The picturesque moment' and *Forms of Life*, pp. 65–89. See also Duckworth, *Improvement of the Estate*, pp. 35–80.
[7] 'die malerischen Aussichten des Parks in einer tragbaren dunklen Kammer aufzufangen und zu zeichnen' (Goethe, *Elective Affinities*, pp. 230, 185). German citations from *Die Wahlverwandtschaften* are from *Goethes Werke*, VI, pp. 430, 392.

of natural beauty, it may end by turning people into figures in a landscape or figures in a painting. Coinciding with a discovery of the natural world, anticipating an imaginative projection of self into the landscape through an act of transport or identification, it assumes an attitude that seems to depend on distance and separation. In so far as it represented a sign of sensibility and taste, the picturesque might be seen as a chapter in the history of aesthetics, a moment of intersection between the histories of literature, painting, and gardening. In so far as it is accompanied by a hint of discomfort, controversy, or excess, however, the picturesque is less a problem in aesthetics than a problem about aesthetics. As such, it represents more than a trend in gardening or a footnote to the history of the sublime; the invention of the picturesque represents a complex and at times paradoxical moment in the evolution of eighteenth-century attitudes about both art and nature.

Pope seems to inaugurate the use of the word in the context of descriptions of nature. In a letter in 1712, he describes lines of verse as being 'what the French call very *picturesque*'[8] – although, as Christopher Hussey points out, 'the French Academy did not admit *pittoresque* till 1732'.[9] Pope's notes to his translation of the *Iliad* contain several instances of the word, usually in the context of praising Homer for embodying the principles of *ut pictura poesis*[10] but including also the newer, more specific sense of a picturesque prospect.[11] The modern sense of the word *picturesque* as applied to landscape and natural beauty was popularized by William Gilpin – who, according to Marianne Dashwood in *Sense and Sensibility*, 'first defined what picturesque beauty was'.[12] In his *Essay on Prints* (1768), Gilpin defines 'Picturesque' as 'a term expressive of that peculiar kind of beauty, which is agreeable in a picture'.[13] The term is used, he writes later in *Three Essays: On Picturesque Beauty; on Picturesque Travel; and on Sketching Landscape*, 'to denote *such objects, as are proper subjects for painting*'. Describing '*picturesque beauty*', Gilpin writes: 'This great object we pursue through the scenery of nature; and examine it by the rules of painting'. Distinguishing between the beautiful and the picturesque, Gilpin makes a distinction between objects 'which please the eye in their *natural state*;

---

[8] Cited in Brownell, *Alexander Pope & the Arts of Georgian England*, p. 104.

[9] Hussey, *The Picturesque*, p. 32.

[10] In a note in Book XIII on the comparison of Achilles shaking the plumes of his helmet, Pope refers to 'a very pleasing Image, and very much what the Painters call Picturesque' (cited in Brownell, *Alexander Pope*, p. 104).

[11] See Pope, *Twickenham Edition*, VIII, p. 234. According to Brownell, 'In all these instances picturesque applied to the description of a scene or to the attitude of a figure against its background means graphic vividness, *enargeia*, or suitability for painting' (*Alexander Pope*, p. 104). See also Hunt, 'Ut pictura poesis', pp. 87–108.

[12] Austen, *Sense and Sensibility, Novels*, I, p. 97.

[13] Gilpin, *An Essay upon Prints*, p. 2.

and those, which please from some quality, capable of being *illustrated in painting*'.[14] Gilpin writes as a 'picturesque traveller', touring Great Britain and Scotland with notebook and sketchbook in hand, describing the varieties of natural scenery available to the 'picturesque eye'. He remarks that 'the picturesque eye is not merely restricted to nature. It ranges through the limits of art. The picture, the statue, and the garden are all objects of its attention.'[15]

Writing in 1794 in his *Essay on the Picturesque*, Price complains, 'There are few words, whose meaning has been less accurately determined than that of the word picturesque.' Rejecting Gilpin's definitions as 'at once too vague, and too confined', Price asserts that the word 'is applied to every object, and every kind of scenery, which has been, or might be represented with good effect in painting'. Price's contribution is to define the picturesque by distinguishing it from the sublime and the beautiful; he intends his treatise to be a kind of pendant to Burke's *Enquiry*, hoping to show 'that the picturesque has a character not less separate and distinct than either the sublime or the beautiful, nor less independent of the art of painting'.[16] Both Price and Gilpin are interested in identifying the properties that make objects in a landscape specifically picturesque, as opposed to beautiful or sublime (or attractive or striking in any other way). They seek to describe the picturesque in order to explain precisely what makes it interesting to the painter and representable in a painting.

Contrasting the picturesque with Burke's category of beauty, which is characterized by smoothness, Gilpin emphasizes the *'roughness'* of the picturesque. The *'smoothness'* of 'an elegant piece of gardening', he writes, although 'as it should be in nature, offends in picture'. However: 'Turn the lawn into a piece of broken ground: plant rugged oaks instead of flowering shrubs: break the edges of the walk: give it the rudeness of a road: mark it with wheel-tracks; and scatter around a few stones, and brushwood; in a word, instead of making the whole *smooth*, make it *rough*; and you make it also *picturesque*'. In the same manner, Palladian architecture loses its elegance and becomes unpleasingly formal when represented in a painting. 'Should we wish to give it picturesque beauty', explains Gilpin, 'we must use the mallet, instead of the chisel: we must beat down one half of it, deface the other, and throw the mutilated members around in heaps. In short, from a *smooth* building we must turn it into a *rough* ruin. No painter, who had the choice of the two objects, would hesitate a moment.' This is why the observer with a 'picturesque eye' prefers 'the elegant relics of ancient architecture; the

---

[14] Gilpin, *Three Essays*, II, p. 42; I, p. 1.
[15] Gilpin, *Three Essays*, II, p. 45.   [16] Price, *Essays*, I, pp. 37, 39, 37, 40.

ruined tower, the Gothic arch, the remains of castles, and abbeys'.[17] As he stakes out 'a station between beauty and sublimity' for the picturesque, Price also emphasizes contrasts of light and shade and roughness; the 'qualities of roughness, and of sudden variation, joined with that of irregularity, are the most efficient causes of the picturesque'.[18] As with Gilpin, ruins are privileged sites of the picturesque.

There are discussions of the problem of defining the term *picturesque* as late as the 1820s; throughout this period, explanations of etymology and translation, laments about ambiguity, complaints about jargon, and the need for neologisms, point to an uncertainty about the referent of the term. The problem of defining the picturesque is from the outset a problem of defining an *idea*. *Picturesque* comes to name a concept in aesthetics and in the theory and practice of gardening and landscape design. It resembles a genre and a style related to the sketch (popularized by Gilpin), landscape painting (as practised especially by Nicolas Poussin, Claude Lorrain, and Salvator Rosa) and certain styles of architecture (from classical to Gothic); yet in these examples it is often identified by thematic content and subject-matter (such as ruins or hermits or bandits). The picturesque was also, as Martin Price suggests, 'an attempt to win traditional sanctions for a new experience'.[19] Barrell describes 'a very different attitude to landscape' – a 'way of looking' that became a 'way of *knowing*' the landscape.[20] More and more in the eighteenth century, as Richard Payne Knight argued (against Uvedale Price) in 1805, the picturesque represented 'modes and habits of viewing'.[21]

To understand the development of the picturesque as a concept in aesthetic theory and practice, one needs to understand what Dallaway called in 1827 'the literary history of gardening'.[22] Gilpin used the term *picturesque* for the most part to appreciate those accidental scenes that might be encountered by the traveller – and increasingly the tourist – passing through the landscape. Both term and concept, however, were developed with a view toward designing landscape as well as appreciating it. Whereas Gilpin wrote essays on 'Picturesque Beauty' and wrote up his tours, Price indicated the practical aspect of his *Essay on the Picturesque* by declaring in his subtitle that his work was also about *the Use of Studying Pictures, for the Purpose of Improving Real Landscape.* In an often quoted remark reported by Spence, Pope declared: 'All gardening is landscape-painting.'[23] In his influential treatise on gardening,

---

[17] Gilpin, *Three Essays*, pp. 5–8, 46.   [18] Price, *Essays*, I, pp. 68, 50.
[19] Price, 'The picturesque moment', p. 259.
[20] Barrell, *The Idea of Landscape*, pp. 50, 59.
[21] Knight, *Analytical Inquiry*, p. 154.
[22] Dallaway, 'Supplementary anecdotes', p. 301.
[23] He referred to 'clumps of trees' on his estate at Twickenham as being 'like the groups in pictures' (Spence, *Observations*, I, p. 252).

William Shenstone declared: 'Landskip should contain variety enough to form a picture upon canvas; and this is no bad test, as I think the landskip painter is the gardiner's best designer.'[24] The tendency to admire natural scenery according to the principles of art, to appreciate a landscape the more it resembled a painting, led a certain class of people to redesign the natural scenery around them in order to reproduce the reproductions of landscape painting.

If the history of the picturesque intersects with the literary history of gardening, these developments in painting, literature, aesthetics, and landscape design themselves intersect with the social and political history of eighteenth-century England. A variety of influences and enabling conditions coincided to form both the literal and the figurative grounds on which the picturesque would be developed and cultivated. Painting gained new prestige and this interest in the visual arts extended to literature as theories of *ut pictura poesis* were reinvigorated and descriptive poetry became popular.[25] John Dyer's topographical poetry and James Thomson's *The Seasons* both reflected and furthered an interest in visual description, nature, and especially landscape. Claude, Rosa, and Poussin were considered ideal landscape painters, and artists such as Wilson and Constable developed their own versions of English landscape painting. Thomson himself (in a familiar trope of *ut pictura poesis*) was known as 'the Claude of poets'.[26]

This investment in the natural world and landscape – and its verbal and visual representations – extended beyond the realm of purely aesthetic appreciation. Hussey links the eighteenth-century appreciation of landscape to the popularity of the Grand Tour, which introduced the aristocracy to both the Alps and Italian landscape painting.[27] With newly acquired or refined tastes for landscape, connoisseurs carried out their acquisition of landscape art outside as well as inside their country houses. Patrons sent artists such as William Kent to Italy to bring back paintings and (as Hunt and Willis remark) their 'grounds steadily assumed the forms the paintings had suggested'.[28] The developing taste for particular forms and styles of landscapes extended from the descriptions imaged in poetry and the perspectives framed on their walls to the prospects framed by their windows and experienced from the privileged points of view enjoyed by landowners who walked their grounds as beholders. This translation from the book and gallery to the estate

---

[24] Shenstone, *Works*, ed. Hunt, XVII, p. 129.
[25] On the relations between *ut pictura poesis* and the picturesque, see Hunt, 'Ut pictura poesis', pp. 87–108. See also Monk, *The Sublime*, p. 203.
[26] Cited in Hussey, *The Picturesque*, p. 33.
[27] Hussey, *The Picturesque*, p. 12.
[28] Hunt and Willis, *The Genius of the Place*, p. 13.

obviously could not have taken place without wealthy landowners, an 'Agricultural Revolution' in which a 'rural professional class' sought to 'control and to manipulate nature',[29] and the enclosure acts, 'which permitted landowners to consolidate their property into large single blocks of land with the house and park at the center'.[30] Over three million acres of land were enclosed through acts of Parliament alone in the course of the eighteenth century, transforming the face of England.[31]

Shaftesbury is often cited for having inspired new responses to and images of nature. In *The Moralists* (1709), the dialogue he subtitles 'A Philosophical Rhapsody', the interlocutors describe natural scenes that open on to the sublime: 'See! with what trembling steps poor mankind tread the narrow brink of the deep precipices, from whence with giddy horror they look down, mistrusting even the ground which bears them, whilst they hear the hollow sound of torrents underneath, and see the ruin of the impending rock, with falling trees which hang with their roots upwards and seem to draw more ruin after them.'[32] The sensibility anticipated here would later thrive on the experience of crossing the Alps; the experience would be codified in Burke's *Enquiry*, the landscape pictured countless times in landscape paintings and Gothic novels. Shaftesbury also is interested in the sort of nature chosen for the human domain. The experience of the natural landscape by a philosophically-minded enthusiast who finds something 'answerable to this in the mind' looks ahead to the *rêveries* of Rousseau and the meditations of the Romantics; and it looks back critically on the formality of seventeenth-century gardens.[33]

'The wildness pleases', insists Shaftesbury's rhapsodist: 'We view [Nature] in her inmost recesses, and contemplate her with more delight than in the artificial labyrinths and feigned wildernesses of the palace.' Evoking 'the genius of the place', Shaftesbury privileges a natural scene 'where neither art nor the conceit or caprice of man has spoiled their genuine order by breaking in upon that primitive state'. His enthusiast pictures a scene that will be reproduced in countless gardens and the descriptions of Gilpin, Price, and Knight: 'Even the rude rocks, the mossy caverns, the irregular unwrought grottos and broken falls of water, with all the horrid graces of the wilderness itself, as representing Nature more, will be the more engaging, and appear with a magnificence beyond the formal mockery of princely gardens.' The attack on

---

[29] Barrell, *The Idea of Landscape*, pp. 60–1.
[30] Addison, *The Spectator*, III, pp. 551–2 (No. 414, 25 June 1712); Streatfield, 'Art and nature', pp. 10, 59.
[31] Hussey, *English Gardens*, pp. 15–16.
[32] Shaftesbury, *Characteristics*, II, p. 123.
[33] Shaftesbury, *Characteristics*, II, p. 271.

the artificiality of the seventeenth-century gardens patterned on French and Dutch models is related to an emerging concept of nature, especially as it impresses itself on the mind, that is accompanied by an avowed preference for nature over art. The enthusiastic character rhapsodizes over 'glorious nature ... whose every single work affords an ampler scene, and is a nobler spectacle than all which ever art presented!'[34] – yet in a gesture that will punctuate virtually all such declarations in the eighteenth century, nature is framed as spectacle and scene.

In the essays on 'the pleasures of the imagination' published in *The Spectator* in 1712, Addison also praises 'the Prospects of an open Champian Country, a vast uncultivated Desart, of huge Heaps of Mountains, high Rocks and Precipices, or a wide Expanse of Waters'. It is not beauty that strikes us but rather 'that rude kind of Magnificence which appears in many of these stupendous Works of Nature'.[35] Contrasting the 'narrow Compass' of the 'Beauties of the most stately Garden or Palace' with 'the wide Fields of Nature' where 'the Sight wanders up and down without Confinement, and is fed with an infinite variety of Images', Addison advocates the 'agreeable Mixture of Garden and Forest, which represent every where an artificial Rudeness' found in France and Italy. 'Our *British* Gardeners, on the contrary', writes Addison, instead of humouring Nature, love to deviate from it as much as possible. Our Trees rise in Cones, Globes, and Pyramids'. Disdaining the 'Neatness and Elegancy' of classical English gardens, he insists: 'I would rather look upon a Tree in all its Luxuriancy and Diffusion of Boughs and Branches, than when it is thus cut and trimmed into a Mathematical Figure.' An 'orchard in Flower' is preferable to 'all the little Labyrinths of the most finished Parterre'.[36]

Pope's 1713 essay in *The Guardian* follows Addison in praising 'the amiable Simplicity of unadorned Nature' in contrast to 'the modern Practice of Gardening' in which 'we seem to make it our Study to recede from Nature, not only in the various Tonsure of Greens into the most regular and formal Shapes, but even in monstrous Attempts beyond the reach of the Art it self: We run into Sculpture, and are yet better pleas'd to have our Trees in the most awkward Figures of Men and Animals, than in the most regular of their own.'[37] Influential in the theory and the practice of gardening (as displayed in his well-known gardens at Twickenham), Pope advised the architect Lord Burlington in his 1731 *Epistle*: 'To build, to plant, whatever you intend, / To rear the Column, or the Arch to bend, / To swell the Terras, or to sink the Grot; / In all,

[34] Shaftesbury, *The Moralists*, II, pp. 122, 125, 98.
[35] Addison, *The Spectator*, III, p. 540 (No. 412, 23 June 1712).
[36] Addison, *The Spectator*, III, p. 541 (No. 412); pp. 549, 551 (No. 414).
[37] Hunt and Willis, *The Genius of the Place*, pp. 205, 207.

let Nature never be forgot. / Consult the Genius of the Place in all.' Like
Shaftesbury, however, Pope expresses his declaration in favour of the
natural in the terms of art. His '*Genius of the Place*' 'scoops in circling
Theatres the Vale', 'varies Shades from Shades', and '*Paints* as you
plant, and as you work, *Designs*'.[38] Here we should recall that Addison's
privileging of the natural over the artificial takes place in the context of
essays about the imagination in which 'the Works of *Nature* and *Art*'
are juxtaposed, in which landscapes are compared with verbal and
visual representations of them. Indeed, although Addison notes that the
poet is always 'in Love with a Country-Life, where Nature appears in
the greatest Perfection', and although he prefers the 'wild Scenes' of
Horace and Virgil to 'any artificial Shows', he insists that 'we find the
Works of Nature still more pleasant, the more they resemble those of
Art'. This is because 'our Pleasure rises from a double Principle; from
the Agreeableness of the Objects to the Eye, and from their Similitude
to other Objects: We are pleased as well with comparing their Beauties,
as with surveying them, and can represent them to our Minds, either as
Copies or Originals'.[39] In comparing works of art and nature in *Spectator* 416, Addison even concludes that despite the disadvantage that
words, unlike painting, must communicate in the arbitrary signs of
language, words, 'when well chosen, have so great a Force in them, that
a Description often gives us more lively Ideas than the Sight of Things
themselves. The Reader finds a Scene drawn in Stronger Colours, and
painted more to the Life in his Imagination, by the help of Words, than
by an actual Survey of the Scene which they describe. In this Case the
Poet seems to get the better of Nature.'[40] In the context of garden
design, nature is preferable to the artificial; yet in the larger context of
the imagination, art seems to get the better of nature. The natural is
simultaneously valued for its avoidance of the artful or artificial and its
resemblance to art.

The picturesque, then, has its origins in this paradoxical grounding of
nature in aesthetic experience. As the history of the picturesque intersects with the literary history of gardening, the garden becomes an
arena in which theoreticians and practitioners display a complex ambivalence about art and nature. Here one can chart the changes in what
Ronald Paulson has called 'the ratio of art to nature'.[41] Rebelling against
the formality, symmetry, and artificial order of the classical garden and
embracing a state of nature with the transports of a new enthusiasm

---

[38] Pope, *Twickenham Edition*, III.ii, pp. 137–9. For Brownell, 'the idea of the
    picturesque is implicit' in these lines (*Alexander Pope*, p. 109).
[39] Addison, *The Spectator*, III, p. 550 (No. 414).
[40] Addison, *The Spectator*, III, p. 560 (No. 416, 27 June 1712).
[41] Paulson, *Emblem and Expression*, p. 20.

that sought out the wild, savage, and sublime, the English developed a new type of garden. Yet created in a context that compared the works of art and nature, privileging unaltered nature by praising its spectacles and scenes, this garden was conceived from the outset with pictures and poetry in mind. Occupying an intermediate stage between formal gardens and the 'places' created by Brown and his followers, it has been called the poetic garden. In gardens such as Twickenham and Stowe, the newly declared taste for unadorned nature coexisted with a desire to create a landscape that resembled a work of art, especially painting. The poetic garden went beyond the accidental resemblances to works of art that Addison noted, and in a sense beyond Pope's concept of gardening as landscape painting, applying the metaphor of the work of art in surprisingly literal ways. This meant that the garden was not only like a work of art; it was a work of art. Furthermore, it was conceived of as a particularly literary work: a poem, a text, a book. The picturesque has its roots in the literary and even verbal forms that emerged as the garden supposedly moved closer to nature. The poetic garden was inscribed *with* writing and *as* writing in both figurative and literal senses. This was in part because of the influence of an iconographic tradition that allowed the garden to be composed (and subsequently read) as a series of emblems, hieroglyphs, and literary allusions.

In this emblematic tradition, architecture (especially imitations of classical architecture with ruins, statues, urns, obelisks, and columns that were often inscribed with mottoes, names, verses and other citations) combined with the visual imagery of paintings and theatre to create complex texts that had to be read and deciphered. The language of such gardens required a knowledge of iconography and allusions, as well as the intellectual ability and the sensibility to reflect on death, virtue, liberty, solitude, or whatever topos or theme was suggested. It also employed puns and sophisticated intertextual references. This play of allusion depended at once on a rich iconographic and literary tradition and on newer principles of association derived from Hobbes and especially Locke.[42] The associations of iconography and classical allusion proved so specific that they became increasingly difficult to read.[43] Dissatisfaction with the inaccessibility of the private language of emblems coincided with a desire for a less intellectual and more affective experience. In his *Observations on Modern Gardening* (1765), Thomas Whately asserts that gardens should make an impression rather than appeal to the intellect. Complaining that 'natural cascades have been

---

[42] See Locke on the 'Connexion of *Ideas* wholly owing to Chance or Custom' (*Essay concerning Human Understanding*, p. 395).

[43] See Hunt and Willis, *The Genius of the Place*, pp. 33–4; and Hunt, 'Ut pictura poesis', pp. 100–1, 98.

disfigured with river gods; and columns erected only to receive quotations', Whately declares: 'All these devices are rather *emblematical* than expressive . . . but they make no immediate impression; for they must be examined, compared, perhaps explained, before the whole design of them is well understood.' Any allusion, he insists, should be 'suggested by the scene . . . and have the force of a metaphor, free from the detail of an allegory'.[44] This move from emblem to expression, from allegory to metaphor, continued to lay the groundwork for the picturesque; like the evolutions and revolutions in landscape design that preceded, it also took place under the sign of nature.

'Capability' Brown, who began as the head gardener at Stowe and became one of the first professional landscape designers, is credited with replacing contrived and ordered allusions with 'more flexible patterns of association', with seeking out 'the forms and shapes of nature' in what he called 'Place-making'.[45] Brown served as a bridge between the academic picturesque of the emblematic or poetic garden and the theories of Gilpin, Price, and Knight. Praised for his part in the rebellion against the symmetry and artificiality of the seventeenth-century garden, called 'a great painter',[46] Brown cleared the way for the picturesque, yet Price and Knight believed that he had cleared away too much, that his 'place-making' had been too radical in the sense that it had literally uprooted the landscape and replaced nature with a new artificiality. Brown and the improvers that followed him – especially Repton – were attacked by the advocates of the picturesque for their expensive and extravagant engineering; in their 'place-making', the improvers seemed to set themselves up as 'geniuses of the place' with licence to move hills and rivers and clear away large sections of the landscape to make lawns and mass-produced forms. The remarkably vitriolic debate between the improvers and the theoreticians of the picturesque once again focused on the ratio of art to nature. To a great extent the debate centred on the status of painting and the adherence of the landscape designer to picturesque principles. However, it was Brown and Repton who were accused of having betrayed the cause of nature.

In his *Letter to Humphry Repton*, Price suggests that 'while Mr Brown was removing old pieces of formality, he was establishing new ones of a more extensive consequence'.[47] Incensed that Repton had 'changed his ground' and renounced the principles of painting, Knight declared that it was 'generally admitted, that the system of picturesque improvement' of Brown and his followers 'is the very reverse of picturesque; all subjects for painting instantly disappearing as they advance'.[48] He called

---

[44] Whately, *Observations on Modern Gardening*, pp. 83–4.
[45] Hunt, *Figure*, pp. 190, 218.   [46] Cited in Hussey, *The Picturesque*, p. 138.
[47] *Letter to Humphry Repton*, *Essays*, III, p. 37.
[48] Knight, *The Landscape*, 2nd edn, pp. 17–18n.

upon Repton to 'quit the school of Mr Brown, and return to that of the great masters in landscape painting'.[49] Perhaps the codification and standardization of lines and forms coincided with changes in convention and perception that altered the sense of what was natural. In the history of literature and painting, changes in the conventions of representation can deny works of art the power of conviction and thereby necessitate new forms that will either fulfil or challenge new notions of verisimilitude; it may be that what at first seemed radically natural in Brown's gardens came to feel artificial to a later generation – just as earlier in the century the once natural-seeming qualities of the poetic garden had begun to feel increasingly archaic and unnatural. In any case, the advocates of the picturesque believed that the improvers had reinstated artificiality and formality because they had abandoned both the forms of nature and the forms of art.

Brown and Repton were derided by Price and Knight for being gardeners[50] yet Repton boasts of having combined the 'powers of the *landscape painter* and the *practical gardener*' in what he terms '*Landscape Gardening*'. Asserting that landscape design cannot be judged by the principles of painting alone, Repton declares (in terms that recall Reynolds's anecdote about Wilson) that Knight 'appears even to forget that a dwelling-house is an object of comfort and convenience, for the purposes of habitation; and not merely the frame to a landscape, or the foreground of a rural picture'.[51] Evoking the excesses of discredited gardening practices of earlier times and pursuing the principles of '*Picture Gardening*' to its logical conclusion, Repton suggests that if 'the painter's landscapes be indispensable to the perfection of gardening, it would surely be far better to paint it on canvas at the end of an avenue, as they do in Holland, than to sacrifice the health, cheerfulness, and comfort of a country residence, to the wild but pleasing scenery of a painter's imagination'.[52] The problem is not simply comfort; at stake is also what it would mean to paint the landscape of nature. What seems threatening here is not the idea that one might design a natural scene as if it were a painting but rather the idea that the scene of painting would have priority over the scene of nature. An actual painting placed in a garden only literalizes the idea that a representation would take the place of nature if landscape gardeners were to copy a natural landscape from the model of painting.

[49] Knight, *The Landscape*, 2nd edn, pp. 99–101.
[50] Knight, *The Landscape*, 2nd edn, pp. 99–101; Price, *Essays*, I, pp. 243–4.
[51] *Landscape Gardening*, p. 99. Repton cites William Wyndham: 'A scene of a cavern, with banditti sitting by it, is the favourite subject of Salvator Rosa; but are we therefore to live in caves, or encourage the neighborhood of banditti?
Gainsborough's country girl is a more picturesque object than a child neatly dressed in a white frock; but is that a reason why our children are to go in rags?' (p. 115).
[52] Repton, *Landscape Gardening*, pp. 114, 104.

Defensive about the relative positions of art and nature in his theory, Price denies that he recommends 'the study of pictures in preference to that of nature, much less to the exclusion of it'.[53] Gilpin also denies having declared '*all beauty* to consist in *picturesque beauty* – and the face of nature to be examined *only by the rules of painting*'. He claims to 'speak a different language. We speak of the grand scenes of nature, tho uninteresting in a *picturesque light*, as having a strong effect on the imagination'[54] – but the problem lies in a language that itself pictures nature in *scenes*, in a point of view that seems to alter the face of nature by designing or merely illuminating it with the rules of painting. Whately had warned in his *Observations on Modern Gardening* that the works of a great painter 'are fine exhibitions of nature' that can teach 'a taste for beauty; but still their authority is not absolute; they must be used only as studies, not as models; for a picture and a scene in nature, though they agree in many, yet differ in some particulars, which must always be taken into consideration, before we can decide upon the circumstances which may be transferred from the one to the other.'[55] Price insists that there are 'reasons for studying *copies* of nature, though the *original* is before us'; he suggests that we look at paintings as 'a set of experiments of the different ways in which trees, buildings, water, &c. may be disposed'.[56] Yet once one enters the picturesque, it is not always easy to make a distinction between the original and the copy, even when the scene of painting is merely a study for the scene of nature. For Whately, gardening is 'as superior to landskip painting, as a reality is to a representation'.[57] However, one might ask what one is looking at when the original of nature is before one, especially when the real scene of nature is regarded as if it were a representation. What does one compose when one designs a landscape, since, as William Marshall noted in 1785, 'Nature scarcely knows the thing mankind call a *land-scape*'?[58] The improvers' counter-attack on Price and Knight is based on common sense rather than a moral or philosophical argument; yet in challenging the priority of painting in the picturesque point of view, it draws upon an undercurrent of anxiety about aesthetic distance that runs throughout the literary history of gardening as well as the aesthetic of the picturesque.

We have seen that from the outset the question of aesthetic distance informs the very concept of the picturesque. Although both theorists and practitioners of landscape design sought to reject the artificial and embrace the natural, by definition the picturesque involved looking at nature as if it were art, using the principles of art to design nature. The

[53] Price, *Essays*, p. 3. [54] *Three Essays*, p. ii. [55] Whately, *Observations*, p. 81.
[56] Price, *Essays*, I, p. 5. [57] Whately, *Observations*, p. 1.
[58] Cited in Andrews, *The Search for the Picturesque*, p. 34.

construction of amphitheatres, the arrangement of trees to frame natural scenes like the wings of a stage, and the use of mirrors to fill the gallery of nature with *tableaux* were only literal manifestations of the point of view the beholder of the picturesque was supposed to internalize. Pope's estate at Twickenham contained a famous grotto that incorporated mirrors in which water, light, and various images would be reflected. In 1747, a visitor offered this description: 'Plates of Looking glass in the obscure Parts of the Roof and Sides of the Cave, where a sufficient Force of Light is wanting to discover the Deception, while the other Parts, the Rills, Fountains, Flints, Pebbles, &c. being duly illuminated, are so reflected by the various profited Mirrors, as, without exposing the Cause, every Object is multiplied, and its Position represented in a surprizing Diversity.'[59] As Brownell notes, citing Pope's own account, the grotto was designed 'to function as a *camera obscura* "on the Walls of which all the objects of the River, Hills, Woods, and Boats, are forming a moving Picture in their visible Radiations"'.[60] Describing the 'very extraordinary Effect' of the 'profusion of Mirrors', Gilpin wrote: 'The prospects without are likewise transferred to the Walls within: And the Sides of the Room are elegantly adorned with landskips, beyond the Pencil of *Titian*.'[61] The visitor explains how, surrounded by these images and reflections, in a 'happy Management of Nature, you are presented with an undistinguishable Mixture of Realities and Imagery'.[62] This indistinguishable mixture, however, is itself part of the aesthetic of the picturesque – which not only compares image and reality, not only looks at nature through the frame of art, not only designs the original after the representation, but finally breaks down the distinction between one and the other.

In the *Spectator* essay in which he asserts that 'the Products of Nature rise in value, according as they more or less resemble those of art' and that 'artificial Works receive a greater Advantage from their Resemblance of such as are natural', Addison offers a remarkable description of an accidental *camera obscura*:

The prettiest Landskip I ever saw, was one drawn on the Walls of a dark Room, which stood opposite on one side to a navigable River, and on the other to a Park. The Experiment is very common in Opticks. Here you discover the Waves and Fluctuations of the Water in strong and proper Colours, with the Picture of a Ship entering at one end, and sailing by Degrees through the whole Piece. On another there appeared the Green

---

[59] Published in *The General Magazine* in 1748, the letter is reprinted in Hunt and Willis, *The Genius of the Place*, pp. 249–50.

[60] Brownell, *Alexander Pope*, p. 129.

[61] Gilpin, *A Dialogue*, cited in Hunt and Willis, *The Genius of the Place*, p. 256.

[62] Hunt and Willis, *The Genius of the Place*, p. 250.

Shadows of Trees, waving to and fro with the Wind, and Herds of Deer among them in Miniature, leaping on the Wall.

Addison suggests that the 'Novelty of such a Sight' may engage the imagination but claims that 'certainly the chief Reason is its near Resemblance to Nature, as it does not only, like other Pictures, give Colour and Figure, but the Motion of the Things it represents'.[63] It is as if Addison has invented (or discovered) motion pictures as he sees images and pictures projected in miniature upon the wall in light and colour. These images are admired for their resemblance to nature; but the other term in the comparison here is not 'other pictures' but rather nature itself. Addison does not appear to be interested in looking out the window or actually stepping into the landscape of nature.

Grottoes like Pope's were not encountered everywhere, but picturesque travellers could arrive on any scene equipped with their own mirrors. Indeed, countless beholders were literally framing their acts of looking with instruments such as the *camera obscura* and especially the Claude-glass. Described as 'a plano-convex Mirror of about four inches diameter on a black foil, and bound up like a pocket-book', the Claude-glass was designed to 'gather every scene reflected in it into a tiny picture';[64] it allowed one to convert the scene of nature into a miniature picture in a way that increased its resemblance to a Claudian landscape or at least to a painting. 'My Convex Mirror', wrote a tourist at Lake Windermere, 'brought every scene within the compass of a picture.'[65] Thus, outside of the borders of the picturesque scenes contained in the garden and the estate, the traveller, tourist, or *promeneur solitaire* in search of natural beauty was not limited to those scenes that accidentally resembled a landscape of Claude. Equipped with a mirror or oval glasses, the picturesque traveller could turn reality into representation; equipped with notebook and sketch pad, he or she could contemplate the natural through its reflection. Indeed, it was through this mimesis that nature could be fully appreciated. This mediation was multiplied by the tendency to visit well-known picturesque landscapes with well-known descriptions of them in hand.[66]

We have seen, however, that the very terms of nature and art are altered by the perspective of the picturesque. Paradoxically, the ancient metaphor of art as a mirror that offered a direct reflection of reality is literally introduced into the landscape. In Pope's grotto, the mirror

---

[63] Addison, *The Spectator*, III, pp. 550–1 (No. 414).

[64] Cited in Andrews, *Search for the Picturesque*, p. 68; and Barrell, *The Idea of Landscape*, p. 23.

[65] Cited by Andrews, *Search for the Picturesque*, p. 68.

[66] See Barrell, *The Idea of Landscape*, p. 43; Hunt and Willis, *The Genius of the Place*, p. 333; and Monk, *The Sublime*, p. 204.

returns the beholder to Plato's cave, regarding a world of images and shadows at several removes. In the shape of a Claude-glass, the mirror inserts mimesis between art and reality, distorting the scene of nature with artistic licence. The *camera obscura*, a prototype of photography meant to create a totally realistic representation of nature, is used as a mechanism that intermixes reality and images and finally turns the picturesque eye from nature. In the frame of the picturesque, the Claude-glass becomes the mirror of art rather than the mirror of nature.

Beyond experiments in optics and the props and machinery of the picturesque, what is crucial here is 'the picturesque eye' – what Knight describes in another context as 'modes and habits of viewing'.[67] Gilpin describes the experience of looking out the window of a chaise through a Claude-glass or convex mirror: 'A succession of high-coloured pictures is continually gliding before the eye. They are like the visions of the imagination, or the brilliant landscapes of a dream. Forms and colours in brightest array fleet before us; and if the transient glance of a good composition happen to unite with them, we should give any price to fix, and appropriate the scene.'[68] In the mind described by Locke and Hume, fleeting images are constantly gliding before the imagination, which is pictured in terms of images. Looking with a picturesque eye, the beholder internalizes the frame and mirror of the Claude-glass and transforms the fleeting images of the world into pictures of art. As so often happens in this period, epistemology and aesthetics become superimposed. Indeed, Gilpin declares that in viewing the picturesque, the 'imagination becomes a camera obscura'. He insists, however, that there is a 'difference' since 'the camera represents objects as they really are; while the imagination, impressed with the most beautiful scenes, and chastened by rules of art, forms its pictures, not only from the most admirable parts of nature; but in the best taste'.[69] This process is not limited to the production of images in the imagination; it appears to take place even when viewing things as they really are in a present scene. In this sense the imagination of the picturesque traveller or beholder becomes a Claude-glass, transforming the scene of nature with the framing perspective of art. The problem of turning objects as they really are into representations by regarding them through the mirror of the picturesque is, of course, compounded when the objects of nature themselves have been designed according to the rules of art – when the landscape before the eye is a vision of the imagination from the outset: the brilliant landscape of a dream of painting.

It was a commonplace in eighteenth-century landscape design that art

---

[67] Knight, *Analytical Inquiry*, I, p. 196.
[68] Gilpin, *Remarks on Forest Scenery*, II, pp. 233–4.
[69] Gilpin, *Three Essays*, II, p. 52.

should be concealed. Knight advocates 'art clandestine, and conceal'd design' in *The Landscape*.[70] Theorists and practitioners such as Whately recognize gardening as one of the 'imitative arts' yet warn that 'the consciousness of an imitation, checks the train of thought which the appearance naturally suggests'. Joseph Spence, who directs the landscape designer to 'follow Nature', writes that 'Gardening is an imitation of "Beautiful nature", and therefore should not be like works of Art. Wherever art appears, the gardener has failed in his execution.'[71] Repton, too, asserts that 'the highest perfection of landscape gardening is, to imitate nature so judiciously, that the interference of art shall never be detected'.[72] According to Price, who cites Tasso's line, 'L'arte che tutto fa, nulla si scopre', in the conclusion to his *Essay on the Picturesque*, 'wherever there is any thing of natural wildness and intricacy in the scene, the improver should conceal himself like a judicious author, who sets his reader's imagination at work, while he seems not to be guiding'. He should be like Homer, who, Price notes (following Aristotle) 'scarcely ever appears in his own person'; Price contrasts this with Fielding's tendency to appear 'sometimes ostentatiously'.[73]

'There are indeed certain words in all languages', writes Price in his conclusion, 'that have a good and a bad sense: such as *simplicity* and *simple*, *art* and *artful*, which as often express our contempt as our admiration.' It is by no means unusual that eighteenth-century theoreticians and practitioners of the picturesque should embrace an ideology that advocated the clandestine use and concealment of art. Yet the literary history of gardening and picturesque aesthetics involves such ambivalence about both nature and art – such contempt as well as admiration – that formulas about the concealment of art cannot be dismissed as mere convention. Furthermore, in so far as the picturesque depends on the *recognition* of art, the insistence that a scene resemble a work of art that either has or might have been composed by an artist, the idea that the art of the design should be invisible becomes complicated.

Knight's theories introduce a further complication since his most important contribution to the theory of the picturesque is his application of associationism. Far from the post-Lockean theories of the proponents of the emblematic garden's obelisks and inscriptions, Knight uses associationism to argue a more radical epistemology of the picturesque that is mostly directed against his friend Price. In his *Analytical Inquiry into the Principles of Taste*, Knight declares:

[70] Knight, *The Landscape*, 1st edn, p. 1.
[71] Hunt and Willis, *The Genius of the Place*, p. 268.
[72] Repton, *Landscape Gardening*, pp. 162, 84.
[73] Price, *Essays*, I, pp. 334–5; *Essay*, p. 287. The criticism of Fielding appears in the first edition but is deleted in the revised and expanded *Essays*. Cf. Tasso, *Gerusalemme liberata* (XVI, 9,8) in *Opere*, p. 449; and Aristotle, *Poetics*, III.ii, p. 11.

The sensual pleasure arising from viewing objects and compositions, which we call picturesque, may be felt equally by all mankind in proportion to the correctness and sensibility of their organs of sight; for it is wholly independent of their being picturesque, or *after the manner of painters*. But this very relation to painting, expressed by the word *picturesque*, is that, which affords the whole pleasure derived from association; which can, therefore, only be felt by persons, who have correspondent ideas to associate; that is, by persons in a certain degree conversant with that art.

Focusing on those who are 'in the habit of viewing, and receiving pleasure from fine pictures', who will 'naturally feel pleasure in viewing those objects in nature, which have called forth those powers of imitation', Knight declares: 'The objects recall to the mind the imitations, which skill, taste, and genius have produced; and these again recall to the mind the objects themselves, and show them through an improved medium – that of the feeling and discernment of a great artist.'[74]

Here again we have a Claude-glass of the imagination; objects in nature remind us of paintings, and we view the objects before our eyes through the medium of an absent representation. What is crucial here is Knight's insistence that objects themselves do not possess picturesque properties independent of the associations of the beholder: 'All these extra pleasures are from the minds of spectators; whose pre-existing trains of ideas are revived, refreshed, and reassociated by new, but correspondent impressions on the organs of sense.' Price's 'fundamental error' is 'seeking for distinctions in external objects, which only exist in the modes and habits of viewing and considering them'.[75] In refusing to locate the picturesque in the 'inherent qualities of the objects',[76] Knight recalls Gilpin's emphasis on the picturesque eye. However, whereas for Gilpin, gardens were 'a very good Epitome of the World: They are calculated for Minds of every Stamp, and give free Scope to Inclinations of every kind',[77] Knight's theory is by definition elitist. Only 'a mind richly stored'[78] will be able to appreciate the picturesque; indeed, to the beholder who is not equipped with the necessary associations, the picturesque will be virtually invisible: 'To all others, however acute soever may be their discernment, or how exquisite soever their sensibility, it is utterly imperceptible'.[79]

Earlier forms of associationism in landscape design were abandoned because they relied on increasingly private and inaccessible codes. Appealing to emotions, moods, and more general acts of imagination, later

---

[74] Knight, *Analytical Inquiry*, pp. 152–3. Cf. Price, *Essays*, II, p. 247.
[75] Knight, *Analytical Inquiry*, p. 196.   [76] Knight, *Analytical Inquiry*, p. 196.
[77] Gilpin, 'A Dialogue upon the Gardens of the Right Honorable the Lord Viscount Cobham at Stow in Buckinghamshire' (1748), in Hunt and Willis, *The Genius of the Place*, p. 258.
[78] Knight, *Analytical Inquiry*, p. 143.   [79] Knight, *Analytical Inquiry*, p. 146.

forms were more inclusive; depending on correspondent ideas, they look forward to the writings of the English Romantics. Yet in the context of the picturesque, Knight's theories raise the possibility of the end of the picturesque. If the picturesque exists only in the mind of the designer or beholder and not in the properties of objects themselves, it is possible that the picturesque might become too invisible. The picturesque depends on an act of recognition; it takes place in the vertiginous space of a comparison that associates a composition in nature with a composition in art in an unending relay of representations, imitations, and reflections. Knight complained that the improvers 'disregarded' art when it was concealed and not ostentatious; but in so far as the picturesque depends on an act of looking that resonates between the absent and the present, between works of art and nature, it is possible that the place between concealment and ostentatiousness might become increasingly difficult to design.

Ironically, perhaps, the fate of the picturesque was to become too recognizable. Depending on a sense of *déjà vu*, the picturesque became recognizable as a style in itself, so that a picturesque landscape – even one accidentally created in and by nature – did not resemble a painting as much as it resembled a picturesque landscape. Once recognized, the picturesque garden, like the earlier poetic garden, risks becoming a stage set. Eighteenth-century garden design is famous for its excesses: the artificial ruins, temples, and even hermitages inhabited by hired and costumed hermits – or, if necessary, 'stuffed dummies that gave the right emblematic effect at twenty yards'.[80] If the picturesque garden aimed to be less theatrical, it aimed no less to be theatre. Like the garden designs and theories that preceded it, then, it also was fated to feel artificial the more its art was recognized and consequently revealed. In a sense, however, it was both the contribution and the curse of the picturesque to inscribe the place of nature in the realm of art. It is precisely in the uncanny wavering between art and artifice as well as between reality and representation that the aesthetics of the picturesque takes place. By hiding or erasing the boundaries between nature and art, by insisting that those boundaries were never very clear to begin with, the picturesque eye changes our view of the world.

[80] Hunt, *Figure*, p. 6. See Streatfield, 'Art and nature', p. 69.

(iii) *Literature and music*
Dean Mace

During the first half of the eighteenth century literary critics in France and England, while accepting the ancient sisterhood of music and poetry, believed music to be an inferior art; by the end of the century they had come to praise music as an art whose condition poetry might aspire to but never reach. This transformation of opinion was a remarkable event in the history of eighteenth-century aesthetics.

The involvement of eighteenth-century literary criticism with music is owing to the fact that opera, which to the eighteenth century was the centre of musical art, looked for its theory and practice and for measurements of its excellence to the spoken drama with its attendant body of theory and criticism. This had been true since the days of the Florentine *Camerata* when literary criticism first began its invasion of musical territory. The content and structure of the Lully–Quinault *tragédie lyrique* were based on literary models, principally plays. The famous operatic reforms of the eighteenth century, the Metastasian libretto, and later the operas of Gluck, were inspired by a respect for literature – the classical drama of Corneille and Racine.

In Paris and London literary critics struck at the opera with satire. Addison's famous pieces in the *Spectator* are typical of the kind save for their superior intelligence and style. He concentrated on questions of verisimilitude. 'People were wonderfully surprized', he wrote in 1711, 'to hear Generals singing the Word of Command'.[1] Some literary critics still take this to be a telling point. But Addison also objected to the stupidity of managers who put real birds in a stage garden, confounding nature and art; or who replaced original Italian words with English words which did not fit the 'passion' or 'affection' of the music. Addison also hated the floridness of the poetry in the Italian librettos, thinking with Boileau that one verse of Virgil was worth all the 'tinsel of Tasso'. Tasso was much blamed for operatic diction.

Between 1711 and 1739 Handel produced thirty-six operas in London, some of them among the dramatic masterpieces of the age. But they were not understood as drama by the English. Even Dr Burney analysed only the *airs* in his account of the Handel operas; yet he understood what the arias were thought to exist for: to express some appropriate 'passion' of the characters at a certain point in the action – whether the passion be rage, love, vengeance, hatred, or whatsoever.[2] The structural principle of the Italian *opera seria* was that the drama

---

[1] Addison, *Spectator*, I, p. 120 (No. 29).
[2] Burney, *General History* II, Bk IV, ch. VI, pp. 672ff.

should consist of a sequence of these arias representing the internal life of the characters as it both responded to and generated the action. The external action was generally left to recitative. This kind of dramatic structure was much ridiculed even in the eighteenth century; yet it is clearly analogous to the structural principle which Dryden described as characteristic of the drama of Corneille and Racine, and which he sets forth in the *Essay of Dramatic Poesy*. French drama is represented there as showing little of the action but brimming with very long speeches (which correspond structurally to arias) in which the characters express their passions. Dryden and others could not see the parallel to opera because they did not accept music as an adequate language of the passions.

Because – like their English colleagues – most French literary critics from the time of Lully had not understood music itself as the essential dramatic language, but as merely a decoration applied to the words of a play, they tended to treat opera as an inferior form of dramatic literature. Quinault became their victim; he was blamed for opera's poor poetry, its excessive appeal to the senses, the frivolities of the *merveilleux*, and the immorality of an art not dedicated to the intellect. Boileau was violently opposed to opera and attacked it for its obsession with love, an obsession which Fénelon saw as already having invaded the drama of Corneille and Racine and thence transmitted to opera. La Bruyère, Dacier, and Saint-Évremond joined Boileau and Fénelon in the attack. Dacier sums up the main objections: the poems of the operas are ridiculous and no one would hear them in the theatre were he not 'enchanted and seduced by one of the greatest musicians who ever lived'.[3] This apparent praise of Lully is in fact a condemnation of music with its provision only for the pleasure of the ear. Such was the ground of Saint-Évremond's real or pretended dislike of opera, which he thought very dangerous because it ruins tragedy 'than which nothing is more proper to elevate the Soul, or more capable to form the Mind'. 'It is vain', he announced while airing his theme, 'to charm the Ears, or gratify the Eyes, if the Mind be not satisfied'.[4] Among early French critics Charles Perrault seems to have been the only one who realized that music was not a mere ornament but rather a dramatic language itself. But Saint-Évremond, not Perrault, was the dominant influence on early eighteenth-century opinion. Not until the Abbé Batteux's *Les Beaux-Arts réduits à un même principe* (1746) would there be a French confession of the superiority of music's place in opera.

The objection that music is unintelligible appeared again and again in French and English literary criticism from Lully's time through the Augustan age. Anthony Motteux in the *Gentleman's Journal* attributed

---

[3] Dacier, *Poétique d'Aristote*, p. 82.   [4] Saint-Évremond, *Letters*, pp. 217, 207.

the creation of those plays with extensive incidental music – such as
Dryden's and Purcell's *King Arthur* – which the English called 'operas'
to the English belief that music could not appeal to the brain.

Our English genius will not relish that perpetual singing ... Our English
Gentlemen, when their Ear is satisfy'd are desirous to have their mind
pleased, and Music and Dancing industriously intermixed with Comedy and
Tragedy.[5]

As John Dennis explains in a miniature comparison of the arts, only
poetry engages all the faculties:

That must be the best and the noblest art, which makes the best Provision
at the same time for the Satisfaction of all the Faculties, the Reason, the
Passions, the Senses. But none of them provides in such a sovereign Manner
as Poetry, for the Satisfaction of the whole man together ... In others the
Passions and the Senses are charm'd, while Reason finds little contentment
in them. Thus Musick by its Harmony raises the Passions, at the same Time
that it Pleases the Ear, and Painting by its Touches moves the Affections, at
the same Time that it charms the Eye. But in a sublime and accomplished
poem, the Reason, and Passions, and Senses are pleased at the same Time
Superlatively.[6]

This opinion was to flourish for a very long time. As late as 1779 James
Beattie could write: 'If I mistake not, the expression of music without
poetry is vague and ambiguous'.[7] Beattie, like many of his contemporaries in England and France, even doubted that music could be
an imitation of nature, despite Aristotle's view to the contrary. While
maintaining that painting and poetry were both imitative arts, Beattie
confessed to 'some unaccountable confusion of thought' whenever he
attempted to explain this ancient doctrine as it applied to music. He
concluded that music pleases not because it is imitative, but 'because
certain melodies and harmonies have an aptitude to raise certain passions, affections, and sentiments in the soul'. This power, alas, is insufficient in Beattie's opinion for the highest missions of art. 'Consequently,
the pleasures we derive from melody and harmony are seldom or never
resolvable into that delight which the human mind receives from the
imitation of nature'.[8] Poetry could represent actions, passions, and, as
no other art could, the workings of the rational mind. Not wishing to
condemn music, Beattie was typical of mid-eighteenth-century wavering
in his opinions about it.

Critics never denied that music was in fact pleasing, that it might be
virtuous and innocent, and that a gentleman might take great delight in

---

[5] Motteux, quoted by Rosenfeld, *Restoration Stage*, p. 454.
[6] Dennis, *Critical Works*, I, p. 263.
[7] Beattie, *Essays*, p. 147.   [8] Beattie, *Essays*, p. 119.

it, but at the same time music was allowed a very minor place among the arts in comparison to poetry. The Boethean commonplaces of the first stanza of Dryden's 1687 St Cecilia's Day ode continued to appear whenever the occasion called for praise of order, and Handel's setting of the poem was much admired. But even in Dryden's time these ideas had come to be merely the material of poetic ceremony.

From the early years of the Restoration and surrounding the life and work of Henry Purcell, Dryden was the dominant English poet and critic, providing the Augustans with many of their favourite views. Apart from dozens of songs in plays and the great odes, Dryden wrote the texts of several popular 'semi-operas' and peppered his essays, prologues, and epilogues with observations on music. He showed the influence of France in his version of the usual charge against music, namely that it was designed to please hearing but not inform the understanding.[9]

Dryden, like Addison later, was clearly put off by what he found to be the artificiality and the lack of verisimilitude in opera, especially the French supply of gods and goddesses. Yet he found the unities and decorums of Corneille and Racine highly verisimilar and he took much trouble to defend the use of rhyme in his own heroic plays. Verisimilitude was then as now an elastic concept. Dryden was at pains to insist that rhyming couplets, though certainly not natural, were nevertheless verisimilar in heroic plays and a true imitation of nature; that is, as he said, they imitated that nature 'wrought up to an higher pitch' which is the 'nature' of an heroic world.[10] As his arguments about rhyme show, Dryden had the sophisticated critical equipment to defend opera as verisimilar. The organization of verse rhythmically and in rhyme depends, like music, on the 'inarticulate'; that is, these are elements of spoken language without denotative meaning. If Dryden found them essential for heightening the drama why did he not – as Augustan critics in general did not – understand that opera, like the heroic play, imitated a 'nature' wrought up to a higher pitch? Why did not the age in fact understand music as a language? A partial answer to this question is to be found in seventeenth-century scientific and philosophical inquiry into the nature of music which supposedly revealed that the art cannot have access to reason.

Some seventeenth-century theorists, reaching back to Pythagorean ideas, tried to justify music as a liberal art or science because it was derived from mathematics; that is, its 'perfect' concords were thought to be invariable sensory images of absolute mathematical ratios: the octave, $1:2$, the fifth, $2:3$, and the fourth, $3:4$. The absolute 'beauty' of

[9] Dryden, *Preface to Albion and Albanius*, in *Essays*, I, p. 271.
[10] Dryden, *An Essay of Dramatic Poesy*, in *Essays*, I, pp. 100–1.

harmony was believed to depend on these ratios. But in the course of researches devoted to discovering the means toward an ideal and perfect musical art (and this was theoretically possible if 'perfection' lies in mathematical intervals) Marin Mersenne found out from the experiments of Vincenzo Galilei that the perfect intervals were by no means invariably derived from the Pythagorean ratios; for example, when weights were hung from strings of equal length and thickness the octave was produced by a ratio of one to four rather than one to two.[11] The Pythagorean ratios pertained only to string length under certain conditions. There was nothing in the nature of number, therefore, which gave to these ratios the exclusive cause of 'perfect' harmony. This, although not often remarked by modern scholarship, was a momentous discovery: it meant that there was no longer the possibility of an objective standard for judging musical beauty. To put it another way, musical pleasure could be determined only by the ear, not by the intellect. In a letter of 1629 Descartes wrote to Mersenne: 'if we judge [the quality of any consonance] by reason, this reason must always assume the ability of our ear'. And again later: 'In order to determine that which is more agreeable, it is necessary to assume the ability of the listener, which changes, like taste, according to each person'.[12] This was literally the birth of the idea of 'taste' as triumphant over rule, an idea so frequently thought to be an eighteenth-century innovation in aesthetics. But it was also the birth of the unfortunate idea that music appeals only to the sense of hearing and not to reason.

How Mersenne's discovery made its way from his heavy books to the polite world is a mystery. But it is undeniable that the late seventeenth-century emphasis on the irrationality of music had roots in philosophical thought which was subjecting old intellectual sciences to the devastating attacks of empiricism. Music plunged downward in the hierarchy of the arts.

Having been detached from reason music would require a new justification if it were to rise again to a high place. Providing this justification in a new aesthetic was the work of the eighteenth century. Its beginnings, however, can also be traced to the speculations of Mersenne who saw the necessity of linking the power of music, not to the mind, which was no longer possible, but to the movements of the passions. In doing this he thought he was returning to ancient doctrine. The seventeenth century was the source of both the abasement of music in the first half of the eighteenth century and its eventual rise in the hierarchy of the arts in the second half of that century.

---

[11] Palisca, 'Scientific empiricism', pp. 127–8, 132.
[12] Descartes, in Mersenne, *Correspondance*, II, p. 228.

Well into the seventeenth century there flourished an idea taken from Augustine's *De Musica* that the poetic feet derived their excellence from their relation to the Pythagorean ratios. In this doctrine the nobility of the iambus, for example, was said to depend on its short–long structure, which equals the Pythagorean ratio of the octave (1:2), the best of the consonances, etc. The spondee was even better – representing equality, another way of understanding unity. Mersenne naturally rejected this tradition, having denied intrinsic value to any proportion, and came to hold the idea that the power of the poetic feet lay in their function as 'images' of the passions and affections. This idea had the advantage of being compatible with ancient theories of poetic rhythm; and in Mersenne's thought it accorded a new power to rhythm in music and in poetry.

The secret of the union of poetry and music so much celebrated by the ancients and so fascinating to seventeenth-century theorists was therefore to be found in common rhythmical structures. The art of *rhythmus* was the art not only of pleasing auditors, but of exciting them to 'some passion and affection, whether of joy or of sadness, of love or of hate, etc.'.[13] This was a way to deal with the weakness of music. It is an early statement of the theory of music as the art of representing the passions and affections – those irrational states of the soul defined by Aristotle in his *Rhetoric* – in musical figures which were analogous to the *loci topici* of rhetoric. The musician should concentrate not on harmony for the mere pleasure of the senses, but on rhythmically animated sound to arouse and represent the passions. Mersenne took a further step in connecting this power – wrongly, as later critics would contend – with the poetic principle that the sound should echo the sense. 'This is why good poets like Virgil have swift movement represented by short syllables, by dactyls, anapests and similar feet, to give to the reader or the hearer a similar motion, or a similar image ... It is certain that these movements, being well regulated and arranged, have a great power upon the mind or on the blood and other humours'.[14] Music could, enter poetry through this 'imitative harmony', as it came to be called, and immeasurably increase the power of poetry. Music would be contained within poetry. Rhythm and sound could both describe and express feeling.

Dryden's St Cecilia odes, with their careful adaptation of imitative metrical patterns to the passion of which the words speak, surely represent some knowledge of and interest on his part in the doctrine of *rhythmus*. Mersenne's principles in this matter were contained in Isaac

[13] Mersenne, *Harmonie Universelle, De l'Art de Bien Chanter*, Partie IV, Prop. XVII, pp. 374–5.
[14] *Ibid.*

Vossius's *De poematum cantu et viribus rhythmi*, a work which Dryden knew and which insisted, at insane lengths, that the celebrated effects of ancient music were based entirely on *rhythmus* rather than on harmony. Whether known directly or indirectly, Mersenne's principles concerning the use of metrical feet had much vogue in the eighteenth century. They underlay the often repeated idea among poets that the sound should echo the sense. This poetic principle paralleled musical thought by insisting that prosodic regularity or 'harmony' in poetry had not so great a value as the power of rhythm to 'represent' things and feelings and to arouse the passions. It is interesting that Pope connects his discussion of sound echoing the sense in the *Essay on Criticism* with Dryden's Timotheus in the 1697 St Cecilia's Day ode and his greatly various metrical schemes. Pope sees the echo of the sound in the sense as proper music, that is, the containment of the powers of music within poetry itself, the realization of the true sisterhood of the arts.[15] Pope castigates mere mellifluousness of sound in poetry, all mere 'harmony' – the 'pleasure of the ear'. To Pope the echo of the sound in the sense is the poetic equivalent of that 'imitative harmony' in music which is descriptive of word meaning – as when the melodic line rises up on the word 'heaven' or at the word 'hell' plunges down again. This 'word painting' was a device much favoured by Purcell and Handel and other eighteenth-century composers (seeming to provide some sense for sound); but by mid-century it had come under severe criticism both as a poetic and as a musical device. Daniel Webb pointed out that a distinction must be made between 'imitation' by movement and 'imitation' by sound. The latter is the imitation of a particular idea in the tone of a word, sound echoing sense. 'In the former, the accord (between idea and expression) springs from an agreement of syllables or sounds no otherwise imitative than as they determine by their succession the nature of the movement.'[16] *Rhythmus* had a higher function than mere description. Through it there was the possibility that music might be in some ways superior to poetry after all. This idea is developed in Webb's *Observations on the Correspondence between Poetry and Music* (1769). Even if Webb's arguments could have had their remote origin in Mersenne they nevertheless revealed a new and specifically eighteenth-century transformation: 'expression' taking precedence over 'imitation' as a fundamental principle of art.

It is Webb's belief that the special power of both music and poetry is 'expression', and expression is made possible by the exploitation of 'accents', that is, the stresses and tones with which we 'naturally' express our passions in the movements of speech. These accents are sounds

---

[15] Pope, *Essay on Criticism*, Part II, ll. 137–83.   [16] Webb, *Observations*, p. 18.

embedded in rhythm. Music, Webb believed, was closer to these accents than was language. Such representative sounds antedate articulate speech and are more accurate than it, because articulate speech is artificial, its meanings established by 'institution' and agreement. If poetry does not contain these accents it can never be anything more than description. It can represent external things but it will never be able to represent feelings, which is its main work.

In judging descriptions, according to Webb, we resort to the rational process of comparing the imitation to the original. But we could only imitate the passions if they were 'of a nature to be reduced into sensible and determined images'. Since they are not, articulate language is not appropriate to them. 'Where passion is concerned, a coincidence of sound and motion, becomes, as it were, the native and proper language of that passion'.[17] This language can only be music.

But how can we judge the success of the imitation? Certainly not by a comparison to the thing imitated. We can judge only by an 'instantaneous feeling'. That is, we judge a representation of a feeling by feeling itself. This is to declare with Hume that 'sentiment is always right'.

Webb takes care to show that 'imitative harmony' like Pope's is not true musical poetry but only description. He does not admire such passages as

> When Ajax strives some rock's vast weight to throw
> The line too labours and the words move slow.

For precisely the same reason Beattie attacked Handel for 'imitating in a trifling way' in his setting of Dryden's *Alexander's Feast*: 'The words "Depth of pains and height of passion" are thrice repeated to different Keys; and the notes of the first clause are constantly deep, and those of the second are regularly high'. He adds, curiously, 'that the poet is not less blamable than the musician'.[18]

Charles Avison also disliked musical 'imitation' of this sort. Composers must not dwell on particular words but rather 'comprehend the Poet's general Drift'.[19] The author of *Remarks on Mr Avison's Essay on Musical Expression* wondered, on the other hand, whether we are 'not in all Cases to make the Sound an Echo to the Sense, as well in setting descriptive Poetry, as such, that is calculated to the more interesting and affecting Purposes?' He claims that Handel, by doing this in his settings of *L'Allegro* and *Il Penseroso*, had managed to achieve in music the 'picturesque'. 'There is not a Scene which Milton describes, were CLAUDE LORRAIN or POUSSIN to paint, could possibly appear in more lively Colours, or give a truer Idea of it, than our GREAT MUSICIAN has by his

---

[17] Webb, *Observations*, p. 50.   [18] Beattie, *Essays*, p. 127.   [19] Avison, *Essay*, p. 69.

picturesque Arrangement of musical Sounds.'[20] In general, however, music
was not allowed to have a role in the doctrine of the picturesque. In the
second half of the eighteenth century sound echoing sense was not held
to be truly musical either in poetry or music.

To Webb true musical poetry is best represented by passages from
Milton such as Satan's expression of the passion of despair:

> Me Miserable! which way shall I fly
> Infinite Wrath, and infinite despair?
> Which way I fly is hell; myself am hell ...

This is musical poetry not because the syllables are 'imitative of a particular idea' but because they 'determine by their succession the nature
of the movement'.

He explains further:

The passions, according to their several natures, do produce certain proper
and distinctive motions in the most refined and subtle parts of the human
body. [The mind] under particular affections, excites certain vibrations in the
nerves, and impresses certain movements on the animal spirits. I shall
suppose, that it is in the nature of music to excite similar vibrations, to
communicate similar movements to the nerves and spirits. For if music owes
its being to motion, and if passion cannot well be conceived to exist
without it, we have a right to conclude, that the agreement of music with
passion can have no other origin than a coincidence of movements.[21]

Avison agrees: 'There are discordant and harmonious Inflections of
musical Sounds when united, and various Modes, or Keys, (besides the
various Instruments themselves) which, like particular Words, or Sentences in Writing, are very expressive of the different Passions, which
are so powerfully excited by the Numbers of Poetry'.[22] The kinship of
poetry with music lay chiefly in the 'numbers'. Neither description nor
imagery gives Satan's lament its emotional power but rather the vibrations which its movements set up in the nerves. England, too, had its
Empfindsamkeit.

Webb uses other passages from Milton to illustrate the principle that by
'various combinations of the primary movements [of rhythm and sound]'
it is possible to 'attain to the expression of almost every passion'.[23] He
is not willing, however, to accept the consequence of his ideas: the
exaltation of music above the other arts. He still ranks poetry above
music because without words, he thinks, along with almost everyone else,
the expression of the passions in music may be vague. Yet his giving so

---

[20] See Avison, *Essay*, pp. 69–70.   [21] Webb, *Observations*, pp. 5–6.
[22] Avison, *Essay*, p. 73.   [23] Webb, *Observations*, p. 23.

much power to rhythm and sound was a challenge to the established aesthetic of the earlier eighteenth century. Boileau had said: 'Rien n'est beau que le vrai.' And to those who followed this principle only the rational word could contain the whole truth.

Webb's speculations nevertheless mark the fundamental change in attitude toward music which had begun to appear among literary men in England and France and, indeed, in Germany about the middle of the century – although one can find earlier anticipations of the change. The change was not to pretend that music could be understood as a rational art, but rather to admit that rational means were not necessarily the best for the expression of feeling. It marked an emphasis on the power of music to express the feelings rather than simply to 'please hearing'. This change was part of deeper currents of thought flowing through philosophy and all speculation about the arts: the glorification of sentiment and the conviction that human nature was as much defined by its capacity to feel as its ability to think. This movement in criticism much more than anything within the development of music itself eventually reversed the early Enlightenment notion that music is inferior to poetry; and in this suggests that criticism sometimes may be useful after all. The change in attitude toward music is to be seen in its most vigorous form in France and particularly in the ideas of the *Encyclopédistes* and Jean-Jacques Rousseau.

Friedrich Grimm in his *Encyclopédie* article 'Poème lyrique' holds not only that each passion has its own kind of melodic expression, but also that the opera excels the spoken drama because language cannot adequately express the passions. Since tragedy presents scenes of passions in conflict, anger, love, hatred, and the like, its natural language is music.[24] The text is necessary only to make the rendering of the passions exact. He understands the essential difference between a text for music and a text for spoken drama.

Rousseau was the most important musical philosopher of the French eighteenth century because he gave popularity to the idea that music is a completely autonomous language of feeling. He naively centred the power of music in melody, but he did so because melody symbolized to him the autonomy of musical sound. He attacked the *déclamation notée* of Lully and Quinault (music subordinated to the rhythm, sounds, and accents of particular words). Music must paint, Rousseau thought, but it does so best in melody, whose emotional meaning is analogous to words rather than imitative of words. Melody cannot represent but causes a mood similar to that suggested by words. Like Grimm he thought that melody expresses feeling and that words only serve to give

---

[24] Grimm, *Encyclopédie*, XII, pp. 823–37.

the feeling precision. Melody must interpret in its own terms whole thoughts – not mere single words.

Rousseau believed that the Italians had understood this principle and that the French had not. This was owing to the nature of the French language, which lacked strong and passionate accents. Italian, on the other hand, was rich in accent. When an Italian is in a passion he 'changes the tone of his voice a thousand times'. Embedded in Rousseau's theory of melody was an element from his theory of language, one which held that the essential basis of linguistic meaning is precisely the non-rational element: not the artificial institution of the word as arbitrary sign, but that part of the word related to the moan, the cry, and the joyous shout.

The ideas of Rousseau about the essential nature of music prevailed in European thought. By the end of the eighteenth century the idea was commonplace that music should be elevated over articulate language. It was in Germany rather than in France or England that the idea came to maturity. As early as 1721 Johann Mattheson had pointed out that music, not having access to reason, belonged to feeling. And he also said that *even* instrumental music should reflect emotion. This was to touch on the principle that underlay the great musical contribution of the German eighteenth century. Recognition of the expressive power of instrumental music independent of the representation of the passions through the voice heralded a new musical era.

Literary and philosophical thought did not catch up with this development until the early nineteenth century. Schopenhauer was the first thinker to set forth the concept that music is not simply a set of devices for expressing emotions, but a language capable of communicating knowledge of the emotions. Not a language as logicians understand it, but an artistic language in which structures of sound symbolize meanings which are accessible only in music.

This view of music was made possible by the speculations of men of letters in the Enlightenment, for it was through their philosophical trials and errors that music, deprived of its basis in science by experiment in the seventeenth century, was to find a new basis as a symbolic language of feeling. At first it had to be subordinated to poetry, later emancipated, and finally set over poetry. This process is the inner history of the eighteenth-century transformation of the role of music in artistic life.

(iv) *Parallels between the arts*
Dean Mace

In the discussions of the Royal Academy of Painting and Sculpture which took place in Paris in the 1660s numerous parallels were drawn by André Félibien, Charles Le Brun, F. Nocret and others between painting and poetry. During the eighteenth century these parallels were extended in both France and England to all the fine arts – which had at last been distinguished from the liberal and the mechanical arts. Dryden wrote *A Parallel of Poetry and Painting* in 1695. Jonathan Richardson declared in 1715 that a painter must 'have the Talents requisite to a good poet';[1] Joshua Reynolds made much of the comparison. Many English critics compared poetry, music, and the other arts, often casually in the manner of Addison; sometimes with more system as in the essays of James Harris or James Beattie. It was in France, however, that the parallel between the fine arts received its fullest and most careful treatment in the eighteenth century. German writers became influential on the subject in the second half of the century with the appearance of Lessing's *Laocoön*.

In his *Réflexions critiques sur la poésie et sur la peinture* (1719) the Abbé Du Bos, perpetual secretary of the French Academy, included music, opera, and drama. His *Dissertation sur les représentations théatrales des Anciens* (Part III of the *Réflexions*) added dance, understood as gesture. He believed as many critics had believed since the Renaissance that the legendary powers of music and dance in antiquity came from their union with poetry. Du Bos's *Réflexions* were translated into English in 1748 and reappeared in both English and French editions throughout the eighteenth century.

In 1746 the Abbé Charles Batteux published *Les Beaux-Arts réduits à un même principe*. This work summed up the accepted opinion of the first half of the century, already set forth by Du Bos, that not only poetry and painting, but indeed all the fine arts are parallel, and they are so because they are all 'imitations'.

Batteux held that the arts exist in three kinds: the necessary or mechanical arts, that is, the arts for use; the fine arts, of which there are four – poetry, painting, music, and dance – whose end is solely to please; and finally the arts combining utility and pleasure: eloquence and architecture.[2]

Human beings, he says, have three means of expressing ideas and sentiments: word, tone of voice, and gesture (p. 336). Of these three the word is best because most versatile, capable of expressing reason allied through tone to sentiment. Tone of voice is the source of all music.

---

[1] Richardson, *Essay on the Theory of Painting*, p. 19.
[2] Batteux, *Les Beaux-Arts*, pp. 24–30.

Gesture is the dance. Despite the superiority of the word, tone of voice and gesture have the great advantage of being 'natural' signs. They are universal. Words, on the other hand, exist only by institution and agreement. They are the organs of reason; tone and gesture are the language of the heart (pp. 337–42).

The appropriate use for an art is largely determined by subject-matter. Clearly a battle and a sentiment must be imitated by different means. A painting or a poem would do for one, music or dance for the other. All comparisons of the arts in the eighteenth century recognized the peculiar means of each, and the philosophers of the parallel between the arts never confused them – as is sometimes believed.

Since some subjects were considered more important than others it was inevitable that a hierarchy of the arts should be set up, even if hierarchy seems to contradict the idea of a parallel. Heroic and historical actions are, for instance, vastly more elevated than the doings of shepherds. The noble epic continued to tower over the lowly pastoral.

In general it may be said that during the first half of the century the arts based on the word were regarded as most worthy, for words are the richest medium for representing heroic actions, thoughts, passions, and lofty morals. In the second half of the century the inarticulate arts – best represented by music – gradually achieved an equal and sometimes superior place. This corresponded – to put it in perhaps an oversimplified way – to the growing eighteenth-century conviction that art is more properly devoted to representing psychological and subjective states of mind than the grand actions of great and significant persons. Essential human nature was increasingly located in mental life rather than in action. Sentiment and feeling came to be considered the essential subjects of art. A sentiment is neither imitated nor expressed best by words or pictures. Being invisible, entirely psychological, its most adequate language is music.

The theory of mimesis in the eighteenth century did not oblige the artist to imitate observed nature. His proper subject was *la belle nature*, nature as it is in its perfection. This 'nature' is bound to be a fiction, even if created from a combination of the best elements from actual nature, and as a fiction it has no true counterpart in reality. Zeuxis' Helen, despite the six beautiful models from which she was fashioned, was a newly made thing. In short, the artist does not make a copy of what is. Rather he creates forms which are essentially works of the imagination. Imagination and imitation are, however the matter is disguised, contradictory ideas. This eventually appears as a problem in the theory of mimesis.

Batteux thought all talk of human creation in the arts an impropriety of speech. All human works are based on models, nature itself being the original and ultimate model. What, then, is this nature? It is the universe itself, 'a magnificent order joined to an infinite variety' (p. 90) with means justly related to ends and causes to effects, where all parts are regular and duly subordinated in a great chain of being. These perfections are to be imitated only with the power of genius (and enjoyed only with the power of taste), the essential if irrational faculty which, working in a state of *enthousiasme*, allows the artist to bridge the gap between ordinary observed nature and *la belle nature* (pp. 51–2).

The principle of the fine arts as imitative of *la belle nature* is traceable to Aristotle's theory of *probability*, which by the eighteenth century had evolved into a principle of artistic form. For two hundred years after the *Poetics* became well known through translations, Italian, French, and even a few English literary critics were mesmerized by Aristotle's belief that, in the search for verisimilitude, poets ought to alter histor-ical fact, to make a story or plot 'probable' by transforming it into what should have happened as opposed to what actually happened. Critical fascination with 'probability' had two consequences. First, it justified basing not only poetry and painting but all the fine arts on an 'idealizing' of observed or 'historical' nature (and rejecting as the basis of art the 'idea' beloved of the neo-Platonists). This idealizing was Batteux's *belle nature*. Second, it produced a universally useful doctrine of artistic form in which the whole was seen as a 'unity' and the parts as carefully subordinated elements. A convenient and accurate image for describing this order is that of the great 'chain', which suggests dependence of lower elements on higher ones, not a 'harmony' – a term frequently suggested because of its general importance in eighteenth-century aesthetics – which is merely an agreeable combination of parts. In epic or tragedy, for example, all lesser parts are to be subordinated to the principal, which is the plot or fable. This plot must be organized in such a way that action, characters, passions, manners (to use neo-classical terms) are all arranged in elaborate subordinations through which the meaning of the whole unfolds. It is this principle which decrees that plots must have beginnings, middles, and ends which are logically related, as indeed the main action and episodes must be.

On the authority of Aristotle himself this principle of form could be adapted to painting as well as poetry, and the eighteenth century easily found it applicable to all the arts – poetry, painting, opera, architecture, all works, indeed, felt to be wholes with constituent parts. It was an idea of form deeply felt because entirely consonant with contemporary notions concerning the structure of the universe itself. The idea was sufficient for legions of eighteenth-century critics to account for the aesthetic appeal, not only of plays, paintings, and epic poems, but indeed of all beautiful objects. This principle not only confirmed the arts as parallel but allowed some to do part of the work of others. An epic or a drama, an opera or a painting could tell a story, represent human actions and passions, and at the same time constitute a perfect formal unity whose visual and narrative elements were all appropriately subordinated. Le Brun's famous analysis of Poussin's *Manna in the Wilderness* shows how an 'historical' picture could be 'read' and also be seen as a purely formal visual object.[3] Thus all the arts could be considered parallel.

The Abbé Du Bos, writing in the earlier part of the century, found that the arts are parallel, not only because they imitate *la belle nature*, but especially because they imitate human passions. In this opinion, although writing earlier, he was more 'modern' than Batteux. Du Bos was preoccupied with what he called 'the natural sensibility of the heart of man', which he thought the 'very basis of society'.[4] It is necessary that human beings be drawn away from their natural propensity to self-love. This cannot be done by reason but only by emotion. Morality has its origin in sentiment.

We are moved by the tears of a stranger, even before we are apprized of the subject of his weeping. The cries of a man, to whom we have no other relation than the common one of humanity, make us fly instantly to his assistance, by a mechanical movement previous to all deliberation. A person that accosts us with joy painted on his countenance, excites in us a like sentiment of joy, even before we know the subject of his contentment.[5]

The highest aim of the fine arts is to move us so deeply as to cause the substitution of good passions for evil ones; this is catharsis. Here we find the conviction of the famously rational eighteenth-century that the essential nature of man is irrational.

Du Bos accepts the conventional hierarchy of the arts. In accordance with the basic rule of mimesis the artist should choose great subjects because an imitation can move only if there is power to move in the original. Du Bos explains that this is why Poussin's *Death of Germanicus* is intrinsically more powerful than a mere landscape, just as the *Aeneid* is more moving than the finest pastoral. 'Nobody stands ... long', he tells us, 'gazing at a basket of flowers' (I, p. 57).

Du Bos, like Batteux later, does not doubt that poetry is capable of the fullest expression of the passions, being vastly superior to painting.

There is no picturesque expression that can articulate, as it were, the words of old Horatius, where he answers the person, who had asked him, what his son was able to do alone against three antagonists? *Qu'il mourût, That he*

---

[3] André Félibien, *Sixième Conférence*, pp. 83–103.
[4] Du Bos, *Critical Reflections*, I, p. 32.
[5] Du Bos, *Critical Reflections*, I, pp. 31–2.

could die. A painter may indeed let us see, that a man is moved with a particular passion tho' he does not draw him in the action of venting it, because there is no one passion of the mind, that is not at the same time a passion of the body. But it is extremely rare, that a painter can express, so as to be sufficiently understood, the particular thoughts produced by anger, according to the proper character and circumstances of each person, or the sublime which it throws out in words adapted to the situation of the personage that speaketh.

(I, p. 70)

Even Poussin's most admired picture must remind us of the superior power of poetry. He illustrates the point so that we may follow him:

Poussin could, in his piece of the death of Germanicus, express all the different sorts and degrees of affliction, wherewith his friends and family were penetrated, when they saw him poisoned, and expiring in their arms; but he was incapable of giving us an account of the last sentiments of this prince, which are so extremely moving. This is left for the poet, who can make him say, *if a death so untimely as mine had snatched me away, even through some mistake of nature, I should yet have a right to complain of the severity of my destiny; but as I fall a victim to treachery and poison, I must exhort you, my friends, to be the avengers of my death, and not to blush to turn informers, to obtain my injured manes satisfaction: The public pity will certainly join with such accusers.* A painter cannot express the greatest part of these thoughts, nor can he exhibit, in a single piece, more than one of such sentiments as he is capable of expressing.

(I, pp. 70–1)

Painting seems to take its rules especially from the drama. Du Bos likens the persons in a picture to actors on a stage and thereby draws the drama into the parallel of the arts. Eighteenth-century writers continued the seventeenth-century tradition of seeing a close relation between the *tableaux* of the theatre and paintings of illustrious historical or mythological actions. Du Bos likens a play to a succession of paintings (I, pp. 328–9). And in painting itself the subordination of character to an action follows the rules of the drama:

Tho' all the spectators in a picture become so many actors, yet the vivacity of their action ought to be in proportion only to the interest they have in the event at which they are present. Thus a soldier, who assists at the sacrifice of Iphigenia, ought to be moved but not near so much as the brother of the victim.

(I, p. 213)

And so on. Music ranks below poetry and painting owing to the problem of probability. Singing in itself is improbable for great persons in a heroic action. Du Bos, however, recalls that the marvellous, which is central to the epic poem, relates the opera to that branch of the poetic art.

The principle of 'imitation' as a basis for the parallel of the arts, however important as the source of *la belle nature* or as a means of representing the passions, was not, as we know, to remain secure and stable in the second half of the century. Some of the reasons for this are already discernible in the writings of Du Bos. His emphasis on the passions as the central subject of the artist leads him to undermine, even if unwillingly, the hierarchy of the arts which placed poetry at the top, for poetry depends on the 'intellectual' word. He admits, for example, that the effects of painting can be stronger than those of poetry. Painting works through the sense of sight; it is not restricted to artificial signs. Poetry can work only gradually because it functions in time, whereas the effect of painting is more or less instantaneous. Words require a multiplicity of operations in the mind which painting does not. Moreover, poetry borrows much from painting. A play may give us fifty *tableaux* (and with the aid of words we may weep as we never do in front of a picture). Dramatic poetry may profit from the visual scene, gesture, and the 'action théâtrale' which mere words cannot in themselves contain.

Music increases the power and energy of words. But even instrumental music has power over the emotions because it can imitate them. Do we not notice that the 'symphonies' (instrumental music) in Lully's operas 'inflame us, calm us, soften us, and in short, operate upon us, as effectually almost as Corneille's or Racine's verses?' (I, p. 366). Precisely how music works is beyond Du Bos's powers of explanation, as it has remained beyond the powers of succeeding ages. He noted that some instrumental music seemed suited to sad and tragic actions; some to happy and joyful actions. The dance, as gesture in the theatre, can assist words and music in the expression of the passions. What composers must avoid is the pleasure of sounds without significance as painters must avoid the mere charms of colour.

In attributing such powerful effects to painting and music Du Bos disturbed the classical hierarchy of the arts and therefore the principle of imitation which upheld it. He was giving to certain powers of music and painting an independent value of their own. They did not have to fit into the hierarchy. Other influences were also tending to dethrone poetry and indeed the whole doctrine of art as imitation. One of these was the agreeable idea that the first duty of art is to please rather than to instruct, a principle espoused by the Abbé Batteux as defining the fine arts. This subordinated *truth* to *effect* as the aim of art; and hence allowed imagination a freedom which no doctrine of mimesis could tolerate.

The doctrine of imitation had always been closely connected to a belief in the power of art to teach, to move a beholder or reader to virtue or to noble thoughts, by representations of things as they ought to be. But there existed other long-received ideas emphasizing a different and competing power in art: that derived from the rhetorical doctrine (essentially Horatian) that art should above all please. Now imitation, bound to the idea that only truth is good, assumed and required a high degree of *verisimilitude*. The power to please did not. The test of the latter power was not faithfulness to nature in imitation, not the power to copy an original, but a capacity to create an agreeable state of mind in the beholder or reader. For the first power there could be, indeed must be, rules. Rules, judiciously used, had to determine what a true 'imitation' is. Their popularity even among the greatest of artists is surprising only to diehard Romantics, since rules were generally understood to be neither rigid nor mechanical. The Abbé Batteux had defined the very idea of art as a collection of rules. If, on the other hand, 'pleasing' or even 'moving' rather than 'imitation' were acknowledged as the chief power of art, it could not be tied to rules. The power of pleasing could rest as effectively on a fantastic illusion as on one based on truth. The eighteenth-century antagonism between Aristotelian *imitation* and the Horatian *power of pleasing* is already – although not to him – evident in the Abbé Du Bos's description of two principles of painting, one of which he calls 'poetic' composition and the other 'picturesque' composition. These terms had much currency and are central in the articles on painting in the *Encyclopédie*.[6] The contrast between them is striking, for they suggest that poetry and painting after all may not be parallel. 'Poetic' composition

is an ingenious disposition of the figures, calculated to render the action it represents, more moving and probable. It requires that all personages be connected by a principal action; for a picture may contain several incidents, provided all these particular actions unite in one principal one, and that, collected all together, they form but one and the same subject. The rules of painting are as much averse to a duplicity of action, as those of dramatic poetry. If painting be allowed to have its episodes like poetry, those episodes ought in pictures, as well as in tragedies, to be connected with the subject; and the unity of action should be equally preserved in the production of a painter as in that of a poet.[7]

Both the Abbé Batteux and conservatives like Sir Joshua Reynolds would have recognized this theory and approved it. Everything is duly subordinated to the unity of the main action. As for 'picturesque' composition, they would have been surprised:

---

[6] *Encyclopédie*, XII, article 'Peinture', pp. 267–75; 'Peinture Moderne', pp. 275–7.
[7] Du Bos, *Critical Reflections*, I, p. 222.

I call picturesque composition, the arrangement of such objects as are to have place in a picture, with regard to the general effect of the piece. A good picturesque composition is that, whereof the first glance produces a great effect, pursuant to the painter's intention, and to the end he had in view. For this purpose a picture ought not to be embarrassed with figures, tho' it would have enough to fill up the picture. The objects ought to be easy to be disintricated; wherefore the figures should not maim one another, by hiding mutually one half of their heads, or of some other parts of the body, which the subject requires to be rendered visible. 'Tis proper also that the groups be well composed; that their light be distributed judiciously; and that the local colors, instead of destroying one another, be disposed in such a manner, as the whole may afford of itself an agreeable harmony to the eye.

(Critical Reflections, I, p. 221)

Now this is an account of painterly form not in any way related to the rules of epic or dramatic poetry. This is painting divorced from poetry. It is visual form whose end is simply to please the eye. The picturesque painter is interested, not in imitation, but in effect. His preoccupation with forms – the distribution of objects, light and shadow – is not like that of the classical poet or painter who correctly *subordinates* actions, manners, passions, etc., but like that of a designer who seeks only a harmonious or beautiful form.

Harmony was understood in eighteenth-century musical thought as a combination of tones existing only for the sake of pleasing, an arrangement which is its own justification. The term itself brings to mind the frequent eighteenth-century criticism of music for being nothing but 'harmony', a mere pleasure for the ear which totally bypasses the intellect. Yet here there is no condemnation, even though 'harmony' in this sense requires no idealization of subject-matter, indeed no particular subject-matter at all. As in the music theory of the later eighteenth century, 'harmony' is now a term associated with the highest aesthetic value. The 'picturesque' and 'poetic' painting described by Du Bos suggest that a crisis was inevitable involving the doctrine of art as an imitation of nature. Although the Abbé – like the *Encyclopédie* after him – apparently does not see 'poetic' and 'picturesque' composition as antagonistic, they are. The 'picturesque' painter is likely to be indifferent to the imitation of nature; he has as his chief aim only pleasing form, and the pleasingness of this form is to be judged only by the sentiment or taste which finds itself pleased. This could allow any sort of departure from nature and a painter could please his public entirely with any illusion he wished to create so long as it were, like Prospero's masque, 'harmonious charmingly'. *La belle nature* is no longer needed. Du Bos does not cross a line toward it, but an independent imagination is at hand, one not linked to anything but its own workings.

Fairly early in the English eighteenth century something similar to Du

Bos's distinction between 'poetic' and 'picturesque' painting was already appearing. One need go no farther than Jonathan Richardson's analysis of Poussin's *Tancred and Erminia* in 1719. Richardson praises the picture as a perfect 'imitation of nature' in the old style. It is a literary picture; it has a story, a hero, a due subordination of persons, but all of this is secondary to the 'harmony' of the picture. He has never seen

> a greater Harmony, nor more Art to produce it in any Picture of what Master soever, whether as to the Easy Gradation from the Principal, to the Subordinate parts, the Connection of one with another, by the degrees of the Lights, and Shadows, and the Tincts of the Colours ... And without considering it as a Story, or the Imitation of any thing in Nature the *Tout-ensemble* of the Colours is a Beautiful, and Delightful Object.[8]

It is scarcely possible to imagine an upholder of the classical parallel of poetry and the visual arts writing this. Richardson is in fact praising the 'beauty' of the picture as something detached from its story and has, apparently unwittingly, separated the visual arts from the verbal arts.

One may also find in Du Bos the suggestion that the function of poetry is distinct from that of music; that these two arts are not parallel nor necessarily related. Poetry for music should contain only sentiments and should not be stocked with images or intellectually complex expression, that is, with characteristic matter of words.[9] This point is significant, for he is allowing articulate language to be subservient to non-articulate expression. This is tantamount to making colour more important in painting than design or story; or in criticism to give a higher place to the Venetians with their colour than to the Roman school with its devotion to history and great subjects. In rhetorical terms it is the reversal of the normal order of *inventio, dispositio,* and *elocutio.* It is to endanger the very principle of imitation as the basis of art, for imitation depends finally on a belief that dignity comes to art from the subject imitated, not from the manner of the imitation.

Lessing fully recognized in 1766 that the power of art does not necessarily rest on 'imitation' but rather on expression. Of course Lessing holds the traditional doctrine of imitation in high esteem, and it appears to be central in his accounts of 'beautiful' works of visual art: Zeuxis' painting of Helen, the image of the Homeric gods in council, whose ideal beauty rests on imitation of what the eye sees. But it is not central in his famous account of the 'significant moment' in the visual arts. That moment was recognized by Du Bos, Batteux, and others as the only subject of the painter, who could not narrate but only suggest action and successive events.

[8] Richardson, *An Essay on the Whole Art of Criticism*, pp. 89–90.
[9] Du Bos, *Critical Reflections*, I, pp. 386–91.

What must the painter or sculptor do with the 'significant moment'? He must excite the imagination: 'Only that which gives free rein to the imagination is effective. The more we see, the more we must be able to imagine. And the more we add in our imaginations, the more we must think we see.'[10] It is not in fact what we actually see in a work of art which is most important but what we imagine. This is surely an account of a complete non-mimetic illusion, for it works in the visual arts by making us attend that which is not visible! The poet makes a similar appeal to the imagination by representing 'things' not in description but by suggesting their existence in narrative actions. The imagination, both in poetry and in the 'significant moment' of a work of visual art, creates for itself what is visible. We do not see Laocoön shriek; we imagine it.

The poet's power lies in his peculiar way of affecting the imagination through a flow of ideas, all of which are related, and all of which depend for their effects on their *temporal* flow.

Although Lessing does not really abandon the idea of the pictorial poem, the relation between poet and painter is not based necessarily on the theory of imitation. The poet is not like the painter because he imitates but because he makes objects seem present. He desires

to make the ideas he awakens in us so vivid that at that moment we believe that we feel the real impressions which the objects of these ideas would produce on us. In this moment of illusion we should cease to be conscious of the means which the poet uses for this purpose, that is, his words.[11]

The poet can paint only by keeping the reader's attention away from his words! To Lessing Homer was the great painter in poetry precisely because he made things themselves instead of words seem present to the reader. Having done so he has seemed to succeed in the impossible task of transforming words from arbitrary signs into natural signs. With this the poet has the most characteristic power of painting without the limitation of mimesis.

Lessing and before him Moses Mendelssohn recognized a distinction in the nature of artistic illusion which had been earlier neglected or not seen by the theorists of imitation.[12] Dryden, Du Bos, and Batteux – all the believers in imitation – were convinced that artistic 'illusion' was a sort of duplication of an object (*belle nature*), and this duplication required the work of art to contain something of the original. 'Ideal' nature rested on 'actual' nature. Lessing and Mendelssohn saw that artistic illusion required no such connection. They grasped that artistic 'illusion' may owe very little to imitation of the object and very much indeed to the imagination of the artist. There is an enormous difference

[10] Lessing, *Laocoön*, III, p. 19.   [11] Lessing, *Laocoön*, XVII, p. 85.
[12] See Wellbery, *Lessing's Laocoon*, p. 61.

between this view and that of the imitators of *la belle nature*. An ideal medium for the latter is one which could make obvious the link between the ideal and the actual. This connection should be highly visible; criticism liked to notice the means by which art improved on nature, by which 'history' was turned into art. Hence the endless eighteenth-century concern with means to achieve *vraisemblance*; hence also the high 'artificiality' of much eighteenth-century art.

A proper medium for creating art as illusion, as Lessing and Mendelssohn understood, should be one in which there is the least necessary mimetic connection between it and the object imitated, a medium which would not interpose itself between the object and the spectator or reader. The desirability of such a medium is behind much later eighteenth-century European scrutiny of the particular powers of each medium. Music was elevated precisely because its connection with its subject is not easy to determine.

In 1779 James Beattie doubted that the arts were all imitative but confesses that his doubts are new:

I apprehend, that critics have erred a little in their determinations ... that Music, Painting, and Poetry, are all imitative arts. I hope at least I may say, without offence, that while this was my opinion, I was always conscious of some unaccountable confusion of thought, whenever I attempted to explain it in the way of detail to others.[13]

Beattie's difficulties stem from his belief that 'pathos', or 'expression', are the chief excellences of music, and that music expresses significant experience. 'Music, therefore, is pleasing, not because it is imitative, but because certain melodies and harmonies have an aptitude to raise certain passions, affections, and sentiments in the soul.' Then in an abrupt and perhaps alarmed shift, he tells us that music can never please as much as an imitation of nature in poetry.

Beattie, even if clinging to the theory of imitation, had clearly separated the arts according to their different natures and different functions. Neither the old parallel nor the old hierarchy could continue to exist if the expression of internal or purely psychological states became more significant than the external world and the actions performed in it. Art as imitation reflects a visible, tangible reality, a reality in which cause and effect are logical and orderly. Art as expression and imagination belongs to worlds whose reality is invisible: the world of sentiments, feelings, intuitions, thoughts, one may say, beyond reason. It is more important for a work of art to strike and to stir the imagination than to reflect truth.

[13] Beattie, p. 119.

The conviction that the fine arts are related easily survived the down-grading of mimesis in European aesthetic theory. Its most profound nineteenth-century expression was Wagner's concept of the *Gesamt-kunstwerk*. Curiously his ideas had been anticipated by no less an eight-eenth-century philosophe than the Abbé Batteux himself. In his chapter 'Sur l'union des beaux arts',[14] he proposed that although the moderns have separated arts which the ancients kept as one (poetry, music, and dance as gesture) the moderns to their great advantage could unite those arts once more in the theatre. Music should reign on the stage, but it should be supported by poetry and by dance. These arts united could represent human actions and passions in front of scenes prepared by architects, painters, and sculptors. This was, in 1746, a remarkable anticipation of nineteenth-century attempts to unite the arts as well as a reflection of the earlier Renaissance belief that the union of the arts was one of the greatest lost secrets of the ancients.

[14] Batteux, *Les Beaux-Arts*, pp. 371ff.

30

Classical scholarship and literary criticism

Glenn W. Most

The hundred years of classical scholarship which elapsed between the careers of Richard Bentley (1662–1742) and Friedrich August Wolf (1759–1824) may not have been as rich in individuals of passionate genius as the first centuries of Renaissance humanism (though, as we shall see, they too were enlivened by their own cranks and lunatics), nor as productive of enduring accomplishments as the well-organized national philological industries of the nineteenth century (though not a few of the editions and reference works published then are indispensable even today). But by working out the implications of some of the insights scattered throughout humanist scholarship, the classical philologists of the eighteenth century finally made it possible to overcome humanism; and by gathering and systematically organizing a vast amount of material and by putting on a firm basis for the first time the ancillary disciplines which were to study it, they laid a secure foundation for the scholars of the next century (who were all too often eager to deny how much there was to learn from them).

The most significant contribution of eighteenth-century classical scholarship to the history of literary criticism is to be found in the 'internal' development of a new set of literary critical methods and concepts within classical scholarship itself rather than in the 'external' relations between the academic study of Greek and Latin texts and contemporary discussions of literary-critical and theoretical issues. For the most part, in this period those 'external' relations were, at best, distant and vague. On the one hand, most eighteenth-century literary critics professed to share with their readers not only a cultivated familiarity with the classic texts but also a gentlemanly disdain for the dusty pedantry of the professors who studied them – Swift's and Pope's attacks on Bentley in such texts as *The Battle of the Books* and *The Dunciad* are two drastic but not unrepresentative examples – and it was only gradually, and especially in the last decades of the century, that some of the professors' insights and terms sifted into the critics' more popular discourse. And, on the other hand, most eighteenth-century classical scholars remained, at least in their scholarship, largely uninvolved in the literary controversies on ancient authors and classical subjects which interested their non-professional contemporaries, and only a few of them were able towards the end of the century to synthesize a hundred years of learned and popular discussion and to draw conclusions from it – conclusions whose repercussions, at the turn of the century and in the following decades, were to go on to reach far beyond classical philology itself.

For his admonition, in the preface to his edition of Horace (1711), not to revere scribes alone but to dare to attain knowledge on the basis of one's own intelligence,[1] Bentley adopted from one of the poet's epistles (1.2.40) a formula, 'sapere aude', which, towards the end of the century, was to return in the first paragraph of Kant's essay 'What is Enlightenment?' (1784) as 'the motto of enlightenment'.[2] The tag, to be sure, can mean many different things,[3] but we may take it as a characteristic expression of one important ideal of classical scholarship in the age of Enlightenment: the reasoned reappropriation of the materials offered by tradition. For if, in the (perhaps somewhat exaggerated) words of a recent historian, in 'the seventeenth century . . . the characteristic scene in most Continental countries was that of self-satisfied polymaths filling enormous volumes with collected antiquities and reproducing in their editions of texts the accumulated notes of the last two centuries' (Pfeiffer, *Classical Scholarship*, p. 143), the activity of the eighteenth-century philologists, like that of many of their intellectual contemporaries in other disciplines, was directed above all no longer towards the mere reaccumulation of the already accumulated but rather towards the collection and especially the rational systematization of large, previously ungathered bodies of evidence. Characteristically, at the age of twenty-nine Bentley had already planned, begun – and abandoned as currently impracticable – a collection of '*The Remains of All of Greek Poetry*, Philosophical, Epic, Elegiac, Dramatic, and Lyric' (*Epistola ad Joannem Millium*, pp. 267, 304–5, ed. Dyce).[4] The collections of the fragments of such poets as Ion of Chios and above all Callimachus

---

[1] 'Noli itaque Librarios solos venerari; sed per te sapere aude, ut singula ad orationis ductum sermonisque genium exigens ita demum pronunties sententiamque feras.'

[2] Immanuel Kant, 'Beantwortung der Frage, Was ist Aufklärung?', *Gesammelte Schriften*, ed. Preussische Akademie der Wissenschaften (Berlin, 1902–), VIII, p. 35: '*Aufklärung ist der Ausgang des Menschen aus seiner selbst verschuldeten Unmündigkeit* . . . Sapere aude! Habe Muth dich deines *eigenen* Verstandes zu bedienen! ist also der Wahlspruch der Aufklärung.'

[3] In Horace it is directed against intellectual sloth which would delay his friend's (and by implication his reader's) decision to study moral philosophy and live rightly; in Bentley, against scholars' blind veneration of manuscript readings simply because they are old; in Kant, against the self-indulgence of any mature rational being who prefers to defer to the intelligence of others decisions he is capable of resolving himself.

[4] It was not until the nineteenth century that such projects were actually carried out – and then they were the fruit of the labours of numerous scholars, each of whom devoted many years to some small portion of the work the young Bentley had planned to do entirely on his own.

which he did publish were of course not the first attempts to gather the remains of untransmitted authors from the indirect tradition of later writers who cited them; but they were the first to be based upon an exhaustive and systematic search of all possible sources of quotations, published and unpublished, and the first to try to arrange the fragments in the order of the works from which they had been drawn and to fit them into hypothetical reconstructions of what had been lost. So, too, Bentley's metrical discoveries were based upon the rational analysis of large quantities of the verses in question, and provided the model for his followers in England at the end of the eighteenth century (R. Porson) and for the Germans who founded the modern study of metrics at the beginning of the nineteenth (G. Hermann, A. Boeckh).

Throughout the eighteenth century, the spirit of enlightenment produced an unprecedented harvest in systematic collections, all the more remarkable as they were almost without exception the result of the labours of individual scholars. The uncritical antiquarian compilations (e.g., Graevius, *Thesaurus Antiquitatum Romanarum*, 12 folio volumes, 1694–9; J. Gronovius, *Thesaurus Antiquitatum Graecarum*, 13 folio volumes, 1697–1702) and the equally uncritical editions *cum notis variorum* of Pieter Burmann not only preceded, but also accompanied them; yet the contrast these new products of a rationalized scholarship present to such more old-fashioned works is unmistakable: in spirit, and often explicitly in language and in choice of models, the philologists of the eighteenth century seem to leap over the seventeenth century and to feel a closer affinity with the critical techniques and the contempt for mere erudition of the great sixteenth-century humanists. In lexicography, Du Cange's dictionaries of medieval Latin (1678) and Greek (1688), which have never been superseded, ushered in a century of notable achievements culminating in Forcellini's *Totius Latinitatis Lexicon* (1771), which replaced the sixteenth-century lexicons in use until then (and has itself still not been entirely replaced by the mammoth collective *Thesaurus Linguae Latinae* after more than a century of preparation and publication), and in J. G. Schneider's *Kritisches griechisches Wörterbuch* (1797f.), the grandfather of the current standard Greek lexicon of Liddell, Scott, and Jones. General encyclopaedias of antiquity were produced by Montfaucon, *L'Antiquité expliquée et représentée en figures* (10 folio volumes, 1719; 5 supplement volumes, 1724), and by J. A. Fabricius, whose *Bibliotheca Latina* (3 volumes, 1697), *Bibliotheca Graeca* (14 volumes, 1705–28), and *Bibliotheca Latina Mediae et Infimae Ætatis* (5 volumes, 1734) provided virtually exhaustive biographies, summaries, and bibliographies for all ancient authors from Homer through the end of the Middle Ages; important topical encyclopaedias were prepared for example by B. Hederich on ancient mythology (1724) and by J. C. G. Ernesti on the terminology of Greek and Latin rhetoric (1795–7, still not superseded). Massive catalogues were compiled: of collections of manuscripts by Montfaucon (*Palaeographia Graeca*, including a listing of more than 11,000 Greek manuscripts, 1708; *Bibliotheca Coisliniana*, 1715; *Bibliotheca Bibliothecarum Manuscriptorum Nova*, 1739) and A. M. Bandini (*Catalogus Codicum Manuscriptorum Bibliothecae Mediceae Laurentianae*, 8 folio volumes, 1764–78); of archaeological collections by the Comte de Caylus (*Recueil d'antiquités*, 7 volumes, 1752–67), P. M. Paciaudi (*Monumenta Peloponnesiaca*, 1761), and G. B. and E. Q. Visconti (*Il Museo Pio-Clementino*, 7 volumes, 1783–1807); of inscriptions by L. A. Muratori (*Novus Thesaurus Veterum Inscriptionarum*, 4 volumes, 1739–42) and S. Maffei (*Museum Veronense*, 1749; *Ars Critica Lapidaria*, 1765); of coins by E. Spanheim (*De Praestantia et Vsu Veterum Numismatum*, 1664) and J. H. Eckhel (*Doctrina Numorum Veterum*, 8 volumes, 1792–8). And over the course of almost two centuries the Benedictines of St Maur published editions of most of the Greek and Latin Church Fathers in hundreds of volumes – massive, often surprisingly critical, and even today not fully superseded.[5] By the end of the eighteenth century, any library that had enough money – and space – could supply scholars with many thousands of large, well-printed tomes which provided extensive, rationally organized guidance to the resources for studying antiquity available in manuscripts, books, and material objects in virtually all of western Europe.

The scholar who approached this intimidating mass of information in the last decade of the eighteenth century was trying to come to grips with what were in certain regards a very different set of questions from those which had busied his predecessors a hundred years earlier. The establishment of the so-called ancillary disciplines – palaeography, codicology, epigraphy, numismatics – during the course of the later seventeenth and early eighteenth centuries had been a response to the crisis in confidence, associated with the scepticism first of the Cartesians at the beginning of the seventeenth century and then of the historical Pyrrhonists at the end, with respect to the possibility of any historical knowledge whatsoever: knowledge of the past was indeed in the end shown to be attainable, but in order to be secure it had to be based upon the unfalsified materiality of ancient witnesses; the trustworthiness of the claims made by a tradition or of the conclusions modern scholars drew from it could on principle never exceed the methodically determined and intersubjectively admitted reliability of its material bearers.

The establishment of scientifically conceived foundational sub-disciplines had repercussions throughout the field of studies of antiquity as

---

[5] The series began with D'Achery's *Indiculus Asceticorum Opusculorum* (1648) and C. Chantelon's *Bibliotheca Patrum Ascetica* (5 volumes, 1661ff.), and was finally closed by the publication in 1840 of the second volume of the edition of Gregory of Nazianzus.

a whole: it was no longer enough simply to read through all the sources
and put the results together, as Casaubon had still hoped; the texts had
become only one, and by no means the most secure, of many sources
of knowledge, and had to be interpreted critically in the light of the
other remains. By the end of the eighteenth century, philology had
become, at least in tendency, merely one specialization within a larger
field of related disciplines, and the familiar classical texts had come
increasingly to seem only a fraction of the remains of antiquity. Much
of the best work of the eighteenth-century philologists was directed not
towards Homer and Virgil, Plato and Livy, but on the one hand towards the ancient lexicographers and grammarians[6] – rebarbative texts,
but ones which transmitted numerous fragments of otherwise vanished
authors and could sharpen the modern scholar's sensitivity to the stylistic niceties of Classical Attic usage, thereby putting him in a better
position to evade the snares unwittingly set by medieval scribes – and
on the other towards the hitherto comparatively neglected Hellenistic
period, in which scholar-poets working under the patronage of enlightened monarchs could provide their modern successors both with a model
and, given their fragmentary transmission, with an endless supply of
problems.[7] At the same time, the non-literary aspects of ancient culture

---

[6] Though seventeenth-century Dutch scholars had already worked on this field (e.g.,
J. Gronovius's Harpocration, 1682, and Stephanus of Byzantium, 1688), it was
above all Bentley who showed the way by the critical use he made in his early
writings of such lexicographers as Hesychius and Pollux. The editions which
followed him included Küster's *Suda* (3 volumes, 1705), Lederlin's and Hemsterhuys's
Pollux (2 volumes, 1706), Valckenaer's Ammonius (2 volumes, 1739), J. Alberti's
and Ruhnken's Hesychius (2 volumes, 1746–66), Ruhnken's Timaeus (1754),
Pierson's Moeris (1756), J. S. Bernard's *Ecloga* of Thomas Magister (1757), Porson's
Photius (edited by Dobree, 1822), Dobree's *Lexicon rhetoricum maximum* (1834),
J. A. Cramer's *Anecdota Graeca* (4 volumes, 1834–7), and finally Gaisford's *Suda*
(3 volumes, 1834), Greek paroemiographers (1836), and *Etymologicum Magnum*
(1848); cf. also, for example, Toup's studies on the *Suda* and Hesychius (4 volumes,
1760–6; 1767; 1775).

[7] Callimachus was studied and/or edited among others by T. Graevius, Spanheim, and
Bentley (1697), Ruhnken (1751, 1761), Reiske (1757–66), J. A. Ernesti (1761),
Bandini (1764), Brunck (1772–6), and Valckenaer (1799); Nicander by Bentley
(1722) and Bandini (1764); Apollonius Rhodius by Ruhnken (1751), Shaw (1777),
and Brunck (1780); Theocritus by Reiske (1765–6), Warton (1770), Brunck (1772–
6), Valckenaer (1773, 1779–81), and Jacobs (1796); Aratus by Bandini (1765) and
Buhle (1793). The Greek Anthology, which contains many epigrams by Hellenistic
poets, was partially edited by Reiske (1754) and Brunck (1772–6) and finally
published completely by Jacobs (1794–1814; 1813–17). Villoison's edition of the
older Homeric scholia (1788) and Wolf's *Prolegomena ad Homerum* (1795) marked
the climax of a century of interest in the philological work of the Alexandrian
scholars. Valckenaer proved that apparent monotheistic fragments of Greek poets
were forgeries by the second-century Alexandrian Jew Aristobulus (1806). Heyne
wrote a fundamental essay on the nature of the Hellenistic age, *De genio saeculi
Ptolemaeorum* (1763, in his *Opuscula Academica Collecta*, I (Göttingen, 1785),
pp. 76–134).

were brought to light for the first time in large-scale systematic excavations whose results were communicated internationally in splendid folio volumes (Herculaneum 1738ff., *Antichità di Ercolano* 1757ff.; Rome 1782ff.); existing monuments which had been forgotten were rediscovered (Paestum 1746); adventurers and epigraphists began to travel through the eastern Mediterranean and send back reports on the archaeological remains and primitive customs they had discovered there (R. Wood, *The Ruins of Palmyra*, 1753; *Essay on the Original Genius and Writings of Homer, with a Comparative View of the Ancient and Present State of the Troad*, 1775; P. A. Guys, *Voyage littéraire de la Grèce, ou lettres sur les Grecs, anciens et modernes, avec une parallèle de leurs moeurs*, 1771; Comte de Choiseul-Gouffier, *Voyage pittoresque en Grèce*, 1782); and learned societies of wealthy amateurs in Italy and England were founded to subsidize further travels, excavations, and publications (Accademia di Cortona, 1726, Società Colombaria, 1735, Accademia di Antichità Profane, 1740, Accademia degli Ercolanesi, 1755; Society of Dilettanti, 1733: J. Stuart and N. Revett, *The Antiquities of Athens Measured and Delineated*, 4 volumes, 1762–1816; R. Chandler, *Ionian Antiquities* 1769–1800, *Inscriptiones Antiquae*, 1774, *Travels in Asia Minor*, 1775, *Travels in Greece*, 1776). The scholar who was looking for an edition of Virgil in a library at the end of the eighteenth century would have found his author in a section which would have seemed far smaller, compared to the many stacks of non-literary works, than it would have a century earlier; and once he had found it he would have discovered that, the more recent the edition, the likelier it was to illustrate the poetic text with coins, sculptures, and other material remains.

The developments in classical scholarship over the course of the eighteenth century can be illustrated briefly in terms of their consequences in three particularly sensitive domains: (1) textual criticism; (2) literary history; and (3) the creation of 'Altertumswissenschaft'.

(1) Before the eighteenth century, most scholars who edited classical texts were content for the most part to reproduce the vulgate which had been established by printed editions before them; only in those passages in which the vulgate seemed for whatever reason unacceptable to them did they feel impelled to intervene in the text, emending it on the basis of their own conjectures or on that of the readings of manuscripts – the oldest ones, the most numerous ones, or simply the ones nearest to hand.[8] By and large, this meant that the fifteenth-century manuscripts which the early printers had taken as the basis for their editions continued to propagate themselves, with their freight of banalizations and

---

[8] The fundamental study of this whole issue is Timpanaro, *La Genesi*.

humanist conjectures, of readings which might not be obviously wrong but were certainly not obviously right. True, some early scholars, especially Politian and Scaliger, had placed particular emphasis upon systematic examination of the manuscripts and had developed in at least a rudimentary form some of the basic concepts of modern textual criticism (the archetype, the classification of manuscripts into families, the elimination of apographs). But it was only when the text at issue was no longer the vulgate of a pagan author, but the *textus receptus* of the New Testament itself, that matters came to a head: for here one pious impulse sought to collect every attested variant while another was terrified at the very thought of any alteration to the canonical text. In an edition of the New Testament like that of Bentley's friend John Mill (1707), in which the same *textus receptus* found in every other edition now throned uneasily over about 30,000 variants collected in thirty years of patient research, the paradox was implicitly posed: what was one to make of all these variants, if they had no impact on the text? and how reliable was a text which was undermined in every passage by such variety? The deists concluded from the mass of variants to the uncertainty of Scripture: Bentley, to confute them, proposed to restore, if not the original text, then at least the oldest attainable one, on the basis of the oldest manuscripts and translations and the indirect tradition. Though Bentley did not fulfil this project,[9] his line of reasoning was pursued in the next decades by a number of Continental theologians, especially by J. A. Bengel, J. J. Wettstein, and J. S. Semler. And by the second half of the eighteenth century the classical philologists had recognized the necessity of applying to their own discipline the doctrines that had been theoretically elaborated by the theologians: the repudiation of the vulgate, the systematic foundation of the edited text at every moment upon the manuscripts, the determination of the genealogical relations among the manuscripts, the refusal to assign independent value to members of the same family. At the end of the century, Wolf began his *Prolegomena ad Homerum* (1795) with a eulogy on systematic recension and an attack upon reliance upon divination alone:

a true recension, attended by the full complement of useful instruments, seeks out the author's true handiwork at every point. It examines in order the witnesses for every reading, not only for those that are suspect. It changes, only for the most serious reasons, readings that all of these approve. It accepts, only when they are supported by witnesses, others that are worthy in themselves of the author and accurate and elegant in their form ... This method certainly has a place for natural talent and the art of

---

[9] In this case too, it was not until a century later that Bentley's plans were fulfilled, by Lachmann and others.

conjecture, but as the credibility of every ancient text rests entirely on the purity of its sources, we must strive above all – and can hardly do so without talent – to examine the properties and individual nature of the sources from which each writer's text is derived: to judge each of the various witnesses, once they are set out by classes and families, by its character; and to learn to follow their voices, and gestures, so to speak, with cunning, but without bias ... And indeed, it is impossible that one who relies on a few codices of the common sort and practices conjecture, however cleverly, can often arrive at the genuine text.

(ch. 1, trans. Grafton et al.)

Wolf himself never put these fine principles into practice, but little matter: his statement of them remained a classic formulation – one which helped shape the thought of the nineteenth-century founder of modern textual criticism, Karl Lachmann – of a position diametrically opposite to the cult of divination (μαντική) which Bentley still practised in his editions and explications of pagan authors: in his edition of Horace, Bentley changed the text in over 700 passages, in well over half of them against the readings of all the manuscripts. At the beginning of the eighteenth century, Bentley's *ratio* had been proudly anti-historical; but by 1795, the very notion of what counted as reason had started to be historicized, and Wolf could implicitly impugn Bentley's contemptuous dismissal of history in the name of reason as a striking example of unreason.

(2) Perhaps the most characteristic form of literary scholarship of the nineteenth century is the literary history, with its fundamental convictions that works of art must be understood within the terms of the period within which they were produced and that the sequence of such periods can be constructed as the logical and chronological skeleton of an identifiable national literature. As such suggested by the gradual historicization of the notion of reason noted in the preceding paragraph, these notions too are acquisitions of the eighteenth century. To be sure, the sense of a development over time within a single literary genre can be traced back at least to Aristotle's *Poetics* (chs. 3–5) and to Cicero's *Brutus* (chs. 25–328), and Joseph Scaliger, in a celebrated letter of 1607 to Salmasius, sketched out in a few sentences a downhill sequence of the four seasons of Greek hexametric poetry (D. Heinsius (ed.), *Iosephi Scaligeri Epistulae* (Leiden, 1627), Nr. 247, pp. 530–1). Moreover, the textual materials upon which any literary history (in the modern sense) had to be based had long been gathered in such compendia as Fabricius's, though these had remained so resolutely bio-bibliographical in character that at most they could function only as a rock quarry for later literary historians. Finally, the study of literary forgeries, a favourite pastime of Renaissance scholars, had focused attention upon what could, and what could not, have been written at any one time. Thus

Bentley introduced his *Dissertation upon the Epistles of Phalaris* (1699) with a characterization of the Hellenistic period, in which the search for valuable manuscripts invited imposture and deceit, and of the activity of the later rhetorical schools, in which students were trained to compose texts of the sort that famous personages of the past could have pronounced under suitable circumstances; and his emphasis, throughout his demonstration of the spuriousness of the epistles, upon chronological rather than merely stylistic considerations demonstrated the usefulness of the application to problems raised by individual texts of a secure framework of Greek institutional and cultural history, within which such diverse facts as the foundation dates of Sicilian cities, the various units of money and measure, the chronology of Athenian tragedy and comedy, and the development of the Attic dialect could all find their place.

But Bentley himself never produced this framework explicitly for its own sake, preferring instead to apply it point by point to individual problems of detail; and it may be doubted whether he would have had much understanding for or interest in the more general issues of artistic and cultural history which became fashionable several generations later. These issues are inseparably connected with the name of J. J. Winckelmann, who in his *Geschichte der Kunst des Altertums* (1764) first provided a convincing model for the detailed interpretation of individual works of art within the terms of historically defined periods and for the narrative of the sequence of these periods as a logic of cultural development. Not only did Winckelmann situate Greek and Roman art historically and geographically within the larger story of the development of art in the ancient eastern Mediterranean as a whole: he also provided an account of the rise and decline of Greek art which satisfied formally for its architectonic simplicity and perspicuity, emotionally for its passionate encomium upon the splendours of the classical and Hellenistic periods and for its pathetic tale of inevitable decline in the aftermath, and historically for the general coincidence of its points of suture with important moments of transition in Greek political history. And above all, he showed how the close analysis of works of art could enormously enrich their meaning by referring them to more encompassing cultural contexts (which were of course largely constructed circularly, on the basis of the interpretation of the very same works of art they were meant to explain).

Conceptually, Winckelmann's innovation presupposed his invention of a notion of historical period to mediate between the atemporal categories of national climate, psychology, and culture on the one hand and the temporally determinate individual works of art on the other, permitting a subtle dialectic between synchronic and diachronic modes; but materially, it also presupposed his acquaintance with the mass of archaeological remains which were just coming to light in these years – Winckelmann wrote back to Germany of his impressions of Herculaneum, and claims to have been the first German ever to see the Doric temples of Paestum. Winckelmann's history of Greek art was immediately recognized as exemplary: Herder demanded that a second Winckelmann apply the same techniques to Greek philosophy and poetry; Friedrich Schlegel explicitly took Winckelmann as his model for his own studies of Greek poetry in the 1790s. By the end of the century, literary histories were not only being produced to accompany university lecture courses on philology, as for example by Wolf for his students in Halle in 1787: they were also providing the conceptual underpinnings for works of scholarship of a new kind – Wolf's *Prolegomena ad Homerum,* whatever else it is, is also a history of Greek literature from the earliest times to the Hellenistic period in terms both of the production and reception of the Homeric poems and of the larger cultural and political context.

(3) Most importantly, the students whom Wolf taught at the end of the eighteenth century were instructed for the first time in a discipline in which the study of antiquity was conceived as a systematically interrelated set of sub-disciplines, all of which had to be understood to a certain degree if any one of them was to be practised competently. To be sure, the full-scale professionalization of the sciences of antiquity, together with that of the other fields of scholarship, which characterized the German universities of the nineteenth century went far beyond anything Wolf or his contemporaries could have imagined: yet the foundations for this development were laid in the course of the eighteenth century. In this regard too, there had been partial precedents among earlier classical scholars, for example in the insistence of Joseph Scaliger and F. Robortello that individual problems had to be seen within the context of an understanding of antiquity as a whole: but the demand that a science, in order to count as such, had to be able, by means of reflection upon itself, to determine the logical interrelation of its components was a characteristically German notion in the later eighteenth century, one which was canonized in Kant's *Critique of Pure Reason* (1781), particularly in the chapter on 'The Architectonic of Pure Reason' (AA III, pp. 538–49), and which led to a new idea of what it meant to practise the study of antiquity as a science.

Wolf christened this new science with the term it still retains in German, 'Altertumswissenschaft', and expounded it to his students in lectures which he gave, starting in 1785, under the title *Encyclopaedia philologica* (anticipated to a certain extent by J. M. Gesner's Göttingen lectures, *Primae Lineae Isagoges in Eruditionem Vniversalem,* published posthumously in 1774) and which he published in 1807 as a programmatic

'Depiction of the Science of Antiquity according to its Concept, Scope, and Purpose' ('Darstellung der Altertumswissenschaft nach Begriff, Umfang und Zweck'). Here he defined his goal as that of 'uniting into an organic whole the various disciplines which partly have been taught in German universities for almost a hundred years, partly must still be developed, so that everything that belongs to the complete knowledge of antiquity can be raised to the dignity of a well-ordered *philosophical– historical science*' (p. 5).[10]

To the new science corresponded a new pedagogical method: the philological seminar, founded by Gesner at Göttingen, developed further by C. G. Heyne at the same university and by Wolf at Halle, and institutionalized at the new University of Berlin by Wilhelm von Humboldt (who was convinced, oddly, that permitting students to participate in scholarly research would make them truly human). In the seminar, students were supposed not to listen passively to the professor's lectures but to propose, in discussion with him and with one another, the results of their own work. The intellectual interchange among persons of differing scholarly interests and capabilities could be seen as a concrete manifestation of the fruitful interrelations among the various sub-disciplines that went to make up 'Altertumswissenschaft'; and those survivors of the institution who did not themselves become university professors were sent out as cadres of school teachers throughout northern Germany, where they regaled their pupils with tales of what they had suffered, and learned, at the university, incidentally transmitting to them ideals of scholarship and a conviction of the unity of the classical world.

As the sheer mass of what the philologist was expected to know increased, the field of philology itself became increasingly specialized: first by differentiating itself increasingly from other fields with which it had been closely associated earlier, like theology[11] and the study of the

---

[10] '... des Verfassers Eifer, die höchsten Gesichtspunkte der alterthümlichen Philologie möglichst genau zu erfassen, und einen Versuch zu machen, wie sich die einzelnen, theils auf deutschen Universitäten seit beinahe hundert Jahren erläuterten, theils noch in der Folge zu bearbeitenden, Doctrinen zu einem organischen Ganzen vereinigen liessen, um alles, was zu vollständiger Kenntniss des gelehrten Alterthums gehört, zu der Würde einer wohlgeordneten *philosophisch-historischen Wissenschaft* emporzuheben.'

[11] Bentley was Chaplain to the King and Regius Professor of Divinity, and most of the other prominent philologists through the mid-eighteenth century had positions in the Church, especially in England, France, and Italy; but Wolf insisted upon inscribing himself, when he matriculated at Göttingen in 1777, as 'studiosus philologiae', while R. Porson, who lost a fellowship at Cambridge in 1792 because of his refusal to take orders, was instead immediately elected Professor of Greek; and it is characteristic of German classical scholarship at the turn of the nineteenth century that Plato comes to take the place next to Homer that the New Testament had occupied earlier.

Oriental languages;[12] and secondly by differentiating itself internally, into specialists in either Latin or, increasingly, Greek philology.[13] The same decades towards the close of the eighteenth century witnessed the development of ancient history in the modern sense, not moralizing and practically directed commentaries on the texts of the ancient historians, but instead independent research on the ancient world, making cautious and suspicious use of these texts but frequent and prominent reference to the material remains; Gibbon's *History of the Decline and Fall of the Roman Empire* (1776–88) provided an extremely successful example of what could be done by wedding the antiquarian tradition of attention to scholarly detail to the philosophical historians' emphasis upon cultural and institutional, rather than political and military history. All these factors led to an increased professionalization of classical scholarship over the course of the eighteenth century, of which one small but unmistakable proof was the opening up of the discipline to poor but talented young men, who could now hope to make a career without joining the Church or enjoying aristocratic patronage – thus Winckelmann, a cobbler's son, born in 1717, still had to convert, but Heyne, a weaver's, born in 1729, did not; and if J. J. Reiske, the celebrated editor of the Athenian orators, was driven by penury to the extremes of studying medicine and even of becoming Professor of Arabic at Leipzig, this was due to one of his many misfortunes, the fact that he was born in 1716, just a few decades too early.

The clearest measure of the difference between classical scholarship at the beginning of the eighteenth century and at its end is provided by the contrast between Bentley's masterpiece, his *Dissertation upon the Epistles of Phalaris* (1699), and Wolf's, his *Prolegomena ad Homerum* (1795). To be sure, the two works have much in common. Bentley's demonstration that Phalaris' letters were not written by Phalaris and Wolf's that

---

[12] Bentley could still discuss competently questions of Syriac semantics and vocalization in his *Epistola ad Millium*, ed. Dyce, pp. 351f.; but the traditional requirement in Holland and Germany that Professors of Greek teach Hebrew and Arabic as well yielded to a split between the two chairs, starting with T. Hemsterhuys in the first half of the eighteenth century, and, though Wolf would go on to apply many of the results of Old Testament scholarship to Homeric problems in his *Prolegomena ad Homerum*, his own relation to studies of the Hebrew texts was entirely passive and derivative, and he explicitly assigns to experts in Arabic literature questions that exceed his own competence; see *Prolegomena*, ch. 35.

[13] Bentley had still been a recognized master of both branches of classical scholarship, and both his collections of the fragments of Greek authors and his editions of transmitted Latin ones were regarded as exemplary; but the Dutch model – separate professorships in the two languages, with Latin assigned to the province of the professor of Eloquence – gradually prevailed, and by the end of the century it became the norm for philologists to devote their research almost exclusively to one language or the other – Wolf's work on Cicero, for example, was of negligible importance compared to his Greek studies.

Homer's epics were not written by Homer are no less typical products of enlightened eighteenth-century anti-traditionalism than Gesner's early proof that the *Philopatris* attributed to Lucian could not be by him (1715) and Valckenaer's brilliant unmasking of the forgeries of Aristobulus (1806) – or, for that matter, than J. Hardouin's lunatic conviction that most of the works transmitted as ancient were really fourteenth-century forgeries (*Chronologiae ex Numis Antiquis Restitutio*, 1693), J. F. Christ's bizarre attempt to prove, by translating Aesop into Latin poetry, that the fables of Phaedrus were forged by the fifteenth-century humanist Niccolò Perotti (*De Phaedro*, 1745; *Uberior Expositio de Phaedro*, 1747; *Phaedri Fabularum Aesopiarum libri II*, 1748), and Wolf's own later demonstration that certain speeches of Cicero, now universally regarded as genuine, were in fact spurious (*Ciceronis quae feruntur IV Orationes*, 1801; *Ciceronis Oratio quae fertur pro Marcello*, 1802).[14] Both works, too, strike the modern reader as a sometimes bewildering mixture of traditionally classicist aesthetic judgements and novel historicist arguments.

But neither such similarities nor Wolf's frequent self-stylization as the only true successor to Bentley should mislead us into construing a linear progression where in fact there is none. For Bentley was not trying to do what Wolf succeeded in accomplishing: in their conception of the methods and purposes of philology, the two works belong to different ages – it is a paradox of the history of classical scholarship that Bentley's *Dissertation* was the first important work in the field to be written in the vernacular, while Wolf's *Prolegomena* was the last book written in Latin to achieve success throughout Europe.

The key difference between the two treatises involves the relation they conceive between historical argumentation and judgements of aesthetic value. Bentley's central purpose is to show that the value of the letters (cited as proof of the superiority of the ancients by an English participant in the *Querelle des anciens et des modernes*, on which see the chapter on Ancients and Moderns by Douglas Patey in this volume) has been over-estimated: the historical demonstration of their spuriousness is subordinated to the judgement that, as late products of the rhetorical schools, they lack the freshness and vigour their admirers had attributed to them. His aim is destructive – as he puts it in his treatise on the letters which passed under the name of Themistocles, 'It will be no unpleasant labour to me, nor, I hope, unprofitable to others, to pull off the disguise from those little Pedants, that have stalked about so long in the apparel of Hero's' (London, 1697, p. 79) – and once he has

---

[14] On the level of individual verses, the same anti-traditionalism is expressed most clearly in the increasing use of athetesis made by such scholars as Bentley (*M. Manilii Astronomicon*, 1739) and Valckenaer (*Euripidis Phoenissae*, 1755).

shown the epistles to be spurious, they lose practically all interest for him: as Wilamowitz pointed out (*Classical Scholarship*, pp. 80, 82), Bentley has remarkably little to say about the intentions and historical context of their real author. Wolf's aim, by contrast, is to write a history of the text of Homer in antiquity: he resorts frequently to judgements on the aesthetic quality of various parts of the Homeric epics, pointing out differences in artistic conception and stylistic level and emphasizing strengths and weaknesses in general structure and in particular detail (especially in chapters 30–1); but he uses the results of these judgements in order to create a vivid account of the historical vicissitudes of the text from its earliest beginnings to the Hellenistic Age. If, in Bentley, historical argumentation is in the service of aesthetic judgment, in Wolf the relation is reversed: precisely what interests Wolf is the question of the intentions and historical contexts of the various personalities who contributed to the creation of the text we know as Homer's. That is why, though both Bentley and Wolf were keenly aware of the differences between Homer's epics and Virgil's, Bentley saw the difference in terms of artistic value, praising the *Aeneid* as the paradigm of organic unity (*Boyle Lectures*, p. 200, ed. Dyce) and dismissing Homer's poems as 'a sequel of Songs and Rhapsodies, to be sung by himself for small earnings and good cheer, at Festivals and other days of Merriment' (*Remarks upon a Late Discourse of Free-Thinking*, 8th edn, Cambridge, 1743, pp. 25–6), while Wolf saw them as the historical results of two very different processes of composition and transmission, and frequently warned his readers not to judge both poems by the same criteria (*Prolegomena*, chs. 11, 12).

In short, eighteenth-century classical scholarship bears a paradoxical relation to literary criticism. On the one hand, familiarity with the classical, especially with the Latin, poets and historians was expected of any eighteenth-century gentleman, and it is not surprising to find literary-critical discussions in this period making frequent allusion to ancient texts. But in general the traces of influence of classical scholarship upon that century's literary criticism are surprisingly infrequent – Dryden's 'Discourse concerning the Original and Progress of Satire' and Pope's Homer translation are important, but only partial, exceptions.[15] And on

---

[15] It is only in the comparatively short section of the 'Discourse' dedicated to the early history of ancient satire that Dryden is largely dependent upon classical scholarship – indeed so dependent that much of this section reads like a paraphrase of André Dacier's 'Preface sur les Satires d'Horace, Où l'on explique l'origine & les progrès de la Satire chez les Romains; & tous les changemens qui lui sont arrivez' (*Les Oeuvres d'Horace traduites en françois*, VI (Paris, 1691)). The importance of this section should not be over-estimated: it is designed essentially to establish Dryden's credentials in order to protect the translations from scholarly attack and to permit him, in the lengthy core of the essay – his relatively original comparison

the other hand, most of the issues of literary theory which obsessed the Enlightenment had little or no impact upon classical philology until the very end of the century (if then): though Longinus' treatise on the sublime was re-edited a number of times during this period,[16] the scholars contributed virtually nothing to the lively discussion which the concept of sublimity provoked among non-professionals; the vast *Querelle des anciens et des modernes* had, at least outside of France, to be reduced to the specific question of the authenticity of the letters of Phalaris before it could become of interest to classical scholarship; Lessing's meditations in *Laokoon* (1766) on the differences between the verbal and the visual arts were admired by Herder and Goethe but ignored by most classicists (with the characteristic exception of Heyne); and it was not until Wolf that the popular eighteenth-century view of Homer as a primitive bard bore philological fruit.[17] By the last quarter of the century, to be sure, some commentators on classical poems had started to supplement the traditional lemmatic line-by-line commentary (which had focused exclusively upon individual grammatical, historical, and textual difficulties) with judgements of taste on the texts' aesthetic quality, demonstrations of their unity and coherence, and praise for their novelty and originality;[18] but these philologists were on the receiving end, and belatedly, of developments in non-professional literary criticism, and they do not seem to have contributed much to wider debates. The crucial development lies elsewhere: in the fact that, by the end of the eighteenth century, classical scholarship had become an organized,

of Horace, Persius, and Juvenal and his depiction of his ideal of satire – to devote himself to what really interests him: a reflection upon the general question of the role of the poet in society. As for Pope, much of his scholarship is tralaticious (derived in this case from Anne Dacier); and it should be noted that his learned commentaries on the *Iliad* are prefaced with an attack upon the lack of literary-critical sensitivity of 'all the Commentators of *Homer*': 'there is hardly one whose principal Design is to illustrate the Poetical Beauties of the Author. They are Voluminous in explaining those Sciences which he made but subservient to his Poetry, and sparing only upon that Art which constitutes his Character ... Hence it has come to pass that their Remarks are rather Philosophical, Historical, Geographical, Allegorical, or in short rather anything than Critical and Poetical ... The chief Design of the following Notes is to comment upon *Homer* as a Poet' (*Twickenham Edition*, VII, p. 82). Neither work provides a convincing example of the fruitful interpenetration of classical scholarship and literary criticism.

[16] The text was edited by J. Tollius (1694), Hudson (1710), Pearce (1724), S. F. N. Morus (1769), Toup (1778), and Bodoni (1793).

[17] Heyne, to be sure, praised Wood's *Essay on the Original Genius and Writings of Homer* in a review and probably arranged for the book to be translated into German; but all in all Wood's views had remarkably little effect upon Heyne's picture of Homer.

[18] In commentaries on Horace the development is first noticeable in Christian David Jani's edition (2 volumes, Leipzig, 1778–82); one of the most celebrated examples in Latin studies is Heyne's oft-reprinted edition of Virgil (4 volumes, Leipzig, 1767–75).

systematic discipline for the study of literature within its historical context, combining close textual analysis with imaginative cultural reconstruction. In the generations that followed, 'Altertumswissenschaft' would come to provide a model first for the medieval, and finally for the modern philologies.

Biblical scholarship and literary criticism

Marcus Walsh

It is a truism that no book was more copiously studied and written about in the late seventeenth century and throughout the eighteenth century than the Bible. The connections between biblical scholarship and literary criticism in the period are multiple and complex, the more so in that many debates about central literary theoretical questions took place within the numerous spheres of biblical discussion, rather than in works of secular literary criticism. This was inevitably the case; at the Restoration secular literary criticism in England was from some points of view in its infancy. There had been no full and systematic theory of poetry since the late sixteenth century, no extended critical analysis or scholarly edition of any English classic. The idea of a secular literary history would begin to take shape only in the eighteenth century.

I shall discuss in this essay, chiefly but not exclusively with reference to the work of British writers, two key themes: the development of appreciation and analysis of the Bible as a literary work, and of its poetic, aesthetic, and rhetorical qualities; and, at least as important to the history of literary criticism, the debates of biblical scholars about the textual and hermeneutic issues raised by the Holy Scriptures. The two themes are not unrelated.

Significant both in itself, and in relation to a number of later issues of literary scholarship, commentary and editing, was the seventeenth-century argument between Roman Catholics and Protestants, particularly Anglicans, concerning the status of the Bible. European and British romanists claimed that tradition, transmitted through the Church, rather than the written Scriptures themselves, must be the rule of faith. If Scripture is to be a rule of faith it must be textually perfect. In fact, however, as the exiled romanist William Rushworth, for example, asserted (*Dialogues*, pp. 244–5), and as Père Richard Simon's massive scholarship demonstrated in his *Critical Histories* of the Old and New Testaments, it had inevitably become faulty in the course of its transmission by human rather than divine agency. As a consequence, John Sergeant amongst others argued, 'the *Certainty* of the Scripture's Significativeness ... is quite lost to all in the Uncertainty of the Letter' (*Sure-Footing*, p. 38). The translations in which Scripture is read are

merely paraphrases, interpretations, of the original words; Simon concluded from his extensive critique of the chief examples that 'it is almost
impossible to translate the Holy Scripture' (*Old Testament*, b1^r). More
radically, as Sergeant, Rushworth, and others claimed, Scripture, even if
read in the original languages, consists only of 'dead letters', which are
themselves no more than an imperfect written paraphrase of Christ's
true and living spoken word. The meaning of Scripture as of any text
is uncertain, founded on equivocal words which signify differently to
every reader. Simon argued that Scripture in particular is opaque,
because of its unfamiliar matter, and because it employs 'terms and
Expressions which we have no knowledge of ... and which the *Jews*
themselves understand not more than we' (*Old Testament*, III, p. 14).
The reader who imagines it might be possible to discover the determinate meaning intended by an author, argued Sergeant, must have an
impossible battery of skills and knowledges: in language, grammar, textual criticism, human and natural history, logic, metaphysics, and divinity (pp. 26–7). For the Roman Catholics therefore the true word of God
cannot be thought to inhere in the bare words of Scripture, but must
be found in those words given sense by the genuine tradition of the
Church (Gother, *Catholic Representer*, p. 50; Bossuet, *Exposition*, p.
162). Scripture, in fact, 'is only to be found in the Church' (Simon, *Old
Testament*, III, p. 166). The text itself is deprived of sacred status.
Indeed, it was a general romanist principle that the text of Scripture,
and any strictly literal interpretation of the text, is secondary not only
to the Church's tradition of oral teaching, but to the explicatory commentaries written on Scripture by the ancient fathers and modern doctors of the Church.

In order to defend the Scripture as a rule of faith, Anglicans had to
argue for the integrity of the text, and the possibility of a standard of
interpretation. Some of the arguments they offered had been familiar in
Protestant discourse since the Reformation. Some were new, developed
in response to the particular charges laid by their Roman adversaries.
Some Anglicans asserted that the text of Scripture had been protected
by God. More cautiously, John Tillotson, though intimating an inclination to believe in such a divine providence, argued in *The Rule of Faith*
(1666) that the text had been transmitted 'without any material corruption or alteration' (*Works*, pp. 660–1). Later Anglican writers, including
Richard Bentley and Jonathan Swift (in their answers to Anthony Collins's
Discourse of Free-Thinking), and Robert Lowth, adopted a position
which would continue to prove tenable as textual criticism increasingly
exposed the fragmentary and derivative nature of the surviving textual
deposits of Scripture; that is, that the Bible, like all other texts, is subject to textual corruption, but remains none the less an authoritative

and reliable means of communicating its essential message. Against accusations that Scripture was equivocal, containing no inherent sense, subject to every man's different reading if not controlled by the interpretative authority of the Church, Anglicans argued that the Scripture text had a determinate, unchanging, intended meaning. John Wilson, in an impressively full and in some important ways representative account of the proper methods of hermeneutics, *The Scripture's Genuine Interpreter Asserted* (1678), insisted that the Scriptures 'had a true sense *Originally* and *Essentially* in themselves, given them by their Author when they were first indited ... the Sense of Scripture is fixt and immutable ... no other than what it always had, and ever will have to the World's end' (p. 5). Taking a familiar position, held by Luther and before him by Augustine, Anglicans reiterated the plainness and comprehensibility of Scripture. All that is 'necessary to be believed', writes Chillingworth in his *Religion of Protestants*, is 'plainly revealed' (p. 92). Tillotson and Wilson among many others offered the essentially humanist arguments that books are 'written to no purpose, if we cannot understand them'; that it is possible to write, as to speak, 'in plain and intelligible words, and such as have a certain sense'; and that the Bible, at least in its vital passages, is so written (Tillotson, *Works*, pp. 674, 688; Wilson, *Interpreter*, pp. 179–80). Hence, the standard of truth is the Scripture, and not tradition or commentary. As Chillingworth had insisted, the apostles' writings 'are the only Rule for us to judge them by', not the imposed 'glosses and interpretations' by which the Pope seeks to maintain his authority (*Religion*, pp. 114, 53).

The defence of these positions led many writers toward partial or extensive statements of a hermeneutic method, and to a greater or lesser degree toward a rational and historical method of interpretation. In his *Tractatus Theologico-Politicus* (1670) Spinoza had argued for a 'true method of interpreting Scripture', which would prefer 'Divine documents' to 'human commentaries', would concentrate on questions of meaning rather than of truth in the Holy Writings, and would assume that the meaning is that intended by its authors. Any scriptural statement, Spinoza asserted, had a 'history', which comprised 'the nature and properties of the language' of the Bible and its authors; an internal analysis of each book and its thematic contents, involving comparison of place with place; and the 'environment', that is, the occasion, period, and audience of original production of the book, the life, conduct, and studies of the author, and the book's reception (*Treatise*, pp. 99, 101–3). The example of two English writers, John Wilson and John Locke, may serve to illustrate some tendencies of English thinking on the interpretation of Scripture. For John Wilson 'the Rule of Interpretation is that which gives us the objective Evidence by which the true Sense of

Scripture is discern'd'. Though Wilson insists on our need for assistance from God 'above our natural Abilities', the 'Means of Interpretation' he lists are operations of the understanding. He divides them into 'remote Means' and 'immediate Means' according to whether they are external or internal to the Scripture itself. 'Remote Means' include knowledge of the specific original language of the Bible; discrimination between literal and figurative expression; knowledge of the original context or 'environment', including the laws, customs, proverbs and rites of Scripture's authors and first audiences; and skill in logic and in natural and moral philosophy. 'Immediate Means' include reference to the local or wider verbal context of any statement; the speaker and his 'scope and design', the antecedents and consequences of the statement, and the comparison of parallel places (*Interpreter*, pp. 6–12). Clearly, there is no essential disagreement between Wilson and such a romanist as Sergeant regarding the essential conditions of an independent rational hermeneutic; what is at issue is the desirability, and the practicability, of such a hermeneutic.

In the preliminary essay to his *Paraphrase and Notes on the Epistles of St Paul* (1706) John Locke presents a cogent set of principles. St Paul's epistles create problems because they are letters, intelligible to the intended recipient in ways they cannot be to us. They are written in a peculiarly Hebraic Greek, on a subject new in itself and therefore requiring the use of terms in a sense different from that which they bear in other discourses. These are, to use Spinoza's term, 'environmental' problems. They must be solved by a rigorous comparison of places genuinely comparable, by reference to Paul's own system of philosophy as it appears in the epistles and not to the prevalent philosophy of later times, and by interpreting each statement in the epistles not as an abstracted verse but in its full original verbal context, for words receive 'a determin'd Sense from their Companions and Adjacents' (p. x). Locke insists that no interpretation or commentary, neither the Pope's nor his own, can replace the 'true Meaning' of the text itself (p. xxiv). Like Spinoza, Locke characterizes commentators as men who would prefer to the true sense of God's sacred word their own conjectures, opinions, and authority.

These movements towards a rational, historical, and increasingly secular hermeneutics were dependent on the possibility of adequate contextualizing knowledge. They were underpinned by a new biblical scholarship, in general more at home in England than in France. Its notable achievements included the biblical commentaries of Matthew Poole and Matthew Henry, Brian Walton's *Biblia Sacra Polyglotta*, the variorum editions of the biblical commentators by Poole and John Pearson, and Edward Leigh's dictionaries of the Hebrew Old Testament and Greek New Testament.

The general principles of interpretative procedure understood by Anglican apologists were widely diffused in eighteenth-century England. A remarkably explicit statement is made by the Independent Isaac Watts in his *Improvement of the Mind* (1741). In chapter 8, 'Of Enquiring into the Sense and Meaning of any Writer or Speaker, and especially the Sense of the Sacred Writings', a recognizably scriptural hermeneutics is delineated, and recommended as appropriate to the reading of all texts. The task of interpretation is to determine what the author meant to communicate, what he 'had in his Mind'. To succeed in this the reader must be 'well acquainted with the . . . *Language* wherein the Author's Mind is exprest'. He must consider not only the verbal context of the words within the text, immediately and by comparison of different places, but also 'the Signification of those Words and Phrases . . . in the *same Nation*, or near the same *Age*, in which that Writer lived'. The '*Scope and Design* of the Writer' must be observed, 'for we suppose a wise and judicious Writer directs his Expressions generally toward his designed End'. Historical texts require a knowledge of the cultural context in which they were produced; obscurities in Scripture sometimes yield to knowledge of '*Jewish* Customs', and of 'ancient *Roman* and *Greek* Times and Manners'. In reading the Bible especially, but in principle in reading any text, we must not warp the sense to our own prejudice or opinion, but practise toward the author a Christian charity, and show a fitting reverence for the sacred or quasi-sacred text:

remember that you *treat every Author, Writer or Speaker, just as you yourselves would be willing to be treated by others*, who are searching out the Meaning of what you write or speak: And maintain upon your Spirit an awful Sense of the Presence of God who . . . will punish those who . . . wilfully pervert the Meaning of the sacred Writers, or even of common Authors.

Improvement, p. 123)

Authorial intention; inherent sense; linguistic and cultural context; the sacred status of the text: these are the essential elements of a received, shared, and confidently stated hermeneutic methodology.

There are connections to be made between biblical scholarship and hermeneutics in the late seventeenth and early eighteenth century, and the beginnings of English editing and annotation of secular literary texts. The procedures of paraphrase and annotation practised in biblical commentaries provided a model perhaps particularly followed in Patrick Hume's edition of *Paradise Lost* (1696). Later editors of Milton increasingly viewed him as a 'divine author', and *Paradise Lost* as a 'divine poem'. Thomas Newton could uncontroversially claim that Milton's epic was the 'best of modern productions' as the Scriptures were 'the best of all ancient ones' (*Paradise Lost*, ed. Newton, II, p. 432). Most eighteenth-century commentators, Zachary Pearce in particular, treated *Paradise Lost* as a sacred text whose true, historical, original and unchanging meaning was to be established by careful scholarship. When Richard Bentley, in his notorious edition of 1732, deviantly treated the poem as a corrupt text, embodying a variety of errors and literary improprieties, which must be corrected by conjectural methods, and accommodated to the tastes and opinions of a later time, his many opponents characterized his edition, and particularly its numerous suggested textual emendations, as an act of 'sacralegious [*sic*] . . . Intrusion' (*Milton Restor'd*, p. viii). It was in similar terms that Spinoza had berated 'those sacrilegious persons who have dared . . . to interpolate the Bible' (*Treatise*, p. 98). As the century progressed Shakespeare too became perceived as a writer of secular scripture. Alexander Pope, as a textual editor of Shakespeare, claimed to have avoided the sectarian heresies of 'Innovation' or 'any indulgence to my private sense or conjecture' (*Works of Shakespeare*, ed. Pope, I, p. xxii). Thomas Edwards, in a letter of 1751, complained of the 'unhallowed hands' with which Warburton had recently profaned Shakespeare in his edition of the Bard.[1]

Such attitudes are related to the arguments about biblical text and interpretation I have outlined. In order to defend the Bible as a rule of faith Anglican apologists had inevitably argued that not only the Bible but all writing in principle embodies a determinate, knowable, authorially intended sense. One of the effects of this was to make it possible to invest written texts other than the Bible with a canonical and quasi-sacred status. Another, connected, effect was to render suspicious, not only to English scholars but also to English satirists, commentaries which seemed to aspire not so much to explain as to overwhelm the text. The parodies of self-serving *scholia* in Swift's *Tale of a Tub*, Pope's *Dunciad*, and Sterne's *Tristram Shandy* of course are in a long-standing humanist tradition of attacks on the over-ingenious glosses of monkish dunces and classical pedants; they also owe something to the more recent debate between Roman Catholics and Anglicans on the relative status of text and commentary.

It is clear that many of the hermeneutic, editorial, and scholarly assumptions and practices of the eighteenth century derived from, and very often were primarily expressed in, biblical scholarship and polemic. Questions of literary aesthetics and poetics were equally profoundly affected by changing attitudes to the Bible. For political and cultural as well as religious reasons the profound implication of the

---

[1] Quoted by Martin Battestin, 'A rationale of literary annotation: the example of Fielding's novels', *Studies in Bibliography*, 34 (1981), 1.

Bible in English literary consciousness which made possible Herbert's *The Temple*, Milton's *Paradise Lost*, or Bunyan's *Pilgrim's Progress* began in the course of the later seventeenth century, and at the beginning of the eighteenth century, to break down. If it is at all possible to generalize coherently about such large trends, then it is necessary to speak of a process by which the Bible came to be seen more and more as a secular text: an 'eclipse of biblical narrative', to use Hans Frei's now well-known phrase, in which Christians no longer 'knew themselves easily and naturally included in that total narration and by means of it in the world it rendered faithfully' (*Eclipse*, p. 49). Through much of the seventeenth century writers had been able familiarly to use a typology by which they could believe the prophecies of the Old Testament fulfilled in the events of the New, and understand the events of their own times as postfigurations within a biblical history. As late as the 1680s John Dryden could naturally, and with a rich and multiple resonance, represent the Exclusion Bill crisis in terms of the revolt of Absalom. Typological handbooks, such as William Guild's *Moses Unvail'd* (1620) or the *Tropologia* of Benjamin Keach (1681) were popular works. In the late seventeenth century and early eighteenth century in England typology as a natural way of thinking began to fade. Perhaps the most dramatic statement, and evidence, of this change is Isaac Watts's insistence that it was no longer possible for a Christian congregation 'to sing the words of *David*, and apply them in our meditation to the things of the new testament'; the 'cloudy and typical expressions' of the Old Testament must now be turned, explicitly, into 'evangelical language' ('Psalmody', pp. 278–81). Typological interpretation continued in the eighteenth century, as might be expected, in sermons and in biblical commentaries and criticism. Such Evangelicals as Martin Madan and John Newton insisted that the New Testament depicts the fulfilment of Old Testament prophecies, that therefore Christ 'is the main scope and subject of every book' (Newton, *Works*, II, p. 335). Indeed, for Evangelicals, our own lives continued to be seen as postfigurations of biblical history, Philip Doddridge for example asserting, in his *Family Expositor*, that 'the Preservation of the Holy Child' (Matthew 2: 13–15) 'may be considered as a Figure of God's Care over his Church, in its greatest Danger'. By the end of the century, however, William Jones of Nayland felt it necessary to present his typological lectures on the *Figurative Language of the Holy Scriptures* (1787) as an attempt to 'revive' (p. 32) a fading and neglected activity. During the course of the eighteenth century typology declined in secular literature. It is easy to find an effective figuralism in *Robinson Crusoe* (1719), where the hero is variously the Prodigal Son, or Jonah saved from the whale. Later novels incorporate typology in redefined, secularizing, and less assimilated ways. The type, abstracted from its scriptural context, became a pattern of behaviour, or a predictive element in narrative structure, or (in the modern sense) a character type. Paul Korshin has provided a full documentation, and analysis, of this process.[2] Less modified kinds of typology survived chiefly in the hymn and in other forms of religious poetry; in the Wesleyan figuring of Britain as Israel, for example, or in Christopher Smart's use of David, in *A Song to David* (1763), as a type not only of Christ but also of the modern poet of religious adoration.

The decline of typology in secular literature represents a profound cultural shift. Inevitably, the early eighteenth century had to begin to renegotiate its aesthetic relation to the Bible. A number of writers made claims for the Bible as a literary model. Some attempted to accommodate the Scriptures to classical standards of style and decorum. Before the turn of the century John Edwards found, in both the Old and the New Testament, that 'the Phrases, Expressions and Modes of Speaking used by the Inspired Writers, are the same with those that we find in the best Classick Authors' (*Discourse*, II, p. 50). Thirty years later, Anthony Blackwall in his *Sacred Classics Defended* (1725) set out to demonstrate, at some length, that the New Testament writers, far from committing solecisms and barbarisms, wrote in a language which is 'incontestably the same with that of the old authentic Grecians' (p. 170), correct, eloquent, above all simple and clear. This insistence has politico-religious as well as literary-critical implications; even at this date Blackwall is aware of the need to defend the Holy Writings against Richard Simon's 'scandalous bigottry, when he speaks against the perspicuity of the sacred writers' (p. 255).

One of the most common literary arguments made for the Bible was that it was characteristically sublime. The claim could be thought to have a classical authority; Longinus' *Peri Hupsous* (*On the Sublime*) had analysed and commended sublimity of style, and had in particular cited as an example of the sublime the Mosaic 'God said, Let there be light: and there was light' (Genesis 1:3). Addison found in the Old Testament 'several Passages more elevated and sublime than any in Homer' (*Spectator* 160, 14 June 1712). Edward Young found in the last chapters of Job (throughout the eighteenth century a favourite *locus* of sublimity) such a 'Force and Vigour of Style, as would have given the great Wits of Antiquity new Laws for the Sublime, had they been acquainted with these Writings' (*Guardian* 86, 19 June 1713). The sacred penmen, of course, had advantages for sublimity in their subject, as well as their style. Addison asserted, as an argument for the return of poetry to sacred subjects, that 'our Idea of the Supreme Being is not only

---

[2] See especially *Typologies*, pp. 34–7, 110–15.

Infinitely more Great and Noble than what could possibly enter into the Heart of an Heathen, but filled with every thing that can raise the Imagination, and give an Opportunity for the Sublimest Thoughts and Conceptions' (*Spectator* 453, 9 August 1712). The most significant if not in the short term the most influential critical writing on the literary qualities of the Bible is to be found in the work of John Dennis, particularly *The Advancement and Reformation of Modern Poetry* (1701) and *The Grounds of Criticism in Poetry* (1704). What Dennis sought to offer was no less than a poetics founded on the sublime, and especially on the biblical sublime. Dennis's fundamental assertion was that poetry is an art which 'attains its End by exciting of Passion' (*Critical Works*, I, p. 336). Lesser poetry (comedy, satire, the elegy, the pastoral) excites ordinary or vulgar passion. Greater poetry (epic, tragic, the high ode), however, excites 'Enthusiastic Passion', 'a Passion ... moved by the Ideas in Contemplation, or the Meditation of things that belong not to common Life' (*Critical Works*, I, p. 338). It is religious ideas, and especially sublime religious ideas, that pre-eminently move men to enthusiastic passion. The ancient poets are sublime because they chose religious subjects, and especially because they wrote of the reigning religion, and hence were in earnest themselves and could move their audience. The Bible is for the same reasons sublime for a Christian readership. Indeed, the sublime representations of an angry God in such passages as Psalms 18:6–15 and Habbakuk 3:3–10 surpass comparable passages in the Greek and Roman classics in their superior poetry, as well as in their superior divinity (*Critical Works*, I, pp. 268, 366–7).

Dennis provided cogent arguments for the choice of religious subjects for poetry and, more particularly, for the turning of modern poetry to Christian subjects. Naturally, Dennis's great exemplar of the possibilities of a new Christian poetry was *Paradise Lost*. Dennis was not of course the first to rediscover Milton's epic after the neglect of the Restoration years. Tonson's folio edition had appeared in 1688. The series of scholarly annotated editions had been initiated by Patrick Hume, and in the *Spectator* Addison developed an extended analysis of the poem, in neo-classical categories, and essentially according to neo-classical rules. It was Dennis, however, who first provided a coherent defence of Milton as the sublime, religious, biblical poet who would be so central a model for eighteenth-century religious verse.

The period's most significant development in the accommodation of biblical criticism and secular poetics took place in the setting of an academic institution. Robert Lowth was Professor of Poetry at Oxford from 1741 to 1750, and from that chair he delivered a series of lectures on the Hebrew sacred poetry. *De sacra poesi Hebraeorum praelectiones* was published in 1753, and translated into English (by G. Gregory) in

1787. In 1778 Lowth published an English translation of the Book of Isaiah, executed according to the critical principles he had outlined in the *Praelectiones*, and reiterated and developed in the Preliminary Dissertation of the *Isaiah* itself. Lowth's work requires extended discussion.

Lowth describes Hebrew poetry as an original poetry, before any rules, characterized by the expression of the emotions of man's first religious contemplations: 'What ideas could so powerfully affect a new-created mind (undepraved by habit or opinion) as the goodness, the wisdom, and the greatness of the Almighty? Is it not probable, that the first effort of rude and unpolished verse would display itself in the praise of the Creator, and flow almost involuntarily from the enraptured mind?' (*Lectures*, I, p. 38). In constantly drawing attention to the prevalence of passionate expression in Hebrew poetry, Lowth implies, and often states, that all poetry is, or should be, characteristically an 'effect of mental emotion' (*Lectures*, I, p. 366). Lowth's theory is mimetic; he describes Aristotle's *Poetics* as 'the great Code of Criticism' (*Isaiah*, p. lx). None the less, positing that poetry 'derives its very existence from the more vehement emotions of the mind' (*Lectures*, I, p. 367), he insists that poetry must be more effective, certainly must be more sublime, when its object of imitation is the mind itself: 'When a passion is expressed . . . the mind is immediately conscious of itself and its own emotions; it feels and suffers in itself a sensation, either the same or similar to that which is described'. Crucial to Aristotelian mimetic theory is recognition of what is imitated, made possible by the faculty of memory. Tellingly and explicitly Lowth assigns to the imitation of externals an inferior role, since 'the understanding slowly perceives the accuracy of the description in all other subjects, and their agreement to their archetypes, as being obliged to compare them by the aid and through the uncertain medium, as it were, of the memory'. Hebrew poetry is valued by Lowth because its mimetic object is directly and immediately the emotion of the mind: 'by far the greater part of the sacred poetry is little else than a continued imitation of the different passions', the passions, that is, of adoration of God, joy in his favour, grief in sin, indignation against God's contemners, terror of divine judgement (*Lectures*, I, p. 368).

Lowth's key achievement was his discovery, explanation, and exemplification of the true verse form of biblical poetry. Previous writers had assumed that with the loss of the original pronunciation, so too had been lost an original accentual system. Lowth, however, noting the Hebrew practice of singing their sacred hymns 'alternately . . . by opposite choirs', demonstrated that the basic metrical form of the Hebrew poetry was based not on accent but on parallel structures (*Lectures*, II, pp. 25–55). Lowth defined three different kinds of parallelism, one or more of which provided an appropriate form for all the different kinds of Hebrew verse. In the *Praelectiones* he exemplified, from Psalms, Judges, Isaiah, and the minor prophets, 'synonymous parallelism, when the same sentiment is repeated in different, but equivalent terms'. Antithetic parallelism, 'when a thing is illustrated by its contrary being opposed to it', Lowth pointed out, was most appropriate in 'adages and acute sayings', in Proverbs for instance. Finally Lowth distinguished a more complex and flexible form, 'Synthetic or Constructive Parallelism', where 'the sentences answer to each other . . . by the form of construction'. Lowth was able to demonstrate this fundamental poetic principle in the prophecies, as well as in books, such as the Psalms, which had long been agreed to be poetical.

Amongst Lowth's most important contributions to the eighteenth-century critical debate were his observations on the poetic language of Hebrew poetry. The classical and neo-classical position was that usage is the proper standard: poetry cannot adopt a special language and should not use words which are either sullied by over-use or unfamiliar. Such poets as Smart and Gray, however, argued for a 'peculiar' language: 'the language of the age', as Thomas Gray wrote in 1742, 'is never the language of poetry' (*Correspondence*, p. 192). Lowth insists repeatedly in the *Praelectiones* that 'The poetry of every language has a style and form of expression peculiar to itself . . . frequently . . . breaking down the boundaries by which the popular dialect is confined' (*Lectures*, I, p. 308). Specifically, the Hebrews 'look upon the language of poetry as wholly distinct from that of common life, as calculated immediately for expressing the passions' (*Lectures*, I, p. 330). Hence they use obsolete or foreign words, irregular word orders and syntax, obscurities of expression, bold figures. Indecorously, from the point of view of a neo-classical aesthetic, the Hebrew poetry sometimes uses terms and images from ordinary life in descriptions of the exertions of divine power: 'the Lord awaked as one out of sleep, and like a mighty man that shouteth by reason of wine' (Psalm 78:65). Lowth explains that it is precisely this startling indecorum which produces the sublime effect:

From ideas, which in themselves appear coarse, unsuitable, and totally unworthy of so great an object, the mind naturally recedes, and passes suddenly to the contemplation of the object itself, and of its inherent magnitude and importance.

(*Lectures*, I, p. 364)

As might be expected, Lowth provides an extensive analysis of the sublime in the Old Testament, taking up, extending, and in some important ways developing already familiar concepts of the religious sublime.

For Lowth the sublime arises at the same time from the divine subject-matter of the Bible, and from the way in which that subject-matter is presented. His distinction between 'sentiment' and 'expression' avowedly follows Longinus' distinction between 'Grandeur of Conception' and 'Vehemence or Enthusiasm of Passion' (*Lectures*, I, pp. 346–7). The Hebrew poets exceed all other writers because their subjects, 'the greatness, the power, the justice, the immensity of God; the infinite wisdom of his works and of his dispensations', are incomparably dignified and important, and 'even exceed the confines of human genius and intellect' (*Lectures*, I, p. 348). In language which anticipates the psychologically based sublime of Burke, Lowth explains that it is precisely the unavailing attempt of the human mind to grasp what is above it which creates the sublime; 'while the imagination labours to comprehend what is beyond its powers, this very labour itself, and these ineffectual endeavours, sufficiently demonstrate the immensity and sublimity of the object' (*Lectures*, I, p. 353). One kind of sublime style is that which immediately represents passion, the 'crouded and abrupt sentences' and 'bold and magnificent expressions' of Job for example. Equally effective however is the brevity and simplicity of God's creating decree 'Let there be light', where our perception of the divine power is allowed to proceed, unimpeded by the verbosity of explanation, 'from the proper action and energy of the mind itself' (*Lectures*, I, pp. 349–50).

Lowth's new poetics of the Hebrew Scriptures represents a development not merely in aesthetics. Blackwall had written about the New Testament, for Protestants the central repository of the truths necessary to salvation, and he had been very much aware of the still recent controversy between Anglicans and Roman Catholics concerning the clarity and stability of Scripture. Naturally, therefore, his aesthetic is classicist, emphasizing the clarity and perspicuity of the sacred books. Lowth, confining himself to the Old Testament, and writing at a greater distance from the political and theological immediacies of the debate between England and Rome, could present an aesthetics which differentiated the Old Testament from classical poetry, stressing its characteristic force and obscurity. The violent transitions natural to the expression of 'vehement affections' occur in Hebrew poetry 'much more frequently, than could be endured in the poetry of the Greeks and Romans, or even in our own'. The modern reader 'will find many of these instances not easy to be understood; the force and design of some of them . . . are indeed scarcely to be explained, or even perfectly comprehended' (*Lectures*, I, p. 329). Lowth insists that Hebrew poetry is often perspicuous, often, indeed, most perspicuous where most sublime; but his is a poetic which includes and values the obscure as well as the clear.

Lowth's views were not wholly revolutionary. In placing poetry among

the 'first fruits of human ingenuity' (*Lectures*, I, p. 97), or considering
it capable of making a 'more forcible impression upon the mind' than
abstract reasoning (*Lectures*, I, p. 80) he enunciated positions familiar
in Renaissance literary criticism, for example in Sidney's *Apology for
Poetry*, a text Lowth surely knew. Lowth's notions of the judgement
and imagination as distinguishing and combining faculties derive, avowedly, from Hobbes and Locke (*Lectures*, I, pp. 263–4 and note), and his
discussion of metaphor (*Lectures*, I, p. 117) has a visual emphasis which
recalls Addison's *Spectator* papers on the Imagination. His insistence
that poetry is an effect of passion had been anticipated by Dennis
among others. None the less, Lowth's extensive characterization of the
literary qualities of the Old Testament provided his contemporaries with
the model and authority of a biblical poetics in many important respects
different from the classics of Greece and Rome. Though Lowth cannot
be simply categorized as a 'pre-romantic', his *Lectures* and *Isaiah* were
none the less key documents in the later eighteenth-century discussion
and reassessment of poetic genre, form, and language, and of the role
of the poet.

Lowth's *Praelectiones* and *Isaiah* were works of secular criticism,
deliberately avoiding all 'theological disquisitions' (*Lectures*, I, p. 41),
and based on an essentially historical scholarship. Lowth's extensive
notes to his translation of Isaiah refer not only to biblical commentators, but also, frequently, to earlier and contemporary observers of life
in the biblical lands. This interest is primarily neither antiquarian nor
anthropological, but founded on the assumption that biblical texts, like
secular texts, can be explicated only with reference to a contextualizing
scholarship. He who would truly understand the Hebrew poetry 'must
imagine himself exactly situated as the persons to whom it was written,
or even as the writers themselves' (*Lectures*, I, p. 114).

The same insistence on the original generation and meaning of the
words of the Old Testament is found in Lowth's textual scholarship. A
key issue here was the masoritic system of pointing the Hebrew of the
Old Testament, brought in by Jewish scholars no earlier than the eighth
century. Earlier Protestant scholars, anxious to assert the integrity of the
Scriptures, had insisted on the perfection of the masoritic text. More
realistically, Lowth agreed with such earlier scholars as Richard Simon
that all texts become corrupt in transmission, and that the Hebrew text
of the Old Testament, being the most ancient, must inevitably contain
many errors. The masoritic system, far from being a divine standard
and preservative of meaning, is in fact, in Lowth's words, no more than
a particular 'Translation' or 'Interpretation' of the Hebrew writings.
The original unpointed Hebrew words were capable of various meanings. In their points, the Jews 'have determined them to one meaning

and construction; and the sense which they thus give is their sense of the passage' (*Isaiah*, p. liv). Lowth is not arguing for a textual, and interpretative, free-for-all; there are, he insists, 'rules of just interpretation', by which may be tested the authority of the masoritic as of any other text. Rather, he is refusing the imposition of a received, 'traditional' interpretation (*masora* means tradition), and appealing to a meticulous textual, and historical, scholarship as the only route to honest and dependable texts and interpretations.

The relations and influence of Lowth's work as biblical scholarship, rather than as aesthetics or poetics, are easier to trace, and at least equally important in the history of literary theory. His work was recognized notably in Germany, the home of the new European critical scholarship. In 1765 he was elected to the Royal Society of Göttingen. In 1770 an edition of the *Praelectiones* was published at Göttingen with notes by J. D. Michaelis. Michaelis himself was an important representative of the rational and academic in German biblical criticism. His *Einleitung in das Neue Testament* (1750) was to have considerable influence in England and America. Michaelis was concerned with the philological and cultural determinants of the Bible rather than with its theology. Realizing that contemporary Arabia had changed little since biblical times, and wishing to forward knowledge of the culture and language which produced the Scriptures, he instigated an expedition to Arabia undertaken by Niebuhr, Forskål, and others (1761–7). As Michaelis had hoped, the expedition was of signal importance for biblical and oriental studies. Michaelis might not have anticipated, however, that it would occasion an answer by an altogether less academic and less rationalist spirit, Johann Georg Hamann. Hamann described his *Aesthetica in Nuce* (1762) as 'a rhapsody in cabbalistic prose'. In its punning, teasing, cryptic, allusive method the *Aesthetica* foreshadows, for an English reader, Blake's *Marriage of Heaven and Hell*. Hamann's targets are rationalist thought, historical scholarship, and Hellenistic criticism. 'The Archangel' Michaelis might be valued for his philologist's knowledge of 'the remains of Canaan's tongue' (p. 141), but the Bible must be understood not literally and objectively, but in the spirit. The true critic cannot be 'a groom of the chamber to the dead letter'; Michaelis's knowledge of the historical contexts of Scripture, his 'copious insight into physical things', cannot control the spirit which 'bloweth where it listeth' (pp. 143–4). A pilgrimage to the East is needed indeed, but it must be a metaphorical and magical journey, not such an anthropological expedition as that sponsored by Michaelis (p. 147). Hamann similarly rejects neo-classicism on the grounds that it is concerned with the historical and aesthetic, rather than with the spiritual. Winckelmann had drawn our attention 'to the monuments of the ancients, to shape our minds through memory' (p. 147); but 'salvation comes from the Jews', not from Greece or Rome.

For Hamann God is 'the poet at the beginning of days' (p. 145), who speaks to man through his creation. The poem which is nature appears to man chaotic, disorganized, incomplete; 'all we have left ... is fragmentary verse and *disjecta membra poetae*'. The scientist and the philosopher can collect and interpret the scattered limbs; the poet, however, is able to 'imitate' and 'adapt' them (p. 142). Hamann has in mind not an Aristotelian but a spiritual imitation. The poet finds the divine unity in apparent disorder, and translates 'from the tongue of angels into the tongue of men'. Truth depends not on empirical or rational apprehension, but on man's sense that he partakes of the divine nature, is made in God's image: 'every impression of Nature in man is not only a memorial, but also a warrant of fundamental truth; who is the LORD'. A truly divine poetry must 'purify the natural use of the senses from the unnatural use of abstractions, which distort our concepts of things' (p. 145). Such a poetry may be found in Homer, in Shakespeare, above all in the Bible. In these productions of a primitive and original genius are to be found passion (as in Job's lament, Job 2:13–3:1ff.), myths (as of Odysseus, for Hamann a mythic forerunner of Christ), the parables which are 'older than reasoning', and images, which are the essential and characteristic property of divine poetry:

The senses and passions speak and understand nothing but images. The entire store of human knowledge and happiness consists in images. The first outburst of Creation, and the first impression of its recording scribe ... are united in the words: Let there be Light! Here beginneth the feeling for the presence of things.

(p. 141)

Much influenced by Hamann, though far more conventional in expression, is Johann Gottfried Herder's *Spirit of Hebrew Poetry* (*Vom Geist der Ebräischen Poesie*, 1782–3). Herder's book finds in the poetry of the Old Testament a model for a developed aesthetic which foreshadows Romanticism.

Hamann had insisted that 'poetry is the mother-tongue of the human race' (p. 141). Herder argues for a similar primitivism. The earliest poetry of the Hebrews was 'the first dawning of the illumination of the world', beginning with the primitive emotions of the human mind, and especially with 'the finest natural theology', 'the purest conceptions of God' (I, pp. 45–6, 54). We must appreciate that the Hebrews wrote with the language and feelings of children, for everything appeared before them 'in the dazzling splendour of novelty' (II, p. 9). The history of poetry tells of decline from pristine energy and innocence. The lyrics of Moses, of Deborah, or of Job are characterized by 'rude strength', 'animated movement', and 'lofty sound' (II, p. 225). By the time of the prophets, language 'had already become more practised, images and sentiments had become more common-place' (II, p. 22). David's Psalms show a movement towards a 'greater gentleness and refinement' (II, p. 225). Our case, in the developed maturity of our civilization, is much worse. Our poetic language is 'weak and facile from a multiplicity of stale and metaphorical expressions'. The facility of our writing is 'the result of experience, the squeamishness and over-refinement of our exhausted and worn out hearts' (II, p. 9).

Like Hamann, Herder argues for a new mimesis, based not on a merely sensory apprehension of external reality, but on man's feelings in face of created things, and on his sense of the divine within him. Hebrew poetry 'had its origin in the union of outward form with inward feeling' (II, p. 5). It is in this sense that the poet becomes divine: 'In ordering all from the impulses of his own inward feeling, and with reference to himself, he becomes an imitator of the Divinity, a second Creator, a true ποιητης' (II, p. 7). Such a poetics has its preferred poetic forms and its preferred poetic qualities. The sung lyric is for Herder the normative form of early Hebrew poetry. It is characterized by 'figurative expressions', animated by 'excited feelings' (II, p. 24). The extended lyric achieves an essential organic coherence, is especially appropriate to the expression of a sense of 'the union of outward form with inward feeling': 'The whole presents itself before us, a picture full of living action. No word can be taken away, no strophe change its place ... the principle of progression [in a lyric poem] must be inward, from the one living fountain of excited emotion' (II, pp. 233, 234).

Hebrew has all the necessary desiderata of a poetic language: 'action, imagery, passion, musick, rhythm' (I, p. 27). The Hebrews wrote in a 'figurative discourse', and especially in the 'plain and simple imagery' proper to a nation in its childhood (II, pp. 9, 26). The lack of adjectives in the Hebrew language, and the abundance of verbs, make it an excellent medium for the 'action and vivid imagery' essential to poetry. Barren in abstract terms, it is rich in synonyms and 'sensuous representations'. Hebrew's single tense is a positive advantage, for to a genuine poetry 'all is present time'. To a rationalist's accusation that parallelism is mere repetition, Herder retorts the examples of dance movement and the choric ode, and insists that 'all that delights the senses in forms and sounds depends on symmetry'. Poetry is addressed not to the understanding alone but 'primarily and chiefly to the feelings'; in the heart overcome by emotions, 'wave follows upon wave, and that is parallelism' (I, pp. 27–41).

Herder begins his book with an acknowledgement of Lowth's 'beautiful and justly celebrated' lectures, but he claims to offer neither a translation nor an imitation of Lowth. Where Lowth had seemed scholarly and analytical, Herder's title itself announces his essential concern with the spirit of biblical verse. He argues that the Hebrew poetry must be seen, not distorted by classical values or classical taxonomies, but in its own terms. As Richard Hurd in England had claimed that the romance could be valued only by reference to its own cultural and social conditions of production (*Letters on Chivalry and Romance*, 1762), so Herder insists that we must ask 'whether, in their own kind, and for their peculiar wants, they had an Homer or an Ossian' (I, p. 28). David's Psalms should not be assessed against a norm derived from Pindar's odes:

in studying these as specimens of art, we must take no examples from other nations and languages, as models, by which to judge of them; [they] must be judged with reference to the peculiar nature of the feelings, sentiments and language, out of which they have grown.

(II, p. 228)

Herder requires that as readers we put off our particular contemporary historical circumstance, and the prejudices and commitments that go with it, and enter into the original spirit of the Hebrew writings:

we must live in their time, in their own country, must adopt their modes of thinking and feeling, must see, how they lived, how they were educated, what scenes they looked upon, what were the objects of their affection and passion, the character of their atmosphere, their skies, the structure of their organs, their dances and their musick.

(I, p. 28)

Herder's book assumes and deploys the scholarship that enables reconstruction of the linguistic and cultural world of the Bible, but he goes beyond a purely historical scholarship to an exemplary insistence on the special and distinctive quality of the writings of the past. We must not look in Hebrew poetry for support for particular modern religious positions. Still less should we imagine that we will find in it 'a model of holy feelings for all men' (II, p. 227). Above all we must not value the productions of the past in the proportion that they succeed in mirroring our own, historical, views and attitudes: 'it seems to indicate either a stupid or a proud presumption to require, that every nation, even of the most ancient times, should think, discourse, feel, and fashion its poetical conceptions in a manner to suit our habits and wants' (II, p. 9).

A similar insistence that the modern reader bring imaginative sympathy to all past writings distinguished the work of Johann Gottfried Eichhorn. Eichhorn, who had been taught by Heyne and Michaelis at Göttingen, succeeded Michaelis as Professor in 1788. Eichhorn regarded the Scriptures as human writings, which had undergone many changes in the first centuries. They must be examined, like any other documents, not by a merely textual criticism, but by a *höhere Kritik*, a higher criticism concerned with their original language and cultural contexts, and their literary characteristics. Using these methods, Eichhorn made pioneering distinctions in the documentary sources of both the Old and New Testaments. In his *Einleitung ins Alte Testament* (Leipzig, 1780–3) he analysed the two narrative strands in the Genesis account of creation. In his *Einleitung in das Neue Testament* (3 vols., Leipzig, 1804, 1810–11, 1812–14) he argued that the four gospels derived from a common Aramaic *Urevangelium*, and that several of the 'Pauline' epistles were by other hands. In his scientific analyses of Scripture Eichhorn was concerned, as Herder had been, that Scripture should be regarded, not through the inappropriate spectacles of modern rationalism or classicism, but with a thorough knowledge of its distinctive historical and cultural character. In a noble and famous passage, Eichhorn urges us to read Genesis:

as two historical works of high antiquity, and thus breathe the air of its age and land. Forget the century you are living in and the knowledge it offers you ... The youth of the world, which it describes, requires that one sink into its depths. The first beams of dawning intelligence will not bear the bright light of the intellect ... Without intimate acquaintance with the customs of pastoral life, without acquaintance with the manner of thinking and imagining among uncultivated peoples gained through the study of the ancient world ... one easily becomes the betrayer of the Book, when one tries to be its rescuer and interpreter.[3]

As the work of Lowth was known to and valued by German writers, so the new German scholarship in its turn affected developments in England. Coleridge's thought and poetry, notably, were substantially influenced by Michaelis, Herder and Eichhorn.[4] Among British biblical scholars, most profoundly influenced by German scholarship was the radical Catholic priest Alexander Geddes. Geddes, who was encouraged by Lowth and corresponded with Eichhorn, carried further than anyone else in England and Scotland the secularizing tendencies of the new textual criticism. Geddes wrote with the confidence and enthusiasm of one who knew he belonged to a new European, and especially English and German, rational scholarship. His views and methods were exemplified in the two volumes he completed of a new translation of the Bible (1792, 1797), and most fully described in his *Prospectus of a New Translation of the Holy Bible* (1786).

---

[3] Quoted by McGann, *Inflections*, pp. 98–9.
[4] See especially Shaffer, '*Kubla Khan*'.

Geddes, like Lowth and Herder, valued the literary qualities of the Bible. He applauded the beauties of Deborah's 'ode' (Judges 5), and of David's 'elegy' on the death of Saul and Jonathan (2 Sam. 1:18–26). (*Holy Bible*, II, pp. xvi–xvii.) In its cosmogonies, its historical narratives, its oratory, and its laws, the Old Testament excelled or at least equalled anything in the classical writings (*Holy Bible*, I, p. i). The Old Testament Scriptures however are secular, their beauties and defects are therefore to be judged like those of 'any other writings of antiquity' (*Critical Remarks*, I, pp. iv–v). Because the Jewish historical writers were not divinely inspired, the substance of their writing, and especially the text itself, must be submitted to the rules of comparative criticism; to distinguish true from false readings is

the task of criticism . . . only: for no authority on earth can make a Text genuine or spurious, that was not such originally: nor can the dross be discriminated from the silver but in the crucible of a severe rational critique: a critique of the very same nature with that by which we ascertain the true or more probable readings of Homer, Virgil, Milton, Shakespeare.

(*Address to the Public*, p. 5)

Geddes claimed that he himself applied rational rules of criticism without 'the smallest deference to inveterate prejudice or domineering authority' (*Critical Remarks*, I, p. iv). In particular, in the opinion of Geddes, as of Lowth, the textual scholarship of the Old Testament had been rendered wholly ineffectual for centuries by a mistaken acceptance of the masoritic system as the inflexible standard and authority. The Jewish scholars, the first teachers of Hebrew, had imposed upon their disciples a subjective canon of interpretation, 'traditionally handed down to them from their great law-giver Moses' (*Prospectus*, p. 5). The editing and interpretation of the text was made an exclusive privilege of those who held that key of knowledge, the *masora*.

Geddes, like Lowth, argued that the abandonment of the false and factitious traditional security of the *masora* need not lead to an uncontrolled ambiguity. The removal of the points allows us to explain the text 'not as we please but as we ought'. It is the 'great object' of biblical criticism, as of criticism of all texts, 'to come at the true signification of every word and sentence', 'the genuine grammatical meaning of a genuine text' (*Prospectus*, pp. 68, 69; *Bible*, II, p. xiii). True readings and true interpretations must be found by the textual methods which scholars had learnt to employ in editing classical texts: the collation of manuscripts, the comparison of parallel places of the text, and in the last resort conjecture, whose aim is to replace human admixture with the word of God (*Prospectus*, pp. 18–58). To these specifically textual procedures must be added a number of higher aids to interpretation:

detailed knowledge of the original language, consultation of lexicons, concordances and commentaries, consideration of the purpose and style of each writer, distinction of the literal from the metaphoric, comparison of passages and of figures of speech (*Prospectus*, p. 71).

Geddes is an appropriate figure with whom to conclude. His work represents a developed form of those tendencies, which I have outlined, towards a rational textual criticism and a historical scholarship of the Bible. To extreme textual conservatives in the English Church, still in the late eighteenth century clinging to the *masora*, and to his superiors in the Roman Church, insisting on the Vulgate and Rheims/Douay translations, Geddes seemed a dangerous radical. Historically, however, he clearly belongs to a European renaissance in biblical scholarship of (in Geddes's own words) 'these last hundred years'. His lineage may be found in earlier continental writers such as Capellus (the first, according to Geddes, to discard the *masora*) and Richard Simon (whose massive and independent historico-textual scholarship finds echoes in the learning and mode of presentation of Geddes's *Prospectus*), and in such English writers of the seventeenth and eighteenth centuries as Hammond, Poole, Patrick, Locke, Lowth, and Kennicott (all of whom Geddes mentions in the *Prospectus*), as well as in the new German scholarship. In the *Prospectus* Geddes described how he saw obfuscating ideological and sectarian prejudices subsiding as the 'learned of all communions' (p. 147) at last joined together in the search for the genuine text, and true meaning, of the Scriptures. Bliss was it, in that textual dawn, to be alive.

Science and literary criticism

Michel Baridon

Science and literary criticism are generally considered to stand so far apart that one cannot analyse their mutual relations without clear definitions of both.

If we assume, as did Ezra Pound, that 'literature is news that stays news', we can consider writers as agents in the transformation of the world-picture of their age. They therefore have something in common with scientists, who keep modifying received ideas by the testing of new paradigms. But their quest for modernity does not always elicit an immediate response on the part of the critics: Thomson's *Seasons* popularized a form of natural sublimity which received its critical status in Burke's *Enquiry* almost thirty years later. Thus, if we wish to consider literary criticism in both its incipient and developed forms, we must include in our corpus the stray remarks, sometimes off the cuff, made by the authors themselves.

The same applies to science. The term must be used in a broad sense, i.e., science as understood by the interested layman. Innovations, whether a writer rejects or favours them, will attract his attention and develop his creative powers, but science, as he apprehends it, is often mediated by philosophy. To use the example of Thomson again, he and Swift held different views about the Royal Society, but the 'new science' was central to their preoccupations. Neither of them had done any work in a laboratory, but both knew about the Boyle Lectures and about the controversies caused by the *Essay concerning Human Understanding*, which relies on the corpuscular theory of matter. The transdisciplinary bridges built by Hobbes, Locke, Hume and Kant supply some of the strongest links between science and literary criticism from the age of Boileau to that of Herder.

Neo-classicism and the geometricians

At the beginning of our period, the spirit of the Renaissance was still abroad in Europe. It was the great age of geometry and algebra. Since the days of Leonardo, Cardano and Tartaglia, the downfall of Aristotelian physics had established new paradigms based on motion, force and space.[1] Geometry and optics enabled the scientist to place objects in relation to an observer and in relation to one another. These two sciences joined forces with mechanics and astronomy because motion could best be observed by studying the movement of celestial bodies. Kepler could never have used a telescope if the propagation of light had not followed the laws of geometry, and it was by coupling this huge eye with his own that he discovered that nature was no longer to be regarded *instar divini animalis* but *instar horologii*. The universe became a machine whose workings could be described by the language of mathematics.

But the size of the machine remained unknown, and the world-image discovered in Galileo's 'great book written in mathematical characters' was deeply disturbing. It led to boundless confidence in the abilities of human reason and yet it generated what Kepler called 'a secret hidden horror'[2] at the idea that man was wandering in boundless space. Hence the power exerted by the scientific imagination over the literature of the period for, while we find Pascal turning to religion to seek protection against the fear 'of infinite spaces', we see Descartes or Spinoza calmly setting out to construct a new world-image. One can read in the *Ethics*: 'I shall consider human actions as if they were lines, planes and solid bodies'[3], and in his *Traité de l'Homme* Descartes explained the nerve impulse by the circulation of animal spirits which, he said, can be compared to the motion of water in the 'fountains playing in the king's garden'. This was the direct application of new cognitive schemes to the exploration of natural phenomena. The anatomist used the laws of hydrostatics and so did the political theorist. In his *Leviathan*, Hobbes described the 'skill of maintaining commonwealths' as consisting 'in certain rules, as doth Arithmetique and Geometry'[4] and he compared individual liberty to water running down an inclined plane,[5] a simile clearly reminiscent of the *catena d'aqua* often found in Renaissance gardens. Such comparisons are not mere illustrations. They are central intuitions demonstrating the possibilities offered by the mechanization of the new world-picture.

The same attitude is traceable in discussions concerning aesthetics. In his *Discourse on Method*, Descartes describes a fine city as one 'regularly laid out on a plain' with straight streets and houses all built in the same style.[6] This bears a strong resemblance to Wren's statement on the

---

[1] Kuhn, *Structure*, pp. 117–18.
[2] Quoted by Koyré, *Closed World*, p. 61.
[3] *Ethics*, Introduction to Book III.   [4] *Leviathan*, p. 261.
[5] 'Liberty and necessity are consistent: As in the water, that hath not only Liberty but a necessity to go down the Channel' (*Leviathan*, p. 263).
[6] *Discours de la Méthode*, in *Oeuvres*, p. 133.

beauty of geometrical forms: 'geometrical figures are naturally more beautiful than other irregular: in this all consent as to a law of nature. Of geometrical figures the square and the circle are most beautiful, next the parallelogram and the oval.'[7] Artists and philosophers were in agreement over the relation of geometrical shapes to artistic expression. Beauty to them was the concordance between abstract knowledge and concrete representation. If mathematics provided the key to the innermost life of things, then outward appearance must be made rationally intelligible. What was true of Hobbes and Descartes was also true of Galileo, whose rejection of mannerism in favour of Raphael's true classicism has been brilliantly analysed by Panofsky.[8] Galileo could, like Hobbes and like Descartes, make connections between the world of scientific observation and the world of aesthetic experience. His method of resolution and composition reduced all phenomena to the bare essentials by stripping them of sensory elements and bringing them as near to mathematics as possible. Once he could decipher the characters in which the great book of nature was written, he tried to discover their overall meaning by testing various mathematical models *ex suppositione*.[9] When the adequate model was found, the great book of nature made sense.

The very language in which literature was written was submitted to a similar process. It was turned into a sort of well-tempered clavier in which every word had a clear meaning accepted by the courtiers and endorsed by the academicians. It seems very strange indeed that Lanson should declare that French neo-classicism owed little to Descartes,[10] for the method of the geometricians is clearly at work in the writings of the great linguists of Port-Royal, as Noam Chomsky has shown.[11] Their *Grammaire générale*[12] (which had to be read with their *Logique*,[13] the authors insisted), presented words as signs which fell into clear-cut categories – verbs expressive of power and motion, substantives standing for substances and adjectives for qualities – and which could be combined into sentences by logical operations. And Port-Royal is a case

---

[7] Cited in Lovejoy, *History of Ideas*, p. 99.   [8] Panofsky, *Galileo*.

[9] A. C. Crombie quotes Galileo as saying 'I argue ex suppositione, imagining a motion'; see 'Experimental science', p. 86. See also his discussion of Galileo's method in *Augustine to Galileo*, II, p. 153, in which he presents abstraction as 'essential to the whole procedure'.

[10] See the many references to Descartes in Lancelot and Arnauld's *Grammaire générale*, whose 1676 edition ends with the following *Avertissement*: 'Mais l'on est bien aise d'avertir que depuis la première impression de ce livre, il s'en est fait un autre intitulé la *Logique ou l'art de penser* qui, estant fondé sur les mêmes principes, peut extremement servir pour l'éclaircir'.

[11] Chomsky, *Cartesian Linguistics*.

[12] Lancelot and Arnauld, *Grammaire générale*.

[13] Arnauld and Nicole, *La Logique*.

in point for, however hostile the Jansenists may have been to the king's religious policy, they played their part, and a very large part it was, in the rationalization of the language. By so doing, they brought into harmony the neo-classical doctrine and the scientific imagination which prevailed in the king's academies. If nothing could be food for thought until it was refined into abstraction, if substance must be shorn of accidents, then language had to be purged of the accretions deposited upon words by archaic or provincial turns of speech. What was archaic smacked of the bizarre and what was provincial seemed offensive to taste. Molière's *précieuses* laughed at a term 'so old that it stinks', and when the *petite noblesse* came to Versailles, they had to teach themselves how to speak a language on which the marks left by space and time were to be erased.

Once language had been processed to provide the substance of literary works, the problem of genres arose, for they too must conform to general principles. The critic saw himself as a designer of archetypes and, like Descartes's architect, he had to conceive forms abstract enough to provide a pattern for individual creations. Hence the discussions of genre and the care with which the epic, the fable, comedy, tragedy and even the eclogue were defined. This accounts for the success of what William K. Wimsatt and Cleanth Brooks call 'the geometric urge' of the French neo-classical critics.[14] But it was more than a mood, it was a method which was at work in the king's privy council and in most of the important intellectual circles. The axiomatic method of the geometricians explains why the second half of the seventeenth century saw the publication of such important critical treatises as Corneille's *Examens et Discours* (1660), Dryden's *Essay of Dramatic Poesy* (1668), Rapin's *Poétique d'Aristote* (1674), Boileau's *Art Poétique* (1674), and Le Bossu's *Du Poème épique* (1675). The French, with their academies and their highly centralized political system, could present themselves as the legislators of Mount Parnassus and propose abstract treatises as ideal models for all literary genres. Rules could be set down because human reason could decide *a priori* on their congruence. Racine's tragedies were acknowledged as models and they served their purpose to perfection because Racine (who had been taught by the Jansenists) complied with the rules.

Tragedy gave the genius of the age ample scope to outshine even the ancients. When Richelieu gave a pension to Chapelain for having derived the much celebrated three unities from Aristotle's *Poetics*, he was in fact rewarding the man who had best understood the direction in which the new theory of knowledge was leading literature. By the three unities,

---

[14] Wimsatt and Brooks, *Literary Criticism*, p. 259.

the vast scene of human affairs was reduced to a three-dimensional frame which turned space into the lighted rectangle of the stage, time into a revolution of the sun, and the complexity of human life into one central crisis ending in death. In truly geometrical fashion, a high level of abstraction had to be reached so as to guarantee the efficient working of the mechanism set into motion by the conflict of passions. Once the three unities were complied with, once the passions were placed in the best possible light, this mechanism acted with the precision of a time-bomb and the compelling power of a demonstration. Hence Rymer's remark on the moderns following Aristotle for 'reasons clear and convincing as any demonstration in mathematics'.[15]

The same method was also at work in the very music of the verse. The regularity of recurring sounds, Boileau's 'juste cadence', kept the reader aware of the fact that time and space remained homogeneous and uniform while the plot gradually unfolded. The regular recurrence of the rhyme created the impression that, however far the reader's imagination might roam, a poem was intelligible within a system created by a code. Dryden underlines this point with superb acumen in his dedication of *The Rival Ladies*: 'But that benefit which I consider most in [rhyme] is, that it bounds and circumscribes the fancy'.[16] No less interesting are the images he uses on other occasions, for they prove the extent to which his world-image was shaped by optics and by geometry. He justifies the unity of place by comparing the stage to a mirror: 'I say not that the less can comprehend the greater but only that it may represent it: as in a glass or a mirror of half a yard diameter a whole room and many persons in it can be seen at once; not that it can comprehend that room or those persons but that it represents them to sight.'[17]

His discussion of the unity of action in the preface to *Troilus and Cressida* is even more perceptive. After stating that the action must be 'one and single', he comments:

The natural reason for this rule is plain; for two different actions distract the attention and concernment of the audience, and consequently destroy the attention of the poet; if his business be to move terror and pity, and one of his actions be comical, the other tragical, the former will divert the people and utterly make void his greater purpose. Therefore, as in perspective, so in Tragedy, there must be a point of sight in which all the lines terminate; otherwise the eye wanders and the work is false.[18]

---

[15] Cited in Spingarn, *Critical Essays*, II, pp. 164–5.
[16] Dedication to *The Rival Ladies*, in *Essays*, I, pp. 7–8.
[17] *A Defense of an Essay of Dramatic Poesy*, in *Essays* II, p. 110.
[18] Preface to *Troilus and Cressida*, 1679, in *Essays*, I, p. 208.

Here again we find Dryden using a comparison which goes to the heart of the epistemology of the mechanistic world-view. In his view, the dramatist has to conform to the same *reductio ad unum* as the artist. The play revolves round a central crisis in which passions act as the prime movers of an all-embracing centripetal system. This was to be seen even in the shape of the theatres which were designed in such a way as to offer the best perspective view to the royal box, and whose scenery was shifted into place along parallel grooves so disposed as to allow less and less free space as the eye of the spectator came nearer to the vanishing point.

Sensibility and the 'new science'

The superb coherence of the world-image of the neo-classicists, the exact correspondence of their aesthetic theory to their cognitive schemes, was not as universal as they thought, however, and the machinery of absolutism did not prove as adaptable to England as the Stuarts wished. Absolutism, however adroitly it had managed to turn the mechanization of the world-picture into political theory,[19] was not on native ground in England. At the same time, the foundation of the Royal Society, and its rapid development in a milieu which knew how to apply the sciences to immediate economic ends, began to popularize a type of epistemology which vindicated the superiority of the 'new science'.

Baconian science did accept the geometrization of the world-picture, but it had its reservations about the *ex suppositione* method of reasoning. Soon after the foundation of the Royal Society, the *Philosophical Transactions* began to advocate a method of scientific observation which rejected the *a priori* method of the geometricians. 'Histories' replaced 'systems'. When Sydenham insisted that the 'history' of a patient's illness should be drawn up, or when Locke compiled a 'register of the weather' for publication in Boyle's *General History of the Air*,[20] they rejected the *a priori* or *ex suppositione* method. To them, a 'history' was a relation providing a full and accurate record of the particular conditions in which an experiment was conducted.[21] It was Boyle who gave the clearest definition of this new cognitive scheme. In one of the very first volumes of the *Philosophical Transactions*[22] he published his 'General

---

[19] Apostolidès, *Le Roi-machine*, ch. II on 'l'Organisation de la culture'.

[20] Dewhurst, *John Locke*, p. 300.

[21] The *OED* defines the scientific meaning of *history* as 'A systematic account (without reference to time) of a set of natural phenomena'. In fact, time indications were essential to experimental scientists.

[22] *Philosophical Transactions*, no. 11, 1666, pp. 222–6.

Heads for the Natural History of a Countrey', a text whose importance is underlined by the fact that Ephraim Chambers reprinted it in his *Cyclopedia* sixty years later. Boyle's purpose was to provide English explorers with a vademecum which would contribute, he hoped, 'to superstruct, in time, a Solid and Useful Philosophy upon', and to this end he recommended what he called 'articles of inquisition about Particulars'. The importance of 'particulars' is also stressed in his instructions to sailors published in the *Philosophical Transactions* a little earlier.[23] In both texts, individualizing features were presented as essential to the establishment of truth and the *a priori, ex suppositione* method was abandoned in favour of a pragmatic approach.

When Newton blamed the Cartesians for having built their physics on metaphysical principles and for sacrificing experience to *a priori* constructions, he rejected their method and their mechanistic world-view. In the very first lines of the *Principia*, he explained:

I wish we could derive the rest of the phenomena of nature by the same kind of reasoning from mechanical principles, for I am induced by many reasons to suspect that they may all depend upon certain forces by which the particles of bodies by some causes hitherto unknown, are either mutually impelled towards one another and cohere in regular figures or are repelled and recede from one another.[24]

Boyle made a similar anti-mechanistic point when he remarked that the big clock in the cathedral of Strasbourg was far simpler than a dog's foot.[25] Systems reproducing the direct action of simple forces appeared more and more reductive and the new, experimental type of physics entered the world of philosophy when Locke invoked the impact of particles on our sense organs to explain the origin of sensations. He created what Voltaire called 'the physics of the soul',[26] and revealed the connection which existed between psychology and 'the operation of insensible particles on our senses'.[27] He also presented mental life as an acquisitive process by which the mind, which is always 'covetous' to be 'furnished' with ideas, gradually conceives 'those sublime thoughts which tower above the clouds and reach as high as heaven itself'. This could only be achieved 'by degrees' and through all 'the alterations that time makes'. Locke was so conscious of his debt towards the 'new science'

---

[23] 'An Appendix to the Directions for Seamen bound for far Voyages', *Philosophical Transactions*, no. 2, 6 Nov. 1665, p. 109.

[24] *Principia*, opening sentence.

[25] Hankins, *Science and the Enlightenment*, p. 3.

[26] 'Tant de raisonneurs ayant fait le roman de l'âme, un sage est venu qui en a fait modestement l'histoire ... Il s'aide partout du flambeau de la physique' (Voltaire, *Lettres philosophiques*, Lettre XIII, Sur M. Locke).

[27] *Essay*, II, viii, para. 13.

that he described his book as having been composed by 'the historical, plain method'.[28]

This was a complete break with the Cartesians, who stressed the synchronic nature of their systems. As Jean Wahl has shown, Descartes's philosophy was 'une philosophie de l'instant'.[29] In the paradigms of the 'new science', things were different. The Newtonian universe suffered a continuous loss of energy counteracted by divine intervention and Locke presented mental life as a process by which sense data were transformed into 'trains of thoughts'. His *Essay concerning Human Understanding* was the very embodiment of the modernity of the age.[30] Feeling, sensation, sense and sentiment became stock terms in the vocabulary of the critics. The Abbé Du Bos spoke of a sixth sense 'affected to the arts' and declared that 'sentiment can grasp' what rational analysis cannot discover.[31] In an often-quoted passage of his *Enquiry concerning Beauty and Virtue*, Hutcheson endowed the nature of man with an aesthetic sense which made it feel 'the greater pleasures of the ideas raised in us which we call by such names as beauty and harmony'. Alexander Gerard began his *Essay on Taste* with an explicit reference to the internal senses; Burke has been called 'the first writer on aesthetics in English to take up the uncompromising sensationist viewpoint';[32] Kames's *Elements* begin with a chapter on 'perceptions and ideas in a train', and as late as 1790, we find Alison grounding his philosophy of taste on the secure basis of sensation. Similar positions can be found in Diderot, who insisted on the necessity for the critic to be absolutely spontaneous because impressions express the true nature of a work of art as they spring to mind. This inevitably lessened the importance once accorded to the rules, which appeared more and more as an antiquated mode of appreciation reminiscent of the *a priori* dicta of neo-classicism. The preference given to subjective impressions over the massive consistency of learned treatises made literary criticism as spontaneous as letter-writing.

Other consequences followed, some of them essential to the elaboration of new criteria. When we read in Locke:

and I ask whether a blind man who distinguished his years either by heat of summer or cold of winter, by the smell of any flower of the spring or taste of any fruit in the autumn, would not have a better measure of time than the Romans had before the reformation of their calendar by Julius Caesar[33]

---

[28] *Essay*, Introduction.   [29] Wahl, *Le Rôle de l'Instant*.
[30] See Maclean, *John Locke*, Introduction.
[31] 'Ce que l'analyse ne saurait trouver, le sentiment le saisit d'abord' (Jean-Baptiste Du Bos, *Réflexions critiques sur la poésie et sur la peinture* (2 vols., Paris, 1770), II, p. 369).
[32] J. T. Boulton, introduction to Burke's *Enquiry* (1958), p. xxxvi.
[33] Locke, *Essay*, II, xiv.

we are at once conscious of a new relation of time to the sensations and to the modes of sensation. Lockean psychology made space and time – 'expansion and duration do mutually embrace and comprehend each other[34] – dependent on the succession of sense impressions. This meant that the old *ut pictura poesis* was no longer valid since the best description in a book could not produce one single coloured sensation, whereas a picture, especially if it aimed at producing the *papillotage* or 'fluttering' effect found in Watteau, Fragonard and Gainsborough, generated an infinite number of direct stimuli. Diderot discussed this problem and, using the 'train of thoughts' theory ('l'âme est un tableau mouvant'), he defined a picture as 'a privileged moment'. Lessing went further and made the distinction between literature and the visual arts central to his *Laokoon*. Chapter XVI, with its brilliant discussion of the contrast between 'consecutive signs' and 'signs arranged in juxtaposition', opened the way for a theory of aesthetics based on the purity of effect rather than the distinction of genres. This discovery, already adumbrated in Baumgarten's *Aesthetica* (1750), explains Goethe's enthusiasm when he read the *Laokoon* for the first time.

The changes which intervened in the early and mid-eighteenth century did not go unopposed, however, and the neo-classicists still held their own against the incoming tide of sensibility. This was partly due to the fact that, in the *Querelle des Anciens et des Modernes*, Cartesianism had its partisans on both sides. Newtonianism, with its 'mysterious forces', could be presented as a resurgence of the Aristotelian occult causes, while the rules of neo-classicism could be presented as a rationalization of the precepts empirically formulated by the classics. Houdart de La Motte, a friend of Voltaire and Rameau, believed that what was taught by Aristotle and Horace had been turned into universal principles by the Moderns, who could use the scientific theory of the passions framed by Descartes.[35] Batteux's *Les Beaux-Arts réduits à un même principe* was an attempt to apply similar criteria to the arts. Despite his declared admiration for Newtonian science, Voltaire agreed with them and this may perhaps explain why he remained faithful to tragedy and why he satirized the sentimentalists. By one of the little ironies of literary history, his adherence to rational criteria made him a conservative in matters of taste. Cassirer rightly notes: 'The development of empirical philosophy from Locke to Berkeley and from Berkeley to Hume represents a series of attempts to minimize the difference between sensation

[34] Locke, *Essay*, II, xv.
[35] 'C'est dans la nature de notre esprit qu'il faut chercher les règles ... La raison générale de l'agrément des choses, prise du rapport qu'elles ont avec notre intelligence, est un principe aussi invariable que la nature même de notre esprit' (Houdart de La Motte, *Discours*, p. 21).

and reflection, and finally to wipe it out altogether.'[36] It was this tendency which Voltaire and Johnson, strange bedfellows as they may seem, tried to oppose. They upheld neo-classical tragedy as a genre. Johnson's comment on *Ossian*, 'Sir, a man might write this stuff for ever, if he would abandon his mind to it',[37] echoes Voltaire's disparaging remarks on the *Esprit des Lois* – 'un cabinet mal rangé' – and on Rousseau's alleged love for 'le déplacé, le faux, le gigantesque'.[38] This also explains Voltaire's about-turn in his appreciation of Shakespeare and the great Cham's solemn prediction '*Tristram Shandy* will not last', or his characterization of the *Vicar of Wakefield* as 'a mere fanciful performance'.

The majority of critics and writers followed a different course. Some of them rejected neo-classicism but still adhered to the classical heritage which Palladianism, they claimed, had rescued from the artificialities of the baroque. Others did not accept this compromise and developed the possibilities offered by empirical epistemology.

Among the Palladians must be counted Pope, Montesquieu and Fielding. They tried to reconcile rationality with the harmony of proportions. Reason, for them, became *ratio* and the Graeco-Roman heritage was preserved by reinjecting a modern dose of pagan sensuality into the figures of the gods. Taste, the key-word of their aesthetics, was a mysterious capacity which virtuosi could acquire by reading the classics, by remodelling the English landscape and by making the temple style of their country houses stand for the virtues of civic humanism. To a certain extent, Shaftesbury had shown the way, since he was an eloquent defender of the classical heritage, but his influence also extends to the Romantic movement with its conception of the poet as a creator whose works harmonize with the forces of nature. More typical of the Palladian revival is Pope's *Essay on Criticism*. At first sight, it looks like a direct transposition of Boileau's *Art Poétique* with its use of the heroic couplet, its definition of art as 'nature methodized' – a direct quotation from Rapin's *Réflexions* – and its constant praise of the classics. Yet it seems clear that Pope's real purpose was to steer away from the formality of the geometrical approach and to give taste the place once allotted to the rules.

Montesquieu went a step further by calling reason 'the most exquisite of our senses', thus claiming that the mind added to our enjoyment of nature by refining our emotions and by relishing the beauty of proportion. The irregular chapters of the *Esprit des Lois*, like those of *Tom Jones*, proved that even the most ambitious books need not affect the cumbrous pomposity of a preconceived order. If knowledge was to be

---

[36] Cassirer, *Philosophy*, p. 100.　　[37] *Life*, p. 1,207.
[38] Quoted by Naves, *Le Goût*, p. 362 and p. 366.

acquired by the 'historical method', the laws of lifemanship, like those of civil government or the layout of an English garden, could be drawn from the observation of the particulars of time and place. Montesquieu thought that uniformity was 'insufferable',[39] just as Pope banished geometry from the English garden, because variety and irregularity corresponded to the cognitive schemes which gave consistency to their world-image. Fielding defined *Tom Jones* as 'a history, not a system'.[40] The Excursion poets held similar views.

Hume tried to provide a philosophical basis for this compromise in his essay 'Of the Standard of Taste'. He was certainly not indifferent to the beauties of neo-classicism[41] but he had to concede that 'strong sense united to delicate sentiment'[42] could play the part once allotted to rules. He attempted to provide a scientific basis for his aesthetic criteria by combining Newtonian physics with the association of ideas. 'Nature', he wrote, 'has bestowed a kind of attraction on certain impressions and ideas, by which one of them, upon its appearance, naturally introduces its correlative'.[43] This enabled him to present the memory of a man of culture as the true fountainhead of critical judgements. If the role of reason had declined to the point where no universals could exist and if, as was the case in Lockean linguistics,[44] words were to be considered as mere signs, no bounds could be ascribed to the freedom of the writer. The standard of taste became a sort of sliding scale. Hume's famous judgement on *Tristram Shandy*[45] proves how consistent he was, and how superior to Johnson in his understanding of contemporary productions. And yet, even if he had enough flair to appreciate the novelties of Sterne, he knew that the success of *Ossian* and of the *Nouvelle Héloïse* was not to his taste. In his last letter to Gibbon he prophesied the 'fall of philosophy and the decay of taste'.[46]

Other critics did not share his pessimism, however, and they resolutely developed all the implications of Lockean epistemology by bypassing the Palladian compromise and by stressing the importance of the particulars of time and space as aesthetic criteria. They followed on the path opened by Addison's interest in popular ballads and by Vanbrugh's attraction to Gothic architecture. 'The fate of things gives a new face to

---

[39] *Essai sur le Goût*, chapter 'Des plaisirs de la variété'.

[40] *The History of Tom Jones, A Foundling*, ed. Martin C. Battestin and Fredson Bowers (Oxford, 1974), p. 651.

[41] His adherence to the standards of neo-classicism is discussed in chapter 10 of this volume.

[42] *Essays*, II, p. 278.

[43] Hume, *Treatise*, p. 289.

[44] See Formigari, *L'Estetica*.

[45] 'The best book that has been written by an Englishman these thirty years (for Dr Franklin is an American) is *Tristram Shandy*, bad as it is' (*Letters of David Hume*, II, p. 269).

[46] *Letters of David Hume*, II, p. 310.

things',[47] said Defoe, as if he wished to provide a motto for the newly-founded Society of Antiquarians. Such mental attitudes explain why the time-scheme played so important a part in the rise of the novel, epis-tolary or otherwise. They also explain why Aaron Hill required the actors of his *Athelstan* to wear furs because 'such was the habit in Saxon times'. Local colour and historicism became the requisites of verisimilitude; they encouraged the vogue for medieval literature and the return to Shakespeare, whose neglect of the genres and whose han-dling of language could be presented as more true to life than the *a priori* views of Dryden. Gray's praise of early English writers is very typical of this new attitude to literary history: 'I am inclined to think (whatever Mr Dryden says) that their measure, at least in serious meas-ures and heroic stanzas, was uniform; not indeed to the eye, but to the ear *when rightly pronounced*.'[48]

Thomas Warton's *Observations on the Fairy Queen* and his *History of English Poetry*, Hurd's *Letters on Chivalry and Romance*, Percy's *Reliques of Ancient Poetry*, Herder's essay *Shakespeare* or his *On the Similarity between Middle English and German Poetry* also aimed at promoting new criteria by historicizing their critical approach. If the reader had the mental capacity to imagine the particulars of time and space revealed by ancient texts, he shared in the discoveries made by the modernity of his own time. He also developed his ability to conceive not only a period of time taken as a whole, but the succession of such periods, each with its own world-image. This led to Horace Walpole's attempts at discriminating between various stages in the history of the Gothic style. It also led to Winckelmann's *Geschichte der Kunst des Altertums*, to Turgot's delineation of world history in his *mappemondes*, and to the triumph of the historical novel. Historicism came to be used as an instrument of investigation over very extended periods of time. Archae-ology, geology and even palaeontology assumed a growing importance in the development of the scientific imagination, giving the concept of sublimity connotations certainly unforeseen by Boileau in his *Réflexions sur Longin*. Vastness, whether in relation to time or to space, identified this new aesthetic category with the modernity of the age of sensibility.

Addison had opened the way. Describing the 'Vastness and Immensity of Nature' in *Spectator* 565, he wrote: 'The noblest and most exalted way of considering this infinite Space is that of Sir Isaac Newton, who calls it the Sensorium of the Godhead.' Natural sublimity thus came to be associated with Newtonianism and with Lockean psychology, making full use of the climates of sensibility familiar to the Protestant Bible-reader who knew the cosmic poetry of the Psalms and who associated God's

[47] *A Tour through the Whole Island of Great Britain*, Introduction.
[48] Quoted by Atkins, *Criticism*, p. 202.

presence in the Creation with the majesty of natural scenes. Recent research has proved that the 'new science' often fused together biblical sources and the Newtonian cosmogony.[49] This may perhaps explain why Dennis or William Smith made use of Boileau's translation of Longinus to demonstrate the poetic quality of the Bible[50] while Robert Lowth, stressing the particulars of time and space, recommended that the Bible should be read 'as the Hebrews had read it'. The public which ensured the sudden success of Thomson was ready to share Dennis's belief that 'the Moderns by joining poetry with religion will have the advantage of the Ancients'.[51]

Burke's *Philosophical Enquiry into the Origin of our Ideas of the Sublime and Beautiful* echoed all these themes. It contained quotations from the Book of Job, and while it always associated the beautiful with human society and with works of art, it often found the causes of the sublime in 'the immense and glorious fabric of the universe'.[52] Its aesthetic categories showed that the vision of the Newtonian cosmos was fully informed by Lockean psychology, thus providing the readers of Thomson, Akenside, Collins and Gray with criteria which corresponded to the modernity of the times. If, as Burke said, 'The true standard of the arts is in every man's power', Hume's definition of taste could no longer hold. One had no need of a good training in the classics to be sensitive to the emotions generated by a landscape or by a moonlit scene.

But it was not only nature that man contemplated when he looked at a landscape. The particulars of time and place also led him to take an interest in ruins, in the monuments of the past as well as in the most transient aspects of universal life. Thomson saw the seasons as the 'Varied God' and meteorological change as the instant manifestation of 'that Power / Who fills, sustains and actuates the whole'.[53] Gray's *Elegy* combined historical time ('yon ivy mantled tower') with the ephemeral life of insects ('the beetle wheels its droning flight') and the immemorial sleep of 'the rude forefathers of the hamlet'. As poets of the age of sensibility, Gray, Shenstone and Thomson made awareness of time inseparable from the growing interest elicited by the life of nature whose mysteries contributed to spread the vogue of the sublime. Book III of Newton's *Opticks* contains descriptions of the tumultuous forces at work in the 'caverns' of the Earth:

Seeing therefore the variety of Motion which we find in the World is always decreasing, there is a necessity of conserving and recruiting it by active Principles such as are the cause of Gravity, by which Planets and Comets keep their Motion in their Orbs, and Bodies acquire great Motion in falling;

---

[49] Copenhaver, 'Jewish theologies', pp. 489–548.
[50] William Smith's translation of Longinus ran to seven editions, Atkins, *Criticism*, p. 187.
[51] Dennis, *Critical Works*, I, p. 509.   [52] Burke, *Enquiry*, p. 69.
[53] *To the Memory of Sir Isaac Newton*, ll. 142–3.

and the cause of Fermentation by which the Heart and the Blood of Animals are kept in perpetual Motion and Heat; the inward parts of the Earth are constantly warmed, and in some Places grow very hot; Bodies burn and shine, Mountains take fire, the Caverns of the Earth are blown up, and the Sun continues violently hot and lucid and warms all things by Light.[54]

If 'the cause of Fermentation' was as important as 'the cause of Gravity' in the 'active Principles' of motion, one can understand why chemistry played such a great part in the development of Newtonian science[55] and why research on the nature of air interested both the physiologist and the geologist in the eighteenth century. Newton, like Shakespeare's colossus, bestrode the world of seventeenth-century mechanics and the world of eighteenth-century chemistry and biology. Natural sublimity is closer to the *Opticks* than to the *Principia*.

Perfectibility and the rise of the Romantic movement

With Turgot, Lavoisier, Mariotte and Buffon in France, Albrecht von Haller in Switzerland, Spallanzani in Italy, Caspar Friedrich Wolff, Winkler, Stahl, Gärtner and Sprengel in Germany, and Priestley, Erasmus Darwin, Black, Hutton and Whitehurst in England, chemistry, physiology and the sciences dealing with what was known as 'the living world' assumed an ever increasing importance in the great debates of ideas. A correlative decline of geometry set in, as Yvon Belaval has shown,[56] for how could one use geometrical figures to explain the growth of plants, the effects of the thunderbolt or the expansibility of gases?

A few years before Burke's *Enquiry* was published, Hartley's *Observations* proved that a radical development of Lockean psychology and of Newtonian physics could lead to a scientific theory of mental life based on physiology. If, he maintained, the impact of particles on the sense-organs provoked vibrations of the nervous system, then it became possible to quantify these vibrations in order to determine how our memory could reactivate the impressions they had caused. By this combination of mathematics and biology, Hartley hoped to show how associationism and sympathy gradually refined our emotions and led men to the pure love of God. A biological process was given teleological significance.

This theory of the mind may have amused Leslie Stephen,[57] but it fired Coleridge's early enthusiasm and it explains why human nature was no longer seen as a fixed entity but as a living organism whose

---

[54] Isaac Newton, *Opticks*, ed. E. Whittaker (New York, 1931), Book III, p. 399.
[55] Metzger, *Newton, Stahl, Boerhaave*, pp. 34–68, on chemistry and attraction.
[56] Belaval, 'La Crise de la géométrisation'.   [57] Stephen, *History*, II, p. 58.

structure and functions were constantly modified by environmental factors. It also explains why psychology was constantly attracted to biology and why the Leibnizian monad, described as an entity moved from within by its own *Kraft*, could appear as the philosophical model best adapted to the scientific movement. In the eyes of writers like Diderot and Herder, it reconciled the action of the external world on the senses (formation from without) with the vital energy possessed by each sentient being (formation from within). Besides, infinitesimal calculus gave philosophy a firm mathematical grasp of the insensible transformations everywhere at work in the living world, and Leibniz's *Theodicy*, by making all monads part of a teleological scheme, applied the historical imagination to the long timescale required by the study of geology and natural history. The Leibnizians, by stressing the biological origins of psychic dynamism and by engaging man in a quest for perfection, could bring together literature, the arts, and the natural sciences, thus making *Naturphilosophie* the agent of a new form of modernity.

Vico is a case in point here, for even if his *Scienza Nuova* does not evidence a great interest in science, it did make use of Baconian empiricism, and it disrupted mechanistic systems by infusing life, continuity and individuality into the history of man. Its comprehensive historicism revealed the appeal of the 'barbaric ages' and it presented poetry as the living voice of primitive man whose fears and enchantments are still part of our feeling for nature. Its rediscovery of the primitive character of the epic, its use of comparative philology and its definition of civilizations as cultural entities heralded the works of Lowth, of Blackwell, of Winckelmann and indeed of Herder himself.

No less important to the development of *Naturphilosophie* was Diderot, whose particular interest was in biology, then in rapid development and heading for full recognition as a science in its own right (1802). Diderot knew Leibniz's works, and he also knew that the monad's self-development as a form of internal growth had drawn attention to embryology. Indeed, it was a Leibnizian, Caspar Friedrich Wolff, whose theory of epigenesis presented the growth of living organisms as a process of germination which did not simply reproduce a pre-existing model. Life, to Diderot, was a shaping force whose fluid energy dynamized the Great Chain of Being.[58] Its very nature made it foreign to the systems of seventeenth-century mechanics, in which, as Jacques Roger stresses, 'since no natural process can give birth to a structure, no embryogeny was conceivable'.[59] Diderot, taking full advantage of the resources offered by the new cognitive structures, launched a series of attacks on

[58] Lovejoy, *Great Chain of Being*, ch. VIII.
[59] Roger, 'Living world', in Rousseau and Porter (eds.), *The Ferment of Knowledge*, p. 271.

neo-classicism in all its forms. In his analyses of paintings, he had no patience with regularity and symmetry. In literature, he disregarded genre-divisions, using the same terms whether he wrote about pictures or about books, and he soon discovered the importance of Richardson in whose work he praised the central function of the time-scheme and the strong power of individuation. He saw Richardson's heroes as 'leaves having each their own particular shade of green', a metaphor in which natural growth is applied metaphorically to the correct delineation of character. The same parallel between vegetable growth and mental energy is to be found in his theory of genius, 'the pure gift of nature', which makes the poet soar above the rules and create his own mode of expression. Young developed similar views in his *Conjectures on Original Composition*. 'An Original', he wrote, 'may be said to be of vegetable nature; it rises spontaneously from the vital root of genius'.[60]

Given the general interest in the sciences of the natural world, Herder could make full use of such concepts as vegetable genius and continuous growth in order to develop the philosophic implications of contemporary biology. From the very start, in the 1760s and in the early 1770s, his *Kritische Wälder* and his *Abhandlung über den Ursprung der Sprache* show that he was trying to combine science and philosophy. He had discovered Vico by reading Cesarotti on *Ossian*.[61] He knew the works of Hartley and of his continuator Priestley.[62] His interest in the natural world was profound; he had read Daubenton, Vicq d'Azyr, Blumenbach, Camper, and Monro, whose *Structure and Physiology of Fishes* he mentions. Though less attracted to mathematics and physics, he knew about the theory of probability, and this may have influenced his conception of evolution, which anticipated Lamarck's views. He considered that 'as the tree from the root, so must the progress of an art be deduced from its origin'. He made a direct application of the theory of epigenesis to literary criticism when he described Homer's lasting influence on his successors: 'Where an epigenesis, i.e., a living additional growth in regular form or power and limbs, should occur, there must be, as the whole of nature shows, a living germ, a shape of nature and art, whose growth all elements joyously favour.'[63] If such was the theory of literary creation, the poet no longer painted nature 'to advantage dress'd'. His 'vegetable' genius could derive from nature the elements which he developed into one single living work. Nature gave the rule to

---

[60] Young, *Conjectures*, p. 12.   [61] Wellek, *History*, I, p. 181.

[62] On Herder and science, see Nisbet, *Herder*, especially pp. 305–18.

[63] 'Wo eine *Epigenese*, d.h. ein lebendiger Zuwachs in regelmäßiger Gestalt an Kräften und Gliedern stattfinden soll, da muß, wie die ganze Natur zeigt, ein *lebendiger Keim*, ein *Natur- und Kunstgebilde* dasein, dessen Wachstum jetzt alle Elemente freudig fördern' (Herder, *Sämtliche Werke*, XVIII, p. 438. Quoted by Wellek, *History*, I, p. 189).

art, not art to nature. This point of view was shared and developed by Goethe, himself a research biologist, who described the man of genius as nature's agent. This theory of genius brought about a new theory of genres and new aesthetic criteria which were discussed and popularized by the great critics of the German school, Herder, Goethe, the Schlegels, Kant and Schelling. Even if, as René Wellek says, 'every one of these philosophers grew out of a different intellectual soil and passed through a different development',[64] there was a great deal of 'symphilosophizing' and the key concepts of aesthetic theory became genius, germ, growth, organic whole, life force, *Naturphilosophie*, expression, empathy and imagination. The new doctrine emerged and made Germany's intellectual life essential to the movement of ideas in Europe.

The Romantic movement began to take shape when Gerstenberg, while he rejected French tragedy, criticized Thomas Warton for being too timid in his reappraisal of Spenser. If the poet was a 'maker', then, as Kant said in his *Critique of Judgement*, the works he created evolved their own individual rules. Genius was the voice of nature whose modes of expression were intuitively apprehended. The critic's task was to describe literary categories in the same way as the botanist described genera. Such categories rested on the spiritual-organic nature of art and they could be considered from more than one angle. Hamann, like Vico, adopted a broad historical perspective. He thought that 'epic and fable are the beginning'. Goethe described the various types of poetry as all descending from an earlier form of *Urpoesie* exactly as he tried to discover the *Urpflanze* when he saw plants 'realizing their form completely' in the public gardens in Palermo. If a distinction between different types of literature was to be preserved, the Schlegels believed, it had to be descriptive and not prescriptive. Poetry, the drama and prose fiction were different species of writing, not different genres.

These different types of literature underwent deep structural modifications around the turn of the century. Prose fiction saw the creation of the historical novel and the development of the *Bildungsroman*, a form which combined the time-scheme of the English *novel of the road* and the psychology of the 'growth of the mind'. The epic received a strong infusion of primitivism; *Ossian*, the Bible, *Minnesang*, Slavic and Scandinavian folk poetry were presented as models by Goethe and Herder, who found in them pure poetry traced back to its origins. Drama saw a bitter struggle between what remained of the neo-classical repertoire and Romantic plays inspired by Shakespeare, the Prometheus who was praised by Herder for having considered the unities as 'chains for our imagination'. But it was in lyrical poetry that the modernity of the Romantics

---

[64] Wellek, *History*, I, p. 228.

found its highest expression. Here the voice of man expressed the very life of ideas, their physical transmission by sounds. Hence the role played by music in German Romanticism, for only sounds could perfectly express the invasion of space and time by energy. Wilhelm Heinse thought that the voice of a singer had an 'all-invading power' because it 'emitted vibratory waves' which 'traversed the body' of the listener.[65] In the same way, Herder thought that with the sounds of lyrical poems 'emerges their spirit, movement, life'.[66] In this new way of appreciating the beauty of a text, one can almost feel the impact of such concepts as fluid, aether, gas, electricity, and 'caloric' on the scientific imagination.

But while the expression of individuality was taken to an extreme in lyrical poetry, the collective aspect of creation was also strongly emphasized. In the same way as Nicole, Arnauld, or the linguists of the Lockean school had contributed to the formation of critical concepts, so Turgot, Rousseau, Condillac, Herder and Wilhelm von Humboldt developed theories of language which fostered the emergence of Romanticism. Herder, developing Leibniz's views on the importance of primitive and popular forms of language,[67] saw that the collective process of language-transmission gave an individual character to the literature of a nation. What Winckelmann had done for the visual arts of the ancients, he did for the literature of his own time. To declare that 'the genius of a language is also the genius of the literature of the nation' is to make the writer a particularizer within a world of collective creation. This conception of language as a projection of individual expression within a process of collective creation was later developed by Wilhelm von Humboldt in his *Über die Verschiedenheit des menschlichen Sprachbaues* (1792) and by Coleridge.[68]

The origin of language and its changes over a long period of time had already become a central problem in the 1760s. Rousseau, like Condillac and like Turgot, saw in language not only the expression of man's feelings and thoughts, but the means by which he continuously transforms his own nature. To give a clear formulation to what appeared to be a completely new concept, Turgot coined the term *perfectibilité*, a word parallel to *expansibilité*, which he had also coined to describe the nature of gases in the *Encyclopédie*. Turgot the linguist clearly worked hand in hand with Turgot the scientist since he also contributed articles

---

[65] Rita Terras, *Wilhelm Heinses Ästhetik* (Munich, 1972), pp. 65–9 and 110–18.

[66] 'So wollen lyrische Gedichte gelesen sein; dazu sind die gearbeitet. Mit dem Klange gehet ihr Geist hervor, Bewegung, Leben' (*Sämtliche Werke*, XXVII, p. 5).

[67] 'Je trouve que de tous les moyens de juger de l'origine ou connexion des peuples, celui des langues est le plus seur [*sic*]' (Leibniz quoted by Aarsleff, *Papers*, p. 393).

[68] On Humboldt and Coleridge, see the last chapter of Chomsky's *Cartesian Linguistics*.

on 'Etymologie', 'Magnétisme', 'Ether' and 'Feu électrique'. Given the vibratory nature of the human voice and given the relation between psychology and physiology, the scientific imagination could represent language as a fluid which expanded the mind by the discoveries of new words transmitted by successive generations. The expansibility of man's psyche became the agent of perfectibility. The word soon gained currency as a philosophical concept encapsulating new cognitive schemes. It was popularized by Rousseau in his *Discours sur l'origine de l'inégalité*, and it was adopted by Price, Priestley, Condorcet, Godwin and Madame de Staël. But it was Kant who saw at once that Rousseau, by using the perfectibility of man as an agent of self-transformation, had made 'a great discovery' totally unknown to the ancients.[69] Rousseau had seen that man can create a language by living in society and that social life shaped his nature and explained his history. 'Deep in the heart of the forest' he had 'unveiled human nature', as he explained in the *Confessions*. The natural world had revealed to him the true nature of man, the *Urform* from which his present existence was derived. Poets could gain an intuitive knowledge of man's true nature because empathy and the intimations revealed by poetic images enabled them to establish pregnant connections between the natural world and their own emotions. Such views, resulting from the study of the origin of language and from the application of the historical imagination to the long time-scale, led to the 'neo-Greek' archaeological renaissance in the visual arts.[70] They also gave a deeper resonance to the Gothic revival and to the rediscovery of popular art forms, which were seen as truer to man's inner nature because they were closer to the origin of literature.

Thus, the naive flavour, the artless repetitive rhythm of the ballad, came to be presented as the fountainhead of the profoundest poetry, and this led to a denunciation of poetic diction. Wordsworth settled this point even before he set about writing the *Prelude*, whose subtitle, it will be remembered, is *The Growth of a Poet's Mind*. In his preface to the *Lyrical Ballads* he wrote: 'The language of such poetry as I am recommending is, as far as is possible, the language really spoken by men'.[71] In other words, the Romantic poet did not believe, as did Gibbon and the upholders of more traditional values, that 'the language of a philosopher would vibrate without effect on the ear of a peasant'.[72] He knew that the peasant had a share in the common language of men and that 'the objects of a poet's thoughts are everywhere'. He also knew

---

[69] Cassirer, *Rousseau, Kant and Goethe*, p. 21.
[70] Rousseau's *Contrat social* presents the legislator as a seer whose 'sublime reason' can make 'the gods speak' (*Oeuvres complètes*, III, p. 384).
[71] Wordsworth and Coleridge, *Lyrical Ballads*, p. 29.
[72] Gibbon, *Decline and Fall*, V, p. 342.

that the poet is entrusted with a 'divine' mission because, while his works bear the individual character of his own voice, they grow with the language and live on with it. 'The poet binds together by passion and knowledge the vast empire of human society, as it is spread over the whole earth and over all time.'[73]

To define the poet's mission in such terms would have appeared very strange, if not preposterous, to Boileau, Pope and even Gray. But many changes had intervened between the age of reason and the age of perfectibility, and these changes explain why a Romantic poet held views so different from those of his predecessors. The relation of literary criticism to the scientific movement sheds some light on the logical character of this evolution. It also explains why the research done by scientists finds an echo in the imaginative powers of those who observe the world by other means.

[73] *Lyrical Ballads*, p. 35.

Bibliography

The institution of criticism

Primary sources and texts

Bacon, Francis, *The Advancement of Learning*, ed. W. A. Wright (Oxford, 1891).

Bayle, Pierre, *Dictionnaire historique et critique* (Rotterdam, 1695–7), trans. *The Dictionary Historical and Critical of Mr Peter Bayle* (5 vols., London, 1731–6).

Blackwell, Thomas, *Letters on Mythology* (London, 1748).

Blair, Hugh, *Lectures on Rhetoric and Belles Lettres* (2 vols., London, 1785).

Boswell, James, *Life of Samuel Johnson*, ed. G. B. Hill and L. F. Powell (6 vols., Oxford, 1934).

Bouhours, Dominique, *The Art of Criticism* (trans. anon., London, 1705).

[Boyer, Abel], *Letters of Wit, Politicks and Morality* (London, 1701).

Brown, John, *A Dissertation on the Rise, Union, and Power, the Progressions, Separations, and Corruptions of Poetry and Music* (London, 1763).

Buhle, J. G., *Grundzüge einer allgemeinen Encyklopädie der Wissenschaften* (Lemgo, 1790).

Burke, Edmund, *A Philosophical Enquiry into the Origin of our Ideas of the Sublime and Beautiful* (1756; ed. James T. Boulton, London, 1958).

Campbell, George, *The Philosophy of Rhetoric* (1776; ed. L. Bitzer, Carbondale IL, 1963).

Dennis, John, *The Critical Works of John Dennis*, ed. Edward Niles Hooker (2 vols., Baltimore, 1939).

Dryden, John, *Of Dramatic Poesy and Other Critical Essays*, ed. George Watson (2 vols., London, 1962).

Du Bos, Jean-Baptiste, *Réflexions critiques sur la poësie et sur la peinture* (1719; 3 vols., Paris, 1755).

Dyer, George, *Poetics: or a Series of Poems, and of Disquisitions on Poetry* (2 vols., London, 1812).

Encyclopédie ou Dictionnaire raisonné des sciences, des arts et des métiers (17 vols., Paris 1751–57 and Neuchâtel, 1765).

Fordyce, David, *Dialogues concerning Education* (London, 1745).

Gibbon, Edward, *An Essay on the Study of Literature* (London, 1764).

Goldsmith, Oliver, *Collected Works of Oliver Goldsmith*, ed. Arthur Friedman (5 vols., Oxford, 1966).

Gottsched, Johann Christoph, *Versuch einer Critischen Dichtkunst* (1730; 2nd edn, Leipzig, 1737).

The Guardian, ed. James Calhoun Stephens (Lexington, 1982).

Harris, James, *Philological Inquiries in Three Parts* (2 vols., London, 1781).

Hobbes, Thomas, 'Answer' to Davenant's Preface to *Gondibert*, in *Critical Essays of the Seventeenth Century*, ed. J. E. Spingarn (Oxford, 1957), II, pp. 54–67.

Hume, David, *The Philosophical Works of David Hume*, ed. T. H. Green and T. H. Grose (3 vols., London, 1882).

Hurd, Richard, *The Works of Richard Hurd, D.D.* (8 vols., London, 1811).

Hutcheson, Francis, *The Works of Francis Hutcheson* (7 vols., London, 1755).

Johnson, Samuel, *A Dictionary of the English Language* (2 vols., London, 1755; 4th edn, 1773).

Lives of the English Poets, ed. G. B. Hill (3 vols., Oxford, 1905).

The Yale Edition of the Works of Samuel Johnson (New Haven, 1958–).

Kames, Henry Home, Lord, *The Elements of Criticism* (3 vols., Edinburgh, 1762).

Kant, Immanuel, *Gesammelte Schriften*, ed. Preussische Akademie der Wissenschaften (Berlin, 1902–).

Le Clerc, Jean, *Ars critica, in qua ad studia linguarum Latinae, Graecae, & Hebraicae via munitur; veterumque emendandorum, & spuriorum scriptorum à genuinis dignoscendorum ratio traditur* (3 vols., Amsterdam, 1697–1700).

Pope, Alexander, *The Twickenham Edition of the Works of Alexander Pope*, ed. John Butt *et al.* (11 vols. in 12, London, 1939–69).

Pope, Alexander, *et al.*, *The Memoirs of Martinus Scriblerus*, ed. Charles Kirby-Miller (New Haven, 1950).

Reid, Thomas, *Thomas Reid's Lectures on the Fine Arts*, ed. Peter Kivy (The Hague, 1973).

Reynolds, Joshua, *Discourses on Art*, ed. Robert Wark, 2nd edn (New Haven, 1975).

Richelet, P., *Dictionnaire françois, contenant les mots et les choses* (2 vols., Geneva, 1680).

Rymer, Thomas, *The Critical Works of Thomas Rymer*, ed. Curt A. Zimansky (New Haven, 1956).

Schiller, Johann Christoph Friedrich von, *Sämtliche Werke*, ed. G. Fricke and H. G. Göpfert (5 vols., Munich, 1958–9).

Shaftesbury, Anthony Ashley Cooper, third Earl of, *Characteristicks of Men, Manners, Opinions, Times* (3 vols., London, 1711).

The Life, Unpublished Letters, and Philosophical Regimen, ed. Benjamin Rand (London, 1900).

Second Characters, or the Language of Forms, ed. Benjamin Rand (Cambridge, 1914).

The Spectator, ed. Donald F. Bond (5 vols., Oxford, 1965).

The Tatler, ed. Richmond P. Bond (3 vols., Oxford, 1987).

Trapp, Joseph, *Lectures on Poetry Read in the Schools of Natural Philosophy at Oxford* (trans. anon., London, 1742).

Voltaire (François-Marie Arouet), *Oeuvres complètes* (52 vols., Paris, 1877–85).

Warton, Joseph, *An Essay on the Genius and Writings of Pope* (2 vols., London, 1756, 1782).

Secondary sources

Abrams, M. H., *The Mirror and the Lamp: Romantic Theory and the Critical Tradition* (New York, 1953).

Adkins, J. W. H., *English Literary Criticism: 17th and 18th Centuries* (New York, 1953).

Bahlman, Dudley W. R., *The Moral Revolution of 1688* (New Haven, 1957).

Barrell, John, *English Literature in History 1730–80: An Equal, Wide Survey* (London, 1983).

    The Political Theory of Painting from Reynolds to Hazlitt (New Haven, 1986).

Basker, James, *Tobias Smollett: Critic and Journalist* (Newark, 1988).

Bate, Walter Jackson, *The Burden of the Past and the English Poet* (Cambridge MA, 1970).

    From Classic to Romantic: Premises of Taste in Eighteenth-Century England (Cambridge MA, 1946).

Berghahn, Klaus L., 'From classicist to classical literary criticism, 1730–1806', in Peter Uwe Hohendahl (ed.), *A History of German Literary Criticism, 1730–1980* (Lincoln, 1988), pp. 13–98.

Burrow, J. W., 'The uses of philology in Victorian Britain', in R. Robson (ed.), *Ideas and Institutions of Victorian Britain: Essays in Honour of George Kitson Clark* (London, 1967), pp. 180–204.

Cannon, John, *Aristocratic Century: The Peerage of Eighteenth-Century England* (Cambridge, 1984).

Cassirer, Ernst, *Die Philosophie der Aufklärung* (Tübingen, 1932); trans. F. Koelin and J. Pettigrove, *The Philosophy of the Enlightenment* (Princeton, 1951).

Caygill, Howard, *Art of Judgement* (Oxford, 1989).

Cohen, Ralph, 'Innovation and variation: literary change and georgic poetry', in *Literature and History* (Los Angeles, 1974), pp. 3–42.

    'John Dryden's literary criticism', in *New Homage to John Dryden* (Los Angeles, 1983), pp. 61–85.

    'Some thoughts on the problems of literary change 1750–1800', *Dispositio*, 4 (1979), 145–62.

Crane, Ronald S., 'Thoughts on writing the history of English criticism, 1650–1800', *University of Toronto Quarterly*, 22 (1953), 376–91.

Darnton, Robert, *The Literary Underground of the Old Regime* (Cambridge MA, 1982).

Darnton, Robert (ed.), *Revolution in Print: The Press in France, 1775–1800* (Berkeley, 1989).

Eagleton, Terry, *The Function of Criticism: From the Spectator to Post-Structuralism* (London, 1984).

Elledge, Scott (ed.), *Eighteenth-Century Critical Essays* (2 vols., Ithaca, 1961).

France, Peter, *Politeness and its Discontents: Problems in French Classical Culture* (Cambridge, 1992).

Gossman, Lionel, 'Literature and education', *New Literary History*, 13 (1982), 341–71.

Griffin, Robert J., *Wordsworth's Pope: A Study in Literary Historiography* (Cambridge, 1995).

Habermas, Jürgen, *Strukturwandel der Öffentlichkeit* (1962), trans. Thomas Burger, *The Structural Transformation of the Public Sphere: An Inquiry into a Category of Bourgeois Society* (Cambridge MA, 1989).

Hirsch, E. D., Jr, *Cultural Literacy: What Every American Needs to Know* (New York, 1987).

Hirschman, Albert O., *The Passions and the Interests: Political Arguments for Capitalism before its Triumph* (Princeton, 1977).

Hohendahl, Peter Uwe, *The Institution of Criticism* (Ithaca, 1982).

Kaiser, Thomas E., 'Rhetoric in the service of the King: the Abbé Dubos and the concept of public judgment', *Eighteenth-Century Studies*, 23 (1990), 182–99.

Kernan, Alvin, *Printing Technology, Letters and Samuel Johnson* (Princeton, 1987).

Klein, Lawrence, *Shaftesbury and the Culture of Politeness: Moral Discourse and Cultural Politics in Early Eighteenth-Century England* (Cambridge, 1994).

Koselleck, Reinhart, *Kritik und Krise: Eine Studie zur Pathogenese der bürgerlichen Welt* (1959); trans. *Critique and Crisis: Enlightenment and the Pathogenesis of Modern Society* (Cambridge MA, 1988).

Leites, Edmund, 'Good humor at home, good humor abroad: the intimacies of marriage and the civilities of social life in the ethic of Sir Richard Steele', in *Educating the Audience: Addison, Steele & Eighteenth-Century Culture* (Los Angeles, 1984), pp. 51–89.

Lough, John, *Writer and Public in France* (Oxford, 1978).

McCarthy, John A., 'The art of reading and the goals of the German Enlightenment', *Lessing Yearbook*, 16 (1984), 79–94.

Meehan, Michael, *Liberty and Poetics in Eighteenth-Century England* (London, 1986).

Morrison, Karl F., *The Mimetic Tradition of Reform in the West* (Princeton, 1982).

Newman, Gerald, *The Rise of English Nationalism: A Cultural History 1740–1830* (New York, 1987).

Parrinder, Patrick, *Authors and Authority: A Study of English Criticism and its Relationship to Culture, 1750–1900* (London, 1977).

Patey, Douglas Lane, 'The eighteenth century invents the canon', *Modern Language Studies*, 18 (1988), 17–37.

Probability and Literary Form: Philosophic Theory and Literary Practice in the Augustan Age (Cambridge, 1984).

Plumb, J. H., 'The public, literature, and the arts in the 18th century', in Paul Fritz and David Williams (eds.), *The Triumph of Culture: 18th Century Perspectives* (Toronto, 1972), pp. 27–48.

Pocock, J. G. A., *Virtue, Commerce, and History: Essays on Political Thought and History, Chiefly in the Eighteenth Century* (Cambridge, 1984).

Rose, Mark, *Authors and Owners: The Invention of Copyright* (Cambridge MA, 1993).

Saintsbury, George, *A History of Criticism and Literary Taste in Europe* (3 vols., London, 1900–4).

Siskin, Clifford, *The Historicity of Romantic Discourse* (New York, 1988).

Staves, Susan, 'Pope's refinement', *The Eighteenth Century: Theory and Interpretation*, 29 (1988), 145–63.

Weinbrot, Howard, '"An ambition to excell": the aesthetics of emulation in the seventeenth and eighteenth centuries', *Huntington Library Quarterly*, 48 (1985), 121–39.

Weinsheimer, Joel, *Imitation* (London, 1984).

Wellek, René, *Concepts of Criticism* (New Haven, 1966).

'The fall of literary history', in Richard E. Amacher and Victor Lange (eds.), *New Perspectives in German Literary Criticism* (Princeton, 1979), pp. 418–31.

A History of Modern Criticism (8 vols., New Haven, 1955–92).

The Rise of English Literary History (Chapel Hill, 1941).

Woodman, Thomas, *Politeness and Poetry in the Age of Pope* (Rutherford, 1989).

Woodmansee, Martha, *The Author, Art, and the Market: Rereading the History of Aesthetics* (New York, 1994).

Ancients and Moderns

Primary sources and texts

Aikin, John, *Letters from a Father to his Son, on Various Topics, Relative to Literature and the Conduct of Life* (1793; 3rd edn, London, 1796).

Aikin, John, and Aikin Anna Laetitia, *Miscellaneous Pieces in Prose* (London, 1773).

d'Alembert, Jean Le Rond, *Discours préliminaire* (1751), trans. Richard N. Schwab and Walter Rex, *Preliminary Discourse to the Encyclopedia of Diderot* (Indianapolis, 1963).

d'Aubignac, François Hédelin, *Conjectures académiques, ou dissertation sur l'Iliade, ouvrage posthume trouvé dans les recherches d'un savant* (Paris, 1715).

Batteux, Charles, *Les Beaux-Arts réduits à un même principe* (Paris, 1746).

Bayle, Pierre, *Dictionnaire historique et critique* (Rotterdam, 1695–7), trans. *The Dictionary Historical and Critical of Mr Peter Bayle* (5 vols., London, 1731–6).

Bergk, Johann Adam, *Die Kunst, Bücher zu lesen: Nebst Bemerkungen über Schriften und Schriftsteller* (Jena, 1799).

Blackwell, Thomas, *An Enquiry into the Life and Writings of Homer* (1735; 2nd edn, London, 1736).

Boileau-Despréaux, Nicolas, *Oeuvres de Boileau*, ed. C. H. Boudhors (7 vols., Paris, 1952).

Boivin, Jean, *Apologie d'Homère, et bouclier d'Achille* (Paris, 1715).

Bonald, Louis de, *Oeuvres de M. de Bonald* (4th edn, 3 vols., Paris, 1882).

Bouhours, Dominique, *La Manière de bien penser dans les ouvrages d'esprit* (Paris, 1687).

Burke, Edmund, *A Philosophical Enquiry into the Origin of our Ideas of the Sublime and Beautiful* (1756; ed. James T. Boulton, London, 1958).

Reflections on the Revolution in France (1790; ed. J. G. A. Pocock, Indianapolis, 1987).

Cartaud de la Villate, François, *Essai historique et philosophique sur le goût* (Amsterdam, 1736).

Charpentier, François, *Deffense de la langue françoise pour l'inscription de l'arc de triomphe* (Paris, 1676).

Dacier, André, *La Poétique d'Aristote* (Paris, 1692); trans. anon., *Aristotle's Art of Poetry* (London, 1705).

Dacier, Anne Lefèvre, *Des Causes de la corruption du goust* (1714; rpt Amsterdam, 1715).

Homère défendu contre l'apologie du R. P. Hardouin ou suite des causes de la corruption du goust (Paris, 1716).

L'Iliade d'Homère, traduite en françois, avec des remarques (5 vols., Paris, 1711); trans. John Ozell, *The Iliad of Homer* (5 vols., London, 1712).

Desmarets de Saint-Sorlin, Jean, *La Comparaison de la langue et de la poésie françoise avec la grecque et la latine, et des poètes grecs, latins, et françois* (Paris, 1670).

Du Bos, Jean-Baptiste, *Réflexions critiques sur la poësie et sur la peinture* (1719; 3 vols., Paris, 1755); trans. Thomas Nugent, *Critical Reflections on Poetry, Painting and Music* (3 vols., London, 1748).

Du Resnel, Jean-François du Bellay, 'Réflexions générales sur l'utilité des belles-lettres; et sur les inconvéniens du goût exclusif, qui paroît s'établir en faveur des mathématiques et de la physique', *Histoire de l'Académie Royale des Inscriptions et Belles-Lettres*, 16 (Paris, 1751), 11–37.

Encyclopédie ou Dictionnaire raisonné des sciences, des arts et des métiers (17 vols., Paris, 1751–7, and Neuchâtel, 1765).

Fontenelle, Bernard le Bovier de, *Digression sur les anciens et les modernes* (1688), in *Oeuvres complètes* (3 vols., Paris, 1818), II, pp. 353–65; trans. John Hughes (1719; rpt in Scott Elledge and Donald Schier (eds.), *The Continental Model* (Ithaca, 1970)), pp. 358–70.

Gibbon, Edward, *An Essay on the Study of Literature* (London, 1764).

Gordon, James, *Occasional Thoughts on the Study and Character of Classical Authors* (London, 1762).

Gravina, Gian Vincenzo, *Della Ragion poetica* (1708); trans. *Raison, ou idée de la poésie, ouvrage traduit de l'italien de Gravina par M. Requier* (2 vols., Paris, 1755).

Hazlitt, William, *The Round Table* (1817; London, 1969).

Herder, Johann Gottfried von, 'Extract from a Correspondence on Ossian and the Songs of Ancient Peoples' and 'Shakespeare' (1773), trans. Joyce P.

Crick, in H. B. Nisbet (ed.), *German Aesthetic and Literary Criticism: Winckelmann, Lessing, Hamann, Herder, Schiller, Goethe* (Cambridge, 1985), pp. 153–76.

Ideen zur Philosophie der Geschichte der Menschheit (1784–91), trans. T. O. Churchill as *Reflections on the Philosophy of the History of Mankind* (1800), abr. Frank Manuel (Chicago, 1968).

Hobbes, Thomas, *Leviathan: Or the Matter, Forme, and Power of a Commonwealth* (1651; ed. Michael Oakeshott, Oxford, 1946).

Huet, Pierre-Daniel, *Huetiana ou pensées diverses de M. Huet, évêque d'Avranches* (Amsterdam, 1723).

Hurd, Richard, *Letters on Chivalry and Romance* (London, 1762).

The Works of Richard Hurd (8 vols., London, 1811).

Hutcheson, Francis, *An Inquiry into the Original of our Ideas of Beauty and Virtue* (London, 1725).

Johnson, Samuel, Preface to *Shakespeare* (1765), in Arthur Sherbo (ed.), *Johnson on Shakespeare*, vols. 7–8 of *The Yale Edition of the Works of Samuel Johnson* (New Haven, 1968), I, pp. 59–113.

Juvigny, Rigoley de, *De la Décadence des lettres et des moeurs, depuis les Grecs et les Romains jusqu'à nos jours* (Paris, 1787).

La Motte, Antoine Houdart de, *Oeuvres de Monsieur Houdart de La Motte* (10 vols., Paris, 1754).

Le Clerc, Jean, *Parrhasiana, ou pensées diverses sur des matières de critique, d'histoire, de morale et de politique* (2 vols., Amsterdam, 1699).

Lefèbvre, Tanneguy, *De futilitate poetices, auctore Tannaquillo Fabro* (Amsterdam, 1697).

Mably, Gabriel Bonnot de, *Observations sur l'histoire de la Grèce* (Paris, 1766).

Montesquieu, Charles Louis de Secondat de, *Oeuvres complètes* (Paris, 1949).

Percy, Thomas, *The Correspondence of Thomas Percy and Evan Evans*, ed. Aneirin Lewis (Baton Rouge, 1957).

Perrault, Charles, *Memoirs of my Life*, trans. J. M. Zarucci (Columbia, 1989).

Parallèle des anciens et des modernes en ce qui regarde les arts et les sciences (4 vols.; 2nd edn, Paris, 1692–96; facs. rpt Geneva, 1979).

Pons, François de, *Oeuvres de monsieur l'abbé de Pons* (Paris, 1738).

Pope, Alexander, *Peri Bathous* (1728), in *The Prose Works of Alexander Pope: Vol. II, The Major Works, 1725–44*, ed. Rosemary Cowler (Oxford, 1986), pp. 171–276.

The Twickenham Edition of the Works of Alexander Pope, ed. John Butt et al. (11 vols. in 12, London, 1939–69).

Pütter, Johann Stephan, *Litteratur des deutschen Staatsrechts* (4 vols., Göttingen, 1776–91).

Richardson, Samuel, *Correspondence*, ed. Anna Laetitia Barbauld (6 vols., London, 1804).

Rollin, Charles, *De la manière d'enseigner et d'étudier les belles lettres, par rapport à l'esprit & au coeur* (1732; Paris, 1741).

Schiller, Friedrich, *Über die aesthetische Erziehung des Menschen* (1795); trans. E. M. Wilkinson and L. A. Willoughby, *The Aesthetic Education of Man* (Oxford, 1967).

Über naive und sentimentalische Dichtung (1796), trans. J. A. Elias, in H. B. Nisbet (ed.), *German Aesthetic and Literary Criticism* (Cambridge, 1985), pp. 179–232.

Schlegel, Friedrich von, *Friedrich Schlegels Briefe an seinen Bruder August Wilhelm*, ed. Oskar Walzel (Berlin, 1980).

Über das Studium der griechischen Poesie: Vorrede 1797, ed. Ernst Behler (2 vols., Weimar, 1962).

Shenstone, William, *Letters of William Shenstone*, ed. Duncan Mallam (Minneapolis, 1939).

The Spectator, ed. Donald F. Bond (5 vols., Oxford, 1965).

Swift, Jonathan, *The Battle of the Books: Eine historisch-kritische Ausgabe*, ed. Hermann Josef Real (Berlin, 1978).

The Battle of the Books: With Selections from the Phalaris Controversy, ed. A. C. Guthkelch (London, 1908).

A Tale of a Tub, ed. A. C. Guthkelch and D. Nichol Smith (2nd edn, Oxford, 1973).

Temple, William, *The Works of Sir William Temple, Bart.* (4 vols., London, 1770).

Terrasson, Jean, *Dissertation critique sur l'Iliade d'Homère, où à l'occasion de ce poëme on cherche les règles d'une poëtique fondée sur la raison, & sur les exemples des Anciens & des Modernes* (2 vols., Paris, 1715); trans. Francis Brerewood, *Critical Dissertations on Homer's Iliad* (2 vols., London, 1746).

La Philosophie applicable à tous les objets de l'esprit et de la raison (Paris, 1754).

Turgot, Anne-Robert-Jacques, Baron de l'Aulne, 'Discours sur les progrès successifs de l'esprit humain', *Oeuvres de M. Turgot, Ministre d'Etat* (9 vols., Paris, 1808), II, pp. 52–92.

Turgot on Progress, Sociology, and Economics, trans. Ronald L. Meek (Cambridge, 1973).

Voltaire (François-Marie Arouet), *An Essay on Epick Poetry*, in *An Essay upon the Civil Wars of France* (London, 1727), pp. 37–130.

Warton, Thomas, *A History of English Poetry* (1774–81; 4 vols., London, 1824).

Winckelmann, Johann Joachim, 'Thoughts on the imitation of the painting and sculpture of the Greeks' (1755), trans. H. B. Nisbet, in Nisbet (ed.), *German Aesthetic and Literary Criticism: Winckelmann, Lessing, Hamann, Herder, Schiller, Goethe* (Cambridge, 1985), pp. 31–54.

Wotton, William, *Reflections upon Ancient and Modern Learning* (London, 1694).

Young, Edward, *Conjectures on Original Composition, in a Letter to the Author of Sir Charles Grandison* (London, 1759).

Secondary sources

Baron, Hans, 'The *querelle* of the Ancients and the Moderns as a problem for Renaissance scholarship', *Journal of the History of Ideas*, 20 (1959), 3–22.

Bergner, Jeffrey, *The Origin of Formalism in the Social Sciences* (Chicago, 1981).

Black, Robert, 'Ancients and Moderns in the Renaissance: rhetoric and history in Accolti's *Dialogue on the Preeminence of Men of His Own Time*', *Journal of the History of Ideas*, 43 (1982), 3–32.

Buck, August, 'Aus der Vorgeschichte der Querelle des anciens et des modernes in Mittelalter und Renaissance', *Bibliothèque d'Humanisme et Renaissance*, 20 (1958), 527–41.

Bury, J. B., *The Idea of Progress: An Inquiry into its Origin and Growth* (1920; New York, 1932).

Butterfield, Herbert, *Man on His Past: The Study of the History of Historical Scholarship* (Cambridge, 1955).

Crane, Ronald S., *The Idea of the Humanities and Other Essays Critical and Historical* (2 vols., Chicago, 1967).

Curtius, Ernst Robert, *European Literature and the Latin Middle Ages* (1948; trans. Willard Trask, Princeton, 1953).

Davidson, Hugh M., 'Fontenelle, Perrault and the realignment of the arts', in C. G. S. Williams (ed.), *Literature and History in the Age of Ideas: Essays on the Enlightenment Presented to George R. Havens* (Athens OH, 1975), pp. 3–13.

Eamon, William, *Science and the Secrets of Nature: Books of Secrets in Medieval and Early Modern Culture* (Princeton, 1994).

Eisenstein, Elizabeth L., *The Printing Press as an Agent of Change: Communications and Cultural Transformation in Early Modern Europe* (2 vols., Cambridge, 1979).

Erskine-Hill, Howard, *The Augustan Idea in English Literature* (London, 1983).

Foerster, Donald M., *Homer in English Criticism: The Historical Approach in the Eighteenth Century* (New Haven, 1947).

Gilbert, Felix, 'Bernardo Ruccelai and the Orti Oricellari: a study of the origin of modern political thought', in *History, Choice and Commitment* (Cambridge MA, 1977), pp. 215–46.

Gillot, H., *La Querelle des Anciens et des Modernes en France* (Paris, 1914).

Gombrich, Ernst, 'The Renaissance conception of artistic progress and its consequences', in *Norm and Form: Studies in the Art of the Renaissance* (Oxford, 1966), pp. 1–10.

Gössman, Elizabeth, 'Antiqui und Moderni im 12. Jahrhundert', *Miscellanea Medievalia*, 9 (1974), 40–57.

Gossman, Lionel, *Medievalism and the Ideologies of the Enlightenment: The World and Work of La Curne de Sainte-Palaye* (Baltimore, 1968).

Grafton, Anthony, 'Renaissance readers and ancient texts: comments on some commentaries', *Renaissance Quarterly*, 38 (1985), 615–49.

Gravelle, Sarah Stever, 'The Latin-vernacular question and humanist theory of language and culture', *Journal of the History of Ideas*, 49 (1988), 367–86.

Hepp, Naomi, *Homère en France au XVIIe siècle* (Paris, 1968).

Howarth, W. D., 'Neo-classicism in France: a reassessment', in D. J. Mossop *et al.* (eds.), *Studies in the French Eighteenth Century Presented to John Lough* (Durham, 1978), pp. 92–107.

Hutchison, Keith, 'Supernaturalism and the mechanical philosophy', *History of Science*, 21 (1983), 297–333.

'What happened to occult qualities in the Scientific Revolution?', *Isis*, 73 (1982), 233–53.

Jauss, Hans Robert, 'Asthetische Normen und geschichtliche Reflexion in der "Querelle des Anciens et des Modernes"', in Jauss (ed.), *Charles Perrault, Parallèle des Anciens et des Modernes* (Munich, 1964), pp. 8–64.

'Schlegels und Schillers Replik auf die "Querelle des Anciens et des Modernes"', in *Literatur als Provokation* (Frankfurt, 1970), pp. 67–106.

Johnson, James William, *The Formation of English Neo-Classical Thought* (Princeton, 1967).

Johnston, Arthur, *Enchanted Ground: A Study of Medieval Romance in the Eighteenth Century* (London, 1964).

Jones, Richard Foster, *Ancients and Moderns: A Study of the Rise of the Scientific Movement in 17th Century England* (1936; 2nd edn, Berkeley, 1961).

Kapitza, Peter K., *Ein bürgerlicher Krieg in der gelehrten Welt: Zur Geschichte der Querelle des Anciens et des Modernes in Deutschland* (Munich, 1981).

Keohane, Nannerl O., 'The Enlightenment idea of progress revisited', in Gabriel Almond *et al.* (eds.), *Progress and its Discontents* (Berkeley, 1977), pp. 21–40.

Kortum, Hans, *Cartaud de La Villate: Ein Beitrag zur Entstehung des geschichtlichen Weltbildes in der französischen Frühaufklärung* (2 vols., Berlin, 1960).

Charles Perrault und Nicolas Boileau. Der Antike-Streit im Zeitalter der klassischen französischen Literatur (Berlin, 1966).

Krauss, Werner, *Fontenelle und die Aufklärung* (Munich, 1969).

Krauss, Werner, and Hans Kortum, *Antike und Moderne in der Literaturdiskussion des 18. Jahrhunderts* (Berlin, 1966).

Kristeller, Paul O., 'The modern system of the arts', *Journal of the History of Ideas*, 12 (1951), 496–527; 13 (1952), 17–46; rpt in *Renaissance Thought II* (New York, 1965), pp. 163–227.

Kroeber, A. L., and Clyde Kluckholn, *Culture* (New York, 1952).

Levine, Joseph M., 'Ancients and Moderns reconsidered', *Eighteenth-Century Studies*, 15 (1981), 72–89.

The Battle of the Books: History and Literature in the Augustan Age (Ithaca, 1991).

'The Battle of the Books and the shield of Achilles', *Eighteenth-Century Life*, 9 (1984), 33–61.

Dr Woodward's Shield: History, Science, and Satire in Augustan England (Berkeley, 1977).

'Giambattista Vico and the Quarrel between the Ancients and the Moderns', *Journal of the History of Ideas*, 52(1991), 55–79.

Humanism and History: Origins of Modern English Historiography (Ithaca, 1987).

Lombard, A., *La Querelle des Anciens et des Modernes: l'Abbé Du Bos* (Neuchâtel, 1908).

Lorimer, J. W., 'A neglected aspect of the "Querelle des Anciens et des Modernes"', *Modern Language Review*, 51 (1956), 179–85.

Macaulay, Thomas Babington, 'Francis Atterbury', in *Miscellaneous Writings* (2 vols., London, 1860), I, pp. 209–26.

McKillop, Alan D., 'Richardson, Young, and the Conjectures', *Modern Philology*, 22 (1925), 391–404.

Margiotta, Giacinto, *Le Origini Italiane della Querelle des anciens et des modernes* (Rome, 1953).

Meek, Ronald L., *Social Science and the Ignoble Savage* (Cambridge, 1976).

Menges, Karl, 'Herder and the "Querelle des Anciens et des Modernes"', in Richard Critchfield and Wulf Koepke (eds.), *Eighteenth-Century German Authors and their Aesthetic Theories: Literature and the Other Arts* (Columbia, 1988), pp. 147–83.

Merton, Robert, *On the Shoulders of Giants: A Shandean Postscript* (New York, 1965).

Meyer, Paul H., 'Recent German studies of the Quarrel between the Ancients and the Moderns in France', *Eighteenth-Century Studies*, 18 (1985), 383–90.

Miller, Henry Knight, 'The Whig interpretation of literary history', *Eighteenth-Century Studies*, 6 (1972), 60–84.

Minnis, A. J., *Medieval Theory of Authorship: Scholastic Literary Attitudes in the Later Middle Ages* (London, 1984).

Moriarty, Michael, *Taste and Ideology in Seventeenth-Century France* (Cambridge, 1988).

Niderst, Alain, *Fontenelle à la recherche de lui-même (1657–1702)* (Paris, 1972).

Patey, Douglas Lane, 'The eighteenth century invents the canon', *Modern Language Studies*, 18 (1988), 17–37.

  Probability and Literary Form: Philosophic Theory and Literary Practice in the Augustan Age (Cambridge, 1984).

  'Swift's satire on "science" and the structure of Gulliver's Travels', *ELH*, 56 (1991), 809–39.

Pigman, G. W., III, 'Imitation and the Renaissance sense of the past: the reception of Erasmus' *Ciceronianus*', *Journal of Medieval and Renaissance Studies*, 9 (1979), 155–77.

Pizzorusso, Arnaldo, 'Antichi e Moderni nella polemica di Madame Dacier', in Pizzorusso (ed.), *Teorie letterarie in Francia* (Pisa, 1968), pp. 16–55.

Plotz, Judith, *Ideas of Decline in Poetry: A Study of English Criticism from 1700 to 1830* (1965; New York, 1987).

Porter, Roy, *Edward Gibbon: Making History* (London, 1988).

Rattansi, P. M., review of R. F. Jones, *Ancients and Moderns*, 2nd edn, *British Journal for the History of Science*, 18 (1968), 250–5.

Reill, Peter Hanns, *The German Enlightenment and the Rise of Historicism* (Berkeley, 1975).

Rigault, Hippolite, *Histoire de la Querelle des Anciens et des Modernes* (Paris, 1859).

Robertson, J. G., *Studies in the Genesis of Romantic Theory in the Eighteenth Century* (Cambridge, 1923).

Ross, Sydney, '"Scientist": the story of a word', *Annals of Science*, 18 (1962), 65–85.

Saisselin, Rémy G., 'Critical reflections on the origins of modern aesthetics', *British Journal of Aesthetics*, 4 (1964), 7–21.

Santangelo, Giovanni Saverio, La 'Querelle des Anciens et des Modernes' nella critica del '900 (Bari, 1975).

Schueller, Herbert M., 'The Quarrel of the Ancients and the Moderns', Music and Letters, 41 (1960), 313–30.

Scouten, Arthur H., 'The Warton forgeries and the concept of preromanticism in English literature', Etudes anglaises, 40 (1987), 434–47.

Seznec, Jean, 'Le Singe antiquaire', in Essais sur Diderot et l'antiquité (Oxford, 1957), pp. 79–96.

Simonsuuri, Kirsti, Homer's Original Genius: Eighteenth-Century Notions of the Early Greek Epic (1688–1798) (Cambridge, 1979).

Snyder, Edward D., The Celtic Revival in English Literature 1760–1800 (Cambridge MA., 1923).

Spadafora, David, The Idea of Progress in Eighteenth-Century Britain (New Haven, 1990).

Starkman, Miriam Kosh, Swift's Satire on Learning in A Tale of a Tub (Princeton, 1950).

Starobinski, Jean, 'From the decline of erudition to the decline of nations: Gibbon's response to French thought', in G. W. Bowerstock et al. (eds.), Edward Gibbon and the Decline and Fall of the Roman Empire (Cambridge MA, 1977), pp. 139–57.

Stephen, Leslie, History of English Thought in the Eighteenth Century (2 vols., London, 1876).

Stone, P. W. K., The Art of Poetry in England, 1750–1820 (London, 1967).

Tilley, Arthur, The Decline of the Age of Louis XIV, or, French Literature 1687–1715 (Cambridge, 1929).

Tinkler, John F., 'The splitting of humanism: Bentley, Swift, and the English Battle of the Books', Journal of the History of Ideas, 49 (1988), 453–72.

Tuveson, Ernest, 'Swift and the world–makers', Journal of the History of Ideas, 11 (1950), 54–74.

Vyverberg, Henry, Human Nature, Cultural Diversity, and the French Enlightenment (New York, 1989).

Wagar, W. Warren, 'Modern views of the origins of the idea of progress', Journal of the History of Ideas, 28 (1967), 55–70.

Watt, Ian, The Rise of the Novel (Berkeley, 1957).

Weinbrot, Howard, Augustus Caesar in 'Augustan' England: The Decline of a Classical Norm (Princeton, 1978).

Wellek, René, 'French classicist criticism', Yale French Studies, 38 (1967), 47–71.

The Rise of English Literary History (Chapel Hill, 1941).

'The term and concept of classicism in Literary history', in Discriminations: Further Concepts of Criticism (New Haven, 1970), pp. 55–89.

Wencilius, L., 'La Querelle des Anciens et des Modernes et l'humanisme', XVIIᵉ Siècle, 9–10 (1951), 15–34.

Williams, David, Voltaire: Literary Critic, vol. 48 of Studies on Voltaire and the Eighteenth Century (Geneva, 1966).

Wolper, Roy S., 'The rhetoric of gunpowder and the idea of progress', Journal of the History of Ideas, 31 (1970), 589–98.

Poetry 1660–1740

Primary sources and texts

Boileau-Despréaux, Nicolas, *Épîtres, Art Poétique, Lutrin*, ed. C. H. Boudhors (Paris, 1952).

Satires, ed. C. H. Boudhors (Paris, 1952).

Works, trans. John Ozell (2 vols., London, 1711–12).

Bouhours, Dominique, *Les Entretiens d'Ariste et d'Eugène*, ed. R. Radouant (Paris, 1920).

La manière de bien penser, trans. anonymously as *The Art of Criticism* (1705): facsimile reproduction (New York, 1981).

Dennis, John, *Critical Works*, ed. E. N. Hooker (2 vols., Baltimore, 1939).

Dryden, John, Boileau's *The Art of Poetry*, trans. Sir William Soames and revised Dryden, in *The Works of John Dryden, II: Poems, 1681–1684*, ed. H. T. Swedenborg, Jr and V. A. Dearing (Berkeley and Los Angeles, 1972).

Of Dramatic Poesy and Other Critical Essays, ed. George Watson (2 vols., London, 1962).

Du Bos, Jean-Baptiste, *Critical Reflections on Poetry, Painting, and Music*, trans. Thomas Nugent (3 vols., London, 1748).

Réflexions critiques sur la poësie et sur la peinture (2 vols., Paris, 1719).

Durham, Willard H. (ed.), *Critical Essays of the Eighteenth Century, 1700–1725* (New Haven, 1915).

Eliot, T. S., *The Use of Poetry and the Use of Criticism* (London, 1933).

Elledge, S. (ed.), *Eighteenth-Century Critical Essays* (2 vols., Ithaca, 1961).

Finch, Robert, and Eugène Joliet (eds.), *French Individualist Poetry, 1686–1760: An Anthology* (Toronto and Buffalo, 1971).

Fontenelle, Bernard le Bovier de, *Discours sur la nature de l'eglogue*, trans. Pierre Anthony Motteux, appended to his translation of Le Bossu's *Treatise of the Epick Poem* (London, 1695).

Gildon, Charles, *The Complete Art of Poetry* (2 vols., London, 1718).

The Guardian, ed. J. C. Stephens (Lexington KY, 1982).

Hepworth, Brian (ed.), *The Rise of Romanticism: Essential Texts* (Manchester, 1978).

La Bruyère, Jean, *Les Caractères*, ed. D. Delafarge (Paris, 1928).

Characters, trans. Jean Stewart (Harmondsworth, 1970).

Le Bossu, René, *M. Bossu's Treatise of the Epick Poem* [and] *A Treatise upon Pastorals by M. Fontenelle*, trans. P. A. Motteux, ed. 'W. J.' (London, 1695).

Traité du poème épique (2 vols., Paris, 1675).

Oldham, John, *Poems*, ed. H. F. Brooks and R. Selden (Oxford, 1987).

Perrault, Charles, *Characters Historical and Panegyrical of the Greatest Men that have appeared in France, during the last Century*, trans. by John Ozell (2 vols., London, 1704–5).

Hommes illustres qui ont paru en France pendent ce siècle (2 vols., Paris, 1696–1700).

Phillips, Edward, *Theatrum Poetarum* (London, 1675).

Pope, Alexander, *The Prose Works of Alexander Pope* (Oxford): vol. I, ed. Norman Ault (1936), vol. II, ed. Rosemary Cowler (1986).

The Twickenham Edition of the Poems of Alexander Pope, general ed. John Butt (11 vols. in 12, London, 1939–69).

Rapin, René, *Dissertatio de Carmine Pastorali* [1681], trans. by Thomas Creech in his *The Idylliums of Theocritus with Rapin's Discourse of Pastorals* (1684; rpt Ann Arbor, 1947).

Refléxions sur la Poétique d'Aristote [1674], trans. by Thomas Rymer (1674), with a new Introduction by P. J. Smallwood (Amersham, 1979).

Rymer, Thomas, *Critical Works*, ed. Curt A. Zimansky (New Haven, 1956).

Saint-Évremond, Seigneur de, *The Works of Mr. de St. Evremont*, trans. from the French (2 vols., London, 1700).

Shawcross, John T. (ed.), *Milton: The Critical Heritage* (London, 1970).

The Spectator, ed. Donald F. Bond (5 vols., Oxford, 1965).

Spence, Joseph, *An Essay on Pope's Odyssey* (London, 1726).

Spingarn, J. E. (ed.), *Critical Essays of the Seventeenth Century* (3 vols., Oxford, 1907).

Temple, Sir William, *Five Miscellaneous Essays by Sir William Temple*, ed. S. H. Monk (Ann Arbor, 1963).

Trapp, Joseph, *Lectures on Poetry*, trans. by William Bowyer and William Clarke (London, 1742).

Vico, Giambattista, *The New Science*, trans. T. G. Berg and M. H. Fisch (Ithaca, 1948).

Principi di una Scienza Nuova (3rd edn, 2 vols., Naples, 1744).

Voltaire (François-Marie Arouet), *An Essay on Epick Poetry*, ed. F. D. White (New York, 1915).

Essay sur la poesie épique, trans. [from the original English by] P. F. G. Desfontaines (Paris, 1728).

Letters concerning the English Nation [1733], ed. C. Whibley (London, 1926).

Lettres philosophiques, ed. G. Lanson (2 vols., Paris, 1924).

Le Temple du goût, ed. E. Carcassonne (Geneva, 1953).

Secondary sources

Anderson, H., and J. S. Shea (eds.), *Studies in Criticism and Aesthetics: Essays in Honour of Samuel Holt Monk* (Minneapolis, 1967).

Barnwell, H. T., *Les idées morales et critiques de Saint-Évremond* (Paris, 1957).

Bate, W. J., *From Classic to Romantic: Premises of Taste in Eighteenth-Century England* (Cambridge MA, 1946).

Borgerhoff, E. B. O., *The Freedom of French Classicism* (Princeton, 1950).

Bredvold, L. I., *The Intellectual Milieu of John Dryden* (Ann Arbor, 1934).

Brody, Jules, *Boileau and Longinus* (Geneva, 1958).

Chapman, Gerald W., *Literary Criticism in England, 1660–1800* (New York, 1966).

Clark, A. F. B., *Boileau and the French Classical Critics in England, 1660–1830* (Paris, 1925).

Congleton, J. E., *Theories of Pastoral Poetry in England, 1684–1798* (Gainesville, 1952).

Elkin, P. K., *The Augustan Defence of Satire* (Oxford, 1973).

Empson, William, 'Wit in the Essay on Criticism', in *The Structure of Complex Words* (London, 1964), pp. 84–100.

Engell, James, *Forming the Critical Mind: Dryden to Coleridge* (Cambridge MA, 1989).

Gilman, M., *The Idea of Poetry in France from Houdar de la Motte to Baudelaire* (Cambridge MA, 1958).

Hagstrum, Jean H., *The Sister Arts: The Tradition of Literary Pictorialism from Dryden to Gray* (Chicago, 1958).

Hipple, W. J., *The Beautiful, the Sublime, and the Picturesque in Eighteenth-Century British Aesthetic Theory* (Carbondale IL, 1957).

Hooker, E. N., 'Pope on Wit: *The Essay on Criticism*', in R. F. Jones *et al.* (eds.), *The Seventeenth Century* (Stanford, 1951), pp. 225–46.

Hume, Robert D., *Dryden's Criticism* (Ithaca, 1970).

Knapp, Steven, *Personification and the Sublime: Milton to Coleridge* (Cambridge MA, 1985).

Litman, T. A., *Le Sublime en France (1660–1714)* (Paris, 1971).

Mahoney, John L., *The Whole Internal Universe: Imitation and the New Defense of Poetry in British Criticism, 1660–1830* (New York, 1985).

Miller, John R., *Boileau en France au XVIIIième siècle* (Baltimore, 1942).

Monk, Samuel H., *The Sublime: A Study of Critical Theories in Eighteenth-Century England*, with a new Preface (Ann Arbor, 1960).

Mornet, Daniel, *Nicolas Boileau* (Paris, 1941).

Morris, D. B., *The Religious Sublime: Christian Poetry and Critical Tradition in Eighteenth-Century England* (Lexington KY, 1972).

Pechter, Edward, *Dryden's Classical Theory of Literature* (Cambridge, 1975).

Peyre, Henri, *Le Classicisme Français* (New York, 1942).

Pocock, Gordon, *Boileau and the Nature of Neo-Classicism* (Cambridge, 1980).

Robertson, J. G., *Studies in the Genesis of Romantic Theory in the Eighteenth Century* (Cambridge, 1923).

Simonsuuri, Kirsti, *Homer's Original Genius: Eighteenth-Century Notions of the Early Greek Epic 1699–1798* (Cambridge, 1979).

Williams, David, *Voltaire: literary critic*, vol. 48 of *Studies on Voltaire and the Eighteenth Century* (Geneva, 1966).

Wimsatt, W. K., and Cleanth Brooks, *Literary Criticism. A Short History* (New York, 1957).

Poetry, after 1740

Primary sources and texts

Addison, Joseph, *et al.*, *The Spectator* (1711–14), ed. Donald F. Bond (5 vols., Oxford, 1965).

Aikin, John, *An Essay on the Application of Natural History to Poetry* (London, 1777).

Akenside, Mark, *The Pleasures of Imagination* (London, 1744).
Poetical Works (London, 1835).

Alison, Archibald, *Essays on the Nature and Principles of Taste* (Edinburgh, 1790).

[Anon.], *The Art of Poetry* (London, 1762).

Arbuckle, James, *Hibernicus's Letters* (2 vols., London, 1729).

Armstrong, John, *Sketches* (1758), in *Miscellanies* (2 vols., London, 1770).

Barbauld, Anna Laetitia, 'Critical Essay' prefixed to Mark Akenside's *The Pleasures of Imagination* (London, 1794).

Batteux, Charles, *Les Beaux-Arts réduits à un même principe* (Paris, 1747).

Beattie, James, *Dissertations Moral and Critical* (London, 1783).

Essays on Poetry and Music, as They Affect the Mind, 2nd edn (Edinburgh, 1778).

Poetical Works (London, 1881).

Beccaria, Cesare, *Ricerche intorno alla natura dello stile* (1770).

Berkeley, George, *Works*, ed. A. A. Luce and T. D. Jessop (9 vols., London, 1948–57).

Blackwell, Thomas, *Enquiry into the Life and Writings of Homer* (London, 1735).

Blair, Hugh, *Critical Dissertation on the Poems of Ossian* (London, 1763, enl. 1765).

Lectures on Rhetoric and Belles-Lettres (2 vols., Edinburgh, 1783); ed. Harold F. Harding (Carbondale IL, 1965).

Blair, Robert, *The Grave* (London, 1743).

Blake, William, *Poetry and Prose*, ed. David Erdman and Harold Bloom (Garden City NY, 1965).

Blanckenburg, Christian Friedrich von, *Litterarische Zusätze zu J. G. Sulzers Allgemeiner Theorie* (Leipzig, 1796–98).

Boswell, James, *Life of Samuel Johnson*, ed. G. B. Hill and L. F. Powell (6 vols., Oxford, 1934–50).

Brown, John, *A Dissertation on the Rise, Union, and Power, the Progressions, Separation and Corruptions of Poetry and Music* (London, 1763).

The History of the Rise and Progress of Poetry, Through Its Several Species (Newcastle, 1764).

Buffon, Georges Louis Le Clerc, Comte de, *Discours sur le style* (Paris, 1753).

Burke, Edmund, *A Philosophical Enquiry into the Origin of Our Ideas of the Sublime and Beautiful* (London, 1757), ed. James T. Boulton (London, 1958).

Chénier, André, *Oeuvres complètes*, ed. Gerard Walter (Bruges, 1940).

Coleridge, S. T., *Biographia Literaria*, ed. James Engell and W. Jackson Bate (Princeton, 1983).

Poems, ed. E. H. Coleridge (2 vols., Oxford, 1912).

Collins, William, *The Works of William Collins*, ed. Richard Wendorf and Charles Ryskamp (Oxford, 1979).

Colman, George, *Prose on Several Occasions* (3 vols., London, 1787).

Condillac, Étienne Bonnot de, *Oeuvres philosophiques*, ed. Georges Le Roy (3 vols., Paris, 1947).

Philosophical Writings, trans. Franklin Philip, with the collaboration of Harlan Lane (2 vols., Hillsdale NJ, 1982).

Cowper, William, *The Letters and Prose Writings of William Cowper*, ed. James King and Charles Ryskamp (5 vols., Oxford, 1979).

Poems, vol. I: 1748–1782, ed. John D. Baird and Charles Ryskamp (Oxford, 1980).

Poetical Works, ed. H. S. Milford (London, 1907; rpt 1967).

Darwin, Erasmus, *The Botanic Garden* (London, 1791); Scolar Press rpt with intro. by Desmond King-Hele (Menston, 1973).

Diderot, Denis, *Oeuvres complètes*, ed. J. Assézat and M. Tourneux (20 vols., Paris, 1875–79).

Dodsley, Robert (ed.), *A Collection of Poems, by Several Hands* (London, 1748).

Drake, Nathan, *Literary Hours*, 2nd edn (2 vols., Sudbury, 1800).

Dryden, John, *Of Dramatic Poesy and Other Critical Essays*, ed. George Watson (2 vols., London, 1962).

Du Bos, Jean-Baptiste, *Réflexions critiques sur la poësie et sur la peinture* (1719; 6th edn, 3 vols., Paris, 1755).

[Duff, William], *Critical Observations on the Writings of the Most Celebrated Writers and Geniuses in Original Poetry* (London, 1770).

An Essay on Original Genius In Philosophy and the Fine Arts, Particularly in Poetry (1767), ed. J. L. Mahoney (Gainesville, 1964).

Enfield, William ('The Enquirer'), *Monthly Magazine* 2 (July, 1796).

Ferguson, Adam, *Essay on the History of Civil Society* (Edinburgh, 1767).

Gerard, Alexander, *An Essay on Genius* (London, 1774); ed. W. J. Hipple (1963); ed. Bernhard Fabian (Munich, 1966).

An Essay on Taste (Edinburgh, 1759; 2nd edn, 1780).

Goethe, J. W. von, *Gedenkausgabe der Werke, Briefe, und Gespräche*, ed. Ernst Beutler (24 vols., Zurich, 1948–60).

The Sorrows of Young Werther and Selected Writings, trans. Catherine Hunter (New York, 1962).

Gray, Thomas, *The Complete Poems of Thomas Gray; English, Latin, and Greek*, ed. H. W. Starr and J. R. Hendrickson (Oxford, 1966).

Correspondence of Thomas Gray, ed. Paget Toynbee and Leonard Whibley (3 vols., Oxford, 1971).

Hamann, J. G., *Sämtliche Werke*, ed. Josef Nadler (6 vols., Vienna, 1949–57).

Hammond, James, *Love Elegies* (London, 1743).

H[arris], J[ames], *Hermes; or, a Philosophical Inquiry Concerning Language and Universal Grammar* (London, 1751).

Three Treatises: The First Concerning Art; the Second Concerning Music, Painting and Poetry; the Third Concerning Happiness (London, 1744; rev. 1765).

Upon the Rise and Progress of Criticism (London[?], 1752).

Hartley, David, *Observations on Man* (2 vols., London, 1749).

Helvétius, Claude Adrien, *De L'Esprit* (Paris, 1758).

De L'Esprit: or, Essays on the Mind and its Several Faculties, anon. English trans. (1759).

Herder, J. G. von, *Essay on the Origin of Language* (with Rousseau's *Essay on the Origin of Language*), trans. John H. Moran and Alexander Gode (New York, 1966).

Sämtliche Werke, ed. Berhard Suphan (33 vols., Berlin, 1877–1913).

Hume, David, *Philosophical Works* (4 vols., Edinburgh, 1854).

Treatise of Human Nature, ed. L. A. Selby-Bigge (London, 1896; rpt 1928).

Hurd, Richard, *Letters on Chivalry and Romance* (Dublin, 1762).

The Works of Richard Hurd, D.D. (8 vols., London, 1811).

Hurdis, James, *Lectures Shewing the Several Sources of That Pleasure Which the Human Mind Receives from Poetry* (Bishopstone, Sussex, 1797).

Johnson, Samuel, *A Dictionary of the English Language* (2 vols., London, 1755).

Lives of the English Poets, ed. G. B. Hill (3 vols., Oxford, 1905).

The Yale Edition of the Works of Samuel Johnson (16 vols., New Haven, 1958–).

Jones, Sir William, *Poems Consisting Chiefly of Translations from the Asiatic Languages; to Which Are Added Two Essays: I, On the Poetry of the Eastern Nations; II, On the Arts Commonly Called Imitative* (Oxford, 1772).

Kames, Henry Home, Lord, *Elements of Criticism* (3 vols., Edinburgh, 1762).

Kant, Immanuel, *Gesammelte Schriften*, ed. Preussische Akademie der Wissenschaften (Berlin, 1902–).

Critique of Judgment, trans. Werner S. Pluhar (Indianapolis, 1987).

Lessing, G. W., *Sämtliche Schriften*, ed. Karl Lachmann and Franz Muncker (23 vols., Stuttgart, 1886–1924).

Locke, John, *An Essay concerning Human Understanding*, ed. Peter H. Nidditch (Oxford, 1975).

Lowth, Robert, *De Sacra Poesi Hebraeorum praelectiones* (Oxford, 1753), trans. as *Lectures on the Sacred Poetry of the Hebrews* (1787).

Maass, Johann G. E., *Versuch über die Einbildungskraft* (Halle and Leipzig, 1792, enl. 1797).

Macpherson, James, *The Poems of Ossian ... Containing Dr. Blair's Three Celebrated Critical Dissertations* (2 vols., London, 1806).

Meiners, Christoph, *Grundriß der Theorie und Geschichte der schönen Wissenschaften* (Lemgo, 1787).

Meister, Leonhard, *Über Aberglauben, Einbildungskraft, und Schwärmerey* (Berne, 1795).

Über die Einbildungskraft in ihrem Einfluß auf Geist und Herz (Zurich, 1795).

Über die Schwärmerei (2 vols., Berne, 1775–7).

Versuch über die Einbildungskraft (Berne, 1778).

Mercier, Louis-Sébastien, *Du Théâtre, ou nouvel essai sur l'art dramatique* (Paris, 1773).

Moir, John, *Gleanings; or, Fugitive Pieces* (2 vols., London, 1785).

Muratori, L. A., *Della forza della Fantasia Umana* (Venice, 1740).

Ogilvie, John, *Philosophical and Critical Observations on the Nature, Character, and Various Species of Composition* (2 vols., London, 1774).

Percy, Thomas, *Reliques of Ancient English Poetry* (3 vols., London, 1765).

Platner, Ernst, *Anthropologie für Aerzte und Weltweise* (Leipzig, 1772, enl. 1790).

Price, Uvedale, *An Essay on the Picturesque, as Compared with the Sublime and Beautiful* (2 vols., London, 1794–8).

Priestley, Joseph, *Course of Lectures on Oratory and Criticism* (Warrington, 1762).

Reynolds, Sir Joshua, *Discourses on Art*, ed. Robert Wark (New Haven, 1975).

Rivarol, Antoine de, *Oeuvres complètes* (5 vols., Paris, 1808).

Schiller, Friedrich, *On the Aesthetic Education of Man*, ed. and trans. E. M. Wilkinson and L. A. Willoughby (Oxford, 1967).

Werke: Nationalausgabe, ed. Julius Petersen, Lieselotte Blumenthal and Benno von Wiese (42 vols., Weimar, 1962–91).

Shaftesbury, Anthony Ashley Cooper, third Earl of, *Characteristicks of Men, Manners, Opinions, Times* (3 vols., London, 1711); ed. J. M. Robertson (2 vols., 1900).

Soliloquy; or, Advice to an Author (London, 1710).

Sharpe, William, *Dissertation upon Genius* (London, 1755); rpt with intro. by William Bruce Johnson (Delmar NY, 1973).

Shenstone, William, *Poetical Works*, ed. George Gilfillan (New York, 1854; rpt 1968).

Smart, Christopher, *Poetical Works*, ed. Marina Williamson and Marcus Walsh (4 vols., Oxford, 1980–7).

Smith, Adam, *The Theory of Moral Sentiments*, ed. D. D. Raphael and A. L. Macfie (Oxford, 1976; rpt with corrections, 1979).

Spence, Joseph, *Observations, Anecdotes, and Characters of Books and Men*, ed. James M. Osborn (Oxford, 1966).

Sulzer, J. G., *Allgemeine Theorie der schönen Künste* (4 vols., Leipzig, 1771–4).

Tetens, Johann Nicolaus, *Philosophische Versuche über die menschliche Natur und ihre Entwicklung* (2 vols., Leipzig, 1776–7).

Thomson, James, *Poetical Works*, ed. J. Logie Robertson (Oxford, 1908; rpt 1965).

Trapp, Joseph, *Lectures on Poetry Read in the Schools of Natural Philosophy at Oxford* (London, 1742, English trans. of Latin text, 1711–19).

Tucker, Abraham, *The Light of Nature Pursued* (7 vols., 1768–77; 2nd edn, rev. and corrected, London, 1805).

Twining, Thomas, *Aristotle's Treatise on Poetry, Translated with Notes and Two Dissertations on Poetical and Musical Imitation* (2 vols., 1789, 1812).

Vico, G., *The New Science of Giambattista Vico*, unabridged trans. of the 3rd edn (1744), trans. Thomas Goddard Bergin and Max Harold Frisch (Ithaca, 1968).

Opere, ed. Fausto Nicolini (Milan, 1953).

Voltaire (François-Marie Arouet), *Oeuvres complètes*, ed. Louis Moland (52 vols., Paris, 1877–83).

Warburton, William, *The Divine Legation of Moses* (London, 1737–8).

Warton, Joseph, *The Enthusiast; or Lover of Nature* (London, 1744).

An Essay on the Genius and Writings of Pope (2 vols., London, 1756, 1782).

Odes on Several Subjects (London, 1746).

ed., *The Works of Virgil* (4 vols., London, 1778).

Warton, Thomas, *History of English Poetry* (4 vols., London, 1774–81).

The Pleasures of Melancholy (London, 1747).

Webb, Daniel, *Observations on the Correspondence Between Poetry and Music* (London, 1769).

Remarks on the Beauties of Poetry (London, 1762).

Wordsworth, William, *Lyrical Ballads*, ed. R. L. Brett and A. R. Jones (New York and Cambridge, 1963).

Prose Works, ed. W. J. B. Owen and J. W. Smyser (3 vols., Oxford, 1974).

Young, Edward, *Complete Works* (2 vols., London, 1854).
Conjectures on Original Composition (London, 1759), ed. E. J. Morley (Manchester, 1918).

Secondary sources

Aarsleff, Hans, *From Locke to Saussure: Essays on the Study of Language and Intellectual History* (Minneapolis, 1882).
The Study of Language in England 1780–1860 (Princeton, 1967).
Abrams, M. H., *The Mirror and the Lamp: Romantic Theory and the Critical Tradition* (New York, 1953).
Arthos, John, *The Language of Natural Description in Eighteenth-Century Poetry* (Ann Arbor, 1949).
Barrell, John, *English Literature in History 1730–80: An Equal, Wide Survey* (New York, 1983).
and Harriet Guest, 'On the use of contradiction: economics and morality in the eighteenth-century long poem', in *The New Eighteenth Century*, ed. Felicity Nussbaum and Laura Brown (London and New York, 1987).
Bate, W. J., *From Classic to Romantic: Premises of Taste in Eighteenth-Century England* (Cambridge MA, 1946).
'The sympathetic imagination in eighteenth-century English criticism', *ELH*, 12 (1945), 144–64.
Beddow, Michael, 'Goethe on genius', in *Genius: The History of an Idea*, ed. Penelope Murray (Oxford, 1989), pp. 98–112.
Berlin, Isaiah, *Vico and Herder: Two Studies in the History of Ideas* (New York, 1976).
Blackall, Eric A., *The Emergence of German as a Literary Language, 1700–1775* (Cambridge, 1959).
Bronson, Bertrand, 'The pre-Romantic or post-Augustan mode', *ELH*, 20 (1953); rpt in *Facets of the Enlightenment* (Berkeley, 1968), pp. 159–72.
Brown, Marshall, 'The urbane sublime', *ELH*, 45 (1978), 236–54.
Butt, John, *English Literature in the Mid-Eighteenth Century*, ed. and completed Geoffrey Carnall (Oxford, 1979).
Chalker, John, *The English Georgic: A Study in the Development of a Form* (London, 1969).
Clark, Robert T., 'Herder, Cesarotti and Vico', *Studies in Philology*, 44 (1947), 645–71.
Cohen, Murray, *Sensible Words: Linguistic Practice in England, 1640–1785* (Baltimore, 1977).
Cohen, Ralph, 'On the interrelations of eighteenth-century literary forms', *New Approaches to the Eighteenth Century*, ed. Philip Harth (New York, 1974), pp. 33–78.
Davie, Donald (ed.), *The Late Augustans: Longer Poems of the Later Eighteenth Century* (London, 1958; rpt 1965).
Purity of Diction in English Verse (London, 1955).
Derrida, Jacques, *The Archaeology of the Frivolous: Reading Condillac*, trans. John P. Leavey, Jr (Lincoln NB, 1980).

Dieckmann, Herbert, 'Diderot's conception of genius', *Journal of the History of Ideas*, 2 (1941), 151–82.

Engell, James, *The Creative Imagination: Enlightenment to Romanticism* (Cambridge MA, 1981).

Feingold, Richard, *Nature and Society: Later Eighteenth-Century Uses of the Pastoral and Georgic* (Hassocks, Sussex, 1978).

Findlay, L. M., 'The genius of the French language: towards a poetics of political reaction during the Revolutionary period', *Studies in Romanticism*, 28 (1989), 531–57.

Frieden, Ken, *Genius and Monologue* (Ithaca, 1985).

Greene, D. J., 'Logical structure in eighteenth-century poetry', *Philological Quarterly*, 31 (1952), 315–36.

Guyer, Paul, *Kant and the Claims of Taste* (Cambridge MA, 1979).

Hartman, Geoffrey, 'Christopher Smart's "Magnificat": toward a theory of representation', *ELH*, 45 (1974); rpt in *The Fate of Reading and Other Essays* (Chicago, 1985).

Hughes, Peter, 'Restructuring literary history: the eighteenth century', *New Literary History*, 8 (1977), 257–77.

Hunter, J. Paul, ' "Peace" and the Augustans: some implications of didactic method and literary form', in *Studies in Change and Revolution*, ed. Paul Korshin (London, 1972).

Johnston, Arthur, 'Poetry and criticism after 1740', in Roger Lonsdale (ed.), *History of Literature in the English Language: Dryden to Johnson* (London, 1971), pp. 257–98.

Land, Stephen, *From Signs to Propositions: The Concept of Form in Eighteenth-Century Semantic Theory* (London, 1974).

Landry, Donna, 'The resignation of Mary Collier: Some problems in feminist literary history', in *The New Eighteenth Century*, ed. Felicity Nussbaum and Laura Brown (London and New York, 1987), pp. 90–120.

Lange, Victor, *The Classical Age of German Literature, 1740–1815* (London, 1982).

Lipking, Lawrence, *The Ordering of the Arts in Eighteenth-Century England* (Princeton, 1970).

Lockwood, Thomas, 'On the relationship of satire and poetry after Pope', *Studies in English Literature*, 14 (1974), 387–402.

Mann, Elizabeth L., 'The problem of originality in English literary criticism, 1750–1800', *Philological Quarterly*, 18 (1939), 97–118.

McLean, Norman, 'From action to image: theories of the lyric in the eighteenth century', in R. S. Crane *et al.* (eds.), *Critics and Criticism Ancient and Modern* (Chicago, 1952).

Menhennet, Alan, *Order and Freedom: German Literature and Society, 1720–1805* (London, 1973).

Miles, Josephine, *The Primary Language of Poetry in the 1740s and 1840s* (Berkeley, 1950).

Monk, Samuel, *The Sublime: A Study of Critical Theories in Eighteenth-Century England* (Ann Arbor, 1935; rpt with a new Preface, 1960).

Natali, Giulio, *Storia Letteraria D'Italia* (2 vols., Milan, 1929).

Nicolson, Marjorie Hope, *Newton Demands the Muse: Newton's 'Opticks' and the Eighteenth Century Poets* (Princeton, 1946).

Nisbet, H. B., *Herder and the Philosophy and History of Science* (Cambridge, 1970).

(ed.), *German Aesthetic and Literary Criticism: Winckelmann, Lessing, Hamann, Herder, Schiller and Goethe* (Cambridge, 1985).

Novak, Maximillian, *Eighteenth Century English Literature* (New York, 1983).

Pascal, Roy, *The German Sturm und Drang* (Manchester, 1953).

Patey, Douglas Lane, 'The eighteenth century invents the canon', *Modern Language Studies*, 18 (1988), 17–37.

Pittock, Joan, *The Ascendancy of Taste: The Achievement of Joseph and Thomas Warton* (London, 1973).

Price, Martin, 'The sublime poem: pictures and powers', *Yale Review*, 58 (1968–69), 194–213.

To the Palace of Wisdom: Studies in Order and Energy from Dryden to Blake (New York, 1964).

Rawson, Claude, *Order from Confusion Sprung: Studies in Eighteenth-Century Literature from Swift to Cowper* (London, 1985).

Schaffer, Simon, 'Genius in Romantic natural philosophy', in Andrew Cunningham and Nicholas Jardine (eds.), *Romanticism and Science* (Cambridge, 1990).

Siskin, Clifford, *The Historicity of Romantic Discourse* (New York, 1988).

Sitter, John, *Literary Loneliness* (Ithaca, 1982).

'Mother, memory, muse and poetry after Pope', *ELH*, 44 (1977), 12–36.

Spacks, Patricia M., *The Poetry of Vision* (Cambridge MA, 1967).

Tillotson, Geoffrey, *Augustan Poetic Diction* (London, 1961; rpt 1964).

Tuveson, Ernest L., *The Imagination as a Means of Grace* (Berkeley and Los Angeles, 1960).

Warnock, Mary, *Imagination* (Berkeley, 1976).

Wasserman, Earl, 'Collins's "Ode on the Poetical Character"', *ELH*, 34 (1967), 92–118.

Wellbery, David E., *Lessing's 'Laocoon': Semiotics and Aesthetics in the Age of Reason* (Cambridge, 1984).

Wellek, René, *A History of Modern Criticism. Vol. I: The Later Eighteenth Century* (New Haven, 1955; paperback edn, Cambridge, 1981).

Wimsatt, W. K., and Cleanth Brooks, *Literary Criticism. A Short History* (New York, 1957; paperback edn, 1967).

Yolton, John, *John Locke and the Way of Ideas* (Oxford, 1956).

Drama, 1660–1740

Primary sources and texts

d'Aubignac, François Hédelin, *La Pratique du théâtre* (1663), ed. Pierre Martino (Algiers and Paris, 1927).

The Whole Art of the Stage (London, 1684; rpt New York, 1968).

Boileau-Despréaux, Nicholas, *Oeuvres*, ed. Antoine Adam (Paris, 1966).

Collier, Jeremy, *A Short View of the Profaneness and Immorality of the English Stage* (1730; rpt Hildesheim, 1969).

Congreve, William, *Letters & Documents*, ed. John C. Hodges (New York, 1964).

Dennis, John, *Critical Works* (2 vols., Baltimore, 1939–43).

Dryden, John, *The Works of John Dryden*, ed. Edward Niles Hooker, Thomas Swedenberg, Maximillian E. Novak *et al.* (Berkeley, 1955–) vol. X.

Du Bos, Jean-Baptiste, *Critical Reflections on Poetry and Painting*, trans. Thomas Nugent (3 vols., London, 1748).

Réflexions critiques sur la poësie et sur la peinture (3 vols., Paris, 1740).

Farquhar, George, *Works*, ed. George Stonehill (2 vols., London, 1930).

The Whole Art of the State (1684) (New York, 1968).

Hughes, John ['Essay on *Othello*'], *The Guardian*, No. 37, ed. John Calhoun Stephens (Lexington KY, 1982).

Le Bossu, René, *Traité du poème épique* (1714), intro. Volker Kapp (Hamburg, 1981).

Pope, Alexander, 'Preface to Shakespeare', *The Prose Works of Alexander Pope*, ed. Rosemary Cowler (Hampden CN, 1986).

Rapin, René, *Réflexions sur la poétique d'Aristote et sur les ouvrages des poètes anciens et modernes* (2 parts, Paris, 1674).

Saint-Évremond, Charles de, *Oeuvres en prose* (2 vols., Paris, 1965).

The Works of Monsieur de St Évremond (London, 1728).

Seades, Colbert (ed.), *Les Sentiments de l'Académie Française sur le Cid* (Minneapolis, 1916).

Shadwell, Thomas, *Works*, ed. Montague Summers (5 vols., London, 1927).

Sorbière, Samuel, *A Voyage to England* (London, 1709).

Sprat, Thomas, 'Observations on Mons. de Sorbière's Voyage into England', in *A Voyage to England*, by Samuel Sorbière (London, 1709).

Steele, Richard, *Plays*, ed. Shirley Kenny (Oxford, 1971).

Secondary sources

Barish, Jonas, *The Antitheatrical Prejudice* (Berkeley, 1981).

Batiffol, Louis, *Richelieu et Corneille* (Paris, 1936).

Brown, Laura, English Dramatic Form, 1660–1760: An Essay in Generic History (New Haven, 1981).

Davis, James Herbert, *Tragic Theory and the Eighteenth-Century Critics*, University of North Carolina Studies in the Romance Languages and Literatures No. 68 (Chapel Hill, 1967).

Gasté, Armand, *La Querelle du Cid* (Paris, 1898).

Hobson, Marion, *The Object of Arts: The Theory of Illusion in Eighteenth-Century France* (Cambridge, 1982).

Hughes, Derek, *Dryden's Heroic Plays* (London, 1981).

Hume, Robert D., *The Development of English Drama in the Late Seventeenth Century* (Oxford, 1976).

Loftis, John, *The Spanish Plays of Restoration England* (New Haven, 1973).

Maurocordato, Alexandre, *La Critique Classique en Angleterre* (Paris, 1964).

Novak, Maximillian E., *William Congreve* (New York, 1971).

Picart, Raymond, *La Carrière de Jean Racine* (Paris, 1961).
Reiss, Timothy, *Tragedy and Truth* (New Haven, 1980).
Scherer, Jacques, *La Dramaturgie Classique en France* (Paris, 1964).

Drama, after 1740

Primary sources and texts

Adams, Henry Hitch, and Baxter Hathaway (eds.), *Dramatic Essays of the Neoclassic Age* (1947; rpt. New York and London, 1965).
d'Aubignac, François Hédelin, *La Pratique du Théâtre*, ed. Pierre Martino (Algiers and Paris, 1927).
Beaumarchais, Pierre Augustin Caron de, *Oeuvres*, ed. Pierre Larthomas (Paris, 1988).
Chapman, Gerald Webster (ed.), *Literary Criticism in England, 1660–1800* (New York, 1966).
Corneille, Pierre, *Théâtre complet*, ed. Maurice Rat (3 vols., Paris, n.d.).
  Trois Discours sur le Poème Dramatique, ed. Louis Forestier (Paris, 1963).
Diderot, Denis, *Oeuvres Esthétiques*, ed. Paul Vernière (Paris, 1959).
Du Bos, Jean-Baptiste, *Réflexions critiques sur la poésie et sur la peinture* (1719; 3 vols., Paris, 1740).
Elledge, Scott (ed.), *Eighteenth-Century Critical Essays* (2 vols., Ithaca, 1961).
Fontenelle, Bernard de Bovier de, *Oeuvres* (11 vols., Amsterdam, 1764).
Gottsched, Johann Christoph, *Schriften zur Literatur*, ed. Horst Steinmetz (Stuttgart, 1972).
Johnson, Samuel, *Johnson on Shakespeare*, ed. Arthur Sherbo, Yale Edition, VII–VIII (New Haven and London, 1968).
Lessing, Gotthold Ephraim, *Sämtliche Schriften*, ed. Karl Lachmann and Franz Muncker (23 vols., Stuttgart, 1886–1924).
Lessing, Gotthold Ephraim, Moses Mendelssohn and Friedrich Nicolai, *Briefwechsel über das Trauerspiel*, ed. Jochen Schulte-Sasse (Munich, 1972).
Lillo, George, *The London Merchant*, ed. William H. McBurney (Lincoln, 1965).
Loewenthal, Erich, and Lambert Schneider (eds.), *Sturm und Drang: Kritische Schriften* (Heidelberg, 1963).
Meier, Georg Friedrich, *Beurtheilung der Gottschedischen Dichtkunst* (Halle, 1747–8).
Mercier, Louis Sébastien, *Du Théâtre ou Nouvel Essai sur L'Art Dramatique* (Amsterdam, 1773; rpt. Hildesheim and New York, 1973).
Pascal, Roy, *Shakespeare in Germany, 1740–1815* (Cambridge, 1937; rpt New York, 1971).
Rousseau, Jean-Jacques, *Lettre à M. d'Alembert*, ed. Michel Launay (Paris, 1967).
Vial, Francisque, and Louis Denise (eds.), *Idées et Doctrines Littéraires du XVIIIᵉ Siècle* (Paris, n.d.).
Vickers, Brian (ed.), *Shakespeare: The Critical Heritage*, IV–VI (London, Henley and Boston, 1976–81).

Voltaire, *Oeuvres complètes*, ed. Louis Moland, V, *Théâtre*, IV (1877; rpt Nendeln, Liechtenstein, 1967).

Secondary sources

Bate, Jonathan, *Shakespearean Constitutions: Politics, Theatre, Criticism 1730–1830* (Oxford, 1989).
Berghahn, Klaus L., 'From classicist to classical literary criticism', in Peter Uwe Hohendahl (ed.), *A History of German Literary Criticism* (Lincoln and London, 1988), pp. 13–98.
Bernbaum, Ernest, *The Drama of Sensibility: A Sketch of the History of English Sentimental Comedy and Domestic Tragedy 1696–1780* (Boston and London, 1915).
Bevis, Richard, *The Laughing Tradition: Stage Comedy in Garrick's Day* (London, 1980).
Borchmeyer, Dieter, *Tragödie und Öffentlichkeit: Schillers Dramaturgie* (Munich, 1973).
Brody, Jules, 'Esthétique et Société chez Molière', in Jean Jacquot (ed.), *Dramaturgie et Société*, vol. 1 (Paris, 1968), pp. 307–26.
Brown, Laura, *English Dramatic Form, 1660–1760: An Essay in Generic History* (New Haven, 1981).
Ermann, Kurt, *Goethes Shakespeare-Bild* (Tübingen, 1983).
Guthke, Karl S., 'Lessing, Shakespeare und die deutsche Verspätung', in *Nation und Gelehrtenrepublik: Lessing im europäischen Zusammenhang*, Sonderband zum Lessing Yearbook, ed. Wilfried Barner and Albert M. Reh (Detroit and Munich, 1984).
McInnes, Edward, *'Ein ungeheures Theater': The Drama of the Sturm und Drang* (Frankfurt am Main, Bern, New York, Paris, 1987).
Martino, Alberto, *Geschichte der dramatischen Theorien in Deutschland im 18. Jahrhundert. I. Die Dramaturgie der Aufklärung* (Tübingen, 1972).
Meisel, Martin, *Realizations: Narrative, Pictorial and Theatrical Arts in Nineteenth-Century England* (Princeton, 1983).
Parker, G. F., *Johnson's Shakespeare* (Oxford, 1989).
Robertson, J. G., *Lessing's Dramatic Theory* (Cambridge, 1939).
Schings, Hans-Jürgen, *Der mitleidigste Mensch ist der beste Mensch* (Munich, 1980).
Sherbo, Arthur, *English Sentimental Drama* (East Lansing MI, 1957).
Smith, David Nichol, *Shakespeare in the Eighteenth Century* (Oxford, 1928).
Szondi, Peter, *Die Theorie des bürgerlichen Trauerspiels im 18. Jahrhundert* (Frankfurt am Main, 1973).
Taylor, Gary, *Reinventing Shakespeare: A Cultural History from the Restoration to the Present* (London, 1990).
van Tieghem, Paul, *Le Préromantisme: Etudes d'Histoire Européenne. III. La Découverte de Shakespeare sur le Continent* (Paris, 1947).
Williams, Simon, *Shakespeare on the German Stage. Vol. 1, 1586–1914* (Cambridge, 1990).
Wolffheim, Hans, *Die Entdeckung Shakespeares* (Hamburg, 1959).

Prose fiction: France

Primary sources and texts

Argens, Jean-Baptiste de Boyer, Marquis d', 'Discours sur les nouvelles', in *Lectures amusantes ou les délassements de l'esprit avec un discours sur les nouvelles* (2 vols., La Haye, 1739), I, pp. 9–69.

Arnaud, François-Marie Baculard d', *Nouvelles historiques* (Paris, 1774).

Aubert de La Chesnaye Des Bois, François Alexandre, *Lettres amusantes et critiques sur les romans en général* (Paris, 1743).

Bougeant, Guillaume-Hyacinthe, *Voyage merveilleux du Prince Fan-Férédin dans la Romancie* (1735), in Charles G. T. Garnier (ed.), *Voyages imaginaires, songes, visions et romans cabalistiques* (Amsterdam and Paris, 1788), XXVI, pp. 1–156.

Charnes, Jean-Antoine de, *Conversations sur la critique de la Princesse de Clèves*, rpt ed. Groupe d'étude du XVIIe siècle de l'Université François Rabelais de Tours, François Weil, Pierre Aquilon, Jacques Chupeau, Jean Lafond and Gérard Maillat (1679; Tours, 1973).

Coulet, Henri, *Le Roman jusqu'à la Révolution*, Collection U (2 vols., Paris, 1968). Vol. I: Histoire du roman en France. Vol. II: Anthologie.

Diderot, Denis, 'Les Deux Amis de Bourbonne', ed. Henri Benac in *Oeuvres romanesques* (Paris, 1962), pp. 780–92.

'Éloge de Richardson', ed. Paul Vernière, in *Oeuvres esthétiques* (Paris, 1959), pp. 29–48.

Du Plaisir, *Sentiments sur les lettres et sur l'histoire avec des scrupules sur le style* (1683); ed. (with original pagination) Klaus Friedrich, in 'Eine Theorie des "Roman nouveau"', *Romanistisches Jahrbuch* 14 (1963), 105–32.

Faydit, l'abbé, *La Télémacomanie, ou la Censure et critique du Roman intitulé, Les Aventures de Telemaque Fils d'Ulysse, ou suite du quatriéme Livre de l'Odyssée d'Homere* (A Eleuterople: chez Pierre Philalethe, 1700).

Huet, Pierre-Daniel, *Lettre-traité sur l'origine des romans*, ed. Fabienne Gégou (Paris, 1971).

Jaquin, Armand-Pierre, *Entretiens sur les romans* (1755; rpt Geneva, 1970).

Lenglet-Du Fresnoy, Nicolas, *De l'usage des romans* (Amsterdam, 1734).

Marmontel, Jean-François, *Essai sur les romans, considérés du côté moral* (1787), in *Oeuvres complètes* (1819; rpt. Geneva, 1968), III, pp. 558–96.

Rousseau, Jean-Jacques, *La Nouvelle Héloïse*, in *Oeuvres complètes*, ed. Bernard Guyon, Jacques Scherer and Charly Guyot, Bibliothèque de la Pléiade (Paris, 1964), II.

Sade, Donatien-Alphonse-François, Marquis de, *Idée sur les romans* (1800), ed. Jean Glastier (Bordeaux, 1970).

Segrais, Regnault de, *Les Nouvelles Françaises, ou les Divertissemens de la princesse Aurélie* (1656; 2 vols., La Haye, 1741).

Staël-Holstein, Anne-Louise Germaine Necker, Baronne de, *Essai sur les fictions* (1795) in *Oeuvres complètes* (Paris, 1844), I, pp. 62–72.

Valincour, Jean Baptiste Henri du Trousset de, *Lettres à Madame la Marquise *** sur le sujet de la Princesse de Clèves*, rpt ed. Groupe d'étude du XVIIe siècle de l'Université François Rabelais de Tours, Jacques Chupeau, Pierre Aquilon, Jean Lafond, François Weil, Gérard Maillat and Augustin Redondo (1678; rpt Tours, 1972).

Secondary sources

Altman, Janet Gurkin, *Epistolarity: Approaches to a Form* (Columbus, 1982).

Alvarez Barrientos, Joaquín, 'Algunas ideas sobre teoría de la novela en el siglo XVIII en Inglaterra y España', *Anales de Literatura Española*, 2 (1983), 5–23.

Barthes, Roland, *S/Z* (Paris, 1970).

Bertana, Emilio, 'Pro e contro i romanzi nel Settecento', *Giornale Storico della Letteratura Italiana*, 37 (1901), 339–52.

Brown, Reginald Francis, *La novela española (1700–1850)* (Madrid, 1953).

Coulet, Henri, *Le Roman jusqu'à la Révolution*, Collection U (2 vols., Paris, 1968). Vol. I: Histoire du roman en France. Vol. II: Anthologie.

Cox, R. Merritt, *Eighteenth-Century Spanish Literature* (Boston, 1979).

DeJean, Joan, *Tender Geographies: Women and the Origins of the Novel in France* (New York, 1991).

Deloffre, Frédéric, *La Nouvelle en France à l'âge classique* (Paris, 1967).

Démoris, René, *Le Roman à la première personne, du classicisme aux Lumières* (Paris, 1975).

DiPiero, Thomas, *Dangerous Truths and Criminal Passions: The Evolution of the French Novel, 1569–1791* (Stanford, 1992).

Ferreras, Juan Ignacio, *La novela en el siglo XVIII* (Madrid, 1987).

Genette, Gérard, *Figures II* (Paris, 1969).

Gevrey, Françoise, *L'Illusion et ses procédés: De 'La Princesse de Clèves' aux 'Illustres Françaises'* (Paris, 1988).

Godenne, René, *Histoire de la nouvelle française aux XVIIe et XVIIIe siècles* (1970; 2nd edn, Geneva, 1977).

Hainsworth, G., *Les 'Novelas exemplares' de Cervantès en France au XVIIe siècle: Contribution à l'étude de la nouvelle en France* (Paris, 1933).

Hobson, Marian. *The Object of Art: The Theory of Illusion in Eighteenth-Century France* (Cambridge, 1982).

Laugaa, Maurice, *Lectures de Madame de Lafayette*, Collection U2 (Paris, 1971).

May, Georges, *Le Dilemme du roman au XVIIIe siècle* (New Haven and Paris, 1963).

Mylne, Vivienne G., *The Eighteenth-Century French Novel: Techniques of Illusion* (1965; 2nd edn, Cambridge, 1981).

Pizzorusso, Arnaldo, *La Poetica del romanzo in Francia (1660–1685)* (Rome, 1962).

Ratner, Moses, *Theory and Criticism of the Novel in France from 'L'Astrée' to 1750* (New York, 1938).

Robert, Raymonde, *Le Conte de fées littéraire en France de la fin du XVIIe à la fin du XVIIIe siècle* (Nancy, 1982).

Showalter, English, Jr, *The Evolution of the French Novel, 1641–1782* (Princeton, 1972).

Spera, Lucinda, 'Il dibattito sul romanzo nel Settecento: Patriarchi e il Traité di P. D. Huet', *Rassegna della Letteratura Italiana*, 90 (1986), 93–103.

Stewart, Philip, *Imitation and Illusion in the French Memoir-Novel, 1700–1750* (New Haven, 1969).

Tieje, Arthur Jerrold, *The Theory of Characterization in Prose Fiction prior to 1740* (Minneapolis, 1916).

Versini, Laurent, *Le Roman épistolaire* (Paris, 1979).

Weil, Françoise, *L'Interdiction du roman et la librairie* (Paris, 1986).

Williams, Charles G. S., *Valincour: The Limits of 'honnêteté'* (Washington, 1991).

Prose fiction: Great Britain

Primary sources and texts

Behn, Aphra, *Love-Letters Between a Noble-Man and His Sister* (London, 1684–7), ed. Janet Todd (Columbus OH, 1993).

Oroonoko (London, 1688), ed. Philip Henderson, in *Shorter Novels: Seventeenth Century* (London, 1962).

Bunyan, John, *The Pilgrim's Progress from This World, to That which is to come* (London, 1678, 1682), ed. N. H. Keeble (Oxford, 1984).

Defoe, Daniel, *The Family Instructor* (London, 1715).

The Life and Strange Surprizing Adventures of Robinson Crusoe, ed. J. Donald Crowley (Oxford, 1981).

Serious Reflections During the Life And Surprising Adventures of Robinson Crusoe (London, 1720).

Fielding, Henry, *The Criticism of Henry Fielding*, ed. Ioan Williams (New York, 1970).

The History of the Adventures of Joseph Andrews (London, 1742), ed. Martin C. Battestin (Oxford, 1967).

The History of Tom Jones, A Foundling (London, 1749), ed. Martin C. Battestin and Fredson Bowers (2 vols., Oxford, 1974).

The Journal of a Voyage to Lisbon (London, 1755), ed. Harold E. Pagliaro (New York, 1963).

The Life of Mr Jonathan Wild the Great, published as *Miscellanies*, Vol. III (London, 1743), ed. A. R. Humphreys and Douglas Brooks (London, 1973).

Godwin, William, *Enquiry concerning Political Justice* (London, 1793).

Fleetwood (London, 1805), Bentley's Standard Novels, No. 22 (London, 1832).

'Of History and Romance' (composed 1797), in M. Hindle (ed.), *Things As They Are; or The Adventures of Caleb Williams* (Harmondsworth, 1988), pp. 359–73.

Haywood, Eliza, *The Female Spectator* (1744–6).

Howes, Alan B. (ed.), *Sterne: The Critical Heritage* (London, 1974).

Knight, Richard Payne, *An Analytical Inquiry into the Principles of Taste* (London, 1805).

McKillop, Alan D. (ed.), *Critical Remarks on Sir Charles Grandison, Clarissa, and Pamela* (1754), Augustan Reprint Society, No. 21, ser. 4, No. 3 (Los Angeles, 1950).

Paulson, Ronald, and Thomas Lockwood (eds.), *Henry Fielding: The Critical Heritage* (London, 1969).

Pope, Alexander, *Peri Bathous: or, of the Art of Sinking in Poetry* (London, 1728).

Rawson, Claude (ed.), *Henry Fielding: A Critical Anthology* (Harmondsworth, 1973).

Reeve, Clara, *The Progress of Romance* (London, 1785).

Richardson, Samuel, *Clarissa, or, the History of a Young Lady* (London, 1747–8), ed. Angus Ross (Harmondsworth, 1985).

Clarissa: Preface, Hints of Prefaces, and Postscript, ed. R. F. Brissenden, Augustan Reprint Society, No. 103 (Los Angeles, 1964).

The Correspondence of Samuel Richardson, ed. Anna Laetitia Barbauld, (6 vols., London, 1804).

Pamela: or, Virtue Rewarded (London, 1740), ed. T. C. Duncan Eaves and Ben D. Kimpel (Boston, 1971).

The Richardson–Stinstra Correspondence, ed. William C. Slattery (Carbondale IL, 1969).

Selected Letters of Samuel Richardson, ed. John Carroll (Oxford, 1964).

Sir Charles Grandison (London, 1753–4), ed. Jocelyn Harris (London, 1972).

Sterne, Laurence, *The Life and Opinions of Tristram Shandy, Gentleman* (1759–67), ed. Melvyn and Joan New (3 vols., Gainesville, 1978–84).

Williams, Ioan (ed.), *Novel and Romance 1700–1800: A Documentary Record* (New York, 1970).

Secondary sources

Armstrong, Nancy, *Desire and Domestic Fiction: A Political History of the Novel* (Oxford, 1987).

Bakhtin, Mikhail M., *The Dialogic Imagination* (trans. Austin, 1981).

Bartolomeo, Joseph F., *A New Species of Criticism: Eighteenth-Century Discourse on the Novel* (Newark DE, 1994).

Bell, Michael D., *The Development of American Romance* (Chicago, 1980).

Belsey, Catherine, *Critical Practice* (London, 1980).

Bender, John, *Imagining the Penitentiary: Fiction and the Architecture of Mind in Eighteenth-Century England* (Chicago, 1987).

Cohn, Dorrit, *Transparent Minds: Narrative Modes for Presenting Consciousness in Fiction* (Princeton, 1978).

Coward, Rosalind, and John Ellis, *Language and Materialism: Developments in Semiology and the Theory of the Subject* (London, 1977).

Davidson, Cathy N., *Revolution and the Word: The Rise of the Novel in America* (Oxford, 1986).

Davis, Lennard J., *Factual Fictions: The Origins of the English Novel* (New York, 1983).

Day, Robert Adams, *Told in Letters: Epistolary Fiction Before Richardson* (Ann Arbor, 1966).

Gilmore, Michael T., 'The literature of the revolutionary and early national periods', in Sacvan Bercovitch (ed.), *The Cambridge History of American Literature* (Cambridge, 1994), I, pp. 539–693.

Hunter, J. Paul, *Before Novels: The Cultural Contexts of Eighteenth-Century English Fiction* (New York, 1990).

Kahler, Erich, *The Inward Turn of Narrative* (1970; trans. Princeton, 1973).

Kay, Carol, *Political Constructions: Defoe, Richardson, and Sterne in Relation to Hobbes, Hume, and Burke* (Cornell, 1988).

Kelly, Gary, *The English Jacobin Novel 1780–1805* (Oxford, 1976).

Lukács, Georg, *The Theory of the Novel*, trans. Anna Bostock (Cambridge MA, 1971).

McKeon, Michael, *The Origins of the English Novel, 1600–1740* (Baltimore, 1987).

McKillop, Alan D., *The Early Masters of English Fiction* (Lawrence KN, 1956).

Martin, Terence, *The Instructed Vision: Scottish Common Sense Philosophy and the Origins of American Fiction* (Bloomington, 1961).

Mullan, John, *Sentiment and Sociability: The Language of Feeling in the Eighteenth Century* (Oxford, 1988).

Napier, Elizabeth R., *The Failure of Gothic: Problems of Disjunction in an Eighteenth-Century Literary Form* (Oxford, 1987).

Orians, G. Harrison, 'Censure of fiction in American romances and magazines, 1789–1810', *Publications of the Modern Language Association of America*, 52 (1937), 195–214.

Ortega y Gasset, José, *Meditations on Quixote* (trans. New York, 1961).

Patey, Douglas L., *Probability and Literary Form: Philosophic Theory and Literary Practice in the Augustan Age* (Cambridge, 1984).

Perosa, Sergio, *American Theories of the Novel: 1793–1903* (New York, 1985).

Ruland, Richard (ed.), *The Native Muse: Theories of American Literature from Bradford to Whitman* (New York, 1976).

Spencer, Jane, *The Rise of the Woman Novelist from Aphra Behn to Jane Austen* (Oxford, 1986).

Starr, G. A., *Defoe and Casuistry* (Princeton, 1971).

Taylor, John T., *Early Opposition to the English Novel: The Popular Reaction from 1760 to 1830* (New York, 1943).

Tompkins, J. M. S., *The Popular Novel in England 1770–1800* (1932; rpt Lincoln, 1961).

Uphaus, Robert W. (ed.), *The Idea of the Novel in the Eighteenth Century* (East Lansing, 1988).

Watt, Ian, *The Rise of the Novel: Studies in Defoe, Richardson and Fielding* (London, 1957).

Prose fiction: Germany and the Netherlands

Primary sources and texts, German

Note: for authors and critics mentioned in the text but not here listed separately, consult the anthology entered below under Lämmert.

Birken, Sigmund von, *Teutsche Redebind- und Dichtkunst* (Nürnberg, 1679).

Blanckenburg, Friedrich von, *Versuch über den Roman. Faksimiledruck der Originalausgabe von 1774*, ed. Eberhard Lämmert (Stuttgart, 1965).

Bodmer, Johann Jacob, *Critische Betrachtungen über die Poetischen Gemählde der Dichter* (Orell/Leipzig, 1741).

Breitinger, Johann Jacob, *Critische Dichtkunst. Faksimiledruck nach der Ausgabe von 1740*, ed. W. Bender, Bd. 1 (Stuttgart, 1966).

Engel, Johann Jakob, *Ueber Handlung, Gespräch und Erzählung. Faksimiledruck der ersten Fassung von 1774*, ed. E. T. Voss (Stuttgart, 1964).

Goethe, Johann Wolfgang, *Wilhelm Meisters Lehrjahre* (1795), in *Goethes Werke*, ed. Erich Trunz (14 vols., Hamburg, 1948–64), vol. VII.

[Goethe, Johann Wolfgang], see [Schiller, Friedrich, *Briefwechsel*].

[Goethe, Johann Wolfgang], *Zeitgenössische Rezensionen und Urteile über Goethes 'Götz' und 'Werther'*, ed. H. Blumenthal (Berlin, 1935).

Gottsched, Johann Christoph, *Versuch einer critischen Dichtkunst*, facs. of the 4th edn, 1751 (Darmstatt, 1962).

Heidegger, Gotthard, *Mythoscopia Romantica, oder Discours von den so benanten Romans. Faksimileausgabe nach dem Originaldruck von 1698*, ed. W. E. Schäfer (Bad Homburg/Berlin/Zürich, 1969).

Hermes, Johann Timotheus, *Sophiens Reise von Memmel nach Sachsen* (1770), ed. F. Brüggemann (Leipzig, 1941).

Huet, Pierre Daniel (trans. Eberhard Guerner Happel), *Traité de l'Origine des Romans. Faksimiledrucke nach der Erstausgabe von 1670 und der Happelschen Uebersetzung von 1682*, ed. Hans Hinterhäuser (Stuttgart, 1966).

Kimpel, Dieter, and Conrad Wiedemann (eds.), *Theorie und Technik des Romans im 17. und 18. Jahrhundert. Band I: Barock und Aufklärung* (Tübingen, 1970).

Theorie und Technik des Romans im 17. und 18. Jahrhundert. Band II: Spätaufklärung, Klassik und Frühromantik (Tübingen, 1970).

Lämmert, Eberhard, *et al.* (eds.), *Romantheorie: Dokumentation ihrer Geschichte in Deutschland 1620–1880* (Köln/Berlin, 1971).

[Neumeister, Erdmann], *Raisonnement über die Romane* (n.p., 1708).

[Schiller, Friedrich], *Der Briefwechsel zwischen Schiller und Goethe*, ed. H. G. Graf and A. Leitzmann (Leipzig, 1912).

Weber, Ernst (ed.), *Texte zur Romantheorie, I (1626–1731)* (Munich, 1973).

Texte zur Romantheorie, II (1732–1780) (Munich, 1981).

Wezel, Johann Carl, *Herrmann und Ulrike* (1780), ed. C. G. von Maassen (Munich, 1919).

Wieland, Christoph Martin, *Die Abenteuer des Don Sylvio von Rosalva* (1764), in *Wielands Werke*, ed. G. Hempel (Berlin, 1867–79).

Geschichte des Agathon (1767), ed. K. Schaefer (Berlin, 1961).

Secondary sources, German

Ansorge, Hans Jürgen, *Art und Funktion der Vorrede im Roman 1750–1900* (Würzburg, 1969).

Bing, S., *Die Nachahmungstheorie bei Gottsched und den Schweizern und ihre Beziehungen zu der Dichtungstheorie der Zeit* (Würzburg, 1934).

Clarke, C., *Fielding und der deutschen Sturm und Drang* (Freiburg, 1897).

Ehrenzeller, H., *Studien zur Romanvorrede von Grimmelshausen bis Jean Paul* (Berne, 1955).

Haas, R., *Die Turmgesellschaft in Wilhelm Meisters Lehrjahren: zur Geschichte des Geheimbundromans und der Romantheorie im 18. Jahrhundert* (Berne, 1975).

Jäger, Georg, *Empfindsamkeit und Roman. Wortgeschichte, Theorie und Kritik im 18. und 19. Jahrhundert* (Stuttgart, 1969).

Kimpel, Dieter, *Der Roman der Aufklärung* (Stuttgart, 1967).

Martens, Wolfgang, *Die Botschaft der Tugend: die Aufklärung im Spiegel der deutschen Moralischen Wochenschriften* (Stuttgart, 1968), part V, ch. 7, 'Der Roman', pp. 492–520.

Matthecka, Gerd, *Die Romantheorie Wielands und seiner Vorläufer* (Tübingen, 1956).

Michelsen, Peter, *Laurence Sterne und der deutsche Roman im 18. Jahrhundert* (Göttingen, 1962).

Montandon, Alain, *La Réception de Sterne en Allemagne* (Clermont-Ferrand, 1985).

Preisendanz, Wolfgang, 'Die Auseinandersetzung mit dem Nachahmungsprinzip in Deutschland und die besondere Rolle der Romane Wielands (*Don Sylvio, Agathon*)', in H. R. Jauss (ed.), *Nachahmung und Illusion: Kolloquium Giessen Juni 1963, Vorlagen und Verhandlungen* (Munich, 1964), pp. 72–95, 196–203.

Sang, J., *Friedrich von Blanckenburg und seine Theorie des Romans* (Munich, 1967).

Scherpe, Klaus, *Gattungspoetik im 18. Jahrhundert. Historische Entwicklung von Gottsched bis Herder* (Stuttgart, 1968).

Schmidt, Erich, *Richardson, Rousseau und Goethe. Zur Geschichte des Romans im 18. Jahrhundert* (Jena, 1875).

Vaget, H. Rudolf, 'Johann Heinrich Merck über den Roman', *Publications of the Modern Language Association of America*, 83 (1968), 347–56.

Vosskamp, Wilhelm, *Romantheorie in Deutschland von Martin Opitz bis Friedrich von Blankenburg* (Stuttgart, 1973).

Wahrenburg, Fritz, *Funktionswandel des Romans und ästhetische Norm: Die Entwicklung seiner Theorie in Deutschland bis zur Mitte des 18. Jahrhunderts* (Stuttgart, 1976).

Weber, Ernst, *Die poetologische Selbstreflexion im deutschen Roman des 18. Jahrhunderts: zu Theorie und Praxis von 'Roman', 'Historie' und pragmatischem Roman* (Stuttgart, Berlin, Mainz, 1974).

Winter, Hans-Gerhard, *Dialog und Dialogroman in der Aufklärung, mit einer Analyse von J. J. Engels Gesprächstheorie* (Darmstadt, 1974).

Wölfel, Kurt, 'Friedrich Schlegels Theorie des Romans', in Reinhold Grimm (ed.), *Deutsche Romantheorien: Beiträge zu einer historischen Poetik des Romans in Deutschland* (Frankfurt am Main/Bonn, 1968), pp. 29–60.

Wolff, Max Ludwig, *Geschichte der Romantheorie, mit besonderer Berücksichtigung der deutschen Verhältnisse* (Nürnberg, 1915).

Primary sources and texts, Dutch

Note: for authors and works not fully cited in the text or notes and omitted below consult the 'Bronnenlijst' in Pol, vol. I, pp. 209–24 and Buisman, *Prozaschrijvers*.

Boekzaal, see [Fielding, H.].

[Defoe, Daniel], *Het Leven en de Wonderbaare Gevallen van Robinson Crusoe* (Amsterdam, 1721).

Dielen, A. J. W. van, *De Onderzoeker*, no. 154 (7 Oct. 1777), 393–400.

Engelen, Cornelis van, *Bloemlezing uit het Werk*, ed. N. C. H. Wijngaards (Zutphen, n.d.).

Feith, Rijnvis, *Het Ideaal in de Kunst*, ed. P. J. Buynsters (The Hague, 1979). *Julia* (1783) and *Ferdinand en Constantia* (1785), reprinted by Het Spectrum (Utrecht, 1981).

[Fielding, H.], Anonymous review of *Historie van den Vondeling Tomas Jones*, *De Boekzaal der Geleerde Wereld*, 73 (Sept. 1751), 284–302.

Kloek, J. J., *Over Werther Geschreven...: Nederlandse Reacties op Goethes Werther 1775–1800* (2 vols., Utrecht, 1985), vol. 2: *Bronnen, Literatuurlijst en Register*.

Nieuwland, Petrus, 'Over gevoeligheid van hart', *Nieuw Algemeen Magazyn*, 2 (1794), ii, 519–52.

Onderzoeker, see Dielen, A. J. W. van.

Pol, L. R., *Romanbeschouwing in Voorredes, een Onderzoek naar het Denken over de Roman in Nederland tussen 1600 en 1755* (2 vols., Utrecht, 1987), Vol. II: *Teksten*.

[Richardson, Samuel], Anon, *De Anti-Pamela of de Valsche Eenvoudigheit, Ontdekt in de Gevallen van Syrena Tricksy...* (Amsterdam, 1743). *Pamela Bespiegeld, of... Pamela, of de Beloonde Deugd... Zedelyk Beschouwd* (Amsterdam, 1741).

Slattery, W. C. (ed.), *The Richardson–Stinstra Correspondence and Stinstra's Prefaces to Clarissa*, ed. W. C. Slattery (London/Amsterdam, 1969).

Smeeks, H., *Beschryvinge van het Magtig Koningryk Krinke Kesmes* (1708), ed. P. J. Buijnsters (Zutphen, n.d.).

Wolff-Bekker, E., *De Gevaaren van de Laster; in eene Briefwisseling tusschen Miss Fanny Springler en haare Vrienden* (The Hague, 1791).

Wolff-Bekker, E., and Deken, A., *Historie van Mejuffrouw Cornelia Wildschut; of de Gevolgen van de Opvoeding* (6 vols., The Hague, 1793–6). *Historie van Mejuffrouw Sara Burgerhart* (1782), ed. P. J. Buijnsters (2 vols., The Hague, 1980). *Historie van Willem Leevend* (8 vols., The Hague, 1784–5).

Secondary sources, Dutch

Berg, W. van den, *De Ontwikkeling van de Term 'Romantisch' en zijn Varianten in Nederland tot 1840* (Assen, 1973).

'Sara Burgerhart en haar derde stem', *Documentatieblad Werkgroep 18e Eeuw*, no. 51/52 (Sept. 1981), 151–207.

Boheemen-Saaf, C. van, 'Fielding and Richardson in Holland: 1740–1800', *Dutch Quarterly Review of Anglo-American Letters*, 14 (1984), 293–307.

'The reception of English literature in Dutch magazines, 1735–85', in J. A. van Dorsten (ed.), *The Role of Periodicals in the 18th Century* (Leiden, 1984).

Buijnsters, P. J., 'Kort geding om *Sara Burgerhart*', *Documentatieblad Werkgroep 18e Eeuw*, 14 (1982), 163–78.

'*Sara Burgerhart* en de ontwikkeling van de Nederlandse roman in de 18e eeuw', in Buijnsters, *Nederlandse Literatuur van de 18e Eeuw* (Utrecht, 1984), pp. 199–222.

Buisman, M., *Populaire Prozaschrijvers van 1600 tot 1815 . . . Alphabetische Naamlijst* (Amsterdam, n.d.).

Buisman-De Savornin Lohman, F. L. W. M., *Laurence Sterne en de Nederlandse Schrijvers van c.1780–c.1840* (Wageningen, 1939).

Kloek, J. J., 'Lezen als levensbehoefte; roman en romanpubliek in de tweede helft van de 18e eeuw', *Literatuur*, 1 (1984) 136–42.

'Meten met twee maten? Johannes Lublink als verdediger van *Werther* en van *Grandison*', *De Nieuwe Taalgids*, 80 (1987), 335–49.

Over Werther Geschreven . . . : Nederlandse Reacties op Goethes Werther 1775–1800 (2 vols., Utrecht, 1985), vol. 1: *Het Onderzoek*.

Mattheij, Th. M. M., *et al.*, 'De ontvangst van Richardson in Nederland (1750–1800)', *Spektator*, 8 (1978/9), 142–57.

'Richardson in Nederland; een bibliografie', *Documentatieblad Werkgroep 18e Eeuw*, no. 40 (Sept. 1978), 19–70.

Nieuweboer, A., 'De populariteit van het vertaalde verhalend proza in 18e-eeuws Nederland en de rol van de boekhandel bij de praktijk van het vertalen', *Documentatieblad Werkgroep 18e Eeuw*, 53/4 (1982), 119–41.

Pol, L. R., *Romanbeschouwing in Voorredes, een Onderzoek naar het Denken over de Roman in Nederland tussen 1600 en 1755* (2 vols., Utrecht, 1987), Vol. I: *Onderzoek*.

Russell, J. A., *Romance and Realism, Trends in Belgo-Dutch Prose Literature* (Amsterdam, 1959).

Slattery, W. C., 'Samuel Richardson and The Netherlands: early reception of his work', *Papers on English Language and Literature*, 1 (1965), 20–30.

Staverman, W. H., *Robinson Crusoe in Nederland, een Bijdrage tot de Geschiedenis van den Roman in de XVIIIe Eeuw* (Groningen, 1907).

Toorn, M. C. van den, 'Sentimentaliteit als grootheid in de literaire terminologie', *De Nieuwe Taalgids*, 57 (1964), 260–71.

Vliet, P. van der, *Wolff en Deken's Brieven van Abraham Blankaart* (Utrecht, 1982).

Voogd, P. J. de, 'Henry Fielding's novels in Dutch', *Dutch Quarterly Review of Anglo-American Letters*, 13 (1983), 179–83.

'Pieter Le Clercq's *Tom Jones*-vertaling', *Documentatieblad Werkgroep 18e Eeuw*, 43 (June 1979), 3–10.

Zwaneveld, A. M., '*De Opmerker/Onderzoeker* als geestverwant van Rijklof Michael van Goens', *Documentatieblad Werkgroep 18e Eeuw*, 18 (1986), 51–64.

Historiography

Primary sources and texts

Alembert, Jean Le Rond d', *Réflexions sur l'Histoire,* in *Oeuvres* (Paris, 1805), IV, p. 195.

Barante, Prosper de, 'De l'Histoire', *Mélanges historiques et littéraires* (Brussels, 1835), II, p. 148.

Bayle, Pierre, *Dictionnaire historique et critique* (Amsterdam, 1697).

Blair, Hugh, *Lectures on Rhetoric and Belles-Lettres* (London, 1783).

Clarendon, Edward Hyde, First Earl of, *History of My Own Time* (London, 1759).

Fontenelle, Bernard le Bovier de, *Oeuvres* (Paris, 1767).
De l'Origine des Fables, ed. Carré (Paris, 1932).

Gibbon, Edward, *Essai sur l'Etude de la Littérature, Miscellaneous Works* (London, 1814), vol. IV, pp. 1–93.
Memoirs of my Life, ed. Bonnard (London, 1956).
The History of the Decline and Fall of the Roman Empire (7 vols., London, 1896–1900).

Herder, Johann Gottfried, *Sämtliche Werke,* ed. B. Suphan (Berlin, 1877–1913).

Hume, David, *Letters,* ed. J. Y. T. Greig (2 vols., Oxford, 1932).
New Letters of David Hume, ed. R. Klibansky and E. C. Mossner (Oxford, 1954).

Lafitau, Jean-François, *Moeurs des Sauvages amériquains* (Paris, 1724).

Le Moyne, Pierre, *De l'Histoire* (Paris, 1670).

Montesquieu, de Secondat, Charles, Baron de la Brède et de, *Oeuvres complètes,* Edition de la Pléiade (Paris, 1956–8).

Robertson, William, *Works* (London, 1827).

Saint-Évremond, Charles de Marguetel de Saint Denys de, *Oeuvres en Prose,* ed. Ternois (Paris, 1962–6).

Smith, Adam, *Lectures on Rhetoric and Belles-Lettres,* ed. J. M. Lothian (London, 1963).

Tillemont, S. Lenain de, *Histoire des Empereurs* (Paris, 1697).

Vico, Giambattista, *Opere,* ed. G. Gentile and F. Nicolini (Bari, 1911–14).

Voltaire (François-Marie Arouet), *Correspondance,* ed. Theodore Besterman (Geneva, 1953–65).
Oeuvres historiques, ed. René Pomeau (Paris, 1957).

Secondary sources

Baridon, Michel, *Gibbon et le Mythe de Rome* (Paris, 1977), pp. 731–826 (on Gibbon's style).

Barthes, Roland, 'Le Discours de l'Histoire', *Informations sur les Sciences sociales,* 6, N°4 (1967), 74.

Becker, Karl L., *The Heavenly City of the Eighteenth-Century Philosophers* (New Haven, 1974).

Bond, Harold L., *The Literary Art of Edward Gibbon* (Oxford, 1960).

Braudy, Leo, *Narrative Form in History and Fiction* (Princeton, 1970).

Brumfitt, J. H., *Voltaire, Historian* (London, 1958).

Canary, Robert H., and Henry Kozicki (eds.), *The Writing of History. Literary Form and Historical Understanding* (Madison WI, 1978).

Clark, Robert T., *Herder, his Life and Thought* (Berkeley and Los Angeles, 1955).

Damon, P., ed., *Literary Criticism and Historical Understanding* (New York, 1967).

Duchet, Michel, 'Discours ethnologique et discours historique: le texte de Lafitau', *Studies on Voltaire and the 18th Century*, 152 (1976), 607–23.

Furet F., and Mona Ozouf, *Lire et Ecrire, L'Alphabétisation des Français de Calvin à Jules Ferry* (Paris, 1977).

Gossman, Lionel, *Medievalism and the Ideologies of the Enlightenment* (Baltimore, 1968).

'History and literature. Reproduction or Signification', in Canary and Kozicki (see above), pp. 13–37.

Gransden, Antonia, *Historical Writing in England* (Ithaca, 1982).

Iggers, George D., *The German Conception of History* (Wesleyan University Press, 1968).

Jogland, H. H., *Ursprünge und Grundlagen der Soziologie bei Adam Ferguson* (Berlin, 1959).

Levine, Joseph M., *Humanism and History, Origins of Modern English Historiography* (Ithaca, 1987).

Louch, A. R., 'History as narrative', *History and Theory*, 8 (1969), 54–70.

Mandelbaum, M., 'A note on history as narrative', *History and Theory*, 6 (1967).

Manuel, Frank E., *The Eighteenth Century Confronts the Gods* (London, 1959).

Martin, Henri-Jean, *Livres, pouvoirs et société au XVIIe siècle* (Geneva, 1967).

Meinecke, Friedrich, *Historism, the Rise of a New Historical Outlook*, trans. J. E. Anderson (London, 1972).

Mink, Louis, 'Narrative form as cognitive instrument', in Canary and Kozicki (eds.), *The Writing of History* (see above).

Pascal, Roy, 'Herder and the Scottish Historical School', *Publications of the English Goethe Society*, new series, 14 (1939), 23–42.

Peardon, T. P., *The Transition in English Historical Writing* (London, 1933).

Pocock, J. G. A., *The Machiavellian Moment* (Princeton, 1975).

Politics, Language and Time (New York, 1971).

Ranum, Orest, *Artisans of Glory. Writers and Historical Thought in Seventeenth-Century France* (Chapel Hill NC, 1980).

Skinner, Quentin, 'Economics and history – The Scottish Enlightenment', *Scottish Journal of Political Economy*, 12 (1965).

Snoeks, R., *L'Argument de tradition dans la Controverse eucharistique entre Catholiques et Réformés français au XVIe siècle* (Gembloux, 1961).

Struever, Nancy S., *The Language of History in the Renaissance* (Princeton, 1970).

Tapié, V. L., *Baroque et Classicisme* (Paris, 1972).

Thompson, James W., *A History of Historical Writing* (New York [1942], 1958).

Tillyard, E. M. W., *The English Epic and its Background* (Oxford, 1966).
Trevor-Roper, Hugh, 'The historical philosophy of the Enlightenment', *Studies on Voltaire and the Eighteenth Century*, 27 (1963), 1,667–87.
Veyne, Paul, *Comment on écrit l'Histoire: Essai d'Epistémologie* (Paris, 1971).
Waszek, Norbert, *Man's Social Nature: A Topic of the Scottish Enlightenment in its Historical Setting* (Berne and New York, 1986).
Williams, David, 'Voltaire's literary criticism', *Studies on Voltaire and the Eighteenth Century*, 48 (1966).

Biography and autobiography

Primary sources and texts

Abbt, Thomas, '161. Literaturbrief', in C. F. Nicolai (ed.), *Briefe, die neueste Literatur betreffend* (Berlin, 1768).
Addison, Joseph, *The Freeholder*, No. 35 (20 April 1716), ed. James Leheny (Oxford, 1979), pp. 193–6.
Annual Register; or, a View of the History, Politicks, and Literature for the Year 1791, vol. I (London, 1792), 475.
Aubrey, John, Letter to Anthony à Wood (15 June 1680), in Andrew Clark (ed.), *Aubrey's Brief Lives*, vol. I (London, 1898), pp. 10–11.
Ballard, George, *Memoirs of Several Ladies of Great Britain Who Have Been Celebrated for their Writings or Skill in the Learned Languages, Arts and Sciences* (London, 1755), rpt in Ruth Perry, ed. (Detroit, 1985).
Biographie universelle ancienne et moderne (52 vols., Paris, 1811–28, and 29 supplementary volumes, 1834–54).
Biographium Faemineum. The Female Worthies: or, Memoirs of the Most Illustrious Ladies of All Ages and Nations (2 vols., London, 1766).
Boswell, James, *Letters of James Boswell*, ed. Chauncey Brewster Tinker (2 vols., Oxford, 1924).
  The Life of Samuel Johnson, LL.D. (London, 1791), ed. George Birkbeck Hill and rev. by L. F. Powell (6 vols., Oxford, 1934–64).
  'On Diaries' [*Hypochondriack* No. 66], *The London Magazine* (March 1783), rpt in Margery Bailey (ed.), *Boswell's Column* (London, 1951).
  'On Imitation' [*Hypochondriack* No. 35], *The London Magazine* (August 1780), rpt in Margery Bailey (ed.), *Boswell's Column* (London, 1951).
Burnet, Gilbert, Preface to *The Life and Death of Sir Matthew Hale, Knight* (London, 1682).
  Preface to *The Memoires of the Lives and Actions of James and William, Dukes of Hamilton and Castleherald, & c.* (London, 1677).
Burney, Charles, *Monthly Review*, 74 (May 1786), 373–4.
Cowley, Abraham, 'Of my self', in *The Works of Abraham Cowley*, ed. Thomas Sprat (5 pts., London, 1668).
D'Israeli, Isaac, *Curiosities of Literature Consisting of Anecdotes, Characters, Sketches and Dissertations* (London, 1791).
  A Dissertation on Anecdotes; by the Author of Curiosities of Literature (London, 1793).

'Some Observations on Diaries, Self-biography, and Self-characters', in *Miscellanies; or, Literary Recreations* (London, 1796), pp. 95–110.

Dryden, John, 'The Life of Plutarch', Preface to *Plutarch's Lives, Translated from the Greek by Several Hands* (1683–6), in Earl Miner, Vinton A. Dearing and George Robert Guffey (eds.), *An Essay of Dramatic Poesy and Shorter Works*, in *Works* (20 vols., Berkeley, 1955–), XVII, pp. 226–88.

Forbes, Sir William, *Life of Beattie* (London, 1806), II, p. 184.

Gally, Henry, 'A Critical Essay on Characteristick Writings', in *The Moral Characters of Theophrastus, translated ... by H.G.* (London, 1725).

Goethe, Johann Wolfgang, *Dichtung und Wahrheit*, ed. Karl Richter and others, *Sämtliche Werke* (24 vols., Munich, 1985), vol. XVI.

Goldsmith, Oliver, Preface to *Plutarch's Lives*, in Arthur Friedman (ed.), *The Works of Oliver Goldsmith*, V, pp. 226–8.

Granger, James, Preface to *A Biographical History of England from Egbert the Great to the Revolution: Consisting of Characters disposed in different Classes, and adapted to a Methodical Catalogue of Engraved British Heads intended as an Essay towards reducing our Biography to System, and a Help to the Knowledge of Portraits* (3 vols., London, 1769–74).

Herder, Johann Gottfried, '5. Humanitätsbrief' (1793), in *Sämtliche Werke*, ed. Bernhard Suphan (33 vols., Berlin, 1877–1913), XVII, pp. 19–25.

Haben wir noch jetzt das Publikum und Vaterland der Alten? (1765), *Sämtliche Werke*, ed. Bernhard Suphan (33 vols., Berlin, 1877–1913), XVII, pp. 284–319.

Preface to *Ueber Thomas Abbts Schriften* (1768), in *Sämtliche Werke*, ed. Bernhard Suphan (33 vols., Berlin, 1877–1913), II, p. 250–57.

Houstoun, William, *Dr Houstoun's Memoirs of His Own Life-Time* (London, 1747).

Johnson, Samuel, *Idler* Nos. 84 (24 November 1759) and 102 (29 March 1760), in W. J. Bate, John M. Bullitt and L. F. Powell (eds.), *The Yale Edition of the Works of Samuel Johnson*, vol. 2 (New Haven, 1963–71).

Lives of the English Poets, ed. George Birkbeck Hill (3 vols., Oxford, 1905).

Rambler No. 60 (13 October 1750), in W. J. Bate and Albrecht Strauss (eds.), *The Yale Edition of the Works of Samuel Johnson* (11 vols., New Haven, 1963–71), vol. III.

Knox, Vicesimus, 'Cursory thoughts on biography', in *Essays Moral and Literary* (London, 1782), II, pp. 48–52.

Winter Evenings; or, Lucubrations on Life and Letters, 2nd edn (2 vols., London, 1790).

'L', 'Memoirs of the Life and Writings of Dr. Samuel Johnson', *Universal Magazine*, 75 (August 1784), 89–97.

Lessing, Gotthold Ephraim, [Review of d'Espiard's *Esprit des Nations*] (1753) in *Sämtliche Schriften*, ed. Karl Lachmann and Franz Muncker (23 vols., Stuttgart, 1886–1924), V, pp. 143–5.

The Life of That Reverend Divine, and Learned Historian, Dr Thomas Fuller (London, 1661).

Mallet, David, *The Life of Francis Bacon, Lord Chancellor of England* (London, 1740).

Martyn, Thomas (ed.), Preface to *Dissertations and Critical Remarks upon the Aeneid of Virgil* (London, 1770).

Mason, William, *Memoirs of the Life and Writings of Mr Gray* (London, 1755), II, p. 40.

Middleton, Conyers, Preface to *The Life and Letters of Marcus Tullius Cicero* (London, 1741).

Niceron, Jean Pierre, Preface to *Mémoires pour servir à l'histoire des hommes illustres dans la république des lettres* (43 vols., Paris, 1729–45).

North, Roger, General Preface to *Life of Dr John North* (St John's College, Cambridge, MS James, No. 613), ed. Peter Millard, *General Preface and Life of Dr John North* (Toronto, 1984).

 Lives of the Right Hon. Francis North, Baron Guilford ... The Hon. Sir Dudley North ... and The Hon. and Rev. Dr. John North (3 vols., London, 1826).

'On Biography', *The Ladies Magazine*, 18 (August, 1787), p. 425.

Public Characters, or Contemporary Biography (London, 1803).

[Review of *Anecdotes of the Late Samuel Johnson, LL.D.*], *The English Review*, 7 (April 1786), 254.

[Review of *Anecdotes of the Late Samuel Johnson, LL.D.*], *Monthly Review*, 64 (May 1786), 373–4.

[Review of *Anecdotes of the Late Samuel Johnson, LL.D.*], *New Annual Register for 1786* (1797), p. 263.

[Review of *General Biography*], *Monthly Review*, n.s. 30 (November 1799), 241–52.

[Review of *Memoirs of the Life and Writings of Percival Stockdale Written by himself*], *Quarterly Review*, 1 (May, 1809), 386.

[Review of *Memoirs of the Life of Peter Daniel Huet*], *Quarterly Review*, 4 (August, 1810), 104.

[Review of *Transactions of the Royal Society of Edinburgh*], *Monthly Review*, ser. 2 (Jan. 1800), 2.

Rousseau, Jean-Jacques, *Les Confessions* (1782), in *Oeuvres Complètes*, Bibliothèque de la Pléiade (5 vols., Paris, 1959–95), I.

 'La première rédaction des *Confessions* (Livres I–IV)', in *Annales de la Société Jean-Jacques Rousseau*, ed. Théophile Dufour (39 vols, Geneva, 1908–77), IV, p. 3.

Ruffhead, Owen [Review of Jortin's life of Erasmus], *Monthly Review*, 19 (October 1758), 385–99.

Schubart, Christian Friedrich Daniel, *Leben und Gesinnungen* (1791), I, p. 120.

Sprat, Thomas, 'An Account of the life and writings of Mr. Abraham Cowley', addressed to Martin Clifford, in *The Works of Abraham Cowley* (5 pts., London, 1668).

Stanfield, James, *Essay on the Study and Composition of Biography* (London, 1813).

[Taylor, William], *Monthly Review*, 2nd series, 29 (1797), 375.

Toland, John, *The Life of John Milton* (London, 1698), Prefatory letter, rpt in *The Early Lives of Milton*, ed. Helen Darbishire (London, 1932), pp. 83–5.

Wakefield, Gilbert, *Memoirs of the Life of Gilbert Wakefield* (London, 1792), p. 6.

[Warton, Thomas], *Idler* No. 33 (2 December 1758), in W. J. Bate, John M. Bullitt and L. F. Powell (eds.), *The Yale Edition of the Works of Samuel Johnson* (11 vols., New Haven, 1963–71).

Whyte, Samuel, *Miscellanea Nova; Containing, Amidst A Variety of Other Matters Curious and Interesting, Remarks on Boswell's Johnson* (Dublin, 1800), pp. vi–vii.

Secondary sources

Browning, J. D. (ed.), *Biography in the Eighteenth Century* (New York, 1980).

Clifford, James, 'Roger North and the Art of Biography', in C. Camden (ed.), *Restoration and Eighteenth-Century Literature: Essays in Honor of Alan D. McKillop* (Chicago, 1963), pp. 275–81.

Clifford, James L. (ed.), *Biography as an Art, Selected Criticism 1560–1960* (New York, 1962).

Daghlian, Philip B. (ed.), *Essays in Eighteenth-Century Biography* (Bloomington, 1968).

May, Georges, 'Biography, autobiography, and the novel in eighteenth-century France', in *Biography in the 18th Century*, ed. J. D. Browning. Publications of the McMaster University Association for 18th-C. Studies (New York and London, 1980), pp. 147–64.

Nussbaum, Felicity A., *The Autobiographical Subject: Gender and Ideology in Eighteenth-Century England* (Baltimore, 1989).

Scheuer, Helmut, *Biographie* (Stuttgart, 1979).

Starobinski, Jean, *Jean-Jacques Rousseau: Transparency and Obstruction*, trans. Arthur Goldhammer, intro. Robert J. Morrisey (Chicago, 1971).

Stauffer, Donald Alfred, *English Biography before 1700* (Cambridge MA, 1930). *The Art of Biography in Eighteenth-Century England* (2 vols., Princeton, 1941).

Criticism and the rise of periodical literature

Primary sources

Acta eruditorum (Leipzig, 1682–1745).

Allgemeine deutsche Bibliothek (Berlin, 1765–1805).

Allgemeine Literatur-Zeitung (Jena and Leipzig, 1785–1803).

Analytical Review (London, 1788–99).

Année littéraire (Amsterdam, 1754–90).

Bibliothèque germanique (Berlin, 1720–40).

Bibliothèque italique (Geneva, 1728–34).

Bibliothèque raisonnée des ouvrages des savants de l'Europe (Amsterdam, 1728–53).

Bibliothèque universelle des romans (1715–89).

British Magazine (London, 1760–7).

Connoisseur (London, 1754–6).

Le Courrier de l'Europe (London and Boulogne, 1776–92).
Covent-Garden Journal (London, 1752).
Critical Review (London, 1756–1817).
English Review (London, 1784–96).
L'Esprit des journaux français et étrangers (Liège, 1772–1818).
Female Spectator (London, 1744–6).
France littéraire (Paris, 1754–84).
Gazette, later *Gazette de France* (Paris, 1631–1792).
General Magazine and Impartial Review (London, 1787–92).
Gentleman's Magazine (London, 1731–1907).
Giornale de' letterati (Florence, 1668–?).
Göttingische Anzeigen von gelehrten Sachen (Göttingen, 1739–52).
Guardian (1713).
Hibernian Magazine (Dublin, 1771–1811).
History of the Works of the Learned (London, 1737–43).
Idler (London, 1758–60).
Journal des dames (1759–78).
Journal des savants (Paris, 1665–1792).
Journal encyclopédique (Paris, 1756–93).
Journal étranger (Paris, 1754–62).
Journal historique et littéraire (Luxembourg, 1773–94).
Journal littéraire (The Hague, 1713–22 and 1729–36).
Ladies Magazine, or, the Universal Entertainer (London, 1749–53).
Lady's Magazine (London, 1770–1819).
Literary Magazine, or Universal Register (London, 1756–8).
London Magazine (London, 1732–85).
Mémoires pour servir à l'histoire des sciences et des arts (Trevoux and Paris, 1701–67).
Memoirs of Literature (London, 1710–17).
Mercure galant, later *Mercure de France* (Paris, 1672–1791).
Monthly Review (London, 1749–1844).
Nouvelles de la République des Lettres (Amsterdam, 1684–9).
Observations sur les écrits modernes (Paris, 1735–43).
Philosophical Transactions of the Royal Society (London, 1665–).
Present State of the Republick of Letters (London, 1728–36).
Rambler (London, 1750–2).
Review of the Affairs of France, later *Review of the State of the English Nation* (London, 1704–13).
Scots Magazine (Edinburgh, 1739–1817).
Spectator (London, 1711–15).
Tatler (London, 1709–11).
Teutsche Merkur, later *Neue Teutsche Merkur* (Weimar, 1773–1810).

Secondary sources

Adburgham, Alison, *Women in Print: Writing Women and Women's Magazines from the Restoration to the Accession of Victoria* (London, 1972).

American Periodicals: A Journal of History, Criticism, and Bibliography, ed. James T. F. Tanner (Denton TX, 1991–).

Basker, James G., *Tobias Smollett, Critic and Journalist* (Newark DE, 1988).

Bedarida, H., 'Voltaire, collaborateur de la *Gazette littéraire de l'Europe*', *Mélanges Baldensperger* (Paris, 1930), I, pp. 24–38.

Bellanger, Claude *et al.* (eds.), *Histoire générale de la presse française*, I, *Des Origines à 1814* (Paris, 1969).

Benhamou, Paul, *Index des jugements sur les ouvrages nouveaux 1744–1746 de Pierre-François Guyot Desfontaines* (Geneva, 1986).

'The periodical press in the *Encyclopédie*', *The French Review*, 59, 3 (February 1986), 410–17.

Birn, Raymond, 'The French-language press and the *Encyclopédie*, 1750–1759', *Studies on Voltaire and the Eighteenth Century*, 55 (1967), 263–86.

Black, Jeremy, *The English Press in the Eighteenth Century* (Philadelphia, 1987).

Blaser, Fritz, *Bibliographie der Schweizer Presse, mit Einschluss des Fürstentums Liechtenstein* (2 vols., Basel, 1956–8).

Bloom, Edward A., ' "Labors of the learned": neoclassic book reviewing aims and techniques', *Studies in Philology*, 54 (1957), 537–63.

Bond, R. P., *Growth and Change in the Early English Press* (Lawrence, 1969).

Bond, R. P. (ed.), *Studies in the Early English Periodical* (Chapel Hill, 1957).

Bond, D. H., and W. R. McLeod (eds.), *Newsletters to Newspapers: Eighteenth-Century Journalism* (Morgantown, 1977).

Botein, S., J. Censor and H. Ritvo, 'The periodical press in eighteenth-century English and French society: a cross-cultural approach', *Comparative Studies in Society and History*, 23 (1981), 464–90.

Brandes, Helga, *Die 'Gesellschaft der Maler' und ihr literarischer Beitrag zur Aufklärung: Eine Untersuchung zur Publizistik des 18. Jahrhunderts.* Studien zur Publizistik. Bremer Reihe – Deutsche Presseforschung, herausgegeben von Elger Bluhm, 22 (Bremen, 1974).

Carlsson, Anni, *Die deutsche Buchkritik von der Reformation bis zur Gegenwart* (Bern, 1969).

Catalogue collectif des périodiques français (Paris: Bibliothèque Nationale, 1978).

Couperus, M. C., *Un Périodique Français en Hollande: Le Glaneur historique 1731–1733* (The Hague, 1971).

Crane, R. S., and F. B. Kaye., *A Census of British Newspapers and Periodicals, 1620–1800* (Chapel Hill, 1927).

Cranfield, G. A., *The Development of the Provincial Newspaper, 1700–1760* (Oxford, 1962).

Darnton, Robert, *The Business of Enlightenment: A Publishing History of the Encyclopédie 1775–1800* (Cambridge MA, 1979).

'The facts of literary life in eighteenth-century France', in *The French Revolution and the Creation of Modern Political Culture* (Oxford, 1987), I, pp. 261–91.

Dehergne, J., 'Une Table des matières de *l'Année littéraire*', *Revue d'Histoire littéraire* (1965), 269–73.

Engell, James, *Forming the Critical Mind: Dryden to Coleridge* (Cambridge MA, 1989).

Fabian, Bernhard, 'English books and their eighteenth-century German readers', in *The Widening Circle: Essays on the Circulation of Literature in Eighteenth-Century Europe*, ed. Paul J. Korshin (Philadelphia, 1976), pp. 117–96.

Fischer, Heinz-Dietrich, *Deutsche Zeitschriften des 17. bis 20. Jahrhunderts* (Munich, 1973).

Forster, Antonia, *Index to Book Reviews in England 1749–1774* (Carbondale IL and Edwardsville, 1990).

Graham, Walter, *The Beginnings of English Literary Periodicals: A Study of Periodical Literature, 1665–1715* (New York, 1926).

English Literary Periodicals (New York, 1930).

Grappin, Pierre, 'Le Groupe de recherches de Metz sur les périodiques de langue allemande au XVIIIième siècle', *Aufklärungen: Frankreich und Deutschland im 18. Jahrhundert*, ed. Gerhard Sauder and Jochen Schlobach (Heidelberg, 1985), I, pp. 235–42.

Hatin, Eugène, *Bibliographie historique et critique de la presse périodique française* (Paris, 1866).

Janssens, Uta, *Matthieu Maty and the Journal britannique 1750–1755* (Amsterdam, 1975).

Journal of Newspaper and Periodical History, ed. Michael Harris and Jeremy Black (London, 1985–).

Kaminski, Thomas, *The Early Career of Samuel Johnson* (New York, 1987).

Kernan, Alvin, *Printing Technology, Letters, and Samuel Johnson* (Princeton, 1987).

Kirchner, Joachim, 'Die Bibliographie der deutschen Zeitschriften bis zur französischen Revolution', *Die Grundlagen des deutschen Zeitschriftenwesens* (Leipzig, 1931).

Bibliographie der Zeitschriften des deutschen Sprachgebiets von den Anfängen bis 1830 (Stuttgart, 1969).

Das deutsche Zeitschriftenwesen: seine Geschichte und seine Probleme: Teil I: Von den Anfängen bis zum Zeitalter der Romantik, 2nd edn (Wiesbaden, 1958).

Kribbs, Jayne, K. (ed.), *An Annotated Bibliography of American Literary Periodicals, 1741–1850* (Boston, 1977).

Martens, Wolfgang, *Die Botschaft der Tugend. Die Aufklärung im Spiegel der deutschen moralischen Wochenschriften* (Stuttgart, 1968).

Martynov, I. F., 'English literature and eighteenth-century Russian reviewers', *Oxford Slavonic Papers*, n.s. 4 (1971), 30–42.

Milford, R. T., and O. M. Sutherland, *A Catalogue of English Newspapers and Periodicals in the Bodleian Library, 1662–1800* (Oxford, 1936).

Mitton, Fernand, *La Presse française*, I: *Des Origines à la Révolution* (Paris, 1943).

Morgan, Bayard Quincy, and A. R. Hohlfeld, *German Literature in British Magazines, 1750–1860* (Madison, 1949).

Mott, Frank Luther, *A History of American Magazines, 1741–1850* (New York, 1930).

Moureau, François, 'La Presse allemande de langue française (1686–1790): Étude statistique et thématique', *Aufklärungen: Frankreich und Deutschland im 18. Jahrundert*, ed. Gerhard Sauder and Jochen Schlobach (Heidelberg, 1985), I, pp. 243–50.

New Cambridge Bibliography of English Literature, ed. George Watson (Cambridge, 1971), II (1660–1800), pp. 1,035–389.

Oppermann, Heinrich Albert, *Die Göttinger gelehrten Anzeigen während einer hundertjährigen Wirksamkeit für Philosophie, schöne Literatur, Politik und Geschichte* (Hanover, 1844).

Paulson, Ronald, and Thomas Lockwood (eds.), *Henry Fielding: The Critical Heritage* (London, 1969).

Reesink, H. J., *L'Angleterre et la littérature anglaise dans les trois plus anciens périodiques français de Hollande, de 1684 à 1709* (Paris, 1931).

Rétat, Pierre (ed.), *Le Journalisme d'ancien régime: questions et propositions* (Lyons, 1983).

Richardson, Lyon N., *A History of Early American Magazines 1741–1789* (New York, 1931).

Roper, Derek, *Reviewing Before the 'Edinburgh' 1788–1802* (Newark DE, 1978).

Ross, Angus (ed.), *Selections from The Tatler and The Spectator of Steele and Addison* (London, 1982).

Saisselin, Remy, *The Literary Enterprise in 18th-Century France* (Detroit, 1979).

Schlobach, Jochen, 'Literarische Korrespondenzen', in *Aufklärungen: Frankreich und Deutschland im 18. Jahrhundert*, ed. Gerhard Sauder and Jochen Schlobach (Heidelberg, 1985), I, pp. 221–32.

Sgard, Jean, *Histoire de France à tràvers les journaux du temps passé: lumières et lueurs du XVIIIᵉ s. 1715–1789* (Paris, 1986).

Sgard, Jean (ed.), *Bibliographie de la presse classique (1600–1789)* (Geneva, 1984).

Dictionnaire des journalistes (1600–1789) (Grenoble, 1976) and Supplements I–V (1980–87).

Dictionnaire des journaux (2 vols., Paris and Oxford, 1991).

Shevelow, Kathryn, *Women and Print Culture: Constructing Femininity in the Early Periodical* (London, 1989).

Sollors, Werner, 'Immigrants and other Americans', in *Columbia Literary History of the United States*, ed. Emory Elliott *et al.* (New York, 1988), pp. 568–88.

Spector, Robert D., *English Literary Periodicals and the Climate of Opinion during the Seven Years' War* (The Hague, 1966).

Sullerot, Evelyne, *Histoire de la presse féminine des origines à 1848* (Paris, 1966).

Sullivan, Alvin (ed.), *British Literary Magazines*, I, *The Augustan Age and the Age of Johnson, 1698–1788*, and II, *The Romantic Age, 1789–1836* (Westport CT, 1983).

Weinreb, Ruth Plaut, 'Madame d'Épinay's Contributions to the *Correspondance littéraire*', *Studies in Eighteenth-Century Culture*, 18 (1988), 389–403.

White, Robert B., Jr, *The English Literary Journal to 1900: A Guide to Information Sources* (Detroit, 1977).

Wiles, R. M., *Freshest Advices: Early Provincial Newspapers in England* (Columbus OH, 1965).

Wilke, Jürgen, *Literarische Zeitschriften des 18. Jahrhunderts (1688–1789)* (2 vols., Stuttgart, 1978).

Theories of language

Primary sources and texts

Astle, Thomas, *The Origin and Progress of Writing* (London, 1784).
Beattie, James, *The Theory of Language* (London, 1788).
Bergier, Nicolas, *Les élémens primitifs des langues* (Paris, 1764).
Berkeley, George, *Alciphron; or the Minute Philosopher* (London, 1732).
   A Treatise concerning the Principles of Human Knowledge (London, 1710).
   Works, ed. A. A. Luce and T. E. Jessop (9 vols., London, 1948–57).
Blair, Hugh, *Lectures on Rhetoric and Belles Lettres* (3 vols., 2nd edn, London, 1785; rpt New York, 1970).
Brosses, Charles de, *Traité de la formation méchanique des langues* (Paris, 1765).
Burke, Edmund, *A Philosophical Enquiry into the Origin of our Ideas of the Sublime and Beautiful* (London, 1757).
Condillac, Etienne Bonnot, de, *Essai sur l'origine des connoissances humaines* (1746), trans. Thomas Nugent (London, 1756; rpt Gainesville, 1971).
   La Logique (Paris, 1780).
   Philosophical Writings, trans. Franklin Philip and Harlan Lane (2 vols., Hillsdale and London, 1982).
Davy, Charles, *Conjectural Observations on the Origin and Progress of Alphabetical Writing* (London, 1772).
Degérando, Joseph Marie, *Des signes et l'art de penser considérés dans leurs rapports mutuels* (4 vols., Paris, 1800).
Diderot, Denis, *Lettre sur les sourds et muets* (Paris, 1751).
Du Bos, Jean-Baptiste, *Critical Reflections on Poetry, Painting, and Music* (1719), trans. Thomas Nugent (5th edn, London, 1748; rpt New York, 1978).
Gébelin, Antoine Court de, *Origine du langage et de l'écriture*, in *Monde primitif, analysé et comparé avec le monde moderne* (9 vols., 2nd edn, Paris, 1777–93), III.
Girard, Gabriel, *Les vrais principes de la langue françoise* (Paris, 1747; rpt Geneva, 1982).
Harris, James, *Hermes; or, a Philosophical Inquiry concerning Language and Universal Grammar* (London, 1751).
Herder, Johann Gottfried, *Abhandlung über den Ursprung der Sprache* (1772), trans. John H. Moran, in John H. Moran and Alexander Gode (eds.), *On the Origin of Language* (Chicago and London, 1966).
   J. G. Herder on Social and Political Culture, ed. and trans. F. M. Barnard (Cambridge, 1969).
Johnson, Samuel, *A Dictionary of the English Language* (London, 1755).
Jones, Rowland, *Hieroglyfic: or a Grammatical Introduction to an Universal Hieroglyfic Language* (London, 1769).

Kames, Henry Home, Lord, *Elements of Criticism* (3 vols., Edinburgh, 1762; rpt New York, 1967).

Leibniz, Wilhelm Gottfried von, *New Essays on Human Understanding* (written *c.* 1703–5; published 1765), trans. Peter Remnant and Jonathan Bennett (Cambridge, 1981).

Locke, John, *An Essay concerning Human Understanding* (1690), ed. Peter H. Nidditch (Oxford, 1975).

Maupertuis, Pierre Louis Moreau de, *Réflexions philosophiques sur l'origine des langues* (1748), in Ronald Grimsby (ed.), *Sur l'origine du language* (Geneva, 1971).

Michaëlis, Johann David, *Beantwortung der Frage vom dem Einfluss der Meinungen in die Sprache und der Sprache in die Meinungen* (Berlin, 1760).

Monboddo, James Burnet, Lord, *Of the Origin and Progress of Language* (Edinburgh, 1773–94; rpt New York, 1973).

Nelme, R. D., *An Essay towards an Investigation of the Origin and Elements of Language and Letters* (London, 1772).

Rapin, René, *Reflections on Aristotle's Treatise of Poesie* (London, 1674).

Reid, Thomas, *An Inquiry into the Human Mind and the Principles of Common Sense* (1764), in *Works*, ed. Sir William Hamilton (Edinburgh, 1863).

Richardson, Jonathan, *Essay on the Theory of Painting* (1715), in *Works* (London, 1792).

Rousseau, Jean-Jacques, *Discours sur l'origine et les fondements de l'inégalité parmi les hommes* (1755), in *The First and Second Discourses*, trans. Victor Gourevitch (New York, 1986).

Essai sur l'origine des langues (1781), trans. Alexander Gode, in John H. Moran and Alexander Gode (eds.), *On the Origin of Language* (Chicago and London, 1966).

Sheridan, Thomas, *A Course of Lectures on Elocution, together with two Dissertations on Language* (London, 1762).

Smith, Adam, *Considerations concerning the First Formation of Languages* (1761), in *Lectures on Rhetoric and Belles Lettres*, ed. J. C. Bryce (Oxford, 1983).

Stewart, Dugald, *Account of the Life and Writings of Adam Smith, LL.D.* (1794), in Adam Smith, *Essays on Philosophical Subjects*, ed. W. P. D. Wightman, J. C. Bryce and I. S. Ross (Oxford, 1980).

Süssmilch, Johann Peter, *Versuch eines Beweises, dass die erste Sprache ihren Ursprung nicht vom Menschen, sondern allein vom Schöpfer erhalten habe* (Berlin, 1766).

Tooke, John Horne, *The Diversions of Purley* (1786) (2 vols., 2nd edn, London, 1798).

Vico, Giambattista, *Principi di scienza nuova d'intorno alla comune natura delle nazioni* (1744), trans. Thomas Goddard Bergin and Max Harold Fisch (Ithaca and London, 1948).

Wachter, Johann, *Naturae et scripturae concordia* (Leipzig and Copenhagen, 1752).

Warburton, William, *The Divine Legation of Moses Demonstrated* (2 vols., London, 1738–41).

Essai sur les hiéroglyphes des Egyptiens, trans. Marc-Antoine Leonard (Paris, 1744).

Wolf, F. A., *Prolegomena to Homer* (1795), trans. James E. G. Zetzel (Princeton, 1985).

Wood, Robert, *An Essay on the Original Genius and Writings of Homer* (London, 1769).

Secondary sources

Aarsleff, Hans, *From Locke to Saussure: Essays on the Study of Language and Intellectual History* (Minneapolis, 1982).

　The Study of Language in England, 1780–1860 (2nd edn, Minneapolis, 1983).

Cohen, Murray, *Sensible Words: Linguistic Practice in England 1640–1785* (Baltimore and London, 1977).

David, Madeleine V.-, *Le débat sur les écritures et l'hiéroglyphe aux XVIIe et XVIIIe siècles* (Paris, 1965).

Derrida, Jacques, *Of Grammatology*, trans. Gayatri C. Spivak (Baltimore and London, 1974).

Formigari, Lia, *Language and Experience in 17th-Century British Philosophy* (Amsterdam and Philadelphia, 1988).

Foucault, Michel, *The Order of Things* (New York, 1970).

Harris, Roy, and Taylor, Talbot J., *Landmarks in Linguistic Thought* (London and New York, 1989).

Howell, Wilbur Samuel, *Eighteenth-Century British Logic and Rhetoric* (Princeton, 1971).

Hudson, Nicholas, *Writing and European Thought, 1600–1830* (Cambridge, 1995).

Knowlson, James, *Universal Language Schemes in England and France 1600–1800* (Toronto and Buffalo, 1975).

Land, Stephen K., *From Signs to Propositions: The Concept of Form in Eighteenth-Century Semantic Theory* (London, 1974).

　The Philosophy of Language In Britain: Major Theories from Hobbes to Thomas Reid (New York, 1986).

Mugnai, Paolo F., *Segno e linguaggio in George Berkeley* (Rome, 1979).

Parret, Herman (ed.), *History of Linguistic Thought and Contemporary Linguistics* (Berlin and New York, 1976).

Robinet, André, *Le Langage à l'âge classique* (Paris, 1986).

Wellbery, David E., *Lessing's Laocoon: Semiotics and Aesthetics in the Age of Reason* (Cambridge, 1984).

The contributions of rhetoric to literary criticism

Primary sources and texts

Bary, René, *La Rhétorique françoise* (Paris, 1659; Amsterdam, 1669).

Batteux, Charles, *Principes de la littérature* (5 vols., Paris, 1764); trans. 'Mr Miller', *A Course of the Belles Lettres, or the Principles of Literature* (London, 1761). 'Traité de la construction oratoire' (1763) is Reel 9, no. 98, in *British and Continental Rhetoric and Elocution* (see below).

Blair, Hugh, *Lectures on Rhetoric and Belles Lettres* (2 vols., London, 1783); rpt with intro. H. F. Harding (Carbondale IL, 1965).

Bouffier, Claude, *Traité de l'éloquence* (Paris, 1732).

Bouhours, Dominique, *La manière de bien penser dans les ouvrages d'Esprit* (Paris, 1687); trans. anonymously as *The Art of Criticism* (London, 1705).

British and Continental Rhetoric and Elocution, 16 microfilm reels of critical and rhetorical treatises of the 16th–18th centuries (Ann Arbor, 1953).

Campbell, George, *The Philosophy of Rhetoric* (2 vols., London, 1776); reprinted with introduction by L. F. Bitzer (Carbondale IL, 1963).

Crevier, J. B. L., *Rhétorique françoise* (2 vols., Paris, 1765) (Reel 11, no. 111, in *British and Continental Rhetoric and Elocution*; see above).

Du Marsais, César Chesneau, *Traité des tropes* (Paris, 1730); avec un commentaire raisonné par M. [Pierre] Fontanier (2 vols., Paris, 1818); reprinted, with an introduction by Gérard Genette (2 vols., Geneva, 1967).

Fénelon, F. de S. de la M., *Dialogues sur l'éloquence en général et la chaire en particulier* (Paris, 1718); trans. William Stevenson, *Dialogues Concerning Eloquence* (London, 1722); trans. with introduction and notes, W. S. Howell, *Fénelon's Dialogues on Eloquence* (Princeton, 1951).

Gibert, Balthazar, *La Rhétorique ou les Regles de l'Eloquence* (Paris, 1730) (Reel 13, no. 119, in *British and Continental Rhetoric and Elocution*; see above).

Gottsched, J. C. *Ausführliche Redekunst* (Leipzig, 1728), ed. P. M. Mitchell, *Ausgewählte Werke*, VII, 1 (Berlin, 1975), pp. 59–326.

Hume, David, 'Of Eloquence', in *Essays, Moral, Political, and Literary* (London, 1741), in *Philosophical Works*, ed. T. H. Green and T. H. Grose (4 vols., London, 1886; rpt Aalen, 1964), III, pp. 163–74.

Kames, Henry Home, Lord, *Elements of Criticism* (3 vols., Edinburgh, 1762; rpt Hildesheim, 1970).

Lamy, Bernard, *De l'Art de parler* (Paris, 1675); anonymous translation, *The Art of Speaking, written in French by Messieurs du Port Royal* (London, 1676); ed. John T. Harwood, *The Rhetorics of Thomas Hobbes and Bernard Lamy* (Carbondale IL, 1986), pp. 131–337.

Lawson, John, *Lectures concerning Oratory* (Dublin, 1758); rpt with intro. E. N. Claussen and K. R. Wallace (Carbondale IL, 1972).

Mayans y Siscar, Gregorio, *Retórica* (Valencia, 1757; 1786), in *Obras completas*, III, ed. A. Mestre Sanchis and J. Gutiérrez (Valencia, 1984), pp. 74–653.

Priestley, Joseph, *A Course of Lectures on Oratory and Criticism* (London, 1777); rpt with intro. David Potter (Carbondale IL, 1965).

Rapin, René, *The Whole Critical Works of Monsieur Rapin*, trans. 'several hands' (2 vols., London, 1706).

Rhetoric of Blair, Campbell, and Whateley, With Updated Bibliographies, The, ed. James L. Golden and Edward P. J. Corbett (Carbondale IL, 1990).

Rollin, Charles, *Traité des études: De la manière d'enseigner et d'étudier les belles-lettres* (4 vols., Paris, 1726–8).

Sheridan, Thomas, *A Course of Lectures on Elocution, Together with Two Dissertations on Language* (London, 1762; rpt New York, 1968).

Smith, Adam, *Lectures on Rhetoric and Belles Lettres* (1762–3), ed. with intro. and notes J. M. Lothian (Carbondale IL, 1963).

Vico, Giambattista, *Institutiones Oratoriae* (Naples, 1711), in *G. B. Vico Opere*, VII, ed. Fausto Nicolini (Bari, 1941).

Ward, John, *A System of Oratory, Delivered in a Course of Lectures Publicly Read at Gresham College* (2 vols., London, 1759).

Witherspoon, John, *Lectures on Moral Philosophy and Eloquence* (Philadelphia, 1801); lectures on rhetoric reprinted in *The Selected Writings of John Witherspoon*, ed. Thomas P. Miller (Carbondale IL, 1990).

Secondary sources

Carr, Thomas M., Jr, *Descartes and the Resilience of Rhetoric: Varieties of Cartesian Rhetorical Theory* (Carbondale IL, 1990).

Conley, Thomas M., *Rhetoric in the European Tradition* (New York, 1990).

Fumaroli, Marc, *L'Age de l'éloquence: Rhétorique et 'res literaria' de la Renaissance au seuil de l'époque classique* (Geneva, 1980).

Genette, Gérard, 'Rhetoric restrained', in *Figures of Literary Discourse*, trans. Alan Sheridan (New York, 1982), pp. 103–26.

Horner, W. B. (ed.), *Historical Rhetoric: An Annotated Bibliography of Selected Sources in English*, 'Part 4: The Eighteenth Century' (Boston, 1980), pp. 187–226.

The Present State of Scholarship in Historical and Contemporary Rhetoric, 4. The Eighteenth Century (Columbia MO, 1983), pp. 101–33.

Howell, W. S., *Eighteenth Century British Logic and Rhetoric* (Princeton, 1971).

Logic and Rhetoric in England, 1500–1700 (Princeton, 1956).

Kennedy, George A., *Classical Rhetoric and Its Christian and Secular Tradition From Ancient to Modern Times* (Chapel Hill, 1980).

McKenzie, Gordon, *Critical Responsiveness: A Study of the Psychological Current in Later Eighteenth-Century Criticism*, Univ. of California Publ. in English, 20 (1949).

Saintsbury, George, *A History of Criticism and Literary Taste in Europe* (3 vols., Edinburgh, 1900–4).

Varga, A. Kibédi, *Rhétorique et littérature: Etudes de structures classiques* (Paris, 1970).

Vickers, Brian, *Classical Rhetoric in English Poetry* (London, 1970).

Francis Bacon and Renaissance Prose (Cambridge, 1968).

In Defence of Rhetoric (Oxford, 1988).

Theories of style

Primary sources and texts

Addison, Joseph, in *The Spectator*, ed. D. F. Bond (5 vols., Oxford, 1965).

Elledge, Scott (ed.), *Eighteenth-Century Critical Essays* (2 vols., Ithaca, 1961).

Harris, James, *Philological Inquiries* (London, 1781).

Johnson, Samuel, *Lives of the English Poets*, ed. G. B. Hill (3 vols., Oxford, 1905).

Kames, Henry Home, Lord, *Elements of Criticism* (6th edn, Edinburgh, 1785).

Secondary sources

Clark, A. F. B., *Boileau and the French Classical Critics in England 1660–1830* (Paris, 1925).

Hagstrum, J. H., *The Sister Arts* (Chicago, 1958).

Probyn, Clive T., *The Sociable Humanist: The Life and Works of James Harris 1709–1780* (Oxford, 1991).

Ross, Ian, *Lord Kames and the Scotland of his Day* (Oxford, 1972).

Saintsbury, George, *A History of Criticism and Literary Taste in Europe* (3 vols., Edinburgh, 1900–4).

Stone, P. W. K., *The Art of Poetry 1750–1800* (London, 1967).

Tillotson, Geoffrey, *Augustan Studies* (London, 1961).

Wimsatt, W. K., and Cleanth Brooks, *Literary Criticism. A Short History* (New York, 1957).

Generality and particularity

Primary sources and texts

Blake, William, *The Complete Poetry and Prose of William Blake*, ed. David V. Erdman (revised edn, New York, 1982).

Boswell, James, *The Life of Samuel Johnson, LL.D.*, ed. G. B. Hill, rev. L. F. Powell (6 vols., Oxford, 1934, 1950).

Campbell, George. *Philosophy of Rhetoric*, 2nd edn (2 vols., London, 1801).

Dennis, John, *The Critical Works of John Dennis*, ed. Edward N. Hooker (2 vols., Baltimore, 1939–43).

Hume, David, *An Inquiry concerning Human Understanding*, ed. C. W. Hendel (Indianapolis, 1955).

Hurd, Richard, *The Works of Richard Hurd* (2 vols., London, 1811).

Johnson, Samuel, *The History of Rasselas, Prince of Abissinia*, ed. Geoffrey Tillotson and Brian Jenkins (Oxford, 1971).

The Lives of the Poets, ed. G. B. Hill (3 vols., Oxford, 1905).

The Yale Edition of the Works of Samuel Johnson, ed. Allen T. Hazen *et al.* (11 vols. to date, New Haven, 1958–).

Kames, Henry Home, Lord, *Elements of Criticism*, 2nd edn (2 vols., Edinburgh, 1763).

Locke, John, *An Essay concerning Human Understanding*, ed. Alexander C. Fraser (2 vols., Oxford, 1894, rpt New York, 1959).

Pope, Alexander, *The Poems of Alexander Pope*, ed. John Butt *et al.* (11 vols., London, 1939–69).

Reynolds, Joshua, *Discourses on Art*, ed. Robert R. Wark (New Haven, 1975).

Scott, John (of Amwell), *Critical Essays of Some of the Poems of Several English Poets* (London, 1785).

Young, Edward, *Conjectures on Original Composition, in a Letter to the Author of Sir Charles Grandison* (London, 1759).

Secondary sources

Abrams, M. H., *The Mirror and the Lamp: Romantic Theory and the Critical Tradition* (New York, 1953).

Adams, Hazard, 'Revisiting Reynolds' *Discourses* and Blake's Annotations', in Robert N. Essick and Donald Pearce (eds.), *Blake in His Time* (Bloomington, 1978), pp. 128–44.

Barrell, John, *The Political Theory of Painting from Reynolds to Hazlitt* (New Haven, 1986).

Basney, Lionel, ' "*Lucidus Ordo*": Johnson and generality', *Eighteenth-Century Studies*, 5 (1971), 39–57.

Crane, R. S., 'English neoclassical criticism: an outline sketch', in Crane *et al.* (eds.), *Critics and Criticism Ancient and Modern* (Chicago, 1952), pp. 372–88.

Damrosch, Leopold, *Symbol and Truth in Blake's Myth* (Princeton, 1980).
The Uses of Johnson's Criticism (Charlottesville, 1976).

Eaves, Morris, *William Blake's Theory of Art* (Princeton, 1982).

Edinger, William, *Samuel Johnson and Poetic Style* (Chicago, 1977).

Elledge, Scott, 'The background and development in English criticism of the theories of generality and particularity', *Publications of the Modern Language Association*, 62 (1947), 147–82.

Hagstrum, Jean H., *Samuel Johnson's Literary Criticism* (Minneapolis, 1952).

Hipple, Walter J., 'General and particular in the *Discourses* of Sir Joshua Reynolds: a study in method', *Journal of Aesthetics and Art Criticism*, 11 (1952), 231–47.

Keast, W. R., 'The theoretical foundations of Johnson's criticism', in R. S. Crane *et al.* (eds.), *Critics and Criticism Ancient and Modern* (Chicago, 1952), pp. 389–407.

Lipking, Lawrence, *The Ordering of the Arts in Eighteenth-Century England* (Princeton, 1970).

Rorty, Richard, *Philosophy and the Mirror of Nature* (Princeton, 1979).

Wasserman, Earl R., *The Subtler Language: Critical Readings of Neoclassical and Romantic Poems* (Baltimore, 1959).

Wellek, René, *A History of Modern Criticism: 1750–1950*, vol. I, *The Later Eighteenth Century* (New Haven, 1955).

Youngren, William, 'Generality, science, and poetic language in the Restoration,' *ELH*, 35 (1968), 158–87.

The sublime

Editions and translations

Dionysius Longinus on the Sublime, trans. William Smith (London, 1739; rpt New York, 1975).

'Longinus' on the Sublime, ed. D. A. Russell (Oxford, 1964).

On Great Writing, trans. G. M. A. Grube (New York, 1957).

Le traité du sublime, trans. Nicolas Boileau-Despréaux (Paris, 1674; rpt New York, 1975).

The Works of Dionysius Longinus, trans. Leonard Welsted (London, 1712; rpt 1724).

Primary texts

Akenside, Mark, *The Pleasures of the Imagination*, in *The Poems of Mark Akenside* (London, 1772).

Alison, Archibald, *Essays on the Nature and Principles of Taste* (2 vols., Edinburgh, 1812).

Ashfield, Andrew, and Peter de Bolla, *The Sublime: A Reader in British Eighteenth-Century Aesthetic Theory* (Cambridge, 1996).

Baillie, John, *An Essay on the Sublime* (London, 1747; rpt Los Angeles, 1953).

Beattie, James, *Dissertations Moral and Critical* (London, 1783; rpt Stuttgart, 1970).

Bentham, Jeremy, *Of Laws In General*, in *Collected Works*, ed. H. L. A. Hart (London, 1970).

Blackwell, Thomas, *An Enquiry into the Life and Writings of Homer* (2 vols., London, 1735).

Blair, Hugh, 'A critical dissertation on the poems of Ossian', in *The Poems of Ossian*, trans. James Macpherson (3 vols., London, 1805).

Lectures on Rhetoric and Belles Lettres (3 vols., London, 1787).

Blake, William, *The Complete Poetry and Prose of William Blake*, ed. David V. Erdman (Berkeley, 1982).

Boileau-Despréaux, Nicolas, *Traité du Sublime ou du Merveilleux* (Paris, 1674; rpt New York, 1975).

Burke, Edmund, *A Philosophical Enquiry into the Origin of our Ideas of the Sublime and Beautiful*, ed. James T. Boulton (Oxford, 1958; rvd 1987).

Reflections on the Revolution in France, in L. G. Mitchell (ed.), *The Writings and Speeches of Edmund Burke*, vol. 8 (Oxford, 1989).

Coleridge, Samuel Taylor, *Biographia Literaria*, ed. J. Shawcross (2 vols., Oxford, 1907).

Miscellaneous Criticism, ed. T. M. Raysor (Cambridge, 1936).

Dennis, John, *The Critical Works of John Dennis*, ed. Edward Niles Hooker (2 vols., Baltimore, 1939).

[Egmont, John Perceval, Earl of], *Faction Detected by the Evidence of the Facts* (London, 1744).

Gerard, Alexander, *An Essay on Genius* (London, 1774; rpt New York, 1970).

An Essay on Taste (London, 1759; rpt Menston, 1971).

Gibbon, Edward, *An Essay on the Study of Literature* (London, 1764; rpt New York, 1970).

Journal to January 28, 1763 (London, 1929).

Godwin, William, *A History of the Life of William Pitt, Earl of Chatham* (London, 1783).

Hartley, David, *Observations on Man, his Frame and Duty and his Expectations* (2 vols., London, 1749; rpt Gainsville, 1966).

Hegel, Georg Wilhelm Friedrich, *Aesthetics*, trans. T. M. Knox (2 vols., Oxford, 1975). Original in: G. W. F. Hegel, *Werke*, ed. Eva Moldenhauer and Karl Markus Michel (20 vols., Frankfurt am Main, 1971), vols. 13–15) (*Vorlesungen uber die Ästhetik*).

Lectures on the Philosophy of Religion, ed. Peter C. Hodgson (2 vols., Berkeley, 1987).

Phenomenology of Spirit, trans. A. V. Miller (Oxford, 1977).

Philosophy of Right, trans. T. M. Knox (Oxford, 1942).

Herder, J. G., *Sämtliche Werke*, ed. Bernhard Suphan (33 vols., Berlin, 1877–1913), esp. vols. 11–12.

The Spirit of Hebrew Poetry, trans. James Marsh (2 vols., Burlington VT, 1833).

Hume, David, *Essays Moral, Political and Literary*, ed. Eugene F. Miller (Indianapolis, 1987).

A Treatise of Human Nature, ed. Ernest C. Mossner (Harmondsworth, 1969).

Johnson, Samuel, *Lives of the English Poets*, ed. George Birkbeck Hill (3 vols., Oxford, 1905).

Kames, Henry Home, Lord, *Elements of Criticism* (2 vols., Edinburgh, 1774).

Kant, Immanuel, *The Failure of all Philosophical Attempts towards a Theodicy*, in *Kant*, ed. Gabrielle Rabel (Oxford, 1963). Original in Kant, *Gesammelte Schriften*, ed. Preussische Akademie der Wissenschaften (Berlin, 1902–), vol. VIII.

Critique of Judgment, ed. James Creed Meredith (Oxford, 1952; rpt 1973); original in *Gesammelte Schriften*, vol. V.

Le Clerc, Jean, *Twelve Dissertations out of Genesis* (London, 1696).

Lessing, Gotthold Ephraim, *Laocoön*, trans. W. A. Steel, in *German Aesthetic and Literary Criticism*, ed. H. B. Nisbet (Cambridge, 1985). Original in Lessing, *Sämtliche Schriften*, ed. Karl Lachmann and Franz Muncker (23 vols., Stuttgart, 1886–1924), IX.

Lowth, Robert, *Lectures on the Sacred Poetry of the Hebrews*, trans. G. Gregory (London, 1847).

Paine, Thomas, *Rights of Man*, ed. Henry Collins (Harmondsworth, 1969; rpt 1983).

Payne Knight, Richard, *Analytical Enquiry into the Principles of Taste* (London, 1805).

Pope, Alexander, *The Art of Sinking in Poetry*, ed. Edna Leake Steeves (New York, 1952).

Poems, ed. John Butt (London, 1963).

Priestley, Joseph, *A Course of Lectures on Oratory and Criticism* (London, 1777; rpt Menston, 1968).

Reynolds, Sir Joshua, *Discourses on Art*, 2nd edn, ed. Robert R. Wark (New Haven, 1975).

Schiller, Friedrich, *Vom Erhabenen*, in *Sämtliche Werke*, ed. Gerhard Fricke and Herbert G. Göpfert, 5 vols. (Munich, 1958–59), X.

On the Sublime, trans. Julius A. Elias (New York, 1966).

Sterne, Laurence, *The Life and Opinions of Tristram Shandy, Gent.* ed. Melvyn New and Joan New (3 vols., Florida, 1978).

Swift, Jonathan, *The Poems of Jonathan Swift*, ed. Harold Williams (3 vols., Oxford, 1937; rpt 1958).

Walpole, Horace, *Memoirs of George II*, ed. John Brooke (3 vols., New Haven, 1985).

Warburton, William, *The Doctrine of Grace* (2 vols., London, 1763).

Wordsworth, William, *The Prose Works of William Wordsworth*, ed. W. J. B. Owen and Jane Worthington Smyser (3 vols., Oxford, 1974).

William Wordsworth, ed. Stephen Gill (Oxford, 1984).

Secondary sources

Abrams, M. H., *The Mirror and the Lamp* (Oxford, 1953).

Altieri, Charles, 'Plato's performative sublime and the ends of reading', *New Literary History*, 12, 2 (1985), 251–73.

Arac, Jonathan, 'The media of sublimity', *Studies in Romanticism*, 26 (1987), 209–20.

Bloom, Harold, *The Anxiety of Influence* (Oxford, 1973).

'Freud and the poetic sublime', in *Freud: A Collection of Critical Essays*, ed. Perry Messel (New Jersey, 1981), 211–31.

Brewer, John, *Party Ideology and Popular Politics at the Accession of George III* (Cambridge, 1976).

Brown, Marshall, 'The urbane sublime', in *Modern Essays in Eighteenth Century Literature*, ed. Leo Damrosch (Oxford, 1988), pp. 426–54.

Caruth, Cathy, 'The force of example: Kant's symbols', *Yale French Studies*, 74 (1988), 17–37.

Clark, Jonathan, *The Dynamics of Change: The Crisis of the 1750s and English Party Systems* (Cambridge, 1982).

Courtine, Jean-François *et al.*, *Du Sublime* (Paris, 1988).

De Bolla, Peter, *The Discourse of the Sublime* (Oxford, 1989).

Deguy, Michel, 'Le Grand-Dire: Pour contribuer à une relecture du pseudo-Longin', *Poétique*, 58 (1984), 197–214.

De Luca, Vincent, 'Blake and the two sublimes', in *Studies in Eighteenth-Century Culture No. 11*, ed. Harry C. Payne (Madison WI, 1982).

De Man, Paul, 'Hegel on the sublime', in *Displacement: Derrida and After*, ed. Mark Krupnick (Bloomington, 1982).

'Phenomenality and materiality in Kant', in *Hermeneutics*, ed. Gary Shapiro and Alan Sica (Amherst, 1984).

Derrida, Jacques, 'Economimesis', *Diacritics* (1981), pp. 3–25.

The Truth in Painting, trans. Geofreey Bennington and Ian McLeod (Chicago, 1987).

Eagleton, Terry, *The Ideology of the Aesthetic* (Oxford, 1990).

Erdman, David V. (ed.), *The Poetry and Prose of William Blake* (New York, 1970).

Escoubas, Eliane, 'Kant ou la simplicité du sublime', *PO&SIE*, 32 (1985), 112–25.

Ferguson, Frances, 'Legislating the sublime', in *Studies in Eighteenth Century Art and Aesthetics*, ed. Ralph Cohen (Berkeley, 1985), pp. 131–44.

Solitude and the Sublime (New York, 1992).

'The sublime of Edmund Burke, or the bathos of experience', *Glyph*, 8 (1981), 62–78.

Commentary on Suzanne Guerlac's 'Longinus and the subject of the sublime', *New Literary History*, 12, 2 (1985), 291–7.

Fry, Paul, 'The possession of the sublime', *Studies in Romanticism*, 26, 2 (1987), 187–207.

The Reach of Criticism (New Haven, 1983).

Guerlac, Suzanne, *The Impersonal Sublime* (Stanford, 1990).

'Longinus and the subject of the sublime', *New Literary History*, 12, 2 (1985), 275–89.

Hebdige, Dick, 'The impossible object: towards a sociology of the sublime', *New Formations*, 1 (1987), 47–76.

Hentzi, Gary, 'Sublime moments and social authority in *Robinson Crusoe* and *Journal of the Plague Year*', *Eighteenth-Century Studies*, 26, 3 (Spring 1993), 419–34.

Hertz, Neil, *The End of the Line: Essays on Psychoanalysis and the Sublime* (New York, 1985).

Hipple, Walter J., *The Beautiful, the Sublime, and the Picturesque in Eighteenth-Century British Aesthetic Theory* (Carbondale IL, 1957).

Johnson, Claudia L., ' "Giant HANDEL" and the musical sublime', *Eighteenth-Century Studies*, 19 (1986), 515–33.

Kay, Carol, 'Burke's fearful reflections', in *Political Constructions* (Ithaca, 1988).

Knapp, Steven, *Personification and the Sublime: Milton to Coleridge* (Cambridge, 1985).

Lacoue-Labarthe, Philippe, 'La vérité sublime', *PO&SIE*, 38 (1986), 83–116.

Lamb, Jonathan, 'Longinus, the dialectic, and the practice of mastery', *ELH*, 60 (1993), 545–67.

'The subject of the subject and the sublimities of self-reference', *Huntington Library Quarterly*, 56, 2 (1993), 191–207.

Leighton, Angela, *Shelley and the Sublime* (Cambridge, 1984).

Levine, Joseph M., *The Battle of the Books* (Ithaca, 1991).

Lloyd, David, 'Kant's examples', *Representations*, 28 (1989), 34–54.

Lyotard, Jean-François, 'The sign of history', in Derek Attridge, Geoff Bennington and Robert Young (eds.), *Poststructuralism and the Question of History* (Cambridge, 1987), pp. 162–80.

'The sublime and the avant-garde', *Artforum*, 22, 8 (April 1984), 36–43.

'Le sublime, à present', *PO&SIE*, 34 (1985), 97–116.

Lessons on the Analytic of the Sublime, trans. Elizabeth Rottenberg (Stanford, 1994).

Mitchell, W. J. T., *Iconology: Image, Text, Ideology* (Chicago, 1986).

Monk, Samuel Holt, *The Sublime in Eighteenth-Century England* (New York, 1935).

Morris, David, B., *The Religious Sublime* (Kentucky, 1972).

Nancy, Jean-Luc, 'L'Offrande sublime', *PO&SIE*, 30 (1984), 76–103.

Paulson, Ronald, *Representations of Revolution* (New Haven, 1983).

Pease, Donald E., 'Sublime politics', *Boundary* 2, 12/13 (1984), 259–79.

Pocock, J. G. A., 'The political economy of Burke's analysis of the French Revolution', in *Virtue, Commerce, Society* (Cambridge, 1985).

Poland, Lynn, 'The Bible and the rhetorical sublime', in *The Bible as Rhetoric*, ed. Martin Warner (London, 1990).

Rosenblum, Robert, *Transformations in Late Eighteenth-Century Art* (New Jersey, 1967).

Saint Girons, Baldine, *Fiat lux: une philosophie du sublime* (Paris, 1992).

Schama, Simon, *Citizens* (Harmondsworth, 1989).

Schor, Naomi, *Reading in Detail: Aesthetics and the Feminine* (London, 1987).

Shapiro, Gary, 'From the sublime to the political', *New Literary History*, 12, 2 (1985), 213–36.

Shell, Marc, *The Economy of Literature* (Baltimore, 1978).

Sitter, John, *Literary Loneliness in Mid-Eighteenth Century England* (Ithaca, 1982).

Tate, Alan, *The Man of Letters and the Modern World* (New York, 1955).

Trussler, Simon, *Burlesque Plays of the Eighteenth Century* (Oxford, 1969).

Weiskel, Thomas, *The Romantic Sublime* (Baltimore, 1976).

Wellek, René, *A History of Modern Criticism 1750–1950: The Later Eighteenth Century* (Cambridge, 1981).

White, Hayden, 'The politics of historical interpretation', in *The Content of the Form* (Baltimore, 1987).

Wimsatt, W. K., and Cleanth Brooks, *Literary Criticism: A Short History* (New York, 1957).

Yaeger, Patricia, 'Toward a female sublime', in *Gender and Theory: Dialogues on Feminist Criticism*, ed. Linda Kauffman (Oxford, 1989).

Žižek, Slavoj, *The Sublime Object of Ideology* (London, 1989).

Sensibility and literary criticism

Primary sources and texts

Alison, Archibald, *Essays on the Nature and Principles of Taste* (London, 1790).

Austen, Jane, *Sense and Sensibility*, ed. R. W. Chapman (1923; rpt Oxford, 1983).

Barnett, George L. (ed.), *Eighteenth-Century British Novelists on the Novel* (New York, 1968).

Beattie, James, *Essays* (London, 1776).

Burke, Edmund, *A Philosophical Enquiry into the Origin of our Ideas of the Sublime and Beautiful*, ed. J. T. Boulton (Oxford, 1987).

Carroll, John (ed.), *Selected Letters of Samuel Richardson* (Oxford, 1964).

Diderot, Denis, *Oeuvres* (Paris, 1951).

Oeuvres philosophiques, ed. P. Verniere (Paris, 1959).

Doktor, Wolfgang, and Gerhard Sauder (eds.), *Empfindsamkeit. Theoretische und kritische Texte* (Stuttgart, 1976).

Elledge, Scott (ed.), *Eighteenth-Century Critical Essays* (2 vols., Ithaca, 1961).

Gerard, Alexander, *An Essay on Taste* (Edinburgh, 1759).

Howes, Alan (ed.), *Sterne. The Critical Heritage* (London, 1974).

Hume, David, *Essays*, ed. E. F. Miller (Indianapolis, 1985; revised edn, 1989).

Kames, Henry Home, Lord, *Elements of Criticism* (3 vols., Edinburgh, 1762).

Lessing, Gotthold Ephraim, *Sämtliche Schriften*, ed. Karl Lachmann and Franz Muncker (23 vols., Stuttgart and Leipzig, 1886–1924).

   G. E. Lessing, Moses Mendelssohn and Friedrich Nicolai, *Briefwechsel über das Trauerspiel*, ed. Jochen Schulte-Sasse (Munich, 1972).

More, Hannah, *Sacred Dramas, Chiefly Intended for Young Persons, to which is added, Sensibility, A Poem* (London, 1782).

Rousseau, J. J., *A Dialogue between a Man of Letters and M. J. J. Rousseau*, in Jean-Jacques Rousseau, *Eloisa, or a series of original letters*, trans. William Kenrick (1803), Woodstock Facsimile reprint (Oxford, 1989).

   A Letter from M. Rousseau, of Geneva, to M. d'Alembert of Paris (London, 1759).

Sauder, Gerhard, *Empfindsamkeit*, Vol. III: *Quellen und Dokumente* (Stuttgart, 1980).

Warton, Joseph, *An Essay on the Genius and Writings of Pope* (London, 1756).

Williams, Ioan (ed.), *Novel and Romance 1700–1800: A Documentary Record* (London, 1970).

Wollstonecraft, Mary, *A Vindication of the Rights of Woman* (London, 1929).

Wordsworth, William, and S. T. Coleridge, *Lyrical Ballads*, ed. R. L. Brett and A. R. Jones (London, 1978).

Secondary sources

Ferriar, John, *Illustrations of Sterne* (London, 1798).

Howes, Alan, *Yorick and the Critics: Sterne's Reputation in England, 1760–1868* (New Haven, 1958).

Mason, John Hope, *The Irresistible Diderot* (London, 1982).

Mullan, John, *Sentiment and Sociability* (Oxford, 1988).

Petriconi, Hellmuth, *Die verführte Unschuld: Bemerkungen über ein literarisches Thema* (Hamburg, 1953).

Sauder, Gerhard, *Empfindsamkeit*, Vol. I: *Voraussetzungen und Elemente* (Stuttgart, 1974).

Schmidt, Erich, *Richardson, Rousseau und Goethe* (Jena, 1875).

Todd, Janet, *Sensibility. An Introduction* (London, 1986).

Wellek, René, *A History of Modern Criticism 1750–1950*, vol. 1 (1955; rpt London, 1966).

Women and literary criticism

Primary sources and texts

Baillie, Joanna, *A Series of Plays: in which it is attempted to delineate the Stronger Passions of the Mind, Each Passion being the Subject of a Tragedy and a Comedy* (London, 1798).

Ballard, George, *Memoirs of Several Ladies of Great Britain, who have been*

Celebrated for their Writings or Skill in the Learned Languages, Arts and Sciences (1752; Detroit, 1985).

Barbauld, Anna Laetitia [Aikin], *The Works of Anna Laetitia Barbauld* (2 vols., London, 1825).

Barbauld, Anna Laetitia [Aikin] (ed.), *The British Novelists; with an Essay, and Prefaces, Biographical and Critical* (50 vols., London, 1810).

The Correspondence of Samuel Richardson (6 vols., London, 1804).

The Female Speaker (London, 1811).

The Pleasures of Imagination by Mark Akenside, M.D. To which is prefixed a critical essay on the poem, by Mrs Barbauld (London, 1795).

The Poetical Works of Mr William Collins. With a prefatory essay by Mrs Barbauld (London, 1797).

Barbauld, Anna Laetitia and John Aikin, *Miscellaneous Pieces in Prose* (London, 1773).

Behn, Aphra, *The Dutch Lover* (London, 1673).

Sir Patient Fancy (London, 1677).

Berger, Morroe (ed. and trans.), *Madame de Staël on Politics, Literature, and National Character* (Garden City NY, 1964).

Brooke, Frances, *The Old Maid by Mary Singleton, Spinster* (1755–6; rev. edn, London, 1764).

Burney, Frances, *Evelina; or The History of a Young Lady's Entrance into the World* (London, 1778).

Carter, Elizabeth (ed. and trans.), *All the works of Epictetus which are now extant; consisting of his Discourses, preserved by Arrian, in four books, the Enchiridion, and fragments. Tr. from the original Greek ... with an introduction and notes, by the translator* (London, 1758).

Letters from Mrs Elizabeth Carter, to Mrs Montagu (3 vols., London, 1817).

A Series of Letters between Mrs Elizabeth Carter and Miss Catherine Talbot (4 vols., 1809; rpt New York, 1975).

Cavendish, Margaret, Duchess of Newcastle, *Nature's Pictures Drawn by Fancies Pencil to the Life* (London, 1656).

CCXI Sociable Letters (London, 1664).

Centlivre, Susannah, *Love's Contrivance; or, Le Médecin Malgré Lui* (London, 1703).

The Perjur'd Husband (London, 1700).

The Platonick Lady (London, 1707).

Cooper, Elizabeth (ed.), *The Muses Library: or, A Series of English poetry, from the Saxons, to the reign of King Charles II, being a general collection of almost all the old valuable poetry extant* (London, 1737).

Dacier, Anne Lefèvre, *Homère défendu contre l'Apologie du R. P. Hardouin; ou suite des causes de la corruption du goust* (Paris, 1716; rpt Geneva, 1971).

Dacier, Anne Lefèvre (ed. and trans.), *L'Iliade d'Homère, traduite en françois, avec des remarques par Madame Dacier* (Paris, 1711).

L'Odyssée d'Homère, traduite en françois, avec des remarques par Madame Dacier (Paris, 1711).

Les Poésies d'Anacréon et de Sapho, traduites de grec en françois, avec des remarques. Par mademoiselle Le Fèvre (Lyon, 1696).

Duncombe, John, *The Feminiad* (London, 1754; rpt Los Angeles, 1981).

Echlin, Elizabeth, Lady, *An Alternative Ending to Richardson's 'Clarissa'* (Berne, 1982).

Eden, Anne, *A Confidential Letter of Albert; from his first attachment to Charlotte to her death. From the Sorrows of Werter* (London, 1790).

Edgeworth, Maria, *Letters for Literary Ladies* (London, 1795).

Elstob, Elizabeth, *An English-Saxon Homily, on the birth-day of St Gregory: Anciently used in the English Saxon Church Giving an Account of the Conversion of the English from Paganism to Christianity, Translated into Modern English, with Notes, etc.* (London, 1709).

The Rudiments of Grammar for the English-Saxon Tongue, first given in English, with an apology for the study of northern antiquities (London, 1715).

Fielding, Henry, *The Covent-Garden Journal* (1751-2; rpt in *The Wesleyan Edition of the Works of Henry Fielding* (Oxford, 1988)).

Tom Jones (1749; rpt in *The Wesleyan Edition of the Works of Henry Fielding* (Middletown, CT and Oxford, 1975)).

Fielding, Sarah, *Remarks on Clarissa* (1749; rpt Los Angeles, 1985).

Francis, Ann, *A Poetical Epistle from Charlotte to Werther* (London, 1788).

Francis, Ann (ed. and trans.), *A Poetical Translation of the Song of Solomon, From the Original Hebrew, with a Preliminary Discourse, and Notes, Historical, Critical and Explanatory* (London, 1781).

Genlis, Stephanie Ducrest de St Aubin, Comtesse de, *De l'Influence des femmes sur la littérature française, comme protectrices des lettres et comme auteurs; ou Précis de l'histoire des femmes françaises les plus célèbres* (Paris, 1811).

Graffigny, Françoise d'Issembourg d'Happoncourt de, *Lettres d'une péruvienne* (Paris, 1752).

Grierson, Constantia (ed.), *Afer Publius Terentius, Comoediae, ad optimorum exemplarium fidem recensitae. Praefixa sunt huic editioni loca Menandri et Apollodori, quae Terentius Latine interpretatus est. Accesserunt emendationes omnes Bentleianae* (Dublin, 1727).

Cornelius Tacitus, Opera quae exstant, ex recensione et cum animadversionibus Theodori Ryckii (3 vols., Dublin, 1730).

Griffith, Elizabeth, *The Morality of Shakespeare's Drama Illustrated* (London, 1775).

Harrison, Elizabeth, *A Letter to Mr John Gay, on His Tragedy Call'd 'The Captives'* (London, 1724).

Haywood, Eliza, *The Female Spectator* (4 vols., 3rd edn, London, 1750).

Inchbald, Elizabeth, *The British Theatre; or, A Collection of Plays, which are acted at the Theatres Royal, Drury Lane, Covent Garden, and Haymarket. Printed under the Authority of the Managers from the Prompt Books. With Biographical and Critical Remarks by Mrs Inchbald* (25 vols., London, 1808).

Johnson, Samuel, *The Adventurer* (no. 115; 11 December 1753), in W. J. Bate, John M. Bullitt and L. F. Powell (eds.), *The Yale Edition of the Works of Samuel Johnson*, II (New Haven, 1963), pp. 456–61.

Lennox, Charlotte [Ramsay], *Shakespear Illustrated: or the Novels and Histories, on which the Plays of Shakespear Are Founded, Collected and Translated from the Original Authors, with Critical Remarks* (2 vols., 1753; rpt New York, 1973).

Madan, Judith, 'The Progress of Poetry', in *The Flower-Piece: A Collection of Miscellany Poems* (London, 1731).

Makin[s], Bathsua [Pell], *An Essay to Revive the Antient Education of Gentlewomen, In Religion, Manners, Arts & Tongues. With an Answer to the Objections against this Way of Education* (1673; rpt Augustan Reprint Society, Los Angeles, 1980).

Mereau, Sophie, *Kalathiskos* (1801–2; rpt Heidelberg, 1968).

Montagu, Elizabeth, *An Essay on the Writings and Genius of Shakespeare, Compared with the Greek and French Dramatic Poets. With Some Remarks upon the Misrepresentations of Mons. de Voltaire. To Which are Added, Three Dialogues of the Dead* (6th edn, London, 1810; rpt New York, 1966).

More, Hannah, *Essays on Various Subjects, principally designed for Young Ladies* (London, 1777).

'Preface to the Tragedies' ['Observations on the Effect of Theatrical Representations with respect to Religion and Morals'], in *The Works of Hannah More*, vol. 2 (London, 1803), pp. 1–27.

Strictures on the Modern System of Female Education (London, 1799), in *The Works of Hannah More*, vol. 4 (London, 1803).

Necker, Suzanne [Curchod], *Mélanges extraits des manuscrits de Mme. Necker* (3 vols., Paris, 1798).

Nicholls, James C. (ed.), *Mme Riccoboni's Letters to David Hume, David Garrick, and Sir Robert Liston, 1764–1783*, in Theodore Besterman (ed.), *Studies on Voltaire and the Eighteenth Century*, 149 (Oxford, 1976).

Reeve, Clara, *The Progress of Romance and the History of Charoba, Queen of Egypt* (1785; rpt New York, 1930).

Riccoboni, Marie-Jeanne [de Heurles de Laboras de Mezières], 'Correspondance de Laclos et de Madame Riccoboni au sujet des *Liaisons dangereuses*', in Choderlos de Laclos, *Oeuvres complètes* (Paris, 1951), pp. 710–22.

Riccoboni, Marie-Jeanne (ed. and trans.), *Un Nouveau théâtre anglais* (Paris, 1768).

Roche, Sophie von La, *Pomona für Teutschlands Töchter* (1783–4; 4 vols., rpt Munich, 1987).

Schurman, Anna Maria van, *Opuscula hebraea, latina, graeca, gallica, prosaica et metrica* (Leiden, 1648).

Seward, Thomas, 'The female right to literature', in Robert Dodsley (ed.), *A Collection of Poems by Several Hands*, vol. 2 (6th edn, London, 1758), pp. 294–300.

Staël-Holstein, Anne Louise Germaine [Necker] de, *De la Littérature, considérée dans ses rapports avec les institutions sociales* (1800; 2 vols., rpt Paris, 1959).

De l'Allemagne (1810; 4 vols., rpt Paris, 1959).

Essai sur les fictions (1795), in *Oeuvres complètes de Mme. la Baronne de Staël*, vol. 2 (Paris, 1820), pp. 173–216.

Swift, Jonathan, *The Battle of the Books* (1704), in A. C. Guthkelch and D. Nichol Smith (eds.), *A Tale of a Tub . . . The Battle of the Books and The Mechanical Operation of the Spirit* (2nd edn, Oxford, 1958).

Wollstonecraft, Mary, 'On poetry and our relish for the beauties of nature', in Janet Todd (ed.), *A Wollstonecraft Anthology* (Bloomington and London, 1977), pp. 170–5.

Secondary sources

Adburgham, Alison, *Women in Print: Writing Women and Women's Magazines From the Restoration to the Accession of Victoria* (London, 1972).

Arendt, Hannah, *Rahel Varnhagen: The Life of a Jewess* (London, 1957).

Backscheider, Paula R., 'Women's influence', *Studies in the Novel*, 11 (1979), 3–22.

Blunt, Reginald, *Mrs Montagu, 'Queen of the Blues'* (2 vols., London, n.d.).

Bowyer, John Wilson, *The Celebrated Mrs Centlivre* (Durham NC, 1952).

Crosby, F. A., *Une romancière oubliée, Mme Riccoboni, sa vie, ses oeuvres* (Paris, 1924).

Curtis, Judith, 'The *Epistolières*', in Samia I. Spencer (ed.), *French Women and the Age of Enlightenment* (Bloomington, 1984), pp. 226–41.

Demay, Andrée, *Marie-Jeanne Riccoboni: ou de la pensée féministe chez une romancière du XVIIIe siècle* (Paris, 1977).

Duffy, Maureen, *The Passionate Shepherdess: Aphra Behn 1640–89* (London, 1977).

Eaves, T. C. Duncan, and Ben D. Kimpel, 'The composition of *Clarissa* and its revision before publication', *Publications of the Modern Language Association of America*, 83 (1968), 416–28.

Samuel Richardson: A Biography (Oxford, 1971).

Ezell, Margaret J. M., *Writing Women's Literary History* (Baltimore and London, 1993).

Ferguson, Moira (ed.), *First Feminists: British Women Writers 1578–1799* (Bloomington and Old Westbury NY, 1985).

Gallagher, Catherine, *Nobody's Story: The Vanishing Acts of Women Writers in the Marketplace 1670–1820* (Berkeley, 1994).

Green, Mary Elizabeth, 'Elizabeth Elstob: the Saxon nymph', in J. R. Brink (ed.), *Female Scholars: A Tradition of Learned Women Before 1800* (Montreal, 1980), pp. 137–60.

Halsband, Robert, 'Addison's *Cato* and Lady Mary Wortley Montagu', *Publications of the Modern Language Association of America*, 65 (1950), 1,122–9.

'Ladies of letters in the eighteenth century', in Earl Miner (ed.), *Stuart and Georgian Moments* (Berkeley and Los Angeles, 1972), pp. 271–91.

The Life of Lady Mary Wortley Montagu (Oxford, 1956).

Hampsten, Elizabeth, 'Petticoat authors: 1660–1720', *Women's Studies*, 7 (1980), 21–38.

Harris, Jocelyn, 'Sappho, souls, and the Salic law of wit', in Alan Charles Kors and Paul J. Korshin (eds.), *Anticipations of the Enlightenment in England, France, and Germany* (Philadelphia, 1987), pp. 232–58.

Haussonville, Gabriel Paul Othenin de Cléron, Comte d', *The Salon of Madame Necker*, trans. Henry M. Trollope (New York, 1882).

Herold, J. Christopher, *Mistress to an Age: A Life of Madame de Staël* (New York, 1958).

Hopkins, Mary Alden, *Hannah More and Her Circle* (New York, 1947).

Irwin, Joyce L., 'Anna Maria van Schurman: The Star of Utrecht', in J. R. Brink (ed.), *Female Scholars: A Tradition of Learned Women Before 1800* (Montreal, 1980), pp. 68–85.

Isles, Duncan, 'Johnson and Charlotte Lennox', *New Rambler*, 19 (1967), 34–8.

Johnson, Reginald Brimley (ed.), *Bluestocking Letters* (London, 1926).

The Letters of Hannah More (London, 1925).

Kavanaugh, Julia, *English Women of Letters* (London, 1862).

Labalme, Patricia (ed.), *Beyond Their Sex: Learned Women of the European Past* (New York, 1980).

Lanser, Susan Sniader, and Evelyn Torton Beck, '[Why] Are there no great women critics? And what difference does it make?', in Julia A. Sherman and Evelyn Torton Beck (eds.), *The Prism of Sex: Essays in the Sociology of Knowledge* (Madison WI, 1979), pp. 79–91.

Lipking, Lawrence, 'Aristotle's sister: a poetics of abandonment', in Robert von Hallberg (ed.), *Canons* (Chicago, 1983), pp. 85–106.

Littlewood, S. R., *Elizabeth Inchbald and her Circle 1753–1821* (London, 1921).

McMullen, Lorraine, *An Odd Attempt in a Woman: The Literary Life of Frances Brooke* (Vancouver, 1983).

Mahl, Mary R., and Helene Koon (eds.), *The Female Spectator: English Women Writers before 1800* (Bloomington and Old Westbury NY, 1977).

Masson, Pierre-Maurice, *Madame de Tencin 1682–1749* (Paris, 1909).

Miller, Nancy K., 'Men's reading, women's writing: gender and the rise of the novel', *Yale French Studies*, 75 (1988), 40–55.

Moore, Catherine E., '"Ladies ... taking the pen in hand": Mrs Barbauld's criticism of eighteenth-century women novelists', in Mary Anne Schofield and Cecilia Macheski (eds.), *Fetter'd or Free: British Women Novelists 1670–1815* (Athens OH, 1986), pp. 383–97.

Needham, Gwendolyn, 'Mrs Frances Brooke: dramatic critic', *Theatre Notebook*, 15 (Winter 1960–1), 47–52.

Reynolds, Myra, *The Learned Lady in England, 1650–1750* (Boston and New York, 1920).

Rogers, Katharine, *Feminism in Eighteenth-Century England* (Urbana IL, 1982).

Schlenther, Paul, *Frau Gottsched und die bürgerliche Komödie* (Berlin, 1886).

Stewart, Joan Hinde, 'The novelists and their fictions', in Samia I. Spencer (ed.), *French Women and the Age of Enlightenment* (Bloomington, 1984), pp. 197–211.

'Vers un "Nouveau Théâtre Anglais", ou la liberté dans la diction', *French Forum*, 9 (1984), 181–9.

Sunstein, Emily W., *A Different Face: The Life of Mary Wollstonecraft* (New York, 1975).

Todd, Janet, *Feminist Literary History* (London, 1988).

The Sign of Angellica: Women, Writing and Fiction, 1660–1800 (London, 1989).

Todd, Janet (ed.), *A Dictionary of British and American Women Writers 1660–1800* (Totowa NJ, 1987).
  A Wollstonecraft Anthology (Bloomington and London, 1977).

Primitivism

Primary and secondary sources

Aarsleff, Hans, *From Locke to Saussure* (Minneapolis, 1982).
  The Study of Language in England 1780–1860 (Minneapolis, 1983).
Bernheimer, Richard, *Wild Men in the Middle Ages* (Cambridge MA, 1952).
Blair, Hugh, *Lectures on Rhetoric and Belles Lettres*, 10th edn (3 vols., London, 1806).
Bond, Richmond, *Queen Anne's American Kings* (Oxford, 1952).
Brown, Roger, *Wilhelm von Humboldt's Conception of Linguistic Relativity* (The Hague, 1967).
Chinard, Gilbert, *L'Amérique et le rêve exotique dans la littérature française au XVIIᵉ et au XVIIIᵉ siècle* (Paris, 1934).
A Collection of Old Ballads (3 vols., London, 1723–5).
Condillac, Étienne Bonnot de, *Essai sur l'origine des connoissances humaines*, in *Oeuvres* (Paris, 1798).
Davenant, Sir William, *Dramatic Works*, ed. James Maidment and William Logan (6 vols., Edinburgh, 1883).
Dudley, Edward, and Maximillian Novak, *The Wild Man Within* (Pittsburgh, 1972).
Fairchild, Hoxie Neal, *The Noble Savage* (New York, 1928).
Farley, Frank Edgar, 'The dying Indian', in *Anniversary Papers by Colleagues and Pupils of ... Kittredge* (Boston, 1913).
Gale, Theophilus, *The Court of the Gentiles* (Oxford and London, 1669–77).
Herder, Johann Gottfried, *Sämtliche Werke*, ed. Bernhard Suphan (33 vols., Berlin, 1877–1913).
Lafitau, Joseph-François, *Moeurs des sauvages américains*, ed. Edna Lemay (2 vols. Paris, 1983).
Lahontan, Louis d'Arce Baron de, *New Voyages to North America* (2 vols., Chicago, 1905).
Lovejoy, Arthur O., *Essays in the History of Ideas* (New York, 1960).
Lovejoy, Arthur O., *et al.*, *A Documentary History of Primitivism* (Baltimore, 1935).
Lowth, Robert, *Lectures on the Sacred Poetry of the Hebrews*, trans. G. Gregory (2 vols., London, 1787).
  A Letter to the Right Reverend Author of the Divine Legation of Moses Demonstrated (Oxford, 1765).
Monboddo, James Burnett, Lord, *Of the Origin and Progress of Language*, 2nd edn (6 vols., Edinburgh, 1774).
Pearce, Roy Harvey, *The Savages of America* (Baltimore, 1953).
Todorov, Tzvetan, *The Conquest of America*, trans. Richard Howard (New York, 1985).

Tuveson, Ernest Lee, *Millennium and Utopia* (Berkeley, 1949).

Vico, Giambattista, *The New Science*, trans. Thomas Bergin and Max Fisch (Ithaca, 1968).

Warburton, William, *The Divine Legation of Moses Demonstrated* (2 vols., London, 1741).

Whitney, Lois, 'English primitivistic theories of epic origins', *Modern Philology*, 21 (1929), 337–78.

    Primitivism and the Idea of Progress in English Popular Literature of the Eighteenth Century (Baltimore, 1934).

Medieval revival and the Gothic

Primary sources and texts

Addison, Joseph, *Miscellaneous Works*, ed. A. C. Guthkelch (2 vols., London, 1914).

Aikin, John, and Anna Laetitia Aikin, *Miscellaneous Pieces in Prose* (London, 1773).

Chatterton, Thomas, *Complete Works*, ed. Donald S. Taylor and Benjamin B. Hoover (2 vols., Oxford, 1971).

Dennis, John, *Critical Works*, ed. Edward Niles Hooker (2 vols., Baltimore, 1939–43).

Dodsley, Robert, *Correspondence*, ed. James E. Tierney (Cambridge, 1988).

    A Select Collection of Old Plays (12 vols., London, 1744–5).

Drake, Nathan, *Literary Hours* (2 vols., London, 1798; 2nd edn 1800).

Dryden, John, *Of Dramatic Poesy and Other Critical Essays*, ed. George Watson (2 vols., London, 1962).

Hazlitt, William, *Complete Works*, ed. P. P. Howe (21 vols., London, 1930–4).

Hurd, Richard, *Letters on Chivalry and Romance*, ed. Hoyt Trowbridge (Los Angeles, 1963).

Johnson, Samuel, *A Journey to the Western Islands of Scotland*, ed. J. D. Fleeman (Oxford, 1985).

    Lives of the English Poets, ed. George Birkbeck Hill (3 vols., Oxford, 1905).

Mathias, Thomas, *The Pursuits of Literature* (London, 1794–7; 10th edn 1799).

Percy, Thomas, *The Correspondence of Thomas Percy and Edmond Malone*, ed. Arthur Tillotson (Baton Rouge, 1944).

    The Correspondence of Thomas Percy and Richard Farmer, ed. Cleanth Brooks (Baton Rouge, 1946).

    Reliques of Ancient English Poetry (3 vols., London, 1765; 4th edn 1794).

Pope, Alexander, *Pastoral Poetry and An Essay on Criticism*, ed. E. Audra and Aubrey Williams (London, 1961).

    Works, ed. William Warburton (9 vols., London, 1770).

Reeve, Clara, *The Old English Baron*, ed. James Trainer (London, 1967).

    The Progress of Romance (2 vols., London, 1785).

Ritson, Joseph, *Ancient English Metrical Romanceës* (3 vols., London, 1802).

Rymer, Thomas, *Critical Works*, ed. Curt A. Zimansky (New Haven, 1956).

Sade, Marquis de, 'Idée sur les romans', in *Oeuvres complètes du Marquis de Sade: Édition Définitive*, X (Paris, 1973); trans. as 'Reflections on the Novel', in *The Marquis de Sade: The 120 Days of Sodom and other Writings*, trans. Austryn Wainhouse and Richard Seaver (New York, 1966).

Sidney, Sir Philip, *An Apology for Poetry*, ed. Geoffrey Shepherd (London, 1965).

The Spectator, ed. Donald F. Bond (5 vols., Oxford, 1965).

Staël, Germaine de, *Essai sur les fictions*, in *Oeuvres complètes de Mme la Baronne de Staël*, II (Paris, 1820); trans. as 'Essay on Fictions', in *An Extraordinary Woman: Selected Writings of Germaine de Staël*, trans. Vivian Folkenflik (New York, 1987).

Turner, Sharon, *The History of the Anglo-Saxons* (4 vols., London, 1799–1805).

Walpole, Horace, *The Castle of Otranto*, ed. W. S. Lewis (Oxford, 1969).
  Correspondence, ed. W. S. Lewis (48 vols., New Haven, 1937–83).
  Works, ed. Mary Berry (5 vols., London, 1798).

Warton, Joseph, *An Essay on the Genius and Writings of Pope* (2 vols., London, 1756–82).

Warton, Thomas, *The History of English Poetry, from the Close of the Eleventh to the Commencement of the Eighteenth Century* (3 vols., London, 1774–81).
  Observations on the Fairy Queen of Spenser (London, 1754; 2nd edn, 2 vols., 1762).

Wordsworth, William, *Prose Works*, ed. W. J. B. Owen and Jane Worthington Smyser (3 vols., Oxford, 1974).

Wright, James, *Historia Histrionica: A Historical Account of the English Stage* (London, 1699).

Secondary sources

Brewer, Derek (ed.), *Chaucer: The Critical Heritage*, vol. I, *1385–1837* (London, 1978).

Bronson, Bertrand H., *Joseph Ritson: Scholar-at-Arms* (2 vols., Berkeley, 1938).

Cooke, Arthur L., 'Some side lights on the theory of the Gothic romance', *Modern Language Quarterly*, 12 (1951), 429–36.

Davis, Bertram H., *Thomas Percy: A Scholar-Cleric in the Age of Johnson* (Philadelphia, 1989).

Frank, Frederick S., *The First Gothics: An Annotated Critical Guide to the English Gothic Novel* (New York, 1987).

Friedman, Albert B., *The Ballad Revival: Studies in the Influence of Popular on Sophisticated Poetry* (Chicago, 1961).

Hadley, Michael, *The Undiscovered Genre: A Search for the German Gothic Novel* (Berne, 1978).

Haywood, Ian, *The Making of History: A Study of the Literary Forgeries of James Macpherson and Thomas Chatterton in Relation to Eighteenth-Century Ideas of History and Fiction* (Rutherford NJ, 1986).

Hooker, Edward Niles, 'The reviewers and the New Criticism, 1754–1770', *Philological Quarterly*, 13 (1934), 189–202.

Johnston, Arthur, *Enchanted Ground: The Study of Medieval Romance in the Eighteenth Century* (London, 1964).

Kinghorn, A. M., 'Warton's *History* and Early English poetry', *English Studies*, 44 (1963), 197–204.

Kliger, Samuel, *The Goths in England: A Study in Seventeenth and Eighteenth-Century Thought* (Cambridge MA, 1952).

Levine, Joseph M., *Humanism and History: Origins of Modern English Historiography* (Ithaca and London, 1987).

Lipking, Lawrence, *The Ordering of the Arts in Eighteenth-Century England* (Princeton, 1970).

Longueil, Alfred E., 'The word "Gothic" in eighteenth-century criticism', *Modern Language Notes*, 38 (1923), 453–60.

McNutt, Dan J. *The Eighteenth-Century Gothic Novel: An Annotated Bibliography of Criticism and Selected Texts* (New York, 1975).

Meyerstein, E. H. W., *A Life of Thomas Chatterton* (London, 1930).

Parreaux, André, *The Publication of 'The Monk': A Literary Event 1796–1798* (Paris, 1960).

Paulson, Ronald, *Representations of Revolution (1789–1820)* (New Haven and London, 1983).

Payne, Richard C., 'The rediscovery of Old English poetry in the English literary tradition', in Carl T. Berkhout and Milton McC. Gatch (eds.), *Anglo-Saxon Scholarship: The First Three Centuries* (Boston, 1982), pp. 149–66.

Pittock, Joan C., *The Ascendancy of Taste: The Achievement of Joseph and Thomas Warton* (London, 1973).

Potter, Robert, *The English Morality Play: Origins, History and Influence of a Dramatic Tradition* (London, 1975).

Sabor, Peter (ed.), *Horace Walpole: The Critical Heritage* (London, 1987).

Spector, Robert Donald, *The English Gothic: A Bibliographic Guide to Writers from Horace Walpole to Mary Shelley* (Westport CT, 1984).

Spurgeon, Caroline F. E., *Five Hundred Years of Chaucer Criticism and Allusion 1357–1900* (3 vols., Cambridge, 1925).

Stafford, Fiona J., *The Sublime Savage: A Study of James Macpherson and the Poems of Ossian* (Edinburgh, 1988).

Summers, Montague, *The Gothic Quest: A History of the Gothic Novel* (London, 1938).

Vance, John A., *Joseph and Thomas Warton* (Boston, 1983).

Varma, Devendra P., *The Gothic Flame* (London, 1957).

Wellek, René, *The Rise of English Literary History* (Chapel Hill, 1941).

Voltaire, Diderot, Rousseau and the *Encyclopédie*

Voltaire

Dictionnaire philosophique, Édition revue et corrigée (Paris, 1967).

Letter to Horace Walpole, 15 July 1768, in Theodore Besterman (ed.), *Voltaire's Correspondence*, vol. 69 (Geneva, 1961), pp. 251–7.

Lettres philosophiques, ed. Raymond Naves (Paris, 1964).

Naves, Raymond, *Le goût de Voltaire* (Paris, 1938).

Pichois, Claude, 'Voltaire et Shakespeare: un plaidoyer', *Shakespeare Jahrbuch*, 98 (1962), 178–88.

Sareil, Jean (ed.), *Voltaire et la critique* (Englewood Cliffs NJ, 1966).

Le Siècle de Louis XIV, ed. Antoine Adam (2 vols., Paris, 1966).

Diderot

Brewer, Daniel, *The Discourse of Enlightenment in Eighteenth-Century France: Diderot and the Art of Philosophizing* (Cambridge, 1993).

Chouillet, Jacques, *La Formation des idées esthétiques de Diderot 1745–1763* (Paris, 1973).

Lettre sur les sourds et muets, ed. Paul Hugo Meyer, in *Diderot Studies*, 7 (Geneva, 1965).

Meyer, Paul H., 'The "Lettre sur les sourds et muets" and Diderot's emerging concept of the critic', in *Diderot Studies*, 6 (1964), 133–55.

Oeuvres esthétiques, ed. Paul Vernière (Paris, 1959).

Oeuvres romanesques, ed. Henri Bénac (Paris, 1962).

Rousseau

Lettre à Mr d'Alembert sur les spectacles, ed. M. Fuchs (Geneva, 1948).

Oeuvres complètes (5 vols., Paris, 1959–95).

L'Encyclopédie, Marmontel, Journalists, Other Writers

Bingham, Alfred J., 'Voltaire and Marmontel', *Studies on Voltaire and the Eighteenth Century*, 55 (1967), 205–62.

Correspondance littéraire, philosophique et critique par Grimm, Diderot, Raynal, Meister, etc., ed. Maurice Tourneur (16 vols., Paris, 1877–82).

Dehergne, Joseph, 'Une table des matières de "L'Année littéraire" de Fréron', *Revue d'Histoire littéraire de la France*, 65, 2 (1965), 269–73.

Delille, Jacques, 'Géorgiques', in *Oeuvres complètes*, vol. 2 (Paris, 1824).

Diderot, Denis and Jean le Rond d'Alembert (eds.), *Encyclopédie, ou Dictionnaire raisonné des sciences, des arts et des métiers* (17 vols., Paris, 1751–65).

Gaudin, Lois Frances, *Les lettres anglaises dans l'Encyclopédie* (New York, 1942).

Kölving, Ulla, and Jeanne Carriat, 'Inventaire de la "Correspondance littéraire" de Grimm et Meister', *Studies on Voltaire and the Eighteenth Century*, vols. 225–7 (1984).

La Harpe, Jean-François de, *Oeuvres* (Paris, 1820–1).

Marmontel, Jean-François, *Oeuvres complètes*. Nouv. éd. (19 vols., Paris, 1818) (*Éléments de littérature* forms vols. 12–15).

Monty, Jeanne, *La critique littéraire de Melchior Grimm* (Geneva, 1961).

Pichois, Claude, 'Préromantiques, rousseauistes et shakespeariens (1770–1778)', *Revue de littérature comparée*, 33 (1959), 348–55.

Rocafort, Jacques, *Les doctrines littéraires de l'Encyclopédie* (Paris, 1890).
Schlobach, Jochen, 'Literarische Korrespondenzen', in Gerhard Sauder and Jochen Schlobach (eds.), *Aufklärungen. Frankreich und Deutschland im 18. Jahrhundert*, vol. 1, pp. 221–33 (Heidelberg, 1985).
Trenard, Louis, 'La Presse française des origines à 1788', in Claude Bellanger, Jacques Godechot, Pierre Guiral and Fernand Terrou (eds.), *Histoire générale de la presse française*, I (Paris, 1969).
Van Tieghem, Paul, *L'Année littéraire comme intermédiaire en France des littératures étrangères* (Paris, 1917).
[Young, Edward], *Les Nuits d'Young, traduites de l'anglois par M. Le Tourneur.* (Nouv. éd., Paris, 1770).

Secondary sources, general

Bénichou, Paul, *Le Sacre de l'écrivain, 1750–1830* (Paris, 1973).
Dictionnaire des lettres françaises (Paris, 1960).
Gilman, Margaret, *The Idea of Poetry in France* (Cambridge, 1958).
Green, Frederick C., *Minuet* (London, 1935).
Hervier, Marcel, *Les écrivains français jugés par leurs contemporains*, vol. 2: *Le Dix-Huitième Siècle* (Paris, 1931).
Houston, John Porter, *The Demonic Imagination. Style and Theme in French Romantic Poetry* (Baton Rouge, 1969).
Wellek, René, *A History of Modern Criticism*, vol. I (New Haven and London, 1955).

German literary theory from Gottsched to Goethe

Primary sources, individual authors

Bodmer, J. J., *Briefwechsel von der Natur des poetischen Geschmacks* (1736). *Critische Abhandlung von dem Wunderbaren in der Poesie* (1740).
Breitinger, J. J., *Critische Dichtkunst* (1740).
Briefe die neueste Literatur betreffend (1759–65).
Bürger, G. A., *Herzensausguß über Volkspoesie* (1776).
Curtius, M. C., *Aristoteles Dichtkunst* (1753).
Engel, J. J., *Anfangsgründe einer Theorie der Dichtarten* (1783).
Goethe, J. W., *Einfache Nachahmung, Manier, Stil* (1789). *Einleitung in die Propyläen* (1798). *Literarischer Sansculottismus* (1795). *Maximen und Reflexionen* (1809ff.). *Der Sammler und die Seinigen* (1799). *Shakespeare und kein Ende* (1816).
Gottsched, J. C., *Beiträge zur critischen Historie der deutschen Sprache, Poesie und Beredsamkeit* (1732–44). *Der Biedermann* (1727–9). *Versuch einer critischen Dichtkunst* (1730).

Hamann, J. G., *Kreuzzüge des Philologen* (1762).
Herder, J. G., *Kritische Wälder* (1769).
   Über die neuere deutsche Literatur. Fragmente (1767).
   Von deutscher Art und Kunst. Einige fliegende Blätter (1773).
Lenz, J. M. R., *Anmerkungen übers Theater* (1774).
G. E. Lessing, *Briefwechsel mit Mendelssohn und Nicolai über das Trauerspiel*
   (1756–7).
   Hamburgische Dramaturgie (1767–9).
   Laokoon oder über die Grenzen der Malerei und Poesie (1766).
   Wie die Alten den Tod gebildet (1769).
Mendelssohn, M., *Briefe über die Empfindung* (1755).
Moritz, K. P., *Über die bildende Nachahmung des Schönen* (1788).
Schiller, F., *Gedanken über den Gebrauch des Gemeinen und Niedrigen in der*
   Kunst (1793).
   Die Horen (1795–7).
   Kallias oder über die Schönheit (1793).
   Die Schaubühne als eine moralische Anstalt betrachtet (1785).
   Über Bürgers Gedichte (1791).
   Über den Gebrauch des Chors in der Tragödie (1803).
   Über die ästhetische Erziehung des Menschen (1795).
   Über Matthissons Gedichte (1794).
   Über naive und sentimentalische Dichtung (1796).
Schlegel, J. E., *Einschränkung der Künste auf einen einzigen Satz* (trans. of
   Batteux, 1751).
   Vergleichung Shakespeares und Andreas Gryphs (1741).
Sulzer, J. G., *Allgemeine Theorie der schönen Künste* (1771–4).
Wieland, C. M., *Der Teutsche Merkur* (1772–1810).
Winckelmann, J. J., *Gedanken über die Nachahmung der griechischen Werke in*
   der Malerei und Bildhauerkunst (1755).
   Geschichte der Kunst des Altertums (1764).

Secondary sources, German Enlightenment

Bruford, W. H., *Germany in the Eighteenth Century: The Social Background of*
   the Literary Revival (Cambridge, 1965).
Cassirer, Ernst, *Die Philosophie der Aufklärung* (Tübingen 1932).
Europäische Aufklärung I, ed. Walter Hinck (Frankfurt, 1974).
Habermas, Jürgen, *Strukturwandel der Öffentlichkeit* (Neuwied, 1962).
Hazard, Paul, *Die Herrschaft der Vernunft. Das europäische Denken im 18.*
   Jahrhundert (Hamburg, 1949).
Kopitzsch, Franklin, *Aufklärung, Absolutismus und Bürgertum in Deutschland*
   (Munich, 1976).
Koselleck, Reinhart, *Kritik und Krise* (Freiburg, 1959).
Kraus, Werner, *Studien zur deutschen und französischen Aufklärung* (Berlin,
   1963).
Literatur im Epochenumbruch. Funktionen europäischer Literaturen im 18. und
   beginnenden 19. Jahrhundert, ed. G. Klotz, W. Schröder and P. Weber
   (Berlin, 1977).

Pütz, Peter, *Die deutsche Aufklärung* (Darmstadt, 1978).
Wehler, Hans Ulrich, *Deutsche Gesellschaftsgeschichte I, 1700–1815* (Munich, 1987).
Wessel, Hans-Friedrich (ed.), *Aufklärung* (Frankfurt, 1984).

Secondary sources, literary life

Balet, L., and E. Gerhard, *Die Verbürgerlichung der deutschen Kunst, Literatur und Musik im 18. Jahrhundert* (Strasbourg, 1936).
Berghahn, Klaus L., 'Das schwierige Geschäft der Aufklärung', in H.-F. Wessel (ed.), *Aufklärung* (Frankfurt, 1984), pp. 32–65.
Haferkorn, Hans Jürgen, 'Der freie Schriftsteller. Eine literatursoziologische Studie über seine Entstehung und Lage in Deutschland zwischen 1750 und 1800', in *Archiv für die Geschichte des Buchwesens*, 5 (1964), 523–711.
Kiesel, H., and P. Münch, *Gesellschaft und Literatur im 18. Jahrhundert* (Munich, 1977).
Kirchner, Joachim, *Die Grundlagen des deutschen Zeitschriftenwesens* (Mit einer Gesamtbibliographie der deutschen Zeitschriften bis zum Jahre 1790), (2 vols., Leipzig, 1928–32).
Martens, Wolfgang, *Die Botschaft der Tugend. Die Aufklärung im Spiegel der deutschen Moralischen Wochenschriften* (Stuttgart, 1968).
Möller, Horst, *Aufklärung in Preußen* (Berlin, 1974).
Prutz, Robert E., *Geschichte des deutschen Journalismus* (Hanover, 1845).
Schenda, Rolf, *Volk ohne Buch. Studien zur Sozialgeschichte der populären Lesestoffe, 1770–1910* (Frankfurt, 1970).
Ungern-Sternberg, Wolfgang von, 'Schriftsteller und literarischer Markt', in *Deutsche Aufklärung bis zur Französischen Revolution, 1680–1789*, ed. Rolf Grimminger (Munich, 1980), pp. 133–185.
Wilke, Jürgen, *Literarische Zeitschriften des 18. Jahrhunderts, 1688–1789* (Stuttgart, 1978).

Secondary sources, German literary theory and criticism

Adler, Hans, *Die Prägnanz des Dunklen. Gnoseologie, Ästhetik, Geschichtsphilosophie Johann Gottfried Herders* (Hamburg, 1990).
Borinski, Karl, *Die Antike in der Poetik und Kunsttheorie. Vom Ausgang des klassischen Altertums bis auf Goethe* (Leipzig, 1921–4).
Boyd, J. S., *The Function of Mimesis and its Decline* (Cambridge, 1968).
Butler, E. M., *The Tyranny of Greece over Germany* (Cambridge, 1935).
Fambach, Oskar, *Ein Jahrhundert deutscher Literaturkritik, 1750–1850* (Berlin, 1957ff.).
Freier, H., *Kritische Poetik: Legitimation und Kritik der Poesie in Gottscheds Dichtkunst* (Stuttgart, 1963).
Gebauer, Gunter (ed.), *Das Laokoon-Projekt* (Stuttgart, 1984).
Herrmann, H. P., *Nachahmung und Einbildungskraft. Zur Entwicklung der deutschen Poetik von 1670 bis 1740* (Bad Homburg, 1970).

Hohendahl, Peter Uwe (ed.), *A History of German Literary Criticism, 1730–1980* (Lincoln NB, 1988), pp. 13–98.

Mayer, Hans (ed.), *Deutsche Literaturkritik I, 1730–1830* (Frankfurt, 1962).

Nachahmung und Illusion, ed. H. R. Jauß (Munich, 1964).

Nivelle, Armand, *Kunst- und Dichtungstheorien zwischen Aufklärung und Klassik* (Berlin, 1971).

Sørensen, Bengt A., *Symbol und Symbolismus in der ästhetischen Theorie des 18. Jahrhunderts und der deutschen Romantik* (Copenhagen, 1963).

Szondi, Peter, 'Antike und Moderne in der Ästhetik der Goethezeit', in Szondi, *Poetik und Geschichtsphilosophie I* (Frankfurt, 1974), pp. 11–266.

Wellek, René, *A History of Modern Criticism, 1750–1950* (New Haven, 1955), vol. I: *The Later Eighteenth Century.*

Wiegmann, Hermann, *Geschichte der Poetik* (Stuttgart, 1977).

The Scottish Enlightenment

Primary sources and texts

Alison, Archibald, *Essay on the Nature and Principles of Taste* (2 vols., Edinburgh, 1790).

Bacon, Francis, *Works,* ed. J. Spedding, R. L. Ellis and D. D. Heath (14 vols., London, 1857–74).

Beattie, James, *Dissertations Moral and Critical* (London and Edinburgh, 1783). *Lectures on Moral Philosophy* (Aberdeen University Library MSS M 165, 1740.18.).

Blackwell, Thomas, *An Enquiry into the Life and Writings of Homer* (London, 1735). *Letters on Mythology* (London, 1747).

Blair, Hugh, *A Critical Dissertation on the Poems of Ossian* (Edinburgh, 1763). *Essays on Rhetoric and Belles Lettres* (Edinburgh, 1783); ed. Harold F. Harding (2 vols., Carbondale, 1965).

Campbell, George, *The Philosophy of Rhetoric* (2 vols., London and Edinburgh, 1776).

Fergusson, Robert, *The Poems of Robert Fergusson,* (Edinburgh, 1773); ed. M. P. McDiarmid, Scottish Text Society vols. 21 and 24 (Edinburgh and London, 1954–6).

Fordyce, David, *Dialogues concerning Education* (2 vols., London, 1747; 3rd edn London, 1757).

Gerard, Alexander, *An Essay on Genius* (London and Edinburgh, 1774). *An Essay on Taste* (London and Edinburgh, 1758); 3rd edn (London and Edinburgh, 1759).

Hume, David, *Essays Moral, Political and Literary,* ed. Eugene F. Miller, rev. edn (Indianapolis, 1987).

Hutcheson, Francis, *Essays on the Nature and Conduct of our Passions and Affections* (Glasgow, 1728). *An Inquiry into the Original of our Ideas of Beauty and Virtue* (Glasgow, 1725).

Johnson, Samuel, *A Journey to the Western Isles of Scotland* (London, 1775).

Kames, Henry Home, Lord, *The Elements of Criticism* (2 vols., Edinburgh, 1762); 4th edn (2 vols., Edinburgh and London, 1769).

Ramsay, Allan, *The Ever Green* (Edinburgh, 1724).

Rollin, Charles, *The Method of Teaching and Studying the Belles Lettres, or an Introduction to Languages, Poetry, Rhetoric, History, Moral Philosophy, Physick, and with reflections on TASTE; and Instructions with regard to Eloquence of the Pulpit, the Bar, and the Stage*, 2nd edn (London, 1737).

Scott, Robert Eden, *Elements of Rhetoric for the Use of the Students of King's College* (Aberdeen, 1802).

Shaftesbury, Anthony Ashley Cooper, third Earl of, *Characteristicks of Men, Manners, Opinions, Times* (3 vols., London, 1708–14).

Smith, Adam, *Lectures on Rhetoric and Belles Lettres*, ed. J. C. Bryce (Oxford, 1983).

Secondary sources

Alexander, Ian, *Two Studies in Romantic Reasonings: Edinburgh Reviewers and the English Tradition*, Salzburg Studies in English Literature, 49 (2 vols., 1976).

Brunius, Teddy, *David Hume on Criticism*, Figura 2, Studies Edited by the Institute of Art History, University of Uppsala (Uppsala, 1952).

Campbell, R. H., and Andrew Skinner, *The Origins and Nature of the Scottish Enlightenment* (Glasgow, 1982).

Carter, J. J., and J. H. Pittock (eds.), *Aberdeen and the Enlightenment* (Aberdeen, 1987).

Cassirer, Ernst, *The Philosophy of the Enlightenment* (Princeton, 1951).

Davie, George E., *The Scottish Enlightenment*, The Historical Association General Series 99 (London, 1981).

Dwyer, John, *Virtuous Discourse: Sensibility and Community in Late Eighteenth-Century Scotland* (Edinburgh, 1987).

Emerson, Roger, 'Scottish universities in the eighteenth century, 1690–1800', *Studies in Voltaire and the Eighteenth Century*, 157 (1977).

Fussell, Paul, *The Rhetorical World of Augustan Humanism* (Oxford, 1965).

Graham, Henry G., *Scottish Men of Letters in the Eighteenth Century* (London, 1901).

Hipple, Walter J., *The Beautiful, the Sublime, and the Picturesque in Eighteenth-Century British Aesthetic Theory* (Carbondale IL, 1957).

Hook, Andrew (ed.), *The History of Scottish Literature*, vol. 2, 1600–1800 (Aberdeen, 1987).

Horner, Winifred J. (ed.), *The Present State of Scholarship in Historical and Contemporary Rhetoric* (Columbia and London, 1983).

Howell, W. B., *Eighteenth-Century British Logic and Rhetoric* (Princeton, 1971).

Lehmann, William C., *Henry Home, Lord Kames, and the Scottish Enlightenment* (The Hague, 1971).

McGuirk, Carol, *Robert Burns and the Sentimental Era* (Athens OH, 1987).

MacQueen, John, *The Enlightenment and Scottish Literature, Progress and Poetry*, vol. 1 (Edinburgh, 1982).

Mooney, Michael, *Vico in the Tradition of Rhetoric* (Princeton, 1985).

Mullan, John, *Sentiment and Sociability: The Language of Feeling in the Eighteenth Century* (Oxford, 1988).

Pittock, J. H., *The Ascendancy of Taste* (London, 1973).

Pittock, J. H., and A. Wear (eds.), *Interpretation and Cultural History* (London, 1991).

Richards, I. A., *The Philosophy of Rhetoric* (New York, 1936).

Sher, Richard, *Church and University in the Scottish Enlightenment* (Princeton and Edinburgh, 1985).

Simonsuuri, Kirsti, *Homer's Original Genius. Eighteenth-Century Notions of the Early Greek Epic* (Cambridge, 1979).

Simpson, Kenneth, *The Protean Scot: the Crisis of Identity in Eighteenth-Century Scottish Literature* (Aberdeen, 1981).

Tytler, Alexander Fraser, *Memoirs of the Life and Writings of Lord Kames* (Edinburgh, 1807).

Wallace, Karl, *Francis Bacon on Communication and Rhetoric* (Chapel Hill, 1948).

Waszek, Norbert, *The Scottish Enlightenment and Hegel's Account of 'Civil Society'* (Dordrecht, Boston, London, 1988).

Canons and canon formation

Primary sources and texts

Blackwell, Thomas, *An Enquiry into the Life and Writings of Homer* (London, 1739, rpt Menston, Yorks., 1972).

Blair, Hugh, *Lectures on Rhetoric and Belles Lettres*, ed. Harold F. Harding (2 vols., Carbondale IL and Edwardsville, 1965).

Boileau-Despréaux, Nicolas, *Oeuvres*, ed. Georges Mongrédien (Paris, 1961).

Bolingbroke, Henry St John, Viscount, *Historical Writings,* ed. Isaac Kramnick (London, 1972).

Dennis, John, 'On the Genius and Writings of Shakespear', in *The Critical Writings of John Dennis*, ed. E. N. Hooker (2 vols., Baltimore, 1939–43).

Descartes, René, *Oeuvres de Descartes*, ed. Charles Adam and Paul Tannery (12 vols., rev. edn, Paris, 1964–76).

Dryden, John, 'Preface. The Grounds of Criticism in Tragedy', in *Of Dramatic Poesy and Other Critical Essays*, ed. George Watson (2 vols., London, 1962).

Edwards, Thomas, *The Canons of Criticism and Glossary: Being a Supplement to Mr Warburton's Edition of Shakespear Collected from the Notes in that Celebrated Work, and Proper to Be Bound up with It*, 7th edn, Reprints of Economic Classics (New York, 1970).

Fielding, Henry, *Amelia*, ed. Martin C. Battestin (Oxford, 1983).

Fontenelle, Bernard, *Oeuvres Diverses* (3 vols., Paris, 1818).

Goldsmith, Oliver, 'An Inquiry into the Present State of Polite Learning', in *Collected Works*, ed. Arthur Friedman (5 vols., Oxford, 1966).

Herder, Johann Gottfried, 'Auszug aus einem Briefwechsel über Ossian und die Lieder alter Völker', in *Sämtliche Werke*, V, pp. 159–207.

'Shakespeare', in *German Aesthetic and Literary Criticism: Winckelmann, Lessing, Hamann, Herder, Schiller, Goethe,* ed. H. B. Nisbet (Cambridge, 1985); original in *Sämtliche Werke*, ed. Bernhard Suphan, 33 vols. (Berlin, 1877–1913), V, pp. 208–31.

Johnson, Samuel, *Johnson on Shakespeare*, vols. VII and VIII of *The Yale Edition of the Works of Samuel Johnson*, ed. Arthur Sherbo (New Haven, 1968).

Lives of the English Poets, ed. G. B. Hill (3 vols., Oxford, 1905).

Lowth, Robert, *Lectures on the Sacred Poetry of the Hebrews*, trans. G. Gregory (London, 1847).

Montfaucon, Bernard de, *Antiquity Explained and Represented in Sculpture* (2 vols., London, 1721–2).

Novalis, *Schriften*, ed. Paul Kluckhorn and Richard Samuel (5 vols., Stuttgart, 1960–75).

Rousseau, Jean-Jacques, *Oeuvres complètes* (5 vols., Paris, 1959–95).

Shaftesbury, Anthony Ashley Cooper, third Earl of, *Characteristics of Men, Manners, Opinions, Times* (New York, 1964).

Smart, Christopher, *Poetical Works*, ed. Karina Williamson and Marcus Walsh (4 vols., Oxford, 1980–7).

Smith, D. Nichol (ed.), *Eighteenth-Century Essays on Shakespeare* (Oxford, 1963).

Stukeley, William, *Stonehenge: A Temple Restor'd to the British Druids* [and] *Avebury: A Temple of the British Druids*, ed. Robert D. Richardson, Jr (New York, 1984).

Swift, Jonathan, 'A Proposal for Correcting the English Tongue', ed. Herbert Davis and Louis Landa, vol. IV of *The Prose Writings of Jonathan Swift*, ed. Herbert Davis *et al.* (14 vols., Oxford, 1939–68), pp. 1–21.

A Tale of a Tub, ed. A. C. Guthkelch and D. Nichol Smith, 2nd edn (Oxford, 1958).

Temple, Sir William, 'An Essay upon the Ancient and Modern Learning', in *Five Miscellaneous Essays by Sir William Temple*, ed. Samuel Holt Monk (Ann Arbor, 1963), pp. 37–71.

Theobald, Lewis, 'Preface to Edition of Shakespeare', in *Eighteenth-Century Essays on Shakespeare*, ed. D. Nichol Smith (Oxford, 1963).

Vico, Giambattista, *The New Science of Giambattista Vico*, trans. Thomas Goddard Bergin and Max Harold Fisch (New York, 1948, rpt 1961).

Opere, ed. Fausto Nicolini (Naples, 1953).

Voltaire, *Le Temple du Goût*, in *Oeuvres Complètes*, ed. Louis Moland (52 vols., Paris, 1877–85).

Warburton, William, 'Preface to Edition of Shakespeare', in *Eighteenth-Century Essays on Shakespeare*, ed. D. Nichol Smith (Oxford, 1963).

Wheeler, Kathleen M., *German Aesthetic and Literary Criticism: The Romantic Ironists and Goethe* (Cambridge, 1984).

Winckelmann, Johann Joachim, *Gedanken über die Nachahmung der griechischen Werke in der Malerei und Bildhauerkunst* (Berlin, 1885; rpt Liechtenstein, 1968).

   Geschichte der Kunst des Altertums, ed. Wilhelm Senff (Weimar, 1964).

   The History of Ancient Art, trans. G. Henry Lodge (2 vols., London, 1881).

   Winckelmann: Writings on Art, ed. David Irwin (London, 1972).

Wordsworth, William, *Lyrical Ballads*, ed. R. L. Brett and A. R. Jones (London, 1965).

Secondary sources

Abrams, M. H., *The Mirror and the Lamp* (New York, 1953).

Belanger, Terry, 'Publishers and writers in eighteenth-century England', in Isabel Rivers (ed.), *Books and Their Readers in Eighteenth-Century England* (Leicester, 1982), pp. 5–25.

Butterfield, Herbert, 'Delays and paradoxes in the development of historiography', in K. Bourne and D. C. Watt (eds.), *Studies in International History* (London 1967), pp. 1–15.

Curtius, E. R., *European Literature and the Latin Middle Ages* (1953, rpt New York, 1963).

Erskine-Hill, Howard, *The Augustan Idea in English Literature* (London, 1983).

Flavell, M. Kay, 'Winckelmann and the German Enlightenment', *Modern Language Review*, 74 (1979), 79–96.

Fokkema, Douwe W., 'The canon as an instrument for problem solving', in János Riesz, Peter Boerner and Bernard Scholz (eds.), *Sensus Communis: Contemporary Trends in Comparative Literature* (Tübingen, 1986).

Gorak, Jan, *The Making of the Modern Canon* (London, 1991).

Hazard, Paul, *La Crise de la conscience européene* (2 vols., Paris, 1935).

Maxwell, J. C., 'Demigods and pickpockets: the Augustan myth in Swift and Rousseau', *Scrutiny*, 11 (1942), 34–9.

Momigliano, Arnaldo, *Studies in Historiography* (London, 1966).

Patey, Douglas Lane, 'The eighteenth century invents the canon', *Modern Language Studies*, 18 (1988), 17–37.

Pfeiffer, Rudolf, *History of Classical Scholarship: From the Beginnings to the End of the Hellenistic Age* (Oxford, 1968).

Rawson, Claude, *Order from Confusion Sprung: Studies in Eighteenth-Century Literature from Swift to Cowper* (London, 1985).

Simon, Fr. Richard, *Histoire Critique du Vieux Testament* (Frankfurt, 1967).

Starobinski, Jean, 'Criticism and authority', *Dedalus*, 106 (1977), 1–16.

   'From the decline of erudition to the decline of nations: Gibbon's response to French thought', *Dedalus*, 105 (1976), 139–57.

Weinbrot, Howard D., *Augustus Caesar in 'Augustan' England: The Decline of a Classical Norm* (Princeton, 1977).

Wellek, René, *A History of Modern Criticism, 1750–1850* (4 vols., Cambridge, 1981), I.

Literature and philosophy

Primary sources and texts

Addison, Joseph, and Richard Steele, *The Spectator*, ed. Donald F. Bond (5 vols., Oxford, 1965).

Alison, Archibald, *Essays on the Nature and Principles of Taste* (2 vols., Edinburgh, 1790).

Berkeley, George, *The Principles of Human Knowledge*, ed. G. J. Warnock (London, 1962).

Blake, William, *The Poetry and Prose of William Blake*, ed. David W. Erdman (New York, 1965).

Burke, Edmund, *A Philosophical Inquiry into the Origin of our Ideas of the Sublime and Beautiful*, ed. J. T. Boulton (Indiana and London, 1958).

Butler, Bishop Joseph, *The Analogy of Religion, Natural and Revealed* ... (1736; London, 1906).

Coleridge, Samuel Taylor, *Biographia Literaria* (1817), ed. James Engell and W. J. Bate, *The Collected Works of Samuel Taylor Coleridge*, gen. ed. Kathleen Coburn (Princeton, 1980–), vol. VII (1983).

Diderot, Denis, *The Encyclopédie of Diderot and D'Alembert*, ed. J. Lough (Cambridge, 1954).

Jacques le fataliste, trans. Michael Henry (Harmondsworth, 1986).

Oeuvres complètes, eds. H. Dieckmann *et al.* (Paris, 1975–).

Oeuvres romanesques, ed. Henri Bénac (Paris, 1962).

Rameau's Nephew and D'Alembert's Dream, trans. L. Tancock (Harmondsworth, 1966).

Goethe, Johann Wolfgang von, *Werke*, Hamburger Ausgabe (14 vols., Hamburg, 1948–64).

Hume, David, *Dialogues concerning Natural Religion*, ed. Norman Kemp Smith (2nd edn, London, 1947).

Essays Moral, Political and Literary (Oxford, 1903).

The Letters of David Hume, ed. J. Y. T. Grieg (2 vols., Oxford, 1932).

A Treatise of Human Nature, ed. L. A. Selby-Bigge, 3rd edn rev. by P. Nidditch (Oxford, 1975).

Hurd, Richard, *Discourse on Poetical Imitation*, in *Works* (8 vols., London, 1811).

Johnson, Samuel, *Rasselas*, ed. J. P. Hardy (Oxford, 1988).

Samuel Johnson, ed. Donald Greene, Oxford Authors Series (Oxford, 1984).

The Yale Edition of the Works of Samuel Johnson, ed. W. J. Bate *et al.* (New Haven, 1958–).

Kames, Henry Home, Lord, *Elements of Criticism*, 9th edn (2 vols., Edinburgh, 1817).

Kant, Immanuel, *The Critique of Aesthetic Judgement*, trans. J. C. Meredith (Oxford, 1928).

The Critique of Practical Reason, trans. K. Abbott (London, 1879).

The Critique of Pure Reason, trans. Norman Kemp Smith (Oxford, 1929).

Werke, ed. Preussische Akademie der Wissenschaften (Berlin, 1902 ff.) (abbreviated as AA).

Locke, John, *An Essay concerning Human Understanding*, ed. P. H. Nidditch (Oxford, 1975).

Newton, Isaac, *Newton's Philosophy of Nature: Selections from his Works*, ed. H. S. Thayer (New York and London, 1953).

Pope, Alexander, *The Twickenham Edition of the Poems of Alexander Pope*, gen. ed. John Butt (11 vols., London, 1939–69):
vol. I, *An Essay on Criticism*, eds. E. Audra and Aubrey Williams (1961);
vol. III (i), *An Essay on Man*, ed. Maynard Mack (1950).

Reynolds, Sir Joshua, *Discourses on Art*, ed. Robert R. Wark, rev. edn (New Haven and London, 1975).

Richardson, Jonathan, *An Essay on the Theory of Painting*, 2nd edn (London, 1725).

Rousseau, Jean-Jacques, *Lettre à M. d'Alembert sur les spectacles*, ed. M. Fuchs (Geneva, 1948).

Oeuvres complètes (5 vols., Paris, 1959–95).

Schlegel, A. W., *Course of Lectures on Dramatic Art and Literature*, trans. J. Black (London, 1846).

Ueber Dramatische Kunst und Litteratur (3 vols., Heidelberg, 1817).

Shaftesbury, Anthony Ashley Cooper, third Earl of, *Characteristicks of Men, Manners, Opinions, Times*, 2nd edn (London, 1714).

Simpson, David (ed.), *The Origins of Modern Critical Thought: German Aesthetic and Literary Criticism from Lessing to Hegel* (Cambridge, 1988).

Smith, Adam, *The Theory of Moral Sentiments*, ed. D. D. Raphael and A. L. Macfie (Oxford, 1976).

Voltaire (François-Marie Arouet), *Candide, ou l'Optimisme* (Paris, 1969).

Letters on England, trans. L. Tancock (Harmondsworth, 1980).

Lettres philosophiques, ed. G. Lanson, rev. A-M. Rousseau (2 vols., Paris, 1964).

Oeuvres complètes, ed. T. Besterman (Geneva, 1968–).

Zadig and other Stories, ed. Haydn Mason (Oxford, 1971).

Secondary sources

Abrams, M. H., *The Mirror and The Lamp: Romantic Theory and the Critical Tradition* (Oxford, 1953).

Natural Supernaturalism: Tradition and Revolution in Romantic Literature (New York, 1971).

Battestin, Martin, *The Providence of Wit* (Oxford, 1974).

Bosker, A., *Literary Criticism in the Age of Johnson*, 2nd edn (Groningen and Djakarta, 1954).

Cassirer, Ernst, *The Philosophy of the Enlightenment*, trans. F. C. A. Koelln and J. P. Pettegrove (Princeton, 1951).

Christensen, Jerome, *Practicing Enlightenment: Hume and the Formation of a Literary Career* (Madison WI, 1987).

Crane, R. S., *The Idea of the Humanities* (2 vols., Chicago and London, 1967).

Damrosch, Leo, *Fictions of Reality in the Age of Hume and Johnson* (Madison WI, 1989).

Engell, James, *The Creative Imagination: Enlightenment to Romanticism* (Cambridge MA and London, 1981).

Fauvel, John, *et al.* (eds.), *Let Newton Be!* (Oxford, 1988).

France, Peter, *Diderot* (Oxford, 1983).

Fussell, Paul, *The Rhetorical World of Augustan Humanism* (Oxford, 1965).

Gay, Peter, *The Enlightenment: An Interpretation* (2 vols., London, 1966–9).

Ginsberg, Robert (ed.), *The Philosopher as Writer* (London and Toronto, 1987).

Grimsley, Ronald, *Jean-Jacques Rousseau* (Brighton, Sussex, 1983).

James, D. G., *The Life of Reason: Hobbes, Locke, Bolingbroke* (London, 1949).

Kuhns, Richard, *Literature and Philosophy: Structures of Experience* (London, 1971).

Levi, Albert W., *Philosophy as Social Expression* (Chicago and London, 1974).

Marshall, David, *The Surprising Effects of Sympathy* (Chicago, 1988).

Mason, Haydn, *Voltaire* (London, 1975).

Potkay, Adam, *The Fate of Eloquence in the Age of Hume* (Ithaca and London, 1994).

Richetti, John J., *Philosophical Writing: Locke, Berkeley, Hume* (Cambridge MA, 1983).

Rosenbaum, S. P. (ed.), *English Literature and British Philosophy* (Chicago and London, 1971).

Sambrook, James, *The Intellectual and Cultural Context of English Literature in the Eighteenth Century, 1700–1789* (London, 1986).

Schaper, Eva (ed.), *Pleasure, Preference and Value: Studies in Philosophical Aesthetics* (Cambridge, 1983).

Scruton, Roger, *Kant* (Oxford, 1982).

Stewart, M. A. (ed.), *Studies in the Philosophy of the Scottish Enlightenment* (Oxford, 1990).

Wellek, René, *A History of Modern Criticism: 1750–1950* (4 vols., London, 1955).

Willey, Basil, *The Eighteenth-Century Background* (London, 1940).

Yolton, John W., *Thinking Matter: Materialism in Eighteenth-Century Britain* (Oxford, 1984).

The psychology of literary creation and literary response

Primary sources and texts

Addison, Joseph, *The Spectator*, ed. D. F. Bond (5 vols., Oxford, 1965).

Burke, Edmund, *A Philosophical Enquiry into the Origin of our Ideas of the Sublime and Beautiful*, ed. J. T. Boulton (London, 1958).

Coleridge, S. T., *Biographia Literaria*, ed. J. Engell and W. J. Bate (2 vols., Princeton, 1983).

Dryden, John, *Of Dramatic Poesy and Other Critical Essays*, ed. George Watson (2 vols., London, 1962).

Duff, William, *An Essay on Original Genius*, ed. J. L. Mahoney (Gainesville, 1964).

Gerard, Alexander, *An Essay on Genius*, ed. B. Fabian (Munich, 1966).

An Essay on Taste, ed. W. J. Hipple (Gainesville, 1963).

Hartley, David, *Observations on Man, his Frame, his Duty, and his Expectations* (5th edn, London, 1810).

Hobbes, Thomas, *Leviathan*, ed. R. Tuck (Cambridge, 1991).

Locke, John, *An Essay concerning Human Understanding*, ed. Peter H. Nidditch (Oxford, 1975).

Newton, Isaac, *Opticks*, ed. E. T. Whittaker (London, 1931).

Shaftesbury, Anthony Ashley Cooper, third Earl of, *Characteristicks of Men, Manners, Opinions, Times* (2nd edn, London, 1714).

Second Characters, ed. B. Rand (Cambridge, 1914).

Spingarn, J. E., *Critical Essays of the Seventeenth Century* (3 vols., Oxford, 1908).

Young, Edward, *Conjectures on Original Composition*, ed. E. J. Morley (Manchester, 1918).

Secondary sources

Abrams, M. H., *The Mirror and the Lamp: Romantic Theory and the Critical Tradition* (Oxford, 1953).

Brett, R. L., *The Third Earl of Shaftesbury: A Study in Eighteenth-Century Literary Theory* (London, 1951).

Elioseff, L. A., *The Cultural Milieu of Addison's Literary Criticism* (Ann Arbor, 1963).

Engell, James, *The Creative Imagination: Enlightenment to Romanticism* (Cambridge MA, 1981).

Fox, Christopher, *Locke and the Scriblerians* (London, 1988).

James, D. G., *The Life of Reason: Hobbes, Locke, Bolingbroke* (London, 1949).

Kallich, Martin, *The Association of Ideas and Critical Theory in Eighteenth-Century England: A History of a Psychological Method in English Criticism* (The Hague, 1970).

MacLean, Kenneth, *John Locke and English Literature of the Eighteenth Century* (New Haven, 1936).

Marsh, Robert, *Four Dialectical Theories of Poetry: An Aspect of English Neo-Classical Criticism* (Chicago, 1965).

Thorpe, C. D., *The Aesthetic Theory of Thomas Hobbes* (Ann Arbor, 1940).

Tuveson, E. L., *The Imagination as a Means of Grace: Locke and the Aesthetics of Romanticism* (Berkeley and Los Angeles, 1960).

Shaftesbury and Addison

Primary sources and texts

Addison, Joseph, *The Letters of Joseph Addison*, ed. Walter Graham (Oxford, 1941).

The Works of the Right Honourable Joseph Addison, ed. Henry G. Bohn (6 vols., London, 1875).

Addison, Joseph, and Richard Steele, *The Guardian*, ed. John Calhoun Stephens (Kentucky, 1982).

The Spectator, ed. Donald F. Bond (5 vols., Oxford, 1965).

The Tatler, ed. Donald F. Bond (3 vols., Oxford, 1987).

Barrell, Rex, A. (ed.), *Anthony Ashley Cooper Earl of Shaftesbury (1671–1713) and 'Le Refuge Français' Correspondence*, Studies in British History, 15 (Lampeter, 1989).

Burke, Edmund, *A Philosophical Enquiry into the Origin of Our Ideas of the Sublime and Beautiful*, ed. James T. Boulton (London, 1968).

Dennis, John, *The Critical Works of John Dennis*, ed. Edward Niles Hooker (2 vols., Baltimore, 1939).

Du Bos, Jean-Baptiste, *Réflexions critiques sur la poésie et sur la peinture* (3 vols., 4th edn Paris, 1740).

Fielding, Henry, *Joseph Andrews and Shamela*, ed. Sheridan Baker (New York, 1972).

Hume, David, *Essays Moral, Political, and Literary*, ed. Eugene F. Miller (Indianapolis, 1985).

Johnson, Samuel, *Lives of the English Poets*, ed. George Birkbeck Hill (3 vols., Oxford, 1905).

Locke, John, *An Essay concerning Human Understanding*, ed. Peter H. Nidditch (2 vols., Oxford, 1975).

Reynolds, Sir Joshua, *Discourses on Art*, ed. Robert R. Wark (New Haven, 1975).

Rousseau, Jean-Jacques, *Oeuvres complètes* (4 vols., Paris, 1964).

Politics and the Arts, Letter to M. d'Alembert on the Theatre, trans. Allan Bloom (Ithaca, 1973).

Shaftesbury, Anthony Ashley Cooper, third Earl of, *Characteristicks of Men, Manners, Opinions, Times* (London, 1711)

Characteristics of Men, Manners, Opinions, Times, etc., ed. John M. Robertson (2 vols., Gloucester MA, 1963).

Letters to a Student at the University (London, 1716).

The Life, Unpublished Letters, and Philosophical Regimen of Anthony, Earl of Shaftesbury, ed. Benjamin Rand (London, 1900).

Second Characters or The Language of Forms, ed. Benjamin Rand (New York, 1969).

Soliloquy: or, Advice to an Author (London, 1710).

Sterne, Laurence, *The Life and Times of Tristram Shandy, Gentleman*, ed. Ian Watt (Boston, 1965).

Taylor, Jeremy, *A Discourse of the Liberty of Prophesying. Shewing the Unreasonableness of Prescribing to Other Men Faith, and the Inequity of Persecuting Differing Opinions* (London, 1648).

Secondary sources

Abrams, M. H., 'From Addison to Kant: modern aesthetics and the exemplary art', in *Studies in Eighteenth-Century British Art and Aesthetics*, ed. Ralph Cohen (Berkeley, 1985), pp. 16–48.

Agnew, Jean-Christophe, *Worlds Apart: The Market and the Theater in Anglo-American Thought, 1550–1750* (Cambridge, 1986).

Aldridge, Alfred Owen, 'Lord Shaftesbury's literary theories', *Philological Quarterly*, 24 (1945), 46–64.

Brett, R. L., *The Third Earl of Shaftesbury: A Study in Eighteenth-Century Literary Theory* (London, 1951).

Cassirer, Ernst, *The Philosophy of the Enlightenment*, trans. Fritz C. A. Koelln and James P. Pettegrove (Princeton, 1951).

Damrosch, Leopold, 'The significance of Addison's criticism', *Studies in English Literature*, 19 (1979), 421–30.

Davidson, James W., 'Criticism and self-knowledge in Shaftesbury's *Soliloquy*', *Enlightenment Essays*, 5 (1974), 50–61.

Eagleton, Terry, *The Function of Criticism from the Spectator to Post-Structuralism* (London, 1984).

 The Ideology of the Aesthetic (Oxford, 1990).

Eisenstein, Elizabeth L., *The Printing Press as an Agent of Change: Communications and Cultural Transformations in Early Modern Europe* (New York, 1979).

Elioseff, Lee Andrew, *The Cultural Milieu of Addison's Literary Criticism* (Austin, 1963).

Fowler, Thomas, *Shaftesbury and Hutcheson* (London, 1882).

Fried, Michael, *Absorption and Theatricality: Painting and Beholder in the Age of Diderot* (Berkeley, 1979).

Fry, Paul, *The Reach of Criticism: Method and Perception in Literary Theory* (New Haven, 1983).

Gay, Peter, 'The spectator as actor: Addison in perspective', *Encounter*, 29 (1967), 27–32.

Grean, Stanley, *Shaftesbury's Philosophy of Religion and Ethics: A Study in Enthusiasm* (Athens OH, 1967).

Habermas, Jürgen, *The Structural Transformation of the Public Sphere: An Inquiry into a Category of Bourgeois Society*, trans. Thomas Burger and Frederick Lawrence (Cambridge, 1989).

Hall, S. C., *Pilgrimages to English Shrines* (New York, 1854).

Hansen, David A., 'Addison on ornament and poetic style', in *Studies in Criticism and Aesthetics, 1660–1800*, ed. Howard Anderson and John S. Shea (Minneapolis, 1967).

Hartman, Geoffrey H., *Minor Prophecies: The Literary Essay in the Culture Wars* (Cambridge, 1991).

Hayman, John G., 'Shaftesbury and the search for a persona', *Studies in English Literature*, 10 (1970), 491–504.

Hipple, Walter John Jr, *The Beautiful, the Sublime, and The Picturesque in Eighteenth-Century British Aesthetic Theory* (Carbondale IL, 1957).

Hohendahl, Peter Uwe, *The Institution of Criticism* (Ithaca, 1982).

Kallich, Martin, 'The association of ideas and critical theory: Hobbes, Locke, and Addison', *ELH*, 12 (1945), 290–315.

Ketcham, Michael G., *Transparent Designs: Reading, Performance, and Form in the Spectator Papers* (Athens GA, 1985).

Kinsley, William, 'Meaning and format: Mr. Spectator and his folio half-sheets', *ELH*, 34 (1967), 482–94.

Klein, Lawrence, 'The third Earl of Shaftesbury and the progress of politeness', *Eighteenth-Century Studies*, 18 (1984–85), 186–214.

Leavis, Q. D., *Fiction and the Reading Public* (Norwood PA, 1977).

Lewis, C. S., *Selected Literary Essays*, ed. Walter Hooper (Cambridge, 1969).

Markley, Robert, 'Sentimentality as performance: Shaftesbury, Sterne, and the theatrics of virtue', in Felicity Nussbaum and Laura Brown (eds.), *The New Eighteenth Century: Theory, Politics, English Literature* (New York, 1987), pp. 210–30.

'Style and philosophical structure: the contexts of Shaftesbury's *Characteristicks*', in Robert Ginsberg (ed.), *The Philosopher as Writer: The Eighteenth Century* (London, 1987), pp. 140–54.

Marsh, Robert, *Four Dialectical Theories of Poetry* (Chicago, 1965).

Marshall, David, *The Figure of Theater: Shaftesbury, Defoe, Adam Smith, and George Eliot* (New York, 1986).

The Surprising Effects of Sympathy: Marivaux, Rousseau, Diderot, and Mary Shelley (Chicago, 1988).

'Arguing by analogy: Hume's standard of taste', *Eighteenth-Century Studies*, 28 (1995), 323–43.

Monk, Samuel H., *The Sublime: A Study of Critical Theories in XVIII-Century England* (Ann Arbor, 1960).

Norton, David Fate, *Shaftesbury and the Two Scepticisms* (Turin, 1968).

Paknadel, Felix, 'Shaftesbury's illustration of the *Characteristics*', *Journal of the Warburg and Courtauld Institutes*, 37 (1974), 290–312.

Paulson, Ronald, *Satire and the Novel in Eighteenth-Century England* (New Haven, 1967).

Plumb, J. H., 'The public, literature, and the arts in the 18th century', in Paul Fritz and David Williams (eds.), *The Triumph of Culture: 18th-Century Perspectives* (Toronto, 1972), pp. 27–48.

Price, Martin, *To The Palace of Wisdom: Studies in Order and Energy from Dryden to Blake* (Carbondale IL, 1970).

Purpus, E. R., 'The "plain, easy, and familiar way": the dialogue in English literature, 1660–1725', *ELH*, 17 (1950), 47–58.

Rogers, Pat, 'Shaftesbury and the aesthetics of rhapsody', *British Journal of Aesthetics*, 12 (1972), 244–57.

Routh, H. V., 'Steele and Addison', in *The Cambridge History of English Literature*, ed. A. W. Ward and A. R. Waller (Cambridge, 1932).

Saccamano, Neil, 'Authority and publication: the works of "Swift"', *The Eighteenth Century*, 25 (1984), 241–62.

'The consolations of ambivalence: Habermas and the public sphere', *MLN*, 106 (1991), 685–98.

'The sublime force of words in Addison's "Pleasures"', *ELH*, 57 (1990), 1–24.

Sherman, Carol, 'In defense of the dialogue: dialogue, Shaftesbury, and Galiani', *Romance Notes*, 15 (1973), 268–73.

Smithers, Peter, *The Life of Joseph Addison* (Oxford, 1954).

Stolnitz, Jerome, '"Beauty": some stages in the history of an idea', *Journal of the History of Ideas*, 22 (1961), 185–204.

'On the origins of "aesthetic disinterestedness"', *Journal of Aesthetics and Art Criticism*, 20 (1961–2), 131–43.

Sweetman, J. E., 'Shaftesbury's last commission', *Journal of the Warburg and Courtauld Institutes*, 19 (1956), 110–16.

Thorpe, Clarence D., 'Addison's contribution to criticism', in Richard Foster Jones *et al.* (eds.), *The Seventeenth Century: Studies in the History of English Thought and Literature from Bacon to Pope* (Stanford, 1951), pp. 316–29.

'Addison's theory of the imagination as "perceptive response"', *Papers of the Michigan Academy of Science, Art, and Letters*, 21 (1936), 509–30.

Townsend, Dabney, 'Shaftesbury's aesthetic theory', *Journal of Aesthetics and Art Criticism*, 41 (1982), 206–13.

Tuveson, Ernest, 'The importance of Shaftesbury', *ELH*, 20 (1953), 267–99.

Uphaus, Robert W., 'Shaftesbury on art: the rhapsodic aesthetic', *Journal of Aesthetics and Art Criticism*, 27 (1969), 341–8.

Voitle, Robert, *The Third Earl of Shaftesbury, 1671–1713* (Baton Rouge, 1984).

Watson, Melvin R., 'The *Spectator* tradition and the development of the familiar essay', *ELH*, 13 (1946), 189–215.

Watt, Ian, 'The consequences of literacy', *Comparative Studies in Society and History*, 5 (1963), 304–45.

'Publishers and sinners: the Augustan view', *Studies in Bibliography*, 12 (1959), 3–20.

Youngren, William H., 'Addison and the birth of eighteenth-century aesthetics', *Modern Philology*, 79 (1982), 267–83.

The rise of aesthetics from Baumgarten to Humboldt

Primary sources and texts

Baumgarten, Alexander Gottlieb, *Aesthetica* (Trajecti cis viadrum [Frankfurt-on-the-Oder], 1750, 1758, rpt Hildesheim, 1961).

Meditationes philosophicae de nonnullis ad poema pertinentibus (Halle, 1735); rpt in *Reflections on poetry. Alexander Gottlieb Baumgarten's Meditationes philosophicae de nonnullis ad poema pertinentibus*, trans. with the original text, and intro. and notes by Karl Aschenbrenner and William B. Holther (Berkeley and Los Angeles, 1954); also in *Philosophische Betrachtungen über einige Bedingungen des Gedichtes*, trans. into German, with the original text, and intro. and notes by Heinz Paetzold, Philosophische Bibliothek, 352 (Hamburg, 1983).

Metaphysica (Halle, 1739; rpt of 7th edn Hildesheim, 1963).

Texte zur Grundlegung der Ästhetik, trans. (into German) and ed. Hans Rudolf Schweizer, Philosophische Bibliothek, 351 (Hamburg, 1983).

Theoretische Ästhetik. Die grundlegenden Abschnitte aus der 'Aesthetica' (1750; 1758), trans. [into German] and ed. Hans Rudolf Schweizer, Philosophische Bibliothek, 355 (Hamburg, 1983).

Burke, Edmund, *A Philosophical Inquiry into the Origin of Our Ideas of the Sublime and Beautiful* (London, 1757).

Diderot, Denis, *Oeuvres complètes de Diderot* (20 vols., Paris, 1875–7).

Goethe, Johann Wolfgang, *Briefe*, ed. Karl Robert Mandelkow (4 vols., Hamburg, 1962–7).

Werke, Sophienausgabe (133 vols., Weimar, 1886–1919).

Werke, ed. Erich Trunz (14 vols., Hamburg, 1949–64) (abbreviated as HA).

Herder, Johann Gottfried, *Sämtliche Werke*, ed. Bernhard Suphan (33 vols., Berlin, 1877–1913) (abbreviated as SW).

Hogarth, William, *The Analysis of Beauty* (London, 1753).

Humboldt, Carl Wilhelm von, *Gesammelte Schriften*, ed. Albert Leitzmann (17 vols., Berlin, 1903–20; rpt Berlin, 1968) (abbreviated as GS).

Hume, David, *Essays Moral, Political and Literary* (Oxford, 1963).

Kant, Immanuel, *Critique of Judgement*, trans. James Creed Meredith (Oxford, 1928).

Gesammelte Schriften, ed. Preussische Akademie der Wissenschaften (Berlin, 1902–) (abbreviated as AA).

Lessing, Gotthold Ephraim, *Laokoon*, ed. Dorothy Reich (Oxford, 1965).

Sämtliche Schriften, ed. Karl Lachmann and Franz Muncker (23 vols., Stuttgart and Leipzig, 1886–1924).

Meier, Georg Friedrich, *Anfangsgründe aller schönen Künste und Wissenschaften* (3 vols., Halle, 1748–50).

Mendelssohn, Moses, *Ästhetische Schriften in Auswahl*, ed. Otto F. Best, Texte zur Forschung, 14 (Darmstadt, 1974).

Gesammelte Schriften, Jubiläumsausgabe, ed. Fritz Bamberger *et al.* (Berlin, 1929; rpt, contd and ed. Alexander Altmann, Stuttgart–Bad Cannstatt, 1971ff.).

Moritz, Karl Philipp, *Schriften zur Ästhetik und Poetik*, ed. Hans Joachim Schrimpf, Neudrucke Deutscher Literaturwerke, N.F. 7 (Tübingen, 1962).

Reynolds, Sir Joshua, *Discourses on Art*, ed. Robert B. Wark (New Haven and London, 1975).

Schiller, Johann Friedrich, *Briefe*, ed. Fritz Jonas (7 vols., Stuttgart, Leipzig, Berlin, Vienna, n.d.).

On the Aesthetic Education of Man, in a Series of Letters, ed., trans. and intro. by Elizabeth M. Wilkinson and L. A. Willoughby (Oxford, 1967).

Schillers Werke, Nationalausgabe, ed. Julius Petersen *et al.* (Weimar, 1943–).

Sulzer, Johann Georg, *Allgemeine Theorie der schönen Künste* (2 vols., Leipzig, 1771–4).

Winckelmann, Johann Joachim, *Sämtliche Werke*, ed. Joseph Eiselein (12 vols., Donaueschingen, 1824–29; rpt Osnabrück, 1965).

Secondary sources

Batley, Edward M., 'On the nature and delineation of beauty in art and philosophy: Lessing's responses to William Hogarth and Edmund Burke', in C. P. Magill, Brian A. Rowley and Christopher J. Smith (eds.), *Tradition and*

Creation. Essays in Honour of Elizabeth Mary Wilkinson (Leeds, 1978), pp. 30–45.

Beck, Lewis White, *Early German Philosophy: Kant and his Predecessors* (Cambridge MA, 1969).

Belaval, Yvon, *L'esthétique sans paradoxe de Diderot* (Paris, 1950).

Bergmann, Ernst, G. F. *Meier als Mitbegründer der deutschen Ästhetik* (Leipzig, 1910).

Cassirer, Ernst, *The Philosophy of the Enlightenment*, trans. Fritz A. Koelln and James P. Pettegrove (Princeton, 1951; German original: *Die Philosophie der Aufklärung*, Tübingen, 1932).

Caygill, Howard, *Art of Judgement* (Oxford, 1989).

Chouillet, Jacques, *Diderot* (Paris, 1977).

L'esthétique des lumières (Littératures Modernes, 4, Paris, 1974).

'Littérature et esthétique', *Studies on Voltaire and the Eighteenth Century*, 264 (1989), 1,035–59.

Cohen, Ted, and Paul Guyer (eds.), *Essays in Kant's Aesthetics* (Chicago and London, 1982).

Coleman, Francis X. J., *The Aesthetic Thought of the French Enlightenment* (Pittsburgh, 1971).

The Harmony of Reason: A Study in Kant's Aesthetics (Pittsburgh, 1974).

Dieckmann, Herbert, *Diderot und die Aufklärung. Aufsätze zur europäischen Literatur des 18. Jahrhunderts* (Stuttgart, 1972).

Ellis, J. M., *Schiller's 'Kalliasbriefe' and the Study of his Aesthetic Theory*, Anglica Germanica, 12 (The Hague and Paris, 1969).

Franke, Ursula, *Kunst als Erkenntnis. Die Rolle der Sinnlichkeit in der Ästhetik Alexander Gottlieb Baumgartens*, Studia Leibnitiana, 9 (Wiesbaden, 1972).

Gilbert, Katharine Everett, and Helmut Kuhn, *A History of Esthetics* (New York, 1939).

Guyer, Paul, *Kant and the Claims of Taste* (Cambridge MA, 1979).

Hatfield, Henry, *Aesthetic Paganism in German Literature from Winckelmann to the Death of Goethe* (Cambridge MA, 1964).

Winckelmann and his German Critics 1755–1781 (New York, 1943).

Haym, Rudolf, *Herder* (2 vols., Berlin, 1880–5; new edn with an introduction by Wolfgang Harich, Berlin, 1954).

Irmscher, Hans Dietrich, 'Zur Ästhetik des jungen Herder', in Gerhard Sauder (ed.), *Johann Gottfried Herder 1744–1803* (Hamburg, 1987), pp. 43–76.

Jaeger, Michael, *Die Ästhetik als Antwort auf das kopernikanische Weltbild. Die Beziehungen zwischen den Naturwissenschaften und der Ästhetik Alexander Gottlieb Baumgartens und Georg Friedrich Meiers*, Philosophische Texte und Studien, 10 (Hildesheim, Zurich, New York, 1984).

Kommentierende Einführung in Baumgartens Aesthetica. Zur Entstehung der wissenschaftlichen Ästhetik des 18. Jahrhunderts in Deutschland (Hildesheim and New York, 1980).

Jolles, Matthijs, *Goethes Kunstanschauung* (Berne, 1957).

Kerry, S. S., *Schiller's Writings on Aesthetics* (Manchester, 1961).

Körner, Stephan, *Kant* (Harmondsworth, 1955).

McCloskey, Mary A., *Kant's Aesthetics* (Basingstoke and London, 1987).

Molbjerg, Hans, *Aspects de l'esthétique de Diderot* (Copenhagen, 1964).

Möller, Uwe, *Rhetorische Überlieferung und Dichtungstheorie im frühen 18. Jahrhundert. Studien zu Gottsched, Breitinger und Georg Friedrich Meier* (Munich, 1985).

Müller-Vollmer, Kurt, *Poesie und Einbildungskraft. Zur Dichtungstheorie Wilhelm von Humboldts. Mit der deutschsprachigen Ausgabe eines Aufsatzes Humboldts für Frau von Staël [Essais Esthétiques* (1799), including French original] (Stuttgart, 1967).

Nisbet, H. B. (ed.), *German Aesthetic and Literary Criticism: Winckelmann, Lessing, Hamann, Herder, Schiller, Goethe* (Cambridge, 1985).

'Laocoon in Germany: the reception of the group since Winckelmann', *Oxford German Studies*, 10 (1979), 22–63.

Nivelle, Armand, *Les Théories esthétiques en Allemagne de Baumgarten à Kant* (Paris, 1955). German trans. *Kunst– und Dichtungstheorien zwischen Aufklärung und Klassik* (Berlin, 1960).

Peters, Hans Georg, *Die Ästhetik A. G. Baumgartens und ihre Beziehung zum Ethischen*, Neuere Deutsche Forschungen, 9 (Berlin, 1934).

Poppe, Bernhard, 'Alexander Gottlieb Baumgarten. Seine Bedeutung und Stellung in der Leibniz-Wolffschen Philosophie und seine Beziehungen zu Kant' (containing a copy of the lecture-notes of Baumgarten's lectures on aesthetics) (Diss. Leipzig, 1907).

Reed, T. J., *The Classical Centre: Goethe and Weimar 1775–1832* (London, 1980).

Reiss, Hans, 'Die Einbürgerung der Ästhetik in der deutschen Sprache des achtzehnten Jahrhunderts oder Baumgarten und seine Wirkung', *Jahrbuch der Deutschen Schillergesellschaft*, 37 (1993), 109–38.

'Georg Friedrich Meier (1718–1777) und die Verbreitung der Ästhetik', in *Geschichtlichkeit und Gegenwart. Festschrift für Hans Dietrich Irmscher zum 65. Geburtstag*, ed. Hans Esselborn and Werner Keller (Cologne, Weimar, Vienna, 1994) pp. 13–34.

'The "naturalisation" of the term "Asthetik" in eighteenth-century German: Alexander Gottlieb Baumgarten and his impact', *Modern Language Review*, 89 (1994), 645–58.

Riemann, Albert, *Die Ästhetik A. G. Baumgartens unter besonderer Berücksichtigung der Meditationes, nebst einer Übersetzung dieser Schrift*, Bausteine zur Geschichte der neueren deutschen Literatur, 21 (Halle, 1928).

Ritter, Joachim, 'Ästhetik, ästhetisch', in Joachim Ritter (ed.), *Historisches Wörterbuch der Philosophie* (Basel and Stuttgart, 1977), I, columns 555–71.

Schaper, Eva, *Studies in Kant's Aesthetics* (Edinburgh, 1979).

Schmidt, Johannes, *Leibniz und Baumgarten. Ein Beitrag zur deutschen Ästhetik* (Halle, 1875).

Schweizer, Hans Rudolf, *Ästhetik als Philosophie der sinnlichen Erkenntnis. Eine Interpretation der 'Aesthetica' A. G. Baumgartens mit teilweiser Wiedergabe des lateinischen Textes und deutscher Übersetzung* (Basel and Stuttgart, 1973).

Sharpe, Lesley, *Friedrich Schiller. Drama, Thought and Politics* (Cambridge, 1991).

Solms, Friedhelm, *Disciplina Aesthetica. Zur Frühgeschichte der ästhetischen Theorie bei Baumgarten und Herder*, Forschungen und Berichte der Evangelischen Studiengemeinschaft, 45 (Stuttgart, 1990).

Strube, Werner, 'Schillers Kallias-Briefe oder über die Objektivität der Schönheit', *Literaturwissenschaftliches Jahrbuch*, 18 (1977), 115–31.

Wellbery, David E., *Lessing's Laocoon. Semiotics and Aesthetics in the Age of Reason* (Cambridge, 1984).

Wellek, René, *A History of Modern Criticism 1750–1950*, vol. I: *The Later Eighteenth Century* (London, 1955).

Wieland, Wolfgang, 'Die Erfahrung des Urteils. Warum Kant keine Ästhetik begründet hat', *Deutsche Vierteljahrsschrift für Literaturwissenschaft und Geistesgeschichte*, 64 (1990), 604–23.

Wilkinson, Elizabeth M., 'Goethe's conception of form', in Elizabeth M. Wilkinson and L. A. Willoughby (eds.), *Goethe. Poet and Thinker* (London, 1962), pp. 167–84.

Ut pictura poesis

Primary sources and texts

Addison, Joseph, *The Spectator*, ed. Donald Bond (5 vols., Oxford, 1965).

Aristotle, *The 'Art' of Rhetoric*, trans. J. H. Freese (Cambridge, 1959).
  The Poetics, trans. W. Hamilton Fyfe (Cambridge, 1973).

Batteux, Charles, *Les Beaux-Arts réduits à un même principe* (Paris, 1747).

Berkeley, George, *Principles, Dialogues, and Philosophical Correspondence*, ed. Colin Murray Turbayne (Indianapolis, 1965).

Blair, Hugh, *Lectures on Rhetoric and Belles Lettres*, ed. Harold F. Harding (2 vols., Carbondale IL, 1965).

Burke, Edmund, *A Philosophical Enquiry into the Origin of Our Ideas of the Sublime and Beautiful*, ed. with an introduction by James T. Boulton (London, 1968).

Caylus, Comte de, *Tableaux tirés de l'Iliade, de l'Odyssée de Homere et de l'Eneide de Virgile: avec des observations générales sur le Costume* (Paris, 1757).

Cicero, *De Oratore*, in *Cicero*, trans. H. Rackham (28 vols., Cambridge MA, 1968).

Diderot, Denis, *Oeuvres complètes* (33 vols., Paris, 1975–).

Diderot, Denis, and Jean le Rond d'Alembert, *Encyclopédie, ou Dictionnaire raisonné des sciences, des arts et des métiers*, vol. III (Paris, 1753).

Dryden, John, *Essays*, ed. W. P. Ker (2 vols., Oxford, 1926).

Du Bos, Jean-Baptiste, *Réflexions critiques sur la poésie et sur la peinture* (3 vols., 4th edn, Paris, 1740).

Du Fresnoy, C. A., *The Art of Painting: With Remarks, trans., with an original Preface, containing a Parallel between Painting and Poetry, By Mr Dryden* (London, 1750).

Dyer, George, *Poetics* (London, 1812) [1796].

Harris, James, *Three Treatises* (London, 1765).

Hobbes, Thomas, *Leviathan Or The Matter, Forme and Power of a Commonwealth Ecclesiasticall and Civil*, ed. Richard Tuck (Cambridge, 1991).

Horace, *Satires, Epistles, Ars Poetica*, trans. H. Rushton Fairclough (Cambridge, 1966).

Hume, David, *Enquiries concerning Human Understanding and concerning the Principles of Morals*, ed. L. A. Selby-Bigge (Oxford, 1975).

Johnson, Samuel, *Selected Poetry and Prose*, ed. with an Introduction by Frank Brady and W. K. Wimsatt (Berkeley, 1977).

Kames, Henry Home, Lord, *Elements of Criticism* (2 vols., New York, 1823).

Lessing, Gotthold Ephraim, *Laocoön: An Essay on the Limits of Painting and Poetry*, trans. with an introduction by Edward Allen McCormick (Indianapolis, 1962).

Laokoon: oder Über die Grenzen der Malerei und Poesie, in *Sämtliche Schriften*, ed. Karl Lachmann and Franz Muncker (Stuttgart, 1886–1924; rpt Berlin, 1968).

Locke, John, *An Essay concerning Human Understanding*, ed. Peter H. Nidditch (Oxford, 1975).

Longinus, *Works*, trans. L. Welsted (London, 1724).

Mendelssohn, Moses, *Gesammelte Schriften*, Jubiläumsausgabe, ed. F. Bamberg *et al.* (17 vols., Stuttgart–Bad Cannstatt, 1971).

Piles, Roger de, *Cours de peinture par principes* (Paris, 1708), trans. 'by a Painter' as *The Principles of Painting* (London, 1743).

Pope, Alexander, 'Preface' to *The Iliad of Homer*, in *Works*, ed. Maynard Mack (New Haven, 1967).

The Twickenham Edition of the Poems of Alexander Pope, ed. John Butt.

Reresby, Tamworth, *A Miscellany of Ingenious Thoughts and Reflections, In Verse and Prose* (London, 1721).

Richardson, Jonathan, *An Essay on the Theory of Painting* (London, 1715).

Two Discourses. I. An Essay on the whole Art of Criticism as it Relates to Painting. II. An Argument in behalf of the Science of a Connoisseur (London, 1719).

Warton, Joseph, *An Essay on the Genius and Writings of Pope* (2 vols., London, 1782).

Secondary sources

Bender, John B., *Spenser and Literary Pictorialism* (Princeton, 1972).

Brownell, Morris R., *Alexander Pope and the Arts of Georgian England* (Oxford, 1978).

Cohen, Ralph, *The Art of Discrimination: Thomson's The Seasons and the Language of Criticism* (Berkeley, 1964).

Folkierski, Wladyslaw, '*Ut pictura poesis* ou l'étrange fortune du *De arte graphica* de Du Fresnoy en Angleterre', *Revue de littérature comparée*, 27 (1953), 385–402.

Fried, Michael, *Absorption and Theatricality: Painting and Beholder in the Age of Diderot* (Berkeley, 1979).

Hagstrum, Jean H., *The Sister Arts: The Tradition of Literary Pictorialism and English Poetry from Dryden to Gray* (Chicago, 1958).

Hollander, John, 'The poetics of *ekphrasis*', in *Word and Image*, 4 (1988) 209–19.

Howard, William G., '*Ut pictura poesis*', *Publications of the Modern Language Association*, 24 (1909), 43–123.

Krieger, Murray, *Ekphrasis: The Illusion of the Natural Sign* (Baltimore, 1992).

Lee, Rensselaer W., '*Ut Pictura Poesis*: the Humanistic theory of painting', *The Art Bulletin*, 22 (1940), 197–269.

Lombard, A., *L'Abbé Du Bos, un initiateur de la pensée moderne* (Paris, 1913).

McGuinness, Arthur E., 'Hume and Kames: the burdens of friendship', *Studies in Scottish Literature*, 6 (1969), 3–19.

Mitchell, W. J. T., *Iconology: Image, Text, Ideology* (Chicago, 1986).

Spacks, Patricia Meyer, *The Poetry of Vision: Five Eighteenth-Century Poets* (Cambridge MA, 1967).

Wellbery, David E., *Lessing's Laocoon: Semiotics and Aesthetics in the Age of Reason* (Cambridge, 1984).

Wellek, René, *A History of Modern Criticism, 1750–1950* (4 vols., New Haven, 1966).

Williams, Robert W., 'Alexander Pope and *Ut Pictura Poesis*', *Sydney Studies in English* (1983–4), 61–75.

Wimsatt, William K. and Cleanth Brooks, *Literary Criticism: A Short History* (New York, 1959).

The picturesque

Primary sources and texts

Addison, Joseph, *The Spectator*, ed. Donald Bond (5 vols., Oxford, 1965).

Aristotle, *The Poetics*, trans. W. Hamilton Fyfe (Cambridge, 1973).

Austen, Jane, *The Novels of Jane Austen*, ed. R. W. Chapman (5 vols., Oxford, 1923; rpt 1966).

Chambers, William, *A Dissertation on Oriental Gardening* (1772; rpt London, 1972).

Dallaway, James, 'Supplementry Anecdotes of Gardening in England' in Horace Walpole, *Anecdotes of Painting in England* (1827; rpt in *The English Landscape Garden*, ed. John Dixon Hunt (vol. 18, New York, 1982).

Fielding, Henry, *The History of Tom Jones, A Foundling*, ed. Fredson Bowers (Oxford, 1975).

Gérardin, R. A., *De la Composition des paysages, ou Des Moyens d'embellir la Nature autour des Habitations, en joignant l'agréable à l'utilité* (Geneva, 1777).

Gilpin, William, *A Dialogue upon the Gardens of the Right Honorable the Lord Viscount Cobham at Stow in Buckinghamshire* (1748).

An Essay upon Prints, Containing Remarks upon the Principles of Picturesque Beauty (London, 1768).

Observations on Several Parts of Great Britain, Particulary the High-Lands of Scotland, Relative Chiefly to Picturesque Beauty Made in the Year 1776 (2 vols., 3rd. edn, London, 1808).

Remarks on Forest Scenery, and Other Woodland Views, Relative Chiefly to Picturesque Beauty (2 vols., London, 1791; rpt The Richmond Publishing Co., 1973).

Remarks on Forest Scenery, and Other Views, ed. Thomas Dick Lauder (2 vols., Edinburgh, 1834).

Three Essays: On Picturesque Beauty; on Picturesque Travel; and on Sketching Landscape (London, 1792).

Goethe, Johann Wolfgang von, *Elective Affinities,* trans. Elizabeth Mayer and Louise Bogan (South Bend, 1963).

Werke, ed. Erich Trunz (14 vols., Hamburg, 1948–1964).

Knight, Richard Payne, *An Analytical Inquiry into the Principles of Taste* (London, 1805; 4th edn, 1808).

The Landscape, A Didactic Poem. In Three Books. Addressed to Uvedale Price, Esq. (London, 1794).

The Landscape, A Didactic Poem. 2nd edn (London, 1795).

Locke, John, *An Essay Concerning Human Understanding,* ed. Peter H. Nidditch (Oxford, 1975).

Mason, George, *An Essay on Design in Gardening* (London, 1768).

Pope, Alexander, *The Twickenham Edition of the Poems of Alexander Pope,* ed. John Butt (10 vols., London, 1961–7).

The Correspondence of Alexander Pope, ed. George Sherburne (5 vols., Oxford, 1956).

Price, Uvedale, *An Essay on the Picturesque, as compared with the sublime and the Beautiful; and on the Use of Studying Pictures, for the Purpose of Improving Real Landscape* (London, 1794).

Essays on the Picturesque as Compared with The Sublime and the Beautiful; and on the Use of Studying Pictures, for the Purpose of Improving Real Landscape (3 vols., London, 1810).

Letter to Humphrey Repton, Esq. on the Application of The Practice as well as the Principles of Landscape-Painting to Landscape-Gardening: Intended as a Supplement to the 'Essay on the Picturesque' (London, 1795).

Repton, Humphrey, *The Landscape Gardening and Landscape Architecture of the Late Humphrey Repton, Esq.,* ed. J. C. Loudon (London, 1860).

Reynolds, Sir Joshua, *Discourses on Art,* ed. Robert R. Wark (New Haven, 1975).

Shaftesbury, Anthony Ashley Cooper, third Earl of, *Characteristics of Men, Manners, Opinions, Times, etc.,* ed. John M. Robertson (2 vols., 1900; rpt Gloucester, 1963).

Shenstone, William, *The Works in Verse and Prose of William Shenstone, Esq.* (2 vols., London, 1764; rpt in *The English Landscape Garden,* ed. John Dixon Hunt, vol. 17 (New York, 1982).

Spence, Joseph, *Observations, Anecdotes, and Characters of Books and Men,* ed. James M. Osborn (2 vols., Oxford, 1966).

Switzer, Stephen, *The Nobleman, Gentleman, and Gardener's Recreation: or, An Introduction to Gardening, Planting, Agriculture, and the Other Business and Pleasures of a Country Life* (London, 1715); reissued in 1718 and 1742 with two additional volumes, as *Ichnographia Rustica: or, The Nobleman, Gentleman, and Gardener's Recreation* (London, 1718; 1742)).

Tasso, Torquato, *Opere* (Turin, 1955).

Whately, Thomas, *Observations on Modern Gardening... to which is added An Essay on the Different Natural Situations of Gardens. With notes by Horace (Late) Earl of Orford* (London, 1801).

Secondary sources

Andrews, Malcolm, *The Search for the Picturesque: Landscape Aesthetics and Tourism in Britain, 1760–1800* (Aldershot, 1989).

Barrell, John, *The Idea of Landscape and the Sense of Place 1730–1840: An Approach to the Poetry of John Clare* (Cambridge, 1972).

Bermingham, Ann, *Landscape and Ideology: The English Rustic Tradition, 1740–1860* (Berkeley, 1986).

Bowie, Karen, *'L'Eclectisme Pittoresque' et l'architecture des gares parisiennes au XIXe siècle* (Thèse pour le Doctorat de IIIe Cycle, Université de Paris I, Sorbonne, 1985).

Brownell, Morris R., *Alexander Pope & the Arts of Georgian England* (Oxford, 1978).

Copley, Stephen, 'Tourists, Tintern Abbey, and the picturesque', *Swiss Papers in English Language and Literature*, 8 (1995), 61–82.

Copley, Stephen and Peter Garside, *The Politics of the Picturesque: Literature, Landscape, and Ideology* (Cambridge, 1994).

Duckworth, Alistair M., *The Improvement of the Estate: A Study of Jane Austen's Novels* (Baltimore, 1971).

Ferguson, Francis, *Solitude and the Sublime: Romanticism and the Aesthetics of Individuation* (New York, 1992).

Hipple, Walter John, Jr, *The Beautiful, the Sublime, and The Picturesque in Eighteenth-Century British Aesthetic Theory* (Carbondale IL, 1957).

Hunt, John Dixon, *The Figure in the Landscape: Poetry, Painting, and Gardening during the Eighteenth Century* (Baltimore, 1976).

'Ut Pictura Poesis, Ut Pictura Hortus, and the Picturesque', *Word and Image*, 1 (1985), 87–108.

Hunt, John Dixon and Peter Willis, *The Genius of the Place: The English Landscape Garden, 1620–1820* (London, 1975).

Hussey, Christopher, *English Gardens and Landscapes 1700–1750* (New York, 1967).

The Picturesque: Studies in a Point of View (1927; rpt London, 1967).

Manwaring, Elizabeth Wheeler, *Italian Landscape in Eighteenth-Century England. A Study Chiefly of the Influence of Claude Lorrain and Salvator Rosa on English Taste 1700–1800* (New York, 1925).

Marshall, David, *The Figure of Theater: Shaftesbury, Defoe, Adam Smith, and George Eliot* (New York, 1986).

'True Acting and the Language of Real Feelings: *Mansfield Park*', *Yale Journal of Criticism*, 3 (1989), 87–106.

Michasiw, Kim Ian, 'Nine revisionist theses on the picturesque', *Representations*, 38 (1992), 76–100.

Samuel H. Monk, *The Sublime: A Study of Critical Theories in XVIII-Century England* (Ann Arbor, 1962).

Paulson, Ronald, *Emblem and Expression: Meaning in English Art of the Eighteenth Century* (Cambridge, 1975).

Price, Martin, *Forms of Life: Character and Moral Imagination in the Novel* (New Haven, 1983).

'The Picturesque Moment', in Frederick W. Hilles and Harold Bloom (eds.), *From Sensibility to Romanticism: Essays Presented to Frederick A. Pottle* (New York, 1965).

Robinson, Sidney K., *Inquiry into the Picturesque* (Chicago, 1991).

Streatfield, David C., 'Art and Nature in the English Landscape Garden: Design Theory and Practice, 1700–1818', in *Landscape in the Gardens and Literature of the Eighteenth Century* (Los Angeles, 1981).

Watkin, David, *The English Vision* (London, 1982).

Williams, Raymond, *The Country and the City* (Frogmore, 1975).

Wiebenson, Dora, *The Picturesque Garden in France* (Princeton, 1978).

Literature and music

Primary sources and texts

Addison, Joseph, *The Spectator*, ed. Donald F. Bond (5 vols., Oxford, 1965).

Avison, Charles, *An Essay on Musical Expression*, 2nd edn (London, 1753).

Beattie, James, *Essays: On Poetry and Music as They Affect the Mind*, 3rd edn (London, 1779).

Boileau, N., *Oeuvres Complètes* (Paris, 1832).

Bonnet, Jacques, *Histoire de la musique* (Paris, 1715).

Brown, Dr John ('Estimate'), *A Dissertation on the Rise, Union, and Power, the Progressions, Separations and Corruptions, of Poetry and Music . . .* (London, 1763).

Burney, Charles, *A General History of Music from The Earliest Ages to the Present Period*, ed. Frank Mercer (2 vols., New York, 1935).

Collier, Jeremy, *Essay on Music* (London, 1702).

Dacier, André (ed.), *La Poétique d'Aristote* (Paris, 1692).

Dennis, John, *The Critical Works of John Dennis*, ed. Edward Niles Hooker (2 vols., Baltimore, 1939).

Dryden, John, *Essays of John Dryden*, ed. W. P. Ker, 2nd edn (2 vols., Oxford, 1926).

Du Bos, Jean-Baptiste, *Critical Reflections on Poetry, Painting, and Music*, trans. Thomas Nugent (3 vols., London, 1748).

Réflexions critiques sur la poésie et sur la peinture (Paris, 1719).

Encyclopédie, vol. XII (Paris, 1765).

Fénelon, François de, *Lettre sur les occupations de l'Académie Française* (3 vols., Paris, 1835).

Gildon, Charles, *The Life of Mr Thomas Betterton . . . with the Judgment of the late Ingenious Monsieur de St Evremond, upon the Italian and French Music and Operas* (London, 1710).

Harris, James, *Three Treatises, The first concerning Art, . . . etc.*, 4th edn (London, 1783).

Hawkins, Sir John, *A General History of the Science and Practice of Music* (2 vols., London, 1875).

Kames, Henry Home, Lord, *Elements of Criticism* (2 vols., New York, 1823).

Mason, John, *An Essay on the Power of Numbers and the Principles of Harmony in Poetical Composition* (London, 1749).

Mersenne, Marin, *Correspondance du P. Marin Mersenne*, ed. Cornelis de Waard in collaboration with René Pintard 17 vols. (Paris, 1932–88).

   Harmonie Universelle (Paris, 1634).

Remarks on Mr Avison's Essay on Musical Expression (London, 1753).

Rousseau, J.-J., *A Complete Dictionary of Music . . .* , trans. William Waring, 2nd edn (London, 1779).

   Dictionnaire de musique (Paris, 1768).

   Lettre sur la musique française . . . (Paris, 1753).

Saint-Évremond, Charles de, *The Letters of Saint-Évremond*, ed. John Haywood (London, 1930).

Schopenhauer, Arthur, *The World as Will and Idea*, trans. R. B. Haldane and J. Kemp (3 vols., London, 1896).

Twining, Thomas, *Aristotle's Treatise on poetry translated with . . . two dissertations on poetical and musical imitation . . .* (London, 1789).

Vossius, Isaac, *De poematum cantu et viribus rhythmi* (London, 1663).

Webb, Daniel, *Observations on the Correspondence between Poetry and Music* (London, 1789).

Secondary sources

Flood, W. H. Gratton, 'An eighteenth-century essayist on poetry and music', *Musical Quarterly*, 2 (1916), 191–8.

Garlington, Aubrey S., Jr, '*Le Merveilleux* and operatic reform in 18th-century French opera', *Musical Quarterly*, 49 (1963), 484–97.

Heartz, Daniel, 'Diderot et le théâtre lyrique: "le nouveau stile" proposé par le Neveu de Rameau', *Revue de Musicologie*, 64 (1978), 6–252.

Kintzler, Catherine, 'De la pastorale ou la tragédie lyrique: quelques elements d'un systeme poétique', *Revue de Musicologie*, 72 (1986), 67–96.

Kivy, Peter, 'Mattheson as philosopher of art', *Musical Quarterly*, 70 (1984), 248–65.

Mace, Dean T., 'Marin Mersenne on language and music', *Journal of Music Theory*, 14 (1970), 2–34.

Oliver, Alfred Richard, *The Encyclopedists as Critics of Music* (New York, 1947).

Palisca, Claude, 'Scientific empiricism in musical thought', in Hedley H. Rhys (ed.), *Seventeenth-Century Science and the Arts* (Princeton, 1961), pp. 91–137.

Rogers, Pat, 'The critique of opera in Pope's *Dunciad*', *Musical Quarterly*, 59 (1973), 15–30.
Rosenfeld, Sybil, 'Restoration stage in newspapers and journals 1660–1700', *Modern Language Review*, 30 (1930), 445–59.
Strauss, John F., 'Jean-Jacques Rousseau: musician', *Musical Quarterly*, 64 (1978), 474–82.

Parallels between the arts

Primary sources and texts

Batteux, Abbé Charles, *Les Beaux-Arts réduits à un même principe* (Paris, 1773; first publ. 1746.
Baumgarten, Alexander G., *Reflections on Poetry*, trans. Karl Aschenbrenner and William B. Holther (Berkeley, 1954).
Beattie, James, *Essays. On Poetry and Music, as they affect the Mind* ... (Edinburgh, 1779; first publ. 1776).
Burke, Edmund, *A Philosophical Enquiry into the Origin of Our Ideas of the Sublime and Beautiful*, ed. J. T. Boulton (London, 1958).
Diderot, Denis, *Essais sur la peinture* ... (Paris, 1795).
Dryden, John, *Essays of John Dryden*, ed. W. P. Ker (2 vols., Oxford, 1926).
Du Bos, Jean-Baptiste, *Critical Reflections on Poetry, Painting and Music* ... , trans. Thomas Nugent (3 vols., London, 1748).
Dissertation sur les représentations théatrales des anciens (Paris, 1736).
Réflexions critiques sur la poésie et sur la peinture (2 vols., Paris, 1719).
Du Fresnoy, Charles Alphonse, *De arte graphica: the art of painting* ... *with remarks* ... (London, 1695).
Encyclopédie, vol. XII (Paris, 1765).
Félibien, André, *Conférences de l'Academie Royale de Peinture et de Sculpture* (Amsterdam, 1706); *Sixième Conférence*, 5 November 1667.
Gilpin, William, *Three Essays: on Picturesque Beauty; on Picturesque Travel, and on Sketching Landscape: to which is added a poem, on Landscape Painting* (London, 1792).
Hogarth, William, *Analysis of Beauty, Written with a View of Fixing the Fluctuating Ideas of Taste* ... (London, 1753).
Lessing, G. E., *Laocoön*, trans. and ed. E. A. McCormick (1962; rpt Baltimore, 1984).
Mendelssohn, Moses, *Gesammelte Schriften*, Jubiläumsausgabe, ed. F. Bamberg *et al.* (17 vols., Stuttgart–Bad Cannstatt, 1971).
Perrault, Charles, *Parallèle des Anciens et des Modernes* (Amsterdam, 1693).
Piles, Roger de, *Cours de peinture par principes* (Paris, 1708), trans. 'by a Painter' as *The Principles of Painting* (London, 1743).
Price, Uvedale, *An Essay on the Picturesque, as compared with the Sublime and the Beautiful* ... (London, 1794).
Reynolds, Sir Joshua, *Discourses on Art*, ed. Robert R. Wark (New Haven, 1975).

Richardson, Jonathan, *An Essay on the Theory of Painting* (1715; London, 1725).

Two Discourses. I. An Essay on the Whole Art of Criticism as it relates to Painting . . . II. An Argument in behalf of the Science of a Connoisseur; . . . (London, 1719).

Spence, Joseph, *Polymetis* (London, 1747).

Webb, Daniel, *Inquiry into the beauties of Painting . . .* (London, 1760).

Winckelmann, J. J., *The History of Ancient Art*, trans. G. H. Lodge (Boston, 1872).

Secondary sources

Allen, Sprague, *Tides in English Taste* (Cambridge MA, 1937).

Folkierski, Wladyslaw, 'Ut pictura poesis ou l'étrange fortune du *De arte graphica* de Du Fresnoy en Angleterre', *Revue de littérature comparée*, 27 (1953), 385–402.

Hagstrum, Jean H., *The Sister Arts* (Chicago, 1958; rpt. 1974).

Howard, W. G., 'Ut pictura poesis', *Publications of the Modern Language Association*, 24 (1909), 40–123.

Hunt, John Dixon, *The Figure in the Landscape: Poetry, Painting, and Gardening during the Eighteenth Century* (Baltimore, 1976).

Kristeller, Paul Oskar, 'The modern system of the arts: a study in the history of aesthetics', *Journal of the History of Ideas*, I, 12 (1952), 496–527; II, 13, 17–46.

Lee, Rensselaer W., 'Ut Pictura Poesis; the humanistic theory of painting', *The Art Bulletin*, 22 (1940), 197–269.

Lombard, A., *L'Abbé du Bos, un initiateur de la pensée moderne* (Paris, 1913).

Manwaring, Elizabeth Wheeler, *Italian Landscape in Eighteenth Century England* (New York, 1925).

Ogden, Henry V. S., and Margaret S. Ogden, *English Taste in Landscape in the Seventeenth Century* (Ann Arbor, 1955).

Rogerson, Brewster, 'The art of painting the passions', *Journal of the History of Ideas*, 14 (1953), 68–94.

Wellbery, David E., *Lessing's Laocoon: Semiotics and Aesthetics in the Age of Reason* (Cambridge, 1984).

Classical scholarship and literary criticism

Primary sources and texts

Bentley, Richard, *A Dissertation upon the Epistles of Phalaris, with an Answer to the Objections of the Honourable Charles Boyle, Esquire* (London, 1699), in *The Works of Richard Bentley, D.D.*, ed. A. Dyce (London, 1836, rpt Hildesheim/New York, 1971), I, pp. xxiii–430, II, pp. 1–237; cited here from R. Bentley, *Dissertations upon the Epistles of Phalaris, Themistocles, Socrates, Euripides, and the Fables of Æsop*, ed. W. Wagner (London, 1883).

Epistola ad Joannem Millium (Oxford, 1691), in *The Works of Richard Bentley, D.D.*, ed. A. Dyce (London, 1836, rpt Hildesheim and New York, 1971), II, pp. 239–365 (rpt Toronto, 1962).

Humboldt, Wilhelm von, *Briefe an Friedrich August Wolf (Im Anhang: Humboldts Mitschrift der Ilias-Vorlesung Christian Gottlob Heynes aus dem Sommersemester 1789)*, ed. P. Mattson (Berlin and New York, 1990).

Schlegel, Friedrich, 'Von den Schulen der griechischen Poesie' (1794), 'Über das Studium der griechischen Poesie' (1795–6), *Geschichte der Poesie der Griechen und Römer* (1798), in Friedrich Schlegel, *Studien des klassischen Altertums*, ed. E. Behler = vol. I of Kritische Friedrich-Schlegel-Ausgabe, ed. E. Behler, J.-J. Anstett and H. Eichner, (Paderborn, Munich and Vienna, 1979).

Winckelmann, Johann Joachim, *Geschichte der Kunst des Altertums* (Dresden, 1764, rpt Vienna, 1934 and Darmstadt, 1972).

Wolf, Friedrich August, 'Darstellung der Alterthums-Wissenschaft', *Museum der Alterthums-Wissenschaft*, I (1807), pp. 1–145 (rpt Berlin, 1985).

Prolegomena ad Homerum (Halle, 1795), Engl. trans. F. A. Wolf, *Prolegomena to Homer 1795*, trans. A. Grafton, G. W. Most and J. E. G. Zetzel (Princeton, 1985).

Wood, Robert, *An Essay on the Original Genius and Writings of Homer: with a Comparative View of the Ancient and Present State of the Troade* (London [1775], rpt Washington, DC, 1973).

Secondary sources

Bolgar, R. R. (ed.), *Classical Influences on Western Thought A.D. 1650–1870* (Cambridge, 1979).

Borghero, Carlo, *La certezza e la storia: cartesianesimo, pirronismo e conoscenza storica* (Milan, 1983).

Brink, C. O., *English Classical Scholarship. Historical Reflections on Bentley, Porson, and Housman* (Cambridge, 1986).

Clarke, G. W. (ed.), *Rediscovering Hellenism. The Hellenic Inheritance and the English Imagination* (Cambridge, 1989).

Clarke, M. L., *Classical Education in Britain. 1500–1900* (Cambridge, 1959). *Greek Studies in England 1700–1830* (Cambridge, 1945).

Constantine, David, *Early Greek Travellers and the Hellenic Ideal* (Cambridge, 1984).

Finsler, Georg, *Homer in der Neuzeit von Dante bis Goethe* (Leipzig and Berlin, 1912).

Fuhrmann, Manfred, 'Die Geschichte der Literaturgeschichtsschreibung von den Anfängen bis zum 19. Jahrhundert', in B. Cerquiglini and H. U. Gumbrecht (eds.), *Der Diskurs der Literatur- und Sprachhistorie. Wissenschaftsgeschichte als Innovationsvorgabe* (Frankfurt a.M., 1983), pp. 49–72.

Grafton, Anthony, *Defenders of the Text* (Cambridge MA, 1991). 'Prolegomena to Friedrich August Wolf', *Journal of the Warburg and Courtauld Institutes*, 44 (1981), 101–29.

Horstmann, A., 'Die "Klassische Philologie" zwischen Humanismus und Historismus. Friedrich August Wolf und die Begründung der modernen

Altertumswissenschaft', *Berichte zur Wissenschaftsgeschichte*, 1 (1978), 51–70.

Irmscher, Johannes (ed.), *Winckelmanns Wirkung auf seine Zeit: Lessing – Herder – Heyne*, Schriften der Winckelmann-Gesellschaft, 7 (Stendal, 1988).

Jebb, R. C., *Richard Bentley* (New York, 1882).

Justi, Carl, *Winckelmann und seine Zeitgenossen* (2 vols., Leipzig, 1923).

Kenney, E. J., *The Classical Text: Aspects of Editing in the Age of the Printed Book* (Berkeley, Los Angeles and London, 1974).

Killy, Walther (ed.), *Geschichte des Textverständnisses am Beispiel von Pindar und Horaz*, Wolfenbütteler Forschungen, 12 (Munich, 1981).

Krauss, Werner, and Hans Kortum (eds.), *Antike und Moderne in der Literaturdiskussion des 18. Jahrhunderts* (Berlin, 1966).

McClelland, C. E., *State, Society and University in Germany, 1700–1914* (Cambridge, 1980).

Momigliano, Arnaldo, *Contributi alla storia degli studi classici (e del mondo antico)* I–IX (Rome, 1955–92).

Most, Glenn W., 'Ansichten über einen Hund: Zu einigen Strukturen der Homerrezeption zwischen Antike und Neuzeit', *Antike und Abendland*, 37 (1991), 144–68.

'Schlegel, Schlegel und die Geburt eines Tragödienparadigmas', *Poetica*, 25 (1993), 155–75.

'The second Homeric Renaissance: allegoresis and genius in early modern poetics', in P. Murray (ed.), *Genius: The History of an Idea* (Oxford, 1989), pp. 54–75.

'Sublime degli Antichi, Sublime dei Moderni', *Studi di estetica* 12: 1–2, N.S. 4/5 (1984), 113–29.

'Zur Archäologie der Archaik', *Antike und Abendland*, 35 (1989), 1–23.

Myres, John L., *Homer and his Critics* (London, 1958).

Pfeiffer, Rudolf, *History of Classical Scholarship from 1300 to 1850* (Oxford, 1976), rev. German trans. *Die Klassische Philologie von Petrarca bis Mommsen* (Munich, 1982).

Reill, P. H., *The German Enlightenment and the Rise of Historicism* (Berkeley, 1975).

Sandys, John Edwin, *A History of Classical Scholarship* I: From the 6th Century BC to the End of the Middle Ages. II: From the Revival of Learning to the End of the Eighteenth Century in Italy, France, England, and the Netherlands. III: The Eighteenth Century in Germany and the Nineteenth Century in Europe and the United States of America (Cambridge, 1903, 1908, 1908).

Shankman, Steven, *Pope's Iliad: Homer in the Age of Passion* (Princeton, 1983).

Simonsuuri, Kirsti, *Homer's Original Genius. Eighteenth-century Notions of the Early Greek Epic (1688–1798)* (Cambridge, 1979).

Timpanaro, Sebastiano, *La Genesi del Metodo del Lachmann*, 3rd edn (Padua, 1985).

Turner, R. S., 'The Prussian universities and the concept of research', *Internationales Archiv für Sozialgeschichte der deutschen Literatur*, 5 (1980), 68–93.

Wilamowitz-Moellendorff, Ulrich von, *History of Classical Scholarship*, trans. A. Harris, ed. H. Lloyd-Jones (London, 1982).

Wohlleben, Joachim, *Die Sonne Homers. Zehn Kapitel deutscher Homer-Begeisterung. Von Winckelmann bis Schliemann* (Göttingen, 1990).

Biblical scholarship and literary criticism

Primary sources and texts

Bentley, Richard, *Remarks upon a Late Discourse of Free-thinking* (London, 1713).

Blackwall, Anthony, *The Sacred Classics Defended and Illustrated* (London, 1725).

Bossuet, Jacques Bénigne, *Exposition de la Doctrine de l'Eglise Catholique* (Paris, 1671).

Burke, Edmund, *A Philosophical Enquiry into the Origin of our Ideas of the Sublime and Beautiful*, ed. James T. Boulton (Oxford, 1987).

Chillingworth, William, *The Religion of Protestants a Safe Way to Salvation* (Oxford, 1638).

Coleridge, Samuel Taylor, *Collected Works* XII: ii (*Marginalia*, Camden to Hutton), ed. George Whalley (London and Princeton, 1984).

Collins, Anthony, *A Discourse of Free-Thinking* (London, 1713).

Dennis, John, *Critical Works*, ed. Edward Niles Hooker (2 vols., Baltimore, 1939, 1943).

Doddridge, Philip, *The Family Expositor: or, a Paraphrase and Version of the New Testament* (6 vols., London, 1739–56).

Edwards, John, *A Discourse concerning the Authority, Stile, and Perfection of the Books of the Old and New Testament* (3 vols., London, 1693–5).

Geddes, Alexander, *Address to the Public, on the Publication of the First Volume of his New Translation of the Bible* (London, 1793).
  Critical Remarks on the Hebrew Scriptures (London, 1800).
  Prospectus of a New Translation of the Holy Bible (Glasgow, 1786).

Geddes, Alexander (trans.), *The Holy Bible* (2 vols., London, 1792, 1797).

Gother, John, *The Catholic Representer* (London, 1687).

Gray, Thomas, *Correspondence*, ed. Paget Toynbee and Leonard Whibley, with corrections and additions by H. W. Starr (3 vols., Oxford, 1971).

The Guardian, ed. John Calhoun Stephens (Lexington KY, 1983).

Guild, William, *Moses Unvail'd* (London, 1620).

Hamann, J. G., *Aesthetica in Nuce*, trans. Joyce P. Crick, with modifications by H. B. Nisbet (ed.), in Nisbet, *German Aesthetic and Literary Criticism* (Cambridge, 1985).

Hammond, Henry, *A Paraphrase, and Annotations upon all the Books of the New Testament* (London, 1653).

Herder, J. G., *The Spirit of Hebrew Poetry*, trans. J. Marsh (2 vols., Burlington VT, 1833).

Jones, William, *A Course of Lectures on the Figurative Language of the Holy Scripture* (London, 1787).

Keach, Benjamin, *Tropologia* (London, 1681).

Kennicott, Benjamin, *Vetus testamentum Hebraicum, cum variis lectionibus* (2 vols., Oxford, 1776).

Leigh, Edward, *Critica Sacra: Philologicall and Theologicall Observations upon all the Words of the New Testament* (London, 1639).

Locke, John, *A Paraphrase and Notes on the Epistles of St Paul* (London, 1706).

Longinus, *On Sublimity*, trans. D. A. Russell (Oxford, 1965).

Lowth, Robert, *Lectures on the Sacred Poetry of the Hebrews*, trans. G. Gregory (2 vols., London, 1787).

    Isaiah. A New Translation (London, 1778).

Mill, John, *Novum Testamentum* (Oxford, 1707).

Milton, John, *Paradise Lost*, ed. Richard Bentley (London, 1732).

    Paradise Lost, ed. Patrick Hume (London, 1696).

    Paradise Lost, ed. Thomas Newton (2 vols., London, 1749).

Milton Restor'd, and Bentley Depos'd (London, 1732).

Newton, John, *Works* (6 vols., London, 1808).

Nisbet, H. B. (ed.), *German Aesthetic and Literary Criticism: Winckelmann, Lessing, Hamann, Herder, Schiller, Goethe* (Cambridge, 1985).

Patrick, Simon, *A Commentary upon the Historical Books of the Old Testament* (3rd edn, London, 1727).

Pearce, Zachary, *A Review of the Text of Milton's Paradise Lost* (3 vols., London, 1732–1733).

Pearson, John, *Critici Sacri* (9 vols., London, 1660).

Poole, Matthew, *Synopsis criticorum aliorumque S. Scripturae interpretum* (4 vols. in 5, London, 1669–76).

Poole, Matthew et al., *Annotations upon the Holy Bible* (2 vols., London, 1683–1685).

Rushworth, William, *The Dialogues of William Richworth* (Paris, 1640).

Sergeant, John, *Sure-Footing in Christianity* (London, 1665).

Shakespeare, William, *Works*, ed. Alexander Pope (6 vols., London, 1725).

Simon, Richard, *A Critical History of the Old Testament . . . translated into English by a Person of Quality* (London, 1682).

    A Critical History of the Text of the New Testament (London, 1689).

Smart, Christopher, *Poetical Works*, ed. Karina Williamson and Marcus Walsh (6 vols., Oxford, 1980–96).

The Spectator, ed. Donald F. Bond (5 vols., Oxford, 1965).

Spinoza, Benedict de, *A Theologico-Political Treatise*, trans. R. H. M. Elwes (New York, 1951).

Swift, Jonathan, *Mr C - - - - ns's Discourse of Free-Thinking, Put into Plain English, by Way of Abstract, for the Use of the Poor* (London, 1713).

Tillotson, John, *The Rule of Faith* (1666); in *Works* (3rd edn, London, 1701).

Walton, Brian, *Biblia Sacra Polyglotta* (London, 6 vols., 1655–7).

Watts, Isaac, *The Improvement of the Mind* (London, 1741).

    'A short essay toward the improvement of psalmody', in *Works* (6 vols., London, 1753), IV, pp. 271–91.

Wesley, Charles and John Wesley, *The Poetical Works of John and Charles Wesley*, ed. G. Osborn (13 vols., London, 1868–72).

Wilson, John, *The Scripture's Genuine Interpreter Asserted* (London, 1678).

Secondary sources

Abrams, M. H., *The Mirror and the Lamp: Romantic Theory and the Critical Tradition* (New York, 1958).

Atkins, J. W. H., *English Literary Criticism: 17th and 18th Centuries* (London, 1966).

The Cambridge History of the Bible (3 vols., Cambridge, 1963–70).

Farrar, Frederic W., *History of Interpretation* (London, 1886).

Frei, Hans W., *The Eclipse of Biblical Narrative: a Study in Eighteenth and Nineteenth Century Hermeneutics* (New Haven, 1974).

Harris, Victor, 'Allegory to analogy in the interpretation of Scriptures', *Philological Quarterly*, 45 (1966), 1–23.

Hepworth, Brian, *Robert Lowth* (Boston, 1978).

Korshin, Paul J., *Typologies in England 1650–1820* (Princeton, 1982).

Kümmel, Werner Georg, *The New Testament: the History of the Interpretation of its Problems* (London, 1983).

McGann, Jerome J., *The Beauty of Inflections: Literary Investigations in Historical Method and Theory* (Oxford, 1985).

Morris, David B., *The Religious Sublime: Christian Poetry and Critical Tradition in 18th-Century England* (Lexington KY, 1972).

O'Flaherty, James C., *J. G. Hamann*, Twayne's World Author Series, 527 (Boston, 1979).

The Quarrel of Reason with Itself: Essays on Hamann, Michaelis, Lessing, Nietzsche, Studies in German Literature, Linguistics, and Culture, 35 (Columbia SC, 1988).

Preston, Thomas R., 'Biblical criticism, literature, and the eighteenth-century reader', *Books and their Readers in Eighteenth-Century England*, ed. Isabel Rivers (Leicester, 1982).

Prickett, Stephen, *Words and The Word: Language, Poetics, and Biblical Interpretation* (Cambridge, 1986).

Roston, Murray, *Prophet and Poet: The Bible and the Growth of Romanticism* (London, 1965).

Shaffer, Elinor S., *'Kubla Khan' and the Fall of Jerusalem: The Mythological School in Biblical Criticism and Secular Literature* (Cambridge, 1975).

Willey, Basil, *The Eighteenth-Century Background* (London, 1962).

Science and literary criticism

Primary sources and texts

Addison, Joseph, *The Spectator*, ed. Donald F. Bond (5 vols., Oxford, 1965).

Arnauld, Antoine, and Pierre Nicole, *La Logique, ou l'art de penser* (Paris, 1662).

Boswell, James, *The Life of Samuel Johnson*, ed. George Birkbeck Hill, rev. L. F. Powell (6 vols., Oxford, 1934–50).

Burke, Edmund, *A Philosophical Enquiry into the Origin of our Ideas of the Sublime and Beautiful* (London, 1757), ed. James T. Boulton (London, 1958).

Burnet, Thomas, *Sacred Theory of the Earth* (London, 1684).

Condorcet, Jean-Antoine-Nicolas Caritat, marquis de, *Esquisse d'un Tableau historique des Progrès de l'Esprit humain* (Paris, An V), ed. O. H. Prior (Paris, 1970).

Dennis, John, *Critical Works*, ed. Edward N. Hooker (Baltimore, 1939–1943).

Descartes, René, *Oeuvres* (Paris, 1953).

Dryden, John, *Essays*, ed. W. P. Ker (2 vols., Oxford, 1926).

Gibbon, Edward, *The History of the Decline and Fall of the Roman Empire* (7 vols., London, 1896–1900).

Goethe, Johann Wolfgang, *Goethes Werke*, ed. Erich Trunz (14 vols., Hamburg, 1948–64).

Hamann, Johann Georg, *Sämtliche Werke*, ed. Josef Nadler (Vienna, 1949–53).

Herder, Johann Gottfried, *Sämtliche Werke*, ed. B. Suphan (Berlin 1877–1913).

Hobbes, *Leviathan* (1651), ed. C. B. Macpherson (Harmondsworth, 1986).

Hume, David, *Essays Moral, Political and Literary*, ed. T. H. Green and E. C. Mossner (2 vols., London, 1922).

Letters of David Hume, ed. J. Y. T. Greig (London, 1932).

New Letters of David Hume, ed. R. Klibansky and E. C. Mossner (London, 1954).

A Treatise of Human Nature, ed. L. A. Selby-Bigge (London, 1964).

Johnson, Samuel, *The Works of Samuel Johnson*, Yale edition (New Haven, 1958–).

Kames, Henry Home, Lord, *Elements of Criticism* (3 vols., Edinburgh, 1762; rpt 1967).

La Motte, Antoine Houdart de, *Discours sur la Fable,* in *Oeuvres complètes*, IX (Paris, 1754).

Lancelot, Claude, and Antoine Arnauld, *Grammaire générale et raisonnée* (Paris, 1660).

Lessing, Gotthold Ephraim, *Sämtliche Werke*, ed. K. Lachmann and F. Muncker (23 vols., Leipzig, 1886–1924).

The Philosophical Transactions of the Royal Society of London.

Rousseau, Jean-Jacques, *Oeuvres complètes* (Paris, 1959–).

Shaftesbury, Anthony Ashley Cooper, third Earl of, *Characteristicks of Men, Manners, Opinions, Times* (London 1711; ed. J. M. Robertson, 2 vols., New York, 1900).

Turgot, Anne-Robert Jacques, *Oeuvres*, ed. Dupont de Nemours (Paris, 1844).

Voltaire, *Oeuvres*, ed. Louis Moland (Paris, 1877–83).

Wordsworth William, and Samuel Taylor Coleridge, *Lyrical Ballads* (1805; ed. Derek Roper, London, 1968).

Young, Edward, *Conjectures on Original Composition* (London, 1759; rpt 1966).

Secondary sources

Aarsleff, Hans, *et al.* (eds.), *Papers in the History of Linguistics* (Amsterdam and Philadelphia, 1987).

Abrams, M. H., *The Mirror and the Lamp: Romantic Theory and the Critical Tradition* (New York, 1953; rpt 1958).

Apostolidès, Jean-Marie, *Le Roi-Machine* (Paris, 1981).

Atkins, J. W. H., *English Literary Criticism, 17th and 18th Centuries* (London, 1951; rpt 1966).

Belaval, Yvon, 'La Crise de la géométrisation de l'univers dans la philosophie des lumières', *Revue internationale de Philosophie*, 6 (1972).

Blumenberg, Hans, *The Legitimacy of the Modern Age*, trans. Robert M. Wallace (Cambridge MA, 1983).

Cassirer, Ernst, *The Philosophy of the Enlightenment* (Princeton, 1951).
Rousseau, Kant and Goethe (Princeton, 1945; rpt 1963).

Chomsky, Noam, *Cartesian Linguistics* (New York, 1966).

Copenhaver, Brian P., 'Jewish theologies of space in the scientific revolution: More, Raphson, Newton and their predecessors', *Annals of Science*, 37, 5 (1980).

Crombie, Alistair C., *Augustine to Galileo* (Harvard, 1952; rpt 1979).
'Experimental science and the rational artist in early modern Europe', *Daedalus* (Summer, 1986).
Science, Optics and Music in Medieval and Early Modern Thought (London, 1990).

Dewhurst, Kenneth, *John Locke, Physician and Philosopher* (London, 1963).

Dijksterhuis, E. J., *The Mechanization of the World-Picture* (Princeton, 1986).

Formigari, Lia, *L'Estetica del Gusto nel Settecento inglese* (Florence, 1962).

Foucault, Michel, *Les Mots et les Choses* (Paris, 1966); English trans. *The Order of Things* (London, 1974).

Hankins, Thomas L., *Science and the Enlightenment* (Cambridge, 1985) with a Bibliographical Essay (pp. 191–203).

Koyré, Alexandre, *Études newtoniennes* (Paris, 1968).
From the Closed World to the Infinite Universe (London, 1962).

Kuhn, Thomas S., *The Structure of Scientific Revolutions* (Chicago, 1962).

Lovejoy, Arthur O., *Essays in the History of Ideas* (Baltimore, 1948).
The Great Chain of Being (Harvard, 1936).

Maclean, Kenneth, *John Locke and English Literature in the Eighteenth Century* (New York, 1962).

Metzger, Hélène, *Newton, Stahl, Boerhaave et la Doctrine chimique* (Paris, 1930).

Naves, Raymond, *Le Goût de Voltaire* (Paris, 1938).

Nicolson, Marjorie H., *Mountain Gloom and Mountain Glory* (Ithaca, 1959; rpt Toronto, 1963).

Nisbet, H. B., *Herder and the Philosophy and History of Science* (Cambridge, 1970).

Panofsky, Erwin, *Galileo as Critic of the Arts* (The Hague, 1954).

Piaget, Jean, *L'Epistémologie génétique* (Paris, 1970).

Piaget, Jean, and R. Garcia, *Psychogenèse et Histoire des Sciences* (Paris, 1983).

Pittock, Joan, *The Ascendancy of Taste. The Achievement of Joseph and Thomas Warton* (London, 1973).

Rhys, Hedley Howell (ed.), *Seventeenth Century Science and the Arts* (Princeton, 1961).

Rousseau, G. S. and Roy Porter, *The Ferment of Knowledge* (Cambridge, 1980).

Schick, Edgar B., *Metaphorical Organicism in Herder's Early Works. A Study of the Relation of Herder's Literary Idiom to his World View*, De Proprietatibus Litterarum, Series Practica, 20 (The Hague and Paris, 1971).

Sebok, Thomas A. (ed.), *Current Trends in Linguistics* (The Hague and Paris, 1975).

Spingarn, J. E., *Critical Essays of the Seventeenth Century* (London, 1908–9).

Stephen, Leslie, *A History of English Thought in the Eighteenth Century* (1876; 2 vols., London, 1962).

Taton, René (ed.), *A General History of the Sciences*, trans. A. J. Pomerans (4 vols., London, 1963–6).

Tuveson, Ernest L., *The Imagination as a Means of Grace. Locke and the Aesthetics of Romanticism* (Los Angeles and London, 1960).

Wahl, Jean, *Le Rôle de l'Instant dans la Philosophie de Descartes* (Paris, 1920).

Wellek, René, *A History of Modern Criticism, 1750–1900* (4 vols., London, 1955; rpt 1970).

Wimsatt, William K. and Cleanth Brooks, *Literary Criticism. A Short History* (New York, 1957; rpt 1970).

Wolf, A., *A History of Science, Technology and Philosophy in the Eighteenth Century* (London, 1952).

A History of Science, Technology and Philosophy in the Sixteenth and Seventeenth Centuries (London, 1950).

Index

Abbt, Thomas 311–12
Abelard, Peter 235
Académie des Inscriptions et Belles-
    Lettres 46n, 59n, 61
Académie Française 34–5, 53, 226,
    350, 562–3, 702, 730
Achery, Jean Luc d' 745n; *Indiculus
    Asceticorum Opusculorum*
    745n
Acta eruditorum 318–19
Addison, Joseph 5–6, 11, 13,
    16–21, 23–4, 27–30, 40n, 41,
    42n, 60, 63, 67, 76, 78,
    99–103, 113–15, 118, 120,
    131–2, 143, 154–5, 158–9, 182,
    258, 303–4, 308–9, 322–3, 332,
    337, 344, 359, 364–71, 373,
    376, 378–80, 385, 414, 426,
    435, 440, 442, 447, 459–62,
    464, 469, 471–4, 482, 546,
    549, 551, 567, 587, 603–4,
    615, 617–22, 626, 628–9,
    632–41, 644–53, 657, 687,
    690–1, 706–9, 713–14, 719,
    722, 730, 765–6, 770, 788–9
'Account of the Greatest English
    Poets' 471
Dialogue upon Medals 646
Cato 435, 442
Essay on Virgil's Georgics 651
Freeholder 308
Remarks on Several Parts of Italy
    651
Spectator (for numbered issues, *see
    also Spectator* entry) 11–13, 17,
    24, 41n, 42n, 67, 76, 78,
    99–103, 114, 132, 143, 154,
    158, 322, 337, 370–1, 378,

385, 414, 426, 447, 459,
461–2, 471–2, 587, 603–4,
618–21, 628–9, 633–40,
643–52, 687, 690, 706–8,
713–14, 719, 765–6, 770, 789
'True and False Wit' 603
Tatler 6n, 633–4, 642–4, 646
Adventurer 132, 250–1, 255, 384,
    435n
    No. 4 255
    No. 16 250–1
    No. 57 132
    No. 99 384
Aelfric 439
*English-Saxon Homily on the
    Birth-day of St Gregory* 439
Aesop 47, 49–50, 495, 542, 754
aesthetic/aesthetics/aestheticism
    10–11, 39, 40n, 45, 63, 67n,
    115, 120, 127, 131, 142, 150,
    155, 163, 166, 173, 184,
    187–9, 200, 216, 234, 262–3,
    295, 300, 355, 367–8, 379,
    381, 388, 390, 393–4, 396,
    400, 407, 411, 414, 426,
    428–9, 431, 456, 489, 495,
    507, 510–11, 519, 524–9, 534,
    536–8, 542–5, 553, 555–7,
    567, 587, 590–2, 599, 603–4,
    607–9, 611, 618, 623–4, 626–7,
    629, 632–63, 665–8, 672–80,
    682, 684–5, 687, 691, 699–702,
    704–5, 708, 712–13, 715–16,
    718–19, 723, 732, 737, 741,
    754–5, 756, 758, 763, 765,
    768–9, 771–2, 779, 780, 783,
    785–8, 790, 794
Aikin, Anna Laetitia (*see* Barbauld)

Aikin, John 43, 66, 146, 251, 440, 482
  Essay on the Application of Natural History to Poetry 146
  Letters from a Father to his Son 43n
  'On Attachment to the Ancients' 43n
  Miscellaneous Pieces in Prose and Verse (with A. L. Barbauld) 440, 482
  'Enquiry into those Kinds of Distress' 482
  'On the Pleasure Derived from Objects of Terror' 482
  Round Table 43n
Ainsworth, Michael 640
Ainsworth, Robert 374
Akenside, Mark 21, 64, 131, 142, 153–6, 165–6, 414, 432, 441, 790
  'Ballance of Poets' 64
  Odes 117
  Pleasures of Imagination 117, 131, 142n, 153–6, 166, 414
Alberti, Joannes 746n
Hesychius (ed. David Ruhnken) 746n
Aldrich, Henry, Dean 547
  Artis Logicae Compendium 547
Alembert, Jean le Rond d' 7n, 39n, 44, 46n, 226, 420, 452, 503n, 504, 506–8, 511, 513–14, 552
  'Discours préliminaire' (*see Encyclopédie*) 504, 511, 514
  'Erudition' (*see Encyclopédie*) 46n
  'Genève' (*see Encyclopédie*) 506, 513
Alexander the Great 93, 565
Algarotti, Francesco 228
Algemeene Oefenschoole 277n
Algemeene Vaderlandsche Letteroefeningen 276n, 277n
Alison, Archibald 26n, 131–2, 367, 412, 428, 432–3, 592–3, 597, 785; *Essays on the Nature and*

Principles of Taste 26n, 132, 412, 432, 592–3, 597
allegory/allegorical 113, 228, 234, 242, 250, 374, 494, 540, 561, 576, 619, 654–6, 682, 710
Allgemeine Deutsche Bibliothek 328, 528
Almanach des Muses 325
Alves, Richard: *Sketches of a History of Literature* 5
American Magazine 325
Ammonius (*see* Valckenaer) 746n
Amyot, Jacques 271
Anacreon (*see* André Dacier) 53
Analytical Review 249, 327, 332, 441, 486
ancienneté 59–60, 65–7
Ancients (classical authors) 32–71, 75, 83, 86, 88–90, 93–9, 103–4, 110, 115, 176–7, 183, 350, 371, 546, 559, 563, 568–9, 579, 581–2, 638, 652, 686, 724, 730, 741, 771, 781, 795–6; Ancients and Moderns (partisans in *querelle*; *see also querelle*) 32–71, 89–90, 93–9, 177, 250, 350, 365, 394, 400, 462, 540, 550, 555, 568–9, 581, 623, 638, 695, 724, 747, 754, 756, 786, 790
Andrewes, Lancelot 581
Anne, Queen of England 397
Année littéraire 515, 516n
Antichità di Ercolano 547
Anti-Pamela (*see* Haywood, Eliza, and Richardson, Samuel)
Anton Ulrich, Herzog 265n
  Aramena 265n
Antoninus, Marcus Aurelius 298
Anton Ulrich, Herzog 265n
  Aramena 265n
Apollonius of Rhodes (*see* eds. Brunck, Ruhnken, Shaw) 746n
Apostolides, Jean-Marie 783n
  Le Roi-machine 783n
  'Organisation de la culture' 783n
Arabian Nights 440

Aratus of Soli (*see* eds. Bandini, Buhle) 746n
Arbuckle, James 152
Arbuthnot, John 374
Arcadian Academies 83, 109
Archaeologia 476–7
Archelaus 5
Aretino, Pietro 228
Argens, Jean-Baptiste de Boyer, Marquis d' 219, 221–2
   'Discours sur les nouvelles' 219
   Lectures amusantes 220
Ariosto, Ludovico 84, 91, 95, 120, 228, 232, 360
Aristarchus of Samothrace 561
Aristobulus (*see* Valckenaer) 746n, 754
Aristophanes (*see* Dacier, André) 53
Aristophanes of Byzantium 561
Aristotle 9, 14–15, 36n, 43, 75–7, 82–4, 88, 94, 96, 98–101, 105, 109, 113–14, 121, 123, 167–70, 173, 177–8, 183–8, 194, 199, 201–3, 205–7, 209, 211, 224, 235–6, 238–9, 254, 256–8, 267, 352, 356, 365, 370, 372, 378, 382, 424, 445, 482, 512, 525, 527, 531–3, 540–3, 562, 569, 579, 595, 619, 645–6, 648, 650, 660n, 678, 716, 721, 724, 732, 736, 749, 767, 772, 778–9, 781–2, 786
   Nicomachean Ethics 41n, 660n, 779
   Poetics 121, 168, 170, 173, 185–7, 201, 531, 678, 686, 716n, 732, 749, 767, 781
   Rhetoric 686, 724
Arnauld, Antoine; and Nicole, Pierre 352n, 795
   Grammaire générale et raisonnée 780
   Logique 352n, 780n
Arriaza, Juan Bautista 83
Artist 244
Art of Poetry (1762) 120

Astle, Thomas 474
   Catalogue of the Harleian Collection 474
Athenian Mercury 249
Attaignant, Gabriel Charles, Abbé de l' 516
Atterbury, Francis 50
Aubignac, François Hédelin, Abbé d' 56, 167–9, 184
   Conjectures académiques 56
   Pratique du théâtre 167–9, 184
Augustan 8–10, 16, 22–4, 40, 47, 50, 70n, 117–18, 120, 145, 366, 371, 566, 575, 720, 722
Augustine, Saint, of Hippo 352, 356, 498, 723, 760, 780n
   De Musica 723
Augustus Caesar 38, 89, 287, 565, 636
Austen, Jane 240, 283, 419–20, 422, 438, 455, 483, 701–2
   Mansfield Park 701
   Northanger Abbey 240, 283, 422, 438, 483
   Sense and Sensibility 419, 702
Avison, Charles 726–7
   Essay on Musical Expression 726–7

'Babes in the Wood' 101, 115, 472
Bacon, Francis 3n2, 23, 33, 39n, 44–5, 48, 136, 285, 290, 293, 298, 302, 310, 336, 350, 374, 468, 546–7, 558–9, 783, 792
   Advancement of Learning 3n2, 23, 44, 350
Baculard d'Arnaud, François-Marie 220, 224–5, 276
   Délassemens de l'homme sensible 225
   'Discours sur le roman' 220, 224
   Nouvelles historiques 224–5
Bage, Robert 246
   Mount Henneth (preface) 246
Baillie, Joanna 442, 447
Baillie, John 412
   Essay on the Sublime 412

Bakhtin, Mikhail 240, 261
ballads 102, 115, 118, 122–3,
    461–4, 469–70, 472–6, 558,
    636, 651, 788, 796
Ballard, George 308, 437n
    *Memoirs of Several Ladies of
    Great Britain* 308
Balzac, Guez de 492
Bandini, Angelo Maria 745, 746n
    Aratus, Callimachus, Nicander
    (edns of) 746n
    *Catalogus Codicum
    Manuscriptorum Bibliothecae
    Mediceae Laurentianae* 745
barbarism 467, 478, 576
Barbauld, Anna Laetitia (née Aikin)
    122, 132, 142, 251, 253, 258,
    440–2, 446, 448–9, 451–2,
    455, 482
    British Novelists 442, 452
    *Correspondence of Samuel
    Richardson* 442, 446, 448–9,
    452
    *Miscellaneous Pieces in Prose and
    Verse* 251, 258, 440, 482 (with
    Aikin, John: 'Enquiry into those
    Kinds of Distress', 482, 'On the
    Pleasure Derived from Objects
    of Terror', 440, 482)
    'On the Origin and Progress of
    Novel-Writing' 253
Barbey, Petrus 60
baroque 83, 289, 294–5, 787
Bary, René 352
    Rhétorique françoise 352
Baskerville, John 475
Batteux, Charles 45, 59, 121, 188,
    207, 368, 532–3, 682, 685,
    720, 730–3, 735–6, 738–9,
    741, 786
    *Les Beaux-Arts réduits à un
    même principe* 45, 59n, 121,
    368, 682, 685, 720, 730, 741,
    786
Battle of the Books 32–4, 46–52,
    55, 321
Baudelaire, Charles 489

Baumgarten, Alexander Gottlieb
    40n, 368, 658–63, 666, 671–2,
    678–9, 786
    Aesthetica 658–61, 786
    Meditationes philosophicae 658,
    660n, 668
Bayle, Pierre 3, 5n, 52, 217, 285–6,
    304, 318–19, 566
    Dictionnaire historique et critique
    5, 52n, 285–6, 304
    'Catius' 5
    'Suétone' 286n
    *Nouvelles de la République de
    Lettres* 318–19
    Pensées sur la Comète 286
Beattie, Gerard 552
    Essay on Truth 552
Beattie, James 141, 152, 250, 253,
    255, 260, 341, 367, 374, 376,
    412, 428, 430–2, 551, 553–5,
    721, 726, 730, 740
    Dissertations Moral and Critical
    374, 412
    'Illustrations on Sublimity'
    412
    Essays on Poetry and Music 152,
    428, 431, 726, 740
    'Of Sympathy' 428
    'Minstrel; or, the Progress of
    Genius' 141, 152, 554–5
    On Fable and Romance 250, 253,
    255, 260
    Theory of Language 341n
Beaumarchais, Pierre Augustin
    Caron de 203–4, 516
    Barbier de Séville 516
    *Essai sur le genre dramatique
    sérieux* 204
    Mariage de Figaro 203
Beaumont, Francis (*see also* Fletcher,
    John) 173
beaux-arts 218, 496
Beauzée, Nicolas 341
    Encyclopédie, 'Langue' 341
Beccaria, Cesare 130
    *Ricerche intorno alla natura dello
    stile* 130

Beethoven, Ludwig van 301
  Eroica (Third Symphony) 301
  Ninth Symphony 301
Behn, Aphra 241–2, 441, 445, 455
  Dutch Lover 441, 445
  'Preface' 445
  *Love-Letters between a Nobleman
    and his Sister* 242
  Oroonoko; or, The Royal Slave 242
belles-lettres 7n, 29, 35, 44–6, 54,
  212, 213n, 303, 315, 320, 324,
  351, 358, 362, 367, 490, 511,
  546–8, 551, 553–5, 557, 562,
  648
Bellori, Giovanni Pietro 110, 115
  *Vite de' pittori, scultori, et
    architetti moderni* 110
Benda, Julien 71n
Bengel, Johann Albanus 748
Bentham, Jeremy 401, 406
  'Of Laws in General' 401
Bentley, Richard 25, 50, 56n, 58–9,
  96, 742–4, 746n, 748–9,
  752–5, 759, 763
  (ed.) Callimachus, Hesychius,
    Nicander, Pollux 746n
  Boyle Lectures 755
  *Dissertation upon the Epistles of
    Phalaris* 50, 750, 753–4
  Epistola ad Joannem Millium 743,
    753n
  M. Manilii Astronomicon 754n
  'Remains of All Greek Poetry' 743
  'Remarks upon a Late Discourse
    of Free-Thinking' 755, 759
Beowulf 124, 479
Berenger, Richard 247
  (*see also* World)
Bergk, Johann 46, 58n
  Kunst 46n, 58n
Berkeley, George 134, 339n, 382,
  392, 591, 606, 686, 688–9,
  786
  *Alciphron; or the Minute
    Philosopher* 339n
  Principles of Human Knowledge
    134, 591

Berlinische Privilegierte Zeitung 326
Bernard, Joannes Stephanus 746n
  Ecloga of Thomas Magister (ed.)
    746n
Bible (*see also* Moses) 5, 65, 84, 101,
  108, 119, 124, 136–7, 180,
  352–3, 356, 404–5, 408–10,
  415–16, 463–8, 480, 491, 495,
  555, 563, 568, 571, 573, 579–80,
  601, 649, 655–6, 748, 752n,
  753n, 758–7, 789–90, 794
  Deuteronomy 353
  Genesis 82, 466, 765, 775
  Habbakuk 766
  Isaiah 767–8, 770–1
  Job 108, 404–5, 408–9, 415–16,
    491, 579–80, 765, 769, 772–3,
    790
  Jonah 764
  Judges 768, 776
  Matthew 764
  New Testament 748, 752n, 758,
    761, 764–5, 769, 771, 775
  Old Testament 84, 101, 108, 415,
    463–9, 495, 571, 573, 579,
    601, 753n, 758, 761, 764–5,
    768–70, 772, 775–6
  Proverbs 768
  Psalms 119, 137, 409–10, 764,
    766, 768, 773–4, 789
  Samuel 776
  Song of Solomon 65, 108, 410,
    439, 579, 649
  Vulgate 747–8, 777
bienséances 491, 513
Bildungsroman 794
Biographia Britannica 304
Biographium Faemineum 308
Birken, Sigmund von 265
  *Teutsche Redebind- und Dicht
    kunst* 265
Blackmore, Sir Richard 35n, 55,
  396, 400
  'Account of the Present
    Controversy concerning Homer's
    Iliad' 55
  Essay upon Epick Poetry 35n

Blackwall, Anthony 765, 769
  Sacred Classics Defended and
    Illustrated 765
Blackwell, Thomas 23–4, 65, 67, 69,
  135–8, 298, 413, 552, 558,
  565, 576, 580–1, 792
  Enquiry into the Life and Writings
    of Homer 135–6, 413n, 558,
    565, 576, 581
  Letters on Mythology 24, 558
Blair, Hugh 29, 45, 121–3, 130,
  137, 139, 146, 248–50, 321,
  342–3, 358, 361–4, 367, 368n,
  374, 412, 467, 479–80, 551,
  554–5, 562, 575, 580, 697–8
  Critical Dissertation on the Poems
    of Ossian 123, 362, 367n, 412,
    467, 479, 555
  Lectures on Rhetoric and Belles
    Lettres 29, 121, 130, 139, 250,
    342, 361–4, 374, 412, 467,
    562, 697
Blair, Robert 117, 133, 136
  Grave 117
Blake, William 122, 124, 137, 166,
  384, 390–3, 413, 584, 590,
  605–6, 612–13, 771
  'Annotations' to Reynolds'
    Discourses 606
  Descriptive Catalogue 391–2
  Jerusalem 392–3
  letter to Rev. John Trussler 166
  Marriage of Heaven and Hell 771
  Songs of Innocence and Experience
    166
  'Tyger' 166
  Urizen 612
  Vision of the Last Judgment 391,
    612
Blanckenburg, Christian Friedrich
  von 161, 269–70
  Litterarische Zusätze zu Johann
    Georg Sulzers allgemeiner
    Theorie der schönen Künste
    161
  Versuch über den Roman 269–70
Blumenbach, Johann Friedrich 793

Boccaccio, Giovanni 228, 471
  Decameron 228
Bodmer, Johann Jacob 30, 66, 266,
  268, 321, 530–2, 541–2
  Kritische Abhandlung von dem
    Wunderbaren in der Poesie 531
  Kritische Betrachtungen über die
    Poetischen Gemälde der Dichter
    266
  Discourse der Mahlern (Discourses
    of the Painters) (with J. J.
    Breitinger) 321, 530
Bodoni, Giambattista 756n
Boeckh, August 744
Boehme, Jakob 465, 467
Boekzaal der Geleerde Wereld 276
Boileau-Despréaux, Nicolas 19–20,
  24, 34–6, 40, 54, 56, 58, 75,
  78–85, 88–9, 95–7, 103,
  105–6, 108–9, 111, 113–14,
  116, 118, 143, 177–8, 185,
  210, 218, 234, 317, 351, 356,
  365, 368, 370, 372, 379,
  394–5, 397–9, 407, 455, 494,
  511, 520, 562, 564, 569,
  645–6, 719–20, 728, 778,
  781–2, 787, 789–90, 797
  Art poétique 35, 78–83, 85, 88,
    116, 118, 185, 356, 366, 564,
    781, 787
  Dialogue des héros de roman 218
  Discours sur la satire 80
  Longinus (trans.) 56n, 82, 789–90
  Lutrin 89
  Réflexions critiques sur quelques
    passages du rhéteur Longin 56n,
    82, 789
  Traité du sublime ou du
    Merveilleux (trans. Longinus)
    394, 397
Boivin, Jean 55, 57
  Apologie d'Homère, et bouclier
    d'Achille 55, 57n
Bolingbroke, Henry St. John, Lord
  570–1
  Letters on the Study and Use of
    History 570–1

Book of Canticles 649

Book of Common Prayer 563

Bos, Lambertus van den 272

Bossu, René Le 24, 37, 54, 75–6, 84, 87–8, 94, 99–100, 102, 107, 113–14, 172, 177, 317, 366, 368, 372, 379, 462, 595, 781

  Traité du poème épique 75, 94, 172n, 366, 781

Bossuet, Jacques Bénigne 113, 282–3, 288–9, 294, 493, 759

  Abrégé de l'Histoire universelle 283

  Adresse à Mgr le Dauphin 282–3

  Discours sur l'Histoire universelle 288n, 289, 493

  Exposition de la Doctrine de l'Eglise Catholique 759

Boswell, James 9n, 143, 303, 305, 307, 309–11, 314, 384, 434, 556, 558, 594, 787

  Hypochondriack No. 66 314

  Letters 310

  Life of Samuel Johnson LLD 9n, 143, 303, 305, 307, 309–11, 594, 787

Bougainville, Louis Antoine, Comte de 191

  'Discours de réception à l'Académie française' 191

Bouhours, Dominique 13, 24, 56, 75, 77–8, 83–4, 94, 103, 109, 215, 366

  Entretiens d'Ariste et d'Eugène 77, 94

  Manière de bien penser 13, 77–8, 109, 366

Boyer, Abel 12, 17

  Letters of Wit, Politicks and Morality 12

Boyle Lectures 755, 778

Boyle, Charles, fourth Earl of Orrery, edn of Phalaris 50

Boyle, Robert, the Hon. 298, 778, 783–5

  'Appendix to the Directions for Seamen bound for far Voyages' (*see also Philosophical Transactions of the Royal Society*) 784n

  'General Heads for the History of a Countrey' 783–4

  General History of the Air 783

Boyle, Roger, first Earl of Orrery 175

Bradshaigh, Dorothy Bellingham, Lady 64, 443–4

Brecht, Bertolt 199, 258

Breitinger, Johann Jacob 30, 266, 268, 530–2

  Discourse der Mahlern (with J. J. Bodmer) 321, 530

  Kritische Dichtkunst 30

Bretonne, Restif de la 516

  Paysan perverti 516

Bridgen, Martha (née Richardson) 483

British Academy 351

British Association for the Advancement of Science 39n

British Critic 486

British Magazine 324–5

British Novelists 442

Brontë, Charlotte 455

Brontë, Emily 455

Brooke, Frances 327, 437, 440–1, 452

  Old Maid 327, 437, 440

Brosses, Charles de 342

  Traité de la formation méchanique des langues 342n

Brown, Charles Brockden 240, 255n

  Edgard Huntly (preface) 240

  Wieland (Advertisement) 255n

Brown, John A. 23, 118, 121–2, 137

  Dissertation on the Power of Poetry and Music 121–2, 137

Brown, Lancelot ('Capability') 709–11

Brown, William Laurence 146

  Essay on Sensibility 146

Browne, Sir Thomas 317, 374, 573
Brunck, Richard Franz Philipp 746n
  (edns of Apollonius of Rhodes,
    Callimachus, Nicander,
    Theocritus) 746n
  Greek Anthology (ed.) 746n
Bryant, Jacob 468
Buckingham, second Duke of (*see*
    Villiers, George)
Büchner, Georg 199
Buffier, Claude 350
Buffon, Georges Louis Le Clerc,
    Comte de 129, 791
  Discours sur le style 129
Buhle, Johann Gottlieb 3, 746n
  Aratus (ed.) 746n
Bulwer, John 351n
  Chirologia and Chironomia 351n
Bunyan, John 242, 250, 253, 360,
    374, 764
  Pilgrim's Progress 242, 250, 253,
    764
Burckhardt, Jacob 571
Bürger, Gottfried August 31, 123,
    325, 529, 534, 543–4
  'Von der Popularität der Poesie' 31
bürgerliches Trauerspiel (*see also*
    tragédie bourgeoise) 193, 201
Burke, Edmund 14, 24, 41, 133–5,
    145, 153, 159, 258, 269, 300,
    328, 339, 361, 368–70, 389,
    403–9, 411, 414, 428–30, 440,
    487, 547, 590, 602, 626–9,
    632, 664n, 671, 681, 703, 706,
    769, 778, 785, 790–1
  *Philosophical Enquiry into the
    Origin of our Ideas of the
    Sublime and Beautiful* 14,
    133–5, 145, 153, 159, 339,
    368–9, 389, 403, 405, 430,
    487, 590, 602, 626–9, 652,
    671, 681, 703, 706, 778, 785,
    790–1
  'On Taste' 429–30, 628
  *Reflections on the Revolution in
    France* 41n, 300, 403, 406
burlesque 197

Burlington, Richard Boyle, third Earl
    of 289, 707
Burmann, Pieter 744
Burnet, Gilbert 303, 309, 360
  *Life and Death of Sir Matthew
    Hale, Knight* (preface) 309
Burnet, Thomas 47
  Sacred Theory of the Earth 47
Burney, Charles B. 719
  General History of Music 719
Burney, Frances (Fanny) 247, 260,
    328, 442
  Evelina 442
Burns, Robert 123, 345, 446, 464,
    557–8
Butler, Samuel 359
  Hudibras 359
Bysshe, Edward 118, 374, 376
  Art of English Poetry 118, 374

Callières, François de 36
  *Histoire poëtique de la guerre
    nouvellement déclarée entre les
    anciens et les modernes* 36
Callimachus (*see* Bandini; Bentley,
    André Dacier, Graevius,
    Spanheim; Brunck; Ernesti,
    J. A.; Reiske; Ruhnken;
    Valckenaer) 53, 743, 746n
Calvinism 142, 284, 286, 288
Calvin, Jean 288n
Campbell, George 23n, 361–2, 367,
    378, 386, 552, 554
  Philosophy of Rhetoric 23n, 361,
    386, 553
Camper, Petrus 793
Canning, George 240–1, 255
  Microcosm 255
canon 7, 25, 149, 246–7, 329–30,
    359, 491, 560–84, 608, 664,
    666, 678, 748, 776
Cappel, Louis (Capellus) 5, 777
  Critica Sacra 5
Cardano, Girolamo 778
Cartaud de la Villate, François 45n
  *Essai historique et philosophique
    sur le goût* 45n

Carter, Elizabeth 439, 444, 446, 453
Cartesianism (see also Descartes,
    René) 40, 54, 60, 285–6, 290,
    296, 298, 352, 498n, 570,
    572–4, 578, 580, 593, 603,
    745, 784–6, 795n
Casaubon, Meric 32, 241, 746
    Of Credulity and Incredulity 241
    Treatise concerning Enthusiasm 32
Castelvetro, Lodovico 113
catharsis 203, 258
Cather, Willa 455
Catherine the Great 331
Cato, Marcus Porcius 395, 563
Cave, Edward (see also Gentleman's
    Magazine) 326
Cavendish, Margaret, Duchess of
    Newcastle 445
Caxton, William 283, 288n
Caylus, Anne-Claude-Philippe de
    Tubières, Comte de 66, 473,
    694–5, 745
    Recueil d'antiquités 745
    Tableaux tirés de l'Iliade 694–5
Centlivre, Susannah 441, 443,
    445–6, 452
    Love's Contrivance (trans. of
    Molière's Médecin Malgré Lui,
    with preface) 441, 446
    The Wonder: A Woman Keeps a
    Secret 452n
Cervantes, Miguel de 210–11, 228,
    232, 240, 266, 268, 323, 360,
    448, 569
    Don Quixote 210–11, 228, 240,
    266, 268
Cesarotti, Melchiorre 124, 793
Chambers, Ephraim 784
    Cyclopedia 784
Chambre, Marin Cureau de la 173,
    179
    Lettre sur la comédie de
    l'imposteur 173, 179
Champaigne, Philippe de 285
Chandler, Richard 747
    Inscriptiones Antiquae 747
    Ionian Antiquities 747

Travels in Asia Minor 747
Travels in Greece 747
Channing, Edward Tyrell 240n
Chantelon, C. 745n
    Bibliotheca Patrum Ascetica 745n
Chapelain, Jean 35, 40, 56, 210,
    781
Chapone, Hester Mulso 444
Chardin, Jean-Baptiste Siméon
    500–1
Charles I 173
Charles II 15, 20, 173, 282, 401,
    456
Charnes, Jean-Antoine de 215
Charpentier, François 36
    Deffense de la langue françoise
    36
Chassiron, Pierre Matthieu Martin
    de 192–3, 195–6, 201
    Réflexions sur le comique
    larmoyant (Reflections on
    Sentimental Comedy) 192
Chateaubriand, François-René 135n,
    148, 519, 584
    Génie du Christianisme 148
Châtelet, Emilie du 444
Chatterton, Thomas 123, 345, 441,
    463–4, 470, 479–81
    'African Eclogues' 464
    Rowley manuscripts 441, 479–80
Chaucer, Geoffrey 92, 115, 359,
    370, 391, 441, 463–4, 470–1,
    473–5, 477–8, 480, 482, 488
    Canterbury Tales 92, 474, 480
    'Wife of Bath's Tale' 474
Chaussée, Pierre Claude Nivelle de
    la 190–1, 194, 196
    La Fausse antipathie (False
    Antipathy) 190
Chénier, André 127–8
Chesnaye Des Bois, Aubert de la
    218, 220, 222
    Lettres amusantes et critiques
    sur les romans en général 220,
    222
Chesterfield, Philip Dormer
    Stanhope, fourth Earl of 245

'Chevy Chase' 102, 115, 323, 370,
　　378, 461–2, 471–2, 475, 551
Cheyne, George (*see also*
　　Richardson, Samuel) 421
Chiari, Pietro 228
Child, Josiah 20
Chillingworth, William 760
　　Religion of Protestants a Safe Way
　　　to Salvation 760
Chirol, J. Louis 247
　　Inquiry 247
Choiseul-Gouffier, Marie Gabriel
　　Auguste Florent, Comte de 747
　　Voyage pittoresque en Grèce 747
Christ, Johann Friedrich 754
　　De Phaedro 754
　　Phaedri Fabularum Aesopiarum
　　　libri II 754
　　Uberior Expositio de Phaedro 754
Churchill, Charles 556
Cibber, Colley 181, 443
　　Love Makes a Man 443
Cicero, Marcus Tullius (Tully) 50,
　　76, 91, 101, 304, 310, 350–3,
　　355–9, 361, 364, 372, 374,
　　460, 490, 549, 645, 652, 684,
　　686, 748, 753n, 754
　　Brutus 748
　　De oratore (*On the Orator*)
　　　355–6, 686
Cincinnatus, Lucius Quinctius 16
Clarendon, Edward Hyde, first Earl
　　of 284, 285n, 360, 374
　　History of My Own Time 285n
classical/classicism 50, 56, 59, 63,
　　67, 69–71, 80, 83, 88, 114–15,
　　120, 156, 171, 184, 200, 202,
　　204, 206, 209–11, 216, 233–4,
　　270, 274, 292, 331, 354–5,
　　358, 361, 363–4, 368–9, 371–2,
　　376, 394, 436, 438, 444, 447,
　　463, 472–3, 482, 491, 495,
　　498n, 500, 502, 515, 518–19,
　　521–2, 524–5, 536–7, 541, 548,
　　560, 572, 577, 581, 583, 599n,
　　601, 634, 673, 678–9, 686,
　　698, 704, 707–9, 719, 735,

　　737–8, 742–57, 763, 765,
　　768–9, 774–6, 780, 787, 790
Claude (Claude Gelée, known as
　　Lorrain) 704–5, 714–15, 717,
　　726
Cleland, William 105–6, 331
Colbert, Jean-Baptiste 20, 35, 46n
Coleridge, Samuel Taylor 22, 127,
　　133, 136–8, 154–5, 158,
　　160–1, 164–5, 183, 208,
　　258–9, 331–2, 370, 412, 433n,
　　455, 484n, 590–1, 608, 611,
　　613, 623–5, 629–31, 775, 791,
　　795, 796n
　　'The Aeolian Harp' 164–5
　　Biographia Literaria 22, 158, 160,
　　　412n, 590, 608, 623–4
　　Critical Review No. 19 (2nd
　　　series) 258
　　'Dejection: An Ode' 591
　　'Frost at Midnight' 154
　　Lyrical Ballads (*see* Wordsworth)
　　　796–7
Colette, Sidonie Gabrielle 455
Collection of Old Ballads 472
Collier, Jeremy 180–1, 189–90, 192
　　Short View of the Profaneness and
　　　Immorality of the English Stage
　　　180, 189
Collier, Mary 127
Collins, Anthony 759
　　Discourse of Free-Thinking 759
Collins, William 117–18, 141, 441,
　　473, 555, 697, 790
　　Odes on Several Descriptive and
　　　Allegorical Subjects 117
　　'Ode on the Political Character'
　　　141
　　Persian Eclogues 117
Colman, George 194
　　English Merchant 194
Columbian Magazine 325
Columbus, Christopher 457
comédie héroïque 186, 188
comédie larmoyante 192, 194–6
commedia dell'arte 172, 178, 185,
　　187

Condillac, Étienne Bonnot de 52,
124, 128, 131–2, 134–5, 137–9,
147–8, 157, 335, 337–43, 345,
347, 466–9, 795
'Art d'écrire' 124, 132
*Essai sur l'origine des
connoissances humaines* 138,
157, 338, 466
Histoire ancienne 52
Logique 339
Traité des Sensations 157
Condorcet, Marie Jean Antoine
Nicolas de Caritat, Marquis de
32, 67, 796
*Esquisse d'un tableau historique
des progrès de
l'esprit humain* 55n
Congreve, William 12, 179–81, 192,
239, 241, 243, 252, 443
'Concerning Humor in Comedy' 12
Double Dealer 180
Incognita (preface) 239, 252
Way of the World 181
Connoisseur 18
Constable, John 705
Constantine (emperor) 287, 293–4
conte 226, 232–3
conte historique 232
conte merveilleux 232
contes moraux 226, 513
conte plaisant 232
Cooper, Elizabeth 441
Muses' Library (ed., intro.) 441
Copernicus 47
Corneille, Pierre 35, 37, 70, 113,
167, 169–70, 175, 182,
185–9, 198, 203, 205, 360,
492–3, 498–9, 511–12, 517,
645, 719–20, 722, 735, 781
Discours de la tragédie 186
Don Sanche d'Aragon 185–6
Epître dédicatoire 185
Examens et Discours 781
Horace 498
Le Cid 167, 175
Pompey 175
Trois discours 170

Correspondance littéraire 331, 498n,
516–17
(*see also* Grimm, Diderot, Meister)
Costantini, Giuseppe Antonio 228
Cotton, Sir Robert 474
Cowley, Abraham 25, 84, 98, 102,
141, 317, 372, 377, 385, 412,
461
Davideis 84
Pindarique Odes 85
Cowley, Hannah 452
Belle's Stratagem 452
Cowper, William 140, 419, 554
The Task 701
Cox, Leonard 352n
Arte or Crafte of Rhetoryke 352n
Craige, John 48
Cramer, John Antony 746n
Anecdota Graeca 746n
Crébillon, Claude Prosper Jolyot de
218–19, 222–3
Crevier, Jean-Baptiste Louis 358n
Rhétorique françoise 358n
Critical Review (*see also* Smollett)
246, 248–9, 327–9, 332, 434,
480, 486
No. 2 249
No. 11 260
No. 16 246
No. 20 248
No. 53 480
No. 70 247
Critical Review (2nd series) 258,
484
No. 11 484
No. 19 (Coleridge) 258
Cromwell, Henry 12
Cromwell, Oliver 302, 456
Crose, Jean de la 318–20
Universal Historical Bibliothèque
318–19
Crowne, John 176
Cudworth, Ralph 624
Cumberland, Richard 195, 258–60,
421, 459
Brothers 195
Henry 259–60

Observer 258
West Indian 195
Curll, Edmund 309

Dacier, André 55–6, 183, 187, 194, 646, 720, 755
  (ed.) Dictys, Florus, Callimachus 53
  (trans.) Anacreon, Aristophanes, Plautus, Sappho, Terence 53
  Les Oeuvres d'Horace traduites en francois 755n
    'Préface sur les Satires d'Horace' 755n
  Poétique d'Aristote, La (ed.) 56, 187, 720
Dacier, Anne Lefèvre 53–4, 56–9, 62–3, 68, 113, 439, 462, 756n
  Homère défendu contre l'Apologie du R. P. Hardouin; ou Suite des causes de la corruption du goust 54, 63n, 439
  L'Iliade d'Homère (trans., preface) 57, 59n, 439
  L'Odyssée d'Homère (trans., remarks) 439
Daguesseau, Henri François 220, 223
Dähnert, Johann Carl 267
Dallaway, James 704
Daniel, Samuel 177, 441
Dante Alighieri 234, 485, 518, 532
  Divine Comedy 518
Danton, Georges Jacques 402
Darwin, Erasmus 127, 131, 152, 613, 791
  Botanic Garden 152, 613
  'Economy of Vegetation' 152
  Loves of the Plants 127
Daubenton, Louis Jean Marie 793
Davenant, Sir William 96, 174–5, 177, 317, 440, 456, 458, 614
  Cruelty of the Spaniards in Peru 458
  Gondibert 96, 175, 440, 614
  'Preface' 614

Defoe, Daniel 65, 241–3, 246, 250, 252–3, 255, 273, 320, 360, 374, 468, 505, 509, 682, 764, 789
  Colonel Jack (preface) 243
  De Arte Graphica (*The Art of Painting*) by Du Fresnoy (verse trans.) 683
  Family Instructor 250
  Moll Flanders (preface) 243, 252
  Review 320
  Robinson Crusoe 242, 250, 253, 255, 273, 505, 509, 764
  Roxana (preface) 243
  Serious Reflections of Robinson Crusoe 243, 250
  Tour of Great Britain 789
Degérando, Joseph Marie 339
  Des signes et l'art de penser considérés dans leurs rapports mutuels 339
Deken, Aagje (*see* Wolff-Bekker, Betje)
Delany, Mary 444
Delaunay (*see* Staal-de Launay)
Delille, Jacques 519–20
  'Preliminary Discourse' to trans. Virgil's *Georgics* 519
Demosthenes 76, 91, 350, 356, 359, 361, 401–2, 408, 460
Denham, Sir John 85–6, 373, 470
Denker, De 277
Dennis, John 11–21, 30–1, 35n, 97–8, 115, 118, 179, 181–2, 190, 366, 370, 372, 382, 396–9, 402–5, 415, 472, 482, 576, 601–2, 647n, 721, 766, 770, 790
  Advancement and Reformation of Modern Poetry 19, 97, 766
  Essay on the Genius and Writings of Shakespeare 181
  Impartial Critick 12, 97
  Large Account 15, 20
  Of the Grounds of Criticism in Poetry 13, 20, 35n, 98, 398, 647n, 766

'Of Simplicity in Poetical
Compositions' 12, 472
'Reflections on *An Essay on
Criticism*' 399
Remarks on Prince Arthur 372,
601-2
'Upon the Roman Satirists' (to
Matthew Prior) 12
Descartes, René 32-3, 37, 42, 48,
54, 60, 62, 81, 285-7, 336,
350, 352n, 493, 498n, 569-70,
572-5, 578, 580, 582, 593,
603, 605, 686, 723, 779-81,
784-6, 795n
Correspondence 723
Discours de la Méthode 285, 350,
779
Traité de l'Homme 779
Traité des passions de l'âme 32
Desmarets de Saint-Sorlin, Jean 35,
37
Clovis 35
*Comparaison de la langue et de la
poésie françoise avec la grecque
et la latine* 35
Desfontaines, Pierre François
218-19, 332
Destouches, Philippe Néricault 190
Philosophe marié 190
determinism 202
Dickinson, Emily 455
Dictys (*see* Dacier, André) 53
Diderot, Denis 119, 134-5, 137,
147, 158, 185, 196-200, 202,
204, 209, 231-3, 276, 331-2,
375, 402, 410-11, 423-4,
443, 459, 490, 495-504, 507,
510-21, 594-7, 609, 624,
662-4, 679-80, 693, 695,
698-9, 785-6, 792, 795
'Ceci n'est pas un conte' 499
Correspondance littéraire 331,
498n, 516-17
Deux amis de Bourbonne 232,
499, 507
Discours de la poésie dramatique
196-7, 499-500, 502

Eloge de Richardson 199, 231-3,
276, 423, 499
Eloge de Terence 499
Encyclopédie (*see also* main entry
Encyclopédie) 4, 7n, 8, 226,
286, 341, 375, 424, 496, 498,
510-21, 680, 695n, 698-9,
728, 736-7, 795
Entretiens sur le fils naturel
196-7, 199-200, 499-502, 699
Essai sur la poésie dramatique
699
Essais sur la peinture 503, 662n
Fils naturel 196-7, 499, 501
Jacques le fataliste et son maître
375, 499-500, 594-5
*Letter on the Blind for the Use of
the Sighted* 496
Lettre sur les Sourds et Muets
134, 496, 497n, 498n, 504,
693n, 695
Neveu de Rameau 375, 402,
410-11, 504
Oeuvres esthétiques 499-500,
501n, 502n
'Essais sur la peinture' 500n
Oeuvres romanesques 500, 594n,
595n
Paradoxe sur le comédien 199n,
424, 500-1, 503, 507
'Pensées sur l'interpretation de la
nature' 423
Père de famille 196, 499
*Recherches philosophiques sur
l'origine et la nature du beau*
662n
*Réfutation suivie de l'ouvrage
d'Helvétius* 147
Rêve de d'Alembert 158, 424,
503n
*Supplément au Voyage de
Bougainville* 459
Salons 496, 500-1, 507, 699
trans. of Shaftesbury, *Inquiry
concerning Virtue and Merit*
498
Dielen, A. S. W. van 277-8

dispositio 738
D'Israeli, Isaac 313–15
Dobree, Peter Paul 746n
  Lexicon rhetoricum maximum
    746n
Doddridge, Philip 764
  Family Expositor 764
Dodsley, Robert 117, 366, 437n,
    473, 476, 547
  Collection of Poems, by Several
    Hands 117
  Correspondence 476
  Miscellany 437n
  Museum 366
  Preceptor 547
  Select Collection of Old Plays 473
  'Short Historical Essay on the Rise
    and Progress of the English
    Stage' 473
Donne, John 581, 615
Dorat, Claude Joseph 225
Douglas, Gavin 479
Drake, Nathan 146, 486
  Literary Hours 146, 486–7
  'Henry Fitzowen' 487
  'Ode to Superstition' 487
  'On Gothic Superstition' 487
Dryden, John 3, 8–9, 14, 16, 22,
    24, 70, 75–81, 85–6, 88–93,
    98, 100–1, 103, 107, 110, 115,
    129, 143, 174–9, 182, 282,
    302, 305, 316–17, 319–20,
    330, 337, 344, 360, 365, 370,
    372–3, 376, 379, 384, 396,
    454, 456, 458, 461, 471, 473,
    475, 488, 493, 549, 562, 615,
    623, 631–2, 683–4, 720–2,
    724–5, 726, 730, 739, 755,
    764, 781–2, 789
  Absalom and Achitophel 89–90
  Alexander's Feast 726
  All for Love 177
  Annus Mirabilis 615
  'Preface' 615
  'Author's Apology for Heroic
    Poetry and Poetic Licence' 88,
    91, 396

Art of Painting (trans. of Du
  Fresnoy: *see* 'Parallel of Poetry
  and Painting') 683–4
Art of Poetry 79–81
'Character [of St Evremond]' 75
Conquest of Granada 91, 176,
  458
Dedication of the *Aeneid* 75, 92
'Defence of the Epilogue' 92
'Defence of an Essay of Dramatic
  Poesy' 782
'Discourse concerning Satire'
  88–9, 755
Evening's Love, An 179
Fables, Ancient and Modern 90,
  92, 471
'Grounds of Criticism in Tragedy'
  75, 77, 88, 177
'Heads of an Answer to Rymer'
  177
Indian Emperor 458
Indian Queen (with Sir Robert
  Howard) 458
King Arthur (with Henry Purcell)
  721
letter to John Dennis 93
'Life of Plutarch' 302, 305
MacFlecknoe 50, 90, 337, 550
Of Dramatic Poesy: An Essay 12,
  75–6, 175–6, 456, 549–50,
  720, 722, 781–2
'Of Heroic Plays: An Essay' 91
'Parallel of Poetry and Painting'
  76, 91, 110, 684, 730
Postscript to the *Aeneid* 90
Preface to *Albion and Albanius* 9,
  722n
Preface to *Fables* 86, 90–2,
  471
Preface to *Ovid's Epistles* 85–6
Preface to *Sylvae* 88
Preface to *Troilus and Cressida*
  782
Rival Ladies 615, 782
Saint Cecilia's Day Odes 722,
  724–5
Spanish Friar 360

State of Innocence 88
'To Roger, Earl of Orrery' 615
'To the Right Honourable My
    Lord Radcliffe' 93
Du Bos, Jean-Baptiste 5, 11, 28, 30,
    39–41, 43, 57–63, 67, 110–12,
    120, 167, 171, 181–3, 187,
    291n, 337, 344, 402, 466–7,
    526, 635, 662, 682–3, 685,
    693, 695, 698, 730, 733–9,
    785
  *Réflexions critiques sur la poésie
    et sur la peinture* 11, 28, 30,
    41, 43, 58–9, 67, 110–12, 120,
    181, 182n, 187, 337, 467, 635,
    682–3, 685, 693, 695, 698,
    730, 733–9, 785
  'Dissertation sur les
    représentations théatrales des
    Anciens' 730
Du Cange, Charles Dufresne 744
Duck, Stephen 127, 324
Duff, William 137, 144–5, 148,
    631–2
  Essay on Original Genius 145,
    631
Du Fresnoy, Charles Alphonse 110,
    683–4, 692
  De Arte Graphica 110, 683–4,
    692
Du Marsais, César-Chesneau 350,
    357
  Traité des tropes 357
Dunbar, William 479
Duncan, William 547
Duncombe, John 437n
Du Plaisir 216–17, 235
  *Sentiments sur les lettres et sur
    l'histoire* 216, 217n
Du Resnel, Jean François du Bellay
    61
  'Réflexions générales sur l'utilité
    des Belles-Lettres' 61
Dyer, George 24, 119
Dyer, John 705
  Fleece 119
  Grongar Hill 119

Echlin, Elizabeth, Lady 444
  *Alternative Ending to Richardson's
    'Clarissa'* 444
Eckhel, Joseph Hilarius 745
  Doctrina Numorum Veterum
    745
Eclectic Review No. 8 247
Eden, Anne 444
Edgeworth, Maria 447
  Letters for Literary Ladies 447
Edinburgh Society 429
Edwards, John 765
Edwards, Thomas 577–8, 763
  *Discourse Concerning the
    Authority, Stile ... of the Old
    and New Testament* 577–8
  *A Supplement to Mr. Warburton's
    Edition* 577, 763
Effen, Justus van 275
  Hollandsche Spectator 275
  *Misantrope of Gestrenge
    Zedenmeester* 275
Egg 246
Egmont, John Perceval, second Earl
    of 401
Eichhorn, Johann Gottfried 774–5
  Einleitung in das Neue Testament
    775
  Einleitung ins Alte Testament
    775
Elibank, Patrick Murray, Lord 556
Eliot, George (pseud. Mary Ann
    Evans) 455
Eliot, Thomas Stearns (T. S.) 71n,
    92, 562, 581
  Use of Poetry 92
Ellis, George 488
elocutio 738
Elstob, Elizabeth 439, 479
  *English-Saxon Homily on the
    Birth-day of St Gregory* 439
    (trans. Aelfric)
  *Rudiments of Grammar for the
    English-Saxon Tongue* 439
Elstob, William 479
Emmery, Willem, Baron de
    Perponcher 279

empiricism/empirical 130–2, 134,
  157, 160, 297–8, 362, 367,
  382, 384, 386, 390–2, 590,
  593, 595–6, 599n, 601–2,
  606–8, 610–12, 653, 666, 668,
  670–1, 674, 687, 786
enargeia 686, 689
energeia 686
Encyclopédie 4, 7n, 8, 226, 286,
  341, 375, 489, 490n, 496, 498,
  504, 506, 510–21, 680–1,
  695n, 698, 723, 737, 772,
  786–7, 792, 795
  Diderot, Denis
    'Art' 498n
    'Beau' 498, 511
    'Composition' 695n, 698
  Alembert, Jean le Rond d' 7n,
    46n, 506, 513–14
    'Discours préliminaire'
      (*Preliminary Discourse*) 504,
      511, 514, 521n
    'Erudition' 7n, 46n
    'Genève' 506, 513
  Beauzée, Nicolas, 'Langue' 341
  Grimm, Friedrich 728
    'Poème lyrique' 728
  Jaucourt, Louis, Chevalier de 8,
    46, 490n, 511, 513, 736
    'Imitation' 8
    'Littérature' 46, 490n
    'Peinture' 736
    'Peinture Moderne' 736
    'Roman' 513
    'Stratford' 513
  Mallet, Edme 521n
    'Critique, s.m.' 521n
  Marmontel, Jean François 226,
    375, 490, 511, 513
    'Critique, s.f.' 4, 511
  Saint-Lambert, Jean François,
    Marquis de 511–12
    'Génie' 511–12
Supplément à l'Encyclopédie 680n
  Turgot, Anne Robert 795
    'Ether' 796
    'Etymologie' 796
'Feu électrique' 796
'Magnétisme' 796
  Voltaire, 'Gens de lettres' 4
Enfield, William 139–40
Engel, Johann Jakob 269
Engelen, Cornelis van 276n, 277
  Philosooph, De No. 42 276n
Enlightenment 4, 10, 32n, 57n, 142,
  144, 159, 189, 233, 263, 271,
  285, 288, 296, 315, 319, 329,
  331, 347, 351, 367, 402,
  460–1, 465, 468–9, 498n,
  523–4, 526, 528–9, 541–3,
  546, 548n, 552, 556, 558–9,
  598, 607, 613, 658, 666, 678,
  682, 687, 728, 742, 744, 756
  German Enlightenment 530, 545,
    729
  Scottish Enlightenment 123, 429,
    546–59
epic (*épopée*) 35–7, 54, 64–5, 75–6,
  80, 87, 89, 98, 120, 123,
  211–15, 234, 238, 240, 247,
  263–6, 269–71, 273, 298, 360,
  365–6, 372, 375, 463, 496,
  503, 515, 518, 555, 561, 576,
  580, 647, 676, 681, 687, 698,
  731–3, 735, 737, 755, 766,
  792, 794
  mock-epic 240
Epicurus 51n, 58
Epictetus 439
Epinay, Louise Tardieu d' 331–2
epistolary (novel) 242–3, 256,
  259–61, 279, 448
Ernesti, Johann August 746n
  edn of Callimachus 746n
Ernesti, Johann Christian Gottlieb
  351n, 744
  *Lexicon technologiae Graecorum
    rhetoricae* 351n, 744
  *Lexicon technologiae Latinorum
    rhetoricae* 351n
*Essay on the New Species of Writing
  founded by Mr. Fielding* 255
Etherege, Sir George 181
  Man of Mode 181

Euripides 359, 492, 511, 581
European Magazine 325, 486
Evans, Evan 65n, 67
  Specimens of the Poetry of the
    Ancient Welsh Bards 67
Evans, Thomas 476
  Old Ballads 476
Evelyn, John 571
  Diary 571

fable, moral 495, 505, 530, 540–2
fable, story or plot 9, 99–101, 108,
  234, 249, 253, 366, 372, 374,
  495, 541, 794
Fabricius, Johann Albert 744,
  749
  Bibliotheca Graeca 744
  Bibliotheca Latina 744
  Bibliotheca Latina Mediae et
    Infimae Aetatis 744
Fagan, Christophe Barthélemi 194
fairy tale 38
Falconer, William 127
  Shipwreck 127
Fanshawe, Sir Richard 85
Farmer, Richard (*see* Percy, Thomas)
  474
Farquhar, George 167, 192
Faydit, Pierre Valentin, Abbé
  218–19
  Télémacomanie 218
Feijóo, Benito Jerónimo
  Teatro crítico universal 114
Feith, Rijnvis 279–80
  Ideaal in de Kunst, Het 280n
  Julia 279
Félibien, André 730, 733n
  Sixième Conférence 733n
feminism/feminist(s) 436, 437n, 443,
  446, 450–2, 454–5
Fénelon, François de Salignac de la
  Mothe 36, 58, 113, 218–19,
  221, 234, 273–4, 355–7, 493,
  720
  Dialogues sur l'éloquence en
    général et la chaire en
    particulier 356–7

Télémaque 36, 218–19, 221, 273,
  493
Ferguson, Adam 25, 122, 137,
  292–3, 556
Fergusson, Robert 557–8
  'Elegy on the Death of Scots
    Music' 557–8
Ferriar, John 422
  Illustrations of Sterne 422
Fichte, Johann Gottlieb 163n, 164,
  332
fictions merveilleuses (*see also* Staël)
  234
Fielding, Henry 65, 180, 229,
  239–41, 243, 246–7, 253–6,
  259–60, 267–70, 273–4,
  276–7, 279–80, 288, 321–4,
  331, 374–5, 378n, 386, 434,
  436, 439, 446, 448–9, 452,
  513, 569, 591, 716, 787–8
  Amelia 276, 569
  Covent-Garden Journal 321, 323,
    434
  Jonathan Wild 259
  Joseph Andrews 254, 273, 276,
    288n, 375, 386
  Joseph Andrews (preface) 239,
    273
  Journal of a Voyage to Lisbon
    (and preface) 260–1
  Shamela 240, 243, 247, 260
  Tom Jones 253, 255–6, 273–4,
    276, 279n, 280, 375, 591,
    787–8
Fielding, Sarah 375n, 440, 452
  Remarks on 'Clarissa' 440
Flaubert, Gustave 217, 230, 450
  Madame Bovary 230, 450
Fletcher, John (*see also* Beaumont,
    Francis) 173–4, 176
Flögel, Karl Friedrich 149
Florus (*see* André Dacier) 53
Fontanier, Pierre 358
  Commentaire raisonné des tropes
    358
  Traité générale des figures du
    discours 358

Fontenelle, Bernard le Bovier de
32–5, 37–9, 40n, 42, 44–5,
47, 49, 55, 60–4, 93–6, 107,
115–16, 192n, 194, 197,
286–7, 290, 296, 569
De l'origine des fables 287
Dialogues des morts 37
*Digression sur les anciens et les
modernes* 36–9, 45, 47, 93–4,
96, 569
Discours sur la nature de l'eglogue
94–5
Poésies pastorales 36
Sur la poésie en general 38n
Sur l'histoire 286
Forcellini, Egidio 744
Totius Latinitatis Lexicon 744
Fordyce, David 12, 547, 552
Dialogues Concerning Education
552
Forskål, Peter 771
Fox, Henry 402
Fragonard, Jean Honoré 786
France littéraire 328
Francis, Ann 439, 444
*Poetical Epistle from Charlotte to
Werther* 444
*Poetical Translation of the Song
of Solomon* 439
Francis, Philip
Eugenia 194
Frankfurter Gelehrte Anzeigen
326
Franklin, Benjamin 321, 788n
Frederick II of Prussia 331
French Revolution (*see* Revolution)
Fréret, Nicolas 61
Fréron, Élie-Catherine 193, 515–16
Année littéraire 515–16
*Lettres sur quelques écrits de ce
temps* 193
Fréron, Stanislas 515
Friedrich Christian, Prince of
Schleswig-Holstein-Augusten-
burg 674n
Fuller, Thomas 302
Furetière, Antoine 210

Gainsborough, Thomas 711n, 786
Gaisford, Thomas 746n
Etymologicum Magnum 746n
Suda 746n
Galanti, Giuseppe Maria 229
Gale, Theophilus 464
Court of the Gentiles 464
Galilei, Vincenzo 723
Galileo Galilei 60n, 779–80
Garrick, David 294, 440, 443
Gärtner, Carl Friedrich 791
Garve, Christian 149, 269, 608
Gassendi, Pierre 493
Gay, John 127, 411–12, 440, 442–3
Beggar's Opera 442–3
Captives 440
Polly 460
Three Hours After Marriage (with
Alexander Pope) 412
Gébelin, Antoine Court de 342
Geddes, Alexander 775–6
Address to the Public ... Bible 776
*Critical Remarks on the Hebrew
Scriptures* 776
Holy Bible (trans.) 775–7
*Prospectus of a New Translation
of the Holy Bible* 775–7
Geisterroman 486
Gellert, Christian Fürchtegott 193–6,
201, 267–8
*Abhandlung für das rührende
Lustspiel* (*An Essay in Defence
of Sentimental Comedy*) 193–4
Die Betschwester (*The Pious
Woman*) 194
Die schwedische Gräfin 267–8
Die zärtlichen Schwestern (*The
Tender Sisters*) 194
Gellius, Aulus 70
General Magazine 327, 713n
Genlis, Stephanie Ducrest de St
Aubin, Comtesse de 438, 450,
452–5
*De l'influence des femmes sur la
littérature française* 450, 452–3
genre sérieux 197–8, 204
Gentleman's Journal 324, 720–1

Gentleman's Magazine 248, 255–6, 260, 320, 324–6, 460, 481
  No. 3 460n
  No. 19 255–6
  No. 40 260
  No. 58 248
Geoffrin, Marie-Thérèse 444
géomètres/geometricians 58–9, 63, 778–83, 787–8
George III 362
Gerard, Alexander 131, 141, 144–5, 148–50, 155, 161–2, 367, 428–9, 547, 548, 551–5, 630–2, 785
  Essay on Genius 144, 149–50, 552, 630–1
  Essay on Taste 141, 144, 148–9, 428–9, 552, 630, 785
  Plan of Education 548, 552
Gerstenberg, Heinrich Wilhelm von 205, 794
  Briefe über Merkwürdigkeiten der Literatur (*Letters on Literary Memorabilia*) 205
Gesner, Johann Matthias 751–2, 754
  Darstellung der Altertumswissenschaft nach Begriff, Umfang und Zweck (*Depiction of the Science of Antiquity according to its Concept . . .*) 752
  Primae Lineae Isagoges in Eruditionem Vniversalem 751
Gespensterroman 486
Gessner, Salomon 330
Giannone, Pietro 296
Gibbon, Edward 3n, 41, 52, 57, 58n, 59n, 62, 69n, 282–91, 293–5, 300, 360, 412–13, 573, 753, 788, 796
  Essai sur l'étude de la littérature 3n, 41, 52, 58n, 62, 69n, 294n, 413
  History of the Decline and Fall of the Roman Empire 52, 291, 293–5, 753, 796
  Journal 412
  Memoirs 282n, 294n, 295

Gildon, Charles 39, 98–9, 255
  Complete Art of Poetry 99
  Epistle to Daniel Defoe 255
Gilpin, William 700, 702–4, 706, 710, 712–13, 715, 717
  'Dialogue' 713
  Dialogue upon the Gardens of the Right Honorable the Lord Viscount Cobham at Stow in Buckinghamshire 717n
  Essay upon Prints 700, 702
  Remarks on Forest Scenery 715
  Three Essays: On Picturesque Beauty 702–4, 715
Ginguené, Pierre Louis 519
Giornale de' letterati 318
Glanvill, Joseph 36n
  Plus Ultra: or, the Progress and Advancement of Knowledge since the Days of Aristotle 36n
Gluck, Christoph Willibald 719
Godwin, William 246, 252, 256–7, 260n, 332, 401, 483–4, 796
  Caleb Williams 260n
  Enquiry concerning Political Justice 256–7
  Fleetwood 260n
  History of the Life of William Pitt 401n
  'Of History and Romance' 246, 252, 256
Goens, Rijklof Michael 277–8
Goethe, Johann Wolfgang von 31, 39n, 70, 123, 125–6, 149–50, 161, 164, 185, 207–8, 235, 270–1, 278, 280, 301, 312, 326, 330–2, 338, 425, 444, 479, 522–4, 529–30, 533–8, 544, 576, 583, 587, 596, 613, 624, 662–3, 673, 676–8, 701, 756, 786, 794, 796n
  Dichtung und Wahrheit 312, 535
  Einfache Nachahmung der Natur, Manier, Stil 535
  Frankfurter Gelehrte Anzeigen (contrib.) 326, 533
  Götz von Berlichingen 149, 207

Hermann and Dorothea 676–7
'Literarischer Sansculottismus' 522
Maximen und Reflexionen 536, 587
On German Architecture 149, 207
Propyläen 536
Wahlverwandtschaften (Elective Affinities) 701n
Werther (Die Leiden des jungen Werthers) 149, 164, 235, 278, 280, 425, 444, 479
West-Östlicher Divan 125
'Naturformen der Dichtkunst' 125
'Noten und Abhandlungen' 125
Wilhelm Meister's Apprenticeship 208, 271, 444, 583
Winckelmann und sein Jahrhundert (Winckelmann and his Century) 663
Zum Shakespeares Tag (On Shakespeare's Name-Day) 207, 673
Golden Age 76, 107, 120, 228, 457–8
Goldoni, Carlo 187, 330
Goldsmith, Oliver 11, 13–14, 16–18, 22, 25, 27–9, 127, 172, 189, 195, 206, 303, 322, 324, 326, 330, 434, 557, 567–8, 787
British Magazine (essay contribution) 324
'Deserted Village' 557
Enquiry into the Present State of Polite Learning in Europe 11, 13, 18, 25, 567, 568
Essay on the Theatre; or A Comparison between Laughing and Sentimental Comedy 189
Good-Natured Man (preface) 189
Plutarch's Lives (preface) 303
She Stoops to Conquer 189, 195
trans. of *Mémoires d'un protestant* 330
Vicar of Wakefield 29, 326, 787
Gomberville, Marin Le Roy 210
Góngora, Luis de 114
Gongorism 83, 114

Gordon, James
Occasional Thoughts on the Study and Character of Classical Authors 69
Gössman, Elizabeth 33n
Gother, John 759
Catholic Representer 759
Gothic/Gothick 65, 66n, 86, 102, 114, 118, 142, 144, 177, 236, 240, 245, 255, 289, 368, 371, 379, 387, 406, 434, 441, 461, 470–88, 551, 577, 704, 706, 788, 796
Göttinger Musenalmanach 325
Göttingische Anzeigen von gelehrten Sachen 328
Gottsched, Johann Christoph 5, 30, 83, 118, 187–8, 193–4, 196, 201, 203, 266–7, 321, 357, 441, 522, 524–7, 530–1, 533, 541–2, 679
Ausführliche Redekunst 357
Beiträge zur kritischen Historie der deutschen Sprache 527
Der Biedermann 527
Der Sterbende Cato (The Death of Cato) 201
Die Vernünftigen Tadlerinnen 321, 441
Versuch einer kritischen Dichtkunst 4, 30, 83, 118, 187, 194, 266–7, 522, 525–7, 530
'On the Good Taste of the Poet' 526
Gottsched, Luise Adelgunde Victoria 441
Gower, John 471, 478
Gozzi, Carlo 229
Gracián, Baltasar
Arte de ingenio 114
Gradus ad Parnassum (reference work) 374, 376
Graevius, Johann Georg 744
Callimachus (ed.) 746n
Thesaurus Antiquitatum Romanorum 744

Graffigny, Françoise d'Issembourg
   d'Happoncourt de 442
   Lettres d'une péruvienne 442
Granger, James 308
   Biographical History of England
   308
Granville, George
   Large Account of the Taste in
   Poetry 12, 19
Gravina, Gian Vicenzo 109, 114, 367
   Della ragion poetica 109, 367
Gray, Thomas 22, 112, 117–18,
   127, 140–1, 300, 307, 323,
   328, 359, 361, 368, 420, 440,
   464, 473–4, 482, 549, 555,
   557, 697, 768, 789–90, 797
   'Bard' 141, 464
   Commonplace Book 474n
   Elegy in a Country Church-yard
   112, 361, 789
   'Ode on a Distant Prospect of
   Eton College' 117, 361, 550
   'Progress of Poetry' 141, 440
Greek Anthology (*see* eds. Brunck,
   Reiske) 746n
Gregory, G. (*see* Lowth) 766
Gregory of Nazianzus, Saint 745n
Grierson, Constantia 439
Griffith, Elizabeth 238, 246, 439–40,
   446, 452
   Delicate Distress 238
   Genuine Letters 246
   Morality of Shakespear's Drama
   Illustrated 440, 446
Griffiths, Isabella 434
Griffiths, Ralph (*see also Monthly*
   Review) 318, 434
Grimm, Friedrich Melchior 331–2,
   516, 728
   Correspondance littéraire 331,
   498n, 516–17
   'Poème lyrique' in *Encyclopédie*
   [ed. Diderot] 728
Gronovius, Jakob 744, 746n
   Harpocration (edn) 746n
   Thesaurus Antiquitatum
   Graecarum 744

Grotius, Hugo 284
Gryzaard (periodical) 276n
Guardian (*see also* Steele) 6n, 16,
   108, 181, 321–2, 707
   No. 12 6n
   No. 34 16
   No. 37 (*see* Hughes) 181
   No. 78 (*see* Pope) 322
   No. 86 108, 765
Guarini, Giovanni Battista
   Il Pastor Fido 85
Guicciardini, Francesco 283, 567
Guild, William 764
   Moses Unvail'd 764
Guilleragues, Gabriel Joseph
   Lavergne, Comte de 219
   Lettres portugaises 219, 235
Gundling, Nicolaus Hieronymous
   266
Guys, Pierre Augustin
   Voyage littéraire de la Grèce 747

Hakewill, George 36n, 39
   Apologie of the Power and
   Providence of God 36n
Hale, Sir Matthew 309
Haller, Albrecht von 270, 330–2,
   791
   Fabius und Cato 270
Halley, Edmund 48
Hamilton, Anthony 232
Hamann, Johann Georg 138, 149,
   162n, 267, 368, 666, 771–3,
   794
   Aesthetica in Nuce 771
   Kreuzzüge des Philologen (*Crusades*
   of the Philologist) 138
Hammond, Henry 777
Hammond, James 117
   Love Elegies 117
Handel, George Frederick 719, 722,
   725–6
Hanmer, Sir Thomas 577
Happel, Eberhard Werner 265
Hardouin, Jean 439, 754
   Chronologiae ex Numis Antiquis
   Restitutio 754

Harleian Manuscripts, Catalogue of
474
Harpocration (*see* Gronovius) 746n
Harrington, James 284, 290
Oceana 284
Harris, James 9, 19, 22–7, 366–7,
369, 373–5, 378–9, 695, 730
*Philological Inquiries in Three
Parts* 19, 22, 366, 375, 378–9
Three Treatises 695
Harrison, Elizabeth 440
*Letter to Mr John Gay, on His
Tragedy Call'd 'The Captives'*
440
Hartley, David 131, 625–6, 632,
791, 793
Observations on Man 625–6,
791
Harvey, William 47
Hau Kiou choaan (Pleasing History)
(*see also* Percy, Thomas) 65
Hawkesworth, John 250–1, 255
Adventurer No. 4 255
No. 16 250–1
Hays, Mary 441
Haywood, Eliza 241, 246, 250–1,
253, 438, 440, 451
Anti-Pamela 275
Female Spectator 251, 253, 440,
451
Tea-Table 250
Hazlitt, William 480
'On Poetry in General' 480
Hebrew (*see also* Bible, Lowth) 69,
108, 115, 119, 124, 137–8,
368, 375, 415, 463, 465, 467,
468n, 579, 758–77, 792
Hédelin (*see* Aubignac)
Hederich, Benjamin 744
Heemskerk, Johan van 272
Hegel, Georg Wilhelm Friedrich 46,
403, 408–11, 414
Aesthetics 408–10
*Lectures on the Philosophy of
Religion* 408–10
Phenomenology of Spirit 409–10
Philosophy of Right 411, 414

Heidegger, Gotthard 265–6, 541
*Mythoscopia Romantica, oder
Discours von den so benannten
Romans* 265, 541
Heinse, Wilhelm 795
Heinsius, Daniel 83
Iosephi Scaligeri Epistulae (ed.)
749
Heliodorus 271
Aethiopica 271
Helvétius, Claude Adrien 146–7
Hemingway, Ernest 450
Hemsterhuys, Tiberius (with
Lederlin) 746n, 753n
Pollux (ed.) 746n
Henry, Matthew 761
Henry, Patrick 361
Herbert, George 764
The Temple 764
Herd, David 476
Ancient and Modern Scots Songs
476
Herder, Johann Gottfried von 25–6,
30–1, 57, 63, 68–9, 119, 122,
124–6, 128, 132, 138–9, 149,
157n, 161–3, 205–7, 271,
298–9, 301, 304, 311–12, 332,
337–9, 344, 346–7, 368,
415–16, 461, 467, 528–30, 534,
543, 576–7, 582, 624, 662,
666–8, 677–8, 751, 756,
772–6, 778, 789, 793–5
*Abhandlung über den Ursprung
der Sprache* 138, 161, 338–9,
344n, 346, 468–9, 793
Adrastea 63
*Fragmente über die neuere
deutsche Literatur* 528
*Haben wir noch jetzt das
Publikum und Vaterland der
Alten?* 304
Humanitätsbriefe 311
*Ideen zur Philosophie der
Geschichte* 68–9
Kalligone 668
Kritische Wälder (Critical Groves)
667, 793

'On the Similarity between Middle English and German Poetry' 789
Plastik (On Plastic Art) 667
'Shakespeare' 789
Spirit of Hebrew Poetry (see Vom Geist der Ebräischen Poesie)
Terpsichore II 161
'Von der Natur und Wirkung der lyrischen Dichtkunst' 161
Über den Ursprung der Sprache (see Abhandlung ... above)
Über die neuere deutsche Literatur (see Fragmente above)
Über Thomas Abbts Schriften 311
Vom Erkennen und Empfinden der menschlichen Seele 149
Vom Geist der Ebräischen Poesie 138, 415, 772–3
Von deutscher Art und Kunst 125
Hermes, Johann Timotheus 268–9
Sophiens Reise von Memel nach Sachsen 268
Herodotus 549, 581
Hesychius (*see also* Alberti, Ruhnken, Toup) 746n
Heyne, Christian Gottlob 65, 746n, 752–3, 756, 774
De genio saeculi Ptolemaeorum 746n
Virgil (ed.) 756n
Hickes, George 479
hieroglyphics 134–5, 465, 468, 497, 693, 709
Hill, Aaron 789
Athelstan 789
histoire galante 215–16
historicism 34, 59, 62, 67n, 68–9, 200, 202, 206
historiography 282–301
Hobbes, Thomas 9, 23, 68, 88, 155, 175, 177, 456, 458–9, 603n, 614–16, 619, 625, 631–2, 641, 686–9, 709, 770, 778–80
Answer to Davenant 9, 23, 614
Leviathan 68, 155, 614–15, 688, 779

Hogarth, William 412–13, 547, 627, 665
Analysis of Beauty 665
The Bathos 413
Holbach, Paul Henri Thiry, Baron d' 600
Hollandsche Pamela 277n
Hölty, Ludwig Christoph Heinrich 325
Homer 8, 14–15, 34–5, 37, 44, 49, 52–9, 62, 64–5, 67, 69, 76, 84, 87, 90–1, 93, 96, 98–101, 104, 108, 110, 113, 115–16, 123, 137–8, 141, 143, 150, 153, 212, 232, 234, 273, 298, 345, 349, 356, 359–60, 366–7, 371–2, 398, 440, 462–3, 465, 467, 480, 490–1, 495, 497, 512, 514, 549, 555, 558, 565, 568, 576, 580–1, 619, 647–50, 694–6, 702, 716, 738–9, 744, 746, 752–6, 765, 772, 774, 776, 793
Iliad 53–4, 57–9, 62, 64n, 93, 101, 113, 371–2, 467, 647, 649–50, 694–6, 702, 756n
Odyssey 93, 467, 495, 772
Hooke, Robert
Philosophical Collections 319
Hoole, John 389n
'Biographical Preface' to works of John Scott of Amwell 389n
Horace/Horatian 13, 19–20, 75–9, 82–3, 85–9, 95–6, 103, 105, 108, 110, 127, 172, 250, 359, 370, 382, 387, 490, 498, 522, 530, 533, 540, 549, 570, 595, 645–6, 681–2, 685, 708, 736, 743, 755n, 756n, 786
Ars Poetica 78, 85–6, 103, 387, 522, 681–2
'ut pictura poesis' 110, 530, 533, 681–2, 685, 786
Horen 331
Hotman, François 284
Franco-gallia 284

Houdart de La Motte, Antoine
   53–5, 58–9, 63, 462, 786
   Discours sur Homère 54
   Discours sur la Fable 786
   Réflexions sur la critique 55
Houdetot, Madame d' 509
Houstoun, William 313
   *Dr Houstoun's Memoirs of His
   Own Life-Time* 313
Howard, Sir Robert 458
   Indian Queen (with John Dryden)
   458
Hudson, John 756n
Huet, Pierre-Daniel 34, 66, 210–13,
   219, 221–4, 226, 228, 230,
   235–6, 250, 264–6, 272–4,
   313, 396, 473
   Huetiana 34n
   *Lettre-traité sur l'origine des
   romans* 66, 211, 228, 250,
   264–5, 272, 473
   Mémoires 313
Hughes, John 181–2, 298, 367
   Guardian No. 37 181
   Short View of Tragedy 181n
Hugo, Victor 510
humanism/humanists 33, 35, 39n,
   50–2, 58, 296, 349, 389, 546,
   551, 742, 744, 787
Humboldt, Wilhelm von 347, 657,
   676–7, 752, 795
   Essais esthétiques 676–7
   *Über die Verschiedenheit des
   menschlichen Sprachbaues*
   795
   *Über Goethes Hermann und
   Dorothea* 676–7
Hume, David 5, 14, 21–2, 69n, 123,
   131, 152, 156–8, 182, 282–3,
   291–5, 315, 319, 328, 361,
   367–9, 371, 382–3, 386, 390,
   400, 406–8, 424, 426–8, 430,
   459, 546, 550–3, 556, 578,
   587–9, 591–7, 599–605,
   607–10, 612–13, 637–9, 663,
   666, 686, 689–92, 726, 778,
   786, 788, 790

*Dialogues concerning Natural
   Religion* 587
*Enquiry concerning the Principles
   of Morals* 428
*Enquiry into the Human
   Understanding* 690–2
History of England 292–3
'My Own Life' 587
'Of the Delicacy of Taste and
   Passion' 428
'Of Eloquence' 69n, 361, 400, 406
'Of the Original Contract' 400
'Of the Standard of Taste' 5, 400,
   426, 551, 596, 599, 637, 788,
   790
Treatise of Human Nature 152,
   156, 428, 591–7, 600–2,
   604, 613, 788
Hume, Patrick (*see* Milton) 762, 766
Hurd, Richard 22n, 41n, 66, 69,
   120–1, 137, 146, 206, 239–40,
   368, 378, 386–7, 470, 473,
   475, 478, 482, 486, 774, 789
'Dissertation on the Idea of
   Universal Poetry' 22n, 239
Letters on Chivalry and Romance
   69n, 120, 470, 475, 478, 486,
   774, 789
Hurdis, James 146
*Lectures Shewing the Several
   Sources … Poetry* 146
Hutcheson, Francis 20–1, 41n, 152,
   424, 546, 587–8, 635, 678, 785
*Inquiry into the Origin of our
   Ideas of Beauty and Virtue* 41n,
   546, 785
System of Moral Philosophy 424
Hutton, James 791
Huyghens, Christiaan 36

illusionism 209
imagination 41–2, 45, 91, 99, 101,
   108–9, 116, 127, 132, 136,
   144, 148, 154–5, 157–8,
   160–6, 168, 210, 232–7,
   247–8, 267, 296–300, 370,
   387, 389, 391–2, 404, 407,

414, 426–7, 430, 433, 466, 474, 478, 486, 488–9, 492, 495, 502–5, 509–13, 515, 519, 524, 530–2, 535, 537–8, 541, 547, 550, 552, 556, 558, 564, 590, 592–3, 595–6, 599, 602–6, 610–16, 618–21, 624–5, 629–32, 637–8, 640, 647–8, 650, 652–3, 660, 664, 670–2, 676–7, 679, 681, 685, 687–9, 691–2, 696–9, 707–8, 711–12, 715–17, 731, 737, 739–40, 766, 770, 781, 789, 794–6
Inchbald, Elizabeth 244, 438, 442–3, 449, 452, 455
  British Theatre (introductory essays) 442, 443n, 452n
  Preface to Cowley's Belle's Stratagem 452n
  Preface to Vanbrugh's Provok'd Wife 449
Inquiry (periodical) 247
inventio 738
Ion of Chios 743
Isocrates 356

Jacob, Giles 11
Jacobi, Friedrich Heinrich 162n
  Über die Lehre des Spinoza 162n
Jacobs, Friedrich Christian Wilhelm 746n
  Theocritus (ed.) 746n
Jago, Richard 131
James II (Stuart), King of England 401
Jani, Christian David 756n
  Horace (ed., commentaries) 756n
Jansenists/Jansenism 282, 285, 781
Jaquin, Armand-Pierre, Abbé 220–1, 231
  Entretiens sur les romans 220
Jaucourt, Louis, Chevalier de (see also Encyclopédie) 8, 46, 490n, 511, 513, 736
  'Imitation' 8
  'Littérature' 46, 490n
  'Peinture' 736

'Peinture Moderne' 736
  'Roman' 513
  'Stratford' 513
Javary, Auguste 32n
  De l'idée du progrès 32n
Jefferson, Thomas 248, 547
  Declaration of Independence 547n
  letter to Nathaniel Burwell, March 1818 248
Jeffrey, Francis 27
je ne sais quoi 77, 83, 114, 116, 635
Jenyns, Soame 9, 331
  Inquiry into the Nature and Origins of Evil 331
Jesus of Nazareth 392, 656
Jesuits (see also Mémoires de Trévoux) 218, 220, 350
Johnson, Samuel, Dr 4–9, 11–12, 16–17, 22, 24–5, 28, 41, 43, 117–18, 129–30, 132–3, 140–3, 145, 153n, 206, 248, 252–3, 258, 303, 305, 307, 309–12, 314–15, 319–20, 322–4, 326, 328, 331, 336, 344–5, 360, 367–8, 371–4, 376–7, 379–81, 383–8, 412, 434–5, 438–9, 442, 446, 455, 464, 472, 479, 481, 547, 551, 555–6, 558, 567, 575, 578, 590, 594–5, 599–601, 604–6, 693, 787
  Adventurer No. 99 384
  Dictionary of the English Language 4, 7–8, 129, 142, 336, 554–5, 599, 601, 604–5
    'Preface' 601
  Idler No. 34 388, 693
    No. 84 303, 314–15
  Journey to the Western Isles of Scotland 345n, 558
  Lectures on Rhetoric and Poetry 248
  Literary Magazine (ed.) 325
  Lives of the English Poets 43, 129, 141–2, 310, 373–4, 377, 379, 383–5, 412, 567
    'Addison' 472
    'Cowley' 412

'Gray' 464
'Milton' 7
'Savage' 303
'London' 133
'Preface to Shakespeare' 28n, 41n, 206, 360, 377, 385–6, 439, 578, 590, 605
Rambler 9n, 17, 117, 141, 248, 252–3, 303, 305, 307, 310, 312, 320, 323, 371, 379, 547, 600, 604
No. 4 248, 252–3, 323, 438
No. 60 303, 305, 307, 310
No. 86 371, 379
No. 88 371
No. 90 371
No. 92 547
No. 93 17
No. 121 141n
No. 125 604
No. 154 9n
No. 156 323
No. 158 117
Rasselas 16, 385, 606
Vanity of Human Wishes 117, 385
Jones, Inigo 289
Jones, Rowland
Hieroglyfic: or a Grammatical Introduction to an Universal Hieroglyfic Language 342
Jones, Sir William 118–19, 122
Essay on the Arts Commonly Called Imitative 122
Jones, William (of Nayland)
Course of Lectures on the Figurative Language of the Holy Scriptures 764
Jonge, Jan Brune de 272
Jonson, Ben 12, 24–5, 85, 173–4, 176, 179, 317, 360, 370, 441, 445
Epicene 176
News from the New World 317
Timber; or, Discoveries 24
Journal des sçavans 653n, 694n
Journal encyclopédique 325, 328
Journal étranger 325, 329
Journal littéraire 218

Julius Caesar 295
Juvenal 76, 87–9, 106, 549, 756n
Juvigny, Rigoley de 61, 62n
Décadence 62n

Kames, Henry Home, Lord 13, 19, 21, 24, 123–4, 130, 133, 146, 158, 205–6, 269, 339, 343, 362, 367–9, 376, 379–80, 386, 430–1, 547, 552, 555–7, 685–7, 692, 697–8, 785
Elements of Criticism 13, 19, 21, 124, 130, 158, 205, 339, 343–4, 362, 368–9, 376–7, 379–80, 386, 430, 555–7, 685–7, 697–8, 785
Kant, Immanuel 3–4, 22, 126, 142, 150–1, 160–4, 208–9, 391, 406–8, 411, 413, 524, 526, 530n, 538, 544–5, 553, 587, 598, 605–11, 624, 662, 665, 668–73, 675–6, 678–80, 743, 751, 778, 794, 796
Anthropologie in pragmatischer Hinsicht 150
Beobachtungen über das Gefühl des Schönen und Erhabenen (*Observations on the Sense of the Beautiful and the Sublime*) 671
Critique of Judgement 22, 142, 150, 162, 406–7, 413, 605, 609, 668–70, 672–3, 794
'Analytic of the Sublime' 150, 406
'Critique of Aesthetic Judgement' 611
Critique of Practical Reason 607, 668
Critique of Pure Reason 3, 391, 524, 587, 607–10, 668, 751
'Architectonic of Pure Reason' 751
'Preface' 524
'Transcendental Dialectic' 391
'Transcendental Doctrine of Method' 608

Failure of all Philosophical Attempts towards a Theodicy 407
Was ist Aufklärung? (What is Enlightenment?) 524, 743
Keach, Benjamin
  Tropologia 764
Kean, Edmund 178
Keats, John 301, 446
  Ode on a Grecian Urn 301
Kennicott, Benjamin 777
Kenrick, William 27n, 421n
  Eloisa (trans. of Rousseau, *Nouvelle Héloïse*) 421n
Kent, William 289, 705, 707
Kepler, Johannes 779
Killigrew, Thomas 174
Klopstock, Friedrich Gottlieb 325, 330
Klotz, Christian Adolf 68n
Knight, Richard Payne 256, 413, 704, 706, 710–12, 715–17
  Analytical Inquiry into the Principles of Taste 256, 413n, 704, 715–18
  The Landscape 710–11, 716
Knox, Vicesimus 248, 308–9
  Essays Moral and Literary 248
  Winter Evenings 308–9
Körner, Christian Gottfried 126, 536, 674
Küster, Ludolf
  Suda 746n

La Beaumelle, Laurent Angliviel de
  Mes Pensées (quoted in Goldsmith) 17
La Bretonne, Rétif de 225
La Bruyère, Jean de 35, 95–6, 493, 509, 720
  Caractères 95–6, 493
La Calprenède, Gautier de Coste de 210
Lachmann, Karl 748–9
Laclos, Choderlos de
  Liaisons dangereuses 219, 438, 443, 450

Lady's Magazine 247
Lady's Museum 441
Lafayette, Marie-Madeleine de 210–11, 213, 217, 221–2, 226, 450, 493
  Princesse de Clèves 210, 213–16, 221–2, 226, 450, 493
  Zaïde 211, 493
Lafitau, Joseph-François 460, 467
  Moeurs des sauvages américains 460
La Fontaine, Jean de 35, 70, 93, 95, 113, 493, 509, 514
  'The Crow and the Fox' 509
  Epître à Huet 95
La Harpe, Jean-François de 517–19
Lahontan, Louis d'Arce, Baron de 459n
  New Voyages to North America 459n
Lamarck, Jean Baptiste de Monet, Chevalier de 793
La Mesnardière, Hippolyte Jules Pilet de 290
La Motte (*see* Houdart de La Motte)
Lamy, Bernard 350, 352–5, 359
  La Rhétorique, ou l'art de parler 352–5
Landois, Paul 197
  Sylvie 197
Langhorne, John 481, 483
Langland, William 441, 471, 476
  Piers Plowman 476
language 3–5, 7–8, 129, 134–5, 137–8, 142, 148, 157, 335–48, 351, 367, 463–9, 496–8, 502, 504, 555, 599, 601, 604–5, 693n, 695, 709, 764, 780–1, 793
La Roche, Marie Sophie von 278, 441, 444, 453
  Geschichte des Fräuleins von Sternheim 278
  Kalathiskos 441
  Pomona für Teutschlands Töchter 441

La Rochefoucauld, François, duc de
   Maximes 493
La Solle, Henri François de 225
Lavoisier, Antoine Laurent 791
Law, William 468
Lawrence, D. H. 450
Lawrence, Herbert 238
   The Contemplative Man 238
Lawson, John 358n
   Lectures Concerning Oratory
   358n
Le Brun, Charles 730, 733
Le Clerc, Jean 3, 35n, 45n, 52, 285,
   396, 399
   Ars Critica 3n
   Parrhasiana, ou pensées diverses
   35n, 45n, 52n
   Twelve Dissertations 399n
Lederlin, Johann Heinrich (with
   Hemsterhuys) Pollux (ed.) 746n
Lee, Nathaniel 177
Lefèvre, Taneguy 45, 53
   De Futilitate poetices 45
Leibniz, Gottfried Wilhelm von 128,
   136, 159, 266, 297–9, 424,
   465–6, 658–60, 792, 795
   New Essays on Human
   Understanding 465n
   Theodicy 792
Leigh, Edward
   Critica Sacra 761
Le Moyne, Pierre 282
Lenglet-Du Fresnoy, Nicolas
   219–22
   De l'usage des romans 219
   Histoire justifiée contre les romans
   220
Lennox, Charlotte 206, 247–8, 252,
   274, 276, 323, 435n, 439, 441,
   452
   Lady's Museum (contrib.) 441
   Female Quixote 247–8, 252, 323
   Life of Harriot Stewart (Dutch
   translation by Verwer, *Het*
   Leven van Henriette Stuart)
   274
   Shakespear Illustrated 439

Lenz, Jakob Michael Reinhold 199,
   205, 533, 543
   Anmerkungen übers Theater
   (*Remarks on the Theatre*) 205
Leonardo da Vinci 778
Lesage, Alain René 219
Lespinasse, Julie de 444
Lessing, Gotthold Ephraim 30, 133,
   159, 185, 188, 194–6, 201–3,
   205–6, 208, 267–8, 305, 326,
   330–2, 340, 368, 416, 424,
   522–3, 527–9, 531–3, 535,
   538, 542–3, 624, 662, 664–6,
   668, 677–8, 681–2, 686, 693–6,
   699, 730, 738–40, 756, 786
   'Bemerkungen über Burkes
   philosophische Untersuchungen
   "Über den Ursprung unserer
   Begriffe vom Erhabenen und
   Schönen"' 664n
   Berlinische privilegierte Zeitung 326
   Beyträge zur Historie und
   Aufnahme des Theaters 195
   Briefe, die neueste Literatur
   betreffend (with Nicolai and
   Mendelssohn) 30, 331, 527–8
   Briefwechsel über das Trauerspiel
   (with Nicolai and Mendelssohn)
   201–3, 424n
   Emilia Galotti 196, 203
   Hamburgische Dramaturgie 30,
   202–3, 205, 424n
   Laokoon 133, 159, 340, 416, 527,
   532, 535, 538, 664–5, 681,
   686, 694–6, 730, 739, 756, 786
   Literaturbriefe 205, 533
   Miss Sara Sampson 201, 424
   Theatralische Bibliothek (ed.) 195
   Über die Quellen und die
   Verbindungen der schönen
   Künste und Wissenschaften 665
L'Estrange, Sir Roger
   Fables 319
Le Tourneur, Pierre 517, 519
   'Preliminary Discourse' to trans.
   Night Thoughts by Edward
   Young 519

Lewis, Matthew 485–6, 488
  Castle Spectre 486
  The Monk 485, 488
Lichtenberg, Georg Christoph 330
Lillo, George 185, 187, 190, 200–1
  London Merchant 185, 187, 190,
    201
Limborch, Philipp van 285
Lipsius, Justus 52
*Literary Magazine, or Universal
  Review* 8, 325, 331
Livy (Titus Livius) 76, 288–9, 360,
  567
Locke, John 29n, 60, 63, 102, 105,
  128–37, 141, 157–8, 285, 298,
  323, 335–9, 341–4, 347–8, 350,
  367, 370, 377, 382–5, 387–8,
  391–2, 459, 466, 468, 546–7,
  588–90, 592, 595, 597,
  599–600, 602–4, 607, 609–10,
  612–13, 616–20, 625, 629,
  647–8, 650–2, 666, 686–9,
  691, 709, 715–16, 746, 760–1,
  770, 777–8, 783–6, 788–9,
  791, 795
  *Essay concerning Human
    Understanding* 129, 135, 158,
    335, 341, 347, 382, 589–90,
    597–8, 600, 603–4, 609,
    616–18, 647–8, 650n, 687–8,
    709, 778, 786
  *Paraphrase and Notes on the
    Epistles of St Paul* 761
  *Third Essay concerning Human
    Understanding* 350
  Two Treatises of Government 29n
London Magazine 324–6
Longinus (*see also* Boileau) 56, 88,
  97, 100, 114, 116, 143, 351,
  355–6, 365, 377, 394–402,
  408, 411–12, 415–16, 426, 464,
  482, 646, 648, 685–6, 756,
  765, 769, 789–90
  On the Sublime (*Peri Hypsous*)
    82, 355, 394, 401, 686, 756,
    765
Lorrain (*see* Claude)

Louis XIV 34, 36–7, 93, 287,
  289–90, 492, 494, 565, 582
Louis XVI 405
Lowth, Robert 118–19, 124,
  137–40, 298, 375, 415–16,
  463, 467, 575, 579–80, 759,
  766–71, 773–7, 790
  *Praelectiones de sacra poesi
    Hebraeorum* (*Lectures on the
    Sacred Poetry of the Hebrews*)
    (trans. G. Gregory) 119, 124,
    137–8, 368, 375, 415, 463,
    468n, 579, 766–70, 792
  Isaiah (trans., 'Preliminary
    Discourse') 767, 770–1
  *Letter to the Right Reverend
    Author of the Divine Legation*
    468n
Lublink, Johannes 280
Lucian 359, 549, 569, 645, 754
Lucretius 153, 512
Lully, Jean-Baptiste 719–20, 727, 735
Luther, Martin 760
Luzac, Elie 275
  Nederlandsche Spectator 275
Luzán, Ignacio de 114
  La Poética, o reglas de la poésia 114
Lydgate, John 471, 474, 479
Lyndsay, David 479

Mabillon, Jean 571, 575
  De Re Diplomatica 571
Mably, Gabriel Bonnot de 51
  *Observations sur l'histoire de la
    Grèce* 51n
Macaulay, Catherine 444
Macaulay, Thomas Babington 32
  'Atterbury' 32n
Machiavelli, Nicolo 283, 284n, 360,
  567
Mackenzie, Henry 208, 248, 257,
  420, 425, 486, 554
  'Account of the German Theatre'
    486
  Lounger No. 20 258
  Man of Feeling 425
  Mirror (articles) 208

Macpherson, James 67n, 123–4,
     138, 140, 292, 344–5, 359,
     362, 367, 376, 412n, 463–4,
     470, 479–81, 486, 555, 557,
     774, 787–8, 793–4
  Fingal 123, 344n, 376, 464
  preface to Fingal: 'Dissertation
     concerning the Antiquity, &c.
     of the Poems of Ossian the
     Son of Fingal' 344n
  Fragments of Ancient Poetry,
     Collected in the Highlands of
     Scotland 67n, 123
  History of Great Britain 292
  Poems of Ossian 344–5, 359,
     362, 376, 463, 467, 479, 486,
     555, 774, 787–8, 793–4
Madan, Judith 440
  'Progress of Poetry' 440
Madan, Martin 764
Maffei, Francesco Scipione
  Ars Critica Lapidaria 745
  Museum Veronense 745
Maintenon, Françoise d'Aubigné,
     Marquise de 453
Makin, Bathsua 436
  Essay to Revive the Antient
     Education 436
Malebranche, Nicolas de 624
Malesherbes, Chrétien Guillaume de
     Lamoignon de 223
Malherbe, François de 80, 95, 373,
     412n, 564
Mallet, David
  Life of Francis Bacon, Lord
     Chancellor of England 310
Mallet, Edme, Abbé
  'Critique, s.m.' in Encyclopédie
     521n
Mallet, Paul-Henri 473
Malone, Edmond 477, 479–80,
     488
  Cursory Observations on the
     Poems Attributed to Thomas
     Rowley 480
Malory, Sir Thomas
  Morte d'Arthur 477

Malpeines, Marc-Antoine Léonard
     des 346n
Mandeville, Bernard 23, 46n, 293,
     340
Manilius, Marcus
  Astronomicon 754n
Manley, Delarivier 241, 254
  Secret History of Queen Zarah
     254
Manuzio (Paulus Manutius) 394
Marie-Antoinette 300, 405
Marinism 83
Marino, Giambattista 109, 114
Mariotte, Edme 791
Marivaux, Pierre Carlet de
     Chamblain de 194, 219, 222–3,
     321, 374–5, 448
  Specateur Français 321
Marlowe, Christopher 360
Marmontel, Jean François 4, 203,
     220, 225–7, 232–3, 277–8, 375,
     490, 510–15, 521
  Contes moraux 226, 513
  'Critique, s.f.' (see Encyclopédie)
     4, 511
  Éléments de littérature 513–15
  'Essai sur le goût' 513
  Essai sur les romans, considérés
     du côté moral 220, 225–7,
     513n
  Mercure de France (ed.) 226
Marot, Clément 113
Marshall, William 712
Martial 102, 461
Martyn, Thomas 304
  Dissertations upon the Aeneids of
     Virgil 304
marvellous 35, 720, 734
Mascov, Johann Jakob 297
Mason, William 117, 307, 310,
     474
  Memoirs of the Life and Writings
     of Mr Gray 307, 310
masora 776–7
Massinger, Philip, and Nathaniel
     Field 195
  Fatal Dowry 195

materialism 152, 157, 232, 423, 589, 594, 612
Mathias, Thomas James 485
Pursuits of Literature 485
Mattheson, Johann 729
Matthisson, Friedrich von 538
Maturin, Charles Robert 488
Bertram 488
Melmoth the Wanderer 488
Maty, Matthieu 325n
Maupertuis, Pierre Louis Moreau de
Réflexions philosophiques sur l'origine des langues 338, 339n
Maurras, Charles 71n
Maximinus, Valerius 582
Mayans y Siscar, Gregorio 357
medieval/medievalism 65–7, 463, 470–88
Meersch, A. A. van de 277
Meier, Georg Friedrich 193, 658, 661–3, 679–80
Anfangsgründe aller schönen Künste 658, 661
Beurtheilung der Gottschedischen Dichtkunst 193
Gedancken von Schertzen 679n, 680n
Meijer, Lodewijk 272
Meinecke, Friedrich 298, 300
Meister, Jacques-Henri 516–17
Correspondance littéraire 331, 498n, 516–17
Meister, Leonhard 160
Versuch über die Einbildungskraft 160
Melanchthon, Philipp 352n
Elementorum Rhetorices Libri Duo 352n
Mémoires de Trévoux (*Mémoires pour l'histoire des sciences et des beaux-arts*) 218, 220
Mémoires d'un protestant (*see* Goldsmith, trans.) 330
Ménage, Gilles 210
Mendelssohn, Moses 30, 201–3, 267, 368, 527–8, 665, 676, 693, 739–40

Briefe, die neueste Litteratur betreffend (*see also* Lessing, Nicolai) 30, 267
Briefwechsel über das Trauerspiel (with Lessing and Nicolai) 201–3, 424n
Morgenstunden oder Vorlesungen über das Dasein Gottes 665
Philosophische Schriften 665
'On the Main Principles of the Fine Arts and Sciences' 665
'Rhapsody, or Additions to the Letters on Sensibility' 665
Menzini, Benedetto
Poetica 83
Merck, Johann Heinrich (*see also Teutsche Merkur*) 270
Mercier, Louis-Sébastien 124, 204–5, 208, 225
Du Théâtre, ou nouvel essai sur l'art dramatique 124, 204
Mercure de France (*see also* Marmontel [ed.]) 226, 518
Mercure galant 218, 318, 324
Mereau, Sophie
Kalathiskos 441
Pomona für Teutschlands Töchter 441
Mersenne, Marin 723–5
Harmonie Universelle, De l'Art de Bien Chanter 724
merveilleux (*see* marvellous)
Metastasio (Pietro Trapassi) 719
Michaelis, Johann David 771, 774–5
Einleitung in das Neue Testament 771
Michelangelo Buonarotti 387
Microcosm (*see* Canning) 255
Middle Ages 33, 47n, 210, 464, 470–88, 514
Middleton, Conyers 304, 310
Life of Cicero 304
Mill, John 748
Mill, John Stuart 48
Millar, John 293
Miller, Henry 450
Milles, Jeremiah 480

Milton, John 22, 25, 35n, 52, 76,
  84–6, 91–2, 98–100, 103, 106,
  113, 115–16, 123, 126, 133,
  143–4, 149, 159, 181, 234,
  294, 306, 317, 320, 360, 366,
  370–1, 375, 379, 389, 398–9,
  404–5, 447, 490, 512, 532,
  583, 618, 627, 638–9, 646–50,
  652–3, 726–7, 762–4, 766, 776
Il Penseroso 726
L'Allegro 726
Lycidas 133
Paradise Lost 22, 24, 76, 86,
  98–100, 113, 126, 143, 159,
  320, 370–1, 398, 618, 627,
  638, 646–50, 727, 762–4, 766
  ed. Patrick Hume 762
  ed. Thomas Newton 762–3
Paradise Regained 98
*Milton Restor'd, and Bentley
  Deposed* 763
mimesis 118, 122, 188, 232, 386,
  391, 395, 397, 399, 411, 530,
  532–8, 684, 687, 689, 714–15,
  731, 733, 735, 739–41, 767,
  773
Minnesang 794
mock-epic 240
modernism 215–16, 263, 394, 397,
  399
Moderns (*see also* Ancients, *querelle*)
  35, 89–90, 92–9, 177, 250,
  269, 350, 365, 394, 400, 437,
  455, 462, 540, 546, 550, 555,
  568–9, 581–2, 623, 638, 741,
  747, 754, 756, 782, 786, 790
Moeris (*see* Pierson) 746n
Moir, Rev. John 145–6
  'Genius of Poetry' 145
  'Originality' 145
Molière (Jean-Baptiste Poquelin) (*see
  also* Centlivre and Chambre,
  Cureau de la) 35, 113, 172–3,
  179, 188–9, 200–1, 322, 441,
  491, 506–7, 516, 781
Bourgeois gentilhomme 189, 201
Le Médecin malgré lui 441

Misanthrope 189, 200, 507
Précieuses Ridicules 781
Tartuffe 173
Monboddo, James Burnett, Lord
  137, 239, 344, 367, 468, 469n
*Of the Origin and Progress of
  Language* 239, 469n
Monro, Alexander
Structure and Physiology of Fishes
  793
Monroe, Thomas 249, 258
Olla Podrida 249, 258
Montaigne, Michel de 37n, 289,
  624
Montagu, Elizabeth 434, 438–40,
  444, 446, 449, 452–3, 455
*Writings and Genius of
  Shakespeare* 434, 439, 446
  'Three Dialogues of the Dead'
  440
Montagu, Mary Wortley 435
Montesquieu, Charles Louis de
  Secondat, Baron de La Brede et
  de 57–8, 221, 286, 288–91,
  294, 296, 325, 330, 525, 552,
  556, 624, 787–8
*Considérations sur les Causes de
  la Grandeur des Romains et de
  leur Décadence* 288–9, 291
Esprit des Lois 289–90, 556, 787
  'Invocation to the Muses' 290
Essai sur le Goût 788
  'Des Plaisirs de la Variété'
  788n
Lettres persanes 288
Mémoires sur les Mines 290
  'Mes pensées' 58n
Montfaucon, Bernard de 3, 571–2,
  575, 744–5
*L'Antiquité expliquée et
  représentée en figures* 571n,
  572, 744
  Preface 571n, 572
*Bibliotheca Bibliothecarum
  Manuscriptorum Nova* 745
Bibliotheca Coisliniana 745
Palaeographia Graeca 3, 745

Monthly Magazine 139, 485
  'Terrorist System of Novel-Writing'
    485
Monthly Mirror
  'On the Absurdities of the
    Modern Stage' 486
*Monthly Papers for Profit and
  Entertainment* 321
Monthly Review 27n, 244, 246–7,
    249, 255, 307, 311, 318,
    327–31, 422n, 434, 441, 475,
    481, 486
  No. 6 244
  No. 27 475
  No. 32 481
  No. 42 259
  No. 48 247
  No. 81 475
  No. 2 (2nd series) 244
  No. 5 (2nd series) 244, 246
  No. 9 (2nd series) 249
  No. 15 (2nd series) 255–6, 259
Moore, John 66
  'Upon the Original of Romances'
    66
morality play 472
Moral Weeklies 523–4, 527
More, Hannah 420, 427, 435, 442,
    444, 450
  'Preface to the Tragedies' 450
  'Observations on the Effect of
    Theatrical Representations
    with respect to Religion and
    Morals' 442
  Sacred Dramas 420n
  Sensibility. A Poetical Epistle. 420
  *Strictures on the Modern System
    of Female Education* 435
Morgann, Maurice 208
  *Essay on the Dramatic Character
    of Sir John Falstaff* 208
Morhof, Daniel Georg 265
Moritz, Karl Philipp 676
Morney, Daniel 71
Morus, Samuel Friedrich Nathanael
    756n
Möser, Justus 297–8

Moses (*see also* Bible) 397–9, 403,
    410, 465, 573, 764–5, 773, 776
Motteux, Anthony 720–1
  Gentleman's Journal 720–1
Mulgrave, third Earl of (*see
    Sheffield, John)
Muratori, Ludovico Antonio
    109–10, 114, 161, 745
  Della forza della Fantasia Umana
    161
  Della perfetta poesia italiana
    109
  *Novus Thesaurus Veterum
    Inscriptionarum* 745
Muses 436, 441

nationalism 92, 139, 347
naturalism 197, 450, 483, 534,
    537
Necker, Suzanne 444
Nelme, R. D. 342n
  *Essay towards an Investigation of
    Language and Letters* 342n
neo-classicism 34, 63, 71, 75–6,
    82–3, 114, 117–21, 124, 126,
    128, 132, 139, 184–5, 187,
    193, 196, 203, 206–9, 290–1,
    294–5, 322–3, 355–6, 362–6,
    381, 384, 387, 394–5, 397,
    400, 402, 439, 445, 489, 519,
    522, 524–6, 530, 533, 540,
    542–3, 556, 564, 567, 578,
    581, 595, 634, 647–8, 732,
    766, 768, 771, 778–83, 785–8,
    793–4
*Neue Bibliothek der schönen
  Wissenschaften und der freyen
  Künste* 269–70
*Neue Zeitungen von Gelehrten
  Sachen* 319
Neumarck, Georg 83
  Poetics 83
Neumeister, Erdmann 266
  Raisonnement über die Romanen
    (attrib.) 266
New Monthly Magazine 487
  No. 16 487

Newton, Sir Isaac 127, 131, 134,
　　290, 296, 370, 397, 546,
　　588–9, 591, 598, 612–13, 617,
　　620, 625, 784–6, 788–91
　Opticks 296, 617, 790–1
　Principia 589, 617, 784, 791
Newton, John 764
Newton, Thomas 762–3
　(ed.) *Paradise Lost* 762
Nibelungenlied 69
Nicander (*see* eds. Bandini, Bentley)
　746n
Nicolai, Friedrich 30, 201–3, 527–8,
　542n
　*Briefe, die neueste Literatur
　　betreffend* 30, 527–8
　(*see also* Lessing, Mendelssohn)
　Briefwechsel über das Trauerspiel
　　(with Lessing and Mendelssohn)
　　201–3, 424n
Nicole, Pierre (*see* Arnauld)
Niebuhr, Karsten 771
Nieuwland, Petrus 280
　'Over gevoeligheid van hart',
　　Nieuw Algemeen Magazyn
　　280n
*Nieuwe Bydragen tot de Opbouw
　der Vaderlandsche Letterkunde*
　277n
Nocret, F. 730
North, Roger 306–9, 312
nouvelle 210–16, 220–1, 224, 228,
　232, 235, 265, 272
　nouveau roman (*see also* roman)
　216
　nouvelles galantes 221
　petite nouvelle 215
　(*see also* histoire galante)
Novalis (Friedrich von Hardenberg)
　271, 577, 582
Nugent, Thomas 110, 466n

Observer No. 27 258
Oddi, Sforza
　Prigione d'amore 189
Oedipus 541
Oeser, Adam Friedrich 673

Ogilvie, John 152
　*Philosophical and Critical
　　Observations on Composition*
　　152
Oldham, John 85
　*Horace's Art of Poetry, imitated in
　　English* 85
Olla Podrida 249, 258
Omeis, Magnus Daniel 265
Onderzoeker (*see* Dielen) 277
Openhertige Juffrow 272
opera/operatic 719–20, 722
Orient 65, 212
orientalism 108, 122
Orsi, Giovanni Giuseppe, Marchese
　109, 114
　Considerazione 109
Ortega y Gasset, José 240, 261
Orwell, George
　Animal Farm 565
Ossian (*see also* Macpherson, James)
　67–9, 122–5, 138, 149, 292,
　295, 344–5, 359, 362, 367,
　368n, 376, 412n, 463–4, 467,
　469, 479–80, 486, 555, 557,
　774, 787–8, 793–4
Otway, Thomas 177, 185
Ovid 85, 92, 101–2, 115–16, 426,
　471, 509, 623
　Epistles 85
　Heroides, Sappho to Phaon 426
　Metamorphoses 101, 623
Ozell, John 93
　*Characters Historical and
　　Panegyrical* (trans. of Perrault)
　　93

Paciaudi, Paulo Maria 745
　Monumenta Peloponnesiaca 745
Palaephatus (Dutch trans. of)
　Van de Ongelooflijcke Historiën
　271
Palladian/Palladio 289–90, 292,
　294–5, 703, 787–8
Pamela Bespiegeld 275
Paracelsus 48
parallelism 767–8, 773

Parnassus/Parnassian 49, 79, 446,
781
Pascal, Blaise 40, 60n, 493, 779
Lettres provinciales 493
pastoral 76, 94–5, 107, 116,
118–19, 121, 184, 264, 321,
360, 459, 731, 733, 766
Patot, Simon Tyssot de 241
*Travels and Adventures of James
Massey* 241
Patriarchi, Gasparo 228
Patrick, Simon 777
Paul, St 761, 775
Pearce, Zachary 756n, 763
*Review of the Text of Milton's
Paradise Lost* 773
Pearson, John
Critici Sacri 761
Pegge, Samuel 476–7
'Observations on Dr Percy's
Account of Minstrels' 476
Pepys, Samuel 461
Percival, Thomas
Moral and Literary Dissertations
146
Percy, Bishop Thomas 65–7, 122–3,
138, 345, 464, 472–7, 479,
488, 789
Correspondence with Richard
Farmer 474
'Essay on the Ancient Minstrels in
England' 122
Four Essays 476
*Reliques of Ancient English
Poetry* 67, 122–3, 464, 475–7,
789
'On the Ancient English
Minstrels' 476–7
'On the Ancient Metrical
Romances' 476
'On the Metre of Pierce
Plowman's Vision' 476
'On the Origin of the English
Stage' 476, 479
'Specimens of the ancient Poetry
of different nations' 65
Perotti, Niccolò 754

Perrault, Charles 34–40, 45, 49,
54–6, 58, 59n, 64, 68, 93–5,
97–8, 396, 522, 720
Cabinet des Beaux-Arts 39n
Le Génie 93
Les Hommes illustres 93
Mémoires de ma vie 34n
*Parallèle des anciens et des
modernes* 36, 39n, 56, 59n,
93
Siècle de Louis le Grand 34, 37
Perrault, Claude 35
Persius 88–9, 756n
Petherham, John 7
Petrarch (Francesco Petrarca) 50
Phalaris (*see also* Bentley) 47, 50–1,
750, 753–4
Philips, Ambrose 106–7, 321
Codrus: or the Dunciad Dissected
106
Phillips, Edward 84–5
Theatrum Poetarum 84
philology 3–5, 22–3, 138, 366, 375,
378–9, 751
Philopatris (attrib Lucian; *see also*
Gesner) 754
Philosooph, De (*see also* Engelen)
277
philosophes 147, 286, 491, 504,
510, 515, 594, 600, 662
Philosophical Collections 318–19
Photius (*see* edns by Dobree,
Porson) 746n
picaresque 221, 228
picturesque (the) 127, 406, 700–18,
736, 738
Pierson, Joannes
Moeris (ed.) 746n
Piles, Roger de (*see also* Du Fresnoy)
683–4, 686, 692–3
Pindar/Pindaric 65, 85, 108, 115,
118, 137, 143, 375, 774
Pinkerton, John 476–7
Scottish Tragic Ballads 476
Piozzi, Hester Lynch Thrale (*see also*
Thrale) 311
Pisistratus 56n

Pitt, William 361, 401, 403, 406, 408, 411
Platner, Ernst
  Anthropologie für Aerzte und Weltweise 160
Plato/Platonism 76, 98, 155, 298, 344, 356, 359, 367, 381, 384–5, 387–9, 391–2, 401, 465, 498, 567, 622–4, 645, 653, 660n, 715, 732, 746, 752n
  Gorgias 401
  Menon 660n
  Phaedrus 344, 356
  Politikos 660n
  Protagoras 401, 623
Plautus (*see* André Dacier) 53
Pliny 560
Plotinus
  Eneads 660n
Plumb, J. H. 27n
Plutarch 302–3, 305, 377, 440, 509, 645, 686
  Lives 302–3, 305
Politian (Angelo Ambrogini) 748
Pollux, Julius (*see* edns by Bentley, Lederlin, Hemsterhuys) 746n
Polybius 296
Pompadour, Jeanne Antoinette Poisson, Marquise de 225
Pons, François, Abbé de 45n, 54
  Dissertation sur le poème épique 45n
Poole, Matthew 761, 777
Pope, Alexander 4–6, 8–9, 11–15, 18–20, 22, 25, 40–1, 43, 46, 50, 51n, 55, 70, 75–7, 98–9, 103–8, 111, 113, 115–16, 118, 127–8, 143, 182, 235, 244–5, 288–9, 292n, 303, 321, 360, 365–8, 370–2, 376, 379, 382, 386, 395, 397–400, 403, 411–12, 425–6, 455, 471, 474, 481–2, 488, 491, 493, 547, 549, 588, 598–9, 613, 615, 624, 632, 695–7, 702, 704, 707–9, 713–14, 725–6, 742, 755–6, 763, 787–8, 797

Brutus 106
'Discourse on Pastoral Poetry' 107
Dunciad 4, 6, 8, 51n, 105–6, 117, 288n, 397, 547, 742, 763
'Elegy on the Death of an Unfortunate Lady' 426
'Eloisa to Abelard' 426
Epilogue to the Satires 106
Epistle of Abelard 235
Epistle to Dr. Arbuthnot 4, 697
Epistle to Augustus 106, 481–2
Epistle to Bathurst 382
Epistle to Burlington 707
'Epitaph. Intended for Sir Isaac Newton' 397n
Essay on Criticism 5, 9, 12, 14–15, 18, 22, 24, 43, 75–6, 99, 103–6, 108, 116, 128, 371, 395, 399, 471, 725, 787
Essay on Man 397, 493, 588, 624
Guardian (contributions to) 321–2, 707
Iliad (trans. and preface) 107, 371–2, 382, 695–6, 702, 755–6
Imitations of Horace 106
Memoirs of Martinus Scriblerus 6n
Odyssey (trans.) 107–8, 755
Peri Bathous, or, Of the Art of Sinking in Poetry 46n, 373, 397–8
Rape of the Lock 50, 397n
Sapho to Phaon 426
Shakespeare (edn of) 763
Three Hours After Marriage (with John Gay) 412
'Windsor-Forest' 397, 696
Popper, Karl 565
  Poverty of Historicism 565
Porée, Charles
  'On Novels' 220–1
Porson, Richard 744, 746n, 752n
  Photius (ed.; *see also* Dobree) 746n
Porta (Franciscus Portus) 394
Port-Royal Logic (*see* Arnauld)
post-modernism 263, 412
Pound, Ezra 778

Poussin, Nicolas 501, 704–5, 726, 733–4, 738
'Death of Germanicus' 733–4
'Manna in the Wilderness' 733
'Paysage au serpent' 501
'Tancred and Erminia' 738
préciosité 83
pre-romanticism 71, 489, 542
Prévost, Antoine François, Abbé 218–19, 221–2, 227, 232, 381
Cleveland 221
Manon Lescaut 221, 227
Price, Richard 406
Price, Uvedale 127, 700–1, 703–4, 706, 710–12, 716, 717, 796
Essay on the Picturesque, As Compared with the Sublime and the Beautiful 127, 700, 703–4, 710, 712, 716–17
letter to Humphry Repton 710–11
Essays on the Picturesque 700
Priestley, Joseph 131, 146, 413, 791, 793
Course of Lectures on Oratory and Criticism 413n
primitivism 101, 122–3, 136–7, 139–40, 156, 456–69, 480, 555, 631, 772, 794, 796
Prior, Matthew (see Dennis) 12, 127, 549
Prometheus 94, 116, 494, 495n, 534, 623–4, 632, 794
Proust, Marcel 619
Prynne, William 180
Ptolemy 60
Public Characters, or Contemporary Biography 303
Pufendorf, Samuel 284, 459
Purcell, Henry 721–2, 725
King Arthur (with Dryden) 721
puritanism 33, 265
Puttenham, George 24–5
Arte of English Poesie 24
Pütter, Johann Stephan 62n
Pyrrhonism 745
Pythagoras 47, 722–4

querelle des anciens et des modernes 32–40, 42, 47–8, 50, 52–71, 97, 365, 394, 462, 522, 540, 754, 756, 786
querelle du merveilleux 35
Quinault, Philippe 113, 719–20, 728
Quintilian 352, 357, 364, 549, 645–6

Rabelais, François 113, 491, 566, 569
Racine, Jean 34–5, 70, 93, 113, 171, 178, 185, 198, 202, 282, 283n, 287, 294–5, 360, 491–3, 507, 511–12, 514–15, 517–18, 520, 549, 565, 719–20, 722, 736, 781
Bérénice 565
Iphigénie 198, 202
Phèdre 185
Radcliffe, Ann 255–6, 259, 407, 483, 487–8
Mysteries of Udolpho 256, 483–4
raillery 88
Raisonnement über die Romanen 266
Raleigh, Sir Walter 319
Arts of Empire 319
Rambouillet, Catherine de Vivonne, Marquise de 453
Rameau, Jean Philippe 375, 402, 410–11, 504, 786
Ramée, Pierre de la (Petrus Ramus) 350
Ramsay, Allan 464, 557–8
Gentle Shepherd 464
Ranke, Leopold von 571
Raphael Sanzio 387, 780
Rapin, René 3, 24, 75–7, 84, 87, 95–6, 104, 107, 114, 116, 171–2, 177, 317, 337, 352, 360, 470, 562, 781, 787
Dissertatio de Carmine Pastorali 76, 95
Réflexions sur la poétique d'Aristote 3, 24, 76–7, 84, 171–2, 337, 470, 781, 787
Réflexions sur l'usage de l'éloquence 352

Raspe, Rudolf Erich 486
  Hermin und Gunilde 486
  'Über die Ritterzeiten und die
    Barbarey derselben' 486
rationalism 11, 13, 132, 135, 167,
    173, 189, 201, 224, 530, 542,
    602, 606–7, 658–60, 662, 666,
    672–3
Räuberroman 486
realism 169, 173, 190, 199, 202,
    224, 231, 244, 249, 252n,
    257–9, 261–3, 267, 306, 374,
    450–1, 459, 481, 499, 502,
    534, 536–7
Reenberg, Toger
  Ars Poetica 83
Reeve, Clara 66, 239–41, 245,
    249–50, 374, 423, 440, 447–9,
    452, 480, 483–5
  Champion of Virtue 483
  *Memoirs of Sir Roger de
    Clarendon* 483–4
  Old English Baron 239, 483
  Progress of Romance 66, 240–1,
    245, 249–50, 374, 423, 440,
    447, 449, 452n, 480
Reformation 21, 47, 284, 565, 759
Reid, Thomas 19, 344, 552, 554
  *Inquiry into the Human Mind and
    the Principles of Common Sense*
    344n
  Lectures on the Fine Arts 19
Reiske, Johann Jakob 746n
  (ed.) Callimachus, Theocritus
    746n
  Greek Anthology (ed. with
    Brunck) 746n
*Remarks on Mr Avison's Essay on
  Musical Expression* 726
Renaissance 3, 16, 22, 33, 35, 36n,
    45, 49, 51, 70, 83, 161, 183,
    210, 264, 305, 349, 354, 373,
    389, 443, 511, 514, 519, 576,
    599n, 662, 682, 730, 741–2,
    749, 770, 777–9
Repton, Humphry 710–11
  Landscape Gardening 711n

Reresby, Tamworth
  *Miscellany of Ingenious Thoughts
    and Reflections* 689n
Resewitz, Friedrich Gabriel 268
Restoration 5, 15, 24, 174, 176,
    178–81, 185, 189–90, 282,
    312, 337, 457, 459, 467,
    470–1, 722, 758, 766
Revett, Nicholas (with Stuart, James)
  Antiquities of Athens 747
Revolution (French) 127–8, 184,
    402, 415, 453, 461, 484–8,
    515, 518, 524, 534, 679
Revolution (of 1688) 401
Reynolds, Sir Joshua 16, 24, 134,
    294, 351, 384, 387–93,
    412–13, 605–6, 636, 679, 683,
    700, 711, 730, 736
  De Arte Graphica (*The Art of
    Painting*) by Du Fresnoy
    (trans., annot.) 683
  Discourses on Art 16, 24, 134,
    294, 351, 387–90, 392, 413,
    605–6, 679
  Ghost of Abel 391
rhetoric 3, 23, 29, 121, 130, 139,
    248, 250, 293, 342, 349–64,
    374, 378, 386, 412, 464, 467,
    546, 562, 686, 697, 724, 744,
    746n
Riccoboni, Luigi 174, 191
  *Lettre sur la comédie de l'École
    des amis* (*Letter on 'The School
    of Friendship'*) 191
Riccoboni, Marie-Jeanne 438, 441,
    443, 450–2, 455
  Nouveau théâtre anglais (ed.,
    trans.) 441
Richardson, Jonathan, the Elder 337,
    599, 692, 698, 730, 738
  Essay on the Art of Criticism 738
  Essay on the Theory of Painting
    599, 692, 698, 730
Richardson, Samuel 64–5, 143, 192,
    218, 222, 229–33, 235, 239,
    241–3, 246, 248, 253–61, 267,
    269, 273–80, 375, 420–3,

425–6, 440, 442–4, 446,
448–9, 451–2, 482–3, 499,
501, 513, 594, 792
Clarissa 218, 253–8, 260, 274–5,
277–80, 421, 423, 425, 440,
443–4, 451, 482, 594
Correspondence (ed. Barbauld)
442, 446, 448–9, 452
letter to George Cheyne 421
Pamela 192, 218–19, 222, 242–3,
253–4, 256, 273–4, 276–7, 422,
594
(*see also Anti-Pamela,
Hollandsche Pamela, Pamela
Bespiegeld*)
Sir Charles Grandison 218–19,
277–8, 280, 483
Richardson, William
*Philosophical Analysis and
Illustration of some of
Shakespeare's Remarkable
Characters* 208
Richelet, César Pierre
Dictionnaire 7n
Richelieu, Armand du Plessis,
Cardinal 168, 563, 781
Richter, Adam Daniel 193
Riedel, Just
'Letters Concerning the Public'
527
Rigault, Hippolyte 32, 34n
Histoire de la Querelle 32
Rist, Johann
Zeit-Verkürtzung 265n
Ritson, Joseph 123, 474, 477–8
*Ancient English Metrical
Romanceës* 477
*Observations on the History of
English Poetry* 477–8
Ritterroman 486
Rivarol, Antoine de 135, 139,
148–9, 497
*Discours sur l'universalité de la
langue française* 135, 148, 497
Robert, Hubert 501
'Grande Galerie éclairée du fond'
501

Robertson, William 20, 283, 291–3
*View of the Progress of Society in
Europe* 20
Robespierre, Maximilien Isidore de
127, 402–3, 411, 485
Robortello, Francesco 394, 751
Rochester, John Wilmot, Earl of 87,
113
Rolli, Paul 567
*Remarks upon M. Voltaire's Essay
on the Epic Poetry of European
Nations* 567
Rollin, Charles 57, 357
*De la manière d'enseigner et
d'étudier les belles-lettres* 58n,
357
roman (*see also nouvelle*) 210–16,
218–20, 222–9, 231–2, 234–5,
264–70, 272, 276–7
romance 66, 228, 239–41, 245,
248, 250, 253–5, 259, 262–4,
266–8, 272–4, 319, 360, 368,
374, 421, 440, 448, 473,
475–8, 481–2, 484, 621
heroic romance 228, 275
romantic/Romantics 8, 70, 101, 118,
123, 129, 132–3, 154, 157,
163, 166, 208, 235, 237, 295,
300, 362, 364, 371, 378–9,
381, 390, 393, 420, 460, 469,
474, 510, 581, 593, 603–5,
608, 611, 613, 622, 629, 706,
718, 736, 787, 794, 796–7
romanticism 7, 71, 163, 233, 271,
330, 355, 412, 447, 521n, 559,
772, 794
Rosa, Salvator 296, 487, 704–5,
711n
Roscommon, Wentworth Dillon, Earl
of 24, 86, 319, 370
Essay on Translated Verse 24, 86
Horace's Art of Poetry 86
Rousseau, Jean-Jacques 67, 119,
122, 128, 135, 158, 200–1,
204, 223, 227, 229–33, 235,
267, 307, 313–14, 325, 332,
335, 337–8, 340–1, 343–5,

347, 374, 402, 420–1, 425,
432, 444, 449, 454, 459,
467–9, 490, 504–10, 513, 521,
549, 582–3, 613, 641, 706,
728–9, 787–8, 795–6
Confessions 267, 307, 313–14,
505, 509, 582–3, 796
Contrat social 796n
*Dialogue between a Man of
Letters and M. J. J. Rousseau*
421n
Discours sur les sciences et les arts
504
*Discours sur l'origine et les
fondements de l'inégalité parmi
les hommes* 201, 338, 341, 469,
505, 796
Emile 459, 505, 508–9
Essai sur l'origine des langues
343–4
First Discourse 505
Julie, ou La Nouvelle Héloïse 223,
227, 229–30, 235, 267, 421,
425, 449, 454, 508–9, 513, 788
*Lettre à M d'Alembert sur les
spectacles* 200, 420, 505,
506–8, 513
Rêveries du promeneur solitaire
432
Rowe, Nicholas 178, 185, 195, 385,
549
Fair Penitent 195
Royal Academy 351, 389–90
Royal Society 48, 94, 96, 290, 312,
318, 783–4
Philosophical Transactions 312,
318–19, 327, 783–4
Royal Society of Edinburgh 486
Rubens, Peter Paul 291
Ruffhead, Owen
Monthly Review 307
Ruhnken, David 560–1, 746n
Apollonius Rhodius (ed.) 746n
Callimachus (ed.) 746n
Hesychius (ed. with Alberti) 746n
*Historia Critica Oratorum
Graecorum* 560–1

*P. Rutilii Lupi: De Figuris
Sententiarum et Elocutionis Duo
Libri* 561n
Timaeus (ed.) 746n
runes, runic 96, 115
Rushworth, William 758–9
Dialogues of William Richworth
758
Rutilius Lupus 561
Rutlidge, John James 518
Rymer, Thomas 3, 13, 84, 87, 115,
172, 177–8, 180–1, 456, 470,
472–3, 569
Edgar 178
Rapin (trans., preface) 3, 172
Short View of Tragedy 84, 470,
473
Tragedies of the Last Age 13, 84,
177

Sabatier de Castres
Siècles de la littérature 67n
Sade, Donatien-Alphonse-François,
Marquis de 225, 235–7,
487–8
Crimes de l'amour 235
'Idée sur les romans' 235–7,
487–8
Saint-Lambert, Jean François,
Marquis de (*see Encyclopédie*,
'Génie')
Sainte-Beuve, Charles Augustin
135n, 489, 498, 521
Sainte-Palaye, J. B. de la Curne de
473, 475
Mémoires sur l'ancienne chevalerie
475
Saint-Évremond, Charles de
Marguetel de Saint-Denis de
75–6, 78, 170–1, 180n, 284,
720
'Dissertation sur le *Grand
Alexandre*' 170
Letters 720n
'Of Ancient and Modern Tragedy'
170
Saint-Just, Louis de 402–3

Saint-Pierre, Charles Irénée Castel, Abbé de 32
Sallo, Denis de 318
Journal des savants 318
salons (art) 496, 500–1, 507
Sand, George (Aurore Dupin, Baronne Dudevant) 455
Sappho 53, 411–12, 416, 426, 436, 652
satire 76, 80, 87–90, 106, 189–90, 195, 755, 786
Scaliger, Joseph Justus 749, 751
Epistulae, ed. Heinsius 749
letter to Salmasius 749
Scaliger, Julius Caesar 24, 37n, 52, 83, 169, 366, 748
Poetices libri septem 37n
Scarron, Paul 210, 221, 232, 493–4
Roman comique 493–4
Virgile travesti 493–4
Schauerroman 486
Schelling, Friedrich Wilhelm Joseph von 163–4, 613, 794
Schelling, Caroline von (formerly Caroline Schlegel) 444
Schiller, Friedrich 5, 31, 45–6, 63, 70, 123, 125–6, 151, 161, 163–4, 185, 203, 207–9, 271, 301, 486, 529, 530n, 534–40, 543–5, 584, 624, 674–8
Aesthetic Letters (see *Letters on the Aesthetic Education of Man*)
Braut von Messina (*The Bride of Messina*) 209, 537
Correspondence (*Briefwechsel*) *between Schiller and Goethe* 271n
Die Räuber 164, 207–8, 486
Die Schaubühne als eine moralische Anstalt betrachtet (*The Theatre Considered as a Moral Institution*) 208, 543, 674
Horen (*The Hours*) 529
Kabale und Liebe (*Intrigue and Love*) 203

Kallias oder über die Schönheit (*Kallias or on Beauty*) 674–5
Letters on the Aesthetic Education of Man (*Ästhetische Briefe*) 45, 46n, 164, 544, 675
letter to Körner 674n
letter to Prince Friedrich Christian 674n
On Naive and Sentimental Poetry 31, 70, 151, 538–9
Über das Pathetische (*On Pathos*) 209
Über den Grund des Vergnügens an tragischen Gegenständen (*On the Source of Pleasure in Tragic Subjects*) 209
Über die ästhetische Erziehung des Menschen, in einer Reihe von Briefen (*On the Aesthetic Education of Man, in a Series of Letters*) 164, 544, 675
Über die tragische Kunst (*On the Art of Tragedy*) 209
Vom Erhabenen (*On the Sublime*) 209
Wallenstein 537
Schlegel, August Wilhelm 332, 347, 577, 613, 794
Schlegel, Dorothea 444, 794
Schlegel, Friedrich 63, 163, 208, 267, 270n, 271, 332, 347, 751, 794
Über das Studium der griechischen Poesie 70
Schneider, Johann Gottlob 744
Kritisches griechisches Wörterbuch 744
Schopenauer, Arthur 729
Schubart, Christian Friedrich Daniel 312
Schurman, Anna Maria van 439
science 38–45, 47–8, 51–2, 54, 56, 60, 62, 64, 778–97
Scots Magazine 319
Scott, John (of Amwell) 389n
Critical Essays 389n
Scott, Robert Eden 546, 551–2
Elements of Rhetoric 546

Scott, Sir Walter 66n, 123, 281,
    442, 488
  Lives of the Novelists 442
Scriblerus, Martinus, and Scriblerians
    (*see also* Arbuthnot, Gay, Pope,
    Swift) 51–2, 76, 373, 396–7
Scudéry, Georges de 210, 271
  Ibrahim (preface) 271
Scudéry, Madeleine de 210
Sedley, Sir Charles 178
Segrais, Regnauld de 210
  Nouvelles françoises 210
Semler, Johann Salomo 748
sensationalist, sensationalism 30,
    135
sensibility 146, 153, 201–2, 232,
    235, 257, 280, 295, 299–300,
    419–33, 503, 542, 551–4, 593,
    610, 624, 663, 702, 706, 709,
    717, 733, 783–91
sentimental/sentimentalism 126, 181,
    187–90, 192, 194–6, 201,
    279–80, 422, 424, 539–40,
    554, 593, 786
Sentimental Magazine 422
Sergeant, John 758–9, 761
  Sure-Footing in Christianity 758
Settle, Elkanah
  Empress of Morocco 176
Sévigné, Marie de Rabutin-Chantal,
    Madame de 452, 493, 514
Seward, Anna 249, 437n
  Variety No. 25 249
Seward, Thomas
  'The Female Right to Literature'
    437n
Shadwell, Thomas 176, 178–9
  Sullen Lovers (preface) 179n
Shaftesbury (Anthony Ashley
    Cooper, third Earl of) 13–14,
    16, 21, 24, 143, 152, 155,
    243–4, 296, 315, 359, 367,
    424, 459, 461–2, 498, 534,
    546, 549, 551, 564, 606–7,
    622–4, 627, 630, 632–46,
    652–7, 678, 694, 706–8,
    787

*Characteristicks of Men, Manners,
    Opinions, Times* 21, 143, 244,
    459, 564, 607, 622–4, 633,
    639, 642, 645, 653–5
  *Inquiry concerning Beauty and
    Merit* (trans. of Diderot) 498
  Letter concerning Design 642
  *Letters to a Student at the
    University* 639–40
  'Miscellaneous Reflections' 622,
    633, 640, 643, 645, 654–5
  *The Moralists, a Philosophical
    Rhapsody* 607, 622–3, 635,
    640, 652n, 653, 706–7
  'Notion of the Historical Draught
    or Tablature of "The Judgement
    of Hercules"' 653, 694n
  *Plastics, or the Original Progress
    and Power of Designing Art*
    624, 642
  Second Characters 624, 635–6,
    640, 642, 653n, 654
  'Picture of Cebes, Disciple of
    Socrates' 654
  Soliloquy; or, Advice to an Author
    24, 143, 623, 633, 641, 644,
    653, 655
Shakespeare, William 25, 68–9, 84,
    98–101, 113, 116, 138, 141,
    143, 149, 174, 176–8, 181–4,
    205–9, 239, 294–5, 322, 331,
    359n, 360, 362–3, 367, 370–1,
    373, 376–8, 384–6, 434, 438,
    440–2, 445–6, 449–50, 456,
    458–9, 470, 487, 491–2, 495,
    512–13, 517–20, 529, 533,
    549, 576–9, 583, 590, 595,
    605, 634, 653, 662, 667, 737,
    763, 772, 776, 782, 787, 789,
    791, 794
  Antony and Cleopatra 178
  Coriolanus 207
  Hamlet 178, 208, 359n, 487, 491,
    583, 653
  Henry IV 99, 442
  Julius Caesar 99, 373, 518
  King Lear 207, 322, 440–1

Othello 84, 178, 181, 491
Tempest 99–100, 174, 207,
    458–9, 737
Troilus and Cressida 177, 782
Sharpe, William 141
    Dissertation upon Genius 141
Shaw, Joannes:
    edn of Apollonius of Rhodes 746n
Sheffield, John, third Earl of
    Mulgrave 24, 87, 370
    Essay upon Poetry 24, 87
Shelburne, William Petty, second
    Earl of 401
Shelley, Mary 488, 623
    Frankenstein 488
Shelley, Percy Bysshe 122, 160, 460,
    623
    Defence of Poetry 460
Shenstone, William 66, 99, 117,
    476, 705, 790
    School-Mistress 117
Sheridan, Frances 194, 452
Sheridan, Richard Brinsley 195,
    199
    The Critic 195, 199
    The Discovery 194
    School for Scandal 195
Sheridan, Thomas 344, 351n
    Course of Lectures on Elocution
    344n, 351n
Shirley, James 173
Sidney, Sir Philip 51, 52n, 271–2,
    770
    *Apologie for Poesie, Defence of
    Poesie* 51, 52n, 271–2
    Arcadia 271–2
Simon, Père Richard 5, 465, 571,
    575, 758–9, 765, 777
    *Critical History of the Text of the
    New Testament* 758
    *Histoire critique du Vieux
    Testament* 5, 465, 571, 758–9,
    770
Simonides of Ceos 681
Sir Gawain and the Green Knight
    124, 471
Skelton, John 479

Smart, Christopher 124, 127, 137,
    374, 570, 765, 768
    'Horatian Canons of Friendship'
    570
    Jubilate Agno 124, 137
    Song to David 137, 765
Smeeks, Hendrik 272
Smith, Adam 16, 25, 123, 141, 152,
    156, 291–3, 337, 340–1, 345,
    347, 358–62, 364, 367–9, 424,
    428, 430, 546, 548–50, 556,
    603
    *Considerations concerning the
    First Formation of Language*
    341
    *Lectures on Rhetoric and Belles
    Lettres* 293
    Theory of Moral Sentiments 141,
    152, 368, 428, 603
    Wealth of Nations 152, 293, 358
Smith, Charlotte 247, 483
Smith, William
    (trans. Longinus) 790
Smollett, Tobias 6n, 206, 246–7,
    256, 321, 324–5, 331, 434,
    448, 482, 557
    British Magazine 324–5
    Critical Review (see separate
    entry)
    Ferdinand Count Fathom 482
    Sir Launcelot Greaves 325
Soames, Sir William 85, 88
    trans. of Boileau's *Art Poétique* 88
Socrates 37n, 298, 395, 654, 656
solipsism 447, 596
Sophocles 68, 295, 366, 492, 579
    Oedipus Tyrannus 579
Sorbière, Samuel 174–6
    *Relation d'un voyage en
    Angleterre* 175n
Sorel, Charles 210
Southerne, Thomas 185
Spallanzani, Lazaro 791
Spanheim, Ezechiel 745
    Callimachus (ed.) 746n
    *De Praestantia et Vsu Veterum
    Numismatum* 745

Spectator (*see also* Addison, Steele)
12–13, 17, 76, 103, 181,
320–3, 370–1, 378, 414, 426,
441, 447, 459, 461–2, 471–2,
587, 603–4, 618–21, 628–9,
633–40, 643–52, 687–8, 690,
706–8, 713–14, 719, 765–6,
788–9
  Nos. 4, 5 647
  No. 10 633
  No. 16 634
  No. 23 102
  No. 29 636
  No. 39 650
  No. 40 322
  No. 44 587
  No. 50 459
  No. 58 634, 639
  Nos. 58–61 102, 337
  No. 61 650
  No. 62 78, 102, 143, 604
  No. 70 636, 651
  Nos. 70, 74 67n, 102, 323, 371,
461, 472
  No. 85 101, 472, 651
  No. 105 644
  No. 119 643
  No. 135 634
  No. 140 636
  No. 159 143
  No. 160 42n, 101, 143, 629, 635,
765
  No. 162 634
  No. 165 634, 651
  No. 169 644
  No. 208 636
  No. 223 651
  No. 253 13n, 99, 102
  No. 267 647
  No. 279 99, 636, 647
  No. 280 636
  No. 285 649
  No. 291 99, 618, 638, 645–7,
649–50
  No. 297 100, 648, 650
  No. 303 648, 652
  No. 321 637, 646, 648

  No. 327 648–9
  No. 328 643
  No. 333 648–9
  No. 339 648
  No. 345 646
  No. 351 648–9
  No. 357 648
  No. 369 100, 648
  No. 409 114, 322, 636, 638, 640,
651
  No. 411 687
  Nos. 411–21 322, 370
  No. 412 619, 628, 707
  No. 413 41n, 620
  No. 414 143, 621, 706–8,
713–14
  No. 416 158, 637, 652, 690, 708
  No. 417 101
  No. 418 621
  No. 419 101, 132, 143, 378
  No. 421 132, 619
  No. 435 634
  No. 453 766
  No. 461 643
  No. 470 644
  No. 565 789
  No. 592 11, 635, 646
Spence, Joseph 108, 118, 367, 704,
716
  Anecdotes, Observations etc. 118,
704n
  Essay on Pope's Odyssey 108
Spenser, Edmund 24, 66, 84–5, 91,
103, 107, 115, 120, 234, 360,
367, 441, 477, 686n, 789,
794
  Faerie Queene 66n, 470, 474,
477–8, 789
Spinoza, Benedict (Baruch) de 162n,
624, 760–1, 763, 779
  Ethics 779
  Tractatus Theologico-Politicus
760, 763
Sprat, Thomas 94, 175–6, 374
  History of the Royal Society 94
Sprengel, Kurt Polykarp Joachim
791

Staal-de Launay, Madame de 53n, 308

Staël, Germaine, Madame de (Anne-Louise Germaine Necker, Baronne de Staël-Holstein) 70, 233–5, 438, 440, 444, 448–9, 453–5, 484–5, 487–8, 519, 523, 676, 796
  Athènes des lettres 523
  De la littérature 453–4
  De l'Allemagne 454
  Essai sur les fictions 233, 440, 448–9, 484
  Réflexions sur la paix 484
  Réflexions sur le procès de la reine 484

Stahl, Georg Ernst 791

Stanfield, James Field 303
  Essay on Biography 303

Stanislaus II (King of Poland) 331

Statius 91

Steele, Joshua 130

Steele, Sir Richard 6, 18–21, 181, 190, 321–2, 332, 447, 459, 639, 644–5, 648
  Conscious Lovers 181, 190
  Guardian 6n, 16, 321, 707
  Spectator 645, 648
  Tatler 6, 18, 320–1, 447, 459, 633, 644

Stein, Gertrude 455

Stendhal (Marie-Henri Beyle) 520, 521n
  Racine et Shakespeare 520, 521n

Stephanus of Byzantium 746n

Sterne, Laurence 9, 229, 243, 246, 278–9, 331, 402, 413, 420, 422, 603, 648, 763, 787–8
  Sentimental Journey 278–9, 422
  Tristram Shandy 243, 278, 331, 402, 413, 422, 603, 648, 763, 787–8

Stewart, Dugald 67, 340
  Life of Adam Smith 340

Stinstra, Johannes 274–7, 280

Stolberg, Friedrich Leopold, Graf zu 325

Stuart, Charles Edward 558

Stuart, James (with Revett, Nicholas)
  Antiquities of Athens 747

Stukeley, William 573–4, 576
  Stonehenge 573
  'Canon of Mosaic Chronology' 573

Sturm und Drang ('Storm and Stress') 30, 122, 125–6, 149–50, 160, 164, 204, 207n, 208, 300, 425, 523–4, 533–4, 542–3, 662

sublime 14, 53, 82, 89, 96, 99–100, 108, 116, 118–19, 123, 127, 133–5, 137, 142, 145, 152–3, 159, 165, 178, 181, 206, 209, 295, 339, 351, 361–2, 365–6, 368–9, 374–5, 377, 389, 394–416, 430, 432, 447, 463–4, 467–8, 480, 482, 486–7, 498, 512, 524, 547, 552, 554, 577, 579, 590–2, 595–6, 602–3, 606, 611, 619, 622, 626–9, 632–3, 639, 648–50, 652–3, 664, 671, 681, 685, 701–6, 709, 721, 734, 756, 765–9, 778, 784–5, 789–91, 796n

Suda (*see* Gaisford, Küster, Toup) 746n

Suetonius 285, 286n

Sulzer, Johann Georg 119, 139, 149, 160–1, 533, 663, 680
  Allgemeine Theorie der schönen Künste 139, 149, 160, 533, 663

supernatural/supernaturalism 33n, 224, 232, 234, 255, 259, 483–5, 530–2

Süssmilch, Johann Peter 341
  Versuch eines Beweises 341n

Swift, Jonathan 34, 44n, 46, 48–53, 58–9, 60n, 61n, 93, 96, 103, 162, 218, 234, 250, 256, 292n, 322, 359–60, 374, 376, 397, 434, 437, 439, 450, 491, 549, 563, 567–9, 742, 759, 763
  Battle of the Books 48–52, 93, 96, 434, 437, 742

'Digression concerning Critics' 49

Gulliver's Travels 49n, 162, 218, 256, 568

'Mr C——ns's Discourse of Free-Thinking' 759

'On Poetry: A Rapsody' 397n

'Proposal for Correcting, Improving and Ascertaining the English Tongue' 563

Tale of a Tub 44n, 48–9, 51n, 52n, 53, 58, 61n, 568–9, 763

Tatler (contribution) 322

Sydenham, Thomas 783

Sylph 245, 258
No. 5 258
No. 19 245

Tacitus 286–7, 439, 549

Tartaglia, Niccoló 778

Tasso, Torquato 81, 91, 95, 103, 109, 113, 120, 228, 232, 649, 716, 719
Gerusalemme liberata 716n

Tassoni, Alessandro 36n, 39
Pensieri diversi 36n

taste (*goût*) 5, 11, 14–22, 27–30, 45, 52, 56, 59, 78, 95–6, 102, 108, 113–14, 116, 122, 132, 167, 249, 256, 287, 295, 331, 363, 400, 413, 419, 426–33, 437, 440–1, 449, 455, 472, 484, 491–3, 495, 497, 500, 504–5, 508, 510–5, 518–22, 527, 529, 533, 546–57, 567–8, 592–3, 596–7, 599, 611–12, 628–9, 633–57, 660, 663–4, 670, 678, 681, 702, 709, 715–17, 723, 732, 756, 785–8, 790

Tate, Nahum 440

Tatler (*see also* Addison, Steele) 18, 320, 322, 447, 459, 634, 642–4, 646
No. 69 642
No. 162 634
No. 165 3, 644

No. 171 459
No. 204 643–4

Taylor, Bishop Jeremy 655
Discourse of the Liberty of Prophesying 655

Taylor, William, of Norwich 680n

Temple, Sir William 34–5, 46–52, 96–7, 108, 284, 310, 320, 563
'An Essay upon the Ancient and Modern Learning' 46, 96
Introduction to the History of England 52n
Memoirs 320
Miscellanea 47n, 96
'Of Poetry' 51n, 96–7, 108
'Some thoughts upon reviewing the essay of Ancient and Modern learning' 49n
'Upon Heroick Virtue' 97

Tencin, Claudine Alexandrine Guérin de 444

Terence (Publius Terentius Afer) (*see also* André Dacier) 53, 366, 439

Terrasson, Jean, Abbé 54–5, 60, 63
Dissertation critique sur l'Iliade 54–5
La philosophie applicable à tous les objets 55n

Tertullian 684

Tetens, Johann Nicolaus 155, 161–2, 164
Philosophische Versuche über die menschliche Natur und ihre Entwicklung 161

Teutsche Merkur, Der 269–70, 331

Theatralische Bibliothek 330

Themistocles 754

Theobald, Lewis 367, 576

Theocritus (*see also* eds. Brunck, Jacobs, Reiske, Valckenaer, Warton) 76, 95, 108, 115, 746n

Thesaurus Linguae Latinae 744

Thirty Years War 184

Thomas, Christian (Thomasius) 265
Monats-Gespräche 265

Thomas Magister (*see* Bernard, J. S.)
Ecloga 746n

Thomson, James 21, 117, 120, 126,
    130-1, 201, 432, 519, 555,
    694, 696, 705, 790
    Castle of Indolence 117
    Seasons 117, 120, 126, 130, 696,
    705, 778
    *To the Memory of Sir Isaac
    Newton* 790n
Thrale, Hester Lynch (*see also*
    Piozzi) 311
Thucydides 76, 360, 374, 567, 581
Thwaites, Edward 479
Thynne, William 474
    (ed.) Chaucer 474
Tickell, Richard 123
Tieck, Ludwig 163
Tillemont, Louis Sébastien le Nain
    de 283-7
    Histoire des Empereurs 285
Tillotson, John 759-60
    Rule of Faith 759
Timaeus (*see also* Ruhnken) 746n
Timpanaro, Sebastiano 747n
    Genesi, La 747n
Tinkler, John F. 52n, 310
Toland, John 306, 310
    Life of John Milton 306
Tollius, Jakob 756n
Tom Thumb, History of 472
Tonson, Jacob 766
Tooke, John Horne 128, 338n
    Diversions of Purley 338n
Torricelli, Evangelista 60n
Toup, Jonathan 746n, 756n
    edn of Hesychius 746n
    edn of *Suda* 746n
Townshend, Charles 406
Tracy, Antoine Louis Claude Destutt
    de 128
tragédie bourgeoise (*see also
    bürgerliches Trauerspiel*) 196,
    198
Trapp, Joseph 8, 10, 13, 16, 108,
    119-20, 194
    Praelectiones Poeticae 10, 119-20,
    194
Troeltsch, Karl Friedrich 267

Trumbull, George
    Treatise on Ancient Painting 351
Trussler, Rev. John (*see* Blake,
    William) 166
Tryal of Skill 11
Tucker, Abraham
    Light of Nature Pursued 131
Tuke, Samuel
    Adventure of Five Hours 175
Tully (*see* Cicero, Marcus Tullius)
Turgot, Anne Robert Jacques, Baron
    de l'Aulne 32, 40, 67, 789, 791,
    795-6
    Discours 40n
    Encyclopédie 795-6
    'Ether' 796
    'Etymologie' 796
    'Feu électrique' 796
    'Magnétisme' 796
Turner, Joseph Mallord William 295
Turner, Sharon 479
    History of the Anglo-Saxons 479
Twining, Thomas 121
Tyrwhitt, Thomas 474, 480
    Canterbury Tales (ed.) 474
    'Vindication of the Appendix to
    the Poems, called Rowley's'
    480

Universal Chronicle 324
Universal Magazine 305
Unwin, Rev. William 140
Upton, John (edn of Spenser) 24
Urevangelium 775
d'Urfé, Honoré 54, 210, 271
    Astrée 271
ut pictura poesis 110, 530, 533,
    535, 681-99, 702, 705, 786

Valckenaer, Lodewyk Kaspar 746n,
    754
    edn of Ammonius 746n
    Aristobulus (writings on forgeries
    by) 746n, 754
    edn of Callimachus 746n
    Euripidis Phoenissae 754n
    edn of Theocritus 746n

Valentine and Orson 458

Valincourt, Jean-Baptiste Henry
 Trousset de 53, 213–16

Vanbrugh, Sir John 190, 192, 449,
 788
 Provok'd Wife 449

Varnhagen, Rahel 444

Variety 249

Vasari, Giorgio 43
 Lives of the Artists 43

Vauvenargues, Luc de Clapiers,
 Marquis de 368

Verdi, Giuseppe 183

Vergier, Jacques 232

verisimilitude (*vraisemblance*) 91,
 169, 211, 214, 215n, 216,
 218–19, 222, 230, 233, 234n,
 254, 265–6, 272, 404, 448–9,
 483, 491–2, 493n, 500n, 525,
 601, 684, 711, 719, 722, 732,
 736, 740, 789

Vernünftigen Tadlerinnen, Die (*see*
 Gottsched) 321, 441

Verwer, J. A. 276

Verwer, Pieter Adriaan 274, 276

Vico, Giambattista 36n, 55, 60n, 65,
 108, 128, 136–7, 161, 296–9,
 335, 340, 345–7, 357, 461,
 464, 556, 572–4, 576–7,
 792–4
 De mente heroica 36n
 Institutiones oratoriae 357
 Scienza nuova 108, 128, 161,
 296–9, 345–6, 357, 461, 556,
 573, 792

Vicq d'Azyr, Félix 793

Vida, Marco Girolamo 24, 37n,
 366, 595
 De arte poetica 37n

Vien, Joseph-Marie 296

Villaroel, Deigo de Torres 228
 Vida 228

Villiers, George, second Duke of
 Buckingham 176, 383
 Rehearsal 176

Villoison, Jean Baptiste Gaspard
 d'Ansse de 746n

Virgil 35, 37–8, 62, 64–5, 76, 81,
 84, 87, 89–91, 95–6, 98–104,
 107–8, 113, 115–16, 120, 123,
 129, 153, 232, 234, 273, 350,
 356, 359, 371, 439, 462–3,
 472, 474, 490, 493–4, 497,
 504, 512, 519–20, 564–5, 576,
 647–9, 651–2, 695–7, 708,
 719, 724, 733, 746–7, 755,
 756n, 776
 Aeneid 65, 75, 101–2, 356, 461,
 472, 490, 504, 564, 647, 696,
 733, 755
 Georgics 62n, 519, 651–2, 697

Visconti, G. B. and E. Q.
 Museo Pio-Clementino 745

Viterbus, Annius 211

Voiture, Vincent 95, 114

Volksgeist 138, 298

Volkspoesie 68–9, 138, 543–4

Volkstümlichkeit 543–4

Voltaire (François-Marie Arouet)
 4–5, 44, 64, 68–9, 71, 109,
 112–14, 139, 147, 174, 182,
 192, 194, 218, 225, 234, 286,
 289–92, 294, 296, 301, 325,
 330, 332, 367, 375, 384, 439,
 459–60, 490–5, 503, 505, 507,
 510, 513–19, 521, 549, 552,
 565–7, 571, 576, 588–9, 595,
 600–1, 784, 786–7
 Candide 490–1, 515, 516n, 600–1
 Catalogue des écrivains 289n
 Dictionnaire philosophique 492,
 494–5
 'Enthousiasme' 492, 494n
 'Fables' 495
 Encyclopédie (*see also* listing
 above) 4, 375, 510
 Essai sur les moeurs 291
 Essay on Epick Poetry 44,
 112–13, 367
 Henriade, La 113
 Histoire de Charles XII 288
 Lettres philosophiques (*Lettres
 Anglaises*) 113, 288, 491–2,
 588, 595, 784

L'Ingénu 459
London Magazine (essay contributions) 325
Nanine 192
Siècle de Louis XIV 289n, 291, 492–4, 565
Taureau blanc 601
Temple du goût 113, 566
Zadig 601n
Vondel, Joost van den 272
Voss, Johann Heinrich 325
Vossius, Gerhard Johann 351
De artium et scientiarum natura ac constitutione 351
Vossius, Isaac 724–5
De poematum cantu et viribus rhythmi 725
vraisemblance (*see* verisimilitude)

Wachter, Johann 342
Naturae et scripturae concordia 342n
Wackenroder, Wilhelm Heinrich 163
Wagner, Heinrich Leopold 204–5
Wagner, Richard 183, 741
Wagstaffe, William 472
Comment upon the History of Tom Thumb 472
Walcherse Robinson 273
Waller, Edmund 86, 98, 102, 373, 470
Walpole, Horace 239, 328, 401n, 402n, 440, 463, 474–5, 479–81, 483–4, 789
Castle of Otranto 440, 470, 479, 481, 483
Correspondence 475
Letter to the Editor of the Miscellanies of Thomas Chatterton 480–1
Memoirs of George II 401n, 402n
Mysterious Mother 479
Walton, Brian 761
Biblia Sacra Polyglotta 761
Walton, Izaak 317
Wanley, Humfrey 479

Warburton, William 134–7, 260, 346, 399–400, 463, 465–9, 478, 481–2, 575–8, 696, 763
Divine Legation of Moses 135, 346n, 465
Doctrine of Grace 399n
Pope's works (ed.) 481
preface to *Clarissa*, vol. III 259–60
edn of Shakespeare 577–8, 763
Warton, Joseph 22, 24, 27, 71n, 118, 120, 130, 132–3, 146, 153, 156, 205, 207, 378, 425–7, 429, 474, 697
Adventurer No. 57 132
The Enthusiast: or the Lover of Nature 117
Essay on Pope 22, 24, 27, 120, 130, 153, 425–6, 474, 697
Odes on Various Subjects 117
'Reflections on Didactic Poetry' 120
edn of Theocritus 746n
'To Fancy' 156
Works of Virgil 120
Warton, Thomas 44–5, 66, 69, 71n, 118, 121, 133, 313–5, 368, 470, 471n, 473–4, 477–8, 480, 482, 575, 789, 794
Enquiry into the Authenticity of the Poems Called Rowley's 480
History of English Poetry 45, 66, 121, 471n, 477–8, 480, 483, 789
Idler No. 33 313
Observations on the Fairy Queen 470, 474, 477–8, 789
Pleasures of Melancholy 117
Watteau, Jean Antoine 172–3, 786
Watts, Isaac 122, 762, 764
Improvement of the Mind 762
'Short essay toward the improvement of psalmody' 762, 764
Webb, Daniel 206, 725–8
Observations on the Correspondence between Poetry and Music 725–7

Webster, Daniel 361
Weekly Memorials of the Ingenious
    318–19
Weil, Françoise 220
Weimar Classicism 31, 208, 524,
    529, 534–6, 545
Weisse, Christian Felix
    Richard III 203
well-made play 199
Welsted, Leonard 367, 394, 396,
    400, 685–6
    Works of Longinus (trans.) 394,
    400n, 685–6
Wesley, John 122, 765
Wettstein, J. J. 748
Wezel, Johann Carl
    Herrmann und Ulrike 270
Wharton, Edith 455
Whately, Archbishop Richard
    Elements of Rhetoric 362
Whately, Thomas 207–8, 709–10,
    712, 716
    *Observations on Modern
    Gardening* 709–10, 712
    *Remarks on some of the Characters
    of Shakespeare* 207–8
Whitehead, William
    School for Lovers 194
Whitehurst, John 791
Whyte, Samuel 311
Wieland, Christoph Martin 150,
    268, 270, 278, 624
    Abenteuer des Don Sylvio 268
    Geschichte des Agathon 268, 270
Wilkes, John 556
Williams, Anna 435n
Wilson, John 760–1
    *Scripture's Genuine Interpreter
    Asserted* 760–1
Wilson, Richard 705, 711
Winckelmann, Johann Joachim 63,
    70, 296, 300–1, 530n, 536,
    572, 576, 581, 624, 663–4,
    666, 673, 679, 750–1, 753,
    771, 789, 792, 795
    Gedanken über die Nachahmung
    663n

    *Geschichte der Kunst des
    Altertums* 300, 664n, 750, 789
Winkler, Johann Heinrich 791
wit 12
Witherspoon, John 358n
    *Lectures on Moral Philosophy and
    Eloquence* 358n
Wolf, Friedrich August 65, 345, 742,
    746n, 748–9, 751–6
    *Ciceronis quae feruntur IV
    Orationes* 754
    *Ciceronis Oratio quae fertur pro
    Marcello* 754
    'Encyclopaedia philologica' 751
    Prolegomena ad Homerum 345n,
    746n, 748, 751, 753–5
Wolff, Caspar Friedrich 791–2
Wolff, Christian 62n, 159, 357, 424,
    658–60
Wolff-Bekker, Betje, and Deken,
    Aagje 278–80
    Gevaaren van de Laster 279n,
    280n
    *Historie van Mejuffrouw Cornelia
    Wildschut* 278n, 280
    *Historie van Mejuffrouw Sara
    Burgerhart* 278, 280
    Historie van Willem Leevend 279
Wollstonecraft, Mary 332, 419–20,
    438, 441
    Analytical Review (contrib.) 441
    Monthly Review (contrib.) 441
    *Vindication of the Rights of
    Woman* 332, 419–20
Wolseley, Robert 87
    Preface to *Valentinian* 87
Woolf, Virginia 323, 455
Wood, Anthony à 320
    Athenae Oxonienses 320
Wood, Robert 65, 345, 747
    *Essay on the Original Genius
    and Writings of Homer* 345n,
    756
    Ruins of Palmyra 747
Wordsworth, William 7, 119, 127,
    129, 131, 133, 136–7, 139–40,
    147, 151, 164–6, 325, 372,

382, 392, 412, 414–16, 433,
447, 455, 488–9, 503n, 554,
562, 583, 605, 608, 612–13,
652, 796, 797n
Essays Upon Epitaphs 415
Excursion 788
Guide to the Lakes 414n
Lyrical Ballads 7, 119, 133, 136,
139, 164–6, 488, 562, 605,
608, 652, 796–7
Preface to *Lyrical Ballads* 7, 139,
147, 151, 433, 503n, 605, 608,
652
Prelude 165, 414, 416, 583,
612–13, 796
'The Sublime and the Beautiful' 414
'Tintern Abbey' 165–6
World No. 79 247
Wotton, William 34, 36n, 39, 42,
47–8, 50–2, 61n, 96, 396
*Defence of the Reflections upon
Ancient and Modern Learning*
49n
History of Rome 51–2
*Reflections upon Ancient and
Modern Learning* 36n, 39n,
42n, 47–8, 50, 61

Wren, Sir Christopher 779
Wright, James 473
Historia Histrionica 473
Wright, Joseph (of Derby) 296
Wycherley, William 189, 491
Country Wife 189
Plain Dealer 189
Wyndham, William 711

Yearsley, Ann 127
Young, Edward 29n, 64, 108, 118,
120, 131, 141–3, 145–6,
148–9, 165–6, 267, 386, 438,
519, 534, 629–32, 765, 793
*Conjectures on Original
Composition* 29n, 64, 141, 143,
146, 148–9, 267, 386, 438,
534, 629–30, 793
Guardian No. 86 765
Night Thoughts 117, 120, 142,
166, 519
Young, William 374

Zeno 58
Zola, Émile 450
Nana 450
Zöllner, Johann Friedrich 524